THE DECIPHERMENT OF
MINOAN LINEAR A

HURRIANS AND HURRIAN IN MINOAN CRETE

VOLUME I, PART II: TEXT AND SUMMARY

by

Peter George van Soesbergen

INGRAMSPARK

To Jan M. Veldhuizen-van Soesbergen
and in remembrance of
Anna M. van Soesbergen-Jurriaans
and Petrus J. van Soesbergen

Second revised edition 2016. ISBN: 9789402157574
printed by BRAVE NEW BOOKS – Amsterdam
Cover: View of the Palace of Phaistos (Crete)
Photograph by the author. Design by Roy Petrie.

Third completely revised and extended edition 2022
ISBN: 9789083275413
Printing and global distribution by INGRAMSPARK
United States, United Kingdom, Australia and printers in countries including: Brazil, China, France, Germany, India, Italy, Japan, Poland, Russia, South Korea and Spain.

Cover: View of the Palace of Phaistos (Crete)
Photograph by the author. Design by Roy Petrie.

Original title of the first edition (Sheffield 1987):

THE ONOMASTICS OF THE 'MINOAN LINEAR A' AND 'LINEAR B' DOCUMENTS AND THEIR HISTORICAL SIGNIFICANCE

Thesis for the degree of Doctor of Philosophy submitted to the Department of Classical Studies of the University of Sheffield, September 1987

Second revised edition 2016

MINOAN LINEAR A - VOLUME I: HURRIANS AND HURRIAN IN MINOAN CRETE

Third completely revised and extended edition 2022

THE DECIPHERMENT OF MINOAN LINEAR A: HURRIANS AND HURRIAN IN MINOAN CRETE

VOLUME I, PART II: TEXT AND SUMMARY

by

Peter George van Soesbergen

INGRAMSPARK 2022

THE MAIN LINEAR A PHONETIC SIGNS (ARRANGED ACCORDING TO THE LINEAR B SYLLABARY)

	a	*e*	*i*	*o*	*u*
d-					
j-					
k-					
m-					
n-					
p-					
q-					
r-					
s-					
t-					
w-					
z-					

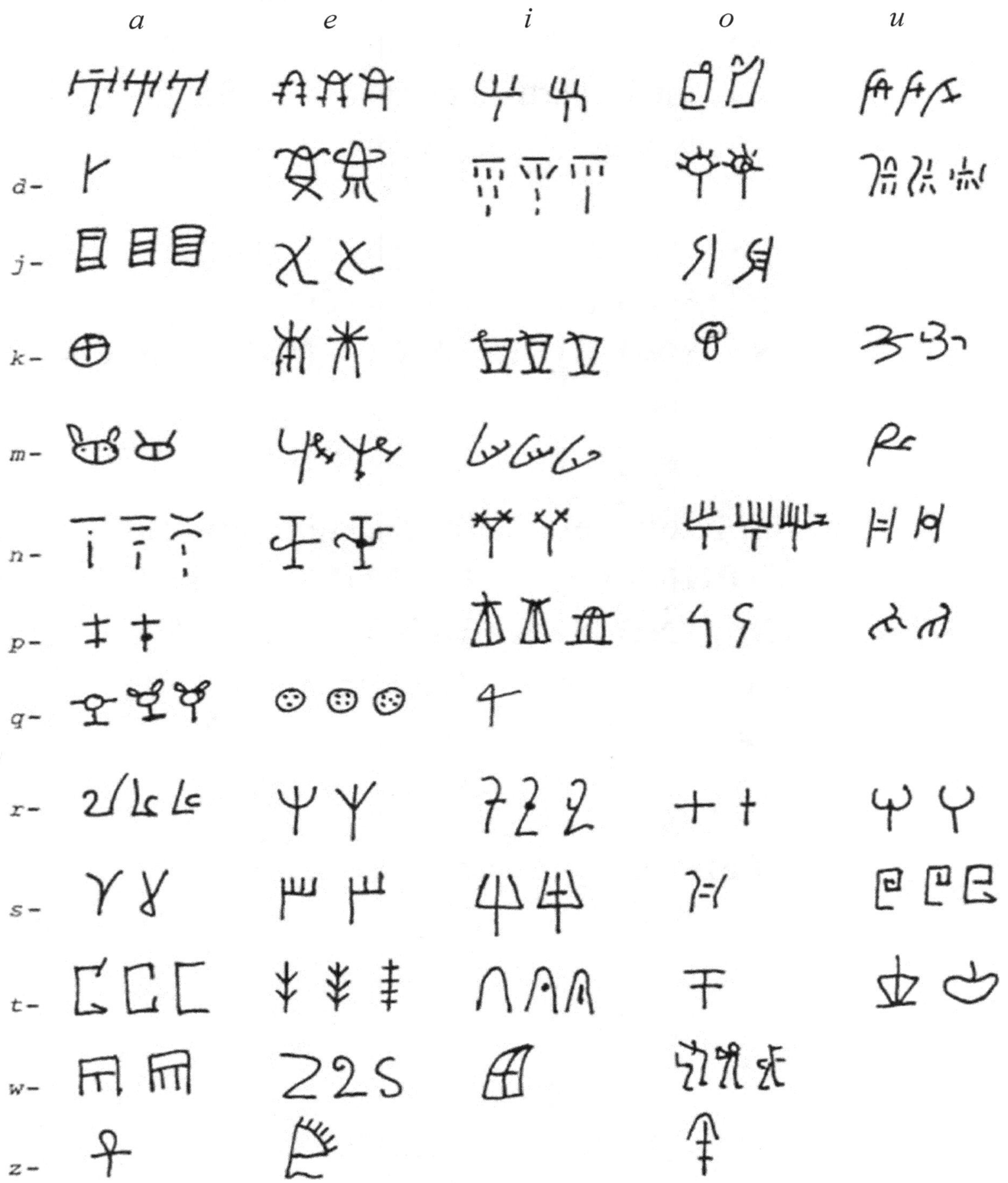

THE MAIN LINEAR A PHONETIC SIGNS SHOWN WITH
THE HURRIAN CUNEIFORM PHONETIC VALUES

	a	*e*	*i*	*o*	*u*
d-					
ḫ-					
j-					
k-					
m-					
n-					
p-					
r-					
s-					
t-					
w-					
z-					

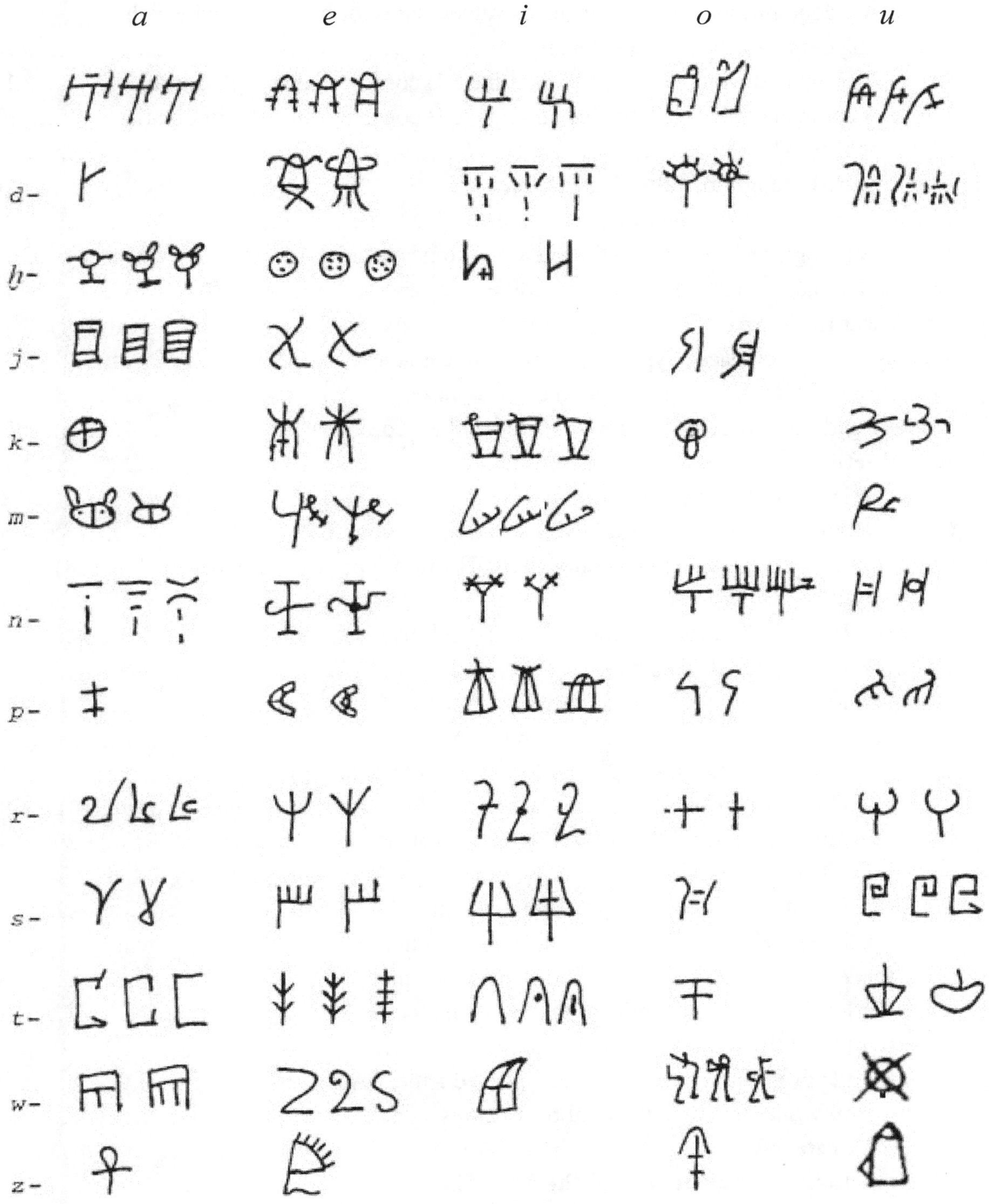

CONTENTS: PAGES

CHAPTER 13

LINEAR A: ONOMASTICA AND LEXICA

Studying the Linear A texts from the archives of Minoan palaces, farmhouses and villas one thing one cannot fail to observe is the fact that normal lexical terms are extremely rare. We encounter so-called transaction terms such as ***ku-ro*** and ***po-to-ku-ro***, ***ki-ro*** (also abbreviated to ***ki***) and ***te***, possibly an abbreviation for ***te+ro*** (HT 104.1). I may add to the repertory very frequent ***sa-ra***$_2$.

Names of commodities are extremely rare in Linear A, even more than in Linear B, because the Minoan scribes used very small page tablets and even smaller nodules, sealings and roundels to keep their records with a kind of shorthand writing that went far beyond what their Mycenaean colleagues were later willing to accept. The Minoan scribes used apart from the normal sequences all sorts of ligatures (in my transliterations rendered with + signs instead of the normal hyphens), but most of all ideograms of men, armed men, women, sheep, goats, oxen, pigs, a great variety of agricultural commodities, arms, among which shields, helmets, cuirasses, lances and chariots, parts of chariots and wheels and tools. Most inventive I consider the ideogram of a *cloud* with the addition of syllabic sign ***pi***, that I describe as NUBES+***pi*** (HT 33.4) and explain as ***Tešup=pi*** 'of Tešub'.

As a result most of the information we receive from the tablets consists of onomastic material, mainly personal names, but also recognizable toponyms and ethnics. One great advantage of Hurrian personal names is that they do not only reveal their clearly Hurrian identity, but that they are themselves complete grammatical formations, whether they are so-called *verbal* or *nominal* 'sentence names' or so-called 'one-word names'. They show that the people registered on the tablets were Hurrian, that they worshipped Hurrian gods and heroes, that they lived in places with Hurrian names, that they used ethnics with Hurrian suffixes and that their vernacular was Hurrian.

I start with a special text that was first published as APPENDIX 2 to the 2016 edition of *MINOAN LINEAR A*, Vol. I, Part II: Linear A ***po-to-ku-ro*** (HT 122b.6; HT 131b.4) : Hurrian ***puttu(-)kuru***.[1] I had chosen to use *Appendices* as an easy solution for the publication of some new identifications and interpretations accomplished after completion of the *indices*. In this way I could avoid altering the order of pages of the original text corresponding with the indices. As a result of my decision to publish a new revised and extended edition it is now possible to incorporate the *Appendices* into the text of this revised edition. My interpretation of Linear A ***po-to-ku-ro*** (HT 122b.6; HT 131b.4) as Hurrian ***puttu(-)kuru*** has led to inclusion into this Chapter.

For the readers convenience I include the texts of the tablets HT 122 and HT 131 from Hagia Triada. For full annotations, bibliographical details and for the *analysed structure* of the texts I refer to my *Corpus of transliterated Linear A texts*.

---

[1] Passages on Linear A *ku-ro* in the Chapter on 'Script and language' (*Minoan Linear A*, Vol I, Part I) are partly repeated in this Chapter, since the discussion on *ku-ro* is closely connected with that on *po-to-ku-ro*.

Starting from A. Kober's observation that Linear A and Linear B employed different words for 'total' in a consistent manner, P. Meriggi pointed out that summations were always preceded by two syllabic signs in Linear A. If these were transliterated with the Ventris's values of their Linear B counterparts, the result would be either ***ku-ro*** or ***ku-lo***, which could represent the common Semitic root ***kl*** meaning 'all'.[2]

The challenge was soon accepted by C.H. Gordon in two articles.[3] He integrated his results into a monograph *Evidence for the Minoan language*, Ventnor, N.J. 1966, in which he changed his allegiance from Akkadian to West Semitic, Phoenician in particular, and compared ***ku-ro*** with Semitic ***kull-*** (e.g. Hebrew כל *kl*) 'all'.[4] Identification of Linear A ***ku-ro*** or ***ku-lo*** with Semitic ***kl*** by P. Meriggi and subsequently by C.H. Gordon seemed attractive on semantic grounds, but Gordon's approach was soon met with criticism, because terms like ***ku-ro*** seem to defy definite conclusions as to the character of the idiom written with Linear A, since the term may be a loan-word just as the English word 'total' is derived from Latin ***totus*** 'entire' [through Middle English, from Old French, from medieval Latin ***totalis***].

E.J.Furnée has offered another etymology for Linear A ***ku-ro***: "Das einzige Wort aus Linear A, dessen Lesung und Bedeutung hundertprozentig sicher erscheinen, nämlich ***ku-ro*** 'Summe', könnte m.E. genauso gut – oder vielleicht sogar besser als bislang geschehen ist [Here he refers to Meriggi, Gordon and Georgiev] – aus dem Vorgriechischen gedeutet werden, wenn man nämlich annimmt, dass ***ku-ro*** für **kuro* steht und auf **ku̯ro-* zurückgeht. Dies könnte dann einen Nebenform von ****kupro-*** sein (vgl. die Hesychglosse *κύπρος* = *κεφάλαιον ἀριθμοῦ*, mit einem im Vorgriechischen nicht ungebräuchlichen Wechsel von ***p*** und ***u̯***. Ich lasse diese Deutung von ***ku-ro*** dahingestellt sein; jedenfalls ist das dem Wort ***κύπρος*** zugrunde liegende vorindogermanische Element ****kup-*** (**kub-*), 'Kopf' für Kreta bezeugt, und zwar in aspirierter Form, vgl. *κύφερον ἢ κυφήν· κεφαλήν. Κρῆτες* (H)." [5]

However, there appears to be one flaw in Furnée's argumentation, since he does not explain how the phonetic development from **ku̯ro-*/**kupro-* > *kuro* could have been completed in the much earlier Linear A form, whereas in the later form *κύπρος* in the gloss of Hesychius of Alexandria the ***/p/*** or ***/w/*** was still fully intact. This is a decisive issue, since an occlusive ***/p/*** was always expressed in consonant clusters and a non-occlusive ***/w/*** preceding sonantic consonants was also expressed in consonant clusters in Linear A and B.

Another etymology for Linear A *ku-ro* was presented by R. Gordesiani: "*Ku-ro* – 'Summe', einziges wort aus Linear A, dessen Lesung and Deutung wir, wie M. Pope bemerkt, für ganz sicher halten konnen. Vgl. georg. *ḳr-* 'sammeln', das in dem Verbalstamm *ḳreb/ḳrib* 'sammeln' (megr. *ḳorob*, tschan. *ḳo(r)ob*) bezeugt ist. Dieser Stamm geht seinerseits auf kartw. *ḳar-/ ḳr-* 'verbinden, verknüpfen, zusammenfügen' zurück." [6]

---

2 P. Meriggi, *Primi Elementi di Minoico A* (Minos Suppl.), Salamanca 1956.

3 C.H. Gordon, 'Notes on Minoan Linear A', *Antiquity 31 (1957)*, 120-130; 'Akkadian tablets in Minoan dress', *Antiquity 31 (1957)*, 237-240.

4 C.H. Gordon, *Evidence for the Minoan language*, Ventnor, N.J. 1966, 27, sub 117.

5 E.J.Furnée, *Die wichtigsten konsonantischen Erscheinungen des Vorgriechischen*, The Hague, Paris 1972, 396.

6 R. Gordesiani, Zu den kaukasisch-ägäischen Beziehungen im II. Jahrtausend v.u.Z.', *Actes*

E. Peruzzi had previously argued in favour of an Indo-European connection. He accepted some of L.R. Palmer's suggestions regarding a possible Luwian interpretation.

He also maintained that morphological evidence for noun declension, meagre though it was, might indicate Greek as the language of the texts. For the Linear A word for 'total' ***ku-ro***, read with Linear B phonetic values, he proposed an Indo-European etymology ****ger-*** 'to collect' (cf. Greek ***ἀγείρω***). For the word that was explained as 'deficit', Linear A ***ki-ro***, he suggested an Indo-European root ****(s)kel-*** 'due', 'owing' (cf. Lithuanian ***skeliu***). Though the evidence was put forward in a comprehensive way, one must conclude that it is too thin. For further criticism of Peruzzi's proposals I may refer to M. Pope's *Aegean writing and Linear A* (SIMA 8), Lund 1964, 6.[7]

In *The historical significance of onomastic data from Linear A and B texts* (Mycenaean Seminar, Institute of Classical Studies, University of London, 28th May 1980, 4) I have explained that Hurrian ***kuru***, which should phonologically be understood as ***/kuro/***, not only provides the exact phonetic equivalent to the Linear A word, but could also be a likely candidate from a semantic point of view. It certainly is one of the most frequent terms in the Tušratta letter. [8] The Hurrian word means 'again'.

E. Laroche, *Glossaire de la langue hourrite*, 156, s.v. ***guru*** 'de nouveau, encore'. "Sens déduit des contextes par Messerschmidt, *Mit. St.*, 26; selon Speiser, *IH,* 71, 91, nom adverbialisé." He gives the examples: ***gu-ru***, Mit. III 15, 39, 55, 93, etc. and *gu-ru-ú-we*, *ib.* IV 42, and *gu-ru-u-u*[, *ib.* I, 45.[9]

E.A. Speiser, *IH*, 91: "***kuru*** 'again, in return': cf. Mit. III 15, 39, 55, etc. The approximate meaning of this adverbial concept has been known since the beginning of Hurrian studies. The word functions as an independent particle when it is not followed by suffixes. The adverbial connotation helps to explain nominal and verbal uses of the root in the sense of 'return'." Cf. also I.M. Diakonoff, *Hurrisch und Urartäisch,* Munich 1971, 147: ***kuru/o*** 'wieder', vgl. ***kur-*** 'zurückkehren'.[10]

---

du VIIe congrès de la F.I.E.C., Vol.II, Budapest 1983, 509.

[7] E. Peruzzi, *Le Iscrizioni Minoiche* (Atti dell' Accademia Toscana di Scienze e Lettere 24), Florence 1960, 32-128.

[8] F.W. Bush, *A grammar of the Hurrian language* (Brandeis University dissertation, Univ. Microfilms Inc.), Ann Arbor 1964, 239-240, sub 'particles exhibiting *-u/-o* stems'. E.A. Speiser, *Introduction to Hurrian, Annual of the American Schools of Oriental research 20 (1940-1941)*, New Haven 1941, 71, 73, 87-88, 91, 183-184, 214.

[9] E. Laroche, *Glossaire de la langue hourrite, Première partie* (A-L), *RHA 34 (1976)*, Paris 1978 and E. Laroche, *Glossaire de la langue hourrite, deuxième partie* (M-Z, Index), *RHA 35 (1977)*, Paris 1979 (reprint Paris 1980), 156.

[10] Cf. F.W. Bush, The relationship between the Hurrian suffixes *-ne/-na* and *-nni/e /-nna*, in: H.A. Hoffner Jr. (ed.), *Orient and Occident. Essays presented to Cyrus H. Gordon on the occasion of his sixty-fifth birthday* (AOAT 22), Kevelaer/Neukirchen -Vluyn 1973, 51^{91}: 'furthermore'.
Cf. M. Dietrich – W. Mayer, Beiträge zum Hurritischen (I), *Ugarit Forschungen 23 (1991)*, 107-126 (especially 116): 'weiter'. Cf. M. Dietrich – W. Mayer, Beiträge zum Hurritischen (II). Die Konjunctive in Mitanni-Hurritischen, *UF 24 (1992)*, 39-58 (esp. 47): 'weiter'. Cf. I. Wegner, *Einführung in die hurritische Sprache*, Wiesbaden 2007^2, 264: 'wieder, wiederum, fernerhin'.

Semantically the usage of Hurrian ***/kuro/*** 'again, in return' can be explained from the mechanism of the scribe's action of counting the numbers just written on the Linear A tablets and recording them *again* in the summation at the bottom, in the sense of: (here are the numbers) *again*, that is in total. The scribes needed a short word that could serve their purpose as the Linear B scribes used ***to-so*** and ***to-sa*** meaning 'so much / so many', which could in the context be perceived as 'so much / so many in total'.

C.H. Gordon offered not only a West Semitic interpretation of Linear A ***ku-ro***, but also of ***po-to-ku-ro***: "HT 122 has a total of 31 (***ku-ro*** 31) on the obverse, and another total of 65 (***ku-ro*** 65) on the reverse. The two totals are combined to form ***po-to-ku-ro*** 96 'grandtotal: 96' (Plate VIII). The meaning 'grandtotal' is fixed by context, but it remains to explain the first element ***po-to***. We know that the word for 'son' was pronounced ***bun-*** in Ugaritic. The feminine ****bunt-*** would become ***butt-*** (with ***nt*** > ***tt***). Tentatively we suggest that ***po-to-ku-ro*** stands for what would appear in Hebrew script as בת כל 'daughter of all' = 'grandtotal'. 'Son' and 'daughter' are often used as the first element of compound nouns in Semitic." [11] Though ingenious, Gordon's interpretation of Linear A ***po-to-ku-ro*** as 'daughter of all' = 'grandtotal' does not appear convincing. So if Hurrian ***kuru***, phonologically ***/kuro/***, with Hurrian ***o***-sound, is an exact phonological equivalent to Linear A ***ku-ro***, it is necessary to examine whether ***po-to-*** may also be interpreted as Hurrian, in particular since it has been established that Hurrian cuneiform ***ú*** represents [***u***] and Hurrian cuneiform ***u*** represents [***o***]. In the Tušratta letter (so in fact in the chancellery of the Royal Palace of *Waššukkanni*, where the letter was written) the orthographic conventions were allegedly strictly applied, but elsewhere the scribes seem to have paid less attention to the rules. Anyway Hurrian [***o***] was probably a close sound.

E. Laroche did not attempt to interpret the form *pu-ud-du-ú-uk-ki-a-šu-u-un-na-a-al-la-an*, Mit. III 60.[12] It is important to realize that double writing of consonants in medial position in cuneiform indicates that a consonant is voiceless (***-t-t-*** or ***-d-d-*** is [***t***]), whereas single writing in medial position shows that a consonant is voiced (so ***-t-*** or ***-d-*** is [***d***]). During the last thirty years much progress has been made. Chr. Girbal interprets Hurrian ***puttukki*** [Mit.] as ***puttu-*** 'Leistung', mit ***-kki***.[13] I. Wegner[14] mentions 'achievement'.

Cf. M. Giorgieri, Schizzo grammaticale della lingua hurrica, *Parola del Passato 55 (2000)*, 171-277 (especially 245): */kuro/u/* 'di nuovo, d'altra parte'.
Cf. G. Wilhelm, Die Absolutiv-Essiv-Konstruktion des Hurritischen, in: Y. Nishina (ed.), *Europa et Asia polyglotta – Sprachen und Kulturen* (Festschrift für Robert Schmitt-Brandt zum 70. Geburtstag), Dettelbach 2000, 199-208 (especially 201[6]).
Cf. D.R.M. Campbell, *Mood and modality in Hurrian*, Dissertation University of Chicago 2007, 35[48], 299, 314: *kur-o* 'again, subsequently'.
Th. Richter, *Bibliographisches Glossar des Hurritischen*, Wiesbaden 2012, 227, s.v. *kur-* III and *kuru* [Mit.].

11 C.H. Gordon, *Evidence for the Minoan language*, Ventnor, N.J. 1966, 27, sub 118.

12 E. Laroche, *Glossaire de la langue hourrite*, *RHA 34-35 (1976-1977)*, Paris 1978-1979 (reprint 1980), 208, s.v. *pu-ud-du-ú-uk-ki-a-šu-u-un-na-a-al-la-an*, Mit. III 60.

13 Chr. Girbal, Der Paragraph 24 des Mitanni-Briefes, *ZA 78 (1988)*, 130.

14 I. Wegner, Suffixaufnahme in Hurrian: Normal cases and special cases, in: F. Plank (ed.), *Double case. Agreement by Suffixaufnahme*, New York – Oxford 1995, 140.

M. Salvini[15] also mentions 'achievement'. M. Giorgieri[16] mentions 'Wert(?)' (***puttū-kki***) and I. Wegner[17] 'Leistung' in her *Einführung in die hurritische Sprache*, Wiesbaden 2007². Th. Richter, who refers to these publications, also mentions a possible relation with the root ***putt-*** II, that might be interpreted as 'ausheben, anwerben.[18]

With regard to a feasible meaning of ***po-to-*** in Linear A ***po-to-ku-ro*** M. Giorgieri's interpretation of 'value' for Hurrian ***puttu-*** 'Wert(?)' in *puttū-kki* would yield the meaning 'value again' for ***po-to-ku-ro***, which is in fact a concept that is expected in the context of the scribe's action of counting several items and giving the total results 'again' (first ***ku-ro***) and 'again' (second ***ku-ro***) and adding the two total numbers together providing 'the *value again*' (***po-to-ku-ro***) in the summation of the two totals. The notion 'value' is emphasized by the high numbers of men and commodities mentioned on both HT 122 and HT 131. This means that the sequence ***po-to-ku-ro*** or the sequences ***po-to ku-ro*** (HT 122b.6 and HT 131b.4) on these accounting tablets from Hagia Triada does or do not mean 'grand total' as most modern scholars had expected, but simply refer(s) to *the scribe's action of counting the results*. Incidentally, even if the scribe wrote *po-to-ku-ro* as one sequence, ***po-to-*** should in my view not be taken as a prefix, because Hurrian is only suffixing, but as a term that was so firmly connected with the usage of ***ku-ro*** that the scribe joined the two terms in one notion. If Linear A ***po-to-ku-ro*** can be identified with Hurrian ***puttu(-)kuru***, one thing is clear: Linear A ***kuro*** and Hurrian ***kuru, /ku-ro/***, is not a loan-word from another language, but a truly Hurrian adverb, when used without suffixes. Comparison with the related Hurrian verbal root ***kur-*** 'to return' and the parallels with Urartian leave no doubt about that.

A parallel example of bookkeeper's terminology is provided by the term 'sum', if used in the sense of 'total amount resulting from addition of items'. Through Middle English and Old French *summe, somme* it is derived from Latin *summa*, feminine of *summus*, 'highest, at the top'. The etymology of 'sum' can thus be explained from the bookkeeper's action of *placing the total amount* resulting from the addition of items *at the top of the page* instead of at the bottom. So the meaning of 'total amount' of the word 'sum' is secondary. The original meaning is 'at the top' and refers to the bookkeeper's action of putting the total number at the top where it can be seen at a glance. If Minoan scribes were not so much interested in using an abstract notion such as our word 'total', but rather focused on the action and result of counting, interpretation of Linear A *po-to-ku-ro* = Hurrian *puttu(-)kuru*, phonologically */po-to ku-ro/*, 'value again' makes sense in the simple conditions of scribal workshops. If this interpretation is accepted, it is a warning, how cautious one should be not to jump to conclusions too readily because of a seemingly obvious assumption. A. Kober's clever observation was only an indication with regard to the semantic sphere of the term *ku-ro* and should not have been taken too literally.

---

[15] M. Salvini, The earliest evidence of the Hurrians before the formation of the Reign of Mittanni, in: G. Buccellati – M. Kelly-Buccellati (ed.), *Urkesh and the Hurrians (Studies in honor of Lloyd Cotsen)*, Bibliotheca Mesopotamica 26, Malibu 1998,103.

[16] M. Giorgieri, Die Beschwörung der 8. Tafel des Šalašu-Rituals, *SCCNH 9 (1998)*, 76[13].

[17] I. Wegner, *Einführung in die hurritische Sprache*, Wiesbaden 2007², 274.

[18] Th. Richter, *Bibliographisches Glossar des Hurritischen*, Wiesbaden 2012, 334.

HT 122a. 1.]*ra-ri* , *u-de-za* 2
2.] 2 *da-si-85* or: *da-si* TAL 2 *pa-*
3. [.]-[.] [ ]-*di* 1 *te-ki* 2
4. *qa-63-i* 3 *ja-mi-da-re* 1
5. *si-da-re* 1 *so-di-ra* 1 *pa-de* 1
6. *ku-pa*$_3$*-nu* 1 *pa-ta-ne* 1 *83a-tu* 1
7. [.]-*du* 1 *ku-pa*$_3$*-nu* 1 *da-we-da* 1
8. *ku-ro* 31 *ku-da* 1

HT 122b.1. *je-di* , CAPSUS , VIR[
2. *83a-ki-ta*$_2$ 7 ' [
3. *a-ra-68* < , > *u-de-za* 2 *qa-qa-*
4. *ru* 2 *di* 2 *da-re* 2
4bis. vacat
5. *ku-ro* 65
6. *po-to-ku-ro* 96 [ ]
7. vacat

Sup. mut.
HT 131a. 1. FIC 62 *ku*[*-ro*
2. 353 *i-qa*
3. TAL GRA 58
4.] OLE 12 J *67* 12 JE

Sup. mut.
HT 131b.1.] ' ' [
2.] FIC 40 [ ]
3. [ ] OLIVA 2 VIN+*sa* [ ]
4. *po-to-ku-ro* 400[
5. 52 J [

HT 6a.1. *ka-pa* , *da-ta-ra*
2. , *te* , FIC, 15 *pi-ta-ja*
3. 24 *ja+ru* (or: *ru+ja*) DD *ma-3*
4. 10 *o-ra*$_2$*-di-ne* 2 *ka-*
5. *pa-qe* 5JE vacat
6. *da-qe-ra* , *qe-pi-ta*
7. 22JE FIC 15J |

HT 6b.1. *wa-du-ni-mi*
2. 3H *ra-ti-se* 1 *ma-*
3. *we-i-no* 3 ,
4. *du-da-ma* 68
5. *me-ki* 3E *sa-ma* 30
6. 5 *pa*$_3$*-ni-na* 17J |

Ad a.2: Punctuation after FIC likely accidental. Ad b.5: Raison-Pope: *me-ki*; *GORILA 1*: *da-ki*.

Linear A tablet Hagia Triada HT 6 (HM 8, 1902-1903) was found in the Villa of Hagia Triada as all tablets from HT 1 to HT 84 were found in that part of the Palace-complex. The other tablets from HT 85 onwards were found in the adjacent part called 'Casa del Lebete' by the Italian excavators. They probably date all from the destruction level at the end of Late Minoan I b.

I shall first discuss texts from Hagia Triada with the sequence ***ka-pa*** (HT 6a.1; HT 8b.4; HT 45a.1; HT 94a.1; HT 102.1; HT 105.1; HT 140.5). HT 6 begins with ***ka-pa*** followed by a word divider separating it from the following sequence ***da-ta-ra***. ***ka-pa*** could well be a toponym appearing in the heading of the text as so often happens with toponyms such as ***ko-no-so*** 'Knossos' and ***pu-ro*** 'Pylos' in the headings of the Linear B tablets from Knossos and Pylos, respectively. This observation may be confirmed by the fact that ***ka-pa*** is one of the Linear A sequences which occur relatively frequently, and what may well be significant, so far only in the Linear A texts from Hagia Triada.

In most cases it also appears as the first entry of the texts as here in HT 6a.1, and in HT 94a.1, HT 102.1, HT 105.1, and possibly in the heavily damaged HT 45a.1, where J. Raison - M. Pope, *Index transnuméré du linéaire A* (BCILL 11), read]*29-2*-[. It also occurs in HT 8b.4 and in HT 140.5. The entry of ***ka-pa*** in HT 94a.1 shows that it cannot refer to one person which excludes the possibility of ***ka-pa*** being a personal name, since it is here followed by the ideogram for VIR ('man') followed by the number 62, which probably means that 62 men are recorded with respect to ***ka-pa***.

Another indication that ***ka-pa*** may well represent a toponym in Linear A is that exactly the same sequence occurs in the Knossos Linear B texts reflecting a toponym as well: ***ka-pa*** (KN E 71). Incidentally, the identification of ***ka-pa*** as a toponym in Linear B does not depend on this tablet where the only entry is: ***ka-pa*** GRA[. The occurrence of the ethnic ***ka-pa-jo*** on another Knossos tablet (KN [X] 5752 + B 7039) proves conclusively the existence of the toponym from which the ethnic is derived. Therefore Linear B ***ka-pa*** has been included in a study on Cretan toponyms by M.V. Cremona, D. Marcozzi, A. Scafa and M. Sinatra, *La toponomastica cretese nei documenti in lineare B di Cnosso* (Incunabula Graeca LXIX), Roma 1978, 18, 28-29. They also point out that many Linear B toponyms are followed by the ideogram GRA: "Esaminando la serie E si osserva che generalmente l'ideogramma GRA è preceduto da indicazioni toponimiche: si potrebbe quindi supporre che anche ***ka-pa*** possa essere un toponimo. Nella tavoletta B 5752 troviamo attestata la forma ***ka-pa-jo***: ***ka-pa-jo / po*** VIR 3. Poiché alla sigla ***po*** (o alla 'scriptio plena' ***po-ku-ta***) si accompagna generalmente un' indicazione toponimica, ne consegue che ***ka-pa-jo*** può essere considerato un etnico. Mettendo a confronto questi due dati sembra dunque lecito ritenere che ***ka-pa*** sia un toponimo, di cui ***ka-pa-jo*** è il relativo etnico." The Linear B suffix ***-jo*** indicates the Greek ethnic suffix ***-yos***.

The observation by the four Italian scholars regarding a connection of Linear B toponyms with the ideogram GRA may be corroborated, if my join of]***-ka-ne*** (AK 3a.1) with ***a***] (AK 1b.1) on a tiny fragment from Arkhanes is correct (*GORILA 3* mentions that AK 1, AK 2 and AK 3 were inscribed by the same *scribe 1*), the resulting sequence ***a***]-***ka-ne*** (AK 3a.1 + AK 1b.1) GRA [represents exactly the toponym *Arkhanes*, where the Villa of Arkhanes was excavated by Yannis and Evi Sakellerakis and where the Linear A Arkhanes-tablets were found.

It corroborates the evidence that the habit of mentioning the place where the tablets were written (preferably at the beginning of a tablet) was probably inherited by the Linear B scribes from their Linear A colleagues. According to Linear A and B orthographic conventions ***-r-*** preceding an occlusive was not expressed in consonant clusters. Eventual final consonants were not expressed either.

The orthographic conventions of Linear B allow several possibilities to interpretion of ***ka-pa***. C.J. Ruijgh, for instance, suggests ***Σκάφᾱ*** for the toponym and ***Σκαφαῖος*** for the ethnic and mentions that *Σκάφη* is attested as a toponym by Suidas. He also refers to *σκάφη* 'bassin' and *σκαφή* 'action de fouir' (cf. C.J. Ruijgh, *EGM,* 227, § 194 and note 87). If, however, ***ka-pa*** in the Linear A texts from Hagia Triada and the Linear B texts from Knossos represents the same toponym, a non-Greek interpretation of the name may be feasible and even preferable. I propose to read ***Ḫalba*** which we know as the Hurrian and later the Hittite designation of 'Aleppo' in Syria, called ***Ḫalab*** in Semitic. It is theoretically possible that Hagia Triada had some overseas connections with Aleppo, the capital of the kingdom of *Yamḫad* in North Syria, whose rulers dominated the kingdoms of Mâri, Alalaḫ and Ugarit among others for a considerable time, or with another place called ***Ḫalba***, but I prefer to see in ***ka-pa*** the designation of the local Cretan toponym referring to Hagia Triada ('Holy Trinity') itself. If this hypothesis is accepted, we should at last have identified the ancient name of the Minoan palace that has yielded the largest number of Linear A texts to date. The Linear B toponym ***ka-pa*** could then be interpreted as ***Χάλβᾱ*** in Mycenaean Greek (= ***Ḫalba*** in Linear A), with correspondence of the Greek aspirate *χ-* [k^h] with the voiceless *initial* velar spirant ***ḫ-*** in the cuneiform syllabary and in alphabetic cuneiform of Ugarit. A voiceless velar spirant in *medial* position would be expressed by double writing ***-ḫḫ-*** in the cuneiform syllabary. Linear B ethnic ***ka-pa-jo*** on another Knossos tablet (KN [X] 5752 + B 7039) may then be ***Χάλβαῖος***. Another suggestion may be pertinent in this respect too. In the list of personal names on HT 6a we see ***ka-pa-qe*** in lines 4-5, if the Linear B phonetic values are applied. The same sequence can possibly be read in HT 140.3.

In 'Relations entre le linéaire B et le linéaire A' in *Études Mycéniennes, Actes du colloque international sur les textes mycéniens*, Gif-sur-Yvette 1956, 265, P. Meriggi remarked: "La langue paraît de type flexionnel. On a l'impression que ***-qe*** s'ajoute à la fin de certains mots (***ku-mi-na/ku-mi-na-qe***; ***ka-pa/ka-pa-qe***; ***sa-ro/sa-ro-qe***; etc.) avec valeur copulative, ce qui inclinerait peut-être, mais non nécessairement, vers l'idée d'une langue indo-européenne." M. Lejeune's reply (*ibidem*, 267) to this remark is pertinent in every respect: "Autre remarque, portant sur la méthode. L'identification d'une copule enclitique ***-qe*** serait, évidemment, d'un haut intérêt. Mais, d'abord, c'est supposer que la langue A a possédé des labiovélaires; il est tout aussi possible que les signes ****qa*** (= ***pa$_2$***) et ***qe*** de B, issus de l'écriture A, aient subi un ajustement au phonétisme grec à partir de valeurs, en A, dont le grec n'avait pas l'emploi. En second lieu, il faudrait que le contexte rendît évident que ce ***-qe***, en A, est une copule et non un suffixe ou une désinence."

It is clear that the sign ***qe*** in Linear B represented a labio-velar sound. It is also clear that Linear B needed its labio-velar signs to represent the labio-velar sounds of Mycenaean Greek. If, however, ***-qe*** in ***ka-pa-qe*** on HT 6a.4-5 represented an enclitic copulative, it would be inexplicable, why the whole list of sequences following ***da-ta-ra***, probably all indicating persons, fails to contain ***-qe*** as its final syllabic sign except ***ka-pa-qe***.

Interpreting final ***-qe*** in ***ka-pa-qe*** as a suffix in Linear A would then be much more feasible than the use of an enclitic copulative only in one item of the list.

In line with M. Lejeune, who had apparently already in 1956 serious doubts about an alleged labio-velar value of the Linear A signs which had a graphic identity with their Linear B counterparts, I propose to read the Linear A sign "***qe***" as a syllable beginning with a voiced velar spirant or fricative, represented by ***-ḫe(-)*** in syllabic cuneiform in medial and final position and in the cuneiform alphabet of Ugarit by ***ġ*** ***(ğ)***, cf. E. Laroche, *GLH,* Paris 1978-1979, 22-24. This sound shares at least the velar characteristics with the labio-velar sounds, which might explain why Linear B scribes may have adopted the Linear A signs with these sounds for the labio-velar series in Linear B. If my view is correct, the Linear A voiced velar spirant, conventionally written ***qe*** (as in Linear B), but in reality reflecting [***ġe***], and the Linear B labio-velar ***qe*** should certainly not be confused with cuneiform emphatic ***qe***. To prevent confusion it may be wise to change the conventional spelling of the Linear A "***q-***" signs officially into ***ḫ-*** signs in the future, see the Linear A grid (Volume I, Part I, page 6).

The voiceless velar spirants are represented in syllabic cuneiform by ***ḫ-*** in initial position, by double writing of ***-ḫḫ-*** in medial position and in alphabetic Ugaritic by ***ḫ*** in all positions.

E. A. Speiser (*Introduction to Hurrian,* New Haven 1941, 48-49, § 58): "In RŠ X 4.10 we find the frase ***tšb ḫlb-x*** which contains a reference to Teshub of Aleppo. [....] The adjectival form, on the other hand is found in the syllabary as ***Ḫalba-ḫi***, cf. J. Friedrich, *Analecta Orientalia 12,* 127, and add the Nuzi name ***Ḫalbaḫi***; cf. SAL *Ḫa-al-pa-ḫi* SMN 345 (= unpublished Nuzi texts, Semitic Museum, Harvard); SAL *Ḫal-pa-a-ḫi* SMN 352. If we take alphabetic ***x*** in the all but generally accepted value of ***ġ*** (voiced velar spirant), the equation ***ḫlb-ġ*** = ***Ḫalba-ḫi*** will satisfy perfectly the phonetic requirements as well as the context." Now the value ***ġ*** in the alphabetic syllabary of Ugarit is generally accepted, but E.A. Speiser (*IH*, 49, § 59) had provided the pertinent evidence: "The independent testimony of RŠ material supports, therefore, the evidence of the syllabary based on the differences between ***-ḫ-*** and ***-ḫḫ-***. These two forms may now be equated with their respective alphabetic equivalents. Single ***ḫ*** in intervocalic position corresponds to alphabetic ***ġ***, as is shown by ***Ḫalbaḫi*** = ***ḫlbġ*** and ***Lubtuḫi*** = ***lbtġ***. Accordingly, intervocalic ***-ḫḫ-*** should appear in RŠ as ***ḫ***. This equation may now be illustrated by a convincing pair of instances. Alongside syllabic ***turuḫḫi(na)*** 'male' and ***aštuḫḫi(na)*** 'female' we get alphabetic ***trḫn*** and ***astḫn*** (RŠ X 4. 55ff). We see, incidentally, that the double writing of the main syllabary has the same purpose in the case of the velars that has previously been noted with the stops, ***s***, ***z*** and ***f***, ***v***: it signifies lack of voice, while single writing marks the respective voiced sound."

If the voiceless velar spirants in Linear A could be represented by the ***k***-series, Linear A ***ka-pa-qe*** can be equated with the ethnic ***Ḫalbaḫe*** in the main cuneiform syllabary and ***ḫlbġ*** in the cuneiform alphabet from Ugarit, meaning 'Man from Ḫalba' with the Hurrian ethnic suffix ***-ḫi/-ḫe***, [***ġe***]. E. Laroche (*GLH*, 22): "Il est légitime, par example, d'interpréter comme ethnique un nom en ***-ḫi/ḫe***, ..." *Ibidem* (p. 90) s.v. ***Ḫalba***: Alep: 1. La métropole syrienne. Nom. ***uru*** ***Ḫal-pa***, KBo XIX 135 III 8. Dat. *uruḪal-pa-(a)-pa,* KUB XLV 84 Ro 13; XLVII 101 IV 5; 2. Ethnique *Ḫalbaḫi* 'Alépin', Sg. *uruḪal-pa-a-ḫi,* KBo VII 61,3.- Pl. *uruḪal-pa-ḫi-n*[*a*], KBo VIII 147,2. - Nom d'homme *Ḫalpaḫi, NH* No. 253. Nom.*m* *Ḫal-pa-ḫi-iš* KBo III 3 IV 4,7 = KUB XIX 44 IV 4,7; 3. Tešub de Ḫalpa, près d'Ugarit. Cf. E. Laroche, *Les Noms des Hittites,* Paris 1966, 273: ***Ḫalbaḫi*** 'Alépin', ethnique hourrite en ***-ḫi***.

E. Laroche assumes that there may have been more than one place called *Ḫalba* in the Near East as he infers from the equation of the Semitic pantheon of Ugarit of *El - Dagan - Baᶜal du Ḫazi/ Ṣapôn* with the Hurrian of *El - Kumarbi - Tešub Ḫalbaḫi*, cf. E. Laroche, 'Notes sur le panthéon hourrite de Ras Shamra', *JAOS 88.2 (1968),* 149-150: "P 2-4, de son côté, énumère *El - Dagan - Baᶜal du Ḫazi/Ṣapôn.* Cela nous ramène à 166 §§ II-III: *El - Kumarbi - Tešub Ḫalbaḫi* et nous invite à conclure que *Kumarbi* = *Dagan* et que *Tešub Ḫalbaḫi* n'est pas le dieu d'Alep, mais celui de Ḫalba du 'Ḫazi/Ṣapôn', conformément à une notice précédemment connue."

I am not convinced that the equation of *Tešub Ḫalbaḫi* with *Baᶜal of Ḫazi/Ṣapôn* implies that there must have been another place *Ḫalba of* '*Ḫazi/Ṣapôn*' to be distinguished from the great city of Aleppo, since the equation could merely refer to the identity of the gods *Tešub of Aleppo* and *Baᶜal of Ḫazi/Ṣapôn.* Equally, if 'Zeus of Olympia' were compared with 'Iupiter of Rome', this would not imply that Olympia and Rome were the same. On the other hand, E. Laroche is right in pointing to the phenomenon that the same or similar toponyms often occur more than once. If the identification of ***ka-pa-qe*** is right and if it should be read as an ethnic name ***Ḫalbaḫe*** or as a personal name derived from the ethnic, it would be the Linear A equivalent to Linear B ***ka-pa-jo***.

If the equation of *ka-pa-qe* with *Ḫalbaḫi* is right, the other sequences mentioned in 1956 by P. Meriggi at Gif-sur-Yvette may be reviewed as well: Could ***-qe*** in Linear A ***sa-ro / sa-ro-qe*** and ***ku-mi-na / ku-mi-na-qe*** have the same or a similar function as ***-qe*** in ***ka-pa / ka-pa-qe*** ? In other words, could ***sa-ro*** be a toponym and ***sa-ro-qe*** an ethnic derived from it, and could ***-qe*** in ***ku-mi-na-qe*** be a suffix indicating an adjectival form of the noun ***ku-mi-na***, if it can be equated with Linear B ***ku-mi-no = κύμῖνον*** 'cumin' ? All answers are affirmative: ***sa-ro*** may very well be a toponym. The Hurrian suffix ***-ḫe*** has an adjectival function in general and can indicate an ethnic in particular. The special aspect of the ethnic suffix is probably derived from the general suffix for the adjective (cf. E.A. Speiser, *IH*, 45, § 56). I shall discuss these forms *infra*, but it may be wise first to continue with other sequences in HT 6.

In the 2016 edition of *Minoan Linear A*, Vol. I, Part I, 70-71, I had mentioned that J.C. Billigmeier (An inquiry into the non-Greek names on the Linear B tablets from Knossos and their relationship to languages of Asia Minor, *Minos 10 (1969)*, 177-183) refers for his identification of Linear A ***da-ta-ra*** (HT 6a.1) as a Lycian name (or a name related to Lycian) to J. Sundwall, *Die einheimischen Namen der Lykier nebst einem Verzeichnisse kleinasiatischer Namenstämme* (Klio. Beiträge zur alten Geschichte, Beiheft XI), Leipzig 1913, 65: ***Δωταρι***, gen.: ***Δωταρις***. Sundwall listed the name elements used by Lycians and their neighbours and abstracted in most cases the roots from the hellenized versions of names appearing in Hellenistic or Roman inscriptions.

Incidentally, L. Zgusta (*Kleinasiatische Personennamen*, Prague, 1964, 156, § 317) mentions s.v. ***Δωταρι***: Pisidia: *Δωταρι Μοσητως*; *Ειη Δωτ*[*α*]*ρις* (Gen.); *Δωταριε Νεις* (Dat. ?), *ArOr 25*, 1957, 608, Nr 1 (epich.). In the 1st millennium B.C. *Πισιδία* (Pisidia) bordered Caria to the west, Lycia to the south, Cilicia to the east and Lycaonia and Phrygia to the north. The land of the Luwians (the *Lukka*-lands) of the 2nd millennium B.C. was no doubt considerably more extensive than Lycia proper was in the 1st millennium B.C.

Remarkably the name of the region *Pisidia* in southern Anatolia seems cognate with that of the village *Πιτσίδια* (Pitsídia) near Kommos and Matala and the palaces of Hagia Triada and Phaistos in southern Crete.

In my view there is now sufficient evidence to cast doubt on identification of Linear A ***da-ta-ra*** (HT 6a.1) and of ***da-ta-re*** (HT 88.6) with Pisidian or Lycian ***Δωταρι*** from the first millennium B.C. or with a postulated Luwian name from the second millennium B.C.

In the 2016 edition I suggested that ***da-ta-ra*** might be a name built on the Hurrian onomastic element ***tant***, cf. P.M. Purves, *NPN*, 262, s.v. ***tant***: e.g. ***Tantakai̯a*** (wr. *Ta-an-ta-qa-a-a*), ***Tantau̯a*** (wr. *Ta-an-ta-ú-a, Ta-ta-ú-a*), ***Tantei̯a***, (wr. *Ta-an-te-ia, Da-an-te-a, Ta-an-ti-ia, Ta-an-te-e-a, Ta-an-te-e, Ta-an-te-a, Ta-a-an-te-ia*).

I think that it is theoretically possible to assume that the form ***Tantei̯a*** is derived from an alleged < *{*tan=d-tei̯a*} 'Tešub celebrates (a festival)', with the root + root-extension ***tan=d-*** 'to celebrate (a festival)', but it is not necessary to assume root + root-extension ***tan=d-*** to explain the personal name ***Tantei̯a***, because ***Tantei̯a*** can be analysed as {*tan-tei̯a*} 'Make / Create (the boy), oh Tešub !' (*Tei̯a* is hypocoristic of *Tešub*), with athematic *imperative* ***tan-***; the personal name ***Tan-atal*** (wr. *ta-na-ta-al*) from Tigunāni, analysis {*tan-adal*}, typology 1.4, lexicon *tan-*, *adal*, has in fact a similar athematic *imperative* formation, but is this time translated as an *indicative* formation by Th. Richter (*VHN*, 297): 'Der Starke machte (Jungen)' ['The strong one made / created (the boy)'].

This root + root-extension ***tan=d-*** is known from the Old Hurrian form ***tan=d=i=b*** (wr. *da-a-an-ti-ip*) in the Hurrian-Hittite bilingual ***Kirenze*** (KBo 32: 13 Vs. 10). To illustrate the context of ***tan=d=i=b*** I quote the transliterated passage (KBo 32: 13 Vs. 8-11) from I. Wegner, *Einführung*, 207 (cf. E. Neu, *StBoT 32*, 220):

8. .... *ḫi-im-za-at-ḫu-u-ši*
9. ᴰ*A-al-la-a-ni* ᴰIM-*up-pa bi-du-úw-wa*$_a$ *a-wi*$_i$*-ta*
10. *e-la wa*$_a$*-aḫ-ru-ša da-a-an-ti-ip ne-ek-ri*
11. *e-še-ni-we*$_e$ ᴰ*A-al-la-a-ni*

The morpheme-analysis (I. Wegner, *ibidem*; cf. E. Neu, StBoT 32, 467):

8. .... *ḫemz=a=tḫ=oš=i*
9. ᴰ*Allani* ᴰ*Teššup=va pid=uff=a av(i)=i=da*
10. *el(i)=a faḫr=o=š(e)=a tan=d=i=b negri*
11. *eše=ne=ve* ᴰ*Allani*

I have rendered her German translation into English (*ibidem*, 207-208; cf. E. Neu, *StBoT 32*, 220; St. de Martino, *PdP*, 304-307):

8. .... She girded herself
9. Allani ('the Lady') (and) for the Stormgod she turned (danced ?).
10. She celebrated a good festival, the bolt
11. of the earth, Allani.

I have used I. Wegner's commentary (*Einführung*, 209-210), cf. Neu, *StBoT 32*, 244f.:

8. ***ḫemz=a=tḫ=oš=i*** corresponding with Hittite *išḫuzii̯ait* (wr. *iš-ḫu-zi-i̯a-it*) 'She girded herself': ***ḫemz-*** 'to bind, gird oneself' + root-extensions ***a*** + ***tḫ*** + suffix ***oš*** indicating perfect or past tense + marker of transitivity ***i***.

9. ***Allani*** 'the Lady' from ***Allai*** 'Lady'. She is in this case not an epithet to *Ḫebat* or *Ištar-Šauška*, but a deity in her own right, 'the Lady of the Nether World'.

She is in that respect comparable with *Kore* (*Κόρη*) 'Girl, Virgin Daughter', common name of the Pre-Greek goddess *Persephone* (*Περσεφόνη, Φερσεφόνη, Περσέφασσα, Περσέφαττα*), daughter of *Demeter* and carried off by *Hades* to rule with him the world of the dead. ^{D}*Allani* (in the *absolutive* case) is subject of the *antipassive* sentence ^{D}*Allani ḫemz=a=tḫ=oš=i* 'the goddess Allani girded herself'.
^{D}***Teššup=va***, name of the Stormgod ***Teššub*** + dative-suffix ***-wa***, phonologically ***/-va/.***
pid=uff=a from ***pid-*** 'to turn (oneself)', probably in the sense of 'to dance' + root-extension ***upp-*** */uff/* (see also I. Wegner, *Einführung*, 89). ***pid=uff=a*** corresponds with Hittite ***weḫatta*** (wr. *ú-e-ḫa-at-ta*), present 3rd pers. sing. med. (root ***weḫ-/waḫ-*** 'to turn').
av(i)=i=da, postposition 'for', refers to the dative ^{D}***Teššup=va***. It corresponds with Hittite *peran* (wr. *pé-ra-an*). The postposition (itself a *directive* form in ***-da***) is always connected with a *dative* or *directive*.
10. ***el(i)=a*** from ***eli-*** 'festival, feast' + *essive* in ***-a***. Theme-vowel ***-i-*** disappears, if *essive* appears. ***el(i)=a*** corresponds with EZEN$_4$-*an* in Hittite text. ***faḫr=o=š(e)=a*** consists of ***faḫr(i)-*** 'good' + derivational vowel ***o*** + adjective-forming morpheme ***š(e)*** + *essive* ***-a***. ***faḫr=o=š(e)=a*** corresponds with Hittite *šanizzin* (wr. *ša-ni-iz-zi-in*).
tan=d=i=b consists of ***tan-*** 'to make' + unclear morpheme ***t*** (phonologically ***/d/***) + marker of transitivity ***i*** + Old Hurrian suffix ***b*** marking the 3rd person singular. Verbal forms in ***=i=b*** allow no object in the *absolutive* case. If an object is mentioned, it is in an oblique case, as here in the *essive* in ***-a***; cf. for *el(i)=a faḫr=o=š(e)=a tan=d=i=b* also I.Wegner, *Einführung*, 122, sub *antipassive* d. The formant ***-t-*** also occurs in Urartian verbal forms, cf. M. Salvini, *SMEA 29*, 1992, 217 ff. The Hurrian sentence ***el(i)=a faḫr=o=š(e)=a tan=d=i=b*** corresponds with Hittite *nu šanizzin* EZEN$_4$-*an iet* (wr. *i-e-et*).
negri '(wooden beam of) bolt', *absolutive* singular.
11. ***eše=ne=ve*** consists of ***eše*** 'earth' + so-called singular article ***ne*** + *genitive* suffix ***ve***. ^{D}***Allani*** 'Goddess *Allani*' in absolutive. The Hurrian sentence ***negri eše=ne=ve*** ^{D}***Allani***, corresponding with Hittite *tagnaš ḫattalwaš tagnaš* ^{D}UTU-*uš* (wr. *ták-na-a-aš ḫa-at-tal-wa-aš ták-na-a-aš* ^{D}UTU-*uš*) 'Die Sonnengöttin der Erde an den Riegeln (Datif Plural) der Erde' (cf. E. Neu, *StBoT 32*, 221) ['The Sun-Goddess of the earth on the bolts (plural *dative*) of the earth'], does grammatically not entirely correlate with the Hittite passage; ***negri eše=ne=ve*** is epithet to ^{D}***Allani***, not a local definition as in the Hittite phrase. Since ***negri*** is a singular *absolutive* form, "Suffixaufnahme" does not occur in the attributive *genitive* ***eše=ne=ve***, because the singular *absolutive* does not have a case-ending. In order to reach more agreement between the Hurrian and Hittite passages, I. Wegner proposes to translate the Hittite phrase as 'The Sun-Goddess of the earth, (the Goddess) of the bolts of the earth', so that *ḫattalwaš* would in this case become a "freely floating" genitive. Hittite *tekan/takn-* (neuter) means 'earth'. Before the Hurrian-Hittite bilingual ***Kirenze*** (KBo 32) was published, one assumed that Hurrian ***eše*** meant 'heaven' and ***ḫaburni / ḫawurni*** 'earth', cf. e.g. E. Laroche, *GLH*, 83-84, s.v. ***eše*** 'ciel': ***eše-ḫaburni*** correspond au hit. AN-***iš*** KI-***paš*** ou ***nebi daganzipas*** des listes divines; cf. Von Brandenstein, *ZA 46*, 85 sq. [...] Thèmes ***eše*** 'ciel' et ***eše-ni*** 'le ciel', etc.; cf. for the old (now obsolete) interpretation of ***ḫaburni / ḫawurni*** e.g. E. Laroche, *GHL*, 99, s.v. ***ḫawurni*** 'terre'. Mot uni et opposé à ***eše*** 'ciel', avec ou sans déterminatif divin; par. ex. ^{d}***e-še-ḫa-bu-ur-ni***, KBo XI 5 I 21. ***ḫaburni / ḫawurni*** is now interpreted as 'heaven'.

However remarkable and confusing it may be in view of the convictions of most scholars in the past, the meanings of ***eše*** and ***ḫaburni / ḫawurni*** have been swapped completely, since the bilingual ***Kirenze*** was published.

Because of the allophonic character of Hurrian consonants I have paid more attention to the existence of the root ***tan-*** + root-extention ***-d-***, especially in Old Hurrian. The orthography of ***da-a-an-ti-ip*** in the bilingual ***Kirenze*** may be suggestive with regard to Linear A ***da-ta-ra*** (HT 6a.1) and of ***da-ta-re*** (HT 88.6), but, as we have seen, the analysis of the sequence yields ***tan=d=i=b*** (with voiced /*d*/), since it is assumed that voicing occurred under influence of the nasal ***-n-***. Of course, we cannot be sure about the degree of voicing of the second dental in ***tan=d=i=b***, because cuneiform orthography of consonant clusters is not conclusive in this respect. We only know that the Linear A forms ***da-ta-re*** and ***da-ta-ra*** show a voiced initial dental ***d-*** and a voiceless second dental ***-t-***.

However, there are other arguments why another Hurrian root appears preferable to ***tan=d***. It is more likely that Linear A ***da-ta-re*** and ***da-ta-ra*** contain the verbal root ***tad- / tatt-*** which is very frequent in personal names.

A. Draffkorn (*HHA*, 55-56) mentioned ***Tat(t)e*** (wr. *ta-at-te*) from Alalaḫ IV (194: 12), which she interpreted as hypocoristic (< *Tad-te*), and ***ᶠTat(t)eya*** (wr. **ᶠTa-at-te-e-ya*), son of Yarim-Lim (?) from Alalaḫ VII (*11:2, 12, 20), which she interpreted as hypocoristic (< *Tad-teya*). She may well be right in both cases, because ***-te*** and ***-teya*** are very frequent hypocoristic forms of ***-teš(š)ub*** in Hurrian personal names, but Th. Richter (*VHN*, 533-534) has a point assuming that the very frequent notion ***tatti*** may well be equated with ***tadi*** 'Liebe' ['love'] and that it may in onomastics mean 'Liebling' ['Beloved one, darling']. He translates ***ᶠAkap-tati*** as 'Der Liebling (das neugeborenes Mädchen) kam herauf (?)' ['The darling (the newborn girl) appeared (?)'] and ***ᶠTaka-tati*** as 'Sei (oder: werde) schön, oh Liebling !' ['Be (or: become) beautiful, oh darling !']. In that case the assumption of a diminutive ***tadakki*** {*tad(i)=a(=)kki*} is also plausible in ***ᶠTatakka***(?).

Th. Richter (*VHN*, 533-534), s.v. ***tad- / tatt-***, confirmed that starting from the variant ***ta-at-t °*** for ***tadubadi*** one may assume that other forms in ***tatt-*** may be connected as well. In accordance with the function of the morpheme-group ***°=o=bade*** one may understand ***tadubadi*** (as well as *ta-at-tu-ba-di*) as 'ungeliebt' ['not loved']. According to I. Wegner (*Einführung*, 59-60 and 137: sub E 'Old Hurrian') the suffix-combination ***-ubad-*** in expressions such as ***naḫḫ=ubad(e)=uš*** 'nicht besiedelt' ['not inhabited'], ***kul=ubad=e*** 'nicht genannt' ['not mentioned'], ***faḫr=ubad=e*** 'ungut' ['not good'] or ***nir=ubad=e*** 'ungut, schlecht' ['not good, bad'] (Ugarit-Vocabulary RS 94-2939, col. V 11', published by B. André-Salvini - M. Salvini, in *SCCNH 9*, 1998, 3 ff. and 14) may be segmented into ***-uw(a)+ade*** and ***-uw(a)*** may reflect the morpheme ***-wa-*** indicating negation. The Tušratta letter, however, also offers abstract forms in ***-ubad-*** without an apparent negative meaning (cf. I. Wegner, Die "genannten" und die "nicht-genannten" Götter in den hethitisch-hurritischen Opferlisten, *Studi micenei ed egeo-anatolici 36 (1995)*, 97 ff.).

The variant root ***tatt-*** occurs frequently: e.g. ***Tattip-papni*** (wr. *ta-at-ti-ip-pa-ap-ni*), at Nuzi (cf. I.J. Gelb, *NPN*, 150), analysis {*tatt=i=b-fabni*} < {*tatt=i=b-pab(a)=ni*}, 'The mountain, it loves the child'. Th. Richter (*VHN*, 533-534); ***ᶠTattiri*** (wr. *ᶠta-at-te-ri*), {*tatt=i=ri*} (Ekalte: WVDOG 192, 75: 19).

Th. Richter also refers (*VHN*, 533, note 789) to a comparable verbal root ***tid-*** 'to attack' that also occurs as ***titt-*** (cf. *BGH*, 464), which may well be significant for the interpretation of Linear A ***ti-ti-ku*** (2 times) and ***ti-ti-ku-ni*** that will be discussed later.

In *Minoan Linear A*, Vol. II: *Corpus of transliterated Linear A texts*, Part I, 17-18, I read (with J. Raison - M. Pope) ***a-si-da-to|-n̲o̲*** (AK 2.2-3) from Arkhanes, but now I think that ***a-si-da-to|-i̲*** (with *GORILA*) is the better reading. Linear A signs ***100a = i*** and ***100b = no*** are similar and can sometimes be confused. It may not be accidental that the Minoan scribe of AK 2 wrote the personal names ***a-si-da-to|-i̲*** (AK 2.2-3) and ***a-su-pu-wa*** (AK 2.5) on the same tablet. He must have been aware of the etymological identity of the first elements of these names. If *GORILA*'s reading of ***-i̲*** in ***a-si-da-to|-i̲*** is correct, the orthographic representation of the element ***-da-to|-i̲*** resembles that of ***a-si-su-po-a*** (KH 9.1), which means that the ending probably represents the sing. genitive suffix ***-wi/-we*** and sing. dative ***-wa***, respectively. This way of writing in Linear A reminds us of cuneiform usage, where the genitive ***-wi/-we*** is, especially after ***-o/u-***, often written as ***-ú-e*** and the dative ***-wa*** as ***-ú-a***: e.g. the genitive KUR *Lu-lu-ú-e*, Nuzi; cf. Lacheman, *BASOR 78*, 22 f; Speiser, *IH*, 51 ff., 89, etc.; cf. E. Laroche, *GLH*, 161, s.v. *Lullu*, pays au Nord-Est de la Mésopotamie. Cf. also *attai-fe* 'my father' and the genitive: *at-ta-iw-wu-ú-e*, Mit. III 35, 37, 71; and the dative: *at-ta-iw-wu-ú-a*, Mit. III 68.

A-si-da-to|-i̲ is ***Azzi-datt=(i>)o/u=(w)i*** or ***Azzi-datt=(a>)o/u=(w)i***, *genitive* (perhaps in the sense of *matronymic*) of the *absolutive* Hurrian ****Azzi-datti*** 'The woman is a darling' or ****Azzi-datt(i)=a*** 'The woman is like a darling', since ***o/u*** in ***-to-*** in ***a-si-da-to|-i̲*** is probably due to ***-w-*** of the *genitive* ***-wi***. The Hurrian feminine personal name ***Allai-tatta*** (wr. ^{f}*Al-la-i-ta-at-ta*) at Nuzi, ***/Allai-datta/*** because of single writing of the first dental, is semantically a parallel to ****Azzi-datta***. ***Azzi*** 'woman' is semantically close to ***allay*** 'lady'. Other names with the element ***-tatta*** (phonologically ***/datta/***) are the names from Nippur ***Ir-me/mi-ta-at-ta*** and ***Ir-me-ta-ta***, Clay, *PNCP*, 93, to be read ***Erme/i-tatta*** (according to P.M. Purves, *NPN*, 263, s.v. *tatt*), i.e. ****Erwi-tatta*** at Nuzi. Cf. also ***Ta-at-ta***, *ibid.*, 138, and ***Ta-ad-du*** at Nuzi, as well as ***˹ta˺-ad-du*** at Boğazköy KUB XXVII 42 obv. 15, 16.

Although the variants ***Ir-me/mi-ta-at-ta*** and ***Ir-me-ta-ta*** from Nippur had made it quite clear that the roots ***tad-*** 'to love' and ***tatt-*** could probably be brought together, my hesitations completely disappeared after publication of Th. Richter's *Vorarbeiten zu einem hurritischen Namenbuch*, Erster Teil, 2016. In *BGH*, 2012, 451, s.v. ***tad-*** [*passim*] he had already casually referred to the variant ***tatt-***, discussed in his Ergänzungen zum hurritischen Wörterbuch, *Altorientalische Forschungen 34 (2007)*, 92[60]. Cuneiform ***tatt-*** may well be significant for the orthography of Linear A ***da-ta-ra*** (HT 6a.1) and of ***da-ta-re*** (HT 88.6), of which the second dental is voiceless, whereas in ***da-du-ma-ta*** (HT 95a.1), ***da-d̲u̲-te*** (HT 34.1) and ***da-du-mi-ne*** (KN Zf 31) the second dental is voiced as in ***tad-***.

I. Wegner (*Einführung*, 88) offers s.v. the *factitive* or *iterative* root-extension ***-ar-*** the examples ***tad=ar-*** 'to love', ***šid=ar-*** 'to curse'; cf. also Th. Richter, *BGH*, 451, s.v. ***tad-*** [*passim*] and ***tad=ar-*** 'lieben'. The Linear A personal name ***da-ta-re*** (HT 88.6), analysed as {*d/tatt=ar=e/i*}, means 'Love again and again !' and consists of the root ***d/tad- / d/tatt-*** 'to love' (frequent in onomastics) + *factitive* or *iterative* root-extension ***-ar-*** + *imperative* 2nd person singular in ***-e/i***, cf. I. Wegner, *Einführung*, 103-104 and Table 9: *The order of suffixes of the positive jussive.*

If Linear A ***da-ta-ra*** (HT 6a.1) is likewise explained and analysed as *{d/tatt=ar=a}*, the form would be intransitive and can perhaps be translated as 'Be loving / Be a loving person again and again !'

Cuneiform ***fTattiri*** (wr. *fta-at-te-ri*), Ekalte: WVDOG 192, 75: 19, is analysed as *{tatt=i=ri}* by Th. Richter (see *supra*), can in principle also be analysed differently as *{tatt=ir=i}*, if we assume that it contains a root-extension ***-ir-*** as mentioned by I.Wegner (*Einführung*, 89, s.v. root-extension ***-ir-***). She tells that the meaning of ***-ir-*** is not yet clear and gives one example: ***maz=ir=i*** (from root ***maz-*** 'helfen' ['to help']), but adds at once that this rare root-extension cannot easily be distinguished from the participial formant ***=i=ri***, cf. *ibidem*, 21 and 113 (sub 5.8), e.g. ***tab=i=ri*** 'der, der gießt, (Metall)gießer' ['someone who casts (metal, copper), coppersmith']. If ***fTattiri*** (wr. *fta-at-te-ri*) is analysed as *{tatt=i=ri}*, as Th. Richter does, the name means 'someone who loves'.

Th. Richter mentions (*VHN*, 533) in his discussion on the personal name ***ta-da-ra*** (Pruzsinsky 2003/1, 240[152]) that it remains uncertain, how we must understand the intransitive forms. *Ibidem* (note 788) he remarks that ***tá-da-ar-ri***, attested at Emar (Pruzsinsky 2003/2, 767), and ***ta-da-ra*** may well only be harmonized on the assumption of a participle ****tadari*** *{tad=a=ri}*, cf. ***tiwarri*** for a comparable formation.

If the evidence for identification of ***ka-pa*** with the toponym ***Ḫalba*** as the ancient Hurrian-Minoan name of Hagia Triada is accepted, it is also attractive to identify the second sequence in the heading ***da-ta-ra*** (HT 6a.1) with ***ta-da-ra*** (R. Pruzsinsky, *Die Personennamen der Texte aus Emar* (*SCCNH 13*, Bethesda 2003/1, 240[152]; Th. Richter, *VHN*, 533, n. 788), so that the tablet starts with registration of place and date (month), which may be expected in a bureaucratic environment. The difference of Linear A ***da-ta-ra*** with cuneiform ***ta-da-ra*** is that the Linear A form contains ***d/tatt-***, whereas the cuneiform example contains ***d/tad-*** 'to love'. Th. Richter has, however, shown that ***tad-*** and ***tatt-*** are essentially equal, cf. Th. Richter, *VHN*, 533, s.v. ***tad-/tatt-***.

Apart from analysis of Linear A ***da-ta-ra*** (HT 6a.1) as *{d/tatt=ar=a}*, explained as intransitive form and translated as 'Be loving / Be a loving person again and again !', which would indeed be quite acceptable for a personal name, or analysis as a participle *{d/tatt=a=r(i)a}*, other explanations must be considered, if ***da-ta-ra*** reflects the name of a month. If Linear A ***da-ta-ra*** is the *comitative* (in ***-ra***) of the divine name ***DTatta***, the marking of the month could reflect 'With ***DTatta/Datta***'. Usage of theonyms in names of months is not unusual, cf. in Roman society *mensis Martius* (Mars), *mensis Iunius* (Iuno).

Linear A ***ta-ta*** (KH 7a.3) at Khania can *prima facie* be compared with the Hurrian personal name ***Tatta*** (wr. *ta-at-ta*) from Mari and Tuttul, and with ***fTatta*** from Mari, analysis *{tatt=a=Ø}*, typology 1.1.1.3.3, lexicon *tad-*, that can be interpreted as a verbal one-word name (*intransitive indicative*) 'He/She is loving' or (*imperative*) 'Be loving ! / Be lovely !' But if it represents a noun in the *essive* form (in ***-a***) of ***tadi / tatti*** 'love', it can be translated as '(He/She is born) like a darling', cf. Th. Richter, *VHN*, 301, s.v. ***Tatta***. Cf. for ***Tatta*** at Mari also J.M. Sasson, Ḫurrians and Ḫurrian names in the Mari texts, *UF 6 (1974)*, 370 and 386: *Ta-at-ta* SY B:v:55, and *Ta-at-ta-a* SY B:iii:73.

The name ***Tatta*** is also embedded in the onomastics of Boğazköy, for instance, as that of a priest of the god of the clouds (LÚ ^{d}U/IM): abs. nom. dat. ^{m}*Ta-(a)-at-ta-(as/an/ti),* KUB VII 22, 3, 11; XXVIII 45 VI 4; XXX 68 Vo 4, and as that of the father of a scribe: abs. ^{m}*Ta-at-ta*, XV 31 IV 41, cf. E. Laroche, *NH,* 181, n° 1301. Names of the type *Kaka, Gaga, Kiki, Kuku, Lala, Lili, Lulu, Mama, Nana, Nini, Nunu, Papa, Baba, Tata, Dada, Tete, Didi, Tutu, Dudu* and *Zuzu* belong according to E. Laroche (*NH*, 240) to the so-called 'Lallnamen'.

However, Hurrian ***Tatta*** is not only a personal name. If Linear A ***ta-ta*** (KH 7a.3) is equated with the Hurrian divine name ^{D}***Tatta***, it corroborates my identification of the sequence ***e-na-si*** (KH 7a.2) in the preceding line as ***ennaše/ši***, that was formerly (e.g. by E. Laroche, *GHL*, 80-82, s.v. ***eni*** 'dieu') analysed as ***en(i)=na=še/ši*** (with plural genitive suffix ***-še / -ši***) = 'of the gods': *e-en-na-a-še*, KUB XXXII 46, 15; KBo XI 19 Vo 15; *e-en-na-a-ši*, KUB XLV 21 bg 1, etc.

In modern literature the plural genitive form is more precisely analysed as ***en(i)=na=aš=(w)e/i***, since it can be proved on the basis of evidence from Nuzi, that ***ennaše/ši*** consists of the root ***en(i)*** + the suffix of the so-called plural definite article ***-na-*** + the pluralizing suffix ***-aš-*** + the genitive suffix ***-we / -wi***. At Nuzi forms such as ***attanašwe*** (cf. E. Laroche, *GLH*, 64: *Attana, attanašwe*, nom d'un mois à Nuzi et à Alalaḫ; cf. *CAD* A II 510; *AW* 87) 'of the fathers' are attested, where ***w*** of the genitive suffix ***-we / -wi*** is preserved, whereas elsewhere ***w*** following ***š*** disappeared in plural genitive forms. According to Th. Richter (*BGH*, 67) the first month at Alalaḫ VII ***attana*** (cf. also ***attannatim*** {*atta(i)=nn(i)=ade*} at Alalaḫ IV), September / October, can be compared with the 7th month at Nuzi ***attanašwe***. He analyses the name of the month ***Attana*** as {*atta(i)=na*} and translates it as 'The fathers', which is in accordance with ***Attanašwe***, analysed as {*attan(i)=n(a)=až=ve*} by G. Wilhelm (*Das Archiv des Šilwa-Teššup*. Heft 3: *Rationenlisten 2*, Wiesbaden 1985, 84) and as {*atta(i)=na=aš=we*} by J.-P. Vita (Zur Menologie und zum Kalender von Alalaḫ, *AoF 27 (2000)*, 298) that can be translated as '(Month) of the fathers'.

E. Laroche assumed that the stem ***Tatta*** or ***Dada*** is the most probable etymology of the divine name ^{d}***Tatta*** (cf. *NH*, 241) and he adds (*NH*, 291): "^{d}*Tatta* ou *Datta*: nom divin auparavant déduit du seul nom propre *Arma*-^{d}U = *Arma-Datta*. Il est maintenant attesté: ^{d}*Tattas*, Bo 3254 Ro 14 = MIO 8, 205. Mais ce texte unique ne dit pas que *Tatta* est un dieu de l'orage."

If Linear A ***ta-ta*** (KH 7a.3) indeed represents the divine Hurrian name ^{d}***Tatta***, it may well be the basis of Linear A ***da-ta-ra*** (HT 6a.1) 'With ^{D}***Tatta/Datta***', marking the month in which tablet HT 6 was written and the transactions described on the tablet took place. If Linear A ***ta-ta*** (KH 7a.3) is a personal name, it might be the name of a priest such as that of the priest of the god of the clouds at Boğazköy. I prefer the first option of the two. Whether initial ***d-*** in ***da-ta-ra*** at Hagia Triada indicates a dialectal difference with initial ***t-*** in ***ta-ta*** at Khania or whether the varying orthographies are due to the allophonic character of consonants in Hurrian, is as yet difficult to say. It is quite conceivable that dialectal differences existed between the *Ḫalba* and *Khania* areas, but we need more evidence to discern a pattern.

Another argument why ***da-ta-ra*** (HT 6a.1) may well represent the *comitative* case is occurrence of the combination of sequences ***da-qe-ra*** **,** ***qe-pi-ta*** (HT 6a.6), followed by 22 JE FIC 15 J | (HT 6a.7) on the same side of the tablet. It can be interpreted as 'with a man for *Ḫebat / Ḫebit*', since ***da-qe-ra*** may be interpreted as Hurrian ***d/taḫe*** 'man' with the Hurrian *comitative* suffix ***-ra***. He may be a 'man' taking part in Ḫebat's cult, possibly a priest. The comitative suffix ***-ra*** in ***da-qe-ra*** expresses 'together with'.

It is justifiable to assume that the same process of assimilation as can be observed with the *genitive* in ***-we/-wi***, also took place with the *dative* in ***-wa***. Consequently on the analogy of the *assimilated* genitive form of ^{d}***Ḫé-bat***: ***Ḫebatti***, ^{d}*Ḫé-pa-at-ti*, KBo XIX 129 Ro 33, etc. < the *unassimilated* form **<** ***Ḫebat-wi***: *^{d}*Ḫé-pa-at-wi*, cf. [^{d}*Ḫé*]*-bat-wi*$_{i}$ KUB XXVII 4. 5 (cf. E.A. Speiser, *IH*, 63, § 82) we may assume that the ending ***-ta*** of Linear A ***qe-pi-ta*** can be explained from ***-t-ta*** < ***-t-wa*** in cuneiform, with the *assimilated* dative form as a result: ***** ^{d}***Ḫé-pa-at-ta*** < *unassimilated* ***** ^{d}***Ḫé-pa-at-wa***.

According to E. Laroche (*GLH*, 100-101) ***Ḫépét*** **/** ***Ḫebat*** is the spouse of *Teš(š)ub*, Hittite Hieroglyphic ^{d}*He-ba-tu* (Yaz. N°. 43). Absolutive, vocative ^{d}*Ḫé-bat*, KBo II 21, 14; KUB XXVII 38 II 9, etc. Alphabetic cuneiform ***Ḫbt***, CTA 166, 56, 60, 62; 170 a 6, 10; 171, 3,5; 176, 5. Ergative: ^{d}*Ḫé-bat-uš*, KUB XXIX 8 III 47; ^{d}*Ḫé-pa-du-uš*, KUB XXVII 42 Vo 11. Genitive: ^{d}*Ḫé-pa-at-ti*, KBo XIX 129 Ro 33, etc. The alphabetic directive form is attested as *Ḫbt-d*, CTA 167 B 14; 172, 10, etc.; cf. *Ugar. V* 525, 535; cf. E. Laroche, *GLH*, 101.

Linear A ***da-qe-ra*** may be analysed as the Hurrian form {*t/daḫe=ra*} = ***d/taḫe*** 'man' (singular absolutive e.g. *da-aḫ-e* = Hitt. LÚ-an, KBo XIX 145 IV 43; KUB XLV 60,3), combined with the Hurrian comitative suffix ***-ra***. Compare for Linear A ***-qe-*** = cuneiform Hurrian ***-ḫe-*** in ***da-ḫe-ra*** the discussion on Linear A ***ka-pa-qe*** *supra*).

The form ***daḫe*** 'man' is opposed to ***ašte/i*** 'woman', cf. *ašti da-a-ḫi-pa da-a-ḫi-it ! ašti-pa* 'a woman for a man, a man for a woman', KBo XX 129+ II 67 (cf. E. Laroche, *GLH*, 251, s.v. ***taḫe*** 'homme'). The alternating orthography of ***-pa/-wa*** for the dative singular in cuneiform is interpreted as [*-va*] in Hurrian, cf. I. Wegner, *Einführung*, 65.

Although E. Laroche (*GLH*, 250) mentions: "***tagi*** 'attribut de Ḫebat', *da-(a)-ki, da-a-ki-it-ti*, KUB XXV 44 II 19; KBo XX 113 IV 16; KUB XXXII 59 II 3; etc.", connection of Linear A ***da-qe-ra*** with the Hurrian root ***d/tag-*** 'beautiful' is excluded, since Linear A ***-qe-*** only represents cuneiform ***-ḫe-*** = ***/ġe/***, not ***/ge/***. But cuneiform *da-(a)-ki* 'beautiful' in this formula can be connected with *GORILA*'s reading of Linear A ***da-ki*** instead of Raison-Pope's reading ***me-ki*** (HT 6b.5) on the *b*-side of the same tablet, see also *infra*.

Since ***da-qe-ra*** may well refer to a 'man' taking part in Ḫebat's cult, some parallels in Linear B may come to mind. On a Pylos tablet occurs ***di-wi-ja do-e-ro*** (PY Cn 1287, 6), *Δίϝyᾱς δόέλος* 'male servant of *Δίϝyᾰ* = *Diwia*' (spouse of Zeus) and ***di-wi-ja do-e-ra*** (PY An 607, 5) *Δίϝyᾱς δοἕλᾱ* 'female servant of *Δίϝyᾰ*'. *Δίϝyᾱς* is genitive of *Δίϝyᾰ*. Mycenaean *δόέλος* later develops to > *δοῦλος*. *Δίϝyᾰ* may be the Indo-European spouse of Zeus, before Hera took her place. Instead of the theonym *Δίϝyᾰ* 'spouse of Zeus' one may also choose the patronymic form *Δίϝyᾱ* (with long *-ᾱ*), 'daughter of Zeus'.

Ἥβη, daughter of Zeus and Hera, is later qualified as *Δία* at Phlius and Sicyon (Strabo, *Geography VIII, 6, 24*): *τιμᾶται δ' ἐν Φλιοῦντι καὶ Σικυῶνι τὸ τῆς Δίας ἱερόν· καλοῦσι δ' οὕτω τὴν Ἥβην* (cf. C.J. Ruijgh, *EGM*, § 108). If the theonym *Ἥβη* was originally derived from the theonym *Ḫebat*, one may wonder, whether she had to become daughter of Zeus instead of his wife, not only because Hera had already taken her place, but also because *ἥβη* means 'youth, vigour, puberty' in Greek.

In the Linear B texts from Pylos ***te-se-u*** is mentioned as ***te-o-jo do-e-ro*** (PY En 74, 5; Eo 276, 4) '***Θησεύς*** (Theseus), servant of a god', which we may probably understand as 'priest of a god'. *Θησεύς* (Theseus) clearly is a Pre-Greek name, since the Indo-European intervocalic ***-s-*** would have changed into ***-h-*** in Mycenaean Greek and would eventually have disappeared. I consider it likely that the name ***Θησεύς*** is in fact derived from the Hurrian hypocoristic name ***Teššui̯a*** (wr. *Te-eš-šu-ia*, *Te-šu-ia*, *Te-iš-šu-ia*, *Ti-iš-šu-ú-ia*, *Te-su-*[*i*]*a*, *Te-eš-su-ia*), attested as the name of 34 persons at Nuzi (cf. I.J. Gelb, *NPN*, 154). ***Teššui̯a*** is in fact a hypocoristic in ***-ya***, derived from a Hurrian theophorous sentence name, of which the theonym ***Teš(š)ub*** is the first onomastic element. I am convinced that the whole 'Theseus – Ariadne – Athena' myth is of Minoan-Hurrian origin. These and many other parallels between Linear A and B show how close Minoan and Mycenaean civilizations were connected.

P.M. Purves, *NPN*, 215-216, writes s.v. ***ḫepet***: "Hurrian female deity mentioned frequently under form *Ḫé-pét* in rituals from Boğazköy, often followed in the Hurrian passages by the epithet *muš(u)ni*, *q.v.* under *muš*. For position of *Ḫepet* in this pantheon, where she seems to be the consort of *Tešup*, see Götze, *Kleinasien*, pp. 58, 123 f., 129. [....] In Ugarit wr. *ḫbt* [....]. Outside of Nuzi *ᶠḪepet-nai̯a*, wr. *ᶠḪé-be-et-na-a-a*, cf. for this element *Um-mi-ᵈḫe-bi-it*, CT XXXIII 41:1, cited by Ungnad, *Subartu*, p. 100, and *ᶠMe-e-na-ḫe-bi* from Nippur, Clay, *PNCP*, p. 106. The form *ḫepa*, commonly taken as variant of *ḫepet*, is found in many personal names; cf. e.g. *ᶠKelu-ḫepa, ᶠPutu-ḫepa, ᶠTatu-ḫepa, ᶠKeluš-ḫepa(š)* and ERUM-*ḫé/ḫe-ba*. Etc." The vowel ***-i-*** of Linear A ***qe-pi-ta*** is attested in forms like *Um-mi-ᵈḫe-bi-it* and *ᶠMe-e-na-ḫe-bi*. The quotation of sentence names with the theophorous element ***-ḫepa*** shows single writing of ***-ḫ-*** indicating a voiced velar spirant. On the analogy of this evidence one may reasonably conclude that initial ***Ḫ-*** of Hurrian ***Ḫebat*** and of *Ḫé-be-et-* in sentence names designates a voiced velar spirant as well. However, this contradicts the current assumption in Hurrian studies that consonants in initial position are always voiceless in Hurrian.

Since voicelessness in medial position is marked by double writing of ***-ḫḫ-*** in the cuneiform syllabary, as in ***Aḫḫiyawa*** in the Hittite texts and ***turuḫḫi(na)*** 'male' and ***aštuḫḫi(na)*** 'female' in Hurrian texts, equally forms such as *ᶠKelu-ḫepa, ᶠPutu-ḫepa, ᶠTatu-ḫepa, Um-mi-ᵈḫe-bi-it* and *ᶠMe-e-na-ḫe-bi*, showing single writing of ***-ḫ-*** in medial and intervocalic position, prove that the theophorous element begins with a voiced velar spirant. It would be anomalous, if the phonetic value of the initial consonant of the same element would change in initial position. The Hurrian name of the Hittite queen ***ᶠPutu-ḫepa***, wife of Ḫattušiliš III, is in all instances of syllabic cuneiform written with single writing of ***-ḫ-*** designating a voiced velar spirant. The alphabetic cuneiform of Ugarit provides ***pdġb*** (RS 17.434) with a voiced velar spirant ***ġ*** in this personal name: cf. Nougayrol, PRU IV 200; Liverani, *Storia di Ugarit*, 51; E. Laroche, *NH*, 151, nº 1063, s.v. ***ᶠPuduḫepa***.

Only the theonym itself provides ***ḫbt*** instead of ***ġbt*** in alphabetic cuneiform of Ugarit suggesting that initial ***ḫ-*** is voiceless (cf. e.g. E. Laroche, *GLH*, 100-101, s.v. *Ḫebat*). The evidence seems ambiguous and inconsistent. The fact that double writing is only possible in medial position, but impossible in initial position in the cuneiform syllabary, makes the phonetic value of an initial consonant *de facto* ambiguous.

Should one say that the name of the Goddess begins with a voiceless *Ḫ-* on account of *ḫbt*, whereas the element *-ḫepa* in *ᶠPuduḫepa* begins with a voiced intervocalic *-ḫ-* on account of single writing in the cuneiform syllabary and on account of *ġ* in *pdġb* in the alphabetic cuneiform ? One must admit that the difference of orthography between *ḫbt* and *pdġb* in alphabetic cuneiform is peculiar, but instead of assuming a different pronunciation of a voiceless velar spirant in initial and a voiced velar spirant in medial position, one might think of the possibility that the use of *ḫ-* in initial position in alphabetic cuneiform may have been a matter of orthographic convention due to scribal habits copied from the cuneiform syllabary, where the use of *ḫ*+vowel was standard in initial position. Taking into account that alphabetic cuneiform is rather late at Ugarit, another approach is that a tendency towards voicelessness of initial consonants may be limited to the Hurrian dialect of Ugarit, maybe even to its latest period.

F.W. Bush (*A grammar of the Hurrian language*, 79-80) has formulated the problems with regard to voiced and voiceless velar fricatives as follows: "One difficulty that either phonemic construction must face is the fact that the adjectival suffix appears as both syllabic *-ḫ-*/ alphabetic *-ġ-* and as syllabic *-ḫḫ-*/ alphabetic *-ḫ-*, with no certain difference in meaning (he refers to E.N. Speiser's observation "Alongside syllabic *turuḫḫi(na)* 'male' and *aštuḫḫi(na)* 'female' we get alphabetic *trḫn* and *astḫn* (RŠ X 4. 55ff)"), nor any discernable phonological conditioning factor that could account for such an alternation. It can only be noted that the interpretation of *-ḫḫ-* as indicating length which is voiceless does open the possibility that the doubling arises from an assimilated element."

After discussing Nougayrol's interpretation of the evidence of the *Foundation Lion Inscription* he continues, 80-81: "If Nougayrol's interpretation is substantiated by future evidence from the Old Akkadian period, then it would appear that there are or were two velar fricative phonemes in the Hurrian of that period. However, the facts are too few and their interpretation is too uncertain to use this construction with any confidence. § 3.74.

Conclusion. As the above discussion shows, the question as to the existence of one or two velar fricative phonemes remains undecided. However, as with the labial fricative, all the evidence that is reasonably clear suggests that the velar fricative has non-phonemic voiced and voiceless positional variants as do the stops and the dental fricative. Although much remains yet ambiguous or uninterpreted, the analogy of the positional variation found above for the other fricatives and the stops is strong. Consequently we shall here so treat it and the symbol [*ḫ*] will be adopted to represent it."

On account of the Linear B values of the syllabic sign ***ka*** one may conclude that it reflects Greek ***κα***, *γα* and ***χα***. Equation of ***χ-*** with the voiceless velar fricative ***ḫ-*** in cuneiform can be comfirmed by comparing Akkadian ***ḫurâṣu***, Hebrew ***ḫarûṣ***, Ugaritic ***ḫrṣ*** with Mycenaean ***ku-ru-so = χρυσός***. As a result rendering cuneiform ***Ḫalba*** into Linear A and B ***ka-pa*** seems normal, as ***Ḫa-*** in ***Ḫalba*** indeed reflects a voiceless velar fricative. Apparently, if the equations are accepted, the following issues can be confirmed:

1. Linear A ***ka*** reflects not only ***/ka/*** and ***/ga/***, but also a voiceless velar fricative ***/ḫa-/*** in initial position and probably also ***/-ḫḫa-/*** in medial position in the cuneiform syllabary.
2. If the interpretation of Linear A ***ka-pa-qe*** is accepted, ***-qe*** would at least represent a voiced velar fricative or spirant ***/-ḫe/*** in medial and final position.
3. If the equation of Linear A ***qe-pi-ta*** with cuneiform ****dḪe-pi-it-ta < *dḪe-pi-it-wa*** is correct, one may conclude that the name of Ḫebat (and its variants) contains either a voiced velar fricative in the Minoan-Hurrian dialect of Crete in initial position in the name of the goddess herself, or, if one maintains that all consonants in all Hurrian dialects are always voiceless in initial position, this would mean that Linear A ***qe-*** can also indicate a voiceless velar fricative, at least in initial position. The theory of voicelessness of all initial consonants in all Hurrian dialects is contradicted by evidence of the series of voiced dental syllabic signs (***da***, ***de***, ***di***, ***do***, ***du***) in Linear A, which also occur in initial position in clearly Hurrian names. Frankly it seems not very likely that this feature is limited to the dentals.

P. Kretschmer (*Glotta XV*, 1926, 76 f.) connected the name ***Hipta*** (in two inscriptions from a Maeonian district) with the element ***-hepa*** of some Mitannian feminine names, which he derived from a goddess ***Hepa***, appearing in the Boğazköy texts under the name of ***Hebe*** or ***Hepit***. In *Hymn. Orph.*, 49, 1-4, ***Hipta*** is called the nurse of Bacchos and ***χθονίη μῆτερ*** (voc.). Proklos, *in Timaeum*, II, 124 C, relates that ***Hipta*** carried the child Dionysos on her head in a *liknon*, surrounded by a snake, cf. M.P. Nilsson, *The Minoan-Mycenaean religion*, 569 and n. 23.

V. Haas, *Hethitische Berggötter und hurritische Steindämonen*, 30 (I translate the German text): "The most famous goddess in North-Syria, venerated during more than three millennia, is ***Ḫebat***. She is already mentioned in the earliest documents of Syria, the texts from Ebla, the city-state near Aleppo, from the end of the thrird millennium; her name appears in the forms ***Ḫeba***, ***Ḫapatu*** und ***Kapatu***. She is the ancestor of the later ***Μήτηρ Ἵππα*** and still occurs in Lycian inscriptions as ***ḫba-ẽni*** 'Mother-*Ḫepa*'. The name is also joined with the Biblical form ***Eva*** via the Semitic form ***Ḥawwat***. As we shall see later, she forms a close couple with the Cilician Mountain God and bull ***Šarrumma***."

Before I continue my analysis of the other sequences on HT 6a, I like to point out that the absolutive of the theonym ***Ḫebat*** appears in ligature writing as ***qe+pa₃*** 100 (HT 33.4) at Hagia Triada. What is even more significant, she seems to be in the company of her consort Tešub. The left top corner of tablet HT 33 is missing and (with this missing part) the first entry that precedes ***sa-ra₂*** (written between word dividers), the only normal sequence of the whole tablet. Linear A ***sa-ra₂*** is one of the most frequent sequences. It is most likely the 3rd person singular of the Hurrian verb ***šar-*** 'to wish, ask, demand' and can be analysed as {*šar=i=(y)a*} 'he wishes, asks, demands', consisting of the verbal root ***šar-*** + the marker of transitivity ***-i-*** + the subject marker ***-a*** of the 3rd person singular of the transitive verb. The subject is probably the missing first entry of the top left corner. This subject may be a personal name, the king or an official, or the palace itself.

Since final consonants are not expressed in Linear A and B, the ligature ***qe+pa₃*** (read from top to bottom) can be interpreted as the theonym ***Ḫebat***, Tešub's consort (see for a discussion about her provenance Th. Richter, *VHN*, 415-416). If the goddess herself is meant, the high number of 100 seems to be in accordance with her dignity.

J. Raison - M. Pope (*Index transnuméré du linéaire A*, Louvain 1977, 56, 276) mention the combination of preceding signs sub ***559*** (HT 33.4), which they analyse as ***49+56a*** = OLIVA+***pi***. Frankly I do not consider their analysis convincing. *GORILA 5*, p. 303, registered it as sign ***341***. An indication is that the number following combination ***559*** is also 100 as in the case of ***qe+pa***$_3$ 100 = ***Ḫebat*** 100. The sign preceding ***pi*** looks like the ideogram NUBES 'cloud' (hapax) and has nothing to do with sign ***49*** = OLIVA.

If the ideogram NUBES 'cloud' refers to the 'Weather God' or 'God of the Clouds', Tešub, it is clear that the consorts Tešub and Ḫebat receive each 100 units. Homer describes Tešub's Greek counterpart, Zeus, likewise: *Iliad* E 631: *Διὸς νεφεληγερέταο* 'of Zeus the cloud-gatherer', and *Odyssey* α 63: *νεφεληγερέτα Ζεύς* 'Zeus the cloud-gatherer'.

The sign ***pi*** following the ideogram NUBES may be the result of assimilation: ***-ub-wi*** > ***uppi***. The process has been adequately described by E.A. Speiser, *IH*, 63, § 82: "The combination of two spirants (evidently voiced) yields the written form ***-pp-***, a doubled sound (evidently voiceless stop). The important fact is that the end-product is a doubled sound. The same result, following assimilation, is obtained when stem-ending ***-b*** combines with ***w-***; cf. ^{d}*Te-e-eš-šu-u-up-pè* Mit. II 72; ^{d}*Te-eš-šu-up-pí* XXV 44 v 6, XXVII 38 ii 14, 20, etc.; with other suffixes added we get ^{d}U^{up}*-pí-na* XXV 44 v 8, XXVII 14 ii 4; ^{d}U^{up}*-pí-na-aš* XXVII 46 iv 2; ^{d}U^{up}*-pí-na-ša* XXVII 42 obv. 36. In all these occurrences the ***-b*** of ***Tešu/ob*** + ***w-*** yield ***-pp-***. That the labial of the case-ending was not lost is shown by its occasional retention in the form ^{d}U^{up}*-wi*$_i$*-na* VII 58 iii 12; XXVII 1 i 72, 74, 75 as against ^{d}U^{up}*-pí-na* (above)."

If the combination NUBES+***pi*** represents the *genitive* ***Tešuppi*** 'of Tešub (the cloud-gatherer)', it reminds us of the use of *phonetic complements* attached to a Sumerogram in cuneiform. If in a Hittite text the Sumerogram EN 'lord, master' was used to express the Hittite word ***išḫaš***, the context made it sometimes clear whether EN indicated the subject, object or indirect object of a verb. But if this was not clear, the Hittite case-endings could be added to the Sumerogram: e.g. ***išḫaš*** is the *nominative* (subject case) of the Hittite word for 'lord', ***išḫan*** the *accusative* (object case) and ***išḫi*** the *dative* (indirect object case). These could be written as EN-*aš*, EN-*an* and EN-*i*, respectively, cf. Th. van den Hout, *The elements of Hittite*, Cambridge 2013^3, 12.

After this brief encounter with ***Ḫebat*** and ***Tešub*** (HT 33.4) we have to return to tablet HT 6a. Since word dividers are normally not used between an ideogram and numeral, punctuation after the ideogram FIC is most likely accidental in HT 6a.2: **, *te* ,** FIC **,** 15. Monosyllabic **, *te* ,** (HT 6a.2) in solitary position is usually preceded and followed by a word divider. It is usually regarded as a "transaction term" in Linear A. The most usual order is that an ideogram follows the "transaction term" ***te*** . It is less usual that an ideogram precedes this "transaction term".

The usual order can be observed in: HT 6a.2: **, *te* ,** FIC; HT 9a.1: **, *te* ,** VIN; HT 14.1: **, *te* ,** GRA; HT 17.1: **, *te* ,** VINa; HT 19.1: **, *te* ,** VINa; HT 21a.1: **, *te* ,** GRA; HT 40+76.1: **, *te* ,** GRA; HT 42[+]59.1: **, *te* ,** OLE+***ki***; HT 44a.1: **, *te*** GRA+F; HT 52a.1: **, *te* ,** '[; HT 62+73.1: **, *te* ,** VIN[; HT 92.1-2: ***te* , *a-du* ,** GRA 680; HT 116a.1: ***u-ta-ro* , *te* , *ku-pa-ja*** GRA; HT 133.1-2: ***a-du* , *te* ,** GRA+***da*** 55.

A reverse (unusual) order can be observed (possibly) in HT 13.2: VINa „ ***te*** ₁ ***re-za*** 5 J[_] (if that is the correct reading); (certainly) in HT 51a.1:] 4 FIC , ***te*** , ***ma***[-; HT 63.1: IUGUM , ***te*** 1; HT 67.3: FIC , ***te*** 400; (possibly) in HT 70+151.1:]FIC/***ni*** , ***te*** 30;

Solitary monosyllables ***te*** occur on 25 nodules from Hagia Triada: HT Wa 1122 - HT Wa 1146; and on one sealing from Phaistos: PH Wb 36.

The function of Linear A ***te*** has often been compared with Linear B ***a-pu-do-si***, Mycenaean Greek ***ἀπύδοσις*** (Att. *ἀπόδοσις*), 'payment, actual delivery'. But verbal terms such as the aorist 3rd person singular ***a-pu-do-ke*** (KN X 681; PY Ma 393, 2) 'he rendered, paid' as well as the augmented aorist ***a-pe-do-ke*** (PY Fr 1184, 1) also occur.

It is, of course, difficult to assess the meaning of this "transaction term" in Linear A, because it probably is an abbreviation of some term and we cannot be sure of which term.

Another frequent Linear A "transaction term" ***ki-ro*** (often abbreviated to ***ki***) can be identified as a Hurrian *imperative* {*kir=o*} 'he/she must redeem his/her debt' from the root ***kir-*** 'to liberate, manumit', known at Ḫattuša from the Hurrian-Hittite bilingual ***Kirenze*** (KBo 32) 'liberation, manumission', but meaning 'redemption of debt' at Nuzi.

One may suspect that Linear A ***te*** is an abbreviation of an *imperative* as well. This makes it attractive to think of a form such as Hurrian ***te-ro*** {*ter=o*} that can be interpreted as an *imperative* of the root ***ter-/tir-*** (see Th. Richter, *BGH*, 461). Th. Richter (*VHN*, 537, note 800) mentions correspondence with the Urartian stem ***ter=u***. Actually, there happens to be a ligature ***te+ro*** as second sequence on HT 104.1 and it is even more intriguing that this ligature is preceded and followed by a word divider, since the first lines read:
HT 104.1-2: ***ta-pa*** , ***te+ro*** , ***da-ku-|se-ne-ti*** 45 J (etc.). So one gets the impression that ***te+ro*** takes the same position as monosyllabic ***te*** (, ***te*** ,) often does, which seems to confirm that Linear A , ***te*** , may well be an abbreviation of the *scriptio plena* , ***te+ro*** , ...

Among the various proposals by several authors such as 'festsetzen, bestimmen' (G.A. Melikišvili, *Die urartäische Sprache*, Studia Pohl 7, Rome 1971, 88; M. Salvini, 1977, 129; B. André-Salvini - M. Salvini, 2002, 19), 'to put, to establish' (I.M. Diakonoff, 1989, 84), the meaning '(Tribut) auferlegen' ['to impose (tribute)'] proposed by Chr. Girbal (Urartäisch *barzani zelde*, *Altorientalische Forschungen 37.1*, 2010, 156) appears to fit very well into the Linear A context. M. Salvini - I. Wegner (*Einführung in die urartäische Sprache*, Wiesbaden 2014, 114) translate Urartian ***ter-*** as 'legen, anlegen (von Gärten); stellen, errichten; bestimmen (von Namen)'. If the Hurrian and Urartian roots ***ter-*** are indeed identical or similar, the *imperative* {*ter=o/u*} may be translated as 'he/she must impose (tribute)' or perhaps simply 'he/she must pay, deliver'.

However, Th. Richter (*VHN*, 541) also mentions another Hurrian verbal root ***ted-/tid-*** 'zählen' ['to count'], cf. Th. Richter (*BGH*, 464), s.v. ***tid-*** I 'to share out, to separate' (Diakonoff/Starostin, 1986, 27; Diakonoff, 1989, 100); 'zählen' ['to count'] (I. Wegner, *Einführung*, 287), which might also provide a good candidate for Linear A monosyllabic ***te***. This root ***ted-/tid-*** I [Boğ.] should not be confused with ***tid-*** II [Boğ.; Mitt.], ***titt-*** / ***te-t°*** [Boğ.] 'angreifen' ['to attack'], cf. *BGH*, 464-465, and *VHN*, 541.

The fact that the sequence , ***te+ro*** , (HT 104.1) is attested in Linear A in the same way as monosyllabic , ***te*** , elsewhere, seems to tip the scales in favour of the root ***ter-***.

Linear A ***pi-ta-ja*** (HT 6a.2) occurs in a list of personal names and can now definitely be identified as a Hurrian personal name containing the Hurrian verbal root ***pitt-***, (trans.) 'to help' or 'to make peace', (intr.) 'to be peaceful'. It can be analysed as *{pitt=a=ja}*, a hypocoristic personal name, consisting of the verbal root ***pitt-*** 'to be peaceful' + the marker of intransitivity ***-a-*** + hypocoristic suffix ***-ya***. Translation: 'He/She is peaceful' (the subject 'He/She' may well be the child or a *numen*).

According to Th. Richter (*BGH*, 319) the (transitive) verbal root ***pitt-*** [Boğ.] means 'helfen' ['to help'], 'Frieden machen' ['to make peace'], (intransitive) 'friedlich sein' ['to be peaceful']. Th. Richter (*VHN*, 486) mentions ***pitt-***, possibly 'to help'. He mentions (*VHN*, 234-235) the following Hurrian personal names with the verbal root ***pitt-***: ***ᶠPittakku*** (wr. *bi-it-ta-ku*) from Mari, analysis *{pitt=a=kk=o}*, typology 1.2.3, and ***Pittun*** (wr. *bi-it-tu-un*) from Šušarrā (Tall Shemshara), analysis *{pitt=o=n(na)}*, typology 1.3.1.1.2.1, 'Hilf ihm (Jungen)' ['Help him (the boy)']. The suffix ***-n(na)*** 'him' marks the enclitic personal pronoun 3rd person singular indicating the object of the transitive verb.

Th. Richter does not accept J.-M. Durand's consideration (*Le culte d'Addu d'Alep et l'affaire d'Alahtum*, Florilegium Marianum 7, Paris 2002, 94[255]) that the names ***ᶠPittakku*** and ***Pittun*** may be connected with Amorite ***bint / bitt*** 'daughter'. In my view forms like ***pitt=ugar-*** [Boğ.], 'to make peace, to thrive, to prosper', analysis *{pitt=uk=ar-}*, and ***pittummi*** [Tušratta letter], analysis *{pitt=ummi}*, definitely prove that the verbal root ***pitt-*** is genuinely Hurrian, cf. Th. Richter, *BGH*, 319. The Hurrian suffix ***-ugar-*** is a verbal root-extension that expresses reciprocity. It can possibly be subdivided into ***-uk+ar-***. For instance, ***ag=ugar-*** 'to send hither', ***kad=ugar-*** 'to speak with each other', ***tad=ugar-*** 'to love each other', cf. I. Wegner, *Einführung*, 88. The Hurrian formant ***-umme*** forms *infinitives* and *nomina actionis*, cf. I. Wegner, *Einführung*, 113.

Since the Hurrian name ***ᶠPittakku*** from Mari provides the closest link with the Pre-Greek name ***Πιττακός*** (***Pittakos***) and with Linear B ***pi-ta-ke-u***, probably ****Πιττακεύς***, I now consider an ultimate derivation of ***Πιττακός*** and ***pi-ta-ke-u*** from names containing the Hurrian verbal root ***pitt-*** more likely than previously alleged derivations from either Luwian or Thracian roots. This means that, for instance, the name ***Πιττακός*** may originally not only be Pre-Greek, but also Pre-Thracian, although it is attested as Thracian: ***Πιττακός*** as a king of the Thracian Edones. Thucydides, IV, 107, 3: *Πιττακοῦ τοῦ Ἠδώνων βασιλέως ἀποθανόντος ὑπὸ τῶν Γοάξιος παίδων καὶ Βραυροῦς τῆς γυναικὸς αὐτοῦ*. ***Πιττακός***, the famous *αἰσυμνήτης* from Mytilènè on Lesbos is already mentioned by Herodotus, I, 27. Suidas also provides interesting information: *Πιττακὸς Μυτιληναῖος, υἱὸς Καϊκοῦ ἢ Ὑρραδίου Θρᾳκός, μητρὸς δὲ Λεσβίας; Ὕρρα παῖς· ὁ Πιττακός, καὶ Ὑρράδιος ὄνομα.*

How should ***-kk-*** in Hurrian ***ᶠPittakku*** from Mari (and in Pre-Greek ***Πιττακός*** and Linear B ***pi-ta-ke-u***, ****Πιττακεύς***) be interpreted ? Th. Richter (*VHN*, 234) does not give an explicit translation of ***ᶠPittakku***, but he analyses it as *{pitt=a=kk=o}*, typology 1.2.3, which is the category of *names with other negative verbal forms*. Th. Richter (*VHN*, 591-593) mentions ***ᶠPittakku*** sub forms with ***°akk-***, c.q. ***°=a=kk-***. I propose to translate 'She (the girl) is/was not peaceful' or 'He/She (a *numen*) was not peaceful'. The suffix ***=kk=o*** marks a negative-intransitive verb (as a result of vowel-harmony ***o > a***, if it precedes ***-tta***, ***-mma***, etc.), cf. I. Wegner, *Einführung*, 99, Tables 6-7. Since the intransitive form 3rd pers. sing. has a ***Ø***-marker instead of enclitic ***-nna***, ***-kko*** does not change to ***-kka***.

Before I continue the analysis of other sequences on HT 6a, it seems wise to discuss first the other Linear A personal names with the Hurrian verbal root ***pitt-***. I start with Linear A ***pi-ta-ka-se*** (HT 21a.1), ***pi-ta-ke-si*** (HT 87.2), ***pi-ta-ra*** (HT 96a.4), ***p̲i̲-ti-sa*** (HT 31.1) from Hagia Triada and shall then move on to ***pi-ti-ne*** (AK 4a.4) from Arkhanes and ***pi-te-za*** (PK Za 11.b) from Mount Petsophas (Palaikastro).

The Lycian names with the element ***Pidda*** or ***Pitta*** were assembled by J. Sundwall, *Die einheimischen Namen der Lykier nebst einem Verzeichnisse kleinasiatischer Namenstämme* (Klio, Elftes Beiheft), Leipzig 1913, 176. E. Laroche, *Recueil d'onomastique hittite,* Paris 1951, 113: "*Pidda-*, *Pitta-* et *Pitti*, éléments fréquents qu'on peut ramener à plusieurs mots hittites homonymiques: *pitta* 'peine, punition', *pidda-* 'creuser', *pittija-* 'fuir', *piddala-* 'abandonner, négliger' (cf. *Pittalija*), *pittejant-* 'fugitif', *pittijaš*, IX 5. 7, etc." The meanings of these forms differ considerably from that of Hurrian ***pitt-***.

Ph. H.J. Houwink ten Cate (*The Luwian population groups of Lycia and Cilicia Aspera during the Hellenistic period*, Leiden, 1965, 116 and 158) compares, s.v. *PITTA*, names from the second millennium B.C. which contain an element *Pidda* or *Pitta,* with Lycian names that had been published in *Tituli Lyciae lingua Lycia conscripti*, Wien 1901:
"A number of names from the second millennium contain an element ***Pidda*** or ***Pitta***, for example ***Pitagatteni*** (E. Laroche, *Onomastique*, no. 565), ***ᶠPitati*** (*Onom.*, no. 566), ***Pidda*** (*Onom.* no. 568), ***Pittaggatalli*** (*Onom.* no. 569), ***Pittaliįa*** (*Onom.*, no. 570), ***Pittanza*** (*Onom.*, no. 571), ***Pittapara*** (*Onom.*, no. 572), ***Pittatta*** (*Onom.*, no. 573), ***Pittazzi*** (*Onom.*, no. 574). Some Lycian names contain an element ***pddẽ***, familiar as preposition and preverbium from the Lycian texts. There is nothing to disprove the hypothesis that ***pddẽ*** is nominal in origin and occurs as nominal element in onomastics. On the other hand it is also possible that it occurs as adverb, in which case this is not the correct place to deal with this element.
pddẽni- (T.L. 106, 1) ***Pitta-anni***; see ***Anni***.
pddakñta (T.L. 15, 2) and ***pddākñta*** (T.L. 13, 2) ***Pitta-ḫanta***; see ***Ḫant(a)***."

E. Laroche (*NH*, Paris 1966, 147-148) mentions the following examples: no. 1025: *Pidda*; no. 1026: *Pittaggatalli*; no. 1027: *⁽ᶠ⁾Pitagatteni*; no. 1028: *Pittaliya*; no. 1029: *Pittanza*; no. 1030: *Pitta/ipara*; no.1031: *Pittatta*; no.1032: *⁽ᶠ⁾Pitati*; no. 1033: *Pittazzi*; no. 1034: *Pithana*; no.1035: *⁽ᶠ⁾Pittiya*; no.1036: *Pitianalga*; no.1037: *⁽ᶠ⁾Pittiyanni*.

Consequently it is not surprising that I at first assumed that Linear A ***pi-ta-ka-se*** (HT 21a.1) and ***pi-ta-ke-si*** (HT 87.2) might contain the Luwian onomastic element ***Pitta-*** that was recognized in Luwian and Lycian personal names.

However, since it is now clear that a transitive and intransitive verbal root ***pitt-*** is also attested in Hurrian, it is no longer necessary and it even seems no longer probable that ***pi-ta-ka-se*** (HT 21a.1) and ***pi-ta-ke-si*** (HT 87.2) contain the Luwian onomastic element ***pitta-***. In fact attestation of Luwian names in the middle of lists with Hurrian names would now appear to be an anomaly, although not entirely inconceivable, since there were areas such as Kizzuwatna (Cilicia), where Luwians and Hurrians probably lived in close contact. It is difficult to assess whether Luwian ***pitta-*** and Hurrian ***pitt-*** were independent and only homonymic or homographic onomastic elements or whether Luwian derived ***pitta-*** (partly ?) from Hurrian ***pitt-***.

In view of the excavation of Urkeš (Tell Mozan) I assume that Hurrians were already indigenous in east Anatolia and the north of Syria and Iraq before the arrival of the Indo-European Hittites and Luwians.

In my view the root ***pent-/bent-*** is not involved in Linear A ***pi-ta-ka-se*** (HT 21a.1) and ***pi-ta-ke-si*** (HT 87.2), because the dental of ***pent-/bent-*** is probably voiced, cf. E. Laroche, *GLH*, 199-200, s.v. ***pend(i)-*** 1. Thème verbal, 2. Divers.

I.J. Gelb (*NPN*, 80-81) and P.M. Purves (*NPN*, 223-224) mention the Hurrian names ***Kase*** (wr. *Qa-si, Qa-si-e*) and ***Kazi*** (wr. *Qa-a-zi, Qa-zi*) at Nuzi. P.M. Purves (*NPN*, 224) mentions s.v. ***kaz***, ***-kazi*** from Nuzi: ***kazuḫḫe*** (wr. *ka-zu-uḫ-ḫe, qa-zu-uḫ-ḫé, qa-zu-uḫ-ḫe*); ***Unnu-kazi*** (wr. *Un-nu-qa-zi*), and s.v. ***-kazzi***: ***Kirrukazzi*** (cf. ***Kirruka***) and ***Taukazzi*** (cf. ***Tauka***), but he thinks that ***-kazzi*** in fact is a compound formative consisting of ***-ka*** and ***-zzi***. If so, the suffix ***-zzi*** might represent the morpheme ***-še/-šše*** forming adjectives. The suffixes ***-(a)=šše*** and ***-(i)=šše*** can also form abstract nouns, cf. I. Wegner, *Einführung*, 54-55.

If ***pi-ta-ka-se*** (HT 21a.1) is to be analysed as *{pitt=a=g/k(k)=a=šše}* and ***pi-ta-ke-si*** (HT 87.2) as *{pitt=a=g/k(k)=e/i=šše}*, we may have to do with names formed as abstract nouns. Compare for the formants ***-kk-*** and ***-g/k(k)-*** I. Wegner, *Einführung*, 56.

If there is not such a segmentation of Linear A ***-ka-se***, it is impossible that we are dealing with the verbal roots ***kaš-*** I or ***kaz-*** II, since ***-ka-se*** in Linear A ***pi-ta-ka-se*** occurs as second element as in ***Unnu-kazi***, ***Kirrukazzi*** and ***Taukazzi*** at Nuzi. It is inconceivable that a Hurrian personal name contains two verbal roots at the same time, ***pitt-*** and ***kaš-*** I {*kaž-*}, occurring as first element in the personal names ***Kašakka*** and ***Kaširazzi*** at Mari, or ***kaz-*** II {*kaž-(?)*}, ***Kazija*** (Mari), ***Kazinna*** (wr. *Ka-zi-in-na*) at Tigunāni {*kaž=i=nna* }. The root ***kaz-*** II reminds of the Nuzi-syntagma ***kaz-umma epēšu***, of which the meaning is not yet known, cf. Th. Richter, *VHN*, 431-432. So if Linear A ***-ka-se*** and ***-ke-si*** do not consist of formants, they probably are nominal onomastic elements

Th. Richter thinks that it is most likely that the 'one-word' personal names ***Kazi*** (wr. *Ka*$_4$*-(a-)zi*) at Nuzi and ***Kazinna*** (wr. *Ka-zi-in-na*) at Tigunāni {*kaž=i=nna*} represent an *imperative*, but he considers it conceivable that ***Kazi*** can be identified with Hurrian ***kazi*** 'Becher' ['beaker, goblet, chalice'].

This word plays an important role in the third parable 'Der Becher und sein Schmied' ['The goblet and its smith'] in the Hurrian-Hittite bilingual ***Kirenze***, KBo 32: 14, 42: *ka-a-zi ta-bal-li-iš ḫe-e-lu-u-wa*$_a$ = *kazi tab=li=ne=š* > *tabal=le=š ḫelov(i)=a* (essive) or *ḫel=o=va* (dative) = 'Einen Becher goß ein (Metall)gießer als Ruhmestat / zum Ruhme' ['A (metal)smith / (copper)smith cast a goblet as an act of fame / to glory'], cf. I. Wegner, *Einführung*, 216-220. Hurrian ***kazi*** (absolutive) is derived from Akkadian ***kāsu(m)*** 'goblet, chalice' and corresponds with Hittite ***teššummi-*** (wr. *te-eš-šum-mi-in*) 'cup, goblet, chalice' in the Hittite version *II*, 42 (E. Neu, *StBoT* 32, 81).

The general rule in Linear B is that non-occlusives [*σ, μ, ν, ρ, λ, ϝ*] preceding non-sonantic consonants [occlusives + *σ*] are usually not expressed in consonant clusters. Since the orthographic conventions of Linear B were probably derived from those of Linear A, ***-r-*** preceding ***-s-*** was not expressed in consonant clusters.

Consequently it is possible that the second onomastic element of Linear A ***pi-ta-ka-se*** (HT 21a.1) contains the theophorous element ***-kar-zi/ši***, since ***ᴰKar-zi/ši*** is attested as a theonym, cf. Van Gessel, 1998, 225; I. Wegner, 2004, 224; Th. Richter, *VHN*, 431, s.v. ***karzi/karši*** {*karži*}. ***ᴰKar-zi/ši*** also occurs in Hurrian context. The word ***karši*** is regarded as the Hurrian designation of 'Lippen' ['lips'], cf. Th. Richter, *BGH*, 190-191; *VHN*, 431; De Martino/Süel, 2015, 75. Th. Richter (*VHN*, 152) mentions ***Karzam*** (wr. *Ka-ar-za-am*) at Šubat-Enlil, analysis {*karž(i)=a*[E]*=m(e/a)*}, typology 3.2.1, lexicon *karzi*, 'Er (Junge) ist mit einer (besonderen) Lippe (geboren)' ['He (the boy) is (born) with a special lip']; ***Karšan*** (wr. *Ka-ar-ša-an*) at Mari, analysis {*karž(i)=a*[E]*=n(na)*}, typology 3.2.1, lexicon *karši*, (idem) 'He (the boy) is (born) with a special lip'. [E] refers to the *essive* case in ***-a***. Since theonyms are usually not connected with enclitics, it is assumed that these 'one-word' names refer to particular features of the lips that were visible after birth of the bearers of the names. The same may apply to the Hurrian personal name ***Karzeya*** (wr. *Qa-ar-ze-ia, Qar-ze-ia, Qa-ar-ze-e-a, Qar-ze-e-a, Qar-ze-e, Kar-ze-ia*) at Nuzi, cf. I.J. Gelb, *NPN*, 80. Since ***-ka-se*** in Linear A ***pi-ta-ka-se*** (HT 21a.1) comprises the second onomastic element and is not followed by enclitics, the theonym ***ᴰKar-zi/ši*** may represent the theophorous element in this name. Since ***pitt=a*** can be either *imperative* or *indicative*, the name can be translated 'Be peaceful, oh (god) ᴰ*Karzi/ši* !' or 'ᴰ*Karzi/ši* is peaceful'.

One may wonder whether Linear A ***pi-ta-ke-si*** (HT 87.2) is a (dialectal ?) variant of ***pi-ta-ka-se*** (HT 21a.1) as seems to be the case in the mountain name ***Kazijar / Kašijar*** and ***Kešijar*** {*Ka/ežijar*} or whether ***kazi / kaši*** and ***kezzi*** are etymologically different forms. According to Th. Richter (*VHN*, 432) the oronym ***Kašijar(i)*** is since M. Streck (Das Gebiet der heutigen Landschaften Armenien, Kurdistân und Westpersien nach den babylonisch-assyrischen Keilinschriften, *ZA 13 (1898)*, 77) identified with the present Ṭūr ᶜAbdīn. The oronym without final ***-i*** is the oldest form. Change from {*Ka/ežijar*} to younger {*Kažijara/i/u*} is in accordance with the general linguistic development of final vowels. ***Kešijar*** and the personal name ***Eḫlip-Kešijar*** are dialectal variants at Tigunāni. Mari has ***Eḫlip-Kazijar***. The mountain name has the function of a (*quasi*) theophorous element in personal names.

Linear A ***pi-ta-ke-si*** (HT 87.2) may only be compared with the Hurrian personal name ***Kezzi*** (wr. *Ge-ez-zi*), and the onomastic element ***Kezzi-*** in ***Kezzi-ḫarpa*** (*Ge-ez-zi-ḫar-pa*) at Nuzi, if ***kezzi*** is nominal, cf. I.J. Gelb, *NPN*, 84, 89; P.M. Purves, *NPN*, 226, s.v. ***kezz, kezzi, Ge-ez-zi***; *NPN*, 228, s.v. ***kiz*** and ***kizz***.

Th. Richter (*VHN*, 441) mentions s.v. ***kiš-*** I {*kiž-*}: ***ᶠKiš-kanazzi, ᶠKišen(?)-ki, Eniš-kiša*** at Mari. The element ***-kiša*** in the latter name reminds of the 'one word' name ***Ki-ša*** (wr. *Ki-ša-a-*) and ***ᶠKisaia*** (wr. *ᶠKi-sa-a-a, ᶠKi-za-a-a*) at Nuzi, cf. I.J. Gelb, *NPN*, 88.

Th. Richter mentions s.v. ***kiz-*** II/***kizz-/kezz-***: (1a) {*kiz-*}: ***Kiza*** (Mari); ***Kizija*** (Mari, Šušarrā); ***ᶠKizi-kanazzi*** (Ašnakkum); ***Kizum*** (Mari); (1b) {*kizz-*}: ***Kizzi*** (Mari, Qaṭṭarā); ***Kizzija*** (Mari, Šubat-Enlil); ***Kizzikan*** (Mari); ***Kizzi-kawari*** (Šubat-Enlil); ***Kizzu*** (Mari, Šubat-Enlil); ***Kizzu-men*** (Mari); ***Kizzunni*** (Mari); ***Kizzutta*** (Mari). Presumably in ***Kizzi-ma*** (Šušarrā); (1c) {*kezz-*}: ***Kezzi*** (Tigunāni); (2) {*kizzazzi*}: ***Kizzazzum*** (Mari); (3) {*kizi*}: ***ᶠŠawanni-kizi*** (Mari); (4) {*kiziġe*}: ***Kizziḫe*** (Tuttul); (5a) {*kizori*}: ***Kizuri*** (Mari); ***Kizurija*** (?) (Šubat-Enlil); (5b) {*kizzori*}: ***Kizzuri*** (Ašnakkum, Mari, Šušarrā); (6a) {*kizo/uzzi*}: ***Kizuzzum*** (Mari); (6b) {*kizzo/uzzi*}: ***Kizzuzzi*** (Mari).

Th. Richter (*VHN*, 441-442) distinguishes ***kiš-*** I {*kiž-*} and ***kiz-*** II / ***kizz-/kezz-***, since it is not yet clear, whether these roots might be just variants. The [***Z***] and [***Š***] series are sometimes used indiscriminately. On account of ***ᶠKiš-kanazzi*** (***kiš-*** I) from Mari and ***ᶠKizi-kanazzi*** (***kiz-*** II/***kizz-/kezz-***) from Ašnakkum, I consider it likely that ***kiš-*** I {*kiž-*} and ***kiz-*** II / ***kizz-/kezz-*** are in fact one and the same root.

For ***pi-ta-ke-si*** (HT 87.2) the best parallels are ***Eniš-kiša*** (***kiš-*** I) at Mari and ***ᶠŠawanni-kizi*** (***kiz-*** II/***kizz-/kezz-***) at Mari, since ***-kiša*** and ***-kizi*** represent the second element in these names, cf. Th. Richter (*VHN*, 105), s.v. ***Eniš-kiša*** (wr. *E-ni-iš-ki-ša*), analysis {*en=i=ž-kiž(i)=a*[E]}, typology 1.3.2.2, lexicon *en-* I, *kiši* (→ *kiš-* I); Th. Richter (*VHN*, 246), s.v. ***Šawanni-kizi*** (wr. *Ša-wa-an-ni-ki-*[*z*]*i*), analysis {*šavanni-kizi*}, typology 2.1, lexicon *šawanni* (→ *ša-*), *kizi* (→ *kiz-* II).

According to Th. Richter (*BGH*, 215) ***kizzu*** [Tušratta] (the ending in ***-u*** is probably an Akkadianizing nominative) means 'a piece of jewelry' and adjectival ***kizziḫi*** [Boğ.; PN], ***kizzi/uḫu*** [Qaṭna], derived from ***kizzi***, means 'ein Schmuckstück(?)' ['an ornament(?)'], 'cult object, temple object', 'a gem', 'a piece of jewelry', 'a designation of a golden pin'.

Th. Richter (*VHN*, 442) considers ***kizziḫe*** {*kizz(i)=i=ġe*} 'Schmuckstück', 'sacrificial term', ***kizzuri*** {*kizz=o=ri*}, ***kizzazzi*** {*kizz(i)=a=zzi*} and ***kiz(z)uzzi*** {*kiz(z)(i)=o/u=zzi*} nominal. If Linear A ***pi-ta-ke-si*** (HT 87.2) is actually analysed as {*pitt=a=kezzi*}, consisting of the verbal root ***pitt-*** 'to be peaceful' + the marker of intransitivity ***-a-*** + nominal term ***kezzi/kizzi*** 'a piece of jewelry', the translation 'The piece of jewelry is peaceful' would be a beautiful name for a newborn child.

Linear A ***pi-ta-ra*** (HT 96a.4) occurs in a list of personal names and can be identified as a Hurrian personal name containing the Hurrian verbal root ***pitt-***, (trans.) 'to help' or 'to make peace', (intr.) 'to be peaceful'. The name can be analysed in different ways as:
1. {*pitt=a=lla*} consisting of the (intr.) verbal root ***pitt-*** 'to be peaceful' + the marker of intransitivity ***-a-*** + the enclitic pronoun ***-lla*** marking the 3rd person plural, indicating the subject of the intransitive verb, translation 'They (scil. *numina*) are/were peaceful'.
2. {*pitt=(i)-alla(i)*} consisting of the transitive verbal root ***pitt-*** 'to help' + the marker of transitivity ***-i-*** that disappeared under influence of following ***-a-*** + the theophorous element ***Allay*** 'Lady', in the *absolutive* case, syntactically in the function of *vocative*, translation 'Help, oh Lady !'.
3. {*pitt=(a)-alla(i)*} consisting of the verbal root ***pitt-*** 'to be peaceful' + the marker of intransitivity ***-a-*** that disappeared under influence of following ***-a-*** + the theophorous element *Allay* 'Lady', in the *absolutive* case, either in the function of *vocative*, translation 'Be peaceful, oh Lady !', or in the function of subject of the intransitive verb, translation 'The Lady is/was peaceful'.
4. {*pitt=(i)-ara*} consisting of the verbal root ***pitt-*** 'to help' + the marker of transitivity ***-i-*** that disappeared under influence of following ***-a-*** + the theophorous element ***Ara***, in the *absolutive* case, syntactically in the function of *vocative*, 'Help, oh *Ara* !'.
5. {*pitt=(a)-ara*} consisting of the verbal root ***pitt-*** 'to be peaceful' + the marker of intransitivity ***-a-*** that disappeared under influence of following ***-a-*** + the theophorous element *Ara*, in the *absolutive* case, either in the function of *vocative*, 'Be peaceful, oh *Ara* !', or in the function of subject of the intransitive verb, '*Ara* is/was peaceful'.

Th. Richter (*VHN*, 378) mentions that in the personal names ***Arum-Ara*** '*Ara* gives / gave' and ***Ḫašip-Ara*** '*Ara* listens / listened' from Tigunāni *°-a-ra* has the function of subject in the *verbal sentence names* and can represent the theonym ᴰ*a-a-ra(°)*, to date only known from Ḫattuša and in CTH 492 attested in an environment of Hurrian gods. 6. *{pitt=(i)-arra}* and 7. *{pitt=(a)-arra}* should perhaps also be mentioned as theoretical possibilities, because Th. Richter (*VHN*, 377-378) mentions a root ***arr-*** that should be distinguished from ***ar-*** 'to give', since it occurs in onomastic elements and 'one-word' names that are completely different. The root ***arr-*** forms verbal and nominal forms. In several personal names *(°)a-ar-ra* can be isolated, representing a noun based on {*arr=i*}. It is not clear, why the *essive* form in ***-a*** is so often involved, e.g. in ***Awiš-arra*** (Mari), ***ᶠŠat-arra*** (Mari), ***ᶠTalp-arra*** (Ašnakkum). He also mentions ***Arruk*** (Šušarrā) and ***Arriwe***(?) (Ašnakkum). Unfortunately the meaning of ***arr-*** is not yet known.

In my view the interpretations with the theophorous element ***Allay*** 'Lady, Queen' are the most likely, both semantically and statistically, because ***alla/allae/allai/alli*** belongs to the most frequent theophorous onomastic elements, cf. e.g. Th. Richter, *VHN*, 369-370. At Nuzi (*NPN*, 199), Alalaḫ (*AT*, 127) and elsewhere the element occurs primarily in names of women, but occasionally also in names of men. Parallel formations such as ***ᶠAllai(-)zu / Ewri(-)zu***, ***ᶠKelum-allai / Keliš-ewri / Kelum-šarri***, ***ᶠArip-alla / Arip-šarri*** show that feminine ***Allay*** matches masculine ***Ewri*** 'Lord, King' and ***Šarri*** 'King of Gods'.

Linear A ***pi-ti-ne*** 1 (AK 4a.4) from Arkhanes, preceded by ***154-te*** 5 (AK 4a.4), is probably a personal name like the other sequences on this tablet that are all followed by a number of units. It can be analysed as {*pitt=i=nne*}, consisting of the Hurrian root ***pitt-*** 'to help' + the marker of transitivity ***-i*** + the suffix ***-nne/i*** marking the *optional allomorphic* enclitic personal pronoun 3rd person singular (instead of ***-nna***) indicating the object of the transitive construction, translation 'Help him /her (the child) (oh *numen*) !'.

Th. Richter (*VHN*, 596, sub 1.3.1.1.2.2) mentions that in 'one-word names' the enclitic suffix ***-tta*** indicating the personal pronoun 1st person singular can sometimes be replaced by the *optional allomorphic* suffix ***-tti***. Likewise the enclitic suffix ***-nna*** indicating the personal pronoun 3rd person singular can be replaced by ***-nne/i*** or ***-nnu*** and the enclitic suffix ***-lla*** indicating the personal pronoun 3rd person plural can be replaced by ***-lle*** or ***-lli***. He gives the example of ***Ullutti*** (wr. *Ul-lu-ut-ti*), analysis {*o/ull=o=tti*}, from Mari and Tigunāni, beside ***Ullutta*** (wr. *Ul-lu-ut-ta*), analysis {*o/ull=o=tta*}, from Šušarrā, 'Destroy me (oh *numen*) !', cf. also Th. Richter, *VHN*, 329.

Th. Richter (*VHN*, 234-235, 486) mentions the Hurrian personal name ***Pittun*** (wr. *bi-it-tu-un*) from Šušarrā (Tall Shemshara), with the verbal root ***pitt-*** 'to help', analysis {*pitt=o=n(na)*}, typology 1.3.1.1.2.1, 'Hilf ihm (Jungen)' ['Help him (the boy)']. The suffix ***-n(na)*** 'him' marks the enclitic personal pronoun 3rd person singular indicating the object of the transitive construction. Hurrian ***Pittun*** (wr. *bi-it-tu-un*) from Šušarrā is in fact a perfect parallel to Linear A ***pi-ti-ne*** (AK 4a.4) from Arkhanes.

Unfortunately the reading of the first sign of ***pi-ti-sa , pu-ko ,*** VASᵈˡ+***ri*** (HT 31.1) from Hagia Triada is uncertain. The first sequence should possibly be read as ***9-ti-sa***, since the first sign may well be identical with the fourth sign of ***ki-de-ma-9-na*** (HT 31.4) on the same tablet. In the past W.C. Brice (*ILA*, 1961) read ***mi-ti-sa***, J. Raison - M. Pope (1994) ***i-ti-sa*** and *GORILA 1* and Meijer [.]***-ti-sa***.

I think that the lower part of the first sign is recognizable as ***pi-*** or as ***L9*** and that the upper part has disappeared or was omitted, since the sign has been written close to the left top corner of the tablet. The readings ***mi-ti-sa*** and ***i-ti-sa*** are certainly not correct. J. Raison - M. Pope (*Études minoennes I*, 1978, 14) wrote about sign ***L9***: "Only on two or three Hagia Triada tablets, and somewhat similar in form to another sign, ***L28***. But a sign very like ***L9*** is now attested once at Khania as a constituant part of a ligature, and once at Kea." I do not agree with them upon the alleged similarity with ***L28*** = ***wi***, but consider ***L9*** a variant of sign ***L56a*** = ***pi*** (in fact only the small horizontal stroke of ***pi*** is missing).

If the reading ***pi-ti-sa*** is correct, it seems *prima facie* equivalent to the Hurrian form *pè-ti-ša-a-tan* in the Tušratta letter, Tuš. III 81, cf. Th. Richter, *BGH*, 320: without translation. But equation of ***pi-ti-sa*** with *pè-ti-ša-a-tan* seems unlikely, because single writing of the Hurrian dentals indicates voicing, whereas the Linear A dental is voiceless.

If ***pi-ti-sa*** (HT 31.1) is an anthroponym, the Hurrian feminine personal name ^{f}***Petteza*** (wr. ^{f}*Be-et-te-ez-a*) from Nuzi seems a perfect equivalent (with double writing of ***-tt-*** and with ***i/e*** alternation, which is common in the Hurrian syllabary), cf. I.J. Gelb, *NPN*, 114.

Linear A ***pi-ti-sa*** (HT 31.1) may be a personal name followed by a toponym ***pu-ko*** that might indicate e.g. *Pyrgos* in the Messara valley, but it can also be a verbal form.

Linear A ***pi-ti-sa*** (HT 31.1) can be analysed as *jussive* form {*pitt=i=š=an*}, consisting of the verbal root ***pitt-*** 'to help' + the *jussive* marker ***-i/e-*** + the pluralizer ***-š-*** for the 1st and 2nd person plural + the syntactical particle ***-an*** (of which the final consonant ***-n*** is not expressed in Linear A), translation 'and we should like to help' or 'and you must help ! (plural *imperative*)'. However, usage of the syntactical particle ***-an*** in the first sequence of the tablet is syntactically not very likely.

Another analysis may be {*pitt=i=šša* < **pitt=i=š=nna*}, 'we should like to help him / her (*-nna*)' or 'you must help him / her ! (plural *imperative*)', cf. I. Wegner, *Einführung*, 103-111 and Table 9: *Order of suffixes of the positive jussive*). Such a verbal form can also be used as a personal 'one-word' name, cf. Th. Richter, *VHN*, *passim*.

The Hurrian-Hittite bilingual ***Kirenze*** (KBo 32: 15 I 18') offers a good example of assimilation of ***-š=nna*** > ***šša*** in another *jussive* form, with the conditional optative formant ***-eva-*** and the object in the absolutive case: *e-ḫi-il-li-wa*$_a$*-aš-ša* ^{D}*Te-eš-šu-up* = {*eḫl=il=eva=š=nna* ^{D}*Teššub*}, translation 'we wish to save him (*-nna*), Teššub', cf. I. Wegner, *Einführung*, 111. She also shows (*ibidem*, 105) that in a form like *it-ti-tén* (Mitt. III 23) = {*itt=i=(i)t=en*} 'they ought to go' ***-i-*** is marker of the *jussive* form and not a marker of transitivity, since the root ***itt-*** 'to go' is intransitive. N.B. ***-(i)t-*** is the pluralizer of the 3rd person plural of the jussive form.

Linear A ***pi-te-za*** (PK Za 11.b) is the sequence following [***du-***]|***pu***$_2$***-re*** on a libation table from Mount Petsophas near Palaikastro. Morphologically it seems equivalent to the Hurrian feminine personal name ^{f}***Petteza*** (wr. *Be-et-te-ez-a*, last sign ***a*** as copied, not ***za***), JEN 507: 11, cf. I.J. Gelb, *NPN*, 114; cf. P.M. Purves, *NPN*, 245, s.v. ***Petteza***. However, since ***pi-te-za*** (PK Za 11.b) is part of the text of a so-called 'libation formula', it appears less likely that it represents a personal name in this text.

In that respect ***pi-te-za*** (PK Za 11.b) differs from ***pi-ti-sa*** (HT 31.1), first entry on a clay tablet from Hagia Triada, that may well be a personal name and perfect match of the Hurrian feminine personal name ***ᶠPetteza*** (wr. *ᶠBe-et-te-ez-a*) from Nuzi (cf. I.J. Gelb, *NPN*, 114), that is (with double writing of ***-tt-***) in accord with the voiceless dental in Linear A ***pi-te-za***. The ***i/e*** alternation of ***pett-/pitt-*** is common in the Hurrian syllabary).

Linear A ***pi-te-za*** (PK Za 11.b) can be analysed as a *jussive* forms {*pitt=i=š=an*}, consisting of the verbal root ***pitt-*** 'to help' + the suffix ***-i/e-*** marking the *jussive* + the pluralizer ***-š-*** for the 1st and 2nd person plural + the syntactical particle ***-an*** (of which the final consonant ***-n*** is not expressed in Linear A), 'and we should like to help' or 'and you must help ! (plural *imperative*)'. Another analysis may be {*pitt=i=šša* < **pitt=i=š=nna*}, 'we should like to help him / her (*-nna*)' or 'you must help him / her ! (plural *imperative*)', cf. I. Wegner, *Einführung*, 103-111 and Table 9: *Order of suffixes of the positive jussive*).

I continue the discussion on tablet HT 6a. Linear A ***ja+ru*** DD (HT 6a.3) can possibly be connected with Hurrian ***ejari / ijari*** [Boğ.] and ***eri*** [Emar] 'Löwe' ['lion'], cf. Th. Richter, *BGH*, 74. Linear A ***ja+ru*** can possibly be analysed as {*(e/i)jar=(i)u*[N.]}, with Akkadianizing *nominative* [N.] in ***-u***. The name can then be interpreted as 'Mister Lion'. There may be a Hamito-Semitic origin of this root. E. Laroche (*GLH*, 119) mentions a series of forms s.v. ***iyar-***, ***eyar-***: *i-ya-ri*, KUB XXVII 42 Ro 17; *e-ya-ar-ri*, KBo VIII 146, 3; *e-ya-ar-ri-we$_e$-na-ma*, KUB XXVII 29 IV 2; *e-ya-ar-ri-e-a*, KBo XIX 139 II 15; *i-ya-ru-e*, Mari 1,15; *e-ya-ru-wa*, KUB XXXII 31, 4, 6; *i-ya-ar-ḫa*, KUB XLV 22 IV 2.

Or ***ja+ru*** can be connected with the transitive root ***iar-/ijar-*** as in ***ia-ru-ḫé-pa***, from which ****jar-*** can be isolated, cf. Th. Richter (*BGH*, 74, s.v. ***iar-/ijar-*** [PN]); M. Popko, Eine "schwarze Tafel" aus Boğazköy (KUB LX 121), *AoF 18 (1991)*, 244 and G. Wilhelm, Name, Namengebung. D. Bei den Hurritern, in: D.O. Edzard (ed.), *Reallexikon der Assyriologie und Vorderasiatischen Archäologie 9/1-2*, Berlin-New York, 1998, 123.

Th. Richter, *BGH*, 73: s.v. ***i-***(?) or ***ij-*** [Mit.] 'taugen, wert sein' or 'Taugliches, Gutes tun'; Th. Richter, *VHN*, 393: s.v. ***ij-*** {*ij-*} or ***i-***, ***ej-*** {*ej-*} 'taugen, wert sein'.

If we assume that ***iar-/ijar-*** consists of a root ***i-*** or ***ij-*** 'to be good' or 'to make good' + *factitive* or *iterative* root-extension ***-ar-***, the Linear A ligature ***ja+ru*** (HT 6a.3) can be analysed as an Old Hurrian past transitive indicative {*i=ar-/ij=ar=o/u=m*}, 'He/She (a *numen*) made (the child) good/worthy', or as an Old Hurrian imperative {*i=ar-/ij=ar=o/u*}, 'Make (the child) good/worthy (oh *numen*) !', or the same form with the enclitic personal pronoun 3rd person singular ***-nna /-n*** {*i=ar-/ij=ar=o/u=n(na)*}, 'Make him/her (the child) good / worthy (oh *numen*) !'. I analyse *ia-ru-ḫé-pa* as {*iar/ijar=u-ḫépa*} 'Ḫebat made (the child) good' or as 'Make (the child) good/worthy, oh *Ḫebat* !'.

Only ***ma-3*** 10 (HT 6a.3-4) cannot yet be analysed, since the value of the rare Linear A sign ***3*** is not yet known. It may represent one of the missing values in the Linear A grid.

Linear A ***o-ra$_2$-di-ne*** 2 (HT 6a.4), preceding ***ka-pa-qe*** 5 JE (HT 6a.4-5), is probably a personal name. Since Linear A sign ***ra$_2$*** is graphically identical with Linear B ***ra$_2$*** = ***ria/rya*** or ***lia/lya***, we may reasonably assume that the phonetic value of Linear A ***ra$_2$*** is identical as well. There is a verbal root ***ull-*** 'to destroy', phonologically probably /***oll-***/, which may serve as the first onomastic element. E. Laroche (*GLH*, 279) also mentions passive-reflexive *ull-ul-* 'to perish'. Since Linear A did not express ***-s-*** before a stop in consonant clusters, I analyse ***o-ra$_2$-di-ne*** as {*o/ull=i-ažd=i=ne*} 'Destroy the woman !'.

The *woman* was in this Cretan context probably not just a woman, but a monstrous one like ***Μέδουσα*** reflecting the feminine form of the present participle ***μέδων*** 'ruling'. Medusa was killed by the Cretan hero Perseus, son of Zeus and Danae. Cuneiform ***ašti***, phonologically ***/aždi/***, means 'woman' in Hurrian; the form ***ašti-ne***, phonologically ***/aždi-ne/***, with the suffix of the so-called definite article ***-ne/-ni***, 'the woman', cf. Laroche, *GLH*, 62. The form may be analysed as {*azd=i=ne*}. Since according to Th. Richter (*VHN* I) many Hurrian personal names contain the 2nd person singular of the *imperative* and ***o/ull=i-*** indeed reflects the singular 2nd person imperative of the root ***o/ull-***, the name can be interpreted as 'Destroy the (monstrous) woman (oh hero) !'.

It may seem awkward that the sign ***ra₂ = lia*** was split up in such a way that one part ***li-*** belonged to the first element ***ulli-*** and the other part ***-a*** to the second element ***-a-di-ne***. But the scribe knew that sign ***ra₂*** was just a way of shorthand writing for the notation of ***li-a*** or ***ri-a*** and he chose the most economic form. In Chapter 1: Linear A and related scripts, I have quoted a short passage from the Classical Cypriot Edalion / Idalium inscription nº 23 (2nd half 5th century B.C.). In lines 2-3 we read: *to-no-na-si-ku-po-*(3)*ro-ne to-ni-ja-te-ra-ne* = *τὸν Ὀνασικύπ*(3)*ρōν τὸν ἴjατῆραν*. We see here that the article *τόν* is twice combined with the first vowels of the next sequences, first with *Ὀνασικύπρōν* and second with *ἴjατῆραν*. The Classical Cypriot text reads first *to-no-* and then *to-ni-*. It even happens to be one of the characteristic orthographic features of that script.

If my interpretation of Linear A ***o-ra₂-di-ne*** is correct, it may well represent the Hurrian prototype of the Greek hero's name ***Περσεύς***, whose name was according to the ancient lexicographers derived from the verb *πέρθω* 'to destroy' (cf. P. Chantraine, *DELG*, 889, s.v. *Περσεύς*). A. Heubeck, *Kadmos IV (1965)*, 142, considered *Περσεύς* a hypocoristic of the compound **Περσίπολις* (or *Περσέπ(τ)ολις* 'destroyer of cities', cf. *πέρθω*). Heubeck's identification as a hypocoristic of a compound is right, but the compound is not *Περσέπ(τ)ολις*, but **Περσέγῦνος* 'destroyer of women', a Greek rendering of Hurrian ****ulli-ašdine***. A parallel of **ulli-ašdine* is *Ullikummi*, the monster created by *Kumarbi* to destroy the city of *Kumme* or *Kummiya*, the kingdom of *Tešub*. *Ullikummi* is also the title of the poem that tells the story of the battle between the gods.

Περσέπ(τ)ολις 'destroyer of cities' has nothing to do with the homonym *Περσέπολις*, ancient capital of Persia and burial place of her kings, also attested as *Περσαίπολις* and *Πέρσαι πόλις* (cf. Liddell & Scott s.v.). According to Greek popular etymology *Πέρσαι* was derived from *Περσεύς*, but the ethnic is, of course, derived from Old Iranian *Pārsa.* P. Chantraine, *DELG*, 889, s.v. *Πέρσαι*: "*Πέρσαι* est emprunté au vieux perse *Pārsa*. On a admis un traitement *Πηρσ-* > *Περσ-*, cf. Meillet-Benveniste, *Gr. du vieux perse*, 28, 49. Mais M. Lejeune, *Phonétique*², § 223 *add.*, préférait *Πᾱρσ-* > *Πᾰρσ-* > *Περσ-*, l'abrégement d'une longue devant sonante semblant plus ancient que le passage de *ᾱ* à *η*. En ce cas il faudrait peut-être supposer une influence du nom de héros *Περσεύς*, d'où les Grecs tiraient le nom *Πέρσαι*."

H.G. Güterbock, *Kumarbi, Mythen vom churritischen Kronos aus den hethitischen Fragmenten zusammengestellt, übersetzt und erklärt*, Zürich - New York 1946, 95, writes (I translate the German text, which is quoted in the *indices*, into English): "Ullikummi, about whom the epos tells, is Kumarbi's son. It is not clear who his mother is, since the beginning of fragment *d* of table I is damaged.

It is certain that he grows upto a supernatural size and that his body consist of diorite (cf. p. 63 f.). The similarity of the second onomastic element with the name of the city of *Kumme* or *Kummiya* is the more remarkable, because in the speech of the father giving a name to his son this city is mentioned in the first place (Table I, fragment D, 20) and etymologizing meanings of names are favoured by all peoples. One would therefore expect a meaning 'Destroyer of Kumme'. Unfortunately the verb is not preserved in the cited passage and a Hurrian word *ull(i/u)*, that belongs to this semantic sphere is to date unknown." E. Laroche (*GLH*, 279) was able to describe the evidence for the pertinent etymology, s.v. *ulli-* 2: Thème verbal. Opt. sg. 3 nég. *ul-li-wa-a-en*, Mit. III 95; cf. KUB XXVII 38 IV 25. Passif *ull-ul-* ?: opt. sg. 3 *ul-lu-li-iš*, KUB XLV 61, 15, v. *Ullikummi.* Speiser, *IH*, 173 n. 281, supposait *ulli-* 'altérer, à partir de *uli-* 'autre', mais les graphies ne concordent pas. – Plutôt *ulli-* 'détruire' et *ull-ul-* 'périr'. - *Ibidem*, s.v. *Ullikummi*:

1. Monstre créé par Kumarbi pour anéantir la royauté de Tešub, et titre du poème qui narre cette théomachie; cf. Güterbock, *JCS 5*, 135-161; *6*, 8-42, *passim*: Hitt. ***^{d}Ul-li-kum-mi*** et ***^{d}Ul-lu-kum-mi***, KUB XXXIII 92 sqq. H. ***ul-li-ku-um-mi-i[n]***, KUB XLV 61, 14.

2. Montagne des listes kiz. (CTH 628). ***U-li-ig-ga-ma***, ***U-li-ka-am-ma***, KBo XV 52 I 49 = 61, 9; cf. MIO I 145; Otten, *ZA 49*, 250; Gonnet, *RHA 83*, 165. ***Ullikummi*** pourrait être la déformation du nom de la montagne, interprété comme "destructeur/ destruction de Kummi"; v. sous ***Kummeni***. – En hitt. "que son nom soit Ullikummi, qu'il écrase Kummiya, la bonne ville"; en hourrite, *Kummi-ni-im ulluliš* "et que Kummi périsse"; cf. Güterbock, ***Kumarbi***, 95; E. Laroche, *NH*, p. 370 et n. 2. Note 2 may be quoted as well: "Jeu de mots étymologique sur ***Ulli-kummi*** 'destructeur de Kummi-(ya)', à en juger par la version hourrite: Bo 9383 II 15 *ku-um-mi-ni-im ul-lu-li-iš* 'et que Kummi(ni) soit détruit!', *ibid.*, 14: *tu-u-we-e te-e-ya ul-li-ku-um-mi-i[n.*"

Another indication that the Linear A name ***o-ra$_2$-di-ne*** may well be interpreted as *{o/ull=i-ažd=i=ne}*, is that Hurrian personal names with the root ***u/oll-*** are quite frequent, cf. e.g. Th. Richter, *VHN* I, 325-329: *Ullaja*, *^{f}Ulli*, *Ullija*, *^{f}Ullen*, *Ullu*, *Ullu-ewri*, *Ulluja*, *Ullukki*, *^{f}Ullum-ki*, *Ullum-tišni*, *Ullum-tišti*, *Ullum-*[...], *Ullun*, *Ullunna*, *Ullunni*, *Ullup-atal*, *Ulluri*, *Ulluš-Taja*, *Ullutta*, *Ullutti*. ***Ullu-ewri*** (*ul-lu-ew-ri, ul-lu-ew-ru*) at Mari, analysis {*o/ull=o-evri, o/ull=o-evr(i)=u*[Akkadianizing nominative]} may be identified with Linear A ***u-re-wi*** (HT 25a.2) = Old Hurrian ***Ull(=u)-erwi*** = Hurrian ***Ull(=i)-erwi***, 'Destroy (the deceased child), oh Lord !', with vowel absorption and with the same (dialectical) metathesis of ***ewri > erwi*** as at Nuzi. Cf. also the Nippur variants ***ermi/irmi***.

The Hurrian root ***ull-***, ***/oll-/***, 'to destroy' in ***Ullikummi*** and Linear A ***o-ra$_2$-di-ne*** {*o/ull=i-ažd=i=ne*} provides a plausible etymology for Pre-Greek ***Ὀλυσσεύς/Ὀδυσσεύς*** (cf. Latin *Ulixes*). The Hurrian hypocoristic name from Nuzi, ***Ulušiịa*** (wr. *Ú-lu-ši-ia*), father of *Am-ma-ku*, HSS V 62:19; *Am-ma-a-ku*, HSS IX 95:4, may be a prototype of this Pre-Greek name. It may be analysed as {*ul(l)=o/u=ž=i=ja*} 'He may destroy', cf. Th. Richter, *VHN*, 601-602, sub 1.3.2.1: verbal forms with $^{o}=V_{owel}=ž$. Compare other Nuzi names such as *Ullunzi* (wr. *Ul-lu-un-zi*), *Uluniki* (wr. *Ú-lu-ni-ki*), *Ulluịa* (wr. *Ul-lu-ia*), *Ulukka* (wr. *Ú-lu-uq-qa, Ú-lu-uk-ka*), *Ululiịa* (wr. *Ú-lu-li-ia, Ú-lu-li-a*), cf. I.J. Gelb, *NPN*, 162-163; P.M. Purves, *NPN*, 271, s.v. *ul*, *ull*; cf. Th. Richter, *BGH*, 486, s.v. *ull-* [Boğ; Mitt; PN]. meanings: 'détruire (?)' (Laroche 1980a: 279 sub *ulli-* 2); 'zerstören' (Salvini 1988b: 158); 'to destroy', d.i. */ull-/* oder */oll-/* (Wilhelm 1991b: 161f.); etc.

Linear A ***ku-mi*** (HT 110a.1) may well be the Minoan-Hurrian toponym ***Kummi***, present *Kommos*, the Minoan harbour of Phaistos and Hagia Triada on the south coast of Crete, recently excavated by G. Cadogan and his team. It can be recognized as the second sequence of the entry ***si-du-69 , ku-mi*** that is followed by HORD+E 20 ***ku-pa*** 1 [ ] (HT 110a.2) and ***ku-ro*** 100 [(HT 110a.3). Linear A ***si-du-69 , ku-mi*** was previously read as ***si-du-69-ku-mi*** (HT 110a.1), because the word divider was difficult to discern on the damaged tablet. However, ***si-du-69 , ku-mi*** (HT 110a.1) is the better reading. The Cretan toponym ***Kummi*** is probably derived from the name of the city of ***Kumma/e/i*** or ***Kummiya*** in Anatolia. Both names may well be derived from the Hurrian root ***kum-*** 'to build / erect / pile up'. If this identification is correct, it would after ***ka-pa*** = ***Ḫalpa*** (present Hagia Triada) be the second Cretan site named after a famous predominantly Hurrian city in the Near East. The theonym ***Kumarbi*** has been connected with the verbal root ***kum-*** 'errichten, auftürmen' ['to build / erect / pile up'] and has been interpreted as ***kum=ar=we*** '(der) des Errichtens / Auftürmens' ['(the one) of building > active as a builder'] or '(quello) di Kumar' ['(the one) of (toponym) Kumar'], cf. Th. Richter, *BGH*, 221-222, s.v. ***kum-*** [EN; Nuzi]. Both etymologies are possible, but in my view not very satisfactory. To me it seems more attractive to interpret ***-bi*** or ***-wi*** in ***Kumarbi / Kumarwi*** not as genitive suffix ***-bi / -wi***, but as part of the Nuzian variant ***erwi*** (as a result of metathesis) of ***ibri / iwri / ebri / ewri*** 'Lord', so that the meaning of ***Kumarbi/wi*** < ****Kum(m)a-erwi*** (result of contraction) is 'Lord of *Kumma*' and that of ***Kumarbi=ni*** is 'The Lord of Kumma'. The variant ***erwi*** may not be limited to Nuzi. One may, for instance, compare ***ermi/irmi*** at Nippur, cf. P.M. Purves, *NPN*, 210-211, s.v. ***erwi-***, ***-erwi***.

In this way the etymology of *Kumarbi* contributes to a better understanding of the mythological struggle between *Kumarbi* as 'Lord of Kumma' and his son *Tešub* who conquered (and mutilated) his father, but also succeeded him as the new Lord of Kumma and is therefore called ***Kummeni***, cf. E. Laroche, *GLH*, 154, s.v. ***Kummeni***: Épithète de Tešub. ^{d}U-*ub* ^{uru}*Arrapḫi-ni* ^{uru}*Kum-me-ni*, KBo XX 128, 8 = XXII 165, 14; cf. KUB XXV 47 I 7 = XXXII 44 Vo 9; - *Tešuba(m) ku-um-me-ni-en*, Mâri 1, 34; - Hitt. ^{uru}*Kummiyas* ^{d}U-*as* 'Tešub de Kummi'. Gén. *alla-ni Ku-um-me-ni-we*, litt. 'la dame de Kummi' (Ḫebat?), RS h. 10, 4 = *Ugar. V*, 467. The name of ***Ullikummi*** (***^{d}Ul-li-kum-mi***) 'Destroyer of Kummi' or (preferably, if ***ulli-*** is interpreted as *imperative* of ***ull-*** 'destroy !') 'Destroy Kummi !' fits very well into this mythological tradition as well. Variant ***Ullukummi*** (***^{d}Ul-lu-kum-mi***) would at present be translated as 'He (the monster) destroyed Kummi' or preferably, if interpreted as an Old Hurrian *imperative*, 'Destroy Kummi (oh monster) !'.

So *Kumma/e/i* plays an essential role in the name of *Kumarbi*, in the epithet of Tešub, *Kummeni*, and in the name of the monster *Ullikummi*. The monster is created by Kumarbi to annihilate the kingdom of Teš(š)ub (Storm-god rules, Kumarbi is displaced, but foments new rebellion using Ullikummi, product of his seed and a rock).

It is historically significant that all three important Minoan sites in the Messara-valley have Hurrian names. I have interpreted the Linear A and B toponym ***ka-pa*** as ***Ḫalba***, the Hurrian name of Aleppo (***Ḫalab*** in Semitic) and have proposed that ***ka-pa*** = ***Ḫalba*** is in fact the ancient name of the palace of Hagia Triada and that the Linear A ethnic ***ka-pa-qe*** is syllabic cuneiform ***Ḫalbaḫe*** = alphabetic cuneiform ***Ḫlbġ*** 'Man of ***Ḫalba***'.

Linear A ***pa-i-to*** occurs in Linear A (not surprisingly) in the archives of the palace of Hagia Triada, only two miles from Phaistos. Linear B ***pa-i-to*** (KN Da 1163+1400, *al.*) reflects the Hellenized form ***Φαιστός*** (*Phaistos*), the name of the palace dominating the Messara-valley.

Observing the Linear B orthography of ***pa-i-to*** (KN Da 1163+1400, *et al.*) ***Φαιστός***, there is absolutely no doubt that Linear B did not express ***-s-*** in consonant clusters before an occlusive. It seems wise to assume that the identical Linear A sequence ***pa-i-to*** also contained the same consonant cluster ***-st-***. Final consonants are not expressed in Linear A and B. The only difference between the Linear A and B forms might be their endings: The (Mycenaean) Greek form ended in ***-ος***, as the later Greek toponym confirms. About the Linear A form ***pa-i-to*** we can be sure that it ended in either ***-o*** or ***-o*** + consonant, not expressed in the script.

In the 2016 edition of *Minoan Linear A* I still reckoned with the possibility that the toponym ***Φαιστός*** was not only Pre-Greek, but also Pre-Hurrian, based on the assumption that at least some Pre-Greek toponymes might go back to Neolithic, Chalcolithic and/or Early Minoan times, i.e. to the period before the alleged arrival of Hurrians in Crete at the beginning of the Middle Minoan period, when the first palaces were built on the island. Doro Levi found pottery of the Chalcolithic period (cf. D. Levi, *The recent excavations at Phaistos*, SIMA XI, Lund 1964, 17, Fig. 5).

However, I also mentioned in the 2016 edition that we cannot be sure that the Linear A toponym ***pa-i-to*** is Pre-Hurrian, for the name probably consists of a theme ***Phai-/Φαι-*** in ***Φαι-στ-ός***, with a formant or cluster ***-st-***.

In Hurrian the element ***Pai-*** or ***Pae(-)*** occurs frequently in onomastics such as *Pa-e, Pa-e-en-ni, Pa-i-šarri, Pa-i-ta-e, Pa-i-te-ia, Pa-i-te-a, Pa-i-te, Pa-i-te-šup, Pa-i-til-la, Pa-i-za-ni, Pa-i-ṣi-na* (cf. I.J. Gelb, *NPN,* 109-110; P.M. Purves, *NPN*, 242; cf. A. Draffkorn, *HHA,* 46: *Pa-i-še-na* on AT 252:15). There is a good chance that the labial occlusive in Minoan-Hurrian ***pai-*** sounded as an *aspirate* labial occlusive in the ears of the Mycenaean Greeks, which may account for the later rendering ***Φαι-***.

Th. Richter (*BGH*, 285) mentions s.v. ***pa-***, ***paḫ-*** II [*passim*] '(er)bauen' ['to build'], in personal names 'schaffen' ['to create']. The root corresponds with Hittite ***weda-/wete-*** (M. Salvini, 1987/88, 181; E. Neu, 1988a, 7, 1996a, 184). Cf. also Th. van den Hout, *The elements of Hittite*, 198, s.v. ***wete*** [Ia] 'to build'.

Th. Richter (*VHN*, 475-476) mentions s.v. ***pa-*** 'bauen' ['to build']: "The root ***pa-*** and the derivation ***pairi*** *{pa=i=ri}* 'einer der gebaut hat' ['someone who has built'] can be regarded as clarified. No doubt ***Pairi*** can also be a theonym, see *BGH*, 285f. The short names ***Pa-i-la*** and ***Pa-i-lu*** belong to and are probably derived from ***paili***, which can probably be connected with the word ***pailija*** that can be interpreted as 'ge-, erbaut' ['built'] and sometimes as 'das, welches ich gebaut habe' ['what I have built'] or 'das von mir Gebaute' ['built by me']. The high frequency of ***Paila*** is remarkable."

The toponym ***pa-i-to*** (HT 97a.3; HT 120.6) can now be analysed as Old Hurrian. In fact the form ***ba-'à-áš-to/um*** 'he has built', attested in the inscription of *Tiš-atal* of Urkeš, the oldest Hurrian inscription, appears to be equivalent to Linear A ***pa-i-to***. The meaning of the toponym is 'He/She (a God or the King) has built (the palace)'.

The provenance of the Tiš-atal tablet was not known for a long time, but it is now generally accepted that it comes from Urkeš (modern Tell Mozān). The inscription (AO 19938) was first edited by A. Parrot - J. Nougayrol, Un document de fondation hourrite, *RA 42 (1948)*, 1-20; and later by I.M. Diakonoff, *Hurrisch und Urartäisch*, München 1971, 110-111, n. 123; 1990, 382. G. Wilhelm provided a German translation in his *Grundzüge der Geschichte und Kultur der Hurriter*, Darmstadt 1982, 15. He also offered a new complete edition: Die Inschrift des Tišatal von Urkeš, in: G. Buccellati - M. Kelly-Buccellati (eds.), *Urkesh and the Hurrians*. Studies in honor of Lloyd Cotsen (Urkesh / Mozan Studies 3), Malibu 1998, 117-143.

I. Wegner (*Einführung in die hurritische Sprache*, Wiesbaden 2007[2], Lektion 14, 232-236) offers the whole transliterated text of 25 lines, a grammatical commentary and a German translation. I discuss here the first sentence of the inscription and translate I. Wegner's comment into English:

1. *ti-iš-a-tal*	Tiš-atal
2. *en-da-an*	endan
3. *ur-kèš*^{ki}	of Urkeš,
4. *pu-ur-li*	a temple
5. ^{D}NERI.GAL	of / for Nergal
6. *ba-'à-áš-tum*	he has built.

1. The personal name *Tiš-atal* is subject of the sentence, however, without grammatical marking of the ergative case [expected for the subject of a transitive verb, PGvS]. The old reading of the name as *Tiš-ari* [e.g. in the 1971 edition of Diakonoff's *HuU*, PGvS] is no longer valid, because the second element is occasionally written in full (*-a-ta-al*).
2. *endan*, title of *Tiš-atal*, is still not completely clarified. The title misses any case-marking. I. Wegner (*Einführung*, 22-24) explains that this Old-Hurrian title of *Tiš-atal*, *Tupkiš* and *Išar-kīnum* was formerly associated with Sumerian *entu* (priestess), but is now interpreted as Hurrian. As a result we often find in early editions the translation "*Tiš-atal,* priestess ? of Urkeš". The element *-tan* is probably equivalent to *-tann / -tenn*, a suffix indicating professions in later texts. The element *en* is derived from either Sumerian EN 'Lord, master' or Hurrian *en(i)* 'God' (see G. Wilhelm, *The Hurrians*, 1989, 11).
3. Urkeš, name of the city. The expected genitive case-ending *-ve* (written *-we*) is hidden behind the heterogram 'UR.KÈŠ^{ki}' according to I.M. Diakonoff.
4. *purli* (cf. the variant form *puruli* in line 7) 'temple' (absolutive singular) is direct object to the transitive-ergative verbal form *pa=ašt=o=m.*
5. Nerigal is an important god from the land east of the Tigris. He belongs to the oldest Gods adopted into Hurrian. This theonym also misses the expected case-ending *-ve* (genitive) [or *-va* (dative), PGvS].
6. ***pa-*** 'to build' + ***V(owel)št*** (root-extension, probably indicating completion of an action) + ***o*** (morpheme of transitive-ergative past / perfect) + ***m*** (indicator of third person singular), cf. I. Wegner, *Einführung*, 88-89, s.v. ***-Všt-***.

In my view Old Hurrian ***ba-'à-áš-tum*** 'he has built' can morphologically be compared with ***ta-wa$_a$-aš-tu-u-um***, mentioned twice in the Hurrian-Hittite bilingual ***Kirenze***, KBo 32: 14 Vs. I 43 (cf. E. Neu, *StBoT 32*, 80), 3rd parable: *The goblet (chalice, cup) and its smith* (KBo 32: 14 Vs. I 42-59).

It consists of the verbal root ***tab/v-*** 'to cast (metal)' + ***V(owel)št*** (root-extension, probably indicating completion of an action) **+ *o*** (morpheme of transitive-ergative past / perfect) **+ *m*** (marker of third person singular), cf. I. Wegner, *Einführung*, 216-221, especially 218.

I am convinced that Linear A ***pa-i-to*** (HT 97a.3; HT 120.6) is a genuine Hurrian toponym meaning 'He/She (a God) has built (the palace)' and equivalent to Old Hurrian ***ba-'à-áš-to/um*** on the Tiš-atal tablet, analysed and normalised as ***pa=ašt=o=m***, and translated as 'He (Tiš-atal) has built (a temple)', cf. also Th. Richter (*BGH*, 285-286), s.v. ***pa-***, *paḫ-* II [*passim*] '(er)bauen' ['to build'], *pa('/h)-*, G. Wilhelm, 1988b, 55.

In my view the following phases of phonetic development are likely: ***ba-'à-áš-to/um* = *pa('/h)=ašt=o=m* > *pa=j=ašt=o=m* > *pa=j=(a)št=o=m* > *pa=j=št=o=m*** (wr. ***pa-i-to*** in Linear A). The transitional glide ***-j-*** distinguished the ***-a*** of the root ***pa-*** from the ***-a-*** of the root-extension ***-ašt-*** and eventually the ***-a-*** of ***-ašt-*** disappeared as a result of *syncope*. For Linear B ***pa-i-to*** (KN Da 1163+1400, *al.*) the Old Hurrian ending in ***=o=m*** had to be changed into a Hellenized form in ***-ος* (*-os*)** : ***Φαιστός*** (Phaistos).

I. Wegner (*Einführung*, 88-89) analyses the form ***ba-'à-áš-to/um*** as {*pa=ašt=o=m*} 'er hat gebaut' ['he has built']. She explains that the vowel in the root-extension ***-Všt-*** is adapted to the vowel in the root, e.g. ***tan=ašt-*** 'machen' ['to make'], ***an- / an=ašt-*** 'sich freuen' ['to enjoy'], ***mad=ašt-*** 'weise sein' ['to be wise'], ***teḫ- / teḫ=ešt-*** 'erhöhen, gross werden' ['to elevate, to grow, to become great'], ***šurv=ušt-*** 'Böses tun' ['to do, to cause, to bring about evil']. This root-extension may have a denominalising character and should not be confused with the intransitive marker of the past tense ***-oš-* + *-t-***. However, there are indications that the formants ***-ol-*** and especially ***-Všt-*** in combination with verbal forms in ***=o=m*** may show other grammatical differentiations (aspect or type of action), cf. G. Wilhelm, *Festschrift Heger*, 1992, 670. The 'Old Hurrian' formant ***-Všt-*** seems to express the end or result of an action, e.g. ***pa=ašt=o=m*** 'he has built'.

Compare also Hurrian forms such as ***paiḫu*** [Nuzi] 'eine Art Feld' ['a sort of field'] (*AHw*, Lieferung 9, 1969, 812), 'building lot' (Maidman, 1976, 376), 'une sorte de terrain' (E. Laroche, *GLH*, 193), ***qaqqaru paiḫu*** 'unbuilt plot' (Zaccagnini, 1979a, 25, 113ff., and others), ***pa=i=ġe*** 'Bauland, Baugrundstück' (G. Wilhelm, 1988b, 55; I. Wegner, *Einführung*, 54, 270, a.o.). Cf. ***pailia / paillija*** [Boğ.; PN(?)] 'gebaut' ['built'] and ***pa=i=ri*** (resultative participle) 'einer, der gebaut hat, Baumeister' ['someone who has built, architect'].

Identification of Linear A ***pa-i-to*** as a genuine Hurrian toponym is corroborated by the fact that the Cretan city of Khania (also with a Minoan palace) bears a name with a similar Hurrian etymology, since Hurrian ***Ḫania*** reflects a Hurrian verbal form {*ḫan=i=a*} 'He/she (a God) (pro)creates, gives / gave birth to (the palace)'.

Linear A ***ka-ni-ja-mi*** (KT Zf 1) occurs as second sequence on a gold pin from Crete. The inscription reads (from left to right): ***a-ma-wa-si , ka-ni-ja-mi , i-ja , qa-ki-se-nu-ti*** or ***za-ki-se-nu-ti , a-ta-de***. It consists of 18 signs in one line on one side of a gold pin of 11 cm, with floral decoration on the other side. Exact provenance uncertain, but probably from Crete. The pin appeared on the European Antiquities Market in 1980 and is now in the Museum of Hagios Nikolaos (inv. nr. 9675).

Interpretation of the second sequence of the Linear A inscription, ***ka-ni-ja-mi***, depends on interpretation of the ending ***-mi***. In principle there are two possibilities:

I) ***-mi*** and ***-me(n)*** can represent hypocoristic forms of ***-min(n)a*** , ***-men(n)a*** or ***-menni*** in Hurrian personal names. This can be demonstrated by parallel formations such as *(f)Aḫar-me* (Mari) beside *fAḫar-menni* (Mari), *fEtim-me* (Mari) beside *fItem-menni* (Mari) beside *fEtem-menni* (Nuzi), *fUnam-me* (Ašnakkum) beside *fUnam-menni* (Middle-Assyrian Nuzi). See for ***-mi*** e.g. *fPaḫar-mi* (Mari), cf. Th. Richter, *VHN*, 457-458.

This means that Linear A ***ka-ni-ja-mi*** can be a personal name consisting of a Hurrian verbal form ***ḫan=i=a*** 'she gives birth (to)' and the nominal element ***-mi / -min(n)a*** 'twin' or (as proposed by Th. Richter) 'sister', meaning 'She (the mother) gives/gave birth to a twin (?) or sister (?)'. The Hurrian personal name ***Ḫanija*** is attested at Ašnakkum, Mari and Šušarrā, where it is the name of men and is translated by Th. Richter (*VHN*, 121-122, 407-408) as 'Sie (Frau) gebar (Jungen)' ['She (woman) gave birth (to a boy)']. The name ***Ḫanija*** also occurs at Emar, Nippur, and Nuzi.

II) If we accept that not only ***pi*** and ***wi***, but also ***mi*** and ***wi*** alternate in some Hurrian texts, since **[*p*]**, **[*m*]** and **[*w*]** are labials and phonetically close, ***ka-ni-ja-mi*** may contain the Hurrian genitive form 'of *Ḫanija*' of the personal name ***Ḫanija*** as at Ašnakkum, Mari and Šušarrā or of the Minoan-Hurrian toponym ***Ḫanija*** (later *Χανιά*) 'of Khania'.

Compare for this ***m/w*** alternation Linear A ***|i-mi-sa-ra*** (HT 27+HT 48a.3), which I have interpreted as the Hurrian personal name ****Irmi/Ermi-šarra*** 'The Lord is King of Gods', which would in fact be equivalent to ***Erwi-šarri*** at Nuzi, ***ibri-šarri*** (***ibri***(EN)-***šarri***(LUGAL), ***ibrḏr / iwrḏr*** at Ugarit and ***ibri-šarri*** [AL 137] at Alalaḫ. Cf. also ***Ir-me/mi-ta-at-ta*** and ***Ir-me-ta-ta*** at Nippur, cf. Clay *PNCP*, 93, to be read ***Erme/i-tatta***, i.e. ****Erwi-tatta***, according to Purves, *NPN*, 263. Since ***Erwi-šarri*** 'the Lord is King of Gods' is the name of 29 persons at Nuzi (cf. I.J. Gelb, *NPN*, 48; P.M. Purves, *NPN*, 211) and since it is also well attested elsewhere, interpretation of Linear A ***i-mi-sa-ra*** as ****Irmi/Ermi-šarra*** is to be preferred to a sentence name with ***Ilmi-/Elmi-***, which is considerably less frequent. This interpretation would offer the Hurrian onomastic element ***ewri/erwi*** in Linear A in the form of ***Irmi/Ermi***, i.e. the form in which the Mycenaean Greeks inherited the name of their god ***Ἑρμῆς*** < ***Ἑρμάάς*** < ***Ἑρμάάς*** (the form with intervocalic ***-h-***), cf. Linear B ***e-ma-a₂ a-re-ja*** (PY Tn 316 r. 7), interpreted as singular dative ***Ἑρμάᾳ Ἀρείᾳ*** 'for ***Ἑρμάάς Ἀρείᾱς***', 'for Hermes the Martial'. Linear A ***|i-mi-sa-ra***, Hurrian ****Irmi/Ermi-šarra***, 'The Lord is like the King of Gods' contains two epithets to Tešub.

If interpretation of ***ka-ni-ja-mi*** as genitive of the toponym ***Ḫanija*** is correct, it is also likely that the gold pin bearing this inscription comes from Khania and that ***Khania*** may well be identified as the ancient Minoan toponym instead of ***Κυδωνίᾱ***. It is theoretically conceivable that the Cretan name ***Khania*** is derived from the name of the land of ***Ḫana*** in the Euphrates and Ḫabur area. The toponym may, however, well reveal a Hurrian verbal form, also known from personal names. Th. Richter (*VHN*, 584-585) shows the following one-word personal names with distinctive verbal endings that can be analysed as subject-markers of the 2nd person singular indicative in ***°=i=o***: ***Ḫaniu*** (wr. *ḫa-ni-ú/ù*) {*ḫan=i=o*} 'You give birth (to the boy)' (Nuzi, see *NPN*, 54. See also Th. Richter, *BGH*, 125, and *VHN*, 407, 585, s.v. ***ḫan-*** 'gebären' ['to give birth'] (one of the most frequent elements at Nuzi; the name ***Ḫaniu*** is the name of 23 men at Nuzi).

The meaning of the root is generally accepted and can be connected with the substantive ***ḫani*** 'child'. The personal name ***Ḫanija***, analysis {*ḫan=i=a*} can be interpreted as 'She gives/gave birth', but can also be interpreted as a hypocoristic with ***ḫani*** 'child' as first element and the hypocoristic suffix ***-ya***, e.g. based on a personal name such as ***ᶠḪa-ni-wa-an-di*** 'The child is right / just / favourable' (Alalaḫ IV, see D.J. Wiseman, *AT*, 135, who reads ***ᶠḪa-ni-wa-aš-di***, 298, 31).

Apart from the question of whether ***ka-ni-ja-mi*** (KT Zf 1) is a Hurrian personal name and a hypocoristic of *Ḫan=i=(j)a-mina*, or genitive of the toponym ***Ḫanija*** 'of *Ḫanija*' or a sort of ethnic '(citizen) of *Ḫanija*', it is not inconceivable that the toponym ***Χανιά*** (Khaniá) is indeed equivalent to Hurrian and Minoan ***Ḫanija*** {*ḫan=i=a*} 'She gives birth'. It is a poetic name commemorative of the birth / creation of a Minoan palace, administrative, social-economic and religious centre.

Κυδωνίᾱ is usually identified with modern Khania, but the many (fragments of) tablets, roundels and noduli which have to date been discovered in the rescue excavations at Khania, have not yet confirmed this identification.

It is probably not entirely accidental that ***i-da-pa₃-i-sa-ri*** (PH 6.4) appears together with ***i-do-ri-ni-ta*** (PH 6.2) on one of the earliest Linear A tablets in Crete, PH 6 (HM 1486), found beneath the concrete of phase 2 in room XXVIII in the south-west section of the Palace of Phaistos and belonging to the end of Doro Levi's local phase 1b of the protopalatial period (2nd architectural period of the First Palace), dated to the transition of MM II a/b. This accounts for Hurrian presence in Crete at a very early date and most interesting apparently even before the zenith of power of the Mitannian Kingdom.

PH 6.1. *i-na-wa* , *a-ri*
PH 6.2. *i-do-ri-ni-ta*
PH 6.3. *a-ri*
PH 6.4. *i-da-pa₃-i-sa-ri*

Prima facie ***i-da-pa₃-i-sa-ri*** seems to consist of the name of mount ***Ida*** combined with the Hurrian personal name ***Pai-šarri*** attested at Nuzi. In Linear B the value ***φα*** (***pha***), with aspirate labial occlusive, has been ascribed to sign ***pa₃***. On the photograph no dot or word divider is visible between ***i-da(-)*** and ***(-)pa₃-i-sa-ri***. Thus we must assume that ***i-da-pa₃-i-sa-ri*** is one sequence.

It is usually thought that the first element ***ida-*** in ***i-da-pa₃-i-sa-ri*** can be identified with the name of the (divine) *Ida*-massif in Crete, mentioned as ***i-da*** in two Linear A texts from Kato Zakro (ZA 21b.1; ZA 27a.1). The mountain name (*oronym*) *Ida* may originally have been a Hurrian verbal form {*id=a*}, consisting of the root ***id-***, (trans.) 'to hit, beat, smash, crush', (intr.) 'to thunder' + the marker of intransitivity ***-a***. Since the intransitive indicative 3rd person singular does not have its own subject marker (no enclitic ***-nna***), the original meaning may be 'He (the Mountain God) thunders'. The intransitive imperative 2nd person singular does not have its own subject marker either, so that {*id=a*} can also mean 'Thunder (oh Mountain God) !'.

The other element has an exact equivalent as a Hurrian personal name attested at Nuzi, ***Pa-i-šarri*** (wr. *Pa-i-šarri*), who is mentioned as son of *Ḫa-ni-ku* (JEN 487), cf. I.J. Gelb, *NPN*, 110; P.M. Purves, *NPN*, 242, s.v. ***Pai-*** + ***-šarri***.

Linear A ***i-da-pa₃-i-sa-ri*** (PH 6.4) is probably morphologically comparable with Linear A ***i-da-ma-te*** on a golden double axe (AR Zf 1) and an identical inscription on a silver double axe (AR Zf 2) from Arkalokhori. It can also be compared with Linear A ***i-da-a*** (KO Za 1.b-c) and | ***i-da-da*** | (KT Zg 2.b). The preferable analysis of ***i-da-ma-te*** is {*id=am=a-te*}, consisting of verbal root ***id-*** + the factitive root-extension ***-am-*** (cf. I. Wegner, *Einführung*, 88) + the indicator of intransitivity ***-a-*** + theophorous element ***-Te*** (hypocoristic of ***-Tešub***) as subject of the verb, 'Tešub thunders, Tešub causes thunder and lightning'. The analysis of ***i-da-a*** is {*id=a=ya*} 'He (the Mountain God) thunders' (with Hurrian hypocoristic suffix ***-ya***) > 'Thunderer', probably hypocoristic of ***i-da-ma-te*** or ****i-da-te*** 'Tešub thunders' or 'Thunder, oh Tešub !' (without root-extension ***-am-***).

If these analyses are correct, ***i-da-pa₃-i-sa-ri*** can be explained as 'Phaišarri thunders', in which case *Phaišarri* appears to take the place of *Tešub* (cf. ***i-da-ma-te***) as a sort of (*quasi*) theophorous element. In this respect it is significant that Hurrian ***šarri*** 'The King of Gods' is, of course, equivalent to *Tešub*. Apart from ***Pa-i-šarri*** (wr. *Pa-i-šarri*) at Nuzi, an 'Old Hurrian' variant ***Paip-šarri*** occurs twice at Mari and once at Tigunāni, cf. Th. Richter, *VHN*, 219: ***Paip-šarri*** (*pa-i-ip-šar-ri, ba-i-ip-šar-ri*), analysis {*pa=i=b-šarri*}, typology 1.1.1.2.1, lexicon *pa-*, *šarri*, translation 'Der Götterkönig baute (Jungen)' ['The King of Gods built / created (the boy)']. Richter compares *pa-i-šar-ri* / *pa-i-*LUGAL at Nuzi (s. *NPN*, 110, *AAN I*, 104), *pa-i-še-na* at Alalaḫ (D.J. Wiseman, *AT* *252: 15), *pá-i-še-en-ni* at Nuzi (s. *SCCNH 6*, 398), *pa/pá-i-te* at Emar and Kurruḫanni, *pa/pá-i-te-sup* at Kurruḫanni, *pa-i-te-sup, ba-i-te-sup, ba-i-ti-sup* at Nuzi, *pa-i-te, ba-i-te, pa-i-te-ia, pa-i-te-a, pa-i-te-e* at Nuzi, *pa-i-til-la* at Nuzi, *ba-il-te-sup* at Nippur, cf. Th. Richter, *VHN*, 219, 475-476, s.v. ***pa-*** 'bauen' ['to build'].

However, though the apparent correlation between Linear A ***i-da-pa₃-i-sa-ri*** (PH 6.4) and the personal name ***Pa-i-šarri*** (wr. *Pa-i-šarri*) at Nuzi seems very convincing, one question troubles me: ***šarri*** can replace *Tešub* in names, but can ***Pai-šarri*** do the same ?

Existence of a Cretan local god called ***Pai-šarri***, possibly originally epithet to *Tešub*, is *a priori* not inconceivable, but it may be a step too far to postulate the existence of such an epithet or deity only on the basis of attestation of Linear A ***i-da-pa₃-i-sa-ri*** (PH 6.4).

So it may be wise to examine, whether correspondence between Hurrian ***Pai-šarri*** and ***i-da-pa₃-i-sa-ri*** might be accidental and whether ***i-da-pa₃-i-sa-ri*** might also be analysed differently. The other sequence ***i-do-ri-ni-ta*** (PH 6.2) may offer a solution.

Linear A ***i-do-ri-ni-ta*** (PH 6.2) on the same tablet from Phaistos can be analysed as {*id=ol=e/in=i=tta*}, consisting of the verbal root ***id-*** + the root-extension ***-ol-*** + the suffix of the *jussive* 3rd person singular ***-e/in-*** + the thematic vowel ***-i-*** + the enclitic personal pronoun 1st person singular ***-tta*** 'me'. Translation: 'May he (the god) hit me violently'.

Can ***i-da-pa₃-i-sa-ri*** (PH 6.4) be analysed likewise ? I think it can. It may well be a sentence name with ***šarri*** as nominal element, analysis {*id=ap(p)=ai-šarri*}, consisting of the root ***id-*** 'to hit, strike violently' + a root-extension ***-ap(p)-*** (possibly comparable with ***-apš-/-epš-*** and ***-upp-***, see I. Wegner, *Einführung*, 88-89) + suffix ***-ai-*** / ***-ae-*** marking the *final debitive* (cf. I. Wegner, *Einführung*, 111-112, and table 12) + the subject ***šarri*** 'King of Gods'. The name can then be translated 'Let the King of Gods hit / strike violently !'.

Even if ***i-da-pa$_3$-i-sa-ri*** does not contain an onomastic element representing an alleged local god called ***Pai-šarri*** that happens to be equivalent to an attested personal name, but has to be analysed as *{id=ap(p)=ai-šarri}*, the scribe of tablet PH 6 seems to have been fond of playing with words and names. I have come across more examples of scribes of Linear A tablets who display a remarkable feeling for poetry: the scribe of tablet ZA 10 from Kato Zakro also used alliteration and rhyme.

The advantage of the latter analysis is that ***a-ri i-do-ri-ni-ta a-ri i-da-pa$_3$-i-sa-ri*** (PH 6.1-4) offers parallel constructions with stylistic harmony of alliteration of ***a-ri ... a-ri*** and ***i-do- ... i-da-*** and names that are formed with non-indicative verbs (*jussive* and *final debitive*), the one as a 'one-word' name, the other as a 'sentence name'.

The scribe has made an effort to write a poetic text worthy of the divine character of the introductory sequence ***i-na-wa*** (PH 6.1) that can be interpreted as a Hurrian *absolutive (vocative)* ***innawwâš*** *{e/in(i)=na=(i)wwâš}* < *{e/in(i)=na=(i)wwa=aš}* 'Our Gods !', consisting of the root ***en(i)-/ in(i)-*** 'god' + the suffix of the so-called plural 'definite article' ***-na-*** + the contracted possessive suffix ***-iwwâš*** of the plural first person, developed from the (singular) possessive suffix of the first person ***-iwwa*** + the pluralizing suffix ***-aš***. In Linear A the final consonant ***-š*** is not expressed as it is not in Linear B.

Tablet PH 6 from Phaistos is indeed a remarkable text, because it does not show any ideogram and units which are usually present in the accounting texts of palatial archives. This fact seems to be in accordance with the religious character of the text, which I have also discussed in the chapter on *'Religious' Linear A inscriptions*.

The first sequences of the entry ***si-du-69 ꞉ ku-mi*** (HT 110a.1) may be interpreted as ***si-du-mina ꞉ ku-mi***, consisting of the Hurrian personal name ***si-du-mina*** followed by the Hurrian toponym ***ku-mi*** = ***Kummi***, Cretan Kommos (excavated by G. Cadogan and his team), the Minoan harbour of Phaistos and Hagia Triada). Linear A sign ***69*** (= Linear B ****34***) probably has a biconsonantal value ***mina***, cf. Linear A doublets such as ***u-mi-na-si*** and ***u-69-si = u-mina-si*** as well as ***]pi-mi-na-te*** and ***pi-69-te = pi-mina-te***.

Linear A ***si-du-mina*** (HT 110a.1) can be analysed as *{šid=u-me/in(n)a}*, of which ***šid=u-*** represents the verbal element and ***-mina / -minna / minni / -mena /-menna / -menni*** the nominal element. I. Wegner (*Einführung*, 52-53) explains that the Hurrian *a*-stems are limited to words indicating congeniality or kinship such as ***šala*** 'daughter', ***šena*** 'brother', ***ela*** 'sister', ***nera*** 'mother', ***mena*** 'twin' (?) or 'sister' (?) as well as some theonyms such as ***Ša(v)uška***, rarely ***Šimiga*** (mostly ***Šimige***) and ***tiša*** 'heart' that does not belong to these categories. She also mentions that some scholars (e.g. G. Wilhelm, *Cambridge Encyclopedia*, Chapter 4, 2004, 105) explain the diphthong-stems in ***-ai*** such as ***allai*** 'Lady', ***attai*** 'father' and ***uštai*** 'hero' as *a*-stems with a 'honorific' ***-i***: ***alla=i***, etc.

According to Th. Richter (*VHN*, 457-458), s.v. ***me/ina*** (etc.) and hypocoristic ***me/mi***, a formation like ***menni*** can be explained from < *{*mena=ni}*, cf. ***šenni*** < *{*šena=ni}*. He also mentions the meaning 'twin sister' (?) for ***mena***. He prefers the meaning 'sister' ('Geschwister'), because the element occurs primarily in names of women, though occasionally in names of men. I prefer the neutral meaning 'twin', though 'twin sister' may be a good option as well, if the child is a girl. The hypocoristics ***-me/-mi*** only occur as second onomastic element.

The doublets ^{f}***Aḫar-me*** (Mari) : ^{f}***Aḫar-menni*** (Mari), ^{f}***Etim-me*** (Mari) : ^{f}***Etem-menni*** (Nuzi), ^{f}***Unam-me*** (Ašnakkum) : ^{f}***Unam-menni*** (Nuzi) prove that they are hypocoristics of ***-mena / -mina***.

P.M. Purves (*NPN*, 234) mentions the following names with ***-menni*** as second element: ***Akam-menni*** (*^{f}A-qa-am-me-en-ni, ^{m}A-qa-am-me-en-ni*), ^{f}***Etem-menni*** (*^{f}E-te-em-me-en-ni*), ^{f}***Ḫalu-menni*** (*^{f}Ḫa-lu-me-en-ni, ^{f}Ḫa-lu-me-ni*), ^{f}***Kašum-menni*** (*^{f}Ka-šu-um-me-en-ni*), ^{f}***Puḫu-menni*** (*^{f}Pu-ḫu-me-en-ni, ^{f}Pu-ḫu-mi-ni, ^{f}Pu-ḫu-mi-en-ni, ^{f}Pu-ḫu-me-ni*), ^{f}***Šatu-menni*** (*^{f}Ša-du-mi-en-ni, ^{f}Ša-du-me-en-ni, ^{f}Ša-du-mi-ni*), ^{f}***Teḫeš-menni*** (*^{f}Te-ḫe-eš-mi-en-ni, ^{f}Te-ḫé-eš-me-en-ni*); with ***menni-*** as first element: ^{f}***Menni-kerаše*** (*^{f}Me-en-ni-ge-ra-še, ^{f}Me-ni-ge-ra-še*), ^{f}***Menni-waše*** (*^{f}Me-en-ni-wa-še, ^{f}Mi-en-ni-wa-še-e, ^{f}Me-ni-wa-še-e, ^{f}Me-ni-wa-še, ^{f}Mi-ni-wa-še*). P.M. Purves (*NPN*, 235): with ***mini- / mina-***: ^{f}***Minen-na*** (*^{f}Mi-ni-en-na*), ^{f}***Minen-naia̯*** (*^{f}Mi-ni-en-na-a-a, Mi-ni-na-a-a, ^{f}Me-ni-na-a-a, ^{f}Me-ni-en-na-a-a*), ^{f}***Mini-kui*** (*^{f}Mi-ni-ku-i*), ^{f}***Minaš-šuk*** (*^{f}Mi-na-aš-šuk, Mi-na-aš-šu-uk, Me-na-aš-šu-uk-ku, Mi-na-šuk*); 'one word' names: ^{f}***Miniku*** (*^{f}Mi-ni-ik-ku, ^{f}Me-ni-ku*), ^{f}***Minuša*** (*^{f}Mi-nu-ša*); hypocoristic: ***Minaia̯*** (*Mi-na-a-a, Me-na-a-a*). See Th. Richter (*VHN*, 458) for a long list of names with ***-mena / -mina, -me/-mi*** (etc.).

According to Th. Richter (*VHN*, 516), s.v. ***šid-*** II, 'verfluchen' [to curse]) the orthography ***ši-d/t°*** allows a distinction from ***šed-*** I 'fett machen, mästen' ['to fatten up, feed'], written ***še-ed°*** in the Hurrian-Hittite bilingual ***Kirenze*** (KBo 32), corresponding with Hittite ***warganu-***. Th. Richter (*BGH*, 398-400) distinguishes ***še/id-*** I [Boğ.; Tiš-atal] 'verfluchen' from ***šed-*** II [Boğ.] 'fett machen, mästen'. [N.B.: root I of *VHN* = root II of *BGH*; and root II of *VHN* = root I of *BGH*.]

Th. Richter ascribes ***Šetija*** at Mari, (wr. *še-di-ja*) to the root ***šed-*** I 'fett machen, mästen' (*VHN*, 279, 516), analysis {*šed=i=ja*}, typology 1.1.1.2.4, lexicon ***šed-*** I, translation 'Er/Sie (scil. ein *Numen*) machte (Jungen) fett(?)' [He/she (scil. a *numen*) made (the boy) fat, c.q. fed (the boy)]. He attributes the following names to the root ***šid-*** II 'verfluchen' (*VHN*, 278-279, 516): ***Šitap-šarri*** (wr. *ši-tap-ša-ri*) at Mari (*TEM-3* VI 64, reading Durant/Marti 2005, 124), typology 1.1.1.3.1, analysis {*šid=a=b-šarri*), lexicon ***šid-*** II, ***šarri***, no translation; ***Šitip-šarri*** at Mari (wr. *ši-di-ip-šar-ri*), typology 1.1.1.2.1, analysis {*šid=i=b-šarri*}, lexicon ***šid-*** II, ***šarri***, translation 'Der Götterkönig verfluchte (verstorbenes Kind)' [The King of Gods cursed (the deceased child)]; ***Šitip-ewri*** (wr. *ši-di-ip-ew-ri*), at Tuttul (Tall Bi'a), analysis {*šid=i=b-evri*), typology 1.1.1.2.1, lexicon ***šid-*** II, ***ewri***, translation 'Der Herr verfluchte (verstorbenes Kind)' [The Lord cursed (the child that passed away)].

Since a nasal ***-n-*** preceding an occlusive in consonant clusters is not expressed in Linear A and B, we must also consider the possibility that Linear A ***si-du-mina*** (HT 110a.1) contains the root ***šind-*** 'seven' or a transitive verbal root ***šind-*** 'to make seven', and the intransitive root 'to be seven', both based on ***šind-*** 'seven'.

Another personal name in Linear A, ***si-di-ja*** (HT 126(+Fr)a.3), can be identified as a Hurrian hypocoristic personal name built on the root ***še/id-*** I or ***šid-*** II, but also on the root ***šind-***. In that case ***Si-di-ja*** (HT 126(+Fr)a.3) can be equated with the Hurrian personal name from Nuzi ***šintia̯***, phonologically ***/šindia̯/***, (wr. *Ši-en-ti-ia, Ši-in-ti-ia*), that P.M. Purves regards as a hypocoristic for ***Šintip-tešup*** (wr. *Ši-in-di-ip-te-šup, Ši-in-ti-ip-te-šup*), since a man of each name is son of *Eḫli-tešup* (*NPN*, 257, s.v. ***šint, šintia̯***).

The dental is considered voiced as the Linear A name confirms. P.M. Purves: "Occurrences as personal name element with ***-p*** added imply verbal use. Yet in *šint-arpu*, e.g. JEN 102:12 and 25, *šint* seems to be primarily a numeral; see Speiser in *AASOR XVI (1936)*, 132, and Oppenheim in *OLZ XL*, cols. 1-6. That *šint* may not necessarily be identical with Hurrian *šin*, 'two', is suggested by J. Friedrich, *KBCG*, 34, who mentions a letter in which Von Brandenstein proposes translation 'seven'." Since publication of the Hurrian-Hittite bilingual ***Kirenze*** (KBo 32) we know that this ***-p/b*** in personal names such as ***Šintip-tešup*** is not a root-complement as E.A. Speiser and P.M. Purves thought, but the Old Hurrian subject-marker ***-b*** (3rd pers. sing.) of the transitive verb, cf. I. Wegner, *Einführung*, 126. E. Laroche, *GLH*, 235-236, distinguishes ***šinti*** 1 and ***šinti*** 2. Sub ***šinti*** 1: compound onomastics: ***šinti(b)-***, ***šinta(l)-***, ***šinta(b)-***, *NPN* 257; *AT* 146; *NH* N° 1154. - Divine names: ***dŠintal-irti***, ***dŠintal-wuri***, cf. ***dŠantaluga***, a divinity in the circle of Ištar, (wr. *dŠa-an-ta-lu-uq-qa*, KUB XXVII 1 II 26; *dŠa-an-da-al-lu-ga*, KUB XXVII 6 I 12).

Hurrian *ši-in-di* Mari 3, 11. - *ši-in-ti-ya-aš-ši*, KUB XXVII 42 Vo 18. - *ši-i-en-te-en*, KUB XLV 8 c 2. - *ši-in-di-i-ni-in*, Msk., etc. Sub ***šinti*** 2 'sept' [seven]: ***šintarbu*** 'de sept ans' [seven years old], Nuzi; cf. Speiser, *AASOR XVI*, 133; *AW* 1243; v. sous *Šidarbu*. - *ši-in-ta-(ta)-a-i* 'par sept, septuple ans' [seven times], KUB XXVII 23 II 10; XLVII 31 I 13, 15; instr. adv. comme *kigatae*. [...] - D'après les parallèles hittites, ***7 widar*** 'les sept eaux / fleuves', on interprête ainsi ***šintatai šiyai***, [According to Hittite parallels, ***7 widar*** 'the seven waters / rivers', one interprets ***šintatai šiyai*** likewise], cf. C.-G. von Brandenstein, *ZA 46*, 94 n.1; E.A. Speiser, *IH*, 82.

Th. Richter (*BGH*, 387, and *VHN*, 512, s.v. ***šind-/šend-***) does no longer distinguish the Hurrian root ***šind-*** 'seven' from the verbal root that is also observed in personal names. He accepts that an intransitive form of the verb can be interpreted as 'to be seven' or 'to be the seventh (child)' and that transitive usage can be interpreted as 'to allow seven (children) to be present' or 'to allow the seventh (child) to be born'.

As a result Linear A ***si-du_mina*** (HT 110a.1), analysed as {*sid=u_mina*}, can be interpreted as: 1. Old Hurrian 'He/She (a *numen*) fed the twin' or 'Feed the twin (oh *numen*) !' (less likely, if ***šed-*** 'to feed, fatten' only contains the phoneme [***e***]); 2. 'He/She (a *numen*) cursed the (deceased) twin' or 'Curse the twin (oh *numen*) !'; 3. analysed as {*sind=u_mina*}, 'He/She (a *numen*) made the twin the seventh (child) (to be born)' or 'Make the twin the seventh (child) (to be born) (oh *numen*) !'.

The comparable Linear A sequence (,) ***si-di-jo-pi*** (,) (KN Zf 13) on a gold signet-ring with long spiral inscription (from edge to centre) from Chambre Tomb IX, E, 1 in the necropolis of Mavro Spilio (east of the Palace of Knossos) can according to Linear A orthography be interpreted as Hurrian {*Šid=i-(j)o/umpi*} 'Curse (the deceased child), oh *O/Umpi* !' or {*Šind=i-(j)o/umpi*} 'Make (the child) the seventh, oh *O/Umpi* !'.

In Linear A the vowel ***-i-*** is commonly followed by the transitional semivowel (glide) ***-j-***, if it is followed by another vowel. The same phenomenon can be observed in Hurrian and it is well-attested in Linear B: e.g. Linear B *i-da-i-jo*, *i-do-me-ni-jo*, *i-ja-wo-ne*[, *i-je-re-u* (next to *i-e-re-u*), *i-je-re-ja*, etc. See the pertinent section for an extensive discussion on the whole Linear A inscription ***a-re-ne_si-di-jo-pi-ke-pa-ja-su-ra-i-te-ra-me-a-ja-ku*** (KN Zf 13) in chapter 10: *Linear A inscriptions on metal objects*.

Linear A ***si-da-te*** (AK 2.1) is the first sequence on tablet AK 2 from Arkhanes. Although a word divider is missing between ***si-da-te*** and following ***ku-ra***, the scribe left much space between the two sequences indicating that they are separate.

The onomastic elements ***-te*** and ***-teya*** are frequent hypocoristics of ***-tešub*** in Hurrian theophorous personal names, cf. the many examples mentioned by P.M. Purves, *NPN*, 264, s.v. ***-te*** and ***-teḭa***, and also 266, s.v. ***-ti***.

However, recent research has made it clear that another possibility has to be taken into account. Many personal names can be identified without a theophorous element. They are described as *names with verbal forms of the Mittani paradigm* by Th. Richter, *VHN*, 2016, 584 ff., s.v. 1.1.2. They are sometimes also described as *'one-word personal names'*.

Th. Richter (*VHN*, 594-595) explains sub 1.3.1.1.2.1, *normal forms*, that the forms in ***°utta***, ***°unna***, ***°ulla*** probably contain the suffixes of the absolutive enclitic personal pronouns ***-tta*** (1st person sg.), ***-nna***, (3rd person sg.), ***-lla*** (3rd person plur.), indicating the object of the transitive and the subject of the intransitive verb. Paradigmatic is the form ***ki-ru-un-na*** in the Hurrian-Hittite bilingual ***Kirenze*** KBo 32, 15 Rs. IV 2, and the parallel formation ***[k]i-ru-un*** in 53 1. Kol. 4' (both Ḫattuša) that can probably be translated as 'release him, set him free, manumit him', containing the verbal root ***kir-*** 'to release, set free, manumit' + the thematic vowel ***-u/o-*** + the enclitic personal pronoun 3rd person singular ***-n(na)***, cf. also Linear A ***ki-ro***. Th. Richter (*VHN*, 595) mentions the following examples of 'one-word names' with enclitic ***-t(ta)***: *fIzzutta*(?) (M); *Ḫalut* (T); *Ḫizzutta* (Š); *Kizzutta* (M); *Kuzzutta* (AŠ); *Nuputta* (M), with variant *Nupatta*; *Ullutta* (Š).

Th. Richter (*VHN*, 596) explains (sub 1.3.1.1.2.2) that the 'one-word names' with enclitic **=tti**, **=nni** / **=nnu**, **=lle** / **=lli** are *optional allomorphic forms* for **=tta**, **=nna**, **=lla**. For example, the Hurrian personal name ***Ullutti*** (wr. *ul-lu-ut-ti*) from Mari and Tigunāni, analysis {*o/ull=u=tti*} with enclitic **=tti** (1st person sg.), lexicon *ull-*, typology 1.3.1.1.2.2, 'Zerstöre mich (oh *Numen*) !', ['Destroy me (oh *numen*) !'], is considered a variant of the personal name ***Ullutta*** (wr. *ul-lu-ut-ta*) from Šušarrā (Tall Shemshara), {*o/ull=u=tta*}, lexicon *ull-*, typology 1.3.1.1.2.1, also 'Zerstöre mich (oh *Numen*) !', ['Destroy me (oh *numen*) !'], with allomorphic suffix ***-tti*** instead of ***-tta***, cf. Th. Richter, *VHN*, 329 and 596.

Consequently we have to seriously reckon with the possibility that the endings ***-te*** and ***-ti*** in Linear A personal names do not always represent the hypocoristic form of ***-tešub***, but can represent the *optional allomorphic form* ***-tte / -tti*** instead of normal ***-tta***. Compare the Linear A personal name ***i̭-du-ti*** (HT 104.2-3) that can be analysed as {*id=u=tti*} 'Beat, hit, strike me (oh *numen*) !'.

We may conclude that thanks to the orthographic conventions of Linear A and B there are several ways to interpret Linear A ***si-da-te***. This was no problem for the scribe, because he knew exactly which name he had in mind, but it is a great problem for us, since (especially in names with consonant clusters containing an occlusive, that can be preceded by another consonant not expressed in the script) the number of possibilities can rise considerably. Moreover, the number of possible root-extension following the root contributes to an even higher number of possibilities.

In my view Linear A ***si-da-te*** cannot be identified as Hurrian ***Šida-te*** {*šid=a-te*}, because translation of the *intransitive* form 'Tešub is fat, well-fed' or 'Tešub is cursed' does not make sense.

Interpretation as ***Šidatte*** *{šid=a=tte}* (instead of ****Šida=tta***) 'I am well-fed' is only possible, if the root ***šed-*** (trans.) 'to feed, fatten', (intr.) 'to be well-fed', can also be ***šid-***. The subject in the intransitive 1st pers. sg. refers to the newborn child. Interpretation as ***Šinda-te*** *{šind=a-te}* 'It is the seventh child, oh Tešub !' is possible and interpretation as ***Šinda-tte*** *{šind=a-tte}* (instead of ****Šinda=tta***), 'I am the seventh child', is conceivable.

If the ***-a-*** in Linear A ***si-da-te*** does not mark the *intransitive* form, but is part of a root-extension, interpretation becomes easier, because the athematic stem can be transitive.

For instance, interpretation as ***Šidar-te***, with *factitive* or *iterative* root-extension ***-ar-***, analysis *{šid=ar=(i)-te}*, can be translated 'Feed (the child), again and again, oh Tešub!' or 'Curse (the deceased child) unceasingly, incessantly, oh Tešub'.

I. Wegner (*Einführung*, 88) gives two examples: ***tad=ar-*** 'lieben' ['to love'] and ***šid=ar-*** 'verfluchen' ['to curse']. The form ***ši-ta-a-ra***, analysis *{šid=ar=a}*, even occurs in the Hurrian-Hittite bilingual ***Kirenze***, KBo 32: 14 Vs. I 46 and 54 (cf. E. Neu, *StBoT 32*, 80), 3rd parable: *The goblet (chalice, cup) and its smith* (KBo 32: 14 Vs. I 42-59).

I. Wegner (*Einführung*, 218) explains the form ***šid=ar=a*** as root ***šid-*** 'to curse' + *iterative* root-extension ***-ar-*** + indicator of the 3rd person singular transitive ***-a***. She explains that ***šid=ar=a*** is a form in the present tense. The obligatory marker of transitivity ***-i-*** of the type ***tad=i=a*** 'he loves' only occurs after unextended roots, but apparently fails after root-extensions such as ***/ar/*** or ***/ol/***. The Hittite translation uses here the supine ***ḫurzakiuan daiš*** [*supine* + 3rd person singular past active] of the *-ske-* verb **ḫurt-ške-* 'he began to curse'. In another passage of the text ***šid=ar=a*** (KBo 32: I 11) corresponds with the Hittite form ***ḫu-ur-za-ki-zi*** (KBo 32: II 13) [*ḫurt-šk-i-zi*] 'he cursed continuously' [I have translated I. Wegner's German comment.].

The fact that the root-extension ***-ar-*** is actually attested in combination with the root ***šid-*** 'to curse', makes ***Šidar-te*** *{šid=ar-te}* 'Curse (the older child that passed away) incessantly, oh Tešub !' or ***Šidarte*** *{šid=ar=tte}* 'Curse me incessantly (oh *numen*) !' probably the most likely equivalents to Linear A ***si-da-te***, cf. also Th. Richter, *BGH*, 398-400, s.v. ***še/id-*** I [Boğ.; Tiš-atal] 'verfluchen' and ***šid=ar-*** [Boğ.] '(unaufhörlich, dauernd) verfluchen', 'maudire plusieurs fois, sans cesse'. D.R.M. Campbell, Split ergativity in Hurrian, *ZA 98 (2008)*, 273: ****šid=ār=i=a*** » ***šid=ār=a***, intensifying function.

Theoretically combination of ***šid-*** with other verbal root-extensions is also feasible: ***Šidal(i)-te*** *{šid=al(=i)-te}* or ***Šidal(i)=tte*** *{šid=al(=i)=tte}*, with root-extension ***-al-*** with unknown meaning, cf. I. Wegner, *Einführung*, 87, s.v. ***-al-***.

Šidan(n)(i)-te *{šid=an(n)(=i)-te}* or ***Šidan(n)(i)=tte*** *{šid=an(n)(=i)=tte}*, with causative root-extension ***-an(n)-***, cf. I. Wegner, *Einführung*, 88, s.v. ***-an(n)-***.

Šidaš(i)-te *{šid=aš(=i)-te}* or ***Šidaš(i)=tte*** *{šid=aš(=i)=tte}*, with intensifying root-extension ***-aš-***, cf. I. Wegner, *Einführung*, 88, s.v. ***-aš-***.

The sequence ***ku-ra*** (AK 2.1) follows ***si-da-te*** immediately. In the next line it is followed by the ideogram VIN*b* and 5 units. Linear A ***ku-ra*** does not only occur on this Linear A tablet from Arkhanes, but also on one from the Palace of Kato Zakro (ZA 20.4), where it is followed by the number 130. Although this number is rather high, ***ku-ra*** is probably not a scribal error for Linear A ***ku-ro***, since attestation at two different sites makes such an assumption less likely and ***ku-ra*** VINb 5 (AK 2.1-2) does certainly not represent a summation.

The Hurrian personal name ***Kurra*** (wr. *Ku-ur-ra*) is attested at Nuzi, cf. I.J. Gelb, *NPN*, 91, s.v. ***Kurra*** (wr. *Ku-ur-ra*), 1. son of *Pu-ḫi-ia*, brother of *Še-la-pa-i*, JEN 257: 2, 8, 14, 18; - 2. father of *Ut-...-en-ni*, *RA* XXIII 19: 4 (*Utḫap-šenni*?); - 3. father of *Ziqa-a-a*, *RA* XXIII 1: 30; cf. P.M. Purves, *NPN*, 230, s.v. ***kurr, kurra***. Cf. also ***Kur-ra*** from Gasur, HSS X 143: 12; 153 v 2; 155 v 1; 211: 11 and 13; an Anatolian personal name ***Ku-ra*** is cited by Stephens, *PNC*, 52 f.

Th. Richter (*BGH*, 226-227) mentions three homographic verbal roots: ***kur-*** I [Nuzi] 'herstellen' ['to make'] (Wilhelm 1992g, 149), ***kur-*** II [Nuzi] 'mästen' ['to fatten (male animals for slaughter)'] and ***kur-*** III 'erwidern' ['to answer, reply'] (Wilhelm 2000, 201; I. Wegner, *Einführung*, 265) and 'to receive in answer' or 'to reply' (Campbell 2007a, 231, 299, 324; 2008, 276). Adverbial ***kuru***, phonologically /***kuro***/, 'again, in return' may well contain a root ***kur-*** identical with ***kur-*** III. See the discussion on Linear A ***ku-ro***.

According to Th. Richter (*VHN*, 450), s.v. ***kur-*** {*ko/ur-*}, it is difficult to assess which of the three homographic verbal roots, mentioned in *BGH*, provides the most plausible interpretation and translation for the Hurrian personal names containing ***kur-***. He mentions ***Kuraiš*** (wr. *ku-ra-i-iš*) from Tigunāni, analysis {*ko/ur=ai=ž*}, typology 1.3.5, lexicon *kur-*; ***ᶠKururze*** from Ašnakkum, reconstruction on the basis of [...*-r*]*u-ur-ze* (*OBTCB* 12 III 30] and *ku-ru-ur-*[...] (*OBTCB* 88 III 25), analysis {*ko/ur=o/u=r=že*}, typology 3.1, lexicon *kururze* (abstract form) (→ *kur-*); and *ku-ru-ri* from Middle-Babylonian Qaṭna (QS 3, 42 Rs. 4), cf. Th. Richter, *VHN*, 180.

Since the Linear B ***k-*** signs represent ***κ-***, ***γ-***, ***χ-***, the corresponding Linear A signs probably represent ***k-***, ***g-***, ***ḫ-*** and ***-ḫḫ-***. This means that Linear A ***ku-ra*** could represent the name of one of the divine bulls guarding *Tešub*, attested as ***ᵈḪu-ur-ra*** at Meskene-Emar (Msk.): the unpublished tablets of the Museum of Aleppo. It is also attested as ***ᵈḪu-u-ur-ra*** at Boğazköy (KBo I 1 rev. 41), in a treaty between Šuppiluliuma I and Mattiwaza. In this text ***ᵈḪurra*** is mentioned alongside with ***ᵈŠeri***. The deities ***ᵈŠer(r)i***, ***ᵈTilla*** and ***ᵈḪurri*** are divine bulls accompanying the Hittite - Hurrian Weather-god. E. Laroche (*GLH*, 115) s.v. ***Ḫurri***: L'un des taureaux de Tešub; v. aussi ***Šerri*** et ***Tilla***. Graphies: *ᵍᵘᵈḫu-(u)-ur-ri, ᵈḪu-(u)-ur-ri*, en contextes akkadiens et hittites: KBo I 1 Vo 41; KBo VI 28+ Vo 32; KUB XXI 1 IV 8; XVII 14 I 10; XXXIII 97 1 12, etc. Msk. *ᵈḪu-ur-ra*.

The theophorous element ***-ḫurra*** also occurs in the Nuzi onomastics, ***Arib-ḫurra*** (wr. *A-ri-ip-ḫur-ra*, *A-ri-ip-ḫu-ur-ra*, *A-rip-ḫur-ra*), cf. I.J. Gelb, *NPN*, 29; P.M. Purves, *NPN*, 218. ***Arib-ḫurra*** can now be analysed as {*ar=i=b-ḫurra*} '*Ḫurri/a*, he gives/gave'.

According to E.A. Speiser (*IH*, § 177) the suffix ***-b***, which he called a 'root-complement', appeared to have an asseverative connotation: e.g. ***Una-b-Tešub*** could be interpreted as 'Arriving-verily is Tešub'. His ingenious argumentation was followed with approval by E. Laroche (*NH*, 347): "E.A. Speiser (*IH*, § 177) enseigne que le suffixe ***-p/b-*** de ***Una-b-Tešub*** a une valeur 'assévérative', renforçant l'affirmation que constitue la phrase nominale: 'Tešub (est) venant assurément'." However, after publication of the Hurrian-Hittite bilingual ***Kirenze*** (KBo 32) the position has changed. Now the suffix ***-b*** can be interpreted as the Old Hurrian marker of the subject of the 3rd person singular of the transitive-(not)ergative verb in ***-i***, and of the intransitive verb in ***-a***, see I. Wegner, *Einführung*, 134 and Table 13: The order of suffixes of the Old Hurrian verb.

The fact that ***ku-ra*** (ZA 20.4) occurs after ***te-65*** (ZA 20.3) = ***te-zu*** (?) = ***Tešub*** on the same tablet may well corroborate the given explanation, because it can hardly be accidental that a sequence interpreted as 'a bull guarding Tešub' occurs together with another that could represent the Storm God himself.

To date the Linear B sign for ***zu*** has not yet been identified. But there is a good chance that the rare Linear A sign ***65*** can be identified with ***zu***, not only because this phonetic value would provide a good explanation for Linear A ***te-65***, but because it would also provide a feasible explanation for Linear A ***ta-i-65***. For if that sequence would be interpreted as ***ta-i-zu***, it could be identified as a Hurrian personal name attested at Nuzi as ***Ta-i-zu***, *manzattuḫlu*, son of *A-ta-a-a* (cf. I.J. Gelb, *NPN*, 145).

The Linear A orthography ***te-zu*** makes sense, if one takes into account that ***š*** is normalized to ***z*** by A. Draffkorn (later Kilmer), *HHA*, 166, s.v. ***Tezu***, e.g. ***Ir-tezu-ba***. Cf. P.M. Purves, *NPN*, 265, s.v. ***tešup***: In Ugarit the name ***Tešup*** is written ***tšb/tθb***; see von Brandenstein in *ZDMG XCI (1937)*, 562 and 570, and Speiser in *JAOS LVIII*, 179.

In accordance with the orthographic conventions of Linear A the final labial occlusive ***-b*** is not expressed in the script. If Linear A sign ***65*** is not ***zu***, it may be ***zi***, because both ***ta-i-zu*** and ***ta-i-zi*** are attested as personal names at Nuzi and the Linear A and B signs for ***zi*** are not yet identified either. But reading ***te-65*** (ZA 20.3) as ****te-zi*** (?) does not make sense. Incidentally, ***Ḫurra*** is also a town in Hurrian territory.

I return to the discussion on tablet HT 6. Linear A ***wa-du-ni-mi*** (HT 6b.1; HT 85b.4-5) from Hagia Triada can now definitely be identified as a Hurrian personal name. The personal name ***Watip***-LUGAL (wr. *Wa-ti-ip*-LUGAL), transliterated as ***Watip-šarri*** (wr. *Wa-ti-ip-šarri*) by I.J. Gelb (*NPN*, 173), is the name of a *judge* at Nuzi, which is significant, since the nominal root ***pand-/wand-*** (var. ***pend-/wend-***) means 'right' and metaphorically 'good, just, favourable', the intransitive verbal root 'to be righteous, just, good' and the transitive verbal root 'to make good, to do justice to someone, to treat someone in a fair way'. ***Watip-šarri*** can be analysed as ***Wad=i=b-šarri***.

Since at Tall Brak the personal name ***Pa-ti-ip***-[LUGA]L^{ri} is attested (Brak 1, p. 41, nr. 3: 1) that can be transliterated as ***Patip-šarri*** [LUGAL certainly equals Hurrian ***šarri*** because of the addition of ^{ri} to Sumerogram LUGAL], ***Watip-šarri*** and ***Patip-šarri*** can be analysed as {*fad=i=b-šarri*}, that can probably be identified with ***Pantip-šarri*** and ***Wantip-šarri***, analysis {*fand=i=b-šarri*}, either as a result of *apocope* of ***-n-*** before ***-d-*** or as a result of assimilation of ***-nd- > -d-***. Since all evidence points to identification of the roots ***pad-/wad-*** with ***pand-/wand-***, both ***Pa(n)tip-šarri*** and ***Wa(n)tip-šarri*** can be translated as 'The King of Gods makes/made (the child) good, just'. Cf. also ***We-en-di-ip***-LUGAL at Emar (Pruzsinszky 2003/2, 666) and ***Be-en-ti-ip***-LUGAL at Ḫattuša (E. Laroche, *NH*, 144, n° 1005). ***Watip-šarri*** and ***Patip-šarri***, analysis {*fad=i=b-šarri*} as well as ***Pantip-šarri*** and ***Wantip-šarri***, analysis {*fand=i=b-šarri*} have led me to the identification of Linear A ***wa-du-ni-mi*** (HT 6b.1; HT 85b.4-5) as a Hurrian personal name. Long ago Linear A ***wa-du-ni-mi*** has been interpreted as ***Badunimi*** from Lycia by P. Meriggi, *Primi Elementi di Minoico A (Minos Suppl.)*, 65. The name *Badunimi* occurs twice on the south side of the enormous Xanthos stele (*Tituli Asiae Minoris I: Tituli Lyciae lingua Lycia conscripti,* Wien 1901, 42, no. 44a, lines 39 and 40; cf. J. Friedrich, *Kleinasiatische Sprachdenkmäler*, Berlin 1932, 64, no. 44a, lines 39-40.).

However, ***Badunimi*** or the element ***wa-du-*** are mentioned by neither Ph.H.J. Houwink ten Cate, *The Luwian populations groups of Lycia and Cilicia Aspera during the Hellenistic period*, Leiden 1965, nor J. Sundwall, *Die einheimischen Namen der Lykier nebst einem Verzeichnisse kleinasiatischer Namenstämme*, Klio, Beiträge zur Alten Geschichte, Elftes Beiheft, Leipzig 1913, nor L. Zgusta, *Kleinasiatische Personen-namen*, Prague 1964. Although *Badunimi* may have been found in Lycian context in the first millennium B.C., it is probably of Hurrian origin.

Linear A ***wa-du-ni-mi*** can be analysed as {*wad=u=n-irmi*} or {*wand=u=n-irmi*}, consisting of the Hurrian verbal root ***p/wad-*** or ***p/wand-*** + the marker of the Old Hurrian transitive past or perfect form ***-u-*** + the suffix of the enclitic personal pronoun 3rd person singular ***-n(na)*** marking the object of the transitive verb + the theophorous element ***irmi* / *ermi*** (at Nippur and in Linear A) = ***erwi*** (at Nuzi) = ***ewri* / *ibri*** (elsewhere, Tušratta letter included) 'Lord', indicating the subject of the verb. Linear A ***wa-du-ni-mi*** can be translated as 'The Lord has made him/her [***-n(na)***] (the child) good'.

The noun ***ewri* / *ibri*** (Tušratta and elsewhere) = ***erwi*** (at Nuzi) = ***irmi* / *ermi*** (at Nippur and in Linear A) can be used as title of a King (e.g. of Mitanni) or as an epithet of Tešub, cf. the *ergative* of the possessive 1st person plural ***eb-ri-iw-wa-šu-uš*** (Mit. IV 118) 'Our Lord'. In that passage King Tušratta addresses *Tešub* as ***dTe-e-eš-šu-pa-aš*** (*ergative*) ... ***eb-ri-iw-wa-šu-uš at-ta-iw-wa-šu-uš*** 'Tešub .. Our Lord, Our Father' (Mit. IV 118), cf. my discussion on Linear A ***a-ta-i-jo-wa-ja*** = Hurrian ****at-ta-(i)-iw-wa-(j)-aš*** 'Our Father', reconstructed *absolutive* (and *vocative*) on the analogy of the attested *absolutive* ***at-ta-a-ar-ti-iw-wa-ašmeš*** {*att(a)=ardi=iwwa=aš*} 'our ancestors, our grandfathers'.

Compare for the interpretation of the ***-n-*** in ***wa-du-ni-mi*** forms like ***Wantin-muša*** {*fand=i=n-muša*} 'Make him [*n(na)*] (the boy) good / just, oh *Muša* !' and ***Wantin-Ugur*** {*fand=i=n-Ugur*} 'Make him [*n(na)*] (the boy) good / just, oh *Ugur* !'. Thus Linear A ***wa-du-ni-mi*** {*fand=u=n(na)-irmi*} means 'Make him/her [*n(na)*] good / just, oh Lord !'. Compare (*supra*) ***Watip-šarri*** and ***Patip-šarri*** as well as ***Pantip-šarri*** and ***Wantip-šarri***.

Linear A]|***du-ne-mi*** 1 (HT 127a.2) occurs on a tablet from Hagia Triada, of which only the lower part is preserved in three parts. The lost preceding line may have contained a syllabic sign to complete the name, for instance, ***wa-***, ***u-*** or ***i-***, so that ****wa-***]|***du-ne-mi*** would be equivalent to ***wa-du-ni-mi***; or as second option: ****u-***]|***du-ne-mi***, analysis {*ud=u=n(na)-ermi*}, consisting of the root ***ud-*** 'to protect' + the marker ***-u-*** of the Old Hurrian transitive past tense + the suffix of the enclitic personal pronoun 3rd person singular ***-n(na)*** marking the object of the transitive verb + the theophorous element ***ermi* / *irmi*** 'Lord', translation 'The Lord protected him/her [*-n(na)*] (the child)' or the Old Hurrian *imperative* 'Protect him/her (the child), oh Lord !'; or as third option ****i-***]|***du-ne-mi*** analysis {*id=u=n(na)-ermi*}, 'The Lord smashed him/her [*-n(na)*] (the deceased child)' or 'Hit/Smash him/her (the deceased child), oh Lord !', with the root ***id-*** 'to hit, beat, strike, smash'. Linear A ***u-di-mi*** (HT 117a.4), {*ud=(e/i)-e/irmi*}, consisting of root ***ud-*** 'to protect' + marker of *transitivity* ***-e/i-*** that contracted with the initial vowel of ***ermi* / *irmi* / *erwi* / *ewri* / *ibri*** 'Lord' (the *imperative* does not have its own marker), translation 'Protect (the child), oh Lord !'. It is almost identical with Linear A ***u***[.]***-de-mi*** (AK 4b.2-3) at Arkhanes, if no sign is missing between ***u***[(AK 4b.2) and]***-de-mi*** (AK 4b.3).

Linear A *ja-re-mi* 1 (HT 87.3) from Hagia Triada is a Hurrian personal name, following *pi-ta-ke-si* 1 (see *supra*) and followed by *di-ki-se* 1 (HT 87.3), *q̱e-su-pu* 1 (HT 87.4), *ku-ru-ku* 1 (HT 87.4), *a-ra-96 a-tu* 1 (HT 87.5).

Linear A *q̱e-su-pu* (HT 87.4) is a 'one-word' Hurrian personal name *Ḫerš=upp=o/u*, consisting of the verbal root *ḫerš- / ḫerz-* (meaning unknown) + root-extension *-upp-* (cf. I. Wegner, *Einführung*, 89), (no marker of transitivity *-i-* after root-extension, cf. I. Wegner, *Einführung*, 90) + subject-marker 2ⁿᵈ pers. sing. *-o/u* (*indicative* or *imperative*) or, since a final consonant is not expressed in Linear A, Old Hurrian *Ḫerš=upp=o/u=m*, consisting of the verbal root *ḫerš- / ḫerz-* + root-extension *-upp-* + Old Hurrian marker of the past tense *-o/u-* + Old Hurrian marker of the subject of action 3ʳᵈ pers. sing. *-m*.

Linear A *ja-re-mi* can be compared with the Hurrian personal name *ia-ru-ḫé-pa*. According to Th. Richter (*BGH*, 74, s.v. *iar-/ijar-* [PN]) the verbal root *iar-/ijar-* (without translation) in *ia-ru-ḫé-pa*, is used in a transitive way. No doubt he refers to the theme-vowel *-u-* that follows the root (cf. M. Popko, Eine "schwarze Tafel" aus Boğazköy (KUB LX 121), *AoF 18 (1991)*, 244; G. Wilhelm, Name, Namengebung. D. Bei den Hurritern, in: D.O. Edzard (ed.), *Reallexikon der Assyriologie und Vorderasiatischen Archäologie*, Berlin-New York, Band 9/1-2, 1998, 121-127, especially 123). As a result it can be analysed as {*iar/ijar=u-ḫé-pa*} 'Ḫebat (transitive verbal form)'.

On the analogy of this name and according to the orthographic conventions of Linear A and B, Linear A *ja-re-mi* can be analysed as {*iar/ijar=(i/o)-ermi*} 'The Lord (transitive verbal form)'. → See also Linear A *ja+ru* DD (HT 6a.3) from Hagia Triada.

The Linear A inscription *te-we-mi* (↓) (PS Zf 1) among the repoussé designs on a bronze tablet from the Dictaean Cave of Psykhro (discussed in chapter 11: *'Religious' Linear A inscriptions*) is probably not a personal name. It can be analysed as {*tew-ermi*}, 'speak, oh Lord !', consisting of *ti-/te- / tiw-/tew-* 'to speak, say words' + *ermi* = *erwi/ewri* 'Lord'. It may well represent the prayer of the dancing supplicant on the tablet.

The Linear A personal name *i-mi-sa-ra* (HT 27+HT 48a.3) from Hagia Triada also contains the theophorous element *Irmi-* 'Lord', though now as first onomastic element. It can be interpreted as the Hurrian personal name **Irmi/Ermi-šarra* 'The Lord is as the divine King', 'The Lord is as the King of Gods', which is in fact almost equivalent to *Erwi-šarri* at Nuzi and to *ibri-šarri*, *ibri*(EN)-*šarri*(LUGAL), *ibrḏr / iwrḏr* at Ugarit; *ibri-šarri* [AL 137] at Alalaḫ. Cf. also *Ir-me/mi-ta-at-ta* and *Ir-me-ta-ta* at Nippur, cf. Clay *PNCP*, 93, to be read *Erme/i-tatta*, i.e. **Erwi-tatta*, according to Purves, *NPN*, 263. Since *Erwi-šarri* 'the Lord is King' is the name of 29 persons at Nuzi (cf. I.J. Gelb, *NPN*, 48; P.M. Purves, *NPN*, 211) and since it is also well attested elsewhere, interpretation of Linear A *i-mi-sa-ra* as **Irmi/Ermi-šarra* is to be preferred to a sentence name with *Ilmi-/Elmi-*, which is considerably less frequent. The ending in *-a* of the element *-šarra* may well be due to the *essive* case, which explains my translation of the Linear A personal name as 'The Lord (is) *like* the divine King' or 'The Lord (is) *like* the King of Gods'.

These interpretations also offer the Hurrian onomastic element *ewri/erwi* in Linear A in the form of *Irmi/Ermi*, i.e. the form in which the Mycenaean Greeks inherited the name of their god Ἑρμῆς < Ἑρμάάς < Ἑρμάάς, cf. Linear B *e-ma-a₂ a-re-ja* (PY Tn 316 r. 7), interpreted as singular dative Ἑρμάᾳ Ἀρείᾳ 'for Ἑρμάάς Ἀρείᾱς', 'for Hermes the Martial'.

If this etymology of the theonym Hermes is correct, it is also conceivable that the Mycenaean theonym ***e-ma-a2*** did not yet contain an initial ***h-***, but only an intervocalic ***-h-*** (Linear B sign ***a2*** represents the phonetic value ***ha = ἁ***). In that case it seems likely that the intervocalic ***-h-*** was drawn to the front of the name after the Mycenaean age and since the remembrance of a connection of the Hellenized theonym with the original Hurrian ***Ewri / Ibri / Erwi / Ermi/e / Irmi*** 'Lord' was lost, a 'popular' etymology deriving the name of ***Ἑρμῆς*** from ***ἕρμα*** 'a pillar of wood or stone (representing the image of the god)' or 'a pile of stones' may have become acceptable. U. von Wilamowitz, *Der Glaube der Hellenen I-II*, Berlin 1931-32, 1960[2], followed by M.P. Nilsson, *Geschichte der griechische Religion I-II*, Munich 1941-1950, 1955-1961[2], proposed an etymological connection between the theonym and the noun, but it is not inconceivable that the ancient Greeks may have considered such a 'popular' etymology themselves as well. However, P. Chantraine, *DELG*, 373-374, s.v. ***Ἑρμῆς***, reminds us that the noun ***ἕρμα*** lacks an etymology as well.

It is significant that the site of the Cretan Peak Sanctuary of Symi Viannou has revealed a remarkable continuity in its cult from Minoan times into the Hellenistic era. Since *Hermes Dendrites* and *Aphrodite* are the gods who were later worshipped at Symi Viannou, the site is now called 'Sanctuary of Hermes and Aphrodite', cf. A. Lebessi, Ἱερὸν Ἑρμοῦ καὶ Ἀφροδίτης εἰς Σύμην Βιάννου, *Πρακτικὰ τῆς ἐν Ἀθήναις Ἀρχαιολογικῆς Ἑταιρείας 1972-2003* (see my bibliography for the pages in *Praktika*); A. Lebessi, Ἱερὸν Ἑρμοῦ καὶ Ἀφροδίτης παρὰ τὴν Κάτω Σύμην Βιάννου, *Ἀρχαιολογικὰ Ἀνάλεκτα ἐξ Ἀθηνῶν (Athens Annals of Archaeology) VI (1973)*, 104-114; A. Lebessi, 'A sanctuary of Hermes and Aphrodite in Crete', *Expedition 18:3* (Spring 1976), 2-13; A. Lebessi, 'The erotic goddess of the Syme sanctuary, Crete', *AJA 113 (2009)*, 521-545; A. Lebessi - P. Metaxa-Muhly, 'The sanctuary of Hermes and Aphrodite at Syme, Crete', *National Geographic, Research 3 (1987)*, 102-113, fig. 1-14; A. Lebessi - P. Metaxa-Muhly, 'Aspects of Minoan cult. Sacred enclosures. The evidence from the Syme sanctuary (Crete)', *AA (1990)*, 315-336, fig. 125; A. Lebessi - P. Metaxa-Muhly - J.-P. Olivier, 'An inscription in the Hieroglyphic script from the Syme sanctuary, Crete (SY Hf 1)', *Kadmos XXXIV (1995)*, 63-67, fig. 1-7, pl. 1; P. Metaxa-Muhly, 'Linear A inscriptions from the sanctuary of Hermes and Aphrodite at Kato Syme', *Kadmos XXIII.2 (1984)*, 124-135, Fig. 1-2, Pl. I-IV; P. Metaxa-Muhly - J.-P. Olivier, 'Linear A inscriptions from the Syme sanctuary, Crete', *Ἀρχαιολογικὴ Ἐφημερίς (2008)*, 197-223.

Interesting are the so-called cylindrical snaketubes found in the Minoan *temenos* of Symi Viannou and in other Minoan peak sanctuaries such as Koumasa (cf. M.P. Nilsson, *The Minoan-Mycenaean Religion*, Lund 1950, 103, fig. 28), which no doubt played a part in the cult of the gods revered. The *κηρύκειον* of Hermes (Latin *caduceus*) with two snakes facing each other may remind us of the snakes seen on either side of the snaketubes found in Minoan Peak Sanctuaries. At Symi Viannou not only an uninterrupted continuity of religious cult appears, but the *κηρύκειον* of Hermes preserves one of the most interesting cultic Minoan features, the snakes on either side of snaketubes. Cylindrical snaketubes are not only found in Crete, but also in the Near East, also in the context of sanctuaries, e.g. at Megiddo and Beth-Shan, cf. N.M.W. de Vries, 'The central sanctuaries at Mallia and Megiddo', in: J.G.P. Best - N.M.W. de Vries (eds.), *Interaction and acculturation in the Mediterranean I*, Amsterdam 1980, 125-134, Fig. 7.

The character of the deities worshipped at the site may have changed in the course of time. Linear B ***e-ma-a_2 a-re-ja*** (PY Tn 316 r. 7) = ***Ἑρμάᾳ Ἀρείᾳ*** = 'for *Ἑρμάας Ἀρείᾱς*' = 'for Hermes the Martial' has revealed the martial character of Hermes in Mycenaean times. A martial aspect has at least been one of his features.

M.P. Nilsson (o.c., 515-516) states: "It is very likely that Hermes has appropriated some Minoan-Mycenaean elements, but he was, more than Artemis, an essentially Greek god." One may, however, wonder, what is essentially Greek about Hermes ? He certainly is a god with many human aspects and features, but is that proof of his Greekness ? Is the Cave of Mount *Κυλλήνη* in southern Arkadia, where he was born according to Greek tradition, proof of his Greekness ? At the time of M.P. Nilsson many scholars still believed that the etymology of his name was Greek. C.J. Ruijgh (*EGM*, § 167, n. 482), however, considered the name Pre-Greek: "… le théonyme *Ἑρμῆς* < *Ἑρμάας* (*e-ma-a_2* PY Tn 316 r 7: dat.), dont la finale est visiblement non grecque [of which the ending is visibly non-Greek.]".

The hypothesis that the theonym ***Ἑρμῆς* < *Ἑρμάας* < **Ἑρμάας*** may be derived from Hurrian ***Ermi-***, variant of ***Erwi-/Ewri*** 'Lord, King', is corroborated by the fact that ***ewri/erwi*** could not only refer to a king of flesh and blood, but also to a deity as is confirmed by the divine names ***^{d}Eb-ri-muša***, KUB XXV 50 II 11 sq.; KBo XXIII 25, 2, 5; and perhaps also ***^{d}Ir-bi-ti-ig(a)***, provided with the divine determinative (cf. E. Laroche, *GLH*, 85-87, s.v. ***ewri*** 'seigneur, roi'). The title ***^{d}Ewri***, if used as a divine name, could refer to a limited number of prominent gods (Tešub in particular), just as the epithet ***Allani*** could refer to *^{d}Ḫébat* or *^{d}Ša-uš-ka* (*Ištar*). ***Allani*** was also a goddess in her own right as queen of the underworld, comparable with Persephone in Greek mythology.

The number and variety of aspects and functions ascribed to Hermes surprised M.P. Nilsson, but the phenomenon may well be explained from the character of the divine name *^{d}Ewri* 'Lord' that could in principle be epithet of any male deity.

Tasks that would have been inappropriate for some specific gods could be attributed to him. At Kato Symi Viannou he could be *Hermes Dendrites*. He has features of a shepherd god, but could also be *Ἀργειφόντης* 'killer of Argos', *ψυχοπομπός* 'companion of souls' to the underworld, god of commerce and thiefs and help gods, heroes and mortals at many occasions.

I take the opportunity to briefly discuss the Linear A personal name ***ku-ru-ku*** (HT 87.4) on the same tablet from Hagia Triada as ***ja-re-mi*** (HT 87.3). Linear A ***ku-ru-ku*** (HT 87.4) may well be identified with the Nuzi personal name ***kuruzku*** (wr. *ku-ru-uz-ku*), which is probably Hurrian, built on the root ***kur-***, cf. I.J. Gelb, *NPN*, 92, s.v. ***Kuruzku***, (wr. *Ku-ru-uz-ku*), son of *Gur-mi-še-en-ni*, HSS IX 27: 24, 33, and P.M. Purves, *NPN*, 230, s.v. ***kur*** and ***kuruzku***. According to Linear A and B orthographic conventions ***-z*** is not expressed in consonant clusters preceding a palatal or other occlusive.

The three homographic verbal roots: ***kur-*** I [Nuzi] 'to make', ***kur-*** II [Nuzi] 'to fatten (male animals for slaughter)' and ***kur-*** III 'to answer, reply' (Th. Richter, *BGH*, 226-227) have just been discussed. Th. Richter (*VHN*, 451[482]) mentions that Richter (2007, 87[39]) and previously Von Brandenstein (1939-1941, 59[14]) suspected that ***-ku*** in personal names may be a shortened form for the theonym ***Kuzuḫ/Kušuḫ*** {*Kužo/uġ*}, the God of the Moon.

Kuzuḫ/Kušuḫ represents one of the frequent theophorous elements in onomastics. Unfortunately confirmation for this attractive hypothesis has not yet been found in the same way as ***-Na*** and ***-Te*** were established as hypocoristics for ***-Naje*** and ***-Tešub*** respectively. Perhaps if ***Arim-Kuzuḫ*** at Mari and ***Arip-ku***[...] at Mari can be equated and if ***Arip-ku***[...] is complete, the existence of a hypocoristic ***-Ku*** for ***-Kuzuḫ*** can be proved. ***Arim-Kuzuḫ*** is analysed as {*ar=i=m(:b)-Kuzo/uġ*}, typology 1.1.1.2.2, '*Kuzuḫ* gab (Jungen)' ['*Kuzuḫ* gave (the boy)'], cf. Th. Richter, *VHN*, 66-68.

Th. Richter (*VHN*, 451) reports that A.L. Oppenheim (Studien zu den nichtsemitischen Nuzi-Namen, *AfO 12*, 1937-1939, 33) was the first to connect syllabic *ku-šu-ḫ°* in non-Semitic personal names from Nuzi with ^{D}EN.ZU-*uḫ/aḫ* from Ḫattuša. Th. Richter (*VHN*, 451[480]) refers for the Hurrian rituals for assistance at birth at Ḫattuša to V. Haas - I. Wegner, *Die Rituale der Beschwörerinnen* ^{SAL}ŠU.GI, ChS I/5, 1988/1, *Die Texte*, 29-30; 1988/2, *Das Glossar*. I propose to analyse Linear A ***ku-ru-ku*** (HT 87.4) as {*kur=o=ž-Ku(žo/uġ)*} and translate the name as 'May *Kuzuḫ/Kušuḫ* answer (the prayers/rituals for a healthy delivery of the baby)'. Th. Richter (*VHN*, 601-602), 1.3.2.1, forms in ***°=o=ž***, at Emar: ^{f}***Aruš-Ḫeba*** (wr. ^{f}*A-ru-uš-ḫé-ba*) {*ar=o=ž- Ḫeba* }, '*Ḫeba* may give (the girl)'.

It may be useful to discuss some other names in Linear A and B containing the Hurrian verbal root ***p/wad-*** or ***p/wand-***. Linear A ***pa-de*** (HT 9a.2; HT 9b.2; HT 122a.5) from Hagia Triada, (cf. also ***pa-de*** in Linear B) occurs in a context of entries that can be identified as lists of names. There is not only some correlation between the *a-* and *b-*sides of HT 9 and HT 122, respectively, but also between HT 9a/b and HT 122a/b themselves, since they have, apart from ***pa-de***, also ***83a-tu*** and ***so-di-ra*** in common:

83a-tu in HT 9a.2, HT 9b.3 and HT 122a.6.
so-di-ra in HT 9a.4, HT 9b.3 and HT 122a.5.
di-na-u in HT 9a.3 and HT 9b.5.
qe-pu in HT 9a.3 and HT 9b.4.
ta-i-65 in HT 9a.4-5 and HT 9b.4.
a-ru in HT 9a.5 and HT 9b.2.
u-de-za in HT 122a.1 and HT 122b.3.

The Hurrian personal name ***Pade-n*** (wr. *Pa-te-in*) from Alalaḫ IV (D.J. Wiseman, *AT*, 181:8), or possibly ****Pade*** without the suffix ***-n*** which A. Draffkorn (*HHA*, 46) called a hypocoristic suffix, probably forms the basis for ***pa-de*** in both Linear A and B. Final ***-n*** would not be expressed according to the orthographic conventions of Linear A and B.

At present final ***-n*** in personal names, based on a verbal root, would be explained as a shortened form of ***-nna***, the enclitic personal pronoun 3rd person sing., cf. I. Wegner, *Einführung*, 76-78. A. Draffkorn (*HHA*, 46) also mentions the hypocoristic name ***Pade-ya*** (wr. *Pa-ti-ya*) at Alalaḫ IV (*AT*, 202:39). The same name ***Patija*** (wr. *Pa-ti-ia*) also occurs at Mari, analysis {*pad=i=ja*}, typology 1.1.1.2.4, lexicon *pad-* (cf. Th. Richter, *VHN*, 229) and may not only be analysed as hypocoristic form in ***-ya***, but also as a transitive (ergative) verbal form, consisting of the verbal root ***pad-*** + the marker of transitivity ***-i-*** + the marker of the 3rd person singular ***-a***, cf. I. Wegner, *Einführung*, 90, e.g. ***tad=i=a*** 'er liebt' ['he loves'}. F. Gröndahl (*PNTU*, 171, 346) mentions ***Padiya*** (wr. ***Pa-di-ya***) and alphabetic cuneiform ***pdy*** at Ugarit.

Th. Richter (*VHN*, 482-483) takes the roots ***pad-*** and ***patt-*** together on the analogy of the variants ***tad-*** and ***tatt-***. He mentions the following personal names s.v. ***pad-/patt-***: (1a) {*pad-*}: *Pataja* (Tuttul); *ᶠPatatte* (Mari); *Patija* (Mari); *ᶠPatul* (Mari); *Patum-atal* (Mari). - (1b) {*patt-*}: *Pattikki*(?) (Tigunāni). - (2) {*pad=all-*}: *Patalla* (provenance not known); *Patallan* (Mari). - (3) {*patti*}: *ᶠPattae* (Mari); [...]*men-pattae* (Mari). - (4) {*padindi*}: *ᶠPatinta* (Mari). Since ***-n-*** preceding an occlusive is according to the orthographic conventions of Linear A and B not expressed in consonant clusters, Hurrian ***Panti*** (wr. *pa-an-di*) at Mari is also a good candidate to be identified with Linear A and B ***Pa-de***. It can be analysed as {*fand=e/i*}, typology 1.3.1.2.1, lexicon *p/wand-*.

Th. Richter (*VHN*, 477-478) takes ***p/wand-*** and ***p/wend-*** {*fa/end-*} together and offers for the adjective ***p/wandi*** the meaning 'rechts' ['right'] with regard to indications of place or direction, cf. Th. Richter, *BGH*, 293ff. In metaphorical sense ***p/wand-*** and ***p/wend-*** means 'gut, günstig' ['good, favourable']. The *intransitive* verbal root ***p/wand- / p/wend-*** 'recht/richtig sein' ['to be right, good, favourable'] is probably derived from the adjective, the *transitive* root means 'recht/richtig machen' ['to make right, good, just, favourable']. Th. Richter (*VHN*, 222) translates the name ***Panti*** (wr. *pa-an-di*) from Mari as 'Make (the boy) good / just (oh *numen*) !'. The Linear A name ***Pa-de*** = ***Pande/i*** can be translated as a nominal form 'Right, Good, Just' or as a verbal form 'Make (the child) good / just (oh *numen*) !'. Compare ****Wandi*** (wr. **Wa-an-di*, *AT* *25:4) at Alalaḫ VII and ***Wandi*** (wr. ZAG-***ti***, *AT* 135:4) at Alalaḫ IV [names from Alalaḫ VII are marked by *], cf. D.J. Wiseman, *AT*, 151; A. Draffkorn, *HHA*, 62. Cf. ***Pendu*** (wr. *pe-en-du*, with Akkadianizing nominative in ***-u***) from Nippur (J.A. Brinkman, *AfO 50 (2003/2004)*, 400).

P.M. Purves (*NPN*, 244-245) wrote, s.v. ***pent-***, that the name of a king of Amurru, ***Be-en-te-ši-na-(an)***, KUB XXIII 1 I 44, and ZAG.ŠEŠ, KBo I 8 obv. 11, 12, and *passim*, with additional var. ZAG.ŠEŠ-*na*, *ibid.* obv. 32, could be compared with the Nuzi name ***Wantiš-šenni***. J. Friedrich (*RHA V, fasc. 35 (1939)*, 99) had already tentatively proposed the meaning 'richtig machen' ['to make just, righteous, good'] for the root ***pent-***.

However, there is a second verbal root ***pend-*** 'schicken' ['to send'] corresponding with Hittite ***appa tarna-*** and Akkadogram *ŠAPĀRU*, which Th. Richter (*BGH*, 311) discusses s.v. ***pe/ind-*** II [Boğ.; Mitt., PN]. I. Wegner (*Einführung*, 110, 236, 273) interprets it as 'zurückschicken, zurückkehren' ['to send back, to return']. So it cannot be excluded that in some personal names the root ***pend-*** should be interpreted as ***pe/ind-*** II 'to send'.

Th. Richter (*VHN*, 222-223) mentions the Hurrian personal name ***Pantia*** (wr. *Pa-an-di-ia, Wa-an-ti-ia*) name of 4 persons at Mari and of 2 persons at Qaṭṭarā, {*fand=i=ja*}, typology 1.1.1.2.4, lexicon *p/wand-*, 'Er/Sie (scil. ein *Numen*) machte (Jungen) gut' ['He/She (scil. a *numen*) made (the boy) good']. Compare also ****Wandi-ya*** (wr. **Wa-an-di-ya*, *AT* *282:5) at Alalaḫ VII, in a text on distribution of rations of barley-flour (ZÌ.DA.ŠE). Total expenditure (ZI.GA) - 93 PA (=*parisi*).

Entries, however, only total 88: 19 to the controller of Kuwan, 27 to *Uwandarama*, 6 to *Kuduru*, 20 to *Wandia* and 16 to *Arip-kušuḫa* (cf. D.J. Wiseman, *AT*, p. 88, nr. *282). ***Wandi-ya*** (wr. ZAG-***ya***, *AT* 202:28), Alalaḫ IV, cf. A. Draffkorn, *HHA*, 63. Cf. ***Pendi-ya*** (wr. *Be-in-diya, mâr bîti*), cf. D.J. Wiseman, *AT*, p. 64, nr. 128:27; cf. A. Draffkorn, *HHA*, 48. E. Laroche (*NH*, 135, n° 929): ***Pantiya*** (wr. *ᵐPa-an-ti-ya-*[*aš*]), XV 12 IV 9. Hourrite; cf. *NPN* 170 sq.; *AT* 189,7; cf. *Bentiya*, *Wantiya*. *Bandišinni*: voir *Bentešina*.

At Kurruḫanni we find *Wa-an-ti-ia*, at Nippur *Pa-an-di-ia*, cf. Th. Richter, *VHN*, 223. At Nuzi 60 persons with the name ***P/Wandia*** are attested, see I.J. Gelb, *NPN*, 170-171, s.v. ***Wantiḭa*** (wr. *Wa-an-ti-ia, Wa-an-di-ia, Pa-an-di-ia*).

Linear A ***wa-di-ni*** (HT Wc 3007, side α; HT Wc 3008, side α) occurs on two roundels from Hagia Triada. The Hurrian 'one-word' name can be analysed as {*wand=i=nni*}, consisting of the root ***pand-/wand-*** (trans.) 'to make good / just / right, to treat in the right way' + marker of transitivity ***-i-*** (the imperative misses its own marker ***Ø***) + the *optional allomorphic* enclitic personal pronoun 3rd person sing. ***-nni*** (instead of ***-nna***) indicating the object of the transitive verb: 'Make him/her (the child) good/just/right (oh *numen*) !' or 'Treat him/her in the right way (oh *numen*) !'. Th. Richter (*VHN*, 477-478) mentions that not only the adjective ***p/wandi*** can mean 'rechts' ['right'], but that the same meaning can be ascribed to Hurrian ***pandani***, which is interesting, since Linear A]***-pa-da-ni*** (KH 79+89.3) occurs at Khania. If it is complete, it can be interpreted as ***Pandani*** 'Right' or 'The right one', but also as ***Pand=a=nni***, consisting of the verbal root ***p/wand-*** + marker of intransitivity ***-a-*** + enclitic personal pronoun 3rd person sing. ***-nna/-nni/-n*** indicating the subject of action of the intransitive verb. The verbal root means 'recht, richtig sein / machen' ['to be right / just, to make right / just']. So Linear A]***-pa-da-ni*** (KH 79+89.3), Hurrian ***Pand=a=nni***, can then be translated as 'He/She (the child) is right / just / good'.

The personal name ***Pantunna*** (wr. *Pa-an-du-un-na*) is attested at Mari, analysis {*fand=o=nna*}, typology 1.3.1.1.2.1, lexicon *p/wand-*, 'Mache ihn [***-nna***] (Jungen) richtig (oh *Numen*) !' ['Make him [***-nna***] (the boy) just, righteous (oh *numen*) !'], cf. Th. Richter, *VHN*, 224. Th. Richter chooses an imperative for his translation, but an indicative is possible as well: 'He/She (scil. a *numen*) made him [***-nna***] (the boy) just, righteous', cf. I. Wegner, *Einführung*, 126: Old Hurrian ***-u-*** in transitive perfect forms.

This name is very interesting, because it allows a Hurrian interpretation of the otherwise inexplicable, Pre-Greek personal name ***wa-du-na*** (KN V(3) 503,3; KN V(7) 1523,1) in the Linear B texts from Knossos (cf. also *Documents*: *Wādunās* ?). Starting from a ***p/w*** alternation in ***p/wand-***, Linear B ***wa-du-na*** is straightforwardly a Hurrian 'one-word' name, ***Wandunna***, analysis {*wand=o/u=nna*}, or ***Wadunna***, {*wad=o/u=nna*}, the latter as a result of *apocope* of ***-n-*** before ***-d-*** or as a result of assimilation of ***-nd-*** > ***-d-***.

The translation is the same as that of ***Pantunna*** at Mari: 'Make him / her [***-nna***] (the child) just, righteous (oh *numen*) !' or 'He/She (scil. a *numen*) made him / her [***-nna***] (the child) just, righteous'. The only difference is that the name at Mari can be identified as a man's name, whereas ***wa-du-na*** from Knossos can theoretically be masculine or feminine, although most other names on the tablets KN V(3) 503 and KN V(7) 1523 are masculine as well. We can also observe some obvious orthographic differences between cuneiform and the Linear scripts of class A and B. Cuneiform had the means of expressing a double consonant by using a sign representing *vowel+consonant* (VC) [***un***] followed by a sign representing *consonant+vowel* (CV) [***na***], whereas Linear A and B used only open syllables, signs for a *single vowel* and signs for *consonant+vowel* (CV) and occasionally signs for consonant+semi-vowel+vowel, e.g. *swi*, ta_2 = *tia/tya*, ra_2 = *ria/rya* or *lia/lya*. Cuneiform used the same method for expressing consonant clusters as for double consonants: it used a sign representing VC followed by a sign representing CV, whereas Linear A and B used special orthographic rules for consonant clusters.

Occlusives (stops) were always expressed in Linear A and B, but a non-occlusive consonant preceding an occlusive was simply not expressed. Consequently ***-n-*** preceding ***-d-*** was not expressed (see for an extensive description the section on '*Orthographic conventions of Linear B*' in *Chapter 1*). As a result Hurrian ***Wandunna*** was written ***wa-du-na*** in Linear (A and) B and could not be distinguished from ****Wadunna***. Cuneiform had also signs for expressing CVC. Since the scripts of Linear A and B were probably only meant for domestic use and not for international correspondence, one could do with a relatively simple script as long as the scribes themselves could read what they had written and knew which persons, products or objects they had described. The Kings of the Empire of Mitanni had to correspond not only with the Kings of foreign powers such as Egypt, but also with the vassal states dependent on Mitanni such as Aleppo (*Ḫalba* in Hurrian, *Ḫalab* in Semitic) and *Alalaḫ* (in Semitic), *Alalḫa* (in Hurrian). They had to resolve legal problems with respect to (persons in) these vassal states as well. Such matters had to be described accurately, so that there was no place for misunderstanding. Their scribes needed a more advanced and complicated script that could be read and understood by their colleagues elsewhere with a minimum of ambiguities.

There are more examples of names with the root ***p/wand-***. Th. Richter (*VHN*, 223) mentions ***Wantip-šenni*** (wr. *Wa-an-di-ip-še-en-ni*), analysis *{fand=i=b-šen(a)=ni}* at Šušarrā, typology 1.1.1.2.1, lexicon *p/wand-*, *šena*, *šeni*, *šenni*, translation 'Der Bruder machte (Jungen) gut' ['The brother made (the boy) good']. At Nuzi 5 persons with the name ***Wantiš-šenni*** (wr. *Wa-an-ti-iš-še-en-ni, Wa-an-ti-še-en-ni, Wa-an-ti-še-ni, Wa-an-ti-iš-še-ni, Ba-an-di-še-en-ni*) are attested, cf. I.J. Gelb, *NPN*, 171. Apparently the hypocoristic name with abbreviated ***-še*** instead of ***-šen(n)i***, ***Wantiš-še*** (wr. *Wa-an-ti-iš-še, Wa-an-di-iš-še*) was even more popular at Nuzi, because 14 persons are attested with that name, cf. I.J. Gelb, *NPN*, 171. Cf. at Ugarit alphabetic cuneiform ***pndd̲n***, cf. F. Gröndahl, *PNTU*, 205, 211, 244, 251, 405. Th. Richter (*VHN*, 223) mentions ***Wantin-muša*** (wr. *Wa-an-ti-in-mu-ša*) at Tigunāni, analysis *{fand=i=n(na)-muž(i)a}*, typology 1.3.1.2.2.1, translation 'Mache ihn (Jungen) gut, Gerechte(r)' ['Make him [***-n(na)***] (the boy) good, sublime/august !']. ***Wanti-muša*** and ***Wadi-muša*** (wr. *Wa-an-ti-mu-ša, Wa-an-di-mu-ša, Wa-di-mu-ša, Wa-an-ti-mu-šá*) are the names of 6 persons at Nuzi, cf. I.J. Gelb, *NPN*, 171; and E. Cassin - J.-J. Glassner, *Anthroponymie et Anthropologie de Nuzi*, Volume I, Malibu 1977, 165. Th. Richter (*VHN*, 223) mentions ***Panti-Išḫara*** (wr. *Pa-an-di-^{D}iš-ḫa-ra*) at Mari, analysis *{fand=i-Išḫara}*, typology 1.3.1.2.1, lexicon *p/wand-*, *Išḫara*, 'Mache (Jungen) gut, oh *Išḫara* !' ['Make (the boy) good, oh *Išḫara* !']. Cf. at Alalaḫ VII ****Wandi-Išḫara*** (wr. **Wa-an-ti-^{D}iš-ḫa-ra* LÚ UŠ.BAR, *AT* *21:3,4) and wr. **Wa-an-di-^{D}iš-ḫa-ra*, *AT* *60:13, cf. A. Draffkorn, *HHA*, 63. See at Alalaḫ VII ****Wandi-Šaw(u)ška*** (wr. **Wa-an-di-ša-uš-ka* LÚ GIŠ.GU.ZA), *AT* *206:7, and (wr. **Wa-an-di-ša-uš-ka*), *AT* *257:16, cf. A. Draffkorn, *HHA*, 63. It can be analysed as *{fand=i-Šaw(u)ška}* 'Make (the boy) good, oh *Šaw(u)ška* !'.

Th. Richter (*VHN*, 224) mentions ***Panti-Ugur*** (wr. *Pa-an-di-^{D}u-gur*) at Mari, analysis *{fand=i-O/Ugo/ur}*, typology 1.3.1.2.1, lexicon *p/wand-*, *Ugur*, 'Mache (Jungen) gut, oh *Ugur* !' ['Make (the boy) good, oh *Ugur* !']. Cf. ***Wantin-Ugur*** (wr. *Wa-an-ti-nu-gur, Wa-an-di-nu-gur*) at Nuzi, cf. I.J. Gelb, *NPN*, 171. The latter name can be analysed as *{fand=i=n(na)-O/Ugo/ur}*, 'Make him [***-n(na)***] (scil. the boy) good, oh *Ugur* !'.

The 'Old Hurrian' form ***Wantip-Ugur*** (wr. *Wa-an-di-pu-ku-ur, Wa-an-di-pu-gur*) is also attested at Nuzi, cf. I.J. Gelb, *NPN*, 171. It can be analysed as *{fand=i=b-O/Ugo/ur}* '*Ugur* made (the boy) good'.

At Nuzi the 'Old Hurrian' personal name ***Wantip-Tilla*** (wr. *Wa-an-ti-ip-til-la*), cf. I.J. Gelb, *NPN*, 171. It can be analysed as *{fand=i=b-Tilla}* '*Tilla* made (the boy) good'.

As to interpretation of Linear B ***Pa-de*** I may quote C.J. Ruijgh (*EGM*, § 67): "Parallèlement à ***a-re*** et ***ar-e-i-***, on rencontre les formes ***pa-de*** (KN Fp 1,4) et ***pa-de-i*** (KN F 953,2), qui ont chance d'appartenir à un théonyme préhellénique de ce type. En interprétant ***pa-d-*** comme ***Πανδ-***, élément préhellénique et asianique attesté dans les anthroponymes ***Πανδάρεος*** et ***Πάνδαρος***, on pourrait lire ***Πάνδῃ*** et ***Πάνδεϊ***, d'un nominatif ****Πάνδης***. Le datif ***pa-de-we*** e.g. ***Πανδήϝει*** (PY Un 219,2) pourrait représenter le thème en ***-ηϝ-*** comparable à ***Ἀρηϝ-***." C.J. Ruijgh's observation that Linear B ***Pa-de*** (KN Fp 1,4) et ***pa-de-i*** (KN F 953,2) may have been a Pre-Greek theonym parallel with ***a-re*** et ***ar-e-i-***, needs confirmation. Anyway, Linear A ***Pa-de*** (HT 9a.2; HT 9b.2; HT 122a.5) is in all cases a personal name.

It seems likely that Linear A and B ***Pa-de*** contain the same root. To date I have not found indications in Hurrian studies that ***pad-/wad-*** or ***pand-/wand-*** might have a theophorous connotation as C.J. Ruijgh suggested. The Hurrian root occurs usually as a verbal root in theophorous personal names, but the theophorous aspect depends on the many theonyms used as onomastic element. Sometimes the nominal element is not theophorous as in the sentence names with ***-šena***, ***-šeni***, ***-šenni*** and ***-še***.

It is conceivable that the hypocoristics in ***-ya***, that are in fact often a shortened form of a theophorous sentence name (as can be proved in the case of one of the Kings of Arrapḫa), the shortened form might have received a touch of divinity as well: ***Itḫi-teš(š)ub***, king of Arrapḫa, cf. I.J. Gelb, *NPN*, 76: *It-ḫi-te-eš-šu-up*, variant *It-ḫi-te-šup*: *šarr* *ᴵAr-ra-ap-ḫi*, son of *Ki-bi-te-eš-šu-up*, HSS X 231:1; SMN 1003; 1466; *šarr ᴵAr-ra-ap-ḫi*, son of *Ki-bi-te-eš-šu-up / Ki-ip-te-šup*, SMN 93, etc. I.J. Gelb refers to the hypocoristic name ***Itḫiḭa***, because he is not only called ***It-ḫi-ia*** (variant ***Ut-ḫi-ia***) *šarr ᴵAr-ra-ap-ḫi* 'King of *Arrapḫa*', but also son of *Ki-bi-te-*[eš]*-šu-up*, SMN 1453. ***Itḫi-teš(š)ub*** and ***Itḫiḭa*** are the same king, since they are the son of apparently the same father.

Linear A ***wa-du-ni-mi*** 3 H (HT 6b.1-2) is followed by ***ra-ti-se*** 1 (HT 6b.2) from Hagia Triada. Remarkably on another tablet (HT 85) from Hagia Triada we observe an almost identical combination, since Linear A ***re-di-se*** 1 (HT 85b.4) is followed by ***wa-du-ni-mi*** 1 (HT 85b.4). Since there are apparently no words or names starting with {L} or {R} that are of demonstrable Hurrian origin, we must assume that the personal names ***ra-ti-se*** (HT 6b.2) and ***re-di-se*** (HT 85b.4) are probably foreign name in the Hurrian world of Minoan Crete. The bearers of the names may be slaves brought from elsewhere to Cretan *Ḫalba*, ***ka-pa*** (HT 6a.1), Hagia Triada. It has been assumed that Linear A ***ra-ti-se*** (HT 6b.2) may be related to (not identical with !) Lycian ***Λατις***, name of a woman appearing in the dative form ***Λατει*** in an inscription from the area of south Phrygia and Lycia. The name ***Λατις*** would have been written as ****ra-ti*** in Linear A and B, because final ***-s*** is not expressed in both scripts. Identification of Linear A ***ra-ti-se*** as a cognate with *Λατις*, with the so-called Pre-Greek formant ***-s(s)-***, would be feasible.

The so-called Pre-Greek formant ***-s(s)-*** may in fact be of Hurrian origin, in which case the Linear A personal name ***ra-ti-se*** may be a hybrid formation with an originally non-Hurrian root and a Hurrian formative. According to I. Wegner (*Einführung*, 54-55) ***-še / -šše*** may be an adjectival morpheme. She offers the following examples: ***talav(i)=o=še*** 'great' [root *tal(mi)-*] (with derivational vowel *o* < *i*); ***šav=o=še*** 'great, high, august'; ***faḫr(i)=o=še*** 'good' [*waḫri {faḫri}* 'good']; ***ker=a=šše*** 'long' [*keri-* 'long']. The suffix ***-(a)+šše*** also forms abstract nouns: ***ašt=a=šše*** 'femininity' [*ašti* 'woman']; ***all=a=šše*** 'ladyship' [*allai-* 'Lady']; ***šarr=a=šše*** 'kingship' [*šarri* 'King']. The suffix ***-(i)+šše*** also forms abstract nouns: ***šar=i=šše*** 'wish' [*šar-* 'to wish']; ***nir=i=šše*** 'goodness' [*niri* 'good']; ***kib=i=šše*** 'being seated (on the throne)' [*kib-/keb-* 'to set, place']. If ***kib=i=šše*** means specifically 'being seated (on the throne)', this may affect the meaning of the root ***ki(b)- / ke(b)-***, that can in general be 'to set, place', but in particular (trans.) 'to place on the throne' and (intr.) 'to be seated on the throne'. This could mean that *Ki-bi-te-eš-šu-up* / *Ki-ip-te-šup*, *šarr* *[l]Ar-ra-ap-ḫi*, King of Arrapḫa to which Nuzi belonged, was born as a crown prince, since his name 'Place (the boy) on the throne, oh Tešub !' actually refers to his future kingship.

Does that mean that the Linear A personal names ***ki-pa-a*** (KN Zb 40.1) on a pithos from Knossos and ***ke-pa-ja*** (KN Zf 13) on a gold signet-ring from Chamber Tomb IX, E 1, at Mavro Spilio, that can be identified as Hurrian hypocoristic names and interpreted as 'He is being seated (on the throne)' refers to kingship, at least of the owner of the gold signet-ring, buried in the Royal Necropolis of Mavro Spilio east of the Palace of Minos ? If so, we may have the name of a real Minoan king of Knossos, King ***ke-pa-ja***, attested in Linear A on a gold signet-ring found in a Royal Chamber tomb. Incidentally, the name of the legendary king *Minos* may be derived from Hurrian ***mina / mena*** 'twin'.

With regard to Linear A ***ra-ti-se*** (HT 6b.2) we also have to take into account that ***-še*** in personal names can be a hypocoristic form of Hurrian ***-šena*** 'brother' or ***-šen(a)=ne/i*** 'the brother' as second element. It depends on the meaning of Linear A ***la-ti- / ra-ti-***, whether we are dealing with this onomastic element or with the formant ***-še / -šše***.

E. Laroche (*GLH*, 159): ***latti***, signe omineux; nom. hitt. ***la-at-ti-iš***, KBo XVI 97 Vo 11; AT 454 I 18, 49; cf. also Th. Richter (*BGH*, 235): ‡ ***latti***, com. [loan-word into Hittite].

Other interpretations are possible, e.g. association with ***Λῆθος*** (< **Lāthos*), son of Teutamos, king of the Pelasgians at Lārīssa (*Iliad* B 843, P 288). Homer also spoke of Pelasgians in Crete, but it is not clear whether he only thought of a vague Pre-Greek population or whether he had a Minoan-Hurrian or a Pre-Hurrian population in mind, if his knowledge really reached that far back, which I doubt.

Association with the theonym ***Λητώ***, Doric ***Λᾱτώ*** (< **Lātō*), *Lātōna* in Latin, is interesting, since she is not only the mother of Apollo and Artemis, but there is also a toponym ***Λᾱτώ*** / *Lātō* in Crete. The modern place *Lātō* lies between Hagios Nikolaos and *Κριτσά / Kritsá*. According to P. Chantraine (*DELG*, 638) the etymology of ***Λητώ***, Doric ***Λᾱτώ*** is obscure. One has tried to find the provenance of this 'Mother Goddess' in Asia Minor and has thought of the Lycian term ***lada*** 'spouse, woman', but the name of ***Λήδη***, mother of Kastōr and Polydeukès (*Odyssey* λ 298), is also derived from that Lycian term. Consequently it is tempting, if ***Λητώ*** and ***Λήδη*** can both be associated with the Lycian term ***lada***, to recognize the same correlation in the Linear A personal names ***ra-ti-se*** (HT 6b.2) and ***re-di-se*** (HT 85b.4), whether the name is originally Lycian or not.

According to M. Ventris - J. Chadwick (*Documents in Mycenaean Greek*, 126) *Apollo* does not appear in the Mycenaean texts. However, the incomplete theonym may be attested at Knossos in the form *]pe-ro₂-[* (KN E 842, 3). C.J. Ruijgh, *EGM*, § 237: "Si on admet la lecture possible ***]pe-ro₂-ne***, il serait tentant de lire ***[a-]pe-ro₂-ne*** et de voir dans cette forme le datif du théonyme ***Ἀπέλγων*** (plus tard dor. ***Ἀπέλλων***, chypr. ***Ἀπείλων***). La forme ***Ἀπόλλων*** peut résulter de l'assimilation régressive de voyelles non contiguës. Une telle interprétation serait corroborée par ***te-o-i*** *θεοῖς* à la ligne 1. De même, ***me-na*** (ligne 2) peut être le datif de ***Μήνᾱ*** 'Lune'."

If Ruijgh's conjecture is correct, the Mycenaean form ***Ἀπέλγων*** is of course the oldest, preserved in Cypriot ***Ἀπείλων*** and Doric ***Ἀπέλλων***. The assembly of Spartan citizens (the *Σπαρτιᾶται* 'Spartiates' or *ὅμοιοι* 'equals' / 'peers') was called ***Ἀπέλλα***, probably because the citizens met in the assembly under the auspices or patronage of *Ἀπέλλων*. A gloss by Hesychius tells: ***ἀπέλλαι · σηκοί, ἐκκλησίαι, ἀρχαιρεσίαι***. The equation with *ἐκκλησίαι* obviously refers to the Lakonian ***Ἀπέλλα***, but that with *σηκοί* 'sheds' may well indicate that ***Ἀπέλγων*** was originally a shepherd god and perhaps also a hunting ****πότνιος θηρῶν*** 'master of wild animals' as his twin sister *Artemis* represented the ***πότνια θηρῶν*** 'mistress of wild animals'. The twins were both armed with bow and arrows.

The root *Ἀπέλ-* can be associated with ***apellu*** 'arrow(head)' at Nuzi, that is suspected to be Hurrian (V. Haas – H.-J. Thiel, 'Die Beschwörungsrituale der Allaituraḫ(ḫ)i und verwandte Texte', *Alter Orient und Altes Testament 31*, *Hurritologische Studien II*, Kevelaer / Neukirchen-Vluyn 1978, 262), cf. Th. Richter, *BGH*, 39. If this etymology is correct, Mycenaean *Ἀπέλγων* is probably originally a Hurrian *hunting god*, worshipped in Crete. M.P. Nilsson, *The Minoan-Mycenaean religion*, 513-516, coined the notion ****πότνιος θηρῶν*** on account of iconographic evidence, arguing that there was no need for two deities with the same function, so that Apollo could move on to other areas important for Greek society, but his original features were never completely wiped out.

The name of *Ἄρτεμις* is represented in the genitive ***a-te-mi-to*** (PY Es 650, 5), *Ἀρτέμιτος* (with East Greek declension in *τ* instead of *δ*) and in the dative ***a-ti-mi-te*** (PY Un 219, 5), *Ἀρτιμίτει* (with *e*/*i* alternation) at Pylos. The form ***]-mi-te*** (KN X 7887, 1) at Knossos is likely to be completed to the dative of the same theonym. Linear A has not yet yielded an equivalent to the Linear B theonym. The *e*/*i* alternation in the Linear B forms *Ἀρτέμιτος* and *Ἀρτιμίτει* make a Greek origin of the theonym unlikely.

P. Chantraine, *DELG*, 117, s.v. ***Ἄρτεμις***: "À la différence du nom d'Apollon, le nom d'Artémis, quelle qu'en soit l'origine, semble bien attesté dans des inscriptions lydiennes: *artimuś ibśimsis* répondrait à *Ἄρτεμις Ἐφεσία* à Larissa du Caystre, etc., cf. Heubeck, *Lydiaka*, 22-25. Il est bien vrai qu'Artémis peut être considérée comme une déesse asiatique (cf. Wilamowitz, *Glaube der Hellenen 1*, 324; M.P. Nilsson, *Gr. Rel. 1*, 451, sqq.). Il est vrai d'autre part qu'elle joue un grand rôle dans le monde dorien, ce qui a conduit à chercher une étymologie illyrienne, d'un illyr. **artos* (M.S. Ruiperez, *Emerita 15*, 1-60, et *Zephyrus 2*, 89 sqq. avec bibliographie). Cette hypothèse qui s'accorde mal avec les données homériques se heurte maintenant à une difficulté, puisque la déesse est connue en mycénien. C'est l'explication par l'Asie Mineure qui semble la plus probable. Les étymologies par le grec reposent toutes plus ou moins sur des jeux de mots.

Le rapprochement avec *ἄρτος* 'ours' se heurte à la difficulté que *ἄρτος* est en grec une forme secondaire. Celui avec *ἄρταμος* 'boucher' est retenue par Kretschmer, *Gl. 27*, 34, mais la graphie *Ἄρταμις* avec le second *α* doit reposer sur une étymologie populaire, cf. Schwyzer, *Gr. Gr. 1*, 256, ce que confirme le mycénien. Quant à un rapprochement avec *ἀρτεμής*, il consiste à expliquer *obscura per obscuriora*. Nous ne savons pas s'il existe un rapport entre ces deux termes, ni lequel des deux serait tiré de l'autre."

The Lydian form *Artimuś* equated with *Ἄρτεμις* may perhaps be compared with the Hurrian name *Ar-ta-mu-zi*, son of *Ut-ḫap-še*, at Nuzi HSS V 69: 22, 24; father of *Ta-a-a*, grandfather of *Ar-ti-ir-wi*, *AASOR XVI* 28:3, cf. I.J. Gelb, *NPN*, 33; P.M. Purves, *NPN*, 203, s.v. *ar-*; 262, s.v. *tamuzi*. Gelb and Purves prefer to divide the name into the elements *ar-* 'give' and *tamuzi*, because Hurrian *tamuzi* (perhaps derived from Akkadian) is identical with the Nuzi month name *Tamuzi*. The name is cognate with Babylonian *dûzu*. The months so named are equated by Gordon and Lacheman in *AOr X (1938)*, 55 and 60.

In principle the division could also be between *arta-* and *-muzi*, since *arta-* and *-muš* are also feasible onomastic elements. At Nuzi: *Ar-ta*, *Ar-ta-tal*, *Ar-ta-ta-al*, *Ar-ta-a-tal* (to be divided into *Arta-atal* or *Ar-tatal*), *Ar-ta-ḫu-ma* (to be divided into *Arta-ḫuma* or *Ar-taḫuma*), *Ar-ta-ḫu-pi* (to be divided into *Arta-ḫupi* or *Ar-taḫupi*), *Ar-ta-še-ni*, *Ar-ta-še-en-ni*, *Ar-ta-še-e-ni* (to be divided into *Arta-šenni* or *Ar-tašenni*), *Ar-ta-tab-bi* (to be divided into *Arta-tappi* or *Ar-tatappi*), and *Ar-ta-a-a*, *Ar-ta-a*, *Ar-ta-ia*. There is also an Indo-Iranian onomastic element *arta-*, but all relatives of "the *Artaia*s" at Nuzi bear Hurrian names. Note also *Ar-ta-ia*, KBo I 1: 44 (twice) at Boğazköy. Compare also at Nuzi *Ari-muše* (wr. *A-ri-mu-še*). If the interpretation of the masculine personal name *Ar-ta-mu-zi* by Gelb and Purves is correct and if the name can be interpreted as 'Give, oh Tamuzi !', we may infer that *Tamuzi* is not only the name of a month at Nuzi, but probably also a theonym. *Ar-ta-mu-zi* is a rare name and it is unknow whether it could also be used as a feminine name. It could explain the ending *-muś* in Lydian *Artimuś*, equated with Greek *Ἄρτεμις*. Th. Richter (*VHN*, 529) mentions that the abstract form ***tammunze*** {*tamm=o/u=n=že*} reminds of *da-a-am-mu-u-zi-*[...] at Ḫattuša (ChS I/5, 88: 6). Cf. ***ᶠTammunze*** (wr. *ᶠTa-am-mu-un-ze*) at Mari, typology 3.1, lexicon *tammunze*, cf. Th. Richter, *VHN*, 297, 529. If *Ar-ta-mu-zi* consists of *arta-* + *-muzi* and if *-muzi* may be equated with adjectival *muš*, *muša-*, *-muša*, *-muše*, *mušu-* and substantival *-mušni*, this element was feminine, if connected with *ᵈHebat*, and masculine, if connected with *ᵈEwri*.

The second *α* in *Ἄρταμις*, already in the earliest Doric inscriptions, may be a matter of dialect. It is conceivable that a Hurrian personal name such as *Ar-ta-mu-zi* was first used as an epithet in Minoan Crete and could have developed into a theonym. Even if the original division of onomastic elements was *Ar-tamuzi*, the Mycenaean Greeks were probably more familiar with the common element *muš* and divided the name into *Arta-muzi*, which made it easier to change *Arta-* into *Arte/i-*. Such a change may have taken place on the analogy of Hurrian *Arte*, hypocoristic of *Artešup* 'Give Teš(š)ub !'. The Lydian form *Artimuś* could have come directly from the Near East to Western Anatolia, but the *-i-* in *Artimuś* may well account for a Cretan provenance of the Lydian theonym in accordance with Mycenaean *Ἀρτιμίτει*. Anyway, my most recent and most simple solution to an etymology of Pre-Greek ***Ἄρτεμις / Ἄρτιμις*** is Hurrian ***Ar-temi*** or ***Ar-timi*** 'Give an oracle (oh Goddess) !' or 'Give a verdict (oh Goddess) !' (see p. 997).

Even if a Hurrian etymology is not accepted, the Mycenaean theonym is at any rate several centuries earlier than the Lydian inscriptions, which makes provenance from Crete more likely than from Anatolia. Since Apollo's name is probably represented in the Linear B texts from Knossos and the name of Artemis in texts from Pylos and Knossos, they likely had a Cretan, possibly Minoan, origin as their mother *Lato*. Provenance from Anatolia is not impossible, but not necessarily preferable.

Linear A ***du-da-ma*** 6<u>8</u> (HT 6b.4) is no doubt a personal name as all the other sequences on HT 6b. The 6<u>8</u> units probably refer to the ideogram FIC, mentioned twice on the *a*-side of the tablet. Th. Richter (*VHN*, 321-323, 547) mentions that the root ***tud-/tutt-*** {*to/ud-*} / {*to/utt-*} is not often attested (cf. *BGH*, 479) and not clear. He tells that only the meaning of ***tudigi*** [Boğ.; PN] 'Abfallhaufen' ['garbage heap'] or 'Lehmgrube' ['loam-pit'] (corresponding with Hittite *ḫuššil(i)-, ḫuššelli-, ḫuššulli-*) is known, in which ***^{o}=i=gi*** may be preserved. He mentions the following personal names with the root {*to/ud-*} / {*to/utt-*}: ***Tutija*** (wr. *Tu-di-ia*) from Šušarrā, analysis {*to/ud=i=ja*}, typology 1.1.1.2.4; cf. *Tu-te-ia* from Emar (Pruzsinszky, 2003/2, 792); ***Tuten*** (wr. *Tu-de-en*) from Mari, {*to/ud=i=n(na)*}, typology 1.3.1.2.2.1; ***Tutinni*** (wr. *Tu-di-in-ni*) from Mari, {*to/ud=i=nni*}, typology 1.3.1.2.2.2; ***Tutunni*** (wr. *Tu-du-un-ni*) from Mari, analysis {*to/ud=o=nni*}, typology 1.3.1.1.2.2; cf. *Tu-ut-tu-un-ni*) from Alalaḫ IV (see D.J. Wiseman, *AT*, 190); cf. *Du-du-nu* from Ugarit (see F. Gröndahl, *PNTU*, 331); ***Tuttu*** (wr. *Tu-ut-tu*) from Mari, {*to/utt=o*}; cf. *Tu/Tù-(ut)-tu* from Alalaḫ IV (see D.J. Wiseman, *AT*, 150; A. Draffkorn, *HHA*, 59); *Tu-ut-tu/te* from Emar (cf. Th. van den Hout, 1995, 171; Pruzsinszky, 2003/2, 792-793); ***Tuttu*** (wr. 1. *Du-du-(u)*; 2. ^{m}*Tu-ut-tu*, 3. ^{m}*Tu-ut-tu*, 4. ^{m}*Tu-(u)-ut-tu-uš*, ^{m}*Du-(du)-du*) from Ḫattuša (see. E. Laroche, *NH*, 192, n° 1390: 1-4); cf. *Tu-ut-*[*t*]*u*, *Tu-ut-ti* (the same person) from Ugarit (see F. Gröndahl, *PNTU*, 358); ^{f}***Tutuk*** (wr. ^{f}*Tu-du-uk,* ^{f}*Tu-tu-uk*), from Mari, {*to/ud=o=g*}, typology 1.2.2.2; ^{f}***Tutu-miš*** (wr. *Tu-du-mi-iš*), from Tigunāni, typology 1.3.1.1.1, {*to/ud=o=miž*}, lexicon *tud-*, *miši*; ^{f}***Tutanap-Šuri*** (wr. ^{f}*Tu-ta-na-ap-šu-ri*) from Mari, {*to/ud=an=a=b-Šo/uri*}, typology 1.1.1.3.1, lexicon *tud-*, *Šuri* (→ *Šuriḫe-*);^{f}***Tutap-irri*** (wr.^{f}*Tu-ta-bi-ir-ri*) from Ašnakkum, {*to/ud=a=b-irri*}, typology 1.1.1.3.1, lexicon *tud-*, (nominal) *irri* (→ *irr-*); ***Tuttaja*** (wr. *Tu-ut-ta-a-ia*) from Qaṭṭarā, typology 1.1.1.3.4, {*to/utt=a=ia*}.

At Nuzi we also find the Hurrian 'sentence name' ***Tutukai̯a*** (wr. *Du-du-qa-a-a*), father of *Du-ra-ri*, cf. I.J. Gelb, *NPN*, 161; P.M. Purves, *NPN*, 270, s.v. ***tut***, cf. ***tutt*** ? This name is also interesting, because it contains ***kai̯a*** as (*quasi* ?) theophorous element. I have already compared Linear A ***ka+ja*** (HT 24b.2) with the 'one-word' Hurrian personal name ***Kai̯a*** (wr. *Qa-a-a, Ka-a-a, Ga-a-a*) at Nuzi (cf. I.J. Gelb, *NPN*, 77; P.M. Purves, *NPN*, 222), which I have compared with the Greek goddess ***Γαῖα*** 'Earth'.

Most interesting I find the orthography of the name of the first wife of the Hittite Emperor *Suppiluliuma I*, ^{f}***Taduḫepa***. E. Laroche, *NH*, 182, n° 1313: ^{f}*Taduḫepa*. Reine hittite, première femme de Suppiluliuma Ier: abs. ^{f}*Da-(a)-du-ḫé-pa*, ^{f}*Du-ú-du-ḫé-pa*, XI 7 + XXXVI 122 Vo 8 = *MDOG 83*, 66; KBo II 15 II 2, 14 = KUB XXV 14 I 28, 46, III 10; XXVI 57 I 9 = *RHA 61*, 125; XXXVI 124 I 8; cf. Otten, *MDOG 83*, 57; Laroche, *Ugar. III*, 101. The name is usually normalized to ^{f}*Taduḫepa*, but the variant writings of ^{f}*Da-(a)-du-* and ^{f}*Du-ú-du-* suggest that ***t/dud-*** may be just a variant of ***t/dad-*** 'to love'.

The indicator of intransitivity ***-a-*** in ***ᶠTutap-irri***, {*to/ud=a=b-irri*}, ***ᶠTutanap-Šuri***, {*to/ud=an=a=b-Šo/uri*}, and ***Tuttaja***, {*to/utt=a=ia*}, shows that the verb can also be intransitive, probably meaning 'to be lovely'.

If we assume identity of ***t/dad-*** and ***t/dud-***, the Linear A 'one-word name' ***du-da-ma*** (HT 6b.4) can be analysed as {*dud=a=mma*}, consisting of the root ***t/dud-*** + the indicator of intransitivity ***-a-*** + the enclitic personal pronoun 2nd person singular ***-mma***, indicating the subject of the intransitive verb, cf. I. Wegner, *Einführung*, 99, Table 6 and 7: *The order of suffixes of the indicative, intransitive-positive and intransitive-negative verb and antipassive verb*. As a result ***du-da-ma*** (HT 6b.4) can be translated as 'You are lovely'.

Other analyses are also feasible, if ***du-da-ma*** (HT 6b.4) is analysed as {*dud=am=a*}, consisting of the root ***t/dud-*** + *factitive* root-extension ***-am-*** (cf. I. Wegner, *Einführung*, 88) + indicator of intransitivity ***-a-***, translation 'He/She (boy/girl) is lovely' (indicative) or 'Be lovely !'. Since a thematic vowel may not be expressed after a root-extension, the final ***-a*** in {*dud=am=a*} may also be the marker of the subject of action 3rd person singular of the transitive verb (position 7 in the chain of suffixes of the indicative, transitive-ergative verb, cf. I. Wegner, *Einführung*, 93, table 4), so that the name can be translated 'He/She (a *numen*) loves/loved (the child) !'. Possibly more evidence will appear in the future, showing whether the root ***t/dud-*** may be equated with ***t/dad-*** 'to love' or not.

The following Linear A personal names will be analysed as well: ***da-du-te*** (HT 34.1); ***da-du-ma-ta*** GRA (HT 95 + HT 149a.1); ***da-ta-ra*** (HT 6a.1); ***da-ta-re*** (HT 88.6); ***ta-ta-pa₃-du*** (PR Za 1a); ***ta-ta*** (KH 7a.3); ***ta-ti*** (HT 26a.2; HT 97a.5). Linear A ***da-du-mi-ne*** (KN Zf 31) on a silver hair-pin from Mavro Spilio may be an expression in context.

I had followed the reading ***me-ki*** 3E (HT 6b.5) by J. Raison – M. Pope (1994, 47-48) in my *Corpus of transliterated Linear A texts*, but I now think that the small scratches, which led them to read ***me-*** are probably due to the fact that the text is palimpsest, so that I now prefer to read ***da-ki*** with *GORILA 1*. Both readings seem to provide acceptable Hurrian personal names.

Th. Richter (*VHN*, 189, 454 + note 489) mentions that there is no doubt about the existence of the verbally used root ***mag-/meg-***, but that the meaning 'schenken' ['to give as a present'], derived from ***maganni*** 'Geschenk' ['present, gift'] is not yet certain, cf. also Th. Richter, *BGH*, 238-239. At Mari the personal name ***ᶠMakija*** occurs with the writing variants *ᶠMa-ki-ja* and *ᶠMe-ki-ja*, analysis {*mag/meg=i=(j)a*}, typology 1.1.1.2.4, translation 'Er/Sie (scil. ein *Numen*) schenkte(?) (Mädchen)' ['He/She (scil. a *numen*) gave(?) (the girl)'], and at Nuzi we find ***Mikkiia*** with the variants *Mi-ik-ki-ia, Mi-ki-ia, Mi-gi-i*[*a*] and [*M*]*e-ek-ki-ia* (cf. I.J. Gelb, *NPN*, 97). Consequently, if Linear A ***me-ki*** (HT 6b.5) is the correct reading, the name can be analysed as an *imperative* {*mag/meg=i*} with the possible meaning 'Give !'.

If *GORILA*'s reading ***da-ki*** 3E (HT 6b.5) is the correct one, we may conclude that this Linear A name is indeed a very popular Hurrian name, which is not surprising in view of its meaning. It can be interpreted as either a nominal name with the meaning 'Beautiful' or as a transitive *imperative* name, analysed as {*dag=i*}, 'Make (the boy/girl) beautiful (oh *numen*) !'.

E. Laroche (*GLH*, 249-250), s.v. ***tagi*** 'beau'. "Lecture du sum. ZALAG; épithète de l'argent. RS voc. II 24 = Ḫḫ II 134 ; sum. ki.lam.zalag.ga = h. MIN *te-gi-še* 'beau prix'; cf. Friedrich, *HW*, 325 : 'schön'. - *inu-me ušḫuni šiḫala ḫišma tagi-ma kiraši-ma* 'comme l'argent (est) pur, brillant, et beau, et long (durable)', KUB XXIX 8 IV 27." He also mentions (*GLH*, 250): "***tagi*** 'attribut de Ḫebat', *da-(a)-ki, da-a-ki-it-ti*, KUB XXV 44 II 19; KBo XX 113 IV 16; KUB XXXII 59 II 3; etc."

The Linear A inscription ***da-ku*** (SE Zf 1) is the only entry on a bronze double axe, bought by Evans at Kritsa near Lato, but reported to be from Selakonos (or rather Selakanos). Since final consonants were not expressed in Linear A and B, Linear A ***da-ku*** can be interpreted as either the Hurrian personal name ***Dagu / Tagu***, ***Dakku / Takku*** or ***Dagu=n(na) / Tagu=n(na)***, ***Dakku=n(na) / Takku=n(na)***. At Nuzi names of seven men are attested s.v. ***Takku*** (wr. *Ta-ak-ku, Ta-a-ku, Ta-ku, Ta-gu, Ták-ku*), cf. I.J. Gelb, *NPN*, 145. It may also be identified as the Hurrian name from Alalaḫ ***Tagu-n*** *(Ta-ku-un)* with ***-n*** suffix (phonologically probably ***/Dagu-n/***) on AT 189: 59, cf. D.J. Wiseman, *AT*, 149; cf. A. Draffkorn, *HHA*, 54, 106. Following Th. Richter one can analyse the name as Old Hurrian {*Dag=u/o=n*}, shortened form of {*Dag=u/o=nna*}; ***-n/-nna*** is in that case the suffix of the personal pronoun 3rd person singular and is the object of transitive ***dag-***. It can then be interpreted as 'He/she (a *numen*) made him/her (the boy/girl) beautiful' or as *imperative* 'Make him / her (the boy/girl) beautiful (oh *numen*) !'. It is also the shortened form of Linear A (and Hurrian) ***da-ku-na*** (HT 103.4).

Linear A ***a-sa|-da-ka*** 1 (MA Wc <5> side a.1-2; side b: GRA+E 4), on a roundel from Mallia. That sequence does not only contain the element ***a-sa-***, which can be identified with Hurrian ***azz- < ažd-*** 'woman', but may also contain the onomastic element ***tak-***, phonologically probably ***/dag-/***, as in Linear A ***da-ka*** (5 times), ***dakuna*** and ***da-ku-se-ne***.

The orthography of Linear A ***a-sa|-da-ka*** is ambiguous, because ***a-sa-*** cannot only represent ***azza- < ažda-*** 'woman', but since ***-r-*** preceding ***-s-*** is not expressed in Linear A and B consonant clusters (to be more precise: since non-occlusives [μ, ν, λ, ρ, σ, *F*] are usually not expressed before non-sonantic consonants [occlusives and σ]), it can also reflect Hurrian and Urartian ***arša- / aršə*** 'young man, boy'. Consequently, if ***a-sa|-da-ka*** is analysed as {*azza-dag=a*}, it can be translated 'The woman is like a beauty'. ***-dag=a*** is the *essive* case in ***-a*** of ***dagi*** 'beauty, beautiful'. If ***a-sa|-da-ka*** is analysed as {*arša-dag=a*}, it means 'The young man/boy is like a beauty'.

In Chapter 11 on *'Religious' Linear A inscriptions* I have eventually concluded that interpretation of ***a-sa-*** as Hurrian ***arša-*** in Linear A ***a-sa-sa-ra-me = *Arša-šarram(m)e***, 'The young boy is Šarru(m)ma', 'The young boy, he is like the King of Gods', is to be preferred to my former interpretation of ***a-sa-*** as Hurrian ***azza-***'woman' in ***a-sa-sa-ra-me***.

Both ***arša-*** and ***-šarra*** are attested as elements in Hurrian personal names: e.g. ***Aršaḫalu*** (wr. *Ar-ša-ḫa-lu*) at Nuzi, JENu 829, cf. I.J. Gelb, *NPN*, 31; ***Arš-apu*** (wr. *Ar-šá-a-pu*), son of *Ip-šá-a-a* at Nuzi, HSS IX 20:44,55, cf. Gelb, *NPN*, 32. The element ***arš*** is not very frequent in Hurrian personal names. P.M. Purves (*NPN*, 205) writes s.v. ***arš***, ***arš-***, ***arša-*** and ***-arša***: "Hurrian in view of occurrence with ***-apu***". Incidentally, the Hurrian name ***Ipšaia*** (wr. *Ip-ša-a-a, Ip-šá-a-a*), just mentioned, is attested as ***i-pa-sa-ja*** (KH 10.3) in Linear A at Khania.

Th. Richter (*BGH*, 48) mentions a possible Hurro-Urartian root ***arš-**, reconstructed by I.M. Diakonoff - S.A. Starostin (*Hurro-Urartian as an Eastern Caucasian language*, Münchener Studien zur Sprachwissenschaft, Beiheft 12, Neue Folge, München 1986, 36) and recognized in Urartian ***ar*****š*****ə*** 'adolescents, young boys'. W.G.E. Watson, Ugaritic onomastics (1), *Aula Orientalis 8 (1990)*, 115, presumes that the alphabetic cuneiform personal name ***åršm*** could mean 'young boy(?)'.

Interesting is the Hurrian name of a woman at Nuzi ***ᶠTa-qa-še*** (*NPN*, 145 and 262). At first sight one might think that the name should be divided into the elements ***Taka- / Daga-*** and ***-še***, frequent hypocoristic of ***-šen(n)i*** in personal names, providing the meaning 'The brother is strong, beautiful'. But this appears very unlikely because of the preceding determinitive that indicates the name of a woman.

The name is actually similar to the name of a female weaver from Mari, mentioned by Th. Richter (*VHN*, 290), s.v. ***ᶠTakazze*** (wr. *da-ga-ze*), typology 3.1, translated 'Schönheit' ['Beauty'], so in fact an appellative based on the abstract noun ***tagišše*** 'beauty', with the suffix ***-šše*** indicating the abstract noun. Th. Richter (*VHN*, 525-526), s.v. ***tag-/takk-***, ***teg***, explains (I translate the German text): "In spite of the voiced initial consonant *da-ga-ze* may well fit in here. It may reflect the same word that - as ***tagašše*** - forms one-word names elsewhere, mainly of women. On the analogy of other *°=a=šše* words (see G/4.2.2.5) 'beauty' may be chosen, although ***tagišše*** already offers a notion of the same type." Th. Richter's analysis of ***ᶠTakazze*** (wr. *da-ga-ze*) from Mari may well be right, but in view of Linear A ***a-sa|-da-<u>ka</u>*** from Mallia another explanation may be feasible, because ***a-sa|-da-<u>ka</u>*** seems to be exactly the same name as ***ᶠTakazze*** (*da-ga-ze*), but with the elements ***/dag=a/*** and ***aše/aša***, ***až(ž)e/až(ž)a*** in reverse order. Linear A ***a-sa|-da-<u>ka</u>*** could be interpreted as 'The woman is beautiful' or, if the final ***-a*** of ***-da-ka*** designates the *essive*, 'The woman is like a beauty'.

Th. Richter (*VHN*, 526) mentions that verbal usage of the root ***tag-*** has been confirmed in more recent literature. The intransitive theme can be interpreted as 'schön sein, (ge)rein(igt) sein' ['to be beautiful / pure / purified'] and the transitive theme as 'schön machen, reinigen, scheinend / leuchtend machen' ['to make beautiful / pure / shining']. This means that ***ᶠTa-qa-še*** from Nuzi and ***ᶠTakazze*** (wr. *da-ga-ze*) from Mari may be interpreted as either {*tag=(i)-azze*} 'Make the woman beautiful / pure / shining' or {*tag=(a)-azze*} 'Be beautiful / pure / shining, oh woman !' or {*tag=(a)=Ø-azze*} 'The woman is beautiful / pure / shining'. As a parallel for the latter can be mentioned ***ᶠTaka-tati*** (wr. *ta-ga-ta-di*) from Mari, typology 1.3.1.3, that Richter translates as 'Sei (oder: werde) schön, oh Liebling !' ['Be / Become beautiful, oh beloved darling !'] or 'Der Liebling ist schön' ['The darling is beautiful'], cf. Th. Richter, *VHN*, 290.

The voiced character of the dental and palatal stops of ***tak***, ***/dag/***, may be deduced from many Hurrian names such as ***ᶠA-wa-ta-ge*** from Nuzi, with single writing of the occlusives. However, we have seen that according to Th. Richter and others the roots ***tag-/takk-***, ***teg*** are basically the same. The distinctions may be due to dialectal or regional variation. The forms like ***da-ka*** and ***da-ku*** with voiced initial dental [***d-***] in Linear A make it quite clear that initial voicing of dentals in the Hurrian dialect of Minoan Crete was as normal as voicing was in medial position (cf. Linear A ***a-du-sa-ra*** = Hurrian ***aždu-šara***).

The evidence deduced from the (later) alphabetic cuneiform texts from Ugarit showing voiceless occlusives in initial position in Hurrian vocabulary and onomastics should only be applied to the Hurrian dialect of Ugarit at the time of those texts. The evidence shown by alphabetic cuneiform shows a peculiar feature of the Hurrian dialect of (the region of) Ugarit and only for the pertinent period. It cannot be applied straight away to other Hurrian dialects and other periods in regions where syllabic cuneiform was the only source. A parallel may be the voiceless initial ***t-*** in High German, where other Germanic languages like English and Dutch use a voiced ***d-***, e.g. High German *Tod* = Dutch *dood* = English *death*.

Linear A ***da-ka*** (HT Wa 1001; HT Wa 1002; HT Wa 1003; HT Wa 1004; HT Wa 1005), inscriptions on 5 nodules from Hagia Triada, may well be identified with a Hurrian personal name from Mari ***Takka*** (wr. *ta-ak-ka*), {*takk=a=Ø*}, typology 1.1.1.3.3, 'Er (Junge) ist schön' ['He (the boy) is beautiful'], or, if the final ***-a*** is explained as *essive*, {*takk(i)=a*(E.)}, 'Er (Junge) ist als Schönling (geboren)' ['He (the boy) is (born) as a beauty'], cf. Th. Richter, *VHN*, 290. In my view the dental and palatal occlusives in Linear A ***da-ka*** are both voiced {*dag=a*}, although that is not certain for the palatal stop.

Linear A ***da-ku-na*** (HT 103.4), followed by 1 unit, precedes ***da-ku-se-ne*** (HT 103.4). The name can be analysed as {*Dag=u/o=nna*}; ***-nna*** is the suffix of the personal pronoun 3rd person singular and is the object of transitive ***dag-***. It can then be interpreted as 'He / She (a *numen*) made him/her (the boy/girl) beautiful' or as 'Make him/her (the boy/girl) beautiful (oh *numen*) !'. An exact equivalent to the name is found in the Cappadocian name ***Dakuna*** (cf. E. Laroche, *NH*, 171, n° 1217) and in the Hurrian name ***Tagu-na*** from Mâri. J.M. Sasson, 'Ḫurrians and Ḫurrian names in the Mari texts', *UF 6 (1974)*, 369, mentions the name twice: *ᶠta-ku-na* SY B: vii: 9 and *ᶠta-ku-na* XIII: 1:viii: 18; cf. *ibidem*, 385, s.v. *tag/k, tag/ku-*. Reading *ᶠta-ku-na* phonologically as ***/Dagu-nna/*** seems preferable, since the initial dental is probably voiced under influence of the following voiced ***/g/***. F.W. Bush, (*GHL*, 283, 288) also discusses Linear A ***da-ku-na*** (HT 103.4).

It is surprising that C.H. Gordon (*Evidence for the Minoan language*, Ventnor N.J. 1966, 31 and 38), who published several articles on Hurrian, was so preoccupied with proving that Linear A recorded West Semitic, that he identified Linear A ***da-ku-se-ne*** (HT 103.2; HT 103.4-5) and ***da-ku-|se-ne-ti*** (HT 104.1-2) as Hurrian, but failed to recognize the same theme ***dag=u-*** in ***da-ku-na*** (HT 103.4). He wrote (p. 31, n° 131): "It is hard to tell whether *da-ku-na* is a personal or a divine name; in any case it is to be compared etymologically with the West Semitic *Dagon* worshipped by the Philistines and Ugaritians." In chapter 6 (*The Hurrian language as a likely candidate: History*) I quoted F.W. Bush, *A grammar of the Hurrian Language*, diss. Brandeis Univ., Ann Arbor 1964, 282-283, who drew attention to an article by J. Nougayrol about the seal of *Daguna*. [C.H. Gordon was chairman of the Dissertation Committee for F.W. Bush's Ph.D.]. F.W. Bush: "Recently, another very suggestive detail has come to light. In 'Documents du Ḫabur ... 2. Le sceau de *Daguna*', *Syria 37 (1960)*, 209-214, Nougayrol has published a cylinder seal, executed in lapis lazuli, so inordinately fine in its workmanship that certain details appear better than in representations on a much larger scale.

The scene represented is a classic 'presentation' scene in which a seated goddess, welcomes with a gesture a cortege which approaches from the right, led by another diety who announced the female supplicant by the words of the appended inscription. The accompanying inscription reads '*Daguna*, the wet-nurse, daughter of *Tiša-dimmuzi*, the royal stewardess'. The name *Daguna* cannot be connected with certainty to any known ethnic or linguistic group [however, it is suggestive that *da-gu-na* occurs immediately before the likely Hurrian name *da-ku-se-né* (i.e. *Takku-Šenni*) in a list of personal names from the Linear A tablets from Hagia Triada on Crete (text No. 103).] However, the name of the mother of *Daguna* is transparently Hurrian, formed from the well attested root *tiš-* and a variant form of the god *Tammuz*. That *Tammuz* had been adopted into the Hurrian pantheon is now seen from the Ug. Quad. Voc. 137 3:33, 4:18, where [*D*]*u-mu-z*[*i*] = ^{d}DUMU.[ZI], see Laroche, *Ugaritica V,* I § 27a. Laroche also refers to the form *dummuzzi* at Boğazköy. Regarding the significance of the presentation of a wet nurse to a goddess, Nougayrol concludes very plausibly that the goddess, seated on a mountain peak, is not just any mountain goddess, but *the* mountain goddess par excellence, the eminent *Ninḫursag*, mother of the gods and the one who nurses royalty with the milk of legitimacy." NIN.ḪUR.SAG is the Sumerian 'Mistress of the mountainlands'.

Linear A ***da-ku-se-ne*** (HT 103.2; HT 103.4-5) is a Hurrian sentence name. E.A. Speiser has suggested that the Ugaritic personal name ***Tgẓn*** might represent Hurrian ****Taki-šenni***, see E.A. Speiser, *JAOS 55 (1935)*, 98 (apud Harris) and *JAOS 58 (1938)*, 191, n. 76. He had to write an asterisk, because he thought that no syllabic parallel for the Ugaritic name was available from elsewhere, but Linear A ***da-ku-se-ne*** (HT 103.2; HT 103.4-5) provides in fact a syllabic equivalent to Ugaritic ***Tgẓn***.

Both elements ***dak=u-*** and ***-šena/-šene/-šeni*** 'brother' and ***-šenne/-šenni*** 'the brother' < ***-šen(a)=ne/ni*** are very frequent in Hurrian personal names. The first, phonologically probably ***/dagu-/***, has been interpreted as 'ferme, dur' by E. Laroche, *NH*, 353 (cf. also P.M. Purves, *NPN*, 261-262, with many examples s.v. ***tak***) or 'beau' by E. Laroche, *GLH*, 259-260: thèmes ***tagi-*** et ***tagu-***. F.W. Bush (*GHL*, 283, 288) transliterates the Hurrian name ***da-ku-se-né*** in a list of personal names (HT 103.4-5) which he normalizes to ***Takku-Šenni***. I should prefer normalization of the Linear A name to ***Dagu-šen(n)e***. It is now possible to interpret ***dag=u-*** as an Old Hurrian transitive *imperative* or *past indicative* of the root ***t/dag/kk-*** 'to make beautiful'.

The second element ***-se-ne*** in ***da-ku-se-ne*** as well as in ***da-ku-|se-ne-ti*** (HT 104.1-2) is probably to be compared with Hurrian ***šen(n)i***. Nuzi offers the longest list of sentence names with this onomastic element, cf. I.J. Gelb, *NPN*, 130-131 and *passim*, and P.M. Purves, *NPN*, 255-256 s.v. ***-šenni***; cf. for Alalaḫ D.J. Wiseman, *AT*, 130, 138, 141, and A. Draffkorn, *HHA*, 103; even Mâri gives some early examples, cf. J.M. Sasson, 'Ḫurrians and Ḫurrian names in the Mari texts', *UF 6 (1974)*, 385, s.v. ***-šeni***: ***Adal-šeni***, ***Kipu-šeni***, ***Turip-šeni***. The name is most likely to be interpreted as 'Firm / beautiful (is) the brother'. Likewise, ***Wanti-šenni*** and ***Bentešina*** mean 'Righteous (is) the brother', ***wanti- = banti- = benti-*** 'just, righteous' (cf. I.J. Gelb, *NPN*, 171, and P.M. Purves, *NPN*, 256: *Wa-an-ti-iš-še-en-ni*, *Wa-an-ti-še-en-ni*, *Wa-an-ti-še-ni*, *Wa-an-ti-iš-še-ni*, *Ba-an-di-še-en-ni*; cf. E. Laroche, *NH*, 350; cf. for ***benti- = banti- = wanti-*** "droit, juste", *ibidem*, 352, and P.M. Purves, *NPN*, 274; cf. for ***Bentešina*** (***-a*** hitt.). E. Laroche, *NH*, 350.).

Since ***šene/i*** was probably originally an ***a***-stem ***šena*** 'brother' like the other words expressing kinship (cf. I. Wegner, *Einführung*, 52-53) such as ***ela*** 'sister', ***nera*** 'mother', ***šala*** 'daughter', ***mena*** 'twin ?' or 'sister ? (Th. Richter)', I prefer normalization of the Linear A name ***da-ku-se-ne*** to ***Dagu-šen(n)e*** that can be analysed as {*dag=u-šen=a/e/i*} or {*dag=u-šen(a)=ne/i*}, the latter with the 'suffix of the definite article' ***-ne / -ni***. The name can be translated as 'He/she (a *numen*) made the brother beautiful' or 'Make the brother beautiful (oh *numen*) !'. See also Th. Richter, *VHN*, 510-512, s.v. ***šena***, ***šen***, ***še***. The meaning 'brother' is confirmed by comparison with Sumerian ŠEŠ and Akkadian ***aḫum***. Th. Richter (*VHN*, 290-293, 525-526) mentions, s.v. ***tag-/takk-***, ***teg-***, the Hurrian names ***Takka*** (Mari), ***Takaja*** (Tigunāni), ***Takkakki*** (Mari), ***ᶠTakazze*** (Mari), ***ᶠTaka-tati*** (Mari), ***Taki*** (Mari, Šušarrā, Šubat-Enlil), ***Ta-(a-)ku*** (Alalaḫ VII and IV), ***Ta-a-gu*** (Emar), ***Takki*** (Mari, Šubat-Enlil), ***Takija*** (Mari, Qaṭṭarā), ***Takkija*** (Mari), ***Taki-ki*** (Mari, Kaniš), ***Taken*** (Šušarrā), ***Takuja*** (Mari), ***Takuzza*** (Mari).

Linear A ***da-ku-|se-ne-ti*** 45 J (HT 104.1-2) from Hagia Triada seems at first sight an extended form of ***da-ku-se-ne*** (HT 103.2; HT 103.4-5). It follows ***ta-pa* ,** ***te+ro* ,** (HT 104.1), see *supra* for the interpretation of the transaction term **, *te+ro* ,** which seems the *scriptio plena* of monosyllabic **, *te* ,** …

The ending ***-ti*** of ***da-ku-|se-ne-ti*** can possibly be explained as a final onomastic morpheme as in ***Šaušgatti***, since E. Laroche (*NH*, 380) describes such a morpheme as a 'finale d'onomastique' that, for instance, occurs in the Hurrian theophorous name ***Šaušgatti*** (cf. *NH,* 161, n° 1142; A. Draffkorn, *HHA*, 102: *Saw(u)ska*, Hurrian name of Ishtar; *ibid.* ***sau*** 'weapon', see also E. Laroche, *JCS 2*, 119). Cf. also E. Laroche, *NH*, 332: Noms en ***-(t)ti-***, ***-ddu-***, ***-tta-***.

As a result of recent research it has become clear that the endings ***-tta*** and ***-tti*** in Hurrian 'one-word' personal names, that contain an initial verbal element, usually represent the suffix indicating the first person singular of the *enclitic* personal pronoun, functioning as subject of the intransitive and as object of the transitive verb. Theoretically it seems possible to interpret the personal name ***Šaušgatti*** as ***Šaušga=tti*** 'I am ***Šaušga***', but that sounds a bit pretentious. Since arrogance might be punished by the god, the less pretentious *essive* ***Šaušg(a)=a***[E.]***=tti*** 'I am *like* ***Šaušga***' may be preferable.

Linear A ***-ti*** in ***da-ku-|se-ne-ti*** occurs in a so-called 'sentence name', of which ***da-ku-*** may well be the verbal element, ***°šen(a)=ne*** the nominal and ***°tti*** the pronominal element. Analysis of ***da-ku-|se-ne-ti*** as a sentence name with a double object seems possible {*dag=u-šen(a)=ne=tti*}, e.g. 'Make me, the brother, beautiful (oh *numen*) !' > 'Make me a beautiful brother (oh *numen*) !'. A sentence name with a double case (subject and object) is also conceivable: 'The (deceased) brother made me beautiful' or (*imperative*) 'Make me beautiful, oh (deceased) brother !'.

It is worth noting that the two names following ***da-ku-|se-ne-ti*** on HT 104 contain an identical final morpheme ***-ti***, with voiceless dental [***t***], ***-tti*** in cuneiform: ***i̱-du-ti*** 20 J̱ (HT 104.2-3) and ***pa-da̱-su-ti*** 29 (HT 104.3-4), analysis {*p/wand=aš=u=tti*}, consisting of the root ***pand-/wand-*** 'to make just, good' + *intensifying* root-extension ***-aš-*** (cf. I. Wegner, *Einführung*, 88), + Old Hurrian marker of the *imperative* ***-u-*** or of the *past indicative* ***-u-*** + the *optional allomorphic* enclitic personal pronoun 1st person singular ***-tti***, translation 'Make me just, good (oh *numen*) !' or 'He/She (a *numen*) made me just, good'.

The Linear A personal name ***i-du-ti*** (HT 104.2-3) can likewise be analysed as Hurrian {*id=u=tti*} 'Beat, hit, strike me (oh *numen*) !', containing the verbal root ***id-*** 'to beat, hit, smash, strike violently', cf. I. Wegner, *Einführung*, 41, 256, s.v. ***id-*** 'schlagen'; Th. Richter, *BGH*, 109-110, s.v. ***id-*** I [Boğ.] and *VHN*, 405, s.v. ***id-*** II, '(zer)schlagen'.

Semantically Linear A ***i-du-ti*** can be compared with the Hurrian personal name ***Ullutti*** (wr. *ul-lu-ut-ti*) from Mari and Tigunāni, analysis {*o/ull=u=tti*}, lexicon *ull-*, typology 1.3.1.1.2.2, 'Destroy me (oh *numen*) !', which is considered a variant of the personal name ***Ullutta*** (wr. *ul-lu-ut-ta*) from Šušarrā (Tall Shemshara), analysis {*o/ull=u=tta*}, lexicon *ull-*, typology 1.3.1.1.2.1, also 'Destroy me (oh *numen*) !', with optional allomorphic suffix ***-tti*** instead of ***-tta***, cf. Th. Richter, *VHN*, 329 and 596. Sub 1.3.1.1.2.1, *normal forms*, Th. Richter (*VHN*, 594-595) explains that the forms in ***°utta***, ***°unna***, ***°ulla*** probably contain the suffixes of the absolutive enclitic personal pronouns ***-tta*** (1st person sg.), ***-nna***, (3rd person sg.), ***-lla*** (3rd person plur.), indicating the object of the transitive verb.

Paradigmatic is the form ***ki-ru-un-na*** in the Hurrian-Hittite bilingual ***Kirenze*** KBo 32, 15 Rs. IV 2, and the parallel formation ***[k]i-ru-un*** in 53 1. Kol. 4' (both Ḫattuša) that can probably be translated as 'release him, set him free, manumit him', containing the verbal root ***kir-*** 'to release, set free, manumit' + the thematic vowel ***-u/o-*** + the suffix of the enclitic personal pronoun ***-n(na)***, cf. Linear A ***ki-ro***. Th. Richter (*VHN*, 595) mentions the following examples of 'one-word names' with enclitic ***-t(ta)***: ^{f}*Izzutta*(?) (Mari); *Ḫalut* (Tigunāni); *Ḫizzutta* (Šušarrā); *Kizzutta* (Mari); *Kuzzutta* (Ašnakkum); *Nuputta* (Mari), with variant *Nupatta*; *Ullutta* (Šušarrā). Th. Richter (*VHN*, 596) explains (sub 1.3.1.1.2.2) that the 'one-word names' with enclitic ***=tti***, ***=nni*** / ***=nnu***, ***=lle*** / ***=lli*** are *optional allomorphic forms* for ***=tta***, ***=nna***, ***=lla***. He mentions ***Ullutti*** (Mari, Tigunāni) as example of a name with the enclitic personal pronoun ***=tti*** (1st person singular).

The Pre-Greek name of the commander of the Cretans during the Trojan War (*Iliad* B 645 ff.), ***Ἰδομενεύς*** (Idomeneus), son of Deukalion and grandson of Minos (N 452), may well contain the same Hurrian verbal rood ***id-***, since there is no trace of an initial digamma (***w-/ϝ-***) in his name. An ultimate Hurrian etymology of this Pre-Greek name, e.g. < ****Id=o=m-en(n)i*** '(The) God struck violently', makes sense for the name of a king, in particular because the formation of the name shows the typical features of so-called Old Hurrian personal names containing a verbal root and verbal endings in ***=i=b***, ***=a=b*** and ***=o=m*** as we know from the Hurrian-Hittite biligual ***Kirenze*** (KBo 32), cf. e.g. I. Wegner, *Einführung*, 34 (I translate the German text): "The Hurrian-Hittite bilingual is in a sense an exceptional case, because the repertory of forms, particularly with regard to the verbs, belongs mainly to the category of so-called 'Old Hurrian'." *Ibidem* (128-129) she gives two examples of *ergative* sentences with the subject in the ergative, the object in the *absolutive* and the verbal form in ***=o=m*** (3rd person singular transitive in ergative construction: ***kazi taballi=š ... tab=ašt=o=m*** (KBo 32: 14 I 42) 'the bronze smith cast a beaker / goblet / cup / bowl (*kazi*)' and ***ur(i)=i=l(la) ... keligel=ešt=o=m*** (KBo 32: 13 Vs. I 5-6) 'he laid his feet high'. The noun ***uri*** means 'foot', cf. I. Wegner, *Einführung*, 291.

Hurrian ****Id=o=m-en(n)i***, which I propose as a Hurrian prototype of ***Ἰδομενεύς*** and its Linear B derivatives ***i-do-me-ne-ja*** (PY Eb 498,1; PY Ep 212,9), ***Ἰδομένεια***, feminine of ***Ἰδομενεύς***, and ***i-do-me-ni-jo*** (PY Gn 428,5; PY Fn 324,7), dative of ***Ἰδομένιος***, are all attestations of names without initial ***w-/ϝ-***.

They show the same formation as Linear A ***da-du-ma-ta*** (HT 95 + 149.1) that can now (thanks to the bilingual ***Kirenze*** and the analysis of Old Hurrian verbal formations) be analysed as ***dad=o/u=m-atta*** 'Father loved the (just born) child and still loves it', with ***atta(i)*** in the double meaning of 'the father of the child', but also of ***eni attanni*** 'God the Father', usually equivalent to the Stormgod Tešub himself.

Likewise Linear A ***da-du-te*** (HT 34.1) can be analyzed as {*dad=o/u=(m)-te*} and translated as 'Tešub loved (the child) and still loves it'. I have put ***-m-*** in brackets, because ***-m-*** preceding an occlusive is not expressed in consonant clusters in Linear A and B. In Hurrian both forms (with and without ***-m-***) are possible. In cuneiform this ***-m-*** (preceding a dental), marking the subject of action 3rd person singular of the transitive-ergative verb, would have been expressed.

If Linear A ***i-da-ma-te*** (AR Zf 1) on a gold double axe-head from the Cave of Arkalokhori (Boston Museum of Fine Arts 58.1009) and (AR Zf 2) on a silver double axe-head from the Cave of Arkalokhori (HM 626) is compared with ***da-du-ma-ta*** and ****Id=o=m-en(n)i***, the analysis could at first sight be †{*id=a=m-atte*} '(God the) Father thunders', with indicator ***-a-*** of the intransitive verb instead of transitive ***-i-*** or ***-o/u-***. A transitive formation, *{*id=o=m-atta*}, would be translated '(God the) Father, he struck (somebody) violently', from the root ***id-*** 'to strike, to hit'. The meaning of ***id=a=m-*** '(he) thunders' seems to be chosen for a good reason: If ***Atta(i)*** in the sense of ***Eni Attanni*** 'God the Father', c.q. Tešub, is subject of alleged intransitive †***id=a=m-*** '(he) thunders', the meaning seems to express exactly the main function of the Head of the Pantheon (Hurrian Tešub and Greek Zeus) and is semantically close to that of transitive ***id=i=b-*** 'he hits, he strikes' and ***id=o=m-*** 'he hit, he struck'.

A problem is though, that - as far as I know - the suffix ***-m*** as subject-indicator of the 3rd person singular agent is to date only attested with certainty in combination with transitive ergative ***-o-*** and not with intransitive ***-a-*** in Old Hurrian verbal forms and personal names, cf. I. Wegner, *Einführung*, 134. This means that the analysis of ***i-da-ma-te*** as †{*id=a=m-atte*} would only be possible, if we accept an exceptional position of Minoan-Hurrian in this respect. That might be a step too far in this stage of research.

Another problem with an analysis as †{*id=a=m-atte*} is that Linear A provides on the golden and the silver double axe-heads final ***-e*** instead of ***-a***. The form ***-atte*** in ***i-da-ma-te*** instead of expected ***-atta*** as in ***da-du-ma-ta*** should then be explained as a shift of ***a > e*** that is indeed sometimes observed in Hurrian, but is in this case less likely, because it would offer confusion with the form ***atte*** 'woman' as variant of ***ašte/ažde*** and ***azze***.

Interpretation of ***i-da-ma-te*** as †{*id=a=m-atte*} depends on the assumption that it is derived from *{*id=a=m-atta*} '(God the) Father thunders' and does not contain ***atte*** 'woman', equivalent to or variant of ***ašte/ažde*** and ***azze***, attested as (onomastic elements of) Hurrian names of women, e.g. ***ᶠAzza*** + nomen, ***ᶠAzza-Naje*** (M), ***ᶠAzze*** (M), ***ᶠAzzu*** (AŠ, M, Q), ***ᶠAzzen*** (Q), ***ᶠAzzue*** (M, Q), ***ᶠAzzuena*** (Q), ***ᶠAzzuāia*** (M), ***ᶠAzzukka*** ([AŠ], M), ***ᶠAzzukki*** (M), ***ᶠAzzunni*** (M), ***ᶠAzzuzari*** (M); ***ᶠAšte*** (M), ***ᶠAšten*** (M), ***ᶠAštu*** (M, TU), ***ᶠAštun*** (M), ***ᶠAštue*** (AŠ, M), ***ᶠAštakka*** (M), ***ᶠAštuḫḫe*** (M), ***ᶠAštuzar*** (AŠ, M); ***ᶠAtte*** (AŠ), ***ᶠAttenan*** (AŠ), ***ᶠAtti*** (M), ***ᶠAttu*** (AŠ, M), ***ᶠAttuāia*** (M), ***ᶠAttue*** (AŠ, M), ***ᶠAttukki*** (AŠ, M), ***ᶠAttuzar*** (M), ***ᶠAttuzari*** (M), cf. Th. Richter, *VHN*, 381-385, 391, s.v. ***azze***, ***azzu***, ***ašte***, ***aštu***, ***atte***, ***atti***, ***attu***.

The fact that, for instance, ^{f}***Azzu***, ^{f}***Aštu***, ^{f}***Attu***, ^{f}***Azzuzari***, ^{f}***Aštuzar***, ^{f}***Attuzar*** and ^{f}***Azzue***, ^{f}***Aštue***, ^{f}***Attue*** all occur at Mari, indicates that these variant writings (and probably variant pronunciations) of ***-zze-***, ***-št-*** and ***-tt-*** can only have been caused by dialectal differences, if the ladies in question originally came from different places with different dialects and were only subsequently stationed in the Palace of Mari and its dependencies keeping their names without any adaptation at all.

Another option is a process of palatalization and assibilation of ***atte*** **[*ate*]** > **[*at*^{y}*e*]** > **[*at*^{s}*e*]** > **[*ase*]**, written ***azze*** in cuneiform and ***a-se*** in Linear A (HT 93a.3; HT 132.1; ZA Zb 3.1), cf. ***a-se-ja*** (HT 115a.4),]***a-se-ja*** (HT 93a.8),]***a-se-re-za***|[(KH 13.2).

Another option may be that the process of assibilation was not completed, but that the stage of **[*at*^{s}*e*]** was subjected to metathesis > **[*aste*]**, written ***ašte*** in cuneiform and ***a-de*** (reflecting [***azde***]) in Linear A, since ***-s/z-*** preceding occlusives was not expressed in consonant clusters in Linear A and B.

A third option may be a sound shift through assimilation from sibilant dental or dental sibilant to either dental (***ašte*** > ***atte***) or sibilant, (***ažde*** > ***azze***), phonologically **[*ase*]**, since double writing indicates voiceless phonemes in syllabic cuneiform. N.B. ***azze*** must always be the last stage in these processes, since a change from ***azze*** > ***ašte/ažde*** and ***atte*** is phonetically impossible.

It seems inconceivable that phonetic changes could have led to a simultaneous usage of ***atte***, ***ašte*** and ***azze*** at Mari (or elsewhere). So it may be a target for future research to examine whether the attestations might show evidence of a difference in time between the three variants. It is also interesting to know, where the people with a dependent status, living in residence in the palace of Mari or outside, originally came from.

Unfortunately Linear A did not use determinatives preceding names as cuneiform did: such as ^{m}□ for names of men, **LÚ**□ for male gender, ^{f}□ for names of women and ^{MUNUS}□ for female gender. This was no problem for Minoan scribes, for they knew whom they described, but it is a great problem for us, since we are missing information that was transparent to the scribes, but which they did not share with us. So we must use every clue to get nearer to the truth.

The double axes from Arkalokhori are considered religious objects, which makes it likely that the identical inscriptions have a religious bearing as well. The violent nature of the root ***id-*** makes it more likely that ***i-da-ma-te*** might be an epithet to a male deity.

Another argument, why ***i-da-ma-te*** probably refers to a male deity, is attestation of the Linear A epithet ***i-da-a*** (KO Za 1.b-c) 'He thunders' > '(The) thunderer', following ***a-ta-i-jo-wa-ja*** , ***tu-ru-sa*** , ***du-pu-re*** (see *sub vocibus*) on a limestone parallelepiped from the Peak Sanctuary of Kophinas. The form ***i-da-a*** {*id=a-ya*} may well be a hypocoristic form of ***i-da-ma-te*** (with the Hurrian hypocoristic suffix ***-ya***), prototype of Linear B ***i-da-i-jo*** (KN K 875,4; PY An 661,2), probably ***Ἰδαῖος***, originally probably with the same meaning as Linear A ***i-da-a*** and ***i-da-ja*** {*id=a-ya*}, '(The) thunderer', but as soon as the Mycenaean Greeks did no longer understand the Minoan-Hurrian etymology of the epithet the meaning changed to 'God of Mount Ida'. The regular variant orthography of Minoan-Hurrian ***i-da-a*** (KO Za 1.b-c) is attested as Linear A ***i-da-ja*** (PK Za 18) on a fragment of a libation table from the Peak Sanctuary of Petsophas near Palaikastro. This kind of orthographic variation is very common in Hurrian hypocoristic names.

Not only the epithet ***i-da-a*** (KO Za 1.b-c) was originally derived from the root ***id-***, but also the name of Mount ***Ida*** itself, twice attested in Linear A as ***i-da*** (ZA 21b.1; ZA 27a.1), since ***Ida*** can be analysed as Hurrian ***id=a=Ø*** 'He (the mountain god) thunders' or 'It (the mountain) thunders', consisting of the root ***id-*** + the indicator of intransitivity ***-a-*** + enclitic personal pronoun as subject indicator 3rd person singular intransitive indicative ***Ø*** (so not ***-nna***), cf. I Wegner, *Einführung*, 99 Table 6 & 7: *The order of suffixes of the indicative, intransitive-positive and intransitive-negative verb and the antipassive verb.*

In fact the Linear A form | ***i-da-da*** | (KT Zg 2.b) proves that Linear A ***i-da*** (ZA 21b.1; ZA 27a.1), though originally a verbal form ***id=a=Ø***, may already have become the designation of the mountain itself in Minoan times, because the Linear A sequence on a perforated black-green steatite sealstone | *da-da-i* | (KT Zg 2.b) [← as read from the sealstone], but | ***i-da-da*** | [→ as read from the seal-impression] shows clear features of a noun, since the Hurrian suffix ***-da*** is the suffix of the directive case-ending ***-da*** 'to', cf. I. Wegner, *Einführung*, 65 (Table 1: *Paradigm of the Hurrian case-endings*). If ***i-da-da*** (KT Zg 2.b) can be analysed as {*ida=da*}, it consists of the name of mount ***Ida*** + the Hurrian directive suffix ***-da*** 'to' and is therefore comparable with Greek ****Ἴδαν-δε***, accusative of ***Ἴδα*** + the directive suffix ***-δε*** 'to Ida'.

However, Linear A ***-da*** can also represent the Hurrian ablative suffix ***-dan*** 'from' (see Wegner, *ibidem*), so that {*ida=dan*} can be compared with Greek ***Ἴδηθεν <*Ἴδᾱ-θεν*** 'from Ida'. The scribe no doubt knew which of the two suffixes he meant, but we do not, because a final consonant is not expressed in Linear A and B.

The genitive ***i-da-mi*** {*Ida=mi/wi*} in the combination]***a-ta-i-jo-wa-ja , i-da-mi , ja-***[(SY Za 1) from the Peak Sanctuary of Symi Viannou makes it quite clear that 'Our Father of (Mount) Ida' can refer to no other god than *Teš(š)ub*.

The same genitive ***i-da-mi*** in]***u-ti-nu , i-na-i-da-mi ,*** [(IO Za 11.2) from Mount Ioukhtas, combined with the plural form ***inna/enna*** 'Gods', 'Bring it (scil. childbirth, childhood) out/forth' {*ušt=i=nnu*}, 'oh Gods (*inna*) {*e/in(i)=na*} of Ida {*Ida=mi/wi*}', shows that not only Tešub, but probably the Holy Trinity of Tešub, Ḫebat and Šarru(m)ma may be regarded as 'Gods of Ida'. Alternation of ***m/w*** is common in Linear A and Hurrian. The genitive ***i-da-mi*** proves that ***i-da*** in Linear is not only verbal, but also nominal.

Returning to ***i-da-ma-te*** (AR Zf 1; AR Zf 2) there is still one option to be discussed: I. Wegner (*Einführung*, 87-89, sub 5.2.1: *Die 1. Position: Die Wurzelerweiterungen*) discusses the so-called 'root-extensions' of the verb, which take the first position in the chain of suffixes, directly following the root. One of these root-extensions is ***-am-*** that expresses the *factitive* aspect of the verb according to G. Wilhelm, *Iraq 53 (1991)*, 12, Anm. 35. I. Wegner offers the example: ***eman-*** 'ten', ***eman=am-***, transitive 'decuple, multiply by ten'; intr. 'increase tenfold'. If we assume that Linear A ***i-da-ma-te*** contains this root-extension ***-am-***, the analysis will be {*id=am=a-te*}, consisting of the root ***id-*** + the *factitive* root-extension ***-am-*** + the marker of intransitivity ***-a-*** [as in ***i-da-a*** (KO Za 1.b-c) and ***i-da-ja*** (PK Za 18)] and the form ***-Te*** (hypocoristic of ***-Tešub***) as subject of the verb: 'Tešub thunders, Tešub causes thunder and lightning'. I conclude that analysis of Linear A ***i-da-ma-te*** as {*id=am=a-te*} 'Tešub causes thunder and lightning' appears to be by far the preferable option from a semantical and grammatical point of view.

The observation that Linear A ***i-du-ti*** (HT 104.2-3), ***i-da-ma-te*** (AR Zf 1; AR Zf 2), ***i-da-a*** (KO Za 1.b-c), ***i-da*** (ZA 21b.1; ZA 27a.1), ***i-da-da*** (KT Zg 2.b), Mycenaean Greek Linear B ***i-da-i-jo*** (KN K 875,4; PY An 661,2) probably ***Ἰδαῖος***, ***i-do-me-ne-ja*** (PY Eb 498,1; PY Ep 212,9), ***Ἰδομένεια***, feminine of ***Ἰδομενεύς***, and ***i-do-me-ni-jo*** (PY Gn 428,5; PY Fn 324,7), dative of ***Ἰδομένιος*** are all attestations of names without initial ***w-/ ϝ-***, is decisive, since Linear A and B faithfully expressed every initial ***w-/ϝ-***. The fact that there is no trace of ***ϝ-*** in ***Ἴδη***, ***Ἴδηθεν***, ***Ἰδαῖος*** in Homer either, proves conclusively that the root ***id-*** in these formations is Pre-Greek and can probably be identified with the Hurrian verbal root ***id-***. If J. Chadwick's and L. Baumbach's association of ***ἴδη*** and Doric ***ἴδᾱ*** 'forest' with Cretan ***Βίδᾱν*** is correct, two distinct roots may have coexisted, one with and one without initial digamma. The name of mount ***Ida*** (***Ἴδη***) and its cognates ***Idaia***, ***Idaios***, ***Idomeneus***, ***Idomeneia***, ***Idomenios***, etc. certainly contained no initial digamma.

Disappearance of the digamma after the time of the Mycenaean Linear B tablets may have caused confusion of the root of the name of mount ***Ida*** with that of the noun ***ἴδη*** (Doric ***ἴδᾱ***) < ****ϝίδᾱ*** 'timber-tree, wood, forest' in popular etymology. P. Chaintraine (o.c.) and H.G. Liddell - R. Scott, *A Greek - English lexicon*, Oxford 1961, do not mention a possible original initial digamma in ***ἴδη*** (Doric ***ἴδᾱ***) 'forest', based on Cretan ***Βίδᾱν*** or Dacian ***ῥαθιβίδα***, which may well account for their association of ***ἴδη*** (Doric ***ἴδᾱ***) 'forest' with the name of mount ***Ida***.

It is an advantage that the Linear A sequence ***sa-ma*** (HT 6b.5, HT 10a.1, HT 52a.1, ZA 10b.3-4) occurs on 4 tablets, 3 from Hagia Triada and 1 from Kato Zakro, so that we can observe the context of each tablet.

The context of the tablet from Kato Zakro is intriguing, because one of the other names in the list of personal names is ***ra***$_2$***-ro-re*** (ZA 10b.5). Linear A ***ra***$_2$***-ro-re*** (ZA 10b.5) may be equated with the name of the Hurrian goddess *Liluri*, with palatalized ***l*** (>l^y) in the first syllable, = ***L***^{y}***al(l)uri*** = ***/L***^{y}***al(l)ore/*** or ***Lial(l)uri*** = ***/Lial(l)ore/*** (with [***o***] and [***e***]).

The goddess is described by E. Laroche, *GLH*, 160, as 'Déesse parèdre de Tešub de Manuziya, au Kizuwatna; fête *ḫišuwaš*, CTH 628, *passim*. Graphies: ^{d}*Li-lu-u-ri, Li-il-lu-ri, Le-el-lu-ri.* Sg. *Lil(l)uri,* KUB XII 12 V 16, 20, VI 7, 15 et dupl.; KUB XXX 40 II 3 sqq.; KUB XXXII 65 I 16 et dupl.; KBo XX 115, 8, etc. – *abate* ^{d}*Liluri* ou ^{d}*Liluri abate,* KUB XII 12 VI 17, 27; KBo XV 37 II 11; KUB XXV 48 III 16, etc.; KBo XVII 98, 12. – Akk. ^{d}*Li-lu-ri,* KBo X 1 Ro 38. Pl. ^{d}*Li-il-lu-ri-in-na* (^{d}*Abatenna tiyarenna),* KUB XXV 42+ II 18, IV 6, 12, V 20.

Linear A ***sa-ma*** (ZA 10b.3-4) may be equated with the name of the Babylonian Sun-god ***Šamaš***, to whom Hurrian ***^{d}Ši-me-ki*** has assimilated (Sumerian ^{d}UTU, Hurrian ***^{d}Ši-me-ki***, ***^{d}Ši-mi-gi-(ni)***, alphabetic ***šmg***, Ugaritic ***šapšu***, Hebrew ***šèmèš***).

The context of Linear A ***sa-ma*** (ZA 10b.3-4) combined with ***ra***$_2$***-ro-re*** (ZA 10b.5) = ***Lial(l)ore*** makes interpretation of ***sa-ma*** as a personal name derived from the theonym ***Šamaš*** attractive, since both names occur in the same list of personal names. Nevertheless it cannot be ruled out that ***sa-ma*** (HT 6b.5, HT 10a.1, HT 52a.1) may be interpreted differently as a homonymic form: ***sa-ma*** 35 (HT 6b.5-6) and ***sa-ma*** 4 **,** ***pa*** (HT 10a.1) are certainly personal names.

A.A. MacRae (*Nuzi Personal Names,* 316) has included names with the theophorous elements ***Šamaš-***, ***Šamša-***, ***-šamaš*** in his 'list of Akkadian elements'. Sentence names such as ^{d}*Šamaš-sarri,* ^{d}*Šamaš-sar-ri* may be hybrid. A.A. MacRae, *NPN*, 294, mentions: "Hybrids are included in this list, if the common noun or verb used is Akkadian, even if a non-Akkadian divine element is involved. Similarly, Akkadian divine elements are to be found in Dr. Purves' list, if they are used with non-Akkadian common elements."

The *b*-side of Linear A tablet HT 24 is quite interesting:

HT 24b.1. .] TAL 1 JE *si+me-ki*
2. TAL 1JE *ka+ja* TAL 1
3-5. vacant

The Hurrian theonym ***^{d}Ši-me-ki*** occurs as Linear A ***si+me-ki*** (HT 24b.1), followed by the ideogram TALENTUM 1 JE, on a tablet from Hagia Triada. It could be a theonym used as a personal name as ***Šimika*** (wr. *Ši-mi-qa, Ši-mi-ga*) at Nuzi, cf. I.J. Gelb, *NPN*, 134), but preferably it refers to the Sun-god himself, since the combination of ***si+me-ki*** TAL 1 JE (HT 24b.1) is followed by ***ka+ja*** TAL 1 (HT 24b.2), which gives the impression that both the Hurrian Sungod ***^{d}Ši-me-ki, ^{d}Ši-mi-gi-(ni)*** attested at Nuzi and the Minoan predecessor of the Goddess ***Γαῖα*** 'Earth' are mentioned in exactly the same way. Linear A ***ka+ja*** (HT 24b.2) can theoretically be interpreted as the Hurrian personal name ***Kaja*** (wr. *Qa-a-a, Ka-a-a, Ga-a-a*) at Nuzi, cf. I.J. Gelb, *NPN*, 77; P.M. Purves, *NPN*, 222.

P. Chantraine, *DELG*, 219, s.v. ***γῆ***: "Ni *γῆ* ni *γαῖα* n'ont d'étymologie établie. On a supposé que *γαῖα* était une contamination de *γῆ* avec *αἶα* (voir ce mot) et *μαῖα*. Simple hypothèse liée à la notion de la 'terre mère'." ["Neither *γῆ* nor *γαῖα* have an established etymology. One has supposed that *γαῖα* was a contamination of *γῆ* with *αἶα* (see that word) and *μαῖα*. Simple hypothesis connected with the notion of 'Mother Earth'."] Certainly many Hurrian personal names are theophorous. So one may wonder whether the Hurrian personal name ***Kaja*** might also be derived from a theonym. E. Laroche (*GLH*, 134) calls ***kai-*** a 'terme d'onomastique théophore' ['theophorous onomastic term'] and refers to *NPN* 222. Compare Th. Richter (*BGH*, 179) for the root ***ka-*** and Linear A ***ka-i-ro*** (ZA 8.6) from Kato Zakro, that I identify as the Hurrian personal name ***Kaillu*** (wr. *Qa-i-el-lu, Ga-i-el-lu, Qa-i-il-lu, Ka-i-il-lu, Qa-i-lu*) from Nuzi, cf. P.M. Purves, *NPN*, 222.

The combination of ***si+me-ki*** (HT 24b.1) and ***ka+ja*** (HT 24b.2) with the ideogram TALENTUM, which represents a high value, seems to make interpretation of both names as theonyms preferable. Unfortunately the left top corner of tablet HT 24b, which may have contained another theonym (?), is broken off. There is only a small trace of a sign/signs or a ligature visible in the top left corner of HT 24.b, but the ideogram TAL 1 JE (HT 24b.1) following this trace is clearly visible. We only know that this sequence was also followed by TAL 1 JE, so that we can conclude that it belonged to the same category as ***si+me-ki*** and ***ka+ja***. One can only speculate about the missing first theonym: Is it ***Kušuḫ***, the God of the Moon, or possibly ***Tešub*** himself, the God of the clouds. We also know that these three entries (and 3x TAL) were the only entries on HT 24b, because that side of the tablet is empty after ***ka+ja*** TAL 1. In Asia Minor ***Šimegi*** follows ***Kušuḫ*** and is represented as a god at Yazılıkaya (cf. H. Otten, *Anatolia 4 (1959)*, 27, n. 4).

Is it merely accidental that Menelaos proposes that the Trojans bring two lambs, a white ram for the Sungod ***Ἥλιος***, a black ewe for the Goddess ***Γῆ***, and that the Greeks bring another lamb for Zeus (*Iliad* Γ 103-104) in order to sacrifice and swear an oath that a combat between Alexandros and himself will bring the Trojan war to an end ?

Interestingly the last line of tablet HT 33 offers the *rebus*-like ideogram NUBES+***pi***, 'cloud'+***pi***, that I interpret as ***Tešup=pi*** 'of Tešub', in the sense of 'belonging to Tešub', with the genitive suffix ***-pi/-wi***, followed by the high number 100 (HT 33.4). Then follows a ligature ***qe+pa₃*** 'Ḫebat', also followed by the high number 100 (HT 33.4). Tablets HT 24b and HT 33 have a lot in common (cf. Chapter 11: *'Religious' Linear A inscriptions*).

Šimigene-m, the Hurrian god of the Sun *Šimige* / *Šimegi* / *Šimigi* (equated with the Egyptian *Amun-Ra*), is attested in Mâri-text 1. 36, with the suffix ***-ne*** of the so-called definite article and the copulative suffix ***-m*** 'and'.

The theophorous onomastic element is in several forms attested at Nuzi: *Ar-ši-mi-qa, Ar-ši-mi-ka* 'Give, oh Sun-god !'; *Ḫa-aš-ši-mi-qa, Ḫa-ši-mi-qa* 'Listen, oh Sun-god !'; Old Hurrian *Ḫu-ti-ip-ši-mi-qa {ḫud=i=b-šimiga}* 'The Sun-god, he blessed (the child)'; *Ḫu-ti-ši-mi-qa {ḫud=i-šimiga}* 'Bless (the child), oh Sun-god !'; *Ḫu-ti-iš-ši-mi-qa {ḫud=i=ž-šimiga}* 'May/Let the Sun-god bless (the child)'; *dŠin-ši-mi-qa* 'Make (the child) the second one, oh Sun-god !'; *Ti-iš-ši-mi-qa, Ti-ši-mi-qa, Ti-iš-ši-me-qa, Ti-eš-ši-me-qa {ti=e=z-šime/iga}* 'The Sun-god may pronounce (the name)', *Zi-iš-ši-mi-qa, Zi-ši-mi-ga*; *Ti-il-ši-mi-qa*; *Tar-mi-iš-ši-mi-ki {tarm=i=ž-šime/iga}* 'May/Let (the child) drink, oh Sun-god !'; *Ši-mi-qa-a-tal, Ši-mi-qa-tal, Ši-mi-ga-tal, Ši-mi-ka-tal, Ši-me-qa-tal, Si-mi-qa-tal {šime/ik(i)-adal}* 'The Sun-god is the strong one' and the hypocoristic names *Ši-mi-ge-ia* and *Ši-mi-ku-ia* (cf. P.M. Purves, *NPN*, 257). I have added some analyses and translations of names [PGvS].

Šimegi 'Sun' also occurs with the suffix of the so-called definite article ***-ni*** in the cuneiform syllabary, ***Šimegi-ni*** 'The Sun' (cf. alphabetic cuneiform ***Šmg-n*** at Ugarit), cf. E. Laroche, *Recherches sur les noms de dieux hittites,* Paris 1947, 59;

E. Laroche (Documents en langue hourrite provenant de Ras Shamra, *Ugaritica V, 1968*, 447-544, especially 508-509, 522) shows the drawing of text Ras Shamra 24.294, (see *chapter 6*) providing a list of divinities in the alphabetic cuneiform of Ugarit. Apart from the suffix representing the definite article ***-n*** in alphabetic cuneiform, which equals ***-ni/-ne*** in the cuneiform syllabary, the list also provides the suffix ***-d*** in alphabetic cuneiform, which equals ***/-da/*** in the cuneiform syllabary (***-ta*** in single writing designating the voiced character of the dental occlusive). E. Laroche (Notes sur le panthéon hourritte de Ras Shamra, *JAOS 88.1, 1968*, 148-150) mentions in his discussion with regard to the list of the Hurrian pantheon of Ugarit that ***-da*** (alphabetic ***-d***) represents the suffix of the singular directive designating 'to, towards, for', whereas ***-šta*** (alphabetic ***-št***) represents that of the plural directive form. According to I. Wegner (*Einführung*, 65, table 1) ***-šta*** < ***-aš=ta*** in fact consists of two suffixes, pluralizing suffix ***-aš-*** + directive suffix ***-d/ta***.

The Hurrians often offered the translation *Šimegi* for the various Sungods of peoples they dealt with, for instance, ***Šimegi-ni*** for *Ra*, following Amon, in the Tušratta's letter to the Egyptian pharao Amenhotep III (*Mit.* I, 76-77). E. Laroche, *GLH*, 232, s.v. *Šimigi* 'soleil': "Lecture du sum. dUTU; Hrozný, *ArchOr. 4*, 119; von Brandenstein, *ZDMG 91*, 563, 570; KUB XXVII p. IV. – Cf. our. *Šiwini* ? Forme habituelle *Šimigi*, rare *Šimiga*.

Graphies: ^{d}UTU-*gi/ki,* $^{(d)}$*ši-mi-(i)-gi-(ni)-,* ^{d}*Ši-me-ki,* alph. *šmg*. RS quadr. 137 IV a 18 = *Ugar. V*, 248: sum. ^{d}UTU = h. *ši-mi-gi* = oug. *šapšu*; cf. Msk. série An N° 30-31: UTU = ^{d}*ši-me-gi,* ^{d}*ši-me-ga*. *Šimigi* = UTU-*gi* désigne, selon les lieux et les occasions: 1. le dieu égyptien *Ra* (Mit.); 2. la déesse cananéenne *Šapaš*; 3. le dieu solaire hourrite, assimilé au babylonien *Šamaš*; 4. la déesse hittite 'Soleil de la terre' (*Ugar V*, 522). Noter que le nom est souvent déterminé par l'article *-ni*, et que *šimigi* paraît avoir été, à l'origine, le nom propre de l'astre plutôt que celui d'une divinité personnelle. Rien n'autorise à supposer un lien étymologique entre *šimigi* et *Šamšu / Šapaš*."

E. Laroche (*GLH*, 213) mentions that Hurrian *ša-am-ša-a-ti*, KBo XVII 86 + II 9, is a Hurrian copy of Akkadian *šamšatu* 'disque solaire' (*AW* 1158); cf. *ib*. 8 *utušuḫḫi.*

If ***pa*** (HT 10a.1, *e.a.*) is monosyllabic, it can be an abbreviation of ***parizi*** = a bushel (a measure, especially of grain = ca. 36,5 litres = ½ Kor) or of ***parizz=ade*** '*parizi*-measure'. It is frequent in Linear A, if it forms a ligature with the ideogram GRA. GRA+***pa*** (HT 43.2; HT 93a.4, 5; HT 102.2, 3; HT 120.2, 4, 6; HT 125b.3; HT 128a.3, 4; KH 27.2; PE 1.3, 4; ZA 6a.5; ZA 6b.1, 3; ZA 11a.1, 4, 5; ZA 11b.1, 3; ZA 18a.1; ZA 28.1).

At Alalaḫ the same abbreviation PA (*parisi*) was used as in Linear A: ****Wandi-ya*** (wr. **Wa-an-di-ya, AT* *282:5) at Alalaḫ VII receives 20 PA of barley-flour, in a text on distribution of rations of barley-flour (ZÌ.DA.ŠE). Total expenditure (ZI.GA) - 93 PA (= *parisi*). Entries, however, only total 88: 19 to the controller of Kuwan, 27 to *Uwandarama*, 6 to *Kuduru*, 20 to *Wandia* and 16 to *Arip-kušuḫa* (cf. D.J. Wiseman, *AT*, p. 88, nr. *282). E. Laroche (*GLH*, 196) mentioned the form *pa-a-ri-zi-ni-wi*$_{i}$*-na-(ma)*, KUB XLVII 1 III 8: pl. du gén. *parizi-ni-wi*. M. Dijkstra, New joins in the Hurrian epic of *Kešši* and their ramifications, *UF 40 (2008)*, 212, now reads this form as: *pa-a-ri-zi-ni-wi*$_{i}$*-na-aš*, cf. Th. Richter, *BGH*, 301, s.v. ***parizi*** [Boğ.] 'bushel' and ***parizzade***, ***parissade*** [Boğ.]: Einheitlich als "½ Kor" und Lw aus akk. *parīsu* gewertet, entspricht sumgr. 1 *PA(-RI-SA)*. [Unanimously rated at "½ Kor" and loan-word from Akkadian, corresponds with Sumerogram 1 PA(-RI-SA).] In alphabetic cuneiform of Ugarit ***prs***.

The term ***parizzade*** occurs in the Hurrian-Hittite bilingual ***Kirenze*** (KBo 32: 15 I 9'), cf. E. Neu, StBoT 32, 288: *pa-ri-iz-za-te ú-bi* [X], analysis {*parizz=ade ubi*} (I. Wegner, *Einführung*, 229-230: "ein halbes Kor Gerste"), one *bushel* (about 36,5 litres) of barley.

According to I. Wegner (*Einführung*, 53) the Hurrian suffix ***-ade*** forms in some cases collectives: ***amm=ade*** 'Großvater' ['grandfather'], ***fir=ade*** 'auswärtiger Gast' ['foreign guest'] (meaning according to G. Wilhelm, *SCCNH 15*, 2005, 175 ff.), ***ḫur=ade*** 'Krieger' ['warrior, soldier'], ***er=ade*** 'Vogel' ['bird']. The suffix often appears in numerals such as ***tumn(i)=ade*** 'je vier' ['four at a time'] or designations of measures such as ***parizz=ade*** '*parīsu*-measure' (derived from Akkadian *parīsu*).

Linear A ***sa-ma , te*** '[(HT 52a.1) occurs as first entry of the tablet, of which only the left top corner is preserved. Theoretically it can be a personal name as well, but in view of the prominent position on the tablet, a toponym is also conceivable.

One may compare the Pre-Greek name of the island of *Samos*, close to *Milete* (*Milawanda / Milawata* in Hittite texts) on the west-coast of Asia Minoar that may well be linked with *Milatos* on the north coast of Crete. In Crete the Gorges of *Samaria* are well-known, reminding of *Samaria* in the Near East.

The names *Samos* and *Samaria* no doubt have a Pre-Greek origin, because an Indo-European initial ***s-*** would have changed into ***h-*** in Greek, cf. Latin ***sex*** : Greek ***ἕξ*** (six) and Latin ***septem*** : Greek ***ἑπτά*** (seven).

E. Laroche, *GLH*, 213, mentions at Boğazköy Hurrian *ša-am-ma*, KUB XXVII 29 IV 15, which might be an exact equivalent. At Ugarit he mentions Hurrian *šam* in alphabetic cuneiform (*CTA* 166, 52). But in both cases he does not provide an interpretation.

Th. Richter (*VHN*, 497-498) mentions, s.v. ***šam-*** I, that ***ša-mu-uk*** (Mari, *RA 36*, 16, Nr. 4: 29) shows the verbal usage of the root. This also applies to other words such as ***ša-ma-ḫa-aš-tu***, analysis {*šam=aġ=ašt-*}, in the incantation texts from Mari and Tuttul (Krebernik, 2001, 158), the definition of a profession or function ***šamaḫule***, analysis {*šam=aġ=o=le*} and ***ša-ma-ḫi-iš*** that all offer a root-extension ***-aġ-***.

He mentions (*VHN*, 245, 498) the personal names ***Šamaḫiš*** (wr. *ša-ma-ḫi-iš*), old slave from Mari, analysis {*šam=aġ-iž*}, typology 1.3.2.2, lexicon *šam-* I; ***Šamaḫul*** (wr. *ša-ma-ḫu-ul, ša-ma-ḫu-li, ša-ba-ḫu-ul*), from Mari and Qaṭṭarā, typology 3.1, analysis {*šam=aġ=o=le*}, lexicon *šamaḫule* (→ *šam-* I), and the variant ***Šemaḫul*** (wr. *še-ma-ḫu-ul*) from Tigunāni, lexicon *šemaḫule*. Cf. also *ša-ma-ḫu-la* at Alalaḫ IV and Emar, *ša-ma-ḫul, ša-ma-ḫu-ul* at Kuruḫanni and *ša/šá-ma-ḫul/ḫu-ul* at Nuzi (*NPN*, 123).

Th. Richter (*VHN*, 245, 498) mentions, s.v. ***zam-*** II, that in spite of single writing of ***-m-*** in the personal name ***Zamal-tuk*** from Mari, the root may be ***zamm-***, c.q. ***samm-***, occurring in the bilingual ***Kirenze*** in the extended Hurrian stem {*zamm=al=ašt-*} that in accordance with the Hittite rendering ***arḫa šakkurija-*** can be translated as 'abreißen' ['to break off, to tear off'] [***arḫa*** adv. 'away (from), off']. The meaning of {*zam(m)=al-*} probably does not differ from {*zamm=al=ašt-*}, cf. also I. Wegner, *Einführung*, 87, s.v. ***zamm=al=ašt-***. In onomastics the meaning may be sought in 'breaking off the navel-string / umbilical cord'. The personal name ***Zamal-tuk*** (wr. *Za-ma-al-du-uk*) from Mari, analysis {*zam=al-to/uk*}, typology 1.4, lexicon *zam-*, *tuk-* (→ *tukki*), can be translated as '*Tuk* broke / tore the navel-string / umbilical cord off'. Th. Richter (*BGH*, 348-349; *VHN*, 497-498) does not mention, whether ***šam-*** I and ***zam(m)-*** II might be the same roots.

Other interesting names are: ***Šamme***, ***Šammena*** [Alalaḫ VII] 'a month-name', cf. partially preserved ***yrḫ šm***[ ] at Ugarit. The toponym ***Šamuḫa*** and the ethnic (URU.) ***Šamuḫaḫi*** [Boğ.], derived from the toponym ***Šamuḫa***. Cf. ^{D}*šá-ma-nu-ḫa ša* ^{URU}*te-di* 'The Sam(an)uḫian [Ištar/Šawuška] of the town *Tedi*' and the theonym ^{D}*ša/sa-ma-an-mi-nu-ḫe/hé*, c.q. ^{D}*ša-am-ma-an-nu-ḫe*, of ***šam(m)an(min)ni*** [Boğ.], cf. Th. Richter, *BGH*, 348-349.

It is conceivable that in (some of) the names ***sa-ma*** (HT 6b.5, HT 10a.1, HT 52a.1, ZA 10b.3-4) and ***sa-ma-|ro*** (HT 88.5-6) the Hurrian verbal root ***šam-*** I or ***zam(m)-*** II is involved. Linear A ***sa-ma-|ro*** 1 (HT 88.5-6) is clearly a personal name in a list of personal names. It can be interpreted as a Hurrian verbal 'one-word' personal name and be analysed as Old Hurrian {*zamm=ar=om*} or {*zamm=al=o=m*}, since Linear A has only one series of syllabic signs for the liquids ***l-*** and ***r-*** and final ***-m*** is not expressed in the script. The formation in ***-o=m*** is in accordance with e.g. ***ba-'à-áš-tum*** 'he has built' in the *Tiš-atal*-inscription (l. 6) from Urkeš (modern Tell Mozan) in Syria (see for an extensive discussion s.v. Linear A ***pa-i-to***, cf. I. Wegner, *Einführung*, 232-236.

If the name ***sa-ma-|ro*** (HT 88.5-6) {*zamm=ar=om*} contains the *factitive* or *iterative* root-extension ***-ar-***, it can be translated as 'He/She (a *numen*) caused the navel-string / umbilical cord to break off', cf. I. Wegner, *Einführung*, 88, s.v. root-extensiom ***-ar-***. The meaning of the root-extension ***-al-*** is not yet clear (cf. I. Wegner, *Einführung*, 87, s.v. ***ḫeš=al-*** 'nackt sein' ['to be naked /to be in the nude'], ***zamm=al=ašt-*** 'abreißen' ['to break off, to tear off'] and ***kab=al-*** '(Feld) plündern' ['to plunder, pillage, loot (a field)'].

Theoretically both root-extensions are possible and the meaning of the forms probably does not differ that much, but since I. Wegner actually provides the attested form ***zamm=al=ašt-*** with a second root-extension ***-V(owel)št-***, that (particularly with the Old Hurrian forms in ***=o=m***) may indicate a special grammatical aspect, e.g. the end or completion of an action as in the example ***pa=ašt=o=m*** 'he has built' (cf. I. Wegner, *Einführung*, 88-89, s.v. root-extension ***-Všt-***; cf. G. Wilhelm, *Festschrift Heger*, 1992, 670), it is most likely that we must choose {*zamm=al=o=m*} as the form the scribe had in mind: 'He/She (a *numen*) has torn off the navel-string / umbilical cord'. See for the Old Hurrian formants 3rd pers. singular in ***=o=m*** I. Wegner, *Einführung*, 34, 96-97, 126-128.

Linear A ***pa₃-ni-na*** 17 J | (HT 6b.6) is the last personal name in the list of personal names on HT 6b. It is difficult to establish on the basis of Linear A and B orthographic conventions, whether it contains the root ***pann-/wann-*** or ***pan-***. The meaning of both roots is not yet known and it is not certain either, whether these roots are cognate or not.

Th. Richter (*VHN*, 222, 477) mentions the name ***Wanni*** (wr. *Wa-an-ni, Pa-an-ni, Wa-an-na*) from Šušarrā, who is a correspondent of Kuwari, analysis {*fann(i)=a*}, typology 3.1, lexicon *wanni*. E. Laroche (*NH*, 204, n° 1489) mentions ***Wanni*** at Ḫattuša: 1. a priest *ᵐWa-an-ni-i-iš* (XII 2 I 24); 2. a priest, absolutive *ᵐWa-an-ni* (XVIII 9 II 22). He also mentions (*NH*, 204, n° 1488) a stonecutter ***Wana*** (wr. *Wa-na-s*) in a Hieroglyphic Luwian inscription (scribe-*la-š*), Karaburun. There is a ***Panni*** (wr. *Pa-an-ni*) at Nippur (see Hölscher, 1996, 166) and ᶠIŠ₈-TÁR-*ba-an-ni* at Alalaḫ VII (*AT* *178 = *UF 38*, 90: 33).

He also mentions (*VHN*, 222, 477) ***Panašḫe*** (wr. *Pa-na-áš-ḫe*) from Mari, a mountain-dweller (LÚ *pabanḫu*) at Ṭāb-salimᴷᴵ. The name can be identified as a noun in *ᵒ=a=šḫe* (Wilhelm/Süel, 2013, 157). He mentions (*VHN*, 40, 477) the sentence name ***ᶠAk[ap-p]anazzi*** (wr. *ᶠAk[ap-p]a-na-zi*) at Mari, analysis {*ag=a=b-panazzi*}, typology 1.1.1.3.1, lexicon *ag-*, *panazzi*, translation '*Panazzi* kam herauf' ['*Panazzi* came up / appeared']. It may be a formation in *ᵒ=a=zzi*, although such forms mainly appear in 'one-word names'.

Interpretation of the Linear A personal name ***pa₃-ni-na*** remains uncertain anyway, also because we do not know, whether the last syllable ***-na*** represents ***-nna*** or, for instance, ***-Na***, the shortened form of the theophorous element ***-Naja/-Naje***. A tentative analysis is ***Pan(n)=i=Na***, '.... (the child) (oh ***Naja / Naje***) !' or ***Pan(n)=i=nna***, '.... him/her [***-nna***] (the child) (oh *numen*)!'.

I shall now discuss some texts with ideograms that can be identified as parts of the chariot. It concerns ideogram ***35*** (CAPSUS) 'chariot-body' (the main part of the chariot), ideogram ***87*** 'chariot-frame', probably covered with linen or leather to protect the charioteer (chariot-warrior) and chariot-driver, and ideogram ***29*** = ROTA 'wheel'.

The identification of the ideograms can be established particularly by the combination of these ideograms in different formations at both Hagia Triada and Khania.

On the tablets HT 8b.5 and HT 26b.4 chariot-frame and chariot-body are written separate from each other, above each other and in *iuxta*-position respectively. On the roundels KH Wc 2056 and Wc 2057 from Khania sign ***87***, the chariot-frame, is written separate from a structure that may be either sign ***35***, the chariot-body, or the pole or even the yoke. Chariot-body and chariot-frame certainly form a unity on KH Wc 2058, KH Wc 2059, KH Wc 2062 and KH Wc 2117b.

The combination of the ideogram of VIR (KH Wc 2117a), indicating an 'armed man', and that of the 'chariot-body' + 'chariot-frame' on the *b*-side is quite suggestive. In this respect J.G. Younger's comparison of KH Wc 2117a: VIR, with KH Wc 2106 is significant, since the latter roundel shows the ideogram of a man armed with a shield. Cf. also my more extensive comment on KH Wc 2056 (*Minoan Linear A*, Volume II: *Corpus of transliterated Linear A texts*).

HT 8 (HM 11, 1902-1903) from the Villa of Hagia Triada. Probably Late Minoan I b.

HT 8a.1. *je-di* OLE+*ki* 10 *pa*$_3$-|
2. *ka-ra-ti* 1J *pa* 3J
3. *te-jo* 2 *qa-63-i*
4. JE *si-ki-ra* E
5. *ki-re-ta-na* J
b. 1. *su-pu*$_2$ *87* (= ideogram of 'chariot-frame') 1
2. vacat
3. 5 *pa*$_3$ *87* 2 *qa-63-*
4. *i* 1 EF *ka-pa* J
5. *pa-ja-re* 1 F *35* (CAPSUS) + *87* (chariot-frame) ↑ J
6. J

HT 140 + 143 + 145 + 148 + 153 + 154 H + Fr. (joins by E.L. Bennett and M. Pope).

1. *u-mina-si* , CAPSUS (or: CURRUS) *si-ni* 1 *je-di* ,
2. OLE+*ki* 1 J , *u-mina-si* CAPSUS *si* TAL+*ka* 3
3. *ka-*[*pa*]*-qe* *u*-[ ] 6
4. OLE+B 3 *ka* or (preferably) ROTA 1 OLE+B 1
5.]*ka* or]ROTA 1 OLE+B 2 *ka-pa* J
6.] OLE+B 6[ ]J
7-8.]vacant

Ad 4: *GORILA*: *ka* pourrait être idéogramme.

Since sign ***29*** (= ***ka*** in syllabic sequences) occurs certainly in solitary position in HT 140.4, one must consider the possibility of the ideogram ROTA 'wheel', especially if it is in the vicinity of e.g. sign ***35*** (= CAPSUS) on the same tablet. Since]***29*** (line 5) is only poorly legible on the edge of a fracture, one cannot be sure whether it is the final syllabic sign of a sequence or again ROTA in solitary position. Compare for the combination of ideogram ***35*** = CAPSUS 'chariot-body' with the frequent occurrence of the ideogram ROTA especially tablet HT 11b, where the evidence is overwhelming.

The *b*-side of tablet HT 8 is interesting because of the ideograms ***35*** (CAPSUS) + ***87***. The scribe writing the third sign of line b.1 seems still to have had sign ***ka*** in mind after having written ***ka*** in ***pa3-ka-ra-ti*** in lines a.1-2, but he realized that he had to write sign ***87***, before he almost closed the 'square' circle. This may explain the strange form of this particular sign ***87*** (HT 8b.1). The sign occurs again in line b.3, after ***pa3*** and is followed by the number 2. In line b.5 it is written above ideogram ***35*** (CAPSUS), but separate from that sign. In HT 26b.4 the combination of sign ***87*** followed by sign ***35*** is attested again at Hagia Triada. If fraction sign J indicates 'a half' (which is proved observing HT 104), the scribe shows that he considers the two parts, sign ***87*** on top of ***35***, followed by two fraction signs JJ, the two halves of a unity ***35+87***, which are temporarily separated from each other.

Linear A ***je-di*** occurs on four tablets from Hagia Triada, three times as first entry (HT 8a.1; HT 36.1; HT 122b.1) and the fourth time also in the heading (HT 140.1), which suggests that it might be a (local) toponym indicating a place near Hagia Triada.
HT 8a.1: ***je-di*** is followed by OLE(um)+***ki*** 10.
HT 36.1-2: ***je-di*** is followed by ***pi-pi*** GRA+*qe* [[20]] 44 J; HT 36.2-3: ***du-do-wa*** 7 J.
HT 122b.1: ***je-di*** **,** is followed by CAPSUS, VIR[, which offers a connection with tablet HT 8b.5-6, where ideograms ***35*** **+** ***87*** (CAPSUS + chariot-frame) are mentioned and HT 8b.1 and HT 8b.3, where ***87*** occurs. A relation of ***je-di*** with chariots and charioteers seems therefore likely. Also ***je-di*** followed by GRA+***qe*** and the high number 44 J may well point to a (local) toponym. If ***je-di*** is not a toponym, it probably refers to an important man. Toponyms sometimes show the same kind of formations as personal names, especially so-called 'one-word' names. Interpretation of Linear A ***je-di*** seems enigmatic.

If ***je-di*** is analysed as *{y(a)/y(e)=edi}*, consisting of the *quasi-proclitic relative pronoun* or *comparative* or *connective particle* ***ya-/ye***, c.q. *ija-, ije-* (cf. Th. Richter, *BGH*, 73, s.v. ***ia*** I ***ija*** I, *ie/ije* [*passim*] 'relative pronoun') + the Hurrian lexeme ***edi/idi*** 'body, person' (cf. Th. Richter, *BGH*, 112, s.v. ***edi/idi*** I 'Körper, Person') and is translated 'as a body / as a person', the exact meaning remains enigmatic. The other sequences on the *a*-side of HT 8 are all personal names. Th. Richter (*VHN*, 405, n. 288) mentions only one personal name, in which ***edi/idi*** 'body, person' may be the second onomastic element: ***A-ga-bi-di*** *{ag=a=b-idi}* 'Der Körper kam herauf' ['The body came up, appeared'] (*JCS 13*, 53; AlT, 298 I 10 [Alalaḫ IV].

However, Th. Richter (*VHN*, 405) also mentions Hurrian personal names with the verbal root ***ed-*** I, of which the meaning is not yet known: ***Eteja*** (Mari), ***fEtim-me*** (Mari), ***fEten-elli*** (Ašnakkum, Mari), ***Etip-ḫuḫ*** (Mari), ***Etip-kirišu*** (Mari). Th. Richter cautiously distinguishes ***ed-*** I from ***id-*** [Boğ.] '(zer)schlagen' ['to hit, strike (violently)'], although he seems to waver because of the (*quasi*) doublets ***fEtim-me*** and ***fItim-menni*** at Mari. It seems unlikely that ***je-di*** *{y(a)/y(e)=edi}* contains an *imperative* 'one-word' name ***Edi***.

Since ***-r-*** preceding an occlusive is not expressed in Linear A and B consonant clusters, it is also possible to analyse Linear A ***je-di*** as *{y(a)/y(e)=erdi}*, which may be translated 'As a tongue', which could be the description of a locality that looks like a tongue. There are also some Hurrian personal names referring to the (peculiar ?) lips of the child. According to Th. Richter (*BGH*, 101) ***e/irde*** [Boğ.] means 'Zunge' ['tongue'] and according to V. Haas (2003a, 151) ***irde paḫrubade*** means 'böse Zunge' ['evil tongue'].

I. Wegner mentions: *edi=v ana=o+l=e=š irde=v urḫ(i)=a tiv(e)=a kad=i+l=e=š* 'dein Körper möge sich freuen (*ana=o+l=e=š*), deine Zunge möge in wahren Worten sprechen (*kad=i+l=e=š*)' ['your body may rejoice, your tongue may speak in true words'], *ChS* I/1 Nr. 9 Rs. III 34-35, cf. I. Wegner, *ZA 85*, 1995, 117; *Einführung*, 113).

Since features of a landscape or locality are sometimes marked by resemblance (of physical parts) of the body, it is not inconceivable that an expression like 'As a tongue' or 'As a body' has become the name of a place. We can only guess which.

Linear A ***pa₃-|ka-ra-ti*** (HT 8a.1-2) can be analysed as a Hurrian personal name *{pag/kk=ar=ašt=i}*, containing two consecutive root-extensions. It consists of the verbal root ***pag-/pakk-*** + *factitive* or *iterative* root-extension ***-ar-*** + root-extension ***-ašt-*** (***-Všt***) indicating ending or completion of an action (as in 'Old Hurrian' ***pa=ašt=o=m*** 'he has built') + the marker of the transitive *imperative* (*jussive*) 2nd person singular in ***-i/e***. See for the *jussive* forms I. Wegner, *Einführung*, 103: Table 9: *The order of suffixes for the positive jussive*. See I. Wegner, *Einführung*, 88-89, s.v. root-extensions ***-ar-*** and ***-Všt-***, cf. G. Wilhelm, *Festschrift Heger*, 1992, 670. See I. Wegner (*Einführung*, 34, 96-97, 126-128) for the Old Hurrian formants 3rd person singular perfect in ***=o=m***. [note: I. Wegner has analysed 'Old Hurrian' ***ba-'à-áš-tum*** in the *Tiš-atal*-inscription as ***pa=ašt=o=m***, translation 'he has built', which may well reflect the Hurrian etymology of Linear A ***pa-i-to*** (HT 97a.3; HT 120.6) 'He (a God) has built (the palace)'.]

At Nuzi the personal names ***Pakka*** (wr. *Pa-aq-qa, Pa-ag-ga, Ba-aq-qa*), ***Pakai̯a*** (wr. *Pa-ka-ia*), ***Pakkai̯a*** (wr. *Pa-aq-qa-a-a, Ba-ak-ka-a-a*), ***Pakkii̯a*** (wr. *Pa-ak-ki-ia*) occur, cf. I.J. Gelb, *NPN*, 110; P.M. Purves, *NPN*, 242. At Alalaḫ VII hypocoristic ***ᶠPaga-ya*** (wr. *ᶠPa-ga-ya*), AT *65: 2, and at Alalaḫ IV ***Pakki-ya*** (wr. *Pa-ak-ki-ya*), s. Amma, AT 121: 2, 9, are attested, cf. A. Draffkorn, *HHA*, 46, 96. Th. Richter (*VHN*, 476-477) mentions ***Pakki*** (wr. *Pa-ak-ki*) at Alalaḫ VII and IV (AT *412; AT 295) and (wr. *Pa-ag-gi*) at Alalaḫ IV (AT 143: 18); ***Pakija*** at Qaṭṭarā; ***Pakkukki*** at Mari; ***Pakkari*** at Mari; ***Pakazzi*** at Mari; ***Pakašti*** at Tigunāni; ***Pakiri*** at Mari; ***Pakuzzi*** at Mari. According to Th. Richter it is justifiable to take the roots with single and double occlusives together on the basis of ***Pakkari*** at Mari (3x *Pa-ka-ri*) and (1x *Pa-ak-ka-ri*). He also mentions that De Martino, Murat and Süel (2013, 143) suspect that a root occurring as *pa-g°* at Ortaköy/Šapinuwa is identical with *{fag-}* 'vertreiben' ['to expel, oust'], which makes a fricative bilabial likely, cf. Th. Richter, *BGH*, 290, s.v. Hurrian ***wag=an-*** [Qaṭna] 'vertreiben' that equals Akkadian ***abāku***. If this meaning can be ascribed to the Hurrian root ***pag-/pakk-*** and ***wag-*** (?), one may in my view think of a difficult delivery of the baby in question, so that the name of the child reminds of the encouragement to the mother or a *numen* to oust the baby from the womb. As a result Linear A ***pa₃-|ka-ra-ti*** (HT 8a.1-2), *{pag/kk=ar=ašt=i}*, may be translated as 'Oust (the baby from the womb, oh woman or oh *numen*) !'.

It is not certain that ***pa₃***| at the end of HT 8a.1 and ***ka-ra-ti*** at the beginning of HT 8a.2 form one sequence ***pa₃|-ka-ra-ti*** (HT 8a.1-2), since the end of a line can sometimes have the same function as a word divider and ***pa₃*** may well be a logogram or an abbreviation as in HT 8b.3, where it precedes the ideogram ***87*** as a monosyllabic logogram (cf. L.C. Meijer's interesting comment, 86-87). Moreover there is some space to the right of ***pa₃***| (HT 8a.1). Linear A ***pa₃*** (HT 8b.3; HT 9b.1; HT 34.6; HT 132.2) is certainly monosyllabic.

Linear A ***pa₃*** may well be distinguished from ***pa*** 3J (HT 8a.2) that may be an abbreviation of ***parizi*** or ***parizzade / parissade*** [Boğ.] 'bushel' = half a kor = ca. 36,5 liter, discussed before.

Since ***pa₃*** is actually the first entry on HT 9b.1, I consider it likely that it represents the toponym ***pa-i-to*** on that tablet. F.M.J. Waanders's view that the phonetic value of Linear B ***pa₃*** may have been derived from Linear A ***[bha]*** (with aspirate voiced labial stop), is very attractive. The complete Linear A sequence ***pa-i-to*** (HT 97a.3; HT 120.6) is attested twice at Hagia Triada. Linear A ***pa-i-to*** may well be the Hurrian name of the Palace of Phaistos ***ba-'à-áš-tum*** 'He/She (a deity) has built (the palace)'. Hagia Triada is only a few miles separated from the Palace of Phaistos. In Mycenaean Greek Linear B ***pa-i-to Φαιστός*** (Phaistos) got the Greek ending in ***-ος***. It may be accidental that the Linear A orthography ****pa₃-i-to*** is not (yet) attested. The attested Linear A spelling ***pa-i-to*** makes it plausible that the ligature VIR+***pa*** refers to 'man from *P(h)aist=o=m*'. The reading of]<u>***pa₃***</u>[(AK 1b.2) from Arkhanes is not certain. *GORILA 3*:]<u>***pa₃***</u>[préférable à]<u>***nu***</u>[. The sign may be part of a sequence. Some scribes had a preference for special signs. The scribe of tablet HT 31 used 3 times special sign ***pa₃*** on one tablet: in ***qa-pa₃***, ***ka-ro-pa₃*** and ***su-pa₃-ra***.

If ***pa₃***| (HT 8a.1) and ***ka-ra-ti*** (HT 8a.2) are separate entries, it has to be examined whether ***ka-ra-ti*** offers a conceivable Hurrian personal name.

Th. Richter (*VHN*, 431, s.v. ***kar-***) mentions that a verbal root ***kar-*** (without root-extension) can be isolated from ***kari(j)e*** 'Vogelfänger' ['bird-catcher, fowler'] (see *BGH*, 190), that may be associated with Urartian ***kar=u-*** 'besiegen' ['to conquer'] (cf. G.A. Melikišvili, *Die urartäische Sprache*, Studia Pohl, Rome 1971, 83; V. Haas, *Rezension zu* Laroche 1980, *Bibliotheca Orientalis 39*, Leiden 1982, 604; I.M. Diakonoff, On some new trends in Urartian philology and some new Urartian texts, *Archäologische Mitteilungen aus Iran. Neue Folge 22*, Berlin 1989, 82[27]; M. Salvini, Die Felsinschrift Argištis I bei Ortakent, Kreis Hanak (Osttürkei), *Orientalia Nova Series 75*, Rome 2006, 75). I may also refer to M. Salvini - I. Wegner, *Einführung in die urartäische Sprache*, Wiesbaden 2014, 110, s.v. ***kar-*** 'besiegen, bezwingen' ['to conquer, to subdue, to control']. Th. Richter thinks that this root offers a good meaning for the Hurrian personal name ***e-ew-ri-ga-ri-im*** {*evri-kar=i=m(: b)*} at Kaniš (cf. Garelli 1963, 156) 'Der Herr besiegte (Feind)' ['The Lord conquered (the enemy)']. Therefore ***kari(j)e*** may originally mean '(Vogel-)Besieger' ['conqueror (of birds)']. Intransitive usage of the root ***kar-*** provides the meaning 'siegen' ['to prevail'].

Linear A ***ka-ra-ti*** (HT 8a.2) can then be analysed as {*kar=a=tti*}, consisting of the verbal root ***kar-*** + the marker of intransitivity ***-a-*** + the *optional allomorphic* enclitic personal pronoun 1st person singular ***-tti*** instead of ***-tta***, subject of the intransitive verb, translation 'I prevail'.

In the past I assumed that Linear A ***te-jo*** (HT 8a.3; HT 98.3) from Hagia Triada might be an expressive personal name reflecting the absolute comparative adjective ****teon*** or superlative ****teol***, related to the Hurrian adjective ***tea*** (wr. *te-a*), Mit. III 42, 69, 94, IV 118, 'great', 'much' or the adverb ***te-on-ae*** (wr. *te-u-un-na-e*), Mit. II 49, 55, 62, 'a great deal' or ***te-ol-ae*** (wr. *te-u-u-la-e*), Mit. IV 130, 'exceedingly much', Speiser, *IH*, 130-132, § 174-175. The final consonants ***-n*** and ***-l*** are not expressed in Linear A orthography.

Since the adverbs in ***-ae*** are probably derived from the singular instrumental forms in ***-ae***, one may deduce ****te-on*** and ****te-ol*** for the absolutive comparative and superlative adjectives, respectively, corresponding with ***te-on-ae*** and ***te-ol-ae***. E. Laroche's reaction (*GLH*, 260, s.v. *tea* 'nombreux'): "Speiser, *IH*, 130 sq., rapproche avec raison l'adjective *tea* de l'adverbe *teunae* 'beaucoup'; il en tire *tea* 'grand'. Mais 'beaucoup' dérive plutôt de 'nombreux'; un *tea* 'multus' conviendrait à *niḫari* 'dot' et à *ḫiayaruḫḫe* 'or'; ainsi *tea, teunae* correspondraient bien à l'akk. *mâdu, mâdiš* d'El Amarna; v. *teunae*."

I. Wegner (*Einführung*, 192, 195) analyses passage Mit. III 73-74 in the Tušratta letter:
ḫi-i̯a-ru-uḫ-ḫa-a-at-ta-a-an te-u-u-na-<e> še-e-ni-íw-wu-uš ge-pa-a-nu-en ... =
ḫiar(i)=o=ḫḫ(e>)=a=tta=ân teona<e> šen(a)=iff=u=š keban=u=en ... =
Viel Gold möge mir mein Bruder schicken = My brother may send me much gold.

Th. Richter, *BGH*, 455-456: ***te-*** II [Mitt] 'ausgedehnt in Größe und Anzahl', ***tea / teja, tei*** [Boğ; Mari; Mitt] 'grande', 'nombreux', corresponding with Akkadian *mādu*; 'much', 'many', *teun(n)a* [Boğ; Mitt] *te=o=nni* 'much'; *teunae* [Mitt] *te=o=nn(i)ae* 'much'.

However, since Th. Richter has shown that the verbal root ***te(j)-/ti(j)- / te(w)-/ti(w)-*** 'to speak, to say names', is quite frequent in personal names, I consider it most likely that Linear A ***te-jo*** (HT 8a.3; HT 98.3) can be analysed as Old Hurrian ***te(j)=o/u=n(na)***, consisting of the verbal root ***te(j)-*** with semivowel ***-j-*** (glide between vowels) + Old Hurrian *imperative* suffix ***-o/u-*** + the absolutive enclitic personal pronoun 3rd pers. sing. ***-n/-nna*** marking the object of the transitive verb, 'Say it (*scil.* the name of the father/mother) (oh child) !' or 'Say it (*scil.* words/names) (oh *numen*) !'.

Linear A ***su-pu$_2$*** (HT 8b.1; HT 63.1) must be regarded in relation with ***ka-ti*** (HT 63.1).
HT 63.1. IUGUM , *te* 1 *ka-ti* 1 *su-pu$_2$* |
2.]-*do* 2 |
3.] vestigia |

If Linear A ***ka-ti*** is a personal name, it may be identified as a Hurrian hypocoristic name ****Ḫaš-ti***, equivalent to ***Ḫaš-te*** (wr. *Ḫa-aš-te-e*), ***Ḫaš-tei̯a*** (wr. *Ḫa-aš-te-ia*) 'Hear (the prayer), oh Tešub !', and comparable with ***Ḫašitte*** (wr. *Ḫa-ši-it-te* < **Ḫašib-te*, *{ḫaš=i=b-te}*) beside ***Ḫašip-tešup*** (wr. *Ḫa-ši-ip-te-šup*) 'Tešub hears, heard (the prayer)', at Nuzi, cf. P.M. Purves, *NPN*, 214-215, s.v. ***ḫaš-***, 'to hear'; *ibid.* 264, s.v. ***-te***, and 266, s.v. ***-ti***. Identification of ****Ḫaš-ti*** with Hurrian ***Ḫaš-te*** is based on comparison of ***-ti*** by P.M. Purves (*NPN*, 266) with ***-te*** (*NPN*, 264) that he considers a hypocoristic form of the theophorous elements ***-tešub*** and ***-tei̯a***. Equation of ***-ti*** with ***-te*** is justifiable, because e.g. ***Ḫui-te*** is written *Ḫu-i-te, Ḫu-i-te-e, Ḫu-e-te* and *Ḫu-i-ti* at Nuzi (*NPN*, 264).

If correct, ***ka-ti*** may be compared with Linear A ***ka+qe*** (HT 37.6), interpreted as Hurrian ****Ḫaš-ḫe***, hypocoristic of ****Ḫaš-ḫepa*** 'Hear (the prayer), oh Ḫebat !'.

However, since ***-tte*** can also be the *optional allomorphic* enclitic personal pronoun 1st person singular ***-tte/i*** instead of ***-tta***, object of the transitive verb, ***Ḫašitte***, *{ḫaš=i=tte}*, consisting of the root ***ḫaš-*** 'to hear' + the marker of transitivity ***-i-*** + ***-tte***, can also mean 'Hear me (oh *numen*) !'. Consequently, if Linear A ***ka-ti*** (HT 63.1) is interpreted as ****Ḫaš-ti***, analysis *{ḫaš=tti}*, it can also be translated 'Ḫear me / Listen to me (oh *numen*) !'.

But Th. Richter (*BGH*, 139) also offers ***ḫašti*** [Boğ.] 'stark' ['strong'], cf. V. Haas/H.J. Thiel, 1978, 249.

Likewise I explain Linear A ***ka-nu-ti*** (HT 97[+]109a.3) as Hurrian ***Ḫanutti***, analysis {*ḫan=o/u=tti*}, consisting of the verbal root ***ḫan-*** 'to give birth to / to create' + the Old Hurrian marker of the transitive perfect ***-u-*** + the *optional allomorphic* enclitic personal pronoun 1st person singular ***-tti*** (instead of normal ***-tta***) (position 9), cf. I. Wegner, *Einführung*, 93 (Table 4), and 126 (Althurritisch), translation 'He/She (a *numen* or the mother) gave birth to me / created me'. Compare for ***-tti*** instead of ***-tta*** Th. Richter, *VHN*, 596, sub 1.3.1.1.2.2. Th. Richter often prefers the Old Hurrian transitive *imperative* to the Old Hurrian transitive *perfect indicative*, cf. *VHN*, 593, sub 1.3.1.1: names with transitive *imperatives* in ***-o***. So he translates (*VHN*, 329; 596) the personal names ***Ullutti*** (wr. *ul-lu-ut-ti*) from Mari and Tigunāni, analysed as {*o/ull=o/u=tti*}, and ***Ullutta*** (wr. *ul-lu-ut-ta*) from Šušarrā (Tall Shemshara), analysis {*o/ull=u=tta*}, as 'Zerstöre mich (oh *Numen*) !' ['Destroy me (oh *numen*) !']. Following Th. Richter I may translate Linear A ***ka-nu-ti*** {*ḫan=o/u=tti*} as 'Give birth to me / Create me (oh *numen*) !'.

Since a sibilant preceding a dental and other occlusives is not expressed in Linear A and B consonant clusters, ***ka-nu-ti*** can *prima facie* also be interpreted as Hurrian ***Ḫanušti***, analysis †{*ḫan=o/uš=tti*}, consisting of the verbal root ***ḫan-*** 'to give birth to / to create' + the suffix ***-oš-*** indicating past or perfect tense (position 2) in 'Mitanni' Hurrian + the enclitic personal pronoun 1st person singular ***-tta*** or allomorphic variant ***-tti*** (position 9), cf. I. Wegner, *Einführung*, 93, Table 4), translation 'He/She (a *numen*) gave birth to me / created me'. An objection to this interpretation is that one would expect the form {*ḫan=o/uš=a=tti*}, with ***-a-*** marking the subject of action 3rd pers. sing. (position 7).

Since Linear A ***ka-ti*** (HT 63.1) appears in the heading of the tablet, it is also possible that it is not a personal name, but a noun and equivalent to Hurrian ***kašti*** 'bow', cf. E. Laroche, *GLH*, 139, s.v. ***kašti*** 'arc': 1. Lecture de gišBAN-*ti*; joint à GI-*ri* 'flèche' et *išpanti* 'carquois'; emprunt à l'akk. *qaštu*; cf. Msk. Série An, No 181. Nom. gišBAN-*ti* (du dieu Nubadig), KUB XXVII 1 II 8; 6 I 11. Com. gišBAN-*ra* et *g/ka-aš-ti-ra* KUB VII 58 IV 11 = dupl. KBo XV 1 IV 23, 34, 37. V. sous *ḫašiyati*. 2. Ug. pl. ***kštġlm***, PRU II 137, 2; V 118, 23. – Lire ****kaštuḫli(m)***, c'est-à-dire 'archers' ou 'fabricants d'arcs'; cf. Dietrich-Loretz, *WO III* 199.

Cf. Th. Richter, *BGH*, 194, s.v. ***kašti*** [Lw/Hu]: Übereinstimmend als 'Bogen' und Lw aus akk. *qaštu* aufgefasst, s. erstmal Haas / Wilhelm 1972: 5, sowie Laroche 1980a: 139, Taracha 2004: 458a, Trémouille 2005: XIX, Campbell 2007a: 258, etc.

If the first entry of HT 63.1, ideogram ***66*** (followed by word divider **,** + transactional term ***te*** + 1 unit) is correctly interpreted as IUGUM 'yoke', ***ka-ti*** 1 (HT 63.1), Hurrian ***kašti*** 'bow', might (also because of its similarity with the form of a 'yoke') be a word belonging to the category 'objects'. Since the ideogram IUGUM 'yoke' and ***ka-ti*** are both followed by 1 unit, it can be excluded that ***ka-ti*** can be interpreted as a description of the ideogram IUGUM. So Linear A ***ka-ti*** (HT 63.1) is either ***kašti*** 'bow' or a personal name.

If the following entry ***su-pu₂***| (HT 63.1) might mean 'chariot-body', that might well be an argument for the specific meaning 'bow' for ***ka-ti*** (HT 63.1). Linear A ***su-pu₂*** also occurs on another tablet from Hagia Triada, where it is followed by ideogram ***87*** 'chariot-frame' (HT 8b.1), which may confirm this meaning. ***Su-pu₂*** could then be a *scriptio plena* equivalent to ideogram ***35*** CAPSUS 'chariot-body', often combined with sign ***87***.

W.C. Brice and L.C. Meijer read Linear A ***su-pu$_2$-ka*** (HT 8b.1), whereas *GORILA 1*, J. Raison – M. Pope (1994, 49) and I read ***su-pu$_2$ 87*** 'chariot-frame'. The last sign of the sequence looks indeed like a mixture of sign ***ka*** and ideogram ***87***, because the 'circle' of sign ***ka*** is not round, but square on the left side and incomplete. According to F.M.J. Waanders the phonetic value ***φυ*** / ***βυ*** of Linear B ***pu$_2$*** may be explained from the Linear A phonetic value [***bhu***] for Linear A ***pu$_2$***. Only if ***su-pu$_2$-ka*** (HT 8b.1) is the correct reading (which I do not believe), the Hurrian personal name ***Šupuga*** (wr. *šu-u-pu-ga-*.[...]) from Boğazköy KUB VII 58 iii 16, can be identified, or ***Šupuk(k)a*** (wr. *Šu-pu-uq-qa*, *Šu-pu-qa*) from Nuzi, cf. I.J. Gelb, *NPN*, 139, s.v. ***Šupukka***, cf. also ***Šupukii̯a*** (wr. *Šu-pu-ki-ia*); cf. Purves, *NPN*, 259, s.v. *šup, šupuka, šupukii̯a, šupukka.* P.M. Purves also mentions that *Šu-pu-ki-ia* might be a variant of ***Šupuka***, since a man of each name is father of ***Ar-tei̯a***.

However, the combination of the ideograms ***35*** + ***87*** (HT 8b.5) is actually written at the end of HT 8b, which confirms the reading ***su-pu$_2$ 87*** (HT 8b.1) by *GORILA 1* and Raison-Pope, instead of the reading ***su-pu$_2$-ka*** by Brice and Meijer, and corroborates the interpretation of ***su-pu$_2$*** as possible *scriptio plena* of ideogram ***35*** (CAPSUS).

It is intriguing that E. Laroche (*GLH*, 308) mentions the noun ***zuppi*** at Boğazköy and translates it with 'an arm, weapon ?': *zu-up-pí*, KUB XXVII 6 I 9 (une arme ?). It is unfortunately not clear whether this arm/weapon might be a chariot-body or not. He also mentions the form with the so-called definite article: *zu-up-pí-ni*, IBoT II39 Ro 44, and the genitive of this form: *zu-up-pí-ni-bi-ni-in*, IBoT II39 Ro 40, cf. also Th. Richter, *BGH*, 417, s.v. ***zuppi*** II [Boğ.] 'une arme ?' (Laroche, *GLH*, 1980, 308); without translation (Wegner, 2004, 78; Campbell, 2007a, 123). Th. Richter, *BGH*, 417, s.v. ***zubinni*** [Ug.] 'a tool', corresponding with Sumerian BA and Akkadian ***supinnu*** (W.H. van Soldt, 1990, 731), see also *zu-bi-*[*i*]*n$^?$-né* (W.H. van Soldt, 1991, 357[224]). It would be interesting to see whether the forms with the voiceless labial occlusive from Boğazköy (s.v. ***zuppi*** II) may correspond with the forms with the voiced labial occlusive from Ugarit (s.v. ***zubinni***).

Th. Richter (*BGH*, 415) mentions, s.v. ***sub-*** I [Boğ.; Mitt.?], and as *sub-ušt-* [Boğ.; Mari] without translation. He also mentions (*BGH*, 421), s.v. ***surw-*** and *surw-ušt-* [Mitt.], the translation 'Schlechtes tun' and 'Böses tun'; and, s.v. ***subi-*** VI [Boğ.; Ug.], 'séparé' ['separated'], corresponding with Ugaritic *ḫarimu* (E. Laroche, *GLH*, 238); corresponding with Sumerian [ḪUL$^?$] and [GUL$^?$], Akkadian *šulputu* 'desecrate(d)', Ugaritic *ġarimu* (Huehnergard 1987a, 89f., 126, Fleming 2000, 181); 'méchant, mauvais' ['naughty, bad'] corresponding with Sumerian ḪUL and Akkadian *lemnu* (André-Salvini/Salvini 1998, 17; 2000, 329); 'evil' (Campbell 2008, 287); s.v. ***surwe-*** I [Mitt.; PN] 'böse, schlecht' ['evil, bad'], 'der Böse' ['the evil one'].

I think that Linear A ***su-pu$_2$*** (HT 8b.1) and ***su-pu$_2$***| (HT 63.1) have to be distinguished from ***su-pu*** (HT 31.2) that is written on top of VASb^1. Content and context of the tablets HT 8 and HT 63 seem to differ completely from HT 31. In the discussion on tablet HT 31 in the 2016 edition I have compared Linear A ***su-pu*** with the Hurrian forms mentioned s.v. ***šubuš-*** by E. Laroche (*GLH*, 239) at Boğazköy. However, Th. Richter (*BGH*, 421) mentions s.v. ***šurbi*** II [Boğ.]: without translation (Laroche, *GLH*, 245 [*šu-ú-úr-pé-e-ni-eš*]; 'eine kathartische Substanz' ['a cathartic substance'] (V. Haas, 2003a, 101[+465]).

Since the liquid ***-r-*** preceding an occlusive is not expressed in Linear A an B consonant clusters, I now consider it likely that Linear A ***su-pu*** on top of VASb[1] (HT 31.2) can be identified with ***šurbi*** II [Boğ.], if the meaning of 'a cathartic substance' is correct. Linear A ***su-pu*** is then Hurrian ***šurbu*** {*šurb(i)=u*}, with Akkadianizing nominative in ***-u***, and may refer to the content of the vase, emphasizing that it is precious. This means that Linear A ***su-pu*** on top of VASb[1] (HT 31.2) can probably not be identified with ***su-pu₂*** (HT 8b.1; HT 63.1).

The Linear A sequence ***pa-ja-re*** (HT 8b.5; HT 29.2; HT 88.5; ZA 10b.5) on three tablets from Hagia Triada and on one from Kato Zakro occurs every time in lists of personal names. It is the last name on HT 8b: ***pa-ja-re*** 1F, followed by *35+87* = CAPSUS + chariot-frame JJ. Th. Richter (*BGH*, 285) mentions s.v. ***pa-***, ***paḫ-*** II [*passim*] '(er)bauen' ['to build'], in personal names 'schaffen' ['to create']. The root corresponds with Hittite ***weda-/wete-*** (M. Salvini, 1987/88, 181; E. Neu, 1988a, 7, 1996a, 184). Linear A ***pa-ja-re*** can be analysed as an *imperative* 'one-word' name {*pa=(j)=ar=e/i*} 'Build (the child) (oh *numen*) !', with *factitive/iterative* root-extension ***-ar-*** and transitional glide ***-j-***.

Perhaps Linear A ***pa-ja-re*** may also be compared with the Hurrian personal name ***Pairi*** (wr. *pa-i-ri*), analysis {*pa=i=ri*}, 2 x at Mari, lexicon *pairi*, typology 3.1, 'Someone who has built / created (the boy)', cf. Th. Richter, *VHN*, 219, s.v. ***Pairi***; 475-476, s.v. ***pa-***.

I. Wegner (*Einführung*, 216-221, 270) interprets ***pa=i=ri*** as a resultative participle 'einer der gebaut hat; Baumeister' ['someone who has built; architect'], belonging to the verbal root ***pa-*** 'to build'. She compares ***pa=i=ri*** morphologically with ***ta-bi-ri-i-ma*** in the Hurrian-Hittite bilingual ***Kirenze***, KBo 32: 14 Vs. I 46 (cf. E. Neu, *StBoT 32*, 80), in the 3rd parable: *The goblet (chalice, cup) and its smith* (KBo 32: 14 Vs. I 42-59) and analyses the form ***tab=i=ri*** as verbal root ***tab/v-*** 'to cast (metal)' + ***i*** (marking transitivity) + ***ri/e*** (participial suffix) 'the one who has cast (metal); smith'. The forms in ***=i=ri/e*** are 'agent oriented resultative participles'. I. Wegner (*Einführung*, 21) points out that before the Akkade-period (2230-2090 B.C., short chronology), ***ta/ibira*** 'copper-worker', for which a plausible Hurrian derivation can be given, occurs in Old Sumerian texts.

The ergative form ***ta-bal-li-iš*** (same parable, lines 42 and 55) is used synonymously to ***tab=i=ri*** (line 46). I. Wegner analyses it as verbal root ***tab/v-*** 'to cast (metal)' + ***li*** (formative indicating professional designations) following the root athemetically (***tab+li***) + the so-called singular article ***ne*** (***tab+li+ne***). If the article is used, *anaptyxis* occurs to make pronunciation easier (development of vowel between two consonants), as well as *apocope* (disappearance of the final vowel) > ***tabal(i)=ne***, so that the ***n*** of the article assimilates to the ***l*** of the stem > ***tabal=le*** '(Metall)gießer = Schmied' ['someone who casts (metal) = smith'] + ergative suffix ***-š***. In the Hittite text it corresponds with the Sumerogram ^{LÚ}SIMUG 'copper-smith'. Morphologically it can be compared with ***kebella*** 'the hunters', analysis ***kebel=la*** < ****keb+li+na***.

Since Linear A sign ***re*** can also be ***le***, comparison with Hurrian ***paili/e*** is also feasible, since according to Th. Richter (*VHN*, 219, 475-476) the frequent name ***Paila*** (wr. *pa-i-la*), 11 times attested at Mari, and (wr. *ba-i-la*) once at Sippar, is derived from ***paili***, analysis {*pail(i)=a*[E.]}, lexicon *paili*, typology 3.2.1, translation 'Er (Junge) ist gemäß des Gebauten (geboren)' ['He (the boy) is (born) like the one that was built / created'].

[E.] refers to the *essive* in ***-a***. Compare also *ba-il-te-sup* at Nippur; ***paili*** can probably be connected with the word ***pailija*** that can be interpreted as 'gebaut, erbaut' ['built'] and sometimes as 'das, welches ich gebaut habe' ['what I have built'] or 'das von mir Gebaute' ['built by me']. The same applies to the personal name ***Pailu*** (wr. *pa-i-lu*) at Mari, lexicon *paili* (→ *pa*), typology 3.1, analysis {*pail(i)=u*[N.]}, translation 'Das Gebaute (≈ Junge) (?)' ['the one that has been built/created (≈ the boy)' (?)]. [N.] refers to the Akkadianizing *nominative* in ***-u***.

Incidentally, in *nomina actoris* with the very productive combination of suffixes ***=o/u=ḫ(e)=li***, graphically ***-uḫli*** or ***-uḫuli*** (the latter is the usual form at Alalaḫ and in the Western Hurrian area), ***-li*** is the true formative indicating professional designations. These designations in ***-uḫli / -uḫuli*** are based on nouns turned into adjectives by use of the suffix ***-ḫe*** (with syncope of final ***-e***), followed by the suffix ***-li***, at Alalaḫ after the derivational vowel ***-o/u-***; elsewhere without this vowel, cf. I. Wegner, *Einführung*, 57-58.

If we read Linear A ***pa-ja-re*** as ***pa-ja-le***, the second ***-a-*** may be due to *anaptyxis* (development of vowel between two consonants, in this case between semivowel ***j*** and ***l***) to make pronunciation easier. As a result a formation like ***paj+li+ne*** > (*anaptyxis*) ***paj=a=li=ne*** > (*apocope*) ***paj=a=l(i)=ne*** > (*assimilation*) ***paj=a=l=le*** is conceivable. Morphologically such a form would be comparable with ***ta-bal-li-iš***, but without the *ergative* ending in ***-š***, because usage of the *absolutive* in lists of personal names is likely.

Etymologically Linear A ***pa-ja-re*** is cognate with the personal name ***pa-ja*** (HT 41a.4) from Hagia Triada and its Hurrian equivalent ***Paia*** (wr. *Pa-a-a, Ba-a-a*), name of 26 persons at Nuzi, cf. I.J. Gelb, *NPN*, 109; P.M. Purves, *NPN*, 242, s.v. ***pai*** and ***paḭa***. For Linear A ***pa-ja*** and ***Paḭa*** at Nuzi two interpretations are possible:
I) It can be a hypocoristic name consisting of the verbal root ***pa-*** 'to build' (in onomastics probably 'to create') + the Hurrian hypocoristic suffix ***-ya***.
II) It can be a so-called 'one-word' name identical with the verbal form {*pa=i=a*) 'He/She (a *numen* or the father/mother) builds / creates or has built/ created (the child)'. The form consists in that case of the verbal root ***pa-*** 'to build' + the marker of transitivity ***-i-*** + the marker of the subject of action ***-a***. ***Pae*** (wr. *Pa-e*) occurs once at Nuzi (cf. I.J. Gelb, *NPN*, 109), analysis (imperative) {*pa=i/e*}, 'Build/Create (the child) (oh *numen*) !'.

Compare the Hurrian personal name at Nuzi, ***Pa-i-šarri*** (wr. *Pa-i-šarri*), who is mentioned as son of *Ḫa-ni-ku* (JEN 487), cf. I.J. Gelb, *NPN*, 110; P.M. Purves, *NPN*, 242, s.v. ***Pai-*** and ***-šarri***. This name can now be translated as 'Build / Create (the boy), oh King of Gods !' or as 'The King of Gods built / created (the boy)'. Compare ***Pa-i-šarri*** at Nuzi also with the 'Old Hurrian' personal name ***Paip-šarri*** (wr. *pa-i-ip-šar-ri, ba-i-ip-šar-ri*) twice at Mari and once at Tigunāni, analysis {*pa=i=b-šarri*}, lexicon *pa-, šarri*, typology 1.1.1.2.1, translation 'The King of Gods built/created (the boy)' (Th. Richter, *VHN*, 219).

At Nuzi the Hurrian element ***Pai- / Pae(-)*** occurs frequently in onomastics such as *Pa-e, Pa-e-en-ni, Pa-i-šarri, Pa-i-ta-e, Pa-i-te-ia, Pa-i-te-a, Pa-i-te, Pa-i-te-šup, Pa-i-til-la, Pa-i-za-ni, Pa-i-ṣi-na* (cf. I.J. Gelb, *NPN,* 109-110; P.M. Purves, *NPN*, 242; cf. A. Draffkorn, *HHA*, 46: *Pa-i-še-na* on AT 252:15).

Since HT 62 and HT 73 have been joined by M. Pope, Linear A ***pa-i-ki***[(HT 62+73.2) from Hagia Triada belongs to a list of personal names on the lower half of the tablet.

If Linear A ***pa-i-ki***[is complete, it may well be cognate with the Hurrian personal name ***Paikku*** attested at Nuzi, with the variant readings *Pa-ik-ku* (son of *Qa-na-a-a*), *Ba-ik-ku* (father of *Tar-mi-ia*), *Pa-i-ik-ku* (father of *Zi-li-ḫa-ma-an-na*), *Pa-a-e-ek-ku* and *Ba-i-ik-ku*, cf. I.J. Gelb, *NPN*, 109; P.M. Purves, *NPN*, 242, s.v. ***paik-***.

One can also maintain that the Linear A name looks even more Hurrian than the name ***Paikku*** from Nuzi, because ***Paikku*** might contain the Akkadianizing *nominative* in ***-u***.

Th. Richter (*VHN*, 588-589) hesitantly analyses ***Paikku*** (wr. *Pa/Pá-(i-)ik-ku*), sub 1.2.1.3: *ungeklärte Bildungen* [*unexplained formations*], differently as {*pa=i=kk=o/u*} with the negation ***-kk-***, and offers the translation 'Er/Sie (scil. ein *Numen*) baute (früher einen Jungen) nicht' ['He/She (scil. a *numen*) did (previously) not build/create (a boy)'].

Since ***pa=i-*** shows in Th. Richter's analysis the marker of transitivity ***-i-*** (position 5) and the marker of the *intransitive* negation ***-kk-*** (position 6) instead of the marker of the transitive negation ***-u(w)/wa-*** (position 6), the form {*pa=i=kk=o/u*} presupposes an *antipassive* construction, which is indeed expected, since no object ('the boy') of the verbal action is mentioned, cf. I. Wegner, *Einführung*, 95: Table 5; and 99: Table 6-7.

Linear A ***pa-i-ki***[, if analysed as {*pa=i=kk=i*}, can likewise be interpreted as a negative *antipassive* construction and be translated in the same way as Th. Richter does with regard to {*pa=i=kk=o/u*}, but ***-ki*** in personal names can also be interpreted otherwise, namely as a hypocoristic or shortened form of Hurrian ***(-)kiaše*** 'sea'.

Th. Richter (*VHN*, 433-434) mentions that ***kijaze / kijaše*** {*kijaže*} 'Meer' ['sea'] and the hypocoristic or shortened form ***ki*** belong to the most frequent *quasi theophorous onomastic elements* (cf. Th. Richter, *BGH*, 200-201). In all sites the writing *(°-)ki-ia-ze* is the most frequent, but *°-ki-ia-še* and *°-ki-ia-ši* also occur at Mari and *°-ki-a-še* is the only writing at Šušarrā and frequent at Nuzi (cf. P.M. Purves, *NPN*, 226). The shortened form ***-ki***, primarily written with [GI], is as frequent. If one observes the long list of personal names with ***-kijaze / -kijaše / -ki*** mentioned by Th. Richter (*VHN*, 434) and with ***-kiaše*** mentioned by P.M. Purves (*NPN*, 226), it may be significant that almost all these names are feminine. I prefer to interpret Linear A ***pa-i-ki***[(HT 62+73.2) as a sentence name. It can be analysed as {*pa=i-ki(aše)*} and be translated as an *imperative*-construction 'Build / Create (the child), oh sea !' or be analysed as {*pa=i=k-ki(aše)* < (Old Hurrian) *pa=i=b-ki(aše)*} and translated as an (Old Hurrian) *indicative* 'The sea built (the child)'.

Linear A orthography does not show whether ***pa-i-ki***[represents cuneiform ***Paiki*** {*pa=i-ki(aše)*} or ***Paikki*** {*pa=i=k-ki(aše)* < (Old Hurrian) *pa=i=b-ki(aše)*}, the latter form with double ***-kk-*** as a result of assimilation < ***-bk-***. Old Hurrian ***pa=i=b-*** contains the marker of the subject of action ***-b***, cf. I. Wegner, *Einführung*, 126-129, especially 128: The transitive verbal form in ***=i=b*** is constructed without object. The subject is in the *absolutive* case. We call this a 'limited *antipassive*' ('eingeschränktes *Antipassiv*').

Remarkably many sentence names with the nominal element ***-kiaše*** at Nuzi contain so-called 'Old Hurrian' verbal constructions with intransitive ***=a=b*** and transitive ***=i=b***. P.M. Purves (*NPN*, 226) mentions at Nuzi: ^{f}***Akap-kiaše*** (wr. ^{f}*A-kap-ki-a-še*, ^{f}*A-qa-ap-ki-a-še*), ^{f}***Ḫašip-kiaše*** (wr. ^{f}*Ḫa-ši-ip-ki-a-še*, ^{f}*Ḫa-ši-ip-ki-a-ši*), ^{f}***Širwip-kiaše*** (wr. ^{f}*Ši-ir-wi-ip-ki-a-še*) next to ^{f}*Ši-ir-wi-ki-a-še*, ^{f}***Zilip-kiaše*** (wr. ^{f}*Zi-lip-ki-a-še*, ^{f}*Zi-li-ip-ki-a-še*). He also mentions ^{f}***Šaš-kiaše*** (wr. ^{f}*Ša-aš-ki-ia-še*, ^{f}*Ša-aš-ki-a-še*) and ^{f}***Unuš-kiaše*** (wr. ^{f}*Ú-nu-uš-ki-a-še*) next to ^{f}***Unu-kiašu*** (wr. ^{f}*Ú-nu-ki-a-šu*).

If ***ka-pa***, Ḫalba, is indeed the toponym indicating the ancient name of Hagia Triada itself, other toponyms could be mentioned in the first entries of texts from other Minoan palaces as well indicating the name of the palace itself.

In the very small group of 7 Linear A tablets found in the Minoan Villa of Arkhanes, south of Knossos, AK 3a.1 mentions: .]-***ka-ne*** GRA[providing exactly the sequence to be expected for *Ἀρχᾶνες*, if the Linear B orthographic conventions are applied to Linear A. According to Linear B orthography ***-r-*** in consonant clusters is not expressed before a palatal stop and the final ***-s*** is not expressed either.

Tablet AK 3 (HM 1675, 1970) from the Villa of Epano Arkhanes, site of Τζαμί, House of Καλπαδάκη, Ὁδός Καπετανάκη (Late Minoan Ib) reads:

AK 3a.1.	.]-*ka-ne* , GRA[
2.	] D OLIVA 3 D VIN*b* 2[
3.	2̲ [[*136* 2̲ vest.]] [
4.	*ki-nu* GRA 13[ ] [
5.	[ ]*t̲e̲* 2[ ] *136* 2 *36* 2 [
6.	]*ku* 3 [
b.1.	]-*ja-pi* GRA 6[
2.	]*pi-163a* GRA 1 [[ ]] O̲L̲E̲[
3.	vacat
4.	] ' 2̲[ ] OLE 4 |
5.	] V̲I̲N̲*a̲* 1 |
6.	] vacat [

Only the sign ***a-***] is missing at the beginning of the text in the left top corner of the tablet. It seems likely that this small fragment can be found in the left top corner of the (reverse) *b*-side of tablet AK 1b.1, which reads according to *GORILA 3* and J. Raison - M. Pope, *Corpus transnuméré du linéaire A* (BCILL 18 and 74): ***a***[ ]***ja-re*** 3[.

Observing the photographs it is not at all evident that the tiny fragment reading ***a***[should really be assigned to AK 1, since that tablet is far from complete and does not provide an irrefutable join with the other fragments. Assigning it to the left top corner of AK 3a would provide the complete sequence ***a***]***-ka-ne*** for *Ἀρχᾶνες*. Another argument that ***a***]***-ka-ne*** could very well represent the local toponym of the palace itself, is the ideogram GRA[mentioned after ***a***]***-ka-ne***, since it has been observed that in Linear B the ideograms of GRANUM and HORDEUM are also frequently preceded by toponyms. It is not certain that the final ***-s*** of *Ἀρχᾶνες* already existed in the Linear A name, since final consonants were not expressed in the script. Occurrence of the toponym 'Arkhane(s)' as the first entry in the heading of one of the few Linear A tablets discovered in the Minoan palace/villa of Arkhanes can hardly be accidental. It is interesting that according to *GORILA 5*, 83, the tablets ARKH 1, ARKH 2 and ARKH 3 are probably all inscribed by scribe 1, which does at least not contradict the assumption that fragment ***a***] belongs to AK 3.

The Linear A toponym ***a***]***-ka-ne*** can actually be analysed as *{ar=ḫane/i}* 'Give a child (oh God / *numen*) !'. Arkhanes lies in the foothills of Mount Ioukhtas and may have been used as a starting point for those who wished to visit the Peak Sanctuary of Ioukhtas to pray to the gods or to bring a 'libation table' with incised prayer.

Some 'libation formulas' from Ioukhtas contain ***u-na-ka-na-si*** (IO Za 2.1; IO Za 9) as well as ***u-na-ru-ka-***[(IO Za 16.b) that can be completed to ***u-na-ru-ka-***[***na-si***. Linear A ***u-na-ka-na-si*** can be interpreted as *{un=a-ḫ(ḫ)an(i)=a=šše/i}* 'come offspring, childhood, childbirth', and ***u-na-ru-ka-***[***na-si*** as *{un=al=u-ḫ(ḫ)an(i)=a=šše/i}* or *{un=ar=u-ḫ(ḫ)an(i)=a=šše/i}* 'bring childhood, childbirth (oh God(s) !', see the chapter on religious Linear A texts.

It seems that the meaning of the toponym *{ar=ḫane/i}* 'Give a child (oh God / *numen*) !' corresponds exactly with the wish / prayer *{un=a-ḫ(ḫ)an(i)=a=šše/i}* 'come offspring, childhood, childbirth', expressed so often on several libation tables.

The formation of Hurrian toponyms is often similar to that of personal names. Compare also my Hurrian interpretation of the toponyms *Khania* and *Phaistos*.

If we assign ***a***[to the left top corner of AK 3a providing a complete sequence ***a***]***-ka-ne*** (AK 3a.1 + fr. AK 1.b1) = *{ar=ḫane/i}*, later ***Ἀρχᾶνες***, we may conclude that]***ja-re*** <u>3</u>[(AK 1b.1) has nothing to do with ***a***[, but may be completed to sequences such as Linear A ***pa-ja-re*** (HT 8b.5; HT 29.2; HT 88.5; ZA 10b.5) and ***pa-ja-<u>re</u>*** (HT 29.2) or ***te-ja-re*** (HT 117a.5) or possibly]**'**, ***pu-te-ja-<u>re</u>*** (PL Zf 1) on a silver hairpin from Tholos A at Platanos in the Messara-valley (HM 498), if read from right to left ←, which can be proved on the basis of the sequence ***ja-sa-sa-ra-<u>me</u>*** (PL Zf 1) on the same hairpin.

A trace of a preceding sign is just visible left of ***-ja-pi***.]**'*-ja-pi*** GRA 6[(AK 3b.1) from Arkhanes. According to *GORILA 3* this sign is not incompatible with sign ***83a*** (value unknown). However, since only one small stroke of the sign is visible, also other signs may be compatible, e.g. ***24 = ke, 44 = e, 78 = ti, 81b = ?, 102a = de***. It does not make sense to speculate. If side b of the tablet is a continuation of the text of side a, there is a good chance that we are dealing with a personal name, but since]**'*-ja-pi*** is the first entry of side b and since it is followed by the GRA ideogram, just like ***a***]***-ka-ne*** GRA[(AK 3a.1 + fr. AK 1.b1), sequence completed with ***a***[(on a tiny fragment probably erroneously assigned to AK 1b.1), providing the name of the palace of ***Ἀρχᾶνες***, the possibility of a toponym must also be taken into account.

It is a pleasant coincidence that, with the join of ***a***] from AK 1b.1 to AK 3a.1, the sequence]***pi-163a*** (AK 3b.1-2) can be completed to [***<u>ki</u>-***]***pi-163a*** (AK 3b.1+fr. AK 1a.1), since ***<u>ki</u>-***] is on the other side of the fragment containing ***a***]. This would offer a personal name with the frequent Hurrian onomastic element ***kip, kipa*** and ***kipi*** in names as ***Kipaia, Kipiia*** at Nuzi (to start with the hypocoristics). I.J. Gelb (*NPN*, 86-88) and P.M. Purves (*NPN*, 227-228) mention the following Hurrian personal names s.v. ***kip, kip-***: *Kip-antil, Kip-apu, Kip-arrapḫe* (cf. *Kipi-arrapḫe*), *Kip-erḫan, Kip-iššuḫri, Kip-kewar, Kip-kušuḫ, Kip-tae, Kip-tali, Kip-talili, Kip-tešup* (cf. *Kipi-tešup*), *Kip-ukur*; s.v. ***kipa-***: *Kipa-kušu* (cf. *Kip-kušuḫ*), *Kipa-šekaše, Kipa-šenni, Kipa-urašše, Kipa-urḫe*; s.v. ***-kipa***: *Alli-kipa, Awiš-kipa, Ir-kipa, Kuš-kipa, Šuḫni-kipa, Tampuš-kipa, Ukur-kipa*; s.v. ***kipal-***: *Kipal-enni, Kipal-rumti, Kipal-zukki, Kipali*; s.v. ***kipan-***: *Kipan-til* or *Kip-antil*(?); s.v. ***kipi-***: *Kipi-arrapḫe, Kipi-tešup, Kipi-tilla*; further *Kipiia, Kipili, Kipukka*. ***Ki-bi-te-eš-šu-up***, father of ***It-ḫi-te-šup***, king of Arrapḫa, *šarr* [l]*Ar-ra-ap-ḫi*, HSS X 231:1; SMN 1003; 1466. The city of Nuzi was part of the Kingdom of Arrapḫa.

P.M. Purves (*NPN*, 227-228), who also indicates that from Ug. Voc. testimony Hurrian ***kip*** seems to correspond to Sumerian GAR and Akkadian ***šakānu***, 'to establish'.

A. Draffkorn, *HHA*, 30, 38, 61-62, 84, s.v. ***kib***, ***kibu-***, ***-kiba***, assumes like P.M. Purves that the onomastic element ***-kiba*** may well be nominal, separate from verbal ***kib***.

At Alalaḫ the Hurrian name ***Kibu-k(k)a***, wr. *Ki-bu-ug-ga* (AT 361,3) with root ***kib*** 'to set, place' is attested, cf. A. Draffkorn, *HHA*, 38, 84. But she assumes a nominal element ***-giba*** in ***Ewari-giba*** (wr. **E-wa-ri-ki-ba* SUKAL), AT *25,8, and **E-wa-ri-ki-ba*, AT *18, 15, corrected from **E-wa-ri-di-ba*; ***Lubar-giba***, wr. (1) **Lu-bar-ki-ba* LÚ ḫazannu (AT *63, 18), (2) **Lu-bar-⌈ki-ba⌉* (AT *204, 10), and ***Wəri-giba***, wr. (1) **Wə-ri-ki-ba* ḫazannu (AT *52, 24), (2) **Wə-ri-ki-ba* LÚ IŠ (AT *253, 25; *256,7), (3) **Wə-ri-ki-ba* QA.ŠU.DU$_8$ (AT *58, 25), (4) **Wə-ri-ki-ba* SANGA (AT *240, 19), (5) **Wə-ri-ki-ba* LÚ SUKAL (AT *27, 9), (6) **Wə-ri-ki-ba* ⌈UGULA⌉ AN.ZA.QAR (AT *96,11), (7) **Wə-ri-ki-ba* (AT *23, 13; *53, 7; *61, 20; *281, 10), cf. A. Draffkorn, *HHA*, 30, 42, 61-62, 84. Documents of level VII are marked * in the *Alalaḫ Texts*, those of level IV without *.

If sign ***163a*** (consisting of 3 parallel undulating lines) is a graphic variant of Linear A sign ***58*** (consisting of 2 parallel undulating lines) = ***ra***$_2$ = ***ria/lia***, Linear A ***[ki-]pi-ria*** would yield a perfect Hurrian name, cf. especially ***Kipali, Kipili, Ki-pa-ri-ia*** at Nuzi.

Linear A ***[ki-]pi-163a*** = ***[ki-]pi-ria*** (AK 3b.1+fr. AK 1a.1) can be analysed as the 'one-word' personal name {*kib=ill=i=a*}, consisting of the verbal root ***kib-*** 'to place' + the Old Hurrian *inchoative* or *ingressive* root-extension ***-ill-*** + the marker of transitivity ***-i-*** + the marker of the subject of action 3rd person singular ***-a***, translation 'He/She (a *numen*) started to place (the child)'. I. Wegner (*Einführung*, 89) offers two examples of forms with the root-extension ***-ill-*** from the Hurrian-Hittite bilingual ***Kirenze*** (KBo 32): *šid=ar=ill=o=m* 'er begann zu verfluchen' ['he began to curse'] and *am=ar=ill=o=m* 'er begann Böses zuzufügen' ['he began to inflict evil'], cf. E. Neu, *Orientalia 59*, 1990, 223-233, and E. Neu, *STBoT 32*, 1996, 104. The analysis {*kib=ir=i=a*} with another root-extension ***-ir-*** is also possible. The meaning of this root-extension is not yet clear, cf. I. Wegner, *Einführung*, 89.

In the Old Babylonian Mâri texts we see the Hurrian anthroponyms ***Kipa-r*** (wr. *ki-ba-ar*), Sûmu-yamam period, cf. G. Dossin, 'Deux listes nominatives du règne de Sûmu-iamam', *Revue d'Assyriologie 65 (1971)*, A. vii,19; ***Kipi-ri*** (wr. *ki-bi-ri*), Sûmu-yamam period, cf. Dossin, *o.c.*, A. iii,77; *Kipu-šenni* (wr. *ki-pu-še-ni*), Zimri-Lim period, cf. G. Dossin, *Archives Royale de Māri*, Paris 1967, VII, 210, rev.10; *Aniš-kipa-l* (wr. *a-ni-iš-ki-ba-al*), Sûmu-yamam period, cf. Dossin, *o.c.*, A. xi, 37, and Zimri-Lim period, cf. M. Birot, 'Textes économiques de Mari (III)', *Revue d'Assyriologie 49 (1955)*, 15-31, vi, 61 (Note: TEM III reads *a-lí-iš-tu-ba-al*). J.M. Sasson, 'Ḫurrians and Ḫurrian names in the Mari Texts', *UF 6 (1974)*, 358, corrects the name *a-lí-iš-tu-ba-al* to *a-ni-iš-ki-ba-al*; *Wari-kipa*, wr. PI-*ri-ki-ba* (Sûmu-yamam and Zimri-Lim periods), cf. G. Dossin, 'Deux listes nominatives du règne de Sûmu-iamam', *Revue d'Assyriologie 65 (1971)*, A. 47, 32, and G. Dossin, *Archives Royales de Māri*, Paris 1967, VII, 120, 11 and VIII, 1, 47. See especially J.M. Sasson, 'Ḫurrians and Ḫurrian names in the Mari Texts', *UF 6 (1974)*, 358, 363, 372 and 379 s.v. *kip/b, kipa-, kipi-, kipu-, -kipa*.

E. Laroche, *GLH*, 145, s.v. ***ki(b)-*** 'mettre, placer'. He equates RS quadr.130 III 10 akkadien ***šakânu*** = hourrite ***ki-um-mi***; cf. *Ugar.V*, 461: *infinitif* en ***-ummi***.

The verbal root ***ki(b)*** 'to place, establish' is extensively discussed with regard to two Linear A hypocoristic names ***ki-pa-a*** and ***u-na-a*** (KN Zb 40.1-2) on a pithoid jar from Knossos.

Remarkably the identical personal name ***Kepai̯a*** also occurs in a Linear A inscription on a gold signet-ring from the cemetery of Mavro Spilio near the Palace of Knossos. Both ***ki-pa-a*** (KN Zb 40.1) and ***ke-pa-ja*** (KN Zf 13) represent intransitive forms.

Linear A (˛) ***ke-pa-ja*** (˛) in ***a-re-ne-si-di-jo-pi-ke-pa-ja-su-ra-i-te-ra-me-a-ja-ku*** (KN Zf 13) can be identified as a Hurrian personal name ***Kepai̯a / Kipai̯a*** {*ke/ib=a-ja*}, with the root ***kib-/ke-***(?) and the hypocoristic suffix ***-ya***. There are at Nuzi 16 male persons bearing the hypocoristic Hurrian name ***Kipai̯a*** (wr. *Ki-pa-a-a, Ki-ba-a-a, Ki-ba-ia*), cf. I.J. Gelb, *NPN*, 86; P.M. Purves, *NPN*, 227-228, s.v. ***Kipai̯a***.

Regarding the orthographic representation of the hypocoristic suffix we observe that Linear A ***ki-pa-a*** (KN Zb 40.1) corresponds with the first and second writing-variants, *Ki-pa-a-a* and *Ki-ba-a-a*, at Nuzi and that Linear A ***ke-pa-ja*** (KN Zf 13) corresponds with the third writing-variant ***Ki-ba-ia*** at Nuzi. Both ***Kepai̯a*** amd ***Kipai̯a*** are also extensively discussed in *chapter 10: Linear A inscriptions on metal objects*.

Th. Richter (*BGH*, 199-200) mentions that the roots ***ke-*** I, ***keb-*** I, ***ḫib-*** III [*passim*] are generally interpreted as 'setzen, stellen, legen', 'to place', cf. E. Laroche, *GLH*, 145, s.v. ***ki(b)-***. Interesting is the form ***kebiri*** [Boğ.] that has been interpreted as 'someone who has set up (a trap)' by G. Wilhelm (1991b, 164) and V. Haas - I. Wegner (1999a, 199), as well as ***kebli***, ***kebeli***, ***kebili*** [Alalaḫ; Boğ.; Mari], explained as 'Jäger' ['hunter'] and 'Fallensteller' ['a trapper'] by several scholars, cf. Th. Richter, *BGH*, 200. He also mentions (*BGH*, 208), s.v. ***keb-*** II [PN], the meanings '(sich) (in eine bestimmte Richtung) bewegen' ['to move (into a certain direction)'], 'bringen' ['to bring'], 'schicken', 'to send'. There is some discussion among scholars, whether all these roots belong together or not. See also Th. Richter, *VHN*, 438-439, s.v. ***kib-*** I, ***ke-***(?).

HT 9 (HM 13, 1902-1903) from the Villa of Hagia Triada. Probably Late Minoan I b.

HT 9a.1.	*sa-ro* , *te* , VIN ,
2.	*pa-de* , 5 JE *83a-tu*
3.	10 *di-na-u* 4 *qe-pu*
4.	2 *so-di-ra* 2 J *ta-*
5.	*i-65* 2 J *a-ru*
6.	4 E *ku-ro* 31 JE
b.1.	*pa*₃ , *wa-ja-pi* 1
2.	*ka-twe* (or rather) ROTA IUGUM ˛ *pa-de* 3 *a-ru*
3.	3 *83a-tu* 8 *so-di-ra* 2
4.	*qe-pu* 2 *ta-i-65* 2
5.	*di-na-u* 4
6.	*ku-ro* 24

It is not likely that ***29-66*** (HT 9b.2) should be read as a syllabic sequence ***ka-twe***, since sign ***29*** can also be the ideogram ROTA = 'wheel', in solitary position, and sign ***66*** can, in solitary position, be interpreted as an ideogram as well: IUGUM = 'yoke' (cf. my note to HT 45a.2, HT 45a.3, HT 45b.3, commenting the analysed structure of the text).

Since wheels and yokes are both parts of vehicles, whether chariots or not, the combination of the two as ideograms is not inconceivable. Moreover, the list of (probably) personal names starting with ***pa-de*** (HT 9a.2) is also preceded by an ideogram, namely VIN. It would not make sense if from ***pa-de*** onwards (HT 9b.2) virtually the same list of entries as on HT 9a would have been repeated, if the b-side of the tablet still counted portions of wine and not another commodity or item.

Counting the units on the b-side of the tablet one must conclude that the total of 25 is not in accordance with the total of 24 given by the scribe. It is, of course, feasible that the scribe did not count very well, but one should not exclude the possibility that either the trace visible at the end of the first line is not a unit but part of another sign, or the scribe used two headings on this side of the tablet (the first in the first line and the second in the second) and started to count the units from line 2 after the line. Possibly the unit of b.1 should be added to the counting of the a-side to complete the total to 31 JE. This may also have been the reason why the scribe ruled the line.

Analysing the text one must wonder whether monosyllabic ***pa***$_3$ (HT 9b.1) takes the same position as ***sa-ro*** (HT 9a.1). If it also has the same function as the toponym ***sa-ro***, ***pa***$_3$ may well be an abbreviation of Linear A (and B) ***pa-i-to***.

HT 62 + 73, join by M. Pope, (HM. 54, 1902-1903) from the Villa of Hagia Triada.

HT 62.1.	*a-du-sa-ra* , *te* , VIN [
2.	*u-na-re* 15 E *ka-ku* 7 [
3.	[ ] 8 *no-ti* 18 *di-* [
4.	4 E *qe-*[ ] vest.[
5.	*je-si* 4 *ko-a* [
6.	*nu* 18 ' [
7.	25 [
HT 73.	Sup. mut.
1.	] *ku* [
2.	] ' , *pa-i-ki* [
3.	] 8 *sa-ro-qe-*[
4.	] 28 ' [
5.	] vest.[

HT 17 (HM 23, 1902-1903) from the Villa of Hagia Triada Probably Late Minoan I b.

HT 17.1-2.	*ra-43-ti* = *ra-swi-ti* , *te* , VIN*a*	38
HT 17.2.	*sa-ro*	10
HT 17.3.	*si-da-re*	5
HT 17.4.	vacat	

HT 19 (HM 26, 1902-1903) from the Villa of Hagia Triada. Probably Late Minoan I b.

Tablet HT 19 from Hagia Triada reads:

HT 19.1-2:	*ra-43-ti* = *ra-swi-ti* , *te* , VIN*a*	30
HT 19.2-3:	*sa-ro*	5 J
HT 19.3-4:	*du-me-di*	43 J
HT 19.5.	vacat	

Ad 1: Linear A sign ***43*** resembles Linear B ****64***, identified as ***swi*** by J. Chadwick.

A good candidate for yielding a toponym in Linear A is ***sa-ro*** (HT 9a.1, HT 17.2, HT 19.2; HT 42.2). W.C. Brice (1961), *ILA*, Pl. II/IIA, L. Godart and J.-P. Olivier, *GORILA 1* (1976), 18-19, and L.C. Meijer (1982), 8 and 57, read the sequence all as ***sa-ro***, whereas J. Raison - M. Pope (1980), 38-39; (1994), 49-50, read ***sa-188*** following J. Sundwall who argued that *188* is a new sign. However, the only difference between Linear A sign ***22*** = ***ro*** and sign ***188*** is a dot at the bottom of the vertical stroke in sign ***188***, which could easily have been caused by extra pressure from the *stilus* of the scribe. It is true that the dot occurs especially in the sequences just mentioned, although it seems to be less clear in HT 19.2. The dot also occurs in the sequence ***wo-188-ja*** on roundel KH Wc 2100, which would be ***wo-ro-ja***, if *188* is only a graphic variant of sign *22*.

The main argument for regarding ***sa-ro*** as a toponym is occurrence of Linear A ***sa-re-96*** (HT 20.4) = ***Ša-re-ḫi*** and ***sa-ro-qe*** (HT 62+73, joined by M. Pope, where it is found on HT 73.3) = ***Ša-ro-ḫe***. Since L. Godart, J.-P. Olivier, J. Raison and M. Pope all read ***sa-ro-qe*** [and no traces of another sign after ***-qe*** can be recognized, ***sa-ro*** and ***sa-ro-qe*** may well be compared with ***ka-pa*** and ***ka-pa-qe***. In that case ***sa-ro-qe*** would be the ethnic name (with the same Hurrian ethnic suffix ***-ḫe***) or an ethnic used as a personal name, derived from the toponym ***sa-ro***, analysis Old Hurrian ***Šar=o*** 'Wish (oh *numen*) !' or ***Šar=o=m*** 'He/She (a *numen*) wished (the village)', from the root ***šar-*** 'to wish, demand'.

Probably ***sa-ro-qe*** belongs to a list of personal names anyway, since the sequence ***pa-i-ki***[in the preceding line (HT 62+73.2) may be cognate with the Hurrian personal name ***Paikku*** from Nuzi with the variant readings *Pa-ik-ku* (son of *Qa-na-a-a*), *Ba-ik-ku* (father of *Tar-mi-ia*), *Pa-i-ik-ku* (father of *Zi-li-ḫa-ma-an-na*), *Pa-a-e-ek-ku* and *Ba-i-ik-ku*, cf. I.J. Gelb, *NPN*, 109, and P.M. Purves, *NPN*, 242, s.v. *paik-* (see *supra*).

If the identification of ***sa-ro*** as a toponym is correct, it probably is a local toponym pointing to a place in the vicinity of Hagia Triada itself. If it had designated another important place in Crete, one would have expected that it would also occur as a toponym in the Linear B tablets from Knossos, although we must realize that ***ka-pa*** itself also occurs only once in the Linear B texts from Knossos.

Could ***sa-ro*** be identified with the Pre-Greek name of the island ***Σάρος*** (now ***Σαρία*** north of ***Κάρπαθος***), also known as the name of a river in Cilicia (Kizzuwatna) ? I gather that ***Ζαρός*** (with lake ***Ζαρός***), north-east of Hagia Triada and Phaistos, may be a better candidate, because it may well have belonged to the area of dominance and power of the rulers of Phaistos and Hagia Triada. An indication could be that *Kamares* and the Cave of *Kamares*, where pottery of the famous Middle-Minoan II *Kamares*-style has been found, are not far west of *Zaros*. Vases belonging to this *Kamares*-style have also been found in the Old Palaces of Phaistos and Knossos.

The roundel KH Wc 2100 from Khania (Khania Museum: inv. 2100, 1974) is found in the Ὀδός Κατρέ 10 (same deposit as KH 5, KH Wc 2006, etc.), Late Minoan 1B.

Linear A ***wo-188c-ja*** (KH Wc 2100, side a) is the only entry on side a of the roundel. Side b: vacat. Side c (edge): 9 seal impressions: two ducks (*Σφραγίσματα*: type 17).

Linear A ***wo-188c-ja*** can be read as ***wo-ro-ja*** (KH Wc 2100, side a), since sign ***188*** is indeed only a graphic variant of ***22***. If one realizes that the sequence would in cuneiform have been written as Old Hurrian ***wu-ru-ja*** or ***wu-lu-ja***, identification is relatively easy.

E. Laroche (*RA 54*, 193 ff.; *GLH*, 298-299) mentions the transitive verb ***wur-*** 1 'voir' ['to see'] and the present 3rd person singular ****wur-ia***: *bu-u-ri-ya*, KBo XI 7 Ro 3; wu_u*-u-ri-ya*, KBo XIX 144 IV 7; KUB XLV 30, 8; 79 Vo 12-14; *bu-u-ri-ya-(an)*, KBo XV 1 IV 13. See *ibidem* for more verbal forms. He also mentions the noun ***wuri*** 'vue' ['view'].

E. Laroche (*GLH*, 205), s.v. ***pur-***, refers to ***wur-*** because of the ***b/w*** alternations.

E. Laroche (*GLH*, 298-299) also mentions a second verbal root ***wur-*** II 'vouloir' ['to wish, desire']. This ***wur-*** II is graphically distinguished from ***wur-*** I: Mit. ***ú-ú-r-***. Gustavs *AfO 8*, 131sq., 'promettre' ['promise']. E.A. Speiser, *IH*, 26, 'to desire'.

Present 1st person sing.: *ú-ú-[r]a-ú* 'I wish, desire' (Mit. IV 112).
Present 3rd sing. *ú-ú-ri-a-a-aš-še-na* = *wur-ya-ššena* 'qu'il veut' ['what he wishes'] (Mit. I 108; III 33, IV 31). The latter is a nominalized form (with nominalizing suffix ***-šše***).

It is attractive to compare Linear A ***wo-ro-ja*** (KH Wc 2100, side a) with Linear A ***pu₂-ra₂*** (ZA 6a.5) from Kato Zakro. Since Linear B sign ***ra₂*** is interpreted as ***ria/rya*** or ***lia/lya*** and Linear B ***pu₂*** (***phu/bu***) may according to F.M.J. Waanders be derived from Linear A ***/bhu/***, Linear A] ***pu₂-ra₂*** (ZA 6a.5), may well be a personal name that can be identified with ***Pu-ri-ia***, a name attested at Nuzi, which I.J. Gelb, *NPN*, 118, compares with ***Pureįa*** (wr. *Pu-re-e-a, Pu-re-ia, Pu-re-e*). P.M. Purves, *NPN*, 247, offers 3 possible etymologies of onomastic element ***pur***: ***pur*** (1) Hurrian. *Pu-ru-uḫ-le-e-a.* Cf. Akkadianized Hurrian ***p/wuruḫlu***, equivalent to Akkadian ***sutānu***, 'south(ern)', since *i-na wu-ru-uḫ-li*, JEN 176:8, corresponds to *i-na su-ta-an-ni*, JEN 524:11, in descriptions of the same piece of real estate, etc., (2) Akkadian ***bûr***, 'son'? or (3) Kassite ***p/bur*** 'lord' (see *purįaš*) ?

I. Wegner (*Einführung*, 59, 274) mentions ***wur-/pur-***, */fur/* 'sehen' ['to see'], but classes 'to wish, desire' sub ***ûr-*** II 'wünschen, wollen' (*Einführung*, 48, 145, 290).

Th. Richter (*BGH*, 325-327) follows the same partition: ***p/wur-*** I [*passim*] 'sehen' ['to see'] (main meaning), other meanings depending on the context: 'herunterblicken' ['to look down'], 'versprechen' ['to promise'], 'trouver' ['to find'], 'to recognize'.

Th. Richter (*BGH*, 496) distinguishes ***ûr-*** II, *wur-* III [Mit.] 'wünschen, wollen'.

According to Th. Richter (*VHN*, 489), s.v. ***pur-*** *{fur-}*, the Hurrian root for 'sehen' is unanimously accepted in recent research. The nouns ***puri*** 'Blick' ['view, look, gaze, glance'] and ***purani*** 'Vorzeichen' ['sign, omen'] are probably derived from the verbal root and the so-called sacrificial term ***puri*** probably has a mantic meaning as well. He mentions (*ibidem*) the following personal names: ***Arip-purani*** (wr. *a-ri-ip-pu-ra-ni*) from Tigunāni, analysis *{ar=i=b-po/urani}*, 'Das Vorzeichen gab (Jungen)' ['The omen gave (the boy)'], cf. *VHN*, 70; ***Purana*** (wr. *pu-ra-na*) from Mari, *{furan(i)=a*[E.]*}*, 'Er (Junge) ist gemäß des Vorzeichens (geboren)' ['He (the boy) is (born) in accordance with the omen'], cf. *VHN*, 239-240. [E.] refers to *essive* in ***-a***. ***Putal-puri*** (wr. *pu-da-al-pu-ri*) from Mari, analysis *{fud=a=l-furi}*. ***Purija*** *{fur-}* from Mari, Šubat-Enlil, Tuttul and Nuzi can be translated as 'He/She sees', identical with Linear A ***pu₂-ra₂*** (ZA 6a.5) from Zakros.

Linear A ***wo-ro-ja*** (KH Wc 2100, side a) may well be an Old Hurrian perfect form and have the meaning 'he has seen, he has inspected' in the bureaucatic context of the roundels. The seal impression on the edge of the roundel may be a distinctive mark of the overseer who has inspected the goods. However, since Hurrian personal names often have the appearance of a verbal form, ***wo-ro-ja*** *{wor=o=ja}* can also be a personal name with the same meaning or it can be a hypocoristic name with the suffix ***-ya***.

Linear A] ***pu$_2$-ra$_2$*** (ZA 6a.5) from Zakros = ***Purija*** can be interpreted as {*pur=i=ja*}, possibly {*bhur=i=ja*}, a hypocoristic personal name (with the hypocoristic suffix ***-ja***) or as {*pur=i=a*}, a (transitive) 'one word' personal name, consisting of the root ***pur-*** 'to see' + the marker of transitivity ***-i-*** + the suffix ***-a*** marking the subject (3rd person singular) of the transitive verb, that can be translated as 'He/She sees'.

Compare also ***Wur-tešup*** (wr. *Wu-ur-te-šup*), 6 persons with that name at Nuzi, and ***Wur-teịa*** (wr. *Wu-ur-te-ia*), 4 persons with that name at Nuzi, which implicates a possible alternation ***pur-/wur-*** (cf. I.J. Gelb, *NPN*, 174).

Since ***ra$_2$*** is not only ***ria/rya***, but also ***lia/lya*** in Linear A and B, **]** ***pu$_2$-ra$_2$*** (ZA 6a.5) can also be interpreted as ***Pu-lia***, attested as *Pu-li-a* in Cappadocia, *PNC* 27 (cf. E. Laroche, *NH,* 149, nº 1045, s.v. *Pulia*).

Th. Richter (*VHN*, 237) mentions the Hurrian personal name ^{f}***Pulija*** (wr. ^{f}*Pu-li-ia,* ^{f}*Pu-li-a*) as name of 4 women at Mari, analysis {*po/ul=i=ja*}, typology 1.1.1.2.4, lexicon *pul-*. ***Pulija*** can be interpreted as a hypocoristic personal name (with the hypocoristic suffix ***-ja***) or as a (transitive) 'one word' personal name, analysis {*po/ul=i=a*}, cf. also ***Pu-lu-ya*** at Mari and Ugarit (cf. F. Gröndahl, *PNTU*, 1967, 348) and *Bu-ul(!)-li-ia = Bu-li-ia* at Middle-Assyrian Assur. ***Pu-lu-ya*** may well be equivalent to Linear A ***wo-ro-ja*** that can be analysed as {*p/wo/ul=o/u=ja*}. He also mentions (*VHN*, 236-237, 488) the hypocoristic names ***Pulaja*** (wr. *Pu-la-ia*) and ^{f}***Pulaja*** (wr. ^{f}*Pu-la-ia*) at Mari, analysis {*po/ul=a=ja*}, typology 1.1.1.3.4; *Pu-la-ia-an* at Alalaḫ IV (*AT* 168: 11); ***Pulukan*** (wr. *Pu-lu-ga-an*) at Mari and Tuttul, analysis {*po/ul=o=kk=o»a=n(na)*}, typology 1.2.2.1, lexicon *pul-*; ^{f}***Pulum*** (wr. ^{f}*Pu-lu-um*) at Ašnakkum, analysis {*po/ul=o=m*}, typology 1.1.1.1.1, lexicon *pul-*; ^{f}***Pulum-kijaze*** (wr. ^{f}*Pu-lu-um-ki-ia-ze*) at Ašnakkum and Mari, analysis {*po/ul=o=m-kiaže*}, typology 1.1.1.1.1, lexicon *pul-, kijaze*; ***Pulum-šarri*** (wr. *Pu-lu-um-šarri*) at Mari, analysis {*po/ul=o=m-šarri*}, typology 1.1.1.1.1, lexicon *pul-, šarri*; ^{f}***Pulum-***[...] (wr. ^{f}*Pu-lu-um-*[...]) at Mari, analysis {*po/ul=o=m-šarri*}, typology 1.1.1.1.1, lexicon *pul-, šarri*; cf. also ***Wul-tešup*** (wr. *Wu-ul-te-šup*) at Nuzi, SMN 347; 518 (cf. I.J. Gelb, *NPN*, 174), which implicates a possible alternation ***pul-/wul-***.

Th. Richter (*VHN*, 488) mentions s.v. ***pul-*** {*po/ul-*} that the root ***pul-*** is attested in the Hurrian-Hittite bilingual ***Kirenze*** (KBo 32: 12 Rs. IV 3') in *pu-lu-uš-d*[*u*...], but that the meaning cannot yet be established, because the Hittite translation is missing. He adds (note 624) that there is no doubt about the Hurricity of the personal names collected by him in spite of the *lemma* on Kassite *pula* in *NPN*, 246, and K. Balkan, *Kassitenstudien. 1. Die Sprache der Kassiten, AOS 37*, 1954, 173.

I have mentioned in my *Corpus of transliterated Linear A texts*, that Linear A sign ***43*** resembles Linear B ****64***, which has been identified as ***swi*** by J. Chadwick. This means that ***ra-43-ti*** (HT 17.1; HT 19.1) can be read as ***ra-swi-ti*** or ***la-swi-ti***. It is tempting to interpret the latter as the original form of ***Lassithi < Laswithi*** (***-ss- < -sw-***).

Since the well-known Cretan *Lassithi*-plateau lies south of *Malia* and its famous Minoan Palace, one would have expected to find the toponym ***Λασ(σ)ίϑι = Lassithi < Laswithi*** in the archives of that palace, rather than at Hagia Triada. However, ***sa-ro*** (HT 19.2), probably ***Ζαρός***, is mentioned after ***r/la-swi-ti*** (HT 17.1; HT 19.1). The 'Plateau of *Nidas*' is north-west of ***Ζαρός***.

Words and names with initial ***l-*** are rare in Hurrian. E. Laroche (*GLH*, 159) mentions Hurrian *la-az-zi* (KUB XLV 21 Vo 21), but does not offer an interpretation, cf. Th. Richter, *BGH*, 235. If ***las-*** in ***r/la-swi-ti*** has the same meaning as Greek ***λᾶας*** 'stone', the toponym '*Laswithi*' > 'Lassithi' can be analysed as {*las=wi=tti*} 'I am of stone, I consist of stone', an expressive name for a mountain-massif. The etymology of *λᾶας* 'stone' is obscure (cf. P. Chantraine, *DELG*, 609-610). So the noun may be Pre-Greek. At Pylos Linear B offers ***ra-e-ja*** (PY Ta 642, 1-3; 713, 1), adjective ***λάειᾱ*** belonging to ***to-pe-za***, ***τόρπεζα*** 'table', nom. sing. fem. of ***λάεγος***, probably < ****λάσ-εγος*** 'of stone' or 'decorated with stone'. Intervocalic ***-s-*** first changed to intervocalic ***-h-*** in Greek (still present in Mycenaean Greek) and disappeared eventually. The adjectives in ***-e-jo / -e-o***, ***-e-ja / -e-a***, with doublet forms in ***-i-jo / -i-ja***, belong to those that indicate material or fabrics.

The Linear B texts from Knossos provide the ethnic ***ra-su-ti-jo*** (KN Lc 761) derived from the toponym ***ra-su-to*** (KN Ai 739,1, *al.*), of which the interpretation is uncertain according to C.J. Ruijgh, *EGM*, § 153. *Ibidem* (note 418) he suggests ***Λάσυστος*** or ***Λάσυνθος*** containing the Pre-Greek theme of ***Λάσος*** (Cretan toponym) and the ending of ***Κάρυστος*** or ***Ὄλυνθος***. Since ***w*** is cognate with ***u***, it is tempting to assume that Linear B ***ra-su-*** = ***Λάσυ-*** is derived from Linear A ***ra-swi-*** = ***Laswi-***. I may add that the ***-th-*** formant occurring in *Lassithi* and *Karpathos* is probably as Pre-Greek as formants ***-nth-*** and ***-st-***.

If the structure of the first lines of HT 17.1-2: ***ra-43-ti = ra-swi-ti , te ,*** VIN*a* 38 ***sa-ro*** 10 and of HT 19.1-3: ***ra-43-ti = ra-swi-ti , te ,*** VIN*a* 30 ***sa-ro*** 5 J, is compared with that of HT 9a.1-2: ***sa-ro , te*** VIN ***, pa-de,*** 5 JE, one gets the impression that both ***ra-swi-ti*** and ***sa-ro*** are toponyms. We have already seen that the ethnic ***sa-ro-qe*** (HT 62+73) is in fact the Hurrian ethnic of toponym ***sa-ro***, with the Hurrian ethnic suffix ***-ḫe***. If ***sa-ro*** (HT 9a.1) is a toponym, it is also tempting to interpret ***pa_3*** (HT 9b.1), which takes approximately the same position as ***sa-ro*** on the *a*-side, as an abbreviation of the toponym ***pa-i-to***, which occurs in full on HT 97a.3 and HT 120.6 as ***pa-i-to*** and, of course, also in the Linear B texts from Knossos, ***pa-i-to*** KN Da 1163+1400b, *et alibi*, *Φαιστός*.

Since I have interpreted ***ra-43-ti = ra-swi-ti*** (HT 17.1; HT 19.1) and ***sa-ro*** (HT 17.2; HT 19.2) as the Cretan toponyms *Laswithi* > *Lassithi* and *Zaros*, respectively, one tends to consider ***si-da-re*** (HT 17.3) a toponym as well. However, ***si-da-re*** (HT 122a.5) occurs certainly in a long list of personal names. This does not automatically mean that ***si-da-re*** (HT 17.3) also has to be a personal name, since there are examples of toponyms that are formed in the same way as anthroponyms. The formation of Linear A ***si-da-re*** has the typical appearance of a 'one-word name' that probably consists of the root ***šed-/šid-*** I 'to fatten up, feed' or ***šid-*** II 'to curse' + the *factitive* or *iterative* root-extension ***-ar-*** + the marker of the transitive *imperative* ***-e/i***. Indeed I. Wegner (*Einführung*, 88) gives the examples ***tad=ar-*** 'lieben' ['to love'] and ***šid=ar-*** 'verfluchen' ['to curse']. She gives (*ibid.*, 53) the example of the noun ***šid=ar=ni*** 'Fluch' ['curse'], with the individualising suffix ***-ni*** (not to be confused with the so-called definite article ***-ni/-ne***).

Since according to Linear A and B orthographic conventions a nasal ***[n]*** preceding an occlusive is not expressed in consonant clusters, Linear A ***si-da-re*** can theoretically also contain the Hurrian root ***šind-*** 'seven' or a verbal root ***šind-*** based on ***šind-*** 'seven'. The *transitive* root ***šind-*** can be interpreted as 'to make seven' > 'to allow a seventh child to be born', whereas the *intransitive* root means 'to be seven' > 'to be the seventh child'.

However, in my view the root-extension ***-ar-*** (certainly if it has an *iterative* aspect) makes it virtually impossible that Linear A ***si-da-re*** reflects the Hurrian form ****šind=ar=e***, because a name meaning 'Allow the seventh child to be born again and again' does not make sense.

If Linear A ***si-da-re*** (HT 17.3; HT 122a.5) contains the root ***šid-*** 'to curse', the name can be translated 'Curse the (deceased) child again and again (oh *numen*) !'. If the root ***šed-*** 'to fatten up, feed' can also be spelled ***šid-***, the name can be translated 'Feed the child again and again (oh *numen*) !'. Both meanings make sense. The root ***šid-*** 'to curse' has the advantage that it is also attested with the root-extension ***-ar-***.

According to Th. Richter (*VHN*, 516, s.v. ***šid-*** II, 'verfluchen' ['to curse']), the orthography ***ši-d/t°*** allows a distinction from ***šed-*** I 'fett machen, mästen' ['to fatten up, feed'], written ***še-ed°*** in the Hurrian-Hittite bilingual ***Kirenze*** (KBo 32), corresponding with Hittite ***warganu-***. Th. Richter, *BGH*, 398-400, distinguishes ***še/id-*** I [Boğ.; Tiš-atal] 'verfluchen' from ***šed-*** II [Boğ.] 'fett machen, mästen'. [N.B.: root I of *VHN* = root II of *BGH*; and root II of *VHN* = root I of *BGH*.]

Th. Richter (*VHN*, 279, 516) ascribes ***Šetija*** at Mari, (wr. *še-di-ja*) to the root ***šed-*** I 'fett machen, mästen', {*šed=i=ja*}, typology 1.1.1.2.4, lexicon ***šed-*** I, translation 'Er/Sie (scil. ein *Numen*) machte (Jungen) fett(?)' ['He/She (a *numen*) made (the boy) fat, c.q. fed (the boy)']. Since ***šed-*** 'to fatten up, to feed' is to date only attested with [***e***] (not yet with [***i***]), we may only reservedly apply this root to Linear A ***si-da-re***. Nevertheless, ***e/i*** alternations are so common in Hurrian that it may be unwise to totally omit it.

Th. Richter (*VHN*, 278-279, 516) attributes the following names to the root ***šid-*** II 'verfluchen': ***Šitap-šarri*** (wr. *ši-tap-ša-ri*) at Mari (*TEM-3* VI 64, reading Durant/Marti 2005, 124), typology 1.1.1.3.1, analysis {*šid=a=b-šarri*}, lexicon ***šid-*** II, ***šarri***; ***Šitip-šarri*** at Mari (wr. *ši-di-ip-šar-ri*), typology 1.1.1.2.1, analysis {*šid=i=b-šarri*}, lexicon ***šid-*** II, ***šarri***, translation 'Der Götterkönig verfluchte (verstorbenes Kind)' ['The King of Gods cursed (the child that died)']; ***Šitip-ewri*** (wr. *ši-di-ip-ew-ri*), from Tuttul (Tall Bi'a), analysis {*šid=i=b-evri*}, typology 1.1.1.2.1, lexicon ***šid-*** II, ***ewri***, translation 'Der Herr verfluchte (verstorbenes Kind)' ['The Lord cursed (the child that passed away)'].

Within Linear A one may compare ***si-da-te*** (AK 2.1), first sequence on a tablet from Arkhanes; ***si-di-ja*** (HT 126(+Fr)a.3) from Hagia Triada; ***si-du-mina , ku-mi*** (HT 110a.1) from Hagia Triada and (,) ***si-di-jo-pi*** (,) (KN Zf 13), the second sequence in a spiral Linear A inscription ***a-re-ne-si-di-jo-pi-ke-pa-ja-su-ra-i-te-ra-me-a-ja-ku*** (KN Zf 13) from the necropolis of Mavro Spilio, east of the Palace of Knossos (see *chapter 10: Linear A inscriptions on metal objects*).

The Linear A personal name ***pa-de*** (HT 9a.2; HT 9b.2; HT 122a.5) has been discussed before as well as the correlation between the *a*- and *b*-sides of HT 9 and HT 122, respectively, but also between HT 9a/b and HT 122a themselves.

Linear A ***di-na-u*** (HT 9a.3; HT 9b.5) from Hagia Triada and many other sequences in Linear A show that an initial voiced dental [***d***] was quite common in the Hurrian dialect of Minoan Crete. I have often expressed the view that it is preferable to limit the apparent evidence for the phenomenon of initial voicelessness (based on the rather late alphabetic cuneiform Hurrian texts from Ugarit) to the area of that city and to that particular period.

There is no solid argument to extend a probably local and late phenomenon over the very large areas of Hurrian presence and over a very long period, where and when Hurrian syllabic cuneiform was the only means of written communication. Since ***di-na-u*** on both sides of tablet HT 9 belongs to lists of names, we may conclude that it is a personal name as well. The ending in ***-au*** is typical for the suffix of the subject-marker of the 1st person singular of transitive indicative verbs. Since publication of Th. Richter (*VHN*, 2016, especially pages 584-587) it has become clear that, what I cautiously considered a theoretical possibility in the 2016 edition of *Minoan Linear A*, namely that some Hurrian personal names seem to have the appearance of verbal forms, is really attested by examples in the Hurrian onomastic material. Richter mentions several examples sub 1.1.2 *Namen mit Verbalformen des Mittani-Paradigmas*: ***Appau*** (wr. *ap-pa-ú*), *{app=av}* at Emar; ***Arau*** (wr. *a-ra-ú*), *{ar=av}* 'Ich gebe (Jungen)' ['I give (boy)'] at Sippar; ***Nanau*** (wr. *na-na-ù*), *{nan=av}* 'Ich schlage (Person(?)) nieder' ['I smash (person(?)) down']; ***Šarau*** (wr. *ša-ra-ú*), *{šar=av}* 'Ich wünsche (Jungen)' ['I wish (boy)'] at Atmannu (*Iraq 70*, 167, nr. 15: 5, see ***šar-*** *BGH*, 355); ***Tappau*** (wr. *tab-ba-ù*), *{tapp=av}* 'Ich mache (Jungen) fest' ['I make (the boy) firm, unwavering'] at Umma. I have only quoted examples of so-called 'one-word' personal names appearing as verbal forms with the suffix ***-au*** of the subject-marker of the 1st person singular transitive indicative.

There are not only parallels in the Near East, but Linear A ***a-mi-da-u*** (ZA 10a.3) and ***a-mi-da-o*** (HT? 170a.5) are also good parallels of the same type of Hurrian personal names: ***a-mi-da-u*** and ***a-mi-da-o*** cannot mean 'I shall *arrive*', because the form cannot be intransitive, since intransitive verbs do not have a suffix ***-e/id-*** (with voiced dental) to indicate the future tense, but ***-e/it-*** (with voiceless dental, written ***-e/itt-*** in cuneiform), cf. e.g. the form ***un=ett=a*** 'he will come', see I. Wegner, *Einführung*, 97: *un-et+t+a* 'er wird kommen' ['he will come']. Moreover, the suffix ***-au*** [***-av/-affu***] is only the marker of the subject of action 1st person singular of transitive-ergative verbs (position 7), cf. I. Wegner, *Einführung*, 93, Table 4. The marker of the subject of action 1st person singular of intransitive verbs is the suffix of the *enclitic absolutive* personal pronoun ***-tta/-t*** (position 9), cf. I. Wegner, *Einführung*, 99, Tables 6-7.

So ***a-mi-da-u*** and ***a-mi-da-o*** may well represent transitive usage of the verb ***amm-*** 'to reach (something)', with the suffix ***-e/id-*** (with voiced dental) indicating the transitive future tense + the suffix of the 1st person singular ***-au***. Starting from the root ***amm-*** 'to reach (something)' ***a-mi-da-u*** and ***a-mi-da-o*** can be analysed as *{amm=e/id=au}* 'I shall reach (something)', 1st person singular future indicative of the verb ***amm-***.

Compare also I. Wegner (*Einführung*, 129) who offers an example of the transitive usage of ***amm-*** II in the Hurrian-Hittite bilingual ***kirenze***: *olvi=ne=ma amm=i=b ommin(i)=ne* (KBo 32: 14 I 19-20), which she translates 'Ein anderes Land aber erreichte es (das Reh)' ['But it (the roe) reached an other land']. This Old Hurrian sentence is antipassive, with a (non-ergative) subject in the *absolutive*, an object in an *oblique* case like ***-a*** (*essive*) or ***-ne***, and with the transitive verbal form in ***=i=b***.

However, if we assume that Linear A ***a-mi-da-u*** and ***a-mi-da-o*** contain the transitive root ***am-*** II [Boğ.] 'ansehen, anschauen, beachten', 'porter son regard sur', 'guardare, osservare, vedere', 'to observe' (Th. Richter, *BGH*, 21-23), the meaning of these personal names would be 'I shall observe', which would also offer a conceivable meaning.

In view of this evidence the Linear A personal name ***di-na-u*** (HT 9a.3; HT 9b.5; HT 16.1-2) may be interpreted as the 1st person singular transitive indicative of the verbal root ***din-*** 'I do, make, build (something)', if it can be equated with ***tin-*** [Ugarit] 'to do, make', cf. Th. Richter, *BGH*, 437-438, s.v. ***tin-*** [Ug.], root in (Sumerian) DÙ.A = (Hurrian) ***ti-ni-šu***: 'faire', for ***tan=uš=a*** (cf. E. Laroche, *GLH*, 254 sub ***tan-***); 'to build, to make' (M.L. Khacikjan, On the typology of the Hurro-Urartian verb, in: M.A. Dandamayev e.a. (eds.), *Societies and languages of the Ancient Near East* (Festschrift I.M. Diakonoff), 1982, 168[7]); corresponds with Sumerian DÙ, probably variant of ***tan-*** 'machen' ['to do, make'] (G. Wilhelm, Die Inschrift des Tišatal von Urkeš, in: G. Buccellati - M. Kelly-Buccellati (eds.), *Urkesh and the Hurrians*. Studies in honor of Lloyd Cotsen (Urkesh / Mozan Studies 3), Malibu 1998, 126[51]; G. Wilhelm, Bemerkungen zu der akkadisch-hurritischen Bilingue aus Ugarit, in: W. Sallaberger - K. Volk - A Zgoll (eds.), *Literatur, Politik und Recht in Mesopotamien*, Festschrift für Claus Wilcke (Orientalia Biblica et Christiana 14), Wiesbaden 2003, 342[8]). See for the form ***tin=i=zə*** 'he made' also M.L. Khacikjan, On some models in Hurrian onomastics, *SCCNH 2*, 1987, 154; see for the 'Ablaut' relation ***tan-*** vs. ***tin-*** I.M. Diakonoff - S.A. Starostin, *Hurro-Urartian as an Eastern Caucasian language* (Münchener Studien zur Sprachwissenschaft, Beiheft 12, Neue Folge), München 1986, 99. Compare ***tn*** (alphabetic cuneiform of Ugarit).

Linear A ***qe-pu*** (HT 9a.3; HT 9b.4) occurs on both sides of the same tablet in similar lists of personal names. The names occur only in a different order on the *a*-side and *b*-side, respectively. A more essential difference is that the *a*-side registers portions of VIN 'wine' for each person and the *b*-side ROTA 'wheels' and IUGUM 'yokes, cross-beams'.

Probably neither Akkadian ***ḫepû(m)*** 'zerbrechen' ['to break (down)'] nor the theonym ***Ḫeba / Ḫebat / Ḫebet*** has anything to do with Linear A ***qe-pu***. The theonym ***Ḫeba(t)*** can be recognized in Linear A ***qe+pa₃*** (HT 33.4), ligature from top to bottom, significantly following the ideogram NUBES+***pi*** (HT 33.4) = ***Tešuppi***. Linear A ***qe-pi-ta*** (HT 6a.6), ***Ḫebitta < Ḫebit=wa*** provides her name in the dative form: 'for Ḫebat' (see *supra*).

Since ***-l-*** preceding an occlusive is not expressed in Linear A and B consonant clusters, it is possible to read ***Ḫelpu*** which would yield a name with the verbal root ***ḫe/ill-***, ***ḫe/il-*** [*passim*] 'to speak, to say (names)', cf. Th. Richter, *BGH*, 147-148. P.M. Purves (*NPN*, 246) considered the ending ***-pu*** a formative in ***Ḫašipu***, but if it is an abbreviation of ***p/wutki*** [Boğ.; Ug.] 'son, child' (cf. Th. Richter, *BGH*, 332-334, s.v. ***p/wud-*** I, *putt-* [Boğ; PN]) 'to procreate', ***Ḫaši-pu*** means 'Listen, oh son !' and ***Ḫel-pu*** 'Speak, oh child !'.

Linear A ***so-di-ra*** (HT 9a.4, HT 9b.3; HT 122a.5) can be interpreted as a Hurrian personal name. Since according to the orthographic conventions of Linear A and B ***-r-*** preceding an occlusive is not expressed in consonant clusters, Linear A ***so-di-ra*** may well be equated with the Hurrian personal name ***Šur-tilla*** (wr. *Šu-ur-til-la*), phonologically ***/Šordilla/***, son of *E-en-na-ma-ti* at Nuzi, HSS IX 7:3, 10, 12, cf. I.J. Gelb, *NPN*, 140; P.M. Purves, *NPN*, 259-260, s.v. ***šur***, cf. also ***Šur-teḭa*** (wr. *Šu-ur-te-e-a*), ***Šur-tešup*** (wr. *Šu-ur-te-šup*, *Šu-ur-te-eš-šu-up*). ***Šur-tilla*** may be analysed as *{šo/ur(=i)-Dilla}*.

Tilla is a Hurrian deity, one of the bulls of Teš(š)ub, according to the Song of *Ullikummi*, cf. KUB XXXVI 12 III 5 = JCS 6, 14. ***Tilla*** is very popular as theophorous element in the onomastics of Nuzi.

If the first element of a name contains a final vowel, the second element ***-tilla*** is written with a single dental indicating that it is voiced. See e.g. *Al-ki-til-la, Ḫu-i-til-la, I-ri-ri-til-la, It-ḫi-til-la, Qa-i-til-la, Ki-bi-til-la, Ku-ul-bi-til-la, Na-i-til-la, Nam-ḫi-til-la, Ni-ir-ḫi-til-la, Ni-im-ki-til-la, Ni-in-ki-til-la, Ni-ra-ri-til-la, Pa-i-til-la, Ba-i-til-la, Še-eḫ-li-til-la, Ši-mi-til-la, Šur-ki-til-la, Ta-i-til-la, Tar-mi-til-la, Te-er-ḫi-til-la, Du-uḫ-mi-til-la, Dup-ki-til-la, Ul-mi-til-la, Ur-ḫi-til-la, Wa-ar-ḫi-til-la*, cf. P.M. Purves, *NPN*, 267.

It is now possible to provide verbal ***šur-*** with the meanings of two different roots. Th. Richter (*BGH*, 418) distinguishes ***šur-*** I [Boğ.] 'schlachten/abstechen (von Kleintieren, von Vieh, von Schafen und Lämmern)' ['to slaughter (small cattle, sheep and lambs)'], also ***šu-ri*** I [Arrapḫa], corresponding with Hittite ***ḫatta***; *trans.* ***šur-*** II [Mit.]: 'eilig gehen lassen, abfertigen' ['to let (somebody) hurry up, to delegate'] (I. Wegner, *Einführung*, 281), 'fortgehen, abreisen lassen' ['to let somebody go, depart'] (E. Neu, 2001, 95), *intr.* ***šurr-*** [Boğ.] 'aller, faire route, se diriger (vers)' ['to go (on his/her way) (to)'] (Catsanicos, 1996, 282), '(hinab)gehen' ['to go down, to descend'] (E. Neu, 2001, 95), 'eilig gehen' ['to go hastily, to hurry'] (M. Salvini - I. Wegner 2004, 181).

In the Hurrian-Hittite bilingual ***Kirenze*** Hurrian *šu-ú-ru-u-um* (KBo 32: 13 Vs. I 17) *{šur=o=m}* 'she slaughtered' corresponds with Hittite *ḫa-at-te-eš* (past 3rd pers. singular active) (II 17, cf. E. Neu, *StBoT 32*, 223, 258f.). Hurrian *šu-ú-ru-u-um* (KBo 32: 13 Vs. I 19) *{šur=o=m}* corresponds with Hittite *ḫa-at-ta-at* (past 3rd pers. singular med.) (II 20, cf. E. Neu, *StBoT 32*, 223, 258f.), cf. I. Wegner, *Einführung*, 210-212.

If Linear A ***so-di-ra*** (HT 9a.4; HT 9b.3; HT 122a.5) is interpreted as Hurrian ***Šur-tilla***, both 'Slaughter (small cattle, sheep and lambs) (for the festival ?), oh Tilla !' and 'Let (the child) hurry up, oh Tilla !' make sense.

Th. Richter (*VHN*, 284, 521) also mentions the personal names ***Šure*** (wr. *Šu-u-re, Šu-re-e*) at Mari and Qaṭṭarā, analysis *{šo/ur=i}*, typology 1.3.1.2.1; cf. *Šu-ri* at Nippur, *Šu-(ú-)re* at Nuzi, *Šu-ri-ia* at Kurruḫanni; ***Šurutta*** (wr. *Šu-ru-ut-ta*) at Alalaḫ IV (AT 128: 23; 189: 24; cf. A. Draffkorn, *HHA*, 52); ***Šurutte*** (wr. *Šu-ru-ut-te*) at Nippur; ***ᶠŠurunna*** (wr. *ᶠŠu-ru-un-na, ᶠŠu-ru-na*) at Mari, analysis *{šo/ur=o=nna}*, typology 1.3.1.1.2.1; ***ᶠŠurunni*** (wr. *ᶠŠu-ru-ni*) at Mari, analysis *{šo/ur=o=nni}*, typology 1.3.1.1.2.2.

Since Th. Richter mentions here a lot of so-called 'one-word' personal names with enclitic personal pronouns ***-tta***, ***-tte*** 'me' and ***-nna***, ***-nni*** 'him/her', with the function of object of action of the transitive verb, the enclitic personal pronoun 1st person plural ***-tilla / -dilla*** 'us' seems equally conceivable. Consequently Linear A ***so-di-ra*** (HT 9a.4; HT 9b.3; HT 122a.5), Hurrian ***Šurtilla*** < *{šo/ur(=i)=dilla}* or *{šo/ur(=o/u)=dilla}*, may perhaps also be interpreted as 'Let us go / depart / hurry up (oh *numen*) !'. Semantically this interpretation is less attractive than *{šo/ur(=i)-Dilla}*, with ***Tilla*** as theophorous element in the personal name as ***Tešup*** is in ***Šur-tešup*** and ***Šur-teḭa***.

Linear A ***ta-i-65*** (HT 9a.4-5; HT 39.1) and ***ta-ḭ-65*** (HT 9b.4) is probably a personal name containing the frequent Hurrian onomastic element ***tai-***, cf. P.M. Purves, *NPN*, 261, s.v. ***tai*** (cf. perhaps ***tae***). The value of sign ***65*** is still unknown, but ***zu*** and ***zi*** may be good candidates, since they are missing in the grid of Linear A phonetic values. ***Taizi*** (wr. *Ta-i-zi*) and ***Taizu*** (wr. *Ta-i-zu*) are attested as Hurrian names at Nuzi (I.J. Gelb, *NPN*, 145; Purves, *NPN*, 277; 279). P.M. Purves calls both ***-zu*** and ***-zi*** formatives.

Apparently a formative. See Oppenheim in *WZKM XLIV*, 206 and *RHA V, fasc. 33 (1938)*, 12. Occurs perhaps in *Apazi, Apizi, Apuzi, Errazi, Ewazi, Ewizi, Karizi, ᶠKirrazi* ?, *Nikazi, Suḫurzi* ?, and *Taizi*. Cf. *ziḭam*: unidentified. Cf. perhaps *Zi-ia-an* from Chagar Bazar, *Iraq VII (1940)*, 42. Cf. *NPN*, 279, s.v. ***-zzi***: Hurrian. Apparently a formative to be found also in *še-en-ni-iw-wu-ú-uz-zi* Tuš. iii 43, and *aš-du-uz-zi,* SMN 2671 (latter a term applied to a garment). Occurs in *Ḫurazzi* (unles Akkadian), *Iuzzi* ?, *Kakkuzzi, Kapazzi, Kinnuzzi, Umpizzi*. *NPN*, 279, s.v. ***-zu***: Hurrian. Apparently a formative; see Oppenheim *WZKM XLIV*, 206. Occurs in *Ḫanizu, Taizu,* and *Wurruzu*. Note also *Kalzu* ?, *Zunzu* and *ᶠZunzu*. Cf. s.v. ***-zzu***, *Ḫanazzu* and *Wantarizzu*.

Sign ***65*** is a rare sign in Linear A. It also occurs in the sequence ***te-65*** (ZA 20.3) at Kato Zakro. If sign ***65*** is ***zu***, the form would yield ***te-zu***, which would make sense, if one takes into account that ***š*** is normalized to ***z*** by A. Draffkorn, *HHA*, 166, s.v. ***Tezu***, e.g. *Ir-tezu-ba*. Cf. also P.M. Purves, *NPN*, 265, s.v. *tešup*, who writes e.g.: In Ugarit the name *Tešup* is written ***tšb/tθb***; see von Brandenstein in *ZDMG XCI (1937)*, 562 and 570, and Speiser in *JAOS LVIII*, 179. As a result Linear A ***te-zu*** (ZA 20.3) could then be *Teš(š)ub*, since in accordance with the orthographic conventions of Linear A and B, the final labial occlusive ***-b*** is not expressed in the script. If identification of ***te-65*** = ***te-zu*** (ZA 20.3) as *Teš(š)ub* can be confirmed, Linear A ***ta-i-65*** (HT 9a.4-5; HT 39.1) and ***ta-i̭-65*** (HT 9b.4) can be identified as the Hurrian personal name ***Ta-i-zu***. Then the value of sign ***65*** can be confirmed as ***zu***. If not, the question is still open whether Linear A sign ***65*** is ***zu*** or ***zi***.

It is unlikely that ***ku-ra*** (ZA 20.4) following ***te-65*** (ZA 20.3) and followed by the high number 130 is a scribal error for ***ku-ro***. It may well represent the name of one of the bulls guarding the Hurrian Weather God *Teš(š)ub*, attested as ***ᵈḪu-ur-ra*** at Meskene-Emar (Msk.): the unpublished tablets of the Museum of Aleppo. It is also attested as ***ᵈḪu-u-ur-ra*** at Boğazköy (KBo I 1 rev. 41), in a treaty between Šuppiluliuma I and Mattiwaza. In this text ***ᵈḪurra*** is mentioned alongside with ***ᵈŠeri***. The deities ***ᵈŠer(r)i***, ***ᵈTilla*** and ***ᵈḪurri*** are divine bulls accompanying the Hittite - Hurrian Weather-god. The theophorous element ***-ḫurra*** also occurs in the Nuzi onomastics, ***Arib-ḫurra*** (wr. *A-ri-ip-ḫur-ra, A-ri-ip-ḫu-ur-ra, A-rip-ḫur-ra*), cf. I.J. Gelb, *NPN*, 29; P.M. Purves, *NPN*, 218. ***Arib-ḫurra*** can be analysed as {*ari=b-ḫurra*} '*Ḫurri/a* gives/gave'. ***Ḫurra*** is also a town in Hurrian territory.

According to E.A. Speiser (*IH*, § 177) the suffix ***-b***, which he called a 'root-complement', appeared to have an asseverative connotation: e.g. ***Una-b-Tešub*** could be interpreted as 'Arriving-verily is Tešub'. His ingenious argumentation was followed by E. Laroche's approval (*NH*, 347): "E.A. Speiser (*IH*, § 177) enseigne que le suffixe ***-p/b-*** de ***Una-b-Tešub*** a une valeur 'assévérative', renforçant l'affirmation que constitue la phrase nominale: 'Tešub (est) venant assurément'." After publication of the Hurrian-Hittite bilingual ***Kirenze*** (KBo 32) the position has changed. Now the suffix ***-b*** can be interpreted as the Old Hurrian marker of the subject of the 3rd person singular of the transitive-(not)ergative verb in ***-i***, and of the intransitive verb in ***-a***, see I. Wegner, *Einführung*, 134 and Table 13: *The order of suffixes of the Old Hurrian verb*.

E. Laroche (*GLH*, 115) s.v. ***Ḫurri***: "L'un des taureaux de Tešub; v. aussi ***Šerri*** et ***Tilla***. Graphies: *ᵍᵘᵈḫu-(u)-ur-ri, ᵈḪu-(u)-ur-ri*, en contextes akkadiens et hittites: KBo I 1 Vo 41; KBo VI 28+ Vo 32; KUB XXI 1 IV 8; XVII 14 I 10; XXXIII 97 1 12, etc. Msk. *ᵈḪu-ur-ra.*– H.: *Šerri Ḫu-ur-ri* GUDᵇⁱᵃ*-ri*, KBo XX 119 I 15, IV 26 = KBo XVII 86+ I 4."

The high number 130 and the position of ***ku-ra*** at the end of the tablet may plead for a scribal error. Possibly the fact that the number 130 following ***ku-ra*** is higher than the number 12 following ***te-65 = te-zu*** ? (ZA 20.3) is not in favour of an interpretation as *Teš(š)ub* and *dḪu-ur-ra* either. On the other hand the fact that these sequences occur together on the same tablet may well corroborate the given explanation, because it would be quite accidental that a sequence that can be interpreted as 'a bull guarding Teš(š)ub' occurs together with another sequence that could be a representation of the Storm God himself. Another argument confirming that Linear A ***ku-ra*** (ZA 20.4) is probably not a scribal error for ***ku-ro***, is that the sequence ***ku-ra*** (AK 2.1) occurs again at Arkhanes, where it certainly cannot be a scribal error for ***ku-ro*** because of its position at the beginning of the tablet. Attestation at two different sites makes such an assumption less likely and ***ku-ra*** VINb 5 (AK 2.1-2) does certainly not represent a summation.

Since the Linear B ***k-*** signs represent ***κ-***, ***γ-***, ***χ-***, the corresponding Linear A signs probably represent ***k-***, ***g-***, ***ḫ-*** and ***-ḫḫ-***. This means that Linear A ***ku-ra*** can in principle not only reflect the name of the divine bull ***dḪu-ur-ra***, but also the Hurrian personal name ***Kurra*** (wr. *Ku-ur-ra*), attested at Nuzi, cf. I.J. Gelb, *NPN*, 91, s.v. ***Kurra*** (wr. *Ku-ur-ra*), 1) son of *Pu-ḫi-ia*, brother of *Še-la-pa-i*, JEN 257: 2, 8, 14, 18; - 2) father of *Ut-...-en-ni*, *RA* XXIII 19: 4 (*Utḫap-šenni*?); - 3) father of *Ziqa-a-a*, *RA* XXIII 1: 30; cf. P.M. Purves, *NPN*, 230, s.v. ***kurr, kurra***. Cf. also ***Kur-ra*** from Gasur, HSS X 143: 12; 153 v 2; 155 v 1; 211: 11 and 13; an Anatolian personal name ***Ku-ra*** is cited by Stephens, *PNC*, 52 f.

Th. Richter (*BGH*, 226-227) mentions three homographic verbal roots: ***kur-*** I [Nuzi] 'herstellen' ['to make'] (Wilhelm 1992g, 149), ***kur-*** II [Nuzi] 'mästen' ['to fatten (male animals for slaughter)'] and ***kur-*** III 'erwidern' ['to answer, reply'] (Wilhelm 2000, 201; I. Wegner, *Einführung*, 265) and 'to receive in answer' or 'to reply' (Campbell 2007a, 231, 299, 324; 2008, 276). Adverbial ***kuru***, phonologically /***kuro***/, 'again, in return' may well contain a root ***kur-*** identical with ***kur-*** III. See also Linear A ***ku-ro***.

According to Th. Richter (*VHN*, 450), s.v. ***kur-*** {*ko/ur-*}, it is difficult to assess which of the three homographic verbal roots, mentioned in *BGH*, provides the most plausible interpretation and translation for the Hurrian personal names containing ***kur-***. He mentions ***Kuraiš*** (wr. *ku-ra-i-iš*) from Tigunāni, analysis {*ko/ur=ai=ž*}, typology 1.3.5, lexicon *kur-*; ***fKururze*** from Ašnakkum, reconstruction on the basis of [...-*r*]*u-ur-ze* (*OBTCB* 12 III 30] and *ku-ru-ur-*[...] (*OBTCB* 88 III 25), analysis {*ko/ur=o/u=r=že*}, typology 3.1, lexicon *kururze* (abstract form) (→ *kur-*); and *ku-ru-ri* from Middle-Babylonian Qaṭna (QS 3, 42 Rs. 4), cf. Th. Richter, *VHN*, 180.

Observing all evidence my conclusion is that the combination of ***te-65 = te-zu*** ? (ZA 20.3) with ***ku-ra*** (ZA 20.4) makes identification of the theonyms ***Teš(š)ub*** and ***dḪurra*** most likely on this tablet from Kato Zakro, but interpretation of ***ku-ra*** VIN*b* 5 (AK 2.1-2) is not so easy. On this tablet from Arkhanes it can represent the Hurrian personal name ***Kurra*** (cf. I.J. Gelb, *NPN*, 91) or ***Ḫura*** (wr. ***Ḫu-ú-ra***), JEN 472: 3, 9, 12 (cf. I.J. Gelb, *NPN*, 63) or (since it is the second entry after ***si-da-te***) it can be a toponym ***Ḫurra*** (as the town attested in Hurrian territory) followed by the ideogram VIN*b* and 5 units. It can also be the theonym ***dḪurra*** as at Kato Zakro. No doubt the scribe knew what was meant.

Three sequences of tablet HT 9 still have to be analysed. Of these ***83a-tu*** (HT 9a.2; HT 9b.3) cannot be analysed, since the phonetic value of the rare sign ***83a*** has not yet been identified. Unfortunately the signs following ***pa**$_3$* , (HT 9b.1) are barely visible. W.C. Brice reads: ***da-su-ra*** 11; J. Raison-M. Pope: ***da-su-pi*** 1; L.C. Meijer: *Lx-su-x*[; *GORILA*: ***wa-ja-pi*** [ ], so it seems wise not to attempt to present an analysis.

Linear A ***a-ru*** (HT 9a.5; HT 9b.2) occurs in the lists of personal names on both sides of HT 9, of which ***pa-de***, ***di-na-u***, ***qe-pu***, ***so-di-ra*** and ***ta-i-65*** have been discussed. Only the order of the 7 identical personal names differs on both sides. Since final consonants are not expressed in the scripts of Linear A and B, ***a-ru*** may well be equivalent to the Hurrian personal name ***Arun*** (wr. *a-ru-un*), {*ar=o=n(na)*}, typology 1.3.1.1.2.1, a *ḫabiru* from Tigunāni (*Prisma* III 47), translation 'Give him (the boy)', cf. Th. Richter, *VHN*, 74. The object 'him' is represented by ***=n***, shortened form of ***=nna***. The full Hurrian name ***Arunna*** (wr. *a-ru-un-na*), {*ar=o=nna*}, with ***=nna*** instead of ***=n***, also occurs, as the name of a *ḫabiru* from Tigunāni (*Prisma* I 21), and as ^{f}***Aruna*** (wr. ^{f}*a-ru-ú-na*) 'Give her (the girl)', girl at Nuzi (*AASOR XVI* 66: 3, 4; cf. I.J. Gelb, *NPN*, 36), cf. Th. Richter, *VHN*, 75. Old Hurrian ***Arum*** {*ar=o/u=m*} 'He/She (a *numen*) gave (the child)' is also possible.

Linear A ***a-si-ja-ka*** is the first sequence in the heading of both HT 28a.1 and HT 28b.1. ***A-si-ja-ka*** (HT 28a.1) is followed by the sequences ***u-mi-na-si*** , ***sa-ra**$_2$* and ideograms GRA 20, OLE+*di* 5, FIC 2, VIN*a* 4 (HT 28a.1-3). J.-P. Olivier and L. Godart (*GORILA 1,* 52-53) have changed the order of the *a* and *b* sides of this tablet. If we analyse ***sa-ra**$_2$* as the Hurrian verbal form {*šar=i=(j)a*} 'he/she demands', since Linear A and B ***ra**$_2$* can be identified as ***ria*** or ***lia***, it is reasonable that ***A-si-ja-ka*** (HT 28a.1) is syntactically the subject of {*šar=i=(j)a*}. The first three lines can be interpreted as: ***A-si-ja-ka*** demands / requests (the following commodities) of the lands (***u-mi-na-si***): GRA 20, OLE+*di* 5, FIC 2, VIN*a* 4. L.C. Meijer (*SAHTT,* 133) already considered ***a-si-ja-ka*** a personal name. If it has the same root as masculine ***Aššiae*** (wr. *Aš-ši-a-e*), son of *Zi-ri-ra*, JEN 79: 20 (cf. I.J. Gelb, *NPN*, 37; P.M. Purves, *NPN*, 206, s.v. ***ašš*** and ***aššiae***), the root ***ašš-*** must be distinguished from that of the frequent names with the root ***azz-*** < ***ažd-*** 'woman'. It may then be a combination of ***Aššiae*** with the formant ***-ka***, cf. P.M. Purves, *NPN*, 221, s.v. ***-ka***, where he mentions: "Hurrian. Apparently a formative in *Apparika, Ḫanuka, Ḫapuka, Ḫarika, Ilmika?, Kanika, Kennuka* (or *Zennuka*?), *Kirruka, Kukkuka, Kurruka, Šimika, Šupuka,* (cf. *Šupukiịa*), *Taika, Tauka, Unnuka, Waruka, Wirrika*, and perhaps in *Aštuaka* ? and *Kirka*. etc...".

Incidentally, the latter name is identical with that of the divine sorceress ***Κίρκη*** (*Kirkè*) from the island of *Aia*, where Odysseus stayed for a year, see Homer's *Odyssey* κ, 135 ff: *Αἰαίην δ' ἐς νῆσον ἀφικόμεθ'· ἔνθα δ' ἔναιε Κίρκη ἐυπλόκαμος, δεινὴ θεὸς αὐδήεσσα,..* So Hurrian ***Kirka*** may well be the prototype of the Pre-Greek and epic name.

The suffix ***-ka*** is often used for the diminutive forms in Hurrian. E. Laroche (*GLH*, 22) remarks: "Il est légitime, par exemple, d'interpréter comme ethnique un nom en ***-ḫi/ḫe***, comme diminutif un nom en ***-ka***, comme nom de métier un dérivé en ***-uḫli***, etc." This does not mean that all the names in ***-ka*** are to be regarded as diminutives. If the theonyms of mighty *Ša(v)uška* and the Sungod *Šimiga* (though more often *Šimige* and *Šimegi*), mentioned as *a*-stems by I. Wegner (*Einführung*, 52), contain this suffix ***-ka***, it can hardly be called *diminutive*. *Honorific* is then more appropriate, cf. I. Wegner, *Einführung*, 56.

Linear A ***a-si-ja-ka*** (HT 28a.1; HT 28b.1) may consist of the hypocoristic name ****a-si-ja-*** with *diminutive* or *honorific* suffix ***-ka***. In principle it can be a *diminutive / honorific* form of Linear A ***a-se-ja*** (HT 115a.4) and ***]a̲-se-ja*** (HT 93a.8) from Hagia Triada, since ***i/e*** alternation is common in Hurrian, but a different approach may be preferable, if ***Aštuaka*** at Nuzi is analysed as *{ašt(=i)=u-ag=a}*, consisting of ***ašt(=i)=u*** 'woman' + root ***ag-/akk-*** 'to come up, to appear' + marker of intransitivity ***-a***, translation (indicative) 'The woman appears / appeared' or (imperative) 'Appear , oh woman !'. Linear A ***a-si-ja-ka*** can likewise be analysed as *{azzi(=j)-ag=a}*, 'The woman appeared' or 'Appear, oh woman!', with intr. ***ag-*** 'to appear' and transitional glide ***-j-*** between two vowels.

Incidentally, although most Hurrian names with ***az-*** or ***azz-*** at Nuzi are clearly feminine, the Hurrian name ***Azii̯a*** (wr. *A-zi-ia*) at Nuzi is masculine, since there is an ***Azii̯a*** (son of *A-ki-pa-pu*, JEN 560:49); ***Azii̯a*** (father of *Ak-ku-le-en-ni*, *AASOR 68*: 11), but I.J. Gelb remarks that, according to P.M. Purves, besides *⸢A⸣-zi-ia*, *[Z]a-zi-ia* is also possible; ***Azii̯a*** (father of *At-ta-a-a*, *AASOR XVI* 97:13); ***Azii̯a***, JEN 412:11. There is also an ***Az-zi-ia*** (father of *A-be-ia*, JEN 418:28), whose name is a misreading, since it should according to Gelb be read *<Pa>-az-zi-ia*, cf. I.J. Gelb, *NPN*, 41. If at least some readings of *A-zi-ia* at Nuzi are correct and if the persons bearing that name were male, one may conclude that there might be another root ***az-*** coexisting beside the more common feminine root ***az(z)-***. Both ***^{f}Azai̯a*** (wr. *^{f}A-za-a-a*) and ***^{f}Az(z)ui̯a*** (wr. *^{f}A-zu-ia* and *^{f}Az-zu-ia*) at Nuzi are certainly feminine, cf. I.J. Gelb, *NPN*, 40-41. Compare for Hurrian ***^{f}Az(z)e*** (wr. *^{f}A-a-ze*, *^{f}A-ze*, *^{f}Az-ze*, *^{f}A-az-ze*, *^{f}A-az-ze-e*, *^{f}Az-ze-e*), ***^{f}Azai̯a*** (wr. *^{f}A-za-a-a*), ***^{f}Az(z)ui̯a*** (wr. *^{f}A-zu-ia*, *^{f}Az-zu-ia*) at Nuzi, P.M. Purves, *NPN*, 208, s.v. ***az(z)***, and for ***^{f}Az-zu*** from Ašnakkum (Tall Šaġīr Bāzār), cf. Gadd, *Iraq VII*, 37; cf. Th. Richter, *VHN*, 80-81.

It is not sure that Linear A ***a-se-ja*** (HT 115a.4) and ***]a̲-se-ja*** (HT 93a.8) can be associated with ***^{f}Azija*** (wr. *^{f}a-zi-ia*), name of women at Mari, typology 1.1.1.2.4, lexicon *az*; ***Azija*** (wr. *a-zi-ia*) at Šušarrā (Tall Shemshara); ***Azija*** (wr. *a-zi-ia*) from Alalaḫ IV (D.J. Wiseman, *AT*, 159: 16; cf. A. Draffkorn, *HHA*, 26: **Azi-ya**, wr. *a-zi-ya*, ŠÀ.TAM LUGAL) and ***Azija*** (wr. *a-zi-ia*) at Emar, cf. Th. Richter, *VHN*, 76. ***^{f}Azziya*** at Boğazköy may be a hypocoristic name in ***-ya***, with ***azzi-*** 'woman' as first onomastic element, cf. E. Laroche, *NH*, 50, N° 217: ***^{f}Azziya***, *^{f}Az-zi-ya-aš*, KBo V 7 Vo 28 = MIO 6, 350.

If Linear A ***a-se-ja*** does not contain the Hurrian nominal root ***azz-*** of ***azze*** < ***ažde*** 'woman' and can be equated with ***Azija*** (wr. *a-zi-ia*) from Nuzi and identical names from Šušarrā, Alalaḫ IV and Emar that are used for names of men and contain a different root ***az-*** (cf. I.J. Gelb, *NPN*, 41; Th. Richter, *VHN*, 76, 381, s.v. ***az-*** *{az- ?}*), some verbal roots must be considered as well, ***aš-*** I [Boğ.] 'to eat' or 'to take away' or ***ašš-*** [Boğ.], also ***aš-*** IV(?) [Boğ.], 'être assis (?)', cf. E. Laroche, *GLH*, 59; (intr.) 'to sit', (trans.) 'to set, put, place', corresponding with Urartian ***aš-***.

However, V. Haas - I. Wegner (Beiträge zum hurritischen Lexikon: Die hurritischen Verben *ušš-* "gehen" und *ašš-* "abwaschen, abwischen", in: J. Klinger e. a. (eds.), *Investigationes Anatolicae: Gedenkschrift für Erich Neu* (*StBoT 52*), Wiesbaden 2010, 97-110) now reject the latter meaning of ***ašš-*** and propose '(ab)waschen, wegwischen, abwischen' ['to wash, to cleanse, wipe off'], cf. also I. Wegner, *Einführung*, 86, 250; cf. Th. Richter, *BGH*, 50-52. If Linear A ***a-se-ja*** (HT 115a.4) and ***]a̲-se-ja*** (HT 93a.8) are analysed as *{ašš=e/i=(j)a}* the meaning may be 'He/She (a *numen*) washed (the child)'.

Linear A ***u-mi-na-si*** (HT 28a.1-2) also occurs in the heading of HT 117a.1-2, where it is preceded by ***ma-ka-ri-te* , *ki-ro*** , and followed by 10 personal names each followed by 1 unit, followed by ***ku-ro*** 10 (HT 117a.6).

Linear A ***u-mi-na-si*** is in both cases a clear Hurrian grammatical form that may well be interpreted as Hurrian ***um(m)innaši***, plural genitive of Hurrian ***umini*** 'land', a word that very frequently occurs in the Tušratta letter and elsewhere. The form ***uminni*** (< **umin(i)-ni*) means 'the land', with the suffix for the so-called singular definite article ***-ni***, whereas the form ***uminna*** (< **umin(i)-na*) means 'the lands', with the suffix for the so-called plural definite article ***-na***, to which (according to older literature) the plural genitive suffix ***-še/ši*** was attached (cf. ***umminnaši*** IBoT II 39 Vo 5; KUB XXVII 18, 6; XXXII 61, 7; alphabetic Ugaritic ***umnž*** genitive or dative, *Ugar.V*, 517 ff.; cf. also E. Laroche, *GLH*, 281-282, s.v. ***umini*** 'pays'). The fact that on HT 28, HT 117 and HT 15 quantities of agricultural commodities are counted and that the quantities of grain mentioned on HT 15 after ***u-mina-si*** are substantial (684 + 570), corroborates the interpretation "of the lands".

E. Laroche, *GLH,* 281, remarks: "***umini*** 'pays'. Lecture du sum. KUR. Sens déjà entrevu par Jensen, *ZA 5,* 190. Équation KUR.KUR^{meš}*-na* = *u(m)minna* établie par von Brandenstein, KUB XXVII p. III. Certains comparent oug. *ebani,* même sens. Les thèmes *umini* 'pays' et *uminni* 'le pays' devraient, en principe, répondre aux graphies *-n- et -nn-*; en fait, *umi(n)ni* et *umi(n)na* s'échangent librement à Boğ. et au Mit. Graphies: KUR *u-u-mi-i-(in)-ni;* Bo. *u-mi-ni, um-mi-ni,* KUR*-ni*, KUR*-mi-ni*, KUR. KUR^{meš}*-ni/na*; RS alph. *Umn.*"

J.G.P. Best, *Talanta 13 (1981),* Middelie 1982, 44, mentions: "Aber in den Haghia Triada-Texten, genau so wie in den ugaritischen, reihen sich an churritische Personennamen churritische Dativendungen auf ***-ti*** an und in der Landwirtschaft wird möglicherweise der churritische Terminus technicus ***u-mi-na-si*** 'land' verwendet." Best does not seem to be aware of the fact that we are dealing here with a typical Hurrian grammatical form with the suffix of the so-called plural definite article and that of the plural genitive form, showing the agglutinative features of Hurrian morphology. Apparently he has forgotten to refer to my paper, read to the London Mycenaean Seminar of 28 May 1980, 6 and note 28, where I have explained this form. The full text of that paper could at the time be obtained from the Secretary of the London Institute of Classical Studies. J.G.P. Best received a copy. An abstract appeared in the *Bulletin of the Institute of Classical Studies 28 (1981)*, 163.

Another point of criticism is Best's erroneous statement about alleged "*churritische Dativendungen auf -ti, die sich an churritische Personennamen anreihen.*" Suffixes designating the Hurrian dative forms are ***-wa*** for the singular and ***-ša*** for the plural forms, respectively, according to E. Laroche, *GLH*, § 11, *Le nom.* In Hurrian personal names ***-te*** (sometimes ***-ti***) is either a shortened form of ***-tešup*** and ***-te̯a*** as final element (cf. e.g. *Al-ki-te, Eḫ-li-te, Ḫu-i-te, Ḫu-i-ti, Ši-il-wa-te*) or perhaps the optional allomorphic enclitic personal pronoun ***-tti*** (instead of ***-tta***) marking the 1st person singular in 'one-word' verbal personal names, indicating the object of the transitive verb or the subject of the intransitive verb.

E. A. Speiser, F.W. Bush, E. Laroche and many others (myself included) used to observe a distinction between the Hurrian singular genitive suffix in ***-we/-wi*** and the plural genitive suffix in ***-še/-ši***, as well as between the Hurrian singular dative suffix in ***-wa*** and the plural dative suffix in ***-ša***.

However, on the basis of evidence, especially from Nuzi, the views on these suffixes have changed in more recent literature, since the ***-š-*** in ***-še/-ši*** (as well as in the plural dative ***-ša***) is no longer regarded as belonging to the plural genitive (c.q. dative) suffix, but as part of the pluralizing suffix ***-aš-***, that is followed by the genitive suffix ***-we/-wi*** (c.q. dative suffix ***-wa***), with subsequent absorption of ***-w-*** in ***-we/i***, c.q. ***-wa***. Analysis: ***=aš=*** (pluralizer) + ***we/wi*** (genitive suffix) or ***wa*** (dative suffix), cf. I. Wegner, *Einführung in die hurritische Sprache*, Wiesbaden 2007[2], 65, (Tafel 1), 75, (Tafel 2), 80 (Tafel 3): plural genitive ***=aš=ve*** (only at Nuzi) > ***=aše*** (elsewhere); (plural dative) ***=aš=va*** > ***=aša***. I. Wegner and her predecessors normalize ***w/p*** to voiced ***v*** and ***ww/pp*** to voiceless ***f***.

I have maintained transliteration of syllabic signs with ***w-*** for Linear A, since it seems preferable to emphasize the continuity from Linear A to Linear B. Moreover, Linear A and B do not use double writing of consonants as a tool for indicating voicelessness like cuneiform does.

It is assumed that for forms like the Hurrian plural genitive ***umminnaši*** the ***-a-*** of the suffix of the so-called plural definite article ***-na-*** is absorbed, if it is followed by the pluralizing suffix ***=aš=***. The ***-w-***, possibly */v/*, in ***=aš=we/i*** is absorbed as well > ***=aš=(w)e/i*** > ***=aš=e/i***.

The translation of ***umminnaši*** 'of the lands' did not change since Speiser, Bush and Laroche, but the whole structure of the chain of suffixes has been extended and improved considerably and has become more coherent as well.

It may be useful to refer to the sequences ***u-69-si*** (HT 15.1; HT 140.1; HT 140.2), which may well represent ***u-mina-si***. This identification should perhaps be followed by a question mark. Although it is probable that special signs with a complex value were not only used in Linear B, but also in Linear A, a bisyllabic value would be exceptional.

Evidence in support of the value ***mina*** for sign ***69***, which may represent a crescent moon and may be compared with Linear B sign ****34*** (LUNA ?), is modest, but attractive. An equation of ***u-69-si*** (HT 15.1, HT 140.1, HT 140.2) with ***u-mina-si*** is relevant for two reasons: I) the position of ***u-69-si*** in the heading of the tablets corresponds with that of ***u-mi-na-si*** (HT 28a.1-2; HT 117a.1-2); II) the value ***mina*** for sign ***69*** would provide another alternation within Linear A: ***]pi-mi-na-te*** (AP Z 2a.2) and ***pi-69-te*** (HT 116a.4), if we take sign ***41*** as the equivalent to sign ***56a*** = ***pi*** following the *communis opinio* on this sign, cf. P.G. van Soesbergen, *The historical significance of onomastic data from Linear A and B texts*, Mycenaean Seminar, London Institute of Classical Studies, 28th May 1980, 20, note 28. Compare also A. Furumark, *Linear A und die altkretische Sprache; Entzifferung und Deutung,* lecture held at the Deutsches Arch. Inst. in Berlin, 10 July 1956, 24 (mimeographed), and D.W. Packard, *Minoan Linear A*, Berkeley - Los Angeles - London, 1974, 107.

Linear A ***sa-ra₂*** (possibly HT 11b.1; possibly HT 15.5; HT 18.2; HT 28a.2; HT 28b.3; HT 30+77.1; HT 32.1; HT 33.1; HT 34.1; HT 56.1: ***<u>sa-ra₂</u>***[; HT 90.1; HT 94a.3; HT 97b.2: ***sa-<u>ra₂</u>***; HT 99a.1; HT 100.4; HT 101.3; HT 102.1; HT 114a.1-2; HT 121.2; HT 125a.4) is certainly one of the most frequent sequences in Linear A.

Sign ***ra₂*** = ***ria / lia*** or ***rya / lya*** is one of the special signs in Linear B (sign ****76***), which corresponds graphically (and probably also phonetically) exactly with Linear A sign ***58***.

Consequently Linear A **sa-ra**$_2$ most likely reflects **sa-ria** (or theoretically **sa-lia**) and replaces a form that would otherwise be written with three syllabic signs, either ***sa-ri-ja*** or ***sa-ri-a***. The scribes were no doubt motivated to use the shortest sequences in order to save writing space on the tablets. This economic motive was most effective in case of frequently used words. As mentioned before, ***sa-ra***$_2$ (HT 28a.2) probably represents the Hurrian verbal form ***šar=i=a*** 'he/she demands, requests, wishes', 3rd person singular indicative of the transitive verbal root ***šar-*** 'to demand, request, wish'. I. Wegner (*Einführung*, 93, Table 4: *The order of suffixes of the indicative of the transitive-ergative, positive verb*), explains the form ***šar=i=a*** as ***šar-*** (position 1: root [+ root-extension, if any]) + ***-i-*** (position 5: marker of transitivity, only in the 2nd and 3rd person singular of the present tense) + ***-a*** (position 7: marker of the subject of action, 3rd person singular).

It is likely that this verbal form occurs especially in the heading of Linear A tablets (as in HT 28a.2) and expresses the ruler's or an official's order, request or demand to deliver certain commodities, persons or livestock to the palace, to a department of the palace or to a place dependent on the palace. Most likely ***sa-ra***$_2$ (HT 28b.3) repeats the same verbal form ***šar=i=a*** as was used on the *a*-side of the same tablet, especially since the subject of the verb, ***a-si-ja-ka*** (HT 28a.1), is also repeated (HT 28b.1) on the *b*-side.

sa-ra$_2$ (HT 11b.1) may well occur as second sequence in the heading of the tablet, if the worn first sign is indeed ***sa-*** as read by W.C. Brice and myself and considered 'pas entierement impossible' ['not entirely impossible'] by *GORILA 1*.

HT 11b.1 reads: **]de-pa**$_3$ **, sa-ra**$_2$ **, , .** The first sign of the first sequence **]de-pa**$_3$ is probably missing, because the left top corner of the *b*-side (= right top corner of the *a*-side) is broken off. Raison-Pope and I read **]de-pa**$_3$. *GORILA* reads ***-nu*** (sign with 2 horizontal strokes) instead of ***-pa***$_3$ (sign with 3 horizontal strokes). If ***sa-ra***$_2$ can be identified with the Hurrian verbal form ***šar=i=a*** 'he / she demands, requests, wishes', the incomplete **]de-pa**$_3$ is probably the subject of this transitive verb and may well be the personal name (in the ergative case) of the person who demands the delivery of the goods summed up in the following lines 2 - 6. The final ***-š*** of the ergative singular is not expressed in Linear A (as in Linear B). For the scribe this was probably no problem, because he no doubt knew that the subject of a transitive verb was in the *ergative* case and the object in the *absolutive*. The *b*-side of this tablet apparently has no clear relation with the *a*-side, since it offers (after the heading) a complete summation of a special category of objects adding up CAPSUS ROTA 40 ROTA 30 ROTA 50 ***si-do-na*** (or: ***sa-do-na***) ROTA 30 ***sa-qe-ri*** , ROTA 30 (HT 11b.2-5), which corresponds exactly with the total of 180 following ***ku-ro*** (HT 11b.5-6).

sa-ra$_2$ (possibly HT 15.5): L.C. Meijer (1982), 9, 91-92, read traces of ***sa-ra***$_2$, whereas all other editors read only erased signs of a surface palimpsest [[vestigia]], cf. *Minoan Linear A*, Vol. II: *Corpus of transliterated Linear A texts*, Part 1: HT 15.5.

sa-ra$_2$ (HT 18.2). Tablet HT 18 is complete, but broken into 4 pieces. The surface is worn. The contents are as follows:

HT 18.1-2: *pa-se* GRA+*qe* 20 OLE+*ki* 2 *67* 3.

HT 18.2-3: *sa-ra*$_2$ GRA 10 FIC 10

HT 18.4-5: vacant

Sign *67* is probably the ideogram of an (as yet) unidentified agricultural commodity. It is quite conceivable that both ***pa-se*** and ***sa-ra₂*** are verbal forms.

I now consider this interpretation preferable, since the meaning of these verbal forms makes sense in view of the bureaucratic context. Since double consonants (indicating voicelessness) in cuneiform are expressed by single writing in Linear A (as in Linear B), Linear A ***pa-se*** can reflect Hurrian ***pašš=e/i*** 'send !' or 'bring in !' (2nd pers. sing. of the *imperative*), consisting of ***pašš-*** (position 1: root) + ***-i/e*** (marker of the *iussive* 2nd person singular) + ***-Ø***, because the *imperative* misses its own marker, whereas e.g. the 1st person singular has the marker ***-l+e*** (voluntative) and the 3rd person singular the marker ***-en***, cf. I. Wegner, *Einführung*, 103, Table 9: *The order of suffixes of the positive iussive*. Th. Richter (*VHN*, 481-482): ***paš-/paz***, {*faž*-(?)}, ***pazz-*** 'to bring in'.

The Hurrian root ***pašš-*** was already correctly identified in 1890 by Peter Jensen (Vorstudien zur Entzifferung des Mitanni, *ZA V*, 197) as 'senden' ['to send'] on the basis of the related form ***paššitḫe*** 'envoy, messenger' in the Tušratta letter, cf. P.M. Purves, *NPN*, 243, s.v. ***pašš***. Th. Richter (*BGH*, 303-304), s.v. ***p/wašš-*** I [Boğ.; Mitt.; PN] 'schicken'; and Th. Richter (*VHN*, 482), s.v. ***paššitḫe***, analysed as {*pašš=id=ġe*} 'Bote, Gesandter', equivalent to Akkadian ***mār šipri***.

If ***pa-se*** (HT 18.1) is a verbal form, ***sa-ra₂*** (HT 18.2) is also likely to be identified with the Hurrian verbal form ***šar=i=a*** 'he/she demands, requests, wishes', since it takes virtually the same position as ***pa-se***. The commodities GRA+*qe* 20 OLE+*ki* 2 *67* 3, following ***pa-se***, as well as GRA 10 FIC 10, following ***sa-ra₂***, are in that case the object of these verbal forms. A problem with reading Linear A in the 21st century is that we do not know for certain whether Linear A ***pa-se*** reflects cuneiform ***paše*** or ***pašše*** and whether Linear A ***sa-ra₂*** always reflects cuneiform ***šar=i=a*** or maybe on some tablets ***šarri-ya***.

In the 2016 edition of *Minoan Linear A*, Vol. I, Part I - II, the possibility that both ***pa-se*** (HT 18.1) and ***sa-ra₂*** (HT 18.2) might be either toponyms or personal names, was also discussed. My arguments were of a more general character and were based on the position of the sequences. The prominent position of ***pa-se*** in the heading could point to its function as a toponym. Also the fact that it is followed by the GRANUM and OLEUM ideograms may corroborate this view, since we have observed that toponyms in the Linear B tablets from Knossos are often followed by the ideograms for GRANUM or HORDEUM and/or those of other agricultural commodities.

Etymologically ***pa-se*** could be explained as Hurrian ***paši*** 'a part of the body', 'une partie du corps', peut-être 'oeil', cf. E. Laroche, *GLH*, 197, s.v. ***paši***, sg. nom. *pa-a-ši*, KUB XXIX 8 IV 24; KUB XXVII 23 III 8; XXXII 24+ II 28; 30, 7. Absolutive (with the suffix ***-ni*** of so-called definite article) *pa-a-ši-e-ni* 'the eye', KUB XLVII 96 Ro 4. According to Hurrian orthography the ending *-ši-e-ni* in *pa-a-ši-e-ni* indicates that the vowel of sign ***-ši-*** should be read as ***-e-***. If ***pa-se*** is a toponym in Linear A, it is not known as such from the Linear B texts from Knossos, which might point to the possibility that it might indicate a local place in the vicinity of Hagia Triada itself. My argument was that semantically a parallel may be provided by the antiquated use of the Dutch word 'oog' = 'eye', which can also be used in the sense of 'island', as is shown in names such as *Schiermonnikoog, Rottumeroog*, two islands in the north of the Netherlands.

Also the village *Callantsoog* on the coast of the North Sea, where I have lived for five years, has been an island during the Middle Ages, cf. P.G. van Soesbergen, *Minoan Linear A*, Vol. I, Part I, 2016, 216-218, 220.

However, M. Salvini, 'Un texte hourrite nommant Zimrilim', *Revue d'assyriologie et d'archéologie orientale 82 (1988)*, 59-69 (especially 63), had his doubts about the meaning 'eye': "la possibilité ne paraît pas s'accorder avec les attestations de Meskéné." and "Le thème *pazi/a* est bien attesté dans les textes hourrites de Meskéné/Emar, où il est souvent précédé du logogramme URU: *pa-za, pa-za-ma, pa-za-la-an, pa-za-al-na, pa-zi-na, pa-zi-da, pa-zi-da-ma, pa-zi-di-ma*." Cf. Th. Richter, *BGH*, 303, s.v. ***paz-*** II [Boğ.; Mari (?); Mitt.; Nuzi (?)] and ***pazi*** (?) [Emar, Nuzi (?)]. Incidentally, it is interesting that the Sumerogram URU designates 'town, city'. The real meaning of ***paši*** has become clear through a passage in *Mari-letter 7+6* (lines 9'-11'), of which I present M. Salvini's transliteration in *RA 82 (1988)*, 6:

9': *še-na-ar-di-ra u[r-ḫ]i-ni-en a-lu-uk-ku ti-zi-in-ni-en*

10': *pa-li pa-z[i-n]i ti-ip-ša-ri ḫi-in-zu-ru-úš ú-gu-u[l-ga-ri* ?]

11': ⌜*e*⌝*-en-na* .... etc.

These lines have been analysed morphologically, translated and commented by I. Wegner, *Einführung in die hurritische Sprache*, Wiesbaden 2007[2], 236-237:

9': *šen(a)=arde=ra urḫi=ne=n al=o=kk=o tiš(a)=i=nni=n*

10': *pali paš(i)=i?=ne tip=šari ḫinzur(i)=uš ugul*[*=ugar?=i?*]

11': *en(i)=na* .... etc.

I translate Ilse Wegner's translation and commentary into English:

9': With the brotherhood he does not speak in a truthful way from his heart.

10': False / unfaithful is the word from his mouth, as an apple-tree he bows/kneels

11': [towards] the gods .....

Comment ad 9': *šen(a)-* 'brother' + *arde* collective suffix + *ra* comitative suffix sing. *urḫi-* 'true' + *ni* + *n*. The formants cannot be explained completely. Segmentation of adverbial *-n(n)i* + *n(na)* is likely. Adverbial, respectively associative, is normally *-nni*, but in the Hurrian Mari-texts the phonematic double writing of intervocalic consonants is often not expressed (see also I. Wegner, *Einführung*, 43 f.).

al(u)- 'say, speak' + *o* intransitive (strictly *-a*) + *kk* suffix for negation of intransitive verbs + *o* intr. (strictly *-a*), see I. Wegner, *Einführung*, 97 f.

tiš(a)- 'heart' + *i* possessive pronoun 3rd person sing. + *nni* adverbial ? + *n(e)* abl.-instr. The word *tiša* is in the Mari-orthography usually written with *z*-signs, e.g. *ti-za-da* 'to the heart' (line 8').

Comment ad 10': *pali* 'false' is the nominal predicate in the *absolute* case. See for sentences with a nominal predicate, that can be either in the *essive -a* or in the *absolutive*, (M. Giorgieri, 'Die hurritische Fassung des Ullikummi-Lieds und ihre hethitische Parallele', in: G. Wilhelm (ed.), *Akten des IV. Internationalen Kongresses für Hethitologie*, Würzburg, 4.-8. October 1999, Studien zu den Boğazköy-Texten 45, Wiesbaden 2001, 145 with note 52.

paz(i) (Mari-orthography) otherwise *paši* 'mouth' + *i* possessive pronoun 3rd person singular + *ne* ablative-instrumental.

tipšari < *tive=šari* 'word' absolutive corresponding with *pali*.

ḫinzur(i) ‘apple-tree’ + *uš* equative.
ugul- ‘to bend, bow, kneel’ + [*ugar* +*i*], the completion of the verbal form is uncertain. A verb *ugul=gar=i* is compared with Hittite *kattan ḫališke-* ‘to kneel repeatedly’ in the Hurrian-Hittite bilingual ***Kirenze*** (KBo 32: 15 Rs. IV 10). The segment *-gar-* possibly reflects the abbreviated suffix of reciprocity *-ugar-*.

Comment ad 11': *en(i)=na* ‘the Gods’ absolutive plural. Since the reading and meaning of the next word are uncertain, it is not clear, whether *enna* is the beginning of a new sentence in line 11' or belongs to the preceding syntagma of line 10'.

In my view the combination of *paš(i)=i ?=ne tip=šari* ‘the word from his mouth’ shows clearly that ***paše/i*** means ‘mouth’ (not ‘eye’). Consequently, my arguments in the 2016 edition of *Minoan Linear A*, Vol. I, based on the previous interpretation of Hurrian ***paše/i*** ‘eye †’, are no longer valid.

However, if Linear A ***pa-se*** (HT 18.1) is Hurrian ***paše/i*** ‘mouth’ and if it is at the same time the designation of a toponym, a place-name like *Portsmouth* might provide a good parallel. The *Oxford Dictionary of British Place Names* gives the Anglo-Saxon name “*Portesmūða*” as late as the 9th century, meaning “mouth [of the harbour called] Portus” (from Latin).

Comparing the sequence ***pa-se*** in HT 18.1 and HT 27+48b.4, we see that ***pa-se*** (HT 18.1) is followed by GRA+*qe* 20, OLE+*ki* 2 and *67* 3, but ***pa-se*** (HT 27+HT 48b.4) is followed by VIN+*wa*, *sa* 4, *re* 70, VINa GRA , *sa* 4, *re*[ ]40.

It is therefore excluded that it is a designation of one of these commodities. Since ***pa-se*** (HT 18.1) takes approximately the same position as ***sa-ra₂*** (HT 18.2) followed by the ideograms GRA and FIC, it probably has the same function as ***sa-ra₂***. So both ***pa-se*** (HT 18.1) and ***sa-ra₂*** (HT 18.2) are either verbal forms or anthroponyms or toponyms, c.q. topographic designations. The question is: Which of these categories is most likely ?

The sequence ***sa-ra₂*** occurs in a lot of HT texts as the sequence preceding either the GRANUM ideogram as in HT 18.2; HT 28a.2; HT 34.1; HT 90.1; HT 93a.4; HT 101.3; HT 102.1; HT 114a.1-2; HT 121.2; HT 125a.4, or the HORDEUM ‘barley’ ideogram as in HT 30+77.1; HT 94+154+Fr.a.3; HT 99a.1; HT 100.4; HT 130.2. Sometimes ***sa-ra₂*** is followed by the ideograms of more commodities as e.g. in HT 18.2; HT 28a.2; HT 28b.3; HT 30+77.1; HT 32.1; HT 33.1; (possibly) HT 49a.1; HT 90.1; HT 99a.1; HT 94+154+Fr.a.3; HT 100.4; HT 101.3; HT 114a.1-2; HT 121.2; HT 125a.4.

This may well be an argument that ***sa-ra₂*** could represent in such cases a toponym or topographical designation, since it has been observed that the GRANUM and HORDEUM ideograms in the Knossos Linear B texts are also frequently preceded by a toponym, cf. for the discussion on ***ka-pa*** GRA[(KN E 71) in Linear B. Cf. also Linear B ***e-ti-wa*** , HORD T 1, *NI* V 3 (KN Fs 19.1) and ***ka-u-da***, HORD , T 1 [(KN Fs 21.1, *et alibi*), see J. Chadwick - L. Godart - J.T. Killen - J.-P. Olivier - A. Sacconi - I.A. Sakellarakis, *Corpus of Mycenaean Inscriptions from Knossos*, Volume I (1-1063), *Incunabula Graeca Vol. LXXXVIII*, Cambridge, London, New York, New Rochelle, Melbourne, Sydney, Roma 1986. N.B. On page X of the preface to this *Corpus* John Chadwick mentions: “Phonetic signs used as ideograms are printed in *ITALIC CAPITALS*.” This means that *NI* represents the ideogram for figs that is in other editions indicated by FIC (abbreviation of FICUS).

The context should always be taken into account. If ***sa-ra₂*** is used at the beginning of a text, there is a very good chance that it signifies the verbal form ***šar=i=a*** 'he/she demands, requests, wishes', for that is exactly the position where such a form is to be expected in the bureaucratic context. But it is important to realize that ***sa-ra₂*** may in other texts reflect a personal name or a toponym or topographical designation, cf. e.g. ***Sariya*** KBo V 6 I 12 = *JCS 10*, 90, toponym, cf. E. Laroche, *NH*, 278, sub 'Rivières et sources'. If the toponym or topographical designation is derived from Hurrian ***šarri*** '(divine) king' or 'King of Gods' and if its meaning is e.g. 'royal palace', an orthography with double writing of ***-rr-*** would be expected in cuneiform.

Consequently, I should have liked to propose that Linear A ***sa-ra₂*** will be analysed as ***šar=i=a***, if its usage as a verbal form is most likely, and that it will be analysed as ***Šarri=ya***, if it is regarded as a proper name, whether toponym or anthroponym, with the theophorous element ***šarri*** 'King of Gods'. Unfortunately this distinction is not altogether evident, since Th. Richter (*VHN*, 584 ff.) has made it quite clear that verbal forms such as ***šar=i=a*** can be used as 'one-word' personal names as well.

Particularly if Linear A ***sa-ra₂*** is mentioned in a list of personal names, identification as a personal name will be feasible. The personal name can then be analysed as a 'one-word' personal name ***Šarii̯a***, analysis {*šar=i=(y)a*}, translation 'He/She (scil. a *numen*) wishes (the child)' or as a hypocoristic personal name ***Šarrii̯a***, analysed as {*šarr=i=ya*}, translation 'He (e.g. *Tešub*) is King of Gods', cf. the Hurrian name ***Šarrii̯a*** (wr. *Šar-ri-ia*, LUGAL^{ri}*-ia* = *Šarri*^{ri}*-a*), 10 times attested at Nuzi, cf. I.J. Gelb, *NPN*, 125. Names such as ***Šar-Tešup*** (attested 21 times at Nuzi) and ***Šar-Tei̯a*** (attested 8 times) may be translated as an *imperative* 'Wish (the child), oh Tešub !', and ***Šar-Tilla*** (attested 4 times at Nuzi) may be translated as 'Wish (the child), oh Tilla !'. ***Šarrii̯a*** may be a hypocoristic personal name based on any theophorous 'sentence name', in which ***šarri*** is an onomastic element.

Theoretically the orthographic conventions may even yield a fourth interpretation of ***sa-ra₂***. Since a final consonant is not expressed in Linear A and B, it is feasible that Linear A ***sa-ra₂*** occasionally reflects Hurrian cuneiform ***šar-ri-ya-aš*** 'their king', IBoT II 39 Ro 48, Vo 4; KBo VIII 145, 6; KUB XXXII 19 III 8, cf. E. Laroche, *GLH*, 217, s.v. ***šarri*** 'roi' and ***šar-ri-ya-aš*** 'leur roi'. The normalized form ***šarr(i)=i=y=aš*** can be analysed as: ***šarr(i)*** (root) + ***-i-*** (suffix of possessive pronoun 3rd person sing.) + ***-y-*** (transitional semivowel between two vowels) + ***aš*** (pluralizing suffix). Compare for the transitional semivowel ***y*** between two vowels also the discussion on Linear A ***a-ta-i-jo-wa-ja***.

P M. Purves, *NPN*, 251-252, s.v. ***šarri***. "Hurrian. Probably a divine epithet; cf. perhaps ***šar-*** (1). Cf. ***šar-ra***, KUB XXVII 38 iv 19 and 21 (etc.)... Hurrian origin, rather than associated with Akkadian ***šarru***, 'king', is claimed by Weidner in *BKS VIII (1923),* 13, n. 7 and by Gustavs in *ZA N.F. II (1925)*, 298 and *MAOG X 3 (1937)*, 50f.; latter derives ***šarri*** from Hurrian ***šar***, 'befehlen, fordern'. (etc.)." Most modern scholars now agree that Hurrian ***šarri*** is eventually a loan-word from Akkadian ***šarrum*** '(divine) king', though the date of borrowing is not clear, cf. Th. Richter, *BGH*, 356, s.v. ***šarri*** I [*passim*]. The meaning is not contested, also because of the reading of the Sumerogram LUGAL in the names in -LUGAL*-ri* instead of the onomastic element ***-šarri***, cf. E. Laroche, *GLH*, 217, s.v. ***šarri*** 'roi'.

E. Laroche (*NH,* 158) mentions the personal name ***Sariya*** at Boğazköy: no.1117. Gén. **^{m}*Ša-ri-ya-aš*, KBo X 10 IV 13. The genitive ^{m}*Ša-ri-ya-aš* at Boğazköy, mentioned by Laroche, is a genitive in Hittite, although the name itself may originally be Hurrian.

****Šar-ri-ya*** occurs at Alalaḫ as a personal name in level VII on AT *34,19, cf. A. Draffkorn, *HHA*, 141. A. Draffkorn indicates all texts from the older level VII (ca. 1640 B.C.) with * to distinguish them from the younger level IV (ca. 1490 B.C.

Th. Richter (*VHN*, 248-250) mentions the names ***Šarraja*** and ***Šarrija*** together (wr. (1) *Šar-ra-ia*, (2) *Šar-ra-a-ia*, (3) *Šàr-ra-a-ia*, (4) *Ša-ar-ra-a*, (5) *Šar-ri-ia*, (6) *Šàr-ri-ia*) from Mari, Ašnakkum, Qaṭṭarā, Šuššarā and Tuttul, analysis (1-4) {*šarr=a=ja*}; (5-6) {*šarr=i=ja*}, typology 1.1.1.3.4, lexicon *šarr-*. In texts from Mari and Qaṭṭarā the King of Razamā^{KI} is called ***Šarraja*** and ***Šarrija***, even partly in the same text. Some scholars have explained the form ***Šarraja*** as Akkadian, e.g. Rasmussen, 1981, 132, 380 (*šarrum* with °*=aya*, °*=ya*, respectively). If both forms are Hurrian, one may interpret ***Šarrija*** as 'He is a (divine) King' and ***Šarraja*** as 'He is like a (divine) King', with ***šarr=a*** (< *šarr(=i)=a*) as the *essive* form in ***-a***, instead of *absolutive* ***šarr=i*** + hypocoristic ***-ya***.

If ***sa-ra₂*** (HT 18.2) could be a personal name such as ****Šar-ri-ya*** at Alalaḫ VII and ***Šarri̯a*** at Nuzi or as ***Sariya*** at Boğazköy, it is also necessary to investigate, whether ***pa-se*** (HT 18.1) might reflect a personal name as well.

I.J. Gelb, *NPN*, 112, mentions the Hurrian personal name ***Pazi*** (wr. *Pa-zi-i*), as father of *Ṭâb-ri-ki-im-šu* from Nuzi. Cognate names such as ***Pazaku*** (wr. *Pa-za-ku*); ***Pazazi*** (wr. *Pa-za-a-zi, Ba-za-zi, Pa-za-zi*); ***Pazi̯a*** (wr. *Pa-zi-ia*); ***Pazzi̯a*** (wr. *Pa-az-zi-ia*); ***Paššii̯a*** (wr. *Pa-aš-ši-ia*), probably hypocoristic for ***Pašši-p-tilla*** (wr. *Pa-aš-ši-til-la, Ba-aš-ši-til-la, Pa-aš-ši-ip-til-la*), for a man of each name is son of ***Pula-ḫali***; ^{f}***Paššišše*** (wr. ^{f}*Pa-aš-ši-iš-še*) are attested at Nuzi as well, cf. also P.M. Purves, *NPN*, 243-244, s.v. ***pašš-*** 'to send', ***paz-*** and ***pazz-***.

The *transitive* meaning of the root was recognized before the *intransitive*. Th. Richter (*BGH*, 302-304), s.v. ***w/paš-*** I [*passim*] *intr.* 'to come in, to enter' (corresponds with Hittite ***andan uwa-***) and *trans.* 'to bring in, to introduce'; s.v. ***p/wašš-*** [Boğ.; Mitt.; PN] 'to send' (corresponding with ***šapâru*** in Akkadian letters from Mitanni, cf. E. Laroche, *GLH*, 197, s.v. ***pašš-***).

According to Th. Richter, *VHN*, 482, s.v. ***paš-/paz-*** {*faž*}, ***pazz-***, the translation 'to enter' for *intr.* {*faž*} is established by the rendering with Hittite ***andan uwa-*** in the bilingual ***kirenze***, by comparisons with Sumerian KU₄ and Akkadian ***erēbu*** in a vocabulary from Ugarit and again with Akkadian ***erēbu*** in a glossary from Qaṭna. Identification of the root ***paz-*** as Hurrian is corroborated by the personal names ***Pa-za-ku*** at Nuzi and ***Pa-za-ka*** at Emar, in which the suffixes ***-ku*** and ***-ka*** represent the morpheme indicating the negation in intransitive verbal forms.

Accordingly the Linear A personal name ***pa-za-ku*** [(ZA 6b.4) at Kato Zakro and the Hurrian names ***Pa-za-ku*** at Nuzi and ***Pa-za-ka*** at Emar can be translated as a *prohibitive* or *apotropaeic* (Greek *ἀποτρόπαιος, ἀποτρέπω*) form 'Do not enter (oh evil *numen*) !'.

According to Th. Richter it is still not completely certain, how ***paz-*** and ***pazz-*** relate to each other, but the geographical spread of personal names with the element ***pazz-*** as well as the context of occurrences make a Hurrian root likely.

The Hurrian-Hittite bilingual *Kirenze* provides a *figura etymologica* ***pa-az-zu-ú-wa pa-az-za*** (KBo 32, 20 Vs I 3), from which E. Neu, *Das hurritische Epos der Freilassung I. Untersuchungen zu einem hurritisch-hethitischen Textensemble aus Ḫattuša*, Studien zu den Boğazköy-Texten (StBoT) 32, Wiesbaden 1996, 441, isolates an (also) transitive usage of the root ***pazz-*** as well as an absolutive ****pazza***, cf. also Th. Richter, *BGH*, 304.

Th. Richter, *VHN* I, 482, mentions the following Hurrian names from Mari: ***ᶠPašaja***, ***Pazi***, ***ᶠPaš-tari***, ***ᶠPazuja***, ***ᶠ⁽?⁾Pazu-ki*** with the root {*faž-*(?)} according to his phonological analysis, and ***Pazza***, to which possibly also ***Pazue*** belongs, with the root {*fazz-*(?)}.

Th. Richter, *ibidem*, 227-228: ***ᶠPašaja*** (wr. *ba-ša-ja*), analysis {*faž-*(?)=*a*=*ja*}, (1) member of the palace (mí é-kál-lim), *Archives Royales de Mari (= ARM) 8*, 88: 12; (2) female worker under *Tatūr-mātum*, J.M Durand - J. Margueron (eds.), *Mari. Annales de recherches interdisciplinaires, Paris (= MARI) 8*, 651 IV 35; (3) female slave of *Aya-turaja* M. 6342a+IV 15; ***Pazi*** (wr. *pa-zi, ba-zi*), analysis{*faž-*(?)=*i*} 'bring (the boy) in !' (1) Tušḫ[umᴷᴵ](?): *ARM 27*, 151: 66 (2); (2) Mari 7744 IV 11. Also Alalaḫ IV: *pa-zi*, D.J. Wiseman, *The Alalakh Tablets (= AT)*, London 1953, 69; A. Draffkorn, *HHA*, 47. Richter also mentions *ba(?)-zi(?)* at Assur and *pa-za-ku, pa/ba-(a-)zi(-i), pa-zi-ia* at Nuzi, *ba-zu* at Assur, *pa-zu* at Emar, *ba-zi-ia* at Kaniš; ***ᶠPaš-tari*** (wr. *pa-aš-ta-ar-e*), analysis {*faž-*(?)*tari*} 'the fire entered' name of female weaver at Mari, Durand - Margueron, *MARI 8*, 653 VI 48'; J.M. Sasson, Ḫurrians and Ḫurrian naames in the Mari texts, *UF 6 (1974)*, 373, cf. *ᶠwa-še-el-li* at Nuzi (*NPN*, 173). ***Pazue***, analysis {*paž(i)*(?)=*ve*}, 'the (boy) of *Pazi*', Mari, Ḫatnumᴷᴵ: Mari 15078, see J.M. Durand, *Archives épistolaires de Mari I/1, ARM 26/1*, 1988, 294 (discussion: either genitive of *pazi* (see *BGH*, 303) or of *paši* 'mouth'. ***ᶠPazuja*** (wr. *pa-zu-ja*), analysis {*faž-*(?)=*o*=*ja*} 'he/she (scil. a *numen*) brought (the girl) in', Mari, *Eqlum-bana*ᴷᴵ, house of *Tašpuš-ulme*: Mari 12382 + III 13. *ᶠ⁽?⁾*'he/she (scil. a *numen*) brought (the girl) in'. ***Pazu-ki*** (wr. *pa-zu-ja*), analysis {*faž*(?)=*o-ki*} 'Bring child in, oh sea !' (*ki* → *kijaze* 'sea'), Mari 15000 Rs. 8'. ***Pazza*** (wr. *pa-az-za*), Mari 10097: 16, analysis{*pažž-*}, cf. Ḫattuša: *Pa-az-zu*, E. Laroche, *NH*, 139, Nr. 961; cf. Nippur: *Pa-as(?)-si*, see M. Hölscher, *Die Personennamen der kassitenzeitlichen Texte aus Nippur*, IMGULA I, Münster 1996, 167; cf. Nuzi: *Pa-az-zi, Pa-az-zi-ia, NPN*, 112.

According to Th. Richter, *VHN* I, 227, "***Pazza*** as well as the personal names from the other archives can be understood as (extended) imperatives, since the root appears not to have formed indicative full names". ***Pašši-p-tilla*** (wr. *Pa-aš-ši-til-la, Ba-aš-ši-til-la, Pa-aš-ši-ip-til-la*), can be analysed as {*pašš*=*i*=*b-Tilla*} and be interpreted as 'Tilla brings / has brought (the boy) in'. Tilla is one of the bulls guarding Tešub.

Pašši-p-tilla belongs to the same category of names as, for instance, ***Ḫazip-Teššup*** (wr. *ḫa-zi-ip-te-eš-šu-up, ḫa-zi-ip-te-eš*₁₅(IŠ)*-šu-up, ḫa-zi-ip-te-šu-up, ḫa-ši-ip-te-šu-up, ḫa-ši-ip-te-eš-šu-up*), 'Teššup heard (person or prayer)', root *ḫaz-* / *ḫaš-*, analysis {*ḫaž*=*i*=*b-Teššob*}, cf. Th. Richter, *VHN* I, 132-133.

Apart from personal names with the verbal roots ***paš- / paz-*** and ***pašš- / pazz-***, also names with the nominal root ***paš- / paz-*** 'mouth' are attested, e.g. ***ᶠUnap-paši*** (wr. *ú-na-ap-pa-aš-e*), analysis {*ún*=*a*=*b-paži*} 'The mouth (of the girl) came', a name from Mari, that can likely be explained as referring to a stage of the birth of the girl, cf. Th. Richter, *VHN* I, 330-331, s.v. ***ᶠUnap-paši***; 482, s.v. ***paši*** {*paži*}.

Whether the sibilants of the verbal roots are presented in double or single writing, semantically the transitive forms indicate 'to bring in, to send' and the intransitive 'to come in, to enter', so it is conceivable that nominal ***paši*** *{paži}* 'mouth' is etymologically derived from the verbal root, because the mouth is *par excellence* the part of the body where food and breath enter and speech and breath leave. The mouth of a river also marks the place where it enters the sea or a lake or where a tributary enters a main river.

HT 102.1-2 reads: ***ka-pa sa-ra₂*** GRA 976. On account of a close connection between ***ka-pa*** and ***sa-ra₂*** in the heading of this tablet I assumed in the 2016 edition that ***sa-ra₂*** might be a special designation of ***ka-pa*** 'Ḫalba' and possibly signify 'the Royal Palace'. The argument seemed plausible, but now I am convinced that the phrase ***ka-pa sa-ra₂*** GRA 976 (HT 102.1-2) is a clear example of a *subject – verb – object construction*, with ***sa-ra₂*** = ***šar=i=a*** as the verbal form. The phrase can be translated as '(The Palace / King of) *Ḫalpa* demands 976 units of grain'. Since one assumes that in Linear B the grain-ideogram GRA followed by numbers probably represents *talents* of grain, it seems likely that the same may be assumed for Linear A: GRA 976 = 976 talents of grain.

Linear A ***sa-ra₂*** (HT 99a.1) occurs in the combination ***a-du*** , ***sa-ra₂*** HORD 6̲[(HT 99a.1), followed by FIC 4[ ]' VINa 1 H GRA+*qe* (HT 99a.2). Line 3:]vestigia vacat. Lines 4-5:] vacant. Linear A ***a-du*** can be compared with the equivalent ***ad(d)u(n)*** (wr. *a-du, a-du-un, a-ad-du, a-du-ú*) in the Old Babylonian grain-distibutions lists at Alalaḫ, especially in relation with barley and emmer; it is also used in relation with various commodities at Mari and oil rations at Nuzi. A. Draffkorn (*HHA*, 1959, 153-154) interprets it as the Hurrian term for 'assigned portion, ration'. The varied spellings may point to a loan-word from either Akkadian or Sumerian. So the tablet starts with essential information: 'assigned portion(s)', followed by the verbal form ***sa-ra₂*** = ***šar=i=a*** 'he demands'. A subject such as in the combination ***ka-pa sa-ra₂*** (HT 102.1) '(The Palace / King of) *Ḫalpa* demands' is missing, but we may perhaps assume that the phrase was so often used that the scribe knew that '(the Palace of) *Ḫalba*' or 'an official of the palace' or even 'the king himself' was the subject of ***šar=i=a*** and did not find it necessary to mention the grammatical subject.

In the Linear A phrase ***da-du̲-te*** , ***si***[ ]***i*** , ***sa-ra₂*** (HT 34.1) the Hurrian personal name ***da-du̲-te*** 'Tešub loved (the child)' may well be the grammatical subject of ***šar=i=a***. The small square brackets in ***si***[ ]***i*** show that there is only a very small gap between the signs ***si*** and ***i*** due to damage to the tablet, small enough to assume that reading ***si-̲i*** may be justifiable. If we compare Linear A ***da-du̲-te*** , ***si***[ ]***i*** , ***sa-ra₂*** (HT 34.1) with ***si*** 4 ***sa-ra₂*** , HORD [ ] 14 J (HT 30+77.1-2) etc., we get *prima facie* the impression that monosyllabic ***si*** (HT 30+77.1) might be the shortened version of ***si***[ ]***i***. Th. Richter (*BGH*, 365) mentions, s.v. ***ši*** I, and/or ***šini***, ***ši'e*** [Boğ.], that the meaning was not yet established at the time of E. Laroche (*GLH*, 224, s.v. ***še-i-e***, KUB XLV 61+ IV 12), but that since E. Neu (1988b, 244f.[+37]) the meaning 'Auge' ['eye'] is confirmed by corresponding Hittite ***šakuwa***.

Incidentally, it is in my view tempting to assume that Hurrian ***šini*** 'two' may etymologically be explained by the fact that not only human beings, but many living creatures have *two eyes*.

Some scholars also consider it likely that the Hurrian term ***šena*** 'brother' may be derived from ***šini*** 'two', because a brother is never the first child, but the second, etc. A parallel may be that the Latin ordinal numeral *secundus* 'second' originally means 'the following' (< **sekʷundus*), from *sequor* 'to follow'.

If this meaning is applicable to Linear A ***si*** (***sa-ra₂*** and ***si-i*** (HT 34.1), 'eye' could perhaps metaphorically be understood as 'overseer, supervisor' and syntactically represent the subject of Linear A ***sa-ra₂*** (HT 30+77.1), equivalent to Hurrian ***ša-ri-(j)a***, analysis {*šar=i=(j)a*}, 'he/she (namely the overseer) demands, wishes'. In my view the meaning 'eye' in the sense of 'overseer, supervisor' seems to be the most likely in the case of ***si-i*** (HT 34.1), since ***si-i*** seems to be in apposition to ***da-<u>du</u>-te***. As a result the phrase ***da-<u>du</u>-te* , *si*[ ]*i* , *sa-ra₂*** (HT 34.1) can be interpreted as ***da-<u>du</u>-te*** 'Tešub loved (the child)', the overseer / supervisor, demands (the following commodities). The verbal form ***ki-ro*** (HT 34.6) 'he must redeem the debt' takes the same syntactical position as ***sa-ra₂***.

However, if ***si*** (HT 30+77.1) has the same function as ***si-i*** (HT 34.1), the number 4 following ***si*** (HT 30+77.1) remains enigmatic. The notion of four eyes / supervisors (or two supervisors, because each has two eyes) as subject of ***sa-ra₂*** does not make sense. The verb should be in the plural, which would yield the Hurrian form {*šar=i=(j)a=š(a)*}, with the ***-a-*** marking the 3rd person singular + the pluralizer ***-ša*** or the shortened form ***-š***, cf. I. Wegner, *Einführung*, 91, sub 5.2.8: *Position 8: the verbal marker of the plural* ***-š(a)-***.

If the Minoan scribe had wanted to write {*šar=i=(j)a=ša*}, he should have written ****sa-ra₂-sa*** instead of ***sa-ra₂***, but if he had wanted to use the shorter form {*šar=i=(j)a=š*}, he could still have written ***sa-ra₂***, because final consonants are not written in Linear A and B. This means that Linear A ***sa-ra₂*** can represent both the singular and plural 3rd person of the transitive verb, although the scribe could make a distinction by using the extended form ****sa-ra₂-sa***, if required. However, although there may orthographically and grammatically be no objection against ***si*** 4 (in the sense of 4 'eyes') as subject of ***sa-ra₂***, the whole idea of more than one supervisor does not make sense in the context.

There may be another solution: The usage of many ligatures in HT 30+77, HT 32, HT 33 and HT 34 shows that the scribe(s) of these tablets seem(s) to have been very fond of shorthand writing. So we may guess what the scribe meant, when he wrote ***si*** 4. Was ***si*** an abbreviation for ***šini*** 'two' instead of ***ši*** I, and/or ***šini***, ***ši'e*** 'eye' and is ***si*** 4 to be interpreted as Hurrian ***sini tumni*** = '2 x 4' ? If so, ***si*** 4 = ***sini tumni*** = '2 x 4' (HT 30+77.1) might be a preliminary announcement of the '4 main commodities', indicated by the ideograms HORD, FIC, VINa and OLE+***ta*** in (I) the list beginning with ***sa-ra₂*** and (II) the list beginning with ***ki-ro***. It may sound too farfetched. Conclusion: *non liquet*.

The tablets HT 30+77, HT 32, HT 33 and HT 34 have, apart from ***sa-ra₂***, some other sequences in common such as ***qa+pu*** (HT 30+77.3,5; HT 32.2 HT 33.2; HT 34.4), ***qa+i*** (HT 32.2; HT 33.2; HT 34.4). They also have a similar structure. The terms ***qa+pu*** D (HT 30+77.3; HT 30+77.5) and ***pa+ro*** 1 (HT 30+77.4; HT 30+77.5) in both lists and probably also ***sa-ra-ra*** J (HT 30+77.3), only occurring in the list following ***sa-ra₂***, may then be minor commodities. But let us first consider all possibilities. The Linear A tablets contain (apart from ideograms and some verbal forms such as frequent ***sa-ra₂*** and ***ki-ro*** and adverbial forms like ***ku-ro***) primarily personal names, some ethnics and some toponyms.

The fact that Linear A and B have only one syllabic series for the ***l-*** and ***r-*** signs, makes several interpretations possible. Consequently ***sa-ra-ra*** (HT 30+77.3) may be explained as three Hurrian theophorous personal names:

1. ***Šal(a)-Alla*** {*šal(a)-alla(i)*}, with the elements ***šala*** 'daughter' and theonym ***Alla(i)***, 'The daughter is (as) *Alla(i) /Allani*'.

2. ***Šar(i)-Alla*** {*šar(i)-alla(i)*}, with the verbal root ***šar-*** 'to wish, demand' and theonym ***Alla(i)***, 'Wish, oh *Alla(i) /Allani* !'. Cf. at Nuzi also ***Šar-teja*** and ***Šar-tešup*** that can be interpreted as either {*šar(i)-tešub*} 'Wish, oh *Tešub* !' or as {*šar(ri)-tešub*} '*Tešub* is King of Gods'.

3. ***Šar(i)-Ara*** {*šar(i)-ara*}, with the verbal root ***šar-*** 'to wish, demand' and theonym ***Ara***, 'Wish, oh *Ara* !'. Cf. Th. Richter (*VHN*, 73) *Arum-Ara* (wr. *A-rum-a-ra*) at Tigunāni, analysis {*ar=o=m-Ara*}, typology 1.1.1.1.1, lexicon *ar-*, *Ara*, 'Ara gave (the boy)'; and (*VHN*, 128) ***Ḫašip-Ara*** (wr. *Ḫa-ši-ip-a-ra*) at Tigunāni, analysis {*ḫaž=i=b-Ara*}, typology 1.1.1.2.1, lexicon *ḫaš*, *Ara*, '*Ara* heard (person of prayer)'.

Th. Richter (*VHN*, 378) mentions sub ***Ara*** that the theonym °*a-a-ra* occurs as subject of verbal sentence names and that the God may well be equivalent to the theonym ᴰ*a-a-ra(°)* known from Ḫattuša (*CTH*, 492), attested in an environment of Hurrian gods. Unfortunately we do not know very much about this god and his function, but Hurrian ᴰ*Ara* may perhaps be the Hurrian prototype of Pre-Greek *Ares*.

However, according to L.C. Meijer (*Eine strukturelle Analyse der Hagia Triada Tafeln*, 1982, 98) ***sa-ra-ra*** J (HT 30+77.3) is a 'Produktbezeichnung' ['commodity'].

One gets the impression that Linear A ***sa-ra-ra*** J belongs to the list of commodities on that tablet indicated by the ideograms of HORD, FIC, VINa and OLE+***ta*** and possibly the ligatures ***qa+pu*** + fraction-sign D (HT 30+77.3; HT 30+77.5) and ***pa+ro*** 1 (HT 30+77.4; HT 30+77.5). One may in that case identify ***sa-ra-ra*** as a grammatical form with the Hurrian *comitative* suffix ***-ra*** '(together) with' (cf. E. Laroche, *GLH*, 26; I. Wegner, *Einführung*, 65) and may compare ***sa-ra-°*** with ***sarabḫu*** at Alalaḫ, according to A. Draffkorn (*HHA*, 198-199) an adjective from the Old Babylonian period with unknown meaning (quality of barley) as observed in the grain distribution lists of Alalaḫ: (x) *pa-ri-si* ŠE *za-ra-ab-ḫu* (24: 5; 241: 12; 245: 2; 247: 15; 249: 4; 252: 20), possibly to be connected with ŠE *za-ra-e* at Nuzi: (x) ANŠE ŠE.MEŠ *za-ra-e ù ḫu-ra-e*, *HSS 14*, 36:1; occurs also *ibidem*: 34: 1, 2; 35: 1, 2. F.W. Bush (*GHL*, 116-118) explains Hurrian ***sarabḫu*** as *sara-p-ḫu,* consisting of the root ***sara-***, a root-complement ***-p-***, combined with ***ḫ*** or perhaps the adjectival suffix ***-ḫe***. Obviously the root-complement ***-p-*** underwent allophonic voicing (> *-b-*). According to E. Laroche, *GLH,* 26, the form ***sarae*** from Nuzi would be that with a 'complément de manière' (or instrumental).

A. Draffkorn (*HHA*, 176), s.v. ***karabḫu***, adjective from Middle Babylonian period 'fallow', also compares adjectival ***sarabḫu*** (*HHA*, 198-199) morphologically with ***karabḫu*** 'fallow'. Th. Richter (*BGH*, 189), s.v. ***karapḫu***, ***karpaḫu*** 'Brachland', 'fallow land', 'fallow', {*k/ḫar=a=ḫḫ(i)=wə*}, loan-word into Akkadian as *karapḫu* 'fallow land, year'. I. Wegner (*Einführung*, 57) mentions (sub 2.1: *the elements forming words, resp. stems*) the ending ***-pḫe***, mainly used for the formation of ethnics. She explains that according to G. Wilhelm (*AdŠ 2*, 1980, 99, 131) /***p***/ reflects an *allomorph* of the genitive-suffix ***-ve*** and that ***-ḫe/i*** is adjectival (***-pḫe*** < ****-ve+-(ḫ)ḫe***).

She mentions the examples ***ninua=p=ḫe*** < ***ninua=v(e)=ḫe*** 'The one (man) of Ninua'; ***pišaiša=p=ḫe*** 'The one (man) of (the mountain) Pišaiša' (theonym).

Th. Richter (*BGH*, 134) mentions Hurrian ***ḫarba*** I [a.o. South-Babylonia] 'Stroh' ['straw'] that may be interesting with respect to Linear A ***qa+pu*** = ***ḫarbu***, possibly ***ḫarba*** with Akkadianizing *nominative* in ***-u***, since the meaning of ***ḫarb/pu*** II [Nuzi] 'a tree' does not seem to be in accordance with usage of the fraction sign D.

I think that the meaning 'fallow land' for ***karapḫu*** can etymologically be derived from the original meaning 'straw land', since after harvesting the grain, the stubble-field of straw is what stays behind. Indeed the original Hurrian form was probably built on ***ḫarb-/ḫarw-***, because the form ***ḫarwara***, phonologically /*ḫarvara*/, 'Stroh' ['straw'] is attested at Nuzi, (cf. G. Wilhelm, 1985a, 93; 1992b, 241[6]; 1998, 175; M. Giorgieri , 2000a, 208: /*ḫarvara*/*i*(?)/; Th. Richter, *BGH*, 134).

Interesting is also (*BGH*, 134) ***ḫarwaraḫḫu*** [loan-word into Akkadian: Mari, Nuzi] 'pitchfork', from ***ḫar(wa)raḫḫe*** that is spelled in four different ways: *ḫa-ar-ra-aḫ-ḫe, ḫa-wa-ra-aḫ-ḫi, ḫa-ar-wa-ra-aḫ-ḫi, ḫa-ar-wa-ra-ḫi*, perhaps 'bundle', according to E.R. Lacheman, Tablets from Arrapḫe and Nuzi in the Iraq Museum, *Sumer 32 (1976)*, 125.

Morphologically the form ***ḫarwara*** (with ending in ***-ara***) is interesting as compared to the formation of Linear A ***sa-ra-ra***. So we may suspect that we are not dealing with a *comitative* in ***-ra***, but with a formation in ***-ar-*** as can be found in ***av=ar=i*** 'Feld' ['field'], ***ped=ar=i*** 'Rind' ['cow, bull, ox'], ***niḫ=ar=i*** 'Geschenk' ['gift'], ***ḫaš=ar=i*** 'Feinöl' ['luxurious, aromatic oil'], ***šid=ar=ni*** 'Fluch' ['curse'] (cf. I. Wegner, *Einführung*, 53).

The 'barley' ideogram HORDEUM occurs twice in this text, first HORD 14 J after ***sa-ra₂*** , (HT 30+77.1-2) and again HORD 8 after ***ki-ro*** , (HT 30+77.4). This fact and the combination with ***qa+pu*** = ***ḫarbu*** (HT 30+77.3) make it likely that Linear A ***sa-ra-ra*** may represent a 'specification of barley' or more likely a 'product made from barley'. The formation analysed as ***šar=ar=(i)=a*** (with *essive* in ***-a***) may corroborate this explanation.

A. Draffkorn (*HHA*, 192) also mentions the adjective ***parabše*** 'cultivated' at Middle-Babylonian Alalaḫ in the combination: 1 *me* A.ŠÀ.MEŠ *ba-ra-ab-še* 80 A.ŠÀ.MEŠ *qa-ra-ab-ḫe ša* PN (218: 1). She says that the meaning of ***parabše*** 'cultivated' is based on the context here, i.e. in opposition to ***karapḫu*** 'fallow'. I may add that the Sumerogram A.ŠÀ means 'field' and MEŠ marks the plural form: A.ŠÀ.MEŠ means 'fields'.

I. Wegner (*Einführung*, 58) mentions (sub 2.1: *the elements forming words, resp. stems*) the root-extension ***-apš-/-epš-***: exact meaning not clear, sometimes with numerals (see also the verbal root-extension in ***šin=apš-*** 'to (ex)change, (inter)change', from ***šin(i)*** 'two'; nominal ***pur=apš=i*** 'priest'; ***taḫapši*** {*taḫ=apš=i*} 'horse-cloth', cf. G. Wilhelm, *Cambridge Encyclopedia*, Chapter 4, 2004, 102. See also ***taḫapše*** 'felt', Th. Richter, *VHN*, 2016, 523).

Comparing Linear A ***qa+pu*** = ***ḫarbu*** (Akkadianizing *nominative* of ***ḫarba***), possibly 'straw', and Linear A ***pa+ro*** with Hurrian ***karapḫu***, ***karpaḫu*** {*k/ḫar=a=ḫḫ(i)=wə*}, at Alalaḫ *qa-ra-ab-ḫe* 'fallow' and ***parabše*** (wr. *ba-ra-ab-še*) 'cultivated', one wonders whether the Linear A terms have the same opposite meanings as the Hurrian forms.

Linear A ***pa+ro*** occurs twice on HT 30+77: the first form ***pa+ro*** 1 (HT 30+77.4) belongs to the series of items following ***sa-ra₂*** and stands between ***sa-ra-ra*** J (HT 30+77.4) and ***ki-ro***; second ***pa+ro*** 1 (HT 30+77.5) belongs to the series of items following ***ki-ro***.

If it belongs to the same category as ***qa+pu*** and is a commodity, it may be a term derived from the Hurrian verbal root ***par-/war-*** III 'backen' ['to bake (bread)'], cf. ***warinni*** [Boğ.] 'Brotbäcker' or 'Bäcker' ['baker (of bread)'], analysis *{far=i=nni}*, cf. G. Wilhelm, 1992f, 663; 2005a, 179; I. Wegner, *Einführung*, 2007[2], 55, 129, 271; Th. Richter, *BGH*, 298. The Old Hurrian verbal form 3rd person sg. ***par=o=m*** 'he baked (bread)' or a *jussive* form ***par=o*** 'he must bake (bread)' does not seem to fit very well in this list of items. So perhaps we are dealing with a noun ***par=u/o*** designating 'some form of bread or pastry', possibly with a nominal ending in ***-n*** (shortened form of ***-nni***), which is as final consonant not expressed in Linear A. The only apparent resemblance between ***par-/war-*** III 'to bake (bread)' and ***parabše*** (wr. *ba-ra-ab-še*) 'cultivated' is a general meaning such as 'to work on, to process, to elaborate'.

The Linear A sequence ***su-re*** 108 ***di*** 65 (HT 32.3) and OLE+***ne*** **1** ***su-re*** 104 ***di*** 53 (HT 32.4) seems to occur twice on tablet HT 32 at Hagia Triada. It reads:

HT 32.1. *pi* , *sa-ra₂* , *90* J OLE+*ne* JK
2. *qa+pu* 1 K *qa+i* 1 *96+ru* 1 vacat
3. *su-re* 108 *di* 65
4. OLE+*ne* 1 *su-re* 104 *di* 53

According to J. Raison - M. Pope (1994), 65, the entry of ***su-re*** in line 3 of this tablet from Hagia Triada appears to be repeated in line 4. The trace ['] preceding ***-re*** in line 4 seems indeed in accordance with ***su-*** as it appears in line 3. Another indication that we are probably dealing with identical entries in lines 3 and 4 seems to be that in both cases very high numbers **108** (line 3) and **104** (line 4) and ***di*** 65 (line 3) and ***di*** 53 (line 4) are following ***su-re*** and ***su-re***. The question is whether Linear A ***su-re*** and ***su-re*** represent a noun or a personal name. Both interpretations seem possible.

At Nuzi the Hurrian personal name ***Šuri*** (wr. ***Šu-ú-ri***) occurs, son of *Ta-a-a* (HSS IX 107: 20, 27; SMN 2609; 2618), cf. I.J. Gelb, *NPN*, 139; cf. P.M. Purves, *NPN*, 259, s.v. ***šur***, ***šuri***, ***šuri-***. It may be a hypocoristic of ***Šuri-ḫaia*** (wr. *Šu-ri-ḫa-a-a*), which may itself be a hypocoristic of ***Šuri-ḫarpa*** (wr. *Šu-ri-ḫar-pa*), see *ibidem.* Cf. also Hurrian names such as ***Šur-teia*** (wr. *Šu-ur-te-e-a*), ***Šur-tešub*** (wr. *Šu-ur-te-šup*, *Šu-ur-te-eš-šu-up*), ***Šur-tilla*** (wr. *Šu-ur-til-la*), see *ibidem*. Cf. also Th. Richter, *BGH*, 418, s.v. ***šur-*** (III) [PN].

Cf. also at Nuzi ***Šuriḫe***, possibly the same as the divine name ***Šuriḫa*** in MacRae's list in *NPN* or comparable with the name of a Hurrian deity **ᵈ*Šuruḫe***, mentioned in KBo I 1 rev. 57; 2 rev. 33; 3 rev. 25, cf. P.M. Purves, *NPN*, 260, s.v. ***Šuriḫe***. A Hurrian sentence name ***Ari-p-šuriḫe*** (wr. *A-ri-ip-šu-ri-ḫe*), consisting of the Hurrian verbal root ***ar-*** 'to give' and the theophorous element ***Šuriḫe***, is attested at Nuzi as well, cf. Purves, *ibidem*. Cf. also Th. Richter, *BGH*, 419, s.v. ***šuruḫḫe*** [Boğ; GN], (GIŠ.)***šuruḫḫa-*** *genus commune* [Lehnwort im Hethitischen], 'ein Epitheton des Wettergottes' (Haas 1971a: 136, Haas/Thiel 1978: 14[25]). If ***su-re*** and ***su-re*** are names, they are verbal or nominal.

Th. Richter (*BGH*, 418), s.v. ***šur-*** I [Boğ] 'schlachten / abstechen (von Kleintieren)' (Neu 1988a: 7[12], Haas 1989a: 267[29], Neu 1989a: 297, Catsanicos 1996: 282, Neu 1996a: 256); 'schlachten (von Schafen und Lämmern)' (Wilhelm 1992a: 134); 'abstechen (von Vieh)' (I. Wegner, *Einführung*, 281; Haas / Wegner 2007: 353); '(Kleintiere) schlachten' (Neu 2001: 95, Campbell 2007a: 43[77]). Entspricht hethitisch ***ḫatta-***.

So it is clear that the verbal root ***šur-*** I means 'to slaughter small cattle, sheep, lambs'.

Th. Richter (*BGH*, 418), s.v. ***šur-*** II, ***šurr-***. Formen mit einfachen und doppeltem {R} wurden gelegentlich zusammengeführt. *šur=am-* [Boğ; Mitt.] o. Ü. = ohne Übersetzung = without translation (E. Laroche, *GLH*, 244 [*šuram-*]); 'eilig gehen lassen' oder 'abfertigen' (I. Wegner, *Einführung*, 281; Görke 2010: 110; 'fortgehen, abreisen lassen' (Neu 2001: 95). *šur=am=ašt-* [Mitt] 'eilen lassen' (Steiner 1978); o. Ü. (E. Laroche, *GLH*, 244 sub *šuram-*), etc. *šurr-* [Boğ] 'aller, faire route, se diriger (vers)' (Catsanicos 1996: 282); [....] Bei zusammensetzung mit ***du-ú-ri*** entspricht hethitisch ***kattanta ijannje-*** (Neu 1992c: 394); 'aller, se rendre en bas » descendre' (Catsanicos 1996: 282). Die Form ***šu-úr-ru-ú*** (KBo 32.13 I 9), entsprechend hethitisch ***i-ia-an-ni-ir*** (zu ***ijannāi-*** 'gehen, marschieren', erfuhr unterschiedliche Bestimmungen (see Richter, *BGH*, 418). See s.v. Linear A ***sa-ta*** (HT 117a.7) and possibly]***sa-ta*** (HT 42[+]59.1) for an extensive discussion on the form ***šu-úr-ru-ú*** (KBo 32.13 I 9) in the Hurrian bilingual ***Kirenze***. So it is clear that the verbal root ***šur-*** II means 'to let go in a hurry, to send out quickly'. So a personal name ***Šure*** {*šur=e/i*} 'Let (the child) hurry up (oh *numen*) !' makes sense.

šur- III [PN], without translation.

Th. Richter, *BGH*, 419, offers nominal forms that may well provide a satisfactory equivalent to the Linear A forms ***su-re*** (HT 32.3) and ***su-re*** (HT 32.4). He mentions s.v. ***šuri-*** II [Boğ], *šuri-* II genus commune, *šurita-* ntr. [Lehnwort im Hethitischen]: von V. Haas 1979a: 59f. zu → *šawuri* (*ša-* I) gestellt, unübersetzt bei Haas 1998a: 243 und Salvini/Wegner 2004: 126. - Lehn: Als (GIŠ.)***šurita-*** 'ball of yarn(?)' Lw im He. (Beckman 1983a: 100), s.a. Strauß 2006: 389 zu (ŠÍG.)***šurita-*** als 'Wollknäuel, Geflecht'. Nach Starke 1990: 209 ist der 'Orakelterminus' als Lehnwort ins He. eingegangen (*šuri=*), aber kaum mit keilschriftluwisch *šurit-* 'Wollknäuel' zu verbinden. **(A)**: 'une marque omineuse' (E. Laroche, *GLH*, 244; de Martino 1992a: 154 [s.a. Popko 1978: 133]); entlehnt zu » he. *šuri-* genus commune 'Geflecht' oder 'Matte', d.i. 'Benennung einer Leberschädigung' (Tischler 2001b: 156); s.a. *HW*² Lfg. 18 [2010] 594f. (Belege). **(B)**: 'Opferterminus: unklar' (Haas/Wilhelm 1974a: 123); 'un arma' (Salvini 1977b: 86); 'attribut divin' (E. Laroche, *GLH*, 244; Wegner 1981: 103f. [der Ištar-Šawuška]); 'Lanze' (Haas 1988a: 295[49]). Th. Richter (*BGH*, 419) ***šu-u-úr-e*** III [Boğ], no translation (E. Laroche, *GLH*, 244). In view of the high numbers, 108 (line 3) and 104 (line 4), mentioned after ***su-re*** (HT 32.3) and ***su-re*** (HT 32.4), respectively, the meaning 'lance' or 'weapon' seems less likely in the context of this Linear A tablet, also since the subject of the text appears to concern 'agricultural commodities' such as OLE+***ne*** (HT 32.1; HT 32.4). Taking into account that the Cretan economy largely depended on the production of wool in Minoan and Mycenaean times, registration of large quantities of 'balls of yarn' or 'balls of winded wool' seems in accordance with the other entries mentioned.

Linear A ***sa-ra₂*** (HT 105.3), followed by VIR 235, seems to take exactly the same contextual position as ***ka-pa*** [.] (HT 105.1) followed by VIR 234. Linear A HT 105 reads:

HT 105.1: *ka-pa* […...] 400 vestigia
HT 105.2: VIR (*99*) 234
HT 105.3: *sa-ra₂* , VIR (*126a*) 235
HT 105.4-5: vacant

Incidentally, *GORILA 1* only reads *vestigia* in the big *lacuna* after ***ka-pa***, since a large part of the upper edge of the tablet is missing except ***ka-pa***. J. Raison – M. Pope (1994) see traces of the lower parts of two small circles (= 2 x 100) and seem to conclude that there may have been another row of two small circles on top of them: result: 400.

In the 2016 edition I argued that ***sa-ra***$_2$ (HT 105.3), followed by VIR 235, seems to take the same contextual position as ***ka-pa*** [.] (HT 105.1) followed by VIR 234, which would make it feasible to interpret ***sa-ra***$_2$ here as a toponym or topographical designation comparable with ***ka-pa***. Indeed interpretation as a toponym is not inconceivable, if we compare the toponym ***Sariya*** KBo V 6 I 12 = *JCS 10,* 90 (cf. E. Laroche, ***NH,*** 278).

Especially the high numbers of men, VIR (***99***) 234 and VIR (***126a***) 235 or MULIER (***126a***) 235, if Raison-Pope (1994) are right, with regard to ***ka-pa*** [....] and ***sa-ra***$_2$, respectively, seemed to make it plausible that ***sa-ra***$_2$ might be a topographic designation on this tablet as ***ka-pa*** certainly is.

However, I now consider it more likely that ***ka-pa*** is the subject of a missing ***sa-ra***$_2$ (or a verbal form like ***sa-ra***$_2$) in the first line, of which 400 ... and VIR 234 are the object, and that ***ka-pa*** is again subject of ***sa-ra***$_2$ = Hurrian ***šar=i=a***, of which VIR (or MULIER) (*126a*) 235 is the object. Translation: '(The Palace of) *Ḫalpa* demands 400 ... and 234 men (VIR = *99*) and 235 men or women (VIR or MULIER = *126a*)', so that the syntactical construction of HT 105 is identical with that of HT 102.1-2, reading: ***ka-pa sa-ra***$_2$ GRA 976 '(The Palace of) *Ḫalpa* demands 976 units of grain'. Since one assumes that in Linear B the grain-ideogram GRA followed by numbers probably represents *talents* of grain, it seems likely that the same may be assumed for Linear A: GRA 976 = 976 talents of grain.

The *a*-side of tablet HT 24 is heavily damaged on the right side. So consequently the *b*-side of tablet HT 24 is heavily damaged on the left side. All lines on the *a*-side contain entries concerning the ligature ***ma+ru*** ↑ (read from bottom to top) signifying LANA = 'wool', in most lines probably followed by ***me***. In fact the addition ***me*** is only clearly visible in line 2. The syllabic sign ***me*** is probably not acrophonic, but onomatopoeic, since it resembles the bleating sound of sheep. The addition ***me*** may confirm that ***ma+ru*** refers to wool of sheep. Linear A ***ma+ru*** is comparable with Linear B ***ma+ro*** ↑ (read from bottom to top), that also signifies LANA.

At first sight one might think that the Linear A ligatures ***ma+ru*** (HT 12.4; HT 24a.1, 2, 3, 4. 5) from Hagia Triada and ***ma+ru*** (PH 3a.3) from Phaistos can be identified with the sequence ***ma-ru*** (HT 117a.3) from Hagia Triada, but that seems unlikely, because Linear A ***ma-ru*** (HT 117a.3) represents a personal name, whereas the Linear A ligatures ***ma+ru*** (HT 12.4; HT 24a.1) and ***ma+ru*** (PH 3a.3) may well designate LANA 'wool' as the Linear B ligature ***ma+ro*** does.

Linear B ***ma+ro*** has been explained as ***μαλλός*** (masc.) 'fleece (of sheep)', which provides a very precise meaning. P. Chantraine (*DELG*, 663), s.v. ***μαλλός*** : "m. 'touffe de laine' (Hés. *Tr.* 234) ......, employé avec *πλόκαμος* pour des cheveux (Eur. *Ba.* 113), cf. Hsch. *μαλλός · τὸ ἔριον καὶ ἡ καθειμένη κόμη*. .. En grec moderne, *μαλλί* signifie 'laine, toison', pluriel *μαλλιά* 'cheveux', *μαλλιαρός* 'poilu, chevelu', etc. Étymologie: Ignorée; voir Pokorny 721, qui pose **ml̥-no-* et rapproche lit. *mìlas* 'drap', lette *mil(n)a* 'drap'."

Since Linear A ***ma+ru*** and Linear B ***ma+ro*** probably signify the same notion, we are likely dealing with the same term and basically with the same root. It is therefore important that Chantraine concludes that the etymology of ***μαλλός*** is unknown (ignorée), so that a clear Indo-European origin is not likely. We may be dealing with a loan-word. According to Th. Richter (*BGH*, 240) there is a Hurrian 'sacrificial term' ***mali*** at Ḫattuša, but it is not yet known, whether it has anything to do with 'a fleece, wool or sheep'. Some scholars see a connection between this Hurrian 'sacrificial term' ***mali*** and the Hittite 'sacrificial term' ***mala***, others do not.

It is a pity that Linear A and B do not distinguish ***-l-*** and ***-r-*** in the script. This is only a problem for us, because we have to examine all possible readings. The scribes knew what they had writen. Because of the satisfactory interpretation of Linear B ***ma+ro*** as ***μαλλός*** 'fleece (of sheep)' we tend to consider this a good explanation for the etymology of ***ma+ro***, although we do not really know from which language the word is ultimately derived. However, it is not likely that Linear A ***ma+ru*** is derived from Linear B ***ma+ro*** or Greek ***μαλλός***. It is more likely that Linear B ***ma+ro*** is derived from Linear A ***ma+ru***.

A. Draffkorn (*HHA*, 183) mentions the Hurrian term ***mardatuǵ(u)li*** at Nuzi and Middle-Babylonian Alalaḫ 'a maker of *mardatu*-textile', which she explains as a loan-word from Akkadian TÚG *mardatu/mardutu.* At Alalaḫ: LÚ.MEŠ *mar-ta-tu-ḫu-li* AT 227: 6; LÚ *mar-ta-tu-ḫu-li* AT 148: 52. At Nuzi: PN *ma-ar-da-du-uḫ-lum HSS* 1 65: 12. Cf. L. Oppenheim, *JNES 11*, 136 ff; E.A. Speiser, *JAOS 74*, 25.

Th. Richter (*BGH*, 246) ‡ ***mardade*** [Qa.] 'Teppich' ['carpet'] is considered a Hurrian term at Qaṭna (Th. Richter, 2005a, 39 ff., 2005c, 118). *CAD* M/I, 1977, 277, assumes a foreign provenance of the Akkadian term 'fabric woven with several colours in a special technique'. At Ugarit ***mrdt(t)*** '*mrdt*-Stoffe', 'garment or carpet'. ***mardaduḫ(u)li*** [Alalaḫ IV; Nuzi; Qa.] 'craftsman making *mardatu*-fabrics', i.e. ***mardatu*** and ***=uḫlu*** CAD M/I, 1977, 278), 'Teppich-Hersteller' ['carpet-maker, carpet-weaver'] (Mayer 1977a, 189); 'un nom professionel' (E. Laroche, *GLH*, 168); 'Teppichknüpfer' (G. Wilhelm, 1992b, 239), etc. It seems most likely that 'craftsman making *mardatu*-fabrics' worked with sheep's wool.

It is remarkable that Linear A ***pa-sa-<u>ri</u>-ja , ma+ru <u>me</u>*** [(HT 24a.4) shows a formation similar to the first entry on the same side of the tablet ***ku-pa₃-<u>ri</u>-ja , ki ma+ru***[(HT 24a.1). This choice of names registered on the same tablet shows that the scribes had a remarkable poetical feeling for rhyming and rhythm and probably also for morphological features. Linear A ***ki*** is probably an abbreviation for ***ki-ro***. That is the most likely and most frequent abbreviation. On the other hand, if ***ki*** preceding the ligature ***ma+ru***, is in that position an abbreviation of ***ḫidāru***, it is quite intriguing that ***ḫidāru*** [Alalaḫ VII; Ug.] means 'eine Wollart' ['a type of wool'] (*Akkadisches Handwörterbuch*, Lfg. 4, 1962 344 [hurritisches Fremdwort]; *CDA*^{2}, 2000, 115 [Hurrian loan-word]; Lauinger, 2007, 101^{+50}); 'ein Textil' ['a textile'] (Waetzoldt, 1980, 30). *CAD* Ḫ (1956, 182) reads ***ḫi-id-ru*** instead „with *ḫidru* ...[as] a native word for wool". See also *Akkadisches Handwörterbuch*, Lfg. 16, 1981, 1561, for $^{GADA!}$*ḫi-da-a-ri* at Ugarit, cf. Th. Richter, *BGH*, 160. Sumerian GADA is 'cloth'. It is possible that ***ki*** is an abbreviation of ***ki-ro*** in ***ki ma+ru***[(HT 24a.1), but the meaning 'a type of wool' for ***ḫidāru*** in combination with ***ma+ru*** = LANA 'wool' is too special to ignore. The scribe may also have been playing with the terms ***ki ma+ru*** and ***ma+ru <u>me</u>***.

Both ***ku-pa$_3$-ri-ja*** (HT 24a.1) and ***pa-sa-ri-ja*** (HT 24a.4) are probably personal names. For Linear A ***pa-sa-ri-ja*** (HT 24a.4) two interpretations are possible:

I) It can be analysed as *{paš(š)=ar=i=ja}*, consisting of the verbal root ***paš-/paz-*** and ***pašš-/pazz-*** (trans.) 'to bring in, to send' + the root-extension ***-ar-*** + the marker of transitivity ***-i-*** + the Hurrian hypocoristic suffix ***-ya***. The root-extension ***-ar-*** expresses a *factitive* and *iterative* aspect according to I. Wegner, *Einführung*, 88.

II) It can be a so-called 'one-word' personal name identical with the verbal form *{paš(š)=ar=i=a}*. The form consists in that case of the verbal root ***paš-/paz-*** and ***pašš-/pazz-*** (trans.) 'to bring in, to send' + the root-extension ***-ar-*** + the marker of transitivity ***-i-*** + the marker of the subject of action ***-a*** of the transitive verb. The name can be translated as 'He/She (a *numen*) brings/brought (the child) in or sends/sent (the child)'. The root ***pašš-*** is equivalent to Akkadian ***šapâru*** 'to send', cf. ***paššiḫi*** 'message' and ***paššitḫi*** 'messenger', 'envoy' = Akkadian ***mâr šipri*** (cf. Jensen, *ZA V (1890)*, 193; E.A. Speiser, *IH, passim*; E. Laroche, *GLH*, 197-198).

Apart from the root-extension ***-ar-*** (with a *factitive* aspect), Linear A ***pa-sa-ri-ja*** (HT 24a.4) does not differ in interpretation and translation from Linear A ***pa-se-ja*** (HT Wc 3001a; HT Wc 3002a) and ***pa-si-a*** (HT 45b.3) and the Hurrian personal names ***Pazii̯a*** (wr. *Pa-zi-ia*), ***Pazzii̯a*** (wr. *Pa-az-zi-ia*) and ***Paššii̯a*** (wr. *Pa-aš-ši-ia*) at Nuzi.

For Linear A ***pa-se-ja*** (HT Wc 3001a; HT Wc 3002a) and ***pa-si-a*** (HT 45b.3) as well as for the Hurrian personal names ***Pazii̯a*** (wr. *Pa-zi-ia*), ***Pazzii̯a*** (wr. *Pa-az-zi-ia*) and ***Paššii̯a*** (wr. *Pa-aš-ši-ia*) from Nuzi two interpretations are possible:

I) They can be hypocoristic personal names consisting of the verbal root ***paš-/paz-*** and ***pašš-/pazz-*** (trans.) 'to bring in, to send' + the marker of transitivity ***-i-*** + the Hurrian hypocoristic suffix ***-ya***: *{paž=i=ya}*. A personal name with the Hurrian verbal root ***pašš-*** 'to send' and the common Hurrian hypocoristic suffix ***-ya*** would be feasible as the name of the owner / sender or receiver of the delivery the roundel was attached to. The sequence ***pa-si-a*** (HT 45b.3) from Hagia Triada must probably also be interpreted as the same Hurrian anthroponym ***Paššii̯a***.

II) They can be a so-called 'one-word' personal name identical with the verbal form *{paš(š)/z(z)=i=a)}*. The form consists in that case of the verbal root ***paš-/paz-*** and ***pašš-/pazz-*** (trans.) 'to bring in, to send' + the marker of transitivity ***-i-*** + the marker of the subject of action ***-a***. The name can be translated as 'He/She (a *numen*) brings/brought (the child) in or sends/sent (the child)'. For Linear A ***pa-se-ja*** (HT Wc 3001a; HT Wc 3002a) on the roundels it is conceivable that the form is not a personal name, but the real verbal form 'he/she sends/sent (namely the delivery going with the roundel)', with the seal-impression on the edge (side c) of the roundel.

If a ***p/w*** alternation is assumed (as in Hurrian ***p/wand-*** and many other Hurrian forms), Linear A ***ku-pa$_3$-ri-ja*** (HT 24a.1) can be compared with the Hurrian personal name ***Kuwarija*** (wr. *ku-wa-ri-ia*) from Mari, partner of *Mašiya* (*ARM 1*, 81: 17), analysis *{ko/uvari=ja}*, typology 3.3, lexicon *kuwari* (*kuw-* II), cf. Th. Richter, *VHN*, 179, 449.

Th. Richter connects ***Kuwarija*** with ***kuwari*** '*kuwari*(-Gerät)' (?) ['*kuwari*(-tool)'] and with the personal names ***Kuwari*** (wr. *Ku-wa-ri, Ku-wa-ri-im*) at Mari, Šušarrā, Alalaḫ VII, Qaṭna, ^{f}***Kuwari*** (wr. ^{f}*Ku-wa-ri,* ^{f}*Ku-ia-ri*) at Ašnakkum and (9x) at Mari, ^{f}*Ku-wa-re-e* at Ugarit (cf. F. Gröndahl, *PNTU*, 341), *Ku-wa-rum* at Old Babylonian Tall Haddad.

He also compares ***Kuari*** at Terqa, *ku-a-ri* at Alalaḫ IV (*AT* 162 = *UF* 34, 860 Vs (?) 26') and ***Kuari*** (wr. *Ku-(ú-)a-ri*) at Nuzi (cf. I.J. Gelb, *NPN*, 89) and ascribes the personal name *ᶠ**Kuwakki*** (wr. *ᶠKu-wa-ak-ki*) at Mari to the root ***kuw-*** II, analysis {*ko/uv=a=kk=i*}, typology 3.1, cf. *VHN*, 178.

Th. Richter (*VHN*, 449) mentions that the 'Opferterminus' ['sacrificial term'] ***kuwari*** (see *BGH*, 225) and the mountain-name *ku-wa-ar-º* (with Hurrian etymology according to V. Haas, 1981b, 643) probably are the same word {*ko/uv=a=ri*} and may well belong to the root ***kuw-***. If {*ko/uv=a=ri*} is nominal, it might in my view belong to the category of words with a nominal root-extension such as ***av=ar=i*** 'Feld' ['field'], ***ped=ar=i*** 'Rind' ['cow, bull, ox'], ***niḫ=ar=i*** 'Geschenk' ['gift'], ***ḫaš=ar=i*** 'Feinöl' ['luxurious, aromatic oil'], ***šid=ar=ni*** 'Fluch' ['curse'] (cf. I. Wegner, *Einführung*, 53). Richter wonders, however, whether the frequent personal name ***Kuwari*** really contains this notion in the sense of a *nominal* 'one-word' name or should be analysed verbally.

I agree that starting from a verbal root ***kub/w-*** another analysis should be considered for Hurrian ***Kuwarija*** and Linear A ***ku-pa₃-ri-ja***, namely {*kub/w=ar=i=a*}, consisting of the verbal root ***kub/w-*** + the root-extension ***-ar-*** + the marker of transitivity ***-i-*** + the indicator of the subject of action 3rd person singular ***-a***. The root-extension ***-ar-*** expresses a *factitive* and *iterative* aspect according to I. Wegner, *Einführung*, 88. Unfortunately the meaning of the root ***kuw-*** is still unknown.

Th. Richter (*VHN*, 448) distinguishes another root ***kub-*** I / ***kupp-*** {*ko/ub- / ko/upp-*} from ***kuw-*** II {*ko/uv-*}, in spite of ***kubaḫi / kuwaḫi*** 'eine Kopfbedeckung' (cf. *BGH*, 225, and *VHN*, 448, n. 465), that is regarded as a 'cultural *Wanderwort*' by some scholars. He mentions that the roots ***kub-*** I and ***kupp-*** show some parallels in onomastics, so that they can be taken together. The personal name *Ku-up-pa-aḫ-*[*ḫ*]*é* at Nuzi (see *SANTAG 4*, 265) may be analysed as {*ko/uppi»a=ḫhe*} with adjectival suffix ***-ḫ(ḫ)e/i***, from which a nominal ****kuppi*** {*ko/upp=i*} can be isolated. Consequently the personal names *ᶠ**Kuppe*** (wr. *ᶠKu-ub-be, ᶠKu-ub-bi*) and ***Kubiįa*** (wr. *Ku-bi-ia*) at Nuzi (cf. I.J. Gelb, *NPN*, 91) and ***Kupi*** (wr. *ku-bi*) at Šušarrā, analysis {*ko/ub=i*}, typology 1.3.1.2.1, ***Kupija*** (wr. *ku-bi-ia*) at Šušarrā, analysis {*ko/ub=i=ja*}, typology 1.1.1.2.4, and ***Kuppija*** (wr. *ku-ub-bi-ia*) at Mari, analysis {*ko/upp=i=ja*}, typology 1.1.1.2.4, may be nominal 'one-word' names, but verbal analyses are equally possible, cf. Th. Richter, *VHN*, 179-180, 448.

Unfortunately the meaning of ***kub-*** I / ***kupp-*** is not yet clarified either. Taking into account the alternation of ***kubaḫi / kuwaḫi***, I should not be surprised, if eventually the roots ***kub-*** I / ***kupp-*** and ***kuw-*** II will appear to be one and the same.

E. Laroche (*GLH*, 157) qualifies ***kuwaḫi*** as 'bonnet, coiffure de Tešub'. According to O. Szemerényi this term, which describes 'a hat' or 'something Tešub wears on his head', maybe 'a crown', comparable with Hebrew ***kōba***ᶜ and with Greek ***κόμβαχος*** (cf. *Die Sprache XI,* 1 ff., and *JHS 94*, 153). One may perhaps add the Hesychius gloss ***κόμβα*** (Polyrrhen.) = ***κορώνη*** 'crown' (cf. H.G. Liddell, R. Scott, e.a., *A Greek-English Lexicon*, Oxford 1961, 975).

It is interesting to see which other personal names in Linear A start with ***ku-pa₃-***: Linear A ***ku-pa₃-nu*** (HT 1a.3; HT 88.5; HT 117a.3; HT 122a.6; HT 122a.7; HT? 170b.3 and possibly also HT 3.6; HT 42.3; HT 49a.6-7) is probably one of the most frequent personal names at Hagia Triada.

The correct reading of this Linear A sequence is ***ku-pa$_3$-nu***, because Linear A sign ***1*** = Linear B sign ****56*** = ***pa$_3$***. Linear B sign ***pa$_3$*** is usually interpreted as ***φα*** (possibly sometimes ***βα***). F.M.J. Waanders considers it likely that Linear A sign ***pa$_3$*** may have represented [***bha***], which may well be the starting point for both [***pha***] and [***ba***].

C.H. Gordon read Linear A sign ***1*** as ***pà***, see C.H. Gordon, *Evidence for the Minoan language*, Ventnor, N.J, 1966, 31, 33, 38, sub ***ku-pà-nu*** (*Gupanu*, Ugaritic *^{m}gu-pa-na, gpn*) and its regular Semitic feminine form ***ku-pà-na-tu*** (Ugaritic *Gupanatu*). *Gupanu* is both a divine and a personal name at Ugarit. ***Gupanu*** is also a messenger of Baal in Ugaritic mythology. Linear A ***ku-pa$_3$-na-tu*** (HT 47a.1-2; HT 119.3) is also attested at Hagia Triada.

F. Gröndahl (*PNTU*, 129) mentions, s.v. ***gupanu*** and alphabetic cuneiform ***gpn***, gemeinsem. 'Strauch, Wein, Rebe' (außer äthiop.) und Name eines Boten des Ba^{c}al, s. Ginsberg, *BASOR 95 (1944)*, 25. However, a word meaning 'bush, shrub, vine' may be a 'cultural *Wanderwort*' as well, so that the eventual provenance of the word remains ambiguous. The many Hurrian names and contextual lexemes with the root(s) ***kub-*** I / ***kupp-*** and ***kuw-*** II may well offer matter to reconsider.

Linear A ***ku-pa$_3$-pa$_3$*** (HT 88.4) is now read by *GORILA 1* (138-139) instead of the former reading ***ku-pa$_3$-nu*** that is also mentioned in the next line, ***ku-pa$_3$-nu*** (HT 88.5). The advantage of this new reading is that the same name is no longer read twice in the same text. Linear A ***ku-pa$_3$-pa$_3$*** can be identified as the Hurrian feminine personal name ***^{f}Kubaba***, that is no doubt derived from the theonym ***^{d}Kubaba*** provided with the divine determinative. Linear A ***ku-pa$_3$-pa$_3$*** (HT 88.4) likely represents the personal name ***Kubaba***, not the theonym, since other names in the list of HT 88 are also anthroponyms.

The personal name ***^{f}Kubaba*** (wr. *^{f}ku-ba-ba*) is attested at Ugarit, cf. also alphabetic ***kbby*** (cf. F. Gröndahl, *PNTU*, 1967, 340, 394) and at Boğazköy, cf. E. Laroche, *NH*, 99, n° 636, ***^{f}Kubaba***: Diverses: abs. nom. *^{f}Ku-ba-ba, ^{f}Ku-pa-(a)-pa-(aš)*, HT 2 III 8 = KBo II 31 Vo 12; KBo IX 142, 3; X 10 III 18; XII 62, 6, 7; fragm. KUB XXXVI 2 c 5. At Alalaḫ IV we find ***^{f}Ku-ba-ba*** (cf. D.J. Wiseman, *AT*, 195 = *ZA 60*, 92, nr. 6: 12).

The personal name ***^{f}Kupapuzi*** (wr. *^{f}ku-ba-pu-zi*) occurs at Mari, lexicon *Kupapuzi*, typology 3.1, '(Göttin) Kubaba angemessen' ['belonging to / pertaining to (goddess) Kubaba'], cf. Th. Richter, *VHN*, 178, 449.

The most significant cult-place of the goddess ***Kubaba*** was Karkemiš in Syria. The goddess was already known in the Ur III period of Hurrian onomastics, e.g. ***Ku-ba-ba-e*** from Puzriš-Dagan, analysis {*kubaba=(v)e*}, 'The one (the boy) of *Kubaba*'. The provenance of ***Kubaba*** cannot be established completely. C.J. Gadd (The tablets from Chagar Bazar and Tall Brak, 1937-38, *Iraq 7 (1940)*, 28) was the first who classified ***Kubaba*** as a Hurrian goddess.

E. Laroche (*NH*, 346 and note 12) mentions that in Hurrian the names reproducing just the name of a deity, without more, are rare. He mentions the example of ***^{f}Kubaba*** in Syria and Anatolia as a personal name that is a copy of the divine name. Virtually all Hurrian theophorous names are compounds of two elements. In the majority of cases the pattern is regressive: attributive - divine name, e.g. ***Talmi-Tešub*** 'Tešub (is) Great', whereas ***^{f}Ḫebat-allani*** 'Ḫebat (is) the Lady', presenting an inverse order, is less common.

E. Laroche (*GLH*, 150) mentions, s.v. ***Kubaba***: Grande déesse de Kargémish, introduite à Ugarit et au Kizuwatna, puis en Anatolie (*Kubêbê*). Dans les listes Kizouvatniennes, avec *Adamma* et *Ḫašuntarḫi*. Graphies: ^{d}*Ku-pa-pa*, KUB XXVII 1 II 53; 8 Ro 14; 13 I 19; KBo XX 113 I 23, etc., ^{d}*Ku-pa-wa*$_{a}$, KBo V 2 III 15 = 1/a 3. - Erg. *Ku-pa-pa-*[*aš*], KUB XXV 42+ V 9. - Gén. *Ku-ba-ba-be*, Msk. - Dir. *kbb-d* = **Kubaba-da*, RS 24.261, 23 = *Ugar. V*, 501, 503. Her name also appears in Kizzuwatna-rituals, cf. Th. Richter, *VHN*, 449.

P.M. Purves (*NPN*, 230) mentions s.v. ***kup***, ***kup-***, the following personal names: ***Kup-arša*** (wr. *Ku-pa-ar-ša, Ḫu-pa-ar-ša, Ku-bar-ša, Ku-ba-ar-ša*). Or ***Kuparša*** ? Interchange of ***k*** and ***ḫ*** suggests non-Hurrian origin; see Purves in *AJSL LVII* 173, n. 51. ***Kup-asa*** (wr. *Ku-ú-ba-a-sa, Ku-ú-ba-sa, Ku-ba-a-sa*). Division uncert. Cf. ^{c}*Ku-ba-sa*, KAJ 143:9. ***Kuperi*** (wr. *Ku-be-ri*). Formed on ***kup*** ? Possibly not Hurrian. L. Oppenheim in *AOF XII*, 35 divides as a divine name ***Kupe*** + formative ***-ri***. But, if so, no other name has this formative preceded by ***e***. Or Akkadian ? He mentions s.v. ***kupp***: ***Kuppe*** (wr. ^{f}*Ku-ub-be*, ^{f}*Ku-ub-bi*.

Th. Richter (*VHN*, 448) mentions, s.v. ***kub-*** I / ***kupp-*** {*ko/ub- / ko/upp-*} that a root ***kub-*** has been isolated in *NPN* 230, on the basis of *Ku-bar/pa-ar-ša/šá* (with variant *Ḫu-pa-ar-ša*) that is certainly the same sequence as ***Kubarze*** {*ko/ub=a=r=ze*} at Šubat-Enlil. Hurrian origin is uncertain. None of the few sequences starting with ***kub-*** I / ***kupp-*** is sufficiently and unanimously defined (morphologically, lexically or semantically), see *BGH*, 225-226. This also applies to forms in context ***ku-pa-a-e*** (Laroche, *GLH*, 150), ***ku-u-bi-ti*** (ChS I/2, 1 Rs. III 4, 31; 4: 2'), ***ku-bi-***x[...] (I/5, 86 Vs 5') and ***ku-u-pu-na-(-)***[...] (98: 7'). Th. Richter (*VHN*, 448) mentions the following personal names: (1a) {*ko/ub-*}: *Kupi* (Šušarrā), *Kupija* (Šušarrā), *Kupe-šaki* (Tigunāni). (1b) {*ko/upp-*}: *Kuppija* (Mari), (2) {*ko/ub=a=r=ze*} *Kubarze* (Šubat-Enlil).

Linear A ***ku-pi*** (ZA 14.3) from Kato Zakro is identical with the Hurrian 'one-word' (*imperative*) personal name ***Kupi*** (wr. *Ku-bi*) from Šušarrā, analysis {*ko/ub=i*}, typology 1.3.1.2.1, cf. Th. Richter, *VHN*, 179. Analysis as {*ḫub=i*} 'Destroy (the deceased child) (oh *numen*) !' is also possible, cf. Th. Richter, *VHN*, 423, s.v. ***ḫub-*** 'to break, destroy'.

Since final ***-m*** is not expressed in Linear A, ***ku-pa-do*** (KH 5.3) from Khania can be analysed as an Old Hurrian verbal 'one-word' name {*ḫub=ad=o=m*}, consisting of the verbal root ***ḫub-*** 'to break, destroy' + root-extension ***-ad-*** (meaning unknown), + the Old Hurrian marker of the past or perfect tense ***-o-*** + the Old Hurrian marker of the subject of the past verb ***-m***, translation 'He/She (a *numen*) destroyed (the deceased child)' or as an Old Hurrian *imperative* {*ḫub=ad=o*} 'Destroy (the deceased child) (oh *numen*) !'.

Although I.J. Gelb (*NPN*, 91) and P.M. Purves (*NPN*, 230) ascribe all variants *Ku-pa-ar-ša, Ḫu-pa-ar-ša, Ku-bar-ša, Ku-ba-ar-ša* to ***Kuparša*** at Nuzi, I have found no explicit evidence that *Ḫu-pa-ar-ša* really is the same person as one of the persons, whose name contains the root ***kub-***. I gather that we are in fact dealing with two different roots: ***kub-*** I / ***kupp-*** and ***ḫup-***, although names built on these roots show the same type of formations as can be observed not only in ***Kuparša*** (wr. *Ku-pa-ar-ša, Ḫu-pa-ar-ša, Ku-bar-ša, Ku-ba-ar-ša*) at Nuzi, but also in ***Ku-up-pa-aḫ-***[***ḫ***]***é*** at Nuzi and ***Ḫupaḫ(ḫ)e*** (wr. *Ḫu-pa-ḫe*) at Tigunāni, typology 3.1, lexicon *ḫupaḫ(ḫ)e* (→ *ḫub-*), cf. Th. Richter, *VHN*, 142.

Alternation of ***k-*** signs with signs for the emphatics ***q-*** is quite normal in cuneiform, but ***k/ḫ*** alternation would be exceptional in Hurrian cuneiform. So I think that it is for a good reason that Th. Richter has kept the roots ***kub-*** I / ***kupp-*** and ***ḫup-*** separate in *BGH* and *VHN*.

Th. Richter (*VHN*, 448, n. 465) cautiously distinguishes ***kub-*** I from ***kuw-*** II {*ko/uv*} in spite of ***kub/waḫi***, cf. *BGH*, 225, s.v. ***kub/waḫi*** [Boğ.], *kupaḫi* com. [loan-word into Hittite], ***qupāḫu*** (?) [Emar]: 'bonnet, coiffure du dieu Teššub' (E. Laroche, *GLH*, 157), 'a sort of head-covering, head-gear' according to many scholars, 'helmet (?)' ***qú/qu-pā-ḫu*** at Emar (Westenholz, 1999, 147; Westenholz *et alii*, 2000, 69).

Th. Richter (*VHN*, 449) identifies the personal names ***ᶠKuwari*** from Ašnakkum, Mari and Šušarrā, ***Kuwarija*** from Mari and ***Kuari*** (note the missing glide ***-w-***) from Terqa with the 'sacrificial term' ***kuwari*** [Boğ.] {*ko/uv=a=ri*}, which he ascribes to the root ***kuw-*** II {*ko/uv*} (cf. also *BGH*, 225), as well as the mountain-name ***ku-wa-ar-º***, see also G.F. del Monte - J. Tischler, *Die Orts- und Gewässernamen der hethietischen Texte, Répertoire géographique des textes cunéiformes 6* (Beihefte zum Tübinger Atlas des Vordern Orients), Wiesbaden 1978, 233; 6/2, 89. It has a Hurrian etymology, cf. V. Haas, *Rezension zu* O. Carruba (ed), *Studia Mediterranea Piero Meriggi dicata*, Pavia 1979, *BiOr 38 (1981)*, 643. V. Haas also calls ***kuwari*** 'eine Materie' (*Materia Magica et Medica Hethitica. Ein Beitrag zur Heilkunde im Alten Orient*, Berlin - New York 2003, 778^{+445}).

It is tempting to compare Linear B ***ku-wa-ni-jo-*** (PY Ta 714, 3: instr. plur. masc.) : ***κυάνιος*** 'in blue enamel', derived from ***ku-wa-no*** = ***κύανος*** (PY Ta 714, 1, *et alibi*: dative-instr. sing.) probably designating *lapis-lazzuli* or a glassy substance that looks like it. The adjective qualifies ***po-ni-ki-pi*** = ***φοίνιχφι***, instr. plur. of ***φοῖνιξ*** 'palm-tree' or 'griffin', designating a decorative element of an armchair. Later ***κυάνεος*** is attested in Homer, cf. C.J. Ruijgh, *EGM*, § 204. Could the mountain-name ***ku-wa-ar-º*** and ***kuwari*** 'eine Materie' ['material'] have anything to do with *lapis-lazzuli* ?

Since the Linear B ***k-*** signs represent ***κ-***, ***γ-***, ***χ-***, the corresponding Linear A signs probably represent ***k-***, ***g-***, ***ḫ-*** and ***-ḫḫ-***. This means that Linear A ***ku-pa*** (HT 110a.2, HT Wa 1020α; ZA 11a.5; ZA 11b.3) and possibly ***ku-pa***[(KH 29.2) from Khania can also reflect Hurrian ***Ḫuba***, analysis {*ḫub=a*}, as ***Ḫu-ba*** attested at UR III.

We may also compare the Linear A personal name ***ku-pa-ja*** GRA 16 (HT 116a.1-2) with the Hurrian personal name ***Ḫu-ba-a*** at Ur III, cf. for ***Ḫu-ba*** and ***Ḫu-ba-a*** at Ur III G.R. Meyer, *AOF XIII (1939/40)*, 148; cf. P.M. Purves, *NPN*, 217, s.v. ***ḫump***, ***Ḫumpa***.

However, since ***-m-*** preceding an occlusive is not expressed in consonant clusters in Linear A and B, interpretation as ***Ḫumpa***, analysis {*ḫumb=a*}, is also possible as the Hurrian personal name ***Ḫumpa*** (wr. *Ḫu-um-pa, Ḫu-um-ba*) at Nuzi (I.J. Gelb, *NPN*, 63). P.M. Purves (*NPN*, 217, s.v. ***ḫump***, ***Ḫumpa***) also considers a development of ***ḫump*** < ***ḫupp*** in view of well-known dissimilation of ***pp*** > ***mp*** and the writing variants of the personal name ***Ḫumpape / Ḫup(p)ape*** (wr. *Ḫu-um-pa-be, Ḫu-pa-be, Ḫu-up-pa-be, Ḫu-um-ba-be, Ḫu-um-pa-bi,* [*Ḫu-um*]*-pa-a-be*) at Nuzi. The Ur III forms are older than those from Nuzi, which makes dissimilation of ***pp*** > ***mp*** indeed more likely than assimilation of ***mp*** > ***pp***. Purves assumes that the underlying form is perhaps exemplified by *ḫu-u-ub-bi*, KUB XXVII 4:2; 8 rev.? 2; 12:13; 21:1; *ḫu-u-ub-bi-in-na*, *ibid.* 12:14.

E. Laroche (*GLH*, 110) mentions, s.v. ***Ḫubušdukarra***, SUKKAL du dieu Ḫešue: [d]*Ḫu-bu-uš-du-kar-ra*, KUB XXVII 1 II 22; cf. onom. ***Ḫubušduka***, *AT* 268, 17.

Th. Richter (*VHN*, 142-143) mentions the following Hurrian personal names with the root ***ḫub-***: ***Ḫupaḫ(ḫ)e*** (wr. *Ḫu-pa-ḫe*) at Tigunāni, typology 3.1, lexicon *ḫupaḫ(ḫ)e* (→ *ḫub-*); *Ḫu-pu-‹uš›-tu-ka* Alalaḫ IV (*AT* 202: 31; A. Draffkorn, *HHA*, 132, without addition); **Ḫu-pu-uš-te-ka* Alalaḫ VII (*AT* *268 = JCS 8, 21: 17, reading Zeeb 2001, 573, *editio princeps* has °*-tu-ka* [cf. E. Laroche, *GLH*, 110]; *Ḫu-up-til-la* at Nuzi (NPN 63); ***Ḫupazzam*** (wr. *Ḫu-ba-az-za-am, Ḫu-bi-iz-za-am*) at Šubat-Enlil, typology 3.2.1, analysis {*ḫo/ubazz(i)=a*[E.]*=m(e)*}, lexicon *ḫubazzi* (→ *ḫub-*); ***Ḫupazzan*** (wr. *Ḫu-ba-za-an, Ḫu-ba-az-za*) at Mari, typology 3.2.1, analysis {*ḫo/ubazz(i)=a*[E.]*=(n(na))*}, lexicon *ḫubazzi* (→ *ḫub-*). [E.] refers to *essive* case. According to Th. Richter (*BGH*, 163-165; *VHN*, 423) the meaning of a verbal root ***ḫub-*** {*ḫo/ub-*} 'to break, destroy' is generally accepted, because it corresponds with Hittite *(arḫa) duwarnai-*, cf. also E. Laroche, *GLH*, 109, s.v. ***ḫub-*** 'briser'. On the other hand, for the nominal form ***ḫupaḫ(ḫ)e*** (in ***°=a=ġ/ḫḫe***) as well as for ***ḫubazzi*** {*ḫo/ubazzi*} a plausible lexical explanation is still failing.

Th. Richter (*VHN*, 142-143) mentions the Hurrian personal name ***Ḫupitam*** (wr. *Ḫu-bi-dam*) at Ašnakkum, Mari, Šubat-Enlil, Tuttul, Ĝirsu (UR III), Kaniš, Nippur (UR III), Umma (UR III), Nuzi, Alalaḫ IV, Dilbat, Ḫattuša, analysis {*ḫo/ubid(i)=a*[E.]*=m(e/a)*}, typology 3.2.1, lexicon *ḫubidi*, translation 'Er (Junge) ist wie ein Kalb' ['He (the boy) is like a calf']. This name is probably derived from Hurrian ***ḫubidi*** {*ḫub=idi*} 'Kalb, Stierkalb' ['calf, bull-calf'], 'Stierkalb (des Teššub)' (I. Wegner, 2004, 30), cf. Th. Richter, *BGH*, 164-165, s.v. ***ḫubidi*** [Boğ.; PN], and *VHN*, 423, s.v. ***ḫubidi***. The meaning is confirmed by correspondences with Sumerogram AMAR(*-ti*) and Akkadian *būru* and a relation with the root ***ḫub-*** is possible (cf. Khacikjan, 1985, 63).

E. Laroche (*GLH*, 108-109): ***ḫubidi*** 'veau'. Lecture du sumérogramme AMAR(*-ti*); cf. Goetze, *RHA 39*, 199 n. 46; Otten, OLZ 1954, 135 n. 2; Laroche, RHA XXVII 67. 1. Épithète de Šarrumma 'veau/garçon de Tešub', ***[d]Teššub-bi ḫu-u-bi-ti [d]Šarrumma-n***, KUB XXVII 38 II 14, 20 = [d]U***-ub-wi*** AMAR***-ti [d]Šarrumma***, KBo XX 119 I 14 = IV 18-19 = KBo XVII 86+ I 3; hiér. hitt. [d]VEAU ***Ti-su-pi*** *[h]****u-pi-ti***, Yaz. 42a. - De même KUB XXV 44 V 6; XXXIV 102 II 8; XXVII 1 I 70; KBo XI 5 I 23. Etc. According to E. Laroche (*GLH*, 229) the meaning 'garçon' ['boy'] is the masculine equivalent to Hurrian ***šiduri*** (wr. *ši-du-ri*) 'jeune fille' ['young girl, daughter'] = Akkadian ***ardâtu***.

Taking this into account and if ***ḫubidi*** is analysed as ***ḫub=idi***, with the nominal element ***-idi*** as in ***tar=idi*** 'pot, pan' from ***tari-*** 'fire' and ***naḫḫ=idi*** 'seat' from ***naḫḫ-*** 'to sit, to sit down', it is conceivable that the personal name *Ḫu-pa-ar-ša* at Nuzi should not be normalized to ***Kuparša*** as P.M. Purves (*NPN*, 230) did, but be analysed as {*ḫub-arša*} 'The young boy is a bull-calf ' or even as {*ḫub=a-arša*} 'The young boy is *like* a bull-calf ', {*ḫub=a-*} in the *essive* case, see Hurrian and Urartian ***aršə*** 'young man, boy', cf. Th. Richter, *BGH*, 48, s.v. ****arš-***. Cf. also Linear A ***a-sa-sa-ra-me*** {*arša-Šarra(m)me*}.

If Linear A ***ti-ni-ta*** (HT 27+48a.1) contains the root ***tin-***, variant of Hurrian ***tan-*** 'to make, do, create' (Th. Richter, *BGH*, 436-438, s.v. ***tan-*** [*passim*], ***tin-*** [Ugarit], 'machen, tun'), Linear A ***ti-ni-ta*** can be analysed as {*tin=i=tta*}, containing ***tin-*** 'to make, create' + marker of transitivity ***-i-*** + enclitic ***-tta*** 'me': 'Make / Create me (oh *numen*) !'.

HT 27 + HT 48 (join by E.L. Bennett), HM 36 + 53 (1902-1903). Late Minoan I b ?

a.1. *ti-ni-ta* , *pi* , VIR 80 [
2. 50 CAPSUS 51 *re* 20 [
3. *i-mi-sa-ra* 43 [
4. *qe* 21 *ki-da-te* [ ] *ma-ki-*
5. *63* , *ku-twe* [ ] *sa-ra-di* 5
6. VIR 42
7. *ku-ro* 355
8. HORD 9 JEB FIC 10 B VINa 7

b.1. . .]-*mi-da* , VIN + *wa* , *sa* 7
2.] VINa , GRA , *sa* 1 *re* 14 VINa , *si* ,
3.] *re* (?) [ ] *pa3* (?)
3bis. vacat
4. *pa-se* , VINa + *wa* , *sa* 4 *re* 70
5. VINa GRA , *sa* 4 *re* [ ] 40
6. vacat

O. Landau, *Mykenisch-griechische Personennamen*, 1958, 271, regarded ***Ti-ni-ta*** as a geographical name. His interpretation as a toponym is attractive for two reasons: the prominent place as first term in the heading of HT 27+48a.1 and the ideogram VIR following the entry, with the high number of 80 (or more) men. Linear A ***ti-ni-ta*** may be a toponym with a formant ***-ta*** as in]***su-ki-ri-ta*** (PH Wa 32, side α), attested at Phaistos.

Linear B ***su-ki-ri-ta*** (KN Db 1324, B; KN Db 1327+ 1345+7681+7992; KN Dn 1092+5379+fr., 2) is a toponym, since the ethnic ***su-ki-ri-ta-jo*** (KN C 911, 3) is also attested in Linear B. The Linear A toponym]***su-ki-ri-ta*** can now be explained as 'one-word' name reflecting an *imperative* {*šugri=tta*}, possibly 'Protect me / Bless me !'.

Linear A ***ti-ni-ta*** (HT 27+48a.1) may also be explained as a *jussive* of a verbal root ***ti-*** I / ***tiw-*** I 'to speak (words), to say names'. Clarification of Linear A ***ti-ni-ta*** (HT 27+48a.1) and ***ti-nu-ja*** (HT 115b.2) is difficult. A solution may be found in the variant writings of the verb ***ti- / tiw-*** 'to speak' and the nominal derivations ***tiwe*** [*passim*] 'word, thing' and ***tie/tije*** [Boğ.], (***ti(j)eni***) 'word, name' and even in the theonym ***Ti(ja)-pa/enti*** 'Er spricht das Gute' ['He says the right / good things'] or ['Say the right / good things'], cf. Th. Richter, *BGH*, 453-455, s.v. ***ti-*** I / ***tiw-*** I 'sprechen'. One gets the impression that both ***-w-*** and ***-j-*** are used as transitional glides between vowels. These glides can be used or omitted in the script. Usage of the glide ***-w-*** in ***tiw=ul-*** [Boğ.] 'to say a word to somebody' can be explained from cognate ***-u-*** of the root-extension ***-ul-***. The process of analogy can then explain the usage of ***-w-*** in ***tiwe*** 'word, thing'.

Anyway Linear A ***ti-ni-ta*** (HT 27+48a.1) can be explained as a *jussive* form of the verb ***ti-***, if the form is analysed as {*ti=(e)n=i=tta < ti=(i)=en=i=tta*}, consisting of the root ***ti-*** + the (syncopated) *jussive* marker ***-i-*** + the indicator of the 3rd person singular of the *jussive* ***-i/en-*** + thematic vowel ***-i-*** + the enclitic personal pronoun 1st pers. sing. ***-tta***, cf. I. Wegner, *Einführung*, 103 and Table 9: *The order of suffixes of the positive jussive*. The form can then be translated as (*voluntative*) 'He/She (scil. a *numen*) wants to name me / wants to give me a name' or (*jussive*) 'He/She (scil. a *numen*) may/must name me / may/must give me a name'.

Linear A ***ti-ni***[(HT 51a.2) is possibly an incomplete personal name. Since the first entry of the *b*-side starts with]***ku-me-ta*** 12[(HT 51b.1), there is a good chance that ***ti-ni***[(HT 51a.2) may be completed to ***ti-ni***[***-ta*** as ***ti-ni-ta*** (HT 27+48a.1) from Hagia Triada.

Linear A]***ku-me-ta*** 12[(HT 51b.1) can be analysed as the Hurrian 'one-word' personal name {*kum=e/i=tta*}, consisting of the Hurrian verbal root ***kum-*** 'to build' + the marker of the transitive imperative ***-e/i-*** + the enclitic personal pronoun 1st person singular ***-tta***, translation 'Build / Create me (oh *numen*) !', cf. Th. Richter, *BGH*, 221-222, s.v. ***kum-*** [EN; Nuzi], 'errichten, auftürmen, erschaffen' ['to erect, build, pile up, create'], cf. the theonym *Kumarbi/Kumarwe* and toponyms *Kumme*, *Kumri*, *Kum(m)anni* and the name of the land *Kummuḫi* (i.e. **Kummi/e=o=ġ/ḫḫe*).

O. Landau (*Mykenisch-griechische Personennamen*, 1958, 271) considered Linear A ***ti-nu-ja*** (HT 115b.2) an ethnic derived from a postulated toponym ****Ti-nu***. Landau's view is obviously based on the Greek masculine ethnic suffix ***-yos*** and feminine ***-ya***. Hurrian has no gender (*genera*). The suffix ***-ya*** in Hurrian is the usual suffix for hypocoristic forms, whereas the Hurrian ethnic suffix is ***-ḫe/ -ḫi***, derived from the adjectival suffix.

Sometimes the suffixes ***-ni/-ne*** for the so-called singular and ***-na*** for the so-called plural definite article can also be used for the ethnic forms. Since KUR ***mašriâ=ni-*** (Mit. II 69) and KUR ***mašria=n(i)=ne*** (Mit. II 71) mean 'the Egyptian land', the suffix ***-(n)ni*** can be called adjectival or perhaps 'adjectivating', but since it also seems to be used in ***maria=nni*** 'charioteer', it can also be substantival, so that we can use the general term 'nominal' or 'nominalizing' suffix (Wegner, *Einführung*, 55; G. Wilhelm, *Double Case*, 1995, 124, examples [48] and [49]. KUR is Sumerogram for 'land' (Hurrian ***umini***).

Linear A ***ti-nu-ja*** (HT 115b.2) can be explained as a Hurrian hypocoristic name with the same *jussive* form {*ti=(e)n-*} as in ***ti-ni-ta*** (HT 27+48a.1), consisting of the root ***ti-*** + the (syncopated) *jussive* marker ***-i-*** + the indicator of the 3rd person singular of the *jussive* ***-en-*** + thematic vowel ***-u-*** + the hypocoristic suffix ***-ya***, translation (*jussive*) 'He/She (the child) may/must speak words' or (*voluntative*) 'He/She wants to say names'.

However, if ***tin-*** (variant of ***tan-***) is involved, Linear A ***ti-nu-ja*** can be explained as a hypocoristic name {*tin=u=ja*} meaning 'He/She (a *numen*) made / created (the child)'.

Linear A ***ki-da-<u>te</u>***[(HT 27+HT 48a.4) from Hagia Triada is probably a personal name. E. Laroche (*GLH*, 146, s.v. ***kid-***) mentions: *ki-ta-pa-a-i*, KUB XXVII 42 Ro 32; *ki-i-ta-a-wa$_a$-e*, KBo XII 80 + IV 9; *ki-tal-li-ip-pa*, KUB XLV 18 Ro 18; *ki-ta-al-lu-wa*, KBo XV 1 IV 27. I.J. Gelb (*NPN*, 89) mentions the personal name ***Kitinti*** (that may according to Gelb perhaps be Akkadian *Qitintu* ?). According to Th. Richter (*VHN*, 443) it probably is Hurrian ***Kidindi***. Th. Richter (*VHN*, 170, 443) also mentions *ᶠ**Kitum-allai*** (wr. *ki-tum-al-la-i*) at Mari, analysis {*kid=u/o=m-allai*}, typology 1.1.1.1.1, lexicon *kid-, allai*; *ᶠ**Kitumze*** (wr. *ki-du-um-ze*) at Mari, analysis {*kid=u/o=m=ze*}, typology 1.3, lexicon *kidumze* (→ *kid-*) that can also be equated with the noun *kidumze*. The root is rare in vocabulary and onomastics. A translation is unfortunately not available, cf. also Th. Richter, *BGH*, 218, s.v. ***kid-***. In Linear A and B ***-n-*** and ***-r-*** preceding an occlusive are not expressed in consonant clusters, so that Linear A ***ki-da-te*** is the expected form to write ***kindarte***. It may be related to the Hurrian personal name ***Kintar*** (wr. *Ki-in-tar, Ki-en-tar*) from Nuzi, phonologically /*kindar*/, /*kendar*/.

According to P.M. Purves (*NPN*, 227) ***kintar*** is Hurrian, possibly formed on ***kint***. Connection with the geographical name ***Kin-da-ri***, LAR I § 236, is suggested. The following sentence names with ***-kintar*** as second element occur at Nuzi: ***Šati-kintar*** (wr. *Ša-ti-ki-in-tar*, *Ša-te-ki-in-tar*, *Ša-di-ki-in-tar*, *Ša-te-ki-tar*, *Šadî-ki-in-tar*, *Šadî-ki*-tar*, *Ša-ti-ki-tar*), ***Turi-kintar*** (wr. *Du-ri-ki-in-tar*, *Tu-ri-ki-tar*, *Du-ri-ki-tar*, *Tu-ri-ki-in-tar*, *Du-ur-ki-in-tar*), ***Ų̯anti-kintar*** (wr. *Ú-an-ti-ki-in-tar* [*ti* might be scribal error for *tar*], ***Wantar-kintar*** (wr. *Wa-an-tar-ki-in-tar*, *Wa-an-tar-ki-tar*, *Ú-an-tar-ki-in-tar*, *Wa-an-da-ri-ki-in-tar*, *Ú-a-an-ta-ri-ki-in-tar*, *Ú-a-an-ta-ar-ki-tar*, *Ú-a-an-tar*-ki-in-tar*), ***Ziwir-kintar*** (wr. *Zi-wi-ir-ki-in-tar*), ***Zu-kitar*** (wr. *Zu-ki-tar*). There is sometimes elision of ***-n-*** (***kintar*** > ***kitar***), so that the single dental becomes intervocalic and voiced. Since ***kintar*** and ***kitar*** occur in the same type of sentence names, the forms ***kind=ar*** (with ***-n-***) and ***kid=ar*** (without ***-n-***) are probably basically the same, although Th. Richter (*BGH*, 207-208, s.v. ***kind-*** [PN] and 217-218, s.v. ***kid-***) and (*VHN*, 437-438, s.v. ***kindiri***, and 443, s.v. ***kid-***) distinguishes the two. It is plausible that ***kind-*** and ***kid-*** are *verbal*, if used as first onomastic element, but *nominal*, if used as second element in personal names.

E. Laroche (*GLH*, 148) mentions *ki-in-da?-ri* at Ugarit (RS h. 3, 11). The *editio princeps* reads *ki-in-na-ri* (RS h. 5: 11), cf. Th. Richter, *VHN*, 438. F. Gröndahl (*PNTU*, 236, s.v. ***kindar***) mentions the personal name *turi*(DUMU)*-ki-in-da-ri* at Ugarit that was read as *bin-kindari* in PRU III 15.09-B-I-20, but corrected by C.H. Gordon, *RA 50 (1957)*, 132-133, on the basis of ***turi/tur-kindar*** at Nuzi (*NPN*, 227).

F. Gröndahl proposes that ***kindari*** can be identified with ***kundari*** 'Göttergemach' ['Residence of the Gods'], cf. E. Laroche, PRU III, 333, and *GLH*, 154, s.v. ***kundari*** 'séjour des dieux'. For the alternation ***i/u*** she refers to M. Berkooz, *The Nuzi Dialect of Akkadian*, Language Dissertations 23 (1937), 34-35, and to E.A. Speiser, *Introduction to Hurrian*, 22. E.A. Speiser's observations (*IH*, 22) are still pertinent: "Since Hurrian ***e***, or at least some forms of it, inclined toward [***i***], the question about the quality of Hurrian ***i*** is in order. Frequent interchange of ***i*** and ***u*** may throw some light on this point. Examples of this variaton are given by Thureau-Dangin (*Syria 12* [1931] 262 - fr. Rš Voc.), Goetze, *Language 14 (1938)*, 139, n. 45, and Berkooz (*op. cit.* 34f. - Nuzi names); cf. P.M. Purves, *AJSL 57 (1940)*, 175, n. 60. It is true that cases like *ti-bu-ša* (Rš Voc. I 21) and *tu-bu-e* (*ibid.* II 23), both from a root meaning 'strong' may indicate no more than a *Shwa* in the first syllable; but *I-ri-ya* alongside *I-ru-ya* (Berkooz, *op. cit.* 35) cannot be dismissed on similar grounds. Berkooz draws, therefore, the conclusion that an underlying sound [***ü***] may have to be assumed in such cases (*ibid.* 35). This assumption seems to be supported by the very interesting iuxta-position of *nu-i-wa$_a$-al-la* XXVII 42 rev. 12 and *nu-u-ya-al* XXIX 8 iii 30, in parallel contexts. The orthographic variants ***-uiwa-*** : ***-uuya-*** favor a sequence [***-ü-a***], or the like. If this supposition is correct, it is probable that Hurrian ***i*** in general was close to the sound [***ü***]. Note also especially the changes listed in [61] and for ***i/unu-***, cf. [127]." He mentions (n. 38): "Another case in point is *^{d}Na-ra-am-zu-un* XXVII 38 iii 18 for Akkadian *Narâm-Sin*. The variant is easily explained on the assumption that the Hurrians pronounced foreign [***i***] as [***ü***], which they would write either ***u*** or ***i***."

Kindari can be analysed as {*ki(n)d=ar=i*}, so that its formation can be compared with forms like ***ḫaš=ar=i*** 'aromatic oil, ointment' from ***ḫaš-*** 'to anoint, to rub with ointment', ***šid=ar=ni*** 'curse' from ***šid-*** 'to curse'.

Haas/Thiel (1978, 166) give the meaning 'Götterwohnstätte' ['Residence of the Gods'] for ***kundari***, Popko (1978, 31) 'eine Art Heiligtum' ['a sort of sanctuary'], Hoffner (1998a, 189) 'a shrine', I. Wegner (2001, 442) 'ein Gemach' ['chamber, room'].

E. Laroche (*GLH*, 154), s.v. ***kundari*** 'séjour des dieux', also mentions ***ku-un-ta-ri purulli*** 'la demeure *k.*', IBoT II 39 Ro 38, 41, and the loan-word into Hittite ***ékuntaras***, *HW* 116, in which Otten (1988, 45) sees 'eine Benennung für die Wohnung des Teššup' ['a name for the residence of Teššub'], cf. Th. Richter, *BGH*, 224-225.

However, even if ***kindari*** can be identified with ***kundari*** 'Residence of the Gods', that does not provide a meaning for a *verbal* form {*kind=ar-*} or {*kund=ar-*} based on the same root ***kind-*** or ***kund-*** and *factitive* or *iterative* root-extension ***-ar-***, cf. I. Wegner, *Einführung*, 88. It seems likely, but is not entirely certain, that the verbal root-extension ***-ar-*** is somehow cognate with nominal ***-ar-***.

If Linear A ***ki-da-te̲***[(HT 27+HT 48a.4) is complete, it may be analysed as Hurrian {*kind=ar-te*} consisting of the verbal onomastic element ***kind=ar-*** (with voicing of the dental because of contiguity with the preceding nasal) + the hypocoristic theophorous element ***-te̲***[, shortened form of ***-tešup*** and ***-teḭa*** as final element. If ***ki-da-te̲***[is not complete, a conjecture of ***ki-da-te̲***[***-su*** or ***ki-da-te̲***[***-zu*** for ****kind=ar-tešup*** or ***ki-da-te̲***[***-ja*** or ***ki-da-te̲***[***-i-ja*** for ****kind=ar-teḭa*** may be possible.

For the hypocoristic theophorous element ***-te̲***[as second and final element in Hurrian personal names one may compare P.M. Purves, *NPN*, 264, s.v. ***te***: Hurrian. Shortened form of ***tešup*** and ***teḭa*** as final element. See L. Oppenheim in *WZKM XLIV*, 203 f., n. 1, and writer in *JAOS LVIII*, 465-467, also genealogies indicated in name list by Dr. Gelb. For names in which ***te*** is a variant of ***teḭa***, see s.v. ***-te***: *Al-ki-te, Eḫ-li-te, Ḫa-iš-te, Ḫu-i-te, Ḫu-i-te-e, Ḫu-e-te, Ḫu-i-ti, In-zi-te, Ma-ar-te, Ša-aḫ-lu-te-e, Ša-aḫ-lu-te, Ša-ḫu-ul-te-e, Še-ḫal-te, Še-ḫa-al-te, Ši-la-ḫi-te, Ši-il-wa-te, Du-ra-ar-te, Ur-ḫi-te*.

The Linear A personal names ***ki-da-ro*** (HT 117a.9) and ***ki-da-r̲o̲***[(HT 47a.4) from Hagia Triada, possibly ****Kindaru***, phonologically /*kindaro*/, are probably related to the Hurrian personal name ***Kintar*** (wr. *Ki-in-tar, Ki-en-tar*) from Nuzi, phonologically /*kindar*/ and /*kendar*/, and the geographical name *Kin-da-ri*, LAR I § 236.

Tablet HT 117 is almost complete and well-preserved. The tablet shows the same handwriting as HT 87 according to Raison-Pope, *Index du linéaire A*, Incunabula Graeca XLI, Rome 1971: scribe III. *GORILA 5*: scribe *9 HT*. Tablet HT 47 is heavily damaged.

After ***ma-ka-ri-te*** , ***ki-ro*** , ***u-mi-na-si*** (HT 117a.1-2) a list of 10 personal names, each followed by 1 unit, is followed by ***ku-ro*** 10 (HT 117a.6) that is underscored with a ruler.

The Linear A orthographic conventions allow two possibly cognate roots: Hurrian ***kid-*** and Hurrian ***kind-*** are both attested in Hurrian personal names. Linear A ***ki-da-ro*** is the expected form to write ***kindaro/u*** that may be related to the Hurrian personal name ***Kintar*** (wr. *Ki-in-tar, Ki-en-tar*) from Nuzi, phonologically /*kindar*/, /*kendar*/. I consider it likely that the form ***kind=ar-*** and ***kid=ar-*** are basically the same.

The Linear A personal name ***ki-da-ro*** 1 (HT 117a.9) and ***ki-da-r̲o̲***[(HT 47a.4) can probably be analysed as {*ki(n)d=ar=o*} 'He/she must ….', cf. I. Wegner, *Einführung*, 138, sub *The jussive and other forms of mood in the bilingual*, 3rd person singular =***u*** [***o***], for instance, ***kud=o*** 'he must fall', 'he must be cut/slashed down', KBo 32: 14 I 57: *ku-ú-du*; ***kir=o*** 'he must be liberated, manumitted, set free', KBo 32: 15 IV 3: *ki-i-ru*.

Compare also the discussion on Linear A ***ki-ro*** {*kir=o*} 'he must redeem his debt'. Th. Richter, *VHN*, 593, sub 1.3.1.1: *Names with transitive imperatives* in {***-o***}, ascribes *imperatives* in *°=**o*** to formations of the 2nd person singular: 'release, liberate, manumit (the boy/girl) !'.

At Hagia Triada we find ***ki-da-ta*** **,** GRA 134[(HT 40+76.2). Tablet HT 40+76 reads:

1. *nu-du-wa* , *te* , GRA 207
2. *ki-da-ta* , GRA 134[
3. *ku-ro*[
4. *ku*[

The Linear B tablets from Knossos show that toponyms are often followed by ideograms for GRANUM or HORDEUM. Remarkably both ***nu-du-wa*** and ***ki-da-ta*** are not only followed by the grain ideogram, but also by high numbers: 207 and 134 units, respectively, which makes it more likely that they may represent toponyms. Another argument for identification of ***nu-du-wa*** as a toponym is its occurrence as first sequence of the tablet. As for ***ki-da-ta*** it is significant that E. Laroche (*NH*, 268-272) mentions indeed the following toponyms in ***-tta*** at Boğazköy: *Haitta* (KUB XXXVI 115 Ro 2; KBo X 20 IV 7; 225/g Ro 4 (oracle), *Assaratta* (KBo II 1 I 40; KUB XXIII 21 III 4, 5), *Halatta* (hapax KUB II 1 I 51: dKal uru*Ḫal-la-at-ta*), *Hurutta* (KBo III 1 + 68 III 30. *Hurutta*, capp.). However, it is not impossible that both ***nu-du-wa*** and ***ki-da-ta*** are personal names in spite of the grain ideograms and high numbers.

In principle there are different options feasible to interpret ***nu-du-wa*** (HT 40+76.1):

1. ***-wa*** is a formant indicating a toponym as in Linear B ***e-ti-wa*** (KN Fs 19,1) with the Greek ethnic ***e-ti-wa-ja-*** (cf. M.V. Cremona, D. Marcozzi, E. Scafa, M. Sinatra, *La toponomastica cretese nei documenti in lineare B di Cnosso*, Incunabula Graeca Vol. LXIX, Roma 1978, 33, 35-37), which occurs in the combination ***pa-i-ti-jo e-ti-wa-ja-qe*** (KN Od 681a.1), which must be considered an ethnic, e.g. ***Ἠτιϝαῖος*** derived from the toponym ***e-ti-wa = Ἠτίϝᾱ***, cf. *Ἦτις / Ἤτεια*, name of a town in Crete according to Pape-Benzeler (cf. C.J. Ruijgh, *EGM*, § 195). The Boğazköy texts provide placenames in ***-wa***, such as the West Anatolian region *Arzawa, Saranduwa* (KBo IV 10 Ro 30) > *Saraduwa,* Cappadocian *Sarawa/Sarama,* with the ethnic **Sarawa-wanni* > *Sarawani, Tuttuwa* (KUB II 1 I 47, III 39; KBo XI 40 I 7; 647/f I 1, 8 = JKF 2, 67) with the ethnic *Tuttuwa-ili, Ankuwa,* perhaps Alişar Höyük: Capp. *A(n)kuwa,* with the ethnic *Ankuwa-ziti* (the Ḫattian name of the city was *Ḫanniku,* with the Hittite ethnic *Ḫanniku-ili*, with the Hittite form ***-ili***, derived from Hattic ***-il***), but also the Assyrian metropolis *Ninuwa* 'Ninive', seat of an Ištar-Šauška cult, popular in the Hittite lands (cf. E. Laroche, *NH*, 268-273).
2. ***-wa*** is the Hurrian singular dative ***-wa***, 'for Nudu' or e.g. 'for Nuda', for the ***-u-*** of ***nu-du-wa*** may be due to the ***-w-*** of ***-wa***.
3. ***-wa*** is the (contracted) Hurrian suffix ***-wwâš*** < ***-wwa-(j)aš*** (plural poss. 1st person), 'our Nudu' or 'our Nuda'.
4. If a ***m/w*** alternation is admitted as in Hurrian ***ilmi-/elwi*** and ***irmi-/erwi***, Linear A ***nu-du-wa*** might be equated with the Hurrian personal name ***Nudumar*** (wr. *Nu-du-mar*) from Nuzi, which probably provides ***nud=u-*** (cf. I.J. Gelb, *NPN*, 109: *Nu-du-mar* am*še-el-li-*[*ta-nu*], TCL IX 10: 3, 7, 8, 10, 11, 14, 21; cf. P.M. Purves, *NPN*, 241: *Nu-du-mar*).

There are many Hurrian personal names (and possibly toponyms as well) consisting of a verbal form. At Mari the name of a woman ^{f}***Nutaja*** (wr. ^{f}*nu-da-a-ia*) is attested, analysis {*no/ud=a=ja*}, typology 1.1.1.3.4, lexicon *nud-*, and the name of a boy (^{lú}*tur*) ***Nutal*** (wr. *nu-da-al*) analysis {*no/ud=a=l*}, typology 1.3.3.3, lexicon *nud-*, which is recognized as a Hurrian verbal root, cf. Th. Richter, *VHN*, 218 and 475. The forms {*no/ud=a=ja*} and {*no/ud=a=l*} are no doubt intransitive, as the marker of intransitivity ***-a-*** shows.

I. Wegner (Phonotaktischer *n*-Verlust in Jussivformen des Boğazköy-Hurritischen, *Orientalia Nova Series 59*, Rome 1990, 298-305 301-302[+10]) has shown that the root is also transitive, e.g. at Boğazköy: *nud=est-, nud=un-, nud=ugar-, nudiduri*, cf. also Th. Richter, *BGH*, 284. Th. Richter (*VHN*, 475) also mentions the Hurrian personal names *nu-tu-ni* at Assur (see OMA I 362) and *nu-du-un-na* at Old Babylonian Kiš (YOS 13, 96: 15). Unfortunately the meaning of this verbal root is still unknown.

Linear A ***ki-da-ta*** (HT 40+76.2) may well be Hurrian ****ki(n)darta***, that probably can be analysed a {*ki(n)d=ar=tta*}, consisting of the verbal root ***kid-*** or ***kind-*** + the *factitive* or *iterative* root-extension ***-ar-*** + the suffix for the enclitic personal pronoun 1st person singular ***-tta*** (position 9) indicating the object of action of the transitive verb, of which the meaning is not yet known. See for the root-extension ***-ar-*** I. Wegner, *Einführung*, 88. See for the suffix of the enclitic pronoun ***-tta*** indicating the object of action of the transitive verb I. Wegner, *Einführung*, 95, Table 5.

Morphologically ***ki-da-ta*** (HT 40+76.2) may well be compared with Linear A] ***su-ki-ri-ta*** (PH Wa 32: side α) on a nodule from Phaistos (HM 1491, 1950). It can be analysed as a Hurrian personal name or rather toponym {*šugr=i=tta*}, 'Protect/bless me !'. The orthographic conventions of Linear A and B require that occlusives in consonant clusters must always be expressed. Consequently the syllable ***-gri-*** must be written as ***-ki-ri-***.

Linear A] ***su-ki-ri-ta*** (PH Wa 32: side α) can be compared with the Linear A personal name ***su-ki-ri-te-i-ja*** (HT Zb 158b) at Hagia Triada, Hurrian ***Šukri-teja̯***, analysis {*šugr=i-teja̯*}, hypocoristic of ***Šukri-tešup*** {*šugr=i-tešub*}, 'Protect/Bless (the child), oh Tešub !'. One may even assume that Linear A ***ki-da-ta*** relates to Linear A ***ki-da-te̲***[(HT 27+48a.4) as Linear A] ***su-ki-ri-ta*** relates to ***su-ki-ri-te-i-ja***, especially since Hurrian ***-te*** and ***-teja̯*** are hypocoristics of ***-Tešub***. The enclitic personal pronoun 1st person singular ***-tta*** 'me' in ***ki-da-ta*** {*ki(n)d=ar=tta*} and] ***su-ki-ri-ta*** {*šugr=i=tta*} is object of the *imperatives* ***ki(n)d=ar(=i)*** and ***šugr=i***, respectively, whereas both ***-te*** and ***-teja̯*** have the function of *vocative* in ***ki-da-te̲***[{*ki(n)d=ar-te*} and in ***su-ki-ri-te-i-ja***, ***Šukri-teja̯*** {*šugr=i-teja̯*}.

On 28 May 1980 I gave my paper *The historical significance of onomastic data from Linear A and B texts* to the Mycenaean Seminar of the Institute of Classical Studies of the University of London. The integral text of the seminar was distributed on request by the Secretary of the Institute. During the seminar I discussed (p. 7) among others the Linear A sequences] ***su-ki-ri-ta*** and ***su-ki-ri-te-i-ja*** and remarked about the latter: "Keeping in mind E. Laroche's statement as regards the character of Hurrian names, we cannot fail to observe the significance of the morphological appearance of this name in Linear A. But even more important is the length of the identified name (six syllabic signs), since it virtually excludes the chance that the equation is just accidental."

Jacques Raison wrote a review on this Mycenaean Seminar in the *Revue des Études Grecques, Tome XCVII, 1984, Bulletin Égéo-Anatolien*, 87, sub 8:

"Du même auteur (Peter G. van Soesbergen), *BICS 28.1981*, p. 163, résume une conférence du 28-5-80 sur le même sujet: *The historical significance of onomastic data from Linear A and B texts* (texte complet fourni sur demande par la revue). ... Sans pousser jusqu'à l'hiéroglyphique, trop mal connu, Van Soesbergen, entre autres preuves, remonte aux origines du linéaire A, dont les traits 'agglutinants' et les caractéristiques orthographiques du syllabaire (inférées de celles du syllabaire B, son héritier) lui paraissent avoir été conçues pour une langue comme celle du Mitanni. Rapprochement de mots du linéaire A et hourrites (assez intéressant, quand ils sont suffisamment longs); essai, finalement, point tellement loin d'une esquisse de déchiffrement partiel."

Linear A] ***su-ki-ri-ta*** (PH Wa 32, side α) is the only entry on a pyramid-shaped nodule (HM 1491, 1950) from the west wing of the Palace of Phaistos, found under the neo-palatial pavement of vano 10, stratum IV, fill-layer of ca. 1 m. between pavement and underlying concrete. Transition Middle Minoan IIb / Middle Minoan III. End of protopalatial period (D. Levi's local phase 3).

PH Wa 32, side α:] *su-ki-ri-ta*

side β: Seal impression: possibly a quadruped.

L. Godart - J.-P. Olivier (*GORILA 2*, 90) read *su-ki-ri-ta* (PH Wa 32) on this nodule from Phaistos. J. Raison - M. Pope (1980), 278, and (1994), 268, read the same nodule, which they labelled PH W 37, as] *su-ki-ṛi-ta*.

Hurrian provides in principle the following feasible interpretations:

I)] ***su-ki-ri-ta*** (PH Wa 32: side α) can be analysed as the Hurrian verbal form {*šugr=i=tta*} 'protect/bless me !' (2nd person singular *imperative*, followed by the suffix of the enclitic personal pronoun 1st person singular ***-tta***), cf. I. Wegner, *Einführung in die hurritische Sprache*, 2007, 103, Table 9: *The order of suffixes for the positive jussive*. The form is based on the root of the transitive ergative verb ***šugr-*** 'to protect, to bless' + the marker of transitivity ***-i-*** (the *imperative* 2nd person singular does not have its own marker) + ***-tta*** 'me' (double writing in cuneiform indicates voicelessness of the dental.). There is a hole for a string visible at the short end. If the nodule was used as an amulet, the inscription may indicate the purpose of the object: protection of the owner against evil. If it served as a label accompanying (precious) goods, the aphorism may have been meant to protect these goods. According to V. Haas, 'Betrachtungen zum Gotte *Tilla*', in: *Festschrift Lacheman*, 1981, 183-188, the verbal root ***šugr-*** in personal names might reflect 'to protect, bless' and the noun ***šugri*** at Boğazköy might be 'Segen, Wünsch' ['blessing, wish']. The term is also deified (*ibidem*, 185, note 11, and 1982a, 357). Most scholars hesitate to translate these forms, cf. also Th. Richter, *BGH*, 409, s.v. ***šugr-*** [PN] and s.v. ***šugri*** [Boğ.]; Th. Richter, *VHN*, 518 + n. 731-732, s.v. ***šugr-*** {*šo/ugr-*}.

II) A category of Hurrian personal names was built exactly in this way, as explained sub I: a 'one-word' name {*šugr=i=tta*} consisting of a verbal element in the *jussive* or *imperative*, followed by the enclitic personal pronoun 1st person sing. ***-tta***, cf. Th. Richter, *VHN*, 136 and 600, where he mentions the example ***Ḫeršitta*** (wr. *ḫe-er-ši-it-ta*) from Qaṭṭarā (Tall ar-Rimaḫ), cf. *ḫé-er-ši-it-ta* from Nuzi (*NPN*, 60), analysis {*ḫerž=i=tta*}, typology 1.3.1.2.2.1, lexicon *ḫerš-*, of which the meaning is unknown.

A. Draffkorn, *HHA*, 1959, 104, called the suffix ***-tta*** in personal names 'either a hypocoristic or formative element', e.g. in ***Šuru-t(t)a*** at Alalaḫ, cf. personal names with the suffix ***-tta*** at Nuzi (P.M. Purves, *NPN*, 268): *Akitta, Arratta, Ḫalutta, Ḫeršitta, Kaitta, Kapatta, Maitta, Pukkitta*. Analysis in more recent literature by I. Wegner (2007), Th. Richter (*VHN*, 2016) and others have clarified the real character of these names and the meaning of the suffixes which are certainly not hypocoristic.

Th. Richter (*VHN*, 600) explains that the enclitic personal pronoun 3rd person singular ***-n/-nna*** occurs more often in personal names than that of the 1st person singular ***-tta***: for instance, ***Ḫerzin***, wr. *ḫe-er-zi-in*, at Mari (Tall Hariri), analysis {*ḫerž=i=n(na)*}, typology 1.3.1.2.2.1, lexicon ***ḫerz-***, see *VHN*, 136 and 600; ***ᶠTawenna*** (wr. *ta-we-en-na*) from Mari and Ašnakkum (Tall Šaġīr Bāzār / „Chagar Bazar"), analysis {*tav=i=nna*}, typology 1.3.1.2.2.1, lexicon *taw-* I, translation 'Cast her (the girl) (oh *numen*) !', see *VHN*, 297, 600. See for the latter name also Linear A ***ta-we-na*** (HT 10b.1-2). This personal name from Hagia Triada is an exact equivalent to the Hurrian personal name ***Tawe-nna*** at Ašnakkum and Mari, cf. also J.M. Sasson, 'Ḫurrians and Ḫurrian names in the Mari texts', *UF 6 (1974)*, 370 and 386: s.v. ***Tawe-nna***.

III) The Linear A form **]** ***su-ki-ri-ta*** (PH Wa 32: side α) is an exact equivalent to Linear B ***su-ki-ri-ta*** (KN Db 1324, B; KN Db 1327+1345+7681+7992; Dw 1325; KN Dn 1092+5379+fr., 2, *et alibi*), identified as a toponym ***Συγρίτᾱ***, because the Linear B ethnic ***su-ki-ri-ta-jo*** (KN C 911, 3: nom. sg. m.), probably ***Συγριταῖος***, is derived from it.

Su-ki-ri-ta has often been equated with the name of the Cretan town ***Συβρίτᾱ***, which is of Pre-Hellenic origin as well, cf. C.J. Ruijgh, *EGM* , § 195, who remarks that ***Συγρίτᾱ*** might be identified with ***Συβρίτᾱ***, a town in Crete, if one admits a doublet ****Συγʷρίτᾱ > Συβρίτᾱ***. But assumption of doublets ***Συγρίτᾱ*** and ****Συγʷρίτᾱ > Συβρίτᾱ*** is not necessary, since ***Συβρίτᾱ*** may well be derived from a different Hurrian root ***šubri-***, wr. *šu-ub-ri* KUB XXXII 21, 6; genitive *šu-ub-ri-bi*, epithet of Tešub, IBoT II 39 Vo 2, 43; - Dative *šu-ub-ri-ba*, KUB XXXII 19 III 2. Pl. *šu-ub-ri-ya-na-*, KUB XXVII 46+ I 25, 31 sqq. 2. theme *šuburri* < *šubri-ni* attribute of Tešub. etc., cf. E. Laroche, *GLH*, 238: Bien que *šubri-bi* soit souvent coordonné à *eḫli-bi* 'du salut', on ne peut l'assimiler, sans plus, à *suḫurri-bi* 'de la vie', v. sous *suḫuri*, cf. E. Laroche, *GLH*, 238; cf. for more references Th. Richter, *BGH*, 417, s.v. ***šubri-*** [Boğ; GN?]: *šubri* 'Terminus des Wohlbefindens' (V. Haas, 1998a: 4); 'Herschafts- oder Vokationsterminus, Epitheton des Teššub' (V. Haas, 1998a: 243); 'Heil(?)' (V. Haas, 2003a: 141+5.

The equation of Linear A **]** ***su-ki-ri-ta*** (PH Wa 32.α) with Linear B ***su-ki-ri-ta*** (KN Db 1324, *et alibi*) makes identification of the Linear A sequence as a toponym attractive. Moreover, as mentioned *supra* with regard to Linear A ***ki-da-ta*** (HT 40+76.2), there are some toponyms with the ending ***-tta*** attested at Boğazköy as well: e.g. ***Haitta***, ***Assaratta***, ***Halatta***, ***Hurutta***, cf. E. Laroche, *NH*, 268-272.

However, since Linear A **]** ***su-ki-ri-ta*** (PH Wa 32.α) is the only syllabic entry on the nodule, there is no conclusive contextual indication, whether we are dealing with **I)** a verbal expression 'protect/bless me !', II) a personal name meaning 'Bless me !' or III) a toponym, also meaning 'Bless me !'. In all three cases the meaning remains the same.

Linear A ***su-ki-ri-te-i-ja*** (HT Zb 158b), Hurrian ***Šugri-teịa***, hypocoristic form of ***Šugri-teš(š)ub***, occurs on the side of a pithos (Her. Mus. 3915) from the Villa of Hagia Triada. The pithos was incised before firing and was found in magazine 5, subjacent to the east foundations of the Mycenaean 'megaron'. The inscription reads:

HT Zb 158a. *tu̲-se-su-ki*

b. *su-ki-ri-te-i-ja*

I agree with J. Raison - M. Pope (1994, 131-132) and *GORILA 4* (64-65) that reading *59-103-72-92-100a-32* = ***su-ki-ri-te-i-ja*** should be preferred to the previous reading by G. Pugliese Carratelli and W.C. Brice as *59-103-72-92-77-32* = ***su-ki-ri-te-se-ja***, since the one but last sign is certainly ***100a = i***, definitely not ***77 = se***, cf. G. Pugliese Carratelli, 'Le iscrizioni preelleniche di Haghia Triada in Creta e della Grecia peninsulare' (*Monumenti Antichi 40*), Roma 1945, 590. Cf. W.C. Brice, *Inscriptions in the Minoan Linear Script of Class A (ILA)*, Oxford 1961, 16, sub II 7 a, b (Her. Mus. 3915) and Plates XXIII/XXIIIa, sub II 7 b.

Regarding the first line of the inscription I had followed the reading [.]-[.]-***no̲-su-ki*** by J. Raison - M. Pope (1994, 131-132) in my *Corpus of transliterated Linear A texts*, but the photograph of *GORILA 4* has convinced me that the reading ***tu̲-se-su-ki*** (HT Zb 158a), proposed by L. Godart and J.-P. Olivier, is to be preferred.

J.G.P. Best (*Some preliminary remarks on the decipherment of Linear A*, Amsterdam 1972, 34, n. 103) has apparently not noticed that C.H. Gordon and St. Alexiou gave in fact a different reading of the same inscription (HM 3915), since he considered the two interpretations of both scholars to be entries in two different inscriptions. Obviously, J.G.P. Best's statement that Gordon's interpretation of ***su-ki-ri-te-se-ja*** as a Hurrian name (Gordon, *Evidence*, 31, no. 128) is supported by the proper name ***su-ki-ri-to-no-ja*** (St. Alexiou, 'Eine neue Linear-A-Inschrift aus Kreta', *Kadmos II*, 16) is not only confusing, but also amusing, if one realizes that one is actually dealing with the same inscription.

Linear A ***su-ki-ri-te-i-ja*** can be identified with Hurrian ***Šugri-teịa***, hypocoristic form of ***Šugri-teš(š)ub***. It offers a perfect and well-attested Hurrian name with ***Šugri-***, perhaps phonologically ***/Sugri-/***, as verbal element (cf. *Šuk-ri, Šuk-ri-šar, Šuk-ri-te-šup, Šuk-ri-ia, Šu-uk-ri-ia, Šuk-ri-a, Šuk-ri-ip-a-pu, Šuk-ri-ip-šarri, Šuk-rip-šarri, Šuk-ri-til-la*, etc.).

I.J. Gelb, *NPN*, 136-137, provides lists of personal names with the element *Šukri-, Šukr-, Šukri-p-, Šukru-m-, -šukru(m)*, which are phonologically likely */sugri-/, /sugr-/, /sugri-b-/, /sugru-m-/, /-sugru(m)/*, respectively. Note the long list of occurrences of the sentence names *Šuk-ri-te-šup*, *Šu-uk-ri-te-šup* and *Šu-gur-te-šup* on page 137.

We now know that names such as *Šuk-ri-ip-a-pu, Šuk-ri-ip-šarri, Šuk-rip-šarri* are in fact 'Old Hurrian' *indicative* sentence names in ***=i=b-***, in which ***=b*** is the Old Hurrian marker of the subject 3rd person singular. 'Old Hurrian' ***šugr=i=b*** 'he protects / blesses' = 'Mitanni' Hurrian ***šugr=i=a***, cf. I. Wegner, *Einführung*, 126-127. A. Draffkorn, *HHA*, 104, *Sugri-ya, Sugrum-alli*. ***Šukrum-Tešub***, King of Elaḫut, mentioned in the Mari texts and at Šubat-Enlil, cf. J.M. Sasson, 'Ḫurrians and Ḫurrian names in the Mari texts', *UF 6 (1974)*, 385; Th. Richter, *VHN*, 281. ***Šukrum-Tešub*** can be analysed as *{šugr=o=m-Tešub}* '*Tešub*, he has blessed / protected (the child)', consisting of the root ***šugr-*** 'to bless, protect' + the Old Hurrian marker of the past tense ***-o/u-*** + the Old Hurrian marker of the acting subject 3rd person singular ***-m***.

Šugri-teia is like ***Šugri-teš(š)ub*** a typical Hurrian theophorous 'sentence name' with the *imperative* of the transitive verb {*šugr=i-*} as first element and ***-teia / -teš(š)up*** as nominal theophorous element in the *vocative*, so that the name can be translated as 'Protect / Bless (the child), oh Teš(š)ub !'. *Teš(š)ub* is, of course, the name of the Hurrian head of the pantheon, 'King of Gods', 'Weather God' or 'God of clouds', who resembles *Ba'al* in Syria, *Iškur* and *Hadad* in Mesopotamia, *Tarhunt* in Anatolia, *Seth* in Egypt and *Zeus* in Greece.

An overwhelming number and a great variety of Hurrian personal names contain a theophorous element referring to ***Tešub*** or ***Teššub***. I give a few examples from the long list of sentence names: *Aki-teš(š)ub, Ari-teš(š)ub, Eḫli-teš(š)ub, Ḫišmi-teš(š)ub, Ḫutu-teš(š)ub, Ini-teš(š)ub, Kili-teš(š)ub, Šukri-teš(š)ub, Talmi-teš(š)ub, Teḫi-teš(š)ub, Tili-teš(š)ub, Tulpi-teš(š)ub, Tuppi-teš(š)ub, Ulmi-teš(š)ub, Urḫi-teš(š)ub*, cf. E. Laroche, *NH*, 348; cf. P.M. Purves, *NPN*, 265-266; cf. A Draffkorn, *HHA*, 108; cf. J.M. Sasson, 'Ḫurrians and Ḫurrian names in the Mari texts', *Ugarit Forschungen* 6 *(1974)*, 386. P.M. Purves, *NPN,* 264-265, gives long lists of examples with comments, s.v. ***-te***, ***-teia***. He remarks with regard to ***-teia*** (the most frequent hypocoristic form of ***-teš(š)ub*** at Nuzi): "***teia***: Hurrian. In most instances demonstrable as hypocoristic form of ***tešup***; a shortened variant is ***te***. Genealogies concerned have been indicated in the name list by Dr. Gelb."

Th. Richter (*BGH*, 409) mentions, s.v. ***šugr-*** [PN], that the meaning 'to protect, bless' was accepted by V. Haas (1981b, 185[11]), whereas other scholars hesitate. V. Haas (*ibidem* and 1982a, 357) also translates the noun ***šugri*** as 'Segen, Wünsch' ['blessing, wish'] and mentions that the term was also deified.

We also find in Linear B a personal name ***su-ki-ri-to*** (KN As 1516, 12), ***Συγρίτος***, which may well be a Hellenized form in ***-ος***, that is either related to the toponym ***su-ki-ri-ta*** (cf. C.J. Ruijgh, *EGM*, § 195 and § 334, n. 84) or may be the shortened Mycenaean rendering of the Linear A personal name ***su-ki-ri-te-i-ja*** and the Hurrian names ***Šugri-teia / Šukri-te***, hypocoristic forms of the 'sentence name' ***Šugri-tešub***.

The fragmentary Linear A inscription]***te-ja***[(PYR Zb 5) on a sherd of a clay vase from the Minoan country house at Pyrgos (Myrtos), now in the Knossos Stratigraphical Museum (MP/71/79), may well be the common theophorous element ***-teya***, hypocoristic of ***-teš(š)ub*** as second element of a Hurrian name. Cf. Linear A ***su-ki-ri-te-i-ja*** (HT Zb 158b) from Hagia Triada and ***o-te-ja*** (PK 1a.4bis) from Palaikastro.

If the reading ***tu-se-su-ki*** (HT Zb 158a), is indeed correct, interpretation of Linear A ***tu-se-su-ki*** (HT Zb 158a) as a Hurrian personal name seems possible. The name is probably a Hurrian sentence name consisting of a verbal first element ***tuš=e-*** and a nominal second element ***šugi*** or ***zuki***. Th. Richter (*VHN*, 321, 547) remarks that the evidence is slight for the roots ***tuš-*** and ***tuz-***, that both can be analysed as {*to/už*} also in the onomastic material. He analyses the personal names ***ᶠTušaja*** (wr. *ᶠTu-ša-ia*) from Mari as {*to/už=a=ja*}, typology 1.1.1.3.4, lexicon *tuš-* (cf. also *Tù-ša* at Kaniš) and ***ᶠTuzija*** (wr. *ᶠTu-zi-ia*) from Ašnakkum as {*to/už=i=ja*}, typology 1.1.1.2.4, lexicon *tuz-*. In note 838 he tells that he is aware of the fact that I.J. Gelb (1980, 646, nr. 6142-6143) interpreted the personal names *tu-za-a* and *tu-za-*[*i*]*a* as Amorite {TU'Z-AJA}.

However, he states that because of the second element in the personal name *ᶠTuza-Naje* (wr. *ᶠTu-za-na-a-ie*) from Mari, analysis *{to/už=a=Ø-Naje}*, typology 1.1.1.3.3, lexicon *tuz-*, *Naje*, and implicitly also in ***ᶠTuza-Na*** (wr. *ᶠTu-za-na*) from Mari, analysis *{to/už=a=Ø-Na}*, typology 1.1.1.3.3, lexicon *tuz-*, *Na* (→ *Naje*), the Hurricity of the roots is very likely, since *Naje/Naja* is a Hurrian deity. Although the meaning of the verbal roots ***tuš- / tuz-*** is unfortunately not yet known, the Hurrian identity is clear. As for the Linear A form *<u>tu</u>-se-su-ki* it is also important that the root can not only be *intransitive* as in *ᶠTuza-Naje, ᶠTuza-Na, ᶠTušaja* and *Tù-ša* (with the indicator of intransitivity ***-a***), but also *transitive* as in *ᶠTuzija* (with the marker of transitivity ***-i***).

According to Th. Richter (*VHN*, 304, 517-518) ***šugi*** I *{šo/ugi}* occurs as second onomastic element in the name ***Teḫes-šuka*** from Šušarrā, *{teġ=i=ž-šo/ug(i)=a*[E.]}, typology 1.3.2.2, lexicon *teḫ-*, *šugi* I, 'Er/Sie (scil. ein *Numen*) möge *šugi* gedeihen lassen' ['He/She (a *numen*) may let *šugi* thrive'], 'Er/Sie (scil. ein *Numen*) möge Jungen retten' ['He/She (scil. a *numen*) may save the boy'], which offers an excellent onomastic meaning. Although he admits that ***šugi*** 'eins' ['one'] (see *BGH*, 406) and ***šugi*** 'Türsturz' ['lintel'] (see *BGH*, 408) cannot be completely excluded, he prefers the translation 'Junge' ['boy']. [E.] refers to the *essive* case in ***-a***. Cf. also the personal name ***Atal-šuku*** (wr. *A-tal-šu-ku*) from Tigunāni, *{adal-šo/ug(i)=u*[N.]}, typology 2.1, lexicon *adal-, šugi* I, cf. Th. Richter, *VHN*, 87, 518. [N.] refers to the Akkadianizing nominative in ***-u***.

Th. Richter (*BGH*, 408; *VHN*, 518) mentions, s.v. ***zugi*** II, that on account of a vocabulary list Hurrian ***zugi*** equals Akkadian ***ṣeḫru*** 'Junge' ['boy'] that is found in so-called 'one-word' names such as ***Zukan*** (Mari), ***Zuki*** (Ašnakkum), ***Zuki-zuki*** (Mari), ***Zuku-zu***[***ku***](?) (Mari), ***Zukašši*** (Mari). *Zu-ga-aš(?)-ši(?)*, *{zo/uga=ašše}*, 'Kleinheit' ['small size'] may well provide a good meaning for a personal name. ***Zuki-zuki*** might represent a superlative 'Der sehr kleine (Junge)' ['The very small (boy)']. Comparing ***šugi*** I and ***zugi*** II it is very likely that we are dealing with variant writings of the same word. As a result the analysis of Linear A of ***<u>tu</u>-se-su-ki*** (HT Zb 158a) offers a personal name that probably contains an *imperative* ***tuš=e/i***, of which ***šugi*** 'the small boy' is the object. The partial translation is: '….. the small boy (oh *numen*) !'.

If Linear A] ***sa-ra-di*** **5** (HT 27+48a.5) is complete, it can be identified with Hurrian ***šalardi***, since in Linear A and B ***-r-*** preceding an occlusive is not expressed in consonant clusters. Hurrian ***šalardi*** is interpreted as a collective form in ***-ardi***.

According to I. Wegner (*Einführung in die hurritische Sprache*, 2007^2, 58, 251, 266, 275, 277) the suffix ***-arde / -ardi*** forms collectives. The thematic vowel disappears, when ***-arde/-ardi*** appears: ***šal(a)=arde*** 'Tochterschaft' ['daughterhood'] from ***šala*** 'daughter'; ***atta(i)=arde*** 'Vorväter, Vorfahren' ['ancestors'] from ***attai*** 'father'; ***šen(a)=arde*** 'Bruderschaft' ['brotherhood'] from ***šena*** 'brother'; ***maria=nn(i)=arde*** 'Streitwagen-kämpfer' ['charioteers'].

In a cuneiform text from Mari the form ***šal(a)=arde*** is combined with the Hurrian numeral ***šindi*** 'seven'. Mari 5: 8-11: ***papan(i)=na=aš=u=uš … Šimige=ne=ve=na šindi šal(a)=arde*** 'the mountains (plural ergative) … the seven daughters of *Šimige*' (cf. I. Wegner, *ibidem*, 92). The collective form in ***-arde/-ardi***, if used in combination with a numeral, apparently indicates 'a *coherent group* consisting of a certain number'.

If this notion is applied to Linear A text HT 27+48, we observe that in the first 6 lines of the *a*-side of this tablet large numbers of men are mentioned (ideogram VIR is even mentioned twice). In line 2 the ideogram CAPSUS appears, followed by the number 51. If ***sa-ra-di*** **5** can indeed be interpreted as 'a *group* of 5 daughters', this would fit in the context of the high number of persons registered in the first 6 lines of the tablet, followed by ***ku-ro*** **355** in line 7. Line 8 of HT 27+48a registers ideograms of commodities, numbers and fractions: HORD 9 JEB FIC 10 B VINa 7, which may possibly be considered rations attributed to the persons just mentioned.

Occurrence of the Linear A term ***a-ta-de*** (KT Zf 1), last sequence of an inscription of 18 Linear A signs in one line on one side of a gold pin of 11 cm, with floral decoration on the other side, that may well be identified with the Hurrian collective form ***atta(i)=arde*** 'ancestors' (see *chapter 10: Linear A inscriptions on metal objects*), seems to corroborate interpretation of Linear A ***sa-ra-di*** as Hurrian ***šalardi***. In view of the precious object (a gold pin), on which the inscription is written, the special meaning of ***attardi*** 'gift for the bride's father' may be pertinent, cf. G. Wilhelm, Hurritische Lexikographie [= review-article on E. Laroche, *Glossaire de la langue hourrite*, Paris 1980], *Orientalia Nova Series 54*, Rome 1985, 491: 'Geschenk für den Brautvater'; cf. also Th. Richter, *BGH*, 67-68, s.v. ***attardi*** [Mitt]. Linear A ***a-ta-de***, interpreted as Hurrian ***attardi*** 'gift for the bride's father' certainly makes sense as last word of the inscription on the gold pin.

In view of the orthographic conventions of Linear A and B, which offer more ambiguities than syllabic cuneiform, another theoretical interpretation must also be considered. Since the preceding sequences ***i-mi-sa-ra*** (HT 27+48a.3) and ***ki-da-<u>te</u>***[(HT 27+48a.4) on the same tablet as ***sa-ra-di*** (HT 27+48a.5) are probably to be interpreted as personal names, it cannot be excluded that ***sa-ra-di*** is a personal name as well. It is conceivable that ***sa-ra-di***, analysed as the abstract collective ***šal(a)=ardi***, can itself be used as a personal name, although I do not know such examples in cuneiform. However, there are comparable examples of personal names with a similar *nominal* suffix: the abstract or collective suffix ***-zari / -šari***.

I. Wegner (*Einführung*, 57) explains ***-zari / -šari*** as a possibly abstract or collective suffix. She offers the examples: ***enzari*** (< ***en(i)*** + ***šari***) 'Gottheit' ['divinity'], derived from ***eni*** 'God'; ***tipšari*** (< ***tiv(e)*** + ***šari***) 'Wort, Sache, Erzählung' ['word, thing, story'], derived from ***tive*** 'Wort' ['word']; ***furulzari*** (< ***fur*** + ***(u)l(i)*** + ***šari***) 'Opferschauer' ['interpreter of sacrifices'], derived from ***fur-*** 'to see' (wr. ***p/wur-***).

Th. Richter (*VHN*, 244, 497) accepts that ***-za-ri / -šari*** indicates abstract or collective forms in ***ᶠŠalanzar*** (wr. *ᶠŠa-la-an-za-ar*), name of 2 women from Qaṭṭarā, and ***ᶠŠalanzari*** (wr. *ᶠŠa-la-an-za-ri, ᶠŠa-la-za-ri*), typology 3.1, lexicon *šalazari* (→ *šala*), translation 'Töchter (?)' ['daughters (?)']. Also in ***ᶠAštuzar*** (wr. *aš-tu-za-ar*), typology 3.1, lexicon *aštuzari* (→ *ašte*), a female weaver from Ašnakkum (Tall Šaġīr Bāzār, 'Chagar Bazar') and a lady from Mari (cf. Th. Richter, *VHN*, 80), and ***ᶠAzzuzari*** (wr. *az-zu*-IZ-*za-ri*), typology 3.1, lexicon *azzuzari* (→ *azze*), Admattum^{KI}, 'wife' of Kulmiš, and female weaver from Mari (cf. Th. Richter, *VHN*, 84), translated as 'Frauen(?)' ['women(?)']. One may add ***ᶠAštuašar*** (wr. *ᶠAš-du-a-šar*) at Nuzi (I. J. Gelb, *NPN*, 37).

I should like to propose the translation 'Womanhood' or 'Woman *par excellence*' for the personal names ***fAštuzar*** at Ašnakkum and Mari, ***fAzzuzari*** at Mari, ***fAš-du-a-šar*** at Nuzi and Linear A ***a-du-sa-ra*** (HT 62+73.1) = ***Ašdu-šara*** or ***Aždu-šara*** (possibly with *essive* ending in ***-a***) at Hagia Triada. I shall later discuss ***a-du-sa-ra*** (HT 62+73.1) more extensively and give another feasible interpretation for the name.

It is theoretically not inconceivable (at least in accordance with the orthographic conventions) that Linear A] ***sa-ra-di*** (HT 27+48a.5) can be interpreted as the personal name ****Šar(=i)-aždi*** 'Wish (the child), oh woman !' or as ****Šal(a)-aždi*** 'The daughter is a woman'. The first is semantically acceptable, but the latter does not make sense, since it is evident that 'a daughter' is female. This does not have to be emphasized.

No doubt the Minoan scribe knew, whether ***sa-ra-di*** on this tablet designates the Hurrian collective term ***šal(a)=arde/i*** 'daughterhood', '(group of) daughters'. Although we cannot be entirely sure, my preference goes to ***šal(a)=arde/i***, since the term is attested in Hurrian cuneiform texts and because it is conceivable that ***sa-ra-di* 5 = *šal(a)=arde/i* 5** = 'a *group* of 5 daughters' can be combined with personal names in the same text.

Moreover, occurrence of the comparable formation Hurrian ***a-ta-de*** (KT Zf 1) ***atta(i)=arde*** 'ancestors' in Linear A makes interpretation of ***sa-ra-di*** (HT 27+48a.5) as ***šal(a)=arde/i* 5** the most likely option. The mentioning of 'a group of daughters' alongside the names of adults reminds us of the Linear B personnel tablets from Pylos, where the women are registered with their names, ethnic provenance or profession, whereas their sons are merely mentioned as ***ko-wo*** and their daughters as ***ko-wa***.

Tablet HT 117a starts with ***ma-ka-ri-te , ki-ro , u-mi-|na-si , u-su*** 1 (HT 117a.1-2), of which ***u-su*** is the first of a series of 10 personal names, all followed by 1 unit: ***mi-tu*** 1 (HT 117a.2), ***ku-ra-mu*** 1 (HT 117a.2-3), ***ma-ru*** 1, ***ku-pa3-nu*** 1 (HT 117a.3), ***tu-|68-ma*** 1 (HT 117a.3-4), ***u-di-mi*** 1 (HT 117a.4), ***mi-ru-ta-ra-re*** 1 (HT 117a.4-5), ***te-ja-re*** 1 ***na-da-re*** 1 (HT 117a.5). After this list of 10 names the *underlined* line 6 offers ***ku-ro*** 10, which clearly is the summation of these 10 units and which can be explained as 'again (in total)'.

In my view Linear A ***ku-ro*** can be identified as the Hurrian particle or adverb ***kuru***, analysis {*kur=o*}, known from the Tušratta letter, 'again'. In the accounting tablets the term can be explained from the action of the scribe who counted the numbers and presented them 'again' (in total) just as the Linear B terms ***to-so*** and ***to-sa*** do not mean 'total', but can be understood as 'so much / many (in total)'. In line 7 a new series begins.

It is remarkable that ***u-su***, ***mi-tu***, ***ku-ra-mu***, ***ma-ru*** and ***ku-pa3-nu*** are all names ending in ***-u***. Apparently the scribe has put these names together on purpose. Possibly rhyme was the main reason. The fact that ***mi-ru-ta-ra-re***, ***te-ja-re*** and ***na-da-re*** are also rhyming may corroborate this view.

Linear A ***ma-ka-ri-te*** (HT 87.1-2; HT 117a.1), attested in the heading of two tablets from Hagia Triada, is probably the name of an important person. It can be analysed as {*mag=ar=i-Te*}, consisting of the verbal root ***mag-*** 'to give (as a present)' + the *factitive* or *iterative* root-extension ***-ar-*** + the marker of *transitivity* (and at the same time of the *imperative*) ***-i-*** + the theophorous element ***-te***, frequent hypocoristic of ***-Tešub***. The name can be translated 'Give (as a present) again and again, oh Tešub !'.

It is also conceivable that we have to do with the Old Hurrian *indicative* in ***=i=b*** {**mag=ar=ib-Te*} that has been assimilated to {*mag=ar=it-Te*}, translation 'Tešub gave again and again'. The unassimilated indicative is impossible, because the labial occlusive ***p/b*** of ***=i=b*** should have been expressed in Linear A. The expected unassimilated form {**mag=ar=ib-Te*} would have been ****ma-ka-ri-pe-te*** in Linear A instead of attested ***ma-ka-ri-te***. See I. Wegner (*Einführung*, 88) for the *factitive* or *iterative* root-extension ***-ar-***.

Compare also Linear A ***ma-ka-i-se*** (ZA 8.4) from Kato Zakro, ***ma-ka-i-ta*** (PK 1.7; ZA 5b.2-3) from Palaikastro and Kato Zakro and ***ma-ki-de-te*** 5 (ZA 10b.3) from Kato Zakro.

Linear A ***u-su*** (HT 117a.1-2) can be identified as a Hurrian 'one-word' personal name. Th. Richter, *BGH*, 502-503, s.v. ***ušš-*** [Boğ.,Mari], ***ušt-, ašt-*** II [Boğ., PN, Ugar.] tells that according to V. Haas - I. Wegner (Beiträge zum hurritischen Lexikon: Die hurritischen Verben ***ušš-*** 'gehen' und ***ašš-*** 'abwaschen, abwischen', in: J. Klinger, E. Rieken, Chr. Rüster [eds.], *Investigationes Anatolicae. Gedenkschrift für Erich Neu (StBoT 52)*, Wiesbaden 2010, 97-109) the root-variants ***ušš-***, ***ušt-***, their derivations and etymology belong together: *intransitive* 'gehen, ausziehen (in den Kampf)' ['to go (to the battlefield)'], *transitive* 'führen, fort-, wegbringen' ['to lead, bring away'].

They completed the verb ***uš-***[...] (corresponding with Sumerian [D]U and Akkadian ***alāku***) to ***uš-[šu-(um-)me]***. Hurrian ***ušš-*** corresponds with Hittite ***ija-*** 'marschieren, gehen' ['to march, to go'] according to I. Wegner, "Haus" und "Hof" im Hurritischen, in: Th. Richter, D. Prechel, J. Klinger (eds.), *Kulturgeschichten. Altorientalische Studien für Volkert Haas zum 65. Geburtstag*, Saarbrücken 2001, 446. One may compare Urartian *intransitive* ***ušta-*** {*ušt=a-*} 'aufbrechen' ['to break up'], *transitive* ***uštu-*** {*ušt=u-*} 'darbringen' ['to bring, offer'], cf. H.-J. Thiel, 'Der Text und die Notenfolgen des Musiktextes aus Ugarit', *Studi micenei ed egeo-anatolici 18 (1977)*, 132; Thiel, 'Zur Gliederung des „Musik-Textes" aus Ugarit', in: *Actes de la XXIVe Rencontre Assyriologique Internationale, Paris 1977: Les Hourrites, RHA 36 (1978)* [1980], 196; cf. V. Haas - I. Wegner, o.c. 2010, 100[21].

After it had been recognized that ***ušš-*** was a verbal root indicating motion, I. Wegner was according to Th. Richter (*VHN* I, 556) the first to advocate the translation 'to go'. V. Haas and I. Wegner then established the meaning extensively (see also *supra*) and marked the form ***úš-še*** in an incantation from Mari as *imperative* 'go !' (*RA 36*, 13 Nr. 3 Rs. 15). Richter considers the same analysis applicable to the personal names for men and women written ***ú-uš-še*** (most frequent), ***ú-úš-še***, ***ú-úš-e*** or ***úš-e***. He sees no basic problems for the variant writings. If we may interpret Linear A ***u-su*** (HT 117a.1-2) as an Old Hurrian *imperative* ***Úššu***, the name can be analysed as {*úšš=o/u*} 'Bring (the child) forth !', but since final consonants are not expressed in Linear A, analysis as {*úšš=o/u=n(na)*}, with the shortened form ***-n*** of the enclitic personal pronoun 3rd person singular ***-nna***, is possible as well, so that we can translate 'Bring him/her (the child) forth !'. Since ***ušš-*** is equivalent to ***ušt-***, we may compare the Linear A name ***u-su*** (HT 117a.1-2) {*úšš=o/u=n(na)*} with the Hurrian personal name ***Uštun*** (wr. *Uš-tu-un*) from Šušarrā, {*ušt=o=n(na)*}, typology 1.3.1.1.2.1, lexicon *ušt-*, 'Bring him (the boy) forth !', cf. Th. Richter, *VHN*, 341.

It is not easy to find an adequate meaning for the Linear A personal name ***mi-tu*** (HT 117a.2). One may possibly think of some Pre-Greek terms known from Linear B.

At Mycenae we find ***mi-ta*** (MY Ge 602, 5B, *et alibi*), ***μίνθα*** (Attic) and ***μίνθη*** (Ionic) 'mint', attested in lists of spices and aromatic plants (cf. Latin *menta*). According to P. Chantraine (*DELG*, 704) ***μίνθη*** is a loan-word from a substrate language, cf. Hester, *Lingua 13 (1965)*, 360; cf. also C.J. Ruijgh, *EGM*, § 271. But why would parents call their child after an aromatic plant or condiment ? Possibly because they were themselves professionally engaged in growing herbs or spices. Names of spices probably belong to the category of 'cultural Wanderwörter' anyway.

Another possibility is ***μίλτος*** 'red paint of mineral origin', 'vermilion, cinnabar'. It occurs, for instance, in the compound ***μιλτοπάρῃος*** 'with vermilion / cinnabar painted cheeks', said about ships (Homer). Interesting is Linear B ***]i-qi-ja , / mi-to-we-sa*** (KN Sd 4416[+fr.].b, *et alibi*) ***ἰκκʷίᾱ μιλτόϝεσσα*** 'vermilion coloured chariot' in the series of the 'chariot' tablets from Knossos, where we also see the 'chariot ideogram' CURRUS.

Confirmation that ***mi-to-we-sa*** is ***μιλτόϝεσσα***, derived from ***μίλτος*** 'vermilion, cinnabar', can be found in the parallel expressions ***i-qi-ja , po-ni-ki-ja*** (KN Sd 4409 + 4481+fr.,b; KN Sd <4450> + 4483.c, *et alibi*) ***ἰκκʷίᾱ φοινίκια*** 'purple-red coloured chariot' in the same series, cf. C.J. Ruijgh, *EGM*, § 204 and note 24. P. Chantraine (*DELG*, 702) mentions that ***μίλτος*** is a technical term and a loan-word according to Schwyzer (*GR. Gr.I*, 503) and Frisk. In Greek the term ***μίλτος*** seems sometimes to be used as an euphemism for 'blood'. If Linear A ***mi-tu*** represents ****miltu***, from which ***μίλτος*** is derived, the name ***mi-tu*** may perhaps refer to a bloody delivery of the baby.

To date it is reasonable to confirm that both ***μίνθα*** (Attic) and ***μίνθη*** (Ionic) 'mint' and ***μίλτος*** 'vermilion, cinnabar' are Pre-Greek substrate terms. Due to our still limited knowledge of Hurrian lexical terms, it cannot yet be confirmed that ***mint(h)-*** and / or ***milt-*** belonged to the Hurrian vernacular or were derived from another vernacular.

For Linear A ***ku-ra-mu*** 1 (HT 117a.2-3) from Hagia Triada we may compare Linear A ***ku-ra*** (AK 2.1; ZA 20.4) from Arkhanes and Kato Zakro. The sequence ***ku-ra*** (AK 2.1) follows ***si-da-te*** immediately. In the next line it is followed by the ideogram VIN*b* and 5 units. ***ku-ra*** does not only occur on this Linear A tablet from Arkhanes, but also on one from the Palace of Kato Zakro (ZA 20.4), where it is followed by the number 130. Although this number is rather high, ***ku-ra*** is probably not a scribal error for Linear A ***ku-ro***, since attestation at two different sites makes such an assumption less likely and ***ku-ra*** VINb 5 (AK 2.1-2) does certainly not represent a summation.

The Hurrian personal name ***Kurra*** (wr. *Ku-ur-ra*) is attested at Nuzi, cf. I.J. Gelb, *NPN*, 91, s.v. ***Kurra*** (wr. *Ku-ur-ra*), 1) son of *Pu-ḫi-ia*, brother of *Še-la-pa-i*, JEN 257: 2, 8, 14, 18; - 2) father of *Ut-...-en-ni*, *RA* XXIII 19: 4 (*Utḫap-šenni*?); - 3) father of *Ziqa-a-a*, *RA* XXIII 1: 30; cf. P.M. Purves, *NPN*, 230, s.v. ***kurr***, ***kurra***. Cf. also ***Kur-ra*** from Gasur, HSS X 143: 12; 153 v 2; 155 v 1; 211: 11 and 13; an Anatolian personal name ***Ku-ra*** is cited by Stephens, *PNC*, 52f. Th. Richter (*BGH*, 226-227) mentions three homographic verbal roots: ***kur-*** I [Nuzi] 'herstellen' ['to make'] (Wilhelm 1992g, 149), ***kur-*** II [Nuzi] 'mästen' ['to fatten (male animals for slaughter)'] and ***kur-*** III 'erwidern' ['to answer, reply'] (Wilhelm 2000, 201; I. Wegner, *Einführung*, 265) and 'to receive in answer' or 'to reply' (Campbell 2007a, 231, 299, 324; 2008, 276). Adverbial ***kuru***, phonologically /***kuro***/, 'again, in return' may contain a root ***kur-*** identical with ***kur-*** III.

According to Th. Richter (*VHN*, 450), s.v. ***kur-*** {*ko/ur-*}, it is difficult to assess which of the three homographic verbal roots, mentioned in *BGH*, provides the most plausible interpretation and translation for the Hurrian personal names containing ***kur-***. He mentions ***Kuraiš*** (wr. *ku-ra-i-iš*) from Tigunāni, analysis {*ko/ur=ai=ž*}, typology 1.3.5, lexicon *kur-*; ***ᶠKururze*** from Ašnakkum, reconstruction on the basis of [...*-r*]*u-ur-ze* (*OBTCB* 12 III 30] and *ku-ru-ur-*[...] (*OBTCB* 88 III 25), analysis {*ko/ur=o/u=r=že*}, typology 3.1, lexicon *kururze* (abstract form) (→ *kur-*); and *ku-ru-ri* from Middle-Babylonian Qaṭna (QS 3, 42 Rs. 4), cf. Th. Richter, *VHN*, 180.

The Linear A 'one-word' personal name ***ku-ra-mu*** (HT 117a.2-3) may be analysed as {*ko/ur=a=mmu*}, consisting of the intransitive verbal root ***kur-*** III 'to return' + marker of intransitivity ***-a-*** + the *optional allomorphic enclitic* personal pronoun 2nd person singular ***-mmu*** (instead of normal ***-mma***) indicating the subject of the intransitive verb, translation 'You return(ed)'. The parents may have recognized features of a deceased child in the newborn baby. However, if the ***-a-*** in ***ku-ra-mu*** belongs to the factitive root-extension ***-am-***, the name can be analysed as a transitive Old Hurrian *imperative* in ***-u***: {*kur=am=o/u*}, containing the root ***kur-*** I 'to make, create', translation 'Create (the child) (oh *numen*) !', or ***kur-*** II 'to feed, nourish', translation 'Nourish (the child) (oh *numen*) !', or ***kur-*** III 'to answer, reply', translation 'Answer (the prayer) (oh *numen*) !'.

Since final consonants are not expressed in Linear A, ***ku-ra-mu*** can also represent {*kur=am=o/u=n*}, shortened form of {*kur=am=o/u=nna*}, in which ***-n*** or ***-nna*** is the enclitic personal pronoun 3rd person singular, indicating the object of the transitive verb, translation 'Create him/her (***-nna***) (namely the child) (oh *numen*) !' or 'Nourish him/her (the child) (oh *numen*) !' or 'Answer it (the prayer) (oh *numen*) !'. No doubt the parents knew which interpretation they had in mind after the child's birth.

Compare for the formation the personal name ***Tadunna*** (wr. *Ta-du-un-na*) from Nuzi, analysis {*tad=o=nna*}, translation 'Love him (the boy) (oh *numen*) !', cf. I.J. Gelb, *NPN*, 150; Th. Richter, *VHN*, 595. Compare also ***ᶠTadun-Naja*** (wr. *ᶠTa-tu-un-na-a-a*) from Nuzi, analysis {*tad=o=n(na)-Naja/e*}, translation 'Love her (the girl) (oh *Naja/e*) !', cf. I.J. Gelb, *NPN*, 150; *AAN* I, 142; Th. Richter, *VHN*, 595.

Linear A ***ma-ru*** (HT 117a.3) is a personal name, since it occurs in a list of 10 personal names on the *a*-side of the tablet, each followed by 1 unit. Since Linear A and B ***ru*** can also represent ***lu***, we cannot be sure, whether Linear A ***ma-ru*** contains the root ***mal-*** or ***mar-***. Both roots are used in Hurrian personal names. The Minoan scribe no doubt knew, with which of the two he was dealing, but we cannot be sure.

Th. Richter (*BGH*, 240), s.v. ***ma-la-še*** [Ug.] and (*VHN*, 454), s.v. ***mal-***, mentions that the vocabulary *SCCNH 9*, 7 IV 12' (Ugarit) offers Sumerian **šeš** = Akkadian ***ma-ra-ru*** = Hurrian ***ma-la-še***, so that the meaning 'Bitterkeit' ['bitterness'] can be assumed for Hurrian ***malaš(š)e***, from which a verbal root ***mal-*** 'to be bitter, to make bitter' can be derived. It cannot yet be established whether this or a homographic root is used in onomastics and whether this or the other is cognate with the purification terms ***mali*** and ***maldi*** in the tradition of Ḫattuša. The personal name ***Malija*** (wr. *Ma-li-ia*) at Emar, Kurruḫanni and Šubat-Enlil, for instance, can be a hypocoristic formation on a verbal or nominal root or a theonym as a one-word name. At Puzriš-Dagan occurs ***Ma-li-a***.

Th. Richter (*VHN*, 189) analyses the name as {*mal=i=ja*}, typology 1.1.1.2.4. The personal name ***Maliia*** (wr. *Ma-li-ia, Ma-li-a*) is the name of 29 persons at Nuzi, cf. I.J. Gelb, *NPN*, 95. The vegetation goddess ***Malija*** belongs to the local pantheon of Kaniš / Neša (modern Kültepe), but the linguistic provenance is not clarified according to Th. Richter, *VHN*, 454, note 494.

Some scholars assume a Luwian origin, but in view of the popularity of the personal name ***Maliia*** at Nuzi I consider a Hurrian identity much more likely than a Luwian, though a homonymic theonym with another identity at Kaniš / Neša cannot be ruled out.

With respect to the qualification of 'vegetation goddess' one readily associates the name with the Greek word ***τὸ μῆλον*** and Doric and Aeolic ***μᾶλον < μᾱλον*** 'apple' and 'each fruit from a tree that resembles an apple', but P. Chantraine (*DELG*, 694) mentions, s.v. 1. *μῆλον*: "Mot méditerranéen qui s'est substitué au nom i.-e. de la pomme, cf. Ernout-Meillet s.v. *Abella*. Il a été emprunté par le latin sous la forme *mālum*, puis *mēlum*, avec *mālinus* et *mēlinus*." Since a commodity is involved, there is a good chance that we are indeed dealing with a so-called 'Wanderwort'.

In the spectrum of onomastics we should not forget that ***Malia*** is also a toponym. It is the name of the Minoan palace (excavated by the French School of Archaeology), a few miles east of the small town of Malia on the north coast of Crete. If the name ***Malia*** is a one-word verbal name, analysis {*mal=i=a*}, consisting of the verbal root ***mal-*** + the marker of transitivity ***-i-*** + the marker of the subject of action 3rd person singular in ***-a***, the name has exactly the same structure as the Hurrian personal name ***Ḫania*** {*Ḫan=i=a*}, translation 'She (the mother) gives/gave birth to the child', and of the name of the Minoan Palace (and the city) of *Khania* that can be translated 'He/She (a God) gave birth to / created (the palace)', a perfect Hurrian name. If ***Malia*** in Crete is called after a goddess ***Malija***, it is not the only toponym formed in that way: There are places in Crete called after the goddesses *Lato* and *Hera* and the great city of Athens is called after Athena (probably Hurrian ***Atta-na / Atta-Naia/e*** 'Naia/e is like her father', a name that can be explained from the myth about the dramatic birth of Athena, born from the head of her father Zeus (Tešub).

Th. Richter (*VHN*, 189) also mentions the personal name ***Mališ-akum*** (wr. *Ma-li-iš-a-gu-um*) at Mari, analysis {*mali=ž-ag=o=m*}, lexicon *mali* (→ *mal-*), *ag-*, typology 1.1.1.1.5, translation '*mali* brachte (Jungen) herauf (?)' ['*mali* brought (the boy) up (?)']. Further the personal name *Arti-maluš* (wr. *Ar-di-ma-lu-úš*) at Mari, typology 1.3.2.1, analysis {*arde-mal=o=ž*}, lexicon *arde* and verbal *mal-*, cf. Th. Richter, *VHN*, 72-73.

The Linear A personal name ***ma-ru*** (HT 117a.3) can be explained as a Hurrian verbal formation {*mal=u/o=ž*} or {*mal=u/o=m*}, of which the final consonant is not expressed in Linear A (and B). Unfortunately the meaning of the verbal root ***mal-*** in personal names remains mysterious.

However, Linear A ***ma-ru*** (HT 117a.3) may also contain the root ***mar-***. At Boğazköy we find ***Tattamaru***, cf. E. Laroche, *NH*, 181, Nr.1303. ***Tattamaru*** 1. Prince: abs. *mTa-at-ta-ma-ru,* KBo IV 10 Vo 30. 2. Divers: abs. nom. *mTa-at-ta-ma-ru-(uš), mTa-ad-da-ma-ru*, XXIII 85, 4, 5; 106 Ro 1 ?; XXVI 43 Ro 5; 92, 10; XXXI 28, 7, 8; 32 Vo 5, 8, 12; XXXVIII 1 I 26 = MIO 8, 181.

Th. Richter (*VHN*, 455) remarks, s.v. ***mar-***, that already Gustavs (1925, 301-302; 1929, 58[1]), considering the etymology of ***marijannu*** (cf. Th. Richter, *BGH*, 245-246), postulated a root ***mar-*** or ***mari-*** (possibly 'besitzen' ['to possess'] or 'nutznießen' ['to hold in usufruct']). Although the etymology remains problematic, the existence of the root cannot be denied. More recent suggestions such as 'von Unreinheit befreien' ['to free from impurities'] or 'töten' ['to kill'] need to be verified. The meaning of the nominal forms is not clear either.

He also discusses the onomastic element ***mari*** that is possibly already known from Mari- and / or Ḫattuša-texts, as well as the new form ***maruḫ(ḫ)e***, {*mari»o=ġ/ḫḫe*}, 'zu mari / Mari gehörig' ['belonging to *mari* / Mari']. Perhaps ***°-mar / -ma-ar-ra*** in the personal name ***ᶠTupi-marra*** at Mari that occurs in the same form at Nuzi can be connected. Th. Richter interprets ***°-mar*** as a shortened form of ***°-ma-ar-ra***. At Nuzi ***Nutu-mar*** (wr. *nu-du-mar*) and ***Itḫi-marra*** (wr. *It-ḫi-mar-ra*) occur, cf. P.M. Purves, *NPN*, 233.

Th. Richter (*VHN*, 190, 455) mentions the personal names: (1) ***Maratilla*** (wr. *ma-ra-di-la*) at Mari, analysis {*mar=a=dilla*}, typology 1.1.1.33.3.1, lexicon; ***Maruš-taḫe*** (wr. *ma-ru-úš-ta-a-ḫe*) at Mari, analysis {*mar=o=ž-taġe*}, typology 1.3.2.1, lexicon *mar-*, *taḫe*. (2) {*marri*}: ***Tupi-marra*** and ***ᶠTupi-marra*** (wr. *tu-bi-mar-ra*, *tu-bi-ma-ar-ra*) at Mari, analysis {*to/ub=i-marr(i)a*}, typology 1.3.1.2.1, lexicon *tub-*, *marri*(?). (3) {*mari»o=ġ/ḫḫe*}: ***ᶠMaruḫ(ḫ)e*** (wr. *ma-ru-*[*ḫ*]*e*) at Mari, analysis {*mari»o=ġ/ḫḫe*}, typology 3.1, lexicon *maruḫ(ḫ)e* (→ *mar-*).

So Linear A ***ma-ru*** (HT 117a.3) can also be explained as the Hurrian personal name ***Maruš*** or ***Marum***, consisting of the verbal formation {*mar=u/o=ž*} or {*mar=u/o=m*}, of which the final consonant is not expressed in Linear A (and B). Unfortunately the meaning of the verbal root ***mar-*** in personal names is not yet clarified and verified.

Linear A ***ku-pa$_3$-nu*** (HT 1a.3; HT 88.5; HT 117a.3; HT 122a.6; HT 122a.7; HT? 170b.3 and possibly also HT 3.6; HT 42.3; HT 49a.6-7) following ***ma-ru*** (HT 117a.3) is one of the most frequent personal names at Hagia Triada. It may together with Linear A ***ku-pa$_3$-na-tu*** (HT 47a.1-2; HT 119.3) be one of the few possibly Semitic personal names in Linear A, although Hurrian interpretations may be more likely.

See for my interpretation of the personal name ***tu-|68-ma*** (HT 117a.3-4) *chapter 12: From undeciphered to deciphered Linear A signs*, where I have proposed the phonetic value ***ḫi*** for Linear A sign ***68***, that shows resemblance with Linear A sign ***96***.

Linear A ***u-de-mi*** (HT 117a.4) may be analysed as {*ud=(e/i)-e/irmi*}, consisting of the root ***ud-*** 'to protect' + marker of *transitivity* ***-e/i-*** (at the same time marker of the *imperative*) that contracted with the initial vowel of ***ermi / irmi / erwi / ewri / ibri*** 'Lord', translation 'Protect (the child), oh Lord !'. It would in that case be equivalent to and almost identical with the Linear A personal name ***u̲***[.]***-de-mi*** (AK 4b.2-3) at Arkhanes, if ***u̲***[.]***-de-mi*** is a complete sequence and if there is no sign missing between ***u̲***[(AK 4b.2) and]***-de-mi*** (AK 4b.3). See Th. Richter (*BGH*, 507), s.v. ***ud-*** I [Boğ.; PN] 'schützen'; *VHN*, 557, s.v. ***ud-*** {*o/ud-*}, 'schützen' ['to protect']. Th. Richter (*VHN*, 342, 557), s.v. ***ud-*** {*o/ud-*}, offers two analyses for the personal name ***ᶠUdulme*** (wr. *ᶠú-du-ul-me*) from Mari: A) {*o/ud=o=l-me*} 'In order that the sister protects (the girl) !', typology 1.3.3.1.

In this analysis he interprets ***-me*** as hypocoristic of ***-mena*** 'Geschwister' ['sister']. I prefer the translation 'twin' instead of 'sister' for ***mena/mina*** and ***-me***, because this onomastic element also occurs in masculine personal names. B) {*o/ud-o/ulme*} 'Let the *ulme*-weapon protect (the girl) !' (Hurrian ***ulme*** = weapon).

If ***u-de-za*** (HT 122a.1; HT 122b.3) is analysed as a form out of context, one may think of the Hurrian *jussive* form {*ud=e=š=an*} consisting of the verbal root ***ud-*** 'to protect' + marker of the *jussive* 2nd person (plural) ***-e-*** + the pluralizing suffix ***-š*** + the suffix of the acting person ***Ø*** (the *imperative* misses this indicator) + the syntactical particle ***-an*** 'and', cf. I. Wegner, *Einführung*, 103 + Table 9: *The order of suffixes for the positive jussive*.

However, the form occurs twice on HT 122, first in the combination]***-ra-ri* , *u-de-za*** 2 (HT 122a.1) in the heading of the *a*-side of the tablet. Due to a big *lacuna*, since the left top corner of the *a*-side (and right top corner of the *b*-side) is missing,]***ra-ri*** is incomplete, for which I propose the conjectural reading ***a***]***-ra-ri* , *u-de-za*** 2.

The second occurrence is the combination]|***a-ra-68 u-de-za*** 2 (HT 122b.3), probably ***a-ra-ḫi u-de-za*** 2. I interpret Linear A ***a-ra-ḫi*** as Hurrian ***Alla(i)=ḫi*** 'belonging to the queen'.

Since Linear A sign ***68*** is probably a variant of sign ***96***, Linear A ***a-ra-96 a-tu*** 1 (HT 87.5) can be interpreted as ***a-ra-ḫi a-tu*** 1 = ***Alla(i)=ḫi aštu*** 1 'one woman belonging to the queen', probably a female servant of the queen.

The context of] ***a-ra-96*** 123 = ***a-ra-ḫi*** 123 (HT 97a+109a.4) is also interesting, because it follows] ***ku-ro*** 129. We may conclude that of the total number of 129 units 123 are 'belonging to the queen'.

Linear A ***a-ra-ḫi*** = ***Alla(i)=ḫi*** may, for instance, be compared on the one hand with the (shortened) variant ***Alḫi*** at Boğazköy (cf. I. Wegner, 2004, 9; De Martino/Giorgieri, 2008, 67; M. Salvini / I. Wegner, 2004, 83) and the theonym ^{D}***Alḫé*** (Van Gessel, 1998/1, 22), on the other with the more common form ***allanuḫḫi*** 'propre à la reine' ['proper to the queen, characteristic of the queen'], *al-la-an-nu-(u)-uḫ-ḫi*, KBo XIV 132 II 6, 9; KBo XX 134 + 9; KBo XX 129 + II 5. Adj. de qualité, dérivé en ***-(u)ḫḫi*** de ***allani***; comparer ***šennuḫḫa***, cf. E. Laroche, *GLH*, 42-43, s.v. ***allai*** 'dame, reine', ***Allani*** 'la Dame'.

Allanuḫḫi analysed as {*alla=nu<ni=(ḫ)ḫi(=ni=ja)*} is epithet to Ḫebat, cf. M. Cl. Trémouille, 1997, 133, 156[+522]; {*alla=n(i)=ō=ḫḫe*}, cf. M. Giorgieri, 1999a, 81[78]; 'belonging to the mistress, queen', cf. Van Gessel, 2001, 174; 'Herrinnenwürde', cf. I. Wegner, *Einführung*, 246. See Th. Richter, *BGH*, 13.

The combination]|***a-ra-68 u-de-za*** 2 (HT 122b.3) is interesting, because ***a-ra-ḫi*** is (unlike the other entries in the list, mainly personal names) not directly followed by a numeral or number of units, but by ***u-de-za*** (HT 122b.3) that is followed by 2 units.

I prefer to analyse ***u-de-za*** (HT 122a.1; HT 122b.3) as {*ud=e=zz(i)=a*}, consisting of the Hurrian verbal root ***ud-*** 'to protect' + the marker of transitivity ***-e/i-*** + the nominal suffix ***-šše/-zze/i*** or adjectival suffix ***-(š)še/-(z)ze/i*** (cf. I. Wegner, *Einführung*, 55, 69) + the suffix of the *essive* ***-a***. She gives some examples of abstract forms in ***-(i)=šše***: ***šar=i=šše*** 'wish' from ***šar-*** 'to wish, demand', Ugarit vocabulary RS 94-2939, col. II 5; ***nir=i=šše*** 'goodness', derived from ***niri*** 'good'; ***kib=i=šše*** 'being seated (on the throne)', derived from ***keb-*** 'to set, put, lay down', cf. *Einführung*, 55.

If this analysis is correct, the lexeme {*ud=e=zze/i*} may have the meaning 'protection' and {*ud=e=zz(i)=a*} may be the *essive* form in ***-a***, that can be translated 'as protection'.

If]***ra-ri*** (HT 122a.1) can be completed to ***a***]***ra-ri***, this conjectural form may be interpreted as Hurrian ***alali*** 'garment, garb, robe (of state)'. Th. Richter (*BGH*, 15) mentions that since publication of the Hurrian-Hittite bilingual ***Kirenze*** (KBo 32), and in particular KBo 32.15 Vs I 12', ***alali*** 'Umhang', 'Gewand' is classified as Hurrian. In the Hittite version it corresponds with (TÚG.)***kušiši-*** ntr.; (GADA.)***alalu-*** ntr. is considered a loan-word into Hittite, cf. (GADA.)***alalu(ša)*** 'ein Tuch, Gewand ?' ['cloth, garment']. I. Wegner, *Einführung*, 142: *a-la-a-la-e* (KBo 32: 15 I 11'), ***alal(i)=ae*** *instr.* 'mit einem Gewand (wollen wir ihn bekleiden)' ['(we want to dress him) with a garment'].

If interpretation of ***a***]***ra-ri*** , ***u-de-za*** (HT 122a.1) as {*al=al=i*} {*ud=e=zz(i)=a*} is correct, the meaning is 'garment/garb/robe as protection'. Likewise]|***a-ra-ḫi u-de-za*** (HT 122b.3), still referring to ***a***]***ra-ri*** (HT 122a.1), can be analysed as [{*al=al=i*}] {*alla(i)=ḫi*} {*ud=e=zz(i)=a*} '[garment] belonging to the queen as protection'. It is justifiable to combine ***a***]***ra-ri*** , ***u-de-za*** (HT 122a.1) with]|***a-ra-ḫi u-de-za*** (HT 122b.3), not only because ***u-de-za*** is repeated, but also because tablet HT 122 is one of the tablets with ***po-to-ku-ro*** (HT 122b.6) 'value again', referring to the grand total, twice preceded by ***ku-ro*** (HT 122a.8) 'again' and ***ku-ro*** (HT 122b.5) 'again (namely the numbers in total)', which means that the *a-* and *b-*sides of the tablet comprise one continuous text.

The Linear A personal name ***mi-ru-ta-ra-re*** (HT 117a.4-5) may be analysed as a sentence name, of which three analyses are possible: I. {*me/il=ušt-alale/i*}, consisting of the verbal root ***mel-*** I 'to expel' (D.R.M. Campbell, *Mood and modality in Hurrian*, diss. Univ. of Chicago, 2007, 90; cf. Th. Richter, *BGH*, 250: *mel=umma* epēšu [Nuzi] '(Tiere) treiben' ['to drive (animals) away, to rouse up (game)'] + the root-extension ***-Všt-*** (cf. I. Wegner, *Einführung*, 88-89) + the noun ***alāli*** [Boğ.] 'cape, mantle, coat' (cf. E. Neu, 1996a, 314+22: 'Umhang'), 'garment, robe, dress' (cf. I. Wegner, *Einführung*, 246: 'Gewand'). It is also a sort of 'travel-cape' for Ḫebat. Since Ḫebat may (like Hera) play a part in the rituals with respect to giving birth, the name-giving may remind of a ritual gesture of throwing away some garment. Translation 'Expell / Throw off the robe !'.

II. {*me/il=ušt=ar-are/i*}, consisting of the verbal root ***mel-*** I 'to expel' + root-extension ***-Všt-*** (cf. I. Wegner, *Einführung*, 88-89) + the *factitive* or *iterative* root-extension ***-ar-*** (cf. I. Wegner, *Einführung*, 88) + the noun (sacrificial term) ***are/i*** 'evil' (cf. Th. Richter, *BGH*, 45: ***ari*** [Boğ.; Mari]; (*VHN*, 380: ***ari*** 'böse, das Böse'). It possibly corresponds with Hittite ***idalu-*** 'böse' ['evil']. Note the divine attribute ***ari mudri*** (wr. *a-(a-)ri mu-ut-ri*) of Tešub, also deified. Translation 'Expell / Drive out the evil !'.

III. As it happens also a reduplicated form of ***ari*** appears to exist in the form ***arari*** [Boğ.], cf. Th. Richter, *BGH*, 45: see V. Haas / H.-J. Thiel, 1978, 309: *a-ra-a-ri-e-ni* KBo 19.145 = ChS I/5 Nr. 40 Rs. 41'; E. Laroche, *GLH*, 53: s.v. *arari* 'maudit' ['cursed'] *a-ra-a-ri-e-ni daḫe* = hit. *alwanzaḫḫantan* LÚ-*an* KBo XIX 145 IV 42, 49; de même , *ib.* IV 41 et 48, ***arare-ni ašta*** 'sa femme maudite' ['his cursed wife']; *a-ra-ri* KUB XXXII 26 III 13; XLVII 26 III 4. – *a-ra-ra-e*[KUB XXXII 41 II 3. Emprunt à l'akk. *arâru* 'maudire' ['to curse']; mais le nom h. *arari-(ni)* 'le maudit' ['the cursed'] est une creation artificielle pour l'akk. *arru*; cf. *CAD* A II, 234, 305.

Th. Richter (*BGH*, 45) mentions that M. Giorgieri, G. Wilhelm and St. de Martino interpret Hurrian ***arari*** as 'Verhexung' ['witchcraft'], M. Savini, I. Wegner, M.-Cl. Trémouille as 'Unheil' ['disaster, calamity'] and D.R.M. Campbell as 'sorcery'.

So Linear A ***mi-ru-ta-ra-re*** (HT 117a.4-5) may be analysed as *{me/il=ušt-arare/i}*, translation 'Expel disaster / witchcraft / sorcery (oh *numen*) !'. The final ***-e*** in ***mi-ru-ta-ra-re*** is even attested in *a-ra-a-ri-e-ni daḫe* and *arare-ni ašta*.

I have mentioned the first analysis *{me/il=ušt-alale/i}*, because it is theoretically possible thanks to the ambiguity of the Linear A (and B) ***r-/l-*** signs, but I prefer the second and third analyses, *{me/il=ušt=ar-are/i}* and *{me/il=ušt-arare/i}*, respectively, not only because they offer semantically the best interpretations, but also because names derived from ***are/i*** 'evil' are actually attested: ***Aruḫḫe*** (wr. *A-ru-uḫ-ḫe*) from Mari, analysis *{aroḫḫe}*, typology 3.1, lexicon *aruḫḫe* (→ *ari*), translation 'Zum Bösen gehörend; Bösartig' ['evil' (adj.)] (cf. Th. Richter, *VHN*, 73, 380), and ***Aruzza*** (wr. *A-ru-uz-za*) from Tigunāni, analysis *{aro/uzz(i)=a*[E.]*}*, typology 3.2.1, lexicon *aruzzi* (→ *ari*), translation 'Er (Junge) ist gemäß einer dem Bösen angemessenen (Person) (geboren)' ['He (the boy) is (born) as an evil person'] (cf. Th. Richter, *VHN*, 75, 380). [E.] refers to the *essive* ***-a***.

The Linear A personal name ***te-ja-re*** (HT 117a.5) can be identified with the Hurrian word ***tiari / tiyari*** [Boğ.; Ugarit], ***/teari/***, that can be explained by lexical comparisons. It also occurs as a divine object associated with *Tešub* and *Lilluri*. E. Laroche (*GLH*, 265-266) mentions s.v. ***tiyari*** 'fuseau' ['bobbin, pivot, spindle of a spinning-wheel']: RS quadr. 137 II 22: Sumerian BAL = Akkadian ***pilakku*** = Hurrian ***te-a-ri*** = Ugaritic ***pilakku***, cf. *Ugar. V*, 242 sq., 455.

1. Nom commun. *ti-ya-ri-iš*, RS h. 13, 4. - *ti-ya-ra*, VBoT 14, 4. - *ti-ya-(a)-ar-ra* (de *Tešub* !), KBo XX 119 I 22 = KBo XVII 86 + I 11. - *ti-ya-a-ri*, KBo XX 119 II 11.

2. Divinisé dans la série kiz. *Lilluri abati tiyari Manuzuḫi* (CTH 628, *passim*): même mot ? - *ti-ya-ri*, KUB XII 12 I 29, 32, VI 17 et dupl.; KBo XV 37 *passim*; KUB XXV 46 III 6; XLV 53 III 6, 9; KBo XI 2 II 5, etc. - *ti-ya-ri-iš*, KUB XXXII 61, 7, 8; 65 II 24 et dupl. - ^{d}*ti-ya-ri-in-na*, KUB XXV 42 + II 19, etc.; KBo XV 48 et dupl., *passim*.

Th. Richter (*BGH*, 456-457) mentions s.v. ***tiari / tijari*** [Boğ.; Ugarit], ***/teari/***, the proposed meanings 'Spindel' ['bobbin, pivot, spindle of a spinning-wheel'], 'Fakkel', also epithet to *Lelluri*, 'torch', also 'deified cult object'.

It also corresponds with Hittite (GIŠ)*zuppari-* ntr., Akkadian *dipāru*, *gizillû* and *zīqu* (V. Haas, 2003a, 170). See also Trémouille, 2005, 336, in Hittite for (GIŠ)*tijarri/a-* 'Ochsenkarren, Spindel'. Also Gamkrelidze / Ivanov, 1995/1, 628, for Sumerogram ^{GIŠ}MAR.GÍD.DA [“possibly of Hurrian origin”]. Ivanov (1999a, 233f.) also points to Hurrian, c.q. North-Caucasian origin, for such a Hittite word for 'military chariot, wheeled vehicle'. Th. Richter (*VHN*, 535) also refers to ^{D}*ti-ia-ar-ra* at Ortaköy / Šapinuwa (cf. Giorgieri / Murat / Süel, 2013, 171, 178).

Th Richter (*VHN*, 305, 535) has recognized the Hurrian personal name ***Tijarnil*** (wr. *Ti-ia-ar-ni-il*) at Tigunāni, analysis *{tijar(i)=ni=l(la)}*, typology 3.1, lexicon *tijari*, translation 'Sie sind ein Spindel'(?) ['They are a bobbin'(?)]. He assumes that in this name the individualising suffix ***-ni*** is used.

Compare Linear B ***te-ja-ro*** (KN V 479 v, 3),]***te-ja-ro*** (KN X 5525) from Knossos.

Comparing Linear A ***pu-te-ja-re*** (PL Zf 1), read from right to left on a silver hairpin from Tholos A at Platanos (Messara-valley), we may assume that the lexeme ***te-ja-re*** can be identified as (*quasi*) theophorous element ***tiari / tiyari, /teari/*** 'torch', connected with *Tešub* and *Lilluri/Lelluri* as a divine object, cf. I. Wegner (2004, 67) for the connection with *Lelluri*. The Linear A and Hurrian element ***-te-ja-re*** is the best recognizable part of the sequence ***pu-te-ja-re*** (PL Zf 1 ←). If the first syllabic sign is also read correctly as ***pu-***, the first verbal element may be Hurrian ***puš-*** as in the personal name ***Puš-teḭa*** (wr. *Pu-uš-te-ia*) from Nuzi (cf. I.J. Gelb, *NPN*, 119; P.M. Purves, *NPN*, 264), since Linear A ***-s-*** is not expressed in consonant clusters before a dental, labial or palatal occlusive, as may be inferred from the Linear B orthographic conventions that were probably inherited from Linear A, cf. e.g. Linear A ***pa-i-to*** *{pa=ašt=o=m}* and Linear B ***pa-i-to***, *Φαιστός*, the name of the famous palace dominating the Messara-valley. The verbal roots ***pur-*** 'to see' (cf. Th. Richter, *VHN*, 489) and ***puš-*** I and ***puz-*** II / ***puzz-*** (cf. Th. Richter, *VHN*, 491-492, s.v. ***puš-*** I *{po/už-}* and ***puz-*** II *{po/uz-}* / ***puzz-*** *{po/uzz-}*) 'to submerge' are equally good candidates: ***pur-teyari/e*** 'see the torch !' and ***puš-teyari/e*** 'submerge the torch !'.

The Linear A personal name ***na-da-re*** 1 (HT 117a.5) from Hagia Triada is not easy to interpret. The formation may be compared with that of ***mi-ru-ta-ra-re*** (HT 117a.4-5), if it is analysed as (I) *{nad=ar=e/i}*, consisting of the *transitive* verbal root ***nad-*** 'to lay (somebody) down to sleep (?)' + the *factitive* or *iterative* root-extension ***-ar-*** (cf. I. Wegner, *Einführung*, 88) + the marker of the transitive *imperative* ***-e/-i***, translation 'Lay (the child) down to sleep (oh *numen*) !' Or (II), if it is analysed as *{nad(=a)-are/i}*, consisting of the *intransitive* stem ***nad=a-*** 'to sleep, to lie down', of which the marker of the *intransitive imperative* ***-a*** is contracted with the initial ***a-*** of ***are/i*** + the noun (sacrificial term) ***are/i*** 'evil' (cf. Th. Richter, *BGH*, 45: ***ari*** [Boğ.; Mari]; (*VHN*, 380: ***ari*** 'böse, das Böse'), translation 'Go to sleep, oh evil *numen* !'.

Th. Richter (*VHN*, 210, 468) mentions 3 Hurrian personal names with the root ***nad-***: ***Natukki*** (wr. *Na-tu-uk-ki*) *ḫabiru* from Tigunāni, analysis *{nad=o=kki}*, typology 1.2.2.3, lexicon *nad-*; *Na-du-ta-al* from Kaniš (cf. K. Balkan, 1965, 148[1]); *Natunuk* (wr. *Na-tu-nu-uk*) from Mari, analysis *{nad=o/un=o=g}*, typology 1.2.2.2, lexicon *nad-*.

Th. Richter (*VHN*, 468) mentions with regard to the root ***nad-*** that one may (apart from the not very clear pair of notions *nadakušri / tanakušri*) refer to Hurrian ***nadi*** [Ugarit] that can be recognized as a loan-word from Akkadian on the basis of comparison with Sumerian [N]A, Akkadian *na-a-du* and Ugaritic *na-du* 'stela' (according to Huehnergard, 1887a, 49, 152), 'waterskin, skin bag for carrying water' (according to W.H. van Soldt, 1990, 731), cf. Th. Richter, *BGH*, 269. He translates (*BGH*, 269) ***nadakušri**, tanakušri* [Nuzi] as 'produce, yield' (Zaccagnini, 1975, 186) and tells that (according to *CAD* T [2006], 168) *tanakušri* may be "metathesis or error for *nadakušri*".

A useful comparison may be found in the meaning of the noun ***natḫe*** 'Bett' ['bed'] that perhaps can be analysed as *{nad=ġe}*. According to V. Haas – G. Wilhelm (1974a, 88) *°=ġe* is often found in loan-words from Akkadian and Sumerian, cf. Th. Richter, *VHN*, 468, n. 550. A. Kammenhuber (1968a, 125) and I.M. Diakonoff (1972, 101[43]) assumed already a derivation from Sumerian ná(d) 'liegen' ['to lie down']. Anyway the meaning 'to lie down' or 'to rest, sleep' for Hurrian ***nad-*** is plausible, cf. Th. Richter, *VHN*, 468[551].

The position of Linear A ***sa-ta*** **,** (HT 117a.7) and]***sa-ta*** (HT 42[+]59.1) from Hagia Triada is prominent. HT 42[+]59.1 reads:]***sa-ta*** **,** ***se+si*** ↓**,** ***te*** **,** OLE+***ki*** 8 OLE+***ro***[.

So ***sa-ta*** **,** (HT 117a.7) is the first sequence following ***ku-ro*** 10, under the line drawn with a ruler. It is followed by a series of 5 personal names (again each followed by 1 unit) on the *a*-side: ***ku-ku-da-ra*** 1 (HT 117a.7), ***ko-sa-ni-|ti*** 1 (HT 117a.7-8), ***da-mi-nu*** 1 (HT 117a.8), ***da-ne-ku-|ti*** 1 (HT 117a.8-9), ***ki-da-ro*** 1 (HT 117a.9) (discussed *supra*).

The text of the *b*-side of the tablet is much shorter. It starts with ***79-tu-ne*** **,** (HT 117b.1), followed by 2 personal names, again each followed by 1 unit: ***ku-re-96*** 1 (HT 117b.1), ***di-ki-se*** (HT 117b.1). The position of ***79-tu-ne*** **,** (HT 117b.1) can be compared with either ***ma-ka-ri-te*** **,** (HT 117a.1) or ***sa-ta*** **,** (HT 117a.7). From ***sa-ta*** onwards the analysis is:

HT 117a.7.	*sa-ta* ,	*ku-ku-da-ra*	1
7-8.		*ko-sa-ni-ti*	1
8.		*da-mi-nu*	1
8-9.		*da-ne-ku-ti*	1
9.		*ki-da-ro*	1
b.1.	*79-tu-ne* ,	*ku-re-96*	1
2.		*di-ki-se*	1

It is significant that ***sa-ta*** is followed by a word divider, not by a sign for a unit, so that ***ku-ku-da-ra*** is the first personal name to be counted:

In search of the possible meaning of ***sa-ta*** it struck me that ***sa-ta*** **,** was followed by 7 personal names and 7 units, one for each person, if the two entries on the *b*-side are included. This might be interesting in view of P.M. Purves's *lemma* (*NPN*, 252) on **satta**: "IE, apparently Indo-Aryan [read: Indo-Iranian] ***saptá*** 'seven'; cf. *šatta-wartanna*, 'seven laps', from the Boğazköy treatise on horse-training, cited by Mironov in *Acta Orientalia XI (1933)*, 208. - Bonfante." It is indeed assumed that this treatise on horse-training contains Indo-Iranian terms.

However, it cannot be confirmed that ***sa-ta*** points to all these seven entries, since the two personal names on the *b*-side seem to depend on preceding ***79-tu-ne*** **,** (HT 117b.1), not on ***sa-ta*** **,** (HT 117a.7). This means that it does not make sense for the scribe to write ***sa-ta*** 'seven'. If ***79-tu-ne*** takes the same position as ***sa-ta***, one would expect that it has a similar relation to ***ku-re-96*** and ***di-ki-se*** as ***sa-ta*** has to the other five entries. Consequently, it seems unlikely that ***sa-ta*** points to all seven entries including the two on the *b*-side. In that case it would not have made sense for the scribe to write ***sa-ta*** 'seven'.

The Hurrian verbal and nominal root ***šatt-*** may be a better candidate. Linear A ***sa-ta*** (HT 117a.7) may be equivalent to Hurrian *ša-a-at-t*[*a*] from Boğazköy, KBo XX 129 + III 1, 3, cf. E. Laroche, *GLH*, 219. P.M. Purves, *NPN*, 252, s.v. ***šatt***: "Bork, *Mitanni-sprache*, 126, translates 'sich einigen', but in his *Mitbr.*, 100, he translates 'helfen'. However, E.A. Speiser, *JAOS LIX (1939)*, 306, n. 52, translates ***šatti*** 'together'." E. Laroche, *GLH*, 219, s.v. ***satt-***, mentions sub 2. Nom. ***šatti-***, *ša-a-at-ti*, Mit. I 23, II 63, 74; KUB XLVII 5 I 9; cf. KBo XXIII 25, 1. *ša-at-ti-ip-pa*, KUB XXXII 19 + II 26. *ša-a-at-t*[*a*], KBo XX 129 + III 1, 3. The root ***satt-*** occurs also in the onomastics of Nuzi in ***Šattu-marti*** (wr. *Ša-ad-du-mar-ti, Ša-at-tu(m)-mar-ti, Ša-at-tu-mar-di*) and in the hypocoristic ***Šattuịa*** (wr. *Ša-at-tu-ia*), cf. I.J. Gelb, *NPN*, 127.

Th. Richter, *BGH*, 364: ***šatti*** II [Boğ; Mit] 'zusammen, gemeinsam'. Th. Richter (*VHN*, 503) distinguishes the verbal root with voiced dental ***šad-*** {*šad-*} '(verstorbenes Kind) ersetzen' ['to replace (the deceased child)'] from that with voiceless dental ***šatt-*** {*šatt-*} '(Kind) ergreifen, packen' ['to take, seize (the child)'] > '(älteres Kind) sterben lassen' ['to let (the older child) die'], although single and double writings of the dentals occur with regard to the same persons. The meaning of transitive ***šatt-*** I (*BGH*, 362-363) could only be established by vocabulary comparison at Ugarit: Sumerian DIB = Akkadian ***ṣabātu*** = Hurrian ***ša(?)-at(?)-tu-um-mi*** 'ergreifen, packen'. The transitive names are replacement-names. The meaning of the intransitive root is not yet clear. The exclusive use of the allophone ***°=m*** instead of ***°=b*** in intransitive constructions is remarkable. He offers the following names as examples: *ᶠŠattam-ki* (Mari); *ᶠŠattam-kiaze* (Mari); *ᶠŠattam-(a)tal* (Mari); *Šattija* (Mari, Ašnakkum, Šubat-Enlil); *Šattiš* (Ašnakkum, [Šušarrā]); *Šattuja(?)* (Šušarrā); *Šattum-arte* ([Mari], [Qaṭṭarā]); *Šattum-atal* (Šubat-Enlil); *ᶠŠattum-ki* (Mari); *ᶠŠattum-kiaze* (Mari); *Šattum-šišni* (Mari). Th. Richter analyses ***Šattum-arte*** (Mari) as {*šatt=o=m-arde*}, typology 1.1.1.1.1, lexicon *šatt-*, *arde*, 'Der Stadt ergriff (Jungen)' ['The city took (the boy)'] > ['The city(-god) let (the older child) die']. This analysis makes it clear that the division ***Šattu-marti*** of the same name at Nuzi by I.J. Gelb (*NPN*, 127) and P.M. Purves should be corrected to ***Šattum-arte***. Although Linear A ***sa-ta*** , (HT 117a.7) can theoretically be an intransitive 'one-word' name ***Šatta*** {*šatt=a*}, this does not seem plausible because of the contextual position of ***sa-ta*** **,** on the tablet.

Possibly the Hurrian-Hittite bilingual ***Kirenze*** (KBo 32) may bring the solution: KBo 32: 13 Vs. I 7-8 (cf. E. Neu, *StBoT 32*, 220, where it is line 9-10):
(7) ᴰIM-*up ša-at-ta(-)ḫa-mu-u-ra šu-úr-ru-ú* (8) *ti-me-er-ri-e e-še-ni du-ú-ri* =
ᴰ*Teššub šatt(=)a(-)ḫam=o=ra šurr=u* (or *šurru*) *timer(i)=ne eše=ni turi* (or: *tur=i*)
'Teššub (ᴰIM, the Storm God) went down / descended together with *Šatta-ḫamu* (I prefer: together with Ḫamu) into the dark earth underneath [into the Dark Underworld].'
The corresponding Hittite version, II 9-10 (cf. E. Neu, *StBoT 32*, 221):
(9) ᴰIM-*aš-kán* ᴰ*šu-wa-li-i̯a-az-za-aš-ša* [N.B. ***-kan*** is a Hittite sentence particle.]
(10) *ka-ta-an-ta ta-an-ku-wa-i ták-ni-i i-i̯a-an-ni-ir*

Translation of the difficult lines 7-8 largely depends on the Hittite version.

I translate the German text of I.Wegner's commentary (*Einführung*, 207-210) in a concise form: (7) It is uncertain whether *ša-at-ta(-)ḫa-mu-u-ra* (*comitative* in ***-ra*** of *šatta(-)ḫa-mu-*) consists of one or two words. The expression corresponds in Hittite with the god *Šuwaliatt-* 'brother of the Weather-God' of the Ullikummi-myth. Analysis: either *šatt=a* (intransitive verbal form) *ḫam=o=ra* (substantive) or *šattaḫam=o=ra*.
The form *šurr=u* is not clear. It is not certain, whether it really corresponds with Hittite *ii̯annir* 'they went'. For the root *surr-* the expression *šurrumma*, attested at Nuzi and Amarna, may perhaps be compared. It means 'promptly, forthwith' (cf. E.A. Speiser, *IH*, 173-174, with note 282), according to *CAD* 'promptly, forthwith, indeed'). Consequently *surru* can be an adverb 'immediately' or a related verbal form 'to set out immediately'. If *surru* is an adverb, the verb of the sentence can only be found in line 8 in the word *du-ú-ri*. According to E. Laroche (*GLH*, 273) *turi* means 'inférieur' ['underneath, deeply down'], cf. ***enna turi-na*** 'dieux infernaux' ['the infernal Gods; the Gods of the Underworld'] = Hittite ***katteres siunes***.

A homographic word [*d*]*u-ú-ri* (KBo 32: 14 I 19) can now be compared with the Hittite verbal form *arḫa ḫuwais* 'he ran away' (KBo 32: 14 II 18). This is confirmed by a sentence in Qaṭna letter MSH02G-i0276 Rs. 41-42: 'Look, now Nuḫašše runs away (*tur=a*) towards your troops', cf. Th. Richter, *AoF 32*, 2005, 36 f.

(8) *timeri-*, adjective 'dark' + the so-called definite article singular *-ne* in locative function: *timeri-ne* > *timerne* > *timerre* (wr. *ti-me-er-ri-e*). The word depends on the next word *eše* 'earth' + *-ne* (also in locative function). The expression *timer(i)=ne eše=ni* corresponds with Hittite *tankuwai tagni* (wr. *ta-an-ku-wa-i ták-ni-i*).

I. Wegner admits that the ending in ***-i*** of a verbal ***tur-*** cannot easily be explained. She does not seem to believe in the suggestion of "a marker of transitivity ***-i*** in antipassive form" and she considers "forms without ***-b***" unlikely for an intransitive verb like ***tur-*** expressing motion.

According to Th. Richter (*BGH*, 418) *trans.* ***sur-*** II [Mit.]: 'eilig gehen lassen, abfertigen' ['to let (somebody) hurry up, to delegate'] (I. Wegner, *Einführung*, 281), 'fortgehen, abreisen lassen' ['to let somebody go, depart'] (E. Neu, 2001, 95), *intr.* ***surr-*** [Boğ.] 'aller, faire route, se diriger (vers)' ['to go (on his/her way) (to)'] (Catsanicos, 1996, 282), '(hinab)gehen' ['to go down, to descend'] (E. Neu, 2001, 95), 'eilig gehen' ['to go hastily, to hurry'] (M. Salvini - I. Wegner 2004, 181).

It is in my view most likely that *du-ú-ri* (KBo 32: 13 Vs. I 8) is not a verbal form, but means 'underneath, deeply down' and may syntactically well belong to the combination *ti-me-er-ri-e e-še-ni*. In that case it is attributive and belongs to the same semantic category as *enna turina*.

However, since ***kattanda*** in the Hittite version means 'down into' and since Hittite *ka-ta-an-ta i-i̯a-an-ni-ir* can according to E. Neu (1992c, 394) also be taken together, parallel Hurrian *šu-úr-ru-ú … du-ú-ri* can also mean 'to go down, to descend', so that *du-ú-ri* is predicative. I. Wegner (*Einführung*, 130) offers examples of *intransitive* verbal endings in ***-u*** that are difficult to explain.

E.A. Speiser (*JAOS LIX (1939)*, 306, n. 52) already translated ***šatti*** as 'together'. Th. Richter (*BGH*, 364), s.v. ***šatti*** II [Boğ.; Mit.] 'zusammen' ['together'] and s.v. ***šatta(-) ḫamu*** [Boğ.; Mit.] mentions that E. Neu (1996a, 244f.) interprets ****ḫamu*** as 'Begleiter, Berater' ['companion, attendant, adviser'] in *ša-at-ta(-)ḫa-mu-u-ra*: ***šatta ḫamō=ra*** 'zusammen mit **ḫamu*' ['together with **ḫamu*']. I. Wegner (*Einführung*, 258) regards *ḫamo* as a noun. V. Haas (2006, 182) interprets it as a proper name.

In fact ***šatta*** 'together with' may be an *essive* form ***šatt(i)=a***, adverbially used and combined with the *comitative* ***ḫamo/u=ra***.

As regards Linear A ***sa-ta*** **,** (HT 117a.7) it is remarkable that the sequence following the word divider is ***ku-ku-da-ra*** 1, in fact the first of the new series of personal names. So one gets the impression that ***ku-ku-da-ra*** might represent the *comitative* of ****ku-ku-da***, but if ***ku-ku-da-ra*** represents a *comitative*, one may logically expect that the other names following ***ku-ku-da-ra*** are also in the same case, but that is not the case.

So I conclude that ***sa-ta*** **,** (HT 117a.7) means 'together with (the 10 persons just mentioned before ***ku-ro*** 10): the following persons …'. This means that the word divider between ***sa-ta*** and ***ku-ku-da-ra*** 1 represents a punctuation mark (**:** in our texts).

Morphologically and syntactically Linear A ***sa-ta*** is used as an adverb and the names ***ku-ku-da-ra*** 1 (HT 117a.7), ***ko-sa-ni-|ti*** 1 (HT 117a.7-8), ***da-mi-nu*** 1 (HT 117a.8), ***da-na-ku-|ti*** 1 (HT 117a.8-9), ***ki-da-ro*** 1 (HT 117a.9) are probably all in the *absolutive* case.

The Linear A personal name ***ku-ku-da-ra*** (HT 117a.7) may consist of two Hurrian elements. In fact ***Ku-ku*** is one of the earliest attested Hurrian names, since it goes back to the Gasur and Ur III periods. P.M. Purves, *NPN*, 229, s.v. ***kukk***: "Hurrian. Oppenheim in *AOF XII*, 34, suggests connection with Elamite *kuk* (meaning unknown). A borrowing by Hurrian from some other non-Semitic language is possible. Cf. *Ku-ku,* HSS X 153 ix 8, 154 v 2, and 155 v16, from Gasur, also Ur III *Ku-ku,* Schneider in *Orientalia*, No. 23 (1927) No. 1841. Other Ur III personal names, *Gu-ú-gu, Gu-ú-gu-a* and *Gu-ú-gu-ga*, listed by Schneider *ibid.* Nos. 614-616, are analogous to Nuzi forms listed here. From Nippur cf. *Ku-uk-ku-ú-a*, Clay, *PNCP*, p.100." At Nuzi: ***ᶠKukku*** (wr. *ᶠKu-uk-ku*), ***Kukkuia*** (wr. *Ku-uk-ku-ia, Ku-ku-ia, Ku-ku-e*), ***ᶠKukkuia*** (wr. *ᶠKu-uk-ku-ia, ᶠKu-ku-ia*), ***ᶠKukkuka*** (wr. *ᶠKu-uk-ku-qa*), ***ᶠKukk-urašše*** (wr. *ᶠKu-uk-ku-ú-ra-aš-še*), I.J. Gelb, *NPN*, 90.

Th. Richter (*VHN*, 443-444) confirms that ***ku-kº*** and ***ku-uk-kº*** occur at Nuzi in names of the same persons, so that ***kug-/kukk-*** {*ko/ug-/ko/ukk-*} are variants (cf. the catalogue ad ***ᶠKukija*** and ***ᶠKukku*** (*VHN*, 170-171). The only context-form seems to be *ku-(uk-)ka-li-ni-na* in texts from Emar (see Th. Richter, *BGH*, 218, 223), if it does not belong to the loan-word ***kukkali/kungalle*** 'Fettschwanzschaf' ['sheep with a fat tail']. For Elamite an interpretation of ***kuk*** as 'Schutz' ['protection'] has been suggested. M. Salvini (2010, 157) has proposed for Urartian ***kug=u-*** '(Stele) aufstellen' ['to erect (a stele)'], but it is not certain that this might also be the meaning of the Hurrian root.

Th. Richter (*VHN*, 444) offers the following personal names: (1a) {*ko/ug-*}: ***ᶠKukija*** (Mari). - (1b) {*ko/ukk-*}: ***ᶠKukki*** (Mari, Šubat-Enlil); ***ᶠKukku*** (Mari); ***Kukku(?)-ewri*** (Mari). - (2) {*ko/ukkori*}: ***ᶠKukkuriān*** (Mari) and ***ᶠKukkurên*** (Mari).

Since according to Th. Richter (*VHN*, 443-444, s.v. ***kug-/kukk-*** {*ko/ug-/ko/ukk-*}) personal names with ***ku-kº*** and ***ku-uk-kº*** also occur in archives such as Alalaḫ, Ḫattuša and Kaniš, where Elamite personal names are very unusual, the existence of a Hurrian root is very likely. In note 443 he remarks that perhaps under influence of Oppenheim 1937-1939a, 34, who defined *kuk* as Elamite, *NPN* 229 suspected a borrowing by Hurrian from some other non-Semitic language. Formations like *ku-uk-ku-ri-a-an* and *ku-uk-ku-re-en* give evidence for a participle ***kukkuri*** {*ko/ukk=o=ri*}. Their mutual relationship can be described by referring to the sound-development {IA} > {Ê} in Old-Babylonian from Mari. There are parallels for this phenomenon in Hurrian vocabulary of that period in two incantation-texts, e.g. *ki-ra-ri-ia-aš* versus *ki-ra-re-eš* and *ḫi-ia-ri-ia-aš* versus *ḫi-ia-ri-iš* (see Krebernik 2001, 158). Richter offers an alternative explanation in note 444: "If Streck (2000, 187 § 2.79) is right that variant writings such as *ki-a-am / ki-e-em* do not reflect contracted forms like **kêm*, but must be interpreted as *kiyam* and *kiyem*, respectively, this indicates existence of a semivowel {J} in Hurrian." [I have translated Richter's German text into English.]

I may add that variant writing of Hurrian hypocoristic names in Hurrian cuneiform and in Linear A proves the existence of this semivowel or at least a glide [*y*], e.g. the writing-variants of ***Kipaia*** {*ke/ib=a=ya*} at Nuzi: *Ki-pa-a-a, Ki-ba-a-a, Ki-ba-ia* (P.M. Purves, *NPN*, 227).

On may also compare Linear A ***ki-pa-a , u-na-a*** (KN Zb 40.1-2) on a pithos from Knossos and ***ke-pa-ja*** (KN Zf 13) {*keb=a=ya*} on a gold ring from Mavro Spilio and the frequent Minoan orthography of Linear A ***a-ta-i-jo-wa-ja*** 'Our Father' as first entry in libation formulas, analysis {*attai(y)=o/uwwa(y)=aš*}, beside the Hurrian reconstructed form ****at-ta-i-iw-wa-aš***, analysis {*attai(y)=iwwa=aš*}, in cuneiform.

In the 2016 edition I compared the second element of Linear A ***ku-ku-da-ra*** with the Hurrian element ***-talla***, e.g. in ***Ḫaš-talla*** (cf. P.M. Purves, *NPN*, 262), with the verbal root ***ḫaš-*** 'to hear', provided that F.W. Bush correctly assumes that allophonic voicing of a dental can take place under influence of liquids and nasals.

The position has changed, because Th. Richter (*VHN*, 412-413) now offers a different analysis of the Hurrian personal name *Ḫa-aš-tal-la* at Nuzi (cf. I.J. Gelb, *NPN*, 58; cf. *Répertoire géographique des textes cunéiformes 10* [= Fincke 1993], 97-98). Richter mentions, s.v. ***ḫašt-***, that {*ḫaš=d-*} probably means 'stark sein' ['to be strong'], but that this meaning needs to be confirmed. He thinks that the Hurrian personal names ***Ḫašta*** (wr. *ḫa-aš-ta*) at Tigunāni, analysis {*ḫašt=a*}, 'He is strong' or 'Be strong !', ***Ḫašten*** (wr. *ḫa-aš-te-en*) at Tigunāni, {*ḫašt=i=n(na)*}, 'Make him strong !', and ***Ḫaštalla*** (wr. *Ḫa-aš-tal-la*) at Nuzi, {*ḫašt=a=lla*}, 'They are strong', may well be verbal forms, with the enclitic personal pronouns ***-n(na)*** 'him/her' (*object* of the *transitive* form) and ***-lla*** 'they' (*subject* of the *intransitive* form), respectively. According to Th. Richter (*BGH*, 139) ***ḫašti*** [Boğ.] means 'stark' ['strong'], cf. V. Haas - H.J. Thiel, 1978, 249.

I think that for ***Ḫaštalla*** (wr. *Ḫa-aš-tal-la*) at Nuzi another analysis is possible as well: either transitive *imperative* {*ḫašt(i)=alla(i)*} 'Make (the boy) strong, oh Allai/Allani !' or intransitive *indicative* {*ḫašt(a)=alla(i)*} 'Allai/Allani (the Lady) is strong'.

Consequently Linear A ***ku-ku-da-ra*** can now also be interpreted along this line. I. Wegner (*Einführung*, 96-97, sub d) mentions that the Hurrian-Hittite bilingual ***Kirenze*** (KBo 32) offers a morpheme ***-ut-*** {*-ud-*} indicating a negation of so-called 'Old Hurrian' verbal forms, to date only attested in the Boğazköy bilingual. She offers examples of the *ergative* 3rd person singular with the formants ***=o=m***: ***fur=ud=o=m*** (KBo 32: 14 I 38) 'er sah nicht (einen zweiten Bezirck)' ['he did not see (a second district, area)'] ***am=ud=o=m*** (KBo 32: 14 I 29) 'er erreichte nicht (das jenseitige Ufer)' ['he did not reach (the other bank of the river)'], cf. Th. Richter, *BGH*, 23-24, s.v. ***amm-*** II [Boğ;Qa] 'ankommen, erreichen' ['to arrive, to reach']. I. Wegner mentions (*Einführung*, 136, sub b) another form *a-mu-du-um* (KBo 32: 19 I 37) 'er sah nicht' ['he did not see'], consisting of root ***am-*** + negation ***-ud-*** + marker of the past tense ***-o-*** + marker of the subject 3rd person singular ***-m***, cf. also Th. Richter, *BGH*, 21-23, s.v. ***am-*** II [Boğ.] 'ansehen, anschauen' ['to see']. I. Wegner adds that E. Neu (*StBoT 32*, 164) proposes to segment ***-ut-*** into ***-u+t-*** : ***am=u***[negation-morpheme]=***t***[formant indicating past tense]***=o=m***.

I consider it likely that the Linear A personal name ***ku-ku-da-ra*** (HT 117a.7) can be analysed as {*kug/kk=ud(=a)-Alla(i)*} '(The Goddess) Allai/Allani did not ….'. (We have to wait for confirmation of the meaning of the verbal root ***kug-/kukk-*** 'to erect/elevate?'). The theophorous element ***Allai*** usually occurs without final ***-i***, if it is used as second onomastic element, cf. e.g. P.M. Purves, *NPN*, 199, s.v. ***all***, ***-alla***.

The personal name ***ko-sa-ni-ti*** 1 (HT 117a.7-8) follows Linear A ***ku-ku-da-ra*** 1 (HT 117a.7). This name can probably be interpreted as a Hurrian 'one-word' verbal name, for which I propose the analysis {*koz(z)=an(n)=i=tti*} and the translation 'Let he/she (scil. a *numen*) hold me back !' or 'Let she (scil. the mother) hold me back !'. The name probably refers to a stage during the process of giving birth.

Th. Richter (*VHN*, 450-451) explains the transitive root ***kuz-*** II/***kuzz*** {*koz-*(?)/*kozz-*(?)} as 'zurückhalten' ['to hold / keep back, to retain']. The intransitive usage cannot yet be explained. The name consists of the verbal root ***koz(z)-*** 'to hold back' + the *causative* root-extension ***-an(n)-*** + the marker of transitivity ***-i-*** + the *optional allomorphic* enclitic personal pronoun 1st person singular ***-tti*** instead of ***-tta***.

Th. Richter (*VHN*, 186) mentions a personal name ***Kuzzutta*** (wr. *Ku-zu-zu-ta*) at Ašnakkum with a similar formation (with the normal enclitic personal pronoun 1st person singular ***-tta***, but without root-extension ***-an(n)-***) that he analyses as {*kozz*(?)=*o*=*tta*} and translates as 'Halte mich zurück !' ['Hold me back !']. According to I. Wegner (*Einführung*, 88) the root-extension ***-an(n)-*** expresses the *causative* aspect: ***ar-*** 'geben' ['to give']; ***ar=ann-*** 'sich geben lassen' ['to let give oneself'].

Th. Richter (*VHN*, 596, sub 1.3.1.1.2.2) mentions that in 'one-word' names the enclitic personal pronoun 1st person singular ***-tta*** can sometimes be replaced by the *optional allomorphic* suffix ***-tti***. Likewise the enclitic personal pronoun 3rd person singular ***-nna*** can be replaced by ***-nne/i*** or ***-nnu*** and the enclitic personal pronoun 3rd person plural ***-lla*** can be replaced by ***-lle*** or ***-lli***. He gives the example of ***Ullutti*** (wr. *Ul-lu-ut-ti*), analysis {*o/ull=o=tti*}, from Mari and Tigunāni, beside ***Ullutta*** (wr. *Ul-lu-ut-ta*), analysis {*o/ull=o=tta*}, from Šušarrā, 'Destroy me (oh *numen*) !', cf. also Th. Richter, *VHN*, 329.

Th. Richter (*VHN*, 181-182, 450-451) mentions that the root ***koz(z)-*** also occurs with the *iterative* root-extension ***-ar-***, which offers the meaning 'weiter zurückhalten' ['to hold / keep back more and more']. As examples of personal names with root-extension ***-ar-*** he mentions the *imperative* forms: ***Kuzar*** (Mari); ***(f)Kuzari*** (Mari, Tuttul); ***Kuzzari*** (Mari, Ašnakkum), all analysed as {*koz(z)=ar=i*}, typology 1.3.1.2.1, and translated as 'Halte (Kind) weiter zurück (oh Frau/*Numen*) !' ['Hold (the child) more and more back (oh woman/*numen*) !']; and the *indicative* form ***Kuzarum*** (Mari), analysis {*koz=ar=o=m*}, typology 1.1.1.1.1, translation 'Er/Sie (*Numen*/Frau) hielt (Kind) weiter zurück' ['He / She (*numen*/woman) held (the child) more and more back'].

Compare also the forms without root-extension: (*imperative*) ***Kuzi*** (Mari, Ekalte, Emar); ***fKuzi*** (Mari, Ḫattuša, KUB 55,54 Vs. I 14, and *passim*); ***Kuzzi*** (Mari, Tigunāni), analysis {*koz(z)=i*}, typology 1.3.1.2.1, translated as 'Halte (Kind) zurück (oh Frau / *Numen*) !' ['Hold (the child) back (oh woman/*numen*) !']; ***Kuzzu*** (Šušarrā, Šubat-Enlil, Tigunāni, Nuzi, cf. I.J. Gelb, *NPN* 94), analysis {*ko/uzz=o*}, typology 1.3.1.1.1, translation 'Halte (Kind) zurück (oh Frau/*Numen*) !' ['Hold (the child) back (oh woman / *numen*) !']; (*indicative*) ***Kuzija*** (Mari, Kaniš, Qaṭna), analysis {*koz*(?)=*i=ja*}, typology 1.1.1.2.4, translation 'Er/Sie (*Numen*/Frau) hielt (Kind) zurück' ['He/She (*numen*/woman) held (the child) back'].

Linear A ***da-mi-nu*** (HT 117a.8) from Hagia Triada follows the personal name ***ko-sa-ni-ti*** 1 (HT 117a.7-8) and precedes ***da-ne-ku-ti*** (HT 117a.8-9).

In my view it can be interpreted as the Hurrian personal name ***Talminnu*** , analysed as {*d/talm=i=nn(a)=u*}, 'Make him (the boy) great, powerful, (oh *numen*) !', consisting of the verbal root ***talm-*** 'to make great, powerful' + the marker of transitivity ***-i-*** (together forming the *imperative* 2nd person sing.) + the suffix of the enclitic personal pronoun 3rd person singular ***-nna*** (him). As discussed before, the enclitic personal pronoun 3rd person singular ***-nna*** can sometimes be replaced by the *optional allomorphic* suffix ***-nni*** or ***-nnu***.

Other Hurrian names with ***Talm=i-*** are, for instance, ***Talmi-Tešub***, that was formerly translated as 'Great is Tešub', but can now probably also be interpreted as 'Make (the boy) great, powerful, oh Tešub !' ***Talmi-Tešub*** is the name of the King of Kargamiš (son of *Ini-Tešub* 'Tešub is God'), mentioned by E. Laroche, *NH*, 172, n° 1230, with references to Boğazköy KBo XII 41 I 5, hieroglyphic seals (*Tal-mi-Tešub*^{ba}), HH I N°s 318, 391, and Ugarit RS 17.226, 1 and cyl. = PRU IV 208. Another clearly Hurrian name is ***Talmi-Šarruma***, name of the Hittite King of Aleppo (grandson of Suppiluliuma I). ***Talmi-Šarruma*** used to be translated as 'Great is Šarruma', but can now also be interpreted as 'Make (the boy) great, powerful, oh Šarruma!': accusative ^{m}*Tal-mi*-LUGAL-*ma-an,* KBo IV 4 III 15, etc. (see *NH*, 172, n° 1229), with the Sumerogram LUGAL instead of *Šarru*. There is an equerry 'master of the horse' called ***Talmiya*** (abs. ^{m}*Tal-mi-ya*, KBo X 10 II 16) and a person mentioned in hieroglyphic ***Tal-mi-ia***, RS 18.263 = Ugar. III 157, with the hypocoristic suffix ***-ya*** (cf. *NH*, 172, n° 1228). Incidentally, it is difficult to distinguish the names with the hypocoristic suffix ***-ya*** from those representing a transitive *indicative* form, 3rd person singular, ***Talmia***, analysis {*talm=i=a*}, 'He makes (the boy) great', cf. Th. Richter, *VHN*, 585 + note 957: "Es ist anzunehmen, daß es daneben PNn mit einer Verbalform der 3PsSg auf ***°=i=a*** gibt; sie können aber nicht von hypokoristischen Bildungen trans. ergativ. Rektion getrennt werden (dazu s. 1.1.1.2.4)[957]."

Compare at Nuzi ***^{f}Allai-talma*** (wr. *^{f}Al-la-i-tal-ma*) 'The Lady is great', ***Erwi-talma*** (wr. *Er-wi-tal-ma, Er-wi-ta-al-ma*) 'The Lord is great', ***Talmu*** (wr. *Da-al-mu*), ***Talmu-šarri*** (wr. *Tal-mu-šarri*), ***Talmuịa*** (wr. *Tal-mu-ia*), cf. P.M. Purves, *NPN*, 262.

The other possible interpretation is ***Tarminnu***, analysed as {*d/tarm=i=nn(a)=u*}, 'Nourish him (the boy), (oh *numen*) !', consisting of the verbal root ***tarm-*** 'to give to drink, to nurse, to nourish, to (breast)feed (a child)' + the marker of transitivity ***-i-*** (together forming the *imperative* 2nd person sing.) + the suffix of the enclitic personal pronoun 3rd person sing. ***-nna*** (him), replaced by the *optional allomorphic* enclitic pronoun ***-nnu***. So ***-nu*** in Linear A ***da-mi-nu*** has nothing to do with ***-ninu*** in the Hurrian anthroponym ***^{f}Tarmin-ninu*** < **^{f}Tarmip(?)-ninu* (wr.*^{f}Tar-mi-in-ni-nu*) at Nuzi, SMN 636 (I.J. Gelb, *NPN*, 149; P.M. Purves, *NPN*, 263; P.M. Purves (*NPN*, 239) s.v. ***ninu-***, ***-ninu***: "*ninu-* in personal names is associated with city Ninua (Niniveh) by Gadd in *RA XXIII* 65; Speiser, *Mes. Or*., 139; Ungnad, *Subartu*, 146; Gustavs, *MAOG X 3 (1937)*, 13 and 50; Speiser, *JAOS LVIII (1938)*, 198."

Th. Richter (*VHN*, 470 + n. 561-562), mentions (s.v. ***Ninu(a)***) [Ortsname = toponym]) that the name of the city of Niniveh, occurs as first element of nominal sentence names, ***ni-nu-(a-)***° at Tigunāni: ***Ninua-šarri*** and ***Ninu(a)-atal***, and that it occurs as second onomastic element elsewhere, e.g. at Nuzi. Niniveh plays a special role in Hurrian mythology and religion.

The centres of the later Assyrian empire, Niniveh and Aššur, had the status of vassal states of Mitanni until the rise of the Hittite empire in the 14th century B.C. under Suppiluliuma I, who reduced his enemy, Mitanni, to a vassal status and occupied the western half of the former Mitannian empire.

The element ***Tarmi-*** has been very popular at Nuzi, since 63 persons with the hypocoristic name ***Tarmiịa*** (wr. *Tar-mi-ia, Ta-ar-mi-ia, Tar-me-ia*) are attested in its archives. ***Tarmiịa*** can also be a 'one-word' name {*tarm=i=a*} 'He/She (a *numen* or the mother) nourishes (the child)'. Compare also at Nuzi ***Tarm-apu*** (wr. *Tar-ma-a-pu*), ***Tarmi-tešup*** (wr. *Tar-mi-te-šup, Tar-mi-te-eš-šup*), ***Tarmi-tilla*** (wr. *Tar-mi-til-la*), ***Tarmi-ẓiẓẓa*** (wr. *Tar-mi-zi-iz-za*), ***Urḫa-tarmi*** (wr. *Ur-ḫa-tar-mi, Ur-ḫa-tar-me*), ***Tarmip-tašenni*** (wr. *Tar-mi-ip-ta-še-ni, Tar-mi-ip-ta-še-en-ni*), ***Tarmiš-šimiki*** (wr. *Tar-mi-iš-ši-mi-ki*), ***Tarmu-šarri*** (wr. *Tar-mu-šarri*), cf. P.M. Purves, *NPN*, 262-263.

A personal name at Mari contains the verbal root ***tarm-*** and *factitive* or *iterative* root-extension ***-ar-*** (cf. I. Wegner, *Einführung* , 88, s.v. ***-ar-***): ***Tarmariš*** (wr. *ta-ar-ma-ri-iš*), analysis {*tarm=ar=i=ž*}, typology 1.3.2.2, lexicon *tarm-*, that Th. Richter (*VHN*, 299, 531) translates as 'Er/Sie (scil. ein *Numen*) möge (Jungen) wiederholt tränken' ['He/She (namely a *numen*) may nurse, nourish, (breast)feed (the boy) repeatedly']. See also ***Tarmuši*** (wr. *tar-mu-ši*) at Šubat-Enlil/Šeḫna (Tall Leilān), analysis {*tarm=o/už=i*}, typology 1.3.1.2.1, lexicon *tarm-*, translation 'Tränke (Jungen) !' ['Nurse / Nourish / (Breast)feed (the boy) !'], cf. Th. Richter, *VHN*, 299, 531. He also mentions the *infinitive* ***tarm-umma*** *epēšu* [Nuzi], cf. Th. Richter, *BGH*, 446.

Since according to P.M. Purves (*NPN*, 262-263) the Hurrian personal name ***Tarmik-kutu*** (wr. *Tar-mi-ik-ku-tu, Tar-mi-ik-ku-du, Tar-mi-ku-du*) consisted of two onomastic elements, ***tarmi-*** and ***-kutu***, and since he proposed that ***-tarni*** in ***Unap-tarni*** (wr. *Ú-na-ap-ta-ar-ni*) may be a phonetic variant of ***tarmi***, it seems *prima facie* attractive to identify Linear A ***da-ne-ku-ti*** (HT 117a.8-9) as ****D/Tarne-kutti***, variant of ***Tarmikkutu***, the name of 4 persons at Nuzi, cf. I.J. Gelb, *NPN*, 149. The Hurrian element ***kut(t)-*** in ***Tarmik-kutu*** can contain a voiced dental (single writing) or voiceless dental (double writing), cf. P.M. Purves, *NPN*, 231, s.v. ***kut***, ***kuti-***, ***kutiịa***, ***-kutu***, ***kutt***, ***kutta-***, ***kutti***. Purves' hypothesis that Hurrian ***tarni-*** in ***Unap-tarni*** (wr. *Ú-na-ap-ta-ar-ni*) may be a phonetic variant of ***tarmi***, is impossible for ***Unap-tarni***, since a Hurrian personal name cannot consist of two verbal elements, in this case ***un-*** 'to come' and ***tarm-*** 'to give to drink, (breast)feed, nourish'. The element ***-tarni*** in ***Unap-tarni*** must be nominal. The meaning of this name may be 'The fire came', analysis {*un=a=b-tar(i)=ni*}. Th. Richter (*BGH*, 444-445) mentions s.v. ***tari*** I [Boğ.; PN] 'Feuer' ['fire'] and s.v. ‡ ***tarni*** [Boğ.], possibly ***tar(i)=ni*** (Görke, 2010,137), cf. also *ta-ri pa-ḫi-ib-wu$_u$-e* 'das Feuer meines Hauptes' ['the fire of my head'] (KBo 27.134 = ChS I/5 Nr. 80 Vs. 14'), cf. De Martino – Giorgieri 2007, 136^{+74}.

According to Th. Richter (*VHN*, 452), s.v. ***kud-/kutt-*** {*kud-*, sometimes *kutt-*}, the verbal onomastic forms with ***kud-*** *intransitive* 'fallen' ['to fall'], transitive 'fallen lassen, fällen, zu Fall bringen' ['to let fall, to overthrow, to bring down'] are equivalent to Hittite ***mauš-*** that can in context be interpreted as 'fallen lassen' ≈ 'gebären' ['to let fall' ≈ 'to bring forth, to give birth to']; Akkadian ***maqātum*** seems to offer the same connotation, cf. Th. Richter, *BGH*, 231-233, s.v. ***kud-***.

However, although ***tarm-*** 'to give to drink, to nurse, to (breast)feed, to nourish (a child)' as well as ***kud-/kutt-*** 'to let fall' ≈ 'to bring forth, to give birth to' fit semantically very well in Hurrian onomastics and are therefore both well attested, a personal name containing *two* verbal roots 'Nourish and give birth !' at the same time, would be quite exceptional and therefore most unlikely.

Since verbal roots are most common as first element in Hurrian personal names, an *imperative* ***tarm=i-*** 'give to drink, nurse, nourish !' would be quite acceptable in Hurrian ***Tarmikkutu***, but cuneiform ***-(k)kutu*** , phonologically ***/-kudu/***, may be nominal and can perhaps be regarded as a (*quasi*) theophorous element. But the meaning of this alleged noun ****kudo/u*** is not clear at all. Comparison with neither the hapax substantive ***kutkūti*** [Boğ.] nor the noun ***kuduni*** [Boğ.] 'neck' offers a solution, cf. Th. Richter, *BGH*, 231-232, s.v. ***kud-*** [Boğ.], ***kutkūti*** [Boğ.] and ***kuduni*** [Boğ.] 'Nacken, Hals (?)'.

Since ***-tarni*** cannot be a variant of ***-tarmi*** in ***Unap-tarni***, it seems preferable to quit the idea that ***tarni*** might be a variant of ***tarmi***, but theoretically it cannot be ruled out that it may be a variant of ***tarmi*** in other personal names, especially if it is the first element.

Consequently, if ***da-ne-ku-ti*** (HT 117a.8-9) is analysed as {*d/tarn/m=e=kku=tti*} replacing {*d/tarn/m=e=kko>a=tta*}, the name can be translated as 'I do not give to drink, (breast)feed, nourish' (semantically not very attractive !), with optional allomorphic ***-tti*** instead of ***-tta*** as subject of the *negative antipassive* verbal form ***d/tarn=e/i-***, alleged variant of ***d/tarm=e/i-***. The antipassive is explained as transitive form without object, but with the same negative suffix ***-kko-*** as in intransitive forms. The transitive negative suffix is ***-u(w)/wa-*** (position 6), cf. I. Wegner, *Einführung*, 95, Table 5. In transitive forms the absolutive enclitic personal pronoun (position 9) indicates the object of the transitive-ergative verb. The enclitic personal pronouns of the *absolutive* (9th position) ***-tta/-t*** (1st pers. sing.), ***-mma/-m*** (2nd pers. sing.), ***Ø*** instead of ***-nna/-n*** (3rd pers. sing.), ***-tilla/-til*** (1st pers. plur.), ***-ffa/-f*** (2nd pers. plur.), ***-lla/-l*** (3rd pers. plur.) are used as markers of the subject, cf. I. Wegner, *Einführung*, 97-99, sub 5.4.1 and Tables 6 and 7: *Die Suffixfolge beim indikativen, intransitiven, negierten und beim antipassivischen Verb*.

However, if the verbal element in ***da-ne-ku-ti*** (HT 117a.8-9) is not ***d/tarn=e/i-***, variant of ***d/tarm=e/i-***, but ***d/tan=e/i-***, and if ***da-ne-ku-ti*** is analysed as {*d/tan=e/i=kku=tti*} replacing {*d/tan=e=kko>a=tta*}, the name can be translated as the *negative antipassive* verbal form 'I do not make, create', from the Hurrian root ***tan-*** 'to make, create'.

Compare the Hurrian personal name ***Tan-atal*** (wr. *Ta-na-ta-al*), *ḫabiru* at Tigunāni (Prisma IV 26), analysis {*tan-adal*}, typology 1.4, lexicon *tan-*, *adal*, translation 'Der Starke machte (Jungen)' ['The strong one made (the boy)']; ***Tanija*** (wr. *Ta-ni-ia*) at Alalaḫ IV (AT 189: 19) and Kurruḫanni, analysis {*tan=i=(j)a*}, 'He/She (a *numen*) makes/made, creates/created (the child)', cf. Th. Richter, *VHN*, 297.

ᶠTanuḫepa is the name of several Hittite queens, cf. E. Laroche, *NH*, 174, nº 1244:

1. Reine, femme de Muwatalli: hiér. [Hieroglyphic Luwian] *Tà-nú-he-pa*, SBo I 42.
2. Reine, femme de *Urḫi-Tešub*: hiér. *Tà-nú-he-pa*, SBo I 43-44.
3. Reine, femme d'un Mursili (II ou III ?): hiér. *Tà-nú-he-pa*, SBo I 24-29.
4. Sources cunéiformes: abs. nom. *ᶠDa/Ta-nu-ḫé-pa-(aš)*, XIV 7 + XXI 19 I 16, 17, 20; XI 33, 19; XXXI 66 III 15. - XV 5 I 7, III 4, 9. - XVI 16 Vo 1; 32 II 1, 4. - KBo IX 151,5.

Sur l'attribution de tous ces textes, cf. Güterbock, SBo I p. 11 sqq.; Laroche, *Ugar. III*, 105. The meaning of Old Hurrian *ᶠ**Tanuḫepa*** may well be (*imperative*) 'Make / Create (the girl), oh Ḫebat !' or (*past indicative*) 'Ḫebat made / created (the girl)'.

Examples of transitive one-word personal names are: Linear A ***ta-na-ti*** (HT 10b.4), analysed as {*tan=an=tti*} replacing {*tan=an=tta*}, with root-extension ***-an-***, translated as an *imperative* 'Practise magic/witchcraft, work charms on me (oh *numen*) !', cf. Th. Richter, *BGH*, 436-438, s.v. ***tan-*** [*passim*], *tin-* [Ugarit], 'machen, tun' ['to make, do'] and ***tan=an-*** [Boğ.], 'verursachen, Zauberei bewirken' ['to cause, practise witchcraft / magic, work charms on']. The suffix ***-tta/-tti*** takes position 9 in the chain of suffixes of the indicative transitive-ergative verb and has syntactically the function of object, cf. I. Wegner, *Einführung*, 93, Table 4.

Linear A ***i̯-du-ti*** (HT 104.2-3), analysis{*id=u=tti*}, 'Beat, hit, strike me (oh *numen*) !'; ***ka-nu-ti*** (HT 97a.3), {*ḫan=u=tti*}, *imperative* 'Give birth to me / create me (oh *numen*)!' or *indicative* 'He/She (a *numen*) created me' or 'She (the mother) gave birth to me'.

The Linear A personal name ***ki-da-ro*** 1 (HT 117a.9) analysed as {*ki(n)d=ar=o*} 'He/she must ….', cf. I. Wegner, *Einführung*, 138, sub *The jussive and other forms of mood in the bilingual*, 3rd person singular ***=u*** [*o*], has already been discussed.

Remarkably – apart from Linear A ***ku-re-96*** (HT 39.2; HT 117b.1), transliterated as ***ku-re-ḫi*** = ***Ḫurr=e=ḫi*** 'Hurrian', twice attested at Hagia Triada – also conventionally transliterated ***qa-ti-96*** 2 (ZA 14.2), that can be interpreted as ***Ḫattiḫi***, analysis ***Ḫatt=i=ḫi***, 'man/woman of the land ***Ḫatti***' = the Hurrian name for 'Hittite' occurs at Kato Zakro, see for an extensive discussion *chapter 12: From undeciphered to deciphered Linear A signs*.

The combination ***79-tu-ne , ku-re-ḫi*** 1 (HT 117b.1) is the first entry of HT 117b. So we may conclude that ***79-tu-ne*** is a personal name followed by the ethnic ***ku-re-ḫi*** = ***Ḫurr=e=ḫi*** 'Hurrian' or 'the Hurrian' followed by 1 unit. Since ***ku-re-ḫi*** follows ***79-tu-ne*** in apposition, it is a real ethnic and not an ethnic used as a personal name. See also ***79-tu-ne*** 1 (HT 7b.1); ***79-tu-ne , ma-ka-|ri-te , pi-ta-ke-si*** 1 (HT 87.1), and possibly ***79-tu***[-***ne***] 1 '[(HT 94b.5). Sign ***79*** is a rare sign, discussed extensively in *chapter 12*.

Linear A ***di-ki-se*** 1 (HT 117b.2), last entry of HT 117b, is no doubt a Hurrian personal name. It is prosopographically significant that ***di-ki-se*** 1 (HT 117b.2) not only occurs in the list of personal names with ***79-tu-ne*** (HT 117b.1) and ***ma-ka-ri-te*** (HT 117a.1) but also in: HT 87.1-2: *79-tu-ne , ma-ka-ri-te , pi-ta-ke-si* 1
3: *ja-re-mi* 1 *di-ki-se* 1 , etc.

Linear A ***di-ki-se*** 1 (HT 87.3; HT 117b.2) contains the root ***tag-/takk-***, ***teg-/tig-***, see Th. Richter (*BGH*, 428-429; *VHN*, 525-526), s.v. ***tag-/takk-***, ***teg-*** 'schön, rein, unbefleckt, glänzend, hell' ['beautiful, immaculate, pure, shining, bright']. He refers to a vocabulary comparison at Ugarit: Hurrian ***tagi*** = Sumerian IZI, Akkadian ***nūru*** 'Licht' ['light'], cf. also (*VHN*, 526-527), s.v. ***Tagidu*** (GNf) [feminine theonym] or ***tagidi***. Th. Richter (*VHN*, 526-527) mentions that *Tagidu* appears among the Hurrian goddesses in the rock-sanctuary of Yazılıkaya. She belongs to the entourage of *Ḫebat*. Ḫebat's epithet ***tagi*** and the combination ***da-(a)-ki***, ***da-a-ki-it-ti*** (E. Laroche) and deified ***ᴰta/da-(a)-ki-(it)-ti*** at Ḫattuša offer an indication that the root ***tag-*** is involved.

The word ***tagidi*** 'beauty, splendour, magnificence' occurs in names at Ugarit probably as an appellative name. ***fTakitu*** occurs at Mari. Compare my interpretation of ***a-di-da-ki-ti*** in ***a-di-da-ki-ti-pa-ku*** (KN Zc 6), *chapter 11: 'Religious' Linear A inscriptions*. In Minoan Linear A the root ***dag-*** has a voiced dental as the personal names ***da-ku-se-ne***, ***da-ku-|se-ne-ti***, ***da-ku-na***, ***da-ku***, ***da-ka*** and ***a-sa|-da-ka*** clearly show (see *supra* in this chapter). The Linear A name ***di-ki-se*** (HT 87.3; HT 117b.2) can be explained as a 'Mitanni' Hurrian variant *{de/ig=i-še(n=a)}* of (Old Hurrian) Linear A ***da-ku-se-ne*** *{dag=o/u-šen(=a)=ne/ni}*, consisting of the (trans.) root ***de/ig-*** (variant of ***dag-***) 'to make beautiful' + marker of transitivity ***-i-*** + ***Ø***-marker of the *imperative* + the abbreviated or hypocoristic form ***še*** of ***šen=a*** 'brother' or ***šen(=a)=ne/ni*** 'the brother', 'Make the brother beautiful (oh *numen*) !' or 'Make (the child) beautiful (oh deceased brother) !'.

However, since a double consonant ***-šš-*** in cuneiform is rendered as single ***-s-*** in Linear A, another interpretation is also possible for Linear A ***di-ki-se***, if Linear A ***-se*** is analysed as the Hurrian suffix ***-šše*** forming abstract nouns, cf. I. Wegner (*Einführung*, 55), who gives, s.v. ***-(i)=šše***, the examples ***šar=i=šše*** 'wish' from ***šar-*** 'to wish, demand', Ugarit vocabulary RS 94-2939, col. II 5; ***nir=i=šše*** 'goodness', derived from ***niri*** 'good'; ***kib=i=šše*** 'being seated (on the throne)', derived from ***keb-*** 'to set, put, lay down'.

Th. Richter (*BGH*, 428-429) mentions, s.v. ***tagiš(š)e*** [Boğ.; Emar(?); Ug.], ***tegiš(š)e*** [Ug.], 'beau' ['beautiful'] or 'beauté' ['beauty'] (E. Laroche, *GLH*, 250, sub ***tagi***); 'Schönheit' ['beauty'], i.e. 'free of anomalies' in liver-omen (De Martino, 1992a, 6, 122); '(stato di) lucentezza', i.e. *tag=i=že* (Giorgieri, 2000a, 204); 'rein' ['pure'] (Haas, 2003a, 236). Vocabulary correspondence between Sumerian ZÁLAG.GA and Hurrian ***te-gi-še*** 'hell, glänzend, rein' ['bright, shining, pure, immaculate']. It is not without significance that Th. Richter (*VHN*, 290, 525-526) also mentions, s.v. ***tag-/takk-***, ***teg-***, the personal names ***fTakazze*** (wr. *Da-ga-ze*) from Mari, ***fTakaše*** (wr. *fTa-qa-še*) from Nuzi (I.J. Gelb, *NPN*, 145), *fTa-ga-ša* from Old-Babylonian Kiš (*YOS 13*, 35: 1), typology 3.1, lexicon ***takazze***, that he compares with ***tagiš(š)e*** 'Schönheit' ['beauty'].

I have argued in *chapter 7* that there is no evidence that the phoneme ***/h/*** existed in the idiom written with Linear A. If my arguments are accepted, interpretation of the Linear A sequence ***a-du*** (HT 85a.1; 86a.4; 88.1; 92.1; 95b.1; 99a.1; 133.1; and perhaps KH 23.1) as the West Semitic theonym *'Haddu'*, as proposed by C.H. Gordon and later by J.G.P. Best, seems unlikely (cf. C.H. Gordon, *Evidence for the Minoan language,* 31; J.G.P. Best, *Some preliminary remarks on the decipherment of Linear A,* 24), even though it has been argued that the 'Casa del Lebete' at Hagia Triada might have been a temple complex. The finds in that complex point to a religious function of the Casa del Lebete (cf. J.W. Jong, 'The religious context of the Linear script A texts found at Hagia Triada near Phaestos in Crete', *Interaction and acculturation in the Mediterranean I,* Amsterdam 1980, 135-141).

An economic function does not dissociate ancient documents from a temple. Temples in the Near East had a strong economic function, especially with regard to the land. The contents of the Linear A tablets, also those from the Casa del Lebete, had primarily an economic purpose and there is in that respect no distinction between the texts found in the Villa and those found in the Villagio. Interpretation in the sphere of agriculture seems preferable, since the Alalaḫ texts provide apparently the best parallel in their grain distribution lists.

Here the substantive term ***ad(d)u(n)*** 'ration', 'assigned portion', is used in connection with emmer wheat (*triticum dicoccum*) and barley in particular. A. Draffkorn (later A. Kilmer), *HHA*, 153: wr. *a-du, a-du-un, a-ad-du, a-du-ú.* In grain distribution lists:

(1) Recipient or purpose undesignated: (vetches) 5 *pa a-na* KASKAL *it-ti* LUGAL 6 *a-na ku-na-te* 3 *a-na a-du-un* (D.J. Wiseman, The Alalakh Tablets, further mentioned as AT, London 1953, text 237 'a': 4, as contrasted to D.J. Wiseman, 'Supplementary copies of Alalakh tablets', Journal of Cuneiform Studies 8,15, text 237 'b'); (vetches) *a-na a-du-un* AT 239: 14; (barley and emmer) *a-na a-du* AT 242: 13; (vetches) *a-na a-ad-du* AT 253: 29; (vetches) *a-ad-du* AT 251: 31; 5 *pa* ZI.AŠ *a-na ku-un-na-te* 30 *a-na a-ad-du* AT 256: 5;

(2) Recipient or purpose designated: (barley) *a-ad-du a-na* NUMUN AT 251: 4; (barley) 24 *a-na ku-un-na-<te>* ŠÀ.GAL GUD.ḪI.A AT 238: 4; (barley) *a-na a-du* ŠÀ.GAL GUD.ḪI.A AT 239: 4; (barley) *a-na a-ad-du* ŠÀ.GAL GUD.ḪI.A AT 245: 3; 15 *pa* ZI.AŠ ŠÀ.GAL GUD.ḪI.A *a-na a-du-un* AT 255: 7; (vetches) 30 *a-du* LÚ APIN 8 *ku-un-na-te* LÚ É UŠ AT 246: 31; (vetches) 8 GÌR *a-du* LÚ APIN AT 247: 24; (vetches) 7 GÌR *ku-un-na-te* 20 GÌR *a-du* LÚ APIN AT 269: 67; (vetches) 6 ŠÀ.GAL GÌR *ku-un-na-te* 20 GÌR *a-du* LÚ APIN AT 269: 73.

The term also refers to rations of various commodities at Mâri and to oil rations at Nuzi, cf. A. Draffkorn, *HHA,* 153-154. At Alalaḫ it designates a common ration of grains for animals and men. A. Draffkorn (*HHA,* 152-153) includes it in her 'Word list A of Hurrian terms'. Her criteria for inclusion are: (1) that the terms are independently established as Hurrian in sources other than those from Alalaḫ; (2) that the terms are provided with demonstrably Hurrian suffixes. These suffixes may be found not only with terms originally Hurrian, but also with loan-words from other languages such as Akkadian and Sumerian. The varied orthographies of ***ad(d)u(n)*** seem to point to a loan-word, so the suggestion of a borrowing from Sumerian is considered, cf. *CAD I pt. 1 (1964)*,135, s.v. ***a-du***; cf. for a discussion on final ***-n***: A. Draffkorn, *HHA,* 120-126. Cf. also S. Davis, *The Decipherment of the Minoan Linear A and Pictographic Scripts,* Johannesburg 1967, 78. The parallels with the Alalaḫ grain distribution lists are too strong to leave any doubt. Here too, the connection of ***ad(d)u(n)*** with emmer wheat and barley prevails. We have seen that the texts from Mâri and Nuzi show that a connection with other commodities is found as well. In view of the connection of ***a-du*** in Linear A with the ideograms of GRANUM and HORDEUM at Khania and Hagia Triada (KH 23.1 and HT 99a.1: with HORDEUM; HT 92.1, HT 95b.1 and HT 133.1: with GRANUM; HT 86a.4: with GRANUM + B), an interpretation of 'ration' or 'assigned portion' is preferable. L.C. Meijer's assignment of the term to the category of 'persons' cannot be accepted.

Let us look at the structure of HT 88:

HT 88.1: *a-du* VIR PARMATUS 20 *re-za* (or to be corrected to *pu*$_2$*-za* ?)

HT 88.2: 6 FIC , *ki-ki-na* 7 (HT 88.3: vacat)

HT 88.4: *ki-ro* , *ku-pa*$_3$*-pa*$_3$ 1 *ka-96* 1

HT 88.5: *ku-pa*$_3$*-nu* 1 *pa-ja-re* 1 *sa-ma-*

HT 88.6: *ro* 1 *da-ta-re* 1 *ku-ro* 6 (HT 88.7: vacat)

We see that ***a-du*** is followed by VIR PARMATUS 'man armed with a small round shield (*parma*)' 20. Then follows ***re-za*** (?) (HT 88.1) (recurring in HT 13.2 ?), followed by 6 units or rather 6 'portions' (***a-du***) of figs indicated by the FIC ideogram + word divider.

Then follows ***ki-ki-na*** (HT 88.2) that may well fit into a long series of Hurrian personal names from Nuzi provided by P.M. Purves (*NPN*, 226) s.v. *kikk*, *kikk-*, *kikki*, *kikkiịa*, *kikkinni*, *kikkiu*. Especially comparison with ***kikkinni*** is interesting. P.M. Purves (*NPN*, 240) a formant ***-nna***: "Hurrian. Apparently a formative in *Ḫašinna*, *Kananna*, *ᶠŠalanna*, *Tatunna*, perhaps *Ḫamanna*". ***ᶠŠalanna*** {*šal=a=nna*} means 'She is a daughter'.

I. Wegner (*Einführung*, 55, s.v. ***-i=nni***: suffix forming adjectives into substantives designating professions) analyses ***p/wandarinni*** as {*fand=ar=i=nni*} 'Koch' ['cook'], {*fand=ar=i=n(n)i=na=ma*}, absolutive plural + particle ***-ma*** (*ibid.* 129, 134, 213-214). She lists (*ibidem*) similar formations such as: {*urb=ar=i=nni*} 'Schlachter' ['butcher'] from ***u(r)b/v-*** 'schlachten' ['to slaughter'] (*ibid.* 211); ***išḫ=ar=i=nni*** 'Bäcker' ['baker'], root ****išḫ-***, Ugarit; ***warin(n)i*** {*far=i=nni*} 'Brotbäcker' ['baker of bread'], root ***par-***, ***/far=/***, {*far=i=nni=na=ma*}, absolutive plural + particle ***-ma*** (*ibid.* 129, 213); ***tabrinni*** < {*tab=(i)=r(i)=i=nni*}, agens-orientated participial form + suffix ***-i=nni*** designating professions, 'Schmied, Metall-Gießer, Kupferschmied' ['(copper)smith'] from ***tab/v-*** '(Metall) gießen' ['to cast (metal)'] (*ibid.* 21, 55-56, 283), cf. ***tab=ašt=o=m***, 3rd person sing. (Old Hurrian), (*ibid.* 128, 216, 218), cf. ***ta/ibira/i*** 'der der gießt, Gießer, Kupfer-arbeiter' ['someone who casts (metal), copperworker'] (*ibid.* 21).

Incidentally, the Hurrian term ***išḫ=ar=i=nni*** 'baker' from ****išḫ=ar=i***, derived from the root ****išḫ-***, with root-extension ***-ar-***, is most interesting, if we compare it with Mycenaean Greek ***e-ka-ra = ἐσχάρā***. Linear B tablet PY Xa 102: ***di-wo-nu-so-jo*** is joined with PY Ea 107:] ***e-ka-ra*** GR 2 T 6, so that the new text offers the combination ***di-wo-nu-so-jo*** , ***e-ka-ra*** GR 2 T 6 = ***Διϝονύσοιο ἐσχάρā*** GR 2 T 6 = 'altar of Dionysos for burnt sacrifices, 2 talents and 6 T of grain'. A Linear B text from Khania: 1. ***di-wi-jo-de di-we***...2. ***di-wo-nu-so…***, ***Δίϝyονδε Διϝεῖ Διϝονύσῳ***, points to 'a sanctuary of Zeus (***Δίϝyον*** + directive suffix ***-δε***, cf. *di-u-jo*, PY Tn 316 v. 8) for Zeus (dative *Διϝεῖ*, cf. *di-we*, PY Tn 316 v. 9, *al.*) and Dionysos, showing that these deities shared a cult and sanctuary at Cretan Khania.

E. Laroche (*GLH*, 125) mentions s.v. ***išḫarini*** 'cuisinier'. RS quadr. 130 Vo 4: akk. *nuḫatimu* = h. *iš-ḫa-ri-ni*. Th. Richter (*BGH*, 102) s.v. ***išḫ-***: o.Ü. [without translation] (Giorgieri 2000a, 211; Wegner 223; *Einführung*, 256: ****išḫ-*** Verbalwurzel [verbal root]). ****išḫari*** 'kitchen' (Diakonoff/Starostin 1986, 39); ***išḫarinni*** [Ug.] 'cuisinier' corresponds with Akkadian *nuḫatimmu* (E. Laroche, *GLH*, 125); 'baker' corresponds with Sumerian [MU], Akkadian *nuḫatimmu*, Ugaritic *'āpiyūma* (*CAD* N/II [1980] 313; Huehnergard 1987a, 52, 108); ***išḫ=ar=i=nni*** 'cuoco' ['cook'] (Giorgieri 2000a, 211); ***išḫ=ar=i=nni*** 'Bäcker' (I. Wegner, *Einführung*, 55, 256).

According to P. Chantraine (*DELG*, 379-380) the exact meaning of Greek *ἐσχάρā*, Ionic *ἐσχάρη*, is 'foyer bas, brasier' ['low hearth, fireplace'], (*Il.*, *Od.*, Ar., etc.), employé notamment pour des foyers de sacrifice, distingués des *βῶμοι* plus élevés [particularly used for sacrificial fireplaces, distinguished from the higher *βῶμοι*]. With regard to the etymology he adds: Terme technique et dans une certaine mesure religieux des plus anciens. Apparemment dérivé en *-ρā* ; pas d'étymologie. Since there is no Greek or I.-E. etymologie, it is not farfetched, if I assume that (Mycenaean) Greek ***e-ka-ra = ἐσχάρā*** that could refer to a charcoal hearth/fireplace in the kitchen or e.g. in the throne-room of the Palace of Nestor at Pylos, where the king could kebab his meat with his guests, but first and foremost the sacrificial altar for burnt sacrifices to propitiate the gods.

I do not believe that ***išḫari*** means 'kitchen', but 'low hearth, fireplace' for domestic and sacrificial usage. It is also most likely that (Mycenaean) Greek ***e-ka-ra*** = ***ἐσχάρᾱ*** is derived from it. I also think that the name of the goddess ***Išḫara*** is derived from it. According to K.R. Veenhof (*Woordenboek der Oudheid*, Bussum 1979, 1508-1509) Babylonian ***Išḫara*** (Akkadian ***išḫara*** < older ***ešḫara***) attested since the Ur III-period, is of unknown provenance. Her qualifications seem to reflect her relation with the altar for burnt sacrifices, for she is the 'Lady of the verdict and the sacrificial altar'. She is also 'Mistress of the inhabited regions / residences' and has some militant features. She was also worshipped by the Hittites and at Ugarit, where her name was also spelled as ***Ušḫara*** and in the list of Hurrian divinities (RS. 24.295) as ***užḫrd***, with the Hurrian directive suffix ***-d*** in alphabetic cuneiform (= ***-da*** in syllabic cuneiform). V. Haas (*Hethitische Berggötter und hurritische Steindämonen, Riten, Kulte und Mythen*, Mainz 1982, 99-102) has dedicated long passages to the Mountain Goddess ***Išḫara***. A sanctuary of ***Išḫara*** was built on the mountain ***Išḫara*** (named after the goddess) in Kizzuwatna near Tarsus, the Hittite city of Tarša. According to V. Haas she is an old Syrian goddess, already in the 3rd millennium B.C. worshipped in North-Syrian Ebla. She came to Mesopotamia from North-Syria and was already venerated at Drehem south of Nippur at the time of the 3rd dynasty of Ur. With increasing influence of religious cults and rites from southeast Anatolia into Ḫattuša the significance of ***Išḫara*** grew in the corresponding documents of the Hittite capital. In the pantheon of Ḫattuša she is mentioned with *Allani* and the goddesses of Fate, ***Ḫudena Ḫudellurra*** = ***ḫdn-št ḫdlr-št*** at Ugarit (cf. E. Laroche, 'Notes sur le panthéon hourrite de Ras Shamra', *JAOS 88,2 (1968)*, 148-150). Her festivals were celebrated in spring and autumn. Here we find peculiar rites: For instance, the sculpture of the goddess was borne through *two fireplaces* for purification, a cathartic ritual that only appears in this festival. Is it accidental that *fireplaces* played such a notorious part in the festival of the goddess, who was herself 'Lady of the verdict and the sacrificial altar' and that ***ἐσχάρᾱ*** means 'low hearth, fireplace, altar for burnt sacrifices', and that the term is attested in Mycenaean Khania, built on top of the Minoan Palace of Khania ?

Whether ***Išḫara*** is originally a Syrian, Sumerian, Akkadian, Hurrian or 'substrate' goddess (cf. Th. Richter, *VHN*, 403-404), she belonged to the Hurrian pantheon. No doubt the Mycenaean Greeks inherited the lexeme *ἐσχάρᾱ* from Minoan-Hurrian in Crete.

Returning to ***ki-ki-na*** (HT 88.2) a suffix ***-e/i=nni*** also occurs in some nouns describing objects, e.g. ***ḫaš=e=nni*** 'ein wertvoller Stein' ['precious stone, gem'], ***kig=i=nni*** 'Dreifuß' ['tripod'], Qaṭna e.a., see also Th. Richter, *AoF 32 (2005)*, 41-42. Hurrian ***kig(e)*** means 'three', cf. I. Wegner, *Einführung*, 81, 206, 262: ***kig(e)*** 'drei'. As as result Linear A ***ki-ki-na* 7** (HT 88.2) seems *prima facie* to mean 'seven tripods', but (apart from the fact that 'seven tripods' may have required the plural form ****ki-ki-ni-na*** instead of ***ki-ki-na*** in Linear A for Hurrian ****kig=i=n(n)i=na***) another argument against that interpretation is that it would have been much easier for the scribe to use the TRIPOD ideogram (Linear A sign *182a*, *182b* or *183*) instead. It would not have been economic to use 3 syllabic signs instead of 1 ideogram, especially because the very small Linear A tablets required the most economic form of writing. Moreover, usage of the ideogram would have left no room for confusion, if the scribe had really meant 'tripods' as utensils.

Linear A ***ki-ki-na*** can also be used as a Hurrian personal name ****Kik(k)inna***, analysis {*kik(k)=i=nn(i)=a*}, since at Mari the Hurrian name ***Kikkinnu*** (wr. *ki-ik-ki-nu*) is attested, analysis {*kikkinn(i)=u*[N]}, lexicon *kikkinni* (→ *kig-/kikk-* 'three'), typology 3.1, translation 'Dreifuß' ['Tripod'], cf. Th. Richter, *VHN*, 156, s.v. ***Kikkinnu***. [N] indicates the Akkadianizing nominative in ***-u***. He also mentions a personal name *ki-ki-nu* at Terqa (Middle-Babylonian period). In fact {*kik(k)=i=nn(i)=a*} would be the *essive* form in ***-a*** of *kikkinni* 'Tripod', which would yield the meaning 'As a tripod', not a very nice name for a child. Semantically I consider this interpretation of the name therefore unlikely.

Th. Richter also mentions another possible interpretation of ***Kikkinnu***, with *optional allomorphic* ***ᵒ=nno/u*** instead of ***ᵒ=nna***, that makes an *imperative* construction possible: {*kikk=i=nnu*} instead of {*kikk=i=nna*}, translation 'Mache ihn/sie (***-nna/-nnu***) dreifach (oh *Numen*) !' ['Triplicate him/her (oh *numen*) !'], in other words 'Let him/her be born as the third child (oh *Numen*) !' Cf. Th. Richter, *VHN*, 156, s.v. ***kig-/kikk-***. The conclusion may well be that Linear A ***ki-ki-na*** reflects the actual regular Hurrian form {*kikk=i=nna*}, not the form with *optional allomorphic* ***ᵒ=nno/u***. In my view this interpretation seems semantically more likely than comparison of a child with a tripod.

Linear A ***ki-ki-ra-ja*** (HT 85b.1) from Hagia Triada is probably a Hurrian personal name followed by either a word divider or the sign for 1 unit. If it indicates 1 unit, the little vertical stroke is shorter than those following all other personal names on HT 85b. The name ***ki-ki-ra-ja*** can be analysed as ***kig=ill=a=ja*** or ***kig=ir=a=ja***, consisting of the verbal root ***kig-/kikk-*** + the Old Hurrian *inchoative* or *ingressive* root-extension ***-ill-*** or Hurrian root-extension ***-ir-*** (aspect not clear) (cf. I. Wegner, *Einführung*, 89) + the marker of intransitivity ***-a-*** + hypocoristic suffix ***-ya***, translation 'He/She (the brother/sister) is the third (child). The hypocoristic suffix ***-ya*** may, for instance, substitute ***šena*** 'brother' or ***ela*** 'sister'. Cf. Th. Richter, *VHN*, 624-625, sub 4.2: 'one-word' names with ***ᵒāja***.

Raison-Pope: ***re-za*** (HT 88.1): ***re-***: sur [[ ]]. However, if the dashes are not the result of palimpsest, but deliberately drawn by the scribe, one may read ***pu₂-za*** instead of ***re-za***. In that case we may be dealing with a Hurrian personal name such as ***Puza*** (wr. *Pu-(ú)-za*) at Nuzi (I.J. Gelb, *NPN*, 119; P.M. Purves, *NPN*, 248), ***Pušan*** (wr. *pu-ša-an*) at Tuttul, analysis {*po/už(i)=a*[E.]*=n(na)*}, typology 3.2.1, lexicon *puši* (→ *puš-* I), cf. ***Pušaja*** (at Mari), ***ᶠPuzakki*** (a woman at Šubat-Enlil), ***Puzzaja*** (a person at Šubat-Enlil), ***Puzi*** (7 persons at Mari), ***ᶠPuzi*** (15 women at Mari, 1 at Ašnakkum), ***Puzzi*** (at Mari and Qaṭṭarā), ***Puzija*** (3 persons at Mari), ***ᶠPuzija*** (2 women at Mari), etc., cf. Th. Richter, *VHN*, 240-242, 491-492, s.v. ***puš-*** I {*po/už-*} and ***puz-*** II/***puzz-*** {*po/uz-*}{*po/uzz-*}, respectively.

Nevertheless it is most likely that ***re-za*** 6 FIC (HT 88.1-2) is the right reading on HT 88, since the sequence occurs again as ***re-za*** 5 J (HT 13.2), which will be discussed later.

The ideogram that I describe as VIR PARMATUS is by most editors interpreted as a ligature VIR+***ka***. If the latter interpretation is correct, ***ka*** in this ligature could, for example, be an abbreviation of Linear A ***ka-pa*** = ***Ḫalba*** (see *sub voce*), the Hurrian equivalent to Semitic ***Ḫalab*** (Aleppo), if it occurs on tablets from Hagia Triada (HT 28b.4; HT 88.1; HT 97a.1; HT 100.1). Since VIR+***ka*** also occurs on 4 roundels from Khania (KH Wc 2029-2032), it could then also be an abbreviation of the toponym *Khania* that may well represent Hurrian ***Ḫania*** 'He/She (a deity) creates /created (the palace)'.

The name is also often used as a Hurrian personal name meaning 'She (the mother) gives birth to (the child)', cf. also the discussion on Linear A ***ka-ni-ja-mi*** (KT Zf 1).

Linear A sign ***29*** can be used in different ways: As a syllabic sign it represents ***ka***, as a solitary ideogram it represents ROTA 'wheel with 4 spokes', in ligature with the ideogram VIR, it may well be an integral part of the ideogram VIR PARMATUS, since it actually looks like a man keeping his round shield on his arm in front of his breast. Interpretation as VIR PARMATUS is actually corroborated by the combination of VIR PARMATUS (HT 100.1) with VIR HASTATUS or ARMATUS 'man armed with a *hasta* (spear)' (HT 100.2). It may also be significant that VIR PARMATUS 82 (HT 97[+]109a.1) is directly followed by AES 33 '33 units of bronze' [[ ]] (HT 97[+]109a.1).

I shall explain why it is evident that the phonetic value ***ka*** for Linear A sign ***29*** and Linear B sign ****77*** is according to the so-called acrophonic principle derived from the Hurrian word ***kargarni*** that means 'round shield'.

Th. Richter (*VHN*, 431, n. 394) provides the meaning 'Panzer, u.ä' ['armour, cuirass, a.o.'] for ***kargarni***. His description of ***kargarni*** [Boğ.], ***kirgirni*** [Mitt.], ***kagani*** [Nuzi] (*BGH*, 190) is much more extensive. He tells that according to M. Salvini (1979a, 308) ***karkarni*** is the Boğazköy-Hurrian and ***kirkirni*** the Mitanni-Hurrian form.

E. Laroche (*GLH*, 137) offers a neutral translation of ***karkarni*** 'une arme':
kar-kar-ni (nuli), KUB XXXII 19 I 18; mais *kir-kir-ni*^{meš} *(nuli*^{meš}*)*, Mit. III 113, 118.
kar-kar-e-ni/ir?[KUB XLVII 100, 4; comit. *kar-kar-ni-ra (nuli-ra)*, KBo XV 1 IV 24. Comparer our. *qarqarani* 'cuirasse'; König, *HGI*, 193; Melikišvili, *Die urartäische Sprache*, 85; Salvini, KUB XLVII, p. VIII. - E. Laroche (*GLH*, 188) qualifies Hurrian *nuli* as 'terme militaire désignant une arme ou une catégorie de soldats'; cf. *karkarni, ḫuradi, mariyani*: *nu-ú-ú-li*^{meš}, Mit. III 113, 118; *nu-ú-li*, KUB XXXII 19 I 17, 18; XXVII 43, 16; comit. *nu-u-li-ra*, KBo XV 1 IV 24, etc.

Most scholars assume a Hurrian origin of ***kargarni*** that corresponds with Urartian *qarqarani*, but F. Zeeb, *Die Palastwirtschaft in Altsyrien nach den spätaltbabylonischen Getreidelieferlisten aus Alalaḫ (Schicht VII)*, Alter Orient und Altes Testament 282, Münster 2001, 403-404, assumes derivation from Akkadian *kakkum* 'eine Waffe' ['an arm, weapon']. Th. Richter (*BGH*, 190) mentions about ***kargarni*** [I translate the German text]: 'a type of shield', probably 'a round shield' (Haas/Thiel 1978, 111f.$^{+}$ [164]); '(a suit) of armour, cuirass' corresponds with urartian *qarqarani* 'cuirasse' (Laroche, 1980a, 137; cf. also Haas 1982b, 604; Salvini, 1991b 176; 1991c, 345), 'a cuirass', i.e. *kar=gar=ni* (Wilhelm, 1987 b, 237[29]; see also 1991a, 44); 'armor (?)' (Campbell, 2007a, 258).

It is in my view conceivable that ***kargarni*** is ultimately derived from the Hurrian root ***kar-*** 'to conquer', in particular if it indeed contains a reduplication of the root. An argument against such a hypothesis is that it is true enough that ***kar-*** and ***kargarni*** are both found in the same semantic sphere of fighting in combat, but that the reconstructed meaning of ***kargarni*** points to the form of the defensive arm, a *round* shield.

The root of Hurrian ***kargarni*** is according to Haas/Thiel (*l.c.*) etymologically cognate with Semitic √KRKR, that may be preserved in (NINDA.)*kakkari*. This leads through *ka-ka*$_4$*-ni* (see *infra*) to *kargarni* .... and, in connection with arrow and bow, it can best be translated as 'round shield'.

In order to confirm the syllabic reading *kir-kir-ni* instead of KIR.KIR.NI they add (*l.c.*) that the vowel *-i-* does not pose a problem, because vowels tend to alternate in Hurrian in syllabic signs of the type consonant-vowel-consonant. They think (*l.c.*, 112[164]) that *ka-*ka_4*-ni-*^{o} in *ka-*ka_4*-ni-aš-we-na* [Nuzi], c.q. the form *kakani-* isolated from it, cannot be distinguished from *kakarni*. If it is connected with *nuli* 'an arm or category of soldiers' (cf. also Th. Richter, *BGH*, 281-282, s.v. *nuli*) as in *kir-kir-ni*^{meš} *(nuli*^{meš}*)* in the Tušratta letter (Mit. III 113, 118), it may well refer to the 'disks (round plates) of the armour'. They also argue that the primary meaning of *kakkaru* may be 'disk'. In research with regard to Akkadian these connections are not found, e.g. 'Kupferteil am Panzer' (*AHw* Lfg. 5 [1963], 421); 'a type of bronze or copper scale for armor' (Kendall 1975, 213); 'part of body armour' (CDA^2 [2000] 141). Usually Linear A research pays tribute to M. Ventris's decipherment of Linear B and to the results of cuneiform studies, Hurrian studies in particular. It rarely happens that Linear A can contribute to Hurrian studies. Linear A syllabic sign ***29*** = ***ka*** (= Linear B sign **77* = ***ka***) is designed as a circle with a cross inside. So it looks like a wheel with four spokes. In Linear A this sign is indeed also used as an ideogram indicating a wheel (ROTA), see the analysed structure of HT 11:

HT 11a.1-2.	*a-ru-ra-ta*[			3
2.	*ka-ro-na*			2 [[*a*]]
3.	[.]-*ri*,			
3.		*ku-ro*		10
3-4.	*a-su-ja* ,			
4-5.	*wo-no*			3
5.	ta_2			15
b.1.	]*de-*pa_3 ,	*sa-*ra_2 ,,		
2.	CAPSUS		ROTA	40
2.			ROTA	30
3.			ROTA	50
3-4.	*si-do-na*		ROTA	30
4-5.	*sa-qe-ri* ,		ROTA	30
5-6.		*ku-ro*		180

Both ***a-ru-ra-ta***[(HT 11a.1-2) and ***ka-ro-na*** (HT 11a.2) may well be Hurrian personal names. If complete, ***a-ru-ra-ta***[can be analysed as a sentence name {*ar=o/ul-atta*}, consisting of the verbal root ***ar-*** 'to give' + root-extension ***-u/ol-*** + ***atta(i)*** 'father'.

According to I. Wegner (*Einführung*, 88) the root-extension ***-u/ol-*** is *reflexive* and causing intransitivity. The exact meaning of the root-extension ***-ol-*** is not yet clear. For instance, Hurrian ***salḫ-*** is 'to hear', but ***salḫ=ol-*** also means 'to hear'; Hurrian ***ar-*** is 'to give', but ***ar=ol-*** also means 'to give', but also 'to bring away', so that the formant might express a spatial relation, cf. E. Neu, *StBoT 32*, 1996, 361: ***-ol-*** 'hin' ['away']. See for the Urartian verbal forms with the formant ***-ul-*** also M. Salvini, *ZA 81 (1991)*, 122 ff.

In my view the subject (or vocative) of this sentence name, ***atta(i)*** 'father', plays a double-role as the father of the child and as ***eni attanni*** 'God the Father' who can probably be identified with the Stormgod Tešub. In the latter role ***atta(i)*** takes the position of a theophorous element. This kind of name-giving combines the domestic and divine sphere in a splendid way. The name can be translated as '(God the) Father gives/gave or brings/brought (the child) away' or 'Give/Bring (the child) away, oh father/Father !'.

In the case of 'bring away' one may think of a so-called replacement-name (the newborn child replaces the child that passed away). Cf. also Linear A ***da-du-ma-ta*** {*dad=o=m-atta(i)*}, '(God the) Father, he loved the child and still loves it', combining the Old Hurrian past tense and the durative aspect, cf. I. Wegner, *Einführung*, 126.

The Linear A personal name ***ka-ro-na*** (HT 11a.2) can be analysed as {*kar=o=nna*}, consisting of the verbal root ***kar-*** + 'to conquer' + the thematic vowel ***-o-*** + the suffix marking the enclitic personal pronoun 3rd person singular ***-nna***, representing the object of action of the verb. The name can be translated as 'Conquer/Control him/her (oh *numen*)!'

Th. Richter (*VHN*, 431, s.v. ***kar-***) mentions that a verbal root ***kar-*** (without root-extension) possibly can be isolated from ***kari(j)e*** 'Vogelfänger' ['bird-catcher, fowler'] (see *BGH*, 190), that may be associated with Urartian ***kar=u-*** 'besiegen' ['to conquer'] (cf. G.A. Melikišvili, *Die urartäische Sprache*, Studia Pohl, Rome 1971, 83; V. Haas, *Rezension zu* Laroche 1980, *Bibliotheca Orientalis 39*, Leiden 1982, 604; I.M. Diakonoff, On some new trends in Urartian philology and some new Urartian texts, *Archäologische Mitteilungen aus Iran.* Neue Folge 22, Berlin 1989, 82[27]; M. Salvini, Die Felsinschrift Argištis I bei Ortakent, Kreis Hanak (Osttürkei), *Orientalia Nova Series 75*, Rome 2006, 75). I may also refer to M. Salvini - I. Wegner, *Einführung in die urartäische Sprache*, Wiesbaden 2014, 110, s.v. ***kar-*** 'besiegen, bezwingen' ['to conquer, subdue, control'].

Th. Richter thinks that this root offers a good meaning for the Hurrian personal name ***e-ew-ri-ga-ri-im*** {*evri-kar=i=m(: b)*} at Kaniš (cf. Garelli 1963, 156) 'The Lord conquered (the enemy)'. Therefore ***kari(j)e*** may originally mean '(Vogel-)Besieger' ['conqueror (of birds)']. Intransitive usage of the root ***kar-*** provides the meaning 'to prevail'. According to Th. Richter (*VHN*, 152, 431) the Hurrian personal name ***Karakka*** (wr. *ka-ra-ak-ka*) at Mari belongs to this verbal root, {*kar=a=kk=a*}, typology 1.2.3, lexicon *kar-*, cf. at Kaniš *kà-ra-ku-na* (see Donbaz, 2006, 275), as well as ***Karija*** (wr. *ga-ri-ia, ka-ri-ia*) at Mari, Šubat-Enlil, Assur, Nippur; (wr. *ka$_4$-ri-a, ka$_4$-ri-ia*) at Kurruḫanni; (wr. *ka$_4$-ri-ia*) at Nuzi, cf. I.J. Gelb, *NPN*, 80, s.v. ***Kariḭa*** (wr. *Qa-ri-ia*), {*kar=i=(j)a*}, 'He conquers (enemy)', typology 1.1.1.2.4. Hurrian ***Karkunni*** (wr. *Qa-ar-ku-un-ni, Ka-ar-ku-un-ni*) at Nuzi (cf. P.M. Purves, *NPN*, 223, s.v. ***kar***) can in my view be analysed as ***kar=kk=o/u=nni*** 'the one who conquers', 'the conqueror'. The meaning is based on the new insights pronounced by I. Wegner regarding the formant ***-kk-*** as nominal element (*nomen actoris* ?). Compare also Linear A ***ka-ru*** (HT 97[+]109a.1) and ***ka-ru[*** (HT 75.1) from Hagia Triada and Linear A ***ka-ku-ne-te*** (ZA 10b.6) from Kato Zakro.

Combination of the ideograms CAPSUS and ROTA (HT 11b.2) is so convincing that reading ***ka*** instead of ROTA is out of the question (cf. for the same combination of CAPSUS and ROTA tablet HT 140). Another consideration is that the contents of this tablet remind us of the Linear B tablets found e.g. in the 'Chariot Tablet Deposit', in the 'North Entrance Passage' and the 'Armoury' or 'Arsenal' of the Palace of Knossos, with the counting of chariots, waggon-bodies of chariots and wheels. Cf. for more extensive commentary on this subject the notes to the roundels from Khania KH Wc 2056 and 2057, and for the combination of 'chariot-body' (CAPSUS) and 'chariot-frame' KH Wc 2058, Wc 2059, Wc 2062 and Wc 2117b. Cf. also HT 8b.5 and HT 26b.4: 35 (CAPSUS) and *87* (chariot-frame); HT 27+48a.2: CAPSUS; HT 45+71a.2: CAPSUS , IUGUM; HT 45+71a.3 and b.3: IUGUM; HT 9b.2: ROTA and IUGUM.

Especially the various combinations of different parts of the chariot (CAPSUS, 'chariot-frame', ROTA, IUGUM) in the Hagia Triada and Khania texts corroborate the evidence that we are indeed dealing with the component parts of chariots. M. Ventris and J. Chadwick (*Documents*, 361) remind us that "Homer makes it clear that it was normal practice to remove the wheels when not in use (*Il.* V, 722), and to place the chariots on stands and cover them with cloths (VIII, 441)." The evidence from Hagia Triada and Khania of ideograms of waggon-bodies with poles, attached or not attached to their chariot-frames, and of chariot wheels, accounts for the existence of a charioteers' aristocracy at the top of Minoan society comparable with the Mitannian, Hittite, Syrian, Babylonian, Egyptian (since the Hyksos occupation) and Mycenaean societies.

The picture is completed with the third usage of Linear A sign ***29***, the combination of the ideogram VIR+***29***, which is by most editors interpreted as VIR+***ka***, but which should in my view be interpreted as VIR 'man' + PARMA 'round shield' or as VIR PARMATUS 'man armed with a round shield', especially because the alleged 'ligature' shows in fact a man holding a round shield to his shoulder. It is evident that the ideograms ROTA and PARMA and syllabic sign ***ka*** are exactly the same. My interpretation of VIR + PARMA, c.q. VIR PARMATUS is corroborated by the first lines of HT 97[+]109a:

HT 97[+]109a.1. *ka-ru* , *pi+pi* , VIR PARMATUS 82 AES
2. 33 [[ ]]
3. *ka-nu-ti* 25 *pa-i-to* 6

Linear A ***ka-ru*** (HT 97[+]109a.1) and (Akkadianized) ***ka-ru***[(HT 75.1) take exactly the same position as first entries on these tablets from Hagia Triada. So ***ka-ru***[(HT 75.1) might well be complete. Hurrian ***kari*** (Boğazköy) and ***karu*** (Alalaḫ IV and Ugarit) 'metal object, probably a weapon, spear (?)' may well be identified with Linear A ***ka-ru*** (HT 97a.1) followed by ***pi+pi*** **,** VIR PARMATUS 82 and AES 'bronze' 33, cf. Th. Richter (*BGH*, 188), s.v. ***kari*** [Boğ.], ***karu*** [Al. IV; Ug.]), 'ein Speer(?)' (cf. J. Sanmartin, '*arbḫ* "vierjährig" (KTU 1.92: 10)', *Ugarit Forschungen 9 (1977)*, 374-375, especially 374[6] [*kar(u)*]). Interpretation of Linear A ***ka-ru*** (HT 97[+]109a.1) as a Hurrian term for 'spear' is attractive because of the following ideogram VIR PARMATUS 'man armed with small round shield' with the high number '82', and the ideogram AES 'bronze' '33'. Occurrence of the ideogram AES 'bronze' and the sequence ***ka-ru*** (HT 97[+]109a.1) 'spear' in the same line as VIR PARMATUS can hardly be accidental.

If this interpretation is correct, could the following Linear A sequence ***ka-nu-ti*** (HT 97a.3), again followed by a high number '25', be related to Hurrian/Hurrianized ****qanu*** 'arrow, shaft', probably derived from Akkadian ***qanû***, cf. Th. Richter, *BGH*, 185, s.v. ***qanuḫḫe*** [Al VII] 'der zum Rohr/Pfeil gehörige' ['the one belonging to the arrow'], d.i. akk. ***qanû*** + ***-ḫḫe***, also Sumerogram LÚ.GI and LÚ.GIŠ.BAN, also 'Bogenmacher' ['bowmaker'] (Zeeb 2001: 438), respectively 'Pfeilschnitzer' ['arrowcutter'] (o.c. 633). The form ***qanuḫḫe*** at Alalaḫ VII contains the Hurrian adjectival suffix ***-ḫḫe***. However, ****qanu*** 'arrow, shaft' only explains the first syllables of Linear A ***ka-nu-ti***. The form ***ka-nu-ti*** can better be explained as a personal name (or possibly a toponym, cf. following ***pa-i-to***) because of the ending ***-ti*** that can be interpreted as the *optional allomorphic* suffix ***-tti*** that can replace ***-tta***. It is equally possible that ***ka-nu-ti*** 25 and following ***pa-i-to*** 6 are both personal names, since they are part of a list of personal names on HT 97[+]109a.

We must not forget that Homer mentions not only the 'town' ***Φαιστός*** in Crete (*Iliad* B 648, *Odyssey* γ 296), but also an ally of the Trojans, called ***Φαῖστος***, son of Bōros from Tarnè, killed by Idomeneus (*Iliad* E 43 ff.). Toponym and anthroponym have different accents. Both names may be derived from Hurrian *ba-'áš-tum* 'he has built' (cf. *Tiš-atal*).

Linear A ***ka-nu-ti*** (HT 97[+]109a.3) can be interpreted as Hurrian ***Ḫanutti***, analysis {*ḫan=o/u=tti*}, consisting of the verbal root ***ḫan-*** 'to give birth to / to create' + the Old Hurrian suffix indicating the *perfect indicative* ***-u-*** + the *optional allomorphic* enclitic personal pronoun 1st person singular ***-tti***, cf. Th. Richter (*VHN*, 596, sub 1.3.1.1.2.2), who mentions that this suffix can replace the enclitic personal pronoun 1st person singular ***-tta*** (position 9 in the chain of verbal suffixes), cf. I. Wegner, *Einführung*, 93 (Table 4), 126. Following I. Wegner I translate 'He/She (a *numen*) gave birth to me / created me'. Following Th. Richter I translate Linear A ***ka-nu-ti*** {*ḫan=o/u=tti*} as an *imperative* form 'Give birth to me / Create me (oh *numen*) !'. Since a sibilant preceding a dental and other occlusives is not expressed in consonant clusters in Linear A and B, ***ka-nu-ti*** can *prima facie* also be interpreted as Hurrian ***Ḫanušti***, analysis †{*ḫan=o/uš=tti*} consisting of the verbal root ***ḫan-*** 'to give birth to / to create' + the suffix indicating past or perfect tense in ***-oš-*** (position 2) in 'Mitanni' Hurrian + the enclitic personal pronoun 1st person singular ***-tta*** or variant ***-tti*** (position 9), cf. I. Wegner, *Einführung*, 93, Table 4), translation 'He/She (a *numen*) gave birth to me / created me' with the allomorphic suffix ***-tti*** instead of ***-tta***, cf. Th. Richter, *VHN*, 329, 596. Objection to this interpretation is that one would expect the form {*ḫan=o/uš=a=tti*}, with the suffix ***-a-*** indicating the subject of action 3rd person singular. Semantically it does not matter, whether the name ***ka-nu-ti*** is an anthroponym or a toponym. Apparently settlements (palaces, villas, cities or vilages) were in a sense regarded as living organisms that could be created like people by divine intervention. For instance, the Hurrian personal name ***Ḫanija*** is attested at Ašnakkum, Mari, Šušarrā, where it is the name of men and is translated by Th. Richter (*VHN*, 121-122, 407-408) as 'Sie (Frau) gebar (Jungen)' ['She (woman) gave birth (to the boy)']. The name ***Ḫanija*** also occurs at Emar, Nippur, and Nuzi (*NPN*, 53). But it is conceivable that the Cretan toponym Khaniá (***Χανιά***) may etymologically be derived from Hurrian {*ḫan=i=a*}, consisting of the verbal root ***ḫan-*** + the indicator of transitivity ***-i-*** that only appears in the present 2nd and 3rd person singular (position 5) + the indicator of the subject of action 3rd person singular ***-a-*** (position 7), 'She gives birth', cf. I. Wegner, *Einführung*, 93 (Table 4). The name Khania (Hurrian ***Ḫania***) might actually date from the time of the foundation of the Minoan palace, partially excavated underneath the modern city. The meaning would then be 'He/she (a God) (pro)creates, gives birth to (the palace)'.

At Nuzi the personal name ***Ḫaniu*** (wr. *ḫa-ni-ú/ù*) occurs as well, analysis {*ḫan=i=o*}, consisting of the verbal root ***ḫan-*** + the marker of transitivity ***-i-*** + the marker of the subject of action 2nd person singular ***-u/o-*** (position 7) 'You give birth (to boy)', cf. Th Richter, 585. At Nuzi 23 persons are called ***Ḫaniu*** (wr. *ḫa-ni-ú/ù*), cf. Gelb, *NPN*, 54).

Another interesting personal name is ***ᶠḪanijatta*** (wr. *ḫa-ni-ia-at-ta*) from Ḫattuša, analysis {*ḫan=i=a=tta*}, 'She bears me, gives birth to me', showing a present transitive formation, in which the enclitic suffix of the personal pronoun ***-tta*** is the object, cf. Th. Richter, *VHN*, 586. Here the personal pronoun ***-tta*** indicates the bearer of the name; the subject of ***ḫan=i=a-*** is the mother.

It is significant that Linear A sign ***29*** derives - in accordance with the so-called acrophonic principle - its phonetic value ***ka*** from ***kargarni***, the Hurrian word for 'round shield' as the Linear A ideogram for VIR + PARMA shows. It also shows that the Hurrian term ***kargarni*** does not mean 'cuirass', but indeed 'round shield' or perhaps basically 'round disk', which makes the meaning of the other Linear A ideogram 'wheel' also feasible. In Hurrian texts, where ***kargarni*** or the variants *kirgirni* or *kagani* seem (according to some authors) to refer to 'a part of a cuirass', it must refer to the 'round plates' or 'disks' as component parts, from which the cuirass is made.

All sequences in HT 88, except ***a-du*** (HT 88.1), ***ki-ro*** (HT 88.4) and ***ku-ro*** (HT 88.6), are probably personal names. ***Re-za*** (or ***pu₂-za*** ?) and ***Ki-ki-na*** are probably important persons, since they receive or contribute 6 and 7 portions of figs, respectively. In line 4 ***ki-ro*** follows (formerly explained as a transactional term meaning 'deficit'), that can now be explained as a Hurrian *imperative* {*kir=o*} 'he must redeem his debt', followed by a word divider, after which 6 personal names are mentioned, each with 1 portion, followed by ***ku-ro*** 'again (in total)' 6. So ***ku-ro*** probably refers to the total of 6 portions mentioned after ***ki-ro***. The 6 persons are: ***ku-pa₃-pa₃*** 1 (HT 88.4), ***ka-96*** 1 (HT 88.4), ***ku-pa₃-nu*** 1 (HT 88.5), ***pa-ja-re*** 1 (HT 88.5), ***sa-ma-|ro*** 1 (HT 88.5-6) and ***da-ta-re*** 1 (HT 88.6).

If we add this deficit to the 6 portions figs of ***re-za*** (or ***pu₂-za*** ?) and the 7 portions of ***ki-ki-na***, the total would be 19, which is one short of the number 20 mentioned after VIR PARMATUS. The conclusion might be that one unit is illegible or the scribe could not count very well or may have been drinking too much wine, since the FIC ideogram is placed on a strange spot in the text after the units instead of before them, as if he realized too late that he should have written the FIC ideogram directly after the first entry ***a-du***.

Of the personal names on HT 88 only ***sa-ma-|ro*** (HT 88.5-6) has not yet been analysed. One is tempted to compare it with Linear A ***sa-ma*** (HT 6b.5, HT 10a.1, HT 52a.1, ZA 10b.3-4), Linear B ***sa-ma-ra*** and ***sa-ma-ri-jo***, Samos and the Gorges of Samaria (Crete).

Th. Richter (*BGH*, 348; *VHN*, 497-498) distinguishes at present two verbal roots: ***šam-*** I [Mari; Tuttul] (without translation). The form ***ša-ma-ḫa-aš-tu*** {*šam=aḫ=ašt=u*} with two root-extensions, occurs in the Old Babylonian incantations from Mari and Tuttul (Krebernik, 2001, 158); ***zam(m)-*** II, *zamm=al-* [Boğ.] and *zamm=al=ašt-* [Boğ.] 'abreißen' 'arracher, détacher' 'to tear off, break off'. The meaning is known because of correspondence with Hittite ***arḫa šakkurija-*** in the bilingual ***Kirenze*** (E. Neu, 1988a, 28/30; 1994, 131; 1996a, 158). Th. Richter is not yet sure, whether ***šam-*** I and ***zam(m)-*** II are basically the same roots. If they are, ***sa-ma-|ro*** (HT 88.5-6), {*zamm=al=o/u*} or {*zamm=ar=o/u*}, with the root-extensions ***-al-*** or ***-ar-*** (cf. I. Wegner, *Einführung*, 87-88), can be translated as 'You must tear off, break off (the umbilical cord) !'. If the analysis is {*zamm=al=o/u=m*} or {*zamm=ar=o/um*}: 'He/She tore off (the umbilical cord) !'.

In my *Corpus of transliterated Linear A texts* I have followed *GORILA*'s numbers and choice of *a*- and *b*-sides with regard to all texts from Zakros. All main editors have attributed different numbers to most tablets from Kato Zakros including ZA 10: ZA 10a (*GORILA 3*, 168-169) = ZA 9b (J. Raison - M. Pope, *Corpus transnuméré du linéaire A*, BCILL 74, 1994, 305-306) = Z 6b (N. Platon and W.C. Brice, *Inscribed tablets and pithos of Linear A system from Zakro*, Athens 1975, 60-61, 122-123).

ZA 10 (HM 1621, 1963) from the Palace of Kato Zakro, room XXVIII, Ceremonial Hall, found on the ground of the fourth rectangle, known as 'Tablet of the double axes', since many sequences begin with sign ***a***, which looks like a double axe. Late Minoan Ib.

ZA 10.a.1. *ta-na-te* 2 *pa* 1 *a-ku-*
2. *mi-na* 1 *a-ta-na-te* 1
3. *a-mi-da-u* 1 *a-du-*
4. *ku-mi-na* 1 *da-i-pi-*
5. *ta* 1 *du-re-za-se* 2
6. vacat

b.1. VINb ? (or: *wa* ?) *pa+i* ↕ 2 *du-re-za-se*
2. VINb 5 *u-120b* 6 *ma-za*
3. 5 *ma-ki-de-te* 5 *sa-*
4. *ma* 5 *a-de* 4 *a-mi-*
5. *ta* 3 *ra*$_2$*-ro-re* 2 *pa-ja-re*
6. 1 *ka-ku-ne-te* J *ta*
7. 2 *du* 1[

Observing the combination of Linear A ***a-du-|ku-mi-na*** 1 (ZA 10a.3-4) in isolation (without taking the context of the tablet into account), one may *prima facie* conclude that one is dealing with registration of 1 'portion' (***a-du***) of 'cumin' (***ku-mi-na***). Although *a-du* and ***ku-mi-na*** may seem separated, since ***a-du*** is written at the end of line 3 and ***ku-mi-na*** at the beginning of line 4, there is no word divider between ***a-du*** and ***ku-mi-na***, so that the two may be one sequence. Since Linear B ***ku-mi-no κύμῑνον*** (MY Ge 602,3 *et alibi*) seems to match with Linear A ***-ku-mi-na*** in ***a-du-|ku-mi-na*** (ZA 10a.3-4), it was generally assumed that Linear A ***-ku-mi-na*** is to be interpreted as 'cumin'. A connection between a term meaning 'portion' and the commodity ***ku-mi-na*** is indeed more plausible than that between ***ku-mi-na*** and a theonym *Haddu*. Observing ***a-ku-|mi-na*** (ZA 10a.1-2) on the same side of the tablet as ***a-du-|ku-mi-na*** (ZA 10a.3-4), one may (again at first sight) think of a scribal error for ***a-<du->ku-mi-na*** or an abbreviated form for which the features of shorthand writing characteristic of Linear A might account. One might even add that a scribal error would be conceivable, since the syllables ***-du-*** and ***-ku-*** contain the same vowel ***u***, so that the scribe might have thought that he had already written ***-du-***, while he was already writing ***-ku-***. If one thinks of a word division at the end of line 1, one must conclude that the division is not between the alleged ***a-<du->*** and ***ku-mi-na*** as in lines 3-4, but between ***a-ku***| and ***mina***.

However attractive comparison between Linear B ***ku-mi-no*** *κύμῑνον* and Linear A ***a-ku-|mi-na*** (ZA 10a.1-2) and ***a-du-|ku-mi-na*** (ZA 10a.3-4) may seem, the context clearly proves that both sequences belong to a list of personal names as ***a-ta-na-te***, ***a-mi-da-u***, ***da-i-pi-ta*** and ***du-re-za-se***, all followed by the same small numbers. The alternative that all these sequences are commodities is very unlikely. If we acknowledge that ***a-ku-|mi-na*** and ***a-du-|ku-mi-na*** are personal names, the advantage is that we do not have to assume that ***a-ku-|mi-na*** is a scribal error for ***a-du-|ku-mi-na***, since they are different personal names and repetition of the same name within the same list would even be unlikely.

If the failing word divider between ***a-du***| and ***ku-mi-na*** is taken seriously, ***a-du-|ku-mi-na*** 1 (ZA 10a.3-4) can be interpreted as Hurrian ***Aštuḫḫu-mina***, phonologically /***aždu****ḫḫ****u-mina***/, that can be translated as 'The twin (twin sister) is female'.

Starting from ****Aštuḫḫi-mina*** a process of progressive assimilation of ***-ḫḫi*** > ***-ḫḫu*** is conceivable with ***Aštuḫḫu-mina*** as a result. A hypocoristic form of such a sentence name is attested at Nuzi as ***ᶠAštuḫḫaia̯*** (wr. *ᶠAš-du-uḫ-ḫa-a-a*), with the hypocoristic suffix ***-ya***, SMN 352, cf. I.J. Gelb, *NPN*, 37; AAN I 36. The personal name ***ᶠAštuḫḫe*** (wr. *ᶠAš-tu-ḫe*) is attested at Mari (M.12608 I 6 (see also Durand 1997b: 602[45]) and (wr. *ᶠAš-du-uḫ-ḫé*) at Nuzi (AAN I 36). Cf. also *ᶠAš-tu-ḫa* at Old Babylonian Sippar (TCL 1, 109: 14) and *ᶠAš-te-ḫé* at Ugarit (cf. F. Gröndahl, *PNTU*, 323), cf. Th. Richter, *VHN*, 80.

It is probably not accidental that the scribe mentioned ***a-du-|ku-mi-na*** (ZA 10a.3-4) and ***a-de*** (ZA 10b.4), Minoan-Hurrian ***ašte***, phonologically ***/ažde/***, 'woman', on the same tablet. In the list of personal names on ZA 10a and b the sequence ***a-de*** is probably not the lexeme ***ašte*** *{ažd=e}*, but the frequently attested personal name ***ᶠAšte***. He must have been aware of the etymological relation between ***ašte*** 'woman' and ***aštuḫḫu-***, ***/ašduḫḫu/*** 'female', that can both be used as Hurrian personal names. ***ᶠAštu*** (wr. *ᶠAš-du*) occurs as 'one-word' personal name at Nuzi (cf. P.M. Purves, *NPN*, 206, s.v. *ašt*) and at Boğazköy as ***ᶠAsdu*** (nom. *ᶠAš-du-uš,* KBo X 10 III 37, cf. E. Laroche, *NH*, 46, nº 182). ***ᶠAšte***, ***ᶠAšten*** and ***ᶠAštun*** occur at Mari and ***ᶠAštu*** at Mari and Tuttul, cf. Th. Richter, *VHN*, 381-385, 391, s.v. ***azze***, ***azzu***, ***ašte***, ***aštu***, ***atte***, ***atti***, ***attu***.

I.J. Gelb (*NPN*, 37) mentions many feminine names containing the root ***ašt-*** 'woman': ***ᶠAštuaka*** (wr. *ᶠAš-du-a-ka*), ***ᶠAštu-anti*** (wr. *ᶠAš-du-a-an-ti*), ***ᶠAštua-šar*** (wr. *ᶠAš-du-a-šar*), ***ᶠAštuia̯*** (wr. *ᶠAš-du-ia*, variant *ᶠAš-du-a-a*), ***ᶠAštun-naia̯*** (wr. *ᶠAš-du-un-na-a-a*), ***ᶠAšta...*** (wr. *ᶠAš-t*[*a....*]), ***ᶠAšta-ḫuta*** (wr. *ᶠAš-ta-ḫu-ta*), ***ᶠAštaia̯*** (wr. *ᶠAš-ta-a-a, ᶠAš-*[*ta*]*-a*), ***ᶠAšta-kanza*** (wr. *ᶠAš-ta-qa-an-za*), ***ᶠAšta-kina*** (wr. *ᶠAš-ta-ki-i-na-a, ᶠAš-ta-ki-na-a, ᶠAš-ta-ki-na*), ***ᶠAšta-meri*** (wr. *ᶠAš-ta-me-ri, ᶠAš-ta-mi-ri*), ***ᶠAšteia̯*** (wr. *ᶠAš-te-e-a*), ***ᶠAšten*** (wr. *ᶠAš-te-en, ᶠAš-te*).

J.M. Sasson (Ḫurrians and Ḫurrian names in the Mari texts, *UF VI (1974)*, 358-359) offers only a few examples of feminine personal names with the root ***ašt***: again the simple 'one-word' name ***Aštu*** (wr. *ᶠAš-tu*) XIII:1:ii:43; and ***Ašta-kuzi*** (wr. *ᶠAš-ta-ku-zi*) XIII:1:v:59; ***Aštua-unna*** (wr. *ᶠAš-tu-a-un-na*) XIII:1:viii:5.

A. Draffkorn (*HHA*, 70) mentions: s.v. ***ašte-*** 'woman, wife': a Hurrian personal name ***Aš-te-mu-šu-ni*** AT 425:14; and hypocoristic ***Ašta-ya*** (wr. *Aš-ta-ya*) AT 148:54 and 194:19, found in Level IV. F. Gröndahl (*Die Personennamen der Texte aus Ugarit (Studia Pohl 1)*, Rome 1967, 221): s.v. ***ašt-*** and (alphabetic cuneiform) ***at̠t***, ***it̠t*** hurrisch 'Frau': "*bn at̠tl*, *bn at̠tyy*, *it̠tl*, ***ašte-ḫe*** (wr. *ᶠAš-te-ḫé*), vgl. ***aštuḫḫe*** 'weiblich' und ***ᶠAštuḫḫaia̯*** [*NPN* 206]; ***ašteḫeiaya*** (wr. *bin-aš-te-ḫé-ia-ya*). In Nuzi sind ***ašt*** immer, ***-menni*** bis auf eine Ausnahme Element in femininen Namen, wogegen ***ašt-*** in Ugarit und ***-menni*** in Ugarit und Alalaḫ auch in männlichen Namen belegt sind; vgl. ***menni***.

E. Laroche, *GLH*, 62-63, s.v. ***ašte*** 'femme' and ***aštuḫḫi*** 'féminin'. The element ***a-du-ku-*** can be explained from Hurrian ***ašduḫḫ(e/i)=u*** 'female', since ***-s-*** before dental is not expressed in Linear A and B consonant clusters (cf. Linear A and B ***pa-i-to***).

We may conclude that the voiceless velar fricative ***-ḫḫ-*** in the cuneiform syllabary (and ***-ḫ-*** in the alphabetic cuneiform of Ugarit) was rendered into ***-k-*** in Linear A and B as is likely, because in Mycenaean Linear B ***a-ka-wi-ja-de*** (KN C 914), accusative of ***Ἀχαιϝίᾱ*** + the directive suffix ***-δε***, 'region of the Achaeans', the ***k-*** sign is rendered into ***-ḫḫ-*** in ***Aḫḫiyawa*** in the Hittite cuneiform texts. ***Ἀχαιϝίᾱ*** is derived from the ethnic ***Ἀχαιϝός***, represented by Linear B ***a-ka-wo*** (KN X 738), ethnic used as a personal name.

Ἀχαιός is later attested as a personal name, cf. F. Bechtel, *Die historischen Personennamen des Griechischen*, 537. C.J. Ruijgh (*EGM*, § 154, n. 420) has explained that it appears more likely that *Ἀχαιϝία* in the Knossos Linear B text reflects a Cretan town than the entire land of the Achaeans, because *Ἀχαία* (< * *Ἀχαιῖα*, cf. Att. *Ἀχαῖα*) is attested as a name of a town in Crete (*Scholion* to Apollonius Rhodius 4, 175).

The personal name ***a-du-|ku-mi-na*** (ZA 10a.3-4) from Kato Zakro may well contain the same element ***-mina*** as can be observed in ***a-ku-mi-na*** (ZA 10a.1-2). Occurrence of ***a-ku-mi-na*** and ***a-du-|ku-mi-na*** so close together on the same side of the tablet appears very significant, because the two persons in question may be twin-sisters. E. Laroche (*GLH*, 170) did not yet offer a translation of ***me-e-na*** (Mit. IV 61, 63, 66), but he already compared it with ***mi-na*** (Mari 6, 19). In fact we read ***me-e-na-a-an*** in the Tušratta-letter IV 61; ***me-e-na-ma-a-an*** 'she is a twin', with the verbal element ***mān(n)*** 'to be', in IV 63; and ***me-e-na-ak-ki*** in IV 66. At first sight one may observe in the latter form ***me-e-na-ak-ki*** and in Linear A ***a-ku-mi-na*** the same onomastic elements, though in reverse order: {*mena-akki*} and {*akku-me/ina*}, but due to orthographic conventions of cuneiform the form ***me-e-na-ak-ki*** may well be read as {*mena=kki*}, with a nominal suffix ***-kki***.

E. Laroche (*GLH*, 170) mentioned that ***-menni*** is the second onomastic element in feminine personal names at Nuzi (*NPN*, 234), but at Alalaḫ and Ugarit also in masculine names (cf. F. Gröndahl, *PNTU*, 240). E. Laroche, *NH*, 163, N° 1154: ***ᶠŠintalimeni***, femme de *Kissi*: abs. *ᶠŠi-in-ta-li-me-ni*, XXXIII 121 II 5; *ᶠŠi-in-ta-mi-in-ni*, XXXVI 61, 2; cf. J. Friedrich, *ZA 49*, 253. - Composé hourrite [Hurrian compound]. (*Kissi* is a personage in a Hurro-Hittite tale; Hurrian ᵐ*Ke-eš-še*, cf. J. Friedrich, *ZA 49*, 234ff.).

If ***a-ku-mi-na*** contains the nominal root ***akki-/akku-*** 'the one or the other of two', ***a-du-ku-mi-na*** may, for instance, be the first-born and ***a-ku-mi-na*** the second-born of twin sisters, mentioned on the tablet. Th. Richter (*VHN*, 368) mentions s.v. ***akki***, that several archives contain (next to certainly or presumably verbal formations with ***akk-***) personal names with ***akk°*** that cannot be interpreted verbally: ***akki*** 'der eine (von beiden)' ['the one (of two)']. He mentions (*VHN*, 48, 368) ***ᶠAkkuwe*** (wr. *ᶠAk-ku-WA*) at Mari, analysis {*akki=ve*}, typology 3.2.2.1, translation 'Das (Mädchen) der/des Einen' ['The one (The girl) of either of the two']; and (*VHN*, 48-49, 368) ***ᶠAkkuzzi*** (wr. *ᶠAk-ku-zi*) at Mari, typology 3.1, 'Der/Dem Einen angemessen' ['The one (The girl) belonging to the one'].

P.M. Purves, *NPN*, 199, wrote about the root ***akk-***: "Hurrian. Cf. *ag-gu-uš a-gu-ú-a*, Tuš. I 81, *ag-gu-uš-ša-a-an a-gu-ú-e*, Tuš. IV 123, and *ag-gu-tan*, Tuš. II 61, tr. 'der eine.... der andere' by Messerschmidt, *Mitanni-Studien*, 37f. and Bork, *Mitannisprache*, 124. However, *a-gu-ú-a* and *a-gu-ú-e* may be forms of verbal root *ak*,..." At any rate the suffixes show that the root is (pro)nominal.

E.A. Speiser, *IH*, 77, § 110: "A pair of correlates paralleling *and^{i}* : *ann^{i}* is *ag^{u}* : *ak(k)^{u}*; cf. *a-gu-ú-a* Mit. I 81 (dat.) and *a-gu-ú-e* Mit. IV 123 (gen.) 'the other of two'; *ag-gu-uš ibid.* I 81 and *ag-gu-uš-ša-a-an ibid.* IV 123 (ag.), *ag-gu-dan ibid.* II 61 (*tan*-form) 'the one of two'. Except for the last-cited instance, these pronouns are employed in juxtaposition; and *ag-gu-dan* is used in a passage where certain objects (tablets) are enumerated, so that here too 'the other of two quantities' is a possible interpretation. For a different term for 'other' cf. [114]." In Speiser's time the term 'agentive' was used, whereas one now preferably uses the term 'ergative', but the term 'agentive' is still used.

E. Laroche, *GLH*, 41, s.v. *a(k)ku* 'autre':
"Erg. *ag-gu-uš* = * *aku-š*, Tuš. I 81, IV 123.
Gén. *a-gu-ú-e* = * *agu-we* Tuš. IV 123.
Dat. *a-gu-ú-a* = * *agu-wa* Tuš. I 81.
Abl. *ag-gu-tan* = * *aku-dan*, Tuš. II 61. Cf. Speiser, *IH*, 26, 77, etc.; Bush, *GHL*, 107. La variante orthographique est inexpliquée."

I. Wegner (*Einführung*, 84, 246) mentions the absolutive pronouns ***akki … agi*** and ***akku … agu*** 'der eine … der andere' ['the one … the other'], e.g. *ak-ki a-ku-ta* (ChS I/1 Nr 52 Rs. 15′) 'der eine … zum anderen' ['the one … to/for the other'], cf. Th. Richter, *BGH*, 8-9, s.v. ***akki*** [*passim*].

Several scholars have recently attributed specific meanings with regard to kinship / congeniality to Hurrian ***mena***, ***mina*** and ***-menni*** that I apply to Linear A ***-mi-na***. G. Wilhelm (Zu den hurritischen Namen der Kültepe-Tafel kt k/k 4, *SCCNH 8 (1996)*, 336); G. Wilhelm (Name, Namengebung. D. Bei den Hurritern, in: *Reallexikon der Assyriologie und Vorderasiatischen Archäologie 9/1-2 (1998)*, 125): 'eine weibliche Verwandtschafts-bezeichnung' ['a meaning with respect to female kinship']; M. Giorgieri (Zu den hurritischen Personennamen in den Amarna-Briefen, *SMEA 41 (1999)*, 79[73]); M. Giorgieri (Schizzo grammaticale della lingua hurrica, *Parola del Passato 55 (2000)*, 199-202); M. Giorgieri (L'onomastica hurritica, *Parola del Passato 55 (2000)*, 284, 289[45]): 'sorella gemella ?' [twin-sister], also for the onomastic element ***-menni***, {*men=ni*}. I. Wegner (*Einführung in die hurritische Sprache*, 2000, 233): 'Zwilling ?' [twin]. Th. Richter, Rezension zu J.-M. Durand (Le culte d'Addu d'Alep et l'affaire d'Alahtum, *Florilegium Marianum 7*, Paris 2002), *Archiv für Orientforschung 51 (2005/06)*, 281; Th. Richter, Ein Ḫurriter wird geboren, … und benannt, in: J. Becker, R. Hempelmann, E. Rehm (eds.), *Kulturlandschaft Syrien - Zentrum und Peripherie* (Festschrift für J.-W. Meyer), *AOAT 371*, Münster 2010, 514: 'Geschwister' [sister].

I. Wegner, *Einführung*, 2007², 52, 162, 267: 'Zwilling ?, Geschwister ?' [twin ? or (according to Th. Richter) sister ?].

Th. Richter, *VHN*, 2016, 457-458, s.v. ***mena*** (usw.) und ***me/mi***, gives the most extensive explanation, especially with regard to the usage in personal names. He emphasizes that the term refers to consanguinity and kinship as is likely on account of the derivation ***minnunni*** {*minn(a/i)=o=nni*} that forms a 'one-word name' *ᶠmime-en-nu-un-ni(-e)* at Nuzi (cf. *NPN*, 97). Formations in ***°unni*** appear to indicate kinship.

Another indication is that the variant ***menni*** is probably derived from {**mena=ni*}, cf. ***ela*** 'sister', ***šala*** 'daughter' and ***šena*** 'brother' for identical formations, as well as the shortened forms ***men*** and ***šen***. Most significant (also with respect to Linear A) is his observation that the shortened forms ***me/mi***, which only occur as second onomastic element, belong to ***mena***, as can be inferred from parallel formations like ***⁽ᶠ⁾Aḫar-me*** vs. ***ᶠAḫar-menni***, ***ᶠEtim-me*** vs. ***ᶠEtem-menni***, ***ᶠ⁽?⁾Unam-me*** vs. ***ᶠUnam-menni*** (Middle-Assyrian Nuzi).

Th. Richter (*VHN*, 195-198) mentions the Hurrian personal names ***Menna*** (wr. *Me-en-na*), without feminine determinative, at Mari and Šubat-Enlil, lexicon *menna*, typology 3.1, that Richter translates as 'Geschwister', cf. *Me-na-a* at Kaniš and Old Babylonian Tall Yalḫi. ***ᶠMenna*** (wr. *ᶠMe-en-na, ᶠMe-en-na-a, ᶠMe-en₆-na-a*) at Mari and Qaṭṭarā.

*ᶠ**Menanna*** (wr. *ᶠMe-na-an-na*) at Mari, analysis {*mena=nna*}, typology 3.2.1, lexicon *mena*, translation 'Es (Mädchen) ist das (wiedergeborene/neue) Geschwister' ['She (the girl) is the (reborn/new) sister'], cf. also *Me-na-an-ni* at Middle-Babylonian Qaṭna.

*ᶠ**Mennazze*** (wr. *ᶠMe-en-na-ze, ᶠMe-na-ze, ᶠMe-en-ni-ze*) at Mari, typology 3.1, lexicon *mennazze* (→ *mena*), translation 'Geschwister' ['sisterhood']. ***Mennatte*** (wr. *Me-en-na-te*), without feminine determinative, at Šušarrā, analysis {*menna=tte*}, typology 3.1, translation 'Ich bin das Geschwister' ['I am the sister'] or analysis {*menn(a)=a*[E.]*=tte*} translation 'Ich bin als Geschwister (geboren)' ['I am (born) as sister']. [E.] refers to the *essive* in ***-a***. Incidentally, ***Mennatte*** {*menna=tte*} may well be equivalent to Linear A ***mi-nu-te*** 20 (HT 86a.5), ***mi-nu-te*** HORD 6 J (HT 106.1), ***mi-nu-te*** 10 (HT 95a.2 HT 95b.2-3), since I have concluded that ***mi-nu-te*** is probably a personal name.

Menni (wr. *Me-en-ni, Me-en-ne*), without feminine determinative, at Šušarrā, analysis {*men(a)=ni*}, typology 3.1, translation 'Geschwister' ['Sister'], cf. *ᶠMe-en-ni* at Alalaḫ VII (AT *409: 7, see A. Draffkorn, *HHA*, 43); *ᶠMe/Mi-en-ni* at Nuzi (AAN I 93). *ᶠ**Minnu*** (wr. *ᶠMi-in-nu*) at Mari, {*minn(a/i)=u*[N.]}, typology 3.1, lexicon *minnu* (→ *mena*), cf. again Linear A ***mi-nu-te***.

*ᶠ**Mennin*** (wr. *ᶠMe-ni-e-en*) at Qaṭṭarā, analysis {*men(a)=ni=n(na)*}, typology 3.1, translation 'Es (Mädchen) ist das (wiedergeborene/neue) Geschwister' ['She (the girl) is the (reborn/new) sister']. *ᶠ**Menninna*** (wr. *ᶠMe-ni-en-na*) at Mari, {*men(a)=ni=nna*}, 'Es (Mädchen) ist das (wiedergeborene/neue) Geschwister' ['He (the boy) is the (reborn/new) sister']. Remarkably Th. Richter translates another ***Menninna*** (wr. *Me-ni-en-na*), without feminine determinative, at Mari, analysis {*men(a)=ni=nna*}, as 'Er (Junge) ist das (wiedergeborene/neue) Geschwister' ['He (the boy) is the (reborn/new) sister']. By adding 'wiedergeborene/neue' [reborn/new] he explains this seemingly contradictory translation as a name that refers to replacement of a deceased sister by the newborn boy. I consider this and some other names with the element ***mena***, but without the feminine determinative, rather a strong argument to prefer the meaning 'twin' to 'sister'.

Moreover, since (as mentioned before) ***-menni*** is used as second onomastic element in feminine personal names at Nuzi (*NPN*, 234), but also in masculine personal names at Alalaḫ and Ugarit (cf. F. Gröndahl, *PNTU*, 240), I consider the gender-neutral meaning 'twin' preferable to that of 'sister'. If the meaning 'twin' is chosen, it is not necessary to assume that ***mena*** and its derivatives are synonymous with Hurrian ***ela*** 'sister'. If that interpretation is right, it is not necessary either to assume that ***a-ku-mi-na*** and ***a-du-ku-mi-na*** are twin-sisters, because it is possible that ***a-du-ku-mi-na*** is a girl (because of ***ašduḫḫu-***), whereas ***a-ku-mi-na*** may also be a boy (because ***akku-*** 'the one', 'the other', is gender neutral as well).

It is, however, possible and probably preferable that Linear A ***a-ku-mi-na*** contains the verbal root ***ag-*** 'to bring, lead, deliver' as first element, with single writing, phonologically ***/ag-/***: e.g. ***aga-***, ***aga-b-***, ***agi-***, ***agi-b-*** and ***agu-*** instead of ***akku-*** 'the one', 'the other'.

The form {*ag=u-*} was formerly considered a passive verbal form in ***-u*** (e.g. E.A. Speiser, E. Laroche, a.o.). For instance, ***Agu-šenni*** (wr. *A-ku-še-en-ni, A-gu-še-en-ni, A-ku-še-ni, A-gu-še-ni*) at Nuzi (cf. I.J. Gelb, *NPN*, 18), used to be interpreted as a passive form 'The brother is brought'.

However, since publication of the Hurrian-Hittite bilingual ***Kirenze*** (KBo 32) forms such as ***Agu-šenni*** are recognized as an 'Old Hurrian' *'active'* transitive *imperative* or *perfect indicative* form, translation 'Bring the brother up (oh *numen*) !' or 'He/She (scil. a *numen*) brought the brother up'. Likewise the Linear A personal name ***a-ku-mi-na*** can be translated as 'Bring the twin up (oh *numen*) !' or 'He/She (scil. a *numen*) brought the twin up'. Since the verbal root ***ag-*** is very frequently used in personal names, this interpretation is in my view also the most likely and therefore preferable.

Linear A orthography does not reveal whether ***a-ku-*** in ***a-ku-|mi-na*** contains a voiced or voiceless palatal. Even if Linear A ***a-ku-|mi-na*** contains a voiceless palatal in the root ***akk-***, this does not necessarily mean that we are dealing with nominal ***akki-/akku-***, for Th. Richter (*VHN*, 366-368) now confirms that the verbal roots ***ag-*** and ***akk-*** are basically identical.

He translates the *intransitive* forms (with the marker of intransitivity ***-a-***) as 'erscheinen' ['to appear'] and 'heraufkommen' ['to come up'] and the *transitive* forms (with the marker of transitivity ***-i-***) as 'heraufbringen' ['to bring up']: e.g. ***ᶠAkap-elli*** 'The sister appeared ≈ was born' and ***Akap-šenni*** and hypocoristic ***Akap-še*** 'The brother appeared ≈ was born'. I.J. Gelb (*NPN*, 12) and P.M. Purves (*NPN*, 198), s.v. *ak, akap-, aki-, akip-, aku-*, and (*ibid.*, 234-235), s.v. *men, menn, menni-, -menni, min, minen-, mini-, miniku, minuša, mina, minaja* mention the Hurrian feminine and masculine personal name from Nuzi ***Akam-menni*** (wr. *ᶠA-qa-am-me-en-ni, ᵐA-qa-am-me-en-ni*) < **Aga-b-menni* [due to assimilation]. This name can now be translated as 'The twin appeared ≈ was born'. E. Laroche (*GLH*, 37) mentions s.v. ***ag-*** 'amener, apporter' the form ***a-ga-mi-na***, KBo VIII 150, 4, that can now be translated as 'The twin appears/appeared ≈ is/was born' or possibly 'Appear, oh twin !'.

Th. Richter (*VHN*, 47) mentions **Akku** (wr. *Ak-ku*) from Mari, analysis {*akk=o*}, typology 1.3.1.1.1, lexicon *akk-*, translation 'Bringe (Jungen) herauf (oh Numen) !' ['Bring (the boy) up (oh numen) !']; ***ᶠAkuja*** (wr. *ᶠA-ku-ia*) from Mari, analysis {*ag=o=ja*}, typology 1.1.1.1.4, lexicon *ag-*, translation 'Er/Sie (scil. ein *Numen*) brachte (Mädchen) herauf' 'He/She (scil. a *numen*) brought (the girl) up']; ***ᶠAkkuja*** (wr. *ᶠAk-ku-ia*) from Ašnakkum, Šubat-Enlil, Kurruḫanni and Alalaḫ IV (AT 214:13), analysis {*akk=o=ja*}, typology 1.1.1.1.4, lexicon *akk-*, translation *idem* as ***ᶠAkuja***. I.J. Gelb (*NPN*, 17-18) and P.M. Purves (*NPN*, 198-199) mention 26 men from Nuzi with the name ***Akkuja*** (wr. *Ak-ku-ia, Ag-gu-ia, Ak-ku-ú-ia, A-ak-ku-ia, Ak-ku-a, A-ku-ia*). The latter names from different sites can also be interpreted as hypocoristics, with hypocoristic ***-ya***. Gelb and Purves also mention 58 men with the name ***Akkul-enni*** (wr. *Ak-ku-le-en-ni, Ak-ku-le-ni, Ak-ku-ul-e-en-ni, Ak-ku-ul-e-ni, Ak-ku-ul-en-ni*); 12 men with the name ***Aku-šenni*** (wr. *A-ku-še-en-ni, A-ku-še-ni, A-gu-še-ni, A-gu-še-en-ni*); 6 men with the name ***Akku-teja*** (wr. *Ak-ku-te-ia, Ak-ku-te-a, Ak-ku-te*); and 5 men with the name ***Akku-tešup*** (wr. *Ak-ku-te-šup*); ***Akku-teni*** (wr. *Ak-ku-te-ni*).

From the many sentence names with ***agi-b-*** I mention a few examples from Nuzi: ***Agi-b-šarri*** was formerly translated as 'The King of Gods is leading'; it is now translated as 'The King of Gods brought (the child) up'; accordingly ***Agi-b-šenni*** can now be translated as 'He/She (a *numen*) brought the brother up' or as 'He, the (deceased) brother brought (the newborn child) up'. In the first interpretation 'the brother' is the newborn child and object of ***ag=i=b***; in the second 'the (deceased) brother' is logical subject of ***ag=i=b*** and a *quasi* theophorous element. ***Agi-b-tešub*** and ***Agi-b-teja*** can now be translated as 'Tešub brought (the child) up', cf. I.J. Gelb, *NPN*, 15-16; P.M. Purves, *NPN*, 198.

E.A. Speiser (*IH*, 1941, 85, § 122) provided pertinent evidence with regard to transitive and intransitive forms: "Some of the verbs employed in onomastic compounds exhibit doublets in *-a+b* : *-i+b*. This is illustrated by *Ag+a+b-* : *Ag+i+b-* (for occurrences cf. *AASOR 16* pp. 145f.). Since *-i-* functions with transitives precisely as *-a-* with intransitives (cf. *Ḫaz-i-b- ibid.* 151, *Tad+i+b ibid.* 164, etc.), it follows that *-a+b* : *-i+b* signalize the same verb as intransitive and transitive respectively. A similar differentiation is apparent in the uncompounded forms of the perfect: *ag+ož+a* Mit. I 87 (trans.) : *ag+ošt+a* VII 58 ii 9, 11 (intrans.); cf. [181]. Inasmuch as *ag-* as a transitive is known to mean 'direct, grant', the intransitive forms of this root may be rendered 'proceed' or the like."

Recent research has brought more fine-tuning to the chain of verbal suffixes. I. Wegner (*Einführung*, 99, tables 6-7) has now split up Speiser's *past intransitive* suffix ***-ošt-*** into two suffixes and attributes *position 2* in the chain of suffixes to the suffixes marking *tense* (***-oš-*** for the past tense) and *position 3* to the suffix ***-t-*** marking absence of an object.

The final ***-a-*** of the transitive perfect ***ag+ož+a*** is marker of the subject of action of the transitive verb 3rd person singular taking *position 7* in the chain of suffixes (*Einführung*, 93, table 4). The final ***-a-*** of the intransitive perfect ***ag+oš+t+a*** is marker of intransitivity and takes *position 5* in the chain of suffixes (the subject of the intransitive verb 3rd person singular has no marker = *Ø*), see I. Wegner (*Einführung*, 99, tables 6-7).

E.A. Speiser interpreted ***-b-*** in intransitive {*ag=a=b-*} and in transitive {*ag=i=b-*} as a root-complement, but since publication of the Hurrian-Hittite bilingual ***Kirenze*** (KBo 32) it has been confirmed that ***-b-*** is the Old Hurrian marker of the subject of action (cf. I. Wegner, *Einführung*, 126): Old Hurrian {*ag=a=b-*} = Mitanni-Hurrian {*ag=a=Ø-*} and Old Hurrian {*ag=i=b-*} = Mitanni-Hurrian {*ag=i=a-*}.

The verbal root ***ag-*** was first recognized as 'darbringen, abliefern' ['to bring in, to deliver'] in the Tušratta-letter by F. Bork, *Die Mitannisprache*, 124. E.A. Speiser (*JAOS LIX (1939)*, 298 and note 36) has comfirmed the meaning of Hurrian ***ag-*** 'guide, direct' by comparing it with Urartian ***agu*** 'guide, direct', for which one may consult J. Friedrich, 'Einführung ins Urartäische', *Mitteilungen der Vorderasiatisch-Ägyptischen Gesellschaft 37.3 (1933),* Leipzig 1933, 25. A. Draffkorn (*HHA*, 66) mentions Hurrian names with the same verbal root ***ag-*** at Alalaḫ: *Aga-n, Agab-keaze, Agab-taġe, Agi-mu, Agi-muzuni, Agi-tešub, Agi-ya* (with hypocoristic suffix *-ya*).

F. Gröndahl (*Die Personennamen der Texte aus Ugarit* (Studia Pohl 1), Rome 1967, 240-241) mentions s.v. *men(n)i, -mn*: Hurrisch, siehe *NPN* 234; in Nuzi, mit einer Ausnahme, nur Element femininer Namen, in Alalaḫ auch häufig in männlichen Namen *Ananu-meni, ninu-meni* [AL 128, 142, 143], in Ugarit bis jetzt nur in männlichen Namen (siehe auch unter *ašt-*). Alphabetischen *-mn* ist nicht zu unterscheiden von dem sem. Suffix *-manu, -munu* (siehe Teil I, Kap. VI § 88): *ag-me-ni*, vergleich *agmn*; *aḫal-me-ni*, vgl. *aġlmn*; *annmn*, vgl. *Ananu-meni* [AL 128]; *pġmn*, vgl. *ᶠpuḫu-meni* [*NPN* 246].

F. Gröndahl (*PNTU*, 215) mentions s.v. *ag/k-, ag*: Hurrisch, *ak-* 'führen, leiten', *NPN* 198; alphabetisch immer *ag*. s.o. § 3: *agdn*, wahrscheinlich **agitenu*, vgl. *aktenu*; *agdṯb*, vgl. *agtṯb*, *agi-tešub*; s.o. § 10; *agytn*, unsicher, vielleicht **agiya+tenu* ?; *ag-me/mi-ni* (G), vgl. *agmn*; *aqammenni* [*NPN* 198]. Siehe aber auch Glossar I unter 'GM; *bn agmz*, vgl. *aki-muša* [*NPN l.c.*]; *a-gap-ḫé*, oder zu *ak-apiḫe* [*NPN l.c.*]; *a-gap-šarri*, vgl. *agpṯr*; *akap-šarru* [AL 126], s.o. §§ 12, 13; *a-gap-te-šub*, vgl. *akip-tešub* [*NPN l.c.*] und s.o.§§ 12, 13;

a-gi₅-tešub; vgl. *agit-tešub*; *a-gi-ia-na* (G), vgl. *agyn*; *akiia* [*NPN* 199, *PNCP* 50, AL 126], *akiian* [AL *l.c.*]; *a-gi₅/git/gi-it-tešub*, aus **agip-tešub*, s.o. § 14; *a-gu-ia*, Kurzform eines Namens wie *agu-šenni* [*NPN* 198]; *agbṯr*, vgl. *agap-šarri*, *agpṯr*; s.o. § 5; *agpṯ*, 2 Element s.u. *šenni*; *agpṯn*, vgl. *akap-šenni* [*NPN* 198, AL 126]; *agyn*, vgl. *agiyanu*; *agynt*, vgl. *akianti*, *ak-ia-an-ti* (G), unsicher, vielleicht *aki* + *anti* [*NPN* 201]; *aqaya*, *bin-a-qa-ya*, unsicher, vgl. *a-qa-a-a* [*NPN* 198]. F. Gröndahl (*PNTU*, 216) mentions s.v. alphabetic cuneiform *ak*, hurrisch *akk-*: *akdṯb*, vgl. *akku-tešub* [*NPN* 199]; *aky*, vgl. *akkuia* [*NPN* 199, AL 127].

E. Laroche, *NH*, 24-25, mentions: n° 15: ***Akiya***. [1. Roi de l'Araḫti: akk. *ᵐA-ki-ya*, KBo I 1 Ro 33, 45; 2 Ro 15, 17 = PD 10]; 2. Homme d'Ismiriga: nom. *ᵐA-ki-ya-aš*, XXIII 68 Vo 19; 3. Médecin: nom. *ᵐA-ki-ya-aš*, XXXIV 45 (+) Ro 12 (Werner); "Seigneur du pays": hiér. *A-ki-i*, SBo II 140; 5 Autres: *ᵐA-ki-y[a]*, KBo V 7 Ro 24 = MIO 6, 345. - *ᵐA-ki-[ya* ?], XXVI 50 Vo 28. Hourrite: cf. Nuzi: *NPN* 14; Alalaḫ: AT p. 126; Ugarit: *PRU* III 238; Qatna: *RA 44*, 112; Capp. *Akia*, EL 67, 18, etc.; EA 30, 3. n° 16: ***Aki-Tešub***: Laroche gives 6 examples of this Hurrian name: 1. Roi du Ni'i ou Neya; 2. Chef mittannien; 3. Prince de Tunip ?; 4. Hittite ? : hiér.; 5. Scribe ou lapicide : hiér.; 6. Autre.

J.M. Sasson, 'Ḫurrians and Ḫurrian names in the Mari texts', *Ugarit Forschungen VI (1974)*, 357, offers the following personal names with the root *ag-* as first element. (Places outside of Mari have an * before a name): "*Aga-tiša-n, *A-ga!-ti-ša-an* VIII:68:3; *Agap-eli, ᶠA-ga-ap-e-li* XIII:1:iv:31; *Agap-tanu, A-ga-ap-ta-nu* VII:176:5; *Aka-ya, ᶠA-ka-ya* SY B:vi:30; *Aki-ya, A-ki-ya* SY A:v:11; *A-ki-ya* I:14:11; *A-ki-ya* VII:139:8; XI:239:6; *Aki-ya-n, *A-ki-ya-an* VII:209:7; *Aki-ra, ᶠA-ki-ra* [H?] IX:291:iv:36; *Akku-ya* (wr. *ᶠAk-ku-a*) IX:294:5; *Aku-ya, ᶠA-ku-ya* SY B:vi:13; vii:17 with the hypocoristic suffix *-ya*." The latter feminine name could be a hypocoristic of e.g. **Agu-elli*, formerly interpreted as 'The sister is brought / granted', but now translated as 'Bring the sister up (oh *numen*) !' or 'He/She (a *numen*) brought the sister up'. The meaning of ***ela/eli*** 'sister' and ***elli*** 'the sister' is deduced from the phrase in Tuš. III 35 ff.: "the daughter of my father (is) my sister ... the daughter of my grandfather (is) the sister of my father." (cf. Messerschmidt, *Mit. St.*, 6; Jensen, *ZA 14*, 173; Speiser, *IH*, 74, 102; E. Laroche, *GLH*, 78, s.v. ***eli*** 'sœur'.

It is tempting to compare the Hurrian onomastic elements ***-mena***, ***-menni***, ***-mina*** and the 'one-word' personal names ***Menna*** at Mari and Šubat-Enlil, ***Menni*** at Šušarrā and ***ᶠMinnu*** at Mari with the name of the legendary King *Minos* of Knossos. Identification is only feasible, if the meaning of the Hurrian lexeme is 'twin' (not 'sister'). Since it is clear that the 'one-word' personal names and the onomastic element in question are not exclusively feminine, I consider the meaning 'sister' unlikely. If the meaning 'twin' is correct, we may conclude that King *Minos* of Knossos and King *Rhadamanthys* of Phaistos were not only brothers, but twins. It is indeed encouraging that the onomastic element ***mina*** is attested in Linear A: ***a-ku-mi-na*** (ZA 10.1-2), ***a-du-|ku-mi-na*** (ZA 10a.3-4) from Kato Zakro, ***da-du-mi-ne*** (KN Zf 31) on a silver hairpin from Knossos and ***mi-nu-te*** (HT 86a.5), ***mi-nu-te*** (HT 106.1), ***mi-nu-te*** (HT 95a.2; HT 95b.2-3) 'It is a twin, oh Tešub !' at Hagia Triada.

It is intriguing that Hurrian, Urartian and Indo-European happen to possess a similar verbal root ***ag-*** 'lead, guide' that is also semantically comparable.

Correspondence between Hurrian and Urartian is expected, because they belong to the same family of agglutinative and ergative languages, but correspondence between Hurrian and Indo-European languages is remarkable, but could be accidental. Correspondence of some Hurrian and Greek lexemes may be explained by the great heritage Minoan society left to the Mycenaean Greeks, but the root of Greek ***ἄγω*** is clearly Indo-European, cf. P. Chantraine (*DELG*, 18): ***ἄγω*** est un vieux présent thématique qui a des correspondants dans skr. ***ájati***, av. ***azaiti***, arm. ***acem***, lat. ***agō***, v. irl. ***aik***, tokh. ***āk-***. On pose une racine ****ə₂eg-*** alternant avec ****ə₂og-*** dans ***ὄγμος***, cf. aussi ***ἀγωγή***.

Intriguing is the Greek verb ***ὄλλῡμι*** 'to destroy', ***-μαι*** 'to destroy oneself, to perish', of which the root ***ὀλ-*** is formally and semantically equal to the Hurrian root ***o/ull-*** 'to destroy'. P. Chantraine, *DELG*, 792-793, s.v. ***ὄλλῡμι***, ***-μαι*** 'perdre, détruire', 'se perdre, périr', mentions about the etymology: "Il faut partir d'un radical ***ὀλ-*** alternant avec ***ὀλε-*** (pour *ὤλεσα, ὄλεθρος, ὀλοός*). On pose donc *ὄλ-νῡ-μι* à côté de *ὤλεσα*, comme *στόρνυμι* à côté de *στορέσαι* : pour ce dernier le skr. fournit un vocalisme zéro, au présent *stṛṇōti*, le vocalisme du grec étant difficile à expliquer, cf. s.v. Celui de *ὄλλῡμι* n'est pas plus clair. .... R. Beekes, *Laryngeals*, 131, 236, pose *ə₃el-ə₁*. Quant à l'aor. *ὠλόμην* on ne peut démontrer qu'il est refait sur un **ὠλέμᾱν*, *ὤλετο* qui serait athématique. Voir encore *οὖλος*. Pas de rapprochement étymologique plausible hord du grec : celui avec lat. *aboleō*, *deleō* est inacceptable. Hypothèses chez Pokorny, 306."

The Hurrian root ***o/ull-*** 'to destroy' may in my view provide a good external etymology for Greek ***ὄλλῡμι***, cf. Th. Richter, *BGH*, 486, s.v. ***ull-*** [Boğ.; Mitt.; PN], 'to destroy', cf. G. Wilhelm, A Hurrian letter from Tell Brak, *Iraq 53 (1991)*, 161-162: /***ull-***/ or /***oll-***/. Etymologically it is also comparable with Urartian ***ul(u)-*** 'vernichten' ['to destroy'], cf. also Hurrian ***ull=ul-*** [Boğ.] 'distruggere' ['to destroy'] with Urartian ***ulu=le-***, see M. Salvini, Sui testi mitologici in lingua ḫurrica, *SMEA 18 (1977)*, 84.

Direct derivation from Minoan-Hurrian into Mycenaean Greek is in my view more likely than derivation from Mitanni-Hurrian or Syrian Hurrian into Greek, the more since Hurrian ***o/ull-*** is attested in Linear A ***o-ra₂-di-ne*** (HT 6a.4) that I have analysed as ***Olli-ašdine*** 'Destroy the woman (oh hero) !', prototype of the name of the Cretan hero Perseus.

Linear A ***a-de*** (ZA 10b.4) can be interpreted as the Hurrian personal name ***ᶠAš-te*** 'Woman' at Nuzi and Mari or ***ᶠAšten*** (wr. *ᶠAš-te-en*) at Nuzi (cf. I.J. Gelb, *NPN*, 37) and Mari (cf. Th. Richter, *VHN*, 78-79), analysis {*ašte=n(na)*}, typology 3.1, 'She (the girl) is a woman'. We may compare Linear A]**'**, ***a-di-ne***[(KH 83.1) from Khania that may well be the lexical term ***aždi-ne*** (with the suffix of the so-called singular definite article ***-ne***) 'the woman' or the personal name ***Aždi-nne*** (with the suffix of the *optional allomorphic* enclitic personal pronoun 3rd person singular ***-nne/-nni***), 'She (the girl) is a woman'. Linear A]***a-di-na*** 5 (KH 59.3) that may be Hurrian ***aždi-na*** 5 'the women 5 (portions)' or '5 women' (with the suffix of the so-called plural definite article ***-na***) or the personal name ***Aždi-nna*** (with the suffix of the enclitic personal pronoun 3rd person singular ***-nna***), 'She (the girl) is a woman', cf. Th. Richter, *BGH*, 59-61, s.v. ***ašte/i***. Cf. also Linear A ***o-ra₂-di-ne*** (HT 6.a.4).

On the basis of the alphabetic cuneiform ***ašt-n-s*** at Ugarit (*CTA* 179, 13, 21, 29, 35), *ergative* of the form with definite article ***-ni-***, = *aš-ti-ni-iš*, Mâri 4, 25 (E. Laroche, *GLH*, 62), one has concluded that Hurrian ***ašt-*** contains a voiceless dental ***-t-***, not voiced dental ***-d-***.

However, F.W. Bush (*GHL*, 52) assumes that positional voicing of the dental stop [*t*] occurs when it is contiguous with *-r-, -l-, -m-, -n-*, but also with other consonants than the liquids and nasals, and he explicitly mentions (sub g) alphabetic Ugaritic ***aṯṯḫ-*** and a personal name ***Aš-tu-a-ta-na*** (*HCP*: 401). There are in my view no clear criteria for the degree of positional voicing of a dental after a sibilant in Hurrian, because the resulting sound was allophonic. Hurrian was spoken and written in a very large area and over a very long period with no doubt many dialectal differences. Syllabic cuneiform was not conclusive with regard to voiced and voiceless consonants in initial position as well as in consonant clusters.

One may assume that adjacent consonants may have influenced the degree of voicing in consonant clusters. My position is that one should not generalize the evidence obtained from the rather late alphabetic cuneiform texts from Ugarit to areas where syllabic cuneiform was the only source, and to periods that were much earlier than the age of alphabetic cuneiform.

This means that Linear A ***a-te*** (ZA 26a.1) at Kato Zakro (if the reading is correct), and ligature ***a+ti*** (HT 94a.2; HT 100.2) at Hagia Triada, may be equated with e.g. Hurrian ***Atti***.. (wr. *At-ti-*.[..]) at Nuzi (*JEN* 539:24) and ***Attiia*** (wr. *At-ti-ia*), son of *In-ni-qa-a-a* (*HSS IX* 126:2, rev.1), with double writing of the dental and therefore voiceless, cf. I.J. Gelb, *NPN*, 39-40. P.M. Purves, *NPN*, 206, s.v. ***ašt***: "Hurrian. Cf. root ***ašt*** in Tuš. and in many word formations in Hurrian texts from Boğazköy. At Nuzi itself *aš-du-uz-zi, SMN* 2671, is a term applied to a garment. On the basis of II R 32, No. 2:24, Jensen in *ZA XIV* 173 f. and in KB VI 1 (1900) p. 381 translates 'Gemahlin' and 'Weib'. Messerschmidt, M.-St., pp. 18 and 123 translates "Gemahlin". Ungnad, *Die älteste Völkerwanderungen Vorderasiens* (*Kulturfragen, Heft 1* [1923]) p. 5, and in *ZA N.F. I* 137 trs. 'Weib'."

E. Laroche, *GLH*, 62, s.v. *ašte* 'femme'. RS bil. 4/9 = PRU III 318: *aš-ta* = akkadien *marḫeta-šu.* KBo XIX 145 IV 41, 48: *aš-ta* = hitt. SAL-*an*, ib. III 41, 48. Etc. 1. Thème *ašte / ašti.* Compare for more examples of all case-endings E. Laroche, *GLH*, 62-63. I agree with Th. Richter (*VHN*, *passim*) that the meaning 'wife' is only applicable with regard to lexemes, but is not likely in personal names, because namegiving probably occurred in antiquity as at present usually soon after a child was born. Only the distinction between a boy or girl, a brother or sister was important, and sometimes the birth of a twin.

If Linear A] ***a-mi-da-o*** (HT? 170a.5) is read correctly, which is not entirely certain since most signs are not very clear, it probably represents the same form as ***a-mi-da-u*** (ZA 10a.3) at Kato Zakro. In HT? 170a.5 the form may well fit into the list of personal names registered on that tablet.] ***a-mi-da-o*** precedes OVIS^{m} 1 in the same way as the other personal names are followed by similar ideograms and numbers. Interpretation of ***a-mi-da-u*** (ZA 10a.3) as a personal name seems likely as well.

In the 2016 edition I mentioned that ***a-mi-da-u*** (ZA 10a.3) and]***a-mi-da-o*** (HT? 170a.5) might contain the element ***-dau / -dai / -dae***, especially since ***da-i-pi-ta*** (ZA 10a.4-5) begins with the onomastic element ***dai-***, but now I am sure that the scribe has in this case only been playing with names like ***da-i-pi-ta*** that indeed display similar sounds, but have nothing to do with each other from an etymological point of view.

I also cited E. Laroche (*GLH*, 46-47) who did not mention Bork's translation of ***amm*** as 'melden' or 'hinschaffen' (cited by Purves, *NPN*, 200), but who cautiously mentioned s.v. ***amm-***: Verbe de sens inconnu. 1. Thème ***amm-***.

Prét. sg. 3 *am-mu-u-u-ša*, Mit. I 95; *a-mu-u-ša*, KUB XXVII 46 IV 17.
Fut. sg. 2 *am-mi-du-ú*, IBoT II 39 Ro 38, 41.
Fut. sg. 3 *am-mi-da*, KBo XX 140, 5.
Opt. sg. 3 *am-mi-en*, KBo VII 70, 5.
Inf. ? *am-mu-um-mi*, KBo XX 130, 10. – *am-mu-um*, KUB XLVII 3,8.
2. Thème (passif ?) *amm-ul-*.
Opt. sg. 3 *a-(am)-mu-le-eš*, KUB XXVII 42 Vo 14, 16; XXIX 8 III 29.
3. Divers: *am-mu-li*, EA 52, 40; KUB XLVII 3, 8; XXVII Ro 14.
– *am-mu-u-la*, KBo XIX 141, 19. – *a-am-ma*, KUB XLV 60, 15.
– *am-mi-im-ba-aš-še*, Mâri 7, 19. – *am-mu-u-ši-e-en-na-(a-an)*, KUB XXXII 46+38, 22.
– *am-mu-ši-ik-ku-un-ne*, KUB XXVII 38 III 20.

In the same edition I wrote: "If *-da-u* / *-da-o* in *a-mi-da-u* / *a-mi-da-o* do not represent the frequent Hurrian onomastic element *tae, tai, tau* (*/dae/, /dai/, /dau/*), *a-mi-da-u* and *a-mi-da-o* could be explained as the Hurrian verbal root **amm-** + the suffix ***-ed-/-id-*** of the future form + the suffix ***-au*** of the 1st pers. sg.: 'I shall *bring a message*' (with Bork's translation of the verb: an appropriate name for e.g. the son of a messenger, born to follow in his father's footsteps) or 'I shall *arrive*', if Th. Richter, *BGH*, 23 (***amm-*** II) is right. See also Th. Richter's *lemmata* of different verbal roots ***am(m)-*** (*BGH*, 19-23). The forms would then serve as appellative personal names.

The *lemma* on **amm-** in E. Laroche, *GLH*, 46-47, shows the future 3rd pers. sg. form ***am-mi-da*** (KBo XX 140, 5) indicating that the Linear A forms ***a-mi-da-u / a-mi-da-o*** can *a priori* be explained as the future 1st pers. sg. form ****am-mi-da-u*** of the Hurrian verb ***amm-*** with the ending ***-au*** of the 1st pers. sg. instead of the ending ***-a*** of the 3rd pers. sg. The context of HT? 170a.5 and ZA 10a.3 leaves no doubt that *a plain verbal form* is not expected in lists of personal names, but an appellative based on such a form might be conceivable. Although interpretation of Linear A ***a-mi-da-u*** and ***a-mi-da-o*** as Hurrian personal names consisting of two frequent onomastic elements seems preferable to appellative names derived from a Hurrian verbal form, a discussion of all feasible possibilities seems useful, because it shows not only the possibilities, but also the problems arising from both Linear A and cuneiform orthographic conventions."

Since publication of Th. Richter, *VHN*, 2016 (especially pages 584-587), it has become clear that, what I cautiously considered a theoretical possibility, is really attested by many examples in the Hurrian onomastic material assembled by Th. Richter.

A correction is necessary: ***a-mi-da-u*** / ***a-mi-da-o*** cannot mean 'I shall *arrive*', because it cannot be intransitive, for intransitive verbs do not have a suffix ***-e/id-*** (with voiced dental) to indicate the future tense, but a suffix ***-e/it-*** (with voiceless dental, written ***-e/itt-*** in cuneiform), cf. e.g. the form ***un=ett=a*** 'he will come', see I. Wegner, *Einführung*, 97: *un-et+t+a* 'er wird kommen' ['he will come'], of which the second ***t*** is now considered the suffix marking the absence of an object (cf. I. Wegner, *Einführung*, 99: tables 6-7).

So ***a-mi-da-u*** and ***a-mi-da-o*** represents transitive usage of the verb ***amm-*** 'to reach (something)', with the suffix ***-e/id-*** (with voiced dental) indicating the transitive future tense + the suffix of the 1st person singular ***-au***. Starting from the root ***amm-*** 'to reach (something)' ***a-mi-da-u*** and ***a-mi-da-o*** can be analysed as {*amm=e/id=au*} 'I shall reach (something)', 1st person sing. future indicative of the verb ***amm-*** 'to reach (something)'.

I. Wegner (*Einführung*, 129) offers an example of the transitive usage of ***amm-*** II in the Hurrian-Hittite bilingual ***kirenze***: *olvi=ne=ma amm=i=b ommin(i)=ne* (KBo 32: 14 I 19-20), which she translates 'Ein anderes Land aber erreichte es (das Reh)' ['But it (the roe) reached an other land']. This Old Hurrian sentence is antipassive, with a (non-ergative) subject in the absolutive, an object in an oblique case like ***-a*** (essive) or ***-ne***, and with the transitive verbal form in ***=i=b***.

However, if we assume that ***a-mi-da-u*** and ***a-mi-da-o*** contain the transitive root ***am-*** II [Boğ.] 'ansehen, anschauen, beachten', 'porter son regard sur', 'guardare, osservare, vedere', 'to observe' (see Th. Richter, *BGH*, 21-23), the meaning of these personal names would be 'I shall observe', which would also offer a conceivable meaning.

The scribe of ZA 10a seems to have been particularly fond of playing with names, because he wrote four names in a row starting with sign ***a-***: ***a-ku-mi-na*** 1, ***a-ta-na-te*** 1, ***a-mi-da-u*** 1, ***a-du-ku-mi-na*** 1. As mentioned in my *Corpus of transliterated Linear A texts*, the tablet is called 'tablet of the double axes', because Linear A sign ***52 = a*** is probably derived from the pictographic or hieroglyphic sign of a double axe.

In the combination of ***ta-na-te*** in line 1 and ***a-ta-na-te*** in line 2 he used rhyme as well as in ***a-ku-mi-na*** and ***a-du-ku-mi-na***. Another example of playing with names is shown by ***a-mi-da-u*** (ZA 10a.3) and ***a-mi-ta*** (ZA 10b.4-5), which may be etymologically related, at least with regard to the Hurrian verbal roots ***amm-*** or ***am-***. The scribe certainly had a poetic feeling for alliteration and displayed his *ars poetica* in a splendid way.

Linear A ***a-mi-ta*** (ZA 10b.4-5) on the b-side of the tablet is certainly a personal name. Whether or not it can be identified with the personal name from Cappadocia ***Amita*** (wr. *A-mì-ta*) is difficult to say, because we cannot define, whether the Cappadocian name is phonologically to be read as ***/A-mì-da/*** *{am=e/id=a}* or as ***/A-mì-ta/***. Cappadocian orthography does not use gemination of the consonants. E. Laroche, *NH*, 240, n. 4: Les noms cunéiformes seront orthographiés selon l'usage cappadocien, sans la gémination consonantique hittite. Par ex.: ***Kuku*** = capp. *Ku-ku-ú,* hitt. *Ku-uk-ku.*

Apart from the status of the name from Cappadocia, Linear A ***a-mi-ta*** (ZA 10b.4-5) can be identified as a Hurrian 'one-word' personal name based on a verbal form. In this case Linear A orthography and Hurrian grammar provide more than one possible interpretation. Linear A orthography does not tell, whether we have to choose a verbal root ***am-*** or ***amm-***, for the Linear A script does not distinguish single and double writing as the cuneiform syllabary (except e.g. the Cappadocian) does.

Hurrian ***am-*** II [Boğ.] 'to observe' (cf. Th. Richter, *BGH*, 21-23). If the Linear A scribe wrote a personal name built on this root, ***a-mi-ta*** (ZA 10b.4-5) can be interpreted as ***Amitta*** and analysed as *{am=(i)=i=tta}* 'Observe me', consisting of (the transitive root) ***am-*** + the transitive theme-vowel ***-i-*** (the *imperative* 2nd person singular does not have its own marker) + (the personal pronoun 1st person singular serving as object in transitive constructions) ***-tta***.

amm- II [Boğ.; Qaṭna]: 'ankommen, gelangen, erreichen', ['to arrive, to reach'], corresponds with Hittite ***ar-*** and Akkadian ***kašādum***, cf. Th. Richter, *BGH*, 23-24. If Linear A ***a-mi-ta*** (ZA 10b.4-5) is built on this root, it can be interpreted as ***Ammitta***, analysis *{amm=i=tta}* 'Reach me !', cf. *supra* the transitive usage of ***amm-*** II in the bilingual ***kirenze***: *olvi=ne=ma amm=i=b ommin(i)=ne.* (KBo 32: 14 I 19-20).

The meaning 'Bring me' for Linear A ***a-mi-ta*** (ZA 10b.4-5), interpreted as ***Ammitta***, can be derived from the interpretation of a parallel Hurrian personal name attested at Mari, with an ending in ***-nna***, representing the suffix of the enclitic personal pronoun 3rd person singular. Th. Richter (*VHN*, 56) mentions ***Amminna*** (wr. *am-mi-na*), name of a man at Mari, analysis {*amm=i=nna*}, typology 1.3.1.2.2.1, lexicon *am(m)*, translation 'Bringe ihn (Junge) her !' ['Bring him (the boy) here !']. The suffix of the personal pronoun ***-nna*** has the function of object as ***-tta*** has in the Linear A name. He also mentions ***^{f}Amminna*** (wr. *am-mi-in-na, a-mi-na*), name of a woman at Mari, 'Bringe es (Mädchen) her !' ['Bring her (the girl) here !'].

There is another interpretation of Linear A ***a-mi-ta*** feasible. If Hurrian ***amm-*** is used as intransitive, the form ***Ammitta*** can be analysed as {*amm=e/it=t=a*} 'He will arrive', consisting of (the intransitive root) ***amm-*** + (the suffix marking the *future* tense) ***-e/it-*** + (the suffix marking absence of an object) ***-t-*** + (the suffix marking *intransitivity*) ***-a-*** + ***Ø*** (in future and past intransitive there is no enclitic pronoun as subject for the 3rd person singular; so no use of ***-nna***). I. Wegner (*Einführung*, 97-99, sub 5.4: *Die Suffixfolge beim indikativen, intransitiven, positiven Verb* (Tabelle 6 und 7)) gives an example of another comparable intransitive form: ***un*** + ***et*** + ***t*** + ***a*** 'er wird kommen' ['He will come'].

The Linear A sequence ***du-re-za-se*** 2 (ZA 10a.5), ***du-re-za-se*** VIN 5 (ZA 10b.1-2), ***du-re-za|-se*** 1 (ZA 20.1-2), occurring on *a*- and *b*-side of tablet ZA 10, and probably again on ZA 20, from Kato Zakro can be identified as a Hurrian personal name of the type 'sentence name'. It may well refer to the same person each time.

The name consists of two nominal elements ***durezza*** and ***-še***. The element ***-še*** is the hypocoristic of ***-šena*** 'brother' or ***-šen(a)=ne/ni*** 'the brother', that is very common in Hurrian personal names. The form ***durezza*** can be compared with two Hurrian names at Mari, ***Turazze*** and ***Turizza***, of which the second bears the closest resemblance to Linear A ***du-re-za-***, cf. Th. Richter, *VHN*, 318-319.

Turazze (wr. *tu-ra-ze*) is a slave at Mari (*MARI 8*, 637 VIII 2), typology 3.1, lexicon *turazze* (→ *turi*), whose name is compared with *tu/tù-ra-ša/šá* and *tu-ra-še* at Nuzi (AAN I, 152). ***Turizza*** (wr. *tu-ri-iz-za*) from Mari (M.5811 II 3'), analysis {*turizz(i)=a*[E.]}, typology 3.2.1, lexicon *turizz(i)* (→ *turi*). [E.] refers to the *essive* form in ***-a***.

According to Th. Richter (*VHN*, 546) the meaning of ***turi*** 'man' has been established by Von Brandenstein (1937, 567), see also Th. Richter, *BGH*, 476. It is not clear, whether or in which way it is to be distinguished from ***taḫe*** 'man'. It is, however, significant that forms of both ***turi*** 'man' and ***taḫe*** 'man' are attested with initial voicing of the dentals in Linear A ***du-re-za-se*** and ***da-qe-ra*** (= Hurrian ***daḫera***, comitative), respectively.

According to Th. Richter (*ibid.*) ***turazze*** can be analysed as {*tur(i)=a=šše*} 'Mannschaft(?)' ['manhood (?)'] (see G/4.2.2.5) beside the formation ***turizzi*** with [*i*] in the second syllable. Parallel formations exist as well: ***ḫani*** 'Kind' ['child'] and ***ḫanazze*** 'Kindschaft(?)' ['childhood (?)]' beside the formation *ḫa-ni-iz-z^o* with [*i*] in the second syllable (see catalogue sub ***Ḫanazzu***).

Consequently I propose to analyse the Linear A personal name ***du-re-za-se*** as {*dure/izz(i)=a-še*} 'The brother is like manhood (?)', consisting of ***dure/izzi*** in the *essive* case in ***-a***, followed by ***-še***, hypocoristic of ***-šena*** 'brother' or ***-šenni*** 'the brother'.

Linear A ***a-ta-na-te*** 1 (ZA 10a.2) and probably ***a-ta-na-[te]*** OVIS+***si*** 2 (ZA 9.4-5) from Kato Zakro can probably be interpreted as a Hurrian personal name. I propose to analyse ***a-ta-na-te*** as *{attann(i)=a*[*essive*]*-Te(šub)}* that can be translated as 'Te(šub) is like (God) the Father'. Or preferably *{att(a)=a*[*essive*]*=nna-Te(šub)}* 'He [*-nna*] (the boy) is/looks like his father, oh Te(šub) !'. The theophorous element ***-te*** is (like ***-teịa***) a frequent hypocoristic form of ***-Tešub*** in Hurrian personal names. The *essive* case in ***-a*** is apparently frequently used in Hurrian personal names, see Th. Richter, *VHN*, *passim*.

Apart from the observation that the scribe was keen on comparing names that have features of sound and orthography in common, it is important for us to examine whether the correspondences are merely a matter of similarity of sounds or not. For instance, is there an etymological relation between ***ta-na-te*** (line 1) and ***a-ta-na-te*** (line 2) ? In other words, is the difference between ***ta-na-te*** and ***a-ta-na-te*** caused by *aphaeresis* of initial ***a-*** in ***a-ta-na-te***, with ***ta-na-te*** as a result ? However suggestive the scribe's presentation may be, I consider an etymological relation between ***ta-na-*** and ***a-ta-na-*** unlikely.

Nevertheless it is worth noting that Th. Richter (*VHN*, 390-391), s.v. ***adana*** *{adana}*, also ***tana*** *{tana}* (?), appears to accept that *aphaeresis* of initial ***a-*** in ***adana*** (i.e. in the forms with voiced ***-d-***, written with single dental in intervocalic position) may be acceptable on the basis of comparable names, although there is no prosopographic evidence to prove the case. He proposes, for instance, to analyse ***Tana-ewri*** (wr. *ta-na-ew-ri*) at Nuzi (HSS 16, 5: 20) as *{(a)dana-evri}* '(A)dana ist Herr' ['(A)dana is Lord']. In note 222 he remarks that, if ***adana*** and ***tana*** have to be distinguished from each other, derivation of ***tana*** from ***tan-***, as proposed by P.M. Purves (*NPN*, 262), has to be considered. In my view it is preferable to keep ***adana*** separate from ***tana***.

Consequently, a personal name ***ta-na-te*** (ZA 10a.1) with a verbal root ***tan-*** 'to make, do' seems preferable. Th. Richter (*BGH*, 436-438), s.v. ***tan-*** [*passim*], ***tin-*** [Ugarit]) 'to make, do', mentions that Hurrian ***tan-*** corresponds with Hittite ***ija-*** 'to make' (Neu 1996a: 421), Akkadian ***epēšu*** and Urartian ***tanu-*** 'to make'. He also mentions that ***tan-*** is usually transitive, but refers to G. Wilhelm (2010a, 632) for an obscure intransitive formation.
I propose that this intransitive meaning is 'to be the Creator'. If we compare ***Tana-ewri*** (wr. *ta-na-ew-ri*) at Nuzi (HSS 16, 5: 20), the analysis is ***{****tan=a-evri****}*** and the proposed translation 'The Lord is the Creator'. If we take ***Tana-ewri*** as a parallel to Linear A ***ta-na-te***, the analysis is *{tan=a-Te(šub)}* 'Te(šub) is the Creator' (with marker of intransitivity ***-a***). The conclusion may be that ***Tana-ewri*** offers a satisfactory parallel to Linear A ***ta-na-te***, the more since ***ewri*** 'Lord' is often used as an epithet to Tešub, also in the Tušratta letter. Tušratta (IV, 118) shows that the *ergatives* ***ew-ri-iw-wa-šu-uš*** 'Our Lord' and ***at-ta-iw-wa-šu-uš*** 'Our Father' are used as epithets of ***^{d}Te-e-eš-šu-pa-aš*** (*ergative* of ***Teš(š)ub***), which means that both ***Ewri*** 'Lord' and ***Eni Attanni*** 'God the Father' refer primarily to ***Teš(š)ub***, see also Linear A ***a-ta-i-jo-wa-ja***, which is equivalent to the reconstructed Hurrian absolutive ****at-ta-i-iw-wa-(j)aš*** 'Our Father !'.

However, since according to Linear A and B orthographic conventions ***-n-*** preceding an occlusive is not expressed in consonant clusters, Linear A ***ta-na-te*** can also reflect *{tan=an-Te(šub)}* 'Practise magic / witchcraft, Work charms, oh Te(šub) !', cf. Th. Richter, *BGH*, 437, s.v. ***tan=an-*** 'Zauberei bewirken, verursachen'. According to I. Wegner (*Einführung*, 88) root-extension ***-an(n)-*** expresses a causative aspect.

Combination of the verbal root ***tan-*** with another root-extension is also feasible. For instance, the Tušratta letter provides 3 examples of the form *ta-a-na-aš-ti-en* (Mit. I 82; III, 75, 78) according to the transliteration by J. Friedrich. E. Laroche (*GLH*, 255) has transliterated it as *ta-a-na-aš-ti-in* and has marked it as *optative* 3rd person singular. He considered ***tan-ašt-*** 'thème d'intensif (?)'.

I. Wegner (*Einführung*, 147) analyses *ta-a-na-aš-ti-en* as ***tan=ašt=i=en***, consisting of the root ***tan-*** 'machen, tun' ['to make, do'] + root-extension ***-ašt-*** + marker of the *jussive* ***-i-*** + the indicator of the 3rd person sing. of the *jussive* ***-en***: 'er möge machen,' ['he may make'].

I. Wegner (*Einführung*, 88) explains that the vowel in the root-extension ***-Všt-*** is adapted to the vowel in the root, e.g. ***tan=ašt-*** 'machen' ['to make'], ***an- / an=ašt-*** 'sich freuen' ['to enjoy'], ***mad=ašt-*** 'weise sein' ['to be wise'], ***teḫ- / teḫ=ešt-*** 'erhöhen, gross werden' ['to elevate, to grow, to become great'], ***šurv=ušt-*** 'Böses tun' ['to do, to cause, to bring about evil']. This root-extension may in some cases have a denominalising character and should not be confused with the intransitive marker of the past tense ***-oš-*** + ***-t-***. However, there are indications that the formants ***-ol-*** and especially ***-Všt-*** in combination with verbal forms in ***=o=m*** may show other grammatical differentiations (aspect or type of action), cf. G. Wilhelm, *Festschrift Heger*, 1992, 670.

The 'Old Hurrian' formant ***-Všt-*** seems to express the end or result of an action, e.g. ***pa=ašt=o=m*** 'he has built', attested in the *Tiš-atal*-inscription, line 6: *ba-'à-áš-tum*.

Since final consonants are not expressed in Linear A and B, it is not entirely certain, whether Linear A ***ta-na-te*** represents ***tan=ašt=i=en*** or whether in that case ****ta-na-ti-e*** would have been expected in Linear A, since ***-i-*** and ***-en*** represent separate suffixes. Contraction of ***-i-en*** > ***-in*** or ***-en*** seems not inconceivable. The easiest solution is, however, that Linear A ***ta-na-te*** does not represent the 3rd person singular of the *jussive* ***tan=ašt=i=en***, but the 2nd person singular of the *jussive*, c.q. the *imperative*, ***tan=ašt=e/i***, since the *imperative* in ***-e*** or ***-i*** misses the marker of the 2nd person (*Ø*), cf. I. Wegner, *Einführung*, 103, Table 9: *The order of suffixes for the positive jussive*. So the Linear A name ***ta-na-te***, analysis ***tan=ašt=e/i***, means 'Make/Create (the child) (oh *numen*) !'.

Since publication of Th. Richter, *VHN*, Wiesbaden 2016, a different approach must be considered as well, since Linear A ***ta-na-te*** can theoretically also be analysed as {*tan=atte*}. Th. Richter (*VHN*, 391) writes, s.v. ***atte/atti*** and ***attu*** {*atto/u*}, that Hurrian ***att^o^*** in the meaning 'father' or sometimes 'direct male ancestor' is known through ***atta*** and the root ***att-***, but that it should be separated from ***atte***, because there is an extensive usage of the same type of feminine personal names built on ***atte*** as on ***azze*** and ***ašte*** (also with a stem in ***-u***). The fact that, for instance, ***^f^Azzu***, ***^f^Aštu***, ***^f^Attu***, ***^f^Azzuzari***, ***^f^Aštuzar***, ***^f^Attuzar*** and ***^f^Azzue***, ***^f^Aštue***, ***^f^Attue*** all occur at Mari, indicates that these variant writings (and probably variant pronunciations) of ***-zze-***, ***-št-*** and ***-tt-*** can only have been caused by dialectal differences, if the ladies in question originally came from different places with different dialects and were only subsequently stationed in the Palace of Mari and its dependencies keeping their names without any adaptation at all. It seems unlikely that phonetic changes could have led to simultaneous usage of ***atte***, ***ašte*** and ***azze*** at Mari (or elsewhere). So it may be a target for future research to examine whether the attestations might show evidence of a difference in time between the three variants.

Linear A ideograms for VIR and MULIER are not always mentioned and the names miss the type of determinatives for *male* and *female* persons which cuneiform personal names have. Typical theophorous elements with a male or female identity or another recognizable lexeme indicating male or female gender such as ***šena / šenni*** 'brother' and ***ela / elli*** 'sister' sometimes give a clue. We must keep in mind that Hurrian nouns do not distinguish gender (*genera*). Hurrian has no separate masculine, feminine and neuter paradigms as, for instance, Indo-European Greek and Latin have.

Against analysis of Linear A ***ta-na-te*** as {*tan-atte*} or {*tan-ašte*} equivalent to {*tan-ažde*} and {*tan-azze*}, lexicon *tan-*, *atte*, *ašte*, 'Make/Create (the child), oh woman !', with *athematic imperative*, I may quote Th. Richter's observation (*VHN*, 381, note 182) that ***ašte***, ***azze*** and ***atte*** primarily occur in 'one-word' names, only occasionally in *nominal* sentence names and never in *verbal* sentence names in his *VHN*-corpus. So it is unlikely that Linear A ***ta-na-ti*** (HT 7a.4; HT 10b.4; HT 49.2; HT 98a.2) from Hagia Triada and ***ta-na-te*** (ZA 10a.1) from Kato Zakro can be identified as {*tan-atte*} or {*tan-ašte*}.

P.M. Purves (*NPN*, 264, s.v. ***-te***; 266, s.v. ***-ti***) assumed that ***-ti*** in personal names could be a variant of ***-te***, hypocoristic of ***-tešub*** and ***teja***. He has probably based his equation of ***-ti*** with ***-te*** on the variant writing of e.g. ***Ḫui-te*** as *Ḫu-i-te*, *Ḫu-i-te-e*, *Ḫu-e-te*, *Ḫu-i-ti*.

1) Linear A ***ta-na-te*** (ZA 10a.1) and ***ta-na-ti*** (HT 7a.4; HT 10b.4; HT 49.2; HT 98a.2) can be analysed as {*tan=an-Te/Ti*} = {*tan=an-Tešub*}, with causitive root-extension ***=an(n)-*** (cf. I. Wegner, *Einführung*, 88; Th. Richter, *BGH*, 437: ***tan=an-*** [Boğ.] 'Zauberei bewirken, verursachen'), 'Practise magic/witchcraft / Work charms, oh Te(šub) !'.

2) Linear A ***ta-na-te*** (ZA 10a.1) and ***ta-na-ti*** (HT 7a.4; HT 10b.4; HT 49.2; HT 98a.2) can be analysed as 2nd person singular of the *imperative*, ***tan=ašt=e/i***, with root-extension ***-Všt-*** (cf. I. Wegner, *Einführung*, 88-89) 'Make/Create (the child) (oh *numen*) !'.

3). Th. Richter (*VHN*, 596, sub 1.3.1.1.2.2) mentions that in 'one-word' names the enclitic personal pronoun 1st person singular ***-tta*** can sometimes be replaced by the *optional allomorphic* suffix ***-tti***. Consequently, if Linear A ***ta-na-ti*** (HT 10b.4) is analysed as {*tan=an=tti*} replacing {*tan=an=tta*}, the name can be translated as an *imperative* 'Practise magic / witchcraft on me, oh *numen* !', 'Work charms on me (oh *numen*) !'.

The personal name ***i-ru-ja*** (HT 7a.2) occurs on the same tablet as Linear A ***ta-na-ti*** (HT 7a.4). It can be interpreted as Old Hurrian ***Iruja***, equivalent to ***Irija*** (wr. *I-ri-ia*) from Mari, Tigunāni, Tuttul, Alalaḫ IV, Ekalte, Emar, Nuzi, (wr. *I-ri-a*) at Middle-Assyrian Tall Brak, analysis {*ir=i=(j)a*}, 'He/She (a *numen*) has given (the boy), cf. Th. Richter, *VHN*, 112, 401. Th. Richter (*VHN*, 401) mentions that in recent literature, starting from the Hurrian-Hittite bilingual *Kirenze*, the root ***er-*** (also ***ir-*** ?) was isolated. Translation 's'accroître' ['to grow'], 'gedeihen' ['to thrive'], 'helfen' ['to help'] and 'schenken' ['to give'] (see also *BGH*, 96). He prefers 'schenken' ['to give'] in the onomastics of *VHN*, e.g. participial ***eriri*** {*er=i=ri*} 'der/die geschenkt hat' ['the one who has given'], cf. the personal name ***Eriri*** (with the same meaning) from Tigunāni. The Linear A names on HT 7 probably refer to men, since the ideogram VIR follows the first entry ***qe-ti*** (HT 7a.1).

Linear A ***qe-ti*** (HT 7a.1) may be an (*imperative*) 'one-word' personal name ***Ḫešt=i***, consisting of the verbal root ***ḫešt-*** 'absperren' (Th. Richter, *BGH*, 159) ['to block, retain'] + the marker of transitivity ***-i***: 'Block/Retain (the baby) (oh *numen*, oh mother) !'.

In Linear A the personal names ***i̱-du-ti*** (HT 104.2-3), analysis Old Hurrian {*id=u=tti*}, 'Beat, hit, strike me (oh *numen*) !', and ***ka-nu-ti*** (HT 97a.3), analysis {*ḫan=u=tti*}, *imperative* 'Give birth to me / Create me (oh *numen*) !' or Old Hurrian past *indicative* {*ḫan=o/u(=m)=tti*} 'He/She (a *numen*) created me' or 'She (the mother) gave birth to me' may in that case be considered good parallels to ***ta-na-ti*** (HT 10b.4),{*tan=an-tti*}.

The sequences]***-nu-ti*** , VIR[(HT 84.2) and]***-nu-ti*** (ZA 9.1) may be personal names or perhaps toponyms, because they may perhaps be completed to either ***ka***]***-nu-ti*** as in Linear A ***ka-nu-ti*** 25 (HT 97a.3) or to ***mi***]***-nu-te*** as in Linear A ***mi-nu-te*** 20 (HT 86a.5), ***mi-nu-te*** HORD 6 J̱ (HT 106.1), ***mi-n̲u̲-te*** 10 (HT 95a.2; HT 95b.2-3).

The reading ***a-ta-na-te*** 1 (ZA 10a.2) is certain, but ***a-ta-na-*[*t̲e̲*]** OVIS+***si*** 2̱ (ZA 9.4-5) is less certain. According to *GORILA 3* (166-167) there are, however, traces at the end of line 4 that can be read as sign ***t̲e̲***. This may be considered likely, since ***a-ta-na-te*** 1 (ZA 10a.2) is clearly attested in a list of personal names on this other tablet from Kato Zakro.

However, if we read ***a-ta-na***(-) instead of ***a-ta-na-*[*t̲e̲*]** OVIS+***si*** 2̱ (ZA 9.4-5), the Hurrian personal name ***Attanna*** may be compared, not in its abbreviated form ***Attan*** as at Tigunāni, but in its fully written form ***Attanna***. The structure of ZA 9 is as follows:

ZA 9.1-2:	]-*nu-ti* , *z̲a̲-*[ ]*ra*	OVIS+*si*	5̱ '[ ]
ZA 9.3-4:	]*p̲a̲-si-ra* [ ]	OVIS+*si*	4̱
ZA 9.4-5:	*a-ta-na-*[*t̲e̲*]	OVIS+*si*	2̱
ZA 9.5:	*p̲u̲$_2$-ma-96*	OVIS^f	2
ZA 9.6:	*wi-ra-re-mi-te*	OVIS^f	1

Th. Richter (*VHN*, 88) analyses ***Attan*** (wr. *at-ta-an*) as {*att=a=n(na)*}, typology 1.1.1.3.3.1, lexicon *att-*, name of 2 *ḫabiru* on *Prisma* II 39 and *Prisma* V 24 at Tigunāni. According to Th. Richter (*VHN*, 386, s.v. ***att-*** {*att-*}) A. Goetze, (1963, 6) was the first to offer evidence for the 'Hurricity' of the verbal root ***att-*** (see Th. Richter, *BGH*, 66, s.v. ***att-*** [Boğ.]). He observed that names with ***att-*** are widely spread, but not very frequent. Names such as *(a)-at-ta-ra/ru* may be based on a noun ***attari*** {*att=a=ri*}. He mentions (*VHN*, 386) the following names: (1) {*att-*}: ***Attaja*** (Mari) [with variant ***Attija***]; ***Attan*** (Tigunāni); ***ᶠAttap-kijaze*** (Ašnakkum); ***ᶠAttap-Na*** (Mari); ***ᶠAttap-Naje*** (Mari, Qaṭṭarā, Šubat-Enlil); ***Attija*** (Mari, Šušarrā); ***Attijān*** (Terqa); [***A***]***ttuja*** (Mari). (2) {*att=a=ri*}: ***Attara*** (Qaṭṭarā, Šubat-Enlil); ***Attaru*** (Šušarrā); (3) {*att=i=zzi*}: ***Attizzi*** (Mari).

In my view the element {*att=a=b-*} in the names ***ᶠAttap-kijaze***, ***ᶠAttap-Na***, ***ᶠAttap-Naje*** clearly shows that ***att-*** is verbal in these names, since ***-b-*** is in Old Hurrian and in archaic or archaizing Hurrian personal names the suffix indicating the subject (3rd person sing.) of the verbal form, for instance, in Old Hurrian ***pašš=i=b*** 'he sends' that would in later Mitanni-Hurrian be ****pašš=i=a***, cf. *pa-aš-ši-a-(ma)*, Mit. IV 55 (present 3rd person sing.); and in Old Hurrian ***un=a=b*** 'he comes' that is in later Mitanni-Hurrian ***un=a=Ø***, cf. I. Wegner, *Einführung*, 126. In view of this evidence one may reasonably infer that Old Hurrian ***ᶠAttap-Na*** {*att=a=b-Na*} and ***ᶠAttap-Naje*** {*att=a=b-Naja/e*} could in Mitanni-Hurrian be ****ᶠAtta-Na*** {*att=a=Ø-Na*} and ****ᶠAtta-Naje*** {*att=a=Ø-Naja/e*}, respectively. The latter names would then also contain the verbal root ***att-***, of which the meaning is unfortunately not yet established.

This might also have consequences for the Pre-Greek theonym ***Ἀθάνᾱ*** and its doublet form ***Ἀθηναίη*** (Attic ***Ἀθηναία***), cf. Hurrian ***-Naia/e*** and ***-Na***. Th. Richter (*BGH*, 66, s.v. ***att-*** [Boğ.]) mentions with hesitation 'to conspire (?)', which is not satisfactory.

Although there are apparently variants attested with single and double writing of the dentals such as ***Ataja / Attaja***, ***Atakku / Attakku***, ***Atija / Attija***, ***Atan / Attan***, and even *a-ta-ia / a-at-ta-a-ia* (Th. Richter, *VHN*, 386, s.v. ***att-***), the verbal roots ***ad-*** and ***att-*** are usually distinguished. To keep on the safe side it is preferable to equate ***Ἀθάνᾱ*** and probably Minoan ***Attana /*Athānā*** only with the Hurrian forms with voiceless dentals. G. Steiner (1978, 184[44]) translates ***ad-*** as 'to protect, guard', cf. Th. Richter, *BGH*, 64. In view of ***adal*** 'strong, the strong one' I should like to propose ***ad-*** (trans.) 'to make strong', (intr.) 'to be strong'. ***Adal*** may contain root-extension ***-al-***. We should not compare the Hurrian month-names ***Attana*** and ***Attanašwe*** with personal names as *a-da-na* at Kaniš, *a-ta-na* at Nuzi (Th. Richter, *VHN*, 390), phonologically ***/adana/***, since single writing of the dentals indicates that they are voiced. The personal name *a-ta-na* seems identical with the toponym *Adana* in south-east Anatolia, cf. also *a-da/ta-(a)-ni*, KUB XXV 44 ii? 5; XXVII 1 ii 31 and 70; XXVII 6 i 31, cf. also P.M. Purves, *NPN*, 207, s.v. *atan*.

This view on ***adana***, already expressed in the 2016 edition of *Minoan Linear A*, Vol. I, is confirmed by Th. Richter, *VHN*, 390, n. 227: "Wegen der konsequenten Einfachschreibung des Dentals kann kaum eine Verbindung mit dem aus Nuzi und Alalaḫ überlieferten MN ***attana / attanašwe*** hergestellt werden, der mit ***atta/attai*** verbunden wird (s. *BGH*, 67)." ["Because of consistent single writing of the dental it is hardly possible to consider a relation with the name of the month ***attana / attanašwe*** attested at Nuzi and Alalaḫ that is connected with ***atta/attai*** (see *BGH*, 66-67)."], cf. E. Laroche, *GLH*, 64, s.v. ***attana***, ***attanašwe***, nom d'un mois à Nuzi et à Alalaḫ, cf. *CAD* A II 510; *AW* 87. The first month at Alalaḫ VII ***attana*** (cf. also ***attannatim*** {*atta(i)=nn(i)=ade*} at Alalaḫ IV), September / October, can be compared with the 7th month at Nuzi ***attanašwe***.

Th. Richter (*BGH*, 67) analyses the name of the month ***Attana*** as {*atta(i)=na*} and translates it as 'The fathers', which is in accordance with ***Attanašwe***, that is analysed as {*attan(i)=n(a)=aš=ve*} by G. Wilhelm (*Das Archiv des Šilwa-Teššup*. Heft 3: *Rationenlisten 2*, Wiesbaden 1985, 84) and as {*atta(i)=na=aš=we*} by J.-P. Vita (Zur Menologie und zum Kalender von Alalaḫ, *AoF 27 (2000)*, 298) that can be translated as '(Month) of the fathers'. Incidentally, this form from Nuzi with the ending ***-na=aš=we*** (consisting of the suffix of the so-called plural definite article ***-na*** + pluralizing suffix ***-aš-*** + the genitive suffix ***-we/-wi***) can also be used to prove that the so-called plural genitive in ***-še / -ši*** (cf. E. Laroche, *GLH*, 26) was actually derived from < ***=(a)š=(w)e/(w)i*** < ***=(a)š=we/wi***.

Although the Hurrian name of the month ***Attana*** at Alalaḫ seems to be explained satisfactorily thanks to comparison with ***attanašwe*** at Nuzi, translation of a personal name or of a theonym ***Attana*** as 'The fathers' does not make sense.

Th. Richter (*VHN*, 88) mentions with regard to ***Attan*** that one may alternatively think of "eine auslautlose Form von ***attani*** 'Vater' (→ ***atta***)" [a form of ***attani*** 'father' without final vowel (→ ***atta***)] or of {*atta(i)=a*[E.]*=n(na)*} 'Er (Junge) ist wie der (verstorbene ?) Vater' ['He (the boy) is like the (deceased ?) father'. [E.] refers to the *essive* case in ***-a***; ***-n(na)*** is then the enclitic personal pronoun 3rd person singular that is the subject 'he' (in the *absolutive* case) of an alleged (intransitive) 'is'.

We have already seen that ***^{f}Atta-Na*** {*att=a-Na*} and ***^{f}Atta-Naje*** {*att=a-Naja/e*} (with single ***-n-***), if compared with ***^{f}Attap-Na*** {*att=a=b-Na*} and ***^{f}Attap-Naje*** {*att=a=b-Naja/e*}, may contain the verbal root ***att-***. To date we have no idea whether there may or may not be an etymological relationship between verbal ***att-*** and nominal ***atta/attai***.

It is, however, conceivable that after loss of the Old Hurrian verbal suffix ***-b-***, the forms ***^{f}Atta-Na*** and ***^{f}Atta-Naja/e*** could easily also be explained on the basis of nominal ***atta/attai***: as {*atta(i)=a*[*essive*]*-Na*} and {*atta(i)=a*[*essive*]*-Naja/e*}, translation '***Nai̯a / Nai̯e*** is like her father'. I am convinced that this analysis explains the real etymology of the Pre-Greek theonym ***Ἀθάνᾱ*** and its doublet form ***Ἀθηναίη*** (Attic ***Ἀθηναία***). The resemblance of the goddess to her father reminds us of her dramatic and spectacular mythological birth. Her father Zeus's severe headache had to be cured by Hephaistos's axe. When the axe cleaved his head, Athena jumped out in full armour. Athena was also her father's darling. The name of ***Ἀθάνᾱ / Ἀθηναία*** (later *Ἀθήνη* with the doublet form *Ἀθηναίη*) in fact tells the myth of her birth in a nutshell. The Minoan-Hurrian etymology of her name may still have been known in Mycenaean times, since the Minoan-Mycenaean religion as well as mythology and iconography had so much in common.

In my view the real *caesura* and serious loss of Minoan-Hurrian traditions probably came only with the end of the Mycenaean era and the arrival of the Dorians in Crete. They came from the north-west of mainland-Greece from areas that had been beyond the sphere of influence of the southern Mycenaean centres, let alone the Minoan civilization. Provenance of the Dorian tribes from the north-west of Greece is not only attested in many ancient Greek sources, but is also proved by the fact that the Doric dialects of the first millennium B.C. resembled the North-West Greek dialects most of all.

We know that in many personal names ***-Na*** is a shortened or hypocoristic form of the theophorous element ***-Nai̯a/-Nai̯e***. This ***-Na*** in Hurrian feminine personal names should not be confused with the frequent suffix ***-na*** of the so-called plural article. P.M. Purves (*NPN*, 236-237, s.v. ***-na***, ***-nai̯a***) already drew attention to this shortened form of ***-nai̯a*** at Nuzi in ***^{f}Aru-na***, ***^{f}Aweš-na*** beside ***^{f}Awiš-nai̯a***, ***^{f}Aze-na***, ***^{f}Minen-na*** beside ***^{f}Minen-nai̯a***, explaining: "Hurrian element apparently found exclusively in feminine personal names. See Speiser in *AASOR XVI (1936)*, p. 75, n. 1, and Oppenheim in *AOF XII (1937-39)*, 36."

P.M. Purves (*NPN*, 237) also offered a list of feminine personal names with the element ***-nai̯a*** at Nuzi: *^{f}Allai-nai̯a, ^{f}Ašmun-nai̯a, ^{f}Aštun-nai̯a* (wr. *^{f}Aš-du-un-na-a-a*) *^{f}Awiš-nai̯a, ^{f}Azun-nai̯a, ^{f}Ḫašun-nai̯a, ^{f}Ḫepet-nai̯a, ^{f}Ḫumer-nai̯a, ^{f}Ilim-nai̯a, ^{f}Imšen-nai̯a, ^{f}Iwin-nai̯a, ^{f}Minen-nai̯a, ^{f}Našmun-nai̯a, ^{f}Nupen-nai̯a, ^{f}Šalḫun-nai̯a, ^{f}Šatum-nai̯a, ^{f}Šeltun-nai̯a, ^{f}Šewir-nai̯a, ^{f}Šinen-nai̯a, ^{f}Šuḫur-nai̯a, ^{f}Šunšun-nai̯a, ^{f}Tatun-nai̯a, ^{f}Teḫeš-nai̯a, ^{f}Teššen-nai̯a, ^{f}Tilun-nai̯a, ^{f}Tulpun-nai̯a, ^{f}Uššen-nai̯a, ^{f}Zilim-nai̯a*.

Th. Richter (*VHN*, 461-462) mentions, s.v. ***Naje*** and ***Na***, that this theonym occurs exclusively in personal names and that it was because of the orthography ***^{o}-na-A-A*** and (rarely) ***^{o}-na-IA*** at Nuzi (*NPN*, 237) mainly read as ***Naja*** in the older literature. However, in several names of women from the Kašijari-area in the Middle-Assyrian period the orthography ***^{o}-na-ie-e*** occurs which is now attested in a wider area and in the Mitanni-period as well. However, variants in space and time cannot be ruled out. ***Naja*** / ***Naje*** and ***Na*** occur mainly in names of women, so it is most likely that we are dealing with a goddess. Th. Richter (*VHN*, 462) offers a long list of names with ***Naje*** and ***Na***:

(1) {*Na*} *ᶠAwiš-Na* (Mari); *ᶠAttap-Na* (Mari); *ᶠIlip-Na* (ŠE); *ᶠElul-Na* (Mari); *ᶠḪazip-Na* (Mari); *ᶠKunuš-Na* (Mari); *ᶠNakaš-Na* (AŠ); *ᶠŠatum-Na* (Mari); *ᶠŠeḫlum-Na* (ŠE); *ᶠŠelwi(?)-Na* (AŠ, Mari); *ᶠŠerwi(?)-Na* (Mari); *ᶠTaḫiz-Na* (Mari); *ᶠTalmeš-Na* (Mari); *ᶠTulup-Na* (Mari); *ᶠTuza-Na* (Mari); *ᶠUniš-Na* (AŠ); *ᶠUnzi-Na* (AŠ); *ᶠUnuš-Na* (Mari). (2) {*Naje*} *ᶠAlla-Naje* (Mari); *ᶠAllum-Naje* (Q); *ᶠAzza-Naje* (Mari); *ᶠAttap-Naje* (Mari, Q, ŠE); *ᶠElip-Naje* (Mari); *ᶠIlip-Naje* (Mari); *ᶠInip-Naje* (Q); *ᶠInnu-Naje* (Mari); *ᶠKanzuš-Naje* (AŠ); *ᶠMaška-Naje* (Mari); *ᶠMemen-Naje* (AŠ); *ᶠNaktum-Naje* (Mari); *ᶠNanip-Naje* (Mari); *ᶠNeniš-Naje* (Mari); *ᶠNupin-Naje* (Mari); *ᶠZazza-Naje* (Mari); *ᶠŠatam-Naje* (Mari); *ᶠŠatum-Naje* ([AŠ], Mari); *ᶠŠatu-Naje* (Mari); *ᶠŠiḫlum-Naje* (Mari); *ᶠŠeḫra-Naje* (Mari); *ᶠŠerum-Naje* (Mari); *ᶠŠunzu-Naje* (AŠ); *ᶠTieš-Naje* (Mari); *ᶠTulup-Naje* (Mari); *ᶠTuza-Naje* (Mari); *ᶠUnuš-Naje* (Mari), and some incomplete names. I have underscored the names with doublets of ***-Na*** and ***-Naja/e***.

In the 2016 edition of *Minoan Linear A* I expressed the view that the month ***Attana*** at Nuzi and Alalaḫ was probably derived from a divine name just as some Roman month-names are derived from Roman theonyms: e.g. (mensis) *Martius* (< Mars), *Iunius* (< Iuno). I also thought that the Pre-Greek theonym *Athena* was probably equivalent to the Hurrian name of the month ***Attana***. If the meaning of the name of the month ***Attana*** at Alalaḫ is, however, 'The fathers', in accordance with ***Attanašwe*** at Nuzi, analysed as {*attan(i)=n(a)=aš=ve*} '(Month) of the fathers', it is less likely that the name of a single goddess is derived from this month-name. But the Hurrian etymology of ***Ἀθάνᾱ*** {*atta(i)=a*[*essive*]*-Na*} / ***Ἀθηναίη*** {*atta(i)=a*[*essive*]*-Naja/e*}, translation '***Naja / Naje*** is like her father' is very convincing, in view of the doublets of these Pre-Greek theonyms and of the doublets in Hurrian onomastics. Since the theonym was in alphabetic Greek written with *theta* (***θ***), the Hurrian voiceless dental may have sounded as a voiceless dental with aspiration **[t^h]** in Greek ears. Since ***Ἀθάνᾱ*** and ***Ἀθηναίη*** are written with single ***-ν-*** (***-n-***) in the Greek alphabetic script, I think that the name of the Hurrian goddess ***Naja/e / Na*** is preserved in Mycenaean and later Greek ***Ἀθάνᾱ*** / ***Ἀθηναίη***, not the enclitic personal pronoun (3rd person singular) ***-nna*** with double ***-nn-***. This mean that the theonym should not be interpreted as the personal name {*atta(i)=a*[E.]*=nna*} '*She* [***-nna***] is like her father', but as ***Ἀθάνᾱ*** {*atta(i)=a*[*essive*]*-Na*} / ***Ἀθηναίη*** {*atta(i)=a*[*essive*]*-Naja/e*}, translation '***Naja / Naje*** is like her father'. The theonym ***Ἀθάνᾱ*** is attested in Linear B ***a-ta-na-po-ti-ni-ja*** (KN V 52+52bis+[X] 8285 Olivier), dative ***Ἀθάνᾳ Ποτνίᾳ*** '(for) the Mistress *Athena*' that may be compared with ***da-pu₂-ri-to-jo po-ti-ni-ja*** (KN Gg 702,2), ***δαβυρίνθοιο Ποτνίᾳ*** 'for the Mistress of the labyrinth'. If the hypothesis that these deities are the same is correct, the goddess *Ἀθάνᾱ* was the deity protecting the labyrinth. Compare also my Hurrian etymologies for the names *Ariadna* and *Theseus*.

Linear A ***da-i-pi-ta*** (ZA 8.5; ZA 10a.4-5) is a Hurrian name occurring on two tablets from Kato Zakro. In the first line of tablet ZA 8 ideogram FIC 'fig' is mentioned. The personal names in the list of names are followed by numbers and signs of fractions, probably indicating the portions of figs attributed to each person. The first sign of ZA 8.4 can in principle be read as ***pa***, but is more likely to be identified with fraction sign A that can be joined with the following fraction sign J, as indicated in the analysed structure of the text in *Minoan Linear A*, Vol. II, *Corpus of transliterated Linear A texts*, Part II, 426.

The easiest approach is to assume that it consists of the Hurrian onomastic element ***tai-/dai-*** followed by the Hurrian element ***-pi-ta***.

P.M. Purves (*NPN*, 260-263, s.v. ***tae***, ***tai*** and ***tau***, see also his note on ***taḫ***) assumed that these elements are probably basically the same or at least cognate. Th. Richter (*BGH*, 426-427), s.v. ***taḫe***, ***ta'e***, does not include ***tau*** in these equations. It is more likely that ***tau-*** can be connected with ***taw-/tab-*** 'to cast (metal)'. So I omit the names with ***tau-***.

At Nuzi occur: *Ta-e, Ta-a-e, Ta-i, Ta-e-na, Ta-i-na, Da-e-na, A-kap-ta-e, A-ka-áp-ta-e, A-ga-ap-ta-e, A-ka-ap-ta-e, A-lu-uš-ta-e, A-ar-ta-e, Ar-ta-e, Ar-ta-a-e, A-ar-da-e, A-da-an-da-e* (possibly scribal error for *Aran-tai,* since a man of each name is father of *Puttu*), *A-wi-iš-ta-e, E-ni-iš-ta-e, E-ni-iš-da-e, I-ni-iš-ta-a-e, Ḫa-wu-*[u]*r-ta-e, Ge-wi-ta-e, Kip-ta-e, Ki-ip-ta-e, Pa-i-ta-e, Pu-i-ta-e, Pu-i-da-e, Pu-i-ta-i, Pu-e-ta-e, Ša-aš-ta-e, Ša-du-ta-e, Ša-tu-ta-e, Ta-mar-ta-e, Ú-na-ap-ta-e, Ú-nap-ta-e, Ú-náp-ta-e, Ú-na-áp-ta-e, Ut-ḫap-ta-e, Ut-ḫa-ap-ta-e, Ut-ḫap-da-e, Wa-aḫ-ra-ta-e, Wa-aḫ-ri-ta-e, Ta-i-ni-ir-še, Ta-i-še-en-ni, Ta-i-še-ni, Da-i-še-en-ni, Ta-a-i-še-en-ni, Da-i-še-ni, Ta-i-te-šup, Ta-i-te-a, Ta-i-til-la, Ta-i-ú-ki, Ta-a-a, Da-a-a, Ta-a-ia, Ta-i-qa, Ta-i-ka, Ta-i-qa-a-a, Ta-i-ku, Ta-i-ma, Ta-a-i-ni, Ta-i-zi, Ta-i-zu* (cf. for the complete list: P.M. Purves, *NPN*, 260-263, s.v. *tae, tai, tau*; cf. I.J. Gelb, *NPN*, 141-145, 150-151).

A single Hurrian dental in intervocalic position indicates voicing of ***/d/*** (cf. e.g. *Pa-i-ta-e, Pu-i-ta-e, Pu-i-da-e, Pu-i-ta-i, Pu-e-ta-e, Ša-du-ta-e*). There is no evidence for an alleged voicelessness of all initial dentals in the Hurrian dialect of Minoan Crete. If the equations with the Linear A forms are correct, initial ***d-*** in Linear A confirms this view. It is anyway difficult to explain, how a single intervocalic dental is considered voiced, whereas the same dental belonging to the same element would become voiceless in initial position.

E. Laroche (*GLH*, 252) calls ***dai*** 'nom de sens inconnue, parfois précédé du dét. divin' ['noun of unknown meaning, sometimes preceded by the divine determinative'] (*CTH* 628, kiz. = Kizzuwatnian dialect). He mentions: *da-a-e*, KUB XXV 42 II 18, IV 5 =XXXII 64+, 12; KBo VIII 137, 7. - *da-i-e*, KUB XLVII 40, 10.
da-a-e-ya, KUB XXVII 8 II 2; 21, 2. - ^{d}*da-a-ya*, KUB XXVII 1 II 60.
da-a-i-ni, KUB XXVII 10 V 5. - *da-in-ni-ya-a*, KUB XII 12 VI 1; cf. XXVII 10 V 10.
da-a-ya-a-na-a, KBo VIII 143, 15. - ^{d}*da-i-ú-ḫi-ni-ša*, KUB XL 102 II 14.

According to Th. Richter (*BGH*, 425) ***daea*** [Boğ.] is called 'Kultgegenstand' ['cultic object'] by M. Popko, *Kultobjekte in der hethitischen Religion (nach keilschriftlichen Quellen)*, Warsaw 1978, 26 [*daeja*], by B.H.L. van Gessel, *Onomasticon of the Hittite pantheon Part III (Handbuch der Orientalistik / Handbook of Oriental Studies I/33.3*, Leiden 2001, 218 [*daje*] and by I. Wegner, *Hurritische Opferlisten aus hethitischen Festbeschreibungen, Teil III: Das Glossar*, Corpus der hurritischen Sprachdenkmäler. I. Abteilung: Die Texte aus Boğazköy (= ChS I/3-3), Rome 2004, 63. For *daei̯a (az)zalli* as Ḫebat's 'divine attribute', see B.H.L. van Gessel, *Onomasticon of the Hittite pantheon Part II (HdO I/33.2)*, Leiden 1998, 1066.

Th. Richter (*VHN*, 525) mentions s.v. ***Taja*** (GN) that the element *-ta-(a-)ia* is certainly identical with the theonym ***Dāja***, sometimes ***dai***, listed by E. Laroche, *GLH*, 252.

The context (KUB 27, 1 = ChS I/3-1, 1 Vs. II 60 and 47, 64 + IBoT 2, 50 = Rs. III 10') consists of descriptions of festivities dedicated to the cult of *Ša(w)uška* of the area of the town *Šamuḫa* (cf. I. Wegner, *Hurritische Opferlisten aus hethitischen Festbeschreib-ungen, Teil I: Texte für Ištar-Ša(w)uška*, Corpus der hurritischen Sprachdenkmäler. I. Abteilung: Die Texte aus Boğazköy (= ChS I/3-1), Rome 1995, 11).

Other names with the theophorous element ***-taia*** are SUM-*ta-ia* at Ugarit (cf. F. Gröndahl, *Die Personennamen der Texte aus Ugarit*, Rome 1967, 258) and possibly *ᶠḪa-bur-ta(?)-ia* at Kār-Tukultī-Ninurta (modern Tulūl ᶜAqīr), cf. H. Freydank - M. Salvini, 'Zu den hurritischen Personennamen aus Kār-Tukultī-Ninurta', *Studi micenei ed egeo-anatolici 24 (1984)*, 50. According to Th. Richter (*VHN*, 525, n. 758) it is conceivable that some personal names at Nuzi with an element ***tai*** or ***-taia*** (P.M. Purves, *NPN*, 261) also belong to this element.

Th. Richter (*VHN*, 523-524) mentions that on the basis of equations with Sumerian and Sumerogram LÚ(*-an*) and Akkadian ***amīlu*** in vocabularies the meaning 'man' is certain for ***taḫe / taḫḫe*** {*taǵ/ḫhe*}, ***ta(')e***, and that a verbally used root has not yet been recognized to date, cf. also Th. Richter, *BGH*, 426-427, s.v. ***taḫe***, ***ta'e*** [*passim*]. He mentions (*VHN*, 523, n. 753) that G. Wilhelm, The Hurrian version [of *The instructions of Šuruppak*], in: B. Alster, *Wisdom of ancient Sumer*, Bethesda 2005, 205[+10], suspects an older form ***taḫa*** (*a*-stem). Cautiously he does not mention the element ***tau*** as equivalent to ***ta(')e*** as P.M. Purves (*NPN*, 261-262) did, but he mentions (*BGH*, 427) that Hurrian ***taḫe***, ***ta'e*** corresponds with Urartian ***ta-ú*** and ***ta***.

Thanks to Th. Richter (*VHN*, 486, s.v. ***pitt-***), the following Hurrian onomastics with the probably verbal root ***pitt-***, possibly 'to help', can now be added: ***ᶠPittakku*** (wr. *bi-it-ta-ku*) from Mari, and ***Pittun*** (wr. *bi-it-tu-un*) from Šušarrā (Tall Shemshara), see *l.c.* 234, s.v. ***ᶠPittakku*** (wr. *bi-it-ta-ku*), analysis {*pitt=a=kko*}, typology 1.2.3; *ibid.* 234-235, s.v. ***Pittun*** (wr. *bi-it-tu-un*), analysis {*pitt=o=n(na)*}, typology 1.2.3; *ibid.* 486 s.v. ***pitt-*** 'helfen' ['to help']; cf. Th. Richter, *BGH*, 319, s.v. ***pitt-*** [Boğ.], 'Frieden machen' ['to make peace'], 'friedlich sein' ['to be peaceful'], 'helfen' ['to help']). Incidentally, Th. Richter does not accept J.-M. Durand's consideration (*Le culte d'Addu d'Alep et l'affaire d'Alahtum*, Florilegium Marianum 7, Paris 2002, 94, note 255) that the names ***ᶠPittakku*** and ***Pittun*** might be connected with Amorite ***bint/bitt*** 'daughter'. In my view forms like ***pitt=ugar-*** [Boğ.], 'Frieden machen, gedeihen' ['to make peace, to thrive, to prosper'], analysis {*pitt=uk=ar-*}, and ***pittummi*** [Tušratta letter], analysis {*pitt=ummi*}, definitely prove that the verbal root ***pitt-*** is genuinely Hurrian, cf. Th. Richter, *BGH*, 319.

Since the Hurrian name ***ᶠPittakku*** from Mari provides the closest link with the Pre-Greek name ***Πιττακός*** (***Pittakos***) and with Linear B ***pi-ta-ke-u***, probably ****Πιττακεύς***, (see *sub voce*), I now consider an ultimate derivation of ***Πιττακός*** and ***pi-ta-ke-u*** from names containing the Hurrian verbal root ***pitt-*** more likely than previously alleged derivations from either Luwian or Thracian roots. This means that the name ***Πιττακός*** may originally not only be Pre-Greek, but also Pre-Thracian, although it is attested as Thracian: ***Πιττακός*** as a king of the Thracian Edones. Thucydides, IV, 107, 3: *Πιττακοῦ τοῦ Ἠδώνων βασιλέως ἀποθανόντος ὑπὸ τῶν Γοάξιος παίδων καὶ Βραυροῦς τῆς γυναικὸς αὐτοῦ.*

Πιττακός, the famous ***αἰσυμνήτης*** from Mytilènè on Lesbos is already mentioned by Herodotus, I, 27. Suidas also provides interesting information: *Πιττακὸς Μυτιληναῖος, υἱὸς Καϊκοῦ ἢ Ὑρραδίου Θρᾳκός, μητρὸς δὲ Λεσβίας; Ὕρρα παῖς· ὁ Πιττακός, καὶ Ὑρράδιος ὄνομα.* Cf. also Linear A ***pi-ta-ja*** (HT 6a.2), which contains the root ***pitt-*** and a probably hypocoristic suffix ***-ya***; Linear A ***pi-ta-ka-se*** (HT 21a.1), ***pi-ta-ke-si*** (HT 87.2); Linear A ***pi-te-za*** (PK Za 11b) and ***pi-ti-sa*** (HT 31.1). But compare also Hurrian ***ᶠPetteza*** (wr. *ᶠBe-et-te-ez-a*) at Nuzi.

Analysis and meaning I: If we choose to divide Linear A ***da-i-pi-ta*** into the Hurrian nominal element ***tai-/dai- = tae-/dae = taḫe/taḫḫe*** 'man' and the Hurrian verbal element ***-pitt=a***, (root ***pitt-*** + marker of intransitivity ***-a***), the meaning of ***da-i-pi-ta*** might be 'The man is peaceful' or 'Be peaceful, oh man !'. If a personal name consists of a verbal and a nominal element, the verbal element is usually the first and the nominal the second. But occasionally the order can be reverse.

Analysis and meaning II: Th. Richter (*BGH*, 425, s.v. ***taḫ-*** [PN]; *VHN*, 523, s.v. ***taḫ-*** {*taġ-*} mentions the form ***taḫ=aš=i=b*** [Boğ.], (wr. *ta-ḫa-ši-i-ib*), KBo 32.12 I 5, see also E. Neu, *Das hurritische Epos der Freilassung. I: Untersuchungen zu einem hurritisch-hethitischen Textensemble aus Ḫattuša* (Studien zu den Boğazköy Texten 32), Wiesbaden 1996, 62f.; E. Neu, Skizze einer Beschreibung der Wurzelstruktur hurritischer Nomina und Verben. Ein Näherungsversuch, in: B. Igla - Th Stolz (eds.), *"Was ich noch sagen wollte". A multilingual Festschrift für Norbert Boretzky on occasion of his 65th birthday* (Studia typologica - Beihefte: Sprachtypologie und Universalienforschung 2), Berlin 2001, 93. This form can only be interpreted as a verbal form (probably used as a personal name) consisting of the root ***taḫ-*** + intensifying root-extension ***-aš-*** + transitivity-marker ***-i-*** + the Old Hurrian subject-marker 3rd person singular ***-b***. Compare for the intensifying root-extension ***-aš-*** I. Wegner, *Einführung*, 88. The meaning of the verbal root ***taḫ-*** is not yet clear. Perhaps ***taḫapše*** 'felt' and ***taḫapšuḫuli*** 'felt-maker' may be connected, so that an activity with regard to the fabrication of textiles may be likely. Th. Richter (*VHN*, 523) thinks that a connection with ***taḫe*** 'man' is less likely. He mentions the following personal names built on the verbal root ***taḫ-***: ***Taḫil*** (Tuttul); ***ᶠTaḫiz-Na*** (Mari); ***Taḫuk*** (Mari); ***Taḫuš*** (Mari).

Th. Richter's view that the verbal root ***taḫ-*** probably has nothing to do with ***taḫe*** 'man' may be crucial, because it will in that case also be less easy to connect the nominal root ***tai-/dai-***, ***tae-/dae-*** or ***ta'e/ da'e*** with a verbal root ***tai-/dai-***, ***tae-/dae-***. Nevertheless it seems possible that verbal forms can be observed in ***da-in-***[...] at Boğazköy (without translation), cf. I. Wegner, *Hurritische Opferlisten aus hethitischen Festbeschreibungen, Teil III: Das Glossar*, Corpus der hurritischen Sprachdenkmäler I: Die Texte aus Boğazköy (= ChS I/3-3), Rome 2004, 63, as well as in ***da-i-bu-un-ni*** KUB XLV 53 III 9 (without translation), cf. E. Laroche, *GLH*, 247, s.v. ***tabuna-***; lexical term in rituals of the *Ḫišuwa*-festival, cf. J. Tischler, *Hethitisches etymologisches Glossar*, Teil III, Lieferung 8, (Innsbrucker Beiträge zur Sprachwissenschaft = IBS 20), Innsbruck 1991, 28; cf. J. Tischler, *Hethitisches Handwörterbuch. Mit dem Wortschatz der Nachbarsprachen* (IBS 102), Innsbruck 2001, 159; see B.H.L. van Gessel, *Onomasticon of the Hittite pantheon Part III (Handbuch der Orientalistik / Handbook of Oriental Studies I/33.3)*, Leiden 2001, 218. See Th. Richter, *BGH*, 425, s.v. ***da-in-***[...] [Boğ.] and s.v. ***taibunna/i*** [Boğ.].

It is wise to take the context of Linear A sequences into account. Linear A ***da-i-pi-ta*** (ZA 8.5) is not the only personal name ending in ***-ta***, that would in cuneiform be rendered as ***-tta*** (with voiceless dental). Linear A ***a-we-||ni-ta*** (ZA 8.2-3) can probably be analysed as {*aw(=i)=en=i=tta*}, consisting of the root ***aw-*** + *jussive* indicator ***-i-*** that probably amalgamated with following ***-en-*** (cf. I. Wegner, *Einführung*, 103ff.) + marker of the *jussive* 3rd person singular ***-en-*** (according to Wegner, *ibid.*) + thematic vowel ***-i-*** + suffix of the enclitic personal pronoun 1st person singular ***-tta*** 'me'. Note that I. Wegner uses the term *jussive*, whereas e.g. E. Laroche (*GLH*, 28) used the terms 'potentiel' ['subjunctive expressing possibility'] and 'optatif' ['optative'] for the suffix ***-en-*** indicating the 3rd person singular of that mood. The translation of Linear A ***a-we-||ni-ta*** (ZA 8.2-3) will then be 'May he/she (a *numen*) save me'. A good parallel, though without the suffix ***-en-***, is a personal name from Ḫattuša ***fḪanijatta*** (wr. *fḫa-ni-ia-at-ta*), analysis {*ḫan=i=a=tta*} 'She gave birth to me', cf. e.g. Th. Richter, *VHN*, 586, where he explains that the enclitic personal pronoun 1st person singular ***-tta*** represents the object (in the absolutive case) of transitive {*ḫan=i=a-*} 'She gives/gave birth'.

It is probably not accidental that ***a-we-||ni-ta*** (ZA 8.2-3), ***ta-i-nu-ma*** (ZA 8.3) and ***da-i-pi-ta*** (ZA 8.5) occur on one and the same Linear A tablet from Kato Zakro. The scribe may well have been conscious of the fact that he inscribed three Hurrian personal names containing transitive verbal forms and the suffix of the enclitic personal pronoun 1st person singular ***-tta*** and of the 2nd person singular ***-mma*** 'you', taking the 9th position in I. Wegner's chain of suffixes of the indicative, transitive-ergative, positive verb (see I. Wegner, *Einführung*, 93, Tabelle 4). The Linear A personal name ***da-i-pi-ta*** (ZA 8.5) can probably be analysed as {*da(i)=i=b=i=tta*} and can be compared with cuneiform ***da-i-bu-un-ni*** KUB XLV 53 III 9, since both forms share {*da(i)=i=b-*} with the Old Hurrian subject-marker of the 3rd person sing. ***-b***, cf. e.g. the personal name ***Arip-atal***, analysis {*ar=i=b-adal*} 'The strong one (*adal*) gives/gave (the boy)', cf. Th. Richter, *VHN*, 579.

Comparing ***da-i-pi-ta*** {*da(i)=i=b=i=tta*} with other Linear A personal names such as ***da-du-te***, ***da-du-ma-ta***, ***da-ku-se-ne*** and ***da-ku-na***, it is worth noting that voicing of initial dental stops occurs in particular when the following intervocalic occlusive is also voiced, at least in the Hurrian dialect of Minoan Crete and perhaps also elsewhere, except in thirteenth-century Ugarit as can be inferred from the evidence provided by alphabetic cuneiform texts at Ugarit. It might be a matter of pattern, cf. the orthography of *Da-(a)-du-ḫe-pa*, *Du-ú-du-ḫe-pa* and *Da-a-ku-u-ya* = */Dagu-ya/* at Boğazköy. This observation may be confirmed by Linear A ***ta-i-nu-ma*** (ZA 8.3) that probably contains the same root ***tai-/dai-*** as ***da-i-pi-ta***, but has a voiceless initial dental, since it is not followed by an intervocalic voiced occlusive. In Hurrian syllabic cuneiform the quality of voiced or voiceless initial consonants is anyway difficult to establish, because they miss in *initial* position the support of double writing which they have in *medial* position to indicate voicelessness.

Since the meaning of the verbal root ***tai-/dai-*** is not yet clear, we can only analyse the structure of the personal name ***da-i-pi-ta*** and offer an approximate translation: 'He/She (the *numen*) … (verbal form in indicative) me'. If we assume that the verbal root ***dai-*** is related to nominal ***dae/tae = daḫe/taḫe/taḫḫe*** 'man', it is plausible that the *transitive* stem means 'to make a man' and the *intransitive* stem 'to be a man'.

Linear A ***da-i-pi-ta*** (ZA 8.5; ZA 10a.4-5), analysis *{da(i)=i=b=i=tta}*, consisting of verbal root ***dai-*** + marker of transitivity ***-i-*** + Old Hurrian subject-marker of the 3rd person sing. ***-b*** + the enclitic personal pronoun 1st person sing. ***-tta***, can then be translated as 'He/She (a *numen*) made me a man'. Cf. Linear A ***da-qe-ra , qe-pi-ta*** (HT 6a.6), which I analyse as ***daḫe=ra Ḫepitta*** < ****Ḫepit-wa*** (assimilation) 'with a man for Ḫebat/Ḫebit'.

Ta-i-nu-ma (ZA 8.3) may theoretically consist of the Hurrian personal name **tain(n)u* (cf. *Ta-e-na*, *Ta-i-na*, *Da-e-na*, 15 persons at Nuzi, cf. I.J. Gelb, *NPN*, 141-142) with the enclitic conjunction ***-ma*** 'and' (cf. E. Laroche, *GLH*, 163, s.v. ***-ma*** 'et'. Conjonction enclitique. Mari, Boğazköy, Msk. ***-ma*** et ***-m***; Ug. alph. ***-m.***). But since three entries follow ***ta-i-nu-ma*** without this so-called enclitic conjunction ***-ma***, this solution is less likely.

Moreover, since ***a-we-||ni-ta*** (ZA 8.2-3) and ***da-i-pi-ta*** (ZA 8.5) on the same tablet show the same structure with the enclitic personal pronoun 1st person singular ***-tta*** 'me', it appears more likely that Linear A ***-ma*** in ***Ta-i-nu-ma*** represents the enclitic personal pronoun of the 2nd person singular ***-mma*** 'you'. ***Ta(i)=i=(e)n=u=mma*** contains the verbal root ***tai-*** + *jussive* marker ***-i-*** + marker of the *jussive* 3rd person singular ***-en-*** + thematic vowel ***-u-*** + ***-mma*** 'you', 'May he/she (a *numen*) make you a man', cf. I. Wegner, *Einführung*, 103, Tabelle 9: *Die Suffixfolge beim positiven Jussiv*.

It is attractive to compare Linear A ***ta-i-65*** (HT 9a.4-5; HT 39.1) and ***ta-i̯-65*** (HT 9b.4) from Hagia Triada. It is probably a personal name containing the frequent Hurrian onomastic element ***tai-***, cf. P.M. Purves, *NPN*, 261, s.v. ***tai*** (cf. perhaps *tae*). The value of Linear A sign ***65*** is to date unknown, but it seems that ***zu*** or ***zi*** may be a good candidate. Both values are missing in the grid of Linear A phonetic values. ***Taizi*** (wr. *Ta-i-zi*), son of *Na-an-te-e-a* (JEN 102: 48) and ***Taizu*** (wr. *Ta-i-zu*), *manzattuḫlu*, son of *A-ta-a-a* (HSS IX 12:30) are both attested as Hurrian personal names at Nuzi (cf. I.J. Gelb, *NPN*, 145; P.M. Purves, *NPN*, 277, 279).

Since ***tae/i*** and ***taḫe*** as well as ***dae/i*** and ***daḫe*** are related, it seems justifiable to equate ***Taizi*** with Hurrian ***taḫuzzi*** *{taġ(e)=o/u=zzi}* 'einem Mann angemessen' ['suitable for a man'], cf. the opposite ***aštuzzi*** 'einer Frau angemessen' ['suitable for a woman'], cf. Th. Richter, *VHN*, 524. ***Taizu*** (with Akkadianizing *nominative* in ***-u***) would have the same meaning as ***Taizi***. If ***ta-i-65*** can be identified with Hurrian ***ta-i-zu*** at Nuzi, then the value of sign ***65*** can be confirmed as ***zu***. If not, Hurrian *ta-i-zu* and *ta-i-zi* have equal chances of providing the correct interpretation and the question is still open whether Linear A sign ***65*** is ***zu*** or ***zi***. If ***te-65*** (ZA 20.3) on a tablet from Kato Zakro is ***te-zu*** (?) and if ***te-zu*** is *Tešub*, of which the final consonant is in accordance with the orthographic conventions of Linear A and B not expressed in the script, then we would have a confirmatory match, especially since ***ku-ra*** (ZA 20.4) following ***te-zu*** (ZA 20.3) on the same tablet can be identified with ***Ḫurra***, attested as ***dḪu-ur-ra*** at Meskene-Emar (Msk.): the unpublished tablets of the Museum of Aleppo. It is also attested as ***dḪu-u-ur-ra*** at Boğazköy (KBo I 1 rev. 41) in a treaty between Mattiwaza and Šuppiluliuma I.

Linear A ***a-re-da-i*** 2 (HT 29.5) from Hagia Triada is an example of a personal name with the Hurrian element ***-dai***. The sequence belongs to a list of personal names, all followed by a number. It can be identified as a Hurrian sentence name consisting of the verbal element ***ar-***, ***are-***, ***ari-*** and the Hurrian nominal onomastic element ***-dae/-dai***.

P.M. Purves, *NPN*, 202-203, s.v. ***ar-***, ***are-***, ***ari-***, ***aran-***. The Hurrian verbal root ***ar-*** was translated by L. Messerschmidt, *Mitanni-Studien,* 18 f. and 123, as 'give'. This view was supported by Urartian ***aru*** 'give', recognized by J. Friedrich, *Einführung ins Urartäische, Mitteilungen der Vorderasiatisch-Ägyptischen Gesellschaft 37.3 (1933)*, Leipzig 1933, 51. The root is very frequent in Hurrian sentence names such as *Ar-te-šup, A-ri-te-šup, A-ri-mu-še*. ***Arinnu*** (I.J. Gelb, *NPN*, 28), {*ar=i=nnu*}, consists of verbal root ***ar-*** 'to give' + marker of transitivity ***-i-*** + *optional allomorphic* enclitic personal pronoun 3rd pers. sing. ***-nnu*** instead of ***-nna*** 'Give him (the boy) (oh *numen*) !'. The name ***Aran-tai*** would now be analysed as {*ar=an-dai*}, consisting of the verbal root ***ar-*** + root-extension ***-an-*** + the nominal element ***dae/i***. According to I. Wegner (*Einführung*, 88) the root-extension ***-an(n)-*** expresses a *causative* aspect and possibly other aspects as well. She translates ***ar=ann-*** as 'sich geben lassen' ['to let give oneself'], from ***ar-*** 'geben' ['to give']. As a result ***Aran-tai*** {*ar=an-dae/i*} would mean 'Let the man give himself !'.

Ar-tae can be analysed as an *athematic imperative* {*ar=(e/i)-dae/i*}, with *syncope* of the suffix ***-e-/-i-*** marking the transitive imperative, 'Give a man !'. The Linear A personal name ***a-re-da-i*** (HT 29.5), {*ar=e/i-dae/i*}, is the regular *thematic* form without syncope of the suffix ***-e-/-i-*** marking the 2nd person singular *jussive* or *imperative* of the transitive verb ***ar-*** + the object ***dai*** (*absolutive* case) and can be translated as 'Give a man !'. The name can be explained as a wish expressed by the parents that a son will be born.

E. Laroche, *GLH*, 52-53, s.v. ***taḫe*** 'homme' ['man']: sg. nom. e.g. *da-aḫ-e* = Hitt. LÚ-*an*, KBo XIX 145 IV 43; KUB XLV 60,3, etc. Most interesting is the proverbial expression (with two dative forms in ***-pa***) ***ašti da-a-ḫi-pa da-a-ḫi-it*** ! ***ašti-pa*** 'the woman for the man, the man for the woman' KBo XX 129+ II 67. According to Th. Richter (*VHN*, 523-524) ***taḫe/i*** {*taġe/i*}, ***taḫḫe/i*** {*taḫḫe/i*}, ***tae/i*** {*tae/i*} or {*ta'e/i*} belong together. The meaning 'man' is confirmed by vocabulary comparison with Sumerian LÚ and Akkadian ***amīlu***. The meaning 'husband', proposed by some scholars, is less likely in names.

Compare also Linear A ***da-qe-ra , qe-pi-ta*** (HT 6a.6) 'with a man for Ḫebat / Ḫebit '; ***da-qe-ra*** may be interpreted as Hurrian ***d/taḫe*** 'man' with the Hurrian comitative suffix ***-ra***. He may be a 'man' taking part in Ḫebat's cult. I have interpreted Linear A ***qe-pi-ta*** as Hurrian dative ****Ḫebitta*** < ****Ḫebit-wa*** that can be compared with the attested genitive ***Ḫebatti*** < ***Ḫebat-wi***: ^{d}*Ḫé-pa-at-ti*, KBo XIX 129 Ro 33, etc. (< the unassimilated form * ^{d}*Ḫé-pa-at-wi*, cf. [^{d}*Ḫé*]*-bat-wi$_{i}$* KUB XXVII 4. 5), cf. E.A. Speiser, *IH*, 63, § 82, and E. Laroche, *GLH*, 100-101. Cf. Linear A ***da-96 = da-ḫi*** (PH 3b.1) 'man' from Phaistos.

Linear A ***a-ma-ta*** 2[(HT 29.1) occurs on a palimpsest tablet from Hagia Triada. Surprisingly the first sign has been misread by all editors as ***ru-*** instead of ***a-***, although the *ductus* is very similar to that of the first sign of ***a-re-da-i*** (HT 29.4).

Since publication of Th. Richter, *VHN*, 2016, especially pages 584-587, section 1.1.2: *Namen mit Verbalformen des Mittani-Paradigmas*, it is clear that, beside the so-called 'Old Hurrian' personal names, there is also a category of names consisting of verbal forms known from the Tušratta letter. Linear A ***a-ma-ta***, followed by a number (2 or more) is the first of a list of personal names. It can be analysed as Hurrian {*amm=a=tta*} 'I come, arrive'. It consists of the verbal root ***amm-*** 'to arrive' + *intr.* theme-vowel ***-a-*** + the enclitic personal pronoun 1st person singular ***-tta***.

It can be compared with the *intransitive* (synonym) verbal form ***unatta*** {*un=a=tta*} 'I come, arrive', consisting of verbal root ***un-*** 'to come' + intr. theme-vowel ***-a-*** + enclitic personal pronoun 1st person singular ***-tta***, cf. I. Wegner, *Einführung*, 97. In this intransitive formation the *absolutive* enclitic personal pronoun ***-tta*** has the function of subject and indicates the bearer of the name. There are, however, also names showing a transitive formation, in which the absolutive enclitic personal pronoun ***-tta*** is the object: e.g. a name from Ḫattuša *f**Ḫanijatta*** (wr. *ḫa-ni-ia-at-ta*), analysis {*ḫan=i=a=tta*} 'Sie zeugt / gebiert mich' ['She bears me, gives birth to me'], cf. Th. Richter, *VHN*, 586. Here the personal pronoun ***-tta*** indicates the bearer of the name; the subject of ***ḫan=i=a-*** is the mother. Incidentally, it is likely that the toponym Khaniá (***Χανιά***) may etymologically be derived from Hurrian ***ḫan=i=a*** 'She gives birth'. The name might actually date from the foundation of the Minoan palace, partially excavated underneath the city: 'He/She (a deity) gives birth to / creates (the palace)'.

Linear A ***a-ma*** (ZA 7b.1) from Kato Zakro can be identified with the Hurrian personal name ***Amma*** (wr. *fAm-ma*), the name of a lady from Nuzi. There are two options: the name contains (I) a nominal or (II) a verbal root. Since Linear A ***a-ma*** (HS Zg 1.2) on a schist plaque from Hagios Stephanos (Lakonia) is the only entry, it can be either a verbal form in context ***amm=a***, *intransitive indicative* 3rd person singular 'he/she arrives' or the *imperative* 'arrive !' or a 'one-word' personal name with the same meaning.

(I) It seems possible to isolate a nominal *a*-stem ***amma°*** from the Hurrian collective term ***ammade*** and from Linear A ***a-ma-wa-si*** (KT Zf 1) first sequence on a gold pin from Crete, that may contain the same ***a***-stem ***amma°*** as occurs in ***ammade*** {*amm(a)=ade*}, that is translated as 'Großvater, Vorfahr', 'ancestor, forefather' by Th. Richter (*BGH*, 25) and 'Großvater' ['grandfather'] by I. Wegner (*Einführung*, 53, 247), comparable with ***attarde*** {*atta(i)=arde*} 'Vorväter, Vorfahren' ['ancestors'] that has more or less the same meaning, cf. I. Wegner, *Einführung*, 58, 251. E. Laroche, *GLH*, 47, s.v. ***ammati*** [***/ammadi/***] 'grand-père, aïeul, ancêtre' = sum. LIBIR, akk. ***labîru***: Messerschmidt, *Mit. St.* 6; Von Brandenstein, *ZA 46*, 110 sq.; Friedrich, *Beiträge* 49; Laroche, *Anat. St. Güterbock* 182. "La fille de mon *ammati*, la sœur de mon père." (Mit. III 37).

Not without significance Hurrian ***attarde*** 'ancestor, forefather' is attested as ***a-ta-de*** (KT Zf 1) at the end of the same inscription that starts with ***a-ma-wa-si*** (KT Zf 1).

According to I. Wegner (*Einführung*, 52) the category of words with an ***a***-stem seems to be limited to terms indicating congeniality or kinship such as: ***šala*** 'daughter', ***šena*** 'brother', ***ela*** 'sister', ***nera*** 'mother', ***mena*** 'twin(?)' or 'sister(?)' (Th. Richter).

According to I. Wegner (*Einführung*, 53) the suffix ***-ade*** in ***ammade*** forms in some cases collectives such as ***amm=ade*** 'Großvater' ['grandfather'], ***wir=ade*** */firade/* (e.g. *fir=ade=na=ân*, plural absolutive + connective) 'auswärtiger Gast' ['foreign guest'] (meaning according to G. Wilhelm, *SCCNH 15*, 2005, 175 ff.), ***ḫur=ade*** 'Krieger' ['warrior, soldier'], ***er=ade*** 'Vogel' ['bird']. The suffix often appears in numerals such as ***tumn(i)=ade*** 'je vier' ['four at a time'] or designations of measures such as ***parizz=ade*** '*parīsu*-measure' (derived from Akkadian *parīsu*). Incidentally, the monosyllybic term ***pa*** that often appears in Linear A texts, especially in ligature with the frequent ideogram GRA+***pa***, might well be an abbreviation of ***parizi*** (= a bushel, a measure, especially of grain = ca. 36,5 litres = ½ Kor) or of ***parizz=ade*** '*parīsu*-measure'.

Linear A ***a-ma-wa-si*** (KT Zf 1) may be interpreted as ****amma=wwâš=(w)i*** < ****amma=(i)wwâš=wi*** < ****amma=iwwa=aš=wi*** 'of our ****amma***'.

The form can be analysed as: ****amma-*** (stem) + ***-iwwa-*** (suffix of the 1st person singular of the possessive pronoun) + ***-aš-*** (plural suffix) + ***-wi-*** (genitive suffix).

M.N. van Loon ('The Euphrates mentioned by Sarduri II of Urartu', in: K. Bittel, Ph.H.J. Houwink ten Cate, E. Reiner (eds.), *Anatolian Studies presented to Hans Gustav Güterbock on the occasion of his 65th birthday*, 192 = *Festschrift H.G. Güterbock I*, Leiden - Istanbul 1974, 187-194), interpreted the Hurrian form ***ammade*** 'ancestor, forefather' as ****amma*** 'mother' + ***ade*** (cf. also Th. Richter, *BGH*, 25, s.v. ***ammade*** 'ancestor, forefather'). If Van Loon's interpretation is correct, he may have identified another term for 'mother' beside Hurrian ***nera*** 'mother'. His observation may be based on the fact that AMA is the Sumerogram for 'mother'. However, whether we are dealing with a derivation from Sumerian or whether the word ***amma*** (with double ***-mm-***) is originally Hurrian itself, both expressions might be onomatopoetic, because they seem to imitate the first sounds / 'word' uttered by a baby towards the mother.

If Van Loon's analysis of ***ammade*** is correct, Linear A ***a-ma-wa-si*** can be translated as 'of our mother'. Perhaps more evidence is needed to confirm Van Loon's hypothesis that the basic meaning of ****amma*** is 'mother', but with the Linear A form ***a-ma-wa-si*** another form beside ***ammade*** has been found in which the nominal stem ****amma*** can be isolated, of which a meaning indicating some form of congeniality is very likely.

If Linear A ***a-ma*** (ZA 7b.1) indeed contains a nominal root, the fact that the personal name ***fAmma*** at Nuzi is the name of a woman seems to confirm Van Loon's hypothesis that ***amma*** means 'mother'. The baby may have received the name ***fAmma*** 'mother', because the child was considered to replace the mother who died giving birth.

However, if ***fAmma*** at Nuzi is based on the verbal root ***amm-***, the determinative f□ has nothing to do with the meaning of the name.

Alternatively in view of ***ammade*** 'ancestor, forefather' and considering the fact that Hurrian already had a word for 'mother', ***nera***, one may think of a different option: According to Th. Richter (*VHN*, 372-373+145) the Amorite lexeme ***cammu*** 'Vatersbruder' ['brother of the father'] is well-known. He explains its usage in hybrid Hurrian-Semitic names from the fact that there was no proper Hurrian lexeme for the notion 'brother of the father' available and that it was one of the most common elements in onomastics of the Semitic world in the second millennium B.C. Moreover, *cammu* could allegedly in contexts also have a more general meaning 'older kinsman, relative', even 'grandfather'.

The latter remark is in my view important with regard to the Hurrian form ***ammade***, analysis {*amm=ade*}, 'grandfather' (cf. I. Wegner, *Einführung*, 53, 'Großvater'; the form {*amm=ad(e)=iff=u-*} 'my grandfather', with the possessive pronoun 1st person singular; the ergative singular {*amm=ad(e)=iff=uš*} (*ibid.* 148, 165, 167); the genitive sg. + enclitic pronoun 3rd person sg. {*amm=ad(e)=iff=u=ve=n(na)*} (*ibid.* 161-162); singular dative {*amm=ad(e)=iff=u=va*} (*ibid.* 192-193); and the absolutive plural {*amatte=na*} (Boğazköy) (*ibid.* 213, 215), of which double writing of ***-tt-*** may be due to a shift of the accent to the vowel before the plural article according to G. Wilhelm, *Orientalia 61*, 1992, 129: *amatte=na enn(i)=na* corresponds with Hittite *karuileš šiuneš* 'die uralten Götter' ['the ancient gods'] in the Hurrian-Hittite bilingual ***kirenze*** (KBo 32).

If ***ammade*** is indeed derived from the Amorite lexeme ***ᶜammu***, the form ***ammade*** with the Hurrian suffix ***-ade*** proves that ***ᶜammu*** has become embedded in the Hurrian vernacular and may have been Hurrianized > ***ammi*** or *a*-stem ***amm=a***. As a result {*amm=ade*} is semantically close to ***attarde***, analysis {*atta(i)=arde*}, 'forefather, ancestor' (cf. I. Wegner, *Einführung*, 58, 251: 'Vorväter, Vorfahren').

(II) Another approach with regard to Linear A ***a-ma*** (ZA 7b.1) is possible as well. It may contain the verbal root ***amm-***, cf. I.J. Gelb, *NPN,* 20, and P.M. Purves, *NPN*, 200, s.v. ***amm***, ***amma***. Since Linear A misses the determinatives ᵐ□ for names of men or ᶠ□ for names of women and the Sumerograms **ᴸᵁ́**□ for male gender or **MUNUS**□ for female gender that cuneiform uses, and since the name does not contain the name of a God or Goddess as theophorous element, we have no tools to determine the gender of Linear A name ***a-ma***, if the root is verbal. The scribe no doubt knew whether ***a-ma*** indicated in this case a man or a woman. For the grammatical analysis it does not matter, since there is no morphological distinction between masculin, feminine or neuter forms in Hurrian.

Thomas Richter describes three Hurrian verbal roots:

am- I, also ***amm-*** I(?) [Boğ.]: Meaning '(völlig) verbrennen', 'embraser complètement, incendier' ['to set on fire, to burn completely'] is confirmed by the Hurrian-Hittite bilingual ***kirenze*** (KBo 32) through the Hittite parallel ***arḫa warnu-***, but by Urartian ***am(=ašt)-*** as well. There may also be connections with some Caucasian languages, cf. Th. Richter, *BGH*, 19-21. A root with this meaning was probably not used in names.

am- II [Boğ.]: 'ansehen, anschauen, beachten', 'porter son regard sur', 'guardare, osservare, vedere', 'to observe', cf. Th. Richter, *BGH*, 21-23.

amm- II [Boğ.; Qaṭna]: 'ankommen, gelangen, erreichen', ['to arrive, to reach'], corresponds with Hittite ***ar-*** and Akkadian ***kašādum***, cf. Th. Richter, *BGH*, 23-24.

Since Linear A orthography does not offer a clue, whether we are dealing with a root ***am-*** or ***amm-***, we have to rely on Hurrian grammar. I. Wegner (*Einführung*, 129) offers an example of transitive usage of ***amm-*** II in the Hurrian-Hittite bilingual ***kirenze***: *olvi=ne=ma amm=i=b ommin(i)=ne* (KBo 32: 14 I 19-20), which has been discussed before. But ***amm-*** II can also be intransitive.

If Linear A ***a-ma*** (ZA 7b.1) is verbal, it is clear that it is intransitive, since it contains the theme-vowel ***-a***. So we can analyse the form as ***amm=a***, which can represent the 3rd person singular of the intransitive *indicative* 'He/she arrives' or the *imperative* 'Arrive !' Both meanings provide plausible Hurrian names for a newborn child. And, more important, the name is attested at Nuzi as a Hurrian name of a woman ***ᶠAm-ma***.

Other names with the same root are: ***Ammanna*** (wr. *am-ma-an-na*) from Mari, analysis {*amm=a=nna*}, typology 1.1.1.3.3.1, lexicon *am(m)-*, 'Er (Junge) kam an' ['He (the boy) arrived'].***ᶠAmmanni*** (wr. *am-ma-an-ni*), name of two ladies from Mari, analysis {*amm=a=nni*}, typology 1.1.1.3.3.1, lexicon *am(m)-*, 'Es (Mädchen) kam an' ['She (the girl) arrived'].***ᶠAmman-eše*** (wr.*ᶠam-ma-an-e-še*), name of 2 ladies from Ašnakkum (Tell Šaġīr Bāzār) / "Chagar Bazar", analysis {*amm=a=n(na)-eže*}, typology 1.1.1.3.3.1, lexicon *am(m)-*, *eše*, 'Der Erde kam an' ['Earth arrived']. ***ᶠAmman-kijaze*** (wr. *am-ma-an-ki-ia-ze*), name of two ladies from Mari, analysis {*amm=a=n(na)-kijaže*}, typology 1.1.1.3.3.1, lexicon *am(m)-*, *kijaze*, 'Das Meer kam an' ['The sea arrived'].

Amman-taḫe (wr. *am-ma-an-ta-ḫe, am-ma-an-ta-aḫ-ḫe, a-ma-an-ta-ḫe*), name of two men from Mari and one from Qaṭṭarā, analysis *{amm=a=n(na)-taġe}*, typology 1.1.1.3.3.1, lexicon *am(m)-*, *taḫe*, 'Der Mann kam an' ['The man arrived'], cf. Th. Richter, *VHN*, 55-56. Cf. also I.J. Gelb, *NPN*, 20, s.v. ***Amante*** (wr. *A-ma-an-te*), father of *Eḫ-li-ia*, JEN 24: 20; father of *Ta-ba-a*-a,* RA XXIII 42: 23 (read so against *Ta-ba-e-a* of copy); father of *Zi-ge*, HSS IX 144: rev.12. This name can now probably be explained as *{amm=a=n(na)-Teš(š)ob}*, 'Teššub, he arrived', or 'He/She (the child) arrived, oh Teššub,' because ***-te*** is a frequent hypocoristic form of ***-Teš(š)ub*** in personal names.

Linear A ***a-ma-ra-ne***[(SK Zb 1) on a fragment of a pithos from Skhoinia / Skhinia (Mirabello). This inscription may well be identified with alphabetic cuneiform ***amrn*** attested at Ugarit, cf. A. Herdner, *Corpus des tablettes en cunéiforme alphabétique* (Mission de Ras Shamra X), Paris 1963, 166, 44-45. E. Laroche has included it in his *Glossaire de la langue hourrite*, 46, without comment on or an analysis of the form.

Since ***a-ma-ra-ne***[(SK Zb 1) is the only entry on this sherd, we cannot be sure whether it just represents a grammatical form or a personal name with the same meaning as the grammatical form. If the identification is correct, we know at least, how alphabetic cuneiform ***amrn*** is to be vocalized. If the sequence is complete, ***-ne***[may well be the enclitic personal pronoun of the 3rd person singular ***-nna***, ***-nni***, ***-nne***.

There is a form *{am=ar-}*, corresponding with Hittite ***idalu takk(i)ški/a-***, consisting of a root ***am-*** + root-extension ***-ar-***, that is interpreted as 'Böses zufügen, (jem.) böse behandeln' ['to bring evil (upon somebody), to treat (somebody) in an evil way'], see Th. Richter, *BGH*, 21, s.v. ***am*** II [Boğ.], cf. also *VHN*, 372.

Since this verb is transitive, Linear A ***a-ma-ra-ne***[(SK Zb 1) can only contain this root ***am-***, if it is followed by two consecutive root-extensions, *factitive* or *iterative* ***-ar-*** + *causative* ***-an(n)-*** (cf. I. Wegner, *Einführung*, 88), so that the form can be analysed as an imperative *{am=ar=an(n)=e}* and can be interpreted as 'bring evil (upon somebody) / treat (somebody) in an evil way!', if it is just a grammatical form, or 'Bring evil (upon somebody) / Treat (somebody) in an evil way (oh *numen*) !', if it is a personal name.

Another option is that ***a-ma-ra-ne***[(SK Zb 1) is analysed as *{amm=ar=a=nne}*, consisting of intransitive ***amm-*** 'to arrive' + the *factitive* or *iterative* root-extension ***-ar-*** + the marker of intransitivity ***-a-*** + the enclitic personal pronoun 3rd person singular ***-nne*** / ***-nni*** (used emphatically), 'He/She (the child) really (***-ar-***) arrived'. But a *transitive* analysis *{amm=ar=a=nne}* 'He/She (the child) reached it [***-nne***] (e.g. the earth)' is also feasible. It may then be a name similar to the personal name of two ladies at Mari, ***ᶠAmmanni*** (wr. *am-ma-an-ni*), analysis *{amm=a=nni}*, typology 1.1.1.3.3.1, lexicon *am(m)-*, 'She (the girl) arrived', cf. Th. Richter, *VHN*, 55. I. Wegner (*Einführung*, 88) mentions the *factitive* or *iterative* root-extension ***-ar-*** and gives the examples ***tad=ar-*** 'lieben' ['to love'] and ***šid=ar-*** 'verfluchen' ['to curse'].

The *jussive* or *imperative* forms ***ar=e*** and ***ar=i*** are each attested twice on Linear A tablets from Hagia Triada and Phaistos. The text of HT 4 from Hagia Triada reads:

HT 4.1:]*-83a̲-ti-ka* ̦ *a̲-r̲e̲* |

HT 4.2:]*t̲a̲-du-we-te* 1 *a̲-re* | (or possibly:]*s̲u̲-du-we-te* 1 *a̲-re* |)

HT 4.3:]*ta-pi-si-di* 1

Since only the right lower part of the tablet is preserved (upper part missing and left side damaged), only 3 lines of the tablet are (partly ?) preserved. So]***ta-pi-si-di*** 1 (HT 4.3) represents the last entry of this Linear A tablet.

The *imperatives* 2nd person singular **, *a-re*** | (HT 4.1) and ***a-re*** | (HT 4.2) 'give !' are forms that one may expect in economic texts. The form also occurs in the Tušratta letter ***a-ri*** (Mit. I 51), cf. e.g. E. Laroche, *GLH*, 52, s.v. ***ar-*** 'donner' and imp. sg. 2 ***a-ri***, Mit. I 51; cf. Th. Richter, *BGH*, 41-44, s.v. ***ar-*** I [*passim*]: "Die Deutung 'geben' ist allgemein akzeptiert." ["The meaning 'to give' is generally accepted."], cf. I. Wegner, *Einführung*, 86, 88-89, 120, 146, 248-249, s.v. ***ar-*** 'geben'. Cf. also Urartian ***aru*** 'to give'. N.B. alternation of ***e/i*** is normal in Hurrian cuneiform orthography and frequent in Linear A.

It is not surprising that an imperative 'give !' is repeated, if more persons are involved. It seems likely that both]***ta-du-we-te*** (or:]***su-du-we-te***) and]***ta-pi-si-di*** refer to different persons.]***-83a-ti-ka*** possibly also refers to a person. Linear A sign ***83a*** is very rare.

The reading]***ta-du-ri-te*** (HT 4.2) by *GORILA* actually offers a perfect Hurrian name, since it can be analysed as {*tad=ul=i=tte*}, consisting of the verbal root ***tad-*** 'to love', this time with an (allophonic) voiceless initial dental, if the reading is correct + the root-extension ***-o/ul-*** + the marker of transitivity ***-i-*** + the *optional allomorphic* personal pronoun 1st person singular ***-tte*** (instead of normal ***-tta***) indicating the object of the transitive verb, translation 'Love me (oh *numen*) !', cf. I. Wegner, *Einführung*, 88.

Instead of the root-extension ***-o/ul-*** Linear A orthography also allows the Old Hurrian root-extension ***-o/ur-***, cf. I. Wegner, *Einführung*, 89. The exact meaning of these root-extensions is not known. I. Wegner presumes a reflexive aspect for ***-o/ul-***. Instead of the optional allomorphic personal pronoun 1st person singular ***-tte*** one can choose to read the hypocoristic theophorous element ***-Te*** (instead of ***-Tešub***). In that case the interpretation of both forms {*tad=ul=i=te*} and {*tad=ur=i=te*} is 'Love (the child), oh *Tešub* !'.

However, in *Minoan Linear A*, Vol. II, Part I, *Corpus of transliterated Linear A texts*, I read]***ta-du-we-te***, because the *dot* in the middle of the sign, which distinguishes sign ***ri*** from ***we***, is lacking, so that I am obliged to read]***ta-du-we-te*** instead of]***ta-du-ri-te***. If]***ta-du-we-te*** is the correct reading, the analysis {*tad=u(w)w(a)=e=tte*} offers a *negative* 'one-word' name, consisting of the verbal root ***tad-*** 'to love' + the marker of the negation of the transitive verb ***-u(w)/w(a)-*** (position 6 in the order of verbal suffixes, cf. I. Wegner, *Einführung*, 91 sub 5.2.6; 94-95) + thematic vowel ***-e/i-*** + the optional allomorphic personal pronoun 1st person singular ***-tte*** (instead of ***-tta***), translation 'Do not love me (oh *numen*) !'. It is not a nice name to give to a child, because it gives the impression that the child was not particularly welcome to the parents. Nevertheless such names exist, for instance, ***Ullutta*** {*ull=u=tta*} at Šušarrā and ***Ullutti*** {*ull=u=tti*} at Mari and Tigunāni that both mean 'Destroy me (oh *numen*) !'. It may be a matter of renouncing a deceased child. If we choose the hypocoristic theophorous element ***-Te*** instead of the optional allomorphic personal pronoun 1st person singular ***-tte***, the name becomes a negative sentence name {*tad=u(w)w(a)=e=Te*}, translation 'Do not love (the deceased child), oh *Tešub* !'. Honesty demands that there is another possibility, though less likely. The first sign of the name, read as]***ta-***, is broken off at the top, exactly on the crucial spot where the distinction between the signs ***ta*** and ***su*** should be observed.

So there is a small chance that we have to read]***su-du-we-te*** instead of]***ta-du-we-te***. There is a verbal root ***šud-*** isolated in Hurrian as we can learn from the form *šu-u-du-uš-ti-i-e-eš* (KBo 15.72 = ChS I/1 Nr. 1 Vs. 5), without translation (cf. E. Laroche, *GLH*, 239; Campbell, 2007a, 150), containing root + root-extension ***šud=ušt-***, cf. Th. Richter, *BGH*, 423, s.v. ***šud-***. Not only the meaning of the root is unknown, it is also very rare, whereas ***tad-*** is very frequent.

Interpretation of]***ta-pi-si-di*** (HT 4.3) seems possible. If the sequence is complete, two Hurrian elements ***tapš-*** and ***-idi*** may be recognized. We may assume that the ***-i-*** in Linear A ***-pi-*** is a mute vowel, since the orthographic conventions of Linear A and B require that a syllable ***psi*** with a consonant cluster ***ps*** should be written ***-pi-si-***, because an occlusive should always be expressed in consonant clusters in the script.

I. Wegner, *Einführung in die Hurritische Sprache*, Wiesbaden 2007^{2}, 49, writes: "Metathesis is attested in the theonym ***Kušuḫ*** (***Kušupḫi*** < ***Kušuḫ*** + ***ve***) (*GLH*, 158) as well as in the verb ***tašp-*** later ***tapš-*** 'to destroy' (see p. 234 f.) and the numeral ***kig*** + ***še*** > ***kiški*** 'third' (see p. 81)." [I have translated the Germen text.] She assumes that the older form ***tašp-*** occurs 3 times in the famous *Tiš-atal* inscription (AO 19938), edited by A. Parrot and J. Nougayrol, *RA 42 (1948)*, 1-20; cf. I.M. Diakonoff, *Hurrisch und Urartäisch*, München 1971, 110f, Anm. 123. 1990, 382. G. Wilhelm, *Grundzüge der Geschichte und Kultur der Hurriter*, Darmstadt 1982, 15, provided a German translation of the text. He offered a completely new edition 'Die Inschrift des Tišatal von Urkeš', in: Buccellati and Kelly-Buccellati (eds.), *Urkeš and the Hurrians - Studies in honor of Lloyd Cotsen* (Bibl. Mes. 26), 1999, 117-143. It is now generally accepted that the inscription comes originally from Urkeš (modern Tell Mozān).

Here follows the transliterated inscription: (1) *Ti-iš-a-tal* (2) *en-da-an* (3) *ur-kèš*^{ki} (4) *pu-ur-li* (5) ^{D}NERI.GAL (6) *ba-'à-áš-tum* (7) *pu-ru-li* (8) *a-ti 'à-al-li* (Diakonoff *ḫà-al-li*) (9) ^{D}*lu-ba-da-ga-áš* (10) *ša-ak-ru-in* (11) *e-me-ni* (12) *da-áš-pi* *'à-al-li* (Diakonoff *ḫà-al-li*) (13) ^{D}*lu-ba-da-ga-áš* (14) *da-áš-pu-in* (15) AN x[ ] (16) *ḫa-˹WA-'à˺-a* (Diakonoff *ḫa-w*-ḫà-a*; E. Laroche, *GLH*, 98: *ḫa-wa-ḫa-a*, AO 19938, 16; cf. Nougayrol *RA 42*, 13. - V. *ḫewad-*.) (17) *ḫa-śu-˹e˺-in* (18) ^{D}NIN *na-gàr*^{ki} (19) ^{D}UTU-*ga-an* (20) ^{D}˹IŠKUR˺ (21) *e-me-ni* (22) *da-áš-pi* *'à-al-li* (Diakonoff *ḫà-al-li*) (23) *in-u-be* (24) *i-na-u-be* (25) *śi-ti-in*. [I have underscored the forms with the root ***tašp-*** in the text.]

According to Th. Richter (*BGH*, 2012, 442-443) most scholars interpret Hurrian ***tapš-*** I [Boğ; Eigenname] (as well as ***tašp-***, with metathesis) as 'to destroy' (comparable to Hittite ***ḫark-*** 'to fight', 'to conquer'). For the possibly comparable personal name in alphabetic cuneiform ***tbšn*** see W.G.E. Watson, *Ugaritic onomastics (4)*, *Aula Orientalis 13* (Sabadell 1995), 228; and *Lexical studies in Ugaritic*, *Aula Orientalis Supplementa 19* (Sabadell 2007), 180. Does ***tbšn*** belong to ***tapš-*** I or ***tapš-*** II ?

Th. Richter, *BGH*, 443: ***tapš-*** II 'gießen' ['to pour, cast']: "Aus der Bilingue heraus deutbare Wurzel für 'gießen'. Cf. e.g. V. Haas, 'Rezension zu *CHD P*, *Fascicle 1*, Chicago 1994', *Orientalische Literaturzeitung 90* (Berlin 1995), 516 and note 9; cf. M.-Cl. Trémouille, *Texte verschiedenen Inhalts*, Corpus der hurritischen Sprachdenkmäler. I. Abteilung: Die Texte aus Boğazköy, Band I/8 (Rome 2005), 325."

The root ***tapš-*** may be divided into ***tap-š-*** and be compared with the root ***tab/w-*** I according to E. Neu, *Das hurritische Epos der Freilassung. I: Untersuchungen zu einem hurritisch-hethitischen Textensemble aus Ḫattuša* (Studien zu den Boğazköy Texten 32), Wiesbaden 1996, 259, and V. Haas, 'Rezension zu *CHD P, Fascicle 1*, Chicago 1994', *Orientalische Literaturzeitung 90* (Berlin 1995), 516 and note 9.

It is difficult to determine, whether we are dealing with the nominal suffix or formant ***-idi*** or with the Hurrian nominal element ***edi / idi*** 'body, person'. I. Wegner (*Einführung*, 59) gives, s.v. ***-idi***, the examples ***tar=idi*** 'Topf' ['pot, pan'] from ***tari-*** 'Feuer' ['fire'] and ***naḫḫ=idi*** 'Sitz' ['seat'] from ***naḫḫ-*** 'sitzen, sich setzen' ['to sit, to sit down']. On the analogy of these examples one may interpret Linear A ***]ta-pi-si-di*** as Hurrian ***tapš=idi*** 'cast, casting'.

However, since ***]ta-du-we-te*** (or: ***]su-du-we-te***) and ***]ta-pi-si-di***, both followed by 1 unit, are probably personal names, I consider it more likely that Linear A ***-idi*** in ***]ta-pi-si-di*** may perhaps be identified with Hurrian ***edi / idi*** 'body, person' known from the Tušratta letter, Boğazköy, Ugarit and Mâri. The personal name ***]ta-pi-si-di*** may then be analysed as {*tapš(i)-e/idi*} and be translated 'Cast the body/person (oh *numen*) !', which is a plausible meaning for a personal name, since it corresponds with the ideas people had in antiquity about the creation of human beings: it could be a matter of assembling all the parts and pieces and putting them together or a matter of casting a model.

One may also compare Linear A ***-e-di-ja*** in the inscription ***]i-ja-re-di-ja i-ja-pa[*** (IO Za 5) from Mount Ioukhtas. It contains the plural *proclitic* relative particle ***ya-lle-***. E.A. Speiser, *IH*, 25, § 32-33: "At the beginning of a syllable ***y*** followed by ***a*** could be expressed by the syllabic sign ***ya***; e.g., ***ya-[a-]la-an*** 'those which' Mit. II 73, 82, 92. The corresponding form ***i-i-al-la/e-*** Mit. I 96, 98, 104, etc. shows that ***y-*** could also be written ***i-i-***. Accordingly, ***i-i-e-ma-a-ni-i-in*** Mit. II 101, IV 27 contains ***ye-***. [...] Medial ***-i-i-*** and ***-i-***, when accompanied by a dissimilar vowel, represents a syllable-closing or ambisyllabic ***y***. E.g., ***at-ta-i-i-wə*** Mit. I 87, 106, ***at-ta-i-wu-uš*** Mit. III 67; ***a-ta-i-ta*** Mâri 5.5; alphabetic ***atynp-*** RŠ X 4.4, all from ***a(t)tay-*** 'father'. The Bogh. form ***at-ta-ya-na-pa*** KUB XLV 21 Ro 9 shows that [***-ay***] could be written ***-a-ya-***, with a silent ***a*** at the end."

E.A. Speiser's latter remarks are illustrative for Linear A ***-jo-*** in ***a-ta-i-jo-wa-ja***, since ***j*** after ***i*** is a syllable-closing semivowel and ***o*** is 'silent'. I have put 'silent' between quotation marks, because a really silent vowel would have adopted its value from the following syllable, whereas ***-jo-*** has received the value ***-o/u-*** from the following ***-w-*** (cognate with ***-u-***). In Linear B the vicinity of ***w*** sometimes causes deviation from strict orthography as well, cf. e.g. ***pe-ru-si-nu-wo o-pe-ro*** (PY Ma 193,2), instead of ****pe-ru-si-no-wo, περυσινϝὸν ὄφελος*** 'the debt of last year'. The rest of the inscription may be clarified as well. If the final vowel ***-e*** of the Hurrian plural *proclitic* relative particle ***i-ja-re*** (= ***i-i-al-le-***) is fused or contracted with the initial vowel of ***-e-di-ja***, one may think of the Hurrian term ***edi / idi*** 'body, person', and in particular of the forms ***ediya*** 'his body' and ***ediyaš*** 'their bodies'.

E. Laroche, *GLH*, 73-74, s.v. ***edi / idi*** 'corps, personne'. Mit. ***edi***; Mâri, RS, Boğ. ***edi*** ou ***idi***; ***idi*** = akk. ***pagru*** 'corps', RS bil. 15-10, 7; cf. PRU III 311, 315. Dir. ***idi-da*** 'à la personne de, à' = akk. ***ana*** 'à, pour': RS 20.149 III 15, [MU] = ***a-na*** = ***idi-da*** = oug. ***le-e***;

cf. Laroche, *Ugar. V* 232, 457; *RA* 54, 198; ***edi-da***, directif postposé au datif: 'à l'égard de, au sujet de'; d'où, par affaiblissement, 'à, pour'. ***ᵈŠimigi-ni-wa e-ti-i-ta*** 'à l'égard du Soleil', Mit. I 106. - ***i-ti pa-a-ḫi*** etc. 'corps, tête' et autres parties du corps; cf. Laroche, *RA 67*, 120.

Unfortunately the Linear A inscription is broken off after ***i-ja-pa-[***, so that we cannot be sure whether the latter sequence can be completed to ***i-ja-pa-[*qe-ja*** = cuneiform ****i-ja-pa-[ḫe-ja(š)***, or to cuneiform ****i-ja-pa-[ḫi-ja(š)***. Because of the vicinity of ***-e-di-ja*** it is tempting, for Linear A ***]i-ja-re-di-ja i-ja-pa-[*ḫe/-ḫi-ja*** would offer a splendid parallel of the Hurrian phrase ***i-ti pa-a-ḫi***, with *quasi*-proclitic ***i-ja-re*** = Hurrian ***ya-lle-*** (wr. ***i-i-al-le-***) and ***i-ja-*** = Hurrian ***ya-*** (wr. ***i-ya*** or ***i-i-a***), and the possessive suffixes ***-i-*** 'his' or ***-i(=y)=as*** 'theirs'. Single writing of ***-t-*** in cuneiform ***e-ti*** / ***i-ti*** shows a voiced dental.

Basically the same *imperatives* 2nd person singular as **,** ***a-re*** | (HT 4.1) and ***a-re*** | (HT 4.2) 'give !' at Hagia Triada recur twice as ***a-ri*** at Phaistos, analysis {*ar=i*}, on one of the earliest Linear A tablets, PH 6 (HM 1486), found in vano (room) XXVIII, in the south-west section of the First Palace of Phaistos, transition Middle Minoan II a/b, end of Doro Levi's local phase 1b, in a vase beneath a concrete floor of phase 2. Tablet PH 6 reads:

PH 6.1: *i-na-wa , a-ri*
PH 6.2: *i-do-ri-ni-ta*
PH 6.3: *a-ri*
PH 6.4: *i-da-pa₃-i-sa-ri*

Since this tablet misses ideograms and numerals characteristic for economic texts and since it starts with the sequence ***i-na-wa***, I consider it a religious text. It is therefore discussed in the Chapter on *Religious Linear A inscriptions*.

Linear A ***a-di*** (HT 37.5) from Hagia Triada could theoretically be identified with the Hurrian word ***ardi / arde*** 'city, town' as opposed to Hurrian ***awari*** 'field', cf. at Ugarit ***ard-n awr-n*** 'city (and) fields', CTA 166, 4 = ***arde-ni awar-ni***, KUB XXVII 1 II 12; KBo XX 129+ II 62-63; cf. RS quadr. 130 Vo 18: [URU] = ***ar-di-na*** = oug. ***qa-ri-tum***, cf. *Ugar. V*, 234, 431 f.; cf. E. Laroche, *GLH*, 54, s.v. ***arde*** 'ville'. However, since ***a-di*** (HT 37.5) occurs in a list of personal names, this identification is not likely. The same applies to ***a-de*** (ZA 10b.4). Theoretically another identification of ***a-di*** is the rare Hurrian name ***Ate / Ati*** (wr. *A-te-e*, and also *A-ti-e*) at Nuzi from the pre-Hurrian Gasur period at Nuzi (HSS X 42: 6), which should be understood as ***/Ade/*** or ***/Adi/*** because of single writing of the dental, cf. P.M. Purves, *NPN*, 206-207, s.v. ***ate***, ***ati***. However, if the reading ***a-di*** is correct, it can most likely be identified as the Hurrian feminine personal name ***Ašti(n)***, analysis {*ažd=i*} 'Woman' or {*ažd=i=n(na)*} 'She (the girl) is a woman'.

Linear A **]', *a-di-ne*[** (KH 83.1) occurs in the heading of an incomplete tablet from Khania. Only part of the top side of Linear A tablet KH 83 is preserved. The surface is palimpsest. The first line only offers **]', *a-di-ne*[** (KH 83.1), in other words: a trace and a word divider precede the sequence ***a-di-ne*[** that may well be complete. Line 2 reads:]' VAS+***a*** 15 VASa²+***ru*** (rest of tablet fails). Since a sibilant ***s/z*** before an occlusive is not expressed in Linear A and B consonant clusters, Linear A **]', *a-di-ne*[** (KH 83.1) can be interpreted as Hurrian ***ašdine***, analysis {*aždi=ne*}, 'the woman', possibly here the lexical form with the suffix ***-ne/-ni*** of the so-called singular definite article.

Linear A]*a-di-na* **5** (KH 59.3) from Khania can be interpreted as Hurrian ***ašdina***, phonologically /*aždina*/, analysis {*aždi=na*}, 'the women 5', a grammatical form with the suffix ***-na*** of the so-called plural definite article. It may well be a lexical term and grammatically represent the plural form of **]', *a-di-ne***[(KH 83.1). The fact that the number 5 is in accordance with usage of the plural ***-na*** may corroborate this interpretation. On the other hand, the number 5, mentioned after]*a-di-na* **5** (KH 59.3), could also refer to the number of portions given to one woman, whose name is ***Ažd=i=nna*** 'She (the girl) is a woman'. It is impossible to make a choice between these possibilities, because the the preceding line only offers]-***no*** 5 (KH 59.3).

We may assume on the basis of the Linear A orthography of ***a-de*** (ZA 10b.4), ***a-di*** (HT 37.5), **]', *a-di-ne***[(KH 83.1),]***a-di-na* 5** (KH 59.3) and ***°-a-di-ne***, second element of Linear A ***o-ra₂-di-ne*** (HT 6a.4), ***a-du-|ku-mi-na*** 1 (ZA 10a.3-4), ***a-du-ni-ta-na*** 41[ ] (AK 5.1), ***a-du-re-za*** (KH 11.1), ***a-du-sa-ra*** (HT 62+73.1) and possibly ***a-du-***[..] (TY 3a.3) that the dental in the consonant clusters is voiced in the Hurrian dialect of Minoan Crete.

Linear A ***a-du-***[..] OLE+***ki*** 51 OLE+***ki+u*** 2 D OLE +***ki+me*** 1 OLE+[ ] 4 J OLIVA 4[(TY 3a.3) on a tablet from Tylissos is probably not complete, since *GORILA 1* mentions: "traces de deux signes après ***a-du-***[." Completion to a personal name such as ***a-du-re-za*** (KH 11.1) or ***a-du-sa-ra*** (HT 62+73.1) is conceivable, but too uncertain.

Linear A ***a-du-re***[(KH 4.1) from Khania can be equated with the Hurrian name ***Ar-dure*** 'Give a man (a boy) (oh *numen*) !', cf. ***Artura*** (wr. *Ar-du-ra, Ar-tu-ra*) at Nuzi (I.J. Gelb, *NPN*, 36), that I prefer to translate as 'Give a man (a boy) (oh *numen*) !'. P.M. Purves (*NPN*, 270) mentions the noun ***turi*** , ***turu*** 'man', onomastic elements ***-turi***, ***-tura***, ***-turu*** and ***turuḫḫe*** 'male'. Cf. Th. Richter, *BGH*, 476-477; *VHN*, 546, s.v. ***tu-ri*** I 'man' and the adjective ***turaḫ(ḫ)e*** [Boğ.; PN] and ***turuḫḫe*** [Boğ., Ug.] 'male' and 'strong, powerful', that can be used as a personal name.

If]***du-re*** 10 (AK 4b.2) at Arkhanes is completed to ***a-***]***du-re*** 10, since there is space for one syllabic sign before]***-du-re***, it yields the same form as ***a-du-re***[(KH 4.1) at Khania. *Arkhanes*, where 7 Linear A tablets were found in a Minoan building excavated by J.A. and E. Sakellarakis, may have been the startingpoint for supplicants and priests to go upto the Peak Sanctuary of Mount Ioukhtas to pray to *Tešub, Ḫebat and Šarru(m)ma* for their help to provide healthy children. Attestation of the Linear A toponym ***a***]***-ka-ne*** as a result of my join of a tiny fragment (AK 1b) containing the syllable ***a***] with]***ka-ne*** on tablet AK 3a, confirms the function of the Minoan building, since Hurrian ***Ar-ḫane***/***Ar-ḫani*** means 'Give a child (oh Gods) !'. Final ***-s*** of the Hellenized toponym was not yet present in the Minoan-Hurrian toponym, because ***ḫane*** / ***ḫani*** 'child' is in the *absolutive* case as object of the transitive verb ***ar-*** 'to give'. The toponym uses the gender-neutral term ***ḫane*** / ***ḫani***, but if the completion ***a-***]***du-re*** (AK 4b.2), Hurrian ***ar-dure***, is correct, the request may be more specific 'give a man (boy) !', and if the sequence is a personal name, 'Give a man !'. Linear A]***du-re*** (AK 4b.2) can equally be completed to ***u***]***-du-re***, equivalent to the Hurrian name ***ᶠUr-duri*** (wr. *ᶠUr-du-ri, ᶠÚ-ur-tu-ri*) at Nuzi (cf. P.M. Purves, *NPN*, 269). The name ***Ur-dure*** means 'Wish a man (a boy) !' and can be analysed as transitive athematic imperative of the root ***ûr-*** 'to wish' + ***dure / ture*** 'man'. Th. Richter (*VHN*, 554) distinguishes (intr.) ***ur-*** I 'to be present, to occur' and (trans.) ***ûr*** II 'to wish'.

It is strange that the name ^{f}***Ur-duri*** at Nuzi seems to have the feminine determinative. Maybe the parents at Nuzi expressed their disappointment that a girl was born instead of a boy. Perhaps they indirectly expressed their hope that their next child would be a boy.

Yet another option is possible, if ***u*]-*du-re*** (AK 4b.2) is analysed as the *imperative* ***ud=ul=e*** or Old Hurrian ***ud=ur=e*** that can both be translated 'Protect (the child) (oh *numen*) !', consisting of the root ***ud-*** 'to protect' + root-extension ***-o/ul-*** or Old Hurrian root-extension ****-o/ur-*** (cf. I. Wegner, *Einführung*, 88-89) + the marker of transitivity ***-i/e*** (the *imperative* misses its own marker ***-Ø***).

The fact that ***a-du-re-za*** (KH 11.1) {*ar-d/tur=izz=(e)=a*} 'Give manhood / virility (oh *numen*) !' or hybrid Hurrian-Akkadian {*aždu-reza*} 'The woman is my helper' and]***a-se-re-za***|[(KH 13.2) are actually attested at Khania just like ***a-du-re***[(KH 4.1), makes completion to ***a-du-re***[***-za*** (KH 4.1) the most likely option.

The scribes, aware of confusion caused by Linear A orthography, may have agreed to use a standard writing of ***a-du*** (HT 85a.1; HT 86a.4; HT 88.1; HT 92.1; HT 95b.1; HT 99a.1; HT 133.1) at Hagia Triada, and ***a-du***[(KH 23.1), followed by HORD '[(KH 23.2) at Khania, for ***ad(d)u(n)***, 'ration', 'assigned portion', but of ***a-de*** or ***a-di*** for {*ažde/i*} 'woman' and of ***a-di-ne*** and ***a-di-na*** for forms with the so-called definite article.

Linear A ***a-da*** (TY 3a.5) from Tylissos is followed by OLE+B 21 OLE+***mi*** 3[ ]J OLE+***ne***[ ]. Both sides of tablet TY 3 contain the registration of portions of OLEUM 'olive-oil' in a great variety and also some portions of OLIVA 'olives'. The syllabic sequences are all personal names, of which ***a-da*** is one. The orthographic conventions of Linear A allow more than one interpretation. The scribe no doubt knew, which he meant.

Since a sibilant preceding a dental is not expressed in consonant clusters, we can read ***Ašda***, analysis {*ažd(e)=a*}, translation 'As a woman', with the *essive* case in ***-a***. However Th. Richter (*VHN*, 384-385) mentions, s.v. ***ašte*** {*ašte*} and ***aštu*** {*ašto/u*} in note 202, that according to Haas/Thiel (1978, 309) an {A}-stem ***ašta*** may have existed, because the forms ***aš-ta-né-eš*** and ***aš-te-ni-iš*** are attested next to each other in two versions of an incantation against the *gergiššum*-disease at Mari and Tuttul. If they are right, ***ašta*** may be comparable with the {A}-stems of words expressing kinship or congeniality such as ***šala*** 'daughter', ***šena*** 'brother', ***ela*** 'sister', ***nera*** 'mother' and ***mena*** 'twin' (or perhaps 'sister'). In that case ***ašta*** does not represent the *essive*, but *absolutive* case.

Since final consonants are not expressed in Linear A and B, the reading ***Ašdan*** is also possible, analysis {*ažd(e)=a=n(na)*}, consisting of the stem *ažd(e)* with absorption of ***-e*** + the suffix of the *essive* ***-a*** + the suffix ***-nna*** of the enclitic personal pronoun 3rd person singular (abbreviated to ***-n***) indicating the subject of the (not expressed) intransitive verb 'to be', translation 'She (the girl) is like a woman', or analysis {*ažda=n(na)*}, translation 'She (the girl) is a woman' (*ažda* interpreted as *absolutive*).

Another possible interpretation of Linear A ***a-da*** (TY 3a.5) from Tylissos is Hurrian ***Adal*** 'Strong' or 'The strong one' derived from the adjectival and substantival noun ***adal*** 'strong' and 'the strong one'. The form was very popular in sentence names as first and (even more) as second element, see Th. Richter (*VHN*, 387-389), s.v. ***adal*** 'stark, der Starke', and his very long list of compounds with ***adal-*** and ***-adal***. He mentions that the meaning has been known for a long time thanks to a vocabulary comparison *a-da-al-lu* = *ga-áš-ru* (cf. *AHw*, 10; *CAD* A/I, 94).

According to Th. Schneider (Eine Vokabel der Tapferkeit. Ägyptisch *tl* – hurritisch *adal*, *UF 31*, 1999, 689) it is even the most frequent onomastic element in Hurrian personal names. Cuneiform orthography of ***adal*** is *(^{o})a-tal(-^{o})*, but also *(^{o})-a-da-al(-^{o})*, cf. Th. Richter, *VHN*, 387. The name ^{f}***Adallašše*** (wr. ^{f}*a-tal-la-aš-še*) at Ašnakkum, typology 3.1, has revealed the otherwise not attested lexeme ***adallašši*** 'strength', with suffix formation ***^{o}=a=šše*** indicating abstract forms, cf. Th. Richter, *VHN*, 389; I. Wegner, *Einführung*, 55, s.v. ***-(a)=šše***. If there is an etymological relation between the noun ***adal*** and the verbal root ***ad-***, one may attribute the meaning 'to make strong, to strengthen' to the *transitive* and 'to be strong' to the *intransitive* form. Comparison with ***adašši*** 'Umwallung der Unterstadt' ['fortification of the lower town'] calls for the meaning 'to fortify' and comparison with ***adani*** 'footstool' calls for the meaning 'to fasten (something to something) underneath' for the verbal root ***ad-***, cf. Th. Richter, *VHN*, 385 and note 204, s.v. ***ad-***. The latter meaning would in my view be very specific, maybe too specific. The meaning 'to support (underneath)' may be preferable.

Anyway Th. Richter (*VHN*, 84-85, 88, 386) ascribes the Hurrian personal name ***Atai*** (wr. *a-da-i*) from Mari, analysis {*ad=ai*}, typology 1.3.5, lexicon *ad-*, translation 'Damit er stark(?) wird' ['Let he be strong'] to that root, as well as ^{f}***Ataja*** (wr. ^{f}*A-da-ia*) from Mari, Alalaḫ IV (AT 222: 4), Kaniš and ***Ataia̯*** (wr. *A-da-a-a, A-ta-a-a, A-ta-a-a-ia, A-ta-a*) from Nuzi (cf. I.J. Gelb, *NPN*, 38), analysis {*ad=a=ja*}, typology 1.1.1.3.4, lexicon *ad-*, and ***Atan*** (wr. *a-da-an*) from Mari and Tuttul, analysis {*ad=a=n(na)*}, typology 1.1.1.3.3.1, lexicon *ad-*, probably 'He is strong'. Consequently Linear A ***a-da*** (TY 3a.5) can theoretically also be interpreted as Hurrian ***Adan*** or as ***Adai***, the latter only if ***-ai*** in {*ad=ai*} is regarded as a diphthong.

Linear A ***a-da-ra*** (KN Zf 31) on a silver hairpin from the Mavro Spelio cemetery at Knossos may well be an exact equivalent to the Hurrian personal name ***Atalla*** (wr. *A-ta-al-la*) at Nuzi, cf. I.J. Gelb, *NPN,* 38. It is phonologically /***Adalla***/ and can be analysed as {*adall(i)=a* < **adal=n(i)=a*}, the *essive* in ***-a*** of the name ***Atalli*** (wr. *A-ta-al-li*) attested at Mari < **adal=ni*, 'The strong one', ***^{o}-lli*** < ***^{o}-l=ni***, with the so-called definite article ***-ni***, cf. also *A-ta-li* at Kaniš (see Balkan, 1974, 36). So ***Adalla*** can be translated as 'Like the strong one'. But since Linear A ***da-du-mi-ne*** (KN Zf 31) {*dad=u/o-min(a)=ni/e*} 'love the twin (oh *numen*) !' and ***a-wa-pi*** (KN Zf 31) {*aw(i)-abi*}, athematic imperative 'save (the deceased person), oh necromantic sacrificial pit !' on the same hairpin from the same Chamber Tomb are forms in context, ***adalla*** may also be a form in context, either nominal *adall(i)=a* 'like the strong one' or verbal ***ad=a=lla*** 'they are strong', consisting of the verbal root ***ad-*** (intr.) 'to be strong' + the marker of intransitivity ***-a-*** + the absolutive enclitic personal pronoun 3rd person plural ***-lla***.

Linear A ***a-da-ro*** (AK 5.2) from Arkhanes may be interpreted as ***Adallo/u***, analysis {*adall(i)=u* < **adal=n(i)=u*}, with Akkadianizing *nominative* in ***-u***, 'The strong one', cf. also the theonym ***Adalur***, a Hurrian mountain god, cf. V. Haas, *Hethitische Berggötter und hurritische Steindämonen*, Mainz 1982, 31. A verbal 'one-word' name is also possible: ***ad=al=o/u*** or ***ad=ar=o/u***, consisting of the root ***ad-*** (trans.) 'to make strong' + root-extension ***-al-*** (not clear) or *factitive* or *iterative* ***-ar-*** + Old Hurrian *imperative* ***-o/u***, 'Make (the child) strong (oh *numen*) !' or Old Hurrian *indicative past tense* ***ad=al=o/u=m*** or ***ad=ar=o/u=m*** 'He/She (a *numen*) made (the child) strong'.

J. Raison – M. Pope (1994, 177) read ***a-ta* , '**[(KH 39.1) on a small fragment of a tablet from Khania, of which only the left top corner is preserved. I agree with L. Godart - J.-P. Olivier (*GORILA 3*) that there is no word divider visible after ***a-ta*** (KH 39.1), so that they read ***a-ta-***[. But there is some space between ***a-ta*** and the traces of an unrecognizable sign (possibly an ideogram). Therefore it is likely, but not entirely sure, that ***a-ta*** (KH 39.1) is complete. The best reading is probably ***a-ta*** -[vestigia]|- (KH 39.1).

On another tablet fragment from Khania L. Godart - J.-P. Olivier (*GORILA 3*) and J. Raison - M. Pope (1994) consider ***a-ta***[and ***a-su***[(KH 73.3) 'également possibles' ['equally possible']. I have followed that view in *Minoan Linear A*, Vol. II, *Corpus of transliterated Linear A texts*, Part II. Indeed Linear A signs ***74*** (***ta***) and ***59*** (***su***) are very similar. So there can sometimes be some doubt, especially if a tablet is damaged or worn.

If we read ***a-ta*** (KH 39.1) and ***a-ta***[(KH 73.3), the sequences can be interpreted as the Hurrian noun ***atta / attai*** 'father', but preferably as the personal name ***Atta /Attai*** 'Father' derived from the noun. I am convinced that the notion ***atta / attai*** has intentionally a double function in Hurrian personal names, not only in sentence names, but also in so-called 'one-word' names: It refers not only to the father of the child, but also to ***eni attanni*** 'God the Father', often epithet of *Teš(š)ub*, but in lists of divinities at Ugarit also a God in his own right. Alongside traditional theophorous personal names, names such as Hurrian ***Attay*** 'Father' show the same affection as the so-called 'Lallnamen', which explains their popularity. Since ***-ai*** in ***Attay*** was probably considered a diphthong, the ***i/y*** did not have to be expressed at the end of the word/name in Linear A, but it had to be expressed in the middle of a sequence such as ***a-ta-i-jo-wa-ja*** in the 'libation formula'.

E. Laroche (*NH*, 1966, 47, n° 193) mentions ***Atta*** as name of a dignitary of Gaggapaha: abs. ^{m}*At-ta-a*, XXXI 44 I 9, and as name of another man: abs. ^{m}*Ad-da-a*, 201/g Vo 10 = MIO 4, 183 n. 10, that can in my view also be normalized as ***Attaya***. He also mentions ***Attai*** (*NH*, 47, n° 195): abs. ^{m}*At-ta-a-i*, XXXVI 111 Ro 9. See also E. Laroche, 'Les noms des Hittites: supplément', *Hethitica IV* (BCILL 21), Louvain-la-Neuve 1981, 11, n° 195: *Attai.* Lire: ^{m}*At-ta-a-i*, KBo XX 34 Vo 12. – Voir aussi KBo XVII 104 II 7, et Bo 2029/g 8 (fragm.). – Nom hourrite *attay* 'père' ??.

The personal name ***Atta*** (wr. *at-ta*) is also attested at Alalaḫ IV, cf. D.J. Wiseman, *AT*, 136: 4, 215: 6. At Mari ***Atta*** (wr. *at-ta, a-at-ta, ad-da, ad-da-a*) is attested as personal name of four men, typology 3.1, lexicon *atta*, translation 'Vater' ['Father'], at Tigunāni as name of two men and at Qaṭṭarā (Tall ar-Rimaḥ) and Terqa (Tall 'Ašara) as name of one man, cf. Th. Richter, *VHN*, 84. See *ibid.*, 84-85, also for other sentence names with the onomastic element ***atta(i)***, such as ^{f}***Attai-nirze*** 'Der Vater ist das Gute' ['The father is the good thing'], ***Attai-šarri*** 'Der Vater ist Götterkönig' ['The Father is King of Gods'] at Šubat-Enlil, ***Attakkuzzi*** 'Einem kleinen Vater angemessen' ['In accordance with a small father'] at Mari, and hypocoristic ***Attaja*** {*att=a=ja*}.

If the reading ***a-su***[(KH 73.3) is correct, it can be identified with the Hurrian noun ***azzu*** (probably < ***aždu***) 'woman', variant of ***aštu/ašdu*** {*aždu*}, or preferably with the personal name ^{f}***Azzu*** 'Woman', variant of Hurrian ^{f}***Ašdu*** {*aždu*} 'Woman', cf. E. Laroche (*NH*, 46, n° 182) at Boğazköy: ^{f}***Ašdu***: ^{f}*Aš-du-uš*, KBo X 10 III 37.

P.M. Purves (*NPN*, 208) mentions s.v. ***az(z)***: ^{f}***Az-zu***, from Chagar Bazar (Gadd, *Iraq VII*, 37). The name ^{f}***Az-zu*** is also attested at Nuzi (AAN I, 39), cf. Th. Richter, *VHN*, 81.

Th. Richter (*VHN*, 80-81) mentions ***fAz-zu*** as Hurrian personal name of 2 women from Ašnakkum (Tall Šaġīr Bāzār / 'Chagar Bazar', cf. also Gadd, *Iraq VII*, 37), of 13 women from Mari and of 3 women from Qaṭṭarā (Tall ar-Rimaḥ), wr. *a-zu, a-az-zu-ú*, typology 3.1, lexicon *azzu* (→ *azze*), 'Frau' ['Woman']. Cf. for more names with the element ***fAštu-*** and ***fAzzu-*** Th. Richter, *VHN*, 75-76, 78-84, 381-385.

Cognate with ***fAz-zu*** is no doubt the Linear A personal name ***a|-su-ja*** (HT 11a.3-4) from Hagia Triada that can be compared with the hypocoristic name ***fAz(z)ui̯a*** at Nuzi, cf. I.J. Gelb, *NPN*, 41, s.v. ***fAz(z)ui̯a*** (wr. *fA-zu-ia, fAz-zu-ia*): 1) SMN 347; (1) (2) 3240; P.M. Purves, *NPN*, 208, s.v. ***az(z)*** and ***fAz(z)ui̯a***. The hypocoristic name can be analysed as {*az(z)o/u-ya*}. Cf. also ***fAzzuāja*** (wr. *az-zu-a-ia*), name of 3 women at Mari, analysis {*azzo/u-āja*}, typology 3.1/4.2, lexicon *azzu* (→ *azze*), cf. Th. Richter, *VHN*, 81.

Cf. also ***fAzziya*** at Boğazköy (E. Laroche, *NH*, 50, n° 217: ***fAzziya***, *fAz-zi-ya-aš*, KBo V 7 Vo 28 = MIO 6, 350, typology 3.1/4.2, lexicon *azzu* (→ *azze*), translation 'woman', cf. Th. Richter, *VHN*, 81.

Linear A ***a-se*** (HT 81.1; HT 93a.3; HT 132.1; ZA Zb 3.1) from Hagia Triada and Epano Zakro can be compared with Hurrian ***fAzze*** (wr. *fA-a-ze, fA-ze, fAz-ze, fA-az-ze, fA-az-ze-e, fAz-ze-e*) from Nuzi (cf. I.J. Gelb, *NPN*, 41; AAN I 39, SANTAG 4, 257) and name of two women from Mari (wr. *fAz-ze*), typology 3.1, translation 'Frau' ['Woman'], cf. Th. Richter, *VHN*, 75-76.

Since final consonants are not expressed in Linear A and B, Linear A ***a-se*** cannot only be compared with Hurrian ***fAzze***, but also with ***fAzzen*** (wr. *fAz-ze-en*), name of a woman from Qaṭṭarā, analysed as {*azze=n(na)*}, typology 3.1, lexicon *azze*, translation 'Es (Mädchen) ist eine Frau' ['She (the girl) is a woman'], cf. Th. Richter, *VHN*, 76.

Compare also ***fAšte*** (wr. *aš-te, áš-te*), name of 4 women from Mari, typology 3.1, translation 'Woman', and ***fAšten*** (wr. *aš-te-en*), name of 4 women from Mari, typology 3.1, analysis {*ašte=en(na)*}, 'Es (Mädchen) ist eine Frau' ['She (the girl) is a woman'], cf. Th. Richter, *VHN*, 78-79.

The series of Linear A sequences starting with ***a-sa-***, ***a-se-***, ***a-si-*** and ***asu-*** may be better understood, if they are compared with Hurrian feminine personal names beginning with ***az(z)-*** that can be equated with Hurrian names beginning with ***ašt-*** {*ažd-*} 'woman': ***a-sa|-da-ka*** (MA Wc <5>a.1-2), ***a-sa-mu-ne*** (ZA Zb 3.1), ***a-sa-ra₂*** (HT 89.1), ***a-sa|-su-ma|-i̯*** (GO Wc 1a.1-3), ***a-se*** (HT 81.1; HT 93a.3; HT 132.1; ZA Zb 3.1), ***a-se-ja*** (HT 115a.4), ***]a-se-ja*** (HT 93a.8), ***]a-se-re-za|***[(KH 13.2), ***a-si-da-to|-i̯*** (AK 2.2-3), ***a-si-ja-ka*** (HT 28a.1; HT 28b.1), ***a-si-ki-ra*** (KH 20.1), ***a-si-su-po-a*** (KH 9.1), possibly ***a-su***[(KH 73.3), ***a|-su-ja*** (HT 11a.3-4),]|***a-su-mi*** TAL[(AK 1a.4), ***a-su-pu-wa*** (AK 2.5).

P.M. Purves, *NPN*, 208, s.v. ***az(z)***: "Hurrian. Stems derived from this root occur in feminine names in forms and combinations analogous to those derived from ***ašt***: ***fAštai̯a*** beside ***fAzai̯a***; ***fAšte*** beside ***fAzze***; ***fAšta-kina*** beside ***fAzze-kena***; ***fAštu-anti*** beside ***fAzu-anti***; ***fAštun-nai̯a*** beside ***fAzun-nai̯a***; ***fAštui̯a*** beside ***fAzzui̯a***. Cf. ***fAzzu***, Gadd in *Iraq VII* 37, from Chagar Bazar. From Nippur cf. ***As-su-e*** and ***fAs-su-me***, Clay, *PNCP*, 59, also ***As-sul-la***, *ibidem*, beside Nuzi ***fAzuli***." We may now add ***fAšten*** at Nuzi beside ***fAzzen*** at Qaṭṭarā (see *supra*).

Here follow the feminine Hurrian names from Nuzi with the onomastic element ***az(z)-*** with the normalized forms as well as those in full writing (P.M. Purves, *NPN*, 208): ***Azaja*** (wr. *fA-za-a-a*); ***Az(z)e*** (wr. *fA-a-ze*, *fA-ze*, *fAz-ze*, *fA-az-ze*, *fA-az-ze-e*, *fAz-ze-e*); ***Azze-kena*** (wr. *fAz-ze-ge-na*); ***Aze-kuja*** (wr. *fA-ze-ku-ia*); ***Azu-ani*** (wr. *A-zu-a-ni*, *fA-zu-a-ni*); ***Azu-anti*** (wr. *fA-zu-an-ti*, *fA-zu-a-an-ti*); ***Azu-ašše*** (wr. *fA-zu-a-aš-še*; *fA-zu-aš-še*); ***Azue*** (wr. *fA-zu-e*); ***Az(z)uja*** (wr. *fA-zu-ia*, *fAz-zu-ia*); ***Azuli*** (wr. *fA-zu-li*, *fA-su-li*); ***Azun-naja*** (wr. *fA-zu-un-na-a-a*, *fA-zu-un-na-a*). The Hurrian name ***Aš-ši-a-e*** from Nuzi has nothing to do with these names, for the name is masculine referring to 'the son of *Zi-ri-ra*', JEN 79:20, cf. I.J. Gelb, *NPN*, 37; cf. P.M. Purves, *NPN*, 206, s.v. ***ašš***.

Th. Richter, *BGH*, 53, s.v. ***azze*** I [PN], "evt. Ein (Dialekt)wort für 'Frau' (Richter 2005b: 155[31]); 'Frau (oder eine bestimmte Gattung von Frauen)' (Richter 2007: 88; 2010b: 517); (MUNUS.) ***azze/inna-*** com. [Lw/He] 'Funktionärin im Kult der IŠTAR / *Šaušga*', wohl aus dem Hu. von Kizzuwatna (*HW*^{2} Lfg.8 [1984] 639."

The possible connection with Kizzuwatna, mentioned by Th. Richter, is interesting, because it brings the parallels between forms with ***azz-*** and those with ***ašt- /ašd/***, detected by Purves in the Nuzi personal names, much closer to Minoan Crete. Although Purves and Richter do not say so, comparing these names, a process of assimilation of ***/ažd/ > /azz/*** is likely, resulting in a whole range of unassimilated forms beside assimilated forms.

Th. Richter (*VHN*, 75-76) mentions several personal names with the element ***azz-***: ***fAzza-Naje*** (wr. *Az-za-na-a-ie*), analysis {*Azz(e)/azz(o/u)=a*[E]-*Naje*}, typology 2.1, lexicon *azza*, *Naje*, 'As a woman is *Naje*'. [E] refers to the *essive* case in ***-a***. However, if ***azza*** has originally a root in ***-a***, this woman from Mari is called 'A woman is *Naje*'.

fAzze (wr. *az-ze*), name of two women from Mari, typology 3.1, lexicon *azze*, 'Woman'. Compare the same name ***Azze*** at Nuzi.

fAzzen (wr. *az-ze-en*), analysis {*Azze=n(na)*}, name of woman from Qaṭṭarā, typology 3.1, lexicon *azze*, translation 'She (the girl) is a woman'. As mentioned *supra*, Linear A ***a-se*** cannot only be identified with Hurrian ***fAzze***, but also with ***fAzzen***, since final consonants are not expressed in Linear A and B.

fAzzu (wr. *a-zu, a-az-zu-ú*), name of 2 women from Ašnakkum, 13 women from Mari and of 3 women from Qaṭṭarā (just discussed *supra*).

In the past I also assumed that ***a-sa-*** in Linear A personal names, identified with Hurrian ***azza- < ažda-*** might also be compared with ***a-sa-*** in the sequence ***a-sa-sa-ra-me*** attested in several Linear A 'libation formulas'. This equation seemed to be confirmed by comparison with the Linear A personal name ***a-du-sa-ra*** (HT 62+73.1) at Hagia Triada, identified as Hurrian ***Aždu-šara*** (possibly with *essive* ending in ***-a***) that can be equated with the personal names ***fAštuzar*** at Ašnakkum and Mari, ***fAzzuzari*** at Mari and ***fAš-du-a-šar*** at Nuzi, that I should like to translate as 'Woman *par excellence*' or 'Womanhood'.

Fortunately I had (in view of the orthographic conventions of Linear A and B) already mentioned that ***a-sa-*** in ***a-sa-sa-ra-me*** could also be identified with the onomastic element ***arš(a)-*** as in ***Ar-šá-a-pu***, ***Ar-ša-ḫa-lu*** and ***Ar-ši-ki-ia***, cf. I.J. Gelb, *NPN*, 31-32. Now I have found sufficient evidence to identify Linear A ***a-sa-sa-ra-me*** as a poetic description of the God *Šarru(m)ma* or *Šarru(m)manni*, since ***a-sa-sa-ra-me*** can be analysed as Hurrian ****Arša-šarr(i)=a=me***, 'The young boy is Šarru(m)ma', literally 'The young boy (***aršə/a***), he is like the King of Gods', see *chapter 11: 'Religious' Linear A inscriptions*.

It is not certain that Linear A ***a-se-ja*** (HT 115a.4) and ***]a-se-ja*** (HT 93a.8) can be associated with ^{f}***Azija*** (wr. ^{f}*A-zi-ia*), name of women from Mari, typology 1.1.1.2.4, lexicon *az-*. The same applies to ***Azija*** (wr. *A-zi-ia*) from Šušarrā (Tall Shemshara), ***Azija*** (wr. *a-zi-ia*) from Alalaḫ IV (D.J. Wiseman, *AT*, 159: 16; cf. A. Draffkorn, *HHA*, 26: ***Azi-ya***, wr. *a-zi-ya*, ŠÀ.TAM LUGAL) and ***Azija*** (wr. *A-zi-ia*) from Emar, cf. Th. Richter, *VHN*, 76. ***Azija*** (wr. *a-zi-ia*) from Nuzi is used for names of men and may well contain a different root ***az-***, cf. I.J. Gelb, *NPN*, 41 and Th. Richter, *VHN*, 76.

Th. Richter (*VHN*, 381) explains that the root ***az-*** {*až-*(?)} in personal names may well be connected with the verbal root ***aš-*** 'essen' ['to eat'], respectively 'wegnehmen' ['to take away'], known from texts at Ḫattuša. In particular the name ***Azip-nan*** (wr. *A-zi-ip-na-an*) from Qaṭṭarā, analysis {*až-*(?)=*i*=*b-nan(i)*}, has a plausible meaning as name of a child that replaces a deceased child: 'Die *nan(i)*-Waffe nahm (Jungen) fort' ['The *nan(i)*-weapon took (the boy) away']. Especially the Old Hurrian verbal form in ***=i=b-*** proves that ***az-*** must be verbal and cannot be associated with the nominal root ***azz-*** 'woman'. As a result it may be wise for the time being to separate the forms ^{f}*A-a-ze* and ^{f}*A-ze* at Nuzi from the other forms ^{f}*Az-ze*, ^{f}*A-az-ze*, ^{f}*A-az-ze-e* and ^{f}*Az-ze-e* that P.M. Purves had put together sub ***azz-***, although I must admit that it remains a dilemma, because some forms with single and double writing of ***-z-*** give the impression of being doublets. If a name is that of a man, it is unlikely that the nominal root ***azz-*** is involved. More prosopographic research on apparent doublets may support the one or the other view.

Anyway ^{f}***Azziya*** at Boğazköy is probably a hypocoristic name in ***-ya***, with ***azzi-*** 'woman' as first onomastic element, cf. E. Laroche, *NH*, 50, n° 217: ^{f}***Azziya***, ^{f}*Az-zi-ya-aš*, KBo V 7 Vo 28 = MIO 6, 350. Possible translation 'She is a woman'.

It is not easy to determine, whether Linear A ***a-se-ja*** (HT 115a.4) and ***]a-se-ja*** (HT 93a.8) should be associated with Hurrian ^{f}***Azija*** (wr. ^{f}*A-zi-ia*) or ^{f}***Azziya***. If double writing of ^{f}***Azziya*** indicates voicelessness of the sibilant, this may well be an argument to equate Linear A ***a-se-ja*** with Hurrian ^{f}***Azziya*** instead of Hurrian ^{f}***Azija***.

However, the picture seems even more complicated, because there appear to be more Hurrian verbal roots that may have to be considered. Th. Richter (*BGH*, 50-52) mentions ***aš-*** I [Boğ.] 'essen' ['to eat'], ***aš-*** II [Boğ.; PN] 'wegnehmen' ['to take away'], ***ašš-*** [Boğ.], also ***aš-*** IV(?) [Boğ.], 'être assis (?)', cf. E. Laroche, *GLH*, 59; (intr.) 'to sit', (trans.) 'to set, put, place', corresponding with Urartian ***aš-***.

V. Haas - I. Wegner (Beiträge zum hurritischen Lexikon: Die hurritischen Verben *ušš-* "gehen" und *ašš-* "abwaschen, abwischen", in: J. Klinger e.a. (eds.), *Investigationes Anatolicae: Gedenkschrift für Erich Neu* (StBoT 52), Wiesbaden 2010, 97-110) reject the latter meaning of ***ašš-*** and propose '(ab)waschen, wegwischen, abwischen' ['to wash, to cleanse, wipe off'], cf. also I. Wegner, *Einführung*, 86, 250.

We have seen that ***a-se*** (HT 81.1; HT 93a.3; HT 132.1; ZA Zb 3.1) is three times attested at Hagia Triada and once at Epano Zakros, where it immediately follows Linear A ***a-sa-mu-ne*** (ZA Zb 3.1). The scribe at Epano Zakro seems consciously and deliberately to have combined ***a-sa-mu-ne*** and ***a-se*** as names that are etymologically connected.

The whole Linear A inscription (ZA Zb.1-3) on a large pithos from the Minoan villa or farmhouse near Epano Zakros (magazine Θ) reads:

ZA Zb 3.1. VINa 32 *di-di-ka-se* , *a-sa-mu-ne* , *a-se*
2. *a-ta-i-jo-de-ka* , *a-re-pi-re-na* , *ti-ti-ku*
3. [[ ]]

Linear A ***a-sa-mu-ne*** (ZA Zb 3.1) is probably a Hurrian personal name consisting of two elements ***asa-*** and ***-mune***. The element ***asa-*** is quite frequent in Linear A and occurs in many personal names. It is equivalent to the more common form ***ašta*** or ***ašte*** 'woman' and can be identified with the frequent Hurrian nominal element ***azza*** as in ***ᶠAzza-Naje*** (Mari), analysed by Th. Richter (*VHN*, 75) as {*azz(e)/azz(u)=a*[E.]-*Naje*} and translated as 'Wie eine Frau ist Naje' ['Like a woman is Naje'], since he assumes that ***-a*** in ***Azza*** may indicate the *essive* form [E.]. However, in the discussion of the same *lemma* he also mentions the possibility that ***azza*** (and ***ašta***) might be '{A}-stämmig' [contain a theme in ***-a***], in which case the translation is 'A woman is Naje'. It is probably not accidental that ***a-sa-mu-ne*** is followed by the sequence ***a-se*** that I have interpreted as the Hurrian name ***ᶠAzze*** 'Woman', equivalent to ***ᶠAšte*** (see s.v. ***a-se***). Theoretically it could represent the noun ***azze*** 'woman', but it seems likely that the whole series of sequences following VINa 32 consists of personal names. The *essive* form ***ᶠAzz=a-*** is acceptable for a name like ***ᶠAzza-Naje***, but in the diminutive name ***ᶠAštakka*** (wr. *aš-ta-ak-ka*), {*ašta=kk(i)=a*[E.]}, translation 'Es (Mädchen) ist wie eine kleine Frau' ['She (the girl) is like a little woman'] (cf. Th. Richter, *VHN*, 78), the *essive* is only likely in the diminutive suffix ***-kk(i)=a*** > ***-kka***, not in ***ašta-*** itself, which may well reflect an original ***a***-stem.

Although the most common forms are ***azze*** < ***aždе*** (wr. ***ašte***, ***ašde***) or ***azzu*** < ***aždu*** (wr. ***aštu***, ***ašdu***) and although ***ašte/i*** is regarded as an ***i/e***-stem by I. Wegner (*Einführung*, 52), one may plead for the possibility that it may originally belong to the category of words with an ***a***-stem, that seems to be limited to words indicating congeniality or kinship such as: ***šala*** 'daughter', ***šena*** 'brother', ***ela*** 'sister', ***nera*** 'mother', ***mena*** 'twin?' or (as Th. Richter proposes) 'sister?', and theonyms such as ***Ša(v)uška*** and ***Šimiga*** which is more rare than ***Šimige***. Hurrian ***tiša*** 'heart' is also an ***a***-stem, although it does not belong to the categories just mentioned.

According to Th. Richter (*VHN*, 459 and notes 507-508) the Hurrian root ***mun-*** {*mo/un-*} has been isolated from *mu-nu-ub-tuk* {*mo/un=o=b(:m)-to/uk(ki)*}, Isin, Old-Babylonian period (*Babylonian inscriptions in the collection of J.B. Nies 9*, New Haven - London - Oxford, 520: 11). Compare for root and derivations Th. Richter, Ergänzungen zum hurritischen Wörterbuch I, *Altorientalische Forschungen 34 (2007)*, 109. Here he had not yet taken into account that *mu-nu-ub-tuk* could also be a Sumerian personal name and that *°-tuku* could be read (see *VHN*, 459, note 507), but he mentions that nevertheless the existence of a Hurrian root ***mun-*** cannot be doubted. The root is mainly nominal in onomastics and ***muni*** can also be found in *eḫ-lam-mu-un* in Alalaḫ IV (cf. D.J. Wiseman, *AT*, 144): {*eġl=a=m(:b)-mo/un(i)*}. The personal names ***Al-muni*** and ***ᶠMunuzzi*** are attested at Mari, cf. also at Ḫattuša ***mu-nu-ši*** (ChS I/1, 47 Rs (?) 6') and ***mu-u-nu-ši*** (ChS I/1, 48: 9'). ***Irim-mun*[*u*]** and ***ᶠAweš-munulu*** occur at Šubat-Enlil / Šeḫna (Tall Leilān). Th. Richter does not yet provide a possible meaning for the root ***mun-***. In search of a suitable meaning for ***-muni*** I had already paid attention to P.M. Purves' proposal that Hurrian ***-mu*** in Nuzi personal names might be a hypocoristic form of ***muš*** and ***muš(u)ni***, before I came across Th. Richter's valuable *lemma* on the root ***mun-***.

According to the orthographic conventions of Linear B the non-occlusives (*σ, μ, ν, ρ, λ, ϝ*) preceding sonantic consonants (*μ, ν, ρ, λ, ϝ, y*) were usually expressed: e.g. ***a-mi-ni-so* = *Ἀμνῖσός*; *de-so-mo* = *δεσμός***. However, *ρ* and *λ* preceding *μ, ν,* and *ϝ* were usually omitted: e.g. ***pe-ma* = *σπέρμα*; *ko-wa* = *κόρϝᾱ***. If we accept that these Linear B conventions were most likely derived from Linear A, we must assume on account of Linear B *de-so-mo* = *δεσμός* that ***-s-*** preceding a nasal (***m*** or ***n***) in Linear A consonant clusters must be expressed. This means that the Linear A form should have been ****-mu-se-ne*** (not ***-mu-ne***) to express Hurrian ***-mušne***. Consequently we have to assume that Linear A ***a-sa-mu-ne*** represents Hurrian ***ᶠAzza-mune***, not ****ᶠAzza-mušne***. Nevertheless a development of ***-mune*** < ***-mušne*** < ***-mušune*** is conceivable. In the 2016 edition I proposed that the personal name ***a-sa-mu-ne*** (ZA Zb 3.1) may well be an abbreviated form of ****Azza-mušuni*** in the same way as the Hurrian personal name ***Enna-mu*** (wr. *En-na-mu, E-en-na-mu*) is compared with ***Enna-muša*** (wr. *En-na-mu-ša, E-en-na-mu-ša, En-mu-ša, En-na-mu-šá*) by P.M. Purves, *NPN*, 235-236, s.v. ***mu*** and ***muš***. Likewise I may compare the Nuzi name ***Arim-mu*** (wr. *A-ri-im-mu*) with ***Ari-muše*** (wr. *A-ri-mu-še*) as well as ***Pentam-mu*** (wr. *Be-en-ta-am-mu, Be-en-ta-am-mu-ú*) with ***Wanti-muša*** (wr. *Wa-an-ti-mu-ša, Wa-an-ti-mu-šá, Wa-an-di-mu-ša, Wa-di-mu-ša*), cf. P.M. Purves, *NPN*, 235-236.

The equation seems corroborated by the fact that the adjectival and substantival element ***muša***, which was translated as 'auguste, sublime' by F. Thureaux-Dangin (*RA XXXVI (1939)*, 22 f.) and as 'reliable, trustworthy, just, true, righteous, pure, sublime, august' in more recent literature, is often combined with the suffix ***-ni*** of the so-called definite article, just as Linear A ***a-sa-mu-ne*** contains the same suffix ***-ne***.

Following Purves' idea I propose that Linear A ***a-sa-mu-ne*** may be interpreted as ****Azza-muni*** < ****Azza-mu-(šu)-ni*** {*azza-mu(šu)=ni*} 'The woman is the trustworthy, true, reliable, just, righteous, pure, sublime, august one', cf. ***ᶠAš-te-mu-šu-ni*** at Alalaḫ IV (cf. D.J. Wiseman, *AT*, 425: 14), cf. Th. Richter, *VHN*, 79, in the *lemma* on ***ᶠAštu-Ala*** (wr. *aš-tu-a-la*) at Mari, lexicon *aštu, a-la* = *allai* / Allai ? 'lady / Lady', cf. Th. Richter, *VHN*, 369, s.v. ***Ala*** (fem. theonym, uncertain), cf. also ***ᶠḪawin-Ala*** and ***ᶠḪawiš-Alla*** at Mari.

P.M. Purves, *NPN*, 235, s.v. ***-mu***: Hurrian. Perhaps shortened form of elements formed on ***muš***; and s.v. ***muš***: "More common in Hurrian texts are occurrences of ***muš(u)ni***, formed on ***muš*** and identical with the personal name element ***mušni***; see Thureaux-Dangin, *loc. cit.* Cf. e.g. *mu-šu-ni*, KUB XII 12 V 33 and VI 20; XXV 32 I 6; XXVII 10 V? 24 and 22 I 1 and 19; *ᵈmu-šu-un-ni*, KUB XXIX 8 II 40; *ᵈmu-šu-un-ni-iš*, *ibid.* I 32; *ᵈmu-šu-ni-iš*, *ibid.* II 44 and 47. A phonetic variant is *mu-uš-ni*, KUB XXVII 1 II 37 and 38; 3 III? 19, 20, 21; 13 I 15; wr. *ᵈmu-uš-ni*, KUB XXVII 33:11. In all these instances ***ᵈmuš(u)ni*** is an epithet of the goddess *Ḫepa*. [ ] Since this word occurs only occasionally with the divine determinative, it must be a divine appellative or epithet, not a deity's name. As F. Thureau-Dangin, *loc. cit.*, proposes, it probably consists of root ***muš*** + demonstrative ***-ni***." ***ᵈMuš(u)ni*** is not only a divine epithet, but is also combined with ***ḫāri*** 'way, road' and with ***šiye-[na]*** 'rivers'. So ***ḫāri ᵈMušuni*** is translated 'la voie droite' ['the right way']. For instance, KBo XXI 34 II 6 offers in Hittite context: *nu* LUGAL-*uš* ᴰUTU *ḫāri* ᴰ*mušuni ekuzi*, which J. Tischler (*Hethitisches etymologisches Glossar*. Teil II, Lfr. 5-6, IBS 20, 1990, 234) translates as 'the King drinks to the Sungod, to the right (= divine) path' [I have translated the German text into English], cf. Th. Richter, *BGH*, 254-256.

E. Neu (Varia Hurritica. Sprachliche Beobachtungen an der hurritisch-hethitischen Bilingue aus Ḫattuša, in: E. Neu - C. Rüster (eds.), *Documentum Asiae Minoris Antiquae*, Festschrift für Heinrich Otten zum 75. Geburtstag, Wiesbaden 1988, 239) was able to confirm the meaning of a Hurrian verbal root ***muz-/muš-*** {*muž-*} 'zurechtstellen' ['to arrange in good order, to make perfect'] on the basis of the Hittite parallel ***ḫandai-*** in the bilingual ***Kirenze***, cf. also Th. Richter, *BGH*, 254-256, and *VHN*, 460-461.

Linear A ***a-sa-ra₂*** (HT 89.1), first entry on this tablet from Hagia Triada, is probably a personal name. Orthographically interpretation as ****Aš(š)alia*** / ****Az(z)alia*** or ****Aš(š)aria*** / ****Az(z)aria*** is possible on the basis of the phonetic value of the identical Linear B sign ***ra₂ = lia/ria***, but starting from e.g. ***azza*** < ***ažda*** 'woman' a nominal root-extension ***-al-*** or ***-ar-*** + the hypocoristic suffix ***-ya*** would have to be assumed. Such a nominal root-extension can be assumed in Hurrian ***awari*** {*av=ar=i*} 'field', ***ped=ar=i*** 'cow, bull, ox', ***niḫ=ar=i*** 'gift', ***ḫaš=ar=i*** 'luxurious, aromatic oil' < ***ḫaš-*** II 'to anoint', ***šid=ar=ni*** 'curse' < ***šid-*** 'to curse'. P.M. Purves (*NPN*, 232, s.v. ***-lli̯a***; 248, s.v. ***-ri̯a***) proposed the existence of compound formatives ***-lli+i̯a*** and ***-ri+i̯a***.

According to the orthographic conventions ****Aršalia*** or ****Aršarria*** are also feasible. At Nuzi ***Ar-šali*** (wr. *Ar-ša-li-(m), Ar-ša-li, Ar-šáli(m)*) 'Give a daughter (oh *numen*) !' and ***Ar-šarri*** (wr. *Ar-šar-ri, Ar-šarri*) 'Give (the child) oh King of Gods !' are attested (cf. I.J. Gelb, *NPN*, 31-32). The verbal root ***ar-*** 'to give' is a frequent onomastic element. Hurrian ***šala*** 'daughter' is originally an *a*-stem, known from the Tušratta letter and from Boğazköy (cf. I. Wegner, *Einführung*, 52-53), cf. *ᶠŠalanna* and hypocoristic *ᶠŠalai̯a*. The onomastic elements ***-šali*** and ***-šalli*** < ***-šal(a)=ni*** (with the so-called definite article ***-ni***) are based on it, cf. P.M. Purves, *NPN*, 250, s.v. *sal* and *sall*). Hurrian ***-šarri*** is usually translated as 'King of Gods'. But these names attested at Nuzi are ending in ***-i***, not ***-i-a***.

A new solution is given recently. There are also verbal roots like ***aš-*** I [Boğ.] 'to eat' or ***aš-*** II [Boğ.; PN] 'to take away' or ***ašš-*** [Boğ.], also ***aš-*** IV(?) [Boğ.], 'être assis', cf. E. Laroche, *GLH*, 59; 'to sit' (intr.), 'to set, put, place' (trans.), corresponding with Urartian ***aš-***. V. Haas - I. Wegner (Beiträge zum hurritischen Lexikon: Die hurritischen Verben *ušš-* "gehen" und *ašš-* "abwaschen, abwischen", in: J. Klinger e. a. (eds.), *Investigationes Anatolicae*, 97-110) reject the latter meaning of ***ašš-*** and propose 'to wash, to cleanse, wipe off', cf. I. Wegner, *Einführung*, 86, 250; Th. Richter, *BGH*, 50-52.

I propose a Minoan etymology for Linear B ***a-sa-mi-to*** (KN Ws 8497) ***ἀσάμινθος*** 'bath-tub' (on a sealing from Knossos, with ideogram of rectangular shape) derived from ***ašš=am=i=(e)n=(i)=tta***, consisting of the verbal root ***ašš-*** + *factitive* root-extension ***-am-*** (cf. I. Wegner, *Einführung*, 88) + *jussive* suffix ***-i-*** + the jussive marker of the acting person ***-en-*** (with syncope of the vowel ***-e-***) + facultative theme-vowel (***-i-***) + the enclitic personal pronoun 1st person sing. ***-tta***, indicating the object of the transitive verb, 'May he/she (a *numen*) wash/ cleanse me !' or 'May it (the bath-tub) wash/ cleanse me !'.

Th. Richter (*VHN*, 381) mentions, s.v. ***az-*** {*až-*(?)}, that in personal names the verbs 'to eat' or 'to take away' often give a good meaning: e.g. ***Azip-nan*** form Qaṭṭara 'The *nan(i)*-weapon took (the boy) away' offers a plausible name indicating substitution of a deceased child. He also mentions ***ᶠAzia*** at Mari and Šušarrā 'He/She eats' or 'He/She (a *numen*) took (the child) away'; ***ᶠAz-mena*** at Mari 'Take the twin away (oh *numen*) !';

ᶠAzum-ki (wr. *a-zu-um-gi*) at Mari, {*az(?)=om-ki*} 'It, the sea, took (the child) away'. Consequently Linear A ***a-sa-ra₂*** (HT 89.1) can be analysed as ***az=ar=i=a***, consisting of the verbal root ***aš-*** I 'to eat' or ***aš-*** II 'to take away' + *factitive* or *iterative* root-extension ***-ar-*** + marker of transitivity ***-i-*** + marker of the subject of action of the transitive verb ***-a***, 'He/She (the child) eats again and again' or 'He/She (a *numen*) took (the child) away'.

Linear A inscription ***a-sa-̲|su-ma-|i̲*** HORD (GO Wc 1a.1-3) on a roundel (HM 83, 1903) from room 25 of house Cf in quarter C on the east slope of Minoan Gournia, reads:

GO Wc 1a.1. *a-sa-̲|*
2. *su-ma-|*
3. *i̲* HORD
GO Wc 1b.1. 11 BOSᵐ 5
2. vacat
GO Wc 1c. 5 seal impressions: type *CMS II*, 6, nº 159: bull.

Linear A ***a-sa-̲|su-ma-|i̲*** HORD (GO Wc 1a.1-3) is written over 3 lines. The *b*-side of the roundel is also interesting: GO Wc 1b.1: 11 BOSᵐ 5; 1b.2: vacat. The reading of the ideogram BOSᵐ 5 seems to be confirmed by the 5 seal impressions of a bull / oxen on the edge of the roundel (GO Wc 1c), type *CMS II*, 6, nº 159: bull. Since the ideogram HORD(eum) 'barley' is not directly followed by a number on the *a*-side, the number 11 at the beginning of the *b*-side indicates the number of portions of barley, followed by the counting of 5 bulls / oxen. Apart from some absolutive forms such as Hurrian ***attay***, ***allay***, ***uštay***, instrumental (and adverbial) singular ***-ae*** and plural ***-aš=ae*** are the only nominal forms in ***-ai/-ae***, cf. E. Laroche, *GLH*, 26, § 11. Le nom: Instrumental: sg. en ***-ae***, pl. en ***-šae*** (?); cf. I. Wegner, *Einführung*, 65. There are, however, also verbal forms in ***-ai***.

A problem for the interpretation of the inscription is that we cannot be entirely sure whether we are dealing with two sequences ***a-sa|*** and ***su-ma-|i̲*** or one ***a-sa-̲|su-ma-|i̲***. So both possibilities have to be examined. Sign ***i̲*** in line 3 can hardly be a separate word, so ***su-ma-|*** and ***i̲*** probably belong together. If Linear A ***a-sa|*** is a separate sequence, it can be identified with Hurrian ***azza*** < ***ažda*** 'woman' that can be used in 'one-word' personal names such as ***Azza***, but also in 'sentence names' such as ***ᶠAzza-Naja/e*** (Mari) that Th. Richter (*VHN*, 75) analyses as {*azz(e)/azz(u)=a*[E]-*Naje*}, 'Wie eine Frau ist Naje' ['Like a woman is Naje'], since he assumes that ***-a*** in ***Azza*** may indicate the *essive* form. But he also mentions the possibility that ***azza*** (and ***ašta***) might contain a theme in ***-a***, in which case the translation would be 'The woman is Naje', as we have discussed before.

Anyway, if Linear A ***a-sa|*** (GO Wc 1a.1) is interpreted as one sequence, it can represent the common word ***azza*** 'woman' or it can be a personal name ***Azza*** 'Woman'. But we have seen that ***a-sa-*** in Linear A ***a-sa-sa-ra-me*** can be interpreted as ***arša*** 'young man, boy'. So it depends on the context which interpretation / meaning is most likely.

Linear A ***su-ma-|i̲*** (GO Wc 1a.2-3) could theoretically be a nominal or verbal form. According to E. Laroche (*GLH*, 242-243) Hurrian ***šummi*** is 'main' ['hand'], based on RS voc. II 3 = Ḫḫ II 113: sum. **šu** = gén. du dét. ***šu-mu-ni-we*** 'de la main' ['of the hand']. Interesting is his remark that the postpositional usage of ***šummi(n)*** is analogous to that of ***abi*** 'devant' ['before'], ***edi*** 'vers' ['to'], ***wuri*** 'face à' ['facing, in front of']: 'à la main de', c'est-à-dire 'avec' ['at the hand of', i.e. 'with'].

If the reading ***su-ma-|i̲*** is correct, it may reflect ***šum(m)ai***, *instrumental* case of ***šum(m)i***, and could according to Laroche be translated as 'with the hand, by hand'.

However, according to I. Wegner (*Einführung*, 47, 84, 217, 219) and Th. Richter (*BGH*, 412-414) ***šummi*** I [Boğ.] is now identified as 'all, ganz, alle' ['all'] and ***šuni*** that was according to E. Laroche (*GLH*, 243) interpreted as 'âme ?' ['soul ?'], is now regarded as the common word for 'hand'. In the third parable '*The cup/beaker/goblet and his smith*' in the Hurrian-Hittite bilingual ***Kirenze*** (KBo 32: 14 Vs. I 48) ***šuni*** {*šoni*} is written ***šu-u-ni*** (cf. E. Neu, *StBoT 32*, 80 and 469) which corresponds with the Hittite nominative singular (genus commune) of the thematic stem ***keššara-š***, written *ki-iš-šar-a*[*š*] (KBo 32: 14 Vs. II 47; cf. E. Neu, *StBoT 32*, 81), cf. I. Wegner, *Einführung*, 217, 219. Both Th. Richter (*BGH*, 413) and I. Wegner (*o.c.*, 219) admit that there is another word for 'hand', ***šum(m)un(n)i***, next to ***šuni*** {*šoni*}.

Th. Richter (*BGH*, 412) also mentions the verbal root ***šumm-*** [Boğ.] 'to assemble(?)' that corresponds with (pro)nominal ***šummi*** 'all'.

Linear A ***su-ma-|i̲*** (GO Wc 1a.2-3) could in that case represent the *final debitive* (in subordinate clauses) or *adhortative* with *jussive* force (in main clauses): ***šumm=ai*** 'in order that he/she assembles' or 'let he/she assemble !'. There are more *adhortative* forms with *jussive* force attested in Linear A: e.g. the Linear A personal names ***ma-ka-i-se*** (ZA 8.4) at Kato Zakro, ***ma-ka-i-ta*** (PK 1.7; ZA 5b.2-3) at Palaikastro and Kato Zakro, and the form ***su-ra-i*** (KN Zf 13) at Mavro Spilio, discussed in *chapter 10.*

F.W. Bush, *GHL*, 1964, 228-229, ascribed 'a definite *jussive* force' to the forms with the suffixes ***-ae / -aen*** and ***-ai / -ain***. The suffixes occur frequently at Boğazköy. The Tušratta letter provides three forms of ***pal-*** 'to know' with the suffixes ***-ae / -aen***, which I quote from J. Friedrich, *Kleinasiatische Sprachdenkmäler*, Berlin 1932, 29 and 31:
še-e-ni-iu̯-u̯u-uš-ša-a-an pal-la-a-en (IV: 56);
še-e-ni-iu̯-u̯u-uš-ša-a-an pal-la-en (IV: 59);
še[*-e-n*]*i-iu̯-u̯u-uš-ša-a-an* [*pa*]*l-la-en* (IV: 108).

F.W. Bush analyses these forms as *šen-iff-ušš+an pal-(i)l+ae+n*, which I translate 'and (copulative ***-an***) in order that My Brother (possessive pron. 1st pers. sg. + *ergative*) knows it'. Analysis ***šen(a)=iff=u=šš=an < šen(a)=iff=u=š=n(na)=an pal=(i)l=ae=n(na)***.

As examples for the formants ***-ai / -ain*** the Tušratta letter can be cited again: DINGIR^{MEŠ} *e-e-ni-iu̯-u̯a-al-la-a-an pal-la-in* (IV: 64); DINGIR^{MEŠ} *e-e-ni-il-la-a-an še-e-ni-iu̯-u̯u-ú-e-na pal-la-i-šal-la-ma-an* (IV: 65), J. Friedrich, *Kleinasiatische Sprachdenkmäler*, 29. The suffixes also occur at Ḫattuša. E. A. Speiser (*Introduction to Hurrian*, § 193) considers them merely an orthographic variant of ***-ae***.

F.W. Bush analyses these phrases as $^{\text{d.m.}}$*en-iff-a+lla+an pal-(i)-l-ai+n* (IV: 64); $^{\text{d.m.}}$*en-i-lla+an šen-iff-u̯e-na pal-(i)-l-ai+ša+lla+man* (IV: 65), which he translates as 'God(s)-my+they+and know (transitive)-voluntative-jussive+cop. God(s)-his+they+and brother-my-of-ones know (trans.)-voluntative-jussive+emphasis(?)+they+conn.', 'and may my gods know it and may the gods of my brother know'. Bush gives more examples with the intransitive root ***itt-*** 'to go', virtually the same as I. Wegner, *Einführung*, 111-112.

I. Wegner (*Einführung*, 111, sub 5.6.4: Die *nicht-indikativen* Formen auf ***-ae / -ai***) interprets the verbal forms with the formants ***-ae / -ai*** as *Debitiv-Finalis* [*final debitive*], semantically similar to the *jussive*, so that a distinction is not always possible.

She refers to F.W. Bush, *GHL*, 1964, 228-229; I.M. Diakonoff, *Hurrisch und Urartäisch*, 1971, 130f.; M.L. Chačikjan, *Churritskij i urartskij jazyki*, Akademija Nauk Armjanskoj SSR, Institut Vostokovedenija, Churrity i Urarty 2, Erevan 1985, 109-110: final optative). I propose to reserve the term *final debitive* (expressing purpose, command or necessity, introduced by *in order to*, *in order that*) for subordinate clauses and to use the term *adhortative* for principal sentences (main clauses) in the sense of 'let somebody do something !'.

I. Wegner presumes an original case ending, the instrumental, in the morpheme ***-ai / -ae***. Just like the forms in ***-eva***, those in ***-ae / -ai*** can be combined with a second formant of the optative ***-il-***, but ***-ae / -ai*** and ***-eva*** exclude each other. As indicator of the plural of the subject of action the pluralizer ***-š(a)*** appears. I. Wegner, *Einführung*, 111, offers Table 12: The order of suffixes for the *final debitive*, of which I present the English translation:

Root+root-extension	formant	formant	pluralizer	enclitic pronoun	syntactic particle
	(-il-)	***-ae/-ai***	***-š(a)***	***-tta***	***-an***, etc.
				-mma	
				-nna, etc.	

She offers the following examples (111-112):

pal + ***(i)l*** + ***-ae*** + ***-n(na)***

(***pal-la-(a-)en*** Mit. IV 56, 59) 'in order that he (My Brother) knows it / may know it'.

pal + ***(i)l*** + ***-ai*** + ***-n(na)***

(***pal-la-in*** Mit. IV 64) 'in order that he may know it'.

itt + ***-ai*** + ***-nna*** + ***-ân***

(***it-ta-in-na-a-an*** Mit IV 53) 'and in order that he may/can go'

pal + ***(i)l*** + ***-ai*** + ***-ša*** + ***-lla***

(***pal-la-i-šal-la*** Mit. IV 65) 'in order that they may know it'.

itt + ***-ai*** + ***-ša*** + ***-lla*** + ***-ân***

(***it-ta-i-šal-la-a-an*** Mit IV 52) 'and in order that they may/can go'

In the Tušratta letter (IV 122) and in some texts from Boğazköy the formant ***-ai*** occurs with other formants such as ***-i-m-*** and ***-i-l-***. G. Wilhelm, *Orientalia 61 (1992)*, 140, ascribes a nominalizing effect to the ***-i-*** in these formants as is to be expected for an (original) case ending (*instrumental*). Grammatically the formants in ***-i-l-ai*** and ***-i-m-ai*** are assigned to the infinite verbal forms of the verbal system. Functionally they can be treated as gerundial forms (cf. e.g. E. Neu, *StBoT 32 (1996)*, 108, 133, 197).

Examples with 'gerund': ***inu=mê=nîn*** ^{D}***Šimige taršuvani=š fur=i=m=ai=n(na) tad=i=a*** (Mit. IV 121-122) 'and just as man / a human being (*taršuvani=š* ergative) loves (*tad=i=a*) the Sun God *Šimige* watching him (*fur=i=m=ai=n(na)*)'.

papani ḫaš=i=m=ai (KBo 32: 14 I 8) 'the mountain hearing (*ḫaš=i=m=ai*) (this)'.

^{I}***Megi=ne tive=na*** ^{D}IM***=u=da kunz=i=m=ai kad=i=a*** (KBo 32: 15 IV 12-13) 'Megi speaks (*kad=i=a*) bowing (*kunz=i=m=ai*) the words (*tive=na*) to the Weather God'. N.B. the subject of action ^{I}*Megi* misses the expected *ergative* morpheme ***-š***; see for this type of sentence I. Wegner, *Altorientalische Forschungen 21 (1994)*, 161f.

^{D}*IŠTAR*-***g[a=]l(la) tive=na*** ^{D}U***=da alu=m=ai=n kad=i=a*** (KBo 12: 80 + KUB 45: 62 Vs. I$^{?}$ 6) 'the Goddess Ištar says (*kad=i=a*) speaking (*alu=m=ai=n*) the words (*tive=na*) to the Weather God'.

Linear A ***su-ma-|i̲*** (GO Wc 1a.2-3) could in that case represent the *final debitive* (in subordinate clauses) or rather *adhortative* with *jussive* force (in main clauses): ***šumm=ai*** 'let he/she assemble !'. As a result the whole Linear A text ***a-sa-̲|su-ma-|i̲*** HORD 11̲ BOS^{m} 5 (GO Wc 1a.1-3 + GO Wc 1b.1) can then be translated:

I. 'Let the woman (***azza***) / Let ***Azza*** / the young boy (***arša***) assemble (***šumm=ai***) 11 portions of barley and 5 bulls / oxen !' or preferably:

II. 'Let the woman (***azza***) / Let ***Azza*** / the young boy (***arša***) assemble (***šumm=ai***) 11 portions of barley (as fodder for ?) 5 bulls / oxen !'

Interpretation with ***azza*** / ***Azza*** / ***arša*** and ***šumm=ai*** as separate sequences makes sense. The option, that ***a-sa-̲|su-ma-|i̲*** might be one sequence and be interpreted as a sentence name, is less attractive, because such a name with the same meaning 'Let the woman / Let the young boy assemble !' does not make sense in onomastics. Moreover, in personal names with a verbal and a nominal element, the verbal element is usually the first and the nominal the second, but there are exceptions. The verbal root ***šumm-*** is probably involved in ***Sum-mi-te-šu-ub***, KAV 30 rev. 5, with variant ***Sum-mi-***^{d}IM, *ibid.* l. 8. Previous reading *Šúm-mi-* for initial element by Ebeling in *MAOG XIII 1 (1939)*, 88, 119, followed by Purves in *AJSL LVII*, 178, is perhaps wrong (cf. P.M. Purves, *NPN*, 259). We also have ***Šummi(š)-šenni*** (wr. *Šu-um-mi-še-ni*, *Šu-um-mi-še-en-ni*, *Šu-um-mi-iš-še-ni*, *Šum-mi-še-ni*, *Šu-um-bi-še-ni*, *Šum-mu-še*-n[i], *Su/Šúm-mu-še-ni*, *Šu-mi-še-ni*, *Šum-mi-še-en-ni*, *Šum-mi-iš-še-ni*) as well as hypocoristic ***Šummii̯a*** (wr. *Šum-mi-ia*, *Šu-um-mi-ia*, *Šu-um-me-ia*, *Šu-mi-ia*, *Šúm-mi-ia*, *Šum-me-ia*, *Šum*^{um}*-me-ia*, *Su-um-mi-ia*), cf. P.M. Purves, *NPN*, 259, s.v. ***šumm***. All these examples show ***šumm-*** as first onomastic element.

I think that the root ***summ-*** 'to assemble' in these names can be interpreted in the sense of 'to put together'. This may well fit into an ancient view of how a human being might be created: a God or a divine power (*numen*) had to assemble all the parts of the body and put them together, so that a human being could be born. The meaning of ***Summ=i-Tešub*** could then be 'Assemble (all parts of the child) and put them together, oh Tešub !' and ***Šummi(š)-šenni*** may mean 'Put (the parts of) the brother together, oh *numen* !'.

Another verbal form with the *final debitive* suffix ***-ai-*** (in subordinate clauses) or *adhortative* suffix with *jussive* force (in main clauses), ***zul(l)=ai***, is attested in Linear A ***su-ra-i*** = Hurrian ***zul(l)=ai*** 'let he connect !' in an inscription on a gold signet-ring from Mavro Spilio: ***a-re-ne-̲si-di-jo-pi-ke-pa-ja-su-ra-i-te-ra-me-a-ja-ku*** (KN Zf 13) that can be read as: ***a-re-ne*** (͵) ***si-di-jo-pi*** (͵) ***ke-pa-ja*** (͵) ***su-ra-i*** (͵) ***te-ra-me*** (͵) ***a-ja-ku***, and analysed as {*Ar-ene=š*} or {*Ar-en(a)=ne=š*} {*Šid=i-j=o/umbi*} or {*Šind=i-(j)o/umpi*} {*Kebaja*} {*zul(l)=ai*} {*Telame*} (*Telame/Talame/Talme*) {*Aya=k(k)=un*}, translated as: 'In order that (the priest) *Aren(n)e* may connect *Ši(n)dijombi* and *Kebaja* (in wedlock with this wedding-ring), oh Great *Ajak(k)un*' or 'Let (the priest) *Aren(n)e* connect *Ši(n)dijombi* and *Kebaja* (in wedlock with this wedding-ring), oh Great *Ajak(k)un* !'.

The inscription allows us a glimpse of a Hurrian wedding-ceremony and offers us an unexpected connection between the Minoan-Hurrian religious rituals, the Mycenaean heroic world and the mythological pedigree of the 'Great Aias', one of the great heroes in Homer's *Iliad*. See for a complete analysis of the inscription § 1 of *Chapter 10*: *Inscriptions on metal objects*.

I return to tablet ZA 10 from Kato Zakro, since not all personal names on that tablet have been discussed. Linear A ***ka-ku-ne-te*** J (ZA 10b.6) is probably a personal name followed by fraction sign J. The first (nominal) element ***ka-ku-ne-*** may be identified with the Hurrian personal name at Nuzi, ***Karkunni*** (wr. *Qa-ar-ku-un-ni*, *Ka-ar-ku-un-ni*), cf. P.M. Purves, *NPN*, 223, s.v. ***kar***; cf I.J. Gelb, *NPN*, 80: *Qa-ar-ku-un-ni*, father of *Ú-na-ap-še*; *Ka-ar-ku-un-ni*, grandfather of *A-qa-we*.

The second element ***-te*** may be identified with the shortened form ***-te*** of the theophorous element ***-tešup*** and ***-teịa*** (cf. e.g. *Al-ki-te, Eḫ-li-te, Ḫa-i-iš-te, Ḫu-i-te, Ḫu-i-te-e, Ḫu-e-te, Ḫu-i-ti, In-zi-te, Ma-ar-te, Ša-aḫ-lu-te-e, Ša-aḫ-lu-te-, Ša-ḫu-ul-te-e, Še-ḫal-te, Še-ḫa-al-te, Ši-la-ḫi-te, Ši-il-wa-te, Du-ra-ar-te, Ur-ḫi-te*), cf. P.M. Purves, *NPN*, 264. According to the orthographic conventions of Linear B, that are probably derived from Linear A, ***-r-*** preceding an occlusive is not expressed in consonant clusters.

Th. Richter (*VHN*, 431, s.v. ***kar-***) mentions that a verbal root ***kar-*** (without root-extension) possibly can be isolated from ***kari(j)e*** 'Vogelfänger' ['bird-catcher, fowler'] (see *BGH*, 190), that may be associated with Urartian ***kar=u-*** 'besiegen' ['to conquer'] (cf. G.A. Melikišvili, *Die urartäische Sprache*, Studia Pohl, Rome 1971, 83; V. Haas, *Rezension zu* Laroche 1980, *Bibliotheca Orientalis 39*, Leiden 1982, 604; I.M. Diakonoff, On some new trends in Urartian philology and some new Urartian texts, *Archäologische Mitteilungen aus Iran. Neue Folge 22*, Berlin 1989, 82[27]; M. Salvini, Die Felsinschrift Argištis I bei Ortakent, Kreis Hanak (Osttürkei), *Orientalia Nova Series 75*, Rome 2006, 75). I may also refer to M. Salvini - I. Wegner, *Einführung in die urartäische Sprache*, 110, s.v. ***kar-*** 'besiegen, bezwingen' ['to conquer, to subdue, to control'].

Th. Richter thinks that this root offers a good meaning for the Hurrian personal name ***e-ew-ri-ga-ri-im*** {*evri-kar=i=m*(: *b*)} at Kaniš (cf. Garelli 1963, 156) 'Der Herr besiegte (Feind)' ['The Lord conquered (the enemy)']. Therefore ***kari(j)e*** may originally mean '(Vogel-)Besieger' ['conqueror (of birds)']. Intransitive usage of the root ***kar-*** provides the meaning 'siegen' ['to prevail']. According to Th. Richter (*VHN*, 152, 431) the Hurrian personal name ***Karakka*** (wr. *ka-ra-ak-ka*) at Mari belongs to this verbal root, analysis {*kar=a=kk=a*}, typology 1.2.3, lexicon *kar-*, cf. at Kaniš *kà-ra-ku-na* (see Donbaz, 2006, 275), as well as ***Karija*** (wr. *ga-ri-ia*, *ka-ri-ia*) at Mari, Šubat-Enlil, Assur, Nippur; (wr. *ka$_4$-ri-a, ka$_4$-ri-ia*) at Kurruḫanni; (wr. *ka$_4$-ri-ia*) at Nuzi, cf. I.J. Gelb, *NPN*, 80, s.v. ***Kariịa*** (wr. *Qa-ri-ia*), analysis {*kar=i=ja*}, typology 1.1.1.2.4, lexicon *kar-*.

Hurrian ***Karkunni*** (wr. *Qa-ar-ku-un-ni*, *Ka-ar-ku-un-ni*) at Nuzi (cf. P.M. Purves, *NPN*, 223, s.v. ***kar***) can be analysed as ***kar=kk=o/u=nni*** 'the one who conquers', 'the conqueror'. The meaning is based on the new insights pronounced by I. Wegner regarding the formant ***-kk-*** as nominal element (*nomen actoris* ?).

E. Laroche (*GLH*, 27) mentioned that the suffix for the assertive negation ***k(k)i*** is attached to the inflected verbal form: "La négation assertive ***-ki*** s'ajoute à la forme verbale fléchie: ***kadi-ki*** 'il ne dit pas', d'où le nom ***kadikku-nni*** 'qui ne parle pas, muet'." [***kadi-ki*** 'he does not speak', from which the noun ***kadikku-nni*** 'the one who does not speak, deaf-mute', is derived.] It is important to realize that this interpretation is only feasible, if one assumes that ***kadi-ki*** and ***kadikku-nni*** are used in antipassive constructions, for the normal negation in transitive constructions is the suffix ***-wa-***, whereas ***-kk-*** is the suffix for negations in intransitive or antipassive constructions.

Now I. Wegner (*Einführung*, 56) does not agree with E. Laroche (and the scholars who followed him in this respect) on this 'negative' interpretation of ***kadikku-nni*** as 'the one who does not speak, deaf-mute'. She points to a nominal element ***-kk-***, often in connection with ***-u/o=nni*** in descriptions of persons: e.g. ***ašḫ=uš=i=kk=o=nni*** 'Opfermandant' ['someone who authorizes sacrifices'] from the root ***ašḫ-*** 'opfern' ['to sacrifice'] (Boğazköy); and ***amumm=i=kk=o=nni*** 'Verwalter' ['estate-steward'] from ***am=om-*** '(hin)sehen, beobachten' ['to observe, to pay attention to'] (Boğazköy).

She bases her analysis on evidence from the Hurrian-Hittite bilingual ***Kirenze*** (KBo 32): "In the Hurrian-Hittite bilingual ***Kirenze*** from Boğazköy (KBo 32: 15 Rs. IV 9) a form ***iš=i=kk=o=nn(i)=a*** (*essive*) occurs that corresponds with a form of Hittite ***wešk-*** 'to lament, wail, moan'. There is no trace of a negation in the Hittite translation. Also in view of Urartian ^{LÚ}***urb=i=ka-*** 'victim, priest ?' (Urartian ***urb-*** 'to slaughter') the Hurrian formant ***-kk-*** (nominal element, *nomen actoris* ?) and the morpheme ***-kkV(vowel)-*** (indicating the negative form of the intransitive and antipassive verb) should be distinguished (cf. already I.M. Diakonoff, *Hurrisch und Urartäisch*, 117^{+129}; now also G. Wilhelm, *SCCNH 15*, 2005, 179^{22}: designation of a person in ***-i=kk(i)=o=nni***)."

If Hurrian ***Karkunni*** (wr. *Qa-ar-ku-un-ni*, *Ka-ar-ku-un-ni*) at Nuzi can indeed be analysed as {*kar=kk=o/u=nni*} 'the one who conquers', 'the conqueror', consequently Linear A ***ka-ku-ne-te*** (ZA 10b.6) can be analysed as {*kar=kk=o/u=nne/i-te*}, consisting of a nominal element ***kar=kk=o/u=nne/i-*** and the theophorous element ***-Te***, hypocoristic of *Tešub*. The name can be translated as 'Tešub (is) the conqueror'. See also the discussion (*supra*) on Hurrian ***kargarni*** 'round shield' and the Linear A and B sign ***ka***.

Actually Linear A provides personal names that may well contain a formation offering a designation of a person in ***-i=kk(i)=o=nni***: namely ***ti-ti-ku*** (HT 35.1; ZA Zb 3.2) and ***ti-ti-ku-ni*** (HT 96a.1). M. Pope has compared these Linear A personal names with Hurrian ***titiku*** and ***titikun*** at Alalaḫ, cf. M. Pope, *Aegean writing and Linear A* (*Studies in Mediterranean Archaeology, Vol. VIII*), Lund 1964, 5.

Linear A ***ti-ti-ku-ni*** can now be analysed as {*titt=i=kk=u=nni*}, based on the root ***tid- / titt-*** and the nominal suffixes ***-kk=u/o=nni***, cf. I. Wegner, *Einführung*, 55-56. This formant ***-kk-*** (often occurring in descriptions of persons: possibly *nomina actoris*) should not be confused with the negation-suffix (***-kk***+vowel) in *intransitive* and *antipassive* verbal forms. ***Titikun*** {*tid=i=kk=u/o=n*}, with a voiced second dental at Alalaḫ, is a shortened form of {*tid=i=kk=u/o=nni*} (root ***tid-***), whereas the Linear A names ***ti-ti-ku*** and ***ti-ti-ku-ni*** have voiceless initial and second dentals (root ***titt-***). Since the Linear A personal names ***ti-ti-ku*** (HT 35.1; ZA Zb 3.2) and ***ti-ti-ku-ni*** (HT 96a.1) as well as ***Titiku*** and ***Titikun*** at Alalaḫ contain the root ***tid-*** II / ***titt-*** 'to attack', it is justifiable to translate them provisionally as 'Attacker', cf. the Urartian parallel ^{LÚ}***urb=i=ka*** 'victim, priest (?)' from Urartian and Hurrian ***urb-*** 'to slaughter, sacrifice' (I. Wegner, *Einführung*, 56).

Linear A ***ma-za*** (ZA 10b.2) at Kato Zakro may be equated with the name of a man ***Masa***, attested at Boğazköy, cf. E. Laroche, *NH*, 115, nº 770. Abs. ^{m}*Ma-ša* (KBo IX 82 Ro 2; fragm. KBo IX 94, 8). E. Laroche, *GLH*, 169 : ***mazeri*** 'aide' ['assistant']: 1. RS quadr. 130 Vo 7: [sum. DAḪ = akk. *re-e-s*]*ú* = h. *ma-zi-ri* = oug. *i-zi-ir-*[*ru*]. 2. Terme d'hépatoscopie hitt.: écrit *ma-zé* ou *ma-zé-eš* ou *ma-zé-re-eš* (*Ugar. V*, 456; *RA 64*, 137).

Th. Richter (*BGH*, 246-247) confirms s.v. ***maz-*** [Mitt.?; PN] and (*VHN*, 456) s.v. ***maz-***, the meaning 'helfen, Hilfe leisten' ['to help, to offer help'] and adds that ***maz-*** in personal names with an intransitive formation can more specifically be interpreted as '(bei der Geburt) Hilfe leisten' ['to offer help at birth, to assist at birth']. The derivation ***mazuri*** {*maz=o=ri*} can be understood as 'Helfender' ['the helping one'], cf. also ***maziri*** {*maz=i=ri*} 'derjenige der hilft' ['the one who helps'] in ^{D}IŠKUR-*ma-zi-ri*.

It is clear that Th. Richter follows I. Wegner's view that we are dealing with the *participial formant* ***=i=ri***, because she mentions (*Einführung*, 89) in her list of verbal root-extensions: ***-ir-***: "Unklar, in ***maz=ir=i*** zu ***maz-*** 'helfen?' ['to help?'] (see for this and the next root-extension ****-o/ur-*** Giorgieri, *SMEA XLI/1*, 1999, 74 with n. 51 [no meaning]). The rare root-extension cannot easily be distinguished the participial formant ***=i=ri*** ."

Th. Richter (*VHN*, 190-191, 456) mentions the Hurrian personal name ***Mazaja*** (wr. *Ma-za-a-ia*) at Tigunāni, analysis {*maz=a=ja*}, lexicon *maz-*, typology 1.1.1.3.4, 'Er/Sie leistete Hilfe' ['He/She offered help, assisted (at birth)']. Since the typology 1.1.1.3.4 refers to *hypocoristic formations* (cf. Th. Richter (*VHN*, 584), it is clear that ***Mazaja*** is a hypocoristic name with the hypocoristic suffix ***-ya***. Transitive formations, such as ***Mazija*** (wr. *ma-zi-ia*) at Emar, can be ambiguous, because that form can be either a hypocoristic name in ***-ya*** or a 'one-word' verbal formation consisting of the verbal root ***maz-*** + the marker of transitivity ***-i-*** + the marker of the subject of action 3rd person singular in ***-a***, cf. I. Wegner, *Einführung*, 93, Table 4.

Th. Richter (*VHN*, 190-191, 456) also mentions the Hurrian personal names ***Mazalla*** (wr. *Ma-za-la*) and ^{f}***Mazalla*** (wr. ^{f}*Ma-za-al-la*) at Mari, analysis {*maz=all=a*}, lexicon *maz-*, typology 1.1.1.3.3; ^{f}***Mazallaja*** (wr. ^{f}*Ma-za-la-a-ia*) at Mari, {*maz=all=a=(a)ia*}, lexicon *maz-*, typology 1.1.1.3.3; ^{f}***Mazallum*** at Mari, analysis {*maz=all=o=m*}, lexicon *maz-*, typology 1.1.1.1.1.

The Linear A personal name ***ma-za*** (ZA 10b.2) represents the *intransitive* form ***maza*** that can be interpreted as either the intransitive *imperative* {*maz=a*} 'Offer help / Assist (at birth) (oh *numen*) !' or the intransitive *indicative* 3rd person singular {*maz=a=Ø*}, 'He/She (a *numen*) offered help / assisted (at birth)', consisting of the verbal root ***maz-*** + the marker of intransitivity ***-a-*** + the marker of the subject of action 3rd person singular in ***-Ø***, cf. I. Wegner, *Einführung*, 99, Table 6 and 7. For example, Hurrian ***una*** means either 'come !' or 'he/she comes'.

According to Linear A and B orthographic conventions ***-n-*** preceding ***-s-*** is not expressed in consonant clusters, cf. Linear B ***ko-ri-si-ja*** (PY Ep 212,4; Eb 347,1; *et alibi*) = ***Κορινσίᾱ***, ethnic of ***ko-ri-to*** (PY Ad 921), ***Κόρινθος***. Therefore an equation of Linear A ***ma-za*** (ZA 10b.2) with the Hurrian form ***ma-an-za*** (KUB XXXII 20.8) could not be excluded in the past, since the meaning was not yet clarified by E. Laroche, *GLH*, 167. However, I. Wegner (*Einführung*, 82-83, sub 3: *The independent pronouns*) and Th. Richter (*BGH*, 242) mention, s.v. ***manella*** (*absolutive* independent personal pronoun 3rd person plural 'they'), that ***manza*** is the plural dative of ***manella*** and can be analysed as {*man=š/z=(v)a*}, so that it can be translated as 'for them (together)'. So we may conclude that ***manza*** cannot represent Linear A ***ma-za*** (ZA 10b.2), because a personal name is required in the list of personal names on ZA 10b, not a personal pronoun. Consequently the Hurrian personal name ***Maza***, {*maz=a*}, is the most likely interpretation of Linear A ***ma-za*** (ZA 10b.2).

Linear A ***ra$_2$-ro-re*** (ZA 10b.5) may be equated with the name of the Hurrian goddess ***Liluri***, with palatalized ***l* (>*l*^{y})** in the first syllable, **= *L^{y}al(l)uri* = /*L^{y}al(l)ore*/** or ***Lial(l)uri*** **= /*Lial(l)ore*/** (with **[*o*]** and **[*e*]**). The goddess is described by E. Laroche, *GLH*, 160, as 'Déesse parèdre de Tešub de Manuziya, au Kizuwatna; fête *ḫišuwaš*, CTH 628, *passim*. Graphies: *^{d}Li-lu-u-ri, Li-il-lu-ri, Le-el-lu-ri.*

Sg. *Lil(l)uri,* KUB XII 12 V 16, 20, VI 7, 15 et dupl.; KUB XXX 40 II 3 sqq.; KUB XXXII 65 I 16 et dupl.; KBo XX 115, 8, etc. – *abate ^{d}Liluri* ou *^{d}Liluri abate,* KUB XII 12 VI 17, 27; KBo XV 37 II 11; KUB XXV 48 III 16, etc.; KBo XVII 98, 12. – Akk. *^{d}Li-lu-ri,* KBo X 1 Ro 38. - Pl. *^{d}Li-il-lu-ri-in-na (^{d}Abatenna tiyarenna),* KUB XXV 42+ II 18, IV 6, 12, V 20; KBo XV 48 II 17, III 23, 42. – Le pluriel *Lillurinna* et le voisinage de *abate(nna) tiyare(nna)* indiquent un appellatif divinisé.

^{d}El-lu-ri, hapax de KBo IV 2 IV 18, 20 (= Murš. Spr. Vo 6, 8), doit être corrigé en *^{d}Li-el-lu-ri,* d'après les dupl. KUB XV 36+ Vo 6, et KUB XLIII 51 Vo 3, 5.

Since there are apparently no words or names starting with {R} and only a few starting with {L} that are of Hurrian origin, we must assume that *^{d}Li-lu-u-ri, Li-il-lu-ri, Le-el-lu-ri* or *^{d}Li-el-lu-ri* was adopted into Hurrian religion and society from elsewhere, possibly from Kizzuwatna. The evidence shows, however, that she was fully embedded in Hurrian religion and society. Since her name is now also attested in Linear A, it cannot be ruled out that her origin was in prepalatial and Pre-Hurrian Crete or in Kizzuwatna (later Cilicia) or other areas in the Near East or Anatolia.

Since ***ra$_2$*** in Linear A ***ra$_2$-ro-re*** in ZA 10b.5 is probably to be interpreted as ***ria/rya*** or ***lia/lya*** as in Linear B, one may think of palatalization of the first ***l-* > *l*^{y}** in the forms with the orthography ***^{d}Li-il-*** and ***^{d}Li-el-*** of the divine name ***Liluri*** attested at Boğazköy.

It is generally assumed that the cuneiform forms with the orthography ***^{d}Li-il(l)-*** and ***^{d}Li-el(l)-*** of the divine name ***Lil(l)uri***, attested at Boğazköy, represent ***Lil(l)-*** or ***Lel(l)-***, but one should realize that it is in fact impossible to distinguish palatalized ***L^{y}il(l)-*** or ***L^{y}el(l)-*** in cuneiform from not-palatalized forms ***Lil(l)-*** or ***Lel(l)-***, if both can appear as ***^{d}Li-il(l)-*** and ***^{d}Li-el(l)-*** in the script.

According to Linear A orthography the Hurrian name attested at Kato Zakro should be read as ***L^{y}al(l)ore*** or ***Lial(l)ore***, which is in accordance with the phonological representation of *^{d}Li-lu-u-ri, Li-il-lu-ri, Le-el-lu-ri* as **/*L^{y}el(l)ore/i*/** or **/*Liel(l)ore/i*/** with **[*o*]** and **[*e*]**. With only one certain example it is difficult to determine, whether possible palatalization of the first ***L-* > *L^y-*** is a feature limited to the name of this goddess or whether it may be a feature of the Minoan-Hurrian dialect and possibly of (some) other Hurrian dialects as well. There are more examples of ***a/e*** alternation in Hurrian, which make alternation of ***L^{y}al(l)-* / *Lial(l)-*** with ***L^{y}el(l)-* / *Liel(l)-*** conceivable.

As can be observed in both Linear A and cuneiform, theonyms such as ***Kubaba***, ***Šamaš*** and ***Šimegi*** can be used as personal names. Since Linear A ***ra$_2$-ro-re*** also occurs in a list of personal names, the divine name ***L^{y}al(l)ore*** or ***Lial(l)ore*** should probably be regarded here as a personal name as well. E. Laroche (*GLH*, 232-233) tells that Hurrian ***Šimigi* / *Šimegi*** assimilated to the Babylonian Sungod ***Šamaš***. The Linear A personal name ***sa-ma*** (HT 6b.5, HT 10a.1, HT 52a.1; ZA 10b.3-4), perhaps representing ***Šamaš*** (see *supra*), occurs on the same side of tablet ZA 10b as ***L^{y}al(l)ore*** or ***Lial(l)ore***. It is likely that both ***Šamaš*** and ***Lial(l)ore*** are theonyms used as personal names on this tablet.

Linear A ***ma-ki-de-te*** 5 (ZA 10b.3) from Kato Zakro, following ***ma-za*** 5 (ZA 10b.2-3) and preceding ***sa-ma*** 5 (ZA 10b.3-4), occurs in a long list of personal names on ZA 10.

There can be no doubt that it is a personal name as well. It can be interpreted as a so-called 'one-word' name that can be analysed as {*mag=e/id=a>e=tte*}, consisting of the verbal root ***mag-*** 'to give (as a present)' + the suffix ***-ed-/-id-*** marking the future tense + the subject marker ***-a > e-*** + the enclitic personal pronoun 1st person singular ***-tta/-tte/-tti*** indicating the object of the transitive verb. It can be translated as 'He/She (scil. a *numen*) will give me (as a present)'. The regular enclitic personal pronoun 1st person singular is ***-tta***, cf. I. Wegner, *Einführung*, 93, table 4. According to Th. Richter (*VHN*, 596, sub 1.3.1.1.2.2) the regular enclitic ***-tta*** in personal names can be replaced by the *optional allomorphic* forms ***-tti/-tte***. Compare: Linear A ***ma-ka-i-ta*** (PK 1.7; ZA 5b.2-3), ***a-mi-ta*** (ZA 10b.4-5), ***a-we-||ni-ta*** (ZA 8.2-3), ***da-i-pi-ta*** (ZA 8.5; ZA 10a.4-5) ***i-do-ri-ni-ta*** (PH 6.2), ***ki-da-ta*** (HT 40+76.2),] ***su-ki-ri-ta*** (PH Wa 32, side α).

The other feasible interpretation is that the name can be analysed as a theophorous 'sentence name', with ***-Tešub*** in its abbreviated or hypocoristic form ***-te*** as subject of the verbal form. The analysis is then {*mag=e/id=a>e=Te*}, consisting of the verbal root ***mag-*** 'to give (as a present)' + the suffix ***-ed-/-id-*** marking the future tense + the subject marker ***-a > e-*** + Te(šub): translation 'Te(šub) will give (the child) (as a present)'.

The Linear A personal name ***ma-ka-i-ta*** (PK 1.7; ZA 5b.2-3) on a tablet at Palaikastro and on one at Kato Zakro shows the same verbal formation as Linear A ***ma-ka-i-se*** (ZA 8.4) at Kato Zakro. Linear A ***ma-ka-i-ta*** can be analysed as {*mag=ai=tta*}, consisting of the root ***mag-*** 'to give (as a present)' + the *final debitive* suffix ***-ai-*** + the suffix of the enclitic personal pronoun 1st person singular ***-tta*** marking the object of action in a transitive construction, translation 'Let he / she (scil. a *numen*) give me (as a present) !' / 'In order that he/she (a *numen*) gives me (as a present)'.

Linear A ***ma-ka-i-se*** (ZA 8.4) at Kato Zakro can be identified as a personal name, since it occurs in a list of names. It can be interpreted as Hurrian ***Magai-še***, hypocoristic form of ***Magai-šena*** or ***Magai-šenni/e***, a perfect name for a newborn boy. Hurrian ***-še*** can be interpreted as a shortened form of ***-šen=a*** 'brother' or ***-šen(=a)=ne/i*** > ***-šenne/i*** 'the brother', which is clear in ***Unap-še*** (wr. *Ú-na-ap-še*, *Ú-nap-še*), because an ***Unap-še*** is son of *Karkunni* and an ***Unap-šenni*** is son of *Qa-ar-*[....] at Nuzi, cf. P.M. Purves, *NPN*, 253. Consequently Linear A ***ma-ka-i-se*** (ZA 8.4) can be analysed as {*mag=ai-še(n=a)*} 'Let he/she (a *numen*) give a brother !' or 'Let the (deceased) brother give (the child) !'.

The word ***maganni*** happens to occur frequently in the Tušratta letter, which may be expected in diplomatic correspondence, in this case about Tušratta's daughter, *Tadu-ḫepa*, who had been given as a wife to Amenhotep III. Tušratta expressed in his letter his wish to receive gifts of gold in return, e.g. a golden statue of his daughter, so that she would always be with him. My hypothesis in the 2016 edition of *Minoan Linear A*, Vol. I, was that the Hurrian form ***maganni***, rendered as 'present, gift', might consist of a noun ****magay*** + the suffix ***-ni*** of the so-called definite article. In other words, ***maganni*** (< **magay-ni*) would be 'the gift, the present'. In fact I proposed that this alleged noun ****magay*** might be a form with a diphthong ending like ***allay*** 'lady' : ***allani*** 'the lady', ***attay*** 'father' : ***attanni*** 'the father' and ***uštay*** (theme ***uštae***) 'hero' : ***uštanni*** 'the hero'.

Anyway, I am now convinced that ***mag=ai-*** in Linear A ***ma-ka-i-se*** (ZA 8.4) and ***ma-ka-i-ta*** (PK 1.7; ZA 5b.2-3) has to be interpreted as a verbal form with the *final debitive* suffix ***-ai-/-ae-***.

E. Laroche, *GLH*, 164: "***maganni*** 'cadeau, présent' (L. Messerschmidt, *Mitanni-Studien*, 25; Speiser, *IH*, 39; *NPN*, 233); *ma-ka-a-an-ni-iw-wu-u-un-na* 'mes présents', Mit. II 15, 54; - *ma-ka-a-an-na* 'son présent', *ibidem* III 58. Sur *maganni, magannuti* à Nuzi et Alalaḫ, cf. *AW*, 574 sq. – Ug. ***mgn*** même sens, *HUS* 178 sq. L'origine indo-arienne (skr. *magha-* + *-nni*), défendue par plusieurs auteurs n'est pas évidente; cf. Von Soden, *JEOL 18*, 339 sq. Il peut s'agir de la racine sém. ***mgn***." It is true that ***mgn*** is 'to give' in Ugaritic, Hebrew, Phoenician and Arabic (cf. F. Gröndahl, *PNTU*, Rome 1967, 156, s.v. ***mgn***), but derivation from Indo-Iranian *magha-* into Hurrian *maganni* into Semitic *mgn* seemed equally plausible. P.M. Purves, *NPN*, 233, s.v. *makannati*: Hurrian? *Ma-qa-an-na-ti, Ma-ga-na-ti*. Cf. *makanni* 'gift', in Tuš., on which see Jensen in *ZA V (1890)*, 196, and Messerschmidt, *Mitanni-Studien*, 25. But personal name *Ma-ga-an-na-ti* also occurs at Susa; see *Mém. XXII*, 192.

Th. Richter (*BGH*, 238-239), s.v. ***mag-*** [PN]: 'offrir (?)' (Faucounau 1980a: 387, Prechel/Richter 2001: 369[210]). [I translate the German text] Etymology: From a Hurrian-Urartian root ****maq-*** 'to reach, to hit' (with derivation ***maganni*** 'present'), see Diakonoff / Starostin 1986: 22. Further: See Faucounau (1980a: 388) ***magu*** 'offert', i.e. *mag-u*, in a Cypro-Minoan text. Richter 2007: 107f. and 2010b: 507; ***maga/i*** [Boğ; Ma] without translation, root cognate with ***maganni*** 'cadeau' (Salvini 1988a: 65); 'Gift' (Görke 2010: 141). E. Laroche (*GLH*, 164) already quoted the Mari-form ***ma-ga-wə***. Etc.

Th. Richter (*VHN*, 189, 454) mentions, s.v. ***mag-/meg-***, the following personal names: ***^{f}Makija*** [with variant ***^{f}Mekija***] (wr. *^{f}Ma-ki-ia; ^{f}Me-ki-ia*), name of 5 ladies at Mari, analysis {*mag/meg=i=ja*}, typology 1.1.1.2.4, lexicon *mag-*, 'Er/Sie schenkte(?) (Mädchen)' ['He/She offered (the girl) as a gift'], cf. *Ma-ku-ia* at Nuzi; ***^{f}Makunta*** (wr. *^{f}Ma-ku-un-da*) at Mari, analysis {*magond(i)=a*[E.]}, typology 3.2.1, lexicon *magundi*; ***^{f}Šeḫrum-makuš*** (wr. *^{f}Še-eḫ-rum-ma-gu-úš*) at Ašnakkum, typology 1.1.1.1.1, analysis {*šeġr=o=m-magoš(še)*}, lexicon *šeḫr-, magušše*, '*maguš* machte (Mädchen) großzügig' ['*maguš* made (the girl) (looking) great'].

Another verbal form with the *final debitive* suffix ***-ai-*** (in subordinate clauses) or *adhortative* suffix with *jussive* force (in main clauses), ***zul(l)=ai***, occurs in a Linear A inscription ***a-re-ne-ṣi-di-jo-pi-ke-pa-ja-su-ra-i-te-ra-me-a-ja-ku*** (KN Zf 13) from Mavro Spilio. I shall not only discuss the form ***zul(l)=ai***, but analyse the whole inscription, which appears to be a complete Hurrian sentence, in § 1 of Chapter 12: *Inscriptions on metal objects*. The inscription allows us a glimpse of a Hurrian wedding-ceremony and offers us an unexpected connection between the Minoan-Hurrian religious rituals, the Mycenaean heroic world and the mythological pedigree of the 'Great Aias', one of the great heroes in Homer's *Iliad*.

After the conclusion that Linear A ***a-ku-mi-na*** and ***a-du-ku-mi-na*** can be interpreted as Hurrian personal names and have nothing to do with the commodity 'cumin', we may wonder, whether this commodity or a form of it, is attested in Linear A. Apparently it is, which is not surprising, since ***ku-mi-no*** (MY Ge 602,3, e.a.) *κύμῑνον* is attested in Linear B.

Two inscriptions offer the same sequence:]***ku-mi-na-qe***[(HT 54a.2) and ***ku-mi-na|-qe*** (HT Wc 3014a-b), the first on a tablet and the second on a roundel from Hagia Triada.

HT 54a.1.] vestigia [
2.] *ku-mi-na-qe* [
3.] *ki-mi-ra2* [
Inf. mut.
Sup. mut.
b.1.] 4 *ki* [
2.] vestigia [
Inf. mut.

HT Wc 3014. Analysed structure of the text:
Sides a-b: | *ku-mi-na|-qe* , CAP
Side c (edge) : three seal impressions: D. Levi: type 81.

Linear A ***-qe*** does not contain the labio-velar sound of Mycenaean Linear B, but the voiced velar fricative or spirant ***-ḫ-***, phonologically ***/ġ/***, of the Hurrian adjectival suffix ***-ḫe / -ḫi***, cf. e.g. E.A. Speiser, *IH*, 47, §57: *paš-ši-ḫi* (Mit. III 54, 57) 'pertaining to sending, shipment' (from *paš* 'send'), described as direct adjectival derivation. Likewise Linear A ***ku-mi-na-qe*** can be analysed as {*kumin=a=ḫe*} and interpreted as 'pertaining to cumin'.

P. Chantraine (*Dictionnaire Étymologique de la Langue Grecque*, Paris 1968, 599), s.v. ***κύμῑνον***: "On admet depuis longtemps un emprunt sémitique, cf. akkad. *kamūnu(m)*, ougar. *kmn*, phénic. *kmn*, hébr. *kammōn*. Voir E. Masson, *Emprunts sémitiques* 51 sq."

However, althought Linear B ***ku-mi-no*** *κύμῑνον* is usually considered a Semitic loan-word, it may well be 'Pre-Greek' in view of ***-īν-***, as in Linear B ***se-ri-no*** = ***σέλῑνον***, and in toponyms as *Σαλαμῑν-*. The Semitic word may have been borrowed from a non-Semitic language, possibly Minoan. It obviously belongs to the category of cultural words that can easily be transmitted from one language to the other. So Latin *cuminum* is probably derived from Greek *κύμῑνον* and the terms for *cumin* in modern Indo-European languages are on their turn derived from Latin.

The identical ethnic suffix ***-ḫe/-ḫi*** in e.g. ***Ḫalbaḫe*** in the cuneiform syllabary and ***Ḫlbġ*** in the alphabetic cuneiform of Ugarit, 'man of Aleppo', is probably derived from the general adjectival suffix. Single ***-ḫ-*** in intervocalic position corresponds to alphabetic ***ġ***, as is shown by ***Ḫalbaḫi*** = ***ḫlbġ***. Accordingly, intervocalic ***-ḫḫ-*** should appear in RŠ as ***ḫ***. This equation is illustrated by a convincing pair of instances. Alongside syllabic ***turuḫḫi(na)*** 'male' and ***aštuḫḫi(na)*** 'female' we get alphabetic ***trḫn*** and ***astḫn*** (RŠ X 4. 55ff).

If the interpretation of Linear A ***a-du-|ku-mi-na*** (ZA 10a.3-4) as ****Aštuḫḫu-mina*** (*supra*) is correct, we can conclude that the voiceless velar fricative or spirant ***-ḫḫ-*** in the cuneiform syllabary and ***-ḫ-*** in the alphabetic cuneiform of Ugarit was rendered by ***-k-*** in Linear A.

Actually the combination of ***ku-mi-na|-qe*** with the ideogram CAP on HT Wc 3014a-b may describe 'goat-cheese or goat-meat flavoured with cumin' rather than 'goat flavoured with cumin'. If the reading **]** ***ki-mi-ra2*** **[** is correct, the combination of] ***ku-mi-na-qe*** [(HT 54a.2) with **]** ***ki-mi-ra2*** [(HT 54a.3) appears to confirm the relation between the adjectival form of 'cumin' and 'goat(s)', for ***ki-mi-ra2*** = ***ki-mi-ria*** may possibly be interpreted as '(small) goats', allegedly ****ḫi-mi-ri-ia*** in cuneiform. Sign ***ra2*** = ***ria / rya*** or ***lia / lya*** in Linear B and probably in Linear A as well.

An interesting gloss is Hesych 476: *χίμαροι· αἶγες χειμέριαι, ἢ τράγοι ἢ ἔριφοι.* Hesych 473 also mentions the *Chimaira*, a trimorphic monster (lion-goat-snake), whose provenance seems to be from Lycia: *Χίμαιρα· τρίμορφον θηρίον, ὃ πρόσθεν μὲν λέων, μέσον δὲ χίμαιρα, ὄπισθεν δὲ δράκων. φασὶν δὲ ἐν Λυκίᾳ γίνεσθαι ὡς κεφαλὴν μὲν λέοντος ἔμπροσθεν, καὶ ἀπὸ στόματος πῦρ ἀποπέμπον, ὄπισθεν δὲ δράκοντος ἔχον κεφαλήν.*

J.-L. Perpillou, who finished the section *χηρωσταί - ὤψ* of P. Chantraine's, *Dictionnaire Étymologique de la Langue Grecque*, Paris 1968, 1260-1261, mentions s.v. *χίμαιρα*: "f., jeune chèvre née à la fin de l'hiver précédent, donc âgée d'un an au moment de sa première mise bas (Hom., etc). Définitions partielles mais claires chez les lexicographes ...... D'autre part, monstre mythologique de formes diverses (différent dans l'*Iliade* et chez Hésiode), mais comportant tête ou corps de chèvre (Hom., Hés, etc.)." Perpillou writes sub étymologie: "le rapport de *χίμαρος* à *χίμαιρα* est discuté. Selon Frisk, *χίμαρος*, qui n'est attesté qu'à partir d'Aristophane, peut être une innovation à partir de *χίμαιρα*, comme *πιερός* de *πίειρα*. La formation pourrait cependant être ancienne, sinon indo-européenne, et *χίμαιρα*, dérivé en *-yă*, lui avoir d'abord servi de féminin (v. Chantraine, *Formation* 226). Formes issues du thème en *r* aussi attesté par les adjectifs *χειμερινός, χειμέριος*, alternant du thème en *n* qui se trouve dans le nom de l'hiver *χειμών, χεῖμα* (voir s.u.). Le vocalisme radical est ici au degré zéro, avec un répondant arménien *jmeȓn* 'hiver' < **ghimer-*." J.-L. Perpillou also mentions an Indo-European etymology (Pokorny) of Greek *χίμαιρα* on account of Old Germanic and Latin, which does not seem convincing: "Emploi ancien dans le vocabulaire de l'élevage, avec des dérivés de forme proche en germanique: ainsi suéd. - norv. dial. *Gimber* (< germ. **gimbrī*) 'brebis qui n'a pas encore eu de petits', et, sans la suffixation **r/n*, avec le latin *bīmus, trīmus, quadrimus* (< **bi-hĭmus*, etc.) appliqué au bétail. Pokorny 426."

The relationship between *χίμαιρα* 'goat' and the adjectives *χειμέριος, χειμερινός* and substantive *χειμών* 'winter' and 'winter(storm)', assumed by the lexicographers *EM* and Hesychius, may well be a typical example of popular etymology.

Derivation of Greek ***χίμαιρα*** (with possible metathesis) from Minoan Linear A ***<u>ki</u>-<u>mi</u>-<u>ria</u>*** seems feasible. If the link between CAP on the roundel HT Wc 3014 from Hagia Triada and ***<u>ki</u>-<u>mi</u>-<u>ria</u>*** on HT 54a.3 can be laid through ***ku-mi-na-qe*** as intermediary in both texts, we may have found the Minoan origin of Greek ***χίμαιρα***, and a Minoan (and possibly Hurrian) word for 'goat'. Provenance of the Chimaira monster from Lycia is of course possible, but it is conceivable that the Mycenaean Greeks learned not only the term ***χίμαιρα*** from the Minoans, but also heard the stories about Chimaira, Minotauros and other monsters directly from the Minoans.

The etymological relationship between Greek *χειμερινός, χειμέριος* and Armenian *jmeȓn* 'hiver' < **ghimer-*, mentioned by Perpillou, is not isolated. There is a large number of 'isoglosses' between Armenian and Greek, which has surprised scholars, because Greeks and Armenians did not live close together in historic times. So it is alleged that they must have lived close together in prehistoric times. Another explanation of the phenomenon might be that these isoglosses are (partly) due to an adstrate or substrate legacy of Hurrian and/or Urartian in Armenian on the one hand and a substrate of Minoan-Hurrian in Greek on the other. Such a theory does not depend on an etymology of Greek *χίμαιρα* from Minoan Linear A ***<u>ki</u>-<u>mi</u>-<u>ria</u>***.

Linear A ***ki-mi-ria*** may be the Minoan word for '(small) goat' surviving in Greek *χίμαρος* (plural: *χίμαροι*) and in the name of the mythological monster *Χίμαιρα*, with the head of a lion (*λέων*), body of a goat (*χίμαιρα*) and a snake (*δράκων*) as its tail.

The Hurrian word for '(small) goat' is not yet confirmed. If the Minoan word is of Hurrian origin, the Hurrian rendering might have been ***ḫimiria*** (written ***ḫi-mi-ri-ia*** in cuneiform). Adaptation of ***ḫimiria*** > ***χίμαιρα*** may be a matter of metathesis.

It is also tempting to compare Hurrian ***ḫawerni*** / ***ḫawirni*** with Linear A ***ki-mi-ra₂*** = ***ki-mi-ria*** = ****ḫimiria*** > ***χίμαιρα***, since ***-w-*** and ***-m-*** sometimes alternate in Hurrian.

Th. Richter (*BGH*, 129) mentions s.v. ***ḫawe/irni*** [Boğ.; PN] that E. Laroche (*GLH*, 88) mentions *ḫa-bi-ir-na-a-e* (KUB XLVII 57 Vo 4) without translation. De Martino (1992a, 8, 12) and Trémouille (2000, 145) translate ***ḫawerni*** / ***ḫawirni*** as 'sheep'. According to Durand (1995) it corresponds with Sumerogram SILA4, which means 'lamb'. According to E. Neu (1996a, 258) it means '(Ziegen-)Bock' ['he-goat, billy-goat'] and corresponds with the Sumerogram MÁŠ.GAL in Hittite texts. According to Catsanicos (1996, 279), De Martino (1999b, 341; 2000, 305[+59]), Wegner (2000, 225; 2007a, 258), Trémouille (2005, 316), Campbell (2007a, 43[77]), Wilhelm (2010a, 631[22]) it means 'agneau', 'agnello', 'lamb'. If a relation between Hurrian ***ḫawerni*** / ***ḫawirni*** [Boğ.; PN] and Linear A ***ki-mi-ria*** can be observed, and if we take the additional evidence of the ideogram CAP 'goat' on roundel HT Wc 3014 from Hagia Triada into account, the meaning 'he-goat, billy-goat' for ***ḫawerni*** / ***ḫawirni*** may be preferred to 'lamb' or 'sheep'.

Reading ***a-du-sa-ra*** **,** ***te*** **,** VIN[(HT 62+73.1) is to be preferred to the rejected reading † ***a-du*** **̦** ***sa-ra*** **,** ***te*** **,** VIN[, see *Minoan Linear A*, Vol. II, *Corpus of transliterated Linear A texts*, Part I, 2016. Although tablet HT 62+73 is damaged, the first signs are probably correctly read as ***a-du-*** by J. Raison - M. Pope (1980, 71; 1994, 82-83). They have probably regarded the little dot between ***-du-*** and ***sa-*** as accidental and I have followed that view. A thin fracture between ***a-du-*** and ***sa-ra*** hampers a sound judgement. L.C. Meijer (*Eine strukturelle Analyse der Hagia Triada Tafeln*, Amsterdam 1982, 107) shares this view. Reading *Lx-x-sa-ra* , *te* , VIN [in the heading he comments: "So lückenhaft auch dieser Text wieder überliefert ist, die Struktur ist dennoch als die von z.B. HT 9a oder 17 erkennbar: eine Weintransaktion mit '*Lx-x-sa-ra*' und '*Lx-ta-re*' bis einschl. ']-*nu*' als beteiligte Parteien."

Only in case ***a-du*** and ***sa-ra*** turn out to be separate sequences, interpretation of *a-du* ̦ *sa-ra* as 'portion(s) of (a quality of) barley' may be considered, although separation of two commodities, barley and wine (VIN), by a transaction term seems very unlikely. Reading ***a-du-sa-ra*** as one sequence remains preferable.

A-du-sa-ra may well represent a Hurrian personal name ***Ašdu-šara*** containing the elements ***aždu-*** 'woman' and ***-šara***, but can Linear A ***-sa-ra*** be compared with ***-sara*** in ***Arip-sara*** (wr. *A-ri-ip-sa-ra*) and ***ᶠArip-sara*** (wr. *ᶠA-ri-ip-sa-ra*) at Nuzi, cf. I.J Gelb, *NPN*, 29 ? The orthography of these Nuzi names differs from frequent ***Arip-šarri*** (LUGAL) 'The King of Gods gives/gave (the boy)', name of 13 men at Nuzi. The element ***-sara*** (with ***s*** instead of ***š***) in *A-ri-ip-sa-ra* and *ᶠA-ri-ip-sa-ra* is nominal, since Old Hurrian ***arip-***, analysis {*ar=i=b-*}, is verbal. Old Hurrian ***-b*** is marker of the subject. Old Hurrian ***ar=i=b-*** = Mitanni-Hurrian ***ar=i=a*** 'he/she gives', cf. I. Wegner, *Einführung*, 126.

The feminine determinative in *ᶠA-ri-ip-sa-ra* does not make it impossible that the parents of the girl thanked *the King of Gods* for the birth of their daughter. The evidence for equation of Hurrian ***-sara*** in ***ᶠArip-sara*** with ***-šarri*** 'King of Gods' seems negative or at least inconclusive: Is ***-sara*** in *A-ri-ip-sa-ra* and *ᶠA-ri-ip-sa-ra* just a divergent spelling of ***-šarri*** as in ***Arip-šarri*** (with an *essive* case in ***-a***) or are we dealing with a different lexeme ? A division into ****Ar-ipsara*** does not help either.

One thing is clear: ***aždu-*** 'woman' in Linear A ***a-du-sa-ra*** can probably not be connected with ***šarri*** 'King of Gods' or the *essive* ***šarr(i)=a*** 'as the King of Gods'.

The West Semitic theonym *(H)adu*, used in hybrid Hurrian names as a borrowed theophorous element, occurs at Alalaḫ only as second element in *Eḫli-adu, Iri-adu, Ir(w)iri-adu, Pendi-adu, Tagi-adu, Tunib-adu, Uḫlab-adu, Uri-adu* and *Wuri-adu*, cf. A. Draffkorn, *HHA*, 65-66. There seems to be no presence of the original /*h*/ in these hybrid Hurrian names at Alalaḫ, which is to be expected in 'Hurrianized' names. At Nuzi the hybrid personal names ***ᵈAdad-šarri*** and ***ᵈAdatteia*** (*ᵈAdad-te-ia*, variants *A-da-te-ia, A-ta-te-e-a, A-ta-an-te-ia*) are attested, cf. I.J. Gelb, *NPN*, 39; A.A. MacRae, *NPN*, 295. If Linear A ***a-du-sa-ra*** represents hybrid ****Adu-šarra***, the construction of the name remains strange, because one would expect two *absolute* forms ****Adu-šarri*** (like in ***Adad-šarri*** 'Adad is King of Gods'), not an *absolutive* + *essive* form 'Adu is like the King of Gods'.

Since Linear A sign ***53*** = ***ra*** can also represent ***la*** as in Linear B, interpretation of Linear A ***a-du-sa-ra*** (HT 62(+73).1) as Hurrian ***Ašdu-šala*** 'The daughter is a woman' is morphologically feasible and would provide a plausible meaning for a personal name. Since ***šala*** 'daughter' belongs to the category of Hurrian *a*-stems, limited to words indicating congeniality or kinship like ***ela*** 'sister', ***nera*** 'mother', ***šena*** 'brother', ***mena/ mina*** 'twin' (or, as proposed by Th. Richter: also 'sister') and a few other words and names (cf. I. Wegner, *Einführung*, 52-53), one may even claim that the ending in ***-a*** is regular, though one should perhaps add: especially, if it is the first element in a personal name. The second element is usually extended with the so-called suffix of the definite article ***-ni*** resulting in ***-šal(a)-ni*** (assimilation) > ***-šalli***, cf. ***šena+-ni*** > ***-šen(a)-ni*** > ***-šenni*** and ***-mena+ni*** > ***-men(a)-ni*** > ***-menni***. P.M. Purves, *NPN*, 250, s.v. ***šall*** and ***-šalli***: "Hurrian. Cf. ***ᶠŠalanna*** and what may be its hypocoristic form, ***ᶠŠalaia***. Since ***-šalli*** occurs exclusively in feminine personal names, cf. probably Tuš. ***šala*** 'daughter'; see Brünnow in *ZA V (1890)*, 211, and Jensen in *ZA V*, 192 f. and *XIV (1899)*, 173. As Hrozný suggests in *MDOG No. 56 (1915)*, 42, cf. also ***ša-a-la*** KBo V 2 ii 22, in passage transliterated by Friedrich, *KASD*, 33. Doubling of final consonant followed by vowel *i* in *-šalli* beside Tuš. *šala* is analogous to that in *-elli* beside Tuš. *ela.* Cf. p.n. *ᶠÚ-nu-úš-ša-li* at Chagar Bazar, *Iraq VII,* 42." Analysis {*un=o=ž-šal(a)=ni*}, 'The (deceased) daughter may bring (the child)'. ***ᶠŠalanna*** can now be analysed as {*šal=a=nna*}, consisting of the *a*-stem ***šal=a*** + the absolutive enclitic personal pronoun ***-nna***, indicating the subject of the (not expressed) intransitive verb ***mann-*** 'to be', translation 'She (*-nna*) is a daughter'.

In the 2016 edition of *Hurrians and Hurrian in Minoan Crete* I already proposed that Linear A ***a-du-sa-ra*** (HT 62(+73).1) may well contain ***ašdu-*** 'woman' and P.M. Purves's ***-šar*** (2) and be compared with the feminine Hurrian names ***ᶠAštua-šar*** (wr. *ᶠAš-du-a-šar*) at Nuzi and ***ᶠAštu-šar*** (wr. *Aš-tu-za-ar*) at Chagar Bazar (*Iraq VII*, 36), cf. P.M. Purves, *NPN*, 206, s.v. *Ašt, Aštu-, Aštua-, Aštun-* and *NPN*, 251, s.v. ***-šar*** (2).

I. Wegner, *Einführung*, 57, explains ***-zari*** / ***-šari*** as a possibly abstract or collective suffix, offering the examples: ***enzari*** (< ***en(i)*** + ***šari***) 'Gottheit' ['deity, divinity'], derived from ***eni*** 'God'; ***tipšari*** (< ***tiv(e)*** + ***šari***) 'Wort, Sache, Erzählung' ['word, thing, story'], derived from ***tive*** 'Wort'; ***furulzari*** (< ***fur*** + ***(u)l(i)*** + ***šari***) 'Opferschauer' ['interpreter of sacrifices'], derived from ***fur-*** (wr. *pur-/wur-*) 'to see'.

Th. Richter (*VHN*, 80) has apparently accepted that ***-za-ri*** reflects this abstract or collective suffix also in personal names such as ^{f}***Aštu-zar*** (wr. *Aš-tu-za-ar*) at Ašnakkum (modern Tall Šaġīr Bāzār / „Chagar Bazar") and Mari (Tall Hariri), typology 3.1, lexicon *aštuzari* (→ *ašte*), which he translates as 'Frauen(?)' ['Women(?)'].

Th. Richter (*VHN*, 384), s.v. ***ašte*** {*ašte*} and ***aštu*** {*ašto/u*}, writes that a formation ^{o}***=o/u=žari*** in ***aštuzari*** {*ašto/u=žari*} 'Frauen(?)' has parallels with ***azze*** and ***atte***. Indeed he mentions (*VHN*, 84) ^{f}***Azzu-zari*** (wr. ^{f}*Az-zu*-IZ-*za-ri*) at Mari, typology 3.1, lexicon *azzuzari* (→ *azze*), 'Frauen(?)', and (*VHN*, 93) ^{f}***Attu-zar*** (wr. ^{f}*At-tu-za-ar*, ^{f}*A-tu-za-ar*) at Mari and ^{f}***Attu-zari*** (wr. ^{f}*At-tu-za-ri*) at Mari, typology 3.1, lexicon *attuzari* (→ *atte*), 'Frauen(?)'. To corroborate these identifications I may add the personal names ^{f}***Šalanzar*** (wr. ^{f}*Ša-la-an-za-ar*) from Qaṭṭarā, and ^{f}***Šalanzari*** (wr. ^{f}*Ša-la-an-za-ri*, ^{f}*Ša-la-za-ri*) from Mari and Šubat-Enlil, typology 3.1, lexicon *šalazari* (→ *šala*), translation 'Töchter(?)' ['Daughters(?)'], cf. Th. Richter, *VHN*, 244.

Since collective forms 'Women(?)' and 'Daughters(?)' as translation of the name of one person is not very satisfactory, I prefer to use the abstract meaning for the suffix ***-zari*** / ***-šari*** and should like to propose a translation 'Womanhood' or 'Woman *par excellence*' for the personal names ^{f}***Aštuzar*** at Ašnakkum and Mari, ^{f}***Azzuzari*** at Mari, ^{f}***Aš-du-a-šar*** at Nuzi and Linear A ***a-du-sa-ra*** (HT 62+73.1) = ***Ašdu-šara*** (possibly with the *essive* ending in ***-a***) at Hagia Triada. Likewise ^{f}***Šalanzar*** from Qaṭṭarā, and ^{f}***Šalanzari*** from Mari and Šubat-Enlil could be translated as 'Daughterhood' or 'Daughter *par excellence*'.

The orthography of ^{f}***Šalanzar*** (wr. ^{f}*Ša-la-an-za-ar*) from Qaṭṭarā, and ^{f}***Šalanzari*** (wr. ^{f}*Ša-la-an-za-ri*) beside ^{f}***Šalazari*** (wr. ^{f}*Ša-la-za-ri*) from Mari and Šubat-Enlil has led me to consider another possibility for interpretation of these names. If ^{f}***Šalanzari*** is the older form and ***Šalazari*** the younger one, we may be dealing with a sentence name ^{f}***Šalanzari*** (syncope of ***-e-***) < ****Šala-enzari***, with a very appropriate meaning 'The daughter is a deity/divinity'.

Likewise the orthography of ^{f}***Aštua-šar*** (wr. ^{f}*Aš-du-a-šar*) at Nuzi < * ^{f}***Aštu-a(n)šar*** < *^{f}***Aštu-enšari*** and the orthography of ^{f}***Azzu-zari*** (wr. ^{f}*Az-zu*-IZ-*za-ri*) = ^{f}***Azzu-izzari*** < *^{f}***Azzu-e/inzari*** at Mari would provide another attractive translation 'The woman is a deity/divinity'. The Linear A personal name ***a-du-sa-ra*** (HT 62+73.1) may then be the *essive* form in ***-a*** of ^{f}***Aštua-šar*** (wr. ^{f}*Aš-du-a-šar*) at Nuzi and of ^{f}***Aštu-zar*** (wr. *Aš-tu-za-ar*) at Ašnakkum and Mari and can be rendered as 'The woman is like a deity/divinity'.

Linear A ***a-sa-sa-ra-me*** (PR Za 1c; possibly PK Za 11b-c, *et alibi*) is one of the most discussed sequences, since it is found on 'Libation Tables' and other religious objects. In view of the religious context I have discussed all attempts of interpretation and theoretical options more extensively in *chapter 11: 'Religious' Linear A inscriptions*. There seemed to be a correlation between ***a-du-sa-ra*** (HT 62+73.1) and ***a-sa-sa-ra-me*** comparable with that of Linear A ***a-du-re-za*** (KH 11.12) next to]***a-se-re-za***|[(KH 13.2), both from Khania.

However, in case of ***a-sa-sa-ra-me***, another interpretation, namely ***Arša-Šarram(m)e***, eventually turned out to provide the best analysis and meaning and appeared to fit best in the context of the holy trinity of *Tešub*, *Ḫebat* and their son *Šarru(m)ma / Šarru(m)manni*, in the Minoan context of the 'Libation Tables' addressed with their epithets and poetic descriptions as ***a-ta-i-jo-wa-ja***, ***a-di-da-ki-ti***, ***a-sa-sa-ra-me*** (mind the alliteration of *A-*, *A-*, *A-*). So finally ***a-sa-sa-ra-me*** turned out to be a male god.

In hindsight it seems that the fascination of scholars with ***a-sa-sa-ra-me*** as a goddess, especially the so-called 'Minoan Mother goddess', started with L.R. Palmer's ingenious reconstruction of Linear A ***a-sa-sa-ra-me*** as the name of „a Luwian goddess" ****Ashassarasmes***, which he translated as 'My Lady' / 'Ma Donna' and compared with Hittite ****Ishassarasmis***. It did not lead to decipherment of the Minoan vernacular written with Linear A as Luwian. The sequences ***a-sa-sa-ra-me*** and ***ja-sa-sa-ra-me***, are to date mainly known from the sacred objects of Minoan 'peak sanctuaries' and from a few other objects such as ***ja-sa-sa-ra-me*** (PL Zf 1) as third sequence on a silver hairpin from Tholos A at Platanos in the Messara-valley, if the inscription is read from right to left.

However, I still think that the correlations between Linear A ***a-sa-***, ***a-se-***, ***a-si-***, ***a-su-*** and ***a-da(-)***, ***a-de***, ***a-di-ne***, ***a-di-na***, ***a-du-*** on the one hand and the Hurrian forms ***azza(-)***, ***azze(-)***, ***azzi(-)***, ***azzu(-)*** beside ***ažda(-)***, ***ažde(-)***, ***aždi(-)***, ***aždu(-)*** are largely valid. The attested Hurrian forms may be explained through the process of assimilation.

Analysis of Linear A ***a-du-re-za*** (KH 11.1) from Khania as *{ar-d/tur=izz=(e)=a}* 'Give manhood / virility (oh *numen*) !' is quite feasible, though the apparent *essive* in ***-a*** does not seem to fit very well as object of the *imperative* ***ar-***, but a construction like 'Give (a child) (as an example of) manhood / virility (oh *numen*) !' is conceivable. Cf. the personal name ***Turizza*** (wr. *Tu-ri-iz-za*) at Mari, analysis *{turizz=(i)=a*[E.]*}*, typology 3.2.1, lexicon *turizzi* (→ *turi*), translation 'Manhood, Virility, Good qualities of a man', cf. Th. Richter (*VHN*, 319, 546), who translates ***turizzi*** and the personal names ***Turizza*** and ***Turazza*** as 'Manschaft' and compares these forms with ***ḫanazze*** 'Kindschaft' ['childhood'] and the personal name ***Ḫanazzu***. Compare also Hurrian ***Artura*** (wr. *Ar-du-ra, Ar-tu-ra*) at Nuzi, possibly *{ar-t/dur=e/i=a}* that may be rendered as 'Give (the child) as a man (oh *numen*) !'. Nuzi provides personal names with ***-d/tura*** as second element: ***Ḫašip-d/tura***, ***Inip-d/tura***, ***Akip-d/tura***, beside names with *absolutive* ***-d/turi***: *Anza-duri*, *ᶠArim-d/turi*, *ᶠŠilwa-d/turi*, *Šurki-duri*, *ᶠUr-d/turi*, *ᶠZilim-d/turi*, cf. P.M. Purves, *NPN*, 269. It is conceivable that ***-d/tura*** is not an *essive* case in these names, but an *a*-stem that exists beside an *i*-stem, just as an *a*-stem ***ažda*** appears to exist beside ***ažde/aždi***.

Likewise Linear A]***a-se-re-za***|[(KH 13.2) from Khania can be analysed as the Hurrian sentence name ***Ar-šerezza***, *{ar-šer=e/i=zz=(e)=a}*, consisting of the *athematic imperative* ***ar-*** of the root ***ar-*** 'to give' + the abstract noun ***šer=i=šše*** 'joy, pleasure' or 'shine, splendour', probably in the *essive* case ***šer=i=šš(e)=a*** / ***šer=i=zz(e)=a***, derived from ***šer-/šir-*** I 'to please, to be pleasant', cf. Th. Richter, *BGH*, 391-392, s.v. ***šer-/šir-*** I 'angenehm sein, genügen, entsprechen' or ***šer-/šir-*** IV 'glänzen' ['to shine']. Polysemy of ***šer-/šir-*** I and ***šer-/šir-*** IV is likely (*VHN*, 513^{+716}). Cf. *aštî=n(na) šen(a)=iff=u=ve ar=oš=av šen(a)=iff=u=ve=NE=n(na) tiša=nna šir=a=šše* (Mit. IV 33-34), 'I have given the wife of my brother that pleases the heart of my brother'; ***šir=a=šše*** (nominalizing suffix ***-šše***).

However, occurrence of]***a-se-re-za***|[(KH 13.2), also at Khania, makes it more likely that ***a-du-re-za*** (KH 11.1) and]***a-se-re-za***|[(KH 13.2) show the same type of formation. These Linear A personal names may well contain the unassimilated nominal element ***ašdu-/aždu-*** (cf. ***ašte***, phonologically /*ažde*/, 'woman') and the assimilated form ***azze-*** as first onomastic element. The second element ***-reza*** may well be equivalent to ***-riša*** in the Hurrian personal name ***Erwi-riša*** (wr. *Er-wi-ri-ša*) at Nuzi (cf. I.J. Gelb, *NPN*, 48: 1. HSS IX 131:5; cf. P.M. Purves, *NPN*, 248). I.J. Gelb adds: "impossible to collate", but ***a-du-re-za*** and]***a-se-re-za***|[may now offer good parallels. The Nuzi onomastic element ***erwi*** (= ***ewri / ibri*** elsewhere) means 'Lord, King'. Coexistence of unassimilated ***a-du-re-za*** and assimilated]***a-se-re-za***|[, attested in the same places, may be explained from the tendency to preserve older forms in onomastics. Likewise we find Old Hurrian personal names with ***=i=b***, ***=a=b*** and ***=u/o=m*** next to the later Mitanni-Hurrian names.

If ***re-za*** 6 FIC (HT 88.1-2) is the right reading on HT 88, since the sequence occurs again as ***re-za*** 5 J (HT 13.2), and if Linear A ***re-za*** is derived from Akkadian ***rēṣu***, it is interesting that Th. Richter (*BGH*, 537) mentions s.v. alphabetic cuneiform ‡ ***rzn*** from Ugarit [loan-word in Hurrian]: 'Helfer' ['help, helper'], i.e. /***rēzenne***/, respectively ***rēz=enne/i***, cf. Dietrich/Mayer 2004a, 28f.

If this identification is right, Linear A ***a-du-re-za*** (KH 11.1) may be analysed as {*aždu-rez=a*} and translated as 'The woman is like somebody who helps' and]***a-se-re-za***|[(KH 13.2) may be analysed as {*azze-rez=a*} and may be translated likewise as 'The woman is like somebody who helps'. Since Akkadian ***rēṣu*** and ***rzn*** (***rēz=enne/i***) from Ugarit as well as Linear A ***re-za*** have a gender neutral meaning, the onomastic element can be used in masculine and feminine names, cf. ***Erwi-riša*** (wr. *Er-wi-ri-ša*) at Nuzi. Incidentally, it is not excluded that]***a-se-re-za***|[(KH 13.2) may be analysed as {*arše-rez=a*} and can be translated as 'The young man, boy is like somebody who helps'. Cf. Akkadian personal name ***Adad-rêṣi*** (wr. *dAdad-re-zi, Ad-re-zi, Ad-re-zu*) next to ***Rîš-Adad*** (wr. *Ri-iš-dAdad*), in reverse order, s at Nuzi, cf. I.J. Gelb, *NPN*, 39, 120; A.A. MacRae, *NPN*, 295, 313.

The Linear A name ***re-za*** (HT 13.2; HT 88.1-2) and the onomastic element ***-re-za***, interpreted as Hurrianized ***(-)rez=a***, may have been the *essive* form {*rez=a*} of *absolutive* ****-rezi***, derived from Akkadian ***rēṣu***. I shall later discuss the possibility that the name of the Cretan goddess ***Ῥέα / Ῥεῖα / Ῥεία***, mother of Zeus, may be the Hurrianized name of a deity ****Reza***, in Linear A attested as a personal name ***re-za***, derived from the theonym.

Other Linear A sequences are equally interesting: ***a-sa|-da-ka*** (MA Wc <5> side a.1-2) on a roundel at Mallia; ***a-sa-mu-ne*** (ZA Zb 3.1) on a pithos in the farmhouse at Epano Zakros; ***a-sa|-su-ma|-i*** or ***a-sa| su-ma|-i*** (GO Wc 1a.1-3) on a roundel at Gournia; ***a-se*** (HT 81.1; HT 93a.3; HT 132.1; ZA Zb 3.1) at Hagia Triada and Epano Zakros; ***a-de*** (ZA 10b.4) and ***a-du-|ku-mi-na*** (ZA 10a.3-4) at Kato Zakro; ***a-di*** (HT 37.5) and ***-a-di-ne***, second element of ***o-ra$_2$-di-ne*** {*olli-aždine*} (HT 6a.4) at Hagia Triada; **]', *a-di-ne***[, (KH 83.1),]***a-di-na* 5** (KH 59.3) at Khania; ***a-se-ja*** (HT 115a.4) and **]*a-se-ja*** (HT 93a.8) at Hagia Triada; ***a-si-da-to|-i*** (AK 2.2-3) at Arkhanes; ***a-si-ja-ka*** (HT 28a.1; HT 28b.1) at Hagia Triada; ***a-si-ki-ra*** (KH 20.1) at Khania; ***a-si-su-po-a*** (KH 9.1) at Khania; ***a-su*[** (KH 73.3) at Khania; ***a|-su-ja*** (HT 11a.3-4) at Hagia Triada;]|***a-su-mi*** TAL[(AK 1a.4) at Arkhanes; ***a-su-pu-wa*** (AK 2.5) at Arkhanes; ***a-du-ni-ta-na*** (AK 5.1) at Arkhanes; ***ta-ta-pa$_3$-du*** (PR Za 1a) at Prassà; and last but not least ***a-du-sa-ra*** (HT 62+73a.1).

The key to a balanced interpretation of Linear A ***a-sa-sa-ra-me*** appeared to be my analysis of the relationship between ***a-di-da-ki-ti-pa-ku*** (KN Zc 6), ***a-di-ki-te-te*** (PK Za 11a), ***a-di-ki-te-[te*** (PK Za 12a), ***ja-di-ki-tu*** (IO Za 2), ***ja-di-ki-te-te*** (PK Za 8a; PK Za 15) on the one hand and ***a-sa-sa-ra-me*** (PR Za 1c), ***a|-sa-sa-ra-me*** (PK Za 11b-c), ***a-sa-sa-ra***[(PK Za 4), ***ja-sa-sa-ra-me*** (PS Za 2c; TL Za 1), ***ja-sa-sa-ra-me*** (PL Zf 1 ←), ***ja-sa-sa-ra***[(IO Za 2), ***ja-sa-[sa-ra-me*** (PK Za 8b), ***ja-sa-sa***[(PK Za 14), ***ja-sa-sa-ra-ma|-na*** (KN Za 10a-b) on the other, especially since these epithets or poetic descriptions of gods sometimes occur in the same inscriptions. Do they refer to the same deities or not ?

Analysis of ***a-di-da-ki-ti-pa-ku*** (KN Zc 6) may offer the solution. There may well be a word division between ***a-di-da-ki-ti*** and ***pa-ku*** as comparison with the other sequences ***a-di-ki-te-te*** (PK Za 11a), ***a-di-ki-te-[te*** (PK Za 12a), ***ja-di-ki-tu*** (IO Za 2), ***ja-di-ki-te-te*** (PK Za 8a; PK Za 15) suggests. Moreover ***-pa-ku-*** seems to recur in KN Zc 6.3. The formation of ***a-di-da-ki-ti*** is the most complete and offers a good Hurrian analysis {*ašdi-dakitti*} 'Woman-Beauty' > 'Beautiful Lady'.

E. Laroche (*GLH*, 70-71), s.v. ***Daru Dakitu***: "Déesse syro-anatolienne, suivante de Ḫebat : Kizuwatna, Yazĭlĭkaya, Ugarit; cf. Laroche, *Ugar. V*, 503. Graphies.

a) *dDa-a-ru, dDa-(a)-ar-ru, dTa-a-ru.* - *dDa-a-ru-du !*, KBo XI 6 Vo 5 (pour *Da-a-ru-da*; cf. aussi *Ḫeba/Ḫebatu*).

b) *dDa-(a)-ki-du, dDa-(a)-ki-tum*, passim; *dDa-ki-da* (KBo XI 6 Vo 5); *dTa-ki-du, dTa-ki-tum*. - Hitt. *dTa-ki-ti-* (KUB XXXIII 106 I 25-30; chant d'Ullikummi).

Contextes hittites: KUB X 27 III 1-2; XXV 46 III 14; XXVII 1 II 41 = 3 III 25; 13 I 17; KBo XV 37 II 5; KBo XVII 98, 14, etc.

Dakitu seule: KBo XXI 34+ III 56, IV 16-19; Kumarbi, l.c.

H.: *dTa-ki-tu*, KUB XLV 68 Ro 10; Yazılıkaya N° 46a = *RHA XXVII* 91; cf. Yaz.[2] 180.

Dir.: [*Ḫ*]*bt-d Dqt-d*, RS 24.261, 19; cf. *ib*. 295, 12; CTA 34, 15; RS 24.291, 7.

Com.: *dTa-a-ki-du-ra*, KUB XXVII 38 II 8.

Daru-Dakitu n'est probablement qu'une seule déesse, nom et surnom; cf. Yazĭlĭkaya. Lire *Takit*, emprunt au sém. *dqt* 'petite'." Of course, the combination **[*Ḫ*]*bt-d dqt-d*** (RS 24.261, 19; cf *ib*. 295, 12; CTA 34, 15; RS 24.291, 7) is most interesting.

Instead of a Semitic etymology ***dqt*** 'petite' ['small'], feminine of ***dq*** 'petit', derivation of ***D/Tagidu / Dakitti*** from the Hurrian root ***dag-/tag-/takk-***, ***teg-*** 'beautiful, splendid, shining, pure' is likely on the basis of ***da-(a)-ki***, ***da-a-ki-it-ti*** , KUB XXV 44 II 19; KBo XX 113 IV 16; KUB XXXII 95 Ro 10; 86, 2; KBo XIX 130 IV 10; KUB XXXII 59 II 3; etc., cf. E. Laroche (*GLH*, 250, s.v. ***tagi***, attribut de *Ḫebat*; Th. Richter (*VHN*, 525-526, s.v. ***tag-/takk-***, ***teg-***; 526-527, s.v. ***Tagidu*** (GNf) [feminine theonym] or ***tagidi*** (unsicher) [uncertain]. Th. Richter (*VHN*, 526-527) mentions that *Tagidu* appears among the Hurrian goddesses in the rock-sanctuary of Yazılıkaya. She belongs to the entourage of *Ḫebat*. Ḫebat's epithet ***tagi*** and the combination ***da-(a)-ki***, ***da-a-ki-it-ti*** (E. Laroche) and deified ***Dta/da-(a)-ki-(it)-ti*** at Ḫattuša indicate that the root ***tag-*** is involved. The word ***tagidi*** 'beauty, splendour, magnificence' occurs in names at Ugarit probably as an appellative name. ***fTakitu*** occurs at Mari. The name of the *Dikta*-mountains in Crete and the theonym *Diktunna* have often been associated with Linear A ***a-di-da-ki-ti(-)*** (KN Zc 6), ***a-di-ki-te-te*** (PK Za 11a), ***a-di-ki-te-[te*** (PK Za 12a), ***ja-di-ki-tu*** (IO Za 2), ***ja-di-ki-te-te*** (PK Za 8a; PK Za 15), lately by G.A. Owens in his doctoral thesis and several other publications.

But none of these Linear A sequences can according to the orthographic conventions of Linear A and B be considered a rendering of *Dikta* or *Diktunna*. ***Dikta*** would have been rendered as ****di-ka-ta*** in Linear A and ***Diktunna*** as ****di-ku-tu-na***, since occlusives in consonant clusters must always be expressed. The first occlusive is expressed by borrowing the vowel of the next syllabic sign, so ***-kta*** is rendered as ***-ka-ta*** and the ***a*** in ***ka*** is mute. In fact the ***a*** of its own syllable ***-kta*** is used. As a matter of fact Linear B ***di-ka-ta-jo*** (KN Fp 1,2) offers the dative singular masculine of the ethnic ***Δικταῖος***, derived from the name of Mount ***Δίκτᾱ***. The adjective ***di-ka-ta-jo*** (KN Fp 1,2) qualifies Linear B ***di-we*** = ***Διϝεῖ***, dative of ***Ζεύς***. The Linear B *directive* ***di-ka-ta-de*** (KN Fp 7,2 *et alibi*) 'to *Dikta*' contains the accusative ***Δίκτᾱν-***, with directive suffix ***-δε***.

The example of Hurrian ***Ipšaia*** (wr. *Ip-ša-a-a, Ip-šá-a-a*), name of 18 persons at Nuzi, that is attested as ***i-pa-sa-ja*** (KH 10.3) in Linear A at Khania, shows that the orthographic conventions of Linear A did not differ from those of Linear B. It can be proved on the basis of prosopographic research that ***Ipšaia*** at Nuzi is a hypocoristic of ***Ipša-ḫalu*** (wr. *Ip-ša-ḫa-lu, Ip-šá-ḫa-lu, Ip-ša-ḫa-a-lu, Ip-sa-ḫa-lu, Ip-šá-ḫa-a-lu*), name of 77 persons at Nuzi, since there are an ***Ipšaia*** and ***Ipša-ḫalu*** son of *Ar-te-ia* and there are an ***Ipšaia*** and ***Ipša-ḫalu*** son of *It-ḫi-iš-ta* (cf. I.J. Gelb, *NPN*, 71-72).

We may conclude that Linear A orthography shows that the element ***-da-ki-ti*** in ***a-di-da-ki-ti(-)*** (KN Zc 6) offers a perfect match with deified ***^{D}ta/da-(a)-ki-(it)-ti*** at Ḫattuša. Linear A orthography also shows that the forms ***a-di-ki-te-te*** (PK Za 11a), ***a-di-ki-te-[te*** (PK Za 12a), ***ja-di-ki-tu*** (IO Za 2), ***ja-di-ki-te-te*** (PK Za 8a; PK Za 15), which may well be related to ***a-di-da-ki-ti(-)*** (KN Zc 6), did not have a consonant cluster ***-kt-*** as can be observed in *Dikta* and *Diktunna*, because the ***-i-*** between ***-k-*** and ***-t-*** is not a mute vowel in the Linear A forms. So if there is any relationship (beyond some similarity of sounds) between Minoan-Hurrian ***a-di-da-ki-ti(-)*** {*ašdi-dakitti*} 'Woman-Beauty' > 'Beautiful Lady' and the forms ***a-di-ki-te-te***, ***a-di-ki-te-[te***, ***ja-di-ki-tu***, ***ja-di-ki-te-te*** on the one hand and the Cretan *Dikta*-mountains and the goddess *Diktunna* on the other, we must assume that all later forms lost ***-i-*** between ***-k-*** and ***-t-*** after the age of Linear A writing.

The formation of ***a-di-da-ki-ti(-)*** is comparable with that of ***a-sa-sa-ra(-me)***, if that is interpreted as ***Azzanšara*** and analysed as {*azza-(e)nšar(i)=a*} 'Woman-Divinity' > 'Divine Lady'. The orthography ***a-di-da-ki-ti(-)*** (KN Zc 6) at Knossos is probably the original complete form, in which both ***aždi*** and ***da-ki-ti*** can easily be recognized.

The easiest explanation for the forms ***a-di-ki-te-te*** (PK Za 11a), ***a-di-ki-te-[te*** (PK Za 12a), ***ja-di-ki-tu*** (IO Za 2), ***ja-di-ki-te-te*** (PK Za 8a; PK Za 15) is the phenomenon of *haplology*, c.q. *haplography*, e.g. in English *Feb'ry* for *February*, and in Linear B ***a-po-re-we*** (MY Ue 611,1) = *ἀμφορῆϝε*, dual nominative of *ἀμφορεύς* 'amphora, two-handled vessel', haplology/haplography for ***a-pi-po-re-we*** (KN Uc 160 r 1), plural nominative of *ἀμφιφορεύς*, a vessel that can be borne on both sides (*ἀμφί* 'on both sides' + *φορεύς* 'carrier' from the verbal root *φερ-/φορ-* 'to bear, carry'). The phenomenon occurs, if long words contain consecutive syllables that sound alike as the Mycenaean examples of ***a-pi-po-re-we*** and ***a-po-re-we*** and the Greek examples of *ἀμφιφορεύς* and *ἀμφορεύς* show. Keeping this in mind one can understand that the syllable ***-da-*** was lost in Linear A ***a-di-da-ki-ti***, especially if the ending ***-ti*** was apparently reduplicated to ***-te-te*** in ***a-di-ki-te-te*** (PK Za 11a), ***a-di-ki-te-[te*** (PK Za 12a) and ***ja-di-ki-te-te*** (PK Za 8a; PK Za 15).

A less easy explanation for ***a-di-ki-te-te*** as compared to ****a-di-<da->ki-te(-te)*** is the possibility that ***a-di-ki-te-te*** can be analysed as *{azz(e/i)-d(a)e/igitte/i=tte(=tte)}*, consisting of ***azz(e/i)-*** 'Woman' (with syncope of ***-e/i***) + ***digitte/i*** < ***dagitte/i*** + suffix/formant ***-tte*** that looks like a (so far not identified) reduplication. The reason, why I consider this solution acceptable is that Th. Richter (*VHN*, 525) takes the roots ***tag-/takk-, teg-*** 'schön, rein, unbefleckt, glänzend, hell' ['beautiful, immaculate, pure, shining, bright'] together. He refers to a vocabulary comparison at Ugarit: Hurrian ***tagi*** = Sumerian IZI, Akkadian ***nūru*** 'Licht' ['light']. Using ***teg-/tig-*** instead of ***tag-*** may be caused by the mechanism of vowel harmony.

I do not think that ***-te-te*** in these forms can be compared with ***-tišti*** in the personal name ***Ullum-tišti*** at Mari, since the first ***-te-*** in ***a-di-ki-te-te*** (etc.) can already be identified with ***-ti*** and ***-tu*** in ***dakiti*** and ***dakitu***, respectively. Th. Richter (*VHN*, 539) mentions anyway that the root of ***tišti*** cannot yet be explained. With regard to the root ***dag/k-/tag/k-*** (etc.) it is clear that in Minoan Hurrian the voiced dentals were preferred to the voiceless dentals, cf. Linear A *da-ku-se-ne, da-ku-|se-ne-ti, da-ku, da-ku-na, a-sa-da-ka*, etc.

The meaning 'Beauty' for ^{D}***Dagitti*** leads us *prima facie* to the Minoan predecessor of Aphrodite that may be ^{D}IŠTAR-*Ša(w)uška*. This seems to be in accordance with what we know about the religious cult of the Peak Sanctuary of Symi Viannou in the south of Crete. It offered complete continuity from the Minoan age to the classical period. The Gods revered in the Classical sanctuary were *Hermes Dendritès* and *Aphodite*, the Greek female goddess of love and beauty. To date the inscriptions from Symi Viannou have not yet shown the names or epithets ***a-di-da-ki-ti(-)*** or its variants and/or ***a-sa-sa-ra(-me)***.

However, since ^{D}***Tagidu*** / ^{D}***Dagitti*** belongs to the entourage of Ḫebat and since Ḫebat herself is often called ***tagi*** / ***dagi*** 'beautiful', I now tend to think that ***a-di-da-ki-ti*** and its variants refer to Ḫebat rather than to ^{D}IŠTAR-*Ša(w)uška*, which is, of course, not such a bad idea, since Ḫebat is Tešub's wife and the epithet 'Our Father' usually refers to Tešub.

For some time I was convinced that ***a-di-da-ki-ti(-)*** and its variants refer to the same divinity as ***a-sa-sa-ra-me***, until I realized that there are inscriptions on Libation Tables such as IO Za 2 from Mount *Ioukhtas*, where we find ***a-ta-i-jo-wa-ja , ja-di-ki-tu , ja-sa-sa-ra***[***-me*** , etc.; PK Za 11: [***a***]***-ta-i-jo-wa-e , a-di-ki-te-te-***[ ] , ... ***a-|sa-sa-ra-me*** , ... etc.; PK Za 12: ***a-ta-i-jo-wa-ja , a-di-ki-te-***[***te***][ ] , ...[ ]***-ra-me*** , etc. from Mount *Petsophas*.

So what are the consequences, if these sequences refer to three different divinities ? One thing is clear: in the three inscriptions just cited ***a-ta-i-jo-wa-e / a-ta-i-jo-wa-ja*** is always mentioned first, then followed by ***ja-di-ki-tu / a-di-ki-te-te*** and ***(j)a-sa-sa-ra-me*** as third. If this reflects the order of importance of the three deities, one readily thinks of the Hurrian divine Trinity of *Tešub*, *Ḫebat* and their son *Šarrumma / Šarrummanni*. The cult and worship of a divine trinity may be in accordance with the discovery of three parallel rooms in the Peak Sanctuary of Ioukhtas by Mrs. Alexandras Karetsou. She mentions that the strong supporting wall of the big terrace simultaneously served as common west-wall of three rooms, parallel from south to north: ... ἐχρησίμευσε ταυτοχρόνως ὡς κοινὸς δυτικὸς τοῖχος τριῶν δωματίων, παραλλήλων ἐκ Νότου πρὸς Βορρᾶν, cf. Ἀ. Καρέτσου, Κρήτη. Ἱερὸν κορυφῆς Γιούχτα, *Τὸ Ἔργον τῆς Ἀρχαιολογικῆς Ἑταιρείας κατὰ τὸ 1975*, σ. 176-178, Εἰκ. 175-176. There are more Minoan sanctuaries with three rooms, for instance, at *Anemospilio*, excavated by Y.A. and E. Sakellarakis.

In Linear B, and probably in Linear A as well, ***-r-*** is not expressed in consonant clusters before ***-s-***; to be more precise: non-occlusives (μ, ν, λ, ρ, σ, F) are usually not expressed before non-sonantic consonants (occlusives and σ). This means that Linear A ***a-sa-*** can also represent ***arša-*** and Linear A ***a-sa-sa-ra-me*** can be interpreted as ****Arša-šarram(m)e***, of which both ***arša-*** and ***-šarra*** are attested as elements in Hurrian personal names: e.g. ***Aršaḫalu*** (wr. *Ar-ša-ḫa-lu*) at Nuzi, JENu 829, cf. I.J. Gelb, *NPN*, 31; ***Arš-apu*** (wr. *Ar-šá-a-pu*), son of *Ip-šá-a-a* at Nuzi, HSS IX 20:44,55, cf. Gelb, *NPN*, 32. The element ***arš*** is not very frequent in Hurrian personal names. The Hurrian name ***Ipšai̯a*** (wr. *Ip-ša-a-a, Ip-šá-a-a*), just mentioned, is attested as ***i-pa-sa-i̯a*** (KH 10.3) in Linear A at Khania.

P.M. Purves, *NPN*, 205, writes s.v. ***arš***, ***arš-***, ***arša-*** and ***-arša***: "Hurrian in view of occurrence with ***-apu***. Cf. perhaps Nippur *Aršii̯enni* (wr. *Ar-ši-ie$_x$(IA)-en-ni*), *Arsi-adrum* or *-addil* (wr. *Ar-si-at/ad-rum/dil*; cf. names on *-antil* under *ant*), *^{f}Arsigu* (wr. *^{f}Ar-si-gu*), *Arsii̯u* (wr. *Ar-si-i̯u$_x$(IA)-u*) in Clay, *PNCP*, 59." At Nuzi he compares *Ar-ši-ki-i̯a*. As example for the use of *-arša* as second element he mentions *Ku-pa-ar-ša, Ḫu-pa-ar-šá, Ku-bar-ša, Ku-ba-ar-ša*. Of these names only *^{f}Arsigu* is feminine, but if this name is divided into the verbal root ***ar-*** 'to give' and ***-zi-g/k^o*** as in the personal names *Zike* (Mari, Qaṭṭarā, Šubat-Enlil), *Zikija* (Qaṭṭarā), *Zikija* (Ašnakkum, Qaṭṭarā), cf. Th. Richter (*VHN*, 505), *^{f}Arsigu* has nothing to do with ***arš-***. If identification of Linear A ***a-sa-sa-ra-me*** with ****Arša-šarram(m)e*** is correct, there is no compelling reason to assume that we are dealing with a Minoan *goddess*.

It is theoretically possible that ***-sa-ra-*** in Linear A ***a-sa-sa-ra-*** represents Hurrian ***-šala*** 'daughter', but we have already seen that this possibility is not very likely. A better candidate is the abstract suffix ***-šar(i)=a***, ***-(e)nšar(i)=a*** 'divinity' or Hurrian ***šarra / šarri*** 'King of Gods' (***šarra*** may be the *essive* in ***-a*** of ***šarri***: 'as the King of Gods'). Anyway it is a puzzle to find the right combination.

Th. Richter (*BGH*, 48) mentions a possible Hurro-Urartian root ****arš-***, reconstructed by I.M. Diakonoff - S.A. Starostin (*Hurro-Urartian as an Eastern Caucasian language*, Münchener Studien zur Sprachwissenschaft, Beiheft 12, Neue Folge, München 1986, 36) and recognized in Urartian ***aršə*** 'adolescents, young boys'. W.G.E. Watson, Ugaritic onomastics (1), *Aula Orientalis 8 (1990)*, 115, presumes that the alphabetic cuneiform personal name ***åršm*** could mean 'young boy(?)'.

No doubt a Minoan scribe knew whether he meant ***azza-*** or ***arša-***, if he wrote ***a-sa-***. That is the main problem with Linear A and B orthographic conventions. Writing and understanding were easy for the scribes, because they knew what to write or what they had written, but we have to take into account which possibilities these conventions allow.

Consequently, if we read ***Arša-šarra(m)me*** for ***a-sa-sa-ra-me***, the meaning may well be 'The young man/boy (is) Šarrumma', and ***ja-sa-sa-ra-ma|-na*** (KN Za 10a-b) may be analysed as {*ia/ya-arša=šarramma=nna*}, consisting of the relative (and interrogative) proclitic particle ***ya- / ye-*** 'in the same way as' > 'as well as' + ***arša*** 'young man/boy' + ***Šarramma*** (< ***Šarrumma***) + ***-nna*** (enclitic personal pronoun 3rd person singular marking the subject of the intransitive verb), translation 'as well as (***ya- / ye-***) "The young boy, he is *Šarrumma*" ', cf. Th. Richter, *BGH*, 356, s.v. ***šarri*** I [*passim*] 'König, Götterkönig (Teššup), vergöttlichter König' ['King, King of Gods (Teššup), deified King'] and ***Šarrumma***, ***Šarrummanni***.

According to E. Laroche (*GLH*, 218) ***Šarru(m)ma*** is a God of Hittite origin forming a triad with Tešub and Ḫebat in Kizzuwatna, in the 14th century imported in Syria. ***Šarrumma*** survived in Asia Minor in the form of *Sarma* and *-zarma* (cf. Laroche, *Syria 40*, 277 ff., and Ph.H.J. Houwink te Cate, *The Luwian population groups of Lycia and Cilicia Aspera during the Hellenistic period*, Leiden 1965, 134 ff.). Orthography: *dŠar-ru-um-ma*, dLUGAL-*ma*; Hieroglyphic Hittite (now: H. Luwian) *dSar(a)-ma*. According to Ph.H.J. Houwink ten Cate (Woordenboek der Oudheid III, 2636) *Šarrummaš* is a young male (Anatolian) Hurrian God, originally the *genius* of a local mountain near *Kummanni* (Comana) in the northeast of Kizzuwatna. In the pantheon of Kummanni he was the son of Tešup and Ḫebat, and brother of Allanzu. In the iconography of Yazılıkaya (No 44 and 81) he appears in the series of female figures following his mother Ḫebat and preceding Allanzu. In Room B he is the god embracing Tudhaliyas IV. At the beginning of the series of male figures he is probably represented as 'bull-calf of Tešub' (No 42a). He is always portrayed as a young male figure standing on a lion or lion-like animal as a pedestal.

The close connection of *Ḫebat – Šarrumma* is visible *passim* in the lists of divinities of Kizzuwatna, e.g. KBo XV 37 II 3; XX 113 II 10, III 9. At Aleppo, HH I No 80.

The connection of *Tešub – Šarrumma* is visible in the expression 'calf/boy of Tešub' ('veau/garçon de Tešub'). E. Laroche (*GLH*, 108-109): ***ḫubidi*** 'veau'. Lecture du suméro-gramme AMAR(*-ti*); cf. Goetze, *RHA 39*, 199 n. 46; Otten, OLZ 1954, 135 n. 2; Laroche, *RHA XXVII*, 67. 1. Épithète de Šarrumma 'veau/garçon de Tešub', ***dTeššub-bi ḫu-u-bi-ti dŠarrumma-n***, KUB XXVII 38 II 14, 20 = dU-***ub-wi*** AMAR-***ti dŠarrumma***, KBo XX 119 I 14 = IV 18-19 = KBo XVII 86+ I 3; hiér. hitt. dVEAU ***Ti-su-pi*** [*h*]***u-pi-ti***, Yaz. 42a. - De même KUB XXV 44 V 6; XXXIV 102 II 8; XXVII 1 I 70; KBo XI 5 I 23. Etc. According to E. Laroche (*GLH*, 229) the meaning 'garçon' ['boy'] is the masculine equivalent to Hurrian ***šiduri*** (wr. *ši-du-ri*) 'jeune fille' ['young girl'] = Akkadian ***ardâtu***.

Th. Richter (*VHN*, 142-143) mentions the Hurrian name ***Ḫupitam*** (wr. *Ḫu-bi-dam*) at Ašnakkum, Mari, Šubat-Enlil, Tuttul, Ĝirsu (UR III), Kaniš, Nippur (UR III), Umma (UR III), Nuzi, Alalaḫ IV, Dilbat, Ḫattuša, analysis {*ḫo/ubid(i)=a*[E.]*=m(e/a)*}, typology 3.2.1, lexicon *ḫubidi*, 'He (the boy) is like a calf'. This name is probably derived from Hurrian ***ḫubidi*** {*ḫub=idi*} 'calf, bull-calf', 'bull-calf (of Teššub)' (I. Wegner, 2004, 30), cf. Th. Richter, *BGH*, 164-165, s.v. ***ḫubidi*** [Boğ.; PN], and *VHN*, 423, s.v. ***ḫubidi***. The meaning is confirmed by correspondences with Sumerogram AMAR(*-ti*) and Akkadian *būru* and a relation with the root ***ḫub-*** is possible (cf. Khacikjan, 1985, 63).

In hindsight I may well have been influenced and involuntarily even prejudiced by the persistent persuasion of many scholars that Linear A ***a-sa-sa-ra-me / ja-sa-sa-ra-me*** represented the so-called 'Mother Goddess'. This 'belief' seemed to be confirmed by the fact that ***a-ta-i-jo-wa-ja*** 'Our Father' turned out to represent the Head of the Hurrian pantheon, Tešub, so that it seemed logical that ***(j)a-sa-sa-ra-me*** might well represent a prominent Goddess. However, the order of three sequences in the inscriptions from Mount Ioukhtas IO Za 2: ***a-ta-i-jo-wa-ja , ja-di-ki-tu , ja-sa-sa-ra***[***-me*** , etc.; and from mount Petsophas PK Za 11: [*a*]***-ta-i-jo-wa-e , a-di-ki-te-te-***[ ] , ... ***a-***|***sa-sa-ra-me*** , ... etc.; PK Za 12: ***a-ta-i-jo-wa-ja , a-di-ki-te-***[***te***][ ] , ...[ ]***-ra-me*** , etc., has convinced me that we are most likely dealing with the divine trinity of *Tešub, Ḫebat* and *Šarrumma*, who may have shared the Peak Sanctuaries of Ioukhtas, Petsophas and perhaps elsewhere.

At Olympia there was not only a temple of Zeus, but also one of Hera. The temple of Juppiter (509 B.C.) on the *mons Capitolinus* in Rome was in fact a temple of *Juppiter, Juno* and *Minerva* and each deity had his/her own cella built parallel to the backwall of that temple.

Orthographically it is possible to read ***a-sa-sa-ra-me*** as ***Azzanšarame***, analysed as {*azza-(e)nšar(i)=a=me*} 'and Woman-Divinity' > 'and the Divine Lady', in which case it might refer to the same goddess as ***a-di-da-ki-ti(-)*** and its variants. However, ***Arša-šarra(m)me*** provides a better meaning for ***a-sa-sa-ra-me***: 'The young man/boy (is) *Šarramma < Šarrumma*', and ***ja-sa-sa-ra-ma|-na*** (KN Za 10a-b), analysed as {*y(a)/y(e)-arša=šarramma=nna*}, may be translated: 'as well as "The young boy, he (is) *Šarramma < Šarrumma*" '. This interpretation of ***ja-sa-sa-ra-ma|-na*** with the enclitic personal pronoun ***-nna*** is logical, if ***Šarrum(m)a*** / (Minoan-Hurrian) ***Šarram(m)a/e*** is taken as the basic form. But usage of ***-nna*** poses a problem, since according to I. Wegner (*Einführung*, 97) the enclitic personal pronouns indeed indicate the subject in intransitive constructions except for the 3rd person singular that has a ***Ø***-indicator (not ***-nna***). One may argue that the intransitive verb is missing in {*y(a)/y(e)-arša-šarramma=nna*} 'as well as "The young boy, he (is) *Šarramma < Šarrumma*" ', which might justify usage of ***-nna***.

However, if ***Šarrummanni*** is the original form of the theonym and ***Šarrumma*** the shortened one, ***Šarrummanni*** may be divided into ***Šarrum-mann=i*** 'He is the King of Gods (because he is Tešub's son)', consisting of the noun ***Šarru(m)*** 'King of Gods' + the root of the irregular verb ***mann-*** 'to be' + theme-vowel ***-i/e***, since ***mann-*** belongs to the group of static verbs (not indicating action or motion) that have an irregular conjugation with the theme-vowel ***-i/e***, cf. I. Wegner, *Einführung*, 101, sub 5.5 Unregelmäßige Verben [irregular verbs]. She mentions ***mann-*** 'sein' ['to be'], ***mann=i*** 'er ist' ['he is']; ***tupp-*** 'vorhanden sein, existieren' ['to be present/available, to exist'], ***tupp=e*** 'ist / war vorhanden' ['is / was present']. The subject of these verbs is in the absolutive case. These verbs miss the suffixes of the past and future tense. However, there are expressions such as ***=lla tupp=a=šše=na*** 'die vorhanden sind' ['they who are present'] with a regular present tense (***tupp=a-***), with the theme-vowel ***-a*** indicating intransitivity.

Indeed if ***ja-sa-sa-ra-ma-na*** is analysed as {*y(a)/y(e)-arša-šarr(i/u)=a(m)=mann=a*} consisting of the relative particle ***y(a)/y(e)-*** + ***arš=e/a*** 'young boy/man' + the *essive* form ***šarr=a*** 'as the King of Gods' instead of *absolutive* ***šarr=i*** or Akkadianizing *nominative* ***šarr=u*** + the regular 3rd person singular ***-mann=a*** instead of irregular ***-mann=i*** 'he is', the sequence can be translated 'as well as "The young boy is like the King of Gods" ', which may as well provide a good etymology for the shortened form ***Šarrumma***: *Šarru(m)=ma < Šarru(m)=mann=i* 'He is the King of Gods'. The expression ***šarr=a*** 'like the King of Gods' (in the *essive* case) is in fact more respectful towards the father than ***Šarru*** in the name ***Šarrumma***, because the son ***Šarrumma*** *is not* 'the King of Gods', because that is the prerogative of his father, but looks like 'the King of Gods'.

Conclusion: If it is difficult to make a choice on linguistic grounds, because the orthographic conventions of Linear A and B allow to read either ***azza-*** or ***arša-*** for Linear A ***a-sa-***, eventually the contextual arguments may prevail. The observation that we may well be dealing with a Holy Trinity of related Gods (Father, Mother, Son) tips the balance in favour of identification of ***a-sa-sa-ra-me*** as 'The young boy *Šarra/u(m)ma*'.

Linear A ***ja-*** is probably equivalent to the Hurrian relative and comparative connective proclitic particle ***ya- / ye-*** in sequences such as ***ja-sa-sa-ra-me***, instead of ***a-sa-sa-ra-me***, and in ***ja-ta-i-jo-u-ja*** , [(AP Za 1.a) 'as well as Our Father' or 'Both Our Father and … and …', next to the very frequent ***a-ta-i-jo-wa-ja*** 'Our Father'. Linear A ***ja-ta-i-jo-u-ja*** , [(AP Za 1.a) happens to be the only preserved entry on that Libation Table.

The same relationship exists between ***a-di-da-ki-ti-pa-ku*** (KN Zc 6), ***a-di-ki-te-te*** (PK Za 11a), ***a-di-ki-te-[te*** (PK Za 12a) on the one hand and ***ja-di-ki-tu*** (IO Za 2), ***ja-di-ki-te-te*** (PK Za 8a; PK Za 15) on the other. In ***ja-ta-i-jo-u-ja***, ***ja-di-ki-tu***, ***ja-di-ki-te-te*** and ***ja-sa-sa-ra-me***, ***ja-sa-sa-ra-ma-na*** we can observe contraction of ***ya- / ye-*** with ***a-*** in ***a-ta-i-jo-wa-ja***, ***a-di-da-ki-ti-pa-ku***, ***a-di-ki-te-te*** and ***a-sa-sa-ra-me***, respectively.

E.A. Speiser, *IH*, § 130: "The relative particle ***ya- / e-*** [112] calls for separate listing because its stem-vowel is ambiguous, being subject to the contrastive alternation ***-a / e*** [115, 254]. The only free occurrence of the stem appears to be ***i-e-e*** Mit. I 54. With the predicative ***-n*** we have both ***i-i-e-e-en*** Mit. II 79 and ***ya-a-an*** III 5, 6."

E. Laroche, *GLH*, 118, s.v. ***ya-/ye-***: "Thème de relatif, souvent en corrélation avec le démonstratif ***anti-***: Mit. I 98-100, 104-106, II 62-63, III 5-9, 55-59, IV 30-31; cf. Messerschmidt, *Mitanni-Studien*, 55, 82; Speiser, *IH*, 94 sq. [.….] ***ya- / ye-*** se comporte comme un adjectif: 'quel …., celui-là'. Plur. ***ya-lla-*** ou ***ya-lle-***. Ex.: ***ya-lla-nin tiwe-na*** 'quae verba, res' (I 98). [……] Premier mot de la phrase, auquelle s'attachent des enclitiques pronominaux et syntaxiques. […] Boğ.: thème ***ya-*** en tête de phrases ou de paragraphes."

Linear A scribes may have used *proclitic* or *quasi-proclitic* constructions in order to avoid confusion of monosyllabic words with abbreviations (e.g. abbreviated transaction terms) or even ideograms. Linear B scribes actually appear to have followed this very special usage of their Linear A colleagues, since Linear B provides comparable examples of this usage, remarkably with respect to the same category of monosyllabic words: ***o-u-di-do-si*** (PY Ma 124,2) = ***οὐ δίδονσι*** 'they do not give', as if ***οὐ*** and ***δίδονσι*** form one sequence; ***o-di-do-si*** (PY Vn 10,1) = ***ὦ δίδονσι*** (***ὦ*** = Hom. ***ὦς***) 'thus / in this way they give'; ***jo-do-so-si*** (PY Jn 829,1) = ***yω δώσονσι*** (***yω*** = Attic ***ώς***) 'as they will give', cf. C.J. Ruijgh, *EGM*, § 9. Especially ***jo-*** in ***jo-do-so-si*** (= ***yω*** in ***yω δώσονσι***) resembles ***ja-*** in ***ja-ta-i-jo-u-ja***, ***ja-di-ki-tu***, ***ja-di-ki-te-te*** and ***ja-sa-sa-ra-me***, ***ja-sa-sa-ra-ma-na*** as *quasi-proclitic* particle, semantically, morphologically and syntactically.

It has to be emphasized that such usage cannot be used as evidence for 'prefixes' in Hurrian, since Hurrian is only suffixing. It is merely a matter of a practical solution 'invented' by the scribes in order to counter a practical problem in the scripts of Linear A and B. So it has nothing to do with the structure of the language as the Linear B examples clearly show.

Th. Richter (*BGH*, 73) shows close correspondence between his *lemma* on ***ia*** I / ***ija*** **I,** ***ie*** I / ***ije*** I [*passim*], Relativpronomen (relative pronoun) 'was (auch immer)' ['what-(ever)'], e.g. ***ja-ti-la-«a»-an*** 'als auch wir' ['as we too'] and that on ***ia*** II / ***ija*** **II,** [Boğ.] 'warum', 'why', 'pourquoi' corresponding with Hittite ***kuwat*** (E. Neu, Zu einigen graphischen Varianten in der hurritischen Fassung der hurritisch-mittel-hethitischen Bilingue aus Ḫattuša, *SMEA 29 (1992)*, 203-216, especially 212[22]; E. Neu, Miscellanea Hurritica, *Studies on the Civilization and Culture of Nuzi and the Hurrians 5 (1995)*, 49ff.

Compare also E. Neu, *Das hurritische Epos der Freilassung I. Untersuchungen zu einem hurritisch-hethitischen Textensemble aus Ḫattuša* (Studien zu den Boğazköy-Texten 32), Wiesbaden 1996, 111, 156.

Th. Richter also points to Urartian ***i-ú*** 'als' ['as'] with regard to the etymology of ***ia*** I / ***ija*** I, ***ie*** I / ***ije*** I and refers to M. Salvini, Die urartäischen Schriftdenkmäler aus Bastam (1977-1978), in: E. Kleiss (ed.), *Bastam II. Ausgrabungen in den urartäischen Anlagen 1977-1978* (Teheraner Forschungen V), Berlin 1988, 125-144, especially 132.

The *(quasi-)proclitic* usage of Linear A ***ja-*** and the *proclitic* usage of ***ia*** I / ***ija*** I, ***ie*** I / ***ije*** I in Hurrian and the *(quasi-)proclitic* usage of Mycenaean Greek Linear B ***jo-*** in ***jo-do-so-si*** offer such strong parallels that accidental correspondence can virtually be ruled out. I think that *(quasi-)proclitic* ***ja-*** in Linear A, especially if it occurs in a combination such as ***a-ta-i-jo-wa-ja , ja-di-ki-tu , ja-sa-sa-ra[-me*** (IO Za 2) from Mount Ioukhtas, can be translated as a sort of conjunction 'as well as'.

As far as I can observe, alternative options for some Hurrian verbal roots do not offer a plausible meaning for ***a-sa-*** in ***a-sa-sa-ra-me***: e.g. ***aš-*** I [Boğ.] 'essen' ['to eat']; ***ašš-*** [Boğ.], also ***aš-*** IV(?) [Boğ.], 'être assis (?)', cf. E. Laroche, *GLH*, 59; 'to sit' (intr.), 'to set, put, place' (trans.), corresponding with Urartian ***aš-***. Incidentally, V. Haas and I. Wegner now reject the latter meaning of ***ašš-*** and propose '(ab)waschen, wegwischen' ['to wash, to cleanse'], cf. I. Wegner, *Einführung*, 86, 250; cf. Th. Richter, *BGH*, 50-52.

We have seen that Linear A and B orthographic conventions have made interpretation of ***a-sa-sa-ra-me*** not easy. In search of an interpretation that is acceptable in all respects I have examined all possibilities that are in accordance with the orthographic conventions of Linear A and B, our present knowledge of Hurrian grammar and onomastics, Hurrian religion and cult and last but not least the archaeological context provided by excavation of Minoan Peak Sanctuaries, in particular of Ioukhtas and Petsophas.

After this long search I think that ***Arša-šarra(m)me*** provides by far the best meaning for ***a-sa-sa-ra-me***: 'The young man/boy (is) *Šarramma < Šarrumma*', and ***ja-sa-sa-ra-ma|-na*** (KN Za 10a-b), analysed as *{y(a)/y(e)-arša=šarramma=nna}* 'as well as "The young boy, he is *Šarramma < Šarrumma*" ' or *{y(a)/y(e)-arša=šarra(m)=mann(i)=a}* 'as well as "The young boy, he is like the King of Gods" '.

The concept of "The young boy, he is *Šarramma < Šarrumma*" or "The young boy, he is like the King of Gods" may also have given rise to the later Greek myths referring to the *infant* Zeus born in Crete, who is in all respects equivalent to Hurrian Tešub, the King of Gods, who is as Mountain God and God of the Clouds (like Zeus) also God of thunder and lightning. The concept of the *son* of Tešub, who may have looked like his father, may (in the mind of the Mycenaean Greeks) have moved to the concept of the *infant* Zeus, miraculously born in Crete. The epithet ***i-da-a*** (KO Za 1b-c) 'The Thunderer' > later 'God of Mount Ida', refers to ***a-ta-i-jo-wa-ja*** 'Our Father'.

I may remind of my identification of the ideogram NUBES+***pi*** 100, followed by ligature ***qe+pa***$_3$ 100 (HT 33.4) on a tablet from Hagia Triada. Since final consonants are not expressed in Linear A and B, the ligature ***qe+pa***$_3$ (read from top to bottom) can be interpreted as the theonym ***Ḫebat***, Tešub's consort (see for a discussion about her provenance Th. Richter, *VHN*, 415-416). If the goddess herself is meant, the high number of 100 units seems to be in accordance with her dignity.

J. Raison - M. Pope (*Index transnuméré du linéaire A*, Louvain 1977, 56, 276) mention the combination of signs sub ***559*** (HT 33.4), which they analyse as ***<u>49</u>+56a*** = <u>OLIVA</u>+***pi***. Frankly I do not consider their analysis convincing. *GORILA 5*, p. 303, registered it as sign ***341***. An indication is that the number following combination ***559*** is also 100 as in the case of ***qe+pa₃*** 100 = ***Ḫebat*** 100. The sign preceding ***pi*** looks like the ideogram NUBES 'cloud' (hapax) and has nothing to do with sign ***49*** = OLIVA.

If the ideogram NUBES 'cloud' refers to the 'Weather God' or 'God of the Clouds', Tešub, it is clear that the consorts Tešub and Ḫebat receive each 100 units. Homer describes Tešub's Greek counterpart, Zeus, likewise: *Iliad* E 631: *Διὸς νεφεληγερέταο* 'of Zeus the cloud-gatherer', and *Odyssey* α 63: *νεφεληγερέτα Ζεύς* 'Zeus the cloud-gatherer'.

The sign ***pi*** following the ideogram NUBES may be the result of assimilation: ***-ub-wi*** > ***uppi***. The process has adequately been described by E.A. Speiser, *IH*, 63, § 82: "The combination of two spirants (evidently voiced) yields the written form ***-pp-***, a doubled sound (evidently voiceless stop). The important fact is that the end-product is a doubled sound. The same result, following assimilation, is obtained when stem-ending ***-b*** combines with ***w-***; cf. ^{d}*Te-e-eš-šu-u-up-pè* Mit. II 72; ^{d}*Te-eš-šu-up-pí* XXV 44 v 6, XXVII 38 ii 14, 20, etc.; with other suffixes added we get ^{d}U^{up}*-pí-na* XXV 44 v 8, XXVII 14 ii 4; ^{d}U^{up}*-pí-na-aš* XXVII 46 iv 2; ^{d}U^{up}*-pí-na-ša* XXVII 42 obv. 36. In all these occurrences the ***-b*** of ***Tešu/ob*** + ***w-*** yield ***-pp-***. That the labial of the case-ending was not lost is shown by its occasional retention in the form ^{d}U^{up}*-wi$_{i}$-na* VII 58 iii 12; XXVII 1 i 72, 74, 75 as against ^{d}U^{up}*-pí-na* (above)."

If the combination NUBES+***pi*** represents the *genitive* ***Tešuppi*** 'of Tešub (the cloud-gatherer)', it reminds us of the use of *phonetic complements* attached to a Sumerogram in cuneiform. If in a Hittite text the Sumerogram EN 'lord, master' was used to express the Hittite word ***išḫaš***, the context made it sometimes clear whether EN indicated the subject, object or indirect object of a verb. But if this was not clear, the Hittite case-endings could be added to the Sumerogram: e.g. ***išḫaš*** is the *nominative* (subject case) of the Hittite word for 'lord', ***išḫan*** the *accusative* (object case) and ***išḫi*** the *dative* (indirect object case). These could be written as EN-*aš*, EN-*an* and EN-*i*, respectively, cf. Th. van den Hout, *The elements of Hittite*, Cambridge 2013³, 12. This *rebus*-like way of writing is also found in the description of 'Šarruma' as ^{D}LUGAL-*ma* = ***Šarru(m)-ma*** in cuneiform (with the Sumerogram LUGAL 'King', equivalent to Akkadian ***šarru(m)***).

Only Linear A ***a-du-ni-ta-na*** 4<u>1</u>[ ] (AK 5.1) is preserved in the heading of this tablet. Tablet AK 5 (HM 1674, 1970) from the Villa of Epano Arkhanes (site of Τζαμί, House of Καλπαδάκη, Ὀδός Καπετανάκη) has the same provenance as AK 1. Only the upper part of the tablet consisting of five fragments and containing three lines is preserved. It reads:

AK 5.1. *a-du-ni-ta-na* 4<u>1</u> [ ]
2. <u>7</u> *a-da-<u>ro</u>* GRA 40 [ ]
3. <u>VIN*b*</u> 6 *a-*[
Inf. mut.

The 7 units at the beginning of the next line probably have to be added to the number of 4<u>1</u>, so that the total number is probably 48. After the 7 units follows another sequence ***a-da-<u>ro</u>*** GRA 40[ ] (AK 5.2), that is followed by VIN*b* 6 (AK 5.3).

According to *GORILA 3* (1976, 17) there is with regard to ***a-du-ni-ta-na*** (AK 5.1) certainly no punctuation between ***-du-*** and ***-ni-***. It is attractive to assume that the incomplete first line of another tablet from Arkhanes, AK 4a.1, of which only the syllables **]-*ni-ta*[** can be read, may represent the same sequence as that of AK 5.1. Morphologically ***a-du-ni-ta-na*** may be compared with Linear A names such as ***a-du-ku-mi-na*** {*ažd=u=ḫḫu-mina*} 'The twin is female' at Kato Zakro, ***a-du-sa-ra*** at Hagia Triada, ***a-du-re-za*** (KH 11.1) and]***a-se-re-za***|[(KH 13.2) at Khania. As most Hurrian personal names, it may consist of two elements: e.g. ***aždu=ni-*** 'the woman' (with singular definite article ***-ni/e***) + ***-tana***. P.M. Purves, *NPN*, 262, s.v. ***tan***, ***tanni***, compares the onomastic element ***-tana*** with the verbal root ***tan*** 'to make': "Hurrian. Cf. ***tanni***. Possibly cognate with ***tan*** translated 'machen' by Messerschmidt, *Mitanni-Studien*, 19 f. In Ur III period the element is *tan* or *tann* cf. *Ú-na-ap-tan*, TCL V 6039 rev. iii 6, which in Nuzi would be **Unap-tanni*. See I.J. Gelb, HS. Cf. Chagar Bazar personal names *ᶠAš-tu-a-ta-na, ᶠSa-aš-tu-a-ta-na* and *Tu-up-ki-ta-na* (*Iraq VII*, 36 and 42 f.)." One might conclude that in view of Linear A ***a-du-sa-ra*** and ***a-du-ni-ta-na*** it can hardly be accidental that *Aštua-šar* (*ᶠAš-du-a-šar*) occurs at Nuzi and *Aštu-šar* (*ᶠAš-tu-za-ar*) at Chagar Bazar (*Iraq VII*, 36), and *ᶠAš-tu-a-ta-na* at Chagar Bazar (ancient Ašnakkum), cf. P.M. Purves, *NPN*, 206, s.v. *Ašt, Aštu-, Aštua-, Aštun-*. Following P.M. Purves one might translate ***a-du-ni-ta-na*** as 'The woman is active, creative', taking ***-tan(n)a*** as an *intransitive* form of ***tan-***. Incidentally, according to Th. Richter (*VHN*, 79, s.v.***ᶠAštu-atana***) *ᶠSa-aš-tu-a-ta-na* is the older reading of *ᶠAš-tu-a-ta-na*. Th. Richter analyses the name as {*ᶠašto/u-adana*}, typology 2.1, lexicon *ᶠaštu, adana*, probably on the basis of single writing of ***-t-*** in *-a-ta-na*, apparently equivalent to (a deity of) the city Adana. ***ᶠAštu-atana*** is attested at Ašnakkum and Mari.

Th. Richter (*VHN*, 80) compares ***ᶠAštun*** (wr. *ᶠAš-tu-un*) from Mari and Nuzi with *ᶠAš-du-un-na* from Nuzi and analyses {*ᶠašto/u=n(na)*} translating 'Es (Mädchen) ist eine Frau' ['She (the girl) is a woman'] and takes ***-n*** in ***ᶠAštun*** and ***-nna*** in ***ᶠAšdunna*** as the enclitic personal pronoun marking the subject of (not expressed) intransitive verb 'to be'. Consequently ***Aštun-naia*** (wr. *ᶠAš-du-un-na-a-a*) at Nuzi (*NPN*, 37) can be analysed as ***Aštu=n(na)-Naia*** and mean 'She (the girl) is a woman, oh *Naia* !'.

If one thinks that ***-ta-na*** in ***a-du-ni-ta-na*** is verbal, the form *Ú-na-ap-tan*, (TCL V 6039 rev. iii 6) from the Ur III period poses a problem, because ***un=a=b-*** in *Ú-na-ap-tan* is certainly verbal, so ***-tan*** needs to be nominal in that name. Th. Richter (*BGH*, 438) may offer a solution s.v. ***tani*** II [Ug.], since Hurrian ***tani*** corresponds with Sumerian [AN$^{?}$], Akkadian [*šarru*$^{?}$], Ugaritic *ma-a-*[*al-ku*$^{??}$] according to E. Laroche, RS 20.189, *UF 1979*, 479. J. Huehnergard (*Ugaritic Vocabulary in syllabic transcription*, Harvard Semitic Series, Atlanta 1987, 28f, 61, 114) corrected and completed the comparison into Sumerian AN/DINGIR, Akkadian *šarru* and Ugaritic *ba*$^{!?}$*-a-*[*lu*$^{?}$]. → **šarri** I.

Since according to Th. Richter (*VHN*, 596, sub 1.3.1.1.2.2) ***-nni*** is considered an optional allomorphic enclitic personal pronoun that can replace ***-nna***, Linear A ***a-du-ni-ta-na*** (AK 5.1) can be analysed as ***aždu=nni-Tana***: 'She is a woman, oh *Tana* / *Tani* !'. Since Hurrian ***Tani*** can according to the Ugaritic Vocabulary RS 20.189 be compared with Akkadian ***šarru*** and consequently with Hurrian ***šarri*** 'King of Gods', it is quite conceivable that nominal ***Tani*** is derived from the verbal root ***tan-*** 'to make' and can be interpreted as 'The Maker, Creator'.

If the reading of Linear A ***a-da-ro*** GRA 40[ ] (AK 5.2), that is followed by VIN*b* 6 (AK 5.3), on the same tablet from Arkhanes is correct, it could be a personal name derived from ***Adalur***, name of the Hurrian mountain god. V. Haas, *Hethitische Berggötter und hurritische Steindämonen*, 31: "Ein lokaler Berggott ist *Adalur*, dessen Name das hurritische Wort *adali* 'stark' enthält." Final ***-r*** of ***Adalur***, phonologically probably /*Adalor*/, would not be expressed in Linear A. Instead of the personal name derived from the theonym ***Adalur*** Linear A ***a-da-ro*** can also represent ***Adallo/u***, analysis {*adall(i)=u* < **adal=n(i)=u*}, 'The strong one', with the Akkadianizing *nominative* in ***-u***.

Linear A ***a-da-ra*** (KN Zf 31) on a silver hairpin from Mavro Spelio (Knossos) is an exact equivalent to the Hurrian personal name ***Atalla*** (wr. *A-ta-al-la*) at Nuzi, cf. I.J. Gelb, *NPN*, 38. It is phonologically /***Adalla***/, since single writing of the dental indicates voicing in syllabic cuneiform. Linear A ***a-da-ra*** can be analysed as {*adall(i)=a* < **adal=n(i)=a*}, 'Like the strong one', the *essive* in ***-a*** of the name ***Atalli*** (wr. *A-ta-al-li*) attested at Mari < **adal=ni*, 'Der Starke' ['The strong one'], ***°-lli*** < ***°-l=ni***, with the so-called definite article ***-ni***, cf. *A-ta-li* at Kaniš (see Balkan, 1974, 36), cf. Th. Richter, *VHN*, 86, s.v. ***Atalli***.

Another analysis of Linear A ***a-da-ra*** (KN Zf 31) and of ***Adalla*** at Nuzi may be that ***Adalla*** can be interpreted as the result of assimilation from < ****Adal-ya***, hypocoristic of e.g. ***Atal-tešup*** (wr. *A-tal-te-šup*, *A-ta-al-te-eš*[*šup*], *A-da-al-te-šup*, *A-da-al-te-šu-up*) from Nuzi, phonologically /*Adal-tešub*/, 'Tešub is the strong one', or ***Atal-ewri*** (wr. *A-tal-ew-ri*) from Mari, analysis {*adal-evri*}, 'Der Starke ist Herr' ['The Strong one is Lord'], or ***Atal-šarri*** (wr. *A-tal-šar-ri*) from Mari or *A-tal*-LUGAL from Kaniš, analysis {*adal-šarri*}, 'Der Starke ist Götterkönig' ['The Strong one is King of Gods'], (etc.), cf. Th. Richter, *VHN*, 86. Linear A ***a-da-ra*** may also be a verbal form in context, ***ad=a=lla*** 'they are strong', with the verbal root ***ad-*** (trans.) 'to make strong', (intr.) 'to be strong'.

Long ago C.H. Gordon observed that there is a connection between the tablets HT 86 and HT 95+149 from Hagia Triada. Comparing HT 86 and HT 95+149 one realizes that both tablets offer lists of sequences (*da-me*, *mi-nu-te*, *ku-ni-su*, *di-de-ru*, *qe-ra$_2$-u* / *qa-ra$_2$-wa*), followed by numbers of portions of grain, expressed by ideogram GRA(NUM).

HT 86a:

1-2.	*a-ka-ru* ,	*ku-ni-su*	GRA+^{KL}	20
2.		*sa-ru*		20
3.		*di-de-ru*		20
3.		*qa-ra$_2$-wa*		10
4.	*a-du* ,	*da-me*	GRA^{+B}	20
5.		*mi-nu-te*		20
6.	vacat			

HT 86b:

1-2.	[[*a-ka-ru* ,	*ku-ni-su*	GRA+^{KL}	20
2.		*sa-ru*		20
3.		*di-de-*[		20
4-6.	vacat]]			

HT 95+149a:

1.	*da-du-ma-ta* ,	GRA	
2.		*da-me*	10
2.		*mi-nu-te*	10
3.		*sa-ru*	20
3-4.		*ku-ni-su*	10
4.		*di-de-ru*	10
4-5.		*qe-ra$_2$-u*	7
6.	vacat		

HT 95+149b:

1-2.	*a-du* ,	*sa-ru*	10	GRA[ ]
2.		*da-me*	10	
2-3.		*mi-nu-te*	10	
3-4.		*ku-ni-su*	10	
4.		*di-de-ru*	10	
4-5.		*qe-ra$_2$-u*	10	
6.	vacat			

A Hurrian interpretation of Linear A ***a-ka-ru*** (HT 2.1; HT 86a.1; HT 86b.1) is feasible. The name may well contain the verbal root ***ag-, akk-***, frequent in personal names (cf. Th. Richter, *VHN*, 366-368), (trans.) 'to bring (up), lead', (remarkably with the same meaning as the Indo-European root ***ag-***); (intr.) 'to appear'. The 'one-word' name may represent an Old Hurrian *imperative* in ***-u*** and be analysed as {*ag=al=u*} or {*ag=ar=u*}, with the root-extension ***-al-*** of unknown meaning (cf. I. Wegner, *Einführung*, 87) or with the *factitive* or *iterative* root-extension ***-ar-*** (cf. I. Wegner, *Einführung*, 88), translation 'Bring (the child) (up) (oh *numen*) !'. Analysis as an Old Hurrian perfect form 3rd pers. sg. {*ag=al=o/u=m*} or {*ag=ar=o/u=m*} is also possible, 'He/She (a *numen*) brought (the child) (up)'.

C.H. Gordon has compared Linear A ***ku-ni-su*** (HT 10a.1, HT 86a.1-2; HT 86b.1-2; HT 95+149a.3; HT 95+149b.3) in combination with the GRANUM ideogram on HT 86a and b, with Akkadian ***kunāšu(m)*** 'emmer wheat'. In HT 10a.1 ***ku-ni-su*** is not followed by an ideogram, but by ***sa-ma*** 4.

The form ***ku(n)nīšu*** (exact equivalent to the Linear A form), that might be considered a variant of 'standard' or 'normal' Akkadian ***kunāšu(m)***, has so far only been found at Ḫattuša (Boğazköy / Boğazkale), where Hurrian influence was important, and at Nuzi (Kirkuk), where the documents show that a predominantly Hurrian population was already present before the date when it may have formed part of Mitanni or may have been subject to this political and military power. In my view it may well be the Hurrian rendering of Akkadian ***kunāšu(m)***. If Gordon's identification of Linear A ***ku-ni-su*** as 'emmer wheat' is correct, all sequences belonging to the lists, in which ***ku-ni-su*** occurs, can logically be identified as commodities of the same category.

A problem is though, that (apart from ***ku-ni-su***) ***sa-ru*** seems to be the only sequence in the series of *da-me*, *mi-<u>nu</u>-te*, *ku-ni-su*, *di-de-ru*, *qe-ra$_2$-u*, c.q. *qa-ra$_2$-wa* that might (with a lot of imagination) indicate a cereal product, if one accepts that it is in some way related to the adjective ***sarabḫu*** of unknown meaning, indicating 'a quality of barley', that occurs in the Old Babylonian grain distribution lists of Alalaḫ (x) ***pa-ri-si*** ŠE ***ẓa-ra-ab-ḫu*** (AT 24.5; 241.12; 245.2; 247.15; 249.4), cf. A. Draffkorn, *HHA*, 198-199.

She compares ***sarabḫu*** at Alalaḫ with ŠE ***ẓa-ra-e*** at Nuzi: (x) ANŠE ŠE.MEŠ *za-ra-e ù ḫu-ra-e*, *HSS 14* 36: 1; occurs also in *ibid*. 34: 1, 2: 35: 1, 2. One may admit that the lack of lexical equivalents may be due to our somewhat fragmentary knowledge of Hurrian lexical terms. Another problem may be that it is sometimes difficult for us to understand the exact relation of an ideogram to adjacent syllabic sequences.

For instance, if Linear A ***ku-ni-su*** meant 'emmer wheat' (and we may assume that the scribe knew that), why did he then also use the ideogram GRA ? One of the two seems superfluous. And if the meaning of Linear A ***sa-ru*** was '(a type or quality of) barley', why did he use the ideogram GRA and not HORD(EUM) with respect to ***sa-ru*** in HT 95+149b.1 ? And to increase the confusion: Why is ***sa-ru*** (HT 123a.4) followed by the ideogram OLIVA and number 16 ? And why does ***sa-ru*** (HT 94b.2) occur in a list of personal names ? For instance, Linear A ***tu-ma*** (HT 94b.1) is equivalent to the Hurrian personal name ***Tumma*** (wr. *Tu-um-ma*) at Nuzi, cf. I.J. Gelb, *NPN*, 157; P.M. Purves, *NPN*, 268. In other words: If ***sa-ru*** is a personal name in HT 94b.1 and HT 123a.4, it is probably also a personal name in HT 86 and HT 95, e.g. an Old Hurrian 'one-word' name.

This 'one-word' name can be analysed as an Old Hurrian *imperative* ***Šar=u*** 'Wish (the child) (oh *numen*) !', consisting of the root ***šar-*** 'to wish' + Old Hurrian *imperative* marker ***-u***. Since final consonants are not expressed in Linear A (and B), the Hurrian personal name ***Šar=u=n(na)*** 'Wish it (the child) (oh *numen*) !' is also an option. ***Šarrun*** (wr. *šar-ru-un*) from Mari is also an exact equivalent, {*šarr=o=n(na)*}, lexicon ***šarr-***, typology 1.3.1.1.2.1, cf. Th. Richter, *VHN*, 251. Th. Richter (*VHN*, 500-501) mentions that the relation between ***šarr-*** and ***šar-*** 'to wish, demand' is not clear. Hurrian ***šarri*** 'King', with the meaning of ***šarri*** 'King of Gods' in personal names, occurs (apart from hypocoristics) usually as second element in personal names, but the personal name ***Šarri-atal*** (referring to the King of Ašlakkā[KI]) at Mari can be analysed as {*šarri-adal*} 'The King of Gods is strong', but in view of ***Šarrip-atal*** (wr. *šar-ri-ip-a-tal*) from Šušarrā (Tall Shemshara), {*šarr=i=b-adal*}, lexicon ***šarr-***, ***adal***, a verbal analysis {*šarr=i-adal*} of the first name is also conceivable, cf. Th. Richter, *VHN*, 250. Observing the large number of sentence names from Nuzi with the element ***šar-*** 'to wish, demand', it seems difficult to draw a sharp line of distinction between the verbal root ***šar-/šarr-*** and the nominal root ***šarr-***: e.g. ***Šar-tešup*** (wr. *Ša-ar-te-šup*, *Šá-ar-te-šup*), 'Wish (the child), oh Tešub !', is the name of 21 persons at Nuzi, and its hypocoristics ***Šar-teia*** and ***Šar-te*** (wr. *Ša-ar-te-e-a*, *Ša-ar-te-e*, *Ša-ar-te-ia*, *Ša-ar-te-a*, *Ša-ar-te*, *Šá-ar-te-e-a*), represent the names of 8 persons at Nuzi, cf. I.J. Gelb, *NPN*, 125. Hypocoristic ***fŠaruia*** (wr. *fŠá-ru-ia*) at Nuzi cannot contain the nominal root ***šarr-*** 'King', since it is the name of a woman. It could, for instance, be the hypocoristic of ***fŠarum-elli*** (wr. *fŠa-ru-me-el-li*), cf. I.J. Gelb, *NPN*, 125. The analysis would then be {*fŠar=u/o=m-elli*), 'The (deceased) sister wished / demanded (the child)' or 'He/She (a *numen*) wished the sister'. But hypocoristic ***Šarriia*** (wr. *Šar-ri-ia*, *Šarri*[ri]*-a*), name of 10 men at Nuzi, can in theory contain either root. Th. Richter, *VHN*, 248-250, also mentions the names ***Šarraia/Šarriia*** (wr. *Šar-ra-ia*, *Šar-ra-a-ia*, *Šàr-ra-a-ia*, *Šar-ar-ra-a*, *Šar-ri-ia*, *Šàr-ri-ia*), analysis {*šarr=a=ia*}, {*šarr=i=ia*}, lexicon *šarr-*, typology 1.1.1.3.4. Both variants are sometimes mentioned in the same text. At Mari it refers to a king of Eluḫḫut[KI], married with Narāmtum, daughter of Zimri-Lim, and to a king of Razamā[KI], also mentioned at Qaṭṭarā (Tall ar-Rimaḫ); it is the name of 5 other persons at Mari, two more at Qaṭṭarā, one at Ašnakkum (Tall Šaġīr Bāzār/'Chagar Bazar') and one at Šušarrā (Tall Shemshara). If ***sa-ru*** is a personal name in HT 86a, HT 86b, HT 95+149a and HT 95+149b, the other sequences are probably names as well. The most likely reason why the same names appear again and again in these tablets, is that the persons in question belonged to the same group of personnel working in the same workshop or department.

Linear A ***tu-pa-di-da*** (HT 123 + 124b.3) is a Hurrian 'one-word' personal name that can be analysed as {*tub/w=ad=id/ed=a*}, consisting of the verbal root ***tub/w-*** 'to conjure, invoke, evoke' + root-extension ***-ad-*** (meaning unknown, cf. I.Wegner, *Einführung*, 88) + the marker of the future tense ***-ed-*** / ***-id-*** + marker of the subject of action 3rd person singular of the transitive verb ***-a***, translation 'He/She (a *numen*) will conjure, invoke, evoke'. Th. Richter, *BGH*, 471, s.v. ***tub-*** I [Boğ. ?] 'beschwören, to conjure, evoke'.

If Linear A ***ku-ni-su*** is a personal name, the first element may be compared with the Hurrian name ***Kunni*** (wr. *ku-un-ni*), lexicon ***kunn-***, analysis {*ko/unn=i*}, typology 1.3.1.2.1, name of an old slave from Mari (*Mari 8*, 642 XI 4), *ku-un-ni* from Alalaḫ VII (cf. D.J. Wiseman, *AT*, *54: 27); *ku-un-ni* from Ugarit, F. Gröndahl, *PNTU*, 1967, 340;

Kunni (wr. *ᵐku-un-ni-iš*) at Boğazköy (XIII 35 III 40), see E. Laroche, *NH*, 98, nr. 629, cf. Th. Richter, *VHN*, 174; cf. ***Kuniš-Na*** (?) or ***Kuniš-naia*** (wr. *ᶠku-ni-iš-na-a* ?), analysis {*ko/un=i=ž-Na* (?)}, typology 1.3.2.2, lexicon *kun-*, *Naje*, a young female musician at Mari, cf. Th. Richter, *VHN*, 174. Compare for the latter name also the frequent Hurrian feminine personal names in ***-na*** and ***-naia*** at Nuzi, cf. P.M. Purves, *NPN*, 258-259, who observed that ***-na*** could often be identified as a shortened form of ***-naia***. The meaning of ***kun-/kunn-*** {*ko/un(n)-*} is not yet known (cf. Th Richter, *VHN*, 446-447).

One may analyse Linear A ***ku-ni-su*** as {*ko/un=i=ž=u=n(na)*} and explain it as an *optative* 'He/She (a *numen*) may ... it (the child)'. According to Th. Richter (*VHN*, 603, sub 1.3.2.2) the verbal forms with ***ᵒ=i=ž*** do not represent an *imperative*, but another modal function, probably the *optative*. He translates the sentence name ***ᶠAweš-tari*** as 'May the fire save ... (the girl)'. The fire may refer to a sacrifice with regard to the child's birth.

Another approach is to divide ***ku-ni-su*** into a first element ***kun(n)i-*** and a second ***-šu***. The second onomastic element ***-su*** in Linear A ***ku-ni-su*** may be equivalent to ***-šu*** in proper names from Ḫattuša that can often be observed in names of female persons, cf. Th. Richter (*VHN*, 517) s.v. (ᵒ)***zu***: "Bei dem Zweitglied ᵒ***-zu*** könnte es sich um das von u.a. Haas, 1971: 139; 1975: 506 und Haas/Wegner, 1988/1: 13 aus Ḫattuša-Eigennamen isolierte ᵒ(=)***šu*** handeln (s.a. E/1.1), das häufig an weiblichen Personennamen zu beobachten ist." He mentions the following examples: ***ᶠAllai(-)zu*** (Mari); ***Ewri(-)zu*** (AŠ); ***Ḫarija(-)zu*** (Mari); ***Nani(-)zu*** (AŠ); ***Nanni(-)zu*** (Mari); ***ᶠPirḫen(-)zu*** (Mari).

Comparison with names with the same first onomastic elements indicates that the second element ᵒ***-zu*** / ᵒ***-šu*** may have been used as a *quasi* theophorous element. If I may embroider on this theme: if ***Ewri-ma*** (wr. *ew-ri-ma*), the name of 3 *ḫabiru* at Tigunāni (cf. Th. Richter, *VHN*, 109-110), is a shortened form of ****Ewri-madi*** (cf. ***Er-wi-ma-du-ni*** at Nuzi, 'The Lord is wise', with metathesis of ***Ewri*** > ***Erwi*** at Nuzi) and if one realizes that ***Madi*** 'wisdom' was sometimes provided with the divine determinative and therefore deified, ***Ewri(-)zu*** at Ašnakkum may perhaps be a shortened form of ****Ewri-šuni*** 'The Lord is the hand (that supports mother and child)', cf. ***A-ri-ip-šu-ni*** 'The hand gave (the boy)' at Emar. The Hurrian-Hittite bilingual ***kirenze*** (KBo 32) offers ***šuni*** 'hand' as parallel of Hittite ***keššar***, cf. Th. Richter, *VHN*, 519, s.v. ***šuni*** {*šoni*}; cf. also Th. Richter, *BGH*, 413-414, s.v. ***šuni*** I [Boğ.; Ug.], perhaps cognate with ***šum(m)un(n)i***.

P.M. Purves (*NPN*, 258) considered ***-šu*** in personal names 'perhaps a formative' in ***Arpišu***, ***Ekammešu*** and ***Kelšu***. However, ***-zu*** in ***Kelzu*** (wr. *ke-el-zu*, *ke-él-zu*), also attested at Mari as name of a bowmaker (*sasinnum*) is analysed differently by Th. Richter (*VHN*, 158), who compares it with the personal name ***Kelze*** (wr. *ke-el-ze*, *ke-él-ze*, *ke-èl*(AN)*-ze*), attested as the name of 6 persons at Mari and 1 person at Tuttul (Tall Bi'a). Both names are translated 'Wohl(?)' ['Healthy']. He analyses ***Kelzu*** as {*kelž(e)=u*} and the ending in ***-u*** as an Akkadianizing nominative in ***-u***. ***Kelze*** and ***Kelzu*** contain the verbal root ***kel-*** (intransitive) 'sich wohl befinden' ['to feel well / thrive / prosper'] and (transitive) 'befriedigen' ['to satisfy'] and 'prosperieren lassen' ['to cause (somebody) to thrive / be successful / prosper']. The word ***keldi*** 'health, well-being' is probably derived from the verbal root and was already analysed as ***kel=d=i*** by A. Gustavs, Bemerkungen zur Bedeutung und zum Bau von Mitanninamen, *Orientalistische Literaturzeitung 15*, Berlin 1912, 302. ***Keldi*** is a divine name. In the tradition of Ḫattuša he is son of ***Aya***.

It is interesting that there may well be a Hurrian and Linear A parallel of Akkadian 'standard', 'normal' Akkadian ***kunāšu(m)*** and Hurrianized (?) ***ku(n)nīšu*** (Nuzi, Ḫattuša).

The Hurrian noun ***utte*** 'emmer' was recognized as Hurrian equivalent to Sumerian [ZÍZ], Akkadian [...]-***šu*** and Ugaritic ***ku-sú-m***[***u***] by W.H. van Soldt, Hurrian *utte* 'emmer', *RA 75*, 1981, 93. His discovery was later confirmed by RS 94-2939 = *SCCNH 9*, 7 V 15': (Sumerian) ZÍZ = (Akkadian) *ku-un-šu* = (Hurrian) *ut-te*, cf. Th. Richter, *VHN*, 557-558. Th. Richter (*BGH*, 508) writes that ***utte*** [Boğ.; PN; Ug.] 'emmer' corresponds with Ugaritic *ku-sú-m*[*u-ma*?] (W.H. van Soldt 1981, 93; J. Huehnergard, 1987b, 724); 'emmer' corresponds with Sumerian [ÁŠ], Akkadian [*ku-na*]-*šu* and Ugaritic *ku-sú-mu* (J. Huehnergard, 1987a, 92, 139; W.H. van Soldt 1990, 732); etc.

Th. Richter (*VHN*, 342, 557-558) analyses the Hurrian personal name ***fUttuzzi*** (wr. *fUt-tu-uz-zi*) from Šubat-Enlil as {*o/utt(e)=o/u=zzi*}, typology 3.1, lexicon *uttuzzi*, and translates it as 'Dem Emmer angemessen' ['Pertaining to emmer'], because it certainly contains the basic lexeme ***utte***.

However, Richter prefers a verbal root in the personal names ***fUtte*** (wr. *fUt-te*) from Ašnakkum, *Ú-ut-ti* from Alalaḫ, Ḫattuša and Nuzi, and *ut-ti* from Emar, analysis {*utt-i*}, typology 1.3.1.2.1, lexicon *utt-*, but cannot fully exclude the possibility that the name is connected with the noun ***utte*** 'emmer', since ***fUtte*** from Ašnakkum happens to be a 'Müllerin' ['female miller or miller's wife']. It might even be a nickname. ***fUtten***, also from Ašnakkum, can eventually also be analysed in this way as {*o/utte=n(na)*} 'Sie (Frau) ist der Emmer' ['She (woman) is emmer'] or name of birth 'Es (Mädchen) ist der Emmer' ['She (the girl) is emmer'].

It may be significant that Linear A ***u-ti*** (HT 10b.1) is the first sequence of the *b*-side of this tablet from Hagia Triada, whereas ***ku-ni-su*** (HT 10a.1) is the first sequence on the *a*-side. Was the scribe playing with words or names ? Linear A ***u-ti*** (HT 10b.1) is certainly a personal name, because it occurs in a list of personal names. Linear A ***ta-we-na*** (HT 10b.1-2) is, for instance, a personal name that can be identified with ***fTawenna*** (wr. *fTa-we-en-na*) from Ašnakkum and Mari, analysis {*tav=i=nna*}, typology 1.3.1.2.2.1, lexicon *taw-* I, translation 'Cast her (the girl) (oh *numen*) !', cf. Th. Richter, *VHN*, 297, 600, already discussed before. The Hurrian personal name ***Ut(t)i*** (wr. *Ú-ut-ti*) is also attested at Alalaḫ on AT 67:3 and AT 108:1, cf. A. Draffkorn, *HHA*, 61, s.v. ***Ut(t)i***, *Ú-ut-ti*. Was the scribe of HT 10 good-humoured and playing with words/names, when he wrote ***ku-ni-su*** and ***u-ti*** respectively as first entry on the *a*- and *b*-sides of the tablet, knowing that both ***ku(n)nīšu*** and ***utte/i*** can be interpreted as 'emmer', but can also have different meanings ?

Linear A ***u-ti*** (MA 2c.2) possibly also occurs on a three-sided bar of clay from Malia. The reading is less certain, since J. Raison - M. Pope (BCILL 18, 252, and BCILL 74, 247-248) read on MA 2c.2:]***ja-ma*** **,** ***u-ti***, whereas L. Godart - J.-P. Olivier, *GORILA 1*, 270-271, read:]***ja-ma-u-ti***.

D.J. Wiseman, *The Alalakh Tablets*, 50, reads the text of tablet 67 as follows: Contract before *Niqmepa* the king. *Enḫuta* buys a slave (LÚ.SAL.TUM) from *Utti* son of *Ṣia*, *Putini* son of *Aduwa*, and *Irteia* son of *Nulu* for 25 (shekels) of silver. Should a legal owner bring a claim (*ušela*) they must settle with him. 4 witnesses. (The tablet bears a seal of *Niqmepa* on the upper obverse. See also *NH* Plate XIX).

D.J. Wiseman, *The Alalakh Tablets*, 58, nº 108. ATT/8/251, Text Obv. reads: (1) *a-na (m) Ú-ut-ti* (2) *um-ma šarru-ma* (3) *ANŠE (meš) ša (m) Niq-me-pa* (4) *ša a-na ša-as-šu i-dab-bu-bu* (5) *muš-šir-šu-nu-ma* (6) *ù mi-ik-sa-šu-nu* (7) *la te-li-ig-gi* (8) *ù e-nu-ma* (9) *(m) Ar-ta-šu-ma-ra* (10) *aš-ra-nu i-il-la-kam* Rev. (11) *ù zu-uk-ki-šu-nu* (12) *ki-i ni-bi-er-ti-šu-nu*. - "To *Utti* thus (says) the king: 'Let go the asses belonging to *Niqmepa* which they have disputed with him, and do not take their toll. When *Artašumara* comes there then clear them according to their transit-tax'." The tablet bears a seal impression on the lower reverse side. The text is a letter from a king to *Utti* asking for exemption from transit-tax for asses belonging to *Niqmepa*. Since the style of the seal is similar to that of *Saušsatar* (14, 74) the sender may be a ruler of that line. Unfortunately only *a*[?......]*-ar* remains of the seal inscription. The name *Arta-šumara* (line 9) recalls the brother of the Mitannian king *Tušratta* who was murdered ca. 1390 B.C.

Th. Richter (*VHN*, 342, 557-558) mentions the following personal names with the root ***utt-*** {*o/utt-*}: ***ᶠUtte*** (Ašnakkum); ***ᶠUtten*** (Ašnakkum); ***ᶠUttazzi*** (Mari); ***Utturi*** (Tuttul).

The Linear A cognate name ***u-ta₂*** (HT 103.1), followed by the FIC (FICUS) ideogram and the number 42, can be interpreted as the Hurrian personal name ***Uttiia*** from Nuzi (wr. *Ú-ut-ti-[i]a, Ú-ti-ia*), cf. I.J. Gelb, *NPN*, 169; P.M. Purves, *NPN*, 273, s.v. *utt* and *uttiia* (Linear A and B sign ***ta₂ = tia***). ***Uttiia*** is a verbal 'one-word' personal name {*utt=i-(j)a*}, consisting of verbal root ***utt-*** + marker of transitivity ***-i-*** + marker of the subject of action 3rd person singular ***-a***, or as a hypocoristic personal name consisting of verbal root ***utt-*** + marker of transitivity ***-i-*** + hypocoristic suffix ***-ya***. Consequently ***u-ti*** (HT 10b.1) at Hagia Triada and possibly ***u-ti*** (MA 2c.2) at Mallia can also be interpreted as an *imperative* of the same verbal root ***utt-***. From a morphological point of view it is not likely that Linear A ***u-ta₂*** (HT 103.1), if interpreted as ***Uttiia***, has anything to do with the noun ***utte*** 'emmer'. All other names (***da-ku-se-ne***, ***da-ku-na*** and ***ki-ra***) mentioned on HT 103 are Hurrian as well. The meaning of the verbal root ***utt-*** has not yet been established, but if ***utt-*** may be identified with ***ud-*** {*o/ud-*}, the meaning may be 'schützen' ['to protect'], cf. Th. Richter, *VHN*, 557, s.v. ***utt-*** {*o/utt*}. Since according to the orthographic conventions of Linear A and B ***-s-*** preceding an occlusive is not expressed in consonant clusters, Linear A ***u-ta₂*** can also be interpreted as Hurrian ***Uštija*** and Linear A ***u-ti*** as Hurrian ***Ušti***.

Many Hurrian nouns are derived from verbal roots. From a morphological and semantic point of view it is likely that this is also the case with ***ušta(i)*** '(war)hero'. If the general meaning ***ušt-*** 'to go out' can also be used in the sense of 'to set out on his way', a special meaning 'to go to war / to the battlefield' may well explain the meaning '(war)hero' for ***ušta(i)*** and 'the hero' for ***uštanni***. Interpretation of Linear A ***u-ta-i-se*** (KH 7b.2) and ***]u-ta-i-si*** (KH 16.2) from Khania will be discussed later. Cf. ***Uštan-šarri*** (*uš-ta-an-šar-ri*) at Mari and Šušarrā, {*ušta=n(na)-šarri*}, 'The hero is king of the gods'.

Th. Richter, *BGH*, 502-503, s.v. ***ušš-*** [Boğ.,Mari], ***ušt-, ašt-*** II [Boğ., PN, Ugar.] tells that according to V. Haas - I. Wegner (Beiträge zum hurritischen Lexikon: Die hurritischen Verben ***ušš-*** 'gehen' und ***ašš-*** 'abwaschen, abwischen', in: J. Klinger, E. Rieken, Chr. Rüster (eds.), *Investigationes Anatolicae. Gedenkschrift für Erich Neu (StBoT 52)*, Wiesbaden 2010, 97-109) the root-variants ***ušš-***, ***ušt-***, their derivations and etymology belong together: intransitive 'gehen, ausziehen (in den Kampf)' ['to go (to the battlefield)'], transitive 'führen, fort-, wegbringen' ['to lead, bring away'].

They completed the verb ***uš-***[...] (corresponding with Sumerian [D]U and Akkadian ***alāku***) to ***uš-[šu-(um-)me***]. Hurrian ***ušš-*** corresponds with Hittite ***ija-*** 'marschieren, gehen' ['to march, to go'] according to I. Wegner, "Haus" und "Hof" im Hurritischen, in: Th. Richter, D. Prechel, J. Klinger (eds.), *Kulturgeschichten. Altorientalische Studien für Volkert Haas zum 65. Geburtstag*, Saarbrücken 2001, 446. One may compare Urartian intransitive ***ušta-*** *{ušt=a-}* 'aufbrechen' ['to break up'], transitive ***uštu-*** *{ušt=u-}* 'darbringen' ['to bring, offer'], cf. H.-J. Thiel, 'Der Text und die Notenfolgen des Musiktextes aus Ugarit', *Studi micenei ed egeo-anatolici 18 (1977)*, 132; Thiel, 'Zur Gliederung des „Musik-Textes" aus Ugarit', in: *Actes de la XXIVe Rencontre Assyriologique Internationale, Paris 1977: Les Hourrites, RHA 36 (1978)* [1980], 196; cf. V. Haas - I. Wegner, o.c. 2010, 100[21]. After it had been recognized that ***ušš-*** was a verbal root indicating motion, I. Wegner was according to Th. Richter (*VHN* I, 556) the first to advocate the translation 'to go'. V. Haas and I. Wegner then established the meaning extensively (see also *supra*) and marked the form ***úš-še*** in an incantation from Mari as imperative 'go !' (*RA 36*, 13 Nr. 3 Rs. 15). Th. Richter considers the same analysis applicable to the personal names for men and women written ***ú-uš-še*** (most frequent), ***ú-úš-še***, ***ú-úš-e*** or ***úš-e***. He sees no basic problems for the variant writings.

According to Th. Richter (*VHN* I, 556-557) all personal names in ***ušt-*** belong to the root ***ušt-*** 'losgehen' ['to dash away'], 'herausgehen, ausziehen' ['to go out/away, to march out'], '(sich aus dem Bett) erheben' ['to get up from bed'], 'to go out (for battle)', see also Urartian ***ušta-*** *{ušt=a-}* 'sich auf den Weg machen' ['to set out on his/her way'], and (transitive) ***uštu-*** *{ušt=u-}* 'schicken' [= 'to send'], cf. G. Wilhelm, 'Die hurritische Ablativ-Instrumentalis */ne/*', *Zeitschrift für Assyriologie 73 (1983)*, 102[20].

Th. Richter (*VHN* I, 341) analyses the Hurrian personal name ***Uštun*** (wr. *Uš-tu-un*) from Šušarrā as *{ušt=o=n(na)}*, typology 1.3.1.1.2.1, lexicon *ušt-* and translates 'Bringe ihn (Jungen) hinaus' [= 'Bring him (the boy) out']. Consequently, we may conclude that Linear A ***u-ta₂***, interpreted as the Hurrian personal name ***Uštija***, can be analysed as a verbal 'one-word' personal name *{ušt=i-(j)a}*, consisting of the verbal root ***ušt-*** + the marker of transitivity ***-i-*** + the marker of the subject of action 3rd person singular ***-a***, or as a hypocoristic personal name consisting of the verbal root ***ušt-*** + the marker of transitivity ***-i-*** + the hypocoristic suffix ***-ya***. Since the meaning of transitive ***ušt-*** is known, we can translate ***Uštija*** as 'He/She (scil. a *numen*) brought him/her (the child) out'. Only the Minoan scribe knew, whether he had the name ***Uttiḭa*** in mind (as at Nuzi) or ***Uštija***.

Linear A ***da-me*** (HT 86a.4; HT 95a.2; HT 95b.2; HT 106.3; HT 120.1) may be interpreted as the Hurrian personal name ***Tame*** (wr. *Da-me*), father of *Ṣa-al-mu* at Nuzi (JEN 408:3), cf. I.J. Gelb, *NPN*, 146; P.M. Purves, *NPN*, 262, s.v. ***tam***, ***tame***; cf. also *ibidem* ***Tamaḭa*** (wr. *Ta-ma-a-a*), ***Tamaku*** (wr. *Ta-a-ma-ku*, *Ta-ma-ku(m)*).

However, in Linear A and B a *liquid* (***r*** or ***l***) preceding ***-m-*** is not expressed, cf. Linear B ***pe-ma*** (PY Er 312, 2, *et alibi*) ***σπέρμα***, and ***pe-mo*** (PY Ep 301, 1, *e.a.*) ***σπέρμο*** 'seed, in particular of wheat'. Consequently Linear A ***da-me*** can also (and probably preferably) be interpreted as the Hurrian personal name ***Talme***, phonologically */Dalme/* in the Hurrian dialect of Minoan Crete, equivalent to Hurrian ***Talm***[***i***...], wr. ***Ta-al-m***[***i***...], at Mari (M.7834), typology 6.2, lexicon ***talm-***, cf. Th. Richter, *VHN*, 294.

The view that Hurrian only had initial voiceless occlusives, is based on relatively late evidence derived from alphabetic cuneiform texts at Ugarit. This evidence can in fact only be applied to the Hurrian dialect of Ugarit at the time of these alphabetic cuneiform texts. The numerous examples of sequences with initial ***d-*** in Linear A provide, however, clear evidence that the much earlier Hurrian dialect of Minoan Crete definitely had initial voiced dentals. The initial voiced dental of Linear A ***da-me*** can be compared with that in another Linear A personal name ***da-du-ma-ta*** (HT 95a.1) that can best be analysed as Hurrian {*dad=u/o=m-atta*} '(God the) Father loved (the boy)', built on the roots ***tad-*** 'to love' and ***-atta*** from ***attai*** 'father'. The personal name ***Talmu*** (wr. *Da-al-mu*), father of *Ar-nu-ur-ḫe* at Nuzi, HSS V 63: 12 (cf. I.J. Gelb, *NPN*, 140; P.M. Purves, *NPN*, 262) probably contains the ending of the Akkadianizing nominative in ***-u***, but is basically equivalent to the Hurrian absolutive ***Talme / Talmi***.

E. Laroche, *GLH*, 253, s.v. ***talmi*** 'grand' ['great'], mentions the reading of Sumerian GAL in the name of ***Talmi-Tešub***, wr. GAL-ᵈU-***ub***, *NH*, Nº 1230. RS voc. II 18 = Ḫ̮ḫ̮ II 130: ki.lam gu.la = MIN ***te-la-ma-e*** 'grand prix'. Thèmes ***talmi*** et ***talami***. Compare also the discussion on Linear A ***te-r̲a̲-me*** (,) ***a-ja-ku*** (KN Zf 13) 'oh Great *A-ya-ku-un*' or 'oh *A-ya-ku-un* the Great' on the gold signet ring from Mavro Spilio.

If my interpretation of ***da-me*** (HT 86a.4; HT 95a.2; HT 95b.2; HT 106.3; HT 120.1) as ***Dalme/Talme*** and of ***te-r̲a̲-me*** = Hurrian ***telame*** as equivalent to ***talame*** and ***talme*** 'great' is correct, these identifications corroborate the observation of *allophones* in Hurrian and Linear A, also at the beginning of a word or name. The meaning 'great' for the variant ***talame*** (e.g. in the Hurrian personal name ***ᶠUmar-talame*** from Mari) is confirmed on the basis of Sumerian MAḪ = Akkadian ***ra-bu-ú*** = Hurrian ***ta-la-am-me***, cf. Th. Richter, *BGH*, 432-433; *VHN*, 527-528.

Since it is suspected that the root ***talm-*** may not only be nominal, but also verbal, the transitive root probably means 'to make great/powerful' and the intransitive 'to be great/ powerful'. Consequently Linear A ***da-me*** and Hurrian ***D/Talme***, analysis {*d/talm=e*}, consisting of the verbal root ***d/talm-*** + the transitive *imperative* suffix ***-i/-e***, can then be translated 'Make (the child) great/powerful (oh *numen*) !'.

Since final consonants are not expressed in Linear A, ***da-me*** can also represent ***D/Talmen***, {*d/talm=e=n*}, shortened form of ***D/Talmenna***, {*d/talm=e=nna*}, consisting of the verbal root ***d/talm-*** + transitive *imperative* suffix ***-i/-e*** + the enclitic personal pronoun 3rd person singular ***-n(na)***, 'Make him/her (the child) great (oh *numen*) !'. Other Hurrian names with ***Talm=i-*** are, for instance, ***Talmi-Tešub***, that was formerly translated as 'Great is Tešub', but can now probably be interpreted as 'Make (the boy) great, powerful, oh Tešub !'. ***Talmi-Tešub*** is the name of the King of Kargamiš (son of *Ini-Tešub* 'Tešub is God'), mentioned by E. Laroche, *NH*, 172, nº 1230, with references to Boğazköy KBo XII 41 I 5, hieroglyphic seals (*Tal-mi-Tešub^ba^*), HH I Nºˢ 318, 391, and Ugarit RS 17.226, 1 and cyl. = PRU IV 208. Another Hurrian name is ***Talmi-Šarruma***, name of the Hittite King of Aleppo (grandson of Suppiluliuma I). ***Talmi-Šarruma*** used to be translated as 'Great is Šarruma', but is now interpreted as 'Make (the boy) great, powerful, oh Šarruma!': accusative *ᵐTal-mi*-LUGAL-*ma-an,* KBo IV 4 III 15, etc. (*NH*, 172, nº 1229), with the Sumerogram LUGAL instead of *Šarru* and the Hittite accusative ending *-an*.

Another interpretation of the Linear A personal name ***da-me*** (HT 86a.4; HT 95a.2; HT 95b.2; HT 106.3; HT 120.1) is also possible, since it can also represent Hurrian ***D/Tarme***, analysis {*d/tarm=e*}, consisting of the transitive verbal root ***d/tarm-*** 'to nurse, nourish, (breast)feed' + the transitive *imperative* suffix ***-i/-e***, 'Nourish (the child, oh *numen*) !' or, since final consonants are not expressed in Linear A, ***D/Tarmen***, {*d/tarm=e=n*}, shortened form of ***D/Tarmenna***, {*d/tarm=e=nna*}, consisting of the verbal root ***d/tarm-*** + transitive *imperative* suffix ***-i/-e*** + enclitic personal pronoun 3rd person singular ***-n(na)***, 'Nourish him/her (the child, oh *numen*) !'.

We have already discussed (*supra*) Linear A ***da-mi-nu*** (HT 117a.8) from Hagia Triada that I have interpreted as the Hurrian personal name ***D/Talminnu*** and analysed as {*d/talm=i=nn(a)=u*}, 'Make him/her (the child) great, powerful, (oh *numen*) !', consisting of the verbal root ***talm-*** 'to make great, powerful' + the marker of transitivity ***-i-*** (together forming the *imperative* 2nd person sing.) + the *optional allomorphic* enclitic personal pronoun 3rd person singular ***-nni/-nnu*** instead of regular ***-nna*** (him/her).

The other possible interpretation is ***D/Tarminnu***, analysed as {*d/tarm=i=nn(a)=u*}, 'Nourish him/her (the child), (oh *numen*) !', consisting of the verbal root ***tarm-*** + the indicator of transitivity ***-i-*** (together forming the *imperative* 2nd person sing.) + the *optional allomorphic* enclitic personal pronoun 3rd person singular ***-nnu*** instead of ***-nna***.

Can ***di-de-ru*** (HT 86a.3; HT 95+149a.4; HT 95+149b.4) and ***di-de-***[(HT 86b.3) also be analysed as a Hurrian personal name ? I think it can. As in many Hurrian personal names the first onomastic element appears to be verbal. According to Th. Richter (*BGH*, 464) there is a verbal root ***tid-*** I [Boğ.] 'to share out, to separate' (cf. I.M. Diakonoff – S.E. Starostin, *Hurro-Urartian as an Eastern Caucasian language* (Münchener Studien zur Sprachwissenschaft, Beiheft 12, Neue Folge), München 1986, 27; I.M. Diakonoff, On some new trends in Urartian philology and some new Urartian texts, *Archäologische Mitteilungen aus Iran. Neue Folge 22*, Berlin 1989, 100) and 'zählen' ['to count'] (cf. I. Wegner, *Einführung in die hurritische Sprache*, 2007², 212, 287).

I. Wegner (*ibid.*, 210-212) analyses ***ti-i-ti-wa$_a$-a-te*** in the Hurrian-Hittite bilingual ***kirenze*** (KBo 32: 13 Vs I 18) as {*tid=i=bade*} and compares it with the Hittite parallel ***kappuwauwar*** (wr. *kap-pu-wa-u-wa-ar-ma*) (KBo 32: 13 II 18) 'das Zählen, das Gezählte' ['count(ing)']; ***tid=i=bade*** consists of the verbal root ***tid-*** 'to count' and the suffix ***-i-bade*** that forms *abstracta*. Compare for ***kappuwauwar*** Th. van den Hout, *The elements of Hittite*, Cambridge 2013³, 192: ***kappuwa(e)-*** 'to count, take care of' ***kappuwauwar***, neut. 'count(ing)'. Wegner also attributes the first element in the personal name ***Tí-tí-na-tal*** {*Titin-adal*} on a tablet from Kültepe (KT 90/k, 223 9) to this verbal root. In my view the Urartian root ***did-*** 'to share?' can also be compared with this Hurrian verbal root (cf. M. Salvini - I. Wegner, *Einführung in die urartäische Sprache*, Wiesbaden 2014, 108). The ending ***-u*** in Linear A ***di-de-ru*** may be an Akkadianizing nominative in ***-u***, so that the underlying Hurrian form is probably ****di-de-ri***. I. Wegner (*Einführung*, 113) mentions sub 5.8 (Partizipien) that ***-i=ri*** is the suffix for transitive and ***-a=uri*** for intransitive participles. For the transitive participles she gives the example ***tab=i=ri*** 'someone who pours/casts (metal, bronze), (bronze)smith'. So ***di-de-ru*** {*did=e/i=r(i)u*} can be translated as 'The one who counts, shares (out), takes care of > caretaker'.

Th. Richter (*BGH*, 464-465) mentions another verbal root ***tid-*** II [Boğ.; Mitt.], ***titt-*** [Boğ.] 'angreifen' ['to attack'] and possibly also ***te-t º***. Th. Richter (*VHN*, 541) mentions s.v. ***ted-/tid-*** that it is uncertain which of the two roots ***tid-*** I 'to count' or ***tid-*** II 'to attack' was used in personal names or whether they were both used. He mentions apart from the personal names from Nuzi (*NPN*, 155 and 268, s.v. *ti-ti*) also: (a) {*ted-*}: ***Tetija*** (Š). (b) {*tid-*}: ***ᶠTita-ki*** (Mari); ***Titikkan*** (Mari); cf. for Mari also J.M. Sasson, 'Ḫurrians and Ḫurrian names in the Mari texts', *UF 6 (1974)*, 370: ***Tidi-ka-n*** (wr. *Ti-di-qa-an*), SY A: viii: 18, 25; *ibidem*, 386: *tid-, tidi-*: *Tidi-ka-n.*

I may for Alalaḫ refer to D.J. Wiseman, *The Alalakh Tablets*, London 1953, 149: *Ti-di-ik-ku* AT 189,44; *Ti-ti-(ik)-ku* AT 147, 10.25.44; AT 173, 17; AT 179, 7; AT 181, 15; AT 188, 11; AT 192, 20; AT 197, 28; AT 307, 4. *Ti-di-ku-un* AT 189, 17; cf. A. Draffkorn, *HHA*, 57 and 109, s.v. *Tidi-k(k)u, Ti-ti-ik-ku.*

M. Pope has compared Linear A ***ti-ti-ku*** (HT 35.1; ZA Zb 3.2) and ***ti-ti-ku-ni*** (HT 96a.1) with the Hurrian names ***titiku*** and ***titikun*** at Alalaḫ, cf. M. Pope, *Aegean writing and Linear A* (*Studies in Mediterranean Archaeology, Vol. VIII*), Lund 1964, 5.

I wrote in the 2016 edition of *Minoan Linear A*, Volume I, Part I, 298: "This identification seems, however, only possible, if one allows for some flaws either in the Hurrian orthography with respect to intervocalic dental stops at Alalaḫ or in the (Hurrian) orthography of Linear A, since according to strict orthographic conventions single writing of an intervocalic dental occlusive indicates ***/d/*** (not ***/t/***) in the cuneiform syllabary, so that one had expected either ***-tt-*** at Alalaḫ (in accordance with Linear A ***ti-ti-ku*** and ***ti-ti-ku-ni***) or ****ti-di-ku*** and ****ti-di-ku-ni*** in Linear A (in accordance with the syllabic cuneiform orthography). (* indicates here hypothetical forms, not provenance from Level VII at Alalaḫ). Since it is exactly at sites such as Nuzi and Alalaḫ, where Hurrian penetration was most pronounced, that Hurrian scribes failed to recognize the difference between voiced and voiceless occlusives and, consequently, used the signs for these stops indiscriminately, we ought to be careful not to dismiss M. Pope's identifications too readily." Now after all I am happy that my judgement on M. Pope's identifications was not too harsh, because there is now evidence for a ***[d]*** / ***[t]*** alternation in the verbal root ***tid-*** II [Boğ.; Mitt.], ***titt-*** [Boğ.] 'angreifen' ['to attack'] that should be distinguished from ***tid-*** I [Boğ.], cf. Th. Richter, *BGH*, 464-465.

Linear A ***ti-ti-ku-ni*** can now be analysed as {*Titt=i=kk=u=nni*}, based on the root ***tid- / titt-*** and the nominal suffixes ***-kk=u/o=nni***, cf. I. Wegner, *Einführung*, 55-56.

She thinks that this formant ***-kk-*** (often occurring in descriptions of persons: possibly *nomina actoris*) should not be confused with the negation-suffix (***-kk***+vowel) in *intransitive* and *antipassive* verbal forms. ***Titikun*** {*tid=i=kk-u/o=n*} at Alalaḫ is the shortened form of {*tid=i=kk=u/o=nni*} (root ***tid-***), with voiced second dental, whereas the Linear A names ***ti-ti-ku*** and ***ti-ti-ku-ni*** have voiceless initial and second dentals (root ***titt-***). It seems justifiable that (because of ***tid- / titt-*** that can be identified with ***tid-*** II / ***titt-*** 'to attack') the Linear A personal names ***ti-ti-ku*** (HT 35.1; ZA Zb 3.2) and ***ti-ti-ku-ni*** (HT 96a.1) as well as ***Titiku*** and ***Titikun*** at Alalaḫ can now provisionally be translated as 'Attacker'. According to I. Wegner (*Einführung*, 56) we find in Urartian ᴸᵁ́***urb=i=ka*** 'victim, priest (?)' from Urartian and Hurrian ***urb-*** 'to slaughter, sacrifice'.

Since final ***-n*** of ***Ti-di-ku-un*** at Alalaḫ (AT 189, 17) would not have been expressed in Linear A, Linear A ***ti-ti-ku*** (HT 35.1; ZA Zb 3.2) can represent *{titt=i=kk=u/o}* or *{titt=i=kk=u/o=n}*. Linear A ***ti-ti-ku-ni*** (HT 96a.1) represents *{titt=i=kk-u/o=nni}*. So Linear A ***ti-ti-ku*** and ***ti-ti-ku-ni*** can both be translated as 'Attacker'.

However, since Linear A ***di-de-ru*** (HT 86a.3; HT 95+149a.4; HT 95+149b.4) and ***di-de-***[(HT 86b.3) clearly contain two voiced dentals, it is preferable to assume that these names are derived from the root ***tid-*** I 'to count'.

Linear A ***mi-nu-te*** 20 (HT 86a.5), ***mi-nu-te*** HORD 6 J̲ (HT 106.1), ***mi-nu-te*** 10 (HT 95a.2; HT 95b.2-3) from Hagia Triada is probably a personal name, since it occurs in lists of personal names, not in lists of commodities. The commodities are indicated by ideograms, not by syllabic sequences. It can be analysed as *{min(=a)=u*[N.]*=tte}* and translated as 'I am a twin'. I prefer the gender-neutral meaning 'twin' to Th. Richter's translation 'Geschwister' ['sister']. The suffix ***-tte/-tti*** (instead of ***-tta***) is the optional allomorphic enclitic personal pronoun 3rd person singular marking the subject of an intransitive construction (or the object of a transitive construction).

Linear A ***mi-nu-te*** is equivalent to the Hurrian personal name ***Mennatte*** (wr. *Me-en-na-te*), without feminine determinative, at Šušarrā, analysis *{menna=tte}*, typology 3.1, that Th. Richter (*VHN*, 196-197) translates as 'Ich bin das Geschwister' ['I am the sister'], or analysis *{menn(a)=a*[E.]*=tte}*, translation 'Ich bin als Geschwister (geboren)' ['I am (born) as sister']. [E.] refers to the *essive* in ***-a***. He also mentions (*VHN*, 197-198) the Hurrian personal name ***ᶠMinnu*** (wr. *ᶠMi-in-nu*) at Mari, *{minn(a/i)=u*[N.]}, typology 3.1, lexicon *minnu* (→ *mena*), that corresponds exactly with Linear A ***mi-nu-*** in ***mi-nu-te***. [N.] refers to the Akkadianizing nominative in ***-u***. Scholars have recently attributed specific meanings with regard to kinship / relationship to Hurrian ***mena***, ***mina***, ***-menni*** that have implications for the interpretation of ***minu-*** in Linear A ***mi-nu-te*** and ***-mi-na*** in ***a-ku-mi-na*** (ZA 10a.1-2) and ***a-du-|ku-mi-na*** (ZA 10a.3-4) from Kato Zakro.

G. Wilhelm, Zu den hurritischen Namen der Kültepe-Tafel kt k/k 4, *SCCNH 8 (1996)*, 336; G. Wilhelm, Name, Namengebung. D. Bei den Hurritern, in: *Reallexikon der Assyriologie und Vorderasiatischen Archäologie 9/1-2 (1998)*, 125: 'eine weibliche Verwandtschaftsbezeichnung' ['a meaning with respect to female kinship']; M. Giorgieri, Zu den hurritischen Personennamen in den Amarna-Briefen, *SMEA 41 (1999)*, 79[73]; M. Giorgieri, Schizzo grammaticale della lingua hurrica, *Parola del Passato 55 (2000)*, 199-202; M. Giorgieri, L'onomastica hurritica, *Parola del Passato 55 (2000)*, 284, 289[45]: 'sorella gemella ?' [twin-sister], also for the onomastic element ***-menni***, *{men(a)=ni}*.

I. Wegner, *Einführung in die hurritische Sprache*, 2000, 233: 'Zwilling ?' ['twin ?']. I. Wegner, *Einführung*, 2007², 52, 162, 267: 'Zwilling?, Geschwister?' ['twin ?, sister ?']. She thinks that ***mena*** belongs to the category of ***a***-stems designating congeniality or kinship like ***šala*** 'daughter', ***šena*** 'brother', ***ela*** 'sister', ***nera*** 'mother'.

Th. Richter, Rezension zu J.-M. Durand (Le culte d'Addu d'Alep et l'affaire d'Alahtum, *Florilegium Marianum 7*, Paris 2002), *Archiv für Orientforschung 51 (2005 / 06)*, 281; Th. Richter, Ein Ḫurriter wird geboren, ... und benannt, in: J. Becker, R. Hempelmann, E. Rehm (eds.), *Kulturlandschaft Syrien - Zentrum und Peripherie* (Festschrift für J.-W. Meyer), *AOAT 371*, Münster 2010, 514: 'Geschwister' ['sister'].

Th. Richter (*VHN*, 2016, 457-458), s.v. ***mena*** (usw.) und ***me/mi***, gives an extensive explanation, especially with regard to the usage in personal names. He emphasizes that the term refers to consanguinity and kinship as is likely on account of the derivation ***minnunni*** {*minn(a/i)=o=nni*}, that forms a 'one-word name' ^{f}*mi/me-en-nu-un-ni(-e)* at Nuzi (cf. *NPN*, 97). Formations in ***°unni*** appear to indicate kinship. Another indication is that the variant ***menni*** is probably derived from {**mena=ni*}, cf. ***ela*** 'sister', ***šala*** 'daughter' and ***šena*** 'brother' for identical formations, as well as the shortened forms ***men*** and ***šen***. Most significant (also with respect to Linear A) is his observation that the shortened forms ***me/mi***, which only occur as second onomastic element, belong to ***mena***, as can be inferred from parallel formations like $^{(f)}$***Aḫar-me*** vs. ^{f}***Aḫar-menni***, ^{f}***Etim-me*** vs. ^{f}***Etem-menni***, $^{f(?)}$***Unam-me*** vs. ^{f}***Unam-menni*** (Middle-Assyrian Nuzi).

Th. Richter (*VHN*, 195-198) mentions the Hurrian personal names ***Menna*** (wr. *Me-en-na*), without feminine determinative, at Mari and Šubat-Enlil, lexicon *menna*, typology 3.1, that Richter translates as 'Geschwister', cf. *Me-na-a* at Kaniš and Old Babylonian Tall Yalḫi. ^{f}***Menna*** (wr. ^{f}*Me-en-na,* ^{f}*Me-en-na-a,* ^{f}*Me-en*$_{6}$*-na-a*) at Mari and Qaṭṭarā. ^{f}***Menanna*** (wr. ^{f}*Me-na-an-na*) at Mari, analysis {*mena=nna*}, typology 3.2.1, lexicon *mena*, translation 'Es (Mädchen) ist das (wiedergeborene / neue) Geschwister' ['She (the girl) is the (reborn / new) sister'], cf. also *Me-na-an-ni* at Middle-Babylonian Qaṭna. ^{f}***Mennazze*** (wr. ^{f}*Me-en-na-ze,* ^{f}*Me-na-ze,* ^{f}*Me-en-ni-ze*) at Mari, typology 3.1, lexicon *mennazze* (→ *mena*), translation 'Geschwister' ['sisterhood']. ***Menni*** (wr. *Me-en-ni, Me-en-ne*), without feminine determinative, at Šušarrā, analysis {*men(a)=ni*}, typology 3.1, translation 'Geschwister' ['Sister'], cf. ^{f}*Me-en-ni* at Alalaḫ VII (AT *409: 7, see A. Draffkorn, *HHA*, 43); ^{f}*Me/Mi-en-ni* at Nuzi (AAN I 93). ^{f}***Mennin*** (wr. ^{f}*Me-ni-e-en*) at Qaṭṭarā, analysis {*men(a)=ni=n(na)*}, typology 3.1, translation 'Es (Mädchen) ist das (wiedergeborene / neue) Geschwister' ['She (the girl) is the (reborn / new) sister']. ^{f}***Menninna*** (wr. ^{f}*Me-ni-en-na*) at Mari, {*men(a)=ni=nna*}, 'Es (Mädchen) ist das (wiedergeborene/neue) Geschwister' ['She (the girl) is the (reborn / new) sister'].

Remarkably Th. Richter translates another ***Menninna*** (wr. *Me-ni-en-na*), without feminine determinative, at Mari, analysis {*men(a)=ni=nna*}, as 'Er (<u>Junge</u>) ist das (wiedergeborene / neue) Geschwister' ['He (the boy) is the (reborn / new) sister']. By adding 'wiedergeborene/neue' [reborn/new] he explains this contradictory translation as a name that refers to replacement of a deceased sister by the newborn boy. I consider this and some other names with the element ***mena***, but without the feminine determinative, a strong argument to prefer the gender-neutral meaning 'twin' to 'sister'.

I have already discussed the personal name ***a-du-|ku-mi-na*** (ZA 10a.3-4) from Kato Zakro, analysis {*aždu=ḫḫu-mina*}, 'The twin is female', that contains the same element ***-mina*** as can be observed in ***a-ku-mi-na*** (ZA 10a.1-2), analysis e.g. {*agu-mina*}, 'Bring the twin up (oh *numen*) !' or 'He/She (scil. a *numen*) brought the twin up'.

The latter name can be compared with ***Agu-šenni***, recognized as an 'Old Hurrian' 'active' transitive *imperative* or *perfect* form, 'Bring the brother up (oh *numen*) !' or 'He/She (scil. a *numen*) brought the brother up'. Occurrence of ***a-ku-mi-na*** and ***a-du-|ku-mi-na*** so close together on the same side of the tablet appears very significant, because the two persons in question are probably twins.

E. Laroche, *GLH*, 170, did not yet offer a translation of ***me-e-na*** (Mit. IV 61, 63, 66), but he already compared it with ***mi-na*** (Mari 6, 19). In fact we read ***me-e-na-a-an*** in the Tušratta-letter IV 61; ***me-e-na-ma-a-an*** 'she is a twin', with the verbal element ***mān(n)*** 'to be', in IV 63; and ***me-e-na-ak-ki*** in IV 66.

E. Laroche (*GLH*, 170) also mentioned that ***-menni*** is the second onomastic element in feminine personal names at Nuzi (*NPN*, 234), but at Alalaḫ and Ugarit also in masculine personal names (cf. F. Gröndahl, *PNTU*, 240). E. Laroche, *NH*, 163, N° 1154: ***ᶠŠintalimeni***, femme de *Kissi*: abs. *ᶠŠi-in-ta-li-me-ni*, XXXIII 121 II 5; *ᶠŠi-in-ta-mi-in-ni*, XXXVI 61, 2; cf. J. Friedrich, *ZA 49*, 253. - Composé hourrite [Hurrian compound]. (*Kissi* is a personage in a Hurro-Hittite tale; Hurrian *ᵐKe-eš-še*, Friedrich, *ZA 49*, 234ff.).

According to M. Pope - J. Raison (Linear A: changing perspectives, in Y. Duhoux (ed.), *Études Minoennes I*, 1978, 20) the sequence ***qa-ra₂-wa*** (HT 86a.3) from Hagia Triada might be a writing variant of ***qe-ra₂-u***, since it is listed alongside the same words as ***qe-ra₂-u*** (HT 1a.1; HT 95+149a.4-5; HT 95+149b.4-5). Both ***qa-ra₂-wa*** and ***qe-ra₂-u*** belong to lists of personal names. Although ***-u*** and ***-wa*** seem occasionally to alternate in Linear A and Hurrian and occurrence of ***qa-ra₂-wa*** and ***qe-ra₂-u*** alongside the same sequences seems a strong argument, it remains difficult to firmly establish that the two similar forms are really identical. Since Linear A and B have no separate series of signs with ***r-*** and ***l-*** and since sign ***ra₂*** can represent ***ria/rya*** or ***lia/lya*** in Linear B and most likely in Linear A as well, Linear A ***qa-ra₂-wa*** can be equated with either Hurrian ***Ḫaliawa*** or Hurrian ***Ḫariawa***. Th. Richter (*BGH*, 119, and *VHN*, 406) mentions a verbal root ***ḫal-*** I [Boğ.] that is (cautiously) translated '(be)singen' ['to sing (of), to celebrate in song, to chant'], which is semantically close to the verbal root ***ḫe/ill-***, *ḫe/il-* II [*passim*]: 'to say, announce, call, inform, tell, to invoke (a God)' (cf. *BGH*, 147-148), discussed s.v. Linear A ***qe-ra₂-u***. Both roots reflect a form of vocal communication. There are not only many examples of alternations of ***e/i*** in Hurrian, but also some of ***a/e***. However, in the present stage of research it may be too early to assume that Linear A ***qa-ra₂-wa*** and ***qe-ra₂-u*** are irrefutable examples of this phenomenon. The roots ***ḫal-*** I and ***ḫe/ill-***, *ḫe/il-* II are treated as different roots in Hurrian, so it is wise to treat them as such at present.

If ***-wa*** in ***qa-ra₂-wa*** replaces ***-u*** as in ***qe-ra₂-u***, an additional argument may be that the Hurrian 1st person singular in ***-au*** of the transitive verb is analysed as {*-av*} in Hurrian studies, but frankly I do not know examples showing that the 1st person in ***-au*** is orthographically expressed as ****-a-wa***. I. Wegner (*Einführung*, 91, 136) mentions, sub 5.2.7: The 7th position, indicator of the 1st person of the transitive-ergative verb: ***-av***, graphically: (consonant)*a-(a)-ú/-ap*, long form *-affu-* [so not **aw-wa* {*-affa-*}]. So at present I prefer to interpret ***qa-ra₂-wa*** as the dative in ***-wa*** of ***Ḫari(y)a*** or ***Ḫali(y)a***.

The meaning of ***ḫal-*** I 'to sing (of), to celebrate in song, to chant' is confirmed by Hurrian ***ḫalmi*** 'chant' ['song'], for according to RS quadr. 137 III 7 Sumerian EZEN = Akkadian ***zammarum*** = Hurrian ***ḫalmi*** = Ugaritic ***šîru***, cf. *Ugar. V*, 246, 455; E. Laroche, *GLH*, 90, s.v. ***ḫalmi***; Richter, *BGH*, 119, s.v. ***ḫalme/i*** [Boğ.; Ug.].

The Linear A name ***qa-ra₂-wa*** (HT 86a.3) can be interpreted as ***Ḫaliawa***, the *dative* in ***-wa*** of a 'one-word' name, ***Ḫalia*** 'He/She (a *numen*) celebrates / celebrated (the child) in song', analysed as {*ḫal=i=(y)a=wa*}.

The name consists of the verbal root ***ḫal-*** I 'to sing (of), to celebrate in song' + the marker of transitivity ***-i-*** + the marker of the 3rd person singular ***-a*** indicating the subject of the transitive verb + the suffix of the singular *dative* ***-wa***, translation 'for ***Ḫalia***'.

However, such a transitive formation can also be interpreted as a hypocoristic personal name ***Ḫal=i=ya***, with the hypocoristic suffix ***-ya***.

Th. Richter (*BGH*, 119) mentions another verbal root ***ḫal-*** II [Boğ.; Qaṭna], probably ***/ḫāl-/*** 'transportieren, forttragen, übertragen, wegschleppen' ['to transport, transfer, to carry off, to drag away'] that corresponds with Akkadian ***naḫālu***. If this root is involved, ***Ḫaliawa*** *{ḫal=i=(y)a=wa}* can be translated as 'for ***Ḫalia***' and the 'one-word' name ***Ḫalia*** can be translated as 'He/She (a *numen*) carried off (the deceased child)' or the hypocoristic name that can be translated likewise. Th. Richter prefers the latter root ***ḫal-*** II as verbal element in personal names in the sense of 'to bring away the (elder) child that passed away', so that the newborn child (the bearer of the name) replaces the elder one.

The root ***ḫal-*** is found as first onomastic element in ***Ḫalu-menni*** (wr. *ᶠḪa-lu-me-en-ni, ᶠḪa-lu-me-ni*), ***Ḫalu-šenni*** (wr. *Ḫa-al-še-en-ni, Ḫa-lu-še-en-ni, Ḫa-al-še-ni, Ḫa-lu(m)-še-ni, Ḫa-lu-še-i*[*n-ni*], *Ḫa-lu-še-ni*), ***ᶠḪaluia*** (wr. *ᶠḪa-lu-ia*), cf. P.M. Purves, *NPN*, 212-213.

Th. Richter mentions (*VHN*, 119-120, 406): ***Ḫalukkan*** (Ašnakkum), ***Ḫalum-atal*** (Mari) 'The strong one carried him/her off (scil. the child that passed away)', ***ᶠḪalunna*** (Mari) 'Carry him/her [***-nna***] (the elder child) off (oh *numen*) !' or 'Celebrate her in song', ***Ḫalaš-tuk*** (Mari, [Šubat-Enlil]), ***Ḫalut*** (Tigunāni) 'Carry me [***-t(ta)***] off (oh *numen*) !' or 'Celebrate me in song', ***Ḫalutil*** (Mari) 'Carry us [***til(la)***] off (oh *numen*) !' or 'Celebrate us in song'.

Th. Richter (*BGH*, 132) also mentions a root ***ḫar-*** [Boğ.; PN], ohne Übersetzung [without translation], in: *ḫa-a-ru-nu-ni-en {ḫar=un=u=n=en}*, cf. V. Haas - H.J. Thiel 1978, Die Beschwörungsrituale der Allaituraḫ(ḫ)i und verwandte Texte, Hurritologische Studien 2, Alter Orient und Altes Testament 31, Kevelaer / Neukirchen-Vluyn 1978, 178.

Richter (*ibid.*) observes the root also in personal names, e.g. in the Nuzi name ***Ḫarap-atal*** (wr. *ḫa-ra-pa-tal*), cf. I.J. Gelb, *NPN*, 55, but also in alphabetic cuneiform ***ḫry*** that corresponds with syllabic cuneiform ***Ḫariya***, 3rd person singular of ***ḫar-***. Hurrian ***Ḫariya*** is the name of two persons at Mari, cf. Th. Richter, *VHN*, 125, s.v. ***Ḫarija*** (wr. *ḫa-ri-ia*), analysis *{ḫar=i=ja}*, lexicon ***ḫar-***, typology 1.1.1.2.4.

Hurrian ***-wa*** is usually case-ending of the *dative* and since the two entries ***di-de-ru*** 20 ***qa-ra₂-wa*** 10 (HT 86a.3) are underscored by a ruler on this tablet, it is *a priori* not inconceivable that ***qa-ra₂-wa*** is the last of the list of names of persons receiving portions of GRA+KL, whereas the following persons, ***da-me*** and ***mi-nu-te*** (HT 86a.4-5), receive each 20 portions (***a-du***) of GRA+B. It might be significant that ***qa-ra₂-wa*** receives only half of the quantity as compared to the others. That may be the reason why he/she is singled out and appears in another case, the *dative* in ***-wa***. The reason for receiving a smaller ration might be that ***Ḫalija*** or ***Ḫarija*** is still a child.

In the Linear B personnel tablets from Pylos we can also observe that the girls (***ko-wa***) and boys (***ko-wo***) receive smaller rations than the adult people, usually their mothers.

Although Linear A ***qe-ra*$_2$*-u*** (HT la.1; HT 95+149a.4-5; HT 95+149b.4-5) is listed alongside the same words as ***qa-ra*$_2$*-wa*** (HT 86a), as suggested by M. Pope - J. Raison, I do not automatically consider it a writing variant of that name, but it may be conceivable that the similarity of sounds was a reason for the scribe to play with words/names as apparently the scribe of tablet ZA 10 from Kato Zakro enjoyed to do.

As can be observed in many Hurrian personal names, the first onomastic element often appears to be verbal, but the sequence ***qe-ra*$_2$*-u*** looks like a complete verbal form, with an ending in ***-au***, which is the Hurrian subject-marker of the 1st person singular indicative. Before publication of Th. Richter's *Vorarbeiten zu einem hurritischen Namenbuch*, Teil I: *Personennamen altbabylonischer Überlieferung vom Mittleren Euphrat und aus dem nördlichen Mesopotamien*, Wiesbaden 2016, such a formation struck me as somewhat unlikely in a personal name. Nevertheless I seriously considered the possibility in case of Linear A ***a-mi-da-u*** (ZA 10a.3) and ***]a-mi-da-o*** (HT? 170a.5), see *supra*.

However, in his section D on *typology* and *morphology* (*VHN*, 584-585), sub 1.1.2: *Namen mit Verbalformen des Mittani-Paradigmas* (Σ = 8), he writes that frequently, also beyond his *Corpus*, one-word names occur that can be described as finite, transitive indicative forms that follow the example of 'Mitanni Hurrian'. For occurrence of verbal forms of 'Old Hurrian' and 'Mitanni Hurrian' formations side-by-side in contexts he refers to V. Haas - I. Wegner, Beiträge zum hurritischen Lexikon: Die hurritischen Verben *ušš-* "gehen" und *ašš-* "abwaschen, abwischen", in: J. Klinger e. a. (eds.), *Investigationes Anatolicae: Gedenkschrift für Erich Neu* (*StBoT* 52), Wiesbaden 2010, 109, and to St. de Martino, The 'Song of Release' twenty-nine years after its discovery, *AoF 39 (2012)*, 209 f.

Th. Richter (*VHN*, 584-585) shows indeed the following one-word personal names with distinctive verbal endings that can be analysed as subject-markers of the 1st person singular transitive indicative in ***°=av***:

Appau (wr. *ap-pa-ú*) {*app=av*} (Emar, s. Pruzsinszky 2003/2: 144f.).

Arau (wr. *a-ra-ú*) {*ar=av*} 'I give (the boy)' (Sippar, Old Babylonian period, cf. L. Dekiere, Old Babylonian real estate documents from Sippar in the British Museum, Mesopotamian history and environment. Series III: texts, Part 6, 917).

Nanau (wr. *na-na-ù*) {*nan=av*} 'I strike/knock (a person) down' (Puzriš-Dagan = Drēḫem, Ur III period, s. Owen 1981, 264).

Šarau (wr. *ša-ra-ú*) {*šar=av*} 'I wish (the boy)' (Atmannu, Middle-Assyrian period, *Iraq 70*, 167, nr. 15: 5. See Th. Richter, *BGH*, 355).

Tappau (wr. *tab-ba-ù*) {*tapp=av*} 'I make (the boy) firm, unwavering' (Umma, Ur III period. See Th. Richter, *BGH*, 440). These names may be regarded as expressions by the father or mother at the time of birth of the child.

Th. Richter (*VHN*, 584-585) also shows the following one-word personal names with distinctive verbal endings that can be analysed as subject-markers of the 2nd person singular indicative in ***°=i=o***:

Ḫaniu (wr. *ḫa-ni-ú/ù*) {*ḫan=i=o*} 'You give birth (to the boy)' (Nuzi, see *NPN*, 54. See also Th. Richter, *BGH*, 125, and *VHN*, 407, s.v. ***ḫan-*** 'gebären' ['to give birth'] (one of the most frequent elements at Nuzi). The meaning of the root is generally accepted and can be connected with the substantive ***ḫani*** 'child'.

Kutiu (wr. *ku-ti-ú*) {*kud=i=o*} 'You let fall (the boy)', 'You delivered (the boy)' (Tall Yalḫi, Old Babylonian period, see Saporetti 1995, 12), from root the ***kud-*** 'to let fall'.
Uriu (wr. *ú-ri-ú*) {*ûr=i=o*} 'You want (the boy)' (Emar, s. Pruzsinszky 2003/2: 809). See ***ûr-*** II 'to want / wish'. Th. Richter (*VHN*, 585) also discusses the one-word personal names with distinctive verbal endings that can be analysed as subject-markers of the 3rd person singular indicative in ***^{o}=i=a***, which are sometimes difficult to distinguish from formations with the hypocoristic suffix ***-ya***.

The personal name ***Ḫanija*** can be interpreted as 'She gives birth', but can also be interpreted as a hypocoristic with ***ḫani*** 'child' as first element and the hypocoristic suffix ***-ya***, based on a personal name such as ***^{f}Ḫa-ni-wa-an-di*** 'The child is right/just/favourable' (Alalaḫ IV, see D.J. Wiseman, *AT*, 135, who reads ***^{f}Ḫa-ni-wa-aš-di***, 298, 31). Actually it is conceivable that the toponym ***Χανιά*** (Khaniá), North-West Crete, is also equivalent to Hurrian and Minoan ***Ḫanija*** 'He/She [scil. a God(dess)] gives / gave birth to [this palace]'. It is a poetic name commemorative of the birth/creation of a Minoan palace and administrative centre.

Actually the Hurrian verbal roots ***ḫan-*** 'to give birth' and ***kud-*** 'to let fall' have almost the same meaning in Hurrian personal names, of which a lot has to do with giving birth.

I have expressed the view that Homer's *Odyssey γ* 291-294 mentions *Κύδωνες* as a people living on both sides of the streams of the Iardanos river in Crete:

ἔνθα διατμήξας τὰς μὲν Κρήτῃ ἐπέλασσεν,
ἧχι Κύδωνες ἔναιον Ἰαρδάνου ἀμφὶ ῥέεθρα –
ἔστι δέ τις λισσὴ αἰπεῖά τε εἰς ἅλα πέτρη,
ἐσχατιῇ Γόρτυνος, ἐν ἠεροειδέι πόντῳ.

The passage in Homer's *Odyssey γ* 292 speaks of *ἧχι Κύδωνες ἔναιον Ἰαρδάνου ἀμφὶ ῥέεθρα* 'where the Kydonians lived on both sides of the streams of the Iardanos'. The passage belongs to the story about part of Menelaos' fleet being shipwrecked on the south coast of Crete in the vicinity of Phaistos, far away from Khania on the north coast of western Crete. Menelaos himself landed with the other part of his fleet in Egypt. It looks as if Homer knew what he was talking about. His reference to Gortyn (*Γόρτυν, Γόρτυνς, Γόρτυς*) in connection with the *Κύδωνες* and the *Ἰάρδανος* river suggests that Homer's *Ἰάρδανος* may be identified with the Messara river and that the region (and/or city ?) of the *Κύδωνες* must primarily be sought in the Messara valley. *Kydonia* may not only be the Mycenaean and Homeric name of the Messara valley, but also the Minoan.

Th. Richter offers (*VHN*, 585) one example of a one-word name with distinctive verbal ending that can be analysed as subject-marker of the 1st person plural indicative in ***^{o}=au=š***: ***Putauš-kate*** (wr. *pu-da-uš-ka₄-de*) from Alalaḫ IV (*UF 1*, 46, nr. 9: 5), analysis {*fud=av=š-kade*}, lexicon *pud-*, *kade*, translation 'We create barley', cf. *BGH*, 197f.

Returning to Linear A ***qe-ra₂-u*** we have to face the fact that Linear A and B have no separate series for signs with ***r-*** and ***l-***. Sign ***ra₂*** can represent ***ria/rya*** or ***lia/lya*** in Linear B and most likely in Linear A as well. For the scribe this obviously did not pose a problem, because he knew the names he had written, but for us it can be a problem. As argued before, the Linear B scribes used Linear A signs for the velar fricatives for their (Indo-European) Mycenaean Greek labio-velar series.

So Linear A ***qe-ra$_2$-u*** can be interpreted as ***Ḫelliau / Ḫilliau***, analysed as {*ḫell=i=au*} 'I say (names ?)' and can be compared with a Hurrian personal name from Tuttul (Tall Bi'a) ***Ḫillija*** (wr. *ḫi-il-li-ja*), analysis {*ḫill=i=a*}, lexicon ***ḫill-***, typology 1.1.1.2.4, 'He/She says/said (names ?)', cf. Th. Richter (*VHN*, 134), who translates the name as 'Er/Sie sagte (Namen(?))'. The ***i/e*** alternation is normal in Hurrian and it is in the case of ***ḫill-/ ḫell-*** also attested, since Th. Richter, *VHN*, 134, also mentions a personal name from Mari ***Ḫellip-atal*** (wr. *ḫe-el-li-pa-tal*), analysis {*ḫell=i=b-adal*}, lexicon ***ḫell-***, typology 1.1.1.2.1, 'The strong one said (names ?)'. Th. Richter (*BGH*, 147-148) offers the following translations for the verbal root ***ḫe/ill-***, *ḫe/il-* II [*passim*]: 'to say, announce, call, inform, tell, to invoke (a God)'.

Since final consonants are not expressed in Linear A, ***qe-ra$_2$-u*** can theoretically also represent the plural form of the 1st person {*ḫell=i=au=š*} 'We say (names ?)', but the plural form does not make sense, because the name most likely refers to the child itself.

Th. Richter (*BGH*, 153-154) also offers the verbal root ***ḫir-*** [Boğ.], 'eintreten' ['to enter']. If this is the root used in the Linear A ***qe-ra$_2$-u***, the Hurrian equivalent would be ***Ḫir=i=au*** and the meaning of the personal name would be 'I enter (the world)', not a bad name for a newborn child either.

The evidence shows that Linear A ***qa-ra$_2$-wa*** (HT 86a) and ***qe-ra$_2$-u*** (HT la.1; HT 95+149a.4-5; HT 95+149b.4-5) probably refer to different persons. If ***qa-ra$_2$-wa*** is indeed a dative in ***-wa***, the real name of the person is probably ***qa-ra$_2$*** = ***Ḫal=i=(j)a*** or ***Ḫar=i=(j)a***.

It is intriguing that Linear A ***qe-ra$_2$-u*** is the first sequence on HT 1a.1. It is followed by ***ki-ro*** 197 (HT 1a.1-2); ***ki-ro*** occurs at least 14 times in Linear A texts.

It has been suggested by several scholars that Linear A ***ki-ro*** might represent a transactional term indicating 'deficit'. Since Linear A and B sign ***ro*** can also be ***lo***, we can *prima facie* not be sure, whether we should read ***ki-ro*** or ***ki-lo***, but the meaning of Hurrian ***kir=o*** appears to be decisive.

The form occurs in the Hurrian-Hittite bilingual text ***kirenze*** (KBo 32). The Hurrian term ***kirenze*** means 'release, liberation, manumission (of slaves)' and corresponds with Hittite ***parā tarnumar***, Akkadian ***(an)durārum*** and Hebrew ***derōr***. ***Kirenze*** is also the title and main subject of text KBo 32. It allegedly means 'a sort of debt-redemption' at Nuzi, cf. Th. Richter, *BGH*, 210-211, s.v. ***ke/ir-*** I [Boğ.; PN(?)] and ***kirenzi*** [Boğ.; Nuzi].

I. Wegner (*Einführung*, 138) mentions in her section E *'Old Hurrian'* sub *'The jussive and other forms of mood in the bilingual'* the form ***kir=o*** (wr. *ki-i-ru*), KBo 32: 15 IV 3, which she translates as 'er soll freigelassen sein/werden' ['he must be set free / released / liberated / manumitted']. In accordance with the usage at Nuzi (and probably also in the bureaucratic setting of the Minoan palace administration expressed through the Linear A tablets) Hurrian ***kir=o***, exact equivalent to Linear A ***ki-ro***, probably also means 'it (the debt) must be redeemed' or 'he must redeem (the debt)', which provides a very adequate meaning of the term in the context of the tablets. There are in principle a few options for interpretation of the combination of ***qe-ra$_2$-u*** **,** ***ki-ro*** 197 (HT 1a.1-2): I) Since ***qe-ra$_2$-u*** is the opening sequence, it could represent the Hurrian verbal form ***ḫelliau / ḫilliau***, analysed as {*ḫell=i=au*} 'I announce, I inform', followed by a list of personal names that are each followed by a number; ***ki-ro*** would then be the first of these personal names containing the same root as ***kir=o*** (wr. *ki-i-ru*), KBo 32: 15 IV 3, just discussed.

It would then be equivalent to the Hurrian name of two persons at Mari, ***Kirru*** (wr. *ki-ir-ru*), analysis {*kirr=o*}, lexicon *kirr-*, typology 1.3.1.1.1, cf. Th. Richter, *VHN*, 166, s.v. ***Kirru***, 'Lasse (Jungen) frei (oh *Numen*)!' ['Set (the boy) free / Release / Liberate / Manumit (the boy) (oh *numen*) !']. The meaning of the name is in that case exactly the same as that of the expression ***kir=o*** (wr. *ki-i-ru*) in KBo 32: 15 IV 3.

II) Another likely option is that ***qe-ra$_2$-u*** (HT 1a.1) has exactly the same function as on HT 95+149a.4-5 and HT 95+149b.4-5, where it is part of a list of anthroponyms.

A) The personal name can be ***Ḫelliau / Ḫilliau*** 'I say (names ?)' or

B) ***Ḫir=i=au*** 'I enter (the world)'. The name is followed by the Hurrian verbal form ***kir=o*** (wr. *ki-i-ru*), KBo 32: 15 IV 3, which I. Wegner translates as 'er soll freigelassen sein/werden' ['he must be set free / released / liberated / manumitted'].

In accordance with the usage at Nuzi Linear A ***ki-ro*** and Hurrian ***kir=o*** can be interpreted as 'it (the debt) must be redeemed' or 'he must redeem (the debt)' which provides an adequate meaning of the term in the context of the tablets, especially since many Mycenologists presumed already for a long time that ***ki-ro*** might have the same function in the Linear A texts as ***o-pe-ro*** has in Mycenaean Linear B. Now this function of ***ki-ro*** as a so-called transactional term can be confirmed and - even more important - it can be firmly established that the language to which this Linear A term belongs is Hurrian. The evidence is provided by the Hurrian-Hittite bilingual ***kirenze*** (KBo 32) and Hurrian texts from Nuzi. And there can be no doubt that the term is Hurrian and nothing else, not even a loan-word, for the form is in fact a very specific grammatical form of a Hurrian verb.

Other examples of 'one-word' personal names comparable with ***qe-ra$_2$-u*** are Linear A ***a-mi-da-u*** (ZA 10a.3) from Kato Zakro and ***]a-mi-da-o*** (HT? 170a.5) probably from Hagia Triada.

I now prefer the reading of Linear A ***qe-ri-ja*** [(HT 3.2) at Hagia Triada to the former reading † ***qe-ra$_2$-ja***. The surface of tablet HT 3 is a bit worn. W.C. Brice, *ILA*, Pl. I/Ia, reads ***qe-ra$_2$-u***[; *GORILA 1* ***qe-ra$_2$-ja***[or ***qe-ri-ja***[. In fact L. Godart and J.P. Olivier read ***qe-ra$_2$-ja***[in their transcription, but write in their note: ***qe-ri-ja*** pas entièrement impossible; J. Raison - M. Pope (1994) ***qe-ra$_2$-ja***[ ]. I think that all editors have involuntarily been influenced by the fact that ***qe-ra$_2$-u*** (HT la.1; HT 95+149a.4-5; HT 95+149b.4-5) occurs three times at Hagia Triada, so that they automatically assumed that they should read ***ra$_2$*** instead of ***ri***.

I followed the reading of Raison-Pope in my *Corpus of transliterated Linear A texts* (*Minoan Linear A*, Vol. II, Part I), but have after close investigation concluded that reading one undulating line (sign ***ri***) instead of two parallel undulating lines (sign ***ra$_2$***) is to be preferred. As a matter of fact the two syllabic signs ***-ri-ja*** offer the same result as Linear A sign ***58*** = ***ra$_2$*** that represents most likely ***ria/rya*** or ***lia/lya*** as in Linear B.

It cannot be ruled out that the sign ***-u*** followed ***qe-ri-ja*** [in the following worn space, in which case ***qe-ri-ja***[***-u***] offers the same result as ***qe-ra$_2$-u*** (= ***Ḫelliau / Ḫilliau*** {*Ḫell=i=au*} 'I say (names ?) / I announce, I inform' or ***Ḫiriau*** {*Ḫir=i=au*} 'I enter (the world)', but that would be pure speculation, because the worn surface after ***qe-ri-ja***[is absolutely illegible.

However, Linear A ***qe-ri-ja*** [(HT 3.2) may be complete. It is in that case completely equivalent to the Hurrian personal name ***Ḫillija*** (wr. *ḫi-il-li-ja*) from Tuttul (Tall Bi'a), analysis {*ḫill=i=ja*}, lexicon ***ḫill-/ḫell-***, typology 1.1.1.2.4, 'He/She says (names ?)', cf. Th. Richter (*VHN*, 134), who translates the name as 'Er/Sie sagte (Namen(?))'. Cf. for the ***i/e*** alternation the personal name ***Ḫellip-atal*** (wr. *ḫe-el-li-pa-tal*) from Mari, analysis {*ḫell=i=b-adal*}, lexicon ***ḫell-***, typology 1.1.1.2.1, 'The strong one said (names ?)', cf. Th. Richter, *VHN*, 134; *BGH*, 147-148. Since Th. Richter (*BGH*, 153-154) also offers the verbal root ***ḫir-*** [Boğ.], 'eintreten' ['to enter'], ***ḫir=ib-*** [SüdB.], 'eintreten lassen (?)' ['to let enter, to allow to enter'], Linear A ***qe-ri-ja***[may perhaps also be equivalent to Hurrian ***Ḫirija*** {*Ḫir=i=ja*}, meaning 'He/She enters (the world)' or 'He/She (scil. a *numen*) allows (the child) to enter (the world)', not a bad name for a newborn child either.

Linear A ***a-du*** (HT 85a.1; HT 86a.4; HT 88.1; HT 92.1; HT 95+ 149b.1; HT 99a.1; HT 103.1) had been interpreted as the West Semitic theonym *Addu* by C.H. Gordon, *Evidence for the Minoan language*, 38. He was followed by J.G.P. Best, *Some preliminary remarks on the decipherment of Linear A*, 24, who interpreted Linear A ***a-du*** as *Haddu*. I have discussed Linear A ***a-du*** already extensively and concluded that it is most likely equivalent to ***ad(d)u(n)***, the Hurrian term for 'ration', 'assigned portion' in the grain distribution lists of Alalaḫ, also used for oil rations at Nuzi and for various commodities in the Old Babylonian Mâri-texts, cf. A. Draffkorn, *HHA*, 153-154, s.v. ***ad(d)u(n)***.

J.G.P. Best (*ibid.*, 24 + n. 59; 34, n. 103) also attempted to identify Linear A ***da-du-ma-ta*** (HT 95+149a.1) with the divine name ***ddmš*** from Ugarit, referring to C.H. Gordon, *Ugaritic Manual* (*AnOr 35*), Rome 1955, 466. To support his interpretation he assumed a shift ***ṯ*** > ***š*** referring to C.H. Gordon, *The present status of Minoan studies*, Incunabula Graeca XXV, Rome 1968, 385. Best calls ***da-du-ma-ta*** a Semitic and female divinity.

Alphabetic ***Ddmš*** is to be identified with syllabic ***Dadmiš*** that is not only embedded in the Semitic, but also in the Hurrian pantheon, providing evidence for the high degree of religious syncretism of the Hurrian and Semitic population of Syria.

E. Laroche includes ***Dadmiš*** in his *Glossaire de la langue hourrite*, 70: "***Dadmiš***. Divinité syrienne d'origine inconnue. ^{d}*Ta-ad-mi-iš*, RŠ 20.24, 27 = alph. *Ddmš*, CTA 29 Vo 6 = *Ugaritica V* 45; dans le pantheon sémitique d'Ugarit. En contextes hourrites: ***Ddmš***, CTA 166, 17 et 21; RŠ 24.269 + 297, 3 = *Ugar. V* 517. - RŠ quadr. 137 IV b 18 = Série An, No 51: sum. ^{d}Šu.zi.an.na = h. *Ta-ad-mi-iš*; cf. Nougayrol, *Ugar. V* 57 sq., 249; Laroche, *Ugar.* 521. Contexte ougar.: RS 24.643 A 8 = Virolleaud, Ugar. V 580."

E. Laroche, 'Documents en langue hourrite provenant de Ras Shamra', *Ugaritica V (1968)*, 521: "*Ddmž* = syll. *Tadmiš* - Le *d-* initial exclut, à mon sens, une 'origine' hourrite; noter justement la graphie *Tadmiš* de la colonne hourrite. I1 n'y a pas trace de cette figure divine (locale?) dans toute la littérature et il n'est pas impossible que cette déesse cananéenne ait été assimilée à l'une des déesses des listes A-D." I agree with E. Laroche that it is difficult to assess the origin of ***Ddmẓ*** = syll. ***Tadmiš***, but I disagree that initial ***d-*** excludes a Hurrian origin. Linear A ***da-du-ma-ta*** does not help in this respect, because I do not believe that it can be identified with ***Ddmẓ*** = syll. ***Tadmiš***.

Apropos of the assumption that voicing of the dental stops did not occur in initial position in Hurrian, E. Laroche seems to follow E.A. Speiser.

The latter stated in his *Introduction to Hurrian* (p. 40) that initially *t* is the rule in the alphabetic texts and in the Akkadianizing syllabary, but doing so he had to assume that *ddmž* was exceptional and suspect (p. 40, n. 87). Accordingly, he thought that alphabetic-syllabic correspondences show that an initial dental is to be interpreted as voiceless in the Hurrian syllabary, even though a given sign may contain *d-*. Note especially Ras Shamra *tr-ḫ-* 'male' = Boğazköy *tu-(u-)ru-uḫ-ḫi-* (VII 56 ii 21, XXVII 3 rev. 17) alongside *du-ru-(uḫ-)ḫi-* (XXVII 1 ii 27 ff., 6 i 28, 14 iii 4). Though the evidence from the alphabetic cuneiform may be suggestive, it is not conclusive.

Orthographically, the main problem is that one misses in the cuneiform syllabary in initial position the clear indications which double writing provides in medial position for the voiceless and single writing for the voiced stops, respectively. Incidentally, one may wonder what the implications would be for occlusives in initial position, if one accepts P.M. Purves's hypothesis (*NPN*, 184) that double writings in medial position are not to be considered the orthographic means of indicating that a stop is voiceless, but are always to be taken at face value as indicators of double sounds, the resultant voicelessness being purely a matter of pattern. One can not assume that the phonetic conditions at the beginning of a word or name can *a priori* be regarded as more favourable for sounds to be voiceless than to be voiced. For instance, within the *linguistic continuum* of Germanic languages one can compare High German *Tod*, Dutch *dood* and English *death*.

F.W. Bush (*GHL*, 52) is less dogmatic in this respect, since he assumes that dental stops could be voiced in initial position in Hurrian, e.g. in alphabetic *trḫ-* at Ugarit (166: 55, 56, 57 etc.), in *ta-di* at Mâri (3:2) and in the name *Ta-gu-uḫ-li* (cf. P.M. Purves, 'The early scribes at Nuzi', *American Journal of Semitic Languages and Literatures 57 (1940),* 172). If one maintains that initial voicing does not exist in Hurrian, the results would be anomalous and irregular, because an onomastic element could only begin with a voiced consonant, when it was used as second element of a compound, written with single writing in intervocalic position, but the same element could begin with a voiceless consonant, when used as first element with single writing. Would not it be logical that, on the analogy of a voiced consonant in medial position, the same consonant belonging to the same element is also voiced when used in initial position ?

If it can be proved that a Cretan dialect of Hurrian was written with Linear A, then that script would provide evidence that initial voicing was present at least in that form of Hurrian. If a phenomenon can allegedly be observed for one particular region and during a particular period of existence of a language, one should be cautious with generalizing such findings with regard to all regions and all periods in which this language was spoken and written, especially if the area in question is very wide and may have hosted many dialects during a long period. The existence of many Hurrian dialects is very likely.

An argument against identification of ***da-du-ma-ta*** with *Dadmiš* is that involvement of this deity in a commercial transaction with grain does not seem likely. The same can be said about Gordon's and Best's interpretation of Linear A ***a-du*** (HT 95b.1) as the theonym *(H)addu*. Decisive is the observation that it is impossible to identify Linear A ***da-du-ma-ta*** (HT 95+149a.1) with ***Dadmiš***, since ***-u-*** in the syllable ***-du-*** cannot be explained as a mute vowel in Linear A orthography, if - as has been argued before - the orthographic conventions of Linear B were inherited from Linear A.

The scribe would have written ***da-di-mi*** to express ***Dadmiš*** or ***da-da-ma*** to express an alleged ***Dadmaṭ***, borrowing the (mute) vowel from the following syllabic sign to express the consonant cluster ***-dm-***. The final consonant ***-š*** in ***Dadmiš*** or ***-ṭ*** in an alleged ***Dadmaṭ*** would not have been expressed according to Linear A and B orthographic conventions, cf. *chapter 5: A 'linguistic' analysis of Linear A*, where Yves Duhoux's conclusion on the question of whether final consonants were expressed in Linear A, is discussed. After providing abundant evidence his conclusion is: *"Such evidence is typical for absence of a notation of final consonants."* Anyway Linear A ***da-du-ma-ta*** can clearly not signify ***Dadmiš***.

Linear A ***da-du-ma-ta*** (HT 95a.1) is probably a Hurrian personal name. In the first edition of *Minoan Linear A* I had interpreted ***da-du-ma-ta*** as a compound personal name with the division between *da-du-* and *-ma-ta*. *Da-du-* could provide an element frequent in Hurrian compound names such as *Tadu-ḫepa*, */Dadu-ḫeba/* (according to F.W. Bush) 'Loved (is) Ḫeba(t)', with the verbal root *tad-* 'to love' and thematic *-u* signifying the 'passive' form of the participle. P.M. Purves *(NPN*, 233) had analysed *Zi-il-li-ma-ar-ta* as ***Zilli-marta***, *Ša-ad-du-mar-ti, Ša-at-tu(m)-mar-ti, Ša-at-tu-mar-di* as ***Šattu-marti***, and *Dur-mar-ti, Tu-ur-mar-ti, Dur-ma-ar-di, Du-ur-mar-ti, Tur-mar-ti* as ***Tur-marti***. So it seemed reasonable to analyse Linear A ***da-du-ma-ta*** as Hurrian ***Dadu-marta***, since ***-r-*** preceding an occlusive is not expressed in consonant clusters in Linear A and B.

ᶠTadu-ḫepa is a well-known Hurrian personal name. King Tušratta of Mitanni sent his daughter ***Tadu-ḫepa*** as a bride to the Egyptian pharaoh Amenhotep III (see EA, p. 1569, cf. P.M. Purves, *NPN*, 263, s.v. *tat*). In his Hurrian letter (EA 24), found at Tell el Amarna, Tušratta paid much attention to the bridal gifts sent with his daughter to the pharaoh and especially to the golden sculpture of her image that he expected in return.

The first wife of the Hittite emperor Suppiluliuma I, had the same name, cf. E. Laroche, *Les Noms des Hittites*, 182, n° 1313: ***ᶠTaduḫepa***. 1. Reine hittite, première femme de Suppiluliuma Ier: abs. ***ᶠDa-(a)-du-ḫé-pa, ᶠDu-ú-du-ḫé-pa***, XI 7 + XXXVI 122 Vo 8 = *MDOG 83*, 66; KBo II 15 II 2, 14 = KUB XXV 14 I 28, 46, III 10; XXVI 57 I 9 = *RHA 61*, 125; XXXVI 124 I 8; cf. Otten, *MDOG 83*, 57; Laroche, *Ugar. III*, 101. – 2. La même ?: hourr. *ᶠTa-du-ḫé-pa-(a)*, XXVII 23 III 2, 3, 6, 11; 24 I 6; XXXII 24 III 3, 4, 6; 25 + III 17-21, IV 10; IBoT II 40 Vo 4, 7; ABoT 37 Ro et Vo passim; KBo XIV 136, 2, 12. Cf. also E. Laroche, 'Les noms hourrites', in *Les Noms des Hittites*, Paris 1966, 353, s.v. *tad-* 'aimer', and E. Laroche, *GLH*, 248, s.v. *tad-* 'aimer'.

For a long time the name, usually normalized to ***ᶠTaduḫepa***, was translated as 'Loved (is) Ḫeba(t)', with transitive verbal root ***tad-*** 'to love' and thematic ***-u-*** signifying the 'passive' participle as reconstructed by E.A. Speiser (*Introduction to Hurrian, passim*).

However, after publication of the Hurrian-Hittite bilingual text ***kirenze*** (KBo 32) the picture changed drastically. It was recognized that many Hurrian names with very characteristic formations probably belong to the category of 'Old Hurrian', cf. I. Wegner, *Einführung in die hurritische Sprache*, Wiesbaden 2007^2, 125. According to M.L. Chačikjan (*Churritskij i urartskij jazyki*, Erevan 1985) ***-u-*** signifies the transitive perfect forms and ***-o-*** the durative aspect.

However, G. Wilhelm (Zum hurritischen Verbal-system, in: S.R. Anschütz (ed.), *Texte, Sätze, Wörter und Moneme*, Festschrift für Klaus Heger zum 65. Geburtstag, Heidelberg 1992, 667 ff.), showed that the 'thematic vowel' of the transitive past or perfect tense is not ***-u-***, but ***-o-***, and that the alleged indicator ***-o-*** of the durative aspect in fact represents the same grammeme. Since differentiation between ***-u-*** and ***-o-*** is in this case no longer necessary, I. Wegner (*o.c.*, 2007, 126) now translates ***Tad=o=ḫepa*** as 'Ḫeba loves (namely the bearer of the name)'. I may add: Parents usually hope that the invoked deity will not only take care of a birth without complications, but also of good fortune in the future. So giving a name to a child was, certainly in antiquity, a significant event as the Latin proverb *nomen est omen* shows. In view of these observations the name *ᶠTaduḫepa* may well combine both aspects: birth and future of the child, suggesting 'Ḫeba(t) loved (the girl at birth) and keeps loving (her)'.

Observing the Linear A personal names ***da-du-ma-ta***, ***da-du-te***, ***da-ku-se-ne*** and ***da-ku-na***, it is worth noting that voicing of initial dental stops occurs in particular when the following intervocalic occlusive is also voiced, at least in the Hurrian dialect of Minoan Crete and perhaps also elsewhere, except in thirteenth-century Ugarit as can be inferred from the evidence provided by alphabetic cuneiform texts at Ugarit. It might be a matter of pattern, cf. the orthography of *Da-(a)-du-ḫe-pa*, *Du-ú-du-ḫe-pa* and *Da-a-ku-u-ya* = */Dagu-ya/* at Boğazköy. An exact equivalent to the Linear A name ***da-ku-na*** (HT 103.4) is found in the Cappadocian name *Dakuna* (cf. E. Laroche, *NH*, 171, nº 1217) and in the Hurrian name *Tagu-na* from Mari. J.M. Sasson (Ḫurrians and Ḫurrian names in the Mari texts, *UF 6 (1974)*, 369) mentions the name twice: *ᶠta-ku-na* SY B: vii: 9 and *ᶠta-ku-na* XIII: 1:viii: 18; cf. *ibidem*, 385, s.v. *tag/k, tag/ku-*. As explained before, reading *ᶠta-ku-na* phonologically as */Dagu-na/* seems preferable, since the initial dental is probably voiced under influence of the following voiced */g/*.

Analysis and translation: Publication of the Hurrian-Hittite bilingual text ***kirenze*** (KBo 32) changed the picture also drastically for Linear A ***da-du-ma-ta*** that can now be analysed as Old Hurrian {*dad=o/u=m-atta*} (***=o=***, written ***-u-***) and translated as '(God) the Father, he loved (the boy)'. It consists of the verbal root ***dad-*** + the Old Hurrian marker of the past tense ***-o/u-*** + the Old Hurrian marker ***-m*** ('he') of the subject of action of the transitive verb + the nominal subject ***atta(y)*** 'father'.

According to Th. Richter (*VHN*, 569-570, sub 1.1.1.1.1: verbal forms in ***ᵒ=o=m***) ***=o=*** is qualified as 'Valenzanzeiger' ['value-indicator', i.e. 'suffix indicating transitivity and ergativity'] and ***=m*** is the subject-marker of the 3rd person singular of the indicative. He remarks (*VHN*, 569, n. 902) that it is apparently important that (according to Khacikjan 1982, 165) *the subject of the transitive verb ... needs no ergative marker* in ***ᵒ=o=m-*** formations in contexts.

The element ***atta(i)*** is in my view often used in a double sense in Hurrian personal names: as a theophorous element ***Atta(y)*** in the sense of ***Eni Attanni*** 'God the Father', often to be identified with Teš(š)ub himself, and at the same time as ***atta(y)*** 'the father (of the child)'. Consequently it cannot be accidental that Linear A ***da-du-ma-ta*** can be compared with Linear A ***da-<u>du</u>-te*** (HT 34.1), {*dad=o/u-te*} 'Tešub loved (the child) and still loves it'. Moreover ***da-du-ma-ta*** (HT 95a.1) and ***da-<u>du</u>-te*** (HT 34.1) take about the same position and are both followed by the ideogram GRA.

As mentioned before, according to Th. Richter (*VHN*, *passim*) verbal forms in ***-u*** in personal names can also be interpreted as Old Hurrian *imperatives*, so that ***da-du-te*** (HT 34.1) can also be translated as 'Love (the child), oh Tešub !' (***-te*** is a common hypocoristic of ***-teš(š)ub***). Only if ***da-du-te*** is analysed as {*dad=o/u=m-te*}, which is conceivable, since ***-m-*** before occlusive is not expressed in Linear A consonant clusters, translating 'Tešub loved (the child) and still loves it' is required.

Another personal name ***Tatip-tešup*** (wr. *Ta-ti-ip-te-šup*) at Nuzi (cf. I.J. Gelb, *NPN*, 150; P.M. Purves, *NPN*, 263, s.v. *tat*, *tatip-*) can now also be recognized as an 'Old Hurrian' formation. Formerly E.A. Speiser (*IH*, 140, § 177) explained the suffix ***-p-*** (phonologically probably ***/b/***) as a 'root-complement' with an 'asseverative' value: "Finally, the suffix ***-b***, which is more common by far in names than all the others combined, appears to have had an asseverative connotation [175 (4)]."

Since publication of the Hurrian-Hittite bilingual *Kirenze* (KBo 32), we know that ***Tatip-tešup*** can be analysed as Old Hurrian {*tad=i=b-tešub*}, consisting of the verbal root ***tad-*** + the marker of transitivity ***-i-*** + the marker of the subject ***-b*** (cf. I. Wegner, *Einführung*, 126), 'He, Tešub, loves (the child)'. This means that Old Hurrian ***tad=i=b*** equals Mitanni-Hurrian ***tad=i=a*** 'he/she loves'. According to Th. Richter (*VHN*, 574-575, sub 1.1.1.2.1: verbal forms in ***°=i=b***) ***=i=*** is qualified as 'Valenzanzeiger' ['value-indicator', i.e. 'suffix indicating transitivity'] and ***=b-*** is the subject-marker of the 3rd person singular of the indicative. He also mentions that the high number of transitive non-ergative indicative names (in the corpus of names in *VHN* I) is due to the fact that some of the most frequent roots are mainly or even entirely built in this way: ***ar-*** 'to give (a child)' (21x); ***eḫl-*** 'to rescue, save (a child)' (12x); ***ḫaš-*** 'to hear (a person), answer (a prayer)' (26x); ***kir-*** 'to liberate, manumit, set free (a slave child) ?' (10x).

The Hurrian personal names ***Tatunna*** (wr. *Ta-du-un-na*) and ***Tatuni*** (wr. *Da-du-ni*) from Nuzi (I.J. Gelb, *NPN*, 150) can be analysed as {*tad=o/u=nna*} and {*dad=o/u=nni*}, respectively, consisting of the verbal root ***d/tad-*** + the Old Hurrian suffix marking the past tense or the Old Hurrian imperative suffix ***-o/u-*** + the enclitic personal pronoun 3rd person singular ***-nna***, c.q. optional allomorphic ***-nni***, indicating the object of the transitive verb.

Another sequence with ***dad=u-*** as first element is Linear A ***da-du-mi-ne*** (KN Zf 31) on a silver hairpin for a woman (HM 540, 1927/1971) from the Minoan Necropolis of Mavro Spilio, east of the Palace of Minos, Chambre Tomb IX, B 2, style Late Minoan 1a (M.S.F. Hood, *Archaeological survey of the Knossos area*, British School at Athens: F 6, point 95). The Linear A inscription continues in one line on one side of the pin. The other side of the pin carries a row of crocus blossoms, cf. E.J. Forskyke, The Mavro Spelio cemetery at Knossos, *BSA XXVIII (1926-1927)*, 267 ff, pl. IXB.2, 289, fig. 38; St. Alexiou – W.C. Brice, A silver pin from Mavro Spelio with an inscription in Linear A: Her. Mus. 540, *Kadmos 11.2 (1072)*, 113-124, pl. I-II, fig. 1-9; cf. L. Godart – J.-P. Olivier, Sur l'épingle de Mavro Spelió, *BCH 100 (1976)*, 309-314; *GORILA 4 (1982)*, XXXIV-XXXV, 154-155: KN Zf 31: Épingle en argent. The silver hairpin was found in the same Chambre Tomb IX as the MM III gold signet ring with spiral Linear A inscription from Mavro Spilio (KN Zf 13). The silver pin came from compartment B 2, whereas the gold ring came from compartment E 1.

Linear A ***da-du-mi-ne*** (KN Zf 31) may well be analysed as {*dad=u/o-min(a)=ni/e*} consisting of the verbal root ***dad-*** + Old Hurrian imperative suffix ***-o/u-*** and nominal element {*min(a)=ni/e*}, object of the verb. Translation: 'love the twin (oh *numen*) !', if it is an *imperative* form in context [like ***a-wa-pi*** (KN Zf 31) {*aw-abi*} 'save (the deceased person), oh necromantic sacrificial pit' on the same silver hairpin] or 'Love the twin (oh *numen*) !', if it is a personal name, The lexeme ***mena / mina*** is an ***a***-stem, since it belongs to the category of Hurrian words designating congeniality or kinship such as: ***šala*** 'daughter', ***šena*** 'brother', ***ela*** 'sister', ***nera*** 'mother', ***mena*** 'twin(?)' or 'sister(?)' (as proposed by Th. Richter), cf. I. Wegner (*Einführung*, 52). I prefer the meaning 'twin' to 'sister', not only because there is already a word for 'sister' in Hurrian, namely ***ela***, but in particular since there are places, where names for men contain ***mena-***, ***mina-***, or ***°men(a)=ne/i***, ***°min(a)=ne/i***. The lexeme with the ***a***-stem is written with single ***-n-*** in cuneiform, whereas the form ending in ***-e/i*** is often written with double ***-nn-***, because the so-called definite article ***-ne/-ni*** is added and the ***-a*** of the ***a***-stem is lost by syncope.

At Mari the personal name ***ᶠTatum-menni*** (wr. *ᶠTa-du-um-me-ni*) is attested, analysis {*tad=o=m-men(a)=ni*}, typology 1.1.1.1.1, lexicon *tad-*, *mena*, 'Das Geschwister liebte (Mädchen)' ['The sister loved (the girl)'], cf. Th. Richter, *VHN*, 303, 533-534, s.v. ***tad-/tatt-***. As argued, I should prefer the translation 'The twin loved (the girl)'. We see here that the writing with double ***-mm-*** in ***ᶠTatum-menni*** shows that we are dealing with an *indicative* construction of which ***-menni*** can be the subject (as can be observed in Th. Richter's translation), but ***-menni*** can also be the object, if we translate 'He/She (***-m***) (a *numen*) loved the twin-sister'. If Linear A ***da-du-mi-ne*** (KN Zf 31) is analysed likewise as an *indicative* construction {*dad=u/o=m-min(a)=ni/e*}, I translate 'He/She (***=m-***) (a *numen*) loved the twin'. The Minoan scribe no doubt knew, whether the name constituted an *imperative* (with single *m* belonging to *min(a)=ni/e*) or an *indicative* construction (with double *m-m*), but Linear A orthography, that only has single writing of consonants, does not show this distinction. In cuneiform the feminine determinative shows that ***ᶠTatum-menni*** was a girl, but Linear A ***da-du-mi-ne*** (KN Zf 31) misses such determinatives.

Since Mavro Spilio may well be a necropolis belonging to the Palace of Minos at Knossos, it seems attractive to identify the Hurrian word ***mina / mena*** 'twin' with the name of the mythical King of Knossos, *Μίνως* (Minōs). If that identification is correct, we may conclude that King *Minos* of Knossos and King *Rhadamanthys* of Phaistos were not only brothers, but probably also twins. It is indeed encouraging that the onomastic element ***mina*** is attested in Linear A: ***a-ku-mi-na*** (ZA 10.1-2), ***a-du-|ku-mi-na*** (ZA 10a.3-4) from Kato Zakro, ***mi-nu-te*** (HT 86a.5; HT 106.1), ***mi-nu-te*** (HT 95a.2; HT 95b.2-3) from Hagia Triada and last but not least ***da-du-mi-ne*** (KN Zf 31) from Mavro Spilio (Knossos).

It must be noted that the orthography of ***da-du-mi-ne*** allows another analysis, namely {*dad=u/o=m-i/eni/e*} 'He/She (***=m-***), *a* God (***ine***), loved (the child)' or {*dad=u/o=m-i/en(i)=ne*} 'He/She (***=m-***), *the* God (***inne***), loved (the child)'. Especially in personal names singular ***ini/e*** 'god' and ***in(i)=ni/e*** 'the god' occur often, whereas in context ***eni/e*** and ***en(i)=ni/e*** are relatively more common. The Minoan scribe no doubt knew, which of these analyses represented the name of the person in question, if ***da-du-mi-ne*** is a personal name and not an expression in context on the silver hairpin (HM 540) at Mavro Spilio.

Since ŠEŠ is the Sumerogram for 'brother', the personal name ***Tati***-ŠEŠ (wr. ^{m}*Ta-ti*-ŠEŠ, XXXI 62 II 10, cf. E. Laroche, *NH*, 182, n° 1309) is equivalent to ***Tati-šen***, ***Tati-šena*** or ***Tati-šen(a)=ne/i*** and can be translated as 'Love the brother (oh *numen*) !'. In the Hurrian names *Še-en-da-da* from Nippur (cf. Clay, *PNCP* 131) and *Še-en-na-ta-ti* and *Še-en-da-ti* from Nuzi (cf. P.M. Purves, *NPN*, 263, s.v. *tat*), the verbal and nominal elements seem to have switched positions as compared to ***Tati***-ŠEŠ. This is possible as ^{f}***Alla-tatum*** (wr. ^{f}*Al-la-ta-dum*) from Mari, {*alla-tad=o=m*}, 'The Lady loved the girl', shows.

But there is also another explanation feasible. Th. Richter (*VHN*, 533-534, s.v. ***tad-/tatt-***) mentions that the lexeme ***tadi*** can mean 'Liebe' ['love'] and in onomastics also 'Liebling' ['darling']. This means that *Še-en-da-da* from Nippur can also be translated as 'The brother is *as* a darling' (***-dada*** *essive* in ***-a***) and *Še-en-na-ta-ti* and *Še-en-da-ti* from Nuzi as 'The brother is a darling'. Th. Richter (*VHN*, 534) mentions the examples ^{f}***Akap-tati*** 'Der Liebling (≈ Neugeborenes Mädchen) kam herauf' ['The darling (≈ the newborn girl) came up'] and ^{f}***Taka-tati*** from Mari, 'Sei (oder: werde) schön, oh Liebling !' ['Be (or: Become) beautiful, oh darling !']. ***Urḫa-tati*** (wr. *Ur-ḫa-ta-ti*) at Nuzi (cf. Purves, *NPN*, 263), phonologically /*Urḫa-dadi*/, 'Be true, oh darling !' may corroborate this view.

After the conclusion (*vide supra*) that Linear A ***da-we-da*** (HT 10a.5; HT 85a.2; HT 93a.7; HT 122a.7), occurring four times, cannot be identified as the Semitic name 'David' (as C.H. Gordon proposed, followed by J.G.P. Best), we need to examine in which way the sequence might be interpreted. Since its final syllabic sign is ***-da***, it may contain the Hurrian *directive* suffix ***-da*** that can be used with nouns, personal names, toponyms and theonyms (see e.g. the lists of Hurrian theonyms combined with this suffix ***-da*** in the cuneiform syllabary and with ***-d*** in alphabetic cuneiform of Ugarit, indicating 'to, towards, for' (cf. E. Laroche, *GLH*, 26; cf. I. Wegner, *Einführung*, 65: Table 1: Paradigm of the Hurrian case-endings).

There is one problem due to the Linear A orthographic rule that final consonants were never expressed: Hurrian had also an *ablative* suffix ***-dan*** indicating 'from' (cf. Laroche, *ibidem*; Wegner, *ibidem*), of which the final ***-n*** is not expressed in Linear A. This did probably not pose any serious problem to the scribes, since they obviously knew what they had in mind, but it does to us, because there is no way for us to distinguish the *directive* form from the *ablative* in Linear A orthography. So if ***da-we-da*** refers to a delivery, we have to live with the fact that we shall never know whether it went to ***da-wa*** or had arrived from it.

The *absolutive* form could be represented as ****da-we-*** on account of ***da-we-da*** (HT 10a.5; HT 85a.2; HT 93a.7; HT 122a.7), but Linear A ***da-wa*** (KN Za 10b) seems preferable on account of its occurrence without the suffix ***-da*** or ***-dan*** on a fragment of a Libation Table of banded limestone (HM 2100, 1923) from the Palace of Knossos: House of the frescoes (north-west of the palace): Survey E 7, point 123.Type: P. Warren, *MSV*: 26. 2B, probably Late Minoan I. The inscription on the Libation Table reads:

KN Za 10a.]-*ta-nu-a-ti* , *ja-sa-sa-ra-ma-*
b. *na* , *da-wa* , [.]-*du-wa-to* , *i-ja*[

The form ***da-we-da*** < ****da-wa-da*** might, for instance, be the result of initial accent. In the Linear B texts from Knossos the toponym ***da-wo*** (KN Ak 621 *et al.*), probably equivalent to Linear A ***da-wa***, is found with its Mycenaean Greek ending in ***-ος*** or ***-ον***.

The Linear B name ***da-wo*** (KN Ak 621 *et al.*) is firmly established as a toponym on the basis of the ethnics ***da-wi-jo*** (KN Am 568, KN Og 427 +8102.1, *et.al.*) and ***da-wi-ja*** (KN Ak 780; KN L 641.2), derived from ***da-wo***, which is included as a toponym in *La toponomastica cretese nei documenti in lineare B di Cnosso* by M.V. Cremona, D. Marcozzi, E. Scafa, M. Sinatra, Incunabula Graeca LXIX, *passim.*

Since I am quite sure that the phonetic value of Linear A sign ***96*** and its variant ***68*** (comparable with Linear B sign ****65***) can be identified as ***ḫi*** (see the great number of confirmative matches in *chapter 12: From undeciphered to deciphered Linear A signs*) it is now also possible to recognize the Linear A ethnic ***da+wa+ḫi*** (TY 2 + fr.) on a Linear A tablet (HM 1374, 1909) from magazine η = room 5 of house A at Tylissos, that is unique and enigmatic, because the main ideograms look like circles bigger than those indicating the number 'hundred' on the same tablet with 'tens' following.

On this tablet a ligature ***da+wa+96 = da+wa+ḫi*** (TY 2.5 + fr.) can be read from top to bottom (↓) to the right of a circular ideogram **309b* in the classification of *GORILA 5*, 291: **309a* indicates a circle without attachments; **309b* shows a circle with an attachment underneath and **309c* a circle within a circle. Could they be the bronze cauldrons, also found in room 5 (cf. J. Hazzidakis, *Les villas minoennes de Tylissos*, Études crétoises III, Paris 1934, 15). Are the numbers too high for one location ? Or could they indicate round shields belonging to an arsenal and could the attachments be leather straps attached to them ? There are more examples of armour in Linear A.

Anyway the Hurrian ethnic ***da+wa+ḫi*** (TY 2.5) is in fact equivalent to the Mycenaean Greek ethnics ***da-wi-jo*** and ***da-wi-ja*** like Linear A ***ka-|pa-qe*** (HT 6a.4-5) = Hurrian ***Ḫalba=ḫe*** 'man of *Ḫalba* (Aleppo)' is equivalent to Mycenaean Greek ***ka-pa-jo*** (KN [X] 5752 + B 7039, Olivier), ethnic of Linear B ***ka-pa*** GRA[(KN E 71).

There may still be one indication significant for the interpretation of ***da-we-da*** (HT 10a.5; HT 85a.2; HT 93a.7; HT 122a.7). In most cases it seems to occur in lists of personal names, which means that ***da-we-da*** does not refer to a delivery to or from ***da-wa***, but to a person, probably from ***da-wa***. This means that ***da-we-da*** could mean 'man/woman (coming) from *Dawa*'. In that case the sequence shows the provenance of the person with the ablative suffix ***-dan***, almost in the same way as an ethnic does. For instance, ***da-we-da*** 1 (HT 122a.7) is preceded by ***ku-pa$_3$-nu*** 1 (HT 122a.7), whereas in the preceding line ***pa-ta-ne*** (HT 122a.6) is preceded by ***ku-pa$_3$-nu*** 1 (HT 122a.6). Linear A ***pa-ta-ne***, that also occurs in HT 94b.1, can be interpreted as 'the one of Sparta' or 'Spartan' (with the 'so-called' definite article, also called individualizing suffix ***-ne/-ni***), since ***s*** preceding ***p***, and ***-r-*** preceding ***-t-*** (in fact non-occlusives preceding occlusives) were according to the orthographic conventions of Linear A and B not expressed in consonant clusters. One may compare Linear B ***pe-mo = σπέρμο*** (PY Ep 301,1 *et alibi*) and ***pe-ma = σπέρμα*** (PY Er 312,2 *e.a.*) 'seed, in particular of grain'. Another Linear A inscription offers a similar parallel, again a combination with ***ku-pa$_3$-nu***. HT(?) 170b.3-4 reads:]' 1 ***ku-pa$_3$-nu*** SUS+***si+re*** 1 ***pa-ta-da*** |] 1. So it seems justifiable to interpret ***pa-ta-da*** as '(the one coming) from *Sparta*'. On a pithos fragment from Hagia Triada ***pa-ta-da du-pu$_2$-re***[(HT Zb 160) is the only preserved entry. Although no word divider is visible between ***-da*** and ***du-***, the distance between the signs is slightly larger than between the others.

Moreover, both ***pa-ta-da*** and ***du-pu₂-re*** occur as separate sequences elsewhere. It is therefore justifiable to treat them here as separate entries as well. Linear A ***du-pu₂-re*** also occurs in some libation formulas.

Since ***pa-ta-da*** |] 1 (HT(?) 170b.3-4) occurs in a list of personal names which makes translation as '(The one) from Sparta' possible (with ablative suffix ***-dan***), the sequence]***ku-du-we*** CAP^{m} 1 (HT(?) 170a.2) on the other side of the tablet offers another parallel, since it can be interpreted as the Hurrian *genitive* in ***-we/-wi*** of Linear A ***ku-da*** 1 (HT 122a.8), that may well be a toponym, since the ethnic ***ku-do-ni*** (HT 13.4; HT 85a.4) and possibly ***ku-do-ni***[(HT 101.4) 'the one of Kuda', 'man/woman of Kuda', derived from *Kuda*, is attested as well. If the reading of]***ku-du-we*** is correct, the change of ***-a-*** > ***-u-*** from ****ku-da-we*** > ***ku-du-we*** can be explained, for ***u*** is cognate with ***w***. Since]***ku-du-we*** refers to a person, the meaning is 'The one of *Kuda*'. Such formations with genitive forms are also attested in Hurrian names written with cuneiform, e.g. ^{f}***Azzue*** (wr. ^{f}*Az-zu-e,* ^{f}*A-zu-e*), name of 11 ladies from Mari and of one from Qaṭṭarā, {*azz(e)/azz(o/u)=ve*}, 'The one (girl) of the woman' (cf. Th. Richter, *VHN*, 81-82), cf. ^{f}***Azue*** (wr. ^{f}*A-zu-(ú-)e*) from Nuzi (cf. I.J. Gelb, *NPN*, 41; *AAN* I 39, *SANTAG* 4, 257), ^{f}***Azue*** (wr. ^{f}*A-zu-e*) from Cappadocia, ICK I 16 A 4, 7, B 3 (cf. E. Laroche, *NH*, 50, n° 219), etc.

Attestation of the ethnic ***pa-ta-qe*** (HT 31.6) 'Spartan' (?), written on top of the ideogram of a vessel VAS^{a1}, with ***-qe*** as the Hurrian adjectival and ethnic suffix ***-ḫe/-ḫi***, makes it very likely that ****pa-ta*** is indeed a toponym. Ideogram VAS^{a1} + ***pa-ta-qe*** is followed by the high number of 3000. Parallel for usage of the ethnic suffix ***-ḫe/-ḫi*** is Linear A ***ka-pa-qe*** (HT 6a.4-5) = Hurrian ***Ḫalbaḫe***, alphabetic cuneiform ***Ḫlbġ***, 'man of *Ḫalba*', derived from the Linear A and B toponym ***ka-pa*** = '*Ḫalba*' (Hurrian name of Aleppo in Syria, called *Ḫalab* in Semitic, but in the Cretan context designating the Hurrian toponym of the Palace of Hagia Triada itself). Compare also the Linear B ethnic ***ka-pa-jo*** **Χαλβαῖος* 'man of *Ḫalba*', provided with the Greek ethnic suffix ***-yos***.

The parallel form ***pa-ta-ne*** (HT 94b.1; HT 122a.6) 'the Spartan one' (with the suffix ***-ne/-ni*** can also be regarded as an ethnic. Both ethnics ***pa-ta-qe*** and ***pa-ta-ne*** are derived from the *substrate* toponym ****pa-ta***, probably 'Sparta'. P. Chantraine (*DELG*, 1033) mentions s.v. *Σπάρτη* that the etymology is obscure. One has attempted to compare *σπείρω*, *σπάρτη* and (more plausibly) the name of a plant *σπάρτος*. He concludes (with A. Heubeck) that a substrate term is most likely.

Compare the parallel usage of the suffixes ***-ne/-ni*** and ***-ḫe*** in the Hurrian ethnics ***Masrianne*** 'Egyptian' **:** ***Ḫurroḫe*** 'Hurrian'. Compare for the usage of the Hurrian ethnic suffix ***-ḫe/-ḫi*** in combination with a non-Hurrian name e.g. the ethnic ***Aggadaḫi*** (wr. ^{uru}*A-ag-ga-da-a-ḫi*) 'Akkadian' KUB XLV 41 III 3, with the *directive* suffix ***-da***, KUR *Ag-ga-tu-ḫé-da* 'to the land of Akkad' KUB VII 31 Ro 7, cf. E. Laroche, *GLH*, 40.

If one accepts the possibility of identification of Linear A ****pa-ta-*** with 'Sparta', one could think of trade of Hagia Triada with Lakonia, Sparta in particular, which was a Mycenaean centre after all. The designation ***pa-ta-qe*** (HT 31.6) 'Spartan' could specify either the 3000 vessels indicated by the ideogram and/or the contents of the vessels.

In view of such trade it may be significant that on the island of Kythera across the Lakonian coast a very small Linear A inscription (KY Zg 1) dating from Middle-Minoan IIIb is visible on a clay weight (Khora Museum, 1965), only with sign ***L100a*** = ***i***, according to *Nestor*, 1-10-1965, 407 and J. Raison - M. Pope, *Corpus transnuméré du linéaire A*, Louvain 1980, 247; 1994, 245. However, L. Godart – J.-P. Olivier (*GORILA 4*, 1982, XXXIV-XXXV; 160) read ***606*** = GRA+E. Since the GRANUM ideogram with fraction sign E appears to suite the purpose of a clay weight better than sign ***i***, identification of GRA+E seems preferable. J.G. Younger reads GRA+E {**581*} and remarks that the fraction E [1/4] presumably refers to the weight of the weight.

Another Linear A inscription, ***da-ma-te*** (KY Za 2), occurs on a serpentine ladle (Piraeus Museum 6588) found in the Peak Sanctuary of Hagios Georgios on Kythera.

Moreover, the Linear A inscription ***a-ma*** (HS Zg 1.2) has been found on a schist plaque from Hagios Stephanos (Lakonia). However, it cannot be ruled out that there was a place called 'Sparta' in Crete as well.

Less probable is another theoretical interpretation of Linear A ***pa-ta-qe*** (HT 31.6) as an equivalent to the Hurrian divinity of Šuta in Mitanni, ***^{d}Pardaḫi***, wr. *^{d}Pár-da-a-ḫi*, KBo I 3 Vo 43 = *^{d}Pa-ar-ta-[ḫi]*, KBo I 1 Vo 57, cf. E. Laroche, *GLH*, 195, s.v. *Pardaḫi*. This interpretation would only be possible, if the dental of *^{d}Pardaḫi* is voiceless, as indicated by ***-ta-*** in Linear A ***pa-ta-qe***, but the dental of *^{d}Pardaḫi* seems voiced. Moreover, if Linear A ***pa-ta-qe*** could be explained as ***^{d}Pardaḫi***, the cross-references with Linear A ***pa-ta-ne*** and ***pa-ta-da*** would no longer make sense. Another problem is that the significance of mentioning a divinity with regard to vessels is not self-evident, unless a temple of this divinity with a cultic function of such vessels was involved. But the high number of 3000 points rather to a merely commercial transaction. So we may conclude that all evidence shows that interpretation of Linear A ***pa-ta-qe*** as {*Sparta=ḫe*} 'Spartan' is to be preferred.

A perforated sealstone (KT Zg 2a-b) of black-green steatite in the form of a bobbin / reel (*CMX* XI, n° 96), donated by R.B. Seager to the Metropolitan Museum in New York (26.31.158), probably from Crete (provenance uncertain) bears a Linear A inscription:

a. | $_2$ ***te-ro-a*** | [← as read from the sealstone] =
 | ***a-ro-te*** $_2$ | [→ as read from the seal-impression]
b. | ***da-da-i*** | [← as read from the sealstone] =
 | ***i-da-da*** | [→ as read from the seal-impression].

I begin with interpretation of Linear A | ***i-da-da*** | (KT Zg 2.b) [→ as read from the seal-impression], because it contains either the Hurrian *directive* suffix ***-da*** or the *ablative* suffix ***-dan*** as ***da-we-da*** and ***pa-ta-da*** just discussed.

The name of Mount ***Ida*** (***Ἴδη***) in central Crete, attested in Linear A as ***i-da*** (PK Za 17; ZA 21b.1; ZA 27a.1) from Mount Petsophas (Palaikastro) and Kato Zakro, can be analysed as Hurrian ***id=a=Ø*** 'He (the mountain god) thunders' or 'It (the mountain) thunders', consisting of the root ***id-*** + the indicator of intransitivity ***-a-*** + enclitic personal pronoun 3rd person singular intransitive indicative ***Ø*** as subject indicator (so not ***-nna***), cf. I Wegner, *Einführung*, 99 (Table 6 and 7: The order of suffixes of the indicative, intransitive-positive and intransitive-negative verb and of the antipassive verb).

In fact the Linear A form | ***i-da-da*** | (KT Zg 2.b) proves that Linear A ***i-da*** (ZA 21b.1; ZA 27a.1), although originally a verbal form ***id=a=Ø***, may already have become the nominal designation of the mountain itself in Minoan times, because the Linear A sequence shows clear features of a noun, since the Hurrian suffixes ***-da*** and ***-dan*** are the *directive* case-ending ***-da*** 'to', and the *ablative* case-ending ***-dan*** 'from', respectively, cf. I. Wegner, *Einführung*, 65 (Table 1: Paradigm of the Hurrian case-endings).

If the form ***i-da-da*** (KT Zg 2.b) is analysed as {*ida=da*}, it may well consist of the name of mount ***Ida*** + the Hurrian directive suffix ***-da*** 'to' and is therefore comparable with Greek ****Ἴδαν-δε***, accusative of ***Ἴδα*** + the directive suffix ***-δε***.

However, since a final consonant is not expressed in Linear A and B, Linear A final ***-da*** in ***i-da-da*** can also represent the Hurrian ablative suffix ***-dan*** 'from', so that {*ida=dan*} can be compared with Greek ***Ἴδηθεν*** <****Ἴδᾱ-θεν***, cf. *Iliad* Γ 276: *Ἴδηθεν* 'from (mount) Ida'. The scribe no doubt knew which of the two suffixes he meant, but we cannot be sure. So it seems that we have to live with this ambiguity (or deficiency) resulting from Linear A (and B) orthographic conventions.

Homer refers to the *Ida*-mountains in the Troad (*Iliad* B 821, B 824, Θ 47 f., 75, 410, 438f., Λ 105, 182 f., 337, M 18-24, 253, N 13, Ξ 283 ff., O 5, 79, 146 ff., Π 666-667, P 594 ff., Y 57-59, 91, 189, 215-218, Φ 449, X 170 f.), where Zeus had his temenos and altar on the highest top *Gargaron* (*Iliad* Θ 47). The name is also known from Phrygia and Mysia. D. Detschew, *Die thrakischen Sprachreste*, Vienna 1957, 214, also mentions a polis ***Ἴδη*** between Kardia and Alopekonnesos on the Thracian Chersonese, mentioned by Scylax 67: *μετὰ δὲ τὸν Μέλανα κόλπον ἐστὶν ἡ Θρᾳκία Χερρόνησος καὶ πόλεις ἐν αὐτῇ αἵδε· Καρδία, Ἴδη, Παιών, Ἀλωπεκόννησος* (cf. also D.A. Hester, 'Pelasgian - a new Indo-European language ?', *Lingua 13 (1965)*, 372-373). However, Linear A ***i-da*** no doubt refers to *Ida* in central Crete.

P. Chaintraine, *Dictionnaire étymologique de la langue grecque*, 455, s.v. ***ἴδη***: "dor. ***ἴδᾱ*** f. 'bois, forêt' (Hdt., Théocr.). Vieux mot qui fournit le toponyme ***Ἴδη***, massif montagneux en Mysie occidentale (Iliade etc.) et en Crète (D.P., Paus.), d'où ***Ἴδηθεν***, ***Ἰδαῖος*** (Iliade etc.). Comme le confirme le toponyme, doit être un terme indigène préhellénique, donc sans étymologie établie."

According to J. Chadwick - L. Baumbach, The Mycenaean Greek vocabulary, *Glotta 41 (1963)*, 157-271, s.v. ***ἴδη***, Doric ***ἴδᾱ*** < * ***ϝίδᾱ*** 'forest', an initial digamma is attested through a Cretan inscription ***Βίδᾱν*** (*Del.* 177, 2). D. Detschew, *Die thrakischen Sprachreste*, 558, mentions ***ῥαθιβίδα*** 'Schamkraut' (Diosc. 4, 119 RV), Dacian name of a plant, which he analyses as Dacian ***ῥαθι-*** from an I.E. root *rēt-*, *rōt-*, *rət-* 'rod, thin tree-trunk / stem' (Walde-Pokorny 2, 368) and ***-βιδα*** from *widh-* 'wood' (cf. *ἴδη ναυπηγήσιμος* 'wood for shipbuilding' (Herodotos V, 23).

According to C.J. Ruijgh (*EGM*, § 188[+44]) the Linear B name ***wi-da-jo*** (KN V 60,3) may be ***Ϝīδαῖος***, ethnic of ****Ϝίδᾱ***, or be derived from ***ϝίδᾱ*** 'wood, forest'. In the latter case the meaning of ***Ϝīδαῖος*** might be 'forester'. He also refers to the probably Pre-Greek personal names ***wi-da-ka-so*** (KN D 1402) and ***wi-da-ma-ro*** (KN Do 919) in Linear B.

However, Linear A ***i-da*** (PK Za 17; ZA 21b.1; ZA 27a.1), | ***i-da-da*** | (KT Zg 2.b), ***i-da-a*** (KO Za 1.b-c), ***i-da-ja*** (PK Za 18), ***i-da-ma-te*** (AR Zf 1; AR Zf 2), ***i̱-du-ti*** (HT 104.2-3) are names without initial ***w-***.

Linear B ***i-da-i-jo*** (KN K 875,4; PY An 661,2), ***Ἰδαῖος***, ***i-do-me-ne-ja*** (PY Eb 498,1; PY Ep 212,9), ***Ἰδομένεια***, feminine of ***Ἰδομενεύς***, and ***i-do-me-ni-jo*** (PY Gn 428,5; PY Fn 324,7), dative of ***Ἰδομένιος***, are also attestations of names without initial ***ϝ-***. This definitely proves that these names had no initial ***w-/ϝ-***, because Linear A and B faithfully expressed that phoneme. The fact that there is no trace of ***ϝ-*** in ***Ἴδη***, ***Ἴδηθεν***, ***Ἰδαῖος*** in Homer either, proves conclusively that the root ***id-*** of ***Ida***, ***Idaia***, ***Idaios***, ***Idomeneus***, ***Idomeneia*** and ***Idomenios*** is Pre-Hellenic and probably Hurrian ***id-***.

The only sound conclusion is: If Chadwick's and Baumbach's association of ***ἴδη*** and Doric ***ἴδᾱ*** 'forest' with Cretan ***Βίδᾱν*** is correct, two distinct roots may have coexisted, one with and one without initial digamma. The name of mount ***Ida*** (***Ἴδη***) and its cognates ***Idaia***, ***Idaios***, ***Idomeneus***, ***Idomeneia*** and ***Idomenios*** certainly contained *no initial digamma*. Disappearance of the digamma after the time of the Mycenaean Linear B tablets may have caused confusion of the root of the name of mount ***Ida*** with that of the noun ***ἴδη*** (Doric ***ἴδᾱ***) < * ***ϝίδᾱ*** 'timber-tree, wood, forest' in popular etymology.

P. Chaintraine (o.c.) and H.G. Liddell - R. Scott, *A Greek - English lexicon*, Oxford 1961, do not mention a possible original initial digamma in ***ἴδη*** (Doric ***ἴδᾱ***) 'forest', based on Cretan ***Βίδᾱν*** or Dacian ***ῥαθιβίδα***, which may well account for their association of ***ἴδη*** (Doric ***ἴδᾱ***) 'forest' with the name of mount ***Ida***.

I have analysed Linear A ***i-da*** (PK Za 17; ZA 21b.1; ZA 27a.1) as Hurrian ***id=a=Ø*** 'He (the mountain god) thunders' or 'It (the mountain) thunders', consisting of the root ***id-*** + the indicator of intransitivity ***-a-*** + enclitic pronoun as subject indicator 3rd person singular intransitive indicative ***Ø***. Usage of the indicator of intransitivity ***-a-*** requires a meaning in accordance with the intransitive aspect of the verb and at the same time a meaning close to that of the transitive form of the root ***id-*** 'to strike, to hit violently' + the indicators of transitivity ***-i-*** or ***-u/o-*** as can, for instance, be found in Linear A ***i-du-ti*** (HT 104.2-3). Thunder and lightning are not only an expression of divine wrath of the Hurrian supreme god Tešub and his Greek counterpart Zeus, but are also associated with the top of a mountain massif where thunderclouds gather and whence these mountain gods hurl their thunderbolts causing great anxiety among the population.

Linear A ***i-du-ti*** (HT 104.2-3) can probably be interpreted as a Hurrian personal name containing the verbal root ***id-*** 'to beat, hit, smash, strike', cf. e.g. I. Wegner, *Einführung*, 41, 256, s.v. ***id-*** 'schlagen'; Th. Richter, *BGH*, 109-110, s.v. ***id-*** I [Boğ.] and *VHN*, 405, s.v. ***id-*** II, '(zer)schlagen' ['to beat, hit, smash, strike violently']. Semantically Linear A ***i-du-ti*** can be compared with the Hurrian personal name ***Ullutti*** (wr. *ul-lu-ut-ti*) from Mari and Tigunāni, analysis {*o/ull=u=tti*}, lexicon *ull-*, typology 1.3.1.1.2.2, 'Zerstöre mich (oh *Numen*) !', ['Destroy me (oh *numen*) !'], which is considered a variant of the personal name ***Ullutta*** (wr. *ul-lu-ut-ta*) from Šušarrā (Tall Shemshara), analysis {*o/ull=u=tta*}, lexicon *ull-*, typology 1.3.1.1.2.1, also 'Zerstöre mich (oh *Numen*) !', ['Destroy me (oh *numen*) !'], with the *optional allomorphic* enclitic personal pronoun 1st person sing. ***-tti*** instead of ***-tta***, cf. Th. Richter, *VHN*, 329 and 596.

Linear A ***i-da-a*** (KO Za 1.b-c) {*id=a-ya*} '(The) thunderer', following ***a-ta-i-jo-wa-ja***, ***tu-ru-sa***, ***du-pu-re*** (see *sub vocibus*) on a limestone parallelepiped from the Peak Sanctuary of Kophinas, is probably epithet to ***a-ta-i-jo-wa-ja*** (= Hurrian reconstructed ****at-ta-i-iw-wa-(y)aš***) 'Our Father', and equivalent to ***i-da-ja*** (PK Za 18) from Petsophas.

The latter inscription used to be read as]***-te*** **,** ***i-da*** **,** ***ja-ja***-['], but should probably be read as]***-te*** **,** ***i-da-ja*** **,** ***ja***-['] and be completed to ***si-ru***]***-te*** **,** ***i-da-ja*** **,** ***ja***-[***di<da>ki-te-te***.

Linear A ***i-da-a*** (KO Za 1.b-c) and ***i-da-ja*** (PK Za 18) may well be a hypocoristic form (with the Hurrian hypocoristic suffix ***-ya***) of Linear A ***i-da-ma-te*** {*id=am=a-te*} 'Tešub is thundering' or 'Thunder, oh Tešub !' and prototype of Linear B ***i-da-i-jo*** (KN K 875,4; PY An 661,2), probably ***Ἰδαῖος***, probably originally with the same meaning as Linear A ***i-da-a*** {*id=a-ya*}, '(The) thunderer'. As soon as the Mycenaean Greeks did no longer understand the Minoan-Hurrian etymology of the epithet, the meaning changed to 'God of Mount Ida', cf. the usual translation of *Zeus Idaios* 'Zeus of Mount Ida'. Like Linear A ***i-da*** (PK Za 17; ZA 21b.1; ZA 27a.1), the epithets ***i-da-a*** (KO Za 1.b-c), ***i-da-ja*** (PK Za 18) and ***i-da-ma-te*** (AR Zf 1; AR Zf 2) contained the root ***id-*** + the marker of intransitivity ***-a-***. However, ***i-da-ma-te*** also contains the root-extension ***-am-*** between the root and the marker ***-a-***. I. Wegner (*Einführung*, 87-89, sub 5.2.1, Position 1: root-extensions) discusses the so-called 'root-extensions' of the verb, which take the first position in the chain of suffixes, directly following the root. One of these root-extensions is ***-am-*** that expresses the *factitive* aspect of the verb according to G. Wilhelm, *Iraq 53 (1991)*, 12, Anm. 35. I. Wegner offers the example: ***eman-*** 'ten', ***eman=am-***, transitive 'decuple, multiply by ten'; intr. 'increase tenfold'.

If we assume that Linear A ***i-da-ma-te*** contains this root-extension ***-am-***, the analysis will be {*id=am=a-te*}, consisting of the root ***id-*** + root-extension ***-am-*** + the indicator of intransitivity ***-a-*** and the form ***-Te*** (hypocoristic of ***-Tešub***) as subject of the verb: 'Tešub thunders, Tešub causes thunder and lightning'. Or ***-Te(šub)*** is a vocative and ***i-da-ma-te*** can be translated 'Cause thunder and lightning, oh Tešub !'.

Theoretically ***i-da-a*** (KO Za 1.b-c) on a limestone parallelipiped (HM 2627, 1962?) from Mount Kophinas could be interpreted as a Hurrian hypocoristic personal name like, for instance, Linear A ***ki-pa-a*** (KN Zb 1) and ***u-na-a*** (KN Zb 2) on a pithoid jar from Knossos (with the Hurrian hypocoristic suffix ***-ya***) or like King Priam's charioteer ***Ἰδαῖος*** (*Iliad* Γ 248; Ω 325) and like a Trojan ***Ἰδαῖος***, son of Dares, saved by Hephaistos (*Iliad* E 11, 20). I have previously suggested that ***i-da-a*** might in that case be the name or title of a priest 'Priest of Ida' or refer to a supplicant, but since it occurs on the limestone parallelipiped from the Peak Sanctuary of Mount Kophinas and especially since it is the third sequence after ***a-ta-i-jo-wa-ja*** 'Our Father', there can in my view be no doubt that it is indeed an epithet to ***a-ta-i-jo-wa-ja*** and that it has exactly the same function as ***Ἰδαῖος*** has in Homer's ***Ζεὺς Ἰδαῖος***, in the combination ***Διὸς ἱρεὺς Ἰδαίου*** 'priest of Zeus Idaios' (*Iliad* Π 604-605) and in ***κελαινεφέϊ Κρονίωνι Ἰδαίῳ*** 'for the son of Kronos, lord of the dark clouds, god of Ida' (*Iliad* Ω 290-291). Moreover, if ***i-da-a*** (KO Za 1.b-c) were a personal name, it would be strange that virtually the same name, ***i-da-ja*** (PK Za 18), was also found in the Peak Sanctuary of Mount Petsophas (Palaikastro).

In the *Iliad* the epithet ***Ἰδαῖος*** may already have lost the original meaning '(The) thunderer', which Linear A ***i-da-a*** and ***i-da-ja*** {*id=a-ya*} probably still had. This is clear, if we compare *Iliad* Ω 308, where Priam prays to Zeus: *"Ζεῦ πάτερ, Ἴδηθεν μεδέων, κύδιστε μέγιστε", "Father Zeus, that rulest from Ida, most glorious, most great"*. Here we see that ***"Ἴδηθεν μεδέων*** *"ruling from Ida"* emphasizes the association of Zeus with Mount Ida, suggesting that ***Ἰδαῖος*** is also to be associated with the mountain.

However, we must not forget that in *Iliad* Ω 290-291, Zeus, the son of Kronos, is not only called ***Ἰδαῖος***, but also 'Lord of the dark clouds'. So the association of Zeus with *thunder and lightning* is never far away. It is also significant that Zeus is called 'Father' in the *vocative* ***Ζεῦ πάτερ*** (*Iliad* Ω 308) in Priam's prayer and that in *Iliad* Θ 31 Athena speaks to him: *"ὦ πάτερ ἡμέτερε Κρονίδη, ὕπατε κρειόντων"*, *"Oh Our Father, thou son of Kronos, high above all lords"*. This reminds us how many Linear A libations formulas start with ***a-ta-i-jo-wa-ja*** (in the *absolutive-vocative*).

Although the absolutive ****at-ta-i-iw-wa-aš*** is not yet attested in cuneiform, the ergative ***at-ta-iw-wa-šu-uš*** is, cf. J. Friedrich, *Kleinasiatische Sprachdenkmäler*, Berlin 1932, 32: ***dTe-e-eš-šu-pa-aš … ip-ri-iu̯-u̯ə-šu-uš at-ta-iu̯-u̯ə-šu-uš*** (Mit. IV, 118) 'Tešub … Our Lord, Our Father', transliterated as ***ew-ri-iw-wa-šu-uš at-ta-iw-wa-šu-uš*** by E.A. Speiser, *Introduction to Hurrian*, New Haven 1941, 103, § 144, n. 105, and E. Laroche, *Glossaire de la langue hourrite*, Paris 1978-79, reprint 1980, 63. They mention that it is the 1st person of the plural possessive ergative, but do not tell that the only time that Tušratta used this form, it refers to Tešub and that this is the closest parallel between the Hurrian Stormgod and ***eni attanni***. It is interesting that in contrast to this usage of the *plural* possessive 'Our Father', Tušratta uses the *singular* forms 'my father' or 'your father', when he speaks about his own father or that of Amenhotep III respectively, so about people of flesh and blood.

It is time to return to the combination | ***a-ro-te*** ₁ | | ***i-da-da*** | (KT Zg 2a-b) → as read from the seal-impression. Since Linear A syllabic sign ***22*** can be ***lo*** or ***ro***, several interpretations of ***a-ro-te*** (KT Zg 2.a.) are feasible:

1) ***a-ro-te*** can be identified with the Hurrian personal name ****Allu-te***. The Hurrian personal name ***Allu-teia̯*** (wr. *Al-lu-te-e-a*) is attested at Nuzi (JEN 518:10; cf. I.J. Gelb, *NPN*, 20, s.v. ***Allu-teia̯***; P.M. Purves, *NPN*, 199, s.v. ***all***, ***allu-***). Since ***-teia̯*** and ***-te*** are both very common hypocoristic forms of ***-tešup*** in Hurrian theophorous sentence names, ****Allu-te*** is equivalent to ***Allu-teia̯***. Phonologically it is probably ***/Allote/***.

According to Th. Richter (*BGH*, 12-14) the verbal root ***all-*** II means 'to rule', cf. Urartian ***alae*** and ***aluse*** 'ruler' and the Urartian root ***al-*** 'to be lord, to rule'. Cf. also Hurrian ***allai*** 'Lady, Mistress' or 'Queen'. If this verbal root is chosen, the whole phrase ***a-ro-te*** ₁ ***i-da-da*** (KT Zg 2.a-b) can be analysed as ***all=o-te ida=dan*** and can be rendered 'Tešub ruled and rules from (Mount) Ida'.

This would again remind us of the Old Hurrian version of Homeric ***Ἴδηθεν μεδέων*** "ruling from Ida" in *Iliad* Ω 308, where Priam prays to Zeus: *"Ζεῦ πάτερ, Ἴδηθεν μεδέων, κύδιστε μέγιστε"*, *"Father Zeus, that rulest from Ida, most glorious, most great"*.

2) Since ***-m-*** preceding an occlusive is not expressed in consonant clusters in Linear A and B, analysis of ***a-ro-te*** as ***all=o=m-te***, consisting of the root ***all-*** + the marker of the Old Hurrian past tense (with durative aspect) ***-o-*** + the Old Hurrian marker of the subject 3rd person singular ***-m*** and the hypocoristic theophorous element ***-te***, is also feasible: 'Tešub, he ruled and rules (from Ida)'. Since there is no object mentioned, we may conclude that the verb is used as an *antipassive*.

3) ***a-ro-te*** can consist of the Hurrian verbal element ***ar=o/u-***, phonologically ***/aro/***, and the hypocoristic theophorous element ***-te***.

After publication of the Hurrian-Hittite bilingual ***kirenze*** (KBo 32) it was recognized that many Hurrian personal names probably belong to the category of 'Old Hurrian', cf. I. Wegner, *Einführung*, 125-126 (sub E 'Althurritisch'). She now translates (*Einführung*, 126) ***Tad=o=ḫepa*** as 'Ḫeba loves (namely the bearer of the name)'. She explains that

-i- is the indicator of the transitive verb without aspect,

-u- is the indicator of the transitive verb in the perfect tense,

-a- is the indicator of the intransitive verb,

-o- is the indicator of a state of being or durative aspect of the verbal element in personal names (type of ***Tad=o=Ḫeba***).

According to M.L. Chačikjan (*Churritskij i urartskij jazyki*, Erevan 1985) ***-u-*** signifies the transitive perfect forms and ***-o-*** the durative aspect. However, G. Wilhelm (Zum hurritischen Verbalsystem, in: S.R. Anschütz (ed.), *Texte, Sätze, Wörter und Moneme*, Festschrift für Klaus Heger zum 65. Geburtstag, Heidelberg 1992, 667 ff.), demonstrated that the 'thematic vowel' of the transitive past or perfect tense is not ***-u-***, but ***-o-***, and that the alleged indicator ***-o-*** of the durative aspect in fact represents the same grammeme.

Differentiation between ***-u-*** and ***-o-*** is in this case no longer necessary. I may add: Parents usually hope that the invoked deity will not only take care of a birth without complications, but also of good fortune in the future. So giving a name to a child was, certainly in antiquity, a significant event as the Latin proverb *nomen est omen* shows. As a result the name *ᶠTaduḫepa* may combine both aspects: birth and future of the child/girl, suggesting 'Ḫeba(t) loved (the girl at birth) and keeps loving (her)'.

In accordance with interpretation of ***Tad=o=Ḫeba***, Linear A ***a-ro-te*** can be analysed as Hurrian ***Ar=o=Te(šub)*** and interpreted as 'Teš(š)ub gave and keeps giving'.

At Nuzi so-called sentence names are attested such as ***Ari-teš(š)up*** (wr. *A-ri-te-šup*), {*ar=i-teš(š)up*}, with transitive imperative ***ar=i-*** + the theophorous element ***-tešup***. At Nuzi one finds at least 52 persons with the name ***Ar-tešup*** (wr. *Ar-te-šup, Ar-te-eš-šup, Ar-te-eš-šu-up, Ar-te-šu-up, A-ar-te-šup, Ar-ᵈte-šup*), which probably represents the *athematic* imperative ***ar-*** + ***-tešup***. Also the hypocoristics with ***-te***, ***-teḭa*** or ***-tešše*** 'Give, oh Teš(š)ub !', are quite common: ***Arte*** (wr. *Ar-te-*, *Ar-te-e*), 58 persons with the name ***Ar-teḭa*** (wr. *Ar-te-ia, Ar-te-e-a, Ar-te-a, Ar-ti-ia, Ar-di-ia*) and 22 persons with the name ***Ar-tešše*** (wr. *Ar-te-eš-še, Ar-te-še, Ar-teš-še*), cf. I.J. Gelb, *NPN*, 34-35; P.M. Purves, *NPN*, 202-204. Old Hurrian ***Ari-p-tešup*** (wr. *A-ri-ip-te-šup*) is also attested at Nuzi, cf. I.J. Gelb, *NPN*, 29. It can be analysed as {*ar=i=b-tešup*}, with the Old Hurrian indicative 3rd person singular *=i=b*, translation 'Tešub gives'. At Alalaḫ *Arib-Tešubi* (wr. **A-ri-ib-te-eš-šu-bi*, *40:7) and *Ari-Tešub* (wr. **A-ri-*ᵈIM DUB.SAR, *6:33) are attested in level VII (* in the Alalaḫ texts), cf. A. Draffkorn, *HHA*, 24, s.v. *Arib-Tešubi* and *Ari-Tešub*. The latter name is also found at Boğazköy, cf. E. Laroche, *NH*, 38, nº 127, s.v. *Ari-Tešub*.

According to I. Wegner (*Einführung*, 125-127) the suffix ***-b-*** is the Old Hurrian marker of the 3rd person singular of transitive and intransitive verbs of action. For instance, the transitive verb ***pašš-*** 'to send', with the marker of transitivity /***i***/, offers the 'Old Hurrian' form ***pašš=i=b*** 'he sends', because it is also a verb of action, whereas the Tušratta-letter would yield ****pašš=i=a*** 'he sends'. The intransitive verb ***un-*** 'to come', with the marker of intransitivity ***-a-***, offers in 'Old Hurrian' the form ***un=a=b*** 'he comes', because it is also a verb of action, whereas the Tušratta-letter yields ***un=a=(Ø)*** 'he comes'.

Incidentally, the personal suffix ***-b-*** occurs with both singular and plural subjects of the 3rd person. In the latter case the plural indicator fails in the verbal form, but the plurality is indicated by the nominal or pronominal subject, cf. G. Wilhelm ('Zum hurritischen Verbalsystem', in: Festschrift für Klaus Heger, 1992, 662); cf. I. Wegner, *Einführung in die hurritische Sprache*, 127. According to I. Wegner (*ibid.*, 125) 'Old Hurrian' shows morphological features differing from the language of the Tušratta letter, which are also structural according to M.L. Chačikjan, *Churritskij i urarartskij jazyki* (Akademija Nauk Armjanskoj SSR, Institut Vostokovedenija, Churrity i Urarty 2), Erevan 1985. See also *chapter 9: Hurrian Grammar (according to I. Wegner).*

4) In *Minoan Linear A*, Vol. I: *Hurrians and Hurrian in Minoan Crete* (edition 2016) I suggested that Linear A ***a-ro-te*** could reflect Hurrian ***aruš-te*** {*ar=oz-te*}, semantically and orthographically representing the perfect form of the transitive verb ***ar-***, with the tense marker and Speiser's agent-suffix ***-uš-***, phonologically */-oz-/*, cf. E.A. Speiser, *IH*, 196, § 225, sub 'suffixes with the verb', perfect ***-oz-***, since according to Linear A and B orthographic conventions ***-s-*** preceding a dental is not expressed in consonant clusters.

An objection to my proposal in the 2016 edition to interpret Linear A ***a-ro-te*** as Hurrian ***Aruš-te*** {*ar=ož-te*} is that the indicator ***-a-*** of the subject of action (position 7 in the chain of suffixes of the indicative, transitive-ergative, positive verb, cf. I. Wegner, *Einführung*, 93, table 4) is missing. The expected form should be {**ar=ož=a-te*} (instead of {**ar=ož-te*}), that can be compared with the personal name ***Arušan*** (wr. *A-ru-ša-an, A-ru-sa-an*) of a *ḫabiru* from Tigunāni and of a soldier from Tuttul (Tall Bi'a), analysis {*ar=ož=a=n(na)*}, typology 1.1.2, translation 'Er/Sie (scil. ein *Numen*) gab ihn (Jungen)' [He/she (scil. a *numen*) gave him (the boy)], cf. Th. Richter, *VHN*, 75. The object 'him' in this name is represented by ***=n***, shortened form of ***=nna***. In his section D on typology and morphology (pp. 584-587), sub 1.1.2, Richter explains that repeatedly, also beyond his *corpus*, 'one-word names' occur that can be described as finite, transitive indicative forms following the example of Mitanni Hurrian (i.e. the vernacular of the Tušratta letter). For the occurrence side by side of 'Old Hurrian' verbal forms and of 'Mitanni Hurrian' formations in contexts he (*VHN*, 584, n. 952) refers to V. Haas - I. Wegner, Beiträge zum hurritischen Lexikon: Die hurritischen Verben *ušš-* "gehen" und *ašš-* "abwaschen, abwischen", in: J. Klinger e. a. (eds.), *Investigationes Anatolicae: Gedenkschrift für Erich Neu* (StBoT 52), Wiesbaden 2010, 109; and S. de Martino, The 'Song of Release' twenty-nine years after its discovery, *Altorientalische Forschungen 39 (2012)*, 209 f.

5) However, Th. Richter (*VHN*, 602) provides s.v. ***Aruš-Ḫeba*** (wr. *a-ru-uš-ḫé-ba*) a form that can be considered parallel to Linear A ***a-ro-te***, interpreted as Hurrian ***Aruš-te***, but the form is analysed in a different way, namely as {*ar=o=ž-Ḫeba*}, and translated '*Ḫeba* möge (Mädchen) geben' ['*Ḫeba* may give (the girl)']. If the theophorous element *-Ḫeba* is exchanged for *-Te*, hypocoristic of *-Teš(š)ub*, the result would be 'May *Teš(š)ub* give (the boy)', quite an acceptable name for a boy.

6) Th. Richter (*VHN*, 593-595), sub 1.3.1.1.1: *Unerweiterte Bildungen* [Unextended formations], mentions that some sentence names can contain an *imperative* in ***^{o}=o*** and a second nominal element in the vocative, e.g.: ***^{f}Talmu-Ḫeba*** at Mari, 'Mache (Mädchen) groß, oh *Ḫeba* !' ['Make (the girl) great, oh *Ḫeba* !'] and ***^{f}Uru-Ḫeba*** at Mari, 'Lasse (Mädchen) vorhanden sein, oh *Ḫeba* !' ['Let (the girl) be present, oh *Ḫeba* !'].

As a result Linear A ***a-ro-te*** can be analysed as *imperative* ***ar=o-Te*** 'give, oh *Tešub* !' and the inscription | ***a-ro-te*** $_2$ | | ***i-da-da*** | (KT Zg 2a-b) 'give, oh *Tešub* from Ida !'.

We are, of course, accustomed to encounter personal names on the Linear A tablets, but since the inscription | ***a-ro-te*** $_2$ | | ***i-da-da*** | occurs on a sealstone, one may choose a real verbal form ***ar=o*** 'give !', combined with the *vocative* 'oh *Tešub* !'. *Tešub* may then grammatically and semantically be connected with the *ablative* **Ida=dan** 'from *Ida*'. „Suffixaufnahme" (suffix-reduplication) is not required in the *absolutive-vocative*, since the *absolutive* is an endingless form, cf. I. Wegner, *Einführung*, 70, e.g. *šen(a)=iff=u=ve ašti* (Mit. III 21) 'the woman (*ašti* absolutive singular) of my brother'.

An objection to this interpretation may be that one would expect that in a real sentence the name of *Tešub* would be fully written and not be abbreviated as in a personal name.

On the other hand the frequent occurrence of ***si-ru-te*** on many libation tables shows that the name *Teš(š)ub* can also be abbreviated in standard expressions. Correspondence of Hurrian ***šilu*** with Hurrian ***šilwa*** in personal names (especially in combination with ***-te*** and ***-tešub***) and with Urartian ***silua*** has convinced me that Linear A ***si-lu-te*** is probably equivalent to a Hurrian proverbial expression often at the close of the prayer.

The libation formula turns out to be a prayer addressing Tešub as 'Our Father' in his role of *eni attanni* 'God the Father' and closing off with 'Tešub is good, benevolent' or rather 'be beneficent, oh Tešub !' or (trans.) 'treat (us) well/benevolently, oh Tešub!', which is semantically close to *Kyrie eleison !* in prayers for God's pity and mercy, and close to '*erbarme dich !*' in J.S. Bach's St. Matthew Passion.

However, it is not impossible that ***a-ro-te*** is not a contextual grammatical form, but just a personal name, probably the name of the owner of the sealstone, 'Give (the child), oh *Tešub* !'. The ablative ***Ida=dan*** 'from *Ida*' could then refer to the provenance of this owner. The problem for us is that Hurrian personal names often show the same formations as grammatical forms in context.

7) Th. Richter (*VHN*, 74) also provides s.v. ***Arum-Te*** (wr. *a-ru-um-te*) a perfect 'Old Hurrian' equivalent to Linear A ***a-ro-te***. According to the orthographic conventions of Linear A and B ***-m-*** preceding a dental stop was not expressed in consonant clusters. The name of the *ḫabiru* ***Arum-Te*** from Tigunāni (*Prisma* II 52) is analysed as {*ar=o=m-Te*}, typology 1.1.1.1.1, lexicon *ar-*, *Te (→Teššub)*, and translated as 'Te(ššub) gave (the boy)', since ***-te*** is a frequent hypocoristic form of ***Teš(š)ub*** in personal names. As a matter of fact the full name ***Arum-Teššub*** (wr. *a-rum-te-eš-šu-up*), analysis {*ar=o=m-Teššob*}, typology 1.1.1.1.1, lexicon *ar-*, *Teššub*, and translated as 'Teššub gave (the boy)', is even attested several times: 1 time at Mari (M. 11405: 28); 6 persons marked *ḫabiru* from Tigunāni (*Prisma* II 46; II 48; III 39; IV 8; VI 39; VI 51).

If Linear A ***a-ro-te*** (KT Zg 2.a.) is a personal name, identification as ***Arum-Te*** seems preferable, since it is itself attested in Hurrian cuneiform and corroborated by attestations of ***Arum-Teššub***, though it must be admitted that the other interpretations are possible and in accordance with the orthographic conventions of Linear A and B as well. Due to the ambiguities caused by the orthographic conventions of Linear A and B, we can conclude that the Minoan scribe, who inscribed the sealstone, and the owner of the sealstone knew exactly which grammatical form or personal name was expressed by the inscription, but we have to take all possibilities into account.

Other personal names with the verbal element ***Arum-***, {*ar=o=m-*}, mentioned by Th. Richter are: ***Arum-Ara***, {*ar=o=m-Ara*} 'Ara gave (boy)'; ***Arum-atal***, {*ar=o=m-adal*} 'The strong one gave (boy)'; ***Arum-Ḫasur***, {*ar=o=m-Ḫasur*} '(*Numen* of) *Ḫasur* gave (boy)'; ***Arum-ḫute***, {*ar=o=m-ḫo/ude*} 'A favourable fortune gave (boy)'; ***Arum-mušni***, {*ar=o=m-mužni*} 'The just/righteous one gave (boy)'; ***Arum-Nawar***, {*ar=o=m-Navar*} '(*Numen* of) *Nawar* gave (boy)'; ***Arum-šar*[*ri*]**, {*ar=o=m-šarri* (?)} 'The King of Gods gave (boy)'; ***Arum-šašar***, {*ar=o=m-šažar(i)*} 'The saw gave (boy)' (the latter name may indicate that giving birth to the boy was fairly unpleasant); ***Arum-šurwit***, {*ar=o=m-šo/urvid(i)*} 'The bad/evil/wicked gave (boy)'; ***Arum-*[...]**, {*ar=o=m-*[...]}'[...] gave (boy)', cf. Th. Richter, *VHN*, 73-74.

The heading of HT 13.1 provides de Linear A sequence ***ka-u-de-ta***, which very much reminds of Linear B ***ka-u-da*** on a tablet from Knossos:

KN Fs 21,1: *ka-u-da* , HORD , T 1 [
KN Fs 21,2: FAR V 1 VIN V 1 [

This text bears a strong resemblance with another tablet from Knossos:

KN Fs 19,1: *e-ti-wa* , HORD T 1 *NI* V 3
KN Fs 19,2: FAR V 1 OLE Z 2 VIN V 1
Verso: *ME* + *RI* Z 1

Since Linear B ***e-ti-wa-ja*** in the combination ***pa-i-ti-jo e-ti-wa-ja-qe*** (KN Od 681a.1), ***Φαίστιοι*** and ***Ἠτιϝαῖαι***, must be considered plural feminine of the ethnic ***Ἠτιϝαῖος*** derived from the toponym ***e-ti-wa*** (KN Fs 19,1) = ***Ἠτίϝᾱ***, cf. *Ἦτις* / *Ἤτεια*, name of a town in Crete according to Pape-Benzeler (cf. C.J. Ruijgh, *EGM*, § 195), there is a good chance that ***ka-u-da*** (KN Fs 21,1) is also a toponym in Linear B. Exactly for this reason M.V. Cremona, D. Marcozzi, E. Scafa and M. Sinatra, *La Toponomastica Cretese nei Documenti in Lineare B di Cnosso,* Incunabula Graeca 69, Rome 1978, 36, have included ***ka-u-da*** in their corpus of Cretan Linear B toponyms. The authors have been able to confirm that toponyms in Linear B are often followed by ideograms of grain or barley, GRA and HORD, and other commodities. This is also the case with Linear A ***ka-u-de-ta*** (HT 13.1), which is followed by the wine ideogram VINa. The toponym can probably be identified with the name of the island ***Γαύδος*** (*Gaudos*) along the south coast of Crete south of the Gorges of Samaria. Today the island can be reached by boat from Chora Sfakion and Palaiochora. There is also a smaller island ***Gaudopoula*** closer to the Cretan coast. In Minoan times these twin islands could be reached by boat from ***Kommos*** (excavated between 1976 and 2005 by Joseph and Maria Shaw, University of Toronto), harbour of Phaistos and Hagia Triada.

Orthographic conventions of Linear A and B allow two possible interpretations for the final syllable ***-ta*** in ***ka-u-de-ta***. Since ***-š-*** preceding ***-t-*** is not expressed in Linear A, it may be either the Hurrian *plural directive* suffix ***-šta*** 'to' or *plural ablative* suffix ***-štan*** 'from' (cf. E. Laroche, *GLH*, 26), now analysed as the *plural* suffix ***-aš-*** + the *directive* suffix ***-ta*** 'to' or the *plural* suffix ***-aš-*** + the *ablative* suffix ***-tan*** 'from' (cf. I. Wegner, *Einführung*, 65-66, sub 2.2.4. Position 4: the case-suffixes). So we encounter the same orthographic problem as with the singular *directive* ***-da*** or the singular *ablative* ***-dan*** in Linear A ***da-we-da***, ***i-da-da*** and ***pa-ta-da*** (*vide supra*). The scribe knew whether he meant a directive or ablative, but we cannot distinguish these cases, since Linear A did not express final consonants. The plural suffix can be explained by the fact that two islands were involved.

Since the toponym ***ka-u-da*** (KN Fs 21,1) occurs in Linear B, it is likely that the Linear A name reflected in ***ka-u-de-ta*** (HT 13.1) was ***ka-u-da*** as well, phonologically probably ***/Gauda/*** with voiced palatal as in the modern Greek name *Gaudos*. It may be a matter of pattern (possibly caused by initial accent) that the final vowel ***-a*** in ***da-wa*** and ***ka-u-da*** changed into ***-e-*** before the following suffixes ***-da(n)*** (see ***da-we-da***) and ***-(a)š=ta(n)*** (see ***ka-u-de-ta***), respectively.

Formerly I also mentioned a third possibility, namely that we might be dealing with a formative ***-ta*** like in the Linear A and probably Hurrian toponym]***su-ki-ri-ta*** (PH Wa 32b) from Phaistos and the identical Linear B toponym ***su-ki-ri-ta*** (KN Db 1324, B; KN Db 1327+ 1345+7681+7992; KN Dn 1092+5379+fr., 2).

However, Linear A]***su-ki-ri-ta*** (PH Wa 32b) from Phaistos can now be identified as a 'one-word' name ***Šugritta*** and be analysed as *{šugr=i-tta}* 'Protect me !', consisting of the verbal root ***šugr-*** 'to protect' + the marker of transitivity ***-i-*** + the enclitic personal pronoun 1st person singular ***-tta*** indicating the object of the transitive verb. Since it cannot be proved that ***gaud-*** is a verbal root, it seems wise to compare Linear A ***ka-u-de-ta*** (HT 13.1) no longer with]***su-ki-ri-ta*** (PH Wa 32b).

It is difficult to assess whether the correct reading after ***ka-u-de-ta*** VINa (HT 13.1-2) is **„ *te* , *re-za*** or **„ *te-re-za*** 5 J[_] (HT 13.2). I present the first 4 lines of Linear A HT 13:

HT 13.1: *ka-u-de-ta*

HT 13.2: VINa „ *te* , *re-za* 5 J[_] (or perhaps VINa „ *te-re-za* 5 J[_] ?)

HT 13.3: *te-tu* 56 *te-ki*

HT 13.4: 27 J *ku-do-ni* 18

Argument for maintaining the reading VINa **„ *te* , *re-za*** is that all editors (me included) read a dot, interpreted as a word divider between ***te*** and ***re-za***, which is justifiable, since monosyllabic ***te*** occurs more often in bureaucratic Linear A texts and is usually regarded as a transaction term. Decisive is that ***re-za*** recurs after VIR PARMATUS 20 in HT 88.1.

Arguments to read VINa **„ *te-re-za*** are: 1) that the clay of the tablets sometimes contains grains of sand that can leave small holes in the tablets, when rubbed out, resembling the dots deliberately inscribed by the scribes. 2) Between the ideogram VINa and syllabic sign ***te*** there are two dots visible (**„** in the transliteration), not in the same line of each other and even smaller than the dot following ***te***. 3) In line 3 we see two sequences ***te-tu*** and ***te-ki*** (possibly personal names) with initial ***te-***, which makes it more likely that we are dealing with a sequence ***te-re-za*** as well containing initial ***te-***. I have observed that many scribes were fond of playing with words and names, often using alliteration as a stylistic form. 4) The most usual order is that an ideogram follows the "transaction term" ***te***. It is less usual that an ideogram precedes this "transaction term".

Anyway considering all arguments I think that **„ *te* , *re-za*** (HT 13.2) must be treated as separate entries and that monosyllabic ***te*** may well be the transaction term, compared with Linear B ***a-pu-do-si***, Mycenaean Greek ***ἀπύδοσις*** (Att. *ἀπόδοσις*), 'payment, actual delivery'. Verbal terms such as the aorist 3rd person singular ***a-pu-do-ke*** (KN X 681; PY Ma 393,2) 'he rendered, paid' as well as the augmented aorist ***a-pe-do-ke*** (PY Fr 1184,1) also occur. We have already seen (*supra*) that the sequence **, *te+ro* ,** (HT 104.1) is attested in Linear A in the same way as monosyllabic **, *te* ,** elsewhere.

Hurrian ***te-ro*** {*ter=o*} can be interpreted as an *imperative* of the root ***ter-/tir-*** (cf. Th. Richter, *BGH*, 461). Comparing **, *te* ,** with the other frequent "transaction term", ***ki-ro*** {*kir=o*}, often abbreviated to monosyllabic ***ki***, that can be identified as a Hurrian *imperative* 'he/she must redeem his/her debt' (see the discussion on Linear A ***ki-ro***), one may suspect that Linear A ***te*** may be an abbreviation of an *imperative* as well. Th. Richter (*VHN*, 537, note 800) mentions correspondence with the Urartian stem ***ter=u***. M. Salvini - I. Wegner (*Einführung in die urartäische Sprache*, Wiesbaden 2014, 114) translate Urartian ***ter-*** as 'legen, anlegen (von Gärten); stellen, errichten; bestimmen (von Namen)'. Among the various proposals by several authors such as 'festsetzen, bestimmen' (G.A. Melikišvili, *Die urartäische Sprache*, Studia Pohl 7, Rome 1971, 88; M. Salvini, 1977, 129; B. André-Salvini - M. Salvini, 2002, 19), 'to put, to establish' (I.M. Diakonoff, 1989, 84), the meaning '(Tribut) auferlegen' ['to impose (tribute)'] proposed by Chr. Girbal (Urartäisch *barzani zelde*, *Altorientalische Forschungen 37.1*, 2010, 156) appears to fit very well into the Linear A bureaucratic context. If the Hurrian and Urartian roots ***ter-*** are indeed identical, the *imperative* {*ter=o/u*} may be translated as 'he/she must impose (tribute)' or perhaps simply 'he/she must pay, deliver'.

Linear A ***re-za*** 5 J[_] (HT 13.2), ***te-tu*** 56 (HT 13.3), ***te-ki*** 27 J (HT 13.3-4) and ***ku-do-ni*** 18 (HT 13.4) are probably all personal names. Of these ***ku-do-ni*** 'Man of *Kuda*' or simply 'Kydonian' is probably an ethnic used as a personal name.

Linear A ***te-tu*** (HT 13.3) may contain the Hurrian verbal root ***tid-*** II [Boğ.; Mitt.], ***titt-*** / ***te-t***^{o} [Boğ.] 'angreifen' ['to attack'], cf Th. Richter (*BGH*, 464-465; *VHN*, 541).

If ***te-tu*** can be identified as a 'one-word' Hurrian personal name ***Tettu*** and be analysed as {*tett=u*}, it can be interpreted as an Old Hurrian *imperative* in ***-u/-o*** and be translated as 'He/She (a *numen*) must attack' or 'Attack (oh *numen*) !' or an Old Hurrian transitive *perfect* 'He/She (a *numen*) attacked (the child)'.

Since final consonants are not expressed in Linear A and B, ***te-tu*** can also reflect ***Tettun***, analysis {*tett=u/o=n(na)*}, consisting of the verbal root ***titt-*** / ***te-t***^{o} 'to attack' + the Old Hurrian *imperative* or transitive *perfect* ***-u/-o*** + the abbreviated enclitic personal pronoun 3rd person singular ***-n*** (instead of ***-nna***), that can be translated as 'Attack him/her/it (oh *numen*) !' or 'He/She (a *numen*) attacked it (the child)'. Possibly we may also compare ***Tette***, name of a ruler of Nuḫašše, *Tetti, Titte* and *Tettii̯a*, wr. *Te-et-ti-ia* (cf. P.M. Purves, *NPN*, 266, s.v. *tett* and *Tettii̯a*). The ruler of Nuḫašše, ***Tette***, is also mentioned by E. Laroche (*NH*, 186, n° 1341): ^{m}*Te-et-te*, KBo I 4 II 17, 21, etc.

It is also conceivable that the Linear A personal name ***te-tu*** can be identified with the name of one of the primordial divinities of the Greek theogony, ***Τηθύς*** (*Tethys*). As daughter of *Ouranos* and *Gaia* and as sister and wife of *Okeanos* she personified the fertile productivity of the sea. *Rhea* entrusted the education of *Hera* to her during *Zeus*' struggle with *Kronos*. *Hera* gratefully reconciled *Tethys* and *Okeanos* who had been at odds, cf. P. Grimal, *The Dictionary of Classical Mythology*, Oxford 1985, 440.

If Linear A ***te-tu*** can be identified with *Tethys*, the form may reflect the *ergative* case in ***-š*** of ***Tettu***. If *Tethys* is originally Hurrian *Tette/Tettu*, we may observe that Hurrian [***t***] may have sounded as aspirated dental [***th***] in Greek ears, cf. the Hurrian prototype ***Teššui̯a*** of (Pre)-Greek ***Θησεύς***.

We may even assume that the original form of ***Τηθύς*** was ****Θηθύς*** and that according to Grassmann's phonetic law the first aspirated dental ***θ-*** lost its aspiration through dissimilation under influence of the second: ****Θηθύς*** > ***Τηθύς***. If a syllable begins and ends with aspirated plosives or if successive syllables begin with such sounds, the first consonant loses its aspiration, cf. L.R. Palmer, *Descriptive and comparative linguistics. A critical introduction*, London 1972, 223. Some examples:

θρίξ [*thrík-s*] 'hair' (nominative sing.) - ***τριχός*** [*trikh-ós*] (genitive sing.).
θρέψω [*thrép-sō*] 'I shall rear' (future) - ***τρέφω*** [*tréph-ō*] 'I rear' (present).
ἕξω [*hék-sō*] 'I shall have' (future) - *ἔχω* [*ékh-ō*] 'I have' (present).

If this reconstruction regarding ****Θηθύς*** > ***Τηθύς*** is correct, we may conclude that a so-called Hellenized Pre-Greek name may have obeyed the same phonetic law(s) as truly Greek forms, if the circumstances were alike.

Since ***te-tu*** can be identified with Hurrian ***Tettu/Tette*** and at the same time with the Pre-Greek Sea-goddess ***Tethys***, it is remarkable that the reading „ ***te*** ₂ ***re-za*** (HT 13.2) may offer an interesting parallel on the same tablet, because ***re-za*** is directly followed by ***te-tu*** and (as we have just observed in the Greek theogony) ***Ῥέα / Ῥεῖα / Ῥείᾳ*** (*Rhea*) entrusted the bringing-up of *Hera* to ***Τηθύς*** (*Tethys*).

Hesiod (*Theogony*, 132-137) also tells: "But afterwards she (*Gaia* = Earth) lay with *Ouranos* (Heaven) and bare deep-swirling *Okeanos, Koios, Krios, Hyperion, Iapetos, Theia, Rhea, Themis, Mnemosyne*, gold-crowned *Phoibe* and lovely *Tethys*."

I suspect that *Theia* is originally a hypocoristic of *Teš(š)ub*, but had to become a sister of *Rhea*, because *Teš(š)ub*'s place had been taken by *Zeus* in the Greek pantheon. *Theia* had to become a goddess, because most words and names in ***-a*** are feminine in Greek.

If Linear A ***re-za*** is the original form of ***Ῥέα / Ῥεῖα / Ῥείᾳ***, we observe that the form followed another phonetic law: Indo-European intervocalic ***-s-*** first changed > ***-h-*** and subsequently disappeared in Greek. We may suspect that the voiced sibilant ***-z-*** in ***re-za*** was indeed so close to the Indo-European intervocalic ***-s-***, that it could undergo the same phonetic development as that intervocalic ***-s-***. If Rhea is derived from ***Reza***, can it be accidental that Hesiod mentions the accusatives ***Ῥείαν*** and ***Τηθύν*** in the same phrase and that Linear A ***re-za*** (HT 13.2) and ***te-tu*** (HT 13.3) follow each other on the same tablet ?

Mycenaean Linear B ***te-se-u, te-o-jo do-e-ro*** (PY En 74, 5; Eo 276, 4) at Pylos can be identified as Pre-Greek '***Θησεύς*** (Theseus), servant of a god', which may be understood as 'priest of a god'. According to my etymological proposal ***Θησεύς*** is derived from Hurrian ***Teššui̯a*** (wr. *Te-eš-šu-ia*, *Te-šu-ia*, *Te-iš-šu-ia*, *Ti-iš-šu-ú-ia*, *Te-su-*[*i*]*a*, *Te-eš-su-ia*), attested as the name of 34 persons at Nuzi (cf. I.J. Gelb, *NPN*, 154). ***Θησεύς*** clearly is a Pre-Greek name, and its non-Indo-European intervocalic ***-s-*** did not change into ***-h-*** in Mycenaean Greek and did not disappear. If Linear A ***re-za*** is the prototype of ***Ῥέα / Ῥεῖα / Ῥείᾳ***, the intervocalic voiced sibilant ***-z-*** differed from ***-šš-*** in ***Teššui̯a***.

It is not certain that Linear A ***re-za*** (HT 13.2) is the name of a woman. The other occurrence of ***re-za*** (HT 88.1) suggests that it is the name of a man on HT 88:

HT 88.1: ***a-du*** VIR PARMATUS 20 ***re-za***
HT 88.2: 6 FIC **,** ***ki-ki-na*** 7

It is unlikely that the ideogram VIR PARMATUS 'man armed with a small round shield' can be combined with registration of women.

Of course we may be dealing with different persons called ***re-za*** on HT 13.2 and HT 88.1. Provided that the reading of ***re-za*** (HT 13.2; HT 88.1) is correct, it is probably a personal name, but can for the same reason not be of Hurrian origin, whether it is derived from the theonym or not. ***Ῥέα / Ῥεῖα / Ῥεία*** is known as a goddess from Crete in Greek mythology, since she is the mother of Zeus, born in Crete. The name itself is probably not of Hurrian origin, since there are no words and names of Hurrian origin attested beginning with ***r-***.

So Cretan ***Ῥέα / Ῥεῖα / Ῥεία*** may be a local Cretan deity of Pre-Hurrian origin or it may be an adstrate name. If it is an adstrate name derived from Linear A ***re-za***, I may refer to Th. Richter (*BGH*, 537) who mentions s.v. alphabetic cuneiform ‡ ***rzn*** from Ugarit [loan-word in Hurrian]: 'Helfer' ['help, someone who helps, gives aid/support'], i.e. ***/rēzenne/***, respectively ***rēz=enne/i***, derived from Akkadian ***rēṣu*** (Dietrich/Mayer 2004a, 28f.). If this etymology of ***Ῥέα / Ῥεῖα / Ῥεία*** is correct, her role of entrusting the bringing-up of *Hera* to *Tethys* may reflect her role as a helping deity.

It is not excluded that ***Rhea*** had to become a goddess in the Greek Pantheon like ***Theia***, because most words and names in ***-a*** are feminine in Greek. If ***Rhea*** is derived from < ***Re^{h}a*** < ***Reza*** and if ***Reza*** and ***Tettu/Tette*** were not only personal names, but also mythological names in Minoan Crete, a reality of which the scribes must have been aware, there was a good reason for the Minoan scribe to mention ***re-za*** (HT 13.2) and ***te-tu*** (HT 13.3) after each other on the same tablet. In that light it is a small wonder that Hesiod mentioned the accusatives ***Ῥεῖαν*** and ***Τηθύν*** in the same sentence in his Theogony about six centuries later.

It is conceivable and perhaps even probable that the Mycenaean Greeks inherited not only the main stories about the Kingdom in Heaven and the Song of Ullikummi from Minoan-Hurrian Crete, but many more aspects of religion and cult, the names of some prominent and minor deities included. Not all details landed undistorted in the traditions preserved by Homer, Hesiod and other authors, in particular the tragedians. Mycenaean religion had, of course, the best chance to inherit integral parts of Minoan traditions, not only because the Mycenaeans conquered Knossos and probably the rest of Crete, but also because they had already been in contact with the Minoan civilization during centuries before they took power in Crete. I am convinced that the Dorians who came from North-West Greece and who had themselves not been in close contact with the Mycenaean civilization caused the most serious breach of continuity of Minoan and Mycenaean traditions. Oral traditions changed during the next centuries of the Dark Ages, but the tales about the creation of the *kosmos* and the struggle between the generations of gods, told in Hesiod's *Theogony*, show that the Minoan-Hurrian religious tradition was deeply embedded in Greek religion and cannot be ascribed to a recent borrowing of these traditions from the Near East during the age of Greek colonisation in the 8th century B.C.

The Linear A names ***te-ki*** (HT 13.3; HT 122a.3) and ***te-ke*** (HT 85a.5) can probably be identified as Hurrian *nominal* ***Tegi/Tagi*** 'Beautiful' or *verbal* 'Make (the child) beautiful (oh *numen*) !'. A perfect equivalent of Linear A ***te-ki*** and ***te-ke*** is Hurrian ***Teki*** (wr. *Te-ki*), son of *Lullu* at Šubat-Enlil, lexicon *tegi* (→ *tag-*), translation 'Schön' ['Beautiful'], cf. Th. Richter, *VHN*, 305; 525-526, s.v. ***tag-/takk-***, ***teg-***.

An interesting name is also ***Tekauš-en*** (wr. *Te-ga-uš-e-in*) at Mari, analysis *{teg=av=š-en(i)}*, typology 1.1.2, lexicon *teg-* (→ *tag-*), *eni*, translation 'Wir machen die Gottheit schön' ['We make the deity beautiful'], cf. Th. Richter, *VHN*, 305; 525-526. See also Th. Richter, *BGH*, 428-429, s.v. ***tag-***, ***teg-*** [*passim*], who shows that the root ***tag-/takk-***, ***teg-*** can be nominal 'beautiful' and verbal 'to make beautiful' (transitive) and 'to be beautiful' (intransitive).

E. Laroche (*GLH*, 249-250, s.v. ***tag-*** 'beau' ['beautiful']) already considered the root ***teg-*** equivalent to ***tag-***, since he wrote: "Lecture du sum. ZALAG; épithète de l'argent. RS voc. II 24 = Ḫḫ II 134: sum. ki.lam.zalag.ga = h. MIN ***te-gi-še*** 'beau prix' ['beautiful price']; cf. Friedrich, *HW*, 325: 'schön' ['beautiful']." He also cited: *inu-me ušḫuni šiḫala ḫišma tagi-ma kiraši-ma* 'comme l'argent (est) pur, brillant, et beau, et long (durable)', KUB XXIX 8 IV 27." He also mentions (*GLH*, 250): "***tagi*** 'attribut de Ḫebat', *da-(a)-ki, da-a-ki-it-ti*, KUB XXV 44 II 19; KBo XX 113 IV 16; KUB XXXII 59 II 3; etc."

If we accept that Linear A ***te-ki*** and ***te-ke*** can be identified with the Hurrian personal name ***Teki*** (wr. *Te-ki*), analysis *{teg=i}*, 'Beautiful' or 'Make (the child) beautiful (oh *numen*) !', we may conclude that Linear A shows that Minoan-Hurrian used both voiced and voiceless initial dentals for the orthography of this common root ***dag-***, ***tag-/takk-***, ***teg-***. I may refer to Linear A ***da-<u>ku</u>*** (SE Zf 1), ***da-ku-na*** (HT 103.4), ***da-ku-se-ne*** (HT 103.2; HT 103.4-5), ***da-ku-|se-ne-ti*** (HT 104.1-2), ***a-sa|-da-<u>ka</u>*** (MA Wc <5> side a.1-2), ***a-di-da-ki-ti(-)*** (KN Zc 6) and ***da-ka*** (HT Wa 1001; HT Wa 1002; HT Wa 1003; HT Wa 1004; HT Wa 1005), discussed before. This ***t/d*** alternation can be ascribed to the tendency to use allophones in Hurrian. In that respect one may expect that it also occurs in Minoan Linear A.

Linear A ***ka-u|-do-ni*** (HT 26b.2-3) 'man of *Gauda*' or '*Gaudian*' is apparently a form with the suffix of the so-called Hurrian singular definite article ***-ne/-ni*** built on the root of the (Linear B) toponym ***ka-u-da*** (KN Fs 21,1). At the same time ***-ne/-ni*** is suspected of having a relational function forming an ethnic, cf. I. Wegner, *Einführung*, 55, s.v. ***-ni***: KUR ***mašriâ=ni-*** 'the Egyptian land' (Mit. II 69); and s.v. ***-nni***: KUR ***mašria=nni-*** 'the Egyptian land' (Mit. II 71) or KUR ***mašria=n(i)=ne***. The Linear A ethnic ***ka-u|-do-ni*** (HT 26b.2-3) may have been used as a personal name.

This usage seems comparable with that in Linear A ***ku-do-ni*** (HT 13.4; HT 85a.4) 'man of *Kuda*', 'Kydonian', and ***]ku-do-na***|[(HT 64.1) 'men of *Kuda*' or 'Kydonians', with the suffix ***-na*** designating the so-called plural definite article or relational suffix.

Hurrian ethnics were usually formed with the adjectival and ethnic suffix ***-ḫe/-ḫi*** as in ***Ḫalbaḫe*** 'man of *Ḫalba* (Aleppo), ***Akkaduḫe*** 'man of *Akkad*', 'Akkadian', ***Ḫurruḫe*** 'Hurrian', ***Ḫattuḫe/ḫi*** 'man of the land *Ḫatti*', 'Hittite', cf. sg. nom. *uruḪa-at-tu-uḫ-e*, KUB XXVII 38 IV 28; *uruḪa-at-tu-ḫi*, KUB XXXII 19 + III 40-41; sg. dative with definite article ***-ni*** and sg. dative suffix ***-wa*** (written as ***-pa***) *uruḪa-at-tu-ḫi-ni-pa*, KUB XII 44 II 17 (see E. Laroche, *GLH*, 98, s.v. *Ḫattuḫi*); cf. also the personal name *Ḫattuḫi* (E. Laroche, *NH*, 65, n° 344, ***Ḫattuḫi***, in Akkadian texts from Ugarit: 'Hittite'(?) d'Ugarit': *Ḫa-(at)-tu-ḫi*, RS 17.28, 4, 9, 27 = PRU IV 109 sq.). Remarkably Linear A ***ku-re-96*** (HT 39.2; HT 117b.1), twice attested at Hagia Triada, can now be transliterated as ***ku-re-ḫi*** = ***Ḫurre=ḫi*** 'Hurrian', see *chapter 12: From undeciphered to deciphered Linear A signs.*

Also conventionally transliterated ***qa-ti-96*** 2 (ZA 14.2) at Kato Zakro can now be interpreted as ***Ḫattiḫi***, analysis ***Ḫatt=i=ḫi***, 'man/woman of the land *Ḫatti*' = the Hurrian name for 'Hittite', see *chapter 12*, where more Linear A ethnics are discussed.

The question as to whether the suffix ***-ne/-ni*** only marks the so-called definite article in Hurrian or whether it also has a relational function, was already answered by E.A. Speiser, *IH*, 98, § 137 (for the sake of clarity he has underlined ***-ne/-ni*** in his text, as well as ***-r-ri-e*** < ****-r-ne***): "In order to determine the meaning of ***-ne*** we have to examine the principal constructions in which this particle may be used. They are represented by the following types: **a)** *ta-še-e-ni-e-we id-du-um-mi* (Mit. I 92f.) "present-*ne*-of going-out" (going-out of the present).
b) K[UR] *Mi-zi-ir-ri-e-we* [66c] KUR *u-u-mi-i-in-ni-e-we al-la-i* (Mit. I 62) "Egypt-*ne*-of land-*ne*-of mistress" (mistress of the land of Egypt).
c) KUR *Ma-a-ás-ri-a-a-an-ni* KUR *u-u-mi-i-in-ni* (Mit. III 7) "Egypt-in-*ne* land" (land of [lit. "in"] Egypt); cf. the parallel phrase *Hur-ru-u-ḫé* KUR *u-u-mi-i-ni* (Mit. III 6) "Hurrian land".
d) [*e-še*]-*ni-bi-ni-iš al-la-a-iš* VII 56 i 27 "heaven-*ne*-of-*ne*-by mistress-by" (by the mistress of heaven). - In all four instances we have attributive constructions. The attribute, always accompanied by ***-ne***, precedes the head. The same word-order is the rule with adjectival concepts marked by the suffix ***-ḫe*** [58]. Indeed the word-order and the parallel ***Masrianne* : *Ḫurroḫe*** (c) indicate that all of the attributes in the above instance have the function of descriptive adjectives."

[N.B. Hurrian ***eše*** was at the time of E.A. Speiser and E. Laroche still translated as 'heaven' and ***ḫaburni / ḫawurni*** as 'earth', but the Hurrian-Hittite bilingual ***Kirenze*** has shown that ***eše*** means 'earth' and ***ḫaburni / ḫawurni*** 'heaven'; [*e-še*]-*ni-bi-ni-iš* can now be analysed as {*eše=ni=vi=****NE****=****š***}. The second ***-ni-*** is not the suffix of the so-called definite article, but the suffix for "Suffixaufnahme" (suffix-reduplication) expressed as =***NE***= in the analysis and taking position 5 in the order of suffixes. So the second ***-ni-*** and ***-š*** in [*e-še*]-*ni-bi-ni-iš* can be recognized as typical examples of "Suffixaufnahme" that are required, since *al-la-a-iš* is in the singular *ergative* case and [*e-še*]-*ni-bi-ni-iš* is the attributive noun belonging to *al-la-a-iš*. The *genitive* suffix ***-we/-wi***, written as ***-bi-***, is normalized to **=*ve*=** in the analysis. The singular *ergative* form has the suffix ***-š***. PGvS.

E.A. Speiser uses here the reconstructed phonological form of the ethnic ***Ḫurruḫe***: /***Ḫurroḫe***/. The equation ***Masrianne* : *Ḫurroḫe*** ('Egyptian' : 'Hurrian') shows that the function of descriptive adjectives (here of ethnics in particular) could be indicated by the suffixes ***-ne/-ni*** and ***-ḫe/-ḫi***. Incidentally, although it is assumed that the writing of *-ni-e*, e.g. in the Tušratta letter, indicates that the actual phoneme was ***-e-*** in ***-ne***, even if it was written as ***-ni***, the cuneiform script seems to use ***-ni*** and ***-ne*** indiscriminately. E.A. Speiser, *IH*, 98, § 136, explains this usage as "no more than orthographic variants".

It is remarkable that Linear A scribes also seem to have adopted this orthographic habit, since many sequences have a final syllabic sign ***-ni*** or ***-ne***. One may suspect that at least some scribes were able to read cuneiform texts and 'followed' this 'cuneiform' example in their Linear A writing. Anyway, the fact that */e/* and */i/* could be interchanged in Hurrian and probably also in Linear A, shows that these vowels were close.

I. Wegner and G. Wilhelm treat the so-called Hurrian suffix of the singular definite article, c.q. relational or ethnic suffix ***-ne/-ni***, likewise sub ***-ni***: KUR *Ma-a-áš-ri-a-a-ni-ma-a-an* (Mit. II 69) 'and the Egyptian land', {*mašri=a=ni=mân*} and sub ***-nni***: KUR *Ma-a-áš-ri-a-an-ni-e-u̯ə* (Mit. II 71) 'of the Egyptian land', {*mašri=a=n(i)=ne=we*} or {*mašri=a=nne=u̯ə*}, cf. I. Wegner, *Einführung*, 55; G. Wilhelm, Suffixaufnahme in Hurrian and Urartian, in: F. Plank (ed.), *Double Case. Agreement by Suffixaufnahme*, New York - Oxford 1995, 124, example [48]. I. Wegner (*Einführung*, 54) mentions the Hurrian adjectival, relational / ethnic suffix ***-ḫe***, e.g. ***Ḫurr=u/o=ḫe*** < ***Ḫurri*** + ***-ḫe*** [with transition from ***i*** > ***o*** or with derivational vowel ***o***] 'Hurrian', ***Ḫatt=u/o=ḫe*** 'Hittite', ***Ebla=ḫe*** 'belonging to Ebla', 'man / citizen of Ebla', etc. If my identification of Linear A ***ku-re-96*** (HT 39.2; HT 117b.1) = ***ku-re-ḫi*** = ***Ḫurr=e=ḫi*** 'Hurrian' and of Linear A ***qa-ti-96*** 2 (ZA 14.2) = ***Ḫattiḫi***, analysis ***Ḫatt=i=ḫi***, 'man/woman of the land ***Ḫatti***' = the Hurrian name for 'Hittite', is correct, we can observe that the Linear A forms preserved here the original forms without transition from ***i /e*** > ***o/u*** or with derivational vowel ***o***.

Linear A offers the following ethnics with the suffixes ***-ni***, ***-qe*** (Hurrian ***-ḫe/-ġ***) and (thanks to the decipherment of Linear A signs ***96*** and ***68***) ***-ḫi***:

ka-u|-do-ni (HT 26b.2-3) 'man of *Gauda*' / '*Gaudian*', derived from toponym ****ka-u-da***, cf. Linear A ***ka-u-de-ta***, indeed attested as ***ka-u-da*** (KN Fs 21,1) '*Gauda*' in Linear B.

ku-do-ni (HT 13.4; HT 85a.4) 'man of *Kuda*' or '*Kydonian*', from ***ku-da*** (HT 122a.8).

]ku-do-na|[(HT 64.1) 'men of *Kuda*' or '*Kydonians*', derived from ***ku-da*** (HT 122a.8).

pa-ta-ne (HT 94b.1; HT 122a.6) 'Man of *Sparta*', derived from ****pa-ta***.

pa-ta-qe (HT 31.6) '*Spartan*', from ****pa-ta***, cf. ***pa-ta-da*** (HT? 170b.3; HT Zb 160).

ka-pa-qe (HT 6a. 4-5; possibly HT 140.3) = Hurrian *Ḫalbaḫe*, 'man of ***ka-pa*** = *Ḫalba*'.

sa-ro-qe (HT 62+73.3) 'man of ***sa-ro*** (possibly Zaros)', derived from the toponym ***sa-ro*** (HT 9a.1, HT 17.2, HT 19.2; HT 42.2), conventionally spelled as ***sa-ro-qe*** as if there is no distinction between Linear A and B.

sa-re-96 (HT 20.4) = ***sa-re-ḫi*** 'man of ***sa-ro*** (possibly Zaros)', equivalent to ***sa-ro-qe[*** (HT 62+73.3). Occurrence of Linear A ***sa-re-ḫi*** (HT 20.4) 'Man of Saro' on the same tablet as Linear A ***ku-ma-96*** = ***ku-|ma-ḫi*** 'Man of *Kumma*' confirms identification of ***sa-re-ḫi*** (HT 20.4) as an ethnic.

ku-ma-96 (HT 20.1-2) = ***ku-|ma-ḫi*** 'Man of *Kumma*', Hurrian ethnic derived from the toponym ***Kumma***, Minoan *Kumma*, now *Kommos*, harbour of Hagia Triada and Phaistos.

da+wa+ḫi (TY 2.5) at Tylissos, ethnic derived from the Linear A toponym ***da-wa*** (KN Za 10b), that is probably equivalent to the Linear B toponym ***da-wo*** (KN Ak 621, *et alibi*) from Knossos. Linear B ***da-wo*** has the Mycenaean Greek ending in ***-οϛ*** or ***-ov.*** Linear B ***da-wo*** (KN Ak 621 *et al.*) is firmly established as a toponym on the basis of the ethnics ***da-wi-jo*** (KN Am 568, KN Og 427 +8102.1, *et.al.*) and ***da-wi-ja*** (KN Ak 780; KN L 641.2), derived from ***da-wo***, which is included as a toponym in *La toponomastica cretese nei documenti in lineare B di Cnosso* by M.V. Cremona, D. Marcozzi, E. Scafa, M. Sinatra, Incunabula Graeca LXIX, *passim*. The acknowledged toponym in both Linear A and B offers a confirmatory identification of the Hurrian ethnic suffix ***-ḫi***. The Hurrian ethnic ***da+wa+ḫi*** (TY 2.5) is in fact equivalent to the Mycenaean Greek ethnics ***da-wi-jo*** and ***da-wi-ja*** like Hurrian ***ka-|pa-qe*** (HT 6a.4-5) is equivalent to the Mycenaean Greek ethnic ***ka-pa-jo*** (KN [X] 5752 + B 7039) derived from Linear B ***ka-pa*** GRA[(KN E 71).

These parallels in Linear A correspond completely with the Hurrian parallels of ***Masrianne*** 'Egyptian' : ***Ḫurruḫe*** 'Hurrian' observed by E.A. Speiser, which on the whole emphasizes the view that grammatical features of Hurrian can be recognized in the Linear A texts. The suffixes ***-ni/-ne*** and ***-na*** could occasionally have a relational or ethnic function comparable to the suffix ***-ḫe/-ḫi*** according to Speiser. The suffixes ***-ni/-ne*** and ***-na*** are the most frequent in Hurrian and appear to be the most frequent final syllabic signs in Linear A as well. Other confirmatory matches are the Minoan-Hurrian ethnics in ***-ḫe/-ḫi*** and the Mycenaean Greeks ethnics in ***-yos*** and ***-ya*** derived from the same toponyms.

The singular Linear A form ***ku-do-ni*** (HT 13.4; HT 85a.4) 'man of *Kuda*' corresponds with the plural form ***]ku-do-na***|['men of *Kuda*' (HT 64.1), with the suffix ***-na*** designating the so-called plural definite article, in this case with a relational (i.c. ethnic) function. Linear A ***ku-da*** 1 (HT 122a.8) appears as last entry on HT 122a.8, after ***ku-ro*** 31. It may be a toponym or personal name, cf. the Hurrian personal name ***Kuda*** at Alalaḫ, cf. A. Draffkorn, *HHA*, 85, ***Kuda***, *Kudi-e* and *Kud-kudanu*, s.v. ***kud*** and ***kud-***.

The fact that ***]ku-do-na***|[(HT 64.1) 'men of *Kuda*' and ***ku-do-ni*** (HT 13.4; HT 85a.4) and possibly ***ku-do-ni***[(HT 101.4) 'man of *Kuda*' also occur at Hagia Triada and can probably be regarded as ethnics derived from ***Kuda***, makes it very likely that Linear A ***ku-da*** represents a toponym indicating either a place in the Phaistos - Hagia Triada area or a region.

The Mari texts offer the Hurrian personal names ^{f}***ku-da-di*** (SY B: iv: 5) and ^{f}***ku-da-di*** (SY B: vii: 29), cf. G. Dossin, 'Deux listes nominatives du règne de Sûmu-iamam', *Revue d'Assyriologie 65 (1971)*, 37-66; cf. J.M. Sasson, 'Ḫurrians and Ḫurrian names in the Mari texts', *UF 6 (1974)*, 363, s.v. ***Kuta-te***. Cf. for occurrences at Nuzi P.M. Purves, *NPN*, 231, s.v. *kut-, kuti-, kuti̯a, -kutu*, etc. All forms are provided with single writing of the dentals which indicates that they are voiced.

According to I. Wegner (*Einführung*, 113, 265) and Th. Richter (*BGH*, 232) Hurrian ***kuduni*** [Boğ] can be interpreted as the noun 'Nacken, Hals(?)' ['neck(?)'], cf. the form *ku-du-ni-ip*, KUB XXIX 8 III 39, analysis {*kuduni=v*}, form with the suffix of the possessive pronoun 2nd person singular ***-v***, 'your neck' (cf. also E. Laroche, *GLH*, 151, without translation). Perhaps ***kuduniwe*** [Lw/A: mA; Nuzi] 'Gespann' (Haas / Thiel 1978, 167); 'designation of yoke-team' (*CDA*^{2} [2000], 171 [HLW]), cf. Th. Richter, *BGH*, 232, can be explained as genitive singular {*kuduni=we*} 'of the neck'. Although the formation of Linear A ***ku-do-ni*** seems to correspond with Hurrian ***kuduni*** 'neck(?)', identification as an ethnic name (or an ethnic name used as a personal name) seems preferable because of the close correspondence with *Κύδων, Κύδωνες Κυδωνίᾱ* and *Κυδώνιος* in Crete and the cognate forms in Linear B. Linear A ***ku-do-ni*** (HT 13.4; HT 85a.4) and probably ***ku-do-ni***[(HT 101.4) 'man of *Kuda*' correspond with the Hellenized ethnic ***Κύδων***. There is probably a correlation between the Linear A plural form ***]ku-do-na***|[(HT 64.1) 'men of *Kuda*' and the plural Hellenized ethnic ***Κύδωνες***.

The Linear B toponym ***ku-do-ni-ja*** (KN Co 904,1; KN C 59,3; KN G 820,1, *et al.*) signifies the place or region ***Κυδωνίᾱ***, later attested as toponym in Crete, derived from the ethnic ***Κύδωνες***. Linear B ***ku-do-ni-ja-de*** (KN L 588, 3) provides the accusative of that toponym with the directive suffix ***-δε***. No doubt Linear B]***ku-do-ni-jo***[(KN X 169) represents the adjective ***Κυδώνιος***, cf. C.J. Ruijgh, *EGM*, § 143.

Inflexional Indo-European languages such as Greek differ basically from agglutinative languages such as Hurrian, so it seems *prima facie* accidental that the Hurrian *directive* suffix ***-da*** resembles the ancient Greek *directive* suffix ***-δε***, particularly since it seems likely that morphological features are less susceptible to transmission from one language into another than, for instance, names of commodities. However, the fact that the Hurrian ablative suffix ***-dan*** 'from' (as in Linear A ***i-da-da***, probably ***Ida=dan*** 'from Mount Ida) also resembles the Greek ablative suffix ***-θεν*** (in ***Ἴδηθεν***, *Iliad* Γ 276, 'from Mount Ida') makes accidental correspondence less likely. Moreover, suffixes such as ***-δε*** and ***-θεν*** are basically anomalous in an inflexional language such as Greek and were largely replaced by prepositions, but they are characteristic for an agglutinative language such as Hurrian. But miracles can happen. For instance, *Κωνσταντινούπολις*, the former *city of Constantine* is now called *Istanbul*. This toponym is derived from *είς τὴν πόλιν* 'to the city'.

The Linear A personal name]***ku-du-we*** (HT? 170a.2) means 'of *Kuda*', analysis {*kud(a)=u=we*}, genitive of toponym or anthroponym ***Ku-da*** (HT 122a.8); ***-u-*** in ***-du-*** is probably due to influence from following ***-w-*** of the genitive suffix ***-we***,.

The same phenomenon can be observed in Linear B e.g. in ***e-nu-wa-ri-jo*** (KN V 52+52bis + [X] 8285,2, join by J.-P. Olivier), theonym in Linear B, ***Ἐνῡαλίῳ***, dative of ***Ἐνῡάλιος***, next to ***e-nwa-ri-jo*** (PY An 724,12). C.J. Ruijgh, *EGM*, § 91, assumes that ***Ἐνῡάλιος*** is derived from a Pre-Hellenic root **Ἐνῡάλο-* (cf. type *Δαίδαλος*), itself derived from a root ****Ἐνῡ-***, cf. the feminine theonym ***Ἐνῡώ*** and the anthroponym ***Ἐνῡεύς*** in Homer. Homer's *Iliad* B 651 offers *Ἐνυαλίῳ ἀνδρειφόντῃ* 'Enyalios, slayer of men', cf. also A. Fournet, *Ἐνυάλιος ἀνδρεϊφόντης*. Poetical code-switching between Hurrian and Greek, *The Macro-Comparitive Journal, Thematic Issue No. 2*, 1-4.

According to A. Fournet *Ἐνυάλιος* contains Hurrian ***eni*** 'God' and the Hurrian verbal root ****wal-*** that he equates with the well-known Hurrian root ***ull-*** 'to destroy'. Greek *ἀνδρεϊφόντης* would then be a translation of the Hurrian compound, cf. e.g. Th. Richter, *BGH*, 486, s.v. ***ull-*** [Boğ.; Mitt.; PN] 'détruire', 'zerstören, unterdrücken, bekämpfen', 'to destroy'. An equation of ***ull-*** with ****wal-*** is not mentioned by Th. Richter, *BGH* and *VHN*, but the hypothesis is worth mentioning. Hurrian ***ull-*** and ***ulluḫ-*** correspond with Akkadian ***kalû*** 'zurückhalten' ['to hold back'] and Hittite ***arḫa anš-*** 'abwischen' ['to clean(se) off'], ***arḫa dā-*** 'wegnehmen' ['to take away'] and ***katta tamašš-*** 'unterdrücken, niederdrücken' ['to oppress'] and Urartian ***ul(u)-*** (trans.) 'to destroy', (intr.) 'to perish'.

Linear A]***ku-du-we*** (HT? 170a.2) and ***te-we*** (HT? 170a.3) are both personal names, since their position can be compared with that of ***we-ru-ma-ti*** (HT? 170a.4).

Linear A ***te-we*** (HT? 170a.3) can be identified as a 'one-word' personal name with the meaning 'Speak (oh child) !' or 'Say names (oh *numen*) !', analysed as an *imperative* 2nd person singular {*tew-e/i*} of the Hurrian verb ***ti-*** I, ***tiw-*** I [*passim*] 'sprechen' ['to speak'], cf. ***tiwe*** 'Wort, Sache' ['word, thing'], theonym ***Ti(ja)-pa/enti*** 'Er spricht das Gute' ['He says the right things / He procures justice'], cf. Th. Richter, *BGH*, 453-455. Cf. also Th. Richter (*VHN*, 534-535), s.v. ***ti-/te-*** and ***ti-***, ***tiw-*** 'sprechen' and personal names such as ***Tieš-Šimika*** at Nuzi (cf. I.J. Gelb, *NPN*, 155): 'May (the Sun-god) *Šimika* speak'.

We may also compare the Linear A inscription ***te-we-mi*** (↓) (PS Zf 1), read from top to bottom, among the repoussé designs on a bronze tablet from the Dictaean Cave of Psykhro, discussed in *chapter 11: 'Religious' Linear A inscriptions*.

The form ***te-we-mi*** (↓) can be analysed as {*tew-ermi*}, 'speak, oh Lord !', consisting of ***ti-/te- / tiw-/tew-*** 'to speak, say words' + ***ermi*** = ***erwi/ewri*** 'Lord'. The element ***-e-mi*** can be interpreted as ***-ermi***, because ***-r-*** preceding ***-m-*** is not expressed in Linear A and B consonant clusters. The *imperative* 'speak, oh Lord !' may well reflect the prayer pronounced by the dancing supplicant / worshipper portrayed on the tablet.

Linear A]***ku-du-we*** (HT? 170a.2) is a personal name with the genitive suffix ***-we*** 'of *Kuda*'. Even if Linear A ***ku-da*** (HT 122a.8) is an anthroponym and not a toponym, the existence of a toponym ***ku-da*** seems very likely, since the Linear A ethnics ***ku-do-ni*** 'the one of *Kuda*' (HT 13.4; HT 85a.4) and]***ku-do-na***|[(HT 64.1) 'men of *Kuda*' are attested.

At first sight a personal name]***ku-du-we*** (HT? 170a.2) in the genitive seems odd, but names in the genitive may have a *possessive* meaning 'belonging to' or a *patronymic* or *metronymic* force 'son or daughter of'. Th. Richter (*VHN*, 620-621) gives many examples of these names in a special category 3.2.2: *Names extended with the genitive morpheme*. Subcategories 3.2.2.1: *Free genitives*; 3.2.2.2: *patro- / metronymic names*. The genitive suffix of these names seems to have a relational value as relational suffix ***-ni***.

Th. Richter (*BGH*, 231-232) mentions that on the basis of correspondences with Hittite ***mauš-*** and ***peššija-*** the Hurrian root ***kud-*** can (since E. Neu 1988a, 31 ; 1988e, 105, 109) be interpreted as (intr.) 'to fall', (trans.) 'to drop, to smash down'. I. Wegner (*Einführung*, 138, 265): (intr.) 'to fall', (trans.) 'to smash down, to throw down'.

Th. Richter (*VHN*, 452), s.v. ***kud-/kutt-***, points out that the verbal personal names with ***kud-*** (intr.) 'fallen' ['to fall'], (trans.) 'fallen lassen, fällen, zu Fall bringen' ['to drop, to smash down'] are indeed analogous with Hittite ***mauš-***, that in context can mean 'fallen lassen' ['to drop'] in the sense of 'gebären' ['to give birth to'] and that Akkadian ***maqātum*** seems to have the same connotation.

Interestingly the root ***kud-/kutt-*** appears to have a special meaning in personal names close to that of the Hurrian root ***ḫan-*** 'to give birth to', from which the toponym *Khania* may well be derived (Hurrian ***Ḫania*** {*ḫan=i=a*} 'He / She (a God / Goddess or the King) gives/gave birth to, creates/created (the Palace)'. *Κυδωνίᾱ* is now usually identified with modern Khania, but the many (fragments of) tablets, roundels and noduli which have to date been discovered in the rescue excavations at Khania have not yet confirmed this identification.

However, I do not believe that *Khania* can be identified with Linear B ***ku-do-ni-ja*** (KN Co 904,1; KN C 59,3; KN G 820,1, *et al.*) ***Κυδωνίᾱ***, derived from the ethnic *Κύδωνες* and attested as a toponym in Crete, because Linear A ***ku-da***, ***ku-do-ni***,]***ku-do-na***|[and]***ku-du-we*** are all attested at Hagia Triada, not at Khania, and the Linear B toponym and ethnics come of course from Knossos.

Moreover, Homer's *Odyssey γ* 292 mentions *ἧχι Κύδωνες ἔναιον Ἰαρδάνου ἀμφὶ ῥέεθρα* 'where the Kydonians lived on both sides of the streams of the Iardanos', in the region of Gortyn (*Γόρτυν, Γόρτυνς, Γόρτυς*) in the Messara valley in Crete. The name of the *Ἰάρδανος* recalls the Jordan in Palestine that is always called *hajjardēn* 'the river', with article, in the Old Testament (except *Job 40, 23* and *Ps 42, 7*). *Kydonia* may not only be the Mycenaean and Homeric name of the Messara valley, but also the Minoan name. Homer's *Ἰάρδανος* may be identified with the river Messara and the region (and / or city?) of the *Κύδωνες* must primarily be sought in the Messara valley.

Ἀχαιοί, Ἐτεόκρητες, Κύδωνες, Δωριέες and *Πελασγοί* are mentioned as inhabiting Crete in Homer's *Odyssey* τ 175-177. The Dorians are, no doubt, a post-Mycenaean interpolation. This passage provides no information on the exact location of the *Κύδωνες*.

Prima facie the term *κυδώνια μῆλα* or *μᾶλα* 'quince-apples' (Stesichorus, Alcman) and *κυδώνιαι μηλίδες* (Ibycus) 'quince-pears' (Pirus Cydonia) may have been derived from the name of the *Κύδωνες*, who may have grown these fruits, or *vice versa* the Kydonians may have been called after the fruits for which they were famous, but P. Chantraine, *Dictionnaire étymologique de la langue grecque*, 596, probably provides the right etymology: *κοδύ-μᾶλον* est la forme la plus anciennement attesté. C'est un arrangement, prenant l'aspect d'un composé (cf. *-μᾶλον*), d'un emprunt à l'Asie Mineure. Puis le grec a créé l'expression *κυδώνια μῆλα* d'après la ville de Kydonia en Crète (La Canée).

The Linear A sequence ***ki-ra*** (HT 103.5, SY Zb 7; ZA 8.1) is found in three sites, on Linear A clay tablets from the Palaces of Hagia Triada and Kato Zakro, but remarkably also on a fragment of a terracotta zoomorphic rhyton (MM IIIb - LM Ia ?) from the Peak Sanctuary of Hermes and Aphrodite at Symi Viannou, south area of the site of Krya Vrysi.

The inscription from Symi Viannou is also remarkable in another respect: If read from left to right, it starts with the sign of 1 unit followed by ***ra-ki* , *wa-ni-e***, which is odd, because units are usually mentioned after sequences. Moreover, sign ***ki*** shows a peculiarity, comparable with sign ***ki*** in the boustrophedon inscription ***ki-pa-a* , *u-na-a*** (KN Zb 40.1-2) from Knossos. Usually sign ***ki*** (which looks like a vessel or rhyton) has its handle on the left side, but here the handle is on the right side suggesting that the direction of reading is 'from right to left' ← (instead of 'from left to right' →). Therefore I propose to read the inscription from right to left: ***e-ni-wa* , *ki-ra*** 1, which offers not only an acceptable order of sequences followed by a number, but also sequences that make sense. If the reading of Linear A ***e-ni-wa*** is correct, it can be analysed as Hurrian:
1. {*eni=wa*} 'for God', consisting of ***eni*** 'God' + the suffix of the singular dative ***-wa***.
2. {*en(i)ni=wa*} 'for the God', consisting of ***eni*** 'God' + the suffix of the so-called singular definite article ***-ni-*** + the suffix of the singular dative ***-wa***.
3. {*en(i)=iwwâš*} contracted form < {*en(i)=iwwa=aš*} 'Our God', consisting of ***eni*** 'God' + the suffix of the possessive pronoun 1st person singular ***-iwwa-/-iwwe-/-iwwə-*** + the pluralizing suffix ***-aš***. N.B. ***-iwwa/e/ə-*** may phonologically be ***/-iffa/e/ə-/***, cf. I. Wegner, *Einführung*, 62-63. Analysis 1 or 2 seems to make more sense than analysis 3 because of following ***ki-ra*** 1 = 'one freedman / one freed woman for (the) God'.

Linear A ***ki-ra*** (HT 103.5) at Hagia Triada is followed by 5 units and a fraction. It is clearly a personal name belonging to a list of personal names. Linear A ***ki-ra*** (ZA 8.1) at Kato Zakro is the first entry of the tablet. The first line reads: ***ki-ra* , *a-ta-re*** , FIC J. The following lines 2-6 contain personal names followed by signs of units and/or fractions.

In the 2016 edition I wrote: "Linear A ***ki-ra*** may be interpreted as the Hurrian personal name ***Kirra-n*** (with ***-n*** suffix), also occurring on tablet *AT 262.4 from Alalaḫ VII, cf. A. Draffkorn, *HHA*, 39, s.v. ***Kirran***, hypocoristic **Ki-ir-ra-an* *262:4. [N.B. * is used by D.J. Wiseman and A. Draffkorn to indicate that the names marked in this way belong to tablets found in the older layer of Level VII at Alalaḫ, whereas the names without * are found in the younger Level IV. So * does not indicate that these names are hypothetical.]

The final ***-n*** in ***Kirran*** provides no problem identifying this name with Linear A ***ki-ra***, since a final consonant is never expressed in the scripts of Linear A and B.

Other personal names at Alalaḫ with the element ***kirr-*** are: ***Kirra-zi*** (*AT 205.3: **Ki-ra-zi*); ***Kirri*** (*AT 8.39; *AT 241.16: **Ki-ir-ri*); ***Kirri-ya*** (hypocoristic) (AT 68.3: *Gi-ri-ya*; AT 181.20: *ki-ri-ya* (both without asterisk, so both from the younger layer IV of Alalaḫ), cf. A. Draffkorn, *HHA*, 39 and 84. At Nuzi occur ***Kirrazi*** (wr. *ᶠKi-i*[*r-r*]*a-zi*) TCL IX 22:26 (see *ᶠKeraše*), ***Kirriịa*** (wr. *Ki-ir-ri-ia*, *Ki-ri-ia*), ***Kirruka*** (wr. *Ki-ir-ru-qa*, *Ki-ru-ú-qa*), ***Kirrukazzi*** (wr. *Ki-ir-ru-ka-*[*az*]*-zi*, *Ki-ir-ru-qa-az-zi*), ***Kirruke*** (wr. *Ki-ir-ru-ge*), *šangû*. Cf. P.M. Purves, *NPN*, 228, s.v. ***kirr***.

Since Linear A ***ra*** can also be read as ***la***, the sequence could also be interpreted as ***Ki-lá*** or ***Ki-il-la*** (cf. E. Laroche, *NH*, 93, n° 574, s.v. ***Kella***, 1. Cappadocia: *Ki-lá*, MAH 16205, 20 (Garelli). 2. Prêtre de Nérik: abs. ᵐ*Ke-el-la*, *Ki-il-la*, KBo III 7 I 1, III 34, IV 30. If these Cappadocian names are related to *Ki-il-li* from Nuzi, they probably may be marked as Hurrian, cf. P.M. Purves, *NPN*, 227, s.v. ***kil***, ***kill*** and ***killi***."

In modern research several roots can be distinguished that have to be considered: Th. Richter (*BGH*, 210-211) mentions ***ke/ir-*** I [Boğ.; PN(?)] 'heraus-, ent- freilassen' ['to release, liberate, manumit (slaves)']. In *VHN* (440) he mentions the same root sub ***kir-*** I / ***kirr-***. The meaning of this root has become clear since publication of the Hurrian-Hittite bilingual ***kirenze*** (KBo 32). Hurrian ***kirenze*** means 'release, liberation, manumission (of slaves)' and corresponds with Hittite ***parā tarnumar***, Akkadian ***(an)durārum*** and Hebrew ***derōr***. ***Kirenze*** is also the title and main subject of text KBo 32. It allegedly means 'a sort of debt-redemption' at Nuzi, cf. Th. Richter, *BGH*, 210-211, s.v. ***ke/ir-*** I [Boğ.; PN(?)] and ***kirenzi*** [Boğ.; Nuzi]. N.B. a certain vocalisation is made impossible by KI-*e-re-en-zé* (KBo 32, 19 Vs. I 11) and KI-*i-re-en-za-am-ma* (KBo 32, 15 Vs. I 4'), cf. Th. Richter, *VHN*, 440, note 430.

It has been mentioned before that several scholars have suggested that Linear A ***ki-ro***, occurring at least 14 times in Linear A, might represent a transactional term indicating 'deficit', equivalent to Linear B ***o-pe-ro*** = Mycenaean Greek ***ὄφελος*** 'debt'. Since Linear A and B sign ***ro*** can also be ***lo***, it was for a long time not clear, whether ***ki-ro*** or ***ki-lo*** should be read. On the basis of evidence from Nuzi and the Hurrian-Hittite bilingual text ***kirenze*** (KBo 32) from Boğazköy it can now definitely be confirmed that Linear A ***ki-ro*** indeed represents Hurrian ***kiro***, analysis {*kir=o*}.

I. Wegner (*Einführung*, 138) mentions in her section E *'Old Hurrian'* sub *'The jussive and other forms of mood in the bilingual'* the form ***kir=o*** (wr. *ki-i-ru*), KBo 32: 15 IV 3, which she translates as 'er soll freigelassen sein/werden' ['he must be set free / released / liberated / manumitted']. Wegner's translation is probably based on E. Neu's analysis of ***ki-ru-un-na***, analysis {*kir=u=nna*} 'er soll freigelassen werden' ['he must be set free, released, liberated, manumitted'], cf. E. Neu, Die hurritischen Pronomina der hurritisch-hethitischen Bilingue aus Ḫattuša, in: G. Beckman et alii (eds.), *Hittite studies in honor of Harry A. Hoffner Jr. on the occasion of his 65th birthday*, Eisenbrauns 2003, 300; cf. also Th. Richter, *BGH*, 210. Th. Richter (*VHN*, 594-595) explains sub 1.3.1.1.2.1, *normal forms*, that the forms in ***°utta***, ***°unna***, ***°ulla*** probably contain the suffixes of the absolutive enclitic personal pronouns ***-tta*** (1st person singular), ***-nna***, (3rd person sg.), ***-lla*** (3rd person plur.), indicating the *absolutive* object of the transitive verb.

Paradigmatic is the form ***ki-ru-un-na*** in the Hurrian-Hittite bilingual ***Kirenze*** KBo 32, 15 Rs. IV 2, and the parallel formation ***[k]i-ru-un*** in 53 1. Kol. 4' (both Ḫattuša) that can probably be translated as 'release him, set him free, manumit him', containing the verbal root ***kir-*** 'to release, set free, manumit' + the thematic vowel ***-u/o-*** + the suffix of the enclitic personal pronoun ***-nna*** and the shortened form ***-n***, respectively, cf. also *VHN*, 440, s.v. ***kir-*** I / ***kirr-***.

There is no semantical distinction between '*he must be set free, released, liberated, manumitted*' and '*release him, set him free, manumit him*', but morphologically there is, since there is allegedly no passive paradigm in Hurrian as the most recent research in Hurrian studies suggests. Therefore Th. Richter's translation in *VHN* is to be preferred.

In view of Th. Richter's transitive translation of ***ki-ru-un-na*** and ***[k]i-ru-un*** 'release him, set him free, manumit him' (KBo 32), and his interpretation (*VHN*, 166) of the Hurrian personal name ***Kirru*** (wr. *ki-ir-ru*) at Mari, analysis {*kirr=o*}, typology 1.3.1.1.1, lexicon *kirr-*, translation 'Lasse (Jungen) frei (oh *Numen*) !' ['Set (the boy) free, Release, Manumit (the boy) (oh *numen*) !'], I consider an *antipassive* interpretation preferable for this personal name (*antipassive* designates usage of a transitive verb without mentioning an object).

Actually Linear A ***ki-ru*** (MI Zb 1) also occurs as a single entry on a potsherd from Phylakopi on the island of Milos. It is now in the National Museum of Copenhagen (Inv. nr. 6960, 1898). Since it is the only entry on this potsherd, the context fails that might have shown, whether Linear A ***ki-ru*** should here be regarded as the verbal form attested in KBo 32: 15 IV 3: *ki-i-ru* {*kir=o*} 'set (the boy / girl) free, release, manumit (the boy / girl) (oh *numen*) !' or as a personal name with the same meaning.

Since final consonants are not expressed in Linear A and B, the Linear A form could also represent ***kir=u/o=n***, shortened form of ***ki-ru-un-na***, {*kir=u/o=nna*}, with the meaning 'set him/her free, release, manumit him/her !'. Th. Richter (*VHN*, 166) interprets the Hurrian personal name ***Kirru*** (wr. *ki-ir-ru*) at Mari, analysis {*kirr=o*}, typology 1.3.1.1.1, lexicon *kirr-*, as 'Lasse (Jungen) frei, (oh *Numen*) !' ['Set (the boy) free, Release, Manumit (the boy) (oh *numen*) !']. However, according to R. Pruzsinsky (*Die Personennamen der Texte aus Emar*, *SCCNH 13*, Bethesda 2003, 243^{+184}) the personal names ***Kirra*** and ***Kirru*** may be interpreted as 'Freigelassener (?)' ['Freedman, Freed woman (?)'], cf. Th. Richter, *BGH*, 211.

It is also conceivable that ***ki-ru*** (MI Zb 1) on the potsherd from Phylakopi has exactly the same economic function as Linear A ***ki-ro*** has on the Linear A clay tablets.

In accordance with the usage at Nuzi (and probably also in the bureaucratic setting of the Minoan palace administration expressed through the Linear A tablets) Hurrian ***kir=o***, exact equivalent to Linear A ***ki-ro***, probably means 'redeem (the debt) !' or 'he must redeem (the debt)'. An advantage is that this *antipassive* usage avoids a (medio-)passive translation. Here should be added again: Since final consonants are not expressed in Linear A and B, the Linear A form could also represent ***kir=u/o=n***, shortened form of ***ki-ru-un-na***, {*kir=u/o=nna*}, with the meaning 'redeem it [*-n(na)*] (namely the debt) !' or 'he must redeem it (namely the debt)'. Since ***=n(na)*** is the object, the form ***kir=u/o=n*** is not antipassive. Monosyllabic ***ki*** may well be a frequent abbreviation of Linear A ***ki-ro***.

This specific verbal form ***ki-ro*** provides a very adequate meaning of the term in the context of the Linear A tablets, especially since it is equivalent to Linear B ***o-pe-ro*** = Mycenaean Greek ***ὄφελος*** 'debt', e.g. at Pylos: *pe-ru-si-nu-wo , o-pe-ro = περυσινϝὸν ὄφελος* 'the debt of last year' (PY Ma 216, 3; PY Ma 330, 2; PY Ma 378, 2; PY Ma 397 [+] 1048, 2); *ὄφελος* from *ὀφείλω < *ὀφέλ-yω* 'to owe someone something'. Also interesting is at Knossos Linear B tablet KN Ga 1530 + 1531, that registers the delivery, ***a-pu-do-si = ἀπύδοσις*** (Att. *ἀπόδοσις*), of aromatics with regard to some ethnic people. First the total is mentioned: ***to-sa*** AROMA 58 = ***τόσ(σ)α*** = so many (plural neuter) AROMA 58 (line 6). Then ***to-sa-de / o-pe-ro*** AROMA 31, i.e. the total of the debt: ***τόσ(σ)α δὲ ὄφελος*** AROMA 31 (line 7).

It is conceivable that Linear A ***ki-ra*** (SY Zb 7), analysis ***kir(r)=a***, can be interpreted as intransitive *indicative* 'he/she is free' or intransitive *imperative* 'be free !'. However, as just mentioned, according to R. Pruzsinsky (*Die Personennamen der Texte aus Emar*, *SCCNH 13*, Bethesda 2003, 243[+184]) the personal names ***Kirra*** and ***Kirru*** may be interpreted as 'Freedman, Freed woman (?)' as well.

Accordingly I propose that Linear A ***e-ni-wa*** **,** ***ki-ra*** 1 (SY Zb 7) from Symi Viannou can be analysed as {*en=i=wa , kir(r)=a*} and interpreted as 'one freedman / freed woman for God' or as {*en(=i)=ni=wa , kir(r)=a*} 'one freedman / freed woman for the God'.

I propose that Linear A ***ki-ra*** (HT 103.5) from Hagia Triada that certainly is a personal name, can be interpreted likewise as 'Freedman, Freed woman'. Since a final consonant is not expressed in Linear A and B, Linear A ***ki-ra*** (HT 103.5) can also represent the personal name ***Kirran***, attested at Alalaḫ VII, wr. **Ki-ir-ra-an* (AT *262:4), that can now be analysed as {*kirr=a=n(na)*}, 'He/She is Freedman /Freed woman'.

Linear A ***ki-ra*** **,** ***a-ta-re*** **,** FIC J (ZA 8.1) from Kato Zakro may be interpreted as 'freedman', ***Aštare*** or ***Attare***, J portion figs. So ***Aštare*** or ***Attare*** may be the name of the freedman. See for a possible interpretation of Linear A ***a-ta-re*** *infra*. Th. Richter (*VHN*, 440) attributes the following names to ***kir-*** I/***kirr-*** (a) {***kir-***}: *Kirija* (Šubat-Enlil); *Kirip-Aranziḫ* (Mari, Tigunāni); *Kirip-atal* (Mari); *ᶠKirip-elli* (Ašnakkum); *Kirip-ewri* (Mari); *Kirip-Kalli* (Tigunāni); *Kirip-šarri* (Mari); *Kirip-šenni* (Mari); *Kirip-Šerriš* (Mari, Šubat-Enlil); *Kirip-Teššup* (Mari); *Kirip-ulme* (Ašnakkum, Mari); *Kir-tuk* (Tigunāni).
(b) {***kirr-***}: *Kirri* (Ašnakkum, Mari); *Kirru* (Mari) and some incomplete names.

Th. Richter (*BGH*, 211-212) mentions s.v. ***ke/ir-*** II [Boğ.; PN(?)] 'andauernd' ['long, lasting'] and 'lang, dauerhaft sein' ['to last for a long time'] and (*VHN*, 440) s.v. ***ker-*** II, *intransitive* 'lang sein' ['to last for a long time'], *transitive* 'lang machen' ['to prolong'], and ***keraš(š)e*** 'lang, dauerhaft' ['long, lasting'] and *ke-ri-(iz-)zi/zu* 'Länge' ['length'], also used in names: (1) {*keraššе*}:***ᶠKerazze*** (Mari). (2) {*kerišše*}: ***Kerizze*** (Mari); ***Kerizzu*** (Mari). ***Kirra-zi*** (*AT 205.3: **Ki-ra-zi*) at Alalaḫ, cf. A. Draffkorn, *HHA*, 39, 84.

Th. Richter (*BGH*, 212) mentions s.v. ***kir-*** III [PN(?)] 'acht (sein)' ['(to be) eight'] and (*VHN*, 440), s.v. ***ker-*** III, intransitive 'acht (sein)' ['(to be) eight'], transitive 'acht vorhanden sein lassen' ['to provide eight'], which could be explained as 'to deliver the eighth child'. However, Richter considers it unlikely that verbalized numerals played an important role in Hurrian personal names, cf. Th. Richter, *VHN*, 440, note 432.

On the other hand ***kirari*** is the Hurrian name of a month at Alalah VII and IV, Emar, Mari and Tuttul, but it is not clear whether it refers to the eighth month of the year.

(EZEN$_4$.)***kirariš*** (name of a festival) is considered a loan-word in Hittite, see for more information Th. Richter, *BGH*, 213, s.v. ***kirari***. According to G. Wilhelm (Nuzi Note 18: A new word in *-arbu*: *kirarbu*, *Studies on the civilization and culture of Nuzi and the Hurrians 8 (1996)*, 347) ***kirarbu*** means 'eight years old'. According to Th. Richter (*BGH*, 212, s.v. ***kir-*** III) the ending ***-u*** in ***kirarbu*** is an Akkadianizing nominative.

Since Linear A and B sign ***ra*** can also be ***la***, we must consider the possibility that Linear A ***ki-ra*** represents ***ki-la***. Th. Richter (*BGH*, 202-204) offers s.v. ***kel-*** I, also *kell-* (?) [*passim*], also ***kil-*** in Ugarit, the intransitive meaning 'aller bien, être en bon état' (E. Laroche, *GLH*, 142-143, s.v. ***kelu-***), 'sich wohl befinden', 'wohl sein', 'to be well', transitive 'befriedigen', 'zufrieden machen', 'faire prospérer', 'to please, make well', 'to satisfy', 'to heal'. Th. Richter prefers (more frequent) ***kel-*** instead of ***kil-***, but admits that in some names, even in case of reference to the same persons, an alternation of [EL] and [IL] occurs, e.g. in ***Kelze*** (Mari 5), ***Kelzu*** (Mari 1), ^{f}***Kelzuzzi*** (Mari 1), see Th. Richter, *VHN*, 435, s.v. ***kel-/kell-***, note 409. The root fits well in personal names [*passim*]. The root is no doubt also found in ***keldi*** 'Gesundheid' ['health'], 'Wohlbefinden' ['wellbeing, comfort']. The theonym or *numen* (divine power) ^{d}***Keldi*** is in the tradition of Ḫattuša, and probably also at Ugarit and Emar, the son of Aya, cf. Th. Richter, *VHN*, $436^{+413-414}$.

Th. Richter (*BGH*, 204-205) also offers s.v. ***ke/il-*** II (*transitive*) '(é)lever, hausser' ['to lift (up), to raise, to elevate'], (*intr.*) 's'élever, se hisser' ['to rise (to a higher level)'].

C.H. Gordon (*Evidence for the Minoan language*, Ventnor N.J. 1966, 32, sub n° 132) compared ***ki-re-ta-na*** (HT 2.3; HT 8a.5; HT 108.1; HT 120.4-5) from Hagia Triada with alphabetic cuneiform ***Krtn*** at Ugarit. However, ***ki-re-ta-na*** does probably not match with Ugaritic hypocoristic ***krtn***, because hypocoristic alphabetic cuneiform ***-n*** does not correspond to Ugaritic syllabic cuneiform ****-na***, but to syllabic cuneiform ***-nu***, cf. ***iln : illanu*** ?; ***b^{c}ln : ba^{c}alanu*** (cf. F. Gröndahl, *PNTU*, 54, § 91).

C.H. Gordon misread ***ki-re-86*** (HT 85b.1-2; HT 129.1) as † ***ki-re-tá*** and ***ki-ri-86*** (HT 114a.1; HT 121.1) as † ***ki-ri-tá*** and compared these sequences with alphabetic cuneiform ***Krt*** at Ugarit. He interpreted the forms as ***Kret*** (variants ***Krit, Kretan***), eponymous hero of Crete, worshipped as a divine king, mortal son of *El* and *Asherah*.

Since Linear A sign ***L86*** is identical with Linear B sign ***66 = ta$_2$ = tia / tya***, ***ki-re-86*** (HT 85b.1-2; HT 129.1) should be read as ***ki-re-ta$_2$*** = ***ki-re-tia***, and ***ki-ri-86*** (HT 114a.1; HT 121.1) as ***ki-ri-ta$_2$*** = ***ki-ri-tia***. Linear A ***ki-re-ta$_2$*** = ***ki-re-tia*** and ***ki-ri-ta$_2$*** = ***ki-ri-tia*** cannot be compared with alphabetic cuneiform ***krt***, but may well match with the Ugaritic hypocoristic ***krty***, since alphabetic cuneiform ***-y*** corresponds with syllabic cuneiform ***-ya***, cf. ***ily : iliya*** and ***b^{c}ly : ba^{c}aliya*** (cf. F. Gröndahl, *ibidem*).

Although there are difficulties with regard to details of C.H. Gordon's comparisons between the *Krt*-epos of Ugarit and the eponymous hero of Crete, I think that they certainly have their merits. David's lifeguard ***k^{e}rētī*** has indeed been associated with ***Κρήτ-*** (in Semitic a vowel must be placed between ***k*** and ***r***, because Semitic words cannot start with a consonant cluster; ***-ī*** can be the old plural ending, later completely replaced by ***-īm***), but I am not convinced that ***Krt*** was originally West-Semitic as Gordon thought. If the name of the legendary founder of Mitanni, ***Kirta***, can be identified with Ugaritic ***Krt*** {*ke/ir=e/i=t(ta)*}, the name of ***Krt***'s bride ***Ḫurrai*** is suddenly revealing.

Kirta may well have a Hurrian etymology, if it is analysed as *{kir=(e/i=)(t)ta}*, consisting of the root ***kir(r)-*** (trans.) 'to liberate/release/manumit' and (intr.) 'to be free', + syncopated marker of the transitive imperative ***-e-/-i-*** + the enclitic personal pronoun 1st person sing. ***-tta*** marking the object of the transitive verb: 'Liberate / Release me !'.

Linear A ***ki-re-ta-na*** (HT 2.3; HT 8a.5; HT 108.1; HT 120.4-5) may be analysed as *{kir=et=t=a=nna}*, consisting of the root ***kir(r)-*** (trans.) 'to liberate', (intr.) 'to be free', + the marker of the future tense ***-ed-*** + the marker of the failing object ***-t-*** + marker of intransitivity ***-a-*** + the enclitic personal pronoun 3rd person singular ***-nna*** (cf. I. Wegner, *Einführung*, 99, tables 6-7), translation: 'He will be free'. According to I. Wegner the marker of the absolutive enclitic personal pronoun 3rd person singular ***-nna***, indicating the subject of the intransitive verb, can be left out. But since the form *{*kir=et=t=a}* 'He will be free' can be confused with *{kir=e/i=tta}* 'Liberate me !', the scribe may have decided to use the spelling ***ki-re-ta-na*** in order to show that *{kir=et=t=a=nna}* 'He will be free' was meant (***=nna*** emphasizes 'he'), but ***ki-re-ta-na*** can also be analysed as transitive *{kir=et=(i)t=a=nna}* 'They (the gods) will liberate him/her', consisting of the root ***kir-*** 'to liberate' + the marker of the future tense ***-ed-/-id-*** + the pluralizer ***-(i)t-*** instead of ***=š(a)-*** (cf. I. Wegner, *Einführung*, 91-92) + thematic ***-a-*** before a next formant, the enclitic personal pronoun 3rd person singular ***-nna*** 'him/her', that refers to the child.

Linear A ***ki-re-tya/tia*** (HT 85b.1-2; HT 129.1) and ***ki-ri-tya/tia*** (HT 114a.1; HT 121.1) can *prima facie* be analysed as *{kir=e/i=tti=an}* 'And liberate me !', consisting of the root ***kir(r)-*** 'to liberate / release / manumit' + marker of the transitive imperative ***-e-/-i-*** + marker of the optional allomorphic enclitic personal pronoun 1st person singular ***-tti*** (instead of ***-tta***) + the enclitic syntactical particle ***-an*** 'and'. This formation would be possible at the end of a sentence, but usage of the enclitic syntactical particle ***-an*** 'and' is odd in a personal name, certainly if it is the first sequence. So *{kir=et=(i)t=ya}* 'They (the gods) will liberate (the child)' conform Ugaritic hypocoristic ***krty*** is preferable.

Linear A ***ta-ti*** 21 (HT 26a.2) precedes ***mi-ki-|se-na*** 15 (HT 26a.2-3) and ***ta-ti*** 2 (HT 97a.5) at Hagia Triada occurs in a list of personal names with Hurrian ***ma-di*** (HT 97a.4) 'wisdom'. The name ***ta-ti*** is probably derived from the Hurrian verbal root ***tad- / tatt-*** 'to love' and ***tadi*** and ***tatti*** in onomastics may well mean 'love' or 'darling'. One may perhaps also compare Linear A ***ta-ta*** (KH 7a.3) = Hurrian ***Tatta***. The Hurrian feminine name ***^{f}Allai-tatta*** from Nuzi (wr. *^{f}Al-la-i-ta-at-ta*), phonologically ***/Allai-datta/*** because of single writing of the first dental, probably contains the same element ***-tatta***, derived from the root ***dad-/tad-/datt-/tatt-***. The final ***-a*** of Linear A ***ta-ta*** and of Hurrian ***Tatta*** and ***Allai-tatta*** from Nuzi may indicate the *essive* case, so that Linear A ***ta-ta*** and Hurrian ***Tatta*** could mean 'He/she (the child) is like a darling' and ***Allai-tatta*** could mean 'The Lady is like a darling'. The same applies to other names with the element ***-tatta*** (phonologically ***/datta/***): e.g. names from Nippur ***Ir-me/mi-ta-at-ta*** and ***Ir-me-ta-ta***, Clay, *PNCP*, 93, to be read ***Erme/i-tatta*** (according to P.M. Purves, *NPN*, 263, s.v. *tatt*), i.e. ****Erwi-tatta***. Cf. also ***Ta-at-ta***, *ibid.*, 138, and ***Ta-ad-du*** at Nuzi, as well as ⌈***ta***⌉***-ad-du*** at Boğazköy KUB XXVII 42 obv. 15, 16. Although the variants ***Ir-me/mi-ta-at-ta*** and ***Ir-me-ta-ta*** from Nippur had shown that the roots ***tad-*** 'to love' and ***tatt-*** might be brought together, my hesitations disappeared after publication of ***tad- / tatt-*** (Th. Richter, *VHN*, 533-534).

In *BGH*, 2012, 451, s.v. ***tad-*** [*passim*] he had (almost casually) referred to the variant ***tatt-*** in his *Ergänzungen zum hurritischen Wörterbuch, Altorientalische Forschungen 34 (2007)*, 92[60]. Th. Richter (*VHN*, 533-534), s.v. ***tad- / tatt-***, confirmed that starting from the variant ***ta-at-t*** *º* for ***tadubadi*** one may assume that other forms in ***tatt-*** may be connected as well. He also refers (note 789) to another comparable verbal root ***tid-*** 'to attack' that also occurs as ***titt-*** (cf. *BGH*, 464), which is interesting for the interpretation of Linear A ***ti-ti-ku*** (2 times) and ***ti-ti-ku-ni*** in Linear A.

The variant root ***tatt-*** occurs frequently: e.g. ***Tattip-papni*** (wr. *ta-at-ti-ip-pa-ap-ni*), analysis {*tatt=i=b-fabni*} at Nuzi (cf. I.J. Gelb, *NPN*, 150); ^{f}***Tattiri*** (wr. ^{f}*ta-at-te-ri*), {*tatt=i=ri*} (Ekalte: WVDOG 192, 75: 19) that may be interesting for a Hurrian interpretation of Linear A ***da-ta-re*** (HT 88.6) and ***da-ta-ra*** (HT 6a.1) from Hagia Triada.

A. Draffkorn (*HHA*, 55-56) mentioned ***Tat(t)e*** (wr. *ta-at-te*) from Alalaḫ IV (194: 12), which she interpreted as hypocoristic (< *Tad-te*), and ^{f}***Tat(t)eya*** (wr. *^{f}*Ta-at-te-e-ya*), son of Yarim-Lim (?) from Alalaḫ VII (*11:2, 12, 20), which she interpreted as hypocoristic (< *Tad-teya*). She may well be right in both cases, because ***-te*** and ***-teya*** are very frequent hypocoristic forms of ***-teš(š)ub*** in Hurrian personal names, but Th. Richter (*VHN*, 533-534) has a good point assuming that the very frequent notion ***tatti*** may well be equated with ***tadi*** 'Liebe' ['love'] and that it may in onomastics mean 'Liebling' ['Beloved one, darling']. Consequently he translates ^{f}***Akap-tati*** {*ag=a=b-tadi*} as 'Der Liebling (das neugeborenes Mädchen) kam herauf (?)' ['The darling (the newborn girl) came up, appeared (?)'] and ^{f}***Taka-tati*** (Mari) as 'Sei (oder: werde) schön, oh Liebling !' ['Be (or: become) beautiful, oh darling !']. In that case a diminutive ***tadakki*** {*tad(i)=a(=)kki*} is also plausible in ^{f}***Tatakka***(?). The meaning would be 'Little darling'.

Linear A ***mi-ki|-se-na*** (HT 26a.2-3) is a personal name, probably with the same elements ***miki-*** or ***milki-*** as in ***|mi-ki-sa-ne[*** (AK la.6). The first element in ***mi-ki|-se-na*** (HT 26a.2-3) could be the Hurrian onomastic element ***mikki-*** as in ***Mikkiḭa*** (wr. *Mi-ik-ki-ja, Mi-ki-ja* and *Mi-gi-i[a]*) at Nuzi. with hypocoristic suffix ***-ya***. One may also compare the personal name *Me-ek-ka-an* from Ašnakkum, formerly referred to as Chagar Bazar, cf. P.M. Purves, *NPN*, 234, s.v. ***mikk***.

If we accept that the orthographic conventions of Linear B may also be applied to Linear A, since they were inherited from Linear A, interpretation of Hurrian ***Milki-šena*** is possible as well, since ***-l-*** preceding ***-k-*** is not expressed in consonant clusters in Linear A and B.

E. Laroche (*GLH*, 170) mentions s.v. ***Melku***: "RS quadr. 137 IVa 15: sum. ^{d}TIŠPAK = h. *mi-il-ku-un-ni* = oug. *gašaru*; *ib*. IVb 12, 14: *mi-il-ku-un* = *gašaru*. - Nom divin *Melku/Milku* à Boğ. et Msk.: hitt. ^{d}*Mi-el-ku-uš*, KUB XII 2 I 20; XXXVIII 16, 9; graphie ^{d}IŠ-*ku-uš* = *Milkuš* (HT 14, 10; KUB XXXVIII 6 I 12, 15, 23, III 5, IV 11, 21) d'après Msk. 74.102, 176: ^{d}*Mil*^{il}*-ku* (textes parallèles). Emprunt au sémitique ***mlk*** 'conseiller, ministre'; cf. ^{d}*Ma-lik*^{meš} = oug. *mlkm*, Panthéon d'Ugarit 32 = *Ugar. V*, 45, 60."

Th. Richter (*BGH*, 25), s.v. ***milgunni*** [Ug.]: "o.Ü. entspricht sum. ^{d}TIŠPAK, ugarit. *ga-š[a-ru]* (Laroche 1980a, 170); 'strong' (Huehnergard 1987a, 117; Pardee 1988, 89; Wyatt 1998, 837[15], Archi 2002, 50). Nach Laroche Lw. aus sem. ***mlk*** 'conseiller, ministre' ['counsellor, councillor, minister']."

Morphologically Hurrian *mi-il-ku-un-ni* has the appearance of an adjective in ***°-o=nni***, cf. I. Wegner, *Einführung*, 55, s.v. ***-o=nni***, e.g. ***mad=o=nni*** 'weise' ['wise'] from ***madi*** 'weisheit' ['wisdom']. I see, however, no obvious semantical correlation between ***milgunni*** 'strong' and Semitic ***mlk*** 'counsellor, councillor, minister'.

I mentioned in the 2016 edition of *Minoan Linear A*, Vol. I, that it is conceivable that ***mikk-*** developed from ***milk-*** through the process of assimilation (***-kk-*** < ***-lk-***). ***Milki-*** is allegedly originally borrowed from Semitic, but certainly very popular as element in Hurrian sentence names such as *Mil-ki-te-šup, Mil-ki-te-eš-šu-up, Mil-ki-dte-šup, En-na-mil-ki, E-en-na-mil-ki, E-na-mil-ki, En-na-mi-il-ki, E-na-mi-il-gi, A-ri-ip-mil-ku, Mil-ku-ma-tal* and *Mi-il-ku-ma-tal* at Nuzi; according to P.M. Purves ***milki-*** and ***milku-*** are grammatical variants, cf. I.J. Gelb, *NPN*, 97, and P.M. Purves, *NPN*, 234-235.

However, Th. Richter (*VHN*, 457) mentions, s.v. ***migi***, that the personal name ***fNan-miki*** (wr. *fNa-an-mi-gi*} from Mari may contain ***°-mi-gi***, that might also be found in the basic lexeme of the sacrificial term ***migiḫi*** (see also *BGH*, 250), {*mig(i)=i=ġe*}. Since he refers to the root ***mag-***, he seems to opt for an equation of ***mig-*** with ***mag-***. If this option is preferred, my hypothesis that ***mikk-*** might be derived from ***milk-/melk-*** through the process of assimilation is no longer tenable. It seems then also more likely that the roots ***milk-/melk-*** and ***mikk-/mig-/meg-*** have a different etymology, if the latter can be identified with ***mag-/meg-*** 'to give/offer as a present'. Anyway, with regard to Linear A ***mi-ki|-se-na*** (HT 26a.2-3) and ***|mi-ki-sa-ne[*** (AK la.6) we must conclude that Linear A and B orthographic conventions allow us to read either ***miki-*** or ***milki-***. The Minoan scribe no doubt knew, which of the two he had in mind, but we cannot be sure. We only know that both roots, ***mik(k)-*** and ***milk-***, were used as elements in Hurrian personal names.

Th. Richter (*VHN*, 189, 454) mentions, s.v. ***mag-/meg-***, the following personal names: ***fMakija*** [with variant ***fMekija***] (wr. *fMa-ki-ia; fMe-ki-ia*), name of 5 ladies at Mari, {*mag/meg=i=ja*}, typology 1.1.1.2.4, lexicon *mag-*, 'Er/Sie schenkte(?) (Mädchen)' ['He/She offered (the girl) as a gift'], cf. *Ma-ku-ia* at Nuzi; ***fMakunta*** (wr. *fMa-ku-un-da*) at Mari, analysis {*magond(i)=a*[E.]}, typology 3.2.1, lexicon *magundi*; ***fŠeḫrum-makuš*** (wr. *fŠe-eḫ-rum-ma-gu-úš*) at Ašnakkum, typology 1.1.1.1.1, {*šeġr=o=m-magoš(še)*}, lexicon *šeḫr-, magušše*, '*maguš* machte (Mädchen) großzügig' ['*maguš* made (the girl) (looking) great'].

If we choose verbal ***meg-/mig-*** (variant of ***mag-***) as first onomastic element, Linear A ***mi-ki|-se-na*** (HT 26a.2-3) can be analysed as {*me/ig=i-šena*}, translation 'Give a brother (oh *numen*) !' and Linear A ***|mi-ki-sa-ne[*** (AK la.6) can probably be analysed as a *jussive* or *optative* 'one-word' name {*me/ig=i=ž=a=nne*}, 'May he/she (a *numen*) give it [***-nne***] (*scil.* the child) !', cf. Th. Richter, *VHN*, 603, sub 1.3.2.2: verbal forms with ***°=i=ž***.

At Boğazkale the name ***Mukišanu*** is attested as 'Vizir de Kumarbi dans la mythologie hourro-hittite', KUB XXVII 1 II 19 et *passim*, *dMu-ú-ki-ša-nu-un*, Hourrite, KUB XLV 62 + IV 15, cf. E. Laroche, *GLH*, 172. It is not very likely that this name is a variant of Linear A ***|mi-ki-sa-ne[*** (AK la.6). If so, the range of vowels from ***muki-*** to ***miki-*** to ***megi-*** to ***magi-*** is very wide indeed. Probably too wide to be true. Moreover, if the analysis {*me/ig=i=z=a=nne*} offers a satisfactory interpretation of Linear A ***|mi-ki-sa-ne[***, there is no need for further speculation.

Incidentally, the issue of frequent alternation of ***-i-*** with ***-u-*** in Hurrian has been discussed by some scholars. F. Gröndahl (*PNTU*, 236, s.v. ***kindar***) mentions the personal name *turi*(DUMU)-*ki-in-da-ri* at Ugarit that was read as *bin-kindari* in PRU III 15.09-B-I-20, but corrected by C.H. Gordon, *RA 50 (1957)*, 132-133, on the basis of ***turi/tur-kindar*** at Nuzi (*NPN*, 227). She also proposes that ***kindari*** can be identified with ***kundari*** 'Göttergemach' ['Residence of the Gods'], cf. E. Laroche, PRU III, 333, and *GLH*, 154, s.v. ***kundari*** 'séjour des dieux'.

For the alternation ***i/u*** she refers to M. Berkooz, *The Nuzi Dialect of Akkadian*, Language Dissertations 23 (1937), 34-35, and to E.A. Speiser, *Introduction to Hurrian*, 22. E.A. Speiser's observations (*IH*, 22) may be pertinent: "Since Hurrian ***e***, or at least some forms of it, inclined toward [***i***], the question about the quality of Hurrian ***i*** is in order. Frequent interchange of ***i*** and ***u*** may throw some light on this point. Examples of this variation are given by Thureau-Dangin (*Syria 12* [1931] 262 - fr. Rš Voc.), Goetze, *Language 14 (1938)*, 139, n. 45, and Berkooz (*op. cit.* 34f. - Nuzi names); cf. also P.M. Purves, *AJSL 57 (1940)*, 175, n. 60. It is true that cases like *ti-bu-ša* (Rš Voc. I 21) and *tu-bu-e* (*ibid.* II 23), both from a root meaning 'strong' may indicate no more than a *Shwa* in the first syllable; but *I-ri-ya* alongside *I-ru-ya* (Berkooz, *o. c.* 35) cannot be dismissed on similar grounds. Berkooz draws the conclusion that an underlying sound [***ü***] may have to be assumed in such cases (*ibid.* 35). This assumption seems to be supported by the very interesting iuxta-position of *nu-i-wa$_a$-al-la* XXVII 42 rev. 12 and *nu-u-ya-al* XXIX 8 iii 30, in parallel contexts. The orthographic variants ***-uiwa-*** **:** ***-uuya-*** favor a sequence [***-ü-a***], or the like. If this supposition is correct, it is probable that Hurrian ***i*** in general was close to the sound [***ü***]. Note also especially the changes listed in [61] and for ***i/unu-***, cf. [127]." In note 38 he mentions: "Another case in point is *^{d}Na-ra-am-zu-un* XXVII 38 iii 18 for Akkadian *Narâm-Sin*. The variant is easily explained on the assumption that the Hurrians pronounced foreign [***i***] as [***ü***], which they would write either ***u*** or ***i***."

We now know that at least part of the forms with ***-u-*** can be ascribed to Old Hurrian.

The second element ***-šena*** of the name ***mi-ki|-se-na*** (HT 26a.2-3) is an ***a***-stem. The Alalaḫ tablets show that ***-šena*** can be found as second element in Hurrian personal names, e.g. AT 64.16: *Kaš-še-na,* and AT 252.15: *Pa-i-še-na*, cf. A. Draffkorn, *HHA,* 38, 45, 103. We may conclude on the basis of the long lists of Hurrian names with the nominal elements ***šena/šen*** and the shortened form ***-še*** at Nuzi and elsewhere that this was one of the most popular nominal onomastic elements, P.M. Purves, *NPN*, 253, s.v. ***še***, ***-še*** ; 255-256, s.v. ***šen***, ***šenna-***, ***šenni***, ***-šenni***. F.W. Bush, *GHL*, 85, sub 'elision of the stem vowel ***-a*** before ***-ne***': "Nominals which end in ***-a*** usually lose their stem vowel before the determining suffix ***-ne*** (and presumably ***-na***), e.g. ***tiθa-***, but ***tiθ-ne*** (Ug. S-H Voc. 2:27), ***θena-***, but ***θen-ne*** (common as a name element), etc." F.W. Bush transliterated ***šena-*** phonetically as ***θena-***. Since nobody else seems to follow his transliterations, I only use it, if I am citing his work. According to Th. Richter (*VHN*, 510-512) ***šena/šen*** and ***še*** 'Bruder' ['brother'] is one of the most frequent anthroponymic words. Its meaning has been known for a long time and is confirmed by comparison with Sumerian ŠEŠ and Akkadian ***aḫu*** (see *BGH*, 384-385, s.v. ***šena*** II [*passim*]). Shortened ***še*** often occurs and ***°-še-en-ni*** can be analysed as {*šen(a)=ni*} (***a***-stem + individualising suffix ***°=ni***).

Since the name |***mi-ki-sa-ne***[(AK la.6) is probably complete, because a dot can be discerned close to the edge of the fragment (The dot is actually visible on the photograph, cf. *GORILA 3*, 2), it is justifiable to investigate whether Linear A ***°-sa-ne*** can be equated with Hurrian ***Šane/Šani*** (wr. *Ša-a-ne/ni*) at Nuzi, father of *Er-wi-šarri*^{ri}, HSS IX 121: rev. 5, cf. I.J. Gelb, *NPN*, 124; P.M. Purves, *NPN*, 250, s.v. ***šan***, ***šani***, ***šani-*** and ***šann***, ***šann-***: Hurrian: *Ša-a-ni*. Cf. ***Sanie***, which can also be ***Sane***; on same basis ***šani*** is perhaps to be read *Ša-a-né*; ***Šani-šuḫ*** (wr. *Ša-ni-šu-uḫ*); ***Šann-apu*** (wr. *Ša-an-na-pu, Ša-an-na-a-pu*).

According to Th. Richter (*VHN*, 498), s.v. ***šan-***, the first element in ***Šan-mata*** (wr. *ša-an-ma-da*) from Ašnakkum and Mari, and in ^{f}***Šan(i)p-atal*** (wr. ^{f}*ša-a-an-ba-tal*) from Šubat-Enlil, may be the same as in the 'one-word' name *Ša-a-ni* at Nuzi (*NPN*, 124, *AAN I*, 118) and Kurruḫanni (Fadhil 1972, 99, nr. 26: 19). The sentence name *Ša?-na-tu-ri* at Kār-Tukultī Ninurta (*Mittelassyrische Rechts- und Verwaltungsurkunden 4*, 131 XI 21) probably contains ***turi*** 'man' and is possibly completely Hurrian. Some personal names at Ugarit with ***°-ša-na/nu*** may also fit in. But if the root ***šan-*** is verbal, as suggested by ^{f}***Šan(i)p-*** {*šan=i=b-*} in ^{f}***Šan(i)p-atal***, Hurrian ***-šane*** cannot be identified with ***-sa-ne*** in Linear A |***mi-ki-sa-ne***[(AK la.6), since a Hurrian name cannot contain two verbal forms at the same time. So analysis as a 'one-word' name {*me/ig=i=ž=a=nne*} is preferable.

I had followed the reading ***me-ki*** 3E (HT 6b.5) by J. Raison – M. Pope (1994, 47-48) in my *Corpus of transliterated Linear A texts*, but I now think that the small scratches, which led them to read ***me-*** are probably due to the fact that the text is palimpsest, so that I now prefer to read ***da-ki*** with *GORILA 1*. Both readings seem to provide acceptable Hurrian personal names. The subject has been explained in the discussion on ***da-ki***. Th. Richter (*VHN*, 189, 454 + note 489) mentions that there is no doubt about the existence of the verbally used root ***mag-/meg-***, but that the meaning 'schenken' ['to give as a present'], derived from ***maganni*** 'Geschenk' ['present, gift'] is not yet certain, cf. also Th. Richter, *BGH*, 238-239. At Mari the personal name ^{f}***Makija*** occurs with the writing variants ^{f}*Ma-ki-ja* and ^{f}*Me-ki-ja*, analysis {*mag/meg=i-ja*}, typology 1.1.1.2.4, translation 'Er/Sie (scil. ein *Numen*) schenkte(?) (Mädchen)' ['He/She (scil. a *numen*) gave(?) (the girl)'], and at Nuzi we find ***Mikkiịa*** with the variants *Mi-ik-ki-ia, Mi-ki-ia, Mi-gi-i*[*a*] and [*M*]*e-ek-ki-ia* (cf. I.J. Gelb, *NPN*, 97). Consequently, if Linear A ***me-ki*** (HT 6b.5) is the correct reading, the name can be analysed as an imperative {*mag/meg=i*} with the possible meaning 'Give (the child, oh *numen*) !'.

Both sides of tablet HT 10 provide lists of personal names. I shall now discuss some personal names on HT 10b. The first entry, ***u-ti*** (HT 10b.1), has already been discussed.

The second entry ***da-re*** (HT 10b.1) also occurs in HT 7a.4; HT 85a.5; HT 122b.4. Further we find either ***pa , da-re*** 16 J or ***pa-da-re*** 16 J (HT 10a.2) from Hagia Triada.

Linear A ***da-re*** (HT 10b.1) is followed by 2 units and is certainly one sequence. On the *a*-side of the tablet *GORILA 1* and Raison-Pope read ***pa , da-re*** 16 J (HT 10a.2), but it is not inconceivable that the little dot between ***pa*** and ***da-re*** is accidental, which makes reading ***pa-da-re*** 16 J possible. The advantage of reading ***pa-da-re*** is that ***da-re*** would otherwise occur twice on the same tablet (HT 10).

The whole text of PK 3 on a four-sided clay bar from Palaikastro is to be read from right to left. W.C. Brice reads]***pa$_3$-da-re*** and J. Raison – M. Pope read ' 72 ***re-da*** 31 ←.

I read ***pa₃-da-re*** (PK 3a.2 ←) in my *Corpus of transliterated Linear A texts*. L. Godart - J.-P. Olivier did not incorporate the bar in *GORILA 1*. They consider it hieroglyphic.

Monosyllabic ***pa*** 3J (HT 10a.2) may well be an abbreviation of ***parizi*** or ***parizzade / parissade*** [Boğ.] 'bushel' = half a kor = ca. 36,5 liter, discussed before.

If, however, ***pa-da-re*** (HT 10a.2) is one sequence and if ***pa₃-da-re*** (PK 3a.2 ←) is the correct reading, they may well be Hurrian personal names. Since ***-n-*** preceding a dental or other occlusive is not expressed in consonant clusters in Linear A (and B), ***pa-da-re*** and ***pa₃-da-re*** can be identified with the Hurrian *appellative* personal name ***Pandare/ri*** 'Cook', cf. Th. Richter, *BGH*, 293-295, s.v. ***p/wand-***, *p/wend-* I [*passim*] 'recht, good (sein), recht, richtig (sein / machen), (to be) right, etc.', and s.v. ***p/wandarinni*** [Boğ.]: "Since E. Neu (Varia Hurritica. Sprachliche Beobachtungen an der hurritisch-hethitischen Bilingue aus Ḫattuša, in: E. Neu - C. Rüster (eds.), *Documentum Asiae Minoris Antiquae*, Festschrift für Heinrich Otten zum 75. Geburtstag, Wiesbaden 1988, 250) interpreted as 'cook', in accordance with Sumerogram (LÚ.) MUḪALDIM, ..., partly normalised as *p/wandarini*. ... recently: 'cook', literally 'someone who is used to professionally achieve the aim that something acquires the right form'." [I have translated the German text into English.]

Since Linear A (and B) ***re*** can also be ***le***, more than one interpretation is possible. Linear A ***da-re*** may be equivalent to the Hurrian name ****Talli***[ ] from Alalaḫ VII on *AT 98.9: *Ta-al-li*[x?], if one accepts voicing of the initial dental (cf. F.W. Bush, *GHL*, 51-52), perhaps under influence of the following liquid sound, cf. A. Draffkorn, *HHA*, 55, 107, but that name may have to be completed to *Ta-al-li*[*a*?], that may be comparable with the Nuzi name ***Taleịa*** (wr. *Ta-le-e-ia, Da-li-ia, Dal-li-ia*), cf. I.J. Gelb, *NPN*, 145; P.M. Purves, *NPN*, 262, s.v. ***tal*** and ***tall***. (* marks provenance from Alalaḫ level VII).

Recent literature offers useful interpretations:

a. (GIŠ.)***tali*** I, {*tāl=i*} (E. Neu, 2001, 93) generally accepted meaning: 'Holz, Baum' ['wood, tree'], lexical comparison with Sumerian [GIŠ], Sumerogram GIŠ-*ru*, Akkadian ***iṣu***, Ugaritic ***iṣṣūma***, cf. E. Laroche, *GLH*, 253, s.v. ***tali*** 'arbre, bois'. RS quadr. 20.149 II 8 = *Ugar. V*, 234; h. ***ta-li*** = oug. ***iṣṣu***; cf. *Ugar V*, 458. Sg. nom. *da-a-li* IBoT II 39 Ro 19, ^{GIŠ}***tali***, Msk. *passim*; KUB XXXII 19 I 14; KBo XX 129+II 33, 46; KBo XX 126+III 46. Plur. nom. *da-a-li-na*, KBo XX 129+II 53. Plur. dat. *da-(a-)li-(e)-na-ša*, IBoT II 39 Ro 25; KBo XX 129+II 55, etc.; cf. Th. Richter, *BGH*, 431, s.v. (GIŠ.)***tali*** I [Boğ. Ug.]; *VHN*, 527, s.v. ***tali***.

b. ***tali*** II 'Opferterminus, Heilsbegriff' ['sacrificial term, wish for salvation'], cf. Th. Richter, *BGH*, 431-432, s.v. ***tali*** II [Boğ.]; Th. Richter, *VHN*, 527, s.v. ***tali***.

c. ***tal-*** I, verbal root '(weg)tragen, (weg)zerren' ['to bring / pull / snatch away'], certain because of equation with Hittite ***parā šallan(n)āi***, since publication of the Hurrian-Hittite bilingual ***Kirenze*** 'liberation, manumission', cf. Th. Richter, *BGH*, 431-432, s.v. ***tal-*** I [Boğ.]; Th. Richter, *VHN*, 527, s.v. ***tal-***.

If we read the Linear A personal name ***da-re*** as ***d/tale***, it could be an appellative based on the Hurrian noun ***tali*** I 'wood, tree' or ***tali*** II 'wish for salvation' or the name could be equivalent to the *imperative* ***dale*** {*d/tal=e/i*} 'Bring / Pull / Snatch (the deceased child) away (oh *numen*) !', based on the verbal root ***d/tal-*** 'to bring / pull / snatch away'.

If Linear A ***da-re*** is read as Hurrian ***d/tare***, more interpretations can be considered:
d. According to Th. Richter, *BGH*, 444, s.v. ***tar-*** [Mitt.] (e.g. Mit. III 30), the meaning 'zusammenkommen (?), sich begegnen (?)' ['to come together (?), to encounter (?)'] has been proposed by I. Wegner, but Th. Richter (*VHN*, 530, note 771) mentions that this meaning remains uncertain and is less plausible in personal names.
e. According to Th. Richter, *BGH*, 444-445, s.v. ***tari*** I [Boğ.; PN] 'Feuer' ['fire'], ***tār=i*** (E. Neu, 2001, 93); corresponds with Sumerian IZI, Akkadian ***išātu***, Hittite ***paḫḫur*** and ***paḫḫuenant-***, Luwian ***pāḫūr***. Also 'Opferterminus, Heilsbegriff' ['sacrificial term, wish for salvation'], especially in *tari tuburburi* (Haas/Wilhelm, 1974a, 98), 'Terminus der Vokation' (Haas, 1998a, 8, 245; Tischler, 2001b, 167). Th. Richter (*VHN*, 530-531, s.v. ***tar-***) mentions that on the basis of ***tari*** 'Feuer' ['fire'] a verbal root ***tar-*** may be conceivable, (transitive) 'jemanden / etwas verbrennen' ['to burn someone / something, to set someone / something on fire'], (intransitive) 'brennen' ['to burn, to be on fire']. This may well provide a good meaning for ***ᶠTarim-Šimika*** (wr. *ta-ri-im-ši-mi-ga*) from Ašnakkum, analysis {*tar=i=m(:b)-Šimiga*}, typology, 1.1.1.2.2, lexicon *tar-*, *Šimiga*, cf. Th. Richter, *VHN*, 298-299. *Ibidem*, 576-577, sub 1.1.1.2.2 (verbal forms in ***ᵒ=i=m***), and note 921, he discusses the view that the formant in ***ᵒ=m*** may be ascribed to the dialect of Urkeš, whereas that in ***ᵒ=b*** may be ascribed to those of Ḫattuša and Babylonia, which makes it likely that the sentence name reflects the *indicative*. He prefers this view to that in which ***ᵒ=m*** is regarded as the enclitic personal pronoun 2nd person singular (***ᵒ=m*** instead of ***ᵒ=mma***). Consequently translation of ***ᶠTarim-Šimika*** as 'Šimika (Sun-god) set (the girl) on fire' is preferred to 'Set (the girl) on fire, oh Šimika (Sun-god) !'.

Incidentally, ****Tar-tari*** 'Burn, oh fire !' may in my view be the Hurrian etymology of Pre-Greek ***Τάρταρος*** / *Tartaros* (plural ***Τάρταρα***), an appropriate description of 'Hell'.
f. According to Th. Richter (*BGH*, 445), s.v. ‡ ***tari*** (II) [Boğ.], and *VHN*, 530, note 771, it is conceivable that a homographic / homonymic Hurrian root ***tar-*** 'stark / mächtig sein' ['to be strong / powerful'] and a noun ***tari*** 'Stärke' ['strength, power'] can be inferred on account of Urartian ***tar=ae=u/oḫe*** '(über)mächtig' ['powerful, superior']. The Linear A name ***da-re*** could then mean either 'Make strong / powerful !' or 'Strength, Power'.

The third entry on HT 10b.1-2 is ***Ta-we-na***, an exact equivalent to the Hurrian personal name ***Tawe-nna***, attested at Mari, cf. J.M. Sasson, 'Ḫurrians and Ḫurrian names in the Mari texts', *UF 6 (1974)*, 370, 386: ***Tawe-nna***. According to J.M. Sasson, 386, ***tawe-*** at Mari may be related to ***tae-*** at Nuzi (cf. Purves *NPN*, 260-261, s.v. ***tae***, ***tai***), but that presupposition is no longer valid, because Th. Richter (*VHN*, 523-524) brings ***taḫe / taḫḫe*** {*taġ/ḫḫe*} and ***ta(')e*** 'man' together, but mentions (*BGH*, 438-440) that the verbal root ***tab-*** I is equivalent to ***taw-*** I '(Metall) gießen' ['to cast / pour out (metal, bronze)'].

According to Th. Richter (*VHN*, 297, 600) the Hurrian personal name ***ᶠTawenna*** (wr. *ᶠTa-we-en-na*) from Ašnakkum (Tall Šaġīr Bāzār / Chagar Bazar) and Mari (Tall Hariri), analysis {*tav=i=nna*}, typology 1.3.1.2.2.1, lexicon *taw-* I, can be translated as 'Gieße es (Mädchen) (oh *Numen*) !' 'Cast her (the girl) (oh *numen*) !'. Th. Richter (*VHN*, 136, 600) explains that the enclitic personal pronoun 3rd person singular ***-n/-nna*** occurs more often in personal names than the enclitic personal pronoun 1st person singular ***-tta***: for instance, ***Ḫerzin*** (wr. *Ḫe-er-zi-in*) at Mari, {*ḫerž=i=n(na)*}, typology 1.3.1.2.2.1, lexicon ***ḫerz-***.

Th. Richter (*VHN*, 529) mentions that the root ***taw-*** I {*tav-*} is known from the Hurrian-Hittite bilingual ***Kirenze*** (KBo 32) as '(Metall) gießen' ['to cast / pour out (metal, bronze)']. According to I. Wegner (*Einführung*, 103, Table 9 (*The order of suffixes of the positive jussive*), the form {*tav=e/i=nna*} consists of the root of the transitive ergative verb ***taw-*** (***/tav-/***) 'to cast' + ***-e/i-*** (marker of transitivity and at the same time indicator of the *iussive* or *imperative* 2nd person singular, because the imperative does not have its own marker) + the suffix of the enclitic personal pronoun 3rd person singular ***-nna*** 'him/her'.

I. Wegner (*Einführung*, 21) mentions that the oldest written evidence for presence of Hurrians and Hurrian in the Near East dates from the Akkade-period (2230-2090 B.C. according to the short chronology; 60 year may be added for the long chronology). But presence of Hurrian in North-Iraq, North-Syria and East-Anatolia may be much earlier, since Old-Sumerian TABIRA/TIBIRA 'Kupferarbeiter' ['copperworker, coppersmith'] can plausibly be derived from Hurrian ***tabiri***, consisting of the root ***tab/v-*** 'gießen' ['to cast, to pour out'] + ***i*** + ***ri***, an agens-orientated resultative participle 'der der gießt' ['someone who casts (metal)'], cf. (*ibidem*, 55, 283) ***tabrinni*** < {*tab=(i)=r(i)=i=nni*} consisting of this resultative participle + the suffixes ***=i=nni*** designating professions, 'Schmied, Metall-Gießer, Kupferschmied' ['(copper)smith'], cf. the verbal form in ***=o=m*** (*ibidem*, 128, 216, 218), ***tab=ašt=o=m***, 3rd person singular past transitive in ergative construction (Old Hurrian) ['he cast (metal)', attested in the third parable 'Der Becher und sein Schmied' ['The goblet and its smith'] in the Hurrian-Hittite bilingual ***Kirenze***, KBo 32: 14, 42-43: *ka-a-zi ta-bal-li-iš ḫe-e-lu-u-wa*$_{a}$ | *ta-wa*$_{a}$*-aš-tu-um* =
kazi tab=li=ne=š > tabal=le=š ḫelov(i)=a (essive) or *ḫel=o=va* (dative) *tab=ašt=o=m*
Einen Becher goß ein (Metall)gießer als Ruhmestat / zum Ruhme'.
['A (metal)smith / (copper)smith cast a goblet as an act of fame / to glory'.].

Hurrian ***kazi*** (absolutive) is derived from Akkadian ***kāsu(m)*** 'cup, goblet, chalice' and corresponds with Hittite ***tešummi-*** 'cup, goblet, chalice' in the bilingual. See the discussion on Linear A ***pi-ta-ka-se*** (HT 21a.1).

I. Wegner (*Einführung*, 216-221, 270) interprets ***pa=i=ri*** as a resultative participle 'someone who has built; architect', belonging to the verbal root ***pa-*** 'to build'. She compares ***pa=i=ri*** morphologically with ***ta-bi-ri-i-ma*** in the Hurrian-Hittite bilingual ***Kirenze***, KBo 32: 14 Vs. I 46 (cf. E. Neu, *StBoT 32*, 80), in the 3rd parable: *The goblet (chalice, cup) and its smith* (KBo 32: 14 Vs. I 42-59) and analyses the form ***tab=i=ri*** as verbal root ***tab/v-*** 'to cast (metal)' + ***i*** (vowel indicating transitivity) + ***ri/e*** (participial suffix) 'the one who has cast (metal); smith'. The forms in ***=i=ri/e*** are 'agensorientierte resultative Partizipien' ['agent orientated resultative participles'].

The ergative form ***ta-bal-li-iš*** (same parable, lines 42 and 55) is used synonymously to ***tab=i=ri*** (line 46). I. Wegner analyses it as verbal root ***tab/v-*** 'to cast (metal)' + ***li*** (formative indicating professional designations) following the root athemetically (***tab+li***) + the so-called singular article ***ne*** (***tab+li+ne***). In case of usage of the article *anaptyxis* (development of vowel between two consonants) occurs to make pronunciation easier, as well as *apocope* (disappearance of the final vowel) > ***tabal(i)=ne***, so that the ***n*** of the article assimilates to the ***l*** of the stem > ***tabal=le*** '(Metall)gießer = Schmied' ['someone who casts (metal) = smith'] + ergative suffix ***š***. In the Hittite text it corresponds with the Sumerogram ^{LÚ}SIMUG 'copper-smith'. Cf. ***kebella*** 'the hunters', ***kebel=la*** < ****keb+li+na***.

Linear A ***ka-sa-ru*** (HT 10b.3) occurs in a list of personal names and may well be a Hurrian personal name consisting of a verbal root ***kaz-*** I, ***kaš-*** II or ***ḫaš-*** + the *factitive* or *iterative* root-extension ***-ar-*** + Old Hurrian marker of transitivity ***-u/o-*** + Old Hurrian marker of the subject 3rd person singular *agens* ***-m***, cf. e.g. I. Wegner, *Einführung*, 134 and table 13. This final ***-m*** is not expressed in Linear A, because final consonants are not expressed in Linear A and B. Hurrian ***Kaš-šena*** is attested at Alalaḫ VII (**AT* 64.16). A. Draffkorn (*HHA*, 38, 83, 103) thinks that ***Kaš-šena*** might phonologically be /*Kaz-sena*/.

Another possible interpretation is that the personal name consists of one of the three verbal roots just mentioned + the theophorous element ***-šarri*** 'King of Gods', with the Akkadianizing nominative in ***-u*** {*šarr(i)=u*}. Cf. Linear B ***ka-sa-ro*** (KN X 1450).

Th. Richter (*BGH*, 191) mentions ***kaz-*** I [Boğ.], e.g. at Nuzi *kaz-umma epēšu*. The meaning of the verbal root is uncertain; proposed are: 'kratzen(?)', 'to scratch(?)', 'to bite(?)', possibly Hurrianized *qāta(m) epēšu* 'to lay hands on', 'schlagen, brechen' ['to beat, break'], 'to wound'; ***kaš-*** II {*kaž-*} without proposed translation.

By far one of the most frequent verbal roots in Hurrian personal names (especially in combination with a theophorous element) is ***ḫaš-*** 'to hear (a prayer)'. Interpretation of Linear A ***ka-sa-ru*** as ***Ḫaš-šarru***, analysis {*ḫaš-šarr(i)=u*}, 'Hear (and answer the prayer) oh King of Gods !' seems to me the most likely option, especially because a good parallel, Old Hurrian ***Ḫazip-šarri*** {*ḫaž=i=b-šarri*} 'The King of Gods heard (and answered the prayer)' is attested at Mari, Nuzi and Tigunāni, cf. Th. Richter, *VHN*, 131.

This analysis is comparable with my interpretation of Linear A ***<u>ka</u>+qe*** (HT 37.6) from Hagia Triada as the Hurrian *athematic* (instead of *thematic* ****Ḫaš=i-ḫe***), hypocoristic name ****Ḫaš-ḫe*** (instead of ****Ḫaš-ḫepa***) 'Hear (the prayer), oh Ḫebat !' (*imperative*), comparable with the Nuzi hypocoristics ***Ḫaš-teia*** (wr. *Ḫa-aš-te-ia*, *Ḫa-aš-te-e*) 'Hear (the prayer), oh Tešub !' and ***Ḫašitte*** (wr. *Ḫa-ši-it-te*) < ****Ḫašip-te***, with Old Hurrian ***-b-***) beside the full name ***Ḫašip-tešup*** (wr. *Ḫa-ši-ip-te-šup*) 'Tešub hears, heard (the prayer)', cf. P.M. Purves (*NPN*, 214-215, s.v. ***ḫaš-*** 'to hear'). Old Hurrian ***ḫašip-***, analysis {*ḫaš=i=b-*} 'he hears, heard'. Another analysis of ***Ḫašitte*** (wr. *Ḫa-ši-it-te*) is {*ḫaš=i=tte*} 'Listen to me (oh *numen*) !', consisting of the root ***ḫaš-*** + the marker of transitivity ***-i-*** + the optional allomorphic enclitic personal pronoun 1st personal singular ***-tte/-tti*** (instead of ***-tta***).

Compare also ***Ḫaš-Šimika*** (wr. *Ḫa-aš-ši-mi-qa*) at Tigunāni and Nuzi, analysis {*ḫaš-Šimiga*}, typology 1.4, 'Hear (the prayer), oh (Sun-God) ***Šimiga*** !' (*imperative*) beside the Old Hurrian *indicative* ***Ḫazip-Šimika*** '***Šimiga*** hears, heard (the prayer)' and ***Ḫazip-Šimike*** '***Šimige*** hears, heard (the prayer)', cf. Th. Richter, *VHN*, 127, 131.

Since the orthographic conventions of Linear A do not tell, whether the cuneiform rendering would have provided single or double writing of the sibilant, Linear A ***ka-sa-ru*** (HT 10b.3) can also be analysed as an Old Hurrian 'one-word' name {*ḫaž=ar=u*}, consisting of the root ***ḫaš-*** 'to hear' + *factitive* and *iterative* root-extension ***-ar-*** + Old Hurrian *transitive imperative* suffix ***-u***, translation 'Listen again and again (oh *numen*) !' or {*ḫaž=ar=o/u=m*}, with the Old Hurrian *past indicative* suffixes 3rd person singular ***°=o/u=m***, translation 'He/She (a *numen*) heard (the prayer) again and again'.

The frequent Linear A name ***ta-na-ti*** (HT 10b.4) is the last sequence of HT 10b. It has been discussed extensively, since it also occurs on other tablets (HT 7a.4; HT 49.2; HT 98a.2) at Hagia Triada and since it may be equivalent to ***ta-na-te*** (ZA 10a.1) at Kato Zakro.

Linear A ***e-na-si*** (KH 7a.2) at Khania can be identified as the Hurrian plural genitive form ***ennaši / ennaše*** 'of the gods' attested as *e-en-na-a-ši* KUB XLV 21 bg 1; *e-en-na-a-še* KUB XXXII 46,15; KBo XI 19 Vo 15; DINGIR^{meš}*-na-a-še* KBo II 21,11; KUB XXVII 42 Ro 14; XXXII 19 I 63, etc.; in alphabetic cuneiform ***enž*** RS 24.643 A 14, 15; 644, 2; CTA 166, 39, 60, 61. Kiz. *E-nu-uš-ši*, KUB XL 103 17 = KBo XVII 98, 25, cf. E. Laroche, *GLH*, 81.

E. Laroche (*GLH*, 80-82), s.v. ***eni*** 'dieu', explained the structure of the plural genitive ***ennaši / ennaše*** as follows: ***eni*** 'god', ***enni*** < ****eni-ni*** 'the god', ***enna*** < ****eni-na*** 'the gods', ***enna-ši/še*** 'of the gods'.

However, evidence from Nuzi has changed this analysis, since older forms have been preserved at Nuzi. The genitive ***ennaši / ennaše*** is now explained as *{en(i)=na=aš=(v)e}* consisting of ***en(i)*** 'god' + the suffix of the so-called plural article ***-na*** + the pluralizing suffix ***-aš*** + the suffix of the (singular) genitive ***-we/-wi***, cf. e.g. I. Wegner, *Einführung*, 65 [sub 2.2.4: the *case-suffixes* (position 4), Table 1], 254.

If the inscription on a fragment of a terracotta zoomorphic rhyton from the Peak Sanctuary of 'Hermes and Aphrodite' of Kato Symi Viannou is read from right to left, we read ***ẹ-ni-wa* , *ki-ra*** 1 (SY Zb 7). Usually Linear A sign ***ki*** (which looks like a 'vessel', 'rhyton') has its handle on the left side, but here the handle is on the right side suggesting that the direction of reading is 'from right to left' (←).

If the inscription is read from left to right, the almost illegible sign following the word divider may be ***wa***, possibly on a palimpsest underground of [[*ia*]]. This sign is followed by ***-ni-*** and possibly the top of sign ***-ẹ***. Another advantage of reading from right to left is that the *hasta* mentioned by J.G. Younger, which may well be a unit, appears at the end of the inscription instead of at the beginning. Therefore the inscription is reversed in the *analysed structure of the text* of *Minoan Linear A*, Vol. II, *Corpus of transliterated Linear A texts*. If this reading is correct, the Linear A sequence ***ẹ-ni-wa*** can be interpreted as the Hurrian singular dative ***eni=wa*** = 'for God', or as the singular dative ***enni-wa*** = 'for the God', with the suffix of the so-called definite article ***-ni-*** + the suffix of the singular dative ***-wa*** < ****en(i)-ni-wa***, cf. I. Wegner, *Einführung*, 65.

However, since a final consonant is not expressed in Linear A and B, the sequence can also represent the Hurrian contracted possessive form of the first person plural ***eni-wwaš*** < ****en(=i)=iwwa/ə=aš***, consisting of the stem ***en=i-*** + the suffix of the possessive pronoun 1st person singular ***-iwwa/ə-*** 'my' + the pluralizing suffix ***-aš***, 'our', translation 'Our God', cf. E.A. Speiser, *IH*, 103, n. 105; cf. E. Laroche, *GLH*, 81-82, s.v. ***eni*** 'dieu'; ***eni-wwaš*** 'notre dieu', cf. I. Wegner, *Einführung*, 62-64: Position 2: *The enclitic possessive pronouns*: ***-iffə/e/u*** + ***aš***.

Identification of Linear A ***e-na-si*** (KH 7a.2) is corroborated by occurrence of the Hurrian (sometimes divine) name ***ta-ta*** (KH 7a.3) in the next line. ***Tatta*** is also attested as a Hurrian personal name at Mari: *Ta-at-ta* SY B:v:55, and *Ta-at-ta-a* SY B:iii:73, cf. J.M. Sasson, 'Ḫurrians and Ḫurrian names in the Mari texts', *UF 6 (1974)*, 370, 386.

According to E. Laroche (*NH*, 240) names of the type *Kaka, Gaga, Kiki, Kuku, Lala, Lili, Lulu, Mama, Nana, Nini, Nunu, Papa, Baba, Tata, Dada, Tete, Didi, Tutu, Dudu* and *Zuzu* belong to the category of 'Lallnamen'.

E. Laroche (*NH*, 239) remarks: "Depuis les travaux de Kretchmer, on sait que l'Asie Mineure est un terrain de choix pour l'étude des 'Lallnamen'. Ces noms apparaissent, à l'aube de l'histoire anatolienne, avec l'onomastique de Cappadoce. Ils abondent à toute époque de la civilisation hittite. Ils se perpétuent et foisonnent encore aux siècles classiques. Mais l'Anatolie n'en a point le privilège exclusif; on en rencontre de multiples exemples en Sumer, en Mésopotamie babylonienne, en Syrie, en Égypte, de même qu'en Grèce, en Italie et en Europe. Il ne s'agit pas là, en effet, d'un mode d'appellation primitif, mais populaire. Il vise, outre la brièveté de l'usage quotidien, à extérioriser des sentiments. On les désigne parfois sous le nom de termes 'câlins' ou 'tendres', tant il est vrai que c'est la façon instinctive, à la fois maternelle et enfantine, d'appeler plutôt que de nommer. Tous les noms de ce niveau onomastique ont ce trait commun d'être dénués de signification discursive et d'être indépendants vis-à-vis des schémas grammaticaux."

At Boğazköy we find ***Tatta***, ***Tattamaru***, ***Tatti*** and ***Tattiya***, cf. E. Laroche, *NH*, 181, nr. 1301. ***Tatta*** 1. Prêtre du dieu de l'orage (LÚ ᵈU/IM): abs. nom. dat. *ᵐTa-(a)-at-ta- (aš / an / ti)*, HT 95, 1, 3, 6; KUB VII 22, 3, 11; XXVIII 45 VI 4; XXX 68 Vo 4; 2. Père de scribe: abs. *ᵐTa-at-ta*, XV 31 IV 41. Nr.1303. ***Tattamaru*** 1. Prince: abs. *ᵐTa-at-ta-ma-ru*, KBo IV 10 Vo 30. 2. Divers: abs. nom. *ᵐTa-at-ta-ma-ru-(uš)*, *ᵐTa-ad-da-ma-ru*, XXIII 85, 4, 5; 106 Ro 1 ?; XXVI 43 Ro 5; 92, 10; XXXI 28, 7, 8; 32 Vo 5, 8, 12; XXXVIII 1 I 26 = MIO 8, 181. Nr. 1304. ***Tatti***, abs. *ᵐTa-at-ti*, XV 30 III 4. 1305. ***Tattiya*** 1. Scribe: abs. *ᵐTa-at-ti-ya*, KBo I 28 Vo 13. 2. Prêtre: *ᵐTa-at-ti-ya-*[*aš*], XII 2 I 2.

He assumes that the stem ***Tatta*** or ***Dada*** is the most probable etymology of the divine name ***ᵈTatta*** (cf. *NH*, 241) and adds (*NH*, 291): "***ᵈTatta*** ou ***Datta***: nom divin auparavant déduit du seul nom propre ***Arma-***ᵈU = ***Arma-Datta***. Il est maintenant attesté: *ᵈTattas*, Bo 3254 Ro 14 = MIO 8, 205. Mais ce texte unique ne dit pas que ***Tatta*** est un dieu de l'orage."

The context of Linear A ***ta-ta*** (KH 7a.3) following ***e-na-si*** (KH 7a.2) makes it likely that ***ta-ta*** (KH 7a.3) represents the divine name ***ᵈTatta***, but if ***ta-ta*** is a personal name, it may be the name of a priest such as that of the priest of the god of the clouds at Boğazköy.

More corroboration comes from the plural genitive of Hurrian ***uštay*** 'hero' in the heading of the *b*-side of the same tablet, just under the line that divides the upper and lower parts: ***u-ta-i-se*** (KH 7b.2) can be identified with ***uštaiše*** < ***uštai=(a)š=(v)e*** < ***uštai=aš=ve*** This interpretation appears to be confirmed by occurrence of a variant orthography on another tablet at Khania,]***u-ta-i-si*** (KH 16.2), representing the same plural genitive form ***uštaiši*** < ***uštai=(a)š=(v)i*** < ***uštai=aš=vi***, but now with the same plural genitive suffix written as ***-ši*** < ***=aš=vi***, with the common ***e/i*** alternation in Hurrian orthography.

The Linear A rendering ***u-ta-i-se*** of the Hurrian form *uštaiše* is the result of Linear A orthographic conventions inherited by Linear B. Comparing the Linear B orthography of ***pa-i-to*** = *Φαιστός* 'Phaistos' (KN Da 1163+1400, al.), there is no doubt that Linear B did not express ***-s-*** before an occlusive in consonant clusters. In the archives of the palace of Hagia Triada, only two miles from Phaistos, Linear A ***pa-i-to*** (HT 97a.3; HT 120.6) is attested. The Linear A form may well represent the Old Hurrian toponym meaning 'He/She (a God) has built (the palace)', equivalent to Old Hurrian ***ba-'à-áš-to/um*** on the Tiš-atal tablet, analysed and normalised as ***pa=ašt=o=m***, and translated as 'He (Tiš-atal) has built (a temple)', cf. I. Wegner, *Einführung*, 232, 234; Th. Richter (*BGH*, 285-286), s.v. ***pa-***, *paḫ-* II [*passim*] '(er)bauen' ['to build'], *pa('/h)-*, G. Wilhelm, 1988b, 55.

E. Laroche (*GLH*, 289-290) compares forms such as ***uštay*** 'hero' with terms as ***allay*** 'lady' and ***attay*** 'father'. I. Wegner (*Einführung*, 52-53) describes them as well as ***šije*** 'water' as *stems* appearing as *diphthongs*. She also mentions that G. Wilhelm (*Cambridge Encyclopedia*, 2004, Chapter 4, 105) and M. Giorgieri (Schizzo grammaticale della lingua hurrica, *PdP 55*, 2000, 199) interpret these stems in ***-ai*** as ***a***-stems with an additional 'honorific' ***-i***: ***alla=i***, etc. I consider this solution very attractive, because it also explains that, for instance, in personal names, in which ***alla=i*** or ***atta=i*** occur as second onomastic element, this 'honorific' ***-i*** can be omitted. This phenomenon can also be observed in the Linear A personal name ***da-du-ma-ta*** (HT 95+149a.1), analysis {*dad=o/u=m-atta*}, '(God) the Father, he loved (the child)' and/or 'The (natural) father, he loved (the child)'.

The meaning of Hurrian ***uštay*** was established by RS quadr. 137 II 24: Sumerian ŠUL = Akkadian ***eṭ-lu*** = Hurrian ***uš-ta-an-ni*** = Ugaritic ***maḫḫurum*** (E. Laroche, *Ugar. V*, 454 sq.; E. Laroche, *GLH*, 289; B. André-Salvini/M. Salvini, Le liste lessicali e i vocabolari plurilingui di Ugarit. Una chiave per l'interpretazione della lingua hurrica, *PdP 55*, 2000, 329; Th. Richter, *BGH*, 503). J. Huehnergard (*Ugaritic vocabulary in syllabic transcription*, Harvard Semitic Studies 32, Atlanta 1987[1], 84, 113; Winona Lake 2008[2], with addenda (375-406) reads the Ugaritic sequence as ***baḫḫuru*** or ***baḫḫuru*** 'youth'. Th. Richter (*VHN*, 556) reads ***ba-aḫ-ḫu-rù*** '(Kriegs)held' ['(war) hero'] and mentions that the meaning has been confirmed by RS 94-2939 = SCCNH 9, 7 V 2'.

Linear A ***u-ta-i-se*** (KH 7b.2) and]***u-ta-i-si*** (KH 16.2) can probably be identified with Hurrian ***uštaiše*** and ***uštaiši*** 'of the heroes', plural genitive of ***uštai/y***, with the plural suffix ***-aš-*** (position 3) and genitive suffix ***-we/i-*** (position 4): ***-(a)š=(w)e / -(a)š=(w)i***.

E.A. Speiser, F.W. Bush, E. Laroche and many others (myself included) used to observe a distinction between the Hurrian singular genitive suffix ***-we/-wi*** and the plural genitive suffix ***-še/-ši***, as well as between the Hurrian singular dative suffix ***-wa*** and the plural dative suffix ***-ša***.

On the basis of evidence, especially from Nuzi, the views on these suffixes have, however, changed in more recent literature, since the ***-š-*** in ***-še/-ši*** (as well as in the plural dative ***-ša***) is no longer regarded as belonging to the plural genitive (c.q. dative) suffix, but as part of the pluralizing suffix ***-aš-***, that is followed by the genitive suffix ***-we/-wi*** (c.q. dative suffix ***-wa***), with subsequent absorption of ***-w-*** in ***-we/i***, c.q. ***-wa***. Analysis: ***=aš=*** (pluralizer) + ***we/wi*** (genitive suffix) or ***wa*** (dative suffix), cf. I. Wegner, *Einführung in die hurritische Sprache*, Wiesbaden 2007[2], 65, (Tafel 1), 75, (Tafel 2), 80 (Tafel 3): plural genitive ***=aš=ve*** (only at Nuzi) > ***=aše*** (elsewhere); (plural dative) ***=aš=va*** > ***=aša***. I. Wegner and her predecessors normalize ***w/p*** to voiced ***v*** and ***ww/pp*** to voiceless ***f***.

I have maintained transliteration of syllabic signs with ***w-*** for Linear A, since it seems preferable to emphasize the continuity from Linear A to Linear B. Moreover, Linear A and B do not use double writing of consonants as a tool for indicating voicelessness like cuneiform does.

It is assumed that for forms like the Hurrian plural genitive ***umminnaši*** 'of the lands', IBoT II 39 Vo 5; KUB XXVII 18, 6; XXXII 61, 7; alphabetic Ugaritic ***umnž*** genitive or dative (*Ugar. V*, 517 ff., E. Laroche, *GLH*, 281-282, s.v. ***umini*** 'pays'), the ***-a-*** of the suffix of the so-called plural definite article ***-na-*** is absorbed, if it is followed by the pluralizing suffix ***=aš=***. The ***-w-***, possibly */v/*, in ***=aš=we/i*** is absorbed as well > ***=aš=(w)e/i*** > ***=aš=e/i***.

The translation of ***umminnaši*** 'of the lands' did not change since Speiser, Bush and Laroche, but the whole structure of the chain of suffixes has been extended and improved considerably and has become more coherent as well. Consequently, following I. Wegner, the analysis of Linear A ***u-ta-i-se*** (KH 7b.2) and ***]u-ta-i-si*** (KH 16.2) is: ***uštai=aš=we/i*** (Hurrian nominal ***uštai*** + pluralizer ***=aš=*** + genitive suffix ***=we/i***) > ***uštai=(a)š=(w)e/i*** (absorption of ***-a-*** and ***-w-***) > ***uštaiše/i***. This seems to be the most likely interpretation in the context of these Linear A texts. Theoretically the forms ***u-ta-i-se*** (KH 7b.2) and ***]u-ta-i-si*** (KH 16.2) can also be interpreted otherwise. Since Linear A orthography (as that of Linear B) always uses single writing, also for forms rendering a double consonant, another possiblitity, the suffix ***-šši / -šše***, would in theory be conceivable. This suffix, which F.W. Bush, *GHL*, 172-173, reads phonologically as ***/-θθe/***, is used with nominals and has a derivational force forming abstract nouns: ***ušta(y)šše***, (Bush) /***uθta(y)θθe***/ 'heroism'. Cf. also T. Richter, *BGH*, 503: ***uštašše*** [Boğ] 'Heldentum'.

E. Laroche (*GLH*, 290) mentions ***uštašši*** 'héroïsme' ['heroism']: *ḫanumašši uš-ta-aš-ši*, KBo XX 119 I 25 = KBo XVII 86 I 15; KBo VIII 86 Ro 15. He compares the form ***uštašši*** with terms as ***allašši*** 'état de reine' ['state of the queen'] and ***šarrašši*** 'royauté' ['kingship'], see *ibidem*, 93, s.v. ***ḫanumašši*** - ***ḫanumpazḫi***:
ḫa-nu-ma-aš-ši (uštašši), KBo XX 119 I 25; KBo VIII 86 Ro 15.
^{d}*ḫa-nu-ma-an-zi* (*uštanzi*), KUB XXVII 1 II 2.
ḫa-nu-(um)-pa-az-ḫi, KBo XX 129+ III 41-42; KBo XX 126+ III 43.
ḫa-nu-um-pa-az-ḫi-ni-ip-pí, KUB XXXII 24+ II 18.
ḫa-nu-um-pa-az-ḫi-ta (*uštaššita*), *ib*. II 5, 6.
Alph. *ḫnn užtn*, RS 24. 643 A 16, 17.

Le binôme *ḫanumašši*/*ḫanumpazḫi* - *uštašši* rappelle le hitt. DUMU-*latar* - *tarḫuilatar* 'fécondité - héroïsme' ['fertility - heroism']; *ḫanumašši* sérait un abstrait à déduire d'un adj.* *ḫanuma/i-* 'fécond' ['fertile'], et à rattacher au verbe *ḫan-* 'enfanter' ['to bear a child, to give birth to a child']. La variante ***-ašši*** / ***-azḫi*** est inexpliquée. Th. Richter (*BGH*, 503), s.v. ***uštašše*** [Boğ.], corresponds with ***uštanzi***, is equivalent to Hittite ***tarḫuilatar***.

I. Wegner (*Einführung*, 55) gives an attractive explanation for the variant ***-azḫi*** and in fact also for the suffix ***-mb-*** in *ḫa-nu-(um)-pa-az-ḫi*, KBo XX 129+ III 41-42; KBo XX 126+ III 43; *ḫa-nu-um-pa-az-ḫi-ni-ip-pí*, KUB XXXII 24+ II 18; *ḫa-nu-um-pa-az-ḫi-ta (uštaššita)*, *ib*. II 5, 6. She explains that the suffix ***-(a)=šše*** forms abstract notions such as ***ašt=a=šše***, ***all=a=šše***, ***šarr=a=šše*** and shows that the combination of suffixes ***-*ambašḫe*** (consisting of the morphemes ***a=mb=aš(še)=ḫ(ḫ)e***) belongs to formations in ***-(a)=šše***.

The suffix-combination builds *attributive* adjectives of abstract forms: e.g. ***alambašḫe*** < ***al=a***(intr.)***=mb***(unknown)***=aš(še)=ḫ(ḫ)e*** 'payment for the delivery of harvesters'; ***teḫambašḫu*** < ***teḫ=a***(intr.)***=mb=aš(še)=ḫ(ḫ)u*** (Akkadianized form in ***-u***) 'salary for upbringing of babies / infants' (Nuzi).

I. Wegner (*Einführung*, 57) mentions, sub ***-(a)=šḫe/i*** (the suffix builds *nomina loci et instrumenti*): ***ašt=a=šḫe*** 'weibliches Attribut' ['attribute for a woman'] from ***ašti*** 'woman'; sub ***-(i)=šḫe/i***: ***an=an=i=šḫe/i*** 'Freude' ['joy'] from ***an-*** 'to rejoice'; ***tur=i=šḫe/i*** 'Okzident' ['occident'] from ***turi-*** 'unten, tief' ['beneath']; sub ***-(u)=šḫe/i***: ***aḫr=u=šḫe/i*** 'Weirauchgefäß' ['censer'] from ***aḫri*** 'Weirauch' ['incense']; ***tiv=u=šḫe/i*** 'Wort, Rede' ['word, speech'] from ***tive*** 'Wort' ['word'].

The suffix ***-ušḫe*** for formation of descriptions of object/tools is in particular known from texts from Nuzi and Alalaḫ. Segmentation of ***-(a)=šḫe/i***, ***-(i)=šḫe/i***, ***-(u)=šḫe/i*** into ***=a=š(še)=ḫe/i***, ***=i=š(še)=ḫe/i***, ***=(u)=š(še)=ḫe/i*** is in my view to be recommended.

With regard to the Linear A forms ***u-ta-i-se*** (KH 7b.2) and ***]u-ta-i-si*** (KH 16.2) it is fair to say that (because of occurrence of ***e-na-si*** (KH 7a.2) 'of the gods') ***u-ta-i-se*** (KH 7b.2) certainly represents the plural genitive form ***uštaiše*** < ***uštai=(a)š=(w)e***. It consists of the stem ***uštai/y*** + the plural suffix ***-aš-*** (position 3) + genitive suffix ***-we*** (position 4).

Only Linear A ***]u-ta-i-si*** (KH 16.2), that misses a morphological and semantic parallel such as the plural genitive ***e-na-si***, can theoretically represent the abstract form ***uštašše*** 'heroism' known from Boğazköy. If so, the abstract form may well be used as a personal name. Nevertheless I consider it more likely that ***]u-ta-i-si*** (KH 16.2) represents the plural genitive form as well. If the abstract form ***uštašši*** 'heroism' is involved, we may conclude that the Linear A form appears to have preserved a more archaic feature: It has preserved the ***-i*** of the diphthong ***-ai*** of ***uštai***, whereas ***uštašše*** from Boğazköy has lost this ***-i***.

Many Hurrian nouns are derived from verbal roots. From a morphological and semantic point of view it is likely that this is also the case with ***ušta(i)*** '(war)hero'. If the general meaning ***ušt-*** 'to go out' can also be used in the sense of 'to set out on his way', a special meaning 'to go to war / to the battlefield' may well explain the meaning '(war)hero' for ***ušta(i)*** and 'the hero' for ***uštanni***.

Th. Richter (*BGH*, 502-503), s.v. ***ušš-*** [Boğ.,Mari], ***ušt-***, ***ašt-*** II [Boğ., PN, Ugar.], tells that according to V. Haas - I. Wegner (Beiträge zum hurritischen Lexikon: Die hurritischen Verben ***ušš-*** 'gehen' und ***ašš-*** 'abwaschen, abwischen', in: J. Klinger, E. Rieken, Chr. Rüster (eds.), *Investigationes Anatolicae. Gedenkschrift für Erich Neu* (StBoT 52), Wiesbaden 2010, 97-109) the root-variants ***ušš-***, ***ušt-***, their derivations and etymology belong together: intransitive 'gehen, ausziehen (in den Kampf)' [= 'to go to war'], transitive 'führen, fort-, wegbringen' [= 'to lead, bring away'].

They completed the verb ***uš-***[…] (corresponding with Sumerian [D]U and Akkadian ***alāku***) to ***uš-***[***šu-(um-)me***]. Hurrian ***ušš-*** corresponds with Hittite ***ija-*** 'marschieren, gehen' ['to go, to march'] according to I. Wegner, "Haus" und "Hof" im Hurritischen, in: Th. Richter, D. Prechel, J. Klinger (eds.), *Kulturgeschichten. Altorientalische Studien für Volkert Haas zum 65. Geburtstag*, Saarbrücken 2001, 446.

One may also compare Urartian intransitive ***ušta-*** {*ušt=a-*} 'aufbrechen' [= 'to break up'], transitive ***uštu-*** {*ušt=u-*} 'darbringen' [= 'to bring, offer'], cf. H.-J. Thiel, 'Der Text und die Notenfolgen des Musiktextes aus Ugarit', *Studi micenei ed egeo-anatolici 18 (1977)*, 132; Thiel, 'Zur Gliederung des „Musik-Textes" aus Ugarit', in: *Actes de la XXIVe Rencontre Assyriologique Internationale, Paris 1977: Les Hourrites, RHA 36 (1978)* [1980], 196; cf. V. Haas - I. Wegner, o.c. 2010, 100[21]. After it had been recognized that ***ušš-*** was a verbal root indicating motion, I. Wegner was according to Th. Richter (*VHN* I, 556) the first to advocate the translation 'to go'. V. Haas and I. Wegner then established the meaning extensively (*supra*) and marked the form ***úš-še*** in an incantation from Mari as imperative 'go !' (*RA 36*, 13 Nr. 3 Rs. 15). Richter considers the same analysis applicable to the names for men and women written ***ú-uš-še*** (most frequent), ***ú-úš-še***, ***ú-úš-e*** or ***úš-e***.

He sees no basic problems for the variant writings. See (*supra*) my interpretion of the Linear A personal name ***u-su*** 1 (HT 117a.1-2) and possibly (Raison-Pope's reading) ***u-su̲***[(HT 58.4) as an Old Hurrian *imperative* ***Úššu***, analysed as {*úšš=o/u*} 'Bring (the child) forth !'. Analysis as {*úšš=o/u=n(na)*}, with the shortened form ***-n*** of the enclitic personal pronoun 3rd person singular ***-nna***, 'Bring him/her (the child) forth !', is also possible or Old Hurrian {*úšš=o/u=m*}, 'He/She (a *numen*) brought him/her (the child) forth, away'.

According to Th. Richter (*VHN* I, 556-557) all names in ***ušt-*** belong to the root ***ušt-*** 'losgehen' ['to dash away'], 'herausgehen, ausziehen' ['to go out/away, to march out'], '(sich aus dem Bett) erheben' ['to get up from bed'], 'to go out (for battle)'. Compare Urartian ***ušta-*** {*ušt=a-*} 'sich auf den Weg machen' ['to set out on his/her way'], and ***uštu-*** {*ušt=u-*} 'schicken' ['to send'], cf. G. Wilhelm, 'Die hurritische Ablativ-Instrumentalis /ne/', *Zeitschrift für Assyriologie 73 (1983)*, 102[20]. Th. Richter (*VHN* I, 341) analyses the Hurrian name ***Uštun*** (wr. *Uš-tu-un*) at Šušarrā as {*ušt=o=n(na)*}, typology 1.3.1.1.2.1, lexicon *ušt-*, and translates 'Bringe ihn (Jungen) hinaus !' [= 'Bring him (the boy) out !'].

Consequently, we may conclude that Linear A ***u-ta₂*** (HT 103.1), interpreted as the Hurrian personal name ***Uštija***, can be analysed as a verbal 'one-word' personal name {*ušt=i-(j)a*}, consisting of the verbal root ***ušt-*** + the marker of transitivity ***-i-*** + the indicator of the subject of action 3rd person singular ***-a***, or as a hypocoristic personal name consisting of the verbal root ***ušt-*** + the marker of transitivity ***-i-*** + hypocoristic suffix ***-ya***. Since the meaning of transitive ***ušt-*** is known, we can translate ***Uštija*** as 'He/She (scil. a *numen*) brought him/her (the child) out'. Only the Minoan scribe knew, whether he had the name ***Uttija*** (as at Nuzi) in mind or ***Uštija***.

The Linear A sequence ***u-ta-ro*** (HT 116a.1) was formerly read as † ***da-ta-ro*** by W.C. Brice and some other authors, but *GORILA 1* and J. Raison - M. Pope (1994) read:

HT 116a.1: *u̲-ta-ro* , *te* , *ku-pa-ja* GRA

HT 116a.2: 16 *pu-ra₂* , GRA 40 OLE+*di* 5

The function and meaning of Linear A monosyllabic ***te*** have already been described extensively as a transactional term to be compared with the Linear A ligature **,** ***te+ro*** **,** (HT 104.1) and Linear B ***a-pu-do-si***, Mycenaean Greek ***ἀπύδοσις*** (Att. *ἀπόδοσις*), 'payment, actual delivery' and verbal forms such as the aorist 3rd person singular ***a-pu-do-ke*** (KN X 681; PY Ma 393, 2) 'he rendered, paid' and augmented aorist ***a-pe-do-ke*** (PY Fr 1184, 1).

If ***u-ta-ro*** (HT 116a.1) is a personal name, it may be the subject of the *imperative* {*ter=o*}, if ***te*** is indeed the abbreviation of that term. Linear A ***u-ta-ro*** **,** ***te*** **,** may then mean: '*U-ta-ro* must impose (tribute)', and if ***ku-pa-ja*** and ***pu-ra₂*** are the object of the verb, they may be the persons who will have to pay the tribute.

Linear A ***u-ta-ro*** (HT 116a.1) may itself be a 'one-word' personal name, Old Hurrian *imperative* in ***=o*** or past indicative in ***=o=m*** (cf. Th. Richter, *VHN*, 593, sub 1.3.1.1, sub 1.1.1.1.3, sub 1.1.1.1.1, and sub 1.3.1.1.2.1). It contains either the verbal root ***ušt-*** or ***utt-*** + the *factitive* or *iterative* root-extension ***-ar-***. Old Hurrian ***ušt=ar=o*** means 'He/She or You (scil. a *numen* or the mother) must bring (the child) out !' and ***ušt=ar=o=m*** 'He/She (scil. a *numen* or the mother) brought (the child) out', cf. I. Wegner, *Einführung*, 126.

The meaning of the verbal root ***utt-*** is not yet established, but if ***utt-*** equals ***ud-*** 'to protect', ***utt=ar=o*** means 'He/She or You (scil. a *numen*) must protect (the child) ! or ***utt=ar=o=m***, 'He/She (scil. a *numen*) protected (the child)'.

Linear A ***ku-pa-ja*** GRA 16 (HT 116a.1-2) can be compared with the Hurrian (Ur III) personal name ***Ḫu-ba-a*** that can be normalised to ***Ḫubaia***, cf. for Ur III ***Ḫu-ba*** and ***Ḫu-ba-a*** G.R. Meyer, *AOF XIII (1939/40)*, 148; cf. P.M. Purves, *NPN*, 217, s.v. ***ḫump***, ***Ḫumpa***. This means that Linear A ***ku-pa*** (HT 110a.2; HT Wa 1020 side α) from Hagia Triada, ***ku-pa[*** (KH 29.2) from Khania and ***ku-pa*** **,** GRA+***pa*** 1 [ ] (ZA 11a.5); ***ku-pa*** **,** GRA+***pa*** 3 (ZA 11b.3) from Kato Zakro can reflect Hurrian ***Ḫuba*** (UR III), wr. *Ḫu-ba*, analysis {*ḫub=a*}. Linear A ***ku-pa*** and ***ku-pa-ja*** have been discussed extensively *supra*.

Linear A ***ku-pa₃-nu*** (read as *ku-pa-nu* by C.H. Gordon) was identified as Ugaritic ***gupanu*** according to the cuneiform syllabary and as ***gpn*** according to alphabetic cuneiform (cf. C.H. Gordon, *Evidence*, 31-39). F. Gröndahl (*Die Personennamen der Texte aus Ugarit*, Rome 1967, 30, 79, 129 and 384) mentions that it is either a theophorous personal name or a divine name designating one of the messengers of Ba'al in Ugaritic mythology. She also mentions that the name is derived from common Semitic *GPN* 'Strauch, Wein, Rebe'.

However, one may wonder, whether 'Wine' or 'Vine' is a likely name for a child. If Linear A ***ku-pa₃-nu*** (HT 1a.3; HT 88.5; HT 117a.3; HT 122a.6; HT 122a.7; HT? 170b.3 and possibly HT 3.6; HT 42.3; HT 49a.6-7) is analysed as Hurrian ***Ḫub=a=nnu***, one of the last possibly Semitic names would disappear from the long list of Linear A personal names. According to Th. Richter (*BGH*, 163-165; *VHN*, 423) the meaning of a verbal root ***ḫub-*** {*ḫo/ub-*} '(zer)brechen, zerstören, vernichten' ['to break, destroy'] is generally accepted, because it corresponds with Hittite ***(arḫa) duwarnai-***, cf. also E. Laroche, *GLH*, 109, s.v. ***ḫub-*** 'briser'. On the other hand, for the nominal form ***ḫupaḫ(ḫ)e*** (in ***°=a=ġ/ḫḫe***) as well as for ***ḫubazzi*** {*ḫo/ubazzi*} a plausible lexical explanation is still failing.

Th. Richter (*VHN*, 142-143) mentions the Hurrian personal name ***Ḫupitam*** (wr. *Ḫu-bi-dam*) at Ašnakkum, Mari, Šubat-Enlil, Tuttul, Ĝirsu (UR III), Kaniš, Nippur (UR III), Umma (UR III), Nuzi, Alalaḫ IV, Dilbat, Ḫattuša, analysis {*ḫo/ubid(i)=a*[E.]*=m(e/a)*}, typology 3.2.1, lexicon *ḫubidi*, translation 'Er (Junge) ist wie ein Kalb' ['He (the boy) is like a calf']. This name is probably derived from Hurrian ***ḫubidi*** {*ḫub=idi*} 'Kalb, Stierkalb' ['calf, bull-calf'], 'Stierkalb (des Teššub)' (I. Wegner, 2004, 30), cf. Th. Richter, *BGH*, 164-165, s.v. ***ḫubidi*** [Boğ.; PN], and *VHN*, 423, s.v. ***ḫubidi***. The meaning is confirmed by correspondences with Sumerogram AMAR(*-ti*) and Akkadian *būru* and a relation with the root ***ḫub-*** is possible (cf. Khacikjan, 1985, 63).

If ***ḫubidi*** is analysed as ***ḫub=idi***, with the nominal element ***-idi*** as in ***tar=idi*** 'pot, pan' from ***tari-*** 'fire' and ***naḫḫ=idi*** 'seat' from ***naḫḫ-*** 'to sit, to sit down', it is conceivable that the personal name *Ḫu-pa-ar-ša* at Nuzi should not be normalized to ***Kuparša*** as P.M. Purves (*NPN*, 230) did, but be analysed as {*ḫub-arša*} 'The young boy is a bull-calf' or even as {*ḫub=a-arša*} 'The young boy is *like* a bull-calf ', {*ḫub=a-*} in the *essive* case, see Hurrian and Urartian ***aršə*** 'young man, boy', cf. Th. Richter, *BGH*, 48, s.v. ****arš-***.

Linear A ***ku-pa₃-nu*** (HT 1a.3; HT 88.5; HT 117a.3; HT 122a.6; HT 122a.7; HT? 170b.3; possibly HT 3.6; HT 42.3; HT 49a.6-7), analysed as ***Ḫub(=i)=a=nnu***, means 'He (the boy) is like a bull-calf', with the *optional allomorphic* enclitic personal pronoun ***-nnu***.

Gordon's identification of Ugaritic '*Gupanu*' in Linear A seems still possible. In the Linear A context I consider interpretation as a theophorous anthroponym more likely than as a divine name. Gordon explains Linear A ***ku-pa-na-tu***, which should be read as ***ku-pa₃-na-tu*** (HT 47a.1-2; HT 119.3), as the regular feminine form of *gupanu*. This explanation is in my view still possible, but it seems no longer the only possibility.

Th. Richter (*VHN*, 625[+1096]) mentions, sub 4.3: *Einwortnamen* mit ***°=atum*** ['one-word' names with ***°=atum***], that several personal names (possibly exclusively of women) show the ending ***°atum*** (inflexion ***°atim***), allegedly with a diminutive function, attached to a verbal form or nominal stem. For this he refers (*ibidem*, o.c., note 1096) to Ranke, 1905, 14ff.; Stamm, 1939, 113f.; Lewy, 1946, 376ff.; Rasmussen, 1981, 187f. ("a feminizing hypocoristic ending ... not very productive in masculine personal names") and Eidem/Læssøe, 2001, 147 (ad *Ḫazipatum*). Streck, (2000, 313ff. §§ 4.7-4.11) has the view that ***°atum*** has for Amorite only a diminutive function in masculine personal names, but indicates the gender of the lady in feminine personal names. However, Huffmon (1965, 133) thinks that ***°atum*** is a "hypocoristic ending" in feminine personal names, but has a "more general, caritative sense" in masculine personal names. The ending ***°atum*** occurs in the following Hurrian names: (A) attached to *finite* verbal forms: ***ᶠḪunzullatum*** (Mari); ***ᶠKuntullatum*** (Mari); (B) attached to hypocoristic verbal forms: ***ᶠ⁽?⁾Akujatum*** (Mari); ***ᶠNanijatum*** (Mari); (C) attached to nominal forms: ***ᶠAzzuatum*** (Mari); ***ᶠMennatum*** (Mari); ***ᶠMinnunnatum*** (Mari); (D) uncertain: ***ᶠŠawlatum*** (Mari, [Tuttul]), cf. Th. Richter, *VHN*, 625.

Consequently, if Linear A ***ku-pa₃-nu*** (HT 1a.3; HT 88.5; HT 117a.3; HT 122a.6; HT 122a.7; HT? 170b.3; possibly HT 3.6; HT 42.3; HT 49a.6-7) is analysed as Hurrian ***Ḫub(=i)=a=nnu***, meaning 'He (the boy) is like a bull-calf', with the *optional allomorphic* enclitic personal pronoun ***-nnu***, Linear A ***ku-pa₃-na-tu*** (HT 47a.1-2; HT 119.3) could be the diminutive or caritative form (with diminutive suffix ***°atum***) of ***Ḫub(=i)=a=nnu*** and be analysed as ***Ḫub=a=n(nu)=atum*** 'He (the boy) is like a *little* bull-calf'.

The following sequence ***pu-ra₂*** (HT 116a.2) also occurs on another tablet (HT 28a.3) from Hagia Triada and may well be compared with Linear A] ***pu₂-ra₂*** (ZA 6a.5) from Kato Zakro. Linear A ***pu-ra₂*** (HT 28a.3; HT 116a.2) represents either ***Puria*** or ***Pulia***. Since Linear B sign ***ra₂*** is interpreted as ***ria/rya*** or ***lia/lya***, the Linear A homographic syllabic sign ***58*** = ***ra₂*** probably has the same phonetic value. Linear A] ***pu₂-ra₂*** (ZA 6a.5), followed by GRA+*pa* or GRA+A, is probably a writing variant of ***pu-ra₂*** and is probably a personal name. Linear B ***pu₂*** (***phu/bu***) may according to F.M.J. Waanders be derived from Linear A /***bhu***/. Linear A ***pu-ra₂*** FIC 6 (HT 28a.3) and ***pu-ra₂*** , GRA 40 OLE+*di* (HT 116a.2) are each followed by ideograms indicating agricultural commodities. They may well be personal names that can be identified with a name attested at Nuzi as ***Pu-ri-ia***, which I.J. Gelb (*NPN*, 118) compares with ***Pureja*** (wr. *Pu-re-e-a, Pu-re-ia, Pu-re-e*).

P.M. Purves (*NPN*, 247) offers 3 possible etymologies for the onomastic element ***pur***: ***pur*** (1) Hurrian. *Pu-ru-uḫ-le-e-a.* Cf. Akkadianized Hurrian ***p/wuruḫlu***, equivalent to Akkadian ***sutānu***, 'south(ern)', since *i-na wu-ru-uḫ-li*, JEN 176:8, corresponds to *i-na su-ta-an-ni*, JEN 524:11, in descriptions of the same piece of real estate, etc., (2) Akkadian ***bûr***, 'son'? or (3) Kassite ***p/bur*** 'lord' (see *purias̆*) ?

Th. Richter (*VHN*, 489) mentions that the meaning 'sehen' ['to see'] for the Hurrian verbal root ***pur-*** *{fur-}* is unanimously accepted in recent research (cf. *BGH*, 325-326). Connected are the Hurrian nouns ***purani*** 'Vorzeichen' ['sign, omen'] and ***puri*** 'Blick' ['view, look, gaze, glance'], although the latter, in case it should be distinguished from ***puri*** 'view, look, gaze, glance', is also known as 'Opferterminus' ['sacrificial term'], cf. *BGH*, 329. Th. Richter mentions the Hurrian personal name ***Purija*** (wr. *Pu-ri-ia*) also at Mari, Šubat-Enlil and Tuttul, and further ***Arip-purani*** at Tigunāni, ***Purana*** at Mari and ***Putal-puri*** at Mari.

Linear A ***pu-ra₂*** (HT 28a.3; HT 116a.2), ***Purija***, can be interpreted as *{pur=i=ja}*, a hypocoristic personal name (with hypocoristic suffix ***-ja***) or as *{pur=i=a}*, a (transitive) 'one word' personal name, consisting of the root ***pur-*** 'to see' + the marker of transitivity ***-i-*** + the suffix ***-a*** marking the subject (3rd person singular) of the transitive verb, that can be translated as 'He/She sees'.

Compare also ***Wur-tešup*** (wr. *Wu-ur-te-šup*), 6 persons with that name at Nuzi, and ***Wur-teḭa*** (wr. *Wu-ur-te-ia*), 4 persons with that name at Nuzi, which implicates a possible alternation ***pur-/wur-*** (cf. I.J. Gelb, *NPN*, 174).

Since ***ra₂*** is not only ***ria/rya***, but also ***lia/lya*** in Linear A and B, ***pu-ra₂*** (HT 28a.3; HT 116a.2) can also be interpreted as ***Pu-lia***, attested as *Pu-li-a* in Cappadocia, *PNC* 27 (cf. E. Laroche, *NH,* 149, nº 1045, s.v. *Pulia*). Th. Richter (*VHN*, 237) mentions the Hurrian personal name ***ᶠPulija*** (wr. *ᶠPu-li-ia, ᶠPu-li-a*) as name of 4 women at Mari, *{po/ul=i=ja}*, typology 1.1.1.2.4, lexicon *pul-*. ***Pulija*** can be interpreted as a hypocoristic personal name (with the hypocoristic suffix ***-ja***) or as a (transitive) 'one word' personal name, analysis *{po/ul=i=a}*, cf. Old Hurrian *Pu-lu-ya* at Mari and Ugarit (cf. F. Gröndahl, *PNTU*, 1967, 348) and *Bu-ul(!)-li-ia* = *Bu-li-ia* at Middle-Assyrian Assur.

Th. Richter (*VHN*, 236-237, 488) also mentions the hypocoristic personal names ***Pulaja*** (wr. *Pu-la-ia*) and ***ᶠPulaja*** (wr. *ᶠPu-la-ia*) at Mari, analysis *{po/ul=a=ja}*, typology 1.1.1.3.4; *Pu-la-ia-an* at Alalaḫ IV (*AT* 168: 11); ***Pulukan*** (wr. *Pu-lu-ga-an*) at Mari and Tuttul, analysis *{po/ul=o=kk=o»a=n(na)}*, typology 1.2.2.1, lexicon *pul-*; ***ᶠPulum*** (wr. *ᶠPu-lu-um*) at Ašnakkum, analysis *{po/ul=o=m}*, typology 1.1.1.1.1, lexicon *pul-*; ***ᶠPulum-kijaze*** (wr. *ᶠPu-lu-um-ki-ia-ze*) at Ašnakkum and Mari, analysis *{po/ul=o=m-kiaže}*, typology 1.1.1.1.1, lexicon *pul-, kijaze*; ***Pulum-šarri*** (wr. *Pu-lu-um-šarri*) at Mari, analysis *{po/ul=o=m-šarri}*, typology 1.1.1.1.1, lexicon *pul-, šarri*; ***ᶠPulum-***[...] (wr. *ᶠPu-lu-um-*[...]) at Mari, analysis *{po/ul=o=m-šarri}*, typology 1.1.1.1.1, lexicon *pul-, šarri*; cf. also ***Wul-tešup*** (wr. *Wu-ul-te-šup*) at Nuzi, SMN 347; 518 (cf. I.J. Gelb, *NPN*, 174), which implicates a possible alternation ***pul-/wul-***.

Th. Richter (*VHN*, 488) mentions s.v. ***pul-*** *{po/ul-}* that the root ***pul-*** is attested in the Hurrian-Hittite bilingual ***Kirenze*** (KBo 32: 12 Rs. IV 3') in *pu-lu-uš-d*[*u*...], but the meaning cannot yet be established, because the Hittite translation is missing. He adds (note 624) that there is no doubt about the Hurricity of the personal names collected by him in spite of the *lemma* on Kassite *pula* in *NPN*, 246, and Balkan, 1954, 173.

Tablet HT 28 (broken into 6 pieces) is written by scribe *14 HT* according to *GORILA 5*, *Scribes*; *a*-side *GORILA* = *b*-side Brice, Raison-Pope, Van Soesbergen and *vice versa.*

Linear A ***a-ru-da-ra*** GRA 5 ***67*** 2 OLE+***di*** 3 (HT 28b.5-6) from Hagia Triada is a Hurrian personal name that can be analysed as {*ar=ud-alla*}, consisting of the verbal root ***ar-*** 'to give' + the Old Hurrian negation-suffix ***-ud-*** + the theophorous element ***Alla(i)*** '(the) Lady', translation 'The Lady did not give' or 'Do not give, oh Lady !'.

According to I. Wegner (*Einführung*, 96-97) ***-ut-*** is an Old Hurrian negation-morpheme known almost exclusively from the Hurrian-Hittite bilingual ***Kirenze*** (KBo 32). She also mentions that E. Neu (StBoT 32, 1996, 164) thinks that ***-u-*** comprises the negation and ***-t-*** the formant marking the past. From the bilingual she offers the following forms with the 3rd person sing. ergative in ***=o=m***: *fur=ud=o=m* 'er sah nicht (einen zweiten Bezirk)' ['he did not see (a second district)'] (KBo 32: 14 I 38); and *am=ud=o=m* 'er erreichte nicht (das jenseitige Ufer)' ['he did not reach (the other bank)'] (KBo 32: 14 I 29).

She adds (n. 83) that (apart from the bilingual) forms like *ḫu-up-pu-ta-aš-ša-a-al-la-a-an* in the Tušratta letter (Mit. II 22) may contain the negation-morpheme ***-ut-*** (V. Haas – I. Wegner, *Festschrift Klengel, AoF 24/2*, 1997, 344 ff.).

The next Linear A sequence ***i-ta-ja*** OLE+***di*** 10 (HT 28b.6) from Hagia Triada is probably a Hurrian hypocoristic personal name. It can be analysed as {*itt=a=ja*}, consisting of the Hurrian verbal root ***itt-*** 'to go' + the marker of intransitivity ***-a-*** + the hypocoristic suffix ***-ya***, translation 'He/She goes'. E. Laroche, *GLH*, 128, s.v. ***idd-*** 'aller' ['to go']: S'oppose à ***un-*** 'venir'; A. Goetze, *Language 15*, 219 sq. cf. E.A. Speiser, *IH*, *passim*. Inf. *id-du-um-mi*, Mit. I 93, II 98. etc. ***ittaranni*** 'coureur, messager ?'.

Th. Richter, *BGH*, 110-111, s.v. ***itt-*** I [Boğ.; Mitt.] 'gehen, losgehen, abgehen, reisen'. (LÚ) ***ittaranni*** [loan-word into Hittite] 'runner, courier' (F.W. Bush, 1973, 44); ***ittummi*** [Mit.] {*itt=ummi*} 'departure', 'andare' ['to go'].

Tablet KH 10 from Khania contains some interesting names:

KH 10.1.		]′	
2.		] vest.	GRA 10
3.	*i-pa-sa-ja* , *qa-85*[ ]	or *qa*	TAL [ ]
3-4.	*a-ki-pi-e-te*		GRA 90

The Linear A personal name ***i-pa-sa-ja*** (KH 10.3) at Khania, is a perfect equivalent to the Hurrian hypocoristic anthroponym ***Ipšaja*** at Nuzi (wr. *Ip-ša-a-a*, *Ip-šá-a-a*), cf. I.J. Gelb, *NPN*, 72; P.M. Purves, *NPN*, 220, s.v. ***ipš***, ***ipša-***, with hypocoristic suffix ***-ya***.

The orthographic conventions of Linear A and B require for the consonant cluster ***-pš-*** in ***Ipšaja*** that the labial occlusive ***-p-*** must always be expressed, which is only possible by usage of a mute vowel ***-a***, borrowed from the syllable to which it belongs. In other words the cluster ***-pša-*** can only be expressed in Linear A by writing ***-pa-sa-***. So the Linear A form offers the spelling that is expected. In fact this form offers an external confirmation of the orthographic conventions as part of the decipherment of Linear B by M. Ventris.

Ipšaja, the name of 18 persons at Nuzi, may well be a hypocoristic of e.g. ***Ipša-ḫalu*** (wr. *Ip-ša-ḫa-lu, Ip-šá-ḫa-lu, Ip-ša-ḫa-a-lu*), the name of 77 persons at Nuzi, cf. I.J. Gelb, *NPN*, 71-72; cf. P.M. Purves, *NPN*, 220. There is an ***Ipša-ḫalu*** son of *Ar-te-ia* and an ***Ipšaja*** son of *Ar-te-ia*. There is an ***Ipša-ḫalu*** son of *Ḫa-ma-an-na* and an ***Ipšaja*** son of *Ḫa-ma-an-na*. There is an ***Ipša-ḫalu*** son of *It-ḫi-iš-ta* and an ***Ipšaja*** son of *It-ḫi-iš-ta*.

The Tušratta letter offers some verbal forms with the root ***ipš-*** (Mit. III 19-20): .... *ú-na-a-la-an* (19) *še-e-ni-íw-wu-ú-a ti-i-ḫa->ni<-níš-ḫa-la-an ip-šu-ši-i-la-an* (20) = *un=a=l(la)=an šen(a)=iff=u=va tîḫan=>ni<=i=šḫ(i>)a=l(la)=an ipš=oš=i=l(la)-an.* I translate I. Wegner's German translation (*Einführung*, 156-157, 160) into English: 'And they (i.e. the things) come to my brother [Amenhotep III] and the indicated (things) have been pleasant.' [The reading concerning *>ni<* is based on the passage *ip-šu-ši-i-in ti-i-ḫa-níš-ḫi-i-in* (Mit. IV 49).] - Commentary: ***un=a=l(la)=an*** consists of the root ***un-*** 'to come' + marker of intransitivity ***-a-*** + shortened suffix ***-l-*** of the enclitic pronoun 3rd person plural ***-lla-*** as marker of the subject of the intransitive sentence + connective ***-an***.

šen(a)=iff=u=va consists of the root ***šen(a)-*** 'brother' + the suffix of the possessive pronoun 1st person singular ***-iff-*** + thematic vowel ***-u-*** + dative suffix ***-va***.

tîḫan=>ni<=i=šḫ(i>)a=l(la) consists of the root ***tîḫan-*** 'to indicate' + ***-i-*** + ***-šḫ(i>)a-*** + ***l(la)*** + ***an***. Derivation of the word is not clear, but it seems to be a substantive in ***-šḫi***, which led to the translation 'the indicated (things)'.

ipš=oš=i=l(la)-an consists of the verbal root ***ipš-*** (meaning unknown, provisionally translated as 'to be pleasant' [German 'gefällen']) + the suffix ***-oš-*** indicating the past or perfect tense + marker of transitivity ***-i-*** + shortened suffix ***-l-*** of the enclitic pronoun 3rd person plural ***-lla-*** as marker of the subject of the intransitive or antipassive sentence + connective ***-an***. The verbal form ***ipš=oš=i=l(la)-an*** is antipassive. Lexically the verb ***ipš-*** has been marked as a transitive form by theme- vowel ***-i-***, but syntactically it is intransitive, since no direct object is expressed. The *absolutive* enclitic personal pronoun 3rd person plural ***-l(la)-*** functions as subject marker, in this case in an antipassive construction.

Another personal name ***a-ki-pi-e-te*** (KH 10.3-4) on the same Linear A tablet from Khania seems to contain the Old Hurrian verbal element {*ag=i=b-*} 'he / she brings' and the theophorous element ***-Te***, hypocoristic of ***-Tešub***, comparable with ***Akip-Tešub*** (wr. *A-kip-te-šub*) and the assimilated form ***Akit-Tešub*** (wr. *A-ki-it-te-šub*) at Nuzi, cf. I.J. Gelb, *NPN*, 16. The unassimilated form ***Akip-Tešub***, analysis {*ag=i=b-Tešub*}, translation 'Tešub, he (***-b-***) brought (the child)', contains the consonant cluster ***-pt-***, which poses no problems in cuneiform writing, since that script has not only syllabic signs of the type consonant+vowel (CV), but also of the types VC and CVC. That is an essential difference with the Aegean syllabic scripts of Class A and B that only have signs for open syllables. A Minoan scribe wishing to write ***Ag=i=b-Te*** with Linear A, had to write "***a-ki-pe-te***", since occlusives always had to be expressed in Linear A and B consonant clusters.

This means that the consonant cluster ***-pt-*** had to be expressed as ***-pe-te***, if ***-e*** is the vowel following ***-t-***. But what could a scribe do, if a syllabic sign for ***pe*** failed in Linear A or if it was so rare that it was hardly ever used. To date a Linear A equivalent of Linear B sign ****72 = pe*** has not yet been recognized.

The rare Linear A sign ***63*** may be a good candidate for the value ***pe***. It is attested at Hagia Triada, Knossos and Kato Zakro, but not yet at Khania, where ***a-ki-pi-e-te*** occurs. The Linear A sequence ***ki-63-re*** (HT 37.4) from Hagia Triada would indeed provide a plausible Hurrian formation ***ki-pe(?)-re***, that can be interpreted as Hurrian ***ki-be-re*** or ***ki-be-le*** 'Jäger, Fallensteller' ['hunter, bird-catcher, fowler'], cf. Th. Richter, *BGH*, 200, s.v. ***ke-bi-ri*** [Boğ.], {*kev=i=ri/e*}, 'someone who has set up (a trap)' (G. Wilhelm 1991b, 164).

Compare I. Wegner – V. Haas (1999a, 199, s.v. ***ke-bi-ri*** [Boğ.]); and ***kebli / kebe/ili*** (?) [Alalaḫ VII; Boğ.; Mari] 'Jäger, Fallensteller' ['hunter, bird-catcher, fowler'], cf. Th. Richter, *VHN*, 439, s.v. ***kebali / kebeli*** (same meaning), from verbal root ***kib-/ke(b)-*** 'to place, set'. The ending ***-i-ri*** marks a participle and the ending ***-li*** indicates a profession.

Could the Minoan scribe from Khania have used the same orthographic solution as cuneiform scribes had at their disposal, if they wanted to make clear that the vowel ***e*** was required, if they had used an ***i***-containing syllabic sign. They could, for instance, write ***pi-e*** to express ***pe***. In cuneiform this orthographic solution was frequently used. The high number of writing variants in cuneiform is partly the result of the habits of scribes and their preferences. It is clear that Minoan scribes tried to use the space on their very small tablets as economically as possible, so if a scribe used a cuneiform-like solution, as I suspect he did in the case of ***a-ki-pi-e-te*** (KH 10.3-4), it must have been out of necessity.

Anyway it cannot be excluded that some scribes have been familiar with reading cuneiform texts, although they did not need that much more complicated script for their bureaucratic administration. We do not know whether the Minoan palaces kept diplomatic relations with rulers in the Near East and possibly with the capital of Mitanni, and if so, whether they corresponded with these rulers. Apart from some Near Eastern seals and the alabaster lid of a vessel with the Egyptian hieroglyphic cartouche of Hyksos pharaoh Chian of the 15th dynasty, found in the Palace of Knossos, there is, as far as I know, no written *cuneiform* evidence found in Minoan Crete. Comparison of ***a-ki-pi-e-*** in Linear A ***a-ki-pi-e-te*** (KH 10.3-4) with cuneiform ***Akipei*** (wr. *A-ki-be-e-i*) at Nuzi (cf. I.J. Gelb, *NPN*, 15; P.M. Purves, *NPN*, 198) does not make sense, since ***Akipei*** is interpreted as a genitive *{agib=e=(w)i}* 'The one (the child) of Agib'. Names such as ***Akipei*** at Nuzi, explained as a genitive *{agib=e=(w)i}* may have a *possessive* or a *patronymic*, c.q. *metronymic*, meaning, cf. Th. Richter, *VHN*, 620-621, sub 3.2.2.

Since the theophorous element ***-te*** is hypocoristic for ***-tešup*** and ***-teia̯***, the name is in fact equivalent to the 'Old Hurrian' Nuzi personal names ***Akip-tešup*** (wr. *A-kip-te-šup*), assimilated ***Akit-tešup*** < ***Akip-tešup*** (wr. *A-ki-it-te-šup*), ***Akip-teia̯*** (wr. [*A-ki*]*p-te-ia*), assimilated ***Akitte*** < ***Akip-te*** (wr. *A-ki-it-te*) and its variant ***Akitti*** (wr. *A-ki-it-ti*), 'Mitanni Hurrian' ***Aki-tešup*** (*A-ki-te-šup*) and ***Aki-teia̯*** (wr. *A-ki-te-ia*), cf. I.J. Gelb, *NPN*, 16-17; P.M. Purves, *NPN*, 198.

The names with single writing of ***-t-***, *A-ki-te-šup* and *A-ki-te-ia*, may be interpreted as *imperative* instead of *indicative*, analysis {*ag=i-Tešub*} and {*ag=i-Teia̯*}, respectively, so that they can be translated as 'Bring (the child), oh Tešub !'.

Th. Richter (*VHN*, 366-368) interprets the *transitive* verbal root ***ag-/akk-*** as '(herauf)-bringen' ['to bring up'] and the *intransitive* root as 'heraufkommen, erscheinen > geboren werden' ['to come up, to appear > to be born'].

The root ***ak-***, /*ag-*/, occurs frequently in the Tušratta letter and was first translated by F. Bork, *Mitannisprache*, 124, as 'darbringen', 'abliefern', by G.R. Meyer, *AOF XII (1937-39)*, 368, as 'bestimmen', but by E.A. Speiser, *JAOS LIX (1939)*, 298 and n. 36, as 'guide', 'direct', on account of comparison with Urartian ***agu*** 'guide', 'direct'.

E.A. Speiser and others regarded ***-p-/-b-*** as a root-complement, but since publication of the Hurrian-Hittite bilingual ***Kirenze*** (KBo 32) ***-b-*** has been recognized as the Old Hurrian marker of the 3rd person singular indicating the subject of the verb.

This element is frequent in Hurrian personal names, with several variants, of which the most frequent are ***akap-*** {*ag=a=b-*} and ***akip-*** {*ag=i=b-*}, e.g. *Akip-apu, Akip-matka, Akip-ninu, Akip-pašaḫ, Akip-šali, Akip-šarri, Akip-šatna, Akip-šenni, Akip-tašenni, Akip-tilla, Akip-tirwi, Akip-tura(e)*, cf. P.M. Purves, *NPN*, 198.

The Linear A name ***a-ki-pi-e-te*** was in the first edition translated 'Tešub is guiding', 'Tešub is directing'. Now I prefer 'Tešub brought (the child)'. Cf. e.g. Th. Richter, *VHN*, 46, s.v. ***Akip-šarri*** (wr. *A-ki-ip*-LUGAL), analysis {*ag=i=b-šarri*}, typology 1.1.1.2.1, lexicon ag-, *šarri*, 'Der Götterkönig brachte (Jungen) herauf' ['The King of Gods brought (the boy) (up)'], name of a weaver at Mari.

If ***a-ki-pi-e-te*** (KH 10.3-4) is indeed a variant writing for *****a-ki-pe-te***, analysed as Old Hurrian {*ag=i=b-Te(šub)*}, as the required Linear A orthography for {*ag=i=b-Te(šub)*}, this interpetation is satisfactory because of the variants ***-Tešub, -Teḭa*** and ***-Te***.

However, another explanation may be possible as well, since it appears that ***-tte*** / ***-tti*** can also be *optional allomorphic* enclitic personal pronouns replacing the normal enclitic personal pronoun ***-tta*** indicating the 1st person singular in 'one-word' personal names, cf. Th. Richter, *VHN*, 595-596. See the variants ***Ullutta*** at Šušarrā and ***Ullutti*** at Mari and Tigunāni, that can be translated as 'Destroy me !'. The *absolutive* suffix ***-tta*** indicates the object of a transitive and the subject of an intransitive verb.

In fact I.J. Gelb (*NPN*, 17) and P.M. Purves (*NPN*, 198) offer the personal name ***Akitta*** (wr. *A-ki-it-ta*) and the variants ***Akitte*** (wr. *A-ki-it-te*) and ***Akitti*** (wr. *A-ki-it-ti*) at Nuzi. These names can be analysed as an *imperative* {*ag=i=tta/e/i*} and be translated as 'Bring me (oh *numen*) !' If ***Akitta*** is an assimilated form < ***Ag=i=b=tta***, ***Akitte*** < ***Ag=i=b=tte***, ***Akitti*** < ***Ag=i=b=tti***, we are dealing with *indicatives* 'He / She (a *numen*) brought me'. Consequently, Linear A ***a-ki-pi-e-te*** (KH 10.3-4) can also be analysed as the *indicative* {*ag=i=b=tte*} and be translated as 'He / She (a *numen*) brought me'.

All editors read the Linear A inscription ***qe-si-te*** $_2$ (MA Ze 11), incised on the (Middle Minoan III ?) south-wall of the northwest court (IV) of the Palace of Malia (northwest corner-stone of wall of room IV 7). Since the Mycenaean Greeks needed Linear B signs representing the Indo-European labio-velar sounds, they probably used Linear A signs representing the (voiced) velar fricatives [***ġ***] for their labio-velar series, cf. the discussion s.v. Linear A ***ka-pa*** and ***ka-pa-qe***. As a result Linear A ***qe-*** represents cuneiform ***ḫe-***.

Linear A ***qe-si-te*** may well be interpreted as a Hurrian sentence name and be analysed as {*ḫerš=i-te(šo/ub)*}, consisting of the verbal root ***ḫerš-*** + the marker of transitivity ***i-*** + the theophorous element ***-te***, that is just as ***-teḭa*** hypocoristic of ***-teš(š)ub*** in Hurrian personal names, cf. Linear A ***a-ki-pi-e-te***, ***da-du-te***, ***si-lu-te***, ***si-da-te***, ***su-ki-ri-te-i-ja***, ***o-te-ja***. Linear A ***qe-si-*** can represent Hurrian ***Ḫerši-***, since ***-r-*** preceding ***-s-*** in consonant clusters was not expressed in Linear A and B.

At Nuzi we find the following 'one word' personal names with the root ***ḫerš-/ḫerz-***: ***Ḫerši*** (wr. *Ḫé-er-ši*), ***Ḫeršiḭa*** (wr. *Ḫé-er-ši-ia, Ḫe-er-ši-ia*), ***Ḫeršitta*** (wr. *Ḫé-er-ši-it-ta*), ***Ḫerzi*** (wr. *Ḫé-er-zi, Ḫe-er-zi*), ***fḪerzikui*** (wr. *fḪe-er-zi-ku-i*), SMN 394, cf. I.J. Gelb, *NPN*, 60; P.M. Purves, *NPN*, 216. ***Ḫerši*** (wr. *Ḫé-er-ši*) at Nuzi is 1. son of *Ḫa-aš*-[....], 2. son of *Ip-šá-a-a*, 3. son of *Na-ni*-i[a]), cf. I.J. Gelb, *NPN*, 60.

Compare Linear A ***i-pa-sa-ja*** (KH 10.3) from Khania (*supra*) with *Ip-šá-a-a*, father of ***Ḫerši*** at Nuzi. Incidentally, I think that ***ᶠḪerzikui***, probably < * *ᶠḪerziku=wi*, may well be a (patronymic ?) genitive of ****ᶠḪerziku***.

For the hypocoristic element ***-te*** in Hurrian personal names one may compare P.M. Purves, *NPN*, 264, s.v. ***te***: Hurrian. Shortened form of ***-tešup*** and ***-te̯ia*** as final element. See L. Oppenheim in *WZKM XLIV*, 203 f., n. 1, and Purves in *JAOS LVIII*, 465-467, also genealogies indicated in name list by Dr. Gelb. For names in which ***te*** is a variant of ***te̯ia***, see s.v. ***-te***: *Al-ki-te, Eḫ-li-te, Ḫa-iš-te, Ḫu-i-te, Ḫu-i-te-e, Ḫu-e-te, Ḫu-i-ti, In-zi-te, Ma-ar-te, Ša-aḫ-lu-te-e, Ša-aḫ-lu-te, Ša-ḫu-ul-te-e, Še-ḫal-te, Še-ḫa-al-te, Ši-la-ḫi-te, Ši-il-wa-te, Du-ra-ar-te, Ur-ḫi-te*. Compare also the long lists of personal names provided by P.M. Purves (*NPN*, 264) s.v. ***-te*** and ***-te̯ia*** with those s.v. ***-tešup*** (*NPN*, 265-266), with many correlations between those names.

A. Draffkorn (*HHA*, 33) mentions, s.v. ***Ḫerze***, 4 persons with the Hurrian personal name **Ḫe-er-še* from Alalaḫ VII (inscriptions from level VII are marked with *):
1) **Ḫe-er-še,* son of *Wullu-ra* AT *375:6; - 2) **Ḫe-er-še,* LÚ ŠU.I, AT *240:3,12;
3) **Ḫe-er-še,* LÚ UŠ.BAR, AT *247:9; - 4) **Ḫe-er-še* AT *33:8; *36:10.

Unfortunately the meaning of the verbal root ***ḫerš-*** and ***ḫerz-*** is not yet known. According to Th. Richter (*VHN, passim*) many theophorous personal names with a verbal root as first element can be interpreted as *imperative*, so that the God addressed in the name is in the *vocative*, in this case 'oh Tešub !'.

Th. Richter (*VHN*, 136-137) mentions ***Ḫerzi*** (wr. *Ḫe-er-zi*), a man living in the mountains (LÚ *pabanḫu*) at Mari and the same name at Nippur (wr. *Ḫe-er-zi*), cf. Clay, *PNCP*, 80, who reads *Ḫi-ir-zi*, analysis {*ḫerž=i*} (imperative), typology 1.3.1.2.1, lexicon *ḫerz-*; ****Ḫerše*** (wr. **Ḫé-er-še*), 4 persons at Alalaḫ VII (cf. D.J. Wiseman, *AT*, 135; A. Draffkorn, *HHA*, 33); ***Ḫersi*** (wr. **Ḫer-si*) at (Middle-Assyrian) Tall Ḫuēra; ***Ḫerzija*** (wr. *Ḫe-er-zi-ia*) at Mari and Qaṭṭarā, analysis {*ḫerž=i=ja*}, typology 1.1.1.2.4, 'one word' name 3rd person singular (indicative) or hypocoristic name with hypocoristic suffix ***-ya*** (imperative); ***Ḫeršitta*** (wr. *Ḫe-er-ši-it-ta*), at Qaṭṭarā, analysis {*ḫerž=i=tta*}, typology 1.3.1.2.2.1; ****Ḫeršulla*** (wr. **Ḫe-er-šu-ul-la*) at Alalaḫ VII (*AT* *43 = *UF 37*, 253: 4), analysis {*ḫerž=u=lla*}; ***Ḫerzin*** (wr. *Ḫe-er-zi-in*) at Mari, typology 1.3.1.2.2.1, analysis {*ḫerž=i=n(na)*}; ***Ḫeršu*** (wr. *Ḫe-er-šu, Ḫé-er-šu*) at Tigunāni and Alalaḫ VII and IV (cf. D.J. Wiseman, *AT*, 135; A. Draffkorn, *HHA*, 33), typology 1.3.1.1.1, analysis {*ḫerž=o*}, lexicon *ḫerš-*; ***Ḫerzuk*** (wr. *Ḫe-er-zu-uk*) at Mari, analysis {*ḫerž=o=g*}, typology 1.2.2.2, lexicon *ḫerz-*; ***Ḫerziḫe*** (wr. *Ḫe-er-zi-ḫe*) at Mari, typology 3.1, analysis {*ḫerž(i)=i=ġe*}, 'zu *ḫerzi* gehörig' ['belonging to *ḫerzi*'], lexicon *ḫerziḫe*.

According to Th. Richter (*VHN*, 471) ***ḫerš-*** and ***ḫerz-*** are the same root. The spelling with {E} is supported by the orthographies with [ḪÉ] at Nuzi, also once at Tigunāni (*Ḫé-er-šu*). To date the root is only found in personal names (Schwemer, 2001, 471), but may also occur in contextual forms as *ḫe-er-ši-t*[*u*(-)...] (ChS I/1, 46 Rs. III 13') and *ḫe-er-šu-uš-š*[*a*(-)...] (KUB 47, 12 Vs. I 6) and *ḫe-er-šu-u*[*š*(-)...] (I 7, all at Ḫattuša. All 'one word' names can be analysed as verbal names, except ***Ḫerziḫe*** that is nominal.

As we have just seen with regard to ***a-ki-pi-e-te*** (KH 10.3-4), ***-te*** cannot only be a hypocoristic of ***-Tešub***, but also the *optional allomorphic* enclitic personal pronoun ***-tte*** / ***-tti*** that can replace ***-tta*** indicating the 1st person singular in 'one-word' personal names.

This interpretation is also a likely possibility, since ***Ḫeršitta*** (wr. *Ḫe-er-ši-it-ta*), analysis {*ḫerž=i=tta*}, is indeed attested at Qaṭṭarā. If ***-te*** is interpreted in this way, the *absolutive* suffix ***-tte*** indicates the object of the transitive *imperative* ***Ḫersi-***.

Linear A ***qe-si-do-e*** 57 (ZA 4a.5; ZA 15a.2) from Kato Zakro seems *prima facie* to be a Hurrian personal name containing ***Ḫerši-*** or ***Ḫerzi-*** as first and ***-do-e*** (cuneiform ***-d/tu-i/e*** or possibly ***-t/du-(w)e/(w)i***) as second onomastic element, but such a division is probably not valid. I consider it most likely that it is a 'one word' personal name in the *genitive* that can be analysed as {*ḫerš=e/id=o/u=(w)e/i*}, consisting of the verbal root ***ḫerš-*** + the temporal suffix ***-ed-/-id-*** marking the future tense (position 2) + the marker of the subject of action 2nd person singular in ***-o*** (position 7) forming the personal name ****qe-si-do*** = {*ḫerš=id=o*}, of which ***qe-si-do-e*** is the *genitive* (with the *genitive* suffix ***-(w)e***), cf. I. Wegner, *Einführung*, 90: ***tad=ed=o*** 'du wirst lieben' ['you will love'] (2nd person singular future), cf. also *ibid*., 93, Table 4.

The formation of ***qe-si-do-e*** 57 (ZA 15a.2) seems similar to ***sa-mi-da-e*** 4 (ZA 15a.6-7) on the same tablet. We may also compare Hurrian ***ᶠḪerzikui*** (wr. *ᶠḪe-er-zi-ku-i*), SMN 394, from Nuzi (cf. I.J. Gelb, *NPN*, 60; P.M. Purves, *NPN*, 216) that may also be a genitive ***ᶠḪerzikui*** (< **ᶠḪerziku=wi*) of ****ᶠḪerziku***, but with the suffix ***-kk-*** indicating the negation of the *intransitive* and *antipassive* verb or with ***-ku*** as abbreviation of ***-Kušuh*** (God of the Moon). Since ***qe-si-do-e*** and ***sa-mi-da-e*** occur in a list of personal names on tablet ZA 15 and the other names show no features of a genitive, I presume that the genitives ***qe-si-do-e*** and ***sa-mi-da-e*** actually represent patronimic names, describing 'The one of / the child of ****qe-si-do***' and 'The one of / the child of ****sa-mi-da***'.

Linear A ***qe-si-do-e*** (ZA 4a.5; ZA 15a.2) and ***sa-mi-da-e*** 4 (ZA 15a.6-7) can in that case be compared with Linear B patronymic adjectives such as ***e-te-wo-ke-re-we-i-jo*** (PY An 654.8-9) = ***Ἐτεϝοκλεϝέίος***, derived from * ***Ἐτεϝοκλέϝης*** (> later ***Ἐτεοκλῆς***) = 'Truly famous', a name that belongs to the wide-spread category of 'expressive' personal names, allegedly expressing some quality of the 'named' person, 'the reality or authenticity of fame', cf. C.J. Ruijgh, *EGM*, § 177; ***ku-sa-me-ni-jo*** (PY An 519,16; 218,4), ***Κυρσαμένιος***, patronymic adjective derived from ****Κυρσαμενός***, cf. C.J. Ruijgh, *EGM,* § 118 + note 214.

The Linear A tablets ZA 4, ZA 5 and ZA 15 from Kato Zakro have much in common, for they register several identical personal names ***qe-si-do-e*** (ZA 4a.5; ZA 15a.2), ***no-nu-ma-re*** (ZA 4a.5-6; ZA 5b.1; ZA 15a.4-5), ***si-pi-ki*** (ZA 4a.6-7; ZA 5b.2; ZA 15a.5), ***ka-di*** (ZA 4a.8; ZA 15b.1) and ***sa-mi-da-e*** (ZA 5a.3; ZA 15a.6-7).

The Linear A personal name ***sa-mi-da-e*** (ZA 5a.3; ZA 15a.6-7) from Kato Zakro can be explained as either a nominal form, if it is based on the noun ***šalmi*** 'ash', or a verbal form, if it is based on the verbal root ***zam-*** II 'abreißen' ['to tear off']. The ambiguity rests on the orthographic conventions of Linear A (and B) that are a greater problem for us than they were for the Minoan scribes who knew which name they registered. In both cases I assume that the ending in ***-e*** probably represents a *genitive* in ****-we*** that may be interpreted as 'the one of …' indicating a patronymic or metronymic name 'the son / daughter of …', in this case 'The one of / the child of ****sa-mi-da***', cf. ***qe-si-do-e*** (ZA 4a.5; ZA 15a.2), just discussed. If we start with the nominal analysis of ***sa-mi-da-e***, {*šalm=i=da=(w)e*} can be explained as 'the son / daughter of **šalm=i=da*' and ****šalm=i=da*** can be interpreted as the *directive* case of ***šalmi*** 'to the ash(es) (of the deceased child or mother)'.

The joy of childbirth was often tempered by the loss of the mother giving birth or the recent death of another child. In Linear A and B a *liquid* preceding ***-m-*** was usually not expressed in consonant clusters.

Th. Richter (*VHN*, 497) mentions s.v. ***šalmuzzi*** {*šalmo/uzzi*} that the meaning of ***šalmi*** 'Asche' ['ash'] is known from the vocabulary from Ugarit RS 94-2939: (Sumerian) dè = (Akkadian) *dì-ik-mé-nu* = (Hurrian) ***šal-mi***, and that the word *ša-al-mu-zi* can be analysed as {*šalm(i)=o/u=zzi* } and be explained as an adjective 'pertaining to ash', cf. *BGH*, 346. Th. Richter (*VHN*, 244) translates the personal name ***ᶠŠalmuzzi*** from Mari, typology 3.1, as 'Der Asche angemessen' ['Pertaining to ash'].

The verbal analysis of ***sa-mi-da-e*** offers {*z/sam=id=a=(w)e*}, consisting of the verbal root ***zam(m)-/sam(m)-*** + the suffix marking the future tense ***-ed-/-id-*** + the suffix ***-a***, indicating the subject of action of the transitive ergative verb 3rd person singular, + the genitive suffix ***-we*** that lost ***-w-*** between two vowels: translation 'The son/daughter of "He/She (a *numen*) will break off / tear off the navel-string / umbilical cord" '.

Th. Richter (*VHN*, 245, 498) mentions, s.v. ***zam-*** II, that in spite of single writing of ***-m-*** in the personal name ***Zamal-tuk*** from Mari, the root may be ***zamm-***, c.q. ***samm-***, occurring in the bilingual ***Kirenze*** in the extended Hurrian stem {*zamm=al=ašt-*} that in accordance with the Hittite rendering ***arḫa šakkurija-*** can be translated as 'abreißen' ['to break off, to tear off']. The meaning of {*zam(m)=al-*} probably does not differ from {*zamm=al=ašt-*}, cf. also I. Wegner, *Einführung*, 87, s.v. ***zamm=al=ašt-***.

In onomastics the meaning may be sought in 'breaking off the navel-string / umbilical cord'. The personal name ***Zamal-tuk*** (wr. *Za-ma-al-du-uk*) from Mari, analysis {*zam=al-to/uk*}, typology 1.4, lexicon *zam-*, *tuk-* (→ *tukki*), can be translated as '*Tuk* broke / tore the navel-string / umbilical cord off'. Th. Richter (*BGH*, 348-349; *VHN*, 497-498) does not mention, whether ***šam-*** I and ***zam(m)-*** II might be the same roots.

The Linear A personal name ***si-pi-ki*** (ZA 4a.6-7; ZA 5b.2; ZA 15a.5) is thrice attested at Kato Zakro. It is identical with Hurrian ***Šipki***, first element in the Hurrian sentence name ***Šipki-Tešup*** (wr. *Ši-ip-ki-te-šup*), son of *Šuk-ri-ia* (*HSS* IX 35:33 and *JEN* 506: 5, 6) at Nuzi, that consists of the theophorous element ***-tešup*** and the onomastic element ***šipki-***, cf. I.J. Gelb, *NPN*, 135; P.M. Purves, *NPN*, 258, s.v. ***šipk***, ***šipki***. If ***šipki-*** {*šipk=i-*} is verbal, as it may well be, it probably can be interpreted as a transitive *imperative*, so that ***-Tešup*** in ***Šipki-Tešup*** can be explained as a *vocative*. Compare also the Hurrian personal name ***Ši-bi-ki-ri*** (AT 194: 5) from Alalaḫ (cf. A. Draffkorn, *HHA*, 141), which gives the impression of a participial ending in ***-i=ri***, cf. I. Wegner, *Einführung*, 21, 113: e.g. ***tab=i=ri*** 'der, der gießt, (Metall)gießer' ['the one who casts, caster (of metal, bronze)']. Th. Richter (*BGH*, 391) mentions with regard to ***šipk-*** [PN]: o.Ü. [without translation] referring to D. Schwemer, *Die Wettergottgestalten Mesopotamiens und Nordsyriens im Zeitalter der Keilschriftkulturen*, Wiesbaden 2001, 472. Incidentally, in ***Ši-bi-ki-ri*** (AT 194: 5) from Alalaḫ the clustering of the consonants ***-p/b-*** and ***-k/g-*** is avoided, probably to make pronunciation easier. Hurrian ***šipki*** can according to the orthographic conventions of Linear A and B only be rendered as ***si-pi-ki*** in Linear A, since the first ***-i-*** in ***ši-*** must be expressed, because it belongs to the root and the second *mute* ***-i-*** in ***-pi-*** is needed, because all occlusives ***-p-*** and ***-k-*** in consonant clusters must always be expressed in the script.

Linear A ***ka-di*** (ZA 4a.8 = HM 1615+ 2 fragm.; ZA 15b.1 = HM 1627) from Kato Zakro can theoretically be explained as either a nominal form, if it is based on the noun ***kade*** 'grain', or a verbal (*imperative*) form {*kad=e/i*} 'Speak !', based on the verbal root ***kad-/katt-*** 'to say, to speak'. Since it occurs on both tablets from Kato Zakro in lists of personal names, it is probably in both cases a so-called 'one-word' personal name.

I start with the least likely interpretation, Hurrian ***kade*** 'grain' ('barley' in particular). It seems significant that the sequence ***ka-di*** on these two tablets occurs both times in connection with the 'wine-ideogram' VIN*a*. The clearest example is on ZA 15b.1, where ***ka-di*** **,** VIN*a* 3 is clearly separated by a word divider. One may get the impression that the scribe wished to indicate that the items, registered by the sequence and the ideogram, belong to the category 'commodities'. The whole first line of ZA 15b is underscored by a line drawn with a ruler. ZA 15b.2 mentions: ***ku-ro*** **,** VIN*a* 78; ZA 15b.3: VIN+***ra*** 17; ZA 15b 4-7: vacant. The total numbers 78 and 17 on the *b*-side clearly refer to the entries on the *a*-side as well. So ***ka-di*** **,** VIN*a* 3 (ZA 15b.1) in fact belongs to the list of personal names on the *a*-side of the tablet.

On the other tablet ***ka-di*** 3 (ZA 4a.8) is the last isolated entry of the last line of the *a*-side. Here we find VIN*a* 104[(ZA 4b.2) at the top of the other side of the tablet. The top of ZA 4 is unfortunately heavily damaged on both sides, but that does not affect the reading of ***ka-di*** 3 (ZA 4a.8) and VIN*a* 104[ ] (ZA 4b.2). The high number of 104 [ ] portions makes it likely that the *vestigia* (traces) in ZA 4b.1 may well contain the sequence ****ku-ro*** indicating the total of 104 (or possibly more) portions of wine. If the combination of ***ka-di*** with the ideogram VIN*a* on both tablets from Zakros is observed in isolation, one might get the impression that this close relation between ***ka-di*** and VINa makes it likely that Linear A ***ka-di*** refers to a commodity, but analysis of the lists, in which ***ka-di*** occurs on both tablets, makes it very clear that it belongs to lists of personal names in both cases.

I have already discussed a similar situation regarding the Linear A personal name ***u-ti*** (HT 10b.1) that is the first sequence of the *b*-side of this tablet from Hagia Triada, whereas ***ku-ni-su*** (HT 10a.1) is the first sequence on the *a*-side. Although Th. Richter prefers a verbal root in the personal names ^{f}***Utte*** (wr. ^{f}*Ut-te*) from Ašnakkum, *Ú-ut-ti* from Alalaḫ, Ḫattuša and Nuzi, and *Ut-ti* from Emar, analysis {*utt-i*}, typology 1.3.1.2.1, lexicon *utt-*, he cannot fully exclude the possibility that the name is connected with the noun ***utte*** 'emmer', since ^{f}***Utte*** from Ašnakkum happens to be a 'Müllerin' ['female miller or miller's wife']. It might even be a nickname. ^{f}***Utten***, also from Ašnakkum, can eventually also be analysed in this way as {*o/utte=n(na)*} 'Sie (Frau) ist der Emmer' ['She (the woman) is emmer'] or name of birth 'Es (Mädchen) ist der Emmer' ['She (the girl) is emmer'].

Likewise, since we do not know, whether ***ka-di*** (ZA 4a.8; ZA 15b.1) might be the (nick)name of a miller or a miller's wife, we cannot exclude the possibility that the personal name ***ka-de*** has indeed the meaning 'Grain'.

According to E. Laroche (*GLH*, 133) Hurrian ***kade*** is 'grain'. He refers to RS voc. II 10: sum. ŠE = h. ***ka-te-ni-we***, gén. du dét. 'du grain'. ^{d}***ga-te-e-na***, pl. KUB XLV 47 III 8: attribut de Nikkal.

Th. Richter, *BGH*, 197-198, s.v. ***kade*** [Boğ; Nuzi] refers for the meaning 'grain' to E. Laroche (*GLH*, 133); B.H.L. van Gessel, *Onomasticon of the Hittite pantheon, Part I* (Handbuch der Orientalistik / Handbook of Oriental Studies I/ 33.1), Leiden 1998, 238.

S. Rösle, Heth. ^{NINDA}***gatai*** 'Gerstenbrot', hurr. ***kade*** 'Gerste', hatt. ***kait*** 'Getreide', und akk. ***kātu(m)***, ***gajjātu(m)*** 'Graupen, Gerste', oder Vom Wandel eines Wanderwortes, *Altorientalische Forschungen 31*, Berlin 2004, 299; I. Wegner, *Hurritische Opferlisten aus hethitischen Festbeschreibungen. Teil III: Das Glossar*, Corpus der hurritischen Sprachdenkmäler. I. Abteilung: Die Texten aus Boğazköy, Rome 2004, I/3-3, 225.

For the meaning 'Gerste, barley' (corresponding to Akkadian ***še'u***) Th. Richter refers to A. Fadhil, Studien zur Topographie und Prosopographie der Provinzstädte des Königreiches Arrapḫa, *Baghdader Forschungen 6*, Mainz 1983, 10; G. Wilhelm, Nuzi Note 28: *aladumma epēšu* 'begleichen; kaufen', *Studies on the Civilization and Culture of Nuzi and the Hurrians 8*, Bethesda 1996, 363; D. Prechel - Th. Richter, Abrakadabra oder Althurritisch. Betrachtungen zu einigen altbabylonischen Beschwörungstexten, in: Th. Richter, D. Prechel, J. Klinger (Hrsg.), *Festschrift Volkert Haas. Kulturgeschichten. Altorientalische Studien für Volkert Haas zum 65. Geburtstag*, Saarbrücken 2001, 364.

There is no *communis opinio* among scholars about the etymology and ultimate provenance of the term ***kade*** and cognate terms in several ancient languages.

E. Neu (Akkadisches Lehnwortgut im Hurritischen, *Archivum Anatolicum / Anadolu Arşivleri 3*, Ankara 1997, 259) mentions ***kade*** as 'eine genuin hurritische Getreidebezeichnung' [a genuinely Hurrian commodity-term] and I.M. Diakonoff regards it as non-Indo-European, but Th.V. Gamkrelidze - V.V. Ivanov, *Indo-European and the Indo-Europeans. A reconstrcution and historical analysis of a proto-language and a proto-culture* (Trends in linguistics. Studies and monographs 80, Part I), Berlin - New York 1995, 779, defend an Indo-European provenance: "Among the cultural terms common to Indo-European, Hattic, and Hurrian and evidently borrowed from Indo-European .. may also be a word for 'grain': PIE **Hat'* 'grain' .. beside Hattic *kait* 'grain; goddess of grain', Hurrian *kad/te* 'barley, grain'."

The first terms for agricultural commodities were probably created during the Neolithic revolution in the Near East and Anatolia, where archaeology provided the first evidence for the change from hunter-gatherer to agricultural societies, domestication of animals and founding of cities, but it is difficult to establish with any certainty, which early language or language-family was the first to create a term for a certain agricultural commodity that became a cultural loan-word (Wanderwort). Archaeology, ethnology (even now with the help of DNA-research), and linguistic research provide incomparable strands of evidence, if one is dealing with prehistoric periods. If the migration and arrival of people speaking a known language or dialect is not well-documented in contemporary sources or in the tradition of later generations, it is difficult, if not impossible, to prove conclusive relations with archaeological and ethnic data. A change of language or dialect in an area can be caused by newcomers, not only if they arrive in large numbers, but also if their numbers are small, provided that they are politically, militarily and / or culturally dominant. Akkadian is usually regarded as dominant, because it was the *lingua franca* used for diplomatic traffic and correspondence between states in the Near East, Egypt and Anatolia, especially during well-documented periods. This superstrate status of the language is often considered the source for providing loan-words. It is often thought that the Hurrians and the Hurrian language may well have taken the position of intermediary because of their central geographical position between South Iraq, Iran, Syria and Anatolia.

It is conceivable that, at the zenith of power of Urkiš and later the Mitannian empire, Hurrian may have taken a superstrate role as well. Anyway, whatever the original provenance of the word may be, it is clear that Linear A ***ka-di*** on the two tablets from Kato Zakro is an exact equivalent to the Hurrian (not the Akkadian or Hattic) term, if it reflects a name derived from the noun ***kade*** and not the *imperative* ***kad=i***.

Since verbal 'one-word' names are common in Hurrian, I consider analysis of ***ka-di*** (ZA 4a.8; ZA 15b.1) as an *imperative* ***kad=i*** 'Speak !' the most likely interpretation. Th. Richter, *BGH*, 195, s.v. ***kad-*** I, ***katt-*** [*passim*] 'sagen, sprechen'; *VHN*, 433, s.v. ***kad-/ katt-*** 'sagen' ['to say, to speak'], especially in onomastics '(Namen) sagen' ['to say (names)'].

A personal name representing the *indicative* 3rd person singular ***Katija*** (wr. *Ka-ti-ia*) is attested at Mari and (wr. *Ka-di(?)-ia*) at Assur, typology 1.1.1.2.4, analysis {*kad=i=ja*}, consisting of the root ***kad-*** + the marker of transitivity ***-i-*** + the marker of the 3rd person singular ***-a*** indicating the subject of action of the transitive verb, translation 'Er/Sie sagte (Namen)' ['He/She said (names)'], cf. Th. Richter, *VHN*, 154. A variant with voiceless dental (wr. *Kat-ti-ia*) is attested at Alalaḫ IV (AT 142 = *UF 34*, 847: 11) and (wr. *Ga-at-ti-ia*) at Middle-Babylonian Qaṭna (*QS 3*, 41:12).

Especially the personal name ***Katiri*** (wr. *Qa-ti-ri, Ka-ti-ri, Qa-di-ri, Ga-ti-ri, Ka-di-ri*) that can be interpreted as a participial formation in ***-i=ri***, is the name of 17 persons at Nuzi (cf. I.J. Gelb, *NPN*, 81) and can be translated as 'The one who has said (names)' or 'The one who has spoken'. Giving names can in this respect relate to two points of concern: 1. Is the child deaf or possibly deaf-mute ? 2. When does it utter the names of the parents ? Th. Richter (*VHN*, 154) also mentions ***Kattiri*** (wr. *Ka-at-ti-ri*) at Tigunāni, typology 3.1, 'Der (Namen) gesagt hat'; *Ka-ti-ri* at Alalaḫ VII (AT *37 = *UF 23*, 424: 12), Assur, Kār-Tukultī-Ninurta, Qaṭṭarā; *Ka-ti-ra* at Emar; *Ka-di-ri* at Nippur. ***Katirḫe*** (wr. *Ka-ti-ir-ḫe*) at Mari and Qaṭṭarā and ***Kattirḫe*** (wr. *Ka-at-ti-ir-ḫe*) at Tiginãni and ***Katterḫe*** (wr. *Ka-at-te-er-ḫé*) at Ḫattuša (E. Laroche, *NH*, 90: N° 549) can be interpreted as an adjectival form (with the adjectival suffix ***-ḫe/-ḫi***) and be translated as 'Zu dem, der (Namen) gesagt hat, gehörig' ['Belonging to the one who has said names'], cf. Th. Richter, *VHN*, 154-155. ***Katam-(a)tal*** (wr. *ka-ta-am-tal*) from Šušarrā, analysis {*kad=a=m(:b)-(a)dal*}, typology 1.1.1.3.2, lexicon *kad-*, *adal*. He does not translate the name, probably since his analysis with {*kad=a=m-*} shows an intransitive construction. This can be avoided, if an analysis with the *factitive* root-extension ***-am-*** is chosen resulting into {*kad=am-(a)dal*}, translation 'The strong one made (the child) say (names)' > 'The strong one encouraged (the child) to say (names)', cf. I. Wegner, *Einführung*, 88, s.v. ***-am-***. See for more examples of names with the root ***kad-***, ***katt-*** Th. Richter, *VHN*, 154-155, 433.

Another name with the verbal root ***kad-*** 'to speak' may be Linear A ***ka-du-ma-ne*** (HT 29.6) from Hagia Triada, but I shall first discuss a previous attempt to explain this name.

C.H. Gordon (*Evidence for the Minoan language*, 36, § 155) has interpreted this sequence, which probably is a personal name, as follows: "As in Ugaritic, many personal names have the suffix ***-an***. The pair ***ki-re-tá*** and ***ki-re-ta-na*** correspond to Ugaritic ***krt*** and ***krtn***. Other Minoan names with ***-an*** are: ***da-na-ne*** = 'Dan' + *-an*; ***ka-du-ma-ne*** = 'Cadm(os)' + *-an*; ***mi-na-ne*** = 'Mino(s)' + *-an* (cf. Ugaritic ***mn*** and ***mnn***)." I have already discussed Linear A ***ki-re-ta-na*** and ***ki-ri-ta*** $_2$ / ***ki-re-ta*** $_2$.

However, it is not as simple as Cyrus Gordon thought, since he ignored the basic orthographic conventions of Linear A and B or to be more precise: the conventions which Linear B most likely inherited from Linear A. These are that Linear A and B did not express a final consonant and that in consonant clusters a dental occlusive preceding ***-m*** would have been expressed by borrowing the vowel of the following syllabic sign (in fact the vowel belonging to its own syllable). A Minoan scribe would have written ****ka-da-ma*** in Linear A to express ***Kadman***, not ***ka-du-ma-ne***. The conclusion is that ***-u-*** in ***-du-*** cannot be a mute vowel, but is a real vowel in ***ka-du-ma-ne***, and ***-ne*** is part of the name as well.

This means that an equation of ***ka-du-ma-ne*** with Ugaritic ***qdm***, gemeinsemitisch 'Vorderseite, Osten', and ***qdmn*** (cf. F. Gröndahl, *PNTU*, 175), would only be conceivable, if the vowels shown in the Linear A sequence could also be traced in the Semitic evidence. However, the comparisons provided by F. Gröndahl are ***qadmī-'el***, ***qedmā*** in the Alalaḫ texts, and ***ᵈqadmu***, Deimel, *Pantheon* Nr. 3002, which are incompatible with Linear A ***ka-du-ma-ne***. The same applies *mutatis mutandis* to other "identifications" by Gordon such as 'other Minoan names' ***da-na-ne*** which he compares with '*Dan*' + the ***-an*** suffix and ***mi-na-ne*** = 'Mino(s)' + ***-an*** (*ibidem*). Calling them 'other Minoan names' he suggests that ***da-na-ne*** and ***mi-na-ne*** are attested in Linear A, but does not refer to the Linear A texts, where he has allegedly found these names. In fact the alleged names do not occur in any Linear A text published to date.

F. Gröndahl (*PNTU*, 283-284) mentions: *minin-*, MNN, anat. ?, s. Goetze, *JCS XVI (1962)*, 49; vgl. *menanim* [*PNC* 58], *menaniya* [*NH* Nr. 801], *minan* [*AL* 142]; *mininu*, *mi-ni-nu* [*NH* Nr. 802]; *mnn*, *bn mnn*: unsicher, siehe auch Glossar I u. MNY.

In search of a feasible interpretation of Linear A ***ka-du-ma-ne***, one may think of alphabetic Ugaritic ***bn qrdmn***, mentioned by F. Gröndahl, *PNTU*, 176-177, s.v. *qrd*, 'Held', vgl. ug. *Aliy qrdm*, Beiname des *Baᶜal*; akkad. *qardu*, *qarrādu*, *quradu*; ug. *ᵈqarrādu* (UR.SAG), *qa-ra-di* (G), *abdi-qarrādi* (ÌR.UR.SAG), *qa-ár-da-na* (G), *bn qrdy*, *bn qrdmn*. Since ***-r-*** preceding a dental in consonant clusters is not expressed in Linear A, this alphabetic cuneiform sequence, not mentioned by Gordon, might in principle be feasible. Unfortunately there is no syllabic equivalent to ***qrdmn*** attested to date, so that the existence of ****Qardumane*** / ****Kardumane*** cannot be proved. However, Akkadian *qardu* would at least cover the first element of that as yet hypothetic name.

Hurrian equivalents to the first element of ***ka-du-ma-ne*** should, however, not be ruled out. E. Laroche, *NH*, 90-91, mentions, sub n° 553, ***Kadu***, abs. *ᵐKa-a-du*, V 13 I 5; sub n° 555, ***Gadudu***, Capp. *Ga-du-du-(ú)*, TCL IV 87, 19 (forgeron). – BIN VI 226, 24; sub n° 556, ***Kaduwa***, Roi de Kargamis: hiér. *ᵐKa-du/dú-wa-s*, A 2, 1 et 3; 3, 1; 11 a 1; 11 b 1; 12, 1; 13 d 1, 5; 23, 1. ***Kadu***, abs. *ᵐKa-a-du*, may be interpreted as an Old Hurrian (*imperative*) 'one-word' name ***Kad=u*** 'Speak ! / Say (names) !'.

It appears to be impossible that ***-ma-*** in ***ka-du-ma-ne*** represents the *negative* morpheme ***-ma*** (also ***-mma***) that may genetically be connected with the negation ***-wa-*** (position 6) in transitive constructions (M.L. Chačikjan, *Churritskij i urartskij jazyki*, Erevan 1985, 95).

According to I. Wegner (*Einführung*, 96, sub c) the negation of the 3rd person singular can be expressed with the *negative* morpheme ***-ma*** (also ***-mma***) that may genetically be connected with the negation ***-wa-*** (position 6) in transitive constructions. She gives the following examples: *pašš* + *i* + *a* + *ma* 'Er schickt nicht' ['He does not send'].

irnoḫ + oš + i + a + ma 'Er hat nicht vergolten' ['He did not repay / give satisfaction'].
ar + i + a + mma (Boğ.) 'Er gibt nicht' ['He does not give'].

In these examples the morpheme ***-ma*** seems to occur, if usage of the suffix ***-wa-*** would lead to a sequence of **i+wa+a* (3rd person transitive). It is to be considered allomorph of ***-wa-***, although ***-ma*** does not take the same position as ***-wa-*** in the chain of suffixes. The suffix ***-wa-*** marking a negation in transitive constructions takes position 6 between the marker of transitivity ***-i-*** and the marker of the 3rd person singular ***-a-***, whereas ***-ma*** follows ***-a-***, cf. also I. Wegner, *Einführung*, 95, Table 5. The *negative* morpheme ***-ma*** is not combined with the associative ***-an*** 'and' in order to avoid confusion with the particle ***-mân*** (*-ma-a-an*, cf. I. Wegner, *Einführung*, 117).

As I. Wegner explains, the *negative* morpheme ***-ma*** / ***-mma*** only replaces ***-wa-*** in very special circumstances, which means that Linear A ***ka-du-ma-ne*** (HT 29.6) cannot be analysed as †{*kad=o/u=m(m)a=nn(a)e/i*}, consisting of the verbal root ***kad-*** + (Old Hurrian) theme vowel marking the perfect tense ***-o/u-*** + the negative suffix ***-m(m)a-*** + the enclitic personal pronoun 3rd person singular ***-nna*** in the allomorphic appearance of ***-nne/i*** (it), indicating the object of action of the verb, 'He/She did not say it'.

Consequently only one possible analysis {*kad=o/u=m=a=nn(a)e/i*} seems to remain, consisting of the verbal root ***kad-*** + (Old Hurrian) theme vowel marking the perfect tense ***-o/u-*** + the Old Hurrian marker of the subject of action ***-m-*** + the theme vowel ***-a-*** preceding the enclitic personal pronoun 3rd person singular ***-nna*** in the allomorphic appearance of ***-nne/i*** (it), indicating the object of the transitive verb, translation 'He/She said it', in the sense of 'He/She pronounced it (namely the name of the father or mother)'.

I. Wegner, *Einführung in die Hurritische Sprache*, 2007², 56, also provides a feasible solution for the ending ***-ka*** in Linear A ***a-<u>ta</u>-i-jo-de-ka*** (ZA Zb 3.2). Text ZA Zb 3 reads:

1. VINa 32 *di-di-ka-se* , *a-sa-mu-ne*, *a-se*
2. *a-<u>ta</u>-i-jo-de-ka* , *a-re-<u>pi</u>-re-na* , *ti-ti-ku*
3. [[ ]]

Whereas all inscriptions with the sequence ***a-ta-i-jo-wa-ja*** are written on religious (stone) objects found in the religious context of Peak Sanctuaries, ***a-<u>ta</u>-i-jo-de-ka*** occurs on a clay pithos in an agricultural and probably commercial context, which is confirmed by occurrence of the wine-ideogram VINa at the beginning, followed by the number 32.

Linear A ***a-<u>ta</u>-i-jo-de-ka*** is probably a Hurrian personal name that can be analysed as {*attai=(j)-o/ud=i/e=k=a*} '(God the) Father as protector'. Since most Hurrian personal names contain a theophorous element and since the *ergative* ***at-ta-iw-wa-šu-uš*** 'Our Father' is directly connected with 'Tešub ... Our Lord', cf. J. Friedrich, *Kleinasiatische Sprachdenkmäler*, Berlin 1932, 32: ***dTe-e-eš-šu-pa-aš … ip-ri-iu̯-u̯ə-šu-uš at-ta-iu̯-u̯ə-šu-uš*** (Mit. IV, 118) 'Tešub ..... Our Lord, Our Father', it seems preferable to interpret the onomastic element ***attay-*** in personal names primarily as a theophorous element referring to '(God the) Father', usually equivalent to *Tešub*. It is, of course, convenient that the element 'father' refers at the same time to the father of the child and head of the family. In a sense the father of flesh and blood is not only the name-giver, but also appears as an intermediary between the Head of the Pantheon and the newborn child.

The ***-o/u-*** of ***-jo-*** in the sequence ***a-ta-i-jo-wa-ja*** 'Our Father' (at the beginning of libation formulas) can probably be explained from the following ***-w-*** of ***-wa-***, but the ***-o/u-*** of ***-jo-*** in the sequence ***a-ta-i-jo-de-ka*** must belong to the second onomastic element of the personal name {*-od=i/e=kk=a*}. This second onomastic element is probably nominal, but contains the verbal root ***ud-/od-***, cf. E. Laroche, *GLH*, 277, s.v. ***ude-***; especially I. Wegner, Zum Namen des *Udibšarri*, *Altorientalische Forschungen 30 (2003)*, 341-344. She was the first to offer the meaning 'schützen' ['to protect'], cf. Th. Richter, *BGH*, 2012, 507, s.v. ***ud-*** I [Boğ., PN] 'schützen'; Th. Richter, *VHN*, 2016, 557, s.v. ***ud-*** {*o/ud-*}.

Concluding: Linear A ***-ka*** in ***a-ta-i-jo-de-ka*** can be explained as the formant ***-kk-***, nominal element (*nomen actoris* ?), in which case the ***-a*** in ***-ka*** may well be the ending in ***-a*** indicating the *essive* case in Hurrian. The meaning of the personal name would then be 'Father as a protector'. The ending in ***-ka*** also reminds of that in Urartian ^{LÚ}***urb=i=ka*** 'Schlachtopfer, Priester (?)' ['victim, priest (?)']. I prefer this solution to the so-called 'honorific' (or 'diminutive') suffix ***-ga / -(k)ka***, cf. I. Wegner, *Einführung*, 56, 59.

Linear A ***no-nu-ma-re*** (ZA 4a.5-6; ZA 5b.1; ZA 15a.4-5) may contain the Hurrian verbal root ***nun-/nunn-*** {*no/un(n)*} mentioned by Th. Richter (*VHN*, 473), who thinks that ***nunn-*** is a variant of ***nun-***, because the Hurrian name ***Nunnakka*** (wr. *Nu-un-na-ak-ka*) from Qaṭṭarā, ***Nunnakka*** (wr. *Nun-na-ak-ka*) from Old Babylonian Tall Muhammad, analysis {*no/unn=a=kk=a*}, typology 1.2.3, lexicon *nunn-*, can hardly be distinguished from ***Nunakka*** (wr. *Nu-na-ak-ka*) from Old Babylonian Kiš, cf. Th. Richter, *VHN*, 213.

He also mentions the personal names ***Nunija*** (wr. *Nu-ni-ia*), analysis {*no/unn=i=ja*} from Emar and Qaṭṭarā, typology 1.1.1.2.4, lexicon *nun-*, and ***Nuni-ki(j)aše/i/u*** (wr. *Nu-ni-ki-a/ia-še/ši/šu*) from Alalaḫ VII, cf. Th. Richter, *VHN*, 213-214, 473.

He mentions (*VHN*, 473[569]), that Urartian *intransitive* ***nun=a-*** means '(her)kommen' ['to come (here)'] and that the meaning 'Bring (the boy) here, oh sea !' is conceivable for a *transitive* construction {*no/un=i-kiaše*}. The Hurrian term ***kiaše*** 'sea' (also abbreviated to ***-ki***) is quite popular in Hurrian personal names. Cf. also M. Salvini – I. Wegner, *Einführung in die urartäische Sprache*, Wiesbaden 2014, 112: ***nun-*** 'kommen' ['to come'].

Analysis of the second element is not easy, because more interpretations are feasible depending on which division is chosen. I shall discuss three possibilities:

1. If we choose an Old Hurrian verbal construction in ***-o/u=m***, analysis of {*non=o/u=m-are*} offers the translation 'The evil / vicious / malicious one, he (***-m***) brought (the child)', since ***ari*** is known as a sacrificial term and/or cult-object, that is translated as 'böse, das Böse' ['evil, the evil power'] by Th. Richter, *BGH*, 45; *VHN*, 380.
2. If we analyse ***no-nu-ma-re*** as an *athematic* verbal construction, {*non-umare*} consists of athematic ***non-*** and nominal ***-umare***. Th. Richter (*VHN*, 551) mentions that the root ***um-*** {*o/um-*} especially occurs in onomastics. It is not certain, whether it is the same root as occurs in the Nuzi-syntagma *um=umm(i)=a epēšu*, translation 'sammeln (?)' ['to assemble (?)'] in *AHw* 1420, see also *BGH*, 488.

   The root also occurs with a root-extension ***um=ar-*** and is according to Richter probably verbal, if it is used as first onomastic element, e.g. in ***Umar-e<lli>***(?) (wr. *Ú-mar-e<-li>*) at Mari, analysis {*o/um=ar-el(a)=ni*} and ^{f}***Umer-elli*** (wr. ^{f}*Ú-me-er-e-li*) at Mari, {*o/um=ir-el(a)=ni*}, typology 1.4, lexicon *um-*, *ela*.

He also mentions ^{f}***Umar-talame*** (wr. ^{f}*Ú-mar-ta-la-am-e,* ^{f}*Ú-mar-ta-lim-e*) at Mari, {*o/um=ar-talame*}. However, ^{f}***Unuš-umar*** (wr. ^{f}*Ú-nu-úš-ú-mar*) from Ašnakkum, analysis {*un=o=ž-o/umar(i)*}, typology 1.3.2.1, lexicon *un-*, *umari*, translation '*umar* möge (Mädchen) bringen' ['*umar* may bring (the girl)'] certainly contains a nominal second element *umar*, because the first element ***unuš-*** is verbal. Nominal ***-umar*** can be explained as a participle ***-o/um=ar=i***, cf. Th. Richter, *VHN*, 336, 551. At Alalah VII we find one and the same person who is called ^{f}***Ḫebat-umara*** (wr. ^{f}*Ḫe-bat-ú-ma-ra*) and ^{f}***Ḫebat-umera*** (wr. ^{f}*Ḫe-bat-ú-me-ra*), cf. Zeeb 2001, 468, 649. See also ^{f}***Šerat-umar*** {*šer=ad-o/umar(i)*} at Mari, cf. Th. Richter, *VHN*, 275, 551.

3. If we choose an Old Hurrian *imperative* construction in ***-o/u***, analysis of {*non=o/u-mare*} offers the translation 'Bring (the child) here, oh charioteer !' or 'Bring the charioteer here, oh *numen* !', since ***mare*** means 'high royal official' in Urartian, cf. Th. Richter, *BGH*, 244-245, s.v. ***marianni / marijanni***, *marijannu* [Nuzi; PN; loan-word in Akkadian; *passim* in the Late Bronze Age] 'charioteer', 'Wagenkämpfer' who are 'officers of the charioteers' in Mitanni and form a class at Alalaḫ. The term is also attested at Boğazköy and Ugarit (***mryn*** in alphabetic cuneiform from Ugarit).

According to E. Laroche and others the origin of ***maryanni*** 'officiers mittanniens, commandant les escadrons de chars de guerre' (*GLH*, 168), is no doubt Indian ***marya-***, but according to Th. Richter (*BGH*, 244-245) a non-Indo-Iranian (so non-Indo-European) etymology seems now plausible because of Urartian ***mare*** 'high royal official'; eventual non-Indo-Iranian origin corresponds with Urartian ***mare*** 'hoher königlicher Angestellter' (M. Salvini 1979a: 309 [similar I.M. Diakonoff 1989: 99; 2000: 50f.[27]]). - Etymology:

(1) For a Hurrian-Urartian (and Caucasian) derivation see Diakonoff / Starostin 1986: 21 (stem ****mari-***) and Diakonoff 1989: 99. 1990: 64, 1993a: 47f.: i.e. ***mari-anne***. For other reasons, e.g. Haas/Thiel (1978, 179) and Boyce (1987, 509) also suspect a Hurrian origin of the word; according to Rubio (2005b, 98) the word is 'perfectly Hurrian'.

(2) Diakonoff (2000, 50f.[27]) suspects correspondence with urartian ***ma-ri-a-ḫe-né*** '*mare*-men' and explains: "A connection with Hurrian *mari-anne* 'charioteer' is possible, but the latter needs no Indo-Iranian (and hence, Indo-European) etymology, which *an und für sich* is not probable when a term is attested in both Hurrian and Urartian, and additionally not only in Mitanni, but also in Alalaḫ and Arrapḫe." Against such considerations G. Wilhelm (1989a: 419), but see yet Diakonoff (1993a, 47).

Remarkably the sequence ***ma-re*** (HT 55a.1; PH 30.2) occurs a few times in Linear A. The inscription on the tablet from Phaistos is even more interesting, for it reads:

PH 30.1: [.]***-ti*** E[

PH 30.2: ***ma-re*** E ***mi-de***[

The latter sequences appear to repeat the sequence ***mi-da-ma-ra***$_2$ (AK Zf 9), but in reverse order: ***ma-re*** E 'charioteer', fraction-sign E, followed by ***mi-de***[= ****mīšde-***, cf. ‡ Hurrian ***mištanni***, Vedic ***mīḍhá-*** and Old Iranian ***mīždа-*** 'reward, pay'. This cross-reference of ***ma-re*** .... ***mi-de***[with ***mi-da-ma-ra***$_2$ also proves that the division in ***mi-da-ma-ra***$_2$ is really between ***mi-da-*** and ***-ma-ra***$_2$. The second element ***-ma-ria/rya*** of Linear A ***mi-da-ma-ra***$_2$ (AK Zf 9) may be compared with ***maryannu/i*** (***mryn*** in alphabetic cuneiform from Ugarit), who are 'officers of the charioteers' in Mitanni.

If my identifications are correct, the whole Linear A inscription ***ja-ki-si-ki-nu* , *mi-da-ma-ra₂*** (AK Zf 9) on the silver hairpin from Arkhanes may be interpreted as: 'which piece of jewelry / hairpin, a reward/payment for an officer of the charioteers' > (in other words): '(this) piece of jewelry / hairpin as a reward/payment for an officer of the charioteers'.

The silver hairpin with the Linear A inscription ***ja-ki-si-ki-nu* , *mi-da-ma-ra₂*** (AK Zf 9) from Arkhanes has no inventory number of the Heraklion Museum, but it was found in a mixed Middle Minoan I - Late Minoan I context in the pillar room of Tholos B at Arkhanes, site of Φουρνὶ Ἀρχανῶν, cf. J.A. Sakellarakis - E. Sakellarakis, *Archanes. Minoan Crete in a new light* (2 vols.), Athens 1997, Vol. I, 169-179 (especially 174-179), 332-333, fig. 296; cf. J.G. Younger, *Linear A texts in phonetic transcription, other texts (not Haghia Triada)*, inaugural date: 1-1-2000 (digital text on internet), 6: ARKH Zf 9. J.G. Younger casually compares ***ja-ki-si-ki-nu*** with ***a-da-ki-si-ka*** (KH 5.1), of which I think he did not realize how lucky a comparison this actually is.

Since I have not yet been able to verify the inscription of AK Zf 9 by autopsy, I do not know yet, whether all signs are legible and the reading of the inscription is beyond doubt. So for the moment it seems wise to offer only a tentative interpretation and to remain reserved until the legibility and a correct reading of the inscription have been established.

If the whole inscription is to be read from left to right as most Linear A texts, ***ja-*** at the beginning of the inscription may well be explained by connection of ****ki-si-ki-nu*** with this Hurrian *(quasi-)proclitic* relative (and interrogative) particle ***ya-/ye-*** as in ***ja-ta-i-jo-u-ja*** (AP Za 1.a) 'What Our Father', 'As Our Father', 'Why Our Father' (beside very frequent ***a-ta-i-jo-wa-ja*** 'Our Father') and ***ja-sa-sa-ra-me*** (beside ***a-sa-sa-ra-me***), with contraction of ***ya-/ye-*** with ***a-*** in ***a-ta-i-jo-wa-ja*** and ***a-sa-sa-ra-me***, respectively.

This *(quasi-)proclitic* usage of ***ja-*** in ***ja-ki-si-ki-nu*** is comparable. Linear A scribes may well have used *proclitic* or *quasi-proclitic* constructions in order to avoid confusion of monosyllabic words with abbreviations (e.g. transaction terms) or even ideograms. Linear B scribes actually appear to have followed this very special usage of their Linear A colleagues, since Linear B provides comparable examples of this usage, remarkably with respect to the same category of monosyllabic words: ***o-u-di-do-si*** (PY Ma 124,2) = ***οὐ δίδονσι*** 'they do not give', as if ***οὐ*** and ***δίδονσι*** form one sequence; ***o-di-do-si*** (PY Vn 10,1) = ***ὧ δίδονσι*** (***ὧ*** = Hom. ***ὧς***) 'thus / in this way they give'; ***jo-do-so-si*** (PY Jn 829,1) = ***yω δώσονσι*** (***yω*** = Attic ***ὡς***) 'as they will give', cf. C.J. Ruijgh, *EGM*, § 9.

It has to be emphasized that such usage cannot be used as evidence for 'prefixes' in Hurrian, since Hurrian is only suffixing. It is merely a matter of a practical solution 'invented' by the scribes in order to counter a practical problem in Linear A and B. So it has nothing to do with the structure of the language as the Linear B examples clearly show.

So if ***ja-*** is equivalent to this quasi-proclitic particle ***ya-/ye-***, Linear A ****ki-si-ki-nu*** may well be compared with Hurrian ***kizziḫi*** [Boğ.; PN] + suffix or formant (?) ***-(n)nu***, cf. ***kizzi/uḫu*** [Qatna], although cuneiform double writting of ***-iḫ-ḫi-*** would probably have been more in accordance with Linear A ***-ki-*** than cuneiform ***-ḫi-***. Actually at the end of his *lemma* on ***kizziḫḫuru*** Th. Richter (*BGH*, 215) mentions ***kiziḫḫi*** as well. Anyway, ***-ḫḫ-*** is also attested in a comparable form ***pizzuḫḫu*** 'garment according to the fashion of ***Bizza/u***', cf. H.P. Adler, *Das Akkadische des Königs Tušratta von Mitanni* (Alter Orient und Altes Testament 201), Kevelaer/Neukirchen-Vluyn 1976, 267.

Th. Richter, *BGH*, 318, s.v. ***pizzuḫḫu*** [Tušr.] 'ein Kleiderstoff, nach der Art von ***Bizza/u***'. I pay attention to these orthographic features, since I assume that in Linear A the Hurrian voiced velar fricatives [*ġ*] are written with ***q-*** signs that are in Linear B reserved for the labio-velar series, whereas the Hurrian voiceless velar fricatives are written with the ***k-*** signs in Linear A, which is in accordance with the fact that the Linear B ***k-*** signs reflect *κ-*, *γ-*, *χ-*. Compare, for instance, the Linear A orthography of ***a-du-|ku-mi-na*** (ZA 10.3-4) from Kato Zakro that I have analysed as {*ašd=u=ḫḫu-mina*} 'The twin is female'.

Th. Richter, *BGH*, 215, s.v. ***kizziḫi*** [Boğ.; PN], ***kizzi/uḫu*** [Qaṭna].

(A) Boğ.: 'ein Schmuckstück(?)' ['piece of jewelry, jewel'], 'Kultgerät; Opferterminus' ['cult-object; sacrificial term'], cf. V. Haas - G. Wilhelm, *Hurritische und luwische Riten aus Kizzuwatna* (Alter Orient und Altes Testament, Sonderreihe 3), Kevelaer/Neukirchen-Vluyn 1974, 108; V. Haas, *Die hurritischen Ritualtermini in hethitischem Kontext*, Corpus der hurritischen Sprachdenkmäler. I. Abteilung: Die Texte aus Boğazköy, Band I/9, Rome 1998, 9, 230; J. Tischler, *Hethitisches Handwörterbuch. Mit dem Wortschatz der Nachbarsprachen* (Innsbrucker Beiträge zur Sprachwissenschaft 102), Innsbruck 2001, 81.

(B) Qaṭna: 'designation of golden pin', cf. J. Black - A. George - N. Postgate, *A Concise Dictionary of Akkadian*, Wiesbaden 2000^2, 163.

The question is: Is it entirely accidental that the Linear A term ***ja-ki-si-ki-nu*** is written on a *silver hairpin* from Arkhanes and that the term ***kizzi/uḫu*** at Qaṭna is the designation of a *golden pin* ? The general meaning 'jewel' fits quite well, but a more specific meaning 'a hairpin of precious metal' would be appropriate as well.

It is significant that Th. Richter (*VHN*, 167, 442) mentions the personal name ***Kizziḫe*** (wr. *Ki-iz-zi-ḫe*) at Tuttul, typology 3.1, translation '*kizziḫe*(-Schmuckstück)', which proves that not only the verbal root ***kiz-*** II / ***kezz-*** and ***kizz-***, but also this specific noun was indeed used in personal names.

Linear A offers not only ***ja-ki-si-ki-nu*** (AK Zf 9), but also the beautiful Hurrian personal name ***a-da-ki-si-ka*** (KH 5.1) at Khania, that can be analysed as {*ažd=a-kizzi=ḫḫ(i)=a*}, consisting of the *a*-stem ***ašd=a*** 'woman' and the *essive* in ***-a*** of ***kizzi=ḫḫi*** 'jewel', so that it can be translated as 'The woman (is / shines) like a piece of jewelry' or more specifically 'The woman (is / shines) like a hairpin of precious metal', if we take into account that ***kizzi/uḫu*** at Qaṭna is the designation of a *golden pin* and that Linear A ***ja-ki-si-ki-nu*** (AK Zf 9) is written on a *silver hairpin* from Arkhanes.

Since a sibilant preceding a dental is not expressed in consonant clusters in Linear A and B, we can read ***Ašda***, analysis {*ažd(e)=a*}, translation 'As a woman', with the *essive* case in ***-a***. The name would then have a double *essive*, because ***kizzi=ḫḫ(i)=a*** is also in the essive case. The translation would then be 'She (the girl) is like a woman, like a jewel'. However, Th. Richter (*VHN*, 384-385, n. 202) mentions, s.v. ***ašte*** {*ašte*} and ***aštu*** {*ašto/u*}, that according to Haas/Thiel (1978, 309) an {A}-stem ***ašta*** may have existed, because the forms ***aš-ta-né-eš*** and ***aš-te-ni-iš*** are attested next to each other in two versions of an incantation against the *gergiššum*-disease at Mari and Tuttul. If they are right, ***ašta*** may be comparable with the {A}-stems of words expressing kinship or congeniality such as ***šala*** 'daughter', ***šena*** 'brother', ***ela*** 'sister', ***nera*** 'mother' and ***mena*** 'twin' (or perhaps 'sister'). In that case ***ašta*** does not represent the *essive*, but *absolutive* case.

Th. Richter (*VHN*, 166-170, 442) mentions more Hurrian personal names with the root ***kiz-*** II / ***kezz-*** and ***kizz-***: ***Kiza*** (wr. *Ki-za*) gardener from Mari, analysis {*kiz=a*}, typology 1.3.1.3; ***Kizza*** (wr. *Ki-iz-za*) from Alalaḫ IV, analysis {*kizz=a*}, typology 1.3.1.3; ***Kezzi*** (wr. *Ge-ez-zi*) from Tigunāni and Nuzi (*NPN*, 84), analysis {*kezz=i*}, typology 1.3.1.2.1; ***Kizzi*** (wr. *Ki-iz-zi*) from Mari, Qaṭṭarā, Emar and Nuzi (*AAN I*, 85), (wr. *Gi/Ki-iz-zi*) Alalaḫ VII and IV, analysis {*kizz=i*}, typology 1.3.1.2.1; ***Kizija*** (wr. *Ki-zi-ia*) from Mari, Qaṭna and Šušarrā, analysis {*kiz=i=ja*}, typology 1.1.1.2.4, ***Giziya*** (wr. *Gi-zi-ia*) from Alalaḫ, registered at Ḫattuša (E. Laroche, *NH*, 95, n° 596); ***Kizzija*** (wr. *Ki-iz-zi-ia, Ki-iz$_x$-zi-ia*) from Mari, Šubat-Enlil, Nuzi and Šušarrā, analysis {*kizz=i=ja*}, typology 1.1.1.2.4; ***Kizzu*** (wr. *Ki-iz-zu*) from Mari, Šubat-Enlil, Nuzi (*NPN*, 89), analysis {*kizz=o*}, typology 1.3.1.1.1; ***Kizum*** (wr. *Ki-zu-m*) from Mari, analysis {*kiz=o=m*}, typology 1.1.1.1.1; ***Kizzikkan*** (wr. *Ki-iz-zi-ga-an*) from Mari {*kizz=i=kk=(i)a=n(na)*}, typology 1.2.1.1; ***^{f}Kizi-kanazzi*** (wr. *^{f}Ki-zi-ka-na-zi*) from Ašnakkum, {*kiz=i-kanazzi*}, typology 1.3.1.2.1, lexicon *kiz-* II, *kanazzi*; cf. ***^{f}Kiš-kanazzi*** (wr. *^{f}Ki-iš-ka-na-zi*) from Mari, {*kiž-kanazzi*}, typology 1.4, lexicon *kiz-* II, *kanazzi*; ***Kizzi-kawari*** (wr. *Ki-iz-zi-ka-wa-ri*) from Šubat-Enlil, analysis {*kizz=i-kavari*}, typology 1.3.1.2.1, lexicon *kizz-*, *kawari*; ***Kizzu-men*** (wr. *Ki-iz-zu-mi-en*) from Mari, analysis {*kizz=o-men*}, typology 1.3.1.1.1; ***Kizzunni*** (wr. *Ki-iz-zu-un-ni*) from Mari, analysis {*kizz=o=nni*}, typology 1.3.1.2.2; ***Kizzutta*** (wr. *Ki-iz-zu-ut-ta*) from Mari, analysis {*kizz=o=tta*}, typology 1.3.1.1.2.1; ***Kizzuri*** (wr. *Ki-iz-zu-ri*) from Ašnakkum, Mari, Šušarrā, typology 3.1, lexicon *kizzuri*; ***Kizuri*** (wr. *Ki-zu-ri*) from Mari, typology 3.1, lexicon *kizuri*; ***Kizurija***(?) (wr. *Ki-zu(?)-ri-ia*) from Šubat-Enlil, analysis {*kizori(?)=ja*}, typology 3.3, lexicon *kizuri*; ***Kizzazzum*** from Mari; etc.

Th. Richter (*VHN*, 167, 587-588) analyses ***Kizzikkan*** (wr. *Ki-iz-zi-ga-an*) from Mari as a negated transitive verbal form + enclitic personal pronoun marking the subject of the verb (typology 1.2.1.1) {*kizz=i=kk=i»a=n(na)*}, but I think that a negative interpretation of the personal name ***Kizzikkan*** (wr. *Ki-iz-zi-ga-an*) can be avoided. Analysing the noun ***kizzi=ḫḫi*** 'jewel', we observe that the suffix ***-ḫḫi*** is the Hurrian adjectival suffix, so that we may conclude that ***kizzi=ḫḫi*** is derived from the substantive ***kizzi***, probably with the same meaning as ***kizzi=ḫḫi***. This means that Hurrian ****kizzi(k)ka*** (mind the orthography *Ki-iz-zi-ga-an*) may represent the form with the so-called honorific or diminutive suffix ***=ga / =(k)ka***, that can express 'kindness' according to I. Wegner, *Einführung*, 56, 59. Cf. E. Laroche (*GLH*, 61-62), s.v. ***aštaga*** (*aš-ta-ka* Msk.; gen. *aš-da-a-ga-bi*, KUB XXIX 8 IV 23) and (*GLH*, 251), s.v. ***taḫe*** 'homme' and ***taḫa(k)ka*** 'homoncule, pauvre homme', RS bil. 15, 18: *ta-aḫ-a-(ak)-ka-an* = Akkadian *amîlu*.

This means that the personal name ***Kizzikkan*** (wr. *Ki-iz-zi-ga-an*) from Mari can also be analysed as {*kizz=i=kka=n(na)*} 'He/She (the child) is a little jewel'. Likewise the formation of Linear A ***a-da-ki-si-ka*** (KH 5.1) from Khania can be analysed as a sentence name ***ašd=a-kizz=i=(k)ka*** 'The woman is a little jewel' or ***ašd=a-kizz=i=(k)ka=n(na)*** 'The woman, she (***-n***) is a little jewel'. But since Linear A ***ka*** can be ***ka***, ***ga*** or ***-ḫḫa***, ***a-da-ki-si-ka*** (KH 5.1) can also be analysed as ***ašd=a-kizzi=ḫḫ(i)=a*** 'The woman is like a jewel', with the *essive* in ***-a*** of ***kizzi=ḫḫi*** 'jewel'. Theoretically Linear A ***ja-ki-si-ki-nu*** can be analysed as {*ja-kizz=i=kki=nnu*}, with a negation of the verbal root ***kiz-*** II / ***kezz-*** / ***kizz-***, but since the sequence is inscribed on a precious silver hairpin, analysis as ***ja-kizz=i=ḫḫi=nnu*** 'As it (***-nnu***, namely the silver hairpin) is a jewel' appears preferable.

Th. Richter (*VHN*, 442) mentions, s.v. ***kiz-*** II/***kezz-*** and ***kizz-***, that the root ***kiz-*** is clearly attested in the term ***kiziḫḫuri*** [Nuzi], analysed as *{kiz=i=ḫḫ(e)=o=ri}*, containing ***=(iḫ)ḫuru/i*** (according to G. Wilhelm 1985a, 119). It designates (according to *BGH*, 215) 'ein Funktionär', 'an official or a profession', 'Berufsbezeichnung' (cf. also I. Wegner, *Einführung*, 58, sub ***-ḫḫuri***), may be compared with ‡ LÚ.*kuzi* [Alalaḫ VII+IV; Amarna; Ugarit] 'Pferdemann' ['groom, hostler']. Recently Von Dassow (2008, 311 ff.) derived Amarna-Akkadian (LÚ.)*ku/ku*$_8$-ZI; (LÚ.)KUŠ$_7$/ŠÙŠ [Alalaḫ IV]; LÚ.)*ka-zi-i-e* [Ugarit] and Egyptian *kṯn/kḏn* from West-Semitic **kāziyu* 'horse-trainer, chariot-driver'.

Th. Richter (*BGH*, 230) gives a survey of various views on possible etymologies and derivations of ‡ LÚ.*kuzi*: (A) Amarna: 'Pferdemann' ['groom, hostler'] corresponds with *kizeḫḫuri* at Nuzi, » Egyptian *kṯ/kḏ, kṯn/kḏn* 'Streitwagenlenker' ['chariot-driver'], also in *ku-u-zu-ib-bi-na* and *ku-zu-zé-ne-e* (V. Haas, 1988d, 123f.). *CAD* G (s.v.), *AHw* Lfg. 4 [1962] 300 ('Stallknecht' ['groom']) and *CDA*^{2} [2000] 97 'stable-lad' favour an Egyptian origin, to which W.A. Ward (Some foreign personal names and loan-words from the Deir el-Medineh ostraca, in: A. Leonard Jr. – B. Beyer Williams (eds.), *Essays in Ancient civilization presented to Helene J. Kantor* (SAOC 47), Chicago 1989, 292^{+38}) objects that "the word has no Egyptian etymology and the variant spellings indicate it is a foreign loan". See "The meaning 'hostler' or 'groom' is required by the context, despite the fact that the Egyptian word from which it derives means 'chariot-driver'. The word is not connected with Akkadian *kizû* 'groom'." To which I should like to add that it is *a priori* not excluded that a groom in the function of horse-trainer might actually be the same person as the 'chariot-driver' who accompanies the 'armed charioteer' in battle. The latter belongs to the class of *mariyanni*, whereas the 'chariot-driver' may well belong to a different class, since he only assists the armed warrior, although he also has to take the risk to be killed in battle. To date the meaning of the verbal root ***kiz-*** II/***kezz-*** and ***kizz-*** is unknown, but the meaning of Hurrian ***kuz-*** [Mit.; PN] was established a long time ago as 'aufhalten' (Steiner, 1978, 183; 1979a, 198); 'retenir, faire attendre' (Faucounau, 1980a, 400); 'garder, retenir' (Laroche, *GLH*, 157); 'zurückhalten' (Girbal, 1990, 99; Dietrich / Mayer, 1992, 51; I. Wegner, *Einführung*, 2007, 265 /***koz-***/; Th. Richter, *BGH*, 229; *VHN*, 450). Th. Richter thinks that the notion of 'zurückhalten' ['to hold/keep back, to retain, to check'] in onomastics may well refer to a stage in the process of giving birth.

The first association one gets with regard to ***kizziḫi*** [Boğ.; PN], ***kizzi/uḫu*** [Qaṭna] 'jewelry, a jewel' is that *it shines*. So one might think that a verbal root ***kiz-*** II / ***kezz-*** and ***kizz-*** might mean 'to shine' (intr.), and 'to make (something/someone) shine' (trans.). But if ***kiz-*** II/***kezz-***/***kizz-*** has the same meaning as ***kuz-*** 'to hold/keep back, to retain, to check', it is obvious that a jewel or rather 'a hairpin of precious metal' or 'a *fibula* for garments' has the function of keeping the hair or garments in place. Semantically 'to hold/keep back, to retain, to check' is also the aim of horse-training, for it is important to keep a tight rein on the horses, so that the chariot-driver keeps them in check. And for the process of giving birth it is important that the mother gets good advice about when she can press on and when she has to hold back as to keep the delivery in check as Th. Richter has pointed out.

Anyway the hypothesis, that ***kiz-*** II/***kezz-***/***kizz-*** may perhaps be interpreted as (trans.) 'to hold/keep back, to retain, to check, to control, to restrain' (comparable with ***kuz-***) and (intr.) 'to be in check, to restrain/control oneself', needs to be verified.

The Linear A sequence ***mi-da-ma-ra₂*** (following ***ja-ki-si-ki-nu ,***) is not easy to interpret. Since Linear A sign ***ra₂*** is graphically identical with Linear B ***ra₂***, it probably represents the same phonetic values ***ria/rya*** and ***lia/lya***. As a result ***mi-da-ma-ria/rya*** or ***mi-da-ma-lia/lya*** can be read.

If the sequence can be divided into two elements, e.g. ***mi-da-*** and ***-ma-ria/rya***, the first might be compared with Vedic ***mīḍhá-*** and Old-Iranian ***mīždа-***. E. Laroche, *GLH*, 171, s.v. ***mištanni***: "sorte de paiement en rachat, AT 3, 19, 34; cf. AW, 661. - Pour une étymologie indienne, cf. Mayrhofer, *Orientalia 24*, 336 sq.; contra: Kammenhuber, *Arier*, 221 sq." Th. Richter, *BGH*, 251-252, s.v. ‡ ***mištannu*** [Al IV]: 'Lohn für Ergreifung', aus vedisch ***mīḍhá-***, zu altiranisch ***mīžda-*** (*AHw* Lfg. 7 [1966] 661); 'reward, pay' (*CAD* M/II, Lfg. 7 [1977], 130) [foreign word]; 'sorte de paiement en rachat' (Laroche 1980a: 171); 'repayment, ransom' (Diakonoff / Starostin 1986:22), etc. (N.B.: ‡ = Hurricity uncertain, respectively, not generally accepted; in secondary entries also: attribution to main entry uncertain, respectively, not generally accepted.)

Although ***mištanni/u*** may well be a Hurrian loan-word derived from Sanskrit ***mīḍhá-*** 'price for a fight' and Old-Iranian ***mīžda-*** 'price, compensation', the root is firmly established in other Indo-European languages as well. Cf. e.g. P. Chantraine, *Dictionnaire étymologique de la langue grecque*, Paris 1974, 705-706, s.v. ***μισθός*** 'récompense, salaire, solde'. [ ] Le mot, qui exprime une notion essentielle, se retrouve en indo-iranien, en germanique et en slave, cf. skr. ***mīḍhá-*** n. 'prix d'un combat', avest. ***mīžda-***'prix, récompense', ossète ***mizd***; en germanique, got. ***mizdo*** f. 'salaire, récompense', v.h.all. ***mēta***, allemand ***Miete*** 'location, loyer', v. sl. ***mīzdá*** 'récompense, rétribution', etc.

The second element ***-ma-ria/rya*** may in that case be compared with ***maryannu/i*** (***mryn*** in alphabetic cuneiform from Ugarit), who are 'officers of the charioteers' in Mitanni.

On a roundel (KH Wc 2005) from Khania we find an interesting Linear A inscription consisting of 4 syllabic signs with an allusion to the name of the Palace and city of Khania, Khania Museum 2005: GSE 1971 TC 43, Plateia Ayia Aikaterini, deposit above room A.

Side a: *ka-na-ni-ti*
Side b: vacat
Side c (edge): 7 seal impressions: 'three monkeys'.

Linear A ***ka-na-ni-ti*** (KH Wc 2005 side a) appears to be a Hurrian 'one-word' personal name that can be analysed as {*ḫan=an(n)=i=tti*}, consisting of the verbal root ***ḫan-*** 'to give birth to' (cf. Th. Richter, *BGH*, 125, and *VHN*, 407, s.v. ***ḫan-*** 'gebären' ['to give birth to'] + causative root-extension ***-an(n)-*** (cf. I. Wegner, *Einführung*, 88) + the *optional allomorphic* enclitic personal pronoun 1st person singular ***-tti*** (instead of normal ***-tta***), translation 'Give birth to me (oh *numen* / oh mother) !'.

The root ***ḫan-*** is one of the most frequent elements at Nuzi. For instance, ***Ḫaniu*** (wr. *ḫa-ni-ú/ù*), analysis {*ḫan=i=o*}, consisting of the verbal root ***ḫan-*** + the indicator of transitivity ***-i-*** that only appears in the present 2nd and 3rd person singular (position 5) + the indicator of the subject of action 2nd person singular ***-u/o-*** (position 7) 'You give birth (to the boy)' is the name of 23 men at Nuzi, cf. I.J. Gelb, *NPN*, 54; cf. also Th. Richter, *VHN*, 122, 407, 585.

The meaning of the verbal root is generally accepted and can be connected with the substantive ***ḫani*** 'child'. The Hurrian personal name ***Ḫanija*** (wr. *Ḫa-ni-ia*), {*ḫan=i=a*} from Mari, Ašnakkum, Šušarrā, Emar, Nippur, Nuzi (cf. Th. Richter, *VHN*, 121) can be interpreted as 'She gives birth', but can also be interpreted as a hypocoristic with ***ḫani*** 'child' as first element and the hypocoristic suffix ***-ya***, e.g. based on a personal name such as ***ᶠḪa-ni-wa-an-di*** 'The child is right/just/favourable' (Alalaḫ IV, see D.J. Wiseman, *AT*, 135, who read ***ᶠḪa-ni-wa-aš-di***, 298, 31). Actually it is not inconceivable that the toponym ***Χανιά*** (Khaniá), North-West Crete, is also equivalent to Hurrian and Minoan ***Ḫanija*** 'He/She [scil. a God(dess)] gives / gave birth to [this palace]'. It is a poetic name commemorative of the birth/creation of a Minoan palace and administrative centre. It can hardly be accidental that the personal name ***ka-na-ni-ti*** is found on a roundel, discovered in the Palace of Khania itself.

Another interesting personal name is ***ᶠḪanijatta*** (wr. *ḫa-ni-ia-at-ta*) from Ḫattuša, analysis {*ḫan=i=a=tta*}, 'She bears me, gives birth to me', showing a present transitive formation, in which the enclitic personal pronoun 1st person singular ***-tta*** is the object, cf. J. Tischler, Beiträge zur hethitischen Anthroponymie, *Serta Indogermanica*, Festschrift G. Neumann 1982, 442; Th. Zehnder, *Die hethitischen Frauennamen*, Dresdner Beiträge zur Hethitologie, 2010, 141f.; Th. Richter, *VHN*, 586. Here the personal pronoun ***-tta*** indicates the bearer of the name; the subject of ***ḫan=i=a-*** is the mother or a *numen*.

If we accept that not only ***pi*** and ***wi***, but also ***mi*** and ***wi*** alternate in some Hurrian texts, since **[*p*]**, **[*m*]** and **[*w*]** are labials and phonetically close, ***ka-ni-ja-mi*** (KT Zf 1), second sequence on a gold pin from Crete (Museum of Hagios Nikolaos 9675), may be identified as ***Ḫanijami/wi***, {*ḫan=i=a=mi/wi*}, 'of *Ḫani(j)a*', containing the Hurrian *genitive* form in ***-wi/-mi*** of the personal name ***Ḫanija***, or of the identical Minoan-Hurrian toponym ***Ḫania*** / *Khania* (later *Χανιά*). The genitive of a personal name can have a possessive or a patronymic / matronymic force.

Linear A ***ka-nu-ti*** (HT 97a.3) from Hagia Triada is morphologically comparable with ***ka-na-ni-ti*** (KH Wc 2005 side a). It misses root-extension ***-an(n)-*** and can be interpreted as Old Hurrian ***Ḫanutti***, analysis {*ḫan=o/u=tti*}, consisting of the verbal root ***ḫan-*** 'to give birth to / to create' + the Old Hurrian suffix indicating the transitive perfect ***-u-*** (cf. I. Wegner, *Einführung*, 126, sub 'Althurritisch') + the enclitic personal pronoun 1st person singular ***-tta*** (position 9, cf. I. Wegner, *Einführung*, 93, Table 4) or suffix ***-tti***, cf. Th. Richter (*VHN*, 596, sub 1.3.1.1.2.2), who mentions that the suffix indicating the enclitic pronoun 1st person singular ***-tta*** can sometimes be replaced by an optional allomorphic suffix ***-tti***, cf. e.g. the personal name ***Ullutti*** (wr. *ul-lu-ut-ti*) from Mari and Tigunāni, analysis {*o/ull=o/u=tti*}, typology 1.3.1.1.2.2, lexicon *ull-*, 'Destroy me (oh *numen*) !', which is considered a variant of the personal name ***Ullutta*** (wr. *ul-lu-ut-ta*) from Šušarrā (Tall Shemshara), {*o/ull=u=tta*}, lexicon *ull-*, typology 1.3.1.1.2.1, also 'Destroy me (oh *numen*) !'. Th. Richter apparently prefers the transitive *imperative* here instead of the transitive *perfect indicative*, cf. Th. Richter, *VHN*, 593, sub 1.3.1.1: names with transitive imperatives in ***-o***. Following Th. Richter we translate Linear A ***ka-nu-ti*** {*ḫan=o/u=tti*} as 'Give birth to me / Create me (oh *numen* or oh mother) !'. Following I. Wegner we can translate 'He/She (a *numen* or my mother) gave birth to me / created me'.

Tablet KH 5 from Khania, starting with ***a-da-ki-si-ka***, is interesting. It reads:

KH 5.1-2:	*a-da-ki-si-ka* , *a-ra-u-*|*da* ,		
KH 5.2:	*wi-sa-sa-ne*	HORD+E 2	VIN*b+9* 2
KH 5.3:	*wi-na-du* ,	OVIS+*na* 1	
KH 5.3-4:	*ku-pa-do*	HORD [ ] 5 A	FIC 2 JB

We have seen that ***a-da-ki-si-ka*** (KH 5.1) represents a beautiful Hurrian name, for it can be analysed as Hurrian {*ašd=a-kizzi=ḫḫ(i)=a*}, consisting of the *a*-stem ***ašd=a*** 'woman' and the *essive* in ***-a*** of ***kizzi=ḫḫi*** 'jewel', so that it can be translated as 'The woman (is/shines) like a jewel' or more specifically 'The woman (is/shines) like a hairpin of precious metal', if we take into account that ***kizzi/uḫu*** at Qaṭna is the designation of a *golden pin* and that Linear A ***ja-ki-si-ki-nu*** (AK Zf 9) is written on a *silver hairpin* from Arkhanes, that I have analysed as {*ya-kizz=i=ḫḫi=nnu*} 'as it is a jewel'.

The second sequence ***a-ra-u-|da*** (KH 5.1-2) is a Hurrian 'one-word' personal name or perhaps a toponym ***Arau*** in the *directive* case, with the *directive* suffix ***-da*** 'to, for', or the *ablative* case, with the ablative suffix ***-dan*** 'from'. The personal name ***Arau*** (wr. *A-ra-ú*), analysis {*ar=av*}, translation 'I give (the boy)', is actually attested at Old Babylonian Sippar (Dekiere 6, 917 Beischrift), cf. Th. Richter, *VHN*, 584-585, sub 1.1.2: *Names with verbal forms of the Mitanni-paradigms*. The scribe no doubt knew, whether he meant the directive or the ablative case, but we do not, because the final ***-n*** is not expressed in Linear A and B. If ***Arau*** designates a toponym, I consider the ablative more likely, since {*ar=av=dan*} could then refer to the provenance of ***a-da-ki-si-ka*** (KH 5.1), but if the tablet is about a transaction between persons, ***a-ra-u-|da*** can mean either 'for Arau' or 'from Arau'.

Th. Richter (*VHN*, 584-585) gives more examples of personal names that show the formation of a transitive verb in the 1st person singular in ***-au*** {*-av*}: ***Appau*** (wr. *ap-pa-ú*), {*app=av*} at Emar; ***Nanau*** (wr. *na-na-ù*), {*nan=av*} 'Ich schlage (Person(?)) nieder' ['I smash (the person(?)) down']; ***Šarau*** (wr. *ša-ra-ú*), {*šar=av*} 'Ich wünsche (Jungen)' ['I wish (the boy)'] at Atmannu (*Iraq 70*, 167, nr. 15: 5, see ***šar-*** *BGH*, 355); ***Tappau*** (wr. *tab-ba-ù*), {*tapp=av*} 'Ich mache (Jungen) fest' ['I make (the boy) firm'] at Umma. I have only quoted examples of so-called 'one-word' personal names appearing as verbal forms with the suffix ***-au*** of the subject-marker of the 1st person singular transitive indicative.

There are not only parallels in the Near East, but Linear A ***a-mi-da-u*** (ZA 10a.3) and ***a-mi-da-o*** (HT? 170a.5) are also good parallels of the same type of Hurrian personal names. ***a-mi-da-u*** and ***a-mi-da-o*** cannot mean 'I shall *arrive*', because the form cannot be intransitive, since intransitive verbs do not have a suffix ***-e/id-*** (with voiced dental) to indicate the future tense, but ***-e/it-*** (with voiceless dental, written ***-e/itt-*** in cuneiform), cf. e.g. the form ***un=ett=a*** 'he will come', see I. Wegner, *Einführung*, 97: *un-et+t+a* 'er wird kommen' ['he will come']. Moreover, the suffix ***-au*** [***-av/-affu***] is only the marker of the subject of action 1st person singular of transitive-ergative verbs (position 7), cf. I. Wegner, *Einführung*, 93, Table 4. The marker of the subject of action 1st person singular of intransitive verbs is the suffix of the enclitic *absolutive* personal pronoun ***-tta/-t*** (position 9), cf. I. Wegner, *Einführung*, 99, Tables 6-7.

So ***a-mi-da-u*** and ***a-mi-da-o*** may well represent transitive usage of the verb ***amm-*** 'to reach (something)', with the suffix ***-e/id-*** (with voiced dental) indicating the transitive future tense + the suffix of the 1st person singular ***-au***. Starting from the root ***amm-*** 'to reach (something)' ***a-mi-da-u*** and ***a-mi-da-o*** can be analysed as {*amm=e/id=au*} 'I shall reach (something)', 1st person singular future indicative of the verb ***amm-***.

However, if we assume that Linear A ***a-mi-da-u*** and ***a-mi-da-o*** contain the transitive root ***am-*** II [Boğ.] 'ansehen, anschauen, beachten', 'porter son regard sur', 'guardare, osservare, vedere', 'to observe' (Th. Richter, *BGH*, 21-23), the meaning of these personal names would be 'I shall observe', which would also offer a conceivable meaning.

The third sequence ***wi-sa-sa-ne*** (KH 5.2) may well be an ethnic used as a personal name, if it can be compared with (D)***p/wiša(i)šapḫi*** [loan-word into Hittite]. According to E. Laroche (*GLH*, 202) ***Piša(i)šapḫi*** is epithet of (D)*Ḫatni*; and ethnic probably derived from the toponym ****Pišaišpa***: d*Ḫatni* d*Pí-ša-(i)-ša-ap-ḫi*, KBo XX 119 IV 13; KBo XI 5 I 20; KBo XXI 50, 6; etc. - *Ḫatni Wi$_i$-ša-a-ša-ap-ḫi*, KUB XXV 48 IV 18; XXXIV 102 II 9, III 28; cf. KUB XXXII 52 III 9; XLV 21 Ro 8, 18. Hurrian context: KUB XXXII 44 Vo 17; 57, 9; 58, 9. – Alphabetic ***Pẓẓpḫ***, CTA 166, 35, 37. With determinative ***Pišašapḫi-ni***, KUB XXVII 42 Ro 31. - Directive: ***Pẓẓpḫ-n-d***, CTA 172, 9; RS 24.261, 18; 295, 9.

E. Laroche, *GLH*, 202, s.v. ***pišaiš***, végétal ? 1. Un fouet en bois (?) de ***pišaiš***, 2. mont ***Pišaiša*** en Syrie, 3. ****Pišaišpa*** toponym; and s.v. ***Piša(i)šapḫi***, épithète de d***Ḫatni***, e.g. d*Ḫatni Pí-ša-(i)-ša-ap-ḫi* and d*Ḫatni Wi$_i$-ša-a-ša-ap-ḫi*. Cf. also Th. Richter, *BGH*, 317-318, s.v. ***pišaiš*** [Boğ.; Mitt.], ***pišaišḫu*** [Nuzi], and s.v. d***p/wiša(i)šapḫi***, divine epithet 'God of Mount *Bišaiša* (North-Syria)' (V. Haas – I. Wegner, *Die Rituale der Beschwörerinnen* SALŠU.GI (ChS I/5), Teil II, *Das Glossar*, 1988, 285), **Pižaiža=ve+ġe » Pižaiža=p+ḫe* (Giorgieri, 2000a, 207) = 'The one of the Mountain *Pišaiša*'. See also Th. Richter, *BGH*, 535, s.v. ***pḏḏpḫ*** and ***pẓẓpḫ***. Here we see that ***-ḏḏ-*** and ***-ẓẓ-*** in alphabetic cuneiform are rendered as ***-ša-ša-*** in syllabic cuneiform.

Comparing Linear A ***wi-sa-sa-ne*** (KH 5.2) with d***P/Wiša(i)šapḫi*** and its analysis **P/Wižaiža=ve+ġe » P/Wižaiža=p+ḫe*, we see that the name of the mountain is ***Piša(i)ša*** or ***Wiša(i)ša*** and that *°=ve+ġe » °=p+ḫe* reflects the genitive suffix + the ethnic suffix. As a result Linear A ***wi-sa-sa-ne*** may well consist of the name of the mountain ***Wišaša / Wišaiša*** + the alternative Hurrian ethnic suffix ***-n(n)i/e*** as we encounter in ***Mašrian(n)i*** 'Egyptian', derived from the country-name *Mašria*. Linear A ***wi-sa-sa-ne*** (KH 5.2) may well be an ethnic used as a personal name, translation 'The one of (Mount) *Wišaša*'.

E. Laroche (*GLH*, 169), s.v. ***Mašrianni*** 'Égyptien'. Sg. KUR *Ma-a-aš/áš-ri-a-an-ni ewir-ni* 'le seigneur égyptien' = le Pharaon (Mit. I 10, II 69, 71, III 117, IV 128. This expression alternates with KUR *Mi-zi-ir-ri-e-we* < **Mišr-ni-we* 'de l'Égypte' (Mit. I 62, 85, III 105), cf. E. A. Speiser, *IH*, 67; F.W. Bush, *GHL*, 335, n. 94; Th. Richter, *BGH*, 247-248. Compare also the personal name *maš-ru-ḫé* 'Égyptien' from Emar (Durand, 1992).

The fourth sequence ***wi-na-du*** (KH 5.3) may be interpreted as the Hurrian sentence-name ***P/Win-ašdu*** and be analysed as {*fin-aždu*} and be translated 'Lift (the child), oh woman !', 'Pick (the child) up, oh woman !'.

Th. Richter (*BGH*, 310-311) mentions s.v. ***pe/in-*** [Boğ.; PN] the translation 'messen, vermessen' ['to measure'] (Deller, 1976, 39); 'hochheben' ['to lift'] (G. Wilhelm apud Röseler, 1999, 398[20] */p/fin-/* or */p/fen-/*, M. Salvini / I. Wegner, 2004, 178; Wilhelm 2005c, 205); 'hochhalten' ['to keep up'], i.e. */fen-/* (V. Haas, 2007a, 346[29]). Corresponds with Hittite ***karp-*** (Wilhelm, l.c.). See also Th. van den Hout, *The elements of Hittite*, Cambridge 2011, 192, s.v. ***karp-*** (Ia) 'to lift, pick up'. Alternatively Linear A ***wi-na-du*** (KH 5.3) may be interpreted as the Hurrian 'one-word' personal name ***P/Winadu*** that can be analysed as *{fin=ad=u}*, consisting of the verbal root ***p/win-*** + the root-extension ***-ad-*** + the Old Hurrian marker of the *imperative* ***-u***, translation 'Lift (the child) !' or Old Hurrian marker of the *past indicative* 3rd pers. singular ***=o=m***, translation 'He/She lifted (the child)'. Maybe such a name refers to the recognition of the child as a legitimate son or daughter. Allegedly the ancient Spartan fathers used such a gesture to show that they acknowledged a child as worthy of living. According to I. Wegner (*Einführung*, 88) the meaning/aspect of the root-extension ***-ad-*** is not clear. She gives the example of ***šir=ad-*** '(be)singen' ['to sing, chant'] and ***am=ad-***, meaning unknown.

As regards Linear A sign ***48b*** corresponding with Linear B ****21*** = ideogram OVIS and syllabogram ***qi***, the correspondence seems only valid for the 'sheep' ideogram, although J. Raison and M. Pope (*Index transnuméré du linéaire A*, 1977, 60) have booked sign ***48b*** as ***qi***. On page 120 of the same book they offer, however, only one sequence with this sign: ***48b-na*** (KH 5.3). In their *Corpus transnuméré du linéaire A*, 1994^{2}, 162, they offer the same sequence, which I have indeed transliterated as ***qi-na*** , (KH 5.3) in my *Corpus of transliterated Linear A texts*. Re-examining the tablet I now consider it more likely that we have to read OVIS+***na*** 1 instead of ***qi-na*** , (KH 5.3) and that Linear A ***48b*** does not represent a syllabogram at all, but only the ideogram OVIS. Since ***wi-sa-sa-ne*** (KH 5.2) and ***ku-pa-do*** (KH 5.3) are also followed by ideograms and numbers, it is more likely in the context that ***wi-na-du*** (KH 5.3) is followed by OVIS+***na*** 1.

The next sequence ***ku-pa-do*** (KH 5.3) is probably also a personal name. Since the Linear B ***k-*** signs represent ***κ-***, ***γ-***, ***χ-***, the corresponding Linear A signs probably represent ***k-***, ***g-***, ***ḫ-*** and ***-ḫḫ-***. This mean that the name can theoretically contain a root ***kub-***, ***kupp-***, ***kurb-***, ***ḫub-***, or ***ḫumb-*** and due to Linear A orthographic conventions with regard to consonant clusters ***°ado*** can, apart from ***-ad=o***, also contain ***-ašdo/u***. This is interesting, because the preceding name ***wi-na-du*** (KH 5.3) has a similar ending and it may be noted that some scribes were fond of playing with words and names. Perhaps ***ku-pa-do*** contains like ***wi-na-du*** a verbal root + the nominal form ***-ašdo/u*** and can be qualified as a sentence name or as a 'one-word' name consisting of verbal root + root-extension ***-ad-*** + the marker of the Old Hurrian transitive *imperative* ***-o/u*** or Old Hurrian *past indicative* 3rd p.s. ***=o=m***.

P.M. Purves (*NPN*, 230) mentions s.v. ***kup***, ***kup-***, the following personal names: ***Kup-arša*** (wr. *Ku-pa-ar-ša*, *Ḫu-pa-ar-ša*, *Ku-bar-ša*, *Ku-ba-ar-ša*). Or ***Kuparša*** ? Interchange of ***k*** and ***ḫ*** suggests non-Hurrian origin; see Purves in *AJSL LVII* 173, n. 51. ***Kup-asa*** (wr. *Ku-ú-ba-a-sa*, *Ku-ú-ba-sa*, *Ku-ba-a-sa*). Division uncertain. Cf. ^{c}*Ku-ba-sa*, KAJ 143:9. ***Kuperi*** (wr. *Ku-be-ri*). Formed on ***kup*** ? Possibly not Hurrian. L. Oppenheim in *AOF XII*, 35 divides as a divine name ***Kupe*** + formative ***-ri***. But, if so, no other name has this formative preceded by ***e***. Or Akkadian ? And s.v. ***kupp***: ***Kuppe*** (wr. ^{f}*Ku-ub-be*, ^{f}*Ku-ub-bi*).

Th. Richter (*VHN*, 448) mentions, s.v. ***kub-*** I / ***kupp-*** {*ko/ub- / ko/upp-*} that a root ***kub-*** has been isolated in *NPN* 230, on the basis of *Ku-bar/pa-ar-ša/šá* (with variant *Ḫu-pa-ar-ša*) that is certainly the same sequence as ***Kubarze*** {*ko/ub=a=r=ze*} at Šubat-Enlil. Hurrian origin is uncertain. None of the few sequences starting with ***kub-*** I / ***kupp-*** is sufficiently and unanimously defined (morphologically, lexically or semantically), see *BGH*, 225-226. This also applies to forms in context ***ku-pa-a-e*** (Laroche, *GLH*, 150), ***ku-u-bi-ti*** (ChS I/2, 1 Rs. III 4, 31; 4: 2'), ***ku-bi-***x[...] (I/5, 86 Vs 5') and ***ku-u-pu-na-(-)***[...] (98: 7') [I have translated the German text into English.].

Incidentally, I wonder, whether another analysis of *Ḫu-pa-ar-ša* as {*ḫub(i)-arša*} may be considered. If ***Ḫub-*** is the root of ***ḫub=idi*** 'calf' (epithet of *Šarruma*), with the nominal ending ***-idi*** as in ***tar=idi*** 'pot, pan' from ***tari-*** 'fire' and ***naḫḫ=idi*** 'seat' from ***naḫḫ-*** 'to sit, to sit down' (cf. I. Wegner, *Einführung*, 59, s.v. ***-idi***), and if ***-ar-ša*** is the noun ***arš=a*** 'young man, boy', *a*-stem of the Hurrian and Urartian root ****arš-***, recognized in Urartian ***aršə*** 'adolescents, young boys' by Diakonoff/Starostin, 1986, 36 (cf. Th. Richter, *BGH*, 48). *Ḫu-pa-ar-ša* {*ḫub(i)-arša*} may then be translated 'The boy is a calf' or {*ḫub(i)=a-arša*} 'The boy is like a bull-calf', with ***ḫub(=i)=a*** as the *essive* of ***ḫub=i***.

Although I.J. Gelb (*NPN*, 91) and P.M. Purves (*NPN*, 230) ascribe all writing variants *Ku-pa-ar-ša*, *Ḫu-pa-ar-ša*, *Ku-bar-ša*, *Ku-ba-ar-ša* to **Kuparša** at Nuzi, I have found no explicit evidence that *Ḫu-pa-ar-ša* really is the same person as one of the persons, whose name contains the root ***kub-***. I therefore gather that it is possible that we are in fact dealing with two different roots: ***kub-*** I / ***kupp-*** and ***ḫup-***, although names built on these roots show the same type of formations as can be observed not only in ***Kuparša*** (wr. *Ku-pa-ar-ša*, *Ḫu-pa-ar-ša*, *Ku-bar-ša*, *Ku-ba-ar-ša*) at Nuzi, but also in ***Ku-up-pa-aḫ-***[***ḫ***]***é*** at Nuzi and ***Ḫupaḫ(ḫ)e*** (wr. *Ḫu-pa-ḫe*) at Tigunāni, typology 3.1, lexicon *ḫupaḫ(ḫ)e* (→ *ḫub-*), cf. Th. Richter, *VHN*, 142. Alternation of ***k-*** signs with signs for the emphatics ***q-*** is quite normal in cuneiform, but ***k/ḫ*** alternation would be exceptional in Hurrian cuneiform. So I think that it is for a good reason that Th. Richter has kept the roots ***kub-*** I / ***kupp-*** and ***ḫup-*** separate in *BGH* and *VHN*. He mentions the following personal names (*VHN*, 448):
(1a) {*ko/ub-*}: ***Kupi*** (Šušarrā), ***Kupija*** (Šušarrā), ***Kupe-šaki*** (Tigunāni). (1b) {*ko/upp-*}: ***Kuppija*** (Mari), (2) {*ko/ub=a=r=ze*} ***Kubarze*** (Šubat-Enlil).

Since the roots ***kub-*** I and ***kupp-*** show parallels in onomastics, Th. Richter has brought them together. Since ***ku-up-pa-aḫ-***[***ḫ***]***é*** (Nuzi: s. SANTAG 4 S. 265), {*ko/uppi»a=ḫḫe*}, also occurs in personal names, a noun ****kuppi-*** {*ko/upp=i*} can be isolated. Consequently the Nuzi name *fKu-ub-be, fKu-ub-bi* (cf. I.J. Gelb, *NPN*, 91) and the names mentioned *supra* sub (1a) and (1b) are probably nominal 'one-word' names. However, verbal analysis is also possible. Cf. Linear A ***ku-pi*** (ZA 14.3) from Kato Zakro that probably is a Hurrian personal name as well. Analysis as ***Ḫub=i*** (without nominal ***=idi***) 'Bull-calf' is possible.

Linear A ***ku-pa*** (HT 110a.2; HT Wa 1020α; ZA 11a.5; ZA 11b.3) can reflect Hurrian ***Ḫuba***, {*ḫub=a*} 'Like a bull-calf' (*essive*). ***Ḫu-ba*** is attested at UR III. Compare the Linear A personal name ***ku-pa-ja*** GRA 16 (HT 116a.1-2), {*ḫub=a=ya*} 'He is like a bull-calf', with the Hurrian personal name ***Ḫu-ba-a*** at Ur III, cf. for ***Ḫu-ba*** and ***Ḫu-ba-a*** at Ur III G.R. Meyer, *AOF XIII (1939/40)*, 148; cf. P.M. Purves, *NPN*, 217, s.v. ***ḫump***, ***Ḫumpa***.

Since ***-m-*** preceding an occlusive is not expressed in Linear A and B consonant clusters, interpretation as ***Ḫumpa***, analysis {*ḫumb=a*}, is also possible as the Hurrian personal name ***Ḫumpa*** (wr. *Ḫu-um-pa, Ḫu-um-ba*) at Nuzi (I.J. Gelb, *NPN*, 63). P.M. Purves (*NPN*, 217, s.v. ***ḫump***, ***Ḫumpa***) also considers a development of ***ḫump*** < ***ḫupp*** in view of well-known dissimilation of ***pp*** > ***mp*** and the writing variants of the personal name ***Ḫumpape / Ḫup(p)ape*** (wr. *Ḫu-um-pa-be, Ḫu-pa-be, Ḫu-up-pa-be, Ḫu-um-ba-be, Ḫu-um-pa-bi,* [*Ḫu-um*]*-pa-a-be*) at Nuzi. The Ur III forms are older than those from Nuzi, which makes dissimilation of ***pp*** > ***mp*** indeed more likely than assimilation of ***mp*** > ***pp***. Purves assumes that the underlying form is perhaps exemplified by *ḫu-u-ub-bi*, KUB XXVII 4:2; 8 rev.? 2; 12:13; 21:1; *ḫu-u-ub-bi-in-na, ibid.* 12:14. But cf. Th. Richter (*VHN*, 422), s.v. ***ḫumb-***.

According to Th. Richter (*BGH*, 163-165; *VHN*, 423) the meaning of a verbal root ***ḫub-*** {*ḫo/ub-*} '(zer)brechen, zerstören, vernichten' ['to break, destroy'] is generally accepted, because it corresponds with Hittite ***(arḫa) duwarnai-***, cf. also E. Laroche, *GLH*, 109, s.v. ***ḫub-*** 'briser'. Since final ***-m*** is not expressed in Linear A, ***ku-pa-do*** (KH 5.3) can be analysed as an Old Hurrian verbal 'one-word' name {*ḫub=ad=o=m*}, with root-extension ***-ad-*** of unknown meaning, 'He/She (a *numen*) destroyed (the deceased child)' or as an Old Hurrian *imperative* {*ḫub=ad=o*} 'Destroy (the deceased child) (oh *numen*) !'.

For the nominal form ***ḫupaḫ(ḫ)e*** (in ***°=a=ġ/ḫḫe***) as well as for ***ḫubazzi*** {*ḫo/ubazzi*} a plausible lexical explanation fails. Th. Richter (*VHN*, 142-143) mentions the following Hurrian names with the root ***ḫub-***: ***Ḫupaḫ(ḫ)e*** (wr. *Ḫu-pa-ḫe*) at Tigunāni, typology 3.1, lexicon *ḫupaḫ(ḫ)e* (→ *ḫub-*); *Ḫu-pu-‹uš›-tu-ka* Alalaḫ IV (*AT* 202: 31; A. Draffkorn, *HHA*, 132, without addition); **Ḫu-pu-uš-te-ka* Alalaḫ VII (*AT* *268 = JCS 8, 21: 17, reading Zeeb 2001, 573, *editio princeps* has *°-tu-ka* [cf. E. Laroche, *GLH*, 110]; *Ḫu-up-til-la* at Nuzi (NPN 63); ***Ḫupazzam*** (wr. *Ḫu-ba-az-za-am, Ḫu-bi-iz-za-am*) at Šubat-Enlil, typology 3.2.1, analysis {*ḫo/ubazz(i)=a*[E.]*=m(e)*}, lexicon *ḫubazzi* (→ *ḫub-*); ***Ḫupazzan*** (wr. *Ḫu-ba-za-an, Ḫu-ba-az-za*) at Mari, typology 3.2.1, {*ḫo/ubazz(i)=a*[E.]*=(n(na))*}, lexicon *ḫubazzi* (→ *ḫub-*); [E.] refers to *essive* case. He also mentions the Hurrian personal name ***Ḫupitam*** (wr. *Ḫu-bi-dam*), {*ḫo/ubid(i)=a*[E.]*=m(e/a)*}, at Ašnakkum, Mari, Šubat-Enlil, Tuttul, Ĝirsu (UR III), Kaniš, Nippur (UR III), Umma (UR III), Nuzi, Alalaḫ IV, Dilbat, Ḫattuša, typology 3.2.1, lexicon *ḫubidi*, translation 'Er (Junge) ist wie ein Kalb' ['He (the boy) is like a calf']. This name is probably derived from Hurrian ***ḫubidi*** {*ḫub=idi*} 'Kalb, Stierkalb' ['calf, bull-calf'], 'Stierkalb (des Teššub)' (I. Wegner, 2004, 30), cf. Th. Richter, *BGH*, 164-165, s.v. ***ḫubidi*** [Boğ.; PN], and *VHN*, 423, s.v. ***ḫubidi***.

The meaning is confirmed by correspondences with Sumerogram AMAR(*-ti*) and Akkadian *būru* and a relation with the root ***ḫub-*** is possible (cf. Khacikjan, 1985, 63).

E. Laroche (*GLH*, 108-109): ***ḫubidi*** 'veau'. Lecture du sumérogramme AMAR(*-ti*); cf. Goetze, *RHA 39*, 199 n. 46; Otten, OLZ 1954, 135 n. 2; Laroche, RHA XXVII 67. 1. Épithète de Šarrumma 'veau/garçon de Tešub', ***ᵈTeššub-bi ḫu-u-bi-ti ᵈŠarrumma-n***, KUB XXVII 38 II 14, 20 = ᵈU***-ub-wi*** AMAR***-ti ᵈŠarrumma***, KBo XX 119 I 14 = IV 18-19 = KBo XVII 86+ I 3; hiér. hitt. ᵈVEAU ***Ti-su-pi*** [***h***]***u-pi-ti***, Yaz. 42a. - De même KUB XXV 44 V 6; XXXIV 102 II 8; XXVII 1 I 70; KBo XI 5 I 23. Etc. According to E. Laroche (*GLH*, 229) the meaning 'garçon' ['boy'] is the masculine equivalent to Hurrian ***šiduri*** (wr. *ši-du-ri*) 'jeune fille' ['young girl, daughter'] = Akkadian ***ardâtu***.

Tablet PK 1 (HM 86), found in 1903 at Palaikastro (house block B, room 13, site of Roussolakkos) is special, since it is one of the few tablets that really answers to the qualification of a _Linear_ A text, because there are indeed 7 horizontal lines drawn with a ruler, probably before the sequences were inscribed between the lines. In Linear B this method of writing between the lines was normal on the page-tablets. Another unusual feature is that the sign **si** is written on the right edge (c). The verso side (b) is uninscribed.

PK 1a.1.   _si-ri̲-ne-ti_ ̣ _ka-qa̲_ 2 | c. (right edge of tablet)

2.   _a-du-za_ 1 _ta₂-ta̲-re_ 1 |

3.   _ta₂-ti-te_ 1 _o-ka-mi-za_ 2̲ |

4.   _i-na_ 1̲ _____ |
4ᵇⁱˢ.   _o-te̲-ja̲_ 1 | _si̲-_

5.   _ra-na-tu-su_ 1̲ _ni̲-mi-tu̲-_ |

6.   _su_ 1̲ _ma-ti-za-i-te_ 1 |

7.   _ma-da-ti_ 1 _ma-ka-i-ta_ 1 |

The reason why sign **si** is written on the edge remains uncertain. If it is part of a sequence, to which sequence should it be added ? The photographs in _GORILA 1_ (p. 280) show that it is written on the same level as **o-te̲-ja** 1, but in their transcription L. Godart - J.-P. Olivier place **si** on the level of line 3 between **o-ka-mi-za** (line 3) and **i-na** (line 4) and read **o-ka-mi-za-si-i-na**. J. Raison – M. Pope put a dot beneath the hyphen after **si̲-** and place **si̲-** to the right of line 4bis. In the 2016 edition I have suggested that **si** might be combined with **i-na**, so that **o-ka-mi-za** **i-na|̲-si** ̣ could be read, which would yield a parallel with **e-na-si** (KH 7a.2), but since **si** in fact follows **o-te̲-ja** 1, I now consider it more likely that it belongs to the next sequence, so that we should read **si̲-|ra-na-tu-su** 1̲ (PK 1c+1a.5), followed by **ni̲-mi̲-tu̲-su** 1̲ (PK1.5-6).

Linear A **si-ri̲-ne-ti** (PK 1a.1), first sequence of the tablet, is followed by **ka-qa** 2̲. This first sequence might contain the Hurrian element **zi-li-** as in _Zi-li-te-ia, Zi-li-te-šup, Ṣill_(MI)_-te-šup, Ṣill_(MI.NI)_-te-šup_, etc., cf. P.M. Purves, _NPN_, 277, s.v. **zil, zili-**, who mentions that the phonetic form is probably **sil** and that some scholars favour the translation 'witness' for **zil** and others translate 'shepherd'. L. Oppenheim (Studien zu den nichtsemitischen Nuzi-Namen, _Altorientalische Forschungen 12 (1937)_, published in 1939, 38) understands **zil** as loan-word from Akkadian **ṣillu**. P.M. Purves does not believe this, but states that it is evident in any event that Hurrian **zil** and Akkadian **ṣillu** were confused by Nuzi scribes, cf. the variant writings of **Zil-tešup, Zili-tešup** on the one hand and **Ṣill-dûri** on the other; **-ne-** in **si-ri̲-ne-ti** may be the suffix for the so-called singular definite article or the individualising suffix in Hurrian, and **-ti/-te** is a hypocoristic form of **Tešub** in personal names, cf. _NPN_, 266, s.v. **-ti**; 264, s.v. **-te**, where P.M. Purves writes: "Hurrian shortened form of **tešup** and **teja** as final element."

The name ***si-ri̱-ne-ti*** (PK 1a.1) can thus be explained as 'Tešub is the witness' or 'Tešub is the shepherd', cf. also Th. Richter, *BGH*, 374-375, s.v. ***zil-*** IV and ***zill-*** I.

Many libation formulas start with ***a-ta-i-jo-wa-ja*** (see *sub voce*) = ****at-ta-i-iw-wa-aš*** 'Our Father', Hurrian *absolutive* form of the possessive 1st person plural of ***attai*** 'Father', reconstructed on the basis of the *ergative* form ***at-ta-i-iw-wa-šu-uš*** (Mit. IV 118), used as epithet of Teš(š)ub in the Tušratta letter, and on the basis of the parallel cognate form ***at-ta-a-ar-ti-iw-wa-aš****meš* (Mit. I 8), 'notre paternité', possessive 1st person plural of ***attardi*** according to E. Laroche, *GLH*, 64, s.v. ***attardi*** 'paternité', cf. also I. Wegner, *Einführung*, 58, 63, s.v. ***atta(i)=arde-*** 'Vorväter, Vorfahren' ['ancestors'].

It is not surprising that the Stormgod himself is invoked as a witness right at the end of the formula with the Linear A sequence ***si-ru-te***, Hurrian ***šilute/zilute*** 'Tešub is witness'.

However, I also referred to P.M. Purves's comparison of Hurrian ***šilu*** (in the personal names *Ši-i-lu* and *Ši-lu-ia*) with ***šilwa*** (in the personal names ***Šilwa-te***, ***Šilwa-tešub***, ***Šilwa-turi*** and ***Šilwai̯a*** at Nuzi. See Linear A ***si-ru-te*** (AP Za 2; IO Za 2; KO Za 1; PK Za 10; PK Za 11; PK Za 12; SY Za 3; TL Za 1; VRY Za 1) in 'libation formulas'.

Th. Richter (*BGH*, 374) offers, s.v. ***šel*** I [Boğ.] and ***šil*** II, 'to be pleasant' and 'good' and, s.v. ***šel=ab-***, ***šel=b-*** 'to treat in a good/kind way', corresponding with Urartian ***silua*** 'to be kind, benevolent, benign'.

Correspondence of Hurrian ***šilu*** with Hurrian ***šilwa*** in personal names (especially in combination with ***-te*** / ***-tešub***) and Urartian ***silua*** has convinced me that Linear A ***si-ru-te*** at the end of libation formulas is probably equivalent to a Hurrian proverbial expression at the close of a prayer. The libation formula turns out to be a prayer addressing Tešub as 'Our Father' in his role of *eni attanni* 'God the Father' and closing off with 'Tešub is good, benevolent' or (transitively) 'treat (us) well / benevolently, oh Tešub !', which is semantically similar to 'be beneficent, oh Tešub !', close to *Kyrie eleison !* in prayers for God's mercy, and close to '*erbarme dich !*' in J.S. Bach's St. Matthew Passion. So Linear A ***si-ri̱-ne-ti*** (PK 1a.1) may be analysed as ***Šil=i=nne-Ti***, consisting of verbal root ***šil-*** II + marker of transitivity ***-i-*** + marker of the *imperative* ***Ø***, since the imperative does not have its own marker + the optional allomorphic enclitic personal pronoun 3rd person sing. ***-nni/e*** instead of ***-nna***, marking the object of the transitive verb + hypocoristic ***-Ti*** instead of ***-Tešub***. Or ***Šil=i=n(na)=e-Ti*** with the shortened enclitic personal pronoun 3rd pers. sing. ***-n*** instead of ***-nna*** + the thematic vowel ***-e-***. The translation is in both cases the same: 'Treat him/her (the child) in a benovolent way, oh Tešub !'. But a *jussive* analysis ***Šil(=i)=en=e-tti*** is also possible: ***šil-*** II + marker of the *jussive* ***-i-*** + marker of the 3rd person of the *jussive* ***-en-*** + theme-vowel ***-e-*** + optional allomorphic enclitic personal pronoun 1st person sing. ***-tti***, 'May he/she (a *numen*) treat me in a benovolent way' (*Einführung*, 103).

Linear A ***ka-qa*** (PK 1.1), following ***si-ri̱-ne-ti***, cannot be equated with the Hurrian personal name ***kanka*** (wr. *Qa-an-qa*, *Ka-an-ka*) at Nuzi (cf. P.M. Purves, *NPN*, 222, s.v. *kak, kakk, kanka*), since the cuneiform emphatics ***q-*** are not equivalent to the Linear A ***q-*** signs that are to be compared with the cuneiform voiced velar fricatives ***-ḫ-***, ***/ġ/***. Compare the discussion on Linear A ***ka-pa*** and ***ka-pa-qe*** (*supra*); ***ka-pa-qe*** may be equated with the Hurrian ethnic ***Ḫalbaḫe*** in the main cuneiform syllabary and with ***ḫlbġ*** in the cuneiform alphabet from Ugarit, 'Man from Ḫalba' with Hurrian ethnic suffix ***-ḫi / -ḫe***.

Alphabetic cuneiform ***ġ*** in ***ḫlbġ*** shows that the syllabic intervocalic ***-ḫ-*** (single writing) in ***Ḫalbaḫe*** represents a voiced velar fricative or spirant in medial position (Linear A ***-qe***) that must be distinguished from the voiceless velar fricative ***ḫ-*** in initial position in syllabic and alphabetic cuneiform and ***-ḫḫ-*** in medial position in syllabic and ***-ḫ-*** in medial position in alphabetic cuneiform.

Identification of Linear A ***ka-qa*** with e.g. Hurrian ****Ḫaš-ḫa*** is possible. ****Ḫaš-ḫa*** may well be a hypocoristic of the Hurrian personal name ***Ḫaš-ḫarpa*** at Nuzi (wr. *Ḫa-aš-ḫar-ba*, *Ḫa-aš-ḫar-me*), cf. P.M. Purves, *NPN*, 214, s.v. ***ḫaš-***, verbal root 'to hear'; s.v. ***-ḫarpa***. P.M. Purves (*NPN*, 212, s.v. ***ḫa***, ***-ḫa***) also mentions about ***Ariḫ-ḫa*** (wr. *A-ri-iḫ-ḫa, A-ri-ḫa*): "Perhaps shortened form of ***Ariḫ-ḫamanna***, for a man of each name is father of *Enna-mati*." Consequently ****Ḫaš-ḫa*** could also be a shortened form of ****Ḫaš-ḫamanna***. According to the orthographic conventions of Linear A and B ***-s-*** preceding an occlusive is not expressed in consonant clusters. It is preferable to choose the verbal root ***ḫaš-*** instead of e.g. ***kar-*** 'to conquer' (cf. Th. Richter, *VHN*, 431, s.v. ***kar-***) that would orthographically also yield a theoretical possibility, since the root ***ḫaš-*** 'to hear' is one of the most popular verbal roots that can be combined with theophorous or *quasi* theophorous elements in Hurrian personal names. The meaning of ***ḫaš-*** in these names seems to be that the prayers to the gods or *numina* 'divine powers' who are addressed, are heard and answered.

P.M. Purves (*NPN*, 214-215) provides a long list of personal names with ***ḫaš-*** or forms of ***ḫaš-*** such as Old Hurrian ***ḫaš=i=b-***, combined with (*quasi*) theophorous elements or hypocoristic forms, e.g. ***Ḫaš-teḭa*** (wr. *Ḫa-aš-te-ia*, *Ḫa-aš-te-e*), probably *imperative* 'Hear (the prayer), oh Tešub !' or *indicative* 'Tešub hears, heard (the prayer)' and ***Ḫašitte*** (wr. *Ḫa-ši-it-te*) < ****Ḫaš=i=b-te***) beside the full name ***Ḫašip-tešup*** (wr. *Ḫa-ši-ip-te-šup*) 'Tešub hears, heard (the prayer)'; ***Ḫašip-tilla*** (wr. *Ḫa-ši-ip-til-la*) 'Tilla hears, heard (the prayer)'; ***Ḫašip-šarri*** (wr. *Ḫa-ši-ip-šarri*) 'The King of Gods hears, heard (the prayer)'; ***Ḫaš-šimika*** (wr. *Ḫa-aš-ši-mi-qa*, *Ḫa-ši-mi-qa*) 'Hear (the prayer), oh ***Šimiga*** !' ['Hear (the prayer), oh Sun-God !'] or '***Šimiga*** hears, heard (the prayer)'; and many more examples.

A very interesting one is ***Ḫašip-ajakke*** (wr. *ᶠḪa-ši-ip-a-a-ag-ge*) at Nuzi (cf. I.J. Gelb, *NPN*, 57), especially because ***te-ra-me a-ja-ku*** (KN Zf 13) = ***telame Ajakkun*** 'oh Great Ajakkun !' is attested in the last two sequences of a Linear A inscription on a gold signet-ring (HM 530, 1927) from the necropolis of Mavro Spilio, Chamber Tomb IX, E 1 (Sinclair Hood, *Archaeological survey*, F 6, point 95), east of the Palace of Minos.

Th. Richter (*VHN*, 126-133) mentions a variety of names with ***ḫaš-*** or Old Hurrian ***ḫaš=i=b-***, e.g. ***Ḫaši*** (wr. *Ḫa-ši*) from Tigunāni and Emar *ḫa-ži*, analysis {*ḫaž=i*}, typology 1.3.1.2.1 (the personal name represents an *imperative* of ***ḫaš-***, lexicon *ḫaš-*, translation 'Erhöre (Person oder Gebet) (oh *Numen*) !' ['Hear (and answer) (person or prayer) (oh *numen*) !']; ***Ḫažija*** (wr. *Ḫa-ži-ia*, *Ḫa-ši-ia*) from Mari, Qaṭṭarā, Šušarrā, Tuttul, Alalaḫ VII and IV, Dūr-Abiešuḫ, Ekalte, Emar, Kurruḫanni, Nuzi, Qaṭna, Sippar, Tall ar-Rimaḥ, Ugarit, analysis {*ḫaž=i=ja*}, typology 1.1.1.2.4, lexicon *haz-*, *ḫaš-*, translation 'Er/Sie (scil. ein *Numen*) erhörte (Person oder Gebet)' ['He/She (scil. a *numen*) heard (and answered) (person or prayer)']. Th. Richter prefers to interpret this name as a verbal form, consisting of the verbal root ***ḫaš- / haz-*** + the marker of transitivity ***-i-*** + the marker of the subject of action 3rd person singular ***-a***, but admits that the form can orthographically not be distinguished from a hypocoristic of a sentence name, with hypocoristic suffix ***-ya***.

Ḫašinna (wr. *Ḫa-ši-in-na*) from Tigunāni and Nuzi, analysis {*ḫaž=i=nna*}, consisting of the verbal root ***ḫaš- / haz-*** + the marker of transitivity ***-i-*** + the suffix of the enclitic pronoun 3rd person sing. ***-nna*** as object of action of the transitive verb, typology 1.3.1.2.2.1, lexicon *ḫaš-*, translation 'Erhöre ihn/sie/es (***-nna***) (Person oder Gebet) (oh *Numen*) !' ['Hear (and answer) him/her/it (***-nna***) (person or prayer) (oh *numen*) !']. The so-called sentence names are the easiest to interpret, e.g. ***Ḫaš-Šimika*** (wr. *Ḫa-aš-ši-mi-qa*) at Tigunāni and Nuzi, analysis {*ḫaš-Šimiga*}, typology 1.4, 'Hear (the prayer), oh ***Šimiga*** !' ['Hear (the prayer), oh Sun-God !'] or '***Šimiga*** hears, heard (the prayer)'; *Ḫašim-Nawar*, *Ḫazip-Nawar*, *Ḫašip-Ara*, *Ḫazip-Aranziḫ*, *Ḫazip-atal*, *Ḫazip-ewri*, *Ḫazip-dIšḫara*, *Ḫazip-Pišapḫe*, *Ḫazip*-IŠTAR, *Ḫazip-Ḫasur*, *Ḫazip-Kuzuḫ*, *Ḫazip-muš*[*ni*] ?, *Ḫazip-Na*, *fḪazip-Šaju*, *fḪazip-šaki*, *Ḫazip-šarri*, *Ḫazip-Šimika*, *Ḫazip-Šimike*, *Ḫazip-tawan*, *Ḫazip-Teš(š)up*, *Ḫazip-dUkur*, *Ḫazip-ulme*.

Linear A ***ka-qa*** (PK 1.1) can theoretically also be interpreted as ****ḫalḫa*** or ****kalḫa***, which might be a Near Eastern prototype of the Greek loan-word ***κάλχη*** '*murex* yielding purple dye' and 'purple dye'. P. Chantraine (*DELG*, 488): ***κάλχη***: "f. '*murex*', coquillage qui fournit la pourpre (Nic., *Al.* 393), 'teinture de pourpre' (Str.), fleur couleur pourpre *Chrysanthemum coronarium* (Alcm. 91 P, Nic., *fr.* 74,60 avec la graphie ***χάλκη***), ….***καλχαίνω*** 'être couleur pourpre' (Nic., *Th.* 641); auparavant ***καλχαίνω*** est attesté au sens d' 'être agité, inquiet'. … Le flottement entre les formes ***κάλχη***, ***χάλκη*** et ***χάλχη***, s'explique par une métathèse d'aspiration." I should like to add: If ****ḫalḫa*** : ***χάλχη*** is the original form, the form ***κάλχη*** is the result of Grassmann's phonetic law in Greek and ***χάλκη*** is the result of metathesis of the aspiration. P. Chantraine mentions (*ibid.*) about the etymology: "On admet que ***κάλχη*** (comme *πόρφυρα*) est un terme d'emprunt, mais l'origine est inconnue. Aucune raison, d'autre part, de rapprocher le nom de ***Κάλχας***." It may be interesting that recent research shows that the famous and precious *murex* was not only found in Phoenicia, but also on the Cretan coasts, probably already in Minoan times.

I disagree with Chantraine that ***κάλχη*** has nothing to do with the name ***Κάλχας***. *Purple dye* has always been a mark of wealth and authority (cf. the *toga* of the Kings of Rome and the wide purple band along the edge of togas of Roman senators and the narrow purple band on the togas of Roman knights (*equites*). It is conceivable that the legendary priest ***Κάλχας***, who played an important role before the departure of the Greek fleet from Aulis to Troy (sacrifice of *Iphigeneia*) and later during the Trojan war, had an appellative name, because he may have been dressed in purple. Correspondence between ***κάλχη / χάλκη / χάλχη*** 'purple dye' and ***χάλκος*** 'bronze' may be due to the purple-red colour and shine of the metal 'bronze', cf. also P. Chantraine, *DELG*, 1243-1244, s.v. ***χαλκός*** : myc. ***ka-ko*** (Pylos), crét. ***καυχός*** de * ***καλχός*** (*I. Cret.* IV, no 162,3, Gortyne, IIIe s. avant J.C.), etc.

Linear A ***a-du-za*** 1 (PK 1.2), following ***ka-qa*** (PK 1.1), is a personal name that can be identified with the Hurrian personal name ***fAštuzar*** (wr. *fAš-tu-za-ar*) at Ašnakkum (Tall Šaġīr Bāzār / „Chagar Bazar") and Mari, typology 3.1, lexicon *aštuzari*, 'Frauen(?)' ['womanhood'] or ['woman *par excellence*'], cf. Th. Richter, *VHN*, 80, 382-383, because the Hurrian suffix ***-šari*** forms according to I. Wegner (*Einführung*, 57) abstracts or collectives. Compare also P.M. Purves (*NPN*, 206, s.v. *Ašt, Aštu-, Aštua-, Aštun-*): ***Aštua-šar*** (wr. *fAš-du-a-šar*) at Nuzi and ***fAštu-šar*** (*fAš-tu-za-ar*) at Chagar Bazar (*Iraq VII*, 36).

Compare also the parallel within Linear A ***a-du-sa-ra*** (HT 62+73.1) from Hagia Triada, that I have interpreted in the same way (see *supra*). Linear A ***a-du-za*** 1 (PK 1.2), Hurrian ^{f}***Aštuzar*** (wr. ^{f}*Aš-tu-za-ar*), can be analysed as {*ažd=u=zar(i)*}, since final consonants are not expressed in Linear A. Linear A ***a-du-sa-ra*** (HT 62+73.1) probably represents the *essive* form in ***-a***, analysis {*ažd=u=zar(i)=a*}, so that the ***-r-*** is expressed in this form. See also the assimilated form ^{f}***Azzuzari*** (wr. ^{f}*Az-zu-*IZ*-za-ri*) Admattum^{KI}, spouse of *Kulmiš* (dam ^{D}*Ku-ul-mi-iš*), then female weaver at Mari, typology 3.1, lexicon *azzuzari*, 'Frauen(?)', cf. Th. Richter, *VHN*, 84, 382-383. See also the forms ^{f}***Attuzar*** (wr. ^{f}*At-tu-za-ar*), name of 6 women at Mari and ^{f}***Attuzari*** (wr. ^{f}*At-tu-za-ri*), Admattum^{KI}, female weaver at Mari, typology 3.1, lexicon *attuzari*, 'Frauen', cf. Th. Richter, *VHN*, 93, 382-383.

I have already discussed the possibility that the orthography of ^{f}***Aštua-šar*** (wr. ^{f}*Aš-du-a-šar*) at Nuzi < * ^{f}***Aštu-a(n)šar*** < *^{f}***Aštu-enšari*** and the orthography of ^{f}***Azzu-zari*** (wr. ^{f}*Az-zu-*IZ*-za-ri*) = ^{f}***Azzu-izzari*** < *^{f}***Azzu-e/inzari*** at Mari would provide another attractive translation 'The woman is a deity/divinity', because ***en=zari*** 'deity/divinity' (< ***eni+šari***) is itself an abstract of ***eni*** 'god', cf. I. Wegner, *Einführung*, 57, s.v. ***-šari***. Since ***-n-*** before ***-s-*** is not expressed in Linear A and B consonant clusters ***a-du-sa-ra*** can be interpreted as {*ažd=u=(e)nzar(i)=a*}, translation 'The woman is *like* (essive) a deity/divinity'.

The sequence ***ta***$_2$***-ta-re*** 1 (PK 1a.2) from Palaikastro is followed by ***ta***$_2$***-ti-te*** 1 (PK 1a.3). Linear A and B ***ta***$_2$ are graphically and phonetically equivalent: ***tia/tya***. The scribe has deliberately combined the personal names ***ta***$_2$***-ta-re*** 1 (PK 1a.2) and ***ta***$_2$***-ti-te*** 1 (PK 1a.3).

Tiam- occurs as first element in Hurrian personal names at Nuzi ***Tiam-pira*** (wr. *Ti-a-am-be-ra, Ti-am-be-ra, Te-em-bi-ra, Te-em-bi-ru*), cf. P.M. Purves, *NPN*, 266, s.v. ***ti*** and ***tiam-***, cf. also Clay, *PNCP*, 138: *Ti-ia-(am)-ma-ḫar-be.*

Since ***-m*** of ***Tiam-*** is not expressed in Linear A and B before an occlusive in consonant clusters, sign ***ta***$_2$ suffices to express ***tiam-*** preceding ***-ta-re*** and ***-ti-te*** as second elements.

It has been observed that many Hurrian verbal roots are followed by a root-extension. So it is now possible to split ***tiam-*** into the verbal root ***te-/ti-*** 'to speak, say' followed by the root-extension ***-am-***, that allegedly has a *factitive* value, cf. I. Wegner, *Einführung*, 88.

Th. Richter (*BGH*, 453-454; *VHN*, 534-535) proposes to connect the verbal root ***ti-/te-*** with ***ti-/tiw-*** 'to speak'. The combination {*ti=am-*} could then be translated as 'to make / let speak'. Compare also Urartian ***ti-*** 'to speak' and ***tini*** 'name' (cf. M. Salvini - I. Wegner, *Einführung in die urartäische Sprache*, Wiesbaden 2014, 114: s.v. ***ti-*** 'sprechen', and s.v. ***tini*** 'Name'. However, next to ***tiam-*** {*ti=am-*} as first element, ***ti=a-*** is also attested, e.g. in the theonym ***Tija-penti*** 'She says the right things / She speaks the truth', cf. Th. Richter, *VHN*, 585, n. 957. He prefers this interpretation to 'Celui/celle qui parle justement / qui dit le juste / le vrai' (Trémouille, 2014), because ***pendi*** (→ ***p/wand***) can be interpreted neither as an adverb nor is there a basis for a relative rendering.

If the first element in Hurrian personal names is verbal, the second is usually nominal. Consequently the second onomastic elements ***-ta-re*** in ***ta***$_2$***-ta-re*** (PK 1.2) and ***-ti-te*** in ***ta***$_2$***-ti-te*** (PK 1.3) are probably nominal. Since Linear A and B sign ***re*** can also be ***le***, the element ***-ta-re*** in ***ta***$_2$***-ta-re*** 1 (PK 1.2) may be compared with the Hurrian onomastic element ***-tali/e*** at Nuzi, occurring as second element of anthroponyms, e.g. ***Kip-tali*** (wr. *Kip-ta-li*), cf. *NPN*, 262.

According to Th. Richter (*BGH*, 431-432) the onomastic element ***tali*** can be identical with the word for 'Holz, Baum' ['wood, tree'], (GIŠ.)***tali*** I [Boğ.; Ug.], or an 'Opferterminus: Heilsbegriff' ['technical term used for sacrifice, good fortune'] ***tali*** II [Boğ.], or a word in an incantation text ***tali*** III [Emar].

Th. Richter (*VHN*, 527) mentions, s.v. ***tali***, that the onomastic element ***tali*** may well have the meaning 'Holz, Baum' ['wood, tree'] or be a sacrificial term (see *BGH*, 431). He mentions (*VHN*, 59, 527) the personal name ***Ani*[*š*(?)]*-tali*** (wr. *a-ni-*[…]*-ta-li*) from Mari, analysis {*an=i*[*=ž*]*-tali*}, typology 1.3.2.2, lexicon *an-*, *tali*, translation 'Der Baum(?) möge erfreuen' ['The tree may delight, make happy'].

If Linear A ***ta$_2$-ta-re*** is to be interpreted as the Hurrian personal name ***Ti=am-tale***, the meaning may be (*imperative*) 'Make / Let (the child) speak, oh wood, tree !'. If Linear A ***ta$_2$-ta-re*** is to be interpreted as the personal name ***Ti(j)=a-tale***, the meaning may be (*indicative*) 'The tree / wood speaks, says words' or perhaps 'He/She (the child) speaks / says words, oh wood, tree !'.

The other possibility is comparison with the Hurrian onomastic element ***-tari/e***. According to Th. Richter (*VHN*, 298-299, 530-531) the Hurrian root ***tar-*** was already isolated by A. Gustavs, Subaräische Namen in einer ägyptischen Liste syrischer Sklaven und ein subaräischer(?) Hyksos-Name, *Zeitschrift für Ägyptische Sprache 67*, Berlin 1929, 56. It might be the same root as in ***tari*** 'fire' (cf. Th. Richter, *BGH*, 444f., s.v. ***tari*** I [Boğ.;PN] 'Feuer') that could as transitive verbal root mean 'to burn, to set on fire (someone / something)', or as intransitive root 'to burn' (not preferred). The name of a female weaver from Ašnakkum (Tall Šaġir Bāzār / 'Chagar Bazar'), ***^{f}Tarim-Šimika*** (wr. *ta-ri-im-ši-mi-ga*), analysis {*tar=i=m(:b)-Šimika*}, typology 1.1.1.2.2, lexicon *tar-* and *Šimiga*, could in that case be meaningful, since *Simeki / Simegi* is the Hurrian name of the Sun-god, which appears at Nuzi as the theonym *^{d}Ši-me-ki, ^{d}Ši-mi-gi-(ni)*, but also as a personal name, written *Ši-mi-qa*, *Ši-mi-ga*. See also the Linear A sequence ***si+me-ki*** (HT 24b.1) that reflects either the theonym or a personal name based on it. Th. Richter, (*BGH*, 444) mentions that Hurrian ***tari*** corresponds with the Sumerogram IZI, Akkadian *isātu*, Hittite *paḫḫuenant-* and *paḫḫur* (ntr.) and Luwian *pāḫūr*.

A verbal root ***tar-*** 'to come together, to meet, to set out for' (cf. I. Wegner (*Einführung*, 48, 175, 178, 284) s.v. ***tar-*** 'zusammen kommen(?), sich begeben(?)') can be excluded as second element in Linear A ***ta$_2$-ta-re***, since the first element ***Ti(j)=a-*** or ***Ti=am-*** is already verbal. The same applies to the verbal root ***tal-***, established since publication of the Hurrian-Hittite bilingual ***Kirenze*** (KBo 32). The rendering of the verbal root ***tal-*** is based on the Hittite parallel ***parā šallan(n)āi-*** 'to snatch away', cf. Th. Richter, *VHN*, 295, 527.

Th. Richter mentions (*BGH*, 445), s.v. ***tari*** II [Boğ.], that V. Haas - H.J. Thiel (Die Beschwörungsrituale der Allaiturahḫi und verwandte Texte, *Hurritologische Studien 2*, Alter Orient und Altes Testament 31, Kevelaer / Neukirchen-Vluyn 1978, 24[58]) observe in *ta-ri pa-ḫi-ib-wu$_ú$-e* (KBo 27.134), because of Urartian *tar=ae=u/oḫe* 'powerful, superior', a word for 'power' as meaning for ***tari*** I. If Linear A ***ta$_2$-ta-re*** is to be interpreted as the Hurrian personal name ***Ti=am-tare***, the meaning may be (*imperative*) 'Make / Let (the child) speak, oh fire / power !'. If Linear A ***ta$_2$-ta-re*** is to be interpreted as the personal name ***Ti(j)=a-tare***, the meaning may be (*indicative*) 'The fire / power speaks' or perhaps 'He/She (the child) speaks / says words, oh fire / power !'.

Linear A ***ta₂-ti-te*** (PK 1a.3) can be interpreted as Hurrian ***Ti=am-titte*** or ***Ti(j)=a-ttitte***. It is doubtful whether ***-ti-te*** in Linear A ***ta₂-ti-te*** can be compared with ***-titi*** in personal names at Nuzi, e.g. *Ar-ti-i-di, Ar-di-i-di, Ar-di-ti* (cf. P.M. Purves, *NPN*, 268, s.v. ***titi*** and ***-titi***), because the Linear A orthography requires voiceless dentals, whereas single writing of the cuneiform examples suggests that we are dealing with voiced dentals. At the same time we know that the distinction between voiced and voiceless occlusives was probably positional rather than phonemic in Hurrian, so that we are often dealing with allophones.

Th. Richter (*BGH*, 464) mentions the verbal root ***tid-*** I [Boğ.] 'zählen' ['to count'], on the basis of comparison of Hurrian ***tidibade*** [Boğ.] (wr. *ti-i-ti-wa$_a$-a-te*) in the Hurrian-Hittite bilingual ***kirenze*** (KBo 32.13 I 18) 'das Zählen, das Gezählte' ['count(ing)'] with Hittite ***kappuwar*** (cf. I. Wegner, 1995b, 102; De Martino 1999b, 341). Cf. Th. van den Hout, *The elements of Hittite*, Cambridge 2013[3], 192, s.v. ***kappuwa(e)*** 'to count, take care of' and ***kappuwauwar*** (neuter) 'count(ing)'. Th. Richter (*BGH*, 464-465) mentions the root ***tid-*** II [Boğ.; Mitt.], ***titt-*** [Boğ.] and possibly ***te-t^o*** 'angreifen' ['to attack'], cf. also ***tid=ugar=umma*** *epēšu* [Nuzi] 'to have a fight, to fight (with) each other'. The advantage of this root is that the variant ***titt-*** with voiceless ***-tt-*** is attested. However, a second verbal form ***titt-*** after verbal ***Ti=am-*** or ***Ti(j)=a-*** within the same personal name is certainly excluded. Since ***-titte*** must be nominal, I may propose that it is a noun, possibly 'attacker' or 'fighter', derived from the verbal root. However, this meaning has to be verified.

Phonologically comparison with names such as ***Tette***, name of a ruler of Nuḫašše, ***Tetti, Titte*** and ***Tettiịa*** (wr. *Te-et-ti-ia*) at Nuzi (cf. P.M. Purves, *NPN*, 266, s.v. ***tett*** and ***Tettiịa***) would be satisfactory, though the element *Te-et-ti-* in the probably hypocoristic *Te-et-ti-ia* is the first and not the second element of the name and is probably verbal.

If Linear A ***ta₂-ti-te*** is interpreted as the Hurrian personal name ***Ti=am-titte***, the meaning may be (*imperative*) 'Make / Let (the child) speak, oh attacker / fighter !'. If Linear A ***ta₂-ti-te*** is explained as the personal name ***Ti(j)=a-ttitte***, the meaning may be (*indicative*) 'The attacker / fighter speaks' or perhaps 'He/She (the child) speaks / says words, oh attacker / fighter !'. In the analysis of ***Ti(j)=a-ttitte*** I use double writing of the intervocalic voiceless dentals because of the orthography ***ta₂-ti-te*** in Linear A.

Within Linear A we may compare the personal names ***ti-ti-ku*** (HT 35.1; ZA Zb 3.2) from Hagia Triada and Epano Zakro and ***ti-ti-ku-ni*** (HT 96a.1) from Hagia Triada. These personal names have been discussed before: ***ti-ti-ku*** can be analysed as *{titt=i=kk-u/o=n}*, shortened form of ***ti-ti-ku-ni***, that can be analysed as *{titt=i=kk=u=nni}*, based on the root ***tid- / titt-*** and the nominal suffixes ***-kk=u/o=nni*** in *nomina actoris* (cf. I. Wegner, *Einführung*, 55-56), translation 'Attacker'.

If the next sequence ***o-ka-mi-za*** (PK 1a.3) is complete, it is probably a personal name consisting of two Hurrian onomastic elements. The last sign ***-za*** is written so close to the edge that only vague traces of possibly two units are just visible. Linear A ***o-ka-*** may represent the Hurrian element ***Urḫa-*** as in ***Urḫa-tarmi*** (wr. *Ur-ḫa-tar-mi* and *Ur-ḫa-tar-me*), ***Urḫa-tati*** (wr. *Ur-ḫa-ta-ti*) at Nuzi. According to Linear A and B orthographic conventions the ***-r-*** is not expressed before an occlusive in consonant clusters. At Nuzi names with ***Urḫi-*** occur: ***Urḫi-kušuḫ, Urḫi-simiịa*** ?, ***Urḫi-šarri, Urḫi-te, Urḫi-tešup, Urḫi-tilla, Urḫi-tirwi*** and hypocoristic ***Urḫiịa***, cf. Purves, *NPN*, 273, s.v. ***urḫ, urḫa-, urḫi***.

There is also a list of names with ***-urḫe*** as second element in Hurrian names. Among these personal names ***Urḫi-tešup*** is the most famous, since it was at Ḫattuša the Hurrian name of birth of the Hittite king *Muršiliš III*, son of the famous *Muwatalli*, who fought the battle of Qadeš with the Egyptian king *Rameses II*. ***Urḫi-tešup*** who took the name of his glorious grandfather *Muršiliš* as his throne-name, was himself after seven years of reign dethroned by his uncle, the great general *Ḫattušiliš III*, who exerted a *damnatio memoriae* on his nephew and kept an intensive correspondence with Rameses II, even about the legitimacy of his own reign. E. Laroche, *NH*, 198-199, N° 1443: ***Urḫi-tešup***, attestations at Boğazköy, Ugarit (RS 17.346, 7, 10 = PRU IV 176) and in hieroglyphic: *Ur-ḫí-Tešub*^{ba}.

E. Laroche (*NH*, 360-361) writes: "Les rois hittites de l'Empire portent un nom de naissance hourrite et un nom de trône anatolien. Les deux noms peuvent être réunis sur le même document hiéroglyphique. Le nom de trône est choisi parmi ceux de rois antérieurs, considérés comme patrons ou éponymes du nouveau souverain. Ainsi Mursili II se réfère à l'ancien Mursili Ier; Mursili III, alias *Urḫi-Tešub*, prend le nom de son grand-père et obéit à la coutume de la papponymie oriëntale. [...] Mais elle cadre avec la situation politique, avec les noms des reines, uniformément hourrites, avec la présence hourrite dans la capitale hittite à partir de Suppiluliuma Ier, avec la prééminence de Tešub, de Ḫebat et de Šarruma dans le panthéon impérial; presque tous les noms royaux et princiers de la dynastie sont des théophores de ces trois divinités. Il est permis d'interpréter ces faits comme le résultat d'un effort conscient, chez les rois du XIVe et XIIIe siècles, pour affirmer la continuité dynastique de Hattuša et la légitimité de leur pouvoir. Ils dévoilent précisément la vérité historique, c'est-à-dire l'origine semi-étrangère, au moins provinciale (Kizzuwatna), des prédécesseurs de Suppiluliuma Ier."

According to E.A. Speiser (132, § 175) the name ***Urḫalenni*** (wr. *Ur-ḫa-le-en-ni*) at Nuzi contains the ***-l-*** "suffix or root-complement" indicating a superlative, 'Very true, truthful, trustworthy (is) the god': "In this connection, some significance may attach also to the fact that *-l-* rather than *-n-* is found in sentence names with *-en(n)i* 'god' [177]. In cases like *Urḫa-l-enni* SMN 652 or *Kiba-l-enni* N 79.2, RA 23 18.2 the superlatives 'most true' and 'most firm' are more suitable than comparatives when referring to a deity." Perhaps ***-l-*** is simply the shortened form of personal pronoun ***-lla***. It is now possible to analyse ***Urḫalenni*** differently, since the root ***urḫ-*** cannot only be nominal, but also verbal and ***-al-*** can be explained as a verbal root-extension, of which the meaning is not yet clear, cf. I. Wegner (*Einführung*, 87): e.g. ***ḫeš=al-*** 'nackt sein' ['to be naked'], ***zamm=al=ašt-*** 'abreißen' ['to tear off, to break off'], ***kab=al*** '(Feld) plündern' ['to plunder (the field)'].

L. Messerschmidt, *Mitanni-Studien* (Mitteilungen der Vorderasiatischen Gesellschaft 4.4, Berlin 1899, 82) translated the root ***urḫ*** in the Tušratta letter as 'authentisch, zuverlässig' ['authentic, trustworthy'] and F. Bork, *Die Mitannisprache* (*Mitteilungen der Vorderasiatischen Gesellschaft 14.1-2*, Berlin 1909, 115, 125) translated 'wahr' ['true'] and later also 'glaubhaft' ['truthful'], cf. P.M. Purves, *NPN*, 273, s.v. ***urḫ***.

E. Laroche (*GLH*, 285) also mentions, s.v. ***urḫi*** 'vrai, fidèle', the equation in RS Voc. II 21: Sumerian GI.NA = Hurrian ***ur-uḫ-zi***, corrupt, read ***ur-uḫ-ḫi*** or ***ur-uḫ-ḫu*** instead. He mentions *u-ur-ḫa* at Boğazköy in KUB XXXII 19 I 4, 28-29, 34, etc.

According to Th. Richter (*BGH*, 497) ***urḫ-*** [Mitt.; PN] can be nominal '(ge)recht' ['true, faithful'] and verbal 'richtig, wahr, treu, zuverlässig sein' ['to be true, faithful].

Etymology: See Diakonoff / Starostin, 1986, 19. There may be a correlation with Urartian ***ulḫ-*** according to M. Salvini, 1976, 30-31. Th. Richter (*BGH*, 498) mentions s.v. ***urḫa*** [Mitt.] 'according to the right', i.e. ***urḫ=â*** (Diakonoff / Starostin, 1986, 80); 'gemäß dem Rechten / wie es richtig ist' ['in accordance with rightiousness / as is right'] (Wegner, 1990, 302); 'wahrheitsgemäß' ['truthful'], i.e. ***urḫ(i)=a*** (Wegner, 1992, 233).

Identification of Linear A ***o-ka-*** with Hurrian ***urḫ=a-*** may give rise to an orthographic discrepancy between my interpretation of Linear A ***u-qe-ti*** (PL Zf 1) as Hurrian ***urḫe-ti*** (expression in context: 'Tešub is faithful' or 'treat (the deceased) faithfully, oh Tešub !') or ***urḫe-tti*** 'treat me (the deceased) faithfully, oh God !' and that of ***o-ka-mi-za*** (PK 1.3-4) as ***Urḫa-miša***. Although this may seem contradictory, we must keep in mind that the Hurrian phonemes [***u***] and [***o***] were close and written as ***u***-sounds (***ú*** and ***u***, respectively) in the cuneiform syllabary, rather consistently in the Tušratta letter, but less consistently elsewhere. See for the use of the vowels [***u***] and [***o***] in Hurrian the chapter on *phonology*. The Linear A ***k-*** signs were the more general signs, since they could represent ***κ-***, ***γ-***, ***χ-*** in Linear B and comparable sounds in Linear A, the voiceless velar fricatives ***ḫ-*** and ***-ḫḫ-*** included. The ***q-*** signs (representing the Linear B labio-velar sounds) were the more specialized signs in Linear A, representing the Hurrian voiced velar spirants or fricatives [***ġ***]. There may actually have existed some orthographic overlap, disregarding the clear distinctions we wish or hope to observe. Especially in consonant clusters one often cannot be sure whether a consonant is voiced or voiceless or to what degree a sound is influenced by an adjacent sound. The scribes may have faced the same problems. Actually I am surprised how much consistency Linear A orthography shows all over Crete.

If identification of Linear A ***o-ka-*** with Hurrian ***urḫ=a-*** is not accepted because of an alleged voiced velar fricative in {*urġ=a-*}, another option is possible. Th. Richter (*BGH*, 482-483; *VHN*, 548) mentions the verbal root ***ug-*** {*o/ug-*} and ***ukk-*** {*o/ukk-*} 'fürchten' ['to fear, to be afraid (of)'] (I. Wegner, *Einführung*, 289), 'to respect' (Campbell, 2007a, 109) that can be inferred from ***ugul-*** {*ug=ul-*} 'craindre' (E. Laroche, *GLH*, 278), 'sich verneigen, niederknien' ['to kneel (down)'] (V. Haas, 1993a, 262f.; E. Neu, 1996a, 355f.). There may also be a relation with the theonym ***Ugur*** {*O/Ugo/ur*} that is also used as theophorous element in personal names, cf. Th. Richter, *BGH*, 483; *VHN*, 549. Cf. for the aspect of kneeling for a God or high authority the tradition of the *proskunesis* still in use at the court of the Great King of the Persian empire many centuries later.

Th. Richter (*VHN*, 323-325, 548) mentions the following personal names with the root ***ug-*** {*o/ug-*} and ***ukk-*** {*o/ukk-*}: (1a) {*o/ug-*}: ***ᶠUki*** (wr. *Ú-gi*) at Qaṭṭarā, explained as *imperative* {*o/ug=i-*}, typology 1.3.1.2.1, 'Fear !' (cf. ***Ú-ge(-e)*** at Nuzi, *NPN*, 162, *AAN I*, 154; and ***Ú-ki*** and ***Ú-ku*** at Kaniš); ***ᶠUkija*** (wr. *Ú-gi-ia*) at Mari, {*o/ug=i=ja*}, typology 1.1.1.2.4 (cf. *Ú-ki-ia* and *Ú-ku$_{(5)}$(ú)ia* at Nuzi, *NPN*, 162, *AAN I*, 154-155); ***Ukun*** (wr. *Ú-gu-un, Ú-ku-un*), boy (***tur***) at Mari, *ḫabiru* at Tigunāni, {*o/ug=o=n(na)*}, typology 1.3.1.1.2.1. (1b) {*o/ukk-*}: ***Ukkannu*** (wr. *Uk-ka-nu*) at Mari and Qaṭṭarā, analysis {*o/ukk=a=nno/u*}, typology 1.1.1.3.3.1; ***Ukku*** (wr. *Uk-ku*) at Šubat-Enlil, analysis {*o/ukk=o*}, typology 1.3.1.1.1; ***Ukkunni*** (wr. *Uk-ku-un-ni*) at Šubat-Enlil, analysis {*o/ukk=o=nni*}, typology 1.3.1.1.2.2; ***Ukkunnu*** (wr. *Úk-ku-un-nu*) at Qaṭṭarā, analysis {*o/ukk=o=nno/u*}, typology 1.3.1.1.2.2; ***Ukkun-enni*** (wr. *Uk-ku-un-e-en-ni*) at Mari, analysis {*o/ukk=o=n(na)-en(i)=ni*}, typology 1.3.1.1.2.1; lexicon *ukk-, eni*.

(2) {*o/ugizzi*}: ***Ugizzan*** (wr. *Ú-ki-za-an*) at Šušarrā, analysis {*o/ugizz(i)=a*[E.]=*n(na)*}, typology 3.2.1. (3) {*o/ukko/urandi*}: ***fUkkuranti*** (wr. *fUk-ku-ra-an-di*) at Mari, typology 3.1, lexicon *ukkurandi* (→ *ukk-*). (4) {*o/ugo/uzzi*}: ***Ukuzzi*** (wr. *Ú-gu-*IZ-*zi*) at Mari, typology 3.1, lexicon *uguzzi* (→ *ug-*). The name ***Ukkannu*** (wr. *Uk-ka-nu*) at Mari and Qaṭṭarā, {*o/ukk=a=nno/u*} shows that ***o/ukk-*** was also used in intransitive constructions {*o/ukk=a-*}, which may well correspond with ***o-ka-*** in Linear A ***o-ka-mi-za*** (PK 1a.3).

The onomastic element ***-mi-za*** in Linear A ***o-ka-mi-za*** (PK 1a.3) may be equated with Hurrian ***-miša*** in *Qar-mi-šá*, (cf. also *Qar-mi-še, Qar-me-še* and *Ka-ar-mi-še*) at Nuzi, cf. P.M. Purves, *NPN*, 223, s.v. ***kar***. P.M. Purves was not yet entirely convinced that ***Karmišá*** should be divided into ***kar-*** and ***-mišá***, and cautiously also mentioned the possibility of a 'one-word' name ***Karmišá***, but Th. Richter (*VHN*, 458) mentions, s.v. ***miš-*** {*miž-*}, that there is no doubt about the 'Hurricity' of the personal names with the root ***miš-***. To illustrate this he points to some Hurrian personal names from Alalaḫ IV: ***fMi-ša-ú*** (D.J. Wiseman, *AT*, 298: 40), ***Mi-ši-ni*** (*AT*, 216: 14), ***Mi-šu-ri*** {*miž=o=ri*} (*AT*, 132: 2; 214: 9; A. Draffkorn, *HHA*, 1959, 137) and ***mi-e***[***š-…***] at Ḫattuša (*ChS I/1*, 41 Vs. II 36).

He mentions (*VHN*, 198, 458) the personal name ***Mišaia*** (wr. *Mi-ša-ia*) at Mari, analysis {*miž=a=ja*}, with the root ***miš-*** {*miž-*}, typology 1.1.1.3.4. And the following names with ***o-miš*** {*miž=e/i*}: ***Nakat-miš*** (wr. *Na-ga-at-mi-iš*), King of Tigunāni^KI, attested at Mari, analysis {*nag=ad-miž(i)*}, typology 1.4, lexicon *nag-*, *miši* (*VHN*, 202, 458); ***Šina-miš*** (wr. *Ši-na-mi-iš*) at Mari, analysis {*šin=a=Ø-miž(i)*}, typology 1.1.1.3.3, lexicon *šin-*, *miši* (*VHN*, 269, 458); ***Tudu-miš*** (wr. *Tu-du-mi-iš*) at Tigunāni, analysis {*to/ud=o-miž*}, typology 1.3.1.1.1, lexicon *tud-*, *miši*, *VHN*, 323, 458.

He also explicitly mentions that we are, with regard to ***o-miš***, probably dealing with the element ***miše*** or ***miši*** {*miž=e/i*}, already isolated from *qar/kar/ka-ar-me/mi-še/šá* at Nuzi (cf. P.M. Purves, *NPN*, 235). Consequently an alternative interpretation of Linear A ***o-ka-mi-za*** as Hurrian †***un-karmišá*** [comparable with Linear A ***o-te-ja*** (PK 4bis) = Hurrian ***Unteja*** 'ComeTešub !'] is no longer needed.

If analysis of ***o-ka-mi-za*** as {*o/ukk=a-miša*} is correct and if we may assume that the first element ***o/ukk=a-*** is verbal, the second element ***-miša*** must be nominal.

Unfortunately the meaning of the Hurrian root ***miš-*** and of the onomastic elements ***miš-o*** and ***o-miš(a/e/i)*** is not yet known. No doubt the Minoan scribe knew, whether he had ***Urḫa-miša*** or ***Uga-miša*** {*o/ug=a-miša*} or ***Ukka-miša*** {*o/ukk=a-miša*} in mind, when he wrote ***o-ka-mi-za*** (PK 1a.3).

Linear A ***i-na*** 1 (PK 1a.4) at Palaikastro is most likely a personal name. In the 2016 edition of *Minoan Linear A*, Vol. II, *Corpus of transliterated Linear A texts*, I read (with J. Raison - M. Pope 1994) a word divider after ***i-na***, but now I think (with *GORILA 1*), that the little vertical stroke may well be the sign of 1 unit, which makes it even more likely that ***i-na*** belongs to the list of personal names on this tablet.

Anyway, comparison with the Hurrian temporal conjunction ***inna*** [Boğ.; Mitt.] 'wenn', 'au moment où, quand', 'quando', ['when'] can be rejected in view of the position of the sequence. Also adverbial 'now' has been suggested as a meaning for ***inna*** (G. Steiner, 1979a, 197), but a term like 'now' does not add valuable information and the scribe usually uses his space on the tablet as economically as possible.

The Akkadogram *INA* that may be attested in cuneiform Hurrian context (e.g. KBo 19.149 = ChS I/8, Nr. 214: 9') seems very unlikely as well, cf. Th. Richter, *BGH*, 86.

I had suggested that the option that sign ***si***, written in the middle of the right edge (side c) of this extraordinary tablet, might be added to the sequence ***i-na***, so that ****i-na-si*** 'of the gods' can be read < *{*e/in(i)=na=aš=(w)i*}. But I already had my doubts, because an expression ****i-na-si*** 'of the gods' does not make sense in the middle of a list of personal names. Now I think that the sign can better be added to the front of ***ra-na-tu-su*** (PK 1a.5), so that ***si-|ra-na-tu-su*** can be read. *GORILA 1* reads the sign ***si*** (on the edge) before ***i-na*** and proposes one long sequence ***o-ka-mi-za|-si-|i̯-na*** (PK 1a.3-4), but I consider that unlikely, because consecutive ***-si-i-*** does not make sense in the script of Linear A.

If the reading ***i-na*** 1 is correct and if the sequence is not part of the preceding sequence (line 3), ***i-na*** could theoretically be identified with the Hurrian plural form ***e/in-na*** < {*e/in(i)=na*} 'the gods', cf. P.M. Purves, *NPN*, 209-210, s.v. ***en*** and 220, s.v. ***in***. The suffix ***-na*** is the Hurrian suffix of the so-called plural definite article. However, mentioning 'the gods' in the middle of a list of personal names seems a bit odd.

It must be admitted though that this scribe has been a bit inaccurate, for it seems that he had forgotten to write ***i-na*** 1 and decided to scribble it a bit higher to the left of ***o-te-ja*** 1 (PK 1a.4bis). A personal name followed by 1 unit is the most likely option anyway. Moreover, orthography of ***in-*** instead of ***en-*** occurs mainly in personal names.

Could Linear A ***i-na*** as such be a personal name ? At Nuzi the singular form ***Inni*** (wr. *In-ni, I-in-ni*) 'The god' is attested as the name of three persons. A personal name in the *essive* case in ***-a*** {*e/in(i)=a*} 'As a god' is conceivable and names in the *essive* case are attested quite frequently (see Th. Richter, *VHN*, *passim*).

Hypocoristic names such as ***Inii̯a*** (wr. *I-ni-ia*), name of 3 persons at Nuzi, and ***Innii̯a*** (wr. *In-ni-ia, I-in-ni-ia*), name of 3 persons at Nuzi, are more common (cf. I.J. Gelb, *NPN*, 70) as well as ***Ennai̯a*** (wr. *En-na-a-a, E-en-na-a-a, E-na-a-a, E-en-na-a, E-en-na-ia*), name of 17 persons at Nuzi, cf. I.J. Gelb, *NPN*, 44. ***E/Innai̯a*** might have been a hypocoristic for sentence names like ***Enna-madi*** (with variants such as *En-na-ma-ti, I-en-na-ma-te, In-na-ma-di-il*), the name of 85 persons at Nuzi, ***Enna-milki***, ***Enna-mu***, ***Enna-muša***, ***Enna-pali***, etc., cf. P.M. Purves, *NPN*, 210.

Th. Richter (*VHN*, 104) mentions ***Innaja*** (wr. *in-na-a-ia*), analysis {*inn=a=ja*}, typology 1.1.1.3.4, lexicon *inn-*, at Šubat-Enlil (Tall Leilān); ^{f}***Innija*** (wr. *i-ni-ia*), analysis {*in=i=ja*}, typology 1.1.1.2.4, lexicon *in-* II, at Ašnakkum; ***Enija*** (wr. *e-ni-ia*), analysis {*en=i=ja*}, typology 1.1.1.2.4, lexicon *en-* I, at Mari. Compare Linear A ***pa-qa*** (PK Za 11.d), if these sequences do not have to be corrected to ***i-di-ja pa-qa***; perhaps also PK Za 12.d) from Mount Petsophas near Palaikastro.

We may conclude that the scribe wrote either deliberately ***i-na*** or, if he had wished to write Linear A ***i-na-a*** or ***i-na-ja*** (Hurrian ***Innaja***), he realized too late that there was virtually no space in line 4 after ***i-na*** to write another sign ***-a*** or ***-ja***, unless he was willing to make an effort to draw very small signs between line 3 and 4. All these considerations are the result of the fact that we tend to think that ***ini*** is always basically a noun equivalent to the very important notion ***eni*** 'god', but some personal names clearly show verbal roots in ^{o}***=i=b-*** (see Th. Richter, *VHN*, 574: typology 1.1.1.2.1). Such names are ***Inip-atal*** (wr. *i-ni-ba-tal*), analysis {*in=i=b-adal*}, typology 1.1.1.2.1, lexicon *in-* II, *adal*.

He also mentions ^{f}***Inip-Naje*** (wr. ^{f}*i-ni-ip-na-ie*), analysis {*in=i=b-Naje*}, typology 1.1.1.2.1, lexicon *in-* II, *Naje*, both from Qaṭṭara. The meaning of the verbal root ***in-*** II is unfortunately not yet clear, but it is important to realize that ***ina*** {*in=a*} could be a 'one-word' personal, either the *intransitive indicative* 3rd person singular or the *intransitive imperative* of verbal ***in-***. The *imperative* can be used as name as many examples in Th. Richter's *corpus* (*VHN*) show. This may well be the most likely solution.

Since in Linear A and B ***-n-*** is not expressed before an occlusive in consonant clusters, Linear A ***o-te-ja*** (PK 1a.4bis) can according to Linear A and B orthographic conventions be identified as the Hurrian theophorous personal name ***Un-tei̯a*** (wr. *Un-te-ia*) at Nuzi, son of *Ḫa-ma-an-na*, HSS V 75:20, hypocoristic of ***Un-tešub*** (wr. *Un-te-šup, Un-te-eš-šup, Ú-te-šup*), name of 3 persons at Nuzi. It can now be analysed as the athematic *imperative* {*un=(a)-tei̯a*} (syncope of ***-a-***), translation 'Come Teš(š)ub !'. Old Hurrian ***Unap-tešub*** (wr. *Ú-na-ap-te-šup, Ú-nap-te-šup, Ú-nap-te-šup*), is 10 times attested at Nuzi, cf. I.J. Gelb, *NPN*, 165; P.M. Purves, *NPN*, 264, s.v. ***-tei̯a***; 266, s.v. ***-tešup***. Analysis {*un=a=b-tešub*}, consisting of the root ***un-*** 'to come' + the marker of intransitivity ***-a-*** + the Old Hurrian indicator of the 3rd person singular *indicative* ***-b*** + the name of the Stormgod *Teš(š)ub*, translation 'Teš(š)ub comes / came', cf. I. Wegner, *Einführung*, 34, 42, 125 ff. P.M. Purves (*NPN*, 272) mentions that the root ***un*** in the Tušratta letter was independently established by Speiser and Götze as 'to come', 'to arrive'.

Theoretically and orthographically it is also possible to interpret Linear A ***o-te-ja*** as Hurrian ***Ur-tei̯a***, *imperative* {*ur=(a)-tei̯a*} (with syncope of ***-a-***), 'Be present, Teš(š)ub !' or {*ur=(o)-tei̯a*} (with syncope of ***-o-***) 'Let (the child) be present, oh Teš(š)ub!', cf. Th. Richter, *BGH*, 495-496, s.v. ***ur-*** I [Boğ.; Mitt.; PN]; *VHN*, 554, s.v. ***ur-*** I 'vorhanden sein, stattfinden', 'to be present, to appear, to occur'. ^{f}***Uru-Ḫeba*** (wr. ^{f}*ú-ru-ḫe-ba*) is attested at Mari, analysis {*ur=o-Ḫeba*}, typology 1.3.1.1.1, 'Lasse (Mädchen) vorhanden sein, oh *Ḫeba* !' ['Let (the girl) be present, appear, oh *Ḫeba* !'] and *Ur-ḫeba* occurs at Emar, analysis {*ur-Ḫeba*}. Nevertheless I consider interpretation as ***Un-tei̯a*** more likely, since the combination of the root ***un-*** + ***-tešub*** / ***-tei̯a***, is more frequent and the Hurrian personal name ***Un-tei̯a*** (wr. *Un-te-ia*) is attested at Nuzi.

As mentioned before, I consider it likely that the sign ***si*** (side c) belongs to the next sequence, so that we should read ***si-|ra-na-tu-su*** 1 (PK 1c+1a.5), followed by the rhyming name ***ni-mi-tu-su*** 1 (PK 1a.5-6). The scribe of PK 1 must have been in a poetic mood showing his *ars poetica* with alliteration in ***ta***$_2$***-ta-re*** (PK 1.2) and ***ta***$_2$***-ti-te*** (PK 1a.3) and at the end of the text with alliteration and rhyme in ***ma-ti-za-i-te*** (PK 1a.6), ***ma-da-ti*** (PK 1a.7) and ***ma-ka-i-ta*** (PK 1a.7).

Comparing ***si-|ra-na-tu-su*** and ***ni-mi-tu-su***, we may conclude that Linear A ***-tu-su*** may well be the second onomastic element in both names. A root ***tuš-*** has been isolated at Ḫattuša in the forms ***tuši*** and ***tušikkae*** {*tuže/i=kk(i)=ae*} (Görke, 2010, 117f.), cf. Th. Richter, *BGH*, 479. Th. Richter (*VHN*, 547) mentions s.v. ***tuš-/tuz*** {***to/už-***} the personal names: ^{f}***Tušaja*** (Mari), ^{f}***Tuza-Na*** (Mari), ^{f}***Tuza-Naje*** (Mari), ^{f}***Tuzija*** (Ašnakkum). ^{f}***Tuza-Naje*** and consequently also ^{f}***Tuza-Na*** are because of the second element ***-Naje*** and its hypocoristic form ***-Na*** probably Hurrian.

Unfortunately the meaning of the root is as yet unknown. Since the root ***tuš-*** in these names is probably verbal and the Linear A element ***-tu-su*** is probably nominal, equation seems doubtful anyway, although we have to admit that some Hurrian roots can be verbal and nominal.

There is, however, a plural noun ***turšena*** [PN; Ugarit] 'les poumons' ['the lungs'], corresponding with Sumerian [ḪAR] and Akkadian *ḫa*-SU-*ú* (B. André-Salvini - M. Salvini, 1999b, 434; 1999c, 145; 2000, 326). Y. Cohen (The West Semitic / peripheral Akkadian term for 'lung', *JAOS 122*, 2002, 826) reads the Akkadian form as *ḫa-sull-ú*. The singular form also occurs at Ḫattuša in the phrase *ú-úr-mi dur-še-e* 'Leber, Lunge' ['liver, lung'] in KBo 27.217 = ChS I/6 Nr. 10 Rs. IV 22', cf. Th. Richter, *BGH*, 478.

At Mari the personal name ***Turzan*** (wr. *Tu-ur-za-an*) is attested as the name of 4 persons, analysis {*to/urž(i)=a*[E.]=*n(na)*}, typology 3.2.1, lexicon *turzi*, cf. Th. Richter, *VHN*, 319, 547. The name can be translated as 'He (*=n(na)*) (namely the boy) is like a lung' (with the *essive* in ***-a***). The name may refer to some birthmark in the form of a lung, maybe a strawberry mark or port-wine mark on the skin. At Nuzi the name seems to refer to toponyms: URU *dur/tu-ur-ša-an* (*RGTC 10*, 305f); URU *dur/du-ur-za-an-zi* (*ibid.*, 312); URU BÀD-*za-am-z*[*i*] (see Fincke 1999), cf. Th. Richter, *VHN*, 319.

We have already discussed the Linear A personal name ***si-ri-ne-ti*** (PK 1a.1), the first in the list of personal names on tablet PK 1, that may be interpreted as 'Treat him/her (the child) in a benovolent way, oh Tešub !'. Linear A ***si-|ra-na-tu-su*** (PK 1c+1a.5) may well contain the same verbal root ***šel*** I [Boğ.] and ***šil*** II, 'angenehm sein' ['to be pleasant'] and 'gut' ['good'] and ***šel=ab-***, ***šel=b-*** 'in gutem Sinne (in Gute) betrachten (behandeln)' ['to treat in a good / kind way'], corresponding with Urartian ***silua*** 'wohlwollend gesinnt sein' ['to be kind, benevolent, benign'], cf. Th. Richter, *BGH*, 374.

If ***si-|ra-na-tu-su*** (PK 1c+1a.5) is analysed as {*šil=an(n)=a-turžu*}, consisting of the root ***šil-*** (*intr.*) 'to be pleasant' + the causative root-extension ***-an(n)-*** (cf. I. Wegner, *Einführung*, 88) + the marker of intransitivity ***-a*** + the noun ***turše*** with Akkadianizing *nominative* in ***-u***, the meaning may be 'Let the lung be pleasant/good (oh *numen*) !' The name may refer to the dramatic moment when the child was born and may have been close to suffocation as a result of a complication.

According to P. Chantraine (*DELG*, 1003) the etymology of the Pre-Greek name ***Σῑληνός***, Doric ***Σῑλανός***, is 'inconnue' ['unknown']. The name is certainly Pre-Greek, because an Indo-European initial ***s-*** would have changed to ***h-*** in Greek. ***Σῑληνός / Σῑλανός*** is companion of Dionysos and the nymphs. He also has a relation with the satyrs (*H. Aphr.* 262, trag., etc.). The form occurs often in the plural. The *Silenes* have an ithyphallic and theriomorphic appearance (cf. M.P. Nilsson, *Gr. Rel.* I^2, 232-233). I propose derivation from the Hurrian root ***šil-***, (*trans.*) 'to please someone', (*intr.*) 'to enjoy oneself, to be happy', which is exactly conform their reputation: {*šil=an(n)=i/e*} 'Please (someone) !' .

Incidentally, there is another verbal root ***šer-*** I / ***šir-*** I [Boğ.(?); Mitt.] in Hurrian with virtually the same meaning as ***šel*** I [Boğ.] and ***šil*** II, 'angenehm sein' ['to be pleasant'] and 'gut' ['good'] and ***šel=ab-***, ***šel=b-*** 'in gutem Sinne (in Gute) betrachten (behandeln)' ['to treat in a good / kind way'], cf. Th. Richter, *BGH*, 391-392. So it is quite conceivable that Linear A ***si-|ra-na-tu-su*** (PK 1c+1a.5) contains that root instead of ***šel*** I [Boğ.] / ***šil*** II. The liquid sounds [***r***] and [***l***] may well have been very close in Hurrian.

This may also have been the reason, why Linear A did not have separate series of syllabic signs for these phonemes. It is in fact quite odd that Linear B has inherited this orthographic feature from Linear A, since distinction between [*l*] and [*r*] is phonemically significant in Greek. There is another verbal root ***šir-*** II, mentioned by Th. Richter (*BGH*, 392), 'zählen, erzählen' ['to count, to tell'], but also 'to sing', and ***šir=ad-*** [Boğ.] 'preisen, erzählen, singen, besingen' ['to praise, to tell, to sing (of), to celebrate in song, to chant']. It is in my view attractive to derive the etymology of the Pre-Greek name ***Σειρήν***, plural ***Σ(ε)ιρῆνες***, from this Hurrian root ***šir-*** II, especially with the meaning 'to sing (of), to celebrate in song, to chant', because these (semi-)divine creatures, the *Sirenes* (*half-bird half-woman*), cast a spell on sailors by their enchanting songs and lured them into death. The spelling with ***σει-*** is found in *IG* II^2, 1629, 687, but ***σιρ-*** on the vases, especially in the plural ***Σιρῆνες***. Compare for attempts to find an Indo-European etymology P. Chantraine, *DELG*, 993-994, s.v. ***Σειρήν***: *Etym.*: Obscure.

Interpretation of Linear A ***ni-mi-tu-su*** 1 (PK 1a.5-6) following ***si-|ra-na-tu-su*** 1 (PK 1c+1a.5) in the list of personal names seems even more difficult, because a clear root ***nim-*** seems not attested. Closest seems the root ***niw-*** I [Boğ.], mentioned by Th. Richter (*BGH*, 274) that is interpreted as 'schreiben, markieren, eindrücken, ritzen' ['to write, mark, impress, incise'] by I. Wegner (*Die hurritischen Körperteilbezeichnungen*, ZA 85, 1995, 121[16]), analysed as ***/niv-/***, but not translated by E. Neu (Skizze einer Beschreibung der Wurzelstruktur hurritischer Nomina und Verben. Ein Näherungsversuch, in: *Festschrift Boretzki*, 2001, 95) and analysed as ***/niv/b-/*** by D.R.M. Campbell (*Mood and modality in Hurrian*, dissertation University of Chicago, 2007, 406, 418).

Since a ***b/w*** alternation is quite common in Hurrian and is also assumed by D.R.M. Campbell in the root ***niv-/nib-***, I consider it possible that the occasional ***b/w/m*** alternation, as attested in ***ibri***, ***ewri***, ***erwi*** (also with metathesis at Nuzi) and ***irmi***, ***ermi*** at Nippur (cf. Clay, *PNCP*, 95; P.M. Purves, *NPN*, 211) and in Linear A ***wa-du-ni-mi*** (HT 6b.1; HT 85b.4-5) that can be analysed as {*wad=u=n-irmi*} or {*wand=u=n-irmi*}, consisting of the Hurrian verbal root ***p/wad-*** or ***p/wand-*** + the marker of the transitive perfect form ***-u-*** + the suffix of the enclitic pronoun 3rd person singular ***-n(na)*** marking the object of the transitive verb + the theophorous element ***irmi*** / ***ermi*** (at Nippur and in Linear A) = ***erwi*** (at Nuzi) = ***ewri / ibri*** (elsewhere, Tušratta letter included) 'Lord', indicating the subject of the verb. Linear A ***wa-du-ni-mi*** can be translated as 'The Lord has made him/her (the child) good, just'. Compare also Linear A ***i-mi-sa-ra*** (HT 27+HT 48a.3) from Hagia Triada that contains the theophorous element ***Irmi-*** 'Lord', though now as first onomastic element. It can be interpreted as the Hurrian personal name ****Irmi/Ermi-šarra*** 'The Lord is as the King of Gods', which is in fact almost equivalent to ***Erwi-šarri*** at Nuzi and to ***ibri-šarri***, ***ibri***(EN)***-šarri***(LUGAL), ***ibrḏr / iwrḏr*** at Ugarit; ***ibri-šarri*** [AL 137] at Alalaḫ.

If this ***b/w/m*** alternation is applicable to the root ***niv-/nib-*** and if I. Wegner's rendering as 'to write, mark, impress, incise' is correct, we may analyse Linear A ***ni-mi-tu-su*** (PK 1a.5-6) as {*nim/w/b=i-turš(e)=u*}, translation 'Mark/Incise the lung (oh *numen*) !'. Since ***-n-*** preceding ***-t-*** in consonant clusters is not expressed in Linear A, the analysis can also be {*nim/w/b=i=n(na)-turš(e)=u*}, so that the name can be translated as 'Mark it [***-n(na)***] (the child), oh lung !' It is not easy for us to grasp, to what event such a meaning refers.

Has it something to do with some ritual during a sacrificial event ? If so, the element ***turš(e)=u*** in ***si-̮|ra-na-tu-su*** (PK 1c+1a.5) may perhaps not refer to a birthmark of the child, but to interpretation of 'liver and lungs' of a sacrificial animal and to rites performed before, during or after the child's birth.

The scribe has not accidentally combined ***ma-ti-za-i-te*** (PK 1a.6) and ***ma-da-ti*** (PK 1a.7), because it has become clear in recent research that the roots ***mad-*** and ***matt-*** are cognate, if not identical. In the past it was thought that the root was only represented with single dental and consequently only voiced. For instance, E. Laroche (*GLH,* 163-164, s.v. ***madi***) emphasized that the nominal themes, written *ma-(a)-ti-, ma-(a)-tu-*, *ma-(a)-ta-*, are never written with double writing of the dental, so that the dental is always voiced */d/* ("avec dentale simple, donc sonore"). See also his discussion on Hurrian ***ma-di***.

Linear A ***ma-da-ti*** (PK 1.7) from Palaikastro is probably a Hurrian personal name with clearly Hurrian onomastic elements. The most simple analysis of Linear A ***ma-da-ti*** (PK 1.7) is as an *intransitive* form {*mad=a=tti*}. But although this form is morphologically possible, a translation 'I am wise/clever' sounds arrogant and is semantically a less likely personal name to give to a child according to modern standards. Fortunately other analyses such as {*mad=aš=tti*} or {*mad=ašt=i*} or {*mad=ašt=i=n(na)*} are possible as well.

E. Laroche (*NH*, 117) mentions three Cappadocian names, n° 786: ***Madala*** (wr. *Ma-da-lá ?-a*, IAV 30, 17), n° 787: ***Madawashi*** (wr. *Ma-da-wa-áš-ḫi*, BIN VI 52, 2), n° 788: ***Madawada*** (wr. *Ma-da-wa-da*, EL 82, 4). Cf. also *ibidem* N° 785 [*Madakina*], [Roi de l'Arman: abs. *ᵐMa-da-ki-na*, KBo III 13 I 13 = ZA 44, 68.]. cf. E. Laroche (*NH*, 117, n° 790): ***Matiya***, prêtre de Ḫebat, abs. *ᵐMa-a-ti-ya*, IX 2 I 1. *Ibidem*, n° 789: ***Mati*** (1), prêtre de Kummanni, abs. *ᵐMa-a-ti-(i)*, XXX 42 IV 20; ABoT 28+29 II 18, 24; KBo VII 74, 5, is according to Laroche perhaps the same person as ***Matiya***, the priest of Ḫebat. ***Matii̯a*** (wr. *Ma-ti-ia*), */madiya/*, is the name of 12 persons at Nuzi (cf. I.J. Gelb, *NPN*, 96-97).

Following P.M. Purves (*NPN*, 264, s.v. ***-te***, and 266, s.v. ***-ti***), who regarded ***-ti*** as equivalent to ***-te*** and ***-tei̯a***, shortened or hypocoristic forms of ***-tešub*** as final element in theophorous sentence names, I assumed almost automatically that interpretation of Linear A ***-ti*** as hypocoristic of ***-tešub*** was the only plausible explanation (cf. the 2016 edition of *Minoan Linear A*, Volume I). Purves' analysis was probably based on variants like ***Ḫu-i-ti***, ***Ḫu-i-te***, ***Ḫu-e-te***, ***Ḫu-i-te-e*** and ***Ḫu-i-te-šup***. His analysis is still relevant.

The Linear A form ***ma-da-ti*** would be a feasible variant of *Ma-at-te-šup, Ma-at-te-eš-šup* and *Ma-at-te-e-a, Ma-at-te-ia, Ma-at-te-a* at Nuzi (cf. P.M. Purves, *NPN*, 264-265) and *Ma-at-tešub* at Ugarit (cf. F. Gröndahl, *PNTU*, Rome 1967, 240). Probably *Ma-at-te-šup* < ****Mad-tešup***, as can be inferred from the same personal name, with the onomastic elements ***madi*** and ***tešup*** in reverse order, *Te-šup-ma-ti = /Tešubmadi/*, (wr. *Te-eš-šu-ma-ti*) at Nuzi (cf. Purves, *NPN*, 265), with voiced dental in ***-madi***.

Th. Richter (*BGH*, 248-249, s.v. ***mad-***, *matt-* [*passim*], cf. *VHN*, 456, s.v. ***mad-***) explains ***mad-*** as '(to be) clever, skilfull' (Diakonoff, 1981a, 86[32]); 'Einsicht/Weisheit zuweisen' (Neu, 1988a, 24[70], 1988e, 111f.), 'to be wise, understand', corresponds with Akkadian *malāku* (Dijkstra 1993b, 168), 'être sage, provident' (Catsanicos 1996, 280), 'weise sein, Einsicht/Weisheit zuweisen' (Wegner 2004, 41); ***mad=ašt-*** [Boğ.; Ug.] 'Einsicht / Weisheit zuweisen', corresponds with Hittite ***ḫattatar šišḫ-*** (Neu, 1988a, 24[70], 1988e, 111), 'weise sein' (V. Haas / I. Wegner 1991b, 385[6], I. Wegner, *Einführung*, 267).

At Emar the variant ***matt-*** occurs in personal names (cf. Pruzsinszky 2003, 251).

In recent research it is now thought that the first element of personal names often consists of a verbal form which means that ***mad-*** in ****Mad-tešup*** is probably verbal, whereas ***-madi*** in *Te-šup-ma-ti*, ***/Tešubmadi/***, is nominal as second onomastic element.

Th. Richter (*VHN*, 191-193, 456) mentions the following Hurrian personal names: ***Matija*** (wr. *ma-di-ia*) at Mari, Dilbat, Emar, analysis {*mad=i=ja*}, typology 1.1.1.2.4, lexicon *mad-*, translation 'Er/Sie (scil. ein *Numen*) wies (dem Jungen) Weisheit zu' ['He / She (scil. a *numen*) made (the boy) wise, clever']; ***ᶠMatazza*** (wr. *ma-ta-az-za*) at Mari, {*madazz(e)=a*[E.]}, typology 3.2.1, lexicon *madazze* (→ *mad-*), 'Es (Mädchen) ist als (Zeichen der) Weisheit (geboren)' ['She (the girl) is (born) as (a sign of) wisdom'] [E. refers to the *essive* form in ***-a***.]; ***ᶠMatunna*** (wr. *ma-du-na*) at Mari, {*mad=o=nna*}, typology 1.3.1.1.2.1, lexicon *mad-*, 'Weise ihm (Mädchen) Weisheit zu (oh *Numen*) !' ['Make her (the girl) wise (oh *numen*) !']; ***ᶠMatunni*** (wr. *ma-du-un-na*) at Mari, {*mad=o=nni*}, typology 1.3.1.1.2.2, lexicon *mad-*, 'Weise ihm (Mädchen) Weisheit zu (oh *Numen*) !' ['Make her (the girl) wise (oh *numen*) !']. ***ᶠMatunna*** and ***ᶠMatunni*** are here explained as verbal forms, but might just as the lexical forms ***madi*** and ***madunni*** {*mad=o=nni*} in context be explained as 'wise', cf. *Er-wi-ma-du-ni* at Nuzi 'The Lord is wise' (see *AAN* I 46, cf. Th. Richter, *VHN*, 456); cf. ***ᶠAllae-mata*** (wr. *ᶠal-la-e-ma-da*) at Mari, {*allae-mad(i)=a*[E.]}, typology 2.1, lexicon *allae*, *madi*, 'Die Herrin ist weise' ['The Lady is wise'] or in order to express the *essive* 'She is like a wise Lady', cf. Th. Richter, *VHN*, 49, 456; cf. ***Šan-mata*** (wr. *ša-an-ma-da*), {*šan-mad(i)=a*[E.]} at Mari and Ašnakkum, typology 1.4, lexicon *šan-*, *madi*, cf. Th. Richter, *VHN*, 245, 456.

If we accept that the Linear A personal name ***ma-da-ti*** (PK 1.7) can be analysed as {*mad=ašt=i*}, the form can be interpreted as *imperative* 'Make (the child) wise / bright (oh *numen* !)'. This interpretation is possible, since ***-s-*** before an occlusive is not expressed in consonant clusters according to the orthographic conventions of Linear A and B.

Since final ***-n*** is not expressed in Linear A, an analysis as {*mad=ašt=i=n(na)*} is also possible: 'Make him/her [*n(na)*] (namely the child) wise / bright (oh *numen* !)'.

I. Wegner (*Einführung*, 88) explains that the vowel in the root-extension ***-Všt-*** is adapted to the vowel in the root, e.g. ***tan=ašt-*** 'machen' ['to make'], ***an- / an=ašt-*** 'sich freuen' ['to enjoy'], ***mad=ašt-*** 'weise sein' ['to be wise'], ***teḫ- / teḫ=ešt-*** 'erhöhen, gross werden' ['to elevate, to grow, to become great'], ***šurv=ušt-*** 'Böses tun' ['to do, to cause, to bring about evil']. This root-extension may in some cases have a denominalising character and should not be confused with the intransitive marker of the past tense ***-oš-*** + ***-t-***. However, there are indications that the formants ***-ol-*** and especially ***-Všt-*** in combination with verbal forms in ***=o=m*** may show other grammatical differentiations (aspect or type of action), cf. G. Wilhelm, *Festschrift Heger*, 1992, 670. The 'Old Hurrian' formant ***-Všt-*** seems to express the end or result of an action, e.g. ***pa=ašt=o=m*** 'he has built', attested in the *Tiš-atal*-inscription: *Tiš-atal*, *endan* of Urkeš, has built a temple for Nergal, etc. (see *supra*). I am convinced that Linear A ***pa-i-to*** (HT 97a.3; HT 120.6) is a genuine Hurrian toponym representing Old Hurrian ***ba-'à-áš-to/um***, meaning 'He/She (a God / the King) has built (the palace)' as attested in the Tiš-atal tablet, analysed and normalised as ***pa=ašt=o=m***, cf. also Th. Richter (*BGH*, 285-286), s.v. ***pa-***, *paḫ-* II [*passim*] '(er)bauen' ['to build'], *pa('/h)-*, G. Wilhelm, 1988b, 55.

A development of ***pa('/h)=ašt=o=m > pa(j)=ašt=o=m > pai=št=o=m*** (wr. ***pa-i-to*** in Linear A) seems likely. For Linear B ***pa-i-to*** the Old Hurrian ending in ***=o=m*** had to be changed into a Hellenized form in ***-ος/-os/***: ***Φαιστός*** (Phaistos).

A slightly different analysis of Linear A ***ma-da-ti*** (PK 1.7) must also be discussed, since I. Wegner (*Einführung*, 88) not only mentions the verbal root-extension ***-Všt-***, but also the *intensifying* root-extension ***-aš-***, e.g. ***ḫaš-*** 'hören' ['to hear'] beside ***ḫaš=aš-*** with the same meaning. This means that Linear A ***ma-da-ti*** (PK 1.7) can also be analysed as {*mad=aš=tti*}, consisting of the verbal root ***mad-*** + root-extension ***-aš-*** + the optional allomorphic suffix ***-tti***, that sometimes replaces the suffix indicating the enclitic personal pronoun 1st person singular ***-tta*** as is demonstrated by recent research in Hurrian studies.

Consequently Linear A ***ma-da-ti*** (PK 1.7), analysed as {*mad=aš=tti*} and interpreted as *imperative* 'Make me wise / bright (oh *numen* !)' would provide a plausible name for a newborn child. One may object that a marker of transitivity ***-i-*** or (Old Hurrian) ***-o/u-*** between ***-aš-*** and ***-tti*** is missing and that one might have expected *{*mad=aš=i=tti*} or *{*mad=aš=o/u=tti*}. There are, however, many examples of an *athematic* imperative in personal names, as we have just observed in the Hurrian personal name ***Un-Teḭa*** at Nuzi and its equivalent ***o-te-ja*** (PK 1a.4bis) in Linear A. Cf. for Hurrian ***-tti*** Linear A ***ka-nu-ti*** (HT 97a.3), ***i-du-ti*** (HT 104.2-3) and ***ta-na-ti*** (HT 7a.4; HT 10b.4; HT 49. 2; HT 98a.2).

Linear A ***ma-ti-za-i-te*** 1 (PK 1a.6) contains the root ***matt-*** (with voiceless dental), whereas preceding ***ma-da-ti*** 1 (PK 1a.7) contains the root ***mad-*** (with voiced dental). At Emar the variant root ***matt-*** occurs in personal names, cf. R. Pruzsinszky, *Die Personennamen der Texte aus Emar* (SCCNH 13), Bethesda 2003, 251; cf. Th. Richter, *BGH*, 248-249, s.v. ***mad-***, *matt-* [*passim*], see *supra*.

The most likely analysis of ***ma-ti-za-i-te*** (PK 1a.6) is {*matt=i=ž=ai=tte*}, consisting of the transitive root ***matt-*** 'to make wise / intelligent, to give wisdom' + the marker of transitivity ***-i-*** + the modal suffix ***-ž-*** probably expressing the *optative* + the modal suffix ***-ai-*** marking the *final debitive* + the optional allomorphic enclitic personal pronoun 1st person singular ***-tte*** instead of normal ***-tta*** indicating the object of the transitive verb. Translation of the 'one-word' name: 'That he/she (a *numen*) may make me clever, give me wisdom !'. If my analysis is correct, {*matt=i=ž=ai=tte*} it contains two consecutive modal suffixes (*optative* and *final debitive*), which is remarkable, because one expects that one of the two is sufficient, but I see at present no better analysis to explain the formation.

As we have often seen, it is also possible that ***-te*** in ***ma-ti-za-i-te*** does not reflect the optional allomorphic enclitic personal pronoun 1st person singular ***-tte***, but the well-known hypocoristic ***-te*** of the theophorous element ***-Tešub***. If so, the 'sentence name' can be analysed as {*matt=i=ž=ai-Te*} and translated as 'That *Tešub* may make (the child) clever'.

Th. Richter (*VHN*, 603-604 and n. 1012-1018) discusses (sub 1.3.2.2) the verbal forms with ***°=i=ž***. He mentions that ***°=i*** and ***°=ž*** show formations indicating transitive plural imperatives and offers the example of *šal-ḫe-eš* {*šalġ=i=ž*} 'hört !' ['hear ! (plural)']. But that offers for {*matt=i=ž=ai=tte*} in the combination of ***=i=ž*** with the final debitive suffix ***=ai*** a problem for the position of ***°=ž***, since according to I. Wegner (*Einführung*, 111-112 + Table 12: *Die Suffixfolge beim sog. Debitiv-Finalis*) the pluralizer ***-š(a)*** is placed after (not before) ***-ae/-ai***.

She compares *pal-la-in* (Mit. IV 64), consisting of root ***pal-*** 'to know' + formant ***-(i)l-*** + *final debitive* suffix ***-ai-*** + enclitic personal pronoun 3rd person singular ***-n(na)*** = 'in order that he may know it', with *pal-la-i-šal-la* (Mit. IV 65) = root ***pal-*** 'to know' + formant ***-(i)l-*** + *final debitive* suffix ***-ai-*** + pluralizer ***-ša-*** + enclitic personal pronoun 3rd person plural ***-lla*** = 'in order that they may know'.

M. Giorgieri (Syntaktische Bemerkungen zu hurritisch *tād=ugār-* und akkadisch *ra'āmu* in den Tušratta-Briefen, in: *Gedenkschrift Emil Orgetorix Forrer*, Dresden 2004, 326[22]) assumes that *°=i=ž* forms are singular in onomastics. Th. Richter agrees with Giorgieri in this respect, for he mentions (*VHN*, 62-63, 603) that the sentence name ***fAweš-tari*** (Mari) can only be translated as 'Das Feuer möge (Mädchen) retten' ['The fire may save (the girl)'], not as 'Rettet (das Mädchen), oh Feuer !' ['Save (plural) (the girl) oh fire!']. He also translates ***Awiš-api*** (wr. *A-wi-iš-a-bi*) from Šušarrā, analysis {*av=i=ž-abi*}, typology 1.3.2.2, lexicon *aw-* II, *abi*, 'Die (Opfer)Grube möge (Jungen) retten' ['The sacrificial pit may save (the boy)'], cf. Th. Richter, *VHN*, 61. I remain surprised about the coexistence of two consecutive modal suffixes in ***ma-ti-za-i-te***. Cf. my interpretation of Linear A ***a-pi*** (KN Ze 16) = Hurrian ***abi*** 'sacrificial pit', inscription incised in the southern door-jamb of the entrance into the circular chamber of a tholos tomb at Kephala (ca. 1,5 Km. north of the Palace of Knossos). Th. Richter (*VHN*, 62) analyses ***fAwiš-Na*** (wr. *fA-wi-iš-na, fA-we-eš-na, fA-wi-iz-na,*) from Mari and ***fAwiš-Na*** (wr. *fA-we-eš-na*) and ***fAwiš-Naja*** (wr. *fA-wi-iš-na-a-a, fA-we-eš-na-a-a*) from Nuzi (I.J. Gelb, *NPN*, 40) as {*av=i=ž-Na*} and {*av=i=ž-Naja/e*}, 'Na(je) möge (Mädchen) retten' ['Na(je) may save (the girl)'].

Linear A ***ma-ka-i-ta*** (PK 1.7; ZA 5b.2-3) is the last personal name on this tablet from Palaikastro and the last on the *b*-side of tablet ZA 5 from Kato Zakro. The geographical position of Palaikastro and Kato Zakro on the east coast of Crete makes it *a priori* likely that there was close contact between these two Minoan sites, of which the palace of Kato Zakro was no doubt the most important. It is therefore not surprising that the same personal names are attested in these two places. It goes too far to speculate whether ***ma-ka-i-ta*** from Palaikastro and ***ma-ka-i-ta*** from Kato Zakro might be the same person. The morphological structure of 'one-word' names such as ***ma-ka-i-ta*** was popular in Hurrian onomastics. Nevertheless it is remarkable that this match between Palaikastro and Kato Zakro occurs on the only well-preserved tablet from Palaikastro discovered to date. The four-sided clay bar PK 3 from Palaikastro is suspected to be hieroglyphic. The text on this bar is probably written from right to left. The other texts from the Palaikastro area are the religious texts from the Peak Sanctuary of mount Petsophas very close to Minoan Palaikastro.

Linear A ***ma-ka-i-ta*** (PK 1.7; ZA 5b.2-3) has already been treated extensively in the discussion on ***ma-ki-de-te*** 5 (ZA 10b.3) from Kato Zakro, that can also be analysed as a 'one-word' name {*mag=e/id=e/i=tte*}, consisting of the verbal root ***mag-*** 'to give (as a present)' + the suffix ***-ed-/-id-*** marking the future tense + the thematic vowel ***-e/i-*** + the enclitic personal pronoun 1st person singular ***-tta/-tte/-tti*** indicating the object of the transitive verb. It can be translated as 'He/She (scil. a *numen*) will give me (as a present)'. The other feasible interpretation is that the name can be analysed as a theophorous 'sentence' name, with ***-Tešub*** in its abbreviated or hypocoristic form ***-te*** as subject of the verbal form. The analysed form {*mag=e/id=e/i=Te*} can then be translated as 'Te(šub) will give (the child) (as a present)'.

The Linear A personal name ***ma-ka-i-ta*** (PK 1.7; ZA 5b.2-3) shows the same verbal formation as Linear A ***ma-ka-i-se*** (ZA 8.4) from Kato Zakro. Linear A ***ma-ka-i-ta*** can be analysed as {*mag=ai=tta*}, consisting of the root ***mag-*** 'to give (as a present)' + the *final debitive* suffix ***-ai-*** + the suffix of the enclitic personal pronoun 1st person singular ***-tta*** indicating the object of action in a transitive construction, so that {*mag=ai=tta*} can be translated as 'Let he / she (scil. a *numen*) give me (as a present) !' or 'In order that he/she (a *numen*) gives me (as a present)'. It is not accidental that the scribe of PK 1 has placed the other form with *final debitive* suffix ***-ai-***, ***ma-ti-za-i-te*** (PK 1a.6) {*matt=i=ž=ai=tte*}, so close to ***ma-ka-i-ta*** (PK 1.7). The scribe was not only in a poetic mood, but must have been aware of the grammatical structure of the names as well. Other Linear A personal names with the enclitic personal pronoun 1st person singular ***-tta*** are ***a-ma-ta*** (HT 29.1), ***a-mi-ta*** (ZA 10b.4-5), ***a-we-||ni-ta*** (ZA 8.2-3), ***da-i-pi-ta*** (ZA 8.5; ZA 10a.4-5), ***i-do-ri-ni-ta*** (PH 6.2), ***ki-da-ta*** (HT 40+76.2),] ***su-ki-ri-ta*** (PH Wa 32.α), ***si-mi-ta*** (HT 96a.2-3).

The Hurrian noun ***magan(n)i*** 'gift, present' occurs for instance in the absolutive plural form as ***maganna*** (wr. *ma-ka-a-an-na*) in the Tušratta letter (Mit. III 58) and can be analysed as {*maga=nna* < *maga=nni* + *na*} 'the gifts, the presents', cf. I. Wegner, *Einführung*, 164-166, 169.

We may also compare ***ma-ka-i-ta*** (PK 1.7; ZA 5b.2-3) with ***ma-ka-i-se*** (ZA 8.4) that shows the same morphological structure, since it can be analysed as the *final debitive* {*mag=ai-še*}, hypocoristic of {*mag=ai-šena*} or {*mag=ai-šen(a)ni*}, and be translated as 'Let he /she (scil. a *numen*) give a/the brother !', 'In order that he/she (scil. a *numen*) gives a/the brother'. Th. Richter (*VHN, passim*) has shown that names referring to replacement of a deceased child by the newborn child play a large role in onomastics. This means that {*mag=ai-še*} can also be interpreted as 'Let the (deceased) brother give (the child) !'.

The Linear A verbal form ***su-ra-i*** = Hurrian ***zul(l)=ai***, with *final debitive* suffix ***-ai-***, has already been discussed extensively in *chapter 10: Linear A inscriptions on metal objects*. The Linear A inscription occurs on a gold signet-ring from Mavro Spilio east of the Palace of Knossos: ***a-re-ne-si-di-jo-pi-ke-pa-ja-su-ra-i-te-ra-me-a-ja-ku*** (KN Zf 13). It can be read as: ***a-re-ne*** (,) ***si-di-jo-pi*** (,) ***ke-pa-ja*** (,) ***su-ra-i*** (,) ***te-ra-me*** (,) ***a-ja-ku***, which can be analysed as {*Ar-ene=š*} {*Šid=i-j=o/umbi*} {*Kebaja*} {*zul(l)=ai*} {*Telame*} [*Telame/Talame/Talme*] {*Aya=k(k)=un*}, that can be translated as: 'In order that (the priest) *Arene* may connect *Šidijombi* and *Kebaja* (in wedlock with this wedding-ring), oh Great *Ajak(k)un*' or 'Let (the priest) *Arene* connect *Šidijombi* and *Kebaja* (in wedlock with this wedding-ring), oh Great *Ajak(k)un* !'.

Linear A ***a-pa-ra-ne*** , (HT 96a.1-2) occurs in a list of personal names on this tablet from Hagia Triada. It follows ***i+ro*** , ***ti-ti-ku-ni*** , (or: ***ti-ti-ku*** FIC 1) (HT 96a.1) and is followed by ***a-65-te*** , (HT 96a.2), ***si-mi-ta*** GRA 5 (HT 96a.2-3), ***r/lu-sa*** 4 ***9*** , ***136*** 1 (HT 96a.3), ***pi-ta-ra*** , 1 ***9*** TRIPUS+***ro*** 1 (HT 96a.4)]***ku-ma-ro*** , ***te*** 20 ˊFICˋ (HT 96a.5). The reading of ***a-pa-ra-ne*** , (HT 96a.1-2) is probably correct, because ***a-pa-ra-ne*** , (HT 96b.1) recurs as first entry on the other side of the tablet. It is not easy to determine, whether ***a-pa-ra-ne*** is a verbal or nominal personal name. The personal names ***ti-ti-ku-ni*** (HT 96a.1) and ***pi-ta-ra*** (HT 96a.4) have been discussed before.

It is not certain, but probable that the root ***ab-*** I / ***app-*** can be equated with the verbal root ***aw-*** II {*av-*}, that may well have the same meaning as the form with root-extension {*av=o/ušk-*} 'retten' ['to save'], cf. Th. Richter, *VHN*, 374-376 and *BGH*, 33 ff. The sentence names ***Awar-tuk*** (wr. *A-wa-ar-du-uk, A-wa-ar-tu-uk*) from Mari and Tigunāni and ***Apar-tuk*** (wr. *A-ba-ar-du-uk*) from Puzriš-Dagan may then be analysed as {*aw/b=ar-to/uk*}, typology 1.4, lexicon *aw-* II, *tuk* (→ *tukki*), '*tuk* rettete (Mutter ?) wiederholt' ['*tuk* saved (the mother ?) again and again'], cf. Th. Richter, *VHN*, 60. These personal names show that the *factitive* and *iterative* root-extension ***=ar=*** that can be observed in Linear A ***a-pa-ra-ne*** is attested in Hurrian onomastics. Since the verbal root ***aw-*** in onomastics is usually attested in transitive *modal forms* in ***°=i=ž*** and *imperatives* in ***-e/-i***, the Linear A name ***a-pa-ra-ne*** may be analysed as {*ab/w=ar=an(n)=e/i*} and have two consecutive root-extensions, *factitive* and *iterative* ***=ar=*** and *causative* ***=an(n)=***, cf. I. Wegner, *Einführung*, 88. The name can be translated 'Save (the child / the mother) again and again'.

The other feasible interpretation of Linear A ***a-pa-ra-ne*** is {*Abar(i)=a=nne*}, consisting of the theonym ^{D}***Abari*** in the *essive* form in ***-a*** + the optional allomorphic enclitic personal pronoun 3rd person singular ***-nne*** instead of normal ***-nna***, indicating the subject of the intransitive verb 'to be', that is usually omitted in personal names. Translation 'She is like (the goddess) ^{D}***Abari***'. Although the theonym also occurs as ***Abara***, I consider it likely that in the personal name ***a-pa-ra-ne*** the *essive* form 'like *Abari*' is used, since that is more polite towards the gods than the *absolutive* 'She is Abara' and avoids human *hybris*. E. Laroche (*GLH*, 33) mentions, s.v. ***abari***: ^{d}***a-ba-ri***, KUB XLIII 51 Vo 3 (on attend ^{d}***Abati***). – Cf. aussi le nom de déesse ***Abara***, de Šamuḫa.

Th. Richter (*VHN*, 376) mentions that the goddess ***Abari*** belongs to the circle of Ištar / *Ša(w)uška* of Šamuḫa and takes the second position after her in the hierarchy, cf. also Th. Richter, *BGH*, 35. The personal name ***Apari*** (wr. *A-ba-ri*) is attested at Mari and Nippur and as *A-ba-ri(-)* [...] at Nuzi (cf. I.J. Gelb, *NPN*, 22). It may be significant that Th. Richter (*VHN*, 60) mentions typology 3.1 and lexicon *abari* (→ *ab-* I) or 'one-word' name ***Abari***.

Linear A ***si-mi-ta*** GRA 5 (HT 96a.2-3) occurs in a list of personal names on this tablet from Hagia Triada. It follows ***i+ro*** $_{1}$ ***ti-ti-ku-ni*** $_{1}$ (or: ***ti-ti-ku*** FIC 1) (HT 96a.1), ***a-pa-ra-ne*** , (HT 96a.1-2) and ***a-65-te*** , (HT 96a.2) and is followed by ***r/lu-sa*** 4 (HT 96a.3).

Linear A ***si-mi-ta*** can be analysed as a Hurrian 'one-word' name {*šim=i=tta*}, consisting of the verbal root ***šim-*** 'to establish ?, determine ?' + the marker of transitivity ***-i-*** + the imperative marker -Ø- + the enclitic personal pronoun 1st person singular ***-tta*** 'me', indicating the object of the verb, translation 'Establish (?) me (oh *numen*) !'.

In many archives personal names with the root ***šim-*** are preserved such as *Ši-mi-ik-ku* at Alalaḫ IV (*AT*, 136: 39), ^{f}***Šimaja*** (wr. ^{f}*Ši-ma-a-a*), ***Šimija*** (wr. *Ši-mi-ia*), ***Šimi-Tilla*** (wr. *Ši-mi-til-la*), ^{f}***Šim-Te*** (wr. ^{f}*Ši-im-Te*, ^{f}*Ši-im-Te-e*), ***Šimšar*** (wr. *Ši-im-šar*) at Nuzi (I.J. Gelb, *NPN*, 134-135). ***Šimšar*** at Nuzi probably correlates with ***Šimšari*** (wr. *Ši-im-ša(?)-ri*), analysis {*šim(i)=žari*}, typology 3.1, at Mari. Attested at Mari are ^{f}***Šima-ewri*** (wr. ^{f}*Ši-ma-ew-ri*), analysis {*šim=a=Ø-evri*}, typology 1.1.1.3.3, ***Šimiš-ewri*** (wr. ^{f}*Ši-mi-iš-ew-ri*, ^{f}*Ši-mi-i-iš-ew-ri*), typology 1.3.2.2, analysis {*šim=i=ž-evri*}, ***Šimiš-šarri*** (wr. *Ši-im-iš-šar-ri*), analysis {*šim=i=ž-šarri*}, typology 1.3.2.2, ^{f}***Šim-kintiri*** (wr. ^{f}*Ši-im-gi-in-di-ri*), analysis {*šim-kindiri*}, typology 1.4 (Th Richter, *VHN*, 267-268, 508, s.v. ***šim-***).

According to Th. Richter (*VHN*, 508) lexical terms based on ***šim-*** are rare (see *BGH*, 378-379). For a great deal they are morphologically and lexically not clear. E. Laroche (*GLH*, 232) booked *ši-mi*$^{!}$(LUM)-*i-ki* (Mit. III 46) as *ši-mi-i-ki* under ***Šimigi*** 'soleil'. Th. Richter (*BGH*, 378) mentions, s.v. ***šim-***, that G. Wilhelm (1985b, 494) offers the analysis ***šim=i=<k>ki*** without translation. According to Dietrich/Mayer (1991, 117) the form is identical with Akkadian ***šiāmu(m)/šâmu*** II 'festsetzen, bestimmen' ['to establish, determine'], but according to G. Wilhelm (1993, 117) the form remains morphologically and semantically obscure. At Ugarit (RS voc. III 13) Hurrian ***ši-ma-ni-šu-ḫi*** is compared with Sumerian MA.NA.LÁ, which suggests a meaning 'hängen (lassen)' ['to (let) hang'] or 'bezahlen' ['to pay'] for ***ši-m***^{o} or ***ši-ma-n***^{o}, but this meaning is not easily applicable elsewhere. Compare also Linear A ***si-ma*** (PH Zb 4) from Phaistos.

Linear A ***ru-sa*** or ***lu-sa*** 4 ***9*** , ***136*** 1 (HT 96a.3) is clearly a personal name in a list of personal names. It is equivalent to two Hurrian personal names attested at Alalaḫ IV:

Lu-uš-ša, mentioned in a list of emmer distributed by *PA* to the men of *Ariante* (15 names), cf. D.J. Wiseman, *AT*, 89 and 141: Text 286, 6; cf. also *JCS 8*, 24 = *JCS 13*, 50.

Lu-uz-za, in a Census List of the forces of (*amêl*) *SA.GAZ* of Šarkuḫe who (captured) the village of Marmaru. The list is subdivided:
(i) 20 armed men (*bêl kakkē(meš)*). Each name is followed by the man's home village, e.g. Qadume, Zaltum, except for 2 names where *Ḫubitta* (l. 16) is called (*amêl*) *šarraku* (cf. 165) and Tulpia (l. 20) is the *bâru*-priest of Išḫara.
(ii) 2 charioteers (*bêl (iṣ)narkabāti*).
(iii) 5 warriors of Eṭir-šarri. One of these is a messenger (*mar ši-ip-ru*).
(iv) 2 ṣabū(meš) maš-ki-en.
Total 29 men, the troops of *amêl SA.GAZ* (*al*) *Šar-ku-ḫe* (*KI*). The remainder is broken, but mentions the city of Ibla, and there appear to be 5(?) additional names, cf. D.J. Wiseman, *AT*, 71 and 141: Text 180, 17.

Th. Richter (*VHN*, 188) mentions these names in comparison with ^{f}***Luzzenna*** (wr. ^{f}*Lu-ze-en-na*) at Mari, analysis {*lo/uzz=i=nna*}, typology 1.3.1.2.2.1, lexicon *luzz-*; *Lu-zi-na* in Old-Assyrian Alişar (OIP 27, 56: 9) and *Lu-zi-na* frequently at Kaniš.

Th. Richter (*VHN*, 453) mentions s.v. ***luzz-*** {*lo/uzz-*} that there is no other etymology possible for *Lu-ze-en-na* than a Hurrian. He considers an allophonic variant of ***nuzz-*** possible. The root may be cognate with ***Lušša / Luzza*** at Alalaḫ IV that he uses as indication for doubling of the sibilant. He also refers to the technical term 3 ^{GIŠ}GU.ZA ^{GIŠ}TASKARIN***lu-uš-še-na*** "3 **lušše**-chairs of box-wood" (Qaṭna, Middle-Babylonian: QS 3, 16: 2).

Linear A]-***ku-ma-ro*** , ***te*** 20 ´FIC` (HT 96a.5) may well be a complete Hurrian personal name. It can be analysed as Old Hurrian {*kum=ar=o=m*}, consisting of the Hurrian verbal root ***kum-*** 'to build, pile up, erect, create' + the *factitive* and *iterative* root-extension ***-ar-*** + the marker of the transitive perfect form ***-o-*** + the Old Hurrian marker of the subject of action ***-m***. This final ***-m*** is omitted in Linear A, because final consonants are not expressed in Linear A and B. Translation 'He / She [***-m***] (scil. the father / mother or a *numen*) has built / created (a child) again and again'.

Another analysis *{kum=ar=o=n(na)}*, with the abbreviated enclitic personal pronoun 3rd person singular ***-n*** instead of ***-nna***, indicating the object of the transitive verb, is also possible. This final ***-n*** is not expressed in Linear A for the same reason as just mentioned. Such ambiguities may be difficult and confusing for us, but the scribe no doubt knew, which final consonant was meant. If we translate 'He / She (scil. the father / mother or a *numen*) has built / created it [***-n(na)***] (scil. a child) again and again', the *iterative* aspect of ***-ar-*** may refer to the fact that many children were born in that family.

Th. Richter (*BGH*, 221-222) mentions, s.v. ***kum-*** [EN (= Eigenname = proper name); Nuzi], 'errichten, auftürmen', also in the theonym Kumarbi «*Kum=ar=we*» '(Der) des Errichtens / Auftürmens' ['(The one) of building' / '(The one) of the piling-up'] (V. Haas, 1994a, 167) or '(quello) di Kumar' ['(The one) of (toponym) Kumar']. Both etymologies are possible, but in my view not very satisfactory.

It seems more attractive to interpret ***-bi*** or ***-wi*** in ***Kumarbi / Kumarwi*** not as the genitive suffix ***-bi / -wi***, but as part of the Nuzian variant ***erwi*** (as a result of metathesis) of ***ibri / iwri / ebri / ewri*** 'Lord', so that the meaning of ***Kumarbi/wi < *Kum(m)a-erwi*** (as a result of contraction) is 'Lord of *Kumma*' and that of ***Kumarbi=ni*** is 'The Lord of Kumma'. The variant ***erwi*** may not be limited to Nuzi. One may, for instance, also compare ***ermi/irmi*** at Nippur, cf. P.M. Purves, *NPN*, 210-211, s.v. ***erw***, *erwi-*, *-erwi*.

It is interesting that the Mari archives offer the personal name ***Kumarwe-ewri*** *{Ko/umarve-evri}*, typology 2.1, translation 'Kumarwe ist Herr' ['Kumarwe is Lord'] and ***Kumarwe-atal*** *{Ko/umarve-adal}*, typology 2.1, 'Kumarwe ist stark' ['Kumarwe is strong'], cf. Th. Richter, *VHN*, 173. ***Kumarwe-ewri***, literally 'The Lord of Kum(m)a is Lord' seems tautological, if my etymology is correct, but was probably not felt as such at Mari, because at Mari ***ewri*** (not ***erwi***) was the normal expression for 'Lord / King' and the theonym ***Kumarwe/Kumarbi*** was possibly already seen as one notion. If my etymology is correct, we may deduce that the theonym may have been created in a region, where the Hurrian dialect used ***erwi*** instead of ***ewri***, perhaps at *Kumma/e* itself, where the mythical struggle between An - Kumarbi - Tešub was situated and concentrated and where *Ullikummi* tried to deprive Tešub of his power on behalf of Kumarbi or/and perhaps at Nuzi, where ***erwi*** was the theophorous element in many personal names. Compare also Linear A ***ku-mi*** (HT 110a.1) at Hagia Triada, discussed before.

The reading of the ligature ***i+<u>ro</u>*** (HT 96a.1) is not entirely certain on HT 96a, but it seems to be repeated more clearly on (HT 96b.2) and again (after SUS and before ***ma-di***) on HT 118.1. If the readings are correct ***i+<u>ro</u>*** can be interpreted as ***ir=o*** or ***il=o***, and since final consonants are not expressed in Linear A an B, also as ***ir=o=m*** or ***il=o=m*** or as ***ir=o=n(na)*** or ***il=o=n(na)***, but also ***irr=o=m*** or ***irr=o=n(na)***.

Th. Richter (*BGH*, 96; *VHN*, 401) mentions, that (thanks to the bilingual *Kirenze*) a root ***er-/ir-*** could be isolated that was translated as "s'accroître" ['to grow'], "gedeihen" ['to thrive'], "helfen" ['to help'] and "schenken" ['to give (as a present)']. A participial form like ***eriri*** *{er=i=ri}* can be interpreted as 'der/die geschenkt hat' ['the one who has given']. He analyses personal names like ***Irija*** (wr. *I-ri-ia*) at Mari, Tigunāni, Tuttul as *{ir=i=ja}* and translates 'He/She (a *numen*) gave (the boy) as a present'; ***Irip-Teššup*** (wr. *Iri-ip-te-eš-šu-up*) at Tigunāni, as *{ir=i=b-Teššob}*, 'Teššub gave (the boy) as a present'.

As a result the ligature ***i+ro*** can be a lexical term in the Old Hurrian *imperative* {*ir=o*} 'give!'. This is indeed semantically a likely option: ***i+ro* , *ti-ti-ku*** FIC 1 (HT 96a.1) could then be interpreted as 'give Tittiku(n) 1 portion figs !'. Theoretically ***i+ro*** can also be a personal name with the same meaning, but a transactional term seems preferable, especially because the scribe chose to use a ligature instead of normal syllabic sequences and the same form was used in HT 96b.2 and HT 118.1.

The other theoretical options are not very promising: According to Th. Richter (*VHN*, 401) it is not yet known whether the root ***irr-*** should be distinguished from ***er-/ir-***. With regard to the root ***el-/il-*** he mentions (*VHN*, 394-395) that there is evidence that the Hurrian root ***il-*** II (*BGH*, 79) corresponds with Akkadian *šūlukum* '(einer Tätigkeit) (nach)gehen lassen' ['to let an activity be checked'], but for ***el-*** the meaning 'zersplittern, zerbrechen' ['to break into splinters / pieces'] was proposed (*ibidem*).

The analysed structure of tablet ZA 8 from the archive-room of the Palace of Kato Zakro (Room XVI A, south niches, like ZA 4, ZA 5, ZA 11, ZA 14, ZA 16, ZA 20) reads:

ZA 8.1.	*ki-ra* , *a-ta-re* ,	FIC		J
2.	*ku-tu-ko-re*			DD
2-3.	*a-we-*‖*ni-ta*		1[ ]	BB
3-4.	*ta-i-nu-ma*‖			AJ
4.	*ma-ka-i-se*		2	EJ
5.	*da-i-pi-ta*		2	J
6.	*ka-i-ro*		4	BB

In the first line of tablet ZA 8 the 'fig' ideogram FIC is mentioned. The personal names in the list of names are followed by numbers and signs of fractions, probably indicating the portions of figs attributed to each person. The first sign of ZA 8.4 can in principle be read as ***pa***, but is more likely to be identified with fraction sign **A** that can be joined with the following fraction sign **J**, as indicated in the analysed structure of the text in *Minoan Linear A*, Vol. II, *Corpus of transliterated Linear A texts*, Part II, 426.

I shall only discuss the remaining personal names of tablet ZA 8 from Kato Zakro. For instance, the first entry ***ki-ra*** (ZA 8.1) and ***ma-ka-i-se*** (ZA 8.4) have already been discussed extensively (*supra*).

In the 2016 edition two possible interpretations of Linear A ***a-ta-re*** (ZA 8.1) as Hurrian personal names were examined. Since both ***-n-*** and ***-s-*** preceding a dental in consonant clusters are not expressed in Linear A, both Hurrian ***antare*** and ***aštare*** were considered feasible options. It is difficult to establish the degree of voicing of the dentals in the consonant clusters of these names. Since voicing was not phonemic in Hurrian, the Hurrian scribes were probably not even aware of using allophonic variants.

The phonological representation of the Hurrian anthroponym ***Antare*** (wr. *An-ta-re, An-ta-re-e*), attested at Nuzi (cf. I.J. Gelb, *NPN*, 22), may well be ***/andare/***, since the dental may well be voiced under influence of the nasal. As a result equation of Linear A ***a-ta-re*** with Hurrian ***Antare*** seems less likely. The phonological representation of the Hurrian personal name ***Aštari*** (wr. *Aš-ta-ri*), attested at Nuzi as son of *Pa-pa-an-te* (HSS IX 13:26), may well be ***/aštare/*** in accordance with Linear A ***a-ta-re***.

Compare also at Nuzi *Aštar-teįa* (wr. *Aš-tar-te-ia, Aš-tar-te-e-a, Aš-tar-te-e*), *Aštar(i)-tešub* (wr. *Aš-tar-te-šup, Aš-ta-ri-te-šu-up, A-aš-ta-ri-te-šup, Aš-ta-ri-te-šup*), *Aštar-tilla* (wr. *Aš-tar-til-la*), see I.J. Gelb, *NPN*, 37.

Ugaritic ***Aštaru*** is equated with the Hurrian Martial God ***Aštabi*** (RS quadr. 137 IV b 16 = *Ugar. V*, 249): *Aš-ta-bi-i[n]* = Ugar. *Aštaru*. ***Aštabi*** is described by E. Laroche (*GLH*, 61) as 'Dieu guerrier, identifié à Ninurta' ['Martial God identified with Ninurta']. In Akkadian texts: ^{D}*Aš-tu-u-bi-nu*, CT XXV 11 II 31; cf. Ungnad, *Subartu*, 65, etc. In Hittite texts: nom. ^{D}*Aštabiš*; acc. ^{D}*Aštabin*; abs. ^{D}*Aš-ta-(a)-bi*, ^{D}*Aš-ta-(a)-wi*; hieroglyphic ^{D}*As-ta-bi*. In Hurrian texts: abs. *Aštb*, CTA 166, 29, 31; Hrozný, *ArchOr. 4*, 123. Dir. *Aštb-d*, *Ugar. V*, 519 ff. Onom.: *AT*, 130 *et passim*; *NH* N° 178. According to Th. Richter (*BGH*, 59) ***Aštabi*** I [Alalaḫ VII] is used as name of a month at Alalaḫ, according to F. Zeeb (*Die Palastwirtschaft in Altsyrien nach den spätaltbabylonischen Getreidelieferlisten aus Alalaḫ (Schicht VII), AOAT 282*, Münster 2001, 163, 653), the second month (October/November).

Ugaritic ***Aštaru*** (RS quadr. 137 IV b 16) has an Akkadianizing *nominative* in ***-u***, whereas the Nuzi personal name ***Aštar(i)-tešub*** (wr. *Aš-tar-te-šup, Aš-ta-ri-te-šu-up, A-aš-ta-ri-te-šup, Aš-ta-ri-te-šup*) shows in *Aš-ta-ri-* the Hurrian *absolutive* ending in ***-i***.

Aštari has certainly nothing to do with Hurrian ***ašta***, ***ašte***, ***ašti***, ***aštu*** 'woman' and the onomastic elements ***ašta-***, ***ašte-***, ***ašti-***, ***aštu-*** in Hurrian feminine personal names as attestation of ***Aštari*** as son of *Pa-pa-an-te* at Nuzi proves as well as the combination with ***-tešub***, ***-teįa***, ***-tilla*** in other masculine personal names. P.M. Purves (*NPN*, 206, s.v. *Aštar, Aštari, Aštar-, Aštari-*) tells that Hurrian *Aštar, Aštari* has nothing to do with *Ištar* and can according to I.J. Gelb possibly be explained by dissimilation: *aštar* < *artar*.

Th. Richter (*BGH*, 58) writes that the transitive verbal root ***ašt-*** I [Boğ.] means 'entsprechen lassen' ['to let agree, correspond with, to let respond, answer, conform to'] and the intransitive root 'entsprechen' ['to agree, correspond with, to respond, answer, conform to'] (De Martino - Giorgieri, 2007a, 142, 2008, 132). According to G. Wilhelm (1991b, 164[34]) ***ašt-*** may be a denominalisation of ***ašte-***, ***ašti-***. According to De Martino - Giorgieri, 2007a, 128[11]) ***ašt-*** should be distinguished from ***ašte-***, ***ašti-***. The meaning of *iterative / frequentative* ***ašt=ar-*** [PN] is 'immer wieder entsprechen lassen' ['to let agree, correspond with again and again, to let respond, answer, conform to again and again'], cf. De Martino - Giorgieri, 2007a, 143f, 2008, 133. See for the *factitive / iterative* root-extension ***-ar-*** I. Wegner, *Einführung*, 88. According to Th. Richter (*BGH*, 58) the anthroponym ***Aštari*** is either a single verbal form without theophorous element [→ see ***ašt=ar-***] or a nominalized form 'Der Entsprechende' ['The (cor)responding one'], 'Die Entsprechung' ['The agreement, correspondence'].

Thanks to Th. Richter's publication *Vorarbeiten zu einem hurritischen Namenbuch*, Erster Teil, Wiesbaden 2016, 89, the Hurrian personal name ****Attari/e*** can now be confirmed on the basis of ***Attara*** (wr. *a-at-ta-ra*), analysis {*Attar(i)=a*[E.]}, typology 3.2.1, lexicon *attari* (→ *att-*) at Qaṭṭara (Tall ar-Rimaḥ) and at Šubat-Enlil / Šeḫna (Tall Leilān), and on the basis of ***Attaru*** (wr. *at-ta-ru*), analysis {*Attar(i)=u*[N.]}, typology 3.1, lexicon *attari* (→ *att-*) at Šušarrā (Tall Shemshara); ***a***[E.] refers to the *essive* case-ending in ***-a***; ***u***[N.] refers to the Akkadian(izing) *nominative* case-ending in ***-u***. According to Th. Richter (*VHN*, 386, s.v. ***att-*** {*att-*}) a noun ***attari*** {*att=a=ri*} can be inferred on the basis of *(a-)at-ta-ra/u* and similar personal names.

Concluding: Linear A ***a-ta-re*** (ZA 8.1) can be identified with the Hurrian personal name ***Aštari*** or ***Attari / Attare***. The scribe no doubt knew, whether he wrote the name of ***Aštari / Aštare*** or of ***Attari / Attare***, but we cannot be sure, since Linear A orthographic conventions offer more than one possibility.

Linear A ***ku-tu-ko-re*** (ZA 8.2) is probably a Hurrian theophorous personal name. Its structure is clear. The first onomastic element is verbal and can be either the Hurrian root ***kud-/kutt-*** or the Hurrian root ***ḫud-/ḫutt-***, since the Linear B ***k-*** signs represent ***κ-***, ***γ-***, ***χ-*** and consequently the corresponding Linear A signs probably ***k-***, ***g-***, ***ḫ-*** and ***-ḫḫ-***.

The second element ***°-u-ko-re*** probably contains the theonym ***Ugur***, cf. Th. Richter, *VHN*, 549, s.v. ***Ugur*** {*O/Ugo/ur*}. Final ***-e/-i*** in ***°-u-ko-re*** may be attested in the feminine Hurrian personal name ***ᶠUk-ku-ri*** at Nuzi, cf. P.M. Purves, *NPN*, 271.

According to Th. Richter (*BGH*, 482; *VHN*, 548-549) a relation between the Hurrian verbal root ***ug-*** {*o/ug-*} / ***ukk-*** {*o/ukk-*} and ***Ugur*** is conceivable, since he refers to ***ugul-*** {*o/ug=o/ul-*}, containing a root ***ug-*** + root-extension ***-o/ul-*** 'niederknien, sich verneigen' ['to kneel down'], derived from ***ug-*** {*o/ug-*} / ***ukk-*** {*o/ukk-*} that may also occur in ***Ugur***.

P.M. Purves (*NPN*, 271) mentions s.v. ***ukur***: "Hurrian. ᵈU.GUR, KUB XXVII 1 i 62 and 13 i 9, which may or may not be ideographic. As a Sumerian deity ***Ukur*** was equated with Akkadian ***namṣaru***, 'sword'; see Tallqvist, *AGE*, 474 and 514. Although the Sumerian form is generally used ideographically for the Akkadian deity ***Nergal***, Dr. Gelb has discovered the Akkadian personal names *Puzur-ù-gur* in Fish, *Catalogue of Sumerian Tablets in the John Rylands Library*, Pl. XLVII vi 23, and *Ú-kur-ṭâb*(DÙG) in an unpublished tablet. These indicate that *Ugur*, as such, was a good Akkadian deity. How and when he was adopted into the Hurrian pantheon still remains a mystery."

According to Th. Richter (*VHN*, 549) there is even in recent research still dispute about reading, linguistic provenance and etymology of the theonym ***Ugur*** {*O/Ugo/ur*}, also in view of the Mesopotamian tradition of ᵈU.GUR in the appearance of *Nergal*. One might be dealing with an accidental homonymic or homographic form, for instance, a plausible Akkadian (popular) etymology ***ᵈu-qur*** = ***uqur*** 'destroy' for ᵈU.GUR (Lambert, 1973, 356) or a tentative Hurrian meaning 'Ständig Unterwerfender' ['Permanently subduing'], cf. *BGH*, 483 [→ ***ug-***]. The name is primarily written as (ᴰ)*u-gur-°*. Only at Šušarrā we find *ú-gur-°* (*Ukur-atal*) and *°u-gu-ur* (*Tar-Ukur*). This orthography shows that the theonym must not be regarded as ideographic. The list of deities from Emar points to the same conclusion: (Sumerian) ᵈu.gur = (Hurrian) *ᵈu-ku-ru-un*, cf. E. Laroche, *GLH*, 278, s.v. Ugur: 1. Msk. série An N° 204.

P.M. Purves (*NPN*, 271) offers the following Hurrian names with ***ukur-*** and ***-ukur***: *Ukur-atal, ᶠUkur-elli, Ukur-kipa, Ukur-šarri, Arip-ukur, Eḫlip-ukur, Ḫašip-ukur, Ḫutip-ukur, Itḫip-ukur, Kelip-ukur, Kip-ukur, Nanip-ukur, Wantin-ukur, Wantip-ukur, Zilip-ukur*.

Th. Richter (*VHN*, 549) mentions the following Hurrian personal names with the theophorous element ***Ugur***: *Awi-Ukur* (Mari); *Arip-Ukur* (Mari); *Ḫazip-Ukur* (Mari); *Panti-Ukur* (Mari); *Tar-Ukur* (Šušarrā); *Tizeḫe*-[*U*]*kur* (Mari); *Ukur-atal* (Šušarrā, Mari, Qaṭṭarā).

We have to return to the first onomastic element in Linear A ***ku-tu-ko-re*** that probably consists of the verbal Hurrian root ***kud-/kutt-*** or the Hurrian root ***ḫud-/ḫutt-***. At Nuzi there are several Hurrian names with the verbal element ***kutt*** such as *Ku-ut-ta, Ku-ut-ta-qa-ni, Ku-ut-ta-an-ni, Ku-ut-ti* and *Ku-ut-ti-in-ni* (cf. I.J. Gelb, *NPN*, 93, and P.M. Purves, *NPN*, 231, s.v. ***kutt***).

Th. Richter (*BGH*, 231-232) mentions that on the basis of correspondences with Hittite ***mauš-*** and ***peššija-*** the Hurrian root ***kud-*** can (since E. Neu 1988a, 31; 1988e, 105, 109) be interpreted as (intransitive) 'fallen' ['to fall'], (transitive) 'fallen lassen, fällen, zu Fall bringen' ['to drop, to smash down']. I. Wegner (*Einführung*, 138, 265): (intr. 'fallen' ['to fall'], (trans.) 'fällen, niederwerfen' ['to smash down, to throw down'].

Th. Richter (*VHN*, 452), s.v. ***kud-/kutt-***, points out that the verbal personal names with ***kud-/kutt-*** (intr.) 'fallen' ['to fall'], (trans.) 'fallen lassen, fällen, zu Fall bringen' ['to drop, to smash down'] are analogous with Hittite ***mauš-*** that in context can be 'fallen lassen' ['to drop'] in the sense of 'gebären' ['to give birth to'] and that Akkadian ***maqātum*** seems to have the same connotation.

As a result Linear A ***ku-tu-ko-re***, interpreted as Hurrian {*kutt(=i)-ugo/ur(e)*}, can be translated as 'Drop / Give birth to (the child) / Let (the child) be born, oh Ugur !'. This would offer a very plausible meaning for the name of a child. The root ***kud-/kutt-*** would then have the same meaning (in case of name-giving) as Hurrian ***ḫan-*** 'to give birth to'.

However, since the Linear A syllable ***ku-*** can also be read as initial ***ḫu-***, another feasible interpretation for Linear A ***ku-tu-ko-re*** must be considered. The form can also be analysed as {*ḫutt(=i)-ugo/ur(e)*}, containing the Hurrian verbal root ***ḫud-/ḫutt-***.

At Nuzi the Hurrian personal names ***Ḫute*** (wr. *ᶠḪu-ú-te, ᶠḪu-te*), and ***Ḫuti*** (wr. *Ḫu-ti, Ḫu-ú-*[*ti*]) are attested (cf. P.M. Purves, *NPN*, 218-219), derived from the root ***ḫut-*** (phonemically ***/ḫud/***), with voiced dental as described s.v. Linear A ***ku-da*** and]***ku-du-we***. The root is certainly verbal because of combination with ***-p-***, phonologically ***/-b-/***, in ***Ḫutip-šarri*** (wr. *Ḫu-ti-ip-šarri, Ḫu-di-ip-šarri*), analysis {*ḫud=i=b-šarri*}, ***Ḫutip-šimika*** (wr. *Ḫu-ti-ip-ši-mi-qa*), next to ***Ḫuti-šimika*** (wr. *Ḫu-ti-ši-mi-qa, Ḫu-ti-iš-ši-mi-qa*), ***Ḫutip-tešup*** (wr. *Ḫu-ti-ip-te-šup, Ḫu-di-ip-te-šup*), next to ***Ḫut-tešup*** (wr. *Ḫu-ut-te-šup*) and many more examples given by I.J. Gelb and P.M. Purves.

P.M. Purves (*ibid.*) also mentioned ***Ḫut-tirwi*** (wr. *Ḫu-ut-ti-ir-wi, Ḫu-ti-ir-wi*). He attributed the second variant *Ḫu-ti-ir-wi* to *Ḫut-tirwi*, but since there is only one ***-t-*** in that name, it could better be read as ***Ḫut-irwi***, with the onomastic element ***irwi*** (Nuzi) = ***erwi*** (Nuzi) = ***ewri / ibri*** (elsewhere) 'Lord'. ***ᵈTirwi*** is a god at Nuzi according to P.M. Purves, *NPN*, 267, cf. also Th. Richter, *VHN*, 537, s.v. ***tirwe*** {*tirve*}, ***tirme***.

P.M. Purves (*NPN*, 218) mentioned, s.v. ***ḫut***, that Gustavs (*OLZ XV*, 1912, cols 244-246) suggested the meaning 'kämpfen, streiten' ['to fight'] on the basis of Tuš. ***ḫutanni***, which Bork translated as 'Soldat' ['soldier'] (see refs. under *ḫutanni-*). See also Gustavs in *ZA N.F. II*, 301, *RLV VIII (1926)*, 225, and *Palästinajahrbuch XXVI (1930))*, 7. He also mentioned that at Ugarit ***ḫud*** might be expressed by alphabetic ***ḫd-*** (see von Brandenstein in *ZDMG XCI*, 571). Cf. ***ᵈḪutena ᵈḪutellura***, occurring as ***ḫdn ḫdlr*** at Ugarit. E. Laroche (1948, 125) proposed 'écrire, marquer' ['to write, to express'] for the root ***ḫud-***, but in his *Glossaire de la langue hourrite*, 110, he abandoned that suggestion, s.v. ***ḫud-***, 'verbe de sens inconnu'.

Th. Richter (*BGH*, 175-177) mentions a long list of feasible interpretations s.v. ***ḫud-*** [*passim*]: '(ver)klagen', entspricht urart. **hutumu* (Mayer 1980: 320); 'bestimmen' (Haas 1981e: 644[12], 1984: 5); 'to determine' (Khacikjan 1987: 155), 'erhöhen, preisen' (Neu 1988e: 111, Salvini 1991a: 128, Wilhelm 1992a: 130, Neu 1996a: 410, Haas 1998c: 138, Wegner 2002: 53[11]); 'beten', 'huldigen, verehren' (Salvini 1988b: 169f. bzw. 172[46]); '(Schicksal) entscheiden' (Wilhelm 1988b: 56); 'segnen' (Haas / Wegner 1995b: 289 [+21], Schwemer 2001: 469, 473); 'faire monter' (Wilhelm 1996g: 181); etc.

Th. Richter (*VHN*, 424-425) mentions, s.v. ***ḫud-*** {*ḫo/ud-*}, that in more recent literature the meaning 'Schicksal entscheiden' ['to destine a fate'] was at first attributed to the root, but that since publication of the Hurrian-Hittite bilingual ***Kirenze*** (KBo 32) ***ḫud-*** can be translated as 'beten, huldigen, erhöhen, preisen, segnen' ['to pray, to pay homage to, to exalt, to praise, to bless'], since it corresponds with Hittite ***šarlāi***. The root is relatively rare in the *VHN*-corpus, but at Nuzi (P.M. Purves, *NPN*, 218-219) and Ugarit (F. Gröndahl, *PNTU*, 233) it is a popular onomastic element.

With regard to Linear A ***ku-tu-ko-re*** (ZA 8.2) the Hurrian personal name ***Ḫuti-p-ukur*** (wr. *Ḫu-ti-pu-gur*, *Ḫu-di-pu-gur*, *Ḫu-ti-ip-ú-kur*, *Ḫu-ti-ip-ù-gur*) at Nuzi (cf. P.M. Purves, *NPN*, 219) is very interesting. Since publication of the Hurrian-Hittite bilingual ***Kirenze*** (KBo 32), the suffix ***-p-***, phonologically /***-b-***/, has been recognized as the Old Hurrian marker of the 3rd person singular indicating the subject of the indicative.

Consequently ***Ḫutip-ukur*** at Nuzi can be analysed as the *indicative* {*ḫud=i=b-Ugur*} and translated as '*Ugur* blessed (the child)', whereas Linear A ***ku-tu-ko-re*** may well represent the *imperative* {*ḫutt(=i)-Ugo/ur*} 'Bless (the child), oh *Ugur* !'. Good parallels are the *indicative* {*ḫud=i=b-*} in ***Ḫutip-tešup*** (wr. *Ḫu-ti-ip-te-šup, Ḫu-di-ip-te-šup*), next to the *imperative* {*ḫud/tt(=i)-*} in ***Ḫut-tešup*** (wr. *Ḫu-ut-te-šup*) at Nuzi, cf. *NPN*, 218-219.

The root ***ḫutt-*** (with voiceless dental), variant of ***ḫud-*** (with voiced dental), is now not only attested at Nuzi, e.g. ***Ḫutta*** (wr. *Ḫu-ut-ta*), but also at Tigunāni, ***Ḫuttan***, probably a variant of ***ᶠḪutan*** at Mari (with single writing of the dental), cf. Th. Richter, *VHN*, 425. Alternation of voiced and voiceless dentals of ***ḫud-/ḫutt-*** and of ***kud-/kutt-*** (see *supra*), respectively, is probably due to the allophonic nature of Hurrian occlusives.

The Minoan scribe knew whether ***ku-tu-ko-re*** reflected {*kutt(=i)-ugo/ur(e)*} 'Drop / Give birth to (the child) / Let (the child) be born, oh *Ugur* !' or {*ḫutt(=i)-ugo/ur(e)*} 'Bless (the child), oh *Ugur* !', but we have to deal with the ambiguities due to the orthographic conventions of Linear A and B. In my view attestation of ***Ḫuti-p-ukur*** at Nuzi seems to tip the scales in favour of the root ***ḫud-/ḫutt-***.

The personal name following ***ku-tu-ko-re*** (ZA 8.2) is ***a-we-||ni-ta*** (ZA 8.2-3) from Kato Zakro that may contain the same first element as ***a-we-su*** (HT 118.3) from Hagia Triada. E.A. Speiser (*JAOS LIX (1939)*, 316, note 77) had already recognized an element ***awisᵒ*** in the Nuzi personal names. I.J. Gelb (*NPN*, 40) and P.M. Purves (*NPN*, 208) mention, s.v. ***aw***, ***awa-***, ***awiš-/aweš-***, at Nuzi: ***Awa*** (wr. *A-wa*), ***Awa-ḫuia*** (wr. *A-wa-ḫu-i*, *A-wa-ḫu-ia*), ***ᶠAwa-šuḫur*** (wr. *ᶠA-wa-šu-ḫu-ur*), ***Awa-šuni*** (wr. *A-wa-šu-ni*), ***ᶠAwa-take*** (wr. *ᶠA-wa-ta-ge*), ***Awiš-kipa*** (wr. *A-wi-iš-ki-pa*), ***ᶠAwiš-muše / Aweš-muše*** (wr. *ᶠA-wi-iš-mu-še*, *ᶠA-we-eš-mu-še*), ***ᶠAweš-na*** (wr. *ᶠA-we-eš-na*), ***ᶠAwiš-naia / ᶠAweš-naia*** (wr. *ᶠA-wi-iš-na-a-a*, *ᶠA-we-eš-na-a-a*), ***Awiš-tae*** (wr. *A-wi-iš-ta-e*), ***Awiš-tuni*** (wr. *A-wi-iš-du-ni*), ***Awiš-ušše*** (wr. *A-wi-iš-uš-še*).

The Hurrian names ***ᶠAwiš-na*** (wr. *ᶠA*-PI-*iš-na*) and ***ᶠAwi-yazi*** (wr. *ᶠA*-PI-*ya-zi*) also occur in the Mâri texts, cf. J.M. Sasson, Hurrians and Hurrian names in the Mari texts, *UF 6 (1974)*, 359, 376. In the older literature the meaning of the root ***aw-*** was not yet known.

W.H. van Soldt (*Studies in the Akkadian of Ugarit. Dating and grammar*, *AOAT 40*, Kevelaer/Neukirchen-Vluyn 1991, 364[250]) has isolated the root ***aw-*** {*av-*} on the basis of *a-wu-ka$_{(4)}$-ru-(u-)ši* at Ugarit, analysed as {*aw(?)=ugar=ož=i*} without translation, cf. Th. Richter, *BGH*, 33, s.v. ***aw-*** I [Boğ.; Mari; Tuttul]. M. Dijkstra (The myth of *apši* "the (sea)dragon" in the Hurrian tradition, *Ugarit-Forschungen 37 (2005)*, 320) writes: "In case of ***awum=***, one is tempted to relate it to ***am=um*** 'to reach somebody (with a message)' and ***amumi = ḫatreššar*** 'message'." Th. Richter (*BGH*, 41) tells that in a quadrilingual comparison (Ugarit) Hurrian ***abuškumme*** is equated with Sumerian KAR, Akkadian ***šūzubu*** and Ugaritic ***pullaṭu*** 'to save', cf. J. Huehnergard, *Ugaritic vocabulary in syllabic transcription* (Harvard Semitic Studies 32), Atlanta 1987[1], 82f., 168; G. Wilhelm, Zum hurritischen Infinitiv in Nuzi, *SCCNH 2 (1987)*, 331[3]. The form ***abuškumme*** can be analysed as {*av=ušk=umme*} consisting of the root ***ab/w-***, root-extension ***-ušk-*** and the Hurrian infinitive-suffix ***-umme***. According to Th. Richter (*VHN*, 375-376), s.v. ***aw-*** II {*av-*}, the root ***aw-*** also occurs in *a-wu-um* {*av=o=m*} at Mari and Tuttul (Tall Bi'a). In onomastics the verbal element ***aw-*** mainly occurs in modal forms in ***ᵒ=i=ž*** and in imperative forms in ***ᵒ=i***. Since *a-wi/mi-iš-ta-e* at Nuzi and *a-bi-iš-ta-e/i* at Ugarit are certainly the same name, orthographies with [W], [M] and [B]/[P] are to be taken into account in accordance with time and place of reference. Richter has brought the root ***aw-*** and the stem ***ab=ušk-*** (= root + root-extension) in ***abuškumme*** together and has proposed that the meaning 'to save', that has been established for ***ab=ušk-***, can also be applied to the root ***aw-*** without root-extension, which fits well in personal names expressing a blessing to the child.

Analysis and meaning: If we take all this into account, the Linear A name ***a-we-||ni-ta*** (ZA 8.2-3) can probably be analysed as {*aw(=i)=en=i=tta*}, consisting of the root ***aw-*** + *jussive* indicator ***-i-*** that probably amalgamated with following ***-en-*** (cf. I. Wegner, *Einführung*, 103ff.) + indicator of the *jussive* 3rd person singular ***-en-*** (according to Wegner, *ibid.*) + thematic vowel ***-i-*** + the suffix of the enclitic personal pronoun 1st person singular ***-tta*** 'me'. Note that I. Wegner uses the term *jussive*, whereas e.g. E. Laroche (*GLH*, 28) used the terms 'potentiel' ['subjunctive expressing possibility'] and 'optatif' ['optative'] for the suffix ***-en-*** indicating the 3rd person singular of that mood. The translation of ***a-we-||ni-ta*** (ZA 8.2-3) will then be 'May he/she (the *numen*) save me'. A good parallel, though without the suffix ***-en-***, is a personal name from Ḫattuša ***ᶠḪanijatta*** (wr. *ᶠḫa-ni-ia-at-ta*), analysis {*ḫan=i=a=tta*} 'She gave birth to me', cf. Th. Richter, *VHN*, 586. Cf. also Linear A ***da-i-pi-ta*** (ZA 8.5) on the same tablet from Kato Zakro.

Th. Richter (*VHN*, 60-63) provides many examples of personal names with the root ***aw-*** as verbal element. I mention a selection of these names: ***Awar-tuk*** (wr. *a-wa-ar-du-uk, a-wa-ar-tu-uk*) at Mari and Tigunāni, analysis {*av=ar-to/uk*}, lexicon *aw-* II, *tuk*, typology 1.4, translation '*tuk* rettete (Mutter ?) wiederholt' ['*tuk* repeatedly saved (mother ?)']. N.B. the root-extension ***-ar-*** adds a *factitive* or *iterative* aspect to the verb. ***Awi-kiriš*** (wr. *a-wi-ki-ri-iš, a-wi-ki-re-eš*) King of Ḫurāza[KI] attested at Mari, and person at Qaṭṭarā, analysis {*av=i-kiriž*}, lexicon *aw-* II, *kirše*, typology 1.3.1.2.1, translation 'Rette (Jungen), oh *kirše* !' ['Save (boy), oh *kirše* !'].

He also mentions ***Awin*** (wr. *a-wi-in*), typology 1.3.1.2.2.1, analysis {*av=i=n(na)*} and ***Awinni*** (wr. *a-wi-ni*), analysis {*av=i=n(ni)*}, typology 1.3.1.2.2.2, both at Mari, lexicon *aw-* II, 'Rette ihn (Jungen) !' ['Save him (boy) !']. ***fAwen-kapi*** (wr. *a-we-en-ga-bi*) at Ašnakkum, analysis {*av=i=n(na)-kabi*}, typology 1.3.1.2.2.1, lexicon *aw-* II, *kabi, kab-*, 'Rette es (Mädchen), oh *kabi* !' ['Save her (girl), oh *kabi* !']. ***fAwiš-muši*** (wr. *a-wi-iš-mu-úš-e*) two ladies at Ašnakkum and two at Mari (one musician), typology 1.3.2.2, analysis {*av=i=ž-muži*}, lexicon *aw-* II, *muši, muš-*, 'Der/Die Gerechte möge (Mädchen) retten' ['The trustful/just one may save (the girl)']. ***fAwiš-Na*** (wr. *a-wi-iš-na, a-we-eš-na, a-wi-iz-na*) five ladies at Mari, typology 1.3.2.2, analysis {*av=i=ž-na*}, lexicon *aw-* II, *Na, Naje*, 'Na(je) möge (Mädchen) retten' ['Na(je) may save (the girl)'], cf. at Nuzi ***fAweš-na*** (wr. *fA-we-eš-na*), ***fAwiš-naja / Aweš-naja*** (wr. *fA-wi-iš-na-a-a* and *fA-we-eš-na-a-a*). ***Awi-Ukur*** (wr. *a-*[w]*i-u-gur*) at Mari, typology 1.3.1.2.1, analysis {*av=i-Ugur*}, lexicon *aw-* II, *Ugur*, 'Rette (Jungen), oh *Ugur* !' ['Save (the boy), oh *Ugur* !']. ***Awiš-teḫupe*** (wr. *a-wi-iš₇-<te/ta>-ḫu-be, a-wi-iš-te-ḫu-x*), two men at Mari, typology 1.3.2.2, analysis {*av=i=ž-teġo/ube*}, lexicon *aw-* II, *teḫube* (→ *taḫube*), '*teḫube* möge (Jungen) retten' ['*teḫube* may save (the boy)']. ***Awi-teḫupe*** (wr. *a-wi-te-ḫu-be*) at Tigunāni, typology 1.3.1.2.1, analysis {*av=i-teġo/ ube*}, lexicon *aw-* II, *teḫube* (→ *taḫube*), 'Rette (Jungen), oh *teḫube* !' ['Save (the boy), oh *teḫube* !']. ***Awiš-api*** (wr. *a-wi-iš-a-bi*) at Šušarrā (Tall Shemshara), typology 1.3.2.2, analysis {*av=i=ž-abi*}, lexicon *aw-* II, *abi, te* 'Die Opfergrube möge (Jungen) retten'. ['The sacificial pit may save (the boy)'].

It seems wise to analyse the cognate Linear A personal name ***a-we-su*** (HT 118.3) from Hagia Triada at once before discussing the other names on tablet ZA 8 from Kato Zakro.

Analysis and meaning: In the past it seemed logical in accordance with P.M. Purves (*NPN*, 208) to split Linear A ***a-we-su*** into the Hurrian onomastic elements ***awiš- / aweš-*** and a suffix ***-u***, since P.M. Purves (*NPN*, 270) mentioned s.v. ***-u***: Hurrian. Apparently a suffix in *Akiju ?, Aniu ?, Atiu, Entiu, Ḫaniu, Ḫašiu, Ikkiu, Kaniu, Kariu, Kikkiu, fKuziu, Metkiu, Zikiu* and possibly in the element *waltiu.* However, in the first edition of *Minoan Linear A*, Vol. I, I already suggested that the Hurrian personal name ***Awa-šuni*** (wr. *A-wa-šu-ni*) at Nuzi (Purves, *NPN*, 208) may be cognate with Linear A ***a-we-su***.

Thanks to modern literature, especially Th. Richter (*VHN*, 584ff.), it has become clear that many of the personal names in ***-iu***, mentioned by P.M. Purves, can be interpreted as so-called 'one-word' names with distinctive verbal endings that can be analysed as subject-markers of the 2nd person singular indicative in ***°=i=o***: ***Ḫaniu*** (wr. *ḫa-ni-ú/ù*) {*ḫan=i=o*} 'You give birth (to the boy)' at Nuzi. See also Th. Richter, *BGH*, 125, and *VHN*, 407, 585, s.v. ***ḫan-*** 'gebären' ['to give birth']. ***Ḫaniu*** is one of the most frequent names. At Nuzi it is the name of 23 men, cf. I.J. Gelb, *NPN*, 54. The meaning of the root ***ḫan-*** is generally accepted and can be connected with the substantive ***ḫani*** 'child'. The personal name ***Ḫašiu*** at Nuzi (cf. I.J. Gelb, *NPN*, 58) can be analysed as {*ḫaš=i=o/u*} and translated as 'You hear' from the root ***ḫaš-*** 'to hear'.

Th. Richter (*VHN*, 63, 375-376) offers two Hurrian personal names that can be equated with Linear A ***a-we-su*** (HT 118.3): ***Awizzu*** (wr. *a-wi-iz-zu*) from Mari may be considered an exact equivalent, analysis {*avišš(e)=u*[N.]}, lexicon *awizze* (→ *aw-* II), typology 3.1, translation 'Rettung' ['Rescue, Salvation, Saving']. [N.] = Akkadianizing nominative ***-u***.

The other is ***Awiš-una*** (wr. *a-wi-iš-ú-na*), name of two men from Mari, that Th. Richter analyses as {*av=i=ž-o/un(i)=a* [E.]}, typology 1.3.2.2, lexicon *aw*- II, *uni*, translation 'Er/Sie (*scil.* ein *Numen*) möge *uni* retten' ['He/she (*scil.* a *numen*) may save *uni*']. [E.] refers to the *essive* case in ***-a***. This analysis is not impossible, but Th. Richter mentions (*VHN*, 553) that the word ***uni*** has to date been isolated neither in context nor in onomastics and that ***Awiš-una*** (Mari) is to date the only possible attestation.

In my view another solution is feasible, if one assumes that ***Awiš-una*** with single writing of ***-n-***, may stand for ***Awišunna*** with double ***-nn-***, which is a phenomenon that occurs more often. The analysis would then be {*av=i=ž=o=nna*}, typology 1.3.1.1.2.1, with an extra thematic vowel ***-o/u-*** between ***-ž-*** and ***-nna***, which might be a means to show that the suffix ***-nna*** is meant distinguishing the 3rd person singular of the personal pronoun 'him' yielding the translation 'He/she (*scil.* a *numen*) may save him (the boy)', from the form ***-Na***, hypocoristic of ***-Naja/-Naje***, as attested in ***fAweš-na*** (wr. *fA*-PI-*iš-na*) at Mari and (wr. *fA-we-eš-na*) at Nuzi, and ***fAwiš-naia / fAweš-naia*** (wr. *fA-wi-iš-na-a-a, fA-we-eš-na-a-a*) at Nuzi, '*Na(je)* möge (Mädchen) retten' ['*Na(je)* may save (the girl)'], cf. Th. Richter, *VHN*, 62. Since a final consonant is not expressed in Linear A and B, Linear A ***a-we-su*** (HT 118.3) may not only represent ***Awešu***, but also ***Awešun***. Since ***-n*** is a very common abbreviation of ***-nna***, ***Awešun*** can then be analysed as {*av=e=ž=o=n(na)*} and also be translated as 'He/she (*scil.* a *numen*) may save him/her (the child)'.

Since ***a-we-||ni-ta*** (ZA 8.2-3) and ***da-i-pi-ta*** (ZA 8.5) on the same tablet show the same structure with the Hurrian suffix ***-tta*** 'me' of the personal pronoun 1st person singular, it appears most likely that Linear A ***-ma*** in ***Ta-i-nu-ma*** (ZA 8.3) indeed represents the suffix of the enclitic personal pronoun ***-mma*** 'you' of the 2nd person singular. In accordance with the analysis of ***da-i-pi-ta*** as {*da(i)=i=b=i=tta*} and the approximate translation 'He/She (the *numen*) made me a man', I propose to analyse the Linear A personal name ***ta-i-nu-ma*** as {*ta(i)=i=(e)n=u=mma*} and translate 'May he/she (the *numen*) make you a man (with *jussive* marker ***-i-*** + marker of 3rd person *jussive* ***-en-***)', cf. I. Wegner, *Einführung*, 103, Tabelle 9: *Die Suffixfolge beim positiven Jussiv*. Since I have already discussed the personal names ***Ta-i-nu-ma*** (ZA 8.3) and ***da-i-pi-ta*** (ZA 8.5) extensively, it is not necessary to repeat all arguments.

Linear A ***ka-i-ro*** (ZA 8.6) is the last entry on this tablet from Kato Zakro. It is probably also a personal name. Those who may have wondered, whether the name of the capital of Egypt is mentioned on this Linear A tablet, must be disappointed, because the sequence ***ka-i-ro*** (ZA 8.6) can be identified as ***Kaillu*** (wr. *Qa-i-el-lu, Ga-i-el-lu, Qa-i-il-lu, Ka-i-il-lu, Qa-i-lu*), a Hurrian personal name attested at Nuzi, cf. P.M. Purves, *NPN*, 222 s.v. ***kai***, *kai-*, *kail-* and ***-lu***, perhaps a shortened form of **kail-lumti* according to Purves. I.J. Gelb, *NPN*, 78, mentions s.v. ***Kail-lu***, that the division of the elements in this name is uncertain. As the Linear A form shows, ***-llu*** may phonologically be ***/-llo/*** in Hurrian.

Comparison with names such as ***Kai-tešup*** (wr. *Qa-i-te-šup, Ka-i-te-šup, Ka-i-te-eš-sup, Ga-i-te-šup, Qa-i-te-šup$_x$*(RUM)) and ***Kai-tilla*** (wr. *Qa-i-til-la, Ka-i-til-la*) at Nuzi (I.J. Gelb, *NPN*, 78; P.M. Purves, *NPN*, 222) seems to justify E. Laroche's qualification of ***kai-*** as a 'terme d'onomastique théophore' (*GLH*, 134).

According to Th. Richter (*BGH*, 179) ***ka-*** [PN] is a root in Nuzi personal names, registered as ***kai-*** and as 'terme d'onomastique théophore' by E. Laroche (*GLH*, 134).

W. Kornfeld (*Onomastica Aramaica aus Ägypten*, Österreichische Akademie der Wissenschaften, Philosophisch-Historisch Klasse, Sitzungsberichte 333, Wien 1978, 115) thinks that the name ***K'*** in the Egyptian Late period belongs to names like ***Ka-a-a*** at Nuzi.

The Hurrian personal name ***Kai̯a*** (wr. *Qa-a-a*, *Ka-a-a*, *Ga-a-a*) at Nuzi is registered by I.J. Gelb (*NPN*, 77) and P.M. Purves (*NPN*, 222). Is it merely accidental that the Linear A ligature ***ka+ja*** (HT 24b.2) at Hagia Triada may well be interpreted as either the Hurrian personal name ***Kai̯a*** at Nuzi or as a theonym, equivalent to the name of the Goddess ***Γαῖα*** 'Earth' ? The latter interpretation seems appropriate, in particular because the Hurrian Sungod ***^{d}Ši-me-ki, ^{d}Ši-mi-gi-(ni)*** is mentioned as the Linear A ligature ***si+me-ki*** on the same side of the tablet, both in the same combination with ideogram TAL(entum): ***si+me-ki*** TAL 1 JE and ***ka+ja*** TAL 1 (HT 24b), see *supra*.

Linear A ***ka-i-ro*** (ZA 8.6), Hurrian ***Kaillu***, may be analysed as the Old Hurrian personal name {*ka=ill=o/u*}, consisting of the verbal root ***ka-*** (meaning unknown) + the Old Hurrian *inchoative* or *ingressive* root-extension ****-ill-*** + the Old Hurrian marker of the *imperative* ***-o-***. According to I. Wegner (*Einführung*, 89) the Old Hurrian root-extension ****-ill-***, marks the *inchoative* or *ingressive* aspect, expressing the beginning of action (only in the Boğazköy bilingual), e.g. *šid=ar=ill=o=m* 'he started to curse'; *am=ar=ill=o=m* 'he began to act in an evil way towards'. If this analysis is correct, the root-extension ****-ill-*** occurred not only in the Hurrian-Hittite bilingual, but also at Nuzi and in Linear A.

Since a final consonant is not expressed in Linear A and B, Linear A ***ka-i-ro*** (ZA 8.6) can also be analysed as Old Hurrian {*ka=ill=o/u=m*}, consisting of the verbal root ***ka-*** + the Old Hurrian *inchoative* or *ingressive* root-extension ****-ill-*** + the Old Hurrian marker of the past tense ***-o-*** + the Old Hurrian marker of the subject of action 3rd person sing. ***-m***.

Incidentally, since the Nuzi personal names also provide the 'one-word' names ***Kaitta*** (wr. *Qa-i-it-ta, Qa-it-ta*), analysis {*kai=tta*} and ***Kainni*** (wr. *Qa-(i)-in-ni, Ga-in-ni*), analysis {*kai=nni*} instead of {*kai=nna*}, a division ***Kai=llu*** (with *optional allomorphic* personal pronoun 3rd person plural ***-llu*** instead of ***-lla, -lli, -lle***) seems conceivable as well.

Linear A tablet HT 31 is an interesting text, because it offers evidence concerning a transaction of a very large quantity of vessels, apparently provided with the names of characteristic types. Another possibility is that the names tell something about the contents of the vessels. The analysed structure of HT 31 is as follows:

HT 31.1-2.	*pi-ti-sa* (or: *9-ti-sa*) , *pu-ko* ,	VAS^{d1} = TRIPUS+*ri*	[ ]5
2.		VAS^{a1} +*qa-pa₃*	10
2.		VAS^{b1}+*su-pu*	10
3.		] VAS^{b2}+*ka-ro-pa₃*	10
3.	*sa-ja-ma*		30
4.			] 10
4-5.	*ki-de-ma-9-na*		4 [[ ]]
5.		VAS^{a}±[	400
5.		VAS^{a1}+*su-pa₃-ra*	300
6.		VAS^{a1}+*pa-ta-qe*	3000
7.	vacat		

Probably ***sa-ja-ma*** and ***ki-de-ma-9-na*** belong to the category of ***<u>pi</u>-ti-sa , pu-ko***. There is a parallel of a Linear B text from Pylos, PY Ta 641, that came to light a short time after Michael Ventris's decipherment of Linear B. It was regarded as a confirmation of the decipherment, because the words referring to the respective ideograms were exact descriptions of the design of these ideograms. For the decipherment of Linear B not merely the matches of ideograms of vessels with corresponding vessel names were decisive, but the accumulation of descriptions that exactly agreed with the designs of the ideograms ('with 4 handles' : ideogram with 4 handles; 'with 3 handles' : ideogram with 3 handles; 'without handles' : ideogram without handles), so that the possibility of accidental coincidence was virtually negligible. It may therefore be useful to quote this Pylos text (cf. M.Ventris - J. Chadwick, *Documents in Mycenaean Greek*, 336; see plate III (b), facing p. 111). I have added the Greek transliterations, translations and some comment.

PY Ta 641.1. ***ti-ri-po-de , a₃-ke-u , ke-re-si-jo , we-ke* *201^{VAS} 2** (N.B. *a₃* = *ai.*)
τρίποδε, Αἰγεὺς / αἰγεύς, Κρησιο-ϝεργής TRIPUS 2
Two tripods, 'Aigeus' / 'aigeus' type, of Cretan workmanship
***ti-ri-po , e-me , po-de , o-wo-we* *201^{VAS} 1**
τρίπως, ἑμεῖ ποδεῖ (> ἑνὶ ποδὶ) οἰϝώϝης TRIPUS 1
One tripod, with one foot/leg, with one ear/handle
\` *ke-re-a₂* ´ *201^{VAS}[
ti-ri-po , ke-re-si-jo , we-ke , a-pu , ke-ka-u-me-no[
τρίπως, Κρησιο-ϝεργής, ἄπυ κεκαυμένος σκέλε^{h}α TRIPUS[
(One) tripod, of Cretan workmanship, burnt off with regard to the legs.

PY Ta 641.2. ***qe-to* *203^{VAS} 3**
χ^{w}έθοι (> κ^{w}έθοι > πίθοι ?) *203^{VAS} 3 = 3 pithoi (?).
***di-pa , me-zo-e , qe-to-ro-we* *202^{VAS} 1**
*δίπας μέζο^{h}ε (< *μέγ-yos-e) k^{w}έτρ-ῶϝες* POCULUM 1
One bigger cup with four ears/handles
***di-pa-e , me-zo-e , ti-ri-o-we-e* *202^{VAS} 2**
δίπα^{h}ε μέζο^{h}ε τρι-ώϝε^{h}ε POCULUM 2
Two bigger cups with three ears/handles
***di-pa , me-wi-jo , qe-to-ro-we* *202^{VAS} 1[**
δίπας μείϝιος k^{w}έτρ-ῶϝες POCULUM 1[
One smaller cup with four ears/handles

PY Ta 641.3. ***di-pa , me-wi-jo , ti-ri-o-we* *202^{VAS} 1**
δίπας μείϝιος τρι-ῶϝες POCULUM 1
One smaller cup with three ears/handles
***di-pa , me-wi-jo , a-no-we* *202^{VAS} 1**
δίπας μείϝιος ἀν-ῶϝες POCULUM 1
One smaller cup without ears/handles.

According to *Grassmann's phonetic law*: $\chi^{w} > \kappa^{w}$ under influence of following aspirate (*θ*). If ***qe-to*** is equated with later ***πίθος***, it is an Aeolism, since only in Aeolic labiovelar > ***π***, whereas in Attic-Ionic labiovelar > ***τ*** (cf. ***k^{w}e > τε***). The *i/e* alternation points to a Pre-Hellenic loan-word, cf. the same phenomenon in following ***δίπας/δέπας***.

C.H. Gordon (*Evidence for the Minoan Language*, 26) does not hesitate to use the term 'virtual bilinguals', comparing Linear B tablet PY Ta 641 with Linear A HT 31, and claims that "out of the five legible pot names on that tablet (HT 31) four are Semitic: ***qa-pà*** = Hebrew כף ***kp*** or Akkadian ***kappu***, ***su-pu*** = Hebrew סף and Ugaritic ***sp***, ***ka-ro-pà*** = Akkadian ***karpu*** (cf. Ugaritic ***krpn***), and ***su-pà-ra*** = Hebrew ספל and Ugaritic ***spl***. Gordon transliterated sign ***pa***$_3$ as ***pà***, whereas this special sign is by scholars in Mycenaean studies regarded as ***βa*** or ***φa***. F.M.J. Waanders presumes a Linear A phonetic value of ***/bha/*** for this sign, comparable with a value ***/bhu/*** for Linear A sign ***pu***$_2$ and Linear B ***pu***$_2$ = ***φυ*** and possibly ***βυ***. It is remarkable that the scribe of HT 31 shows a preference for using the special sign ***pa***$_3$ instead of ***pa***. C.H. Gordon (*ibidem*, 30) translates ***su-pu*** (HT 31.2) as 'jar', ***qa-pà*** (HT 31.2) as 'pan, vessel', ***ka-ro-pà*** (HT 31.3) as 'vase' and ***su-pà-ra*** (HT 31.5) as 'pot'. He mentions in his note 50: "The second vowel of ***ka-ro-pà*** is dropped in Akkadian ***karpu*** like all short unaccented vowels between single consonants in Akkadian." This remark is apparently meant to prevent criticism that Akkadian ***karpu*** would not have been written as ***ka-ro-pa***$_3$ in Linear A, but as ****ka-pu***, because Linear A (as Linear B) does not express a liquid ***r*** preceding occlusive ***p*** in consonant clusters. However, Gordon does not explain how a probably younger Linear A text from Hagia Triada dating from ca. 1400 B.C. could still contain '***-o-***', while the probably older Akkadian term had already lost the vowel '***-u-***'. What Gordon actually did, is only comparing the Linear A 'vessel' names with possible Akkadian, Hebrew and Ugaritic pot names, forgetting that in the Linear B text of tablet PY Ta 641, which he compared, the plain vessel names were not the essential information given by the scribe, since such information was sufficiently provided by the ideograms. More important was specific information like 'Aigeus/aigeus' type, 'of Cretan workmanship', whether they were intact or damaged, how many handles the vessels had, whether they were 'bigger' or 'smaller'.

There is a more satisfactory Hurrian alternative for interpreting Linear A ***ka-ro-pa***$_3$ (HT 31.3). I think that Hurrian ***ka-ru-bi*** and the Hurro-Hittite derivation ***karuba=ḫi*** are more satisfactory alternatives for Gordon's interpretation of Linear A ***ka-ro-pa***$_3$ (HT 31.3).

E. Laroche (*GLH*, 137) mentions: ***ka-ru-bi*** 'grenier'. RS voc II 9: ***ka-ru-bi*** = sum. Ì.DUB = akkadien ***ispiku*** (*CAD* I 258 sq.). Gén. *ka-ri !-bi-ni-we* = **karubi-ni-we, ibidem* II 8. Dér. hitt. É ***karubaḫi*** 'entrepôt'; cf. Laroche, *RA 54*, 198. The attested genitive form is provided with the Hurrian 'definite article' suffix ***-ni*** and Hurrian genitive suffix ***-we***.

The Hurro-Hittite derivation ***karubaḫi*** represents in fact an exact equivalent to the Linear A sequence ***ka-ro-pa***$_3$, with the adjectival suffix ***-ḫi***.

E. Laroche (*GLH*, 18) explains how we should understand Hurrian glosses in Hittite texts: "À Boğazköy la situation est plus complexe. En effet, en Asie Mineure hittite, au cours du 13ème siècle, se produisirent des événements politiques dont la conséquence fut l'importation au cœur du Hatti d'une religion provinciale de langue hourrite, celle du Kizzuwatna (Cilicie). La littérature qui l'exprime est caractérisée par des termes techniques d'origine hourrite et syrienne; l'accord avec les sources ougaritiques le prouve clairement. Le scribe anatolien s'efforce de naturaliser ces termes. Il n'y parvient qu'à demi. Ce qui est arrivé avec la louvite, langue provinciale d'Anatolie, se produit, parallèlement, avec le hourrite: on voit naître une littérature mixte, de langue hittite, imprégnée d'une masse lexicale étrangère.

On la dénomme hourro-hittite; elle se présente sous un vêtement grammatical peu correct (morphologie flottante, syntaxe relâchée), et les dictionnaires du hittite l'incorporent au vocabulaire général, ainsi que les assyriologues le font du 'nouzien'. Par leur nombre et leur variété, les documents de Boğazköy sont devenus la source première et comme le moteur de la philologie hourrite. ...."

As regards Linear A ***ka-ro-pa₃*** (HT 31.3) we may observe whether the meaning of Hurrian ***ka-ru-bi*** 'granary', ***karubaḫi*** 'entrepôt' and in general 'place to store grain' is suitable to signify or specify a jar or pithos as presented by the ideogram to which it clearly belongs. The sequence is actually written on top of the ideogram of a pithos. A designation of 'pithoi to store grain' or 'storage-jars for grain' would be useful information specifying the items administered by the scribe. The *pithos* ideogram tells that *pithoi* are registered, but ***ka-ro-pa₃*** gives essential additional information, namely that 'storing grain' (not olive-oil or another liquid commodity) is the purpose of the pithoi. Obviously Minoan and Mycenaean palaces did not store their dry and liquid commodities just in the large magazines, but used huge pithoi, that could be sealed well, to store their valuable goods and to protect them from mice or rats, and, of course, to transport them in the easiest way.

Th. Richter (*BGH*, 188-189), s.v. ***kar-*** and ***kar-ul-umma*** *epēšu* [Nuzi], 'speichern, einlagern' ['to store'] (Fincke 1998a: 42f. [s.a. 1991: 202], Neu 2001: 93 [*kar=u/ol-*]). (É.)***karupaḫi*** [Lw / Hethitisch] 'entrepôt' (E. Laroche, *GLH*, 137) sub ***karubi***, Košak 1982: 42, Singer 1983a: 110[66]); 'Lager-, Vorratshaus' (Tischler 1980: 528f. [s.a. Siegelova 1986: 90, 600]); 'warehouse' (Bernabé 1988: 119); 'store, storage, granary', hu. Lw. (vgl. ***karubi*** 'store, granary', entspricht akk. ***išpiku***, sum. Ì.DUB) (Puhvel 1997: 115, ähnlich Weeks 1985: 118). Th. Richter (*BGH*, 189), s.v. ***karuwe*** [Al. IV], Hurrian, 'a metal object, probably a weapon' (*CAD* K [1971] 240 [FOW]); Lw aus akk. ***karû*** 'grain heap, granary', das letztlich von sum. GURU₇ herstammt (Hoffner 1974: 37 [*karubi*]; 'grenier', entspricht sum. Ì.DUB, akk. ***išpiku*** (Laroche 1980a: 137 [*karubi*]); d.i. ***kar-u-we***, entspricht sum. Ì.DUB 'Vorratsspeicher, -krug' (Fincke 1998a: 42[+4]); 'Getreidehaufen, Getreidespeicher', zu akk. *karû* « sum. GURU₇, enthält *-o/ub/vi* (Akdoğan / Wilhelm 2003: 220[13]). - Etym.: Nach Haas 1982b: 604 ist urart. ***karu-*** 'besiegen, überwältigen' anzuschliessen; s.a. Diakonoff/Starostin 1986: 48. - Sonstiges: Sanmartin 1977: 374[6] ('eine Art Waffe', evtl. 'ein Speer' [im Anschluss an *CAD* K]).

It seems preferable to divide the *lemmata* in Th. Richter, *BGH*, 188-189, s.v. ***kar-, kari***, ***karu***, (É.)***karupaḫi***, ***karubi***, ***karuwe***, into two homonymic, but etymologically different roots, e.g. ***kar-*** I, to which ***kari*** [Boğ.] and ***karu*** [Al. IV; Ug.] 'a metal object, probably a weapon, spear (?)' belong, etymologically related to Urartian ***karu-*** 'conquer, overpower'; and ***kar-*** II, to which (É.)***karupaḫi*** and ***karubi*** 'granary, storage-jar, pithos' can be attributed, etymologicaly related to Hurrian ***kar-ul-umma*** *epēšu* [Nuzi], 'speichern, einlagern' (Fincke 1998a: 42f. [s.a. 1991: 202], Neu 2001: 93 [*kar-u/ol-*]). The same distinction can be made between Linear A ***ka-ru*** (HT 97a.1) on the one hand (see *supra*), as a Hurrian term for 'metal weapon, spear (?)' combined with the ideograms for VIR PARMATUS and AES (Hurrian ***kar-*** I); and on the other Linear A ***ka-ro-pa₃*** (HT 31.3) 'jar / pithos for storing grain', written on top of the ideogram of a pithos (Hurrian ***kar-*** II).

Keeping in mind that the Linear B scribe of text PY Ta 641 mentioned that three tripods were ***Κρησιο-ϝεργής*** 'of Cretan workmanship', in other words 'made in Crete', it is clear that the provenance of the product, in this case Crete, was also worth mentioning, cf. the discussion on the bronze cauldron (MY Zf 2) from Grave Circle A at Mycenae, Shaft Grave IV, probably imported from Crete, possibly with the Linear A inscription ***ai***, perhaps indicating ***ai-ke-u*** 'Aigeus-type' or aigeus-type.

Th.G. Palaima (*Briciaka*, 190-191): "In the first fascicle of *Kadmos I (1962)*... Ernst Grumach presented a general photograph (figure 1a) of a bronze cauldron with vertical raised handles, attached by rivets, coming from Grave Circle A at Mycenae, Shaft Grave IV, and published by Karo as no. 576. This cauldron stands 19.5 cm. high and has a diameter of 35-37 cm. In the later cleaning of the bronze cauldron was discovered a Linear sign inscribed on the attachment flange which secures one of its handles to the body of the vessel. Grumach drew attention to the sign (figure 1b). He compared the vessel itself to Linear A ideographic signs *Lc 43* and *45*, which according to Pugliese Carratelli's classification of Linear A signs, represented respectively a bronze 'lebete' (with phonetic sign *L 52* surjoined), which we here refer to as a cauldron, and a 'lebete tripodato' (with phonetic sign *L 81* surjoined), or what we call simply a tripod. These ideographic images help to confirm what is known from the archaeological record: neopalatial Minoan Crete manufactured and exported large bronze vessels." On page 195 he argues for reading *ai*: "The virtue of the identification of the Shaft Grave cauldron sign as a sign corresponding to Linear B ***ai*** (whether the sign belongs to Linear A or Linear B) is that it is a sign that *could* have existed in a script designed to represent the Minoan language(s)."

His proposal of the hypothesis (p. 197-199) that ***ai*** on MY Zf 1 might be an akrophonic abbreviation of ***ai-ke-u*** 'Aigeus' type, mentioned in the Ta series of Linear B tablets from Pylos, is quite attractive, especially since the term is at Pylos a specification of valuable tripods of Cretan workmanship as, for instance, PY Ta 641.1 clearly shows:

ti-ri-po-de , ai-ke-u , ke-re-si-jo , we-ke *201^{VAS} 2
τρίποδε, Αἰγεὺς / αἰγεὺς, Κρησιο-ϝεργής TRIPUS 2
Two tripods, 'Aigeus' / 'aigeus' type, of Cretan workmanship.
(Linear B sign *ai* was originally identified as a_3.)

Other possibilities: If the inscription is Hurrian and written with Minoan Linear A and if it is complete, ***ai*** could be *temporal* and *conditional* 'when' or 'if', cf. Th. Richter, *BGH*, 1, s.v. ***ai/aj*** I [Boğ.; Mitt.].

If the inscription is not complete, it could e.g. be completed to ***ai=man*** 'and if', which introduces a series of hepatoscopic observations at Emar, cf. Th. Richter, *BGH*, 1, s.v. ***ai=man*** [Emar].

Or it could perhaps be an abbreviation of ***aiwa***, the Hurrian designation for 'eine Kornart' ['a sort of corn / grain'], cf. *AHw*, Lfg. 1, 1959, 26 [hurritisches Fremdwort]; 'a foodstuff prepared from emmer', cf. *CAD* A/I, 1964, 218 [hurritisches Wort / Hurrian word]; 'ein Nahrungsmittel' ['foodstuff'], cf. G.G.W. Müller, *Londoner Nuzi-Texte*, SANTAG. Arbeiten und Untersuchungen zur Keilschriftkunde 4, Wiesbaden 1998, 92, ***/aiwe/***); 'a cereal foodstuff' CDA^2, 2000, 9 [hurritisches Lehnwort / Hurrian loan-word]); see also *AHw*, Lfg. 16, 1981, 1542; cf. Th. Richter, *BGH*, 1, s.v. ***aiwa*** [Nuzi].

C.H. Gordon's interpretation of Linear A ***qa-pa₃*** (HT 31.2) as Semitic ***qa-pà*** = Hebrew כף ***kp*** or Akkadian ***kappu*** 'pan, vessel' (*Evidence*, 26) is not very likely, because the information concerning vessels was already provided by the ideogram of a vessel on the tablet, even showing the form of the vessel. However, a decisive argument against identification of Linear A ***qa-pa₃*** (HT 31.2) with Semitic ***qa-pà*** = Hebrew כף ***kp*** or Akkadian ***kappu*** is that the Linear A ***q-*** signs cannot be equated with the cuneiform emphatics ***q-*** or the normal ***k-*** signs, but probably represented the ***ḫ-*** signs for the voiced velar fricatives. The Linear A transliteration with ***q-*** signs is inherited from the successful decipherment of Linear B. The ***q-*** signs in Linear B are used for the labio-velar series.

Unfortunately this has in the case of the ***q-*** signs caused confusion for Linear A, because one is used to attribute the same phonetic values to the Linear A signs showing graphic identity with their Linear B counterparts. In most cases this is justifiable, but it is not in case of the Linear B labio-velar series, since the Minoan-Hurrian language written with Linear A did not have labio-velar sounds. The Linear B scribes needed a special series of signs to express the Indo-European and Mycenaean Greek labio-velar sounds and used Linear A signs for the ***ḫ-*** sounds for this purpose. Normally the voiced velar fricatives are written with ***-ḫ-*** in medial position with single writing in syllabic cuneiform and with ***ġ*** in the cuneiform alphabet of Ugarit, whereas the voiceless velar fricatives are written with ***-ḫḫ-*** in medial position with double writing in syllabic cuneiform and with ***ḫ*** in the alphabetic cuneiform of Ugarit. This can be observed in the ethnic ***Ḫalbaḫe*** 'Man of Aleppo' in syllabic and ***Ḫlbġ*** in alphabetic cuneiform. Likewise I have identified regular Linear A ***ka-pa*** with ***Ḫalba*** 'Aleppo' and Linear A ***ka-pa-qe*** (HT 6a.4-5; possibly HT 140.3) with ***Ḫalbaḫe*** / ***Ḫlbġ***. The Linear B ***k-*** series represents *κ-*, *γ-*, *χ-*. The voiceless Greek aspirate ***χ*** came probably close to the cuneiform voiceless ***ḫ-*** in initial position and ***-ḫḫ-*** in medial position. ***Ḫalbaḫe / Ḫlbġ*** could be written with Linear A as ***ka-pa-qe***.

Compare also ***Aḫḫiyawa*** in the Hittite syllabic cuneiform texts vs. Mycenaean Linear B ***a-ka-wi-ja-de*** (KN C 914), accusative of ***Ἀχαιϝίᾱ*** + the directive suffix ***-δε***, 'region of the Achaeans'. The Mycenaean ***k-*** sign is rendered into ***-ḫḫ-*** in ***Aḫḫiyawa*** in the Hittite texts. ***Ἀχαιϝίᾱ*** is derived from the ethnic ***Ἀχαιϝός*** that appears to be represented by Linear B ***a-ka-wo*** (KN X 738), which may be an ethnic used as a personal name (***Ἀχαιός*** is later attested as a personal name, cf. F. Bechtel, *Die historischen Personennamen des Griechischen*, 537). C.J. Ruijgh (*EGM*, § 154, n. 420) has explained that it appears more likely that ***Ἀχαιϝίᾱ*** in the Knossos Linear B text reflects a Cretan town than the entire land of the Achaeans, because ***Ἀχαίᾱ*** (< * ***Ἀχαιΐᾱ***, cf. Att. ***Ἀχᾱΐᾱ***) is attested as a name of a town in Crete (*Scholion* to Apollonius Rhodius 4, 175).

The Linear A *hapax* ***qa-pa₃*** (HT 31.2) is probably an exceptional writing variant of Linear A ***ka-pa***, which occurs frequently in Linear A, but only at Hagia Triada (with in this case ***qa*** representing a voiced velar fricative also in initial position and with the special sign ***pa₃ = ba / pha < bha***). The initial voiced dentals [***d-***] in Linear A show that Minoan-Hurrian did have voiced initial occlusives. The orthography of ***qa-pa₃*** (HT 31.2) shows that this may also be the case with (some) velar fricatives.

If both ***ka-pa*** and ***qa-pa₃*** designate ***Ḫalba***, ***ka-pa*** is the regular form and ***qa-pa₃*** the exception with an initial voiced allophone. ***Ḫalba*** is the Hurrian name of Aleppo in Syria, alphabetic cuneiform ***Ḫlb***, *Ḫalab* in Semitic (cf. E. Laroche, *GLH*, 90, s.v. *Ḫalba* Alep).

Linear A ***ka-pa*** = ***Ḫalba*** could theoretically refer to the famous Syrian city, capital of the primarily Hurrian kingdom of Yamḫad, but more likely, it may designate the ancient place-name of Hagia Triada itself.

At any rate Linear A ***qa-pa₃*** (HT 31.2) agrees better with the consonants and vocalism of the Linear A toponym than Akkadian *kappu*. If the identification of ***qa-pa₃*** is correct, it may well refer to the provenance of the 10 vessels (indicated by the ideogram VAS[al] and the number 10) as being manufactured at ***Ḫalba***, modern Hagia Triada ('Holy Trinity') itself, or it could refer to the special type for which the palace was famous.

Some arguments for identification of Linear A ***ka-pa*** as a toponym:

A. ***ka-pa*** is first entry of HT 6a.1, HT 94a.1, HT 102.1, HT 105.1, and possibly in (damaged) HT 45a.1. It also occurs in HT 8b.4 and HT 140.5.

B. ***ka-pa*** is one of the most frequent sequences in Linear A, but significantly it only occurs in the Linear A tablets of Hagia Triada.

C. ***ka-pa*** GRA[(KN E 71) also occurs in the Linear B texts from Knossos and has been identified as a toponym because of occurrence of the Linear B ethnic ***ka-pa-jo / po*** VIR 3 (KN [X] 5752 + B 7039), with the Greek ethnic suffix ***-yos***.

D. Many Linear B tablets from Knossos start with the sequence ***ko-no-so*** and many Linear B tablets from Pylos (Greek mainland) begin with ***pu-l/ro***, indicating the actual place, where the palace-archives were stationed and traffic of people and goods was registered.

E. It has been observed in Linear B that toponyms are often followed by the grain ideogram GRA, e.g. ***ka-pa*** GRA[(KN E 71), and sometimes by ideograms of other commodities as well. This pattern is confirmed in Linear A: e.g. ***ka-pa sa-ra₂*** GRA 976 (HT 102.1-2).

F. If my identification of ***ka-pa-qe*** (HT 6a. 4-5) on the same tablet that starts with ***ka-pa*** (HT 6a.1), and possibly again on HT 140.3, is correct and if it should be read as the Hurrian ethnic name ***Ḫalbaḫe*** or as a personal name derived from the ethnic, it would be the Linear A equivalent to Linear B ***ka-pa-jo***. ***ka-pa-qe*** may be equated with the Hurrian ethnic ***Ḫalbaḫe*** in the main cuneiform syllabary and with ***ḫlbġ*** in the cuneiform alphabet from Ugarit, 'Man from Ḫalba' with Hurrian ethnic suffix ***-ḫi/-ḫe***, cf. E. Laroche, *GLH*, 22. Alphabetic cuneiform ***ġ*** in ***ḫlbġ*** shows that the syllabic intervocalic ***-ḫ-*** (single writing) in ***Ḫalbaḫe*** represents a voiced velar fricative or spirant in medial position (Linear A ***-qe*** according to Linear B orthography) that must be distinguished from the voiceless velar fricative ***ḫ-*** in initial position in both syllabic and alphabetic cuneiform.

G. If my join of]***ka-ne*** (AK 3a.1) with ***a***] (AK 1b.1) on a tiny fragment from Arkhanes is correct (*GORILA 3* mentions that AK 1, AK 2 and AK 3 were inscribed by the same *scribe 1*), the resulting sequence ***a***]***-ka-ne*** (AK 3a.1 + AK 1b.1) GRA [represents exactly the toponym *Arkhane(s)*, where the Villa of Arkhanes was excavated by Yannis and Evi Sakellerakis and where the Linear A Arkhanes-tablets were found. This corroborates the evidence that the habit of mentioning the place where the tablets were written (preferably at the beginning of a tablet) was probably inherited by the Linear B scribes from their Linear A colleagues. According to Linear A and B orthographic conventions ***-r-*** preceding an occlusive was not expressed in consonant clusters. An eventual final consonant was not expressed either in the scripts of Linear A and B. However, in my view Linear A ***a***]***-ka-ne*** did not yet have a final ***-s*** like the modern Greek toponym Arkhanes, because it probably represents Hurrian ***Ar=ḫane/i*** meaning '(Please) give a child (oh *numen*) !'.

Linear A ***pa-ta-qe*** (HT 31.6) is written on top of ideogram VAS^{a1}, followed by the high number 3000. Since according to the orthographic conventions of Linear A and B ***s-*** preceding ***-p-***, and ***-r-*** preceding ***-t-*** (in fact non-occlusives preceding occlusives) were not expressed in consonant clusters, Linear A ***pa-ta-qe*** (HT 31.6) can represent ***Spartaḫe*** and be analysed as {*Sparta=ḫe*} 'Spartan', containing the Hurrian adjectival and ethnic suffix ***-ḫe/-ḫi***. The ethnic ***pa-ta-qe*** is derived from the toponym ****pa-ta*** 'Sparta'. With regard to the orthography one may compare Linear B ***pe-mo = σπέρμο*** (PY Ep 301,1 *et alibi*) and ***pe-ma = σπέρμα*** (PY Er 312,2 *e.a.*) 'seed, in particular of grain'.

A useful parallel for usage of the ethnic suffix ***-ḫe / -ḫi*** is Linear A ***ka-pa-qe*** (HT 6a.4-5) = Hurrian ***Ḫalbaḫe***, alphabetic cuneiform ***Ḫlbġ***, 'man of *Ḫalba*', just discussed.

Linear A ***pa-ta-ne*** (HT 94b.1; HT 122a.6) may well be considered a parallel of Linear A ***pa-ta-qe*** (HT 31.6), because both forms may be regarded as ethnics. Since ***pa-ta-ne*** (HT 94b.1) and ***pa-ta-ne*** (HT 122a.6) occur in lists of personal names on both Linear A tablets, they are in that context probably ethnics used as personal names.

The form ***pa-ta-ne*** (HT 94b.1; HT 122a.6) 'the Spartan one' contains the suffix of the 'so-called' definite article, ***-ne/-ni*** or the individualizing suffix, that can occasionally have an ethnic or relational function. Attestation of these distinctive Hurrian ethnics ***pa-ta-qe*** and ***pa-ta-ne*** in Linear A makes derivation from a substrate toponym ****pa-ta***, probably 'Sparta', very likely, cf. also Linear A ***pa-ta-da***|[(HT? 170b.3) and ***pa-ta-da*** (HT Zb 160) from Hagia Triada. Linear A ***pa-ta-da*** can be interpreted as either 'to Sparta', with the Hurrian directive suffix ***-da***, or 'from Sparta', with the ablative suffix ***-dan***.

I have already argued that the sequence ***pa-ta-da*** |] 1 (HT(?) 170b.3-4) may well refer to a person's provenance, because it occurs in a list of personal names, which makes translation as '(The one) from Sparta' possible (with the ablative suffix ***-dan***). As a good parallel I have mentioned]***ku-du-we*** CAP^{m} 1 (HT(?) 170a.2) on the other side of the tablet, that can be interpreted as the Hurrian *genitive* in ***-we/-wi*** of Linear A ***ku-da*** 1 (HT 122a.8), that may well be a toponym, since the ethnic ***ku-do-ni*** (HT 13.4; HT 85a.4) and possibly ***ku-do-ni***[(HT 101.4) 'the one of Kuda', 'man/woman of Kuda', derived from *Kuda*, is attested as well. If the reading of]***ku-du-we*** is correct, a change of ***-a-*** > ***-u-*** from ****ku-da-we*** > ***ku-du-we*** can be explained, because ***u*** is cognate with ***w***. Since]***ku-du-we*** refers to a person, the meaning is probably 'The one of *Kuda*'. Such formations with genitive forms are also attested in Hurrian personal names written with cuneiform, e.g. ***^{f}Azzue*** (wr. *^{f}Az-zu-e, ^{f}A-zu-e*), name of 11 ladies from Mari and of one from Qaṭṭarā, analysis {*azz(e)/azz(o/u)=ve*}, translation 'Das (Mädchen) der Frau' ['The one (girl) of the woman'] (cf. Th. Richter, *VHN*, 81-82), cf. ***^{f}Azue*** (wr. *^{f}A-zu-(ú-)e*) from Nuzi (cf. I.J. Gelb, *NPN*, 41; *AAN* I 39, *SANTAG* 4, 257), ***^{f}Azue*** (wr. *^{f}A-zu-e*) from Cappadocia, ICK I 16 A 4, 7, B 3 (cf. E. Laroche, *NH*, 50, n° 219), etc.

P. Chantraine (*Dictionnaire étymologique de la langue grecque IV-1*, Paris 1977, 1033) mentions s.v. ***Σπάρτη*** that the etymology is obscure. One has attempted to compare *σπείρω*, *σπάρτη* and (more plausibly) the name of a plant *σπάρτος*. He concludes (with A. Heubeck) that a substrate term is most likely: "Comme pour beaucoup de toponymes, étymologie obscure. On a tenté de rapprocher le mot de *σπείρω*, de *σπάρτη*, ou, ce qui serait plus plausible, du nom de plante *σπάρτος*, cf. Bölte, *RE* II 3, 1272; Heubeck, *Beiträge zur Namenforschung 1,1949-1950*, 280, pose plutôt un terme de substrat."

Compare the parallel usage of the suffixes ***-ne/-ni*** and ***-ḫe/-ḫi*** in the Hurrian ethnics ***Masrianne*** 'Egyptian' **:** ***Ḫurroḫe*** 'Hurrian'. Compare for the usage of the Hurrian ethnic suffix ***-ḫe/-ḫi*** in combination with a non-Hurrian name e.g. the ethnic ***Aggadaḫi*** (wr. *uruA-ag-ga-da-a-ḫi*) 'Akkadian' KUB XLV 41 III 3; and with the *directive* suffix ***-da***, KUR *Ag-ga-tu-ḫé-da* 'to the land of Akkad' KUB VII 31 Ro 7, cf. E. Laroche, *GLH*, 40.

The Hurrian adjectival suffix ***-ḫe/-ḫi*** occurs in ***paš-ši-ḫi*** 'pertaining to sending, shipment', *pa-aš-ši-ḫi-iw-wə* 'my shipment(s)' Mit. III 54, 57, *e-ew-ri-iš-ši-ḫi-* 'pertaining to lordship' (KUB XXVII 42 rev. 5-6 ff.), analysis {*ewri=šši=ḫi-*}, *šar-ra-aš-ši-ḫi-* 'pertaining to kingship' *ibidem* 9, 15 ff. (cf. E.A. Speiser, *IH*, 45-50, § 56-61.) and in Linear A in ***ku-mi-na|-qe*** (HT Wc 2014a-b) and ***]ku-mi-na-qe***[(HT 54a.2), cf. *supra*.

If one accepts the possibility of identification of Linear A ****pa-ta-*** with 'Sparta', one could think of trade of Hagia Triada with Lakonia and with Sparta in particular, which was a Mycenaean centre after all. The designation ***pa-ta-qe*** (HT 31.6) 'Spartan' could specify either the 3000 vessels indicated by the ideogram or the contents of the vessels. In view of such trade it may be significant that on the island of Kythera across the Lakonian coast a small Linear A inscription <u>GRA</u> E (KY Zg 1) dating from Middle-Minoan IIIb has been found. In the Peak Sanctuary of Hagios Georgios on Kythera a Linear A inscription ***da-ma-te*** (KY Za 2) was found on a serpentine ladle. Moreover, on a schist plaque from Hagios Stephanos, a bronze age settlement in South-Lakonia, trench Λ 1 (1973), a Linear A inscription ***a-ma*** (HS Zg 1.2) was found in a not-stratified surface deposit (LH I-IIa and LH IIIa-b). The object possibly belongs to the first of these periods.

Although it cannot be ruled out that there was a place called 'Sparta' in Crete as well, the high number of 3000 vessels points to an important commercial transaction, probably with a place called Sparta on the Peloponnese. We do not know whether this was Hagios Stephanos or possibly the Menelaion (Μενελάειον). Mansion 1 is the original building of the Menelaion facing south assembling three parallel units, of which the central unit is considered a megaron. It was according to H.W. Catling built about 1450 BC and soon destroyed possibly by an earthquake. Hagios Stephanos seems to be the best candidate, but other settlements may be involved as well. Anyway we may conclude that all evidence shows that interpretation of Linear A ***pa-ta-qe*** as {*Sparta=ḫe*} 'Spartan' is to be preferred.

According to C.H. Gordon (*Evidence*, 26, 30) Linear A ***su-pu*** (HT 31.2) equals Hebrew סף and Ugaritic ***sp*** 'jar', and ***su-pa₃-ra*** (HT 31.5) Hebrew ספל and Ugaritic ***spl*** 'pot'. Unfortunately only the consonants of the Hebrew and Ugaritic words are known, so that it cannot be confirmed whether the vowels approach the Linear A vowels or not.

According to Ch.-F. Jean and J. Hoftijzer, *Dictionnaire des inscriptions sémitiques de l'ouest*, Leiden 1965, 315, ***šp*** (I), sing. abs. in Aramaic, probably means 'partie d'un bateau' and ***šp*** (II), sing. abs. in Aramaic, probably means 'mesure de longueur'. They add that ***šp*** (I) and ***šp*** (II) are probably not identical.

Unfortunately our knowledge of the Hurrian vocabulary is still far from complete. Of some attested words or forms we only have a vague idea in what sphere they were used. Often the exact meaning remains unknown or uncertain. E. Laroche gives many examples of such words and forms in his *Glossaire de la langue hourrite*. In the discussion on tablet HT 31 in the 2016 edition I have compared Linear A ***su-pu*** with several Hurrian forms mentioned, s.v. ***šubuš-***, at Boğazköy and Mari by E. Laroche (*GLH*, 239).

Its consonants and vowels correspond exactly with Linear A ***su-pu***, but we have no idea whether its meaning corresponds as well. Th. Richter (*BGH*, 415) mentions, s.v. ***sub-*** I [Boğ.; Mitt.?], some of these forms such as *sub-ušt-* [Boğ.; Mari] without translation.

Th. Richter (*BGH*, 421) mentions, s.v. ***surw-*** and *surw-ušt-* [Mitt.], 'Schlechtes tun' and 'Böses tun'; and, s.v. ***subi-*** VI [Boğ.;Ug.], 'séparé' ['separated'], corresponding with Ugaritic *ḫarimu* (Laroche, *GLH*, 238); corresponding with Sumerian [ḪUL$^?$], [GUL$^?$], Akkadian *šulputu* 'desecrate(d)', Ugaritic *ġarimu* (Huehnergard 1987a, 89f., 126, Fleming 2000, 181); 'méchant, mauvais' ['naughty, bad'] corresponding with Sumerian ḪUL and Akkadian *lemnu* (André-Salvini/Salvini 1998, 17; 2000, 329); 'evil' (Campbell 2008, 287); s.v. ***surwe-*** I [Mitt.; PN] 'böse, schlecht' ['evil, bad'], 'der Böse' ['the evil one']. Cf. also Th. Richter, *VHN*, 520-521, s.v. ***sub-*** {*so/ub-*}, ***surw-*** {*so/urv-*}. However, these forms do not provide a satisfactory meaning with regard to the vase, VASb^1, on top of which Linear A ***su-pu*** (HT 31.2) is written.

Th. Richter (*BGH*, 421) mentions, s.v. ***šurbi*** II [Boğ.], that E. Laroche (*GLH*, 245), s.v. *šu-ú-úr-pé-e-ni-eš* (Ibo T II 39 Vo 35), does not provide a translation. However, V. Haas (*Materia magica et medica Hethitica. Ein Beitrag zu Heilkunde im alten Orient*, Berlin – New York 2003, 101^{+465}) offers the translation 'eine kathartische Substanz'. Since the liquid ***-r-*** preceding an occlusive is according to the orthographic conventions of Linear A and B not expressed in consonant clusters, ***šurbi*** II [Boğ.], 'a cathartic substance' offers the most likely meaning for Linear A ***su-pu*** (HT 31.2) on top of VASb^1. Linear A ***su-pu*** (HT 31.2) is then Hurrian ***šurbu*** {*šurb(i)=u*}, with Akkadianizing nominative in ***-u***, and may refer to the contents of the vase, emphasizing that the contents are precious.

This means that Linear A ***su-pu*** on top of VASb^1 (HT 31.2) can probably not be identified with ***su-pu$_2$*** (HT 8b.1; HT 63.1), cf. Linear A ***su-pu$_2$*** (HT 8b.1; HT 63.1) *supra*.

Linear A ***su-pa$_3$-ra*** (HT 31.5) was interpreted by C.H. Gordon (*Evidence*, 26, 30) as Hebrew ספל and Ugaritic ***spl*** 'pot'. In my view the meaning 'pot' does not really add to the information that the scribe already provided by incising the ideogram of a vessel of the type VAS^{a1} under the sequence ***su-pa$_3$-ra***. Even stranger is the fact that the following sequence ***pa-ta-qe*** (HT 31.6) is written on top of an identical VAS^{a1}-ideogram. This shows that the general meaning 'pot' is unlikely for ***su-pa$_3$-ra***, because ***su-pa$_3$-ra*** and ***pa-ta-qe*** obviously offer specific meanings referring to type, function, provenance or contents of the identical vessels. I tend to interpret ***su-pa$_3$-ra*** (HT 31.5) in line with the approach of ***qa-pa$_3$*** (HT 31.2) = ***Ḫalba*** and ***pa-ta-qe*** (HT 31.6), ***Spartaḫe***, analysed as {*Sparta=ḫe*} 'Spartan' as a name that might designate the provenance of the vessels in question or of the contents of those vessels or in line with function or type of the vessel as in the case of ***ka-ro-pa$_3$*** (HT 31.3), cf. Hurrian ***ka-ru-bi*** 'granary', ***karubaḫi*** 'entrepôt' and in general 'place / pithos to store grain'. If interpretation of ***su-pa$_3$-ra*** as ***Subara*** is correct, one might think of either pots of a 'Subarian' type (from *Subaru*) or agrarian commodities designated as 'Subarian', cf. *Giš-ma Su-bir$_4^{KI}$* = *Su-bur-ri-tu* (LTBA I 62: 15; cf. Sumerian only in *Syria XII* [1931] Pl. XLVI i 26), 'Subarian fig'; *giš-šennur-kur-ra* = *Su-bur-r*[*i-tu*] (*Recueil de travaux relatifs à la philologie et à l'archéologie ég. et assyr. XXXVI* [1914] 188: 10), 'Subarian plum (or medlar ?)'; [*nu-úr-ma Su-bir$_4^{KI}$*] = *Su-bur-r*[*i-tu*] (LTBA I 58 v 1), 'Subarian pomegranate', cf. I.J. Gelb, *Hurrians and Subarians*, 29, n. 43.

There are, of course, many ways to give names to various types of earthenware and now also porcelain. One of them is 'china' for the fine porcelain coming from China and we have the 'delft' or 'delftware' for the Dutch imitation of blue 'china', that is produced in the city of Delft (Holland) since the 17th century. The name of a very common Roman pottery is red 'terra sigillata', but the finest and oldest variant is called *Aretine* ware, because it was first produced at Arretium, later Arezzo (Etruria) from ca. 25 B.C..

However, more interpretations of Linear A ***su-pa$_3$-ra*** (HT 31.5) seem possible. In view of the common ***b/w*** alternation in Hurrian words and names, it is conceivable that ***su-pa$_3$-ra*** (HT 31.5), ***/su-b^{h}a-ra/*** may be an orthographic, c.q. phonetic, variant of ***šuwala*** and the theonym ^{D}***Šuwala***. The alternation is, however, not yet attested in the term ***šuwala*** and in the theonym ^{D}***Šuwala***.

Th. Richter (*BGH*, 416) mentions, s.v. ***šuwali*** [Boğ.;GN], that it may refer to *šu-u-wa-la-aš* 'vin' ['wine'] (R. Lebrun, *Samuha. Foyer religieux de l'empire Hittite* (Publications de l'Institut Orientaliste de Louvain 11), Louvain-la-Neuve 1976, 235; M.-Cl. Trémouille, 2000, 167^{+213}); without translation (E. Laroche, *GLH*, 245 [***šuwala***], I. Wegner, 2004, 62); without translation, not 'wine' (A. Kammenhuber, 1986, 106, 123); 'wine(?)' (D.R.M. Campbell, *Mood and modality in Hurrian*, Diss. Univ. of Chicago 2007, 202^{+186}).

E. Laroche, *GLH*, 245-246, s.v. ***šuwala***: "1. ^{D}***Šuwala***; v. sous *Nabarbi*. 2. *šu-u-wa-a-la*, KBo XXIII 12 + *passim*; XIX 136 I 4; KUB XXXII 47+74 III 8-9, etc.; XLV 15, 2; 5 III 13; XLVII 45, 15. *šu-u-wa-a-la-aš*, KBo XXIII 34 I 19. Erg ? *šu-u-wa-le-e-eš*, KUB XII 12 V 7, 10 sq.; XLV 59 Vo 5, 8 (kiz.). Laroche, *RHA XXVIII*, 71, a proposé 'vin', en se fondant sur les contextes hittites." Here we see, that E. Laroche states that he had already proposed the meaning 'wine', based on Hittite contexts in *RHA XXVIII (1970)*, 71.

If an equation of ***/su-b^{h}a-ra/*** with ***šuwala*** is correct and if the meaning is indeed 'wine', Linear A ***su-pa$_3$-ra*** may refer to the contents and consequently also the function of the vessels: to contain or store wine. Semantically it may then be comparable with ***ka-ro-pa$_3$*** (HT 31.3), Hurrian ***ka-ru-bi*** 'granary', ***karubaḫi*** 'entrepôt' and in general 'place to store grain' or 'big jar/pithos to store grain'. This analysis of ***su-pa$_3$-ra*** is also an attractive proposition depending on an alleged ***b/w*** alternation that needs to be verified for this term.

I do not think that writing of the name of the goddess ^{D}***Šuwala*** makes sense in the context of registrations of pots.

Th. Richter (*BGH*, 416) also mentions (GIŠ.)***zup(p)ari*** I, *zupḫuri*, *zupuḫri* [Boğ.], *zuppari* ntr. [loan-word into Hittite ?] 'eine Zedernart' ['a sort of cedar'] (V. Haas, 2003a, 281-282), possibly connected with Akkadian *dipāru* and Hittite (GIŠ.)*zup(p)ari*- 'Fackel' ['torch']. According to D.M. Weeks (Hittite Vocabulary: An Anatolian appendix to Buck's 'Dictionary of selected synonyms in the principlal Indo-European languages', Diss. Univ. of California, Los Angeles 1985, 115) a previously suspected Indo-European etymology (Sanskrit *kṣúbhyati*) is unlikely. According to Haas/Wilhelm (1974b, 89) the cultural word for 'torch', attested in Hittite (GIŠ.)*zuppari* ntr. and Akkadian *dipāru* (with neither Akkadian nor Sumerian etymology) can go back to Hurrian ***zupari***, frequently attested as *zu-u-pa-ra* and *zu-u/ú-pa-a-ri* in ChS I/1-Texts. Other meanings such as 'Kiefernholz (?)' ['fir-wood, pine-wood (?)'] are mentioned. Although comparison of Linear A ***su-pa$_3$-ra*** with Hurrian *zu-u-pa-ra* seems orthographically possible, the context of the list of pottery excludes meanings such as 'cedar-wood' or 'fir-/pine-wood'.

E. Laroche (*GLH*, 246) also mentions s.v. ***šuwari***: *šu-ú-wa-ri*, Mari 2, 13, 17.
Plur. gén. dét. *šu-wa-ra-še-na*, KUB XXVII 1 III 1; cf. 3 IV 10.
šu-wa-ar-ri-iš-ša-an, KUB XXVII 29 IV 12 = KBo XIX 139 III 19.
šu-bar-ša-e, KUB XXXII 19 + IV 37.

P.M. Purves (*NPN*, 260) also mentions the first three sequences s.v. ***šuwar***. Hurrian. He also mentions *šu-ú-wa-ru-ta-nam*, KUB XXVII 38 iii 13. If E. Laroche has placed *šu-bar-ša-e* correctly in his *lemma*, a ***b/w*** alternation can be confirmed at least for ***šuwari***.

Th. Richter (*BGH*, 416) also mentions ***šuwari*** II [Boğ.; Mari], which may make sense in the context, if the meaning 'ein pflanzliches Produkt zum Verspritzen von geweihten Flüssigkeiten im Kult' ['a vegetable product for the spraying of sacred liquids in a cult'] according to J. Tischler (*Hethitisches etymologisches Glossar*, Teil II, Lieferung 14, IBS 20, 1234), most often *šu-u/ú-°*, (without etymology) is correct. It would be interesting, if the 300 vessels marked with the VAS^{al}-ideogram and qualified as ***su-pa$_3$-ra*** (HT 31.5) could be identified as vessels meant for some precious vegetable liquids sprayed out during some ritual, but in my view the large quantity of 300 vessels makes this identification less likely. I consider an interpretation as 'pots of a "Subarian" type' or 'agrarian commodities described as "Subarian" ' more likely as well as ***šuwala*** 'wine'.

Before we continue to interpret the remaining sequences on HT 31, I should like to discuss Linear A ***su-wa-|re-su*** (HT 37.1-2) from Hagia Triada. It may well be a personal name comparable with the feminine Hurrian names ***^{f}Šuwar-ḫepa*** (wr. *^{f}Šu-wa-ar-ḫé-pa*, *^{f}Šu-wa-ar-ḫé-pa-a*), ***^{f}Šuwar-ninu*** (wr. *^{f}Šu-wa-ar-ni-nu*) and ***^{f}Šuwar-zizza*** (wr. *Šu-wa-ar-zi-iz-za*) at Nuzi, cf. P.M. Purves, *NPN*, 260.

P.M. Purves (*NPN*, 260) mentions s.v. ***šuwar***: "Hurrian. Cf. *šu-wa-ra-še-na*, KUB XXVII 1 iii 1; [*šu-w*]*a-ra-a-si-na, ibidem* 3 iv? 10; *šu-ú-wa-ri*, Mari 2: 13 and 17; *šu-wa-ar-ri-iš-ša-am*, KUB XXVII 29 iv 12; *šu-ú-wa-ru-ta-nam*, *ibidem* 38 iii 13. C.G. von Brandenstein (*ZDMG XCI*, 560) considers *šuwar* represented in Ugarit ***ś/θwrm***. L. Oppenheim (*AOF XII* 31 f., n. 10) classifies *šuwar* as a non-divine element and suggests an ultimate Indo-European origin [Indo-Aryan *súvar-* 'sun', later 'sky', is indeed found in the Amarna personal name *Šuwar-data*, as noted by Mironov in *Acta Orientalia XI (1933)*, 179f. – Bonfante]. The occurrences of ***šuwar*** in the Hurrian texts cited above, also its use in Nuzi names in combination with Hurrian elements only, indicate either borrowing from Indo-Aryan, as suggested above, or accidental phonetic resemblance." N.B. the term 'Indo-Aryan' is widely used, but linguistically Indo-Iranian is the correct term.

Linear A ***su-wa-|re-su*** (HT 37.1-2) shows some similarity with *šu-wa-ar-ri-iš-ša-am*, attested at Boğazköy KUB XXVII 29 IV 12, also mentioned by E. Laroche, *GLH*, 246. The ***e/i*** alternation is quite common in Hurrian. Possibly the second element of the Linear A name contains the onomastic element ***ezu***, as in the Hurrian personal names from Nuzi *E-zu-ú-a* and *^{f}E-zu-i*, cf. P.M. Purves, *NPN*, 212, s.v. *ezu, ezua, ezui*. Cf. the Hurrian names *Iz-zi-ia* and *Iz-zu-ú-ia* from Nuzi, see P.M. Purves, *NPN*, 221, s.v. *izz, izziḭa, izzuḭa*.

If the reading is correct and if it is one sequence, ***su-wa-|re-su*** (HT 37.1-2) may contain the onomastic element ***šuwar-*** that is either Hurrian on account of combinations with other Hurrian elements or ultimately Indo-Iranian, cf. P.M. Purves, *NPN*, 260, s.v. ***suwar*** and ***suwar-***, who considers both options feasible.

In the 2016 edition of *Minoan Linear A*, Vol. I: *Hurrians and Hurrian in Minoan Crete*, I wrote: "If we are dealing with Indo-Iranian ***súvar-*** 'sun', later 'sky', it seems almost too accidental that Hurrian ***eše*** means 'heaven'/ 'sky' as well, so that the Linear A name ***su-wa-|re-su*** (HT 37.1) may almost be considered an Indo-Iranian - Hurrian bilingual in a nutshell 'sun / sky (is) heaven', comparable to the hybrid Akkado-Hurrian personal name ***Adad-teḭa*** (wr. *ᵈAdad-te-ia, A-da-te-ia, A-ta-te-e-a*, etc.) 'Adad (is) Tešub' at Nuzi, cf. e.g. A.A. MacRae, *NPN*, 295.

E. Laroche, *GLH*, 83-84, s.v. ***eše*** 'ciel': ***eše-ḫaburni*** correspond au hit. AN-***iš*** KI-***paš*** ou ***nebi daganzipas*** des listes divines; cf. Von Brandenstein, *ZA 46*, 85 sq. [...] Thèmes ***eše*** 'ciel' et ***eše-ni*** 'le ciel', etc. If ***su-wa-|re-su*** is a hybrid Indo-Iranian - Hurrian name, the person in question may have been of high rank, possibly a royal, since the Hurrian kings of Mitanni also bore Indo-Iranian names."

However, the interpretation of ***eše*** 'heaven' is no longer valid and consequently there is no bilingual in a nutshell 'sun / sky (is) heaven' either. According to Th. Richter (*BGH*, 103-104), s.v. ***eše*** II [*passim*], the previously generally accepted meaning 'Himmel' [heaven] has been given up, since G. Wilhelm, apud J. Huenergard, 1987a, 61, established the meaning 'Erde' [earth], cf. also E. Neu, *Das Hurritische: Eine altorientalische Sprache in neuem Licht*, Akademie der Wissenschaften und der Literatur Mainz, 1988/3, 26-27. Cf. also Th. Richter, *VHN*, 403, s.v. ***eše***. Although E. Laroche mentioned that ***eše-ḫaburni*** corresponds with Hittite AN-***iš*** KI-***paš*** or ***nebi daganzipas*** in lists of divinities, publication of the Hurrian-Hittite bilingual ***kirenze*** (KBo 32) shows that ***nepiš***, 'heaven' in Hittite, turns out to refer to Hurrian ***ḫaburni*** 'heaven', not to Hurrian ***eše*** 'earth', which corresponds with Hittite ***tekan/takn-*** (ntr.) 'earth'. An important observation by Laroche (*ibidem*) is that ***eše-ḫaburni*** occurs with or without divine determinative, e.g. *ᵈe-še-ḫa-bu-ur-ni*, KBo XI 5 I 21; *ᵈe-še ᵈḫa-wu-ur-ni*, KBo XX 119 I 9 = IV 14 = KBo XXI 50, 10; KBo VIII 79 Ro 18. - *e-še ḫawurni*, KBo XVII 96 I 11; KUB XLV 3 I 47; XXXIV 102 II 16; XXXII 52 III 7; XXV 44 V 4; *eše ḫawurunni*, KBo XX 129 + II 4, 59. Compare for the same usage *with and without divine determinative* Hurrian ***šimigi / šimegi*** 'sun': E. Laroche, *GLH*, 232, s.v. ***Šimigi*** 'soleil'. See also Linear A ***si+me-ki*** (HT 24b.1).

Th. Richter (*BGH*, 415) mentions several roots and themes s.v. ***šub-*** I [Boğ.; Mitt.(?)], without translation; (possibly) ***šuw-*** II [Boğ.] 'tagen, Tag werden' ['to dawn']; ***šuwi*** or ***šuwa*** [Boğ.] 'Tag' ['daylight, dawn']; ***zub-*** III, *zub=umma epēšu* [Nuzi] 'zurückgeben, erstatten' ['to give back, return, restitute'].

Of these ***šuw-*** II [Boğ.] 'tagen, Tag werden' ['to dawn']; ***šuwi*** or ***šuwa*** [Boğ.] 'Tag' ['daylight, dawn'] is most interesting, since it is conceivable that Linear A ***su-wa-|re-su*** (HT 37.1-2) contains the verbal root ***šuw-*** II 'to dawn' + root-extension ***-al-*** (cf. I. Wegner, *Einführung*, 87, meaning of ***-al-*** not clear) or the *factitive* or *iterative* root-extension ***-ar-*** (cf. I. Wegner, *Einführung*, 88). The *iterative* aspect of ***-ar-*** may well be significant, since *dawn* returns every morning. So if we analyse Linear A ***su-wa-|re-su*** (HT 37.1-2) as ***šuw=ar-eš(e)=u*** (with Akkadianizing nominative in ***-u***), the meaning of the name would be 'Dawn again and again, oh Earth !', 'Let dawn return every day, oh Earth !'.

Th. Richter (*BGH*, 415) mentions, s.v. ***šuwi*** or ***šuwa*** [Boğ.], 'Tag' ['day'] (V. Haas / I. Wegner, 1996b, 287-288 [i.e. possibly */šuove/* or */šouve/*], E. Neu, 2001, 94[34] [i.e. ***šuv=i***], see also 1996a, 416). The word is an {A}-stem according to G. Wilhelm 1998b, 179-180.

Starting point is *ši-in-ti-šu-ú-wa-at šu-u-ú-wa* (a.o. KBo 32.19 I 22-23) with the Hittite translation ***nu nam-ma*** UD.7.KAM-[(***az***)] (II 22-23). Sumerogram UD(.KAM) = Hittite ***šiwatt-*** com. 'day'; ***nu*** is a Hittite connective and ***namma*** means 'then, subsequently'. According to V. Haas – I. Wegner (1996b, 288) the Hurrian phrase can be analysed as *šindi=š(še)=uwe=a*[Essive]*=t(ta) šūw*(vowel)*=a* 'am siebten Tag' ['on the 7th day'].

Since Linear A and B sign ***ra*** can also be ***la***, it is also possible to interpret Linear A ***su-wa-|re-su*** as ***Šuw=al-eš(e)=u***, of which I presume that the translation does not differ very much from that of ***šuw=ar-eš(e)=u***. The theonym ***dŠuwala*** and the theophorous element in personal names ***Šuwala*** {*Šo/uvala*} may well contain the extended stem ***šuw=al-***.

P.M. Purves (*NPN*, 258) mentions s.v. ***šual*** at Nuzi the personal names ***Ar-šuala*** (wr. *Ar-šu-a-la*) 'Give, oh Šuwala !' and hypocoristic ***fŠualiịa*** (wr. *fŠu-a-li-ia*), analysis {*šuv=al=i=a*}, 'She dawns'. He mentions at Boğazköy *dŠu-u-wa-u-la*, KBo V 2 iii 13; *(d)Šu-u-wa-la*, KUB XXVII 1 ii 51 and 8 obv.(?) 11; *dŠu-wa-la*, KUB XXVII 13 i 18; *dŠu-wa-li-ia-ti*, KUB XXIX 8 i 15, and in the Tell Brak tablets *Šu-a-la*KI, s. Gadd, *Iraq VII*, 43.

E. Laroche (*GLH*, 174) mentions D***Šuwala*** s.v. ***Nabarbi***, déesse parèdre de Ninurta = *Suwaliyat*, cf. Ungnad, *Subartu*, 67. Graphies: D*Na-(a-)bar-bi*, D*Na-(a-)bar-wi*i. [.......]
2. Au Kizuwatna. (a) D*Na-(a-)bar-bi* D*Šuwala*, KBo V 2 III 13; XX 113 I 20; IBoT II, 26, 10; KUB XXVII [I 11; XXXII 93 I 5; XLVII 101 IV 12; *Nabarbi* et *Šuwala*, KUB XXVII 1 II 51; 13 I 18 = dupl. KBo XIV 142 I 29, etc.

Th. Richter (*VHN*, 116, 521) mentions ***fIšmen-Šuwala*** (wr. *fIš-me-en-šu-wa-la*), a female weaver from Ašnakkum, {*išm=i=n(na)-Šo/uvala*}, typology 1.3.1.2.2.1, as a name with the theophorous element ***-Šuwala***. At Alalaḫ IV we find ***Ḫašip-Šuwala*** (wr. *Ḫa-ši-ip-šuwala*), {*ḫaž=i=b-Šo/uvala*} '*Šuwala* heard (the prayer)' (AT 177: 29). According to Th. Richter (*VHN*, 521) the goddess ***Šuwala*** {*Šo/uvala*} is sometimes associated with the God of War ***Aštabi*** (V. Haas, *Geschichte der hethitischen Religion*, Handbuch der Orientalistik 1/15, Leiden 1994, 861). In the Hittite period she belongs to the circle of *Ḫebat* and is attested in the *ḫišuwa*-festivities of Kizzuwatna. In religious texts of Kizzuwatnan origin she is connected with *Nabarbi*, in Emar with *Nergal*. She may originally come from North-West Syria, because her main cult-place *Mardaman* is mentioned next to *Ebla* and *Ḫalab* (Aleppo). This relation is obvious in D*šu-u-wa-a-la* URU*ma-ar-ta-ma-an-ḫi* 'Mardamanian Šuwala' (I. Wegner, *Hurritische Opferlisten aus hethitischen Festbeschreibungen*, Teil III: *Das Glossar*, Corpus der hurritischen Sprachdenkmäler. I. Abteilung: Die Texte aus Boğazköy (= ChS I/3-3), Rome 2004, 234. Already in the older sources the city is connected with Hurrian onomastics. So the relations with Kizzuwatna are secondary. Accordingly the name may well be Hurrian. An interpretation is not possible according to Th. Richter.

I should not be surprised, if D***Šuwala*** {*Šo/uvala*} is the 'Goddess of Dawn' (the deity who announces the new day) and that her name can be derived directly from ***šuwi*** or ***šuwa*** 'day'. That is also the reason, why I hesitate to accept the meaning 'wine' for ***šuwali*** and eventually for Linear A ***su-pa3-ra*** (HT 31.5), for which 'Subarian' may be the most appropriate meaning after all. The meaning 'wine' for ***šuwali*** seems only possible, if we are dealing with homonymic lexemes, cf. also Th. Richter, *VHN*, 521[742]. If D***Šuwala*** is the 'Goddess of Dawn', she is the Hurrian counterpart of Homer's ***Ἠώς*** 'Goddess of Dawn' (*Iliad* B 48f., Θ 1, Λ 1, Ψ 227, 243-246; *Odyssey* ε 1, 121, μ 3, ο 250) < ****ἀϝώς*** < I.-E. ****āusōs*** (cf. Latin ***Aurōra***), cf. P. Chantraine, *DELG*, 394-395.

The first sequence of ***pi*-*ti-sa* , *pu-ko* ,** VAS^{d1}+***ri*** (HT 31.1) from Hagia Triada should possibly be read as ***9*-*ti-sa***, since the first sign may well be identical with the fourth sign of ***ki-de-ma-9-na*** (HT 31.4) on the same tablet. In the past W.C. Brice (*ILA*, 1961) read ***mi*-*ti-sa***, J. Raison - M. Pope (1994) ***i*-*ti-sa*** and *GORILA 1* and Meijer [.]-***ti-sa***. I think that the lower part of the first sign is recognizable as ***pi-*** or as ***L9*** and that the upper part has disappeared or was omitted, since the sign has been written close to the left top corner of the tablet. The readings ***mi*-*ti-sa*** and ***i*-*ti-sa*** are certainly not correct. J. Raison - M. Pope (*Études minoennes I*, 1978, 14) wrote about sign ***L9***: "Only on two or three Hagia Triada tablets, and somewhat similar in form to another sign, ***L28***. But a sign very like ***L9*** is now attested once at Khania as a constituant part of a ligature, and once at Kea." I do not agree with them upon the alleged similarity with ***L28* = *wi***, but consider ***L9*** a variant of sign ***L56a* = *pi*** (in fact only the small horizontal stroke of ***L56a* = *pi*** is missing).

If ***pi*-*ti-sa*** is an anthroponym, the Hurrian feminine personal name ***ᶠPetteza*** (wr. *ᶠBe-et-te-ez-a*) from Nuzi seems a perfect equivalent (with double writing of ***-tt-*** and with ***i/e*** alternation, which is common in the Hurrian syllabary), cf. I.J. Gelb, *NPN*, 114.

One may think of abstract forms in ***-(i)šše*** such as ***šar=i=šše*** 'wish, desire' from ***šar-*** 'to wish, desire, demand', ***nir=i=šše*** 'the good' from ***niri*** 'good', ***kib=i=šše*** 'sitting on the throne', 'taking place on the throne' from ***ke/ib-*** 'to set, place' (cf. I. Wegner, *Einführung*, 55) and ***tag=i=šše*** 'beauty' (cf. Th. Richter, *VHN*, 526: ***tag=i=šše*** 'Schönheit').

According to Th. Richter (*BGH*, 319) the (transitive) verbal root ***pitt-*** [Boğ.] means 'helfen' ['to help'], 'Frieden machen' ['to make peace'], (intransitive) 'friedlich sein' ['to be peaceful']. Th. Richter (*VHN*, 486) mentions ***pitt-***, possibly 'to help'. Consequently an abstract ***pitt=i=šše***, derived from a verbal root ***pitt-***, could mean 'help' or perhaps 'peace'. There are many examples of Hurrian personal names representing such abstract forms, e.g. ***ᶠTagazze*** (wr. *ᶠDa-ga-ze*) from Mari, typology 3.1, 'Schönheit' ['Beauty'], *Ta-ga-si* = *Ta-ga-zi* from Middle-Assyrian Atmannu (*Iraq 70*, 174, nr 24E: 8; 175, nr. 24T: 7), ***ᶠTakaše*** (wr. *ᶠTaqaše*) from Nuzi (cf. I.J. Gelb, *NPN*, 145) and ***ᶠTakaša*** (with the *essive* form in ***-a***) from Old Babylonian Kiš. These are all variant forms of ***tag=i=šše*** 'beauty'.

The *essive* form is very popular in Hurrian names. As a result Linear A ***pi*-*ti-sa*** can be analysed as such an abstract *essive* form *{pitt=i=šš(e)=a}* and can be translated as 'Like peace' or '(The child) looks like peace'.

Th. Richter (*VHN*, 234-235) mentions the following Hurrian personal names with the verbal root ***pitt-***: ***ᶠPittakku*** (wr. *bi-it-ta-ku*) from Mari, analysis *{pitt=a=kk=o}*, typology 1.2.3, and ***Pittun*** (wr. *bi-it-tu-un*) from Šušarrā (Tall Shemshara), typology 1.3.1.1.2.1, analysis *{pitt=o=n(na)}*, 'Hilf ihm (Jungen)' ['Help him (the boy)']. The suffix ***-n(na)*** 'him' marks the enclitic personal pronoun 3rd person singular indicating the object of the transitive construction. Old Hurrian ***Pittun*** (wr. *bi-it-tu-un*) from Šušarrā is in fact a perfect parallel to Linear A ***pi-ti-ne*** (AK 4a.4) from Arkhanes. The enclitic suffix ***-nna*** indicating the personal pronoun 3rd person singular can be replaced by the optional allomorphic suffix ***-nne/i*** or ***-nnu***, cf. Th. Richter (*VHN*, 596, sub 1.3.1.1.2.2). Compare also other Linear A forms with the root ***pitt-*** such as ***pi-te-za*** (PK Za 11.b) from the Peak Sanctuary of Mount Petsophas near Palaikastro, ***pi-ta-ja*** (HT 6a.2), ***pi-ta-ka-se*** (HT 21a.1), ***pi-ta-ke-si*** (HT 87.2) and ***pi-ta-ra*** (HT 96a.4) from Hagia Triada (discussed *supra*).

Linear A ***pi-ti-sa*** (HT 31.1) can theoretically also be analysed as a *jussive* form *{pitt=i=š=an}*, consisting of the verbal root ***pitt-*** 'to help' + the *jussive* marker ***-i/e-*** + the pluralizer ***-š-*** for the 1st and 2nd person plural + the syntactical particle ***-an*** (of which the final consonant ***-n*** is not expressed in Linear A), translation 'and we should like to help' or 'and you must help ! (plural *imperative*)'. However, usage of a syntactical particle ***-an*** in the first sequence of the tablet is syntactically not very likely.

A better analysis may be *{pitt=i=šša < *pitt=i=š=nna}*, 'we should like to help him / her (*-nna*)' or 'you must help him / her ! (plural *imperative*)', cf. I. Wegner, *Einführung*, 103-111 and Table 9: *Order of suffixes of the positive jussive*). Such a verbal form can also be used as a personal 'one-word' name, cf. Th. Richter, *VHN, passim.*

The Hurrian-Hittite bilingual ***Kirenz***e (KBo 32: 15 I 18') offers a good example of assimilation of ***-š=nna*** > ***šša*** in another *jussive* form, with the conditional optative formant ***-eva-*** and the object in the absolute case: *e-ḫi-il-li-wa*$_{a}$*-aš-ša* ^{D}*Te-eš-šu-up* = *{eḫl=il=eva=š=nna* ^{D}*Teššub}*, translation 'we wish to save him (*-nna*), Teššub', cf. I. Wegner, *Einführung*, 111. She also shows (*ibidem*, 105) that in a form like *it-ti-tén* (Mitt. III 23) = *{itt=i=(i)t=en}* 'they ought to go' ***-i-*** is marker of the *jussive* form and not a marker of transitivity, since the root ***itt-*** 'to go' is intransitive. N.B. ***-(i)t-*** is the pluralizer of the 3rd person plural of the *jussive* form.

If ***-nt-*** assimilated > ***-tt-***, a voiceless dental indicated by double writing may be the result, cf. Th. Richter (*VHN*, 482-483) on ***pad-/patt-*** and ***p/wand-***. If the reading of ***pi-ti-sa*** (HT 31.1) is correct, it is conceivable that also ***pett-/pitt-*** are the result of assimilation from ***pent-/bent-***, cf. E. Laroche, *GLH*, 199-200, s.v. ***pend(i)***- 1. Thème verbal, 2. Divers: *pé-en-ti-ša* KUB XXVII 46 + I 28; P.M. Purves, *NPN*, 244-245, s.v. ***pent***: *bi-en-ti-ša* KUB XXVII 46 I 22. It is feasible that the feminine Hurrian name ^{f}***Petteza*** (wr. ^{f}*Be-et-te-ez-a*) from Nuzi (cf. I.J. Gelb, *NPN*, 114) in fact shows the assimilated form of *pé-en-ti-ša* and *bi-en-ti-ša* from Boğazköy. But this hypothesis needs verification.

Tablet HT 31.1 starts with ***pi-ti-sa* , *pu-ko*** , VAS^{d1}***+ri*** = TRIPUS+*ri* (HT 31.1). So Linear A ***pu-ko*** (HT 31.1) is the second entry of the tablet. Since the ideogram is only mentioned after the second entry, there is a good reason to assume that these entries have different functions, for instance, a personal name ***pi-ti-sa*** followed by a transaction term or a toponym ***pu-ko***. However, since the formation of Hurrian toponyms is often similar to that of personal names, it is also conceivable that ***pi-ti-sa*** is the toponym and ***pu-ko*** the personal name. There is no basic difference, if the abstract *essive* form *{pitt=i=šš(e)=a}* is used for the name of a child 'He/She (the child) looks like peace' or for the name of a place 'It (the place) looks like peace'. Although two consecutive personal names cannot be ruled out either, that option seems less likely to me. All options have to be examined.

If ***pu-ko*** is a personal name, it may be compared with Hurrian personal names with the root ***pug-*** as in *Pu-ku-an-ta, Pu-ku-un-ta,* ^{f}*Pu-ku-li*, cf. also *Pu-qa-an-ta* and *Pu-uk-li* at Nuzi (cf. I.J. Gelb, *NPN*, 118; P.M. Purves, *NPN*, 246, s.v. ***puk***) or with Hurrian personal names with the element ***pukk***, cf. I.J. Gelb, *NPN*, 118; P.M. Purves, *NPN*, 246, s.v. ***pukk***: ***Pukkiḭa*** (wr. *Pu-uk-ki-ia, Pu-ki-ia, Pu-uk-ki-a*), ***Pukkitta*** (wr. *Pu-uk-ki-it-ta*).

Th. Richter (*BGH*, 323) mentions that the root ***wug-*** I [Boğ.] may have the meaning 'zeigen (?)' ['to indicate, show (?)'] according to E. Neu (1996a, 268[106]), but 'lang sein, machen (?)' ['to be, make long/tall (?)'] according to M. Salvini - I. Wegner (2004, 178).

The latter meaning seems according to Th. Richter (*VHN*, 488) the most appropriate for the verbal root ***pug-*** {*fug-*} in personal names.

Th. Richter (*VHN*, 236) mentions ***Pukija*** (wr. *Pu-ki-ia, Pu-gi-ia*) at Ašnakkum and Mari, analysis {*fug=i=ja*}, typology 1.1.1.2.4, lexicon *pug-*, 'Er/Sie (scil. ein *Numen*) hat (Jungen) lang gemacht' ['He/She (scil. a *numen*) has made (the boy) tall'].
Pukiri (wr. *Pu-gi-ri*) at Šušarrā, typology 3.1, lexicon *pugiri* (→ *pug-*), 'Der/Die (Kind) lang machte' ['He/She who made (the child) tall'], with participial ending in ***-iri***.
Pukuḫl[***e***] (wr. *Pu-ku-uḫ-l*[*e*]) at Šubat-Enlil, lexicon *puguḫle* (→ *p/wug-*), typology 3.1, discussion: professional designations in ***-uḫle*** form complete 'one-word' names.

If we analyse ***Pukkitta*** (wr. *Pu-uk-ki-it-ta*) from Nuzi as {*pukk=i=tta*}, the translation may well be 'Make me tall (oh *numen*) !'.

If Linear A ***pu-ko*** (HT 31.1) is a personal name containing the root ***pug-***, it can be analysed as an Old Hurrian *jussive* 3rd person singular {*pug=o*} 'He/She (a *numen*) must make (the child) tall'. Indeed such a meaning only makes sense in the context, if it is a personal name. It can be compared with Old Hurrian ***kud=o*** 'Er soll fallen', 'Er soll gefällt sein' ['He must fall'], 'He must be smashed down' in the Hurrian-Hittite bilingual ***Kirenze*** 'Liberation, release (especially of slaves)', KBo 32: 14 I 57: *ku-ú-do*. And ***kir=o*** 'Er soll freigelassen sein/werden' ['He must be set free / liberated / manumitted / released'] KBo 32: 15 IV 3 in the Boğazköy context, cf. I. Wegner, *Einführung*, 138.

If Linear A ***pu-ko*** represents a real verbal form (with the function of a transaction term), a *jussive* form ***pug=o***, morphologically comparable with ***kud=o*** and ***kir=o***, would only make sense, if the meaning is 'he must indicate/show(?)', cf. E. Neu's interpretation of ***p/wug-***. Linear A ***pi-ti-sa , pu-ko*** may then be interpreted as '*Pittišša* must indicate /show', perhaps in the sense of '*Pittišša* must give indications, directions, instructions'. This would mean that *Pittišša* acts as a sort of supervisor of the transaction recorded on HT 31.

A third option is that ***pu-ko*** (HT 31.1) is a toponym, which is feasible in the heading of a tablet. It is conceivable that the common (probably Pre-Hellenic) place-name ***Pyrgos*** is mentioned, since (according to the orthographic conventions of Linear A and B) ***-r-*** preceding an occlusive is not expressed in consonant clusters. Since final consonants are not expressed in Linear A and B, it is not certain that the final ***-s*** of later ***Πύργος*** or another consonant or no final consonant belonged to the Minoan sequence.

There is a place called Pyrgos about 30 kilometers east of Hagia Triada in the Messara valley. It is likely that the whole Messara valley was administered from the palaces of Phaistos and Hagia Triada. There are more places called Pyrgos such as Myrtos Pyrgos on the south coast of Crete, where Linear A was found by G. Cadogan, but the finds of Linear A there could also mean that Myrtos Pyrgos was itself a small economic and administrative centre in Minoan times, independent of other palaces. Pyrgos in the Messara valley seems then the better candidate. Some toponyms might date from prepalatial times. So they might not only be Pre-Hellenic, but also Pre-Hurrian.

P. Chantraine (*DELG III*, 958) writes about the etymology of ***πύργος***: "Le mot fait penser évidemment à allem. ***Burg***, got. ***baurgs*** 'tour, château, ville' et Kretschmer, *Gl. 22, 1934*, 100 sq., a supposé que le mot venait du germanique par l'intermédiaire d'une langue balkanique, p. ex. le macédonien. C'est d'autre part un des rares termes qui pourraient fournir quelque fondement à la théorie pélasgique.

On rapproche ainsi ***Πέργαμος, -ον, -α***, qui répondrait à l'allemand **Berg** (i.-e. ***bhr̥gh-o-**, ***bhergh-**), voir Heubeck, *Praegraeca* 63-65 sq. avec la bibliographie, selon qui le mot serait emprunté à une langue i.-e. d'Asie Mineur: il évoque hitt. ***parku-*** 'haut', ***parkeššar*** 'hauteur'; en outre les gloses d'Hsch. ***φύργος · τεῖχος*** et ***φ<ο>ύρκορ · ὀχύρωμα***. Sur ce point, cf. aussi Pisani, *Rev. intern. étym. balk. 3*, 22, n. 1. Voir encore Hester, *Lingua 13, 1965*, 363."

It seems unlikely that the Hurrian root ***purḫ-/wurḫ-*** (meaning unknown) occurring in the Hurrian names ***Purḫunni*** (wr. *ᶠPu-ur-ḫu-u-ni* and *ᵐPur-ḫu-u-ni*) at Nuzi (cf. I.J. Gelb, *NPN*, 118), ***Wurḫe*** (wr. *Wu-ur-ḫe*) at Nuzi (cf. I.J. Gelb, *NPN*, 174) and ***Wurḫaš(š)i*** (wr. *Wu-úr-ḫa-ši*) at Qaṭṭarā (cf. Th. Richter, *VHN*, 240, 491) has anything to do with Linear A ***pu-ko*** (HT 31.1) or with the glosses just mentioned with regard to ***πύργος***.

Linear A ***sa-ja-ma*** 30[ ]10 (HT 31.3-4) from Hagia Triada may be either complete or has to be read as ***sa-ja-ma-di*** (?)+ numbers. I shall discuss both options.

If Linear A ***sa-ja-ma*** (HT 31.3) is complete, it can be identified as a Hurrian personal name that can be analysed as *{sa(j)=a=mma}*, consisting of the verbal root ***sa(j)- / sa(w)-*** (intr.) 'to be great, excellent', (trans.) 'to make great, excellent' + marker of *intransitivity* ***-a-*** + the *enclitic* personal pronoun 2nd person singular ***-mma / -m***, indicating the absolutive subject of the intransitive verb. The meaning of the name is 'You are great, excellent'.

Th. Richter (*VHN*, 494) mentions, s.v. ***ša-***, ***šaw-*** I *{šav-}*, that in recent research the *intransitive* root ***ša-***, resp. ***šaw-***, is usually translated as 'groß sein' ['to be great'] and the *transitive* root as 'groß machen' ['to make great'], cf. *BGH*, 340-341. He proposes to translate 'hervorragend machen' ['to make excellent'] in order to distinguish the root from ***talm-/talb-***. He adds (note 645) that it is difficult to imagine that the theonym ***Ša(w)uška*** only alludes to the physical size of the goddess. He remarks that the fricative labial spirant *{v}* in *{šav=o=m-°}* is not expressed at Šubat-Enlil and that orthographies vary at Mari. Such varying orthographies also occur in ***šawuri*** *{sav=o=ri}*: *na-ni-ip-ša-wu/ú-ri* (Mari). It is not clear whether the notion is to be considered a *quasi* theophorous element or 'a certain weapon', similar to an appellative. In the tradition of Ḫattuša the word refers to 'the weapon of *Ša(w)uška*', with whose name it has the root in common, cf. ***šau*** 'weapon', cf. also E. Laroche, *GLH*, 219, s.v. ***šauri*** 'arme'.

The element ***šawuri*** occurs in the onomastics of Kaniš and Alalaḫ, not at Nuzi. Th. Richter (*VHN*, 246-248, 261, 494) mentions the following personal names with this root: ***ᶠŠawanni-kizi*** (wr. *ᶠŠa-wa-an-ni-ki[z]i*) at Mari, *{šavanni-kizi}*, typology 2.1, lexicon *šawanni* (→ *ša-*), *kizi* (→ *kiz-*); ***Šap-Namar*** (wr. *Ša-ap-na-mar*) at Šubat-Enlil, *{ša=a=b-Namar}*, typology 1.1.1.3.1, lexicon *ša-*, *Namar* (→ *Nawar*), '(*Numen* von) Nawar ist hervorragend' ['(The *numen* of) Nawar is excellent']; if one reads *{šav-Namar}*, reading *Ša-áw-na-mar*, one can translate '(*Numen* von) Nawar machte (Jungen) hervorragend' ['(The *numen* of) Nawar made (the boy) excellent']; ***Šaum-Namar*** (wr. *Ša-ú-um-na-mar, Ša-um-na-mar*) at Šubat-Enlil, *{ša=o=m-Namar}*, typology 1.1.1.1.1, lexicon *ša-*, *Namar* (→ *Nawar*), '(*Numen* von) Nawar machte (Jungen) hervorragend' ['(The *numen* of) Nawar made (the boy) excellent']; ***Šawum*** (wr. *Ša-wu-ú-um*) at Mari, analysis *{šav=o=m}*, typology 1.1.1.1.1, lexicon *šaw-* I, 'Er/Sie (scil. ein *Numen*) machte (Jungen) hervorragend' ['He/She (a *numen*) made (the boy) excellent'];

Šau (wr. *Ša-ú*) at Šušarrā, analysis {*šav=o*}, typology 1.3.1.1.1, lexicon *ša-*, 'Mache (Jungen) hervorragend (oh *Numen*) !' ['Make (the boy) excellent (oh *numen*) !']; cf. *ᶠ*Ša-a-ú* at Alalaḫ VII, analysis {*šav=o*}, typology 1.3.1.1.1, lexicon *ša-*, 'Make (the girl) excellent (oh *numen*) !'; ***Šaun*** (wr. *Ša-ú-un*) at Tigunāni, analysis {*šav=o=n(na)*}, typology 1.3.1.1.2.1, lexicon *ša-*, 'Mache ihn (Jungen) hervorragend (oh *Numen*) !' ['Make (the boy) excellent (oh *numen*) !']; ***ᶠŠawum-nirze*** (wr. *ᶠŠa-wu-ú-um-ni-ir-ze*), wife of Zimrī-Lim at Mari, analysis {*šav=o=m-nirze*}, typology 1.1.1.1.1, lexicon *šaw-* I, *nirze* (→ *nir-*), 'Das Gute machte (Mädchen) hervorragend' ['Goodness made (the girl) excellent']; ***Šawu-muru*** (wr. *Ša-wu-mu-ru*), old slave at Mari, analysis {*šav=o-mur(i)=u*[N.]}, typology 1.3.1.1.1, lexicon *šaw-* I, *muri* (→ *mur-*), 'Mache (Jungen) hervorragend, oh *muri* !' ['Make (the boy) excellent, oh *muri* !'], [N.] refers to Akkadianizing nominative; alternative analysis {*šav=o=m-ur(i)=u*[N.]}; ***Šaum-uri*** (wr. *Ša-ú-um-ú-ri*), at Šubat-Enlil, analysis {*ša=o=m-uri*}, typology 1.1.1.1.1, lexicon *ša-*, *uri*, 'Der Fuß machte (Jungen) hervorragend' ['The foot made (the boy) excellent']; *Šá-um-ši-en* at Urkeš, from Old Akkadian period (*RA 9*, 2 r. Rd.).

If Linear A ***sa-ja-ma*** 30[ ]10 (HT 31.3-4) is complete, it can be analysed as a perfect Hurrian name, but if it is incomplete and ***sa-ja-ma-di*** can be read instead, it is conceivable to compare it with the feminine Hurrian name ***Šai̯u(m)-madi***, mentioned by P.M. Purves at Nuzi. The only difference would be that the name at Nuzi is transitive, whereas the Linear A name is intransitive.

The tablet is broken just after sign ***-ma*** at the end of ***sa-ja-ma*** (HT 31.3-4) and the fracture shows even a hole just at the crucial spot after ***-ma***. All editors read traces of numbers after ***-ma***. One argument in favour of reading ***sa-ja-ma-di*** is that the missing sign ***-di*** consists of one horizontal and four vertical strokes which can easily be misread as numerals. This conjecture remains hypothetical, since only ***sa-ja-ma*** is legible with certainty, but the possibility that ***sa-ja-ma-di*** might be the correct reading, should be mentioned, especially since the top horizontal stroke of sign ***di*** is visible just above the hole in the tablet. If ***sa-ja-ma-di*** is the correct reading, it can be translated as '*Madi* is excellent'. Hurrian ***madi*** means 'wisdom, intelligence' and is used as a theophorous onomastic element, cf. Th. Richter, *BGH*, 248f.; *VHN*, 456. Cf. also frequent Linear A ***ma-di*** (HT 3.7, HT 69.2, HT 85b.5, HT 97a.4, HT 118.1, HT? 170b.2 (Raison-Pope) = PH? 31b.2 (Godart-Olivier) = Her. Mus. 1609. The transitive verbal root ***mad-*** means 'to grant wisdom / intelligence (to somebody)', and the intransitive root 'to be intelligent / wise'. Compare also Linear A ***ma-da-ti*** (PK 1.7).

Th. Richter (*VHN*, 453) mentions, s.v. ***(ᵒ)ma***, that the Hurrian personal name ***ew-ri-ma***, attested on the *prisma* from Tigunāni, is not clear in analysis and meaning. I should like to propose the hypothesis that ***(ᵒ)ma*** can be a hypocoristic of the frequent theophorous onomastic element ***-madi*** as ***(ᵒ)mu*** is for ***-muša***, ***-mušni***, ***-te*** for ***-tešup*** and ***-še*** for ***-šena***, ***-šenni***. I consider the hypothesis justifiable, since e.g. the personal name ***Enna-madi*** (wr. *En-na-ma-ti, E-en-na-ma-ti, E-na-ma-ti, En-na-ma-di, E-en-na-ma-di, E-na-ma-di, I-en-na-ma-te, En-na-a-ma-ti, En-na-ma-dil, In-na-ma-di-il*) is the name of 85 persons at Nuzi, cf. I.J. Gelb, *NPN*, 44-46; P.M. Purves, *NPN*, 234. The meaning of ***Enna-madi*** 'The Gods are wisdom' or 'The Gods are wise' is not far away from ***ew-ri-ma(-di)*** 'The Lord is wise'.

P.M. Purves (*NPN*, 249) mentions, s.v. ***šai̯u, šai̯um-*** and (*NPN*, 233-234), s.v. ***mat*** and ***-ma-ti***: ***Šai̯u(m)-madi*** (wr. *ᶠŠa-a-ú-um-ma-ti, ᶠŠá-a-ú-ma-ti, ᶠŠa-a-ú-mâ-ti*[ti]*, ᶠŠa-a-ú-ma-ti*) at Nuzi and (*NPN*, 249), s.v. ***-šai̯a, -šai̯u*** as second element in Hurrian personal names: ***ᶠḪašip-šai̯a*** (*ᶠḪa-ši-ip-ša-a-a, ᶠḪa-ši-ip-šá-a-a*), ***ᶠḪašip-šai̯u*** (*ᶠḪa-ši-ip-ša-a-ú, ᶠḪa-ši-ip-šá-a-ú*); ***ᶠMušup-šai̯a*** (*ᶠMu-šu-up-šá-a-a*), ***ᶠMušup-šai̯u*** (*ᶠMu-šu-up-šá-i-ú, ᶠMu-šu-up-ša-ú*), ***ᶠŠurkup-šai̯u*** (*ᶠŠur-ku-up-ša-a-ú, ᶠŠur-kum-ša-i-ú*).

Interpretation of the sequence ***ki-de-ma-9-na*** (HT 31.4) is not easy. First the question has to be answered, whether Linear A sign ***9*** belongs to the signs that may represent one of the missing phonetic values in the grid of Linear A or whether it is just a variant of Linear A sign ***56a = pi***, in which only the top horizontal stroke is missing as I have assumed reading ***pi-ti-sa*** instead of ***9-ti-sa*** (HT 31.1), first sequence of the same tablet.

E. Laroche (*GLH*, 146, s.v. ***kid-***) mentions: *ki-ta-pa-a-i*, KUB XXVII 42 Ro 32; *ki-i-ta-a-wa*$_a$*-e*, KBo XII 80 + IV 9; *ki-tal-li-ip-pa*, KUB XLV 18 Ro 18; *ki-ta-al-lu-wa*, KBo XV 1 IV 27. I.J. Gelb (*NPN*, 89) mentions the personal name ***Kitinti*** (that may according to Gelb perhaps be Akkadian *Qitintu* ?).

According to Th. Richter (*VHN*, 443) ***Kitinti*** from Nuzi probably is Hurrian ***Kidindi***. Th. Richter (*VHN*, 170, 443) also mentions ***ᶠKitum-allai*** (wr. *ki-tum-al-la-i*) at Mari, analysis {*kid=u/o=m-allai*}, typology 1.1.1.1.1, lexicon *kid-, allai*; ***ᶠKitumze*** (wr. *ki-du-um-ze*) at Mari, analysis {*kid=u/o=m=ze*}, typology 1.3, lexicon *kidumze* (→ *kid-*) that can also be equated with the noun *kidumze*. The root is rare in vocabulary and onomastics. A translation is unfortunately not available, cf. also Th. Richter, *BGH*, 217-218, s.v. ***kid-***.

Th. Richter cautiously distinguishes the root ***kid-*** (*BGH*, 217-218; *VHN*, 443) from the root ***kind-*** [PN] (*BGH*, 207-208; *VHN*, 437-438). He considers ***kindiri*** (*VHN*, 438) in personal names a participle in ***°=i=ri***, built on the root ***kind-***, and offers the personal names ***Šelwi***(?)***-kin***[***tiri***](?) (wr. *Še-el-*WA*-gi-in-*[…]) from Mari, analysis {*šelv=i-kin*[*diri*](?)}, typology 1.3.1.2.1, lexicon *šelw-, šilw-, kindiri* (?); ***Šim-kintiri*** (wr. *Ši-im-gi-in-di-ri*) from Mari, analysis {*šim-kindiri*}, typology 1.4, lexicon *šim-, kindiri*; ***Šuše-kin***[***tiri***](?) (wr. *Šu-še-gi-in(-)*[(…)] from Mari, analysis {*šo/už-kin*[*diri*](?)}, typology 1.3.1.2.1, lexicon *šuš-* I, *kindiri* (?). I consider it likely that the roots ***kid-*** and ***kind-*** are basically the same and that the development from ***kind=ar*** to ***kid=ar*** is the result of elision of ***-n-***.

Especially the names from Nuzi with ***-kintar*** and ***-kitar***, phonologically ***/-kindar/*** and ***/-kidar/***, show that we are dealing with the same onomastic element ***kind=ar / kid=ar***. The following sentence names with ***-ki(n)tar*** as second element are attested at Nuzi: ***Šati-ki(n)tar*** (wr. *Ša-ti-ki-in-tar, Ša-te-ki-in-tar, Ša-di-ki-in-tar, Ša-te-ki-tar, Šadî-ki-in-tar, Šadî-ki*-tar, Ša-ti-ki-tar*), ***Turi-ki(n)tar*** (wr. *Du-ri-ki-in-tar, Tu-ri-ki-tar, Du-ri-ki-tar, Tu-ri-ki-in-tar, Du-ur-ki-in-tar*), ***U̯anti-kintar*** (wr. *Ú-an-ti-ki-in-tar* [*ti* might be scribal error for *tar*]), ***Wantar-ki(n)tar*** (wr. *Wa-an-tar-ki-in-tar, Wa-an-tar-ki-tar, Ú-an-tar-ki-in-tar, Wa-an-da-ri-ki-in-tar, Ú-a-an-ta-ri-ki-in-tar, Ú-a-an-ta-ar-ki-tar, Ú-a-an-tar*-ki-in-tar*), ***Ziwir-kintar*** (wr. *Zi-wi-ir-ki-in-tar*), ***Zu-kitar*** (wr. *Zu-ki-tar*), cf. P.M. Purves, *NPN*, 227.

I consider it likely that ***kindari*** can be analysed as {*ki(n)d=ar=i*}, so that its formation can be compared with forms like ***ḫaš=ar=i*** 'Feinöl' ['aromatic oil, ointment'] from ***ḫaš-*** 'salben' ['to anoint, to rub with ointment'], ***šid=ar=ni*** 'Fluch' ['curse'] from ***šid-*** 'verfluchen' ['to curse'].

Haas/Thiel (1978, 166) give the meaning 'Götterwohnstätte' ['Residence of the Gods'] for ***kundari***, Popko (1978, 31) 'eine Art Heiligtum' ['a sort of sanctuary'], Hoffner (1998a, 189) 'a shrine' and I. Wegner (2001, 442) 'ein Gemach' ['a chamber, room']. E. Laroche (*GLH*, 154), s.v. ***kundari*** 'séjour des dieux', also mentions ***ku-un-ta-ri purulli*** 'la demeure *k.*', IBoT II 39 Ro 38, 41, and the loan-word into Hittite ^{é}***kuntaras***, *HW* 116, in which H. Otten (1988, 45) sees 'eine Benennung für die Wohnung des Teššup' ['a name for the residence of Teššub'], cf. Th. Richter, *BGH*, 224-225.

However, even if ***kindari*** {*kind=ar=i*} can be identified with ***kundari*** {*kund=ar=i*} 'Residence of the Gods', that does not provide a meaning for the root ***kind-*** or ***kund-***, cf. also the discussion on Linear A ***ki-da-ta*** (HT 40+76.2), ***ki-da-te***[(HT 27+ 48a.4), ***ki-da-ro*** (HT 117a.9) and ***ki-da-ro***[(HT 47a.4) from Hagia Triada.

HT 118.1.	SUS , *i+ro* ,		
1-2.	*ma-di*	15	*ki* 10
2-3.	*qa-qa-ru*	6	*ki* 4
3-4.	*a-we-su*	4	*ki* 1
4.	*we-ru-ma*	10	
5.	*ku-ro*	30	*ki* 15[

Linear A tablet HT 118.1 starts with the ideogram SUS 'pig'. The scribe probably made an error in counting the total after *ku-ro*, which should have been 35 instead of 30. The total of *ki* 15 is correct. The scribe may have been an expert in handwriting, but a less successful accountant.

Linear A ***ma-di*** (HT 3.7, HT 69.2, HT 85b.5, HT 97[+]HT 109a.4, HT 118.1, HT? 170b.2 [Raison-Pope] = PH? 31b.2 [Godart-Olivier] = Her. Mus. 1609) is at least six times attested as a personal name at Hagia Triada. The ligature ***ma+di*** (KN Zg <21>) perhaps also occurs on a weight or seal-stone from Knossos (HM, 1957; excavation-number HH/[19]57/52) according to J. Chadwick (in: J. Chadwick - M.S.F. Hood, 'Two Linear A inscriptions from Knossos', *BSA LVII (1962)*, 73-74, pl. XX), whereas Raison-Pope, 1994, 232 (KN Z 21) and *GORILA 4*, 164, read ***si+di***, which is probably the correct reading.

In Linear B we find the masculine personal name ***ma-di*** in KN As(1) 603+8157+fr.,2 (join J.T. Killen) before VIR 1 among several personal names, in KN Db 1168+7168+fr.b before ***e-ko-so*** (toponym) ***we-we-si-jo-jo***. The identification of ***ma-di*** in the Linear B texts from Knossos as a masculine personal name confirms identification of the same sequence as a (masculine) personal name in the Linear A texts from Hagia Triada.

It is also useful that ***ma-di*** is recognized as a Pre-Greek name in Linear B. C.J. Ruijgh, *EGM*, § 188, note 41: "Il peut s'agir d'un nom dont l'élément ***ma-d-*** est préhellénique; cf. les anthroponymes ***ma-di*** (KN As 603, 2), ***ma-di-qo*** (KN B 806,4),]***ma-da-ro*** (KN Db 1368), ***ma-du-ro*** (PY Cn 655,18)." The fact that the personal name ***ma-di*** occurs in both Linear A and B may be considered a confirmation of the phonetic value of signs ***ma*** and ***di*** that are graphically identical in Linear A and B. The same applies, for instance, to the signs ***pa***, ***i*** and ***to*** in the Linear A and B toponym ***pa-i-to***.

The only obvious exception to graphic and phonetic identity of Linear A and B signs is the series of signs for the Linear B labio-velar sounds, required for (Indo-European) Mycenaean Greek. Hurrian did not have labio-velars, but it had (voiced) velar fricatives.

Ma-di occurs as a Hurrian 'one-word' name at Alalaḫ, cf. A. Draffkorn, *HHA*, 43, 89: ***Ma-di*** NAGAR (*AT* 224: r.10). Theophorous names with the same element occur at Alalaḫ: ***madi-eni*** (wr. *ma-ti-e-ni*), *AT* 159,14, ***Eǵlum-mada***, ***Kušam-madi*** < ***Kušaǵ-***, ***Šaum-madi*** < ***Šaub-***, ***Tanne-madi***, ***Iri-madu***, cf. A. Draffkorn, *HHA*, 89-90.

At Nuzi a large number of sentence names with the element ***ma-di*** is mentioned by P.M. Purves, *NPN*, 233-234, s.v. ***mat-***, ***-mati***: ***Mat-teja*** (wr. *Ma-at-te-e-a, Ma-at-te-ia, Ma-at-te-a*), hypocoristic of ***Mat-tešup*** (wr. *Ma-at-te-šup, Ma-at-te-eš-šup, Ma-at-te-sup*), ***Enna-mati*** (wr. *En-na-ma-ti, E-en-na-ma-ti, E-na-ma-ti, En-na-ma-di, E-en-na-ma-di, E-na-ma-di, I-en-na-ma-te, En-na-a-ma-ti, En-na-ma-dil, ᶠE-en-na-ma-a-ti, I-na-ma-di-il*), ***Nawar-mati*** (wr. *ᶠNa-wa-ar-ma-ti*); ***Ninum-mati*** (wr. *ᶠNi-nu-um-ma-ti*), ***Šajum-madi*** (wr. *ᶠŠa-a-ú-um-ma-ti, ᶠŠá-a-ú-ma-ti, ᶠŠa-a-ú- ma-ti^{ti}, ᶠŠa-a-ú-ma-ti*), ***Tešup-mati*** (wr. *Te-šup-ma-ti, Te-eš-šu-ma-ti*), ***Mati-p-tešup*** (wr. *Ma-ti-ip-te-šup*), ***Mati-ya*** (wr. *Ma-ti-ia*), with hypocoristic suffix ***-ya*** according to Purves, but see *infra* for a verbal interpretation of *{mad=i=(j)a}* by Th. Richter. ***Ma-at-te-šup*** and ***Tešup-mati*** occur at Ugarit, cf. F. Gröndahl, *Die Personennamen der Texte aus Ugarit*, 240.

There used to be disagreement on the meaning and etymology of the theme ***mad-***. L. Oppenheim, 'Studien zu den nichtsemitischen Nuzi-Namen', *Archiv für Orientforschung 12 (1937)* [1939], 32, n. 14: ***mati*** erscheint noch im Frauennamen *Na-wa-ar-ma-ti* (Nu 531, 10) (dazu s. S. 35) "Der Gott (von) Namar ist *mati*". Hier wie in ***Ena-mati*** (s. im Text) ist ***mati*** sicherlich Adjektivum. C.-G. von Brandenstein, 'Ein arisches und ein semitisches Lehnwort im Churrischen', *Archiv für Orientforschung 13 (1939)*, 60, considered ***mat*** in the form ***mati*** a loan-word from Indo-European: 'Denken', 'Meinung', 'Verstand', synonymous with Akkadian ***uznu*** 'Ohr', in the sense of 'Verstand', 'Sinn'.

A. Draffkorn, *HHA*, 89, s.v. *mad* 'wisdom', and F. Gröndahl, *PNTU*, 240, 'Verstand', both followed this view. P.M. Purves (*NPN*, 233-234) regarded names as ***Mati-p-Tešup***, with suffix ***-p-***, which he (like E.A. Speiser) interpreted as a verbal root-complement, as evidence for use of ***mat*** as a verb in anthroponyms and he adds: "Furthermore, the personal name *Ša$_x$ (SÁ)-dar-ma-at* on the bronze Samarra tablet, *RA IX (1912)*, 1-4, is evidently analogous to Nuzi ****Satar-mati***. For equation of ***-mat*** in the Samarra personal name with ***-mati*** in Hurrian personal names from Nuzi see Speiser, *Mes. Or.*, p. 144. Since the Samarra tablet probably antedates the Ur III period, it also antedates very likely the contact between Indo-European and Hurrian linguistic groups." Since the arguments given by Purves are sound, we must accept that an Indo-Iranian etymology of ***madi*** is unlikely and that the term is probably Hurrian. Recognition of occurrence of a verbal root ***mad-*** was important. Since publication of the Hurrian-Hittite bilingual ***Kirenze*** the suffix ***-b-*** appeared to represent the Old Hurrian marker of the subject of the verb 3rd person singular.

E. Laroche (*GLH,* 163-164, s.v. ***madi***) reminds us that the nominal themes, written *ma-(a)-ti-, ma-(a)-tu-* and *ma-(a)-ta-*, which are very frequent in theophorous personal names, are never written with double writing of the dental, so that we must conclude that the dental is always voiced ***/d/*** ("avec dentale simple, donc sonore"). He mentions that ***madi*** is a frequent attribute of the god Ea in Asia Minor: *ᵈÉ.A-an-na ma-a-ti-ni-bi abin* (IBoT II 39 Ro 43) "*Ea* of the *madi*". He also mentions *ᵈÉ.A-ma-ti-ni-bi wurulli* 'temple of *Ea-madi*' (KUB XXXII 26 II 13 = KBo XV 75 Vo 4; cf. KUB XLVII 10, 10; 59, 12-13) and the divine name ***Madu-Šauška*** (wr. *ᵈMa-a-tu-uš-ša-uš-ga/qa*), KUB XXV 48 IV 11, 17.

E. Laroche, *GLH*, 164: "Le sens du mot n'est pas connu. On a souvent supposé qu'à côté de ***ḫazzizzi*** 'entendement' (akk. ***ḫasisu***), ***mati*** 'sagesse' serait un attribut de Ea, analogue au hitt. 'Ea seigneur de sagesse (***hattannas***)'. On compare alors skr. ***matiḥ*** 'pensée', et l'on déduit ***matunni*** 'sage'. Mais: 1. Le pluriel ***mate-na*** indique plutôt un objet; 2. L'onomastique attribue ***mati-*** à beaucoup de dieux et déesses; 3. La graphie exclut l'identité avec skr. ***mati-***. – Le sens réel est à trouver; il ne s'agit pas d'un terme technique emprunté, mais d'un concept religieux qui va au-delà du ***ḫazzizzi*** hourro-mittanien. L'origine indo-arienne est peu vraisemblable; *NPN* 234; Mayrhofer, *Annali Napoli 1*, 3 sqq.; *Die Sprache V*, 87 sq.; Indo-Arier, *passim*; contra: Kammenhuber, *Arier im vorderen Orient*, *passim*."

In recent research it is now thought that the first element of personal names often consists of a verbal form which means that ***mad-*** in ****Mad-tešup*** is probably verbal, which is confirmed by forms like ***Mati-p-tešup***, analysis {*mad=i=b-tešup*}, whereas ***Tešub-madi*** (wr. *Te-šup-ma-ti*) probably contains nominal ***-madi*** as second onomastic element.

Th. Richter (*BGH*, 248, s.v. ***mad-***, *matt-* [*passim*]; *VHN*, 456, s.v. ***mad-***) explains ***mad-*** as '(to be) clever, skilfull' (Diakonoff, 1981a, 86[32]); 'Einsicht/Weisheit zuweisen' (Neu, 1988a, 24[70], 1988e, 111f.), 'to be wise, understand', corresponds with Akkadian *malāku* (Dijkstra 1993b, 168), 'être sage, provident' (Catsanicos 1996, 280), 'weise sein, Einsicht/ Weisheit zuweisen' (Wegner 2004, 41). At Emar the variant ***matt-*** occurs in names (cf. Pruzsinszky 2003, 251). Th. Richter (*BGH*, 248-249) s.v. ***madi***: Bei Kammenhuber 1976a: 175 und Laroche 1980a: 163 ungedeutet, sonst als 'Verstand' (u.a. Haas/Thiel 1979: 349) bzw. 'Einsicht, Klugheit, Weisheit (u.ä.)' (Haas 2003a: 259, Wegner 2004: 41, Trémouille 2005: 319, Campbell 2007a: 245, Wegner 2007a: 266), zuweilen (zusätzlich) in adj. Sinn als 'sage' (Lebrun 1976: 234) oder 'verständig' (Haas 1978b: 60[3]); 'weise, Weisheit' (Wilhelm 1992b: 241[6]), Salvini/Wegner 2004: 175). .... Gleichung: Die Deutung ist seit Neu 1987: 180 auch aufgrund der hethitische Entsprechung ***ḫattātar*** gesichert (*passim* in neuerer Literatur); entspricht auch akk. ***ḫasīsu*** (Archi 1993a: 29). Derivation of Hurrian ***madi*** from Old-Indian ***matí-*** is no longer assumed.

Th. Richter (*VHN*, 191-193, 456) mentions the following Hurrian personal names: ***Matija*** (wr. *Ma-di-ia*) at Mari, Dilbat, Emar and (wr. *Ma-ti-ia*) at Nuzi, analysis {*mad=i=ja*}, typology 1.1.1.2.4, lexicon *mad-*, translation 'Er/Sie (scil. ein *Numen*) wies (dem Jungen) Weisheit zu' ['He/She (scil. a *numen*) made (the boy) wise, clever']; ***ᶠMatazza*** (wr. *Ma-ta-az-za*) at Mari, analysis {*madazz(e)=a*[E.]}, typology 3.2.1, lexicon *madazze* (→ *mad-*), 'Es (Mädchen) ist als (Zeichen der) Weisheit (geboren)' ['She (the girl) is (born) as (a sign of) wisdom'], [E. refers to the *essive* in ***-a***.]; ***ᶠMatunna*** (wr. *Ma-du-na*) at Mari, {*mad=o=nna*}, typology 1.3.1.1.2.1, lexicon *mad-*, translation 'Weise ihm (Mädchen) Weisheit zu (oh *Numen*) !' ['Make her (the girl) wise (oh *numen*) !']; ***ᶠMatunni*** (wr. *Ma-du-un-ni*) at Mari, {*mad=o=nni*}, typology 1.3.1.1.2.2, lexicon *mad-*, 'Weise ihm (Mädchen) Weisheit zu (oh *Numen*) !' ['Make her (the girl) wise (oh *numen*) !']. ***ᶠMatunna*** and ***ᶠMatunni*** are here explained as verbal forms, but might just as the lexical forms ***madi*** and ***madunni*** {*mad=o=nni*} in context be explained as 'wise', cf. *Er-wi-ma-du-ni* at Nuzi 'The Lord is wise' (see *AAN* I 46, cf. Th. Richter, *VHN*, 456). Th. Richter (*VHN*, 49, 456) also mentions ***ᶠAllae-mata*** (wr. *ᶠAl-la-e-ma-da*) at Mari, {*allae-mad(i)=a*[E.]}, typology 2.1, lexicon *allae*, *madi*, 'Die Herrin ist weise' ['The Lady is wise'].

In order to express the *essive* a translation 'She is like a wise Lady' seems preferable. Th. Richter (*VHN*, 245, 456): ***Šan-mata*** (wr. *Ša-an-ma-da*), analysis {*šan-mad(i)=a*[E.]} at Mari and Ašnakkum, typology 1.4, lexicon *šan-*, *madi*.

Concluding: Linear A and B ***ma-di*** may be interpreted as a Hurrian one-word *nominal* personal name ***Madi*** (subst.) 'Wisdom / Intelligence' or (adj.) 'Wise / Intelligent' or as a *verbal* (trans. *imperative*) name {*mad=i*} 'Make (the child) wise, intelligent (*numen*) !' Both interpretations are plausible. See also Linear A ***ma-da-ti*** (PK 1.7) from Palaikastro.

Linear A ***qa-qa-ru*** (HT 93a.4-5; HT 111a.3; HT 118.2-3; HT 122b.3-4) from Hagia Triada has at first sight the appearance of Akkadian ***kakkaru*** (*CAD* K 49 ff.). However, since the sequence apparently occurs in lists of personal names, it seems likely that ***qa-qa-ru*** is a personal name as ***ma-di*** (HT 118.1), ***a-we-su*** (HT 118.3), ***we-ru-ma*** (HT 118.4), ***te-ki, ja-mi-da-re, si-da-re, so-di-ra, pa-de, ku-pa₃-nu*** and ***pa-ta-ne*** (HT 122).

If one *prima facie* thinks of the Hurrian roots ***kakk-*** and ***kank-***, one must realize that signs of the Linear A ***q-*** series reflect neither the Mycenaean labio-velar ***q-*** nor the cuneiform emphatic ***q-***, but the Hurrian voiced velar fricative ***ḫ-*** and ***-ḫ-***.

Consequently Linear A ***qa-qa-ru*** may be interpreted as a Hurrian sentence name ***Ḫaš-ḫalu***, consisting of the Hurrian verbal root ***ḫaš-*** and the onomastic element ***-ḫalu***. It is evident that ***-ḫalu*** must be nominal in the names, where the first element is verbal. The root ***ḫaš-*** was first described by L. Messerschmidt, *Mitanni-Studien*, 22, 125, as 'hören'. The meaning 'to hear' is now generally accepted. At Nuzi we find the names ***Ḫaš-ampa*** (wr. *Ḫa-ša-am-pa*) beside ***Ḫašip-ampa*** (wr. *Ḫa-ši-pa-am-pa*), ***Ḫaš-ḫarpa*** (wr. *Ḫa-aš-ḫar-ba, Ḫa-aš-ḫar-me*), ***Ḫaš-šimika*** (wr. *Ḫa-aš-ši-mi-qa, Ḫa-ši-mi-qa*), ***Ḫaš-teįa*** (wr. *Ḫa-aš-te-ia*) beside ***Ḫašip-tešup*** (wr. *Ḫa-ši-ip-te-šup*), cf. P.M. Purves, *NPN*, 214-215. Purves's ***Ḫaš-talla*** (wr. *Ḫa-aš-tal-la*) can now be analysed as {*ḫašt=a=lla*}, 'They are strong'.

The Hurrian onomastic element ***-ḫalu*** is found in ***Arša-ḫalu*** (wr. *Ar-ša-ḫa-lu*), ***Eniš-ḫalu*** (wr. *ᶠE-ni-iš-ḫa-lu, ᶠE-ni-eš-ḫa-lu*), ***Ipša-ḫalu*** (wr. *Ip-ša-ḫa-lu, Ip-šá-ḫa-lu, Ip-ša-ḫa-a-lu, Ip-sa-ḫa-lu, Ip-šá-ḫa-a-lu*), ***Išip-ḫalu*** (wr. *I-ši-ip-ḫa-lu, I-zi-ip-ḫa-lu*), *NPN*, 213.

Ḫalu- is found as first onomastic element in ***Ḫalu-menni*** (wr. *ᶠḪa-lu-me-en-ni, ᶠḪa-lu-me-ni*), ***Ḫalu-šenni*** (wr. *Ḫa-al-še-en-ni, Ḫa-lu-še-en-ni, Ḫa-al-še-ni, Ḫa-lu(m)-še-ni, Ḫa-lu-še-i*[*n-ni*], *Ḫa-lu-še-ni*), ***ᶠḪaluįa*** (wr. *ᶠḪa-lu-ia*), cf. P.M. Purves, *NPN*, 212-213.

It is clear that ***Ḫalu-*** is verbal as first element in personal names and can be analysed as {*ḫal=o/u-*}. Th. Richter (*BGH*, 119; *VHN*, 406) mentions two verbal roots:

ḫal- I [Boğ.] '(be)singen' ['to sing (of), to celebrate in song, to chant'], cf. ***ḫalme/i*** [Boğ., Ug.] 'Gesang, Lied' ['chant, song'], corresponds with Sumerian EZEN, Akkadian *zammarum*, Ugaitic *šîru*, see E. Laroche (*GLH*, 90), s.v. ***ḫalmi*** 'chant'. RS quadr. 137 III 7: sum. EZEN = akk. *zammarum* = h. *ḫal-mi* = oug. *šîru*, cf. *Ugar. V*, 246, 455.

ḫal- II [Boğ., Qaṭna] 'to transport, to bring away, to carry off, to drag away', corresponds with Akkadian ***naḫālu***. Th. Richter prefers this root as verbal element in personal names in the sense of 'to bring away a (deceased) child'. He mentions (*VHN*, 119-120, 406): ***Ḫalaš-tuk*** (Mari, [Šubat-Enlil]), ***Ḫalukkan*** (Ašnakkum), ***Ḫalum-atal*** (Mari) 'The strong one carried him (the deceased boy) off', ***ᶠḪalunna*** (Mari) 'Carry her off (oh *numen*) !' or 'Celebrate her in song', ***Ḫalut*** (Tigunāni) 'Carry me off (oh *numen*) !' / 'Celebrate me in song', ***Ḫalutil*** (Mari) 'Carry us off (oh *numen*) !' / 'Celebrate us in song'.

It is conceivable that a noun ****ḫali*** existed as a variant of ***ḫalmi*** 'chant'. The personal name ****Ḫaš-ḫali*** may in that case be interpreted as 'Hear the chant (oh *numen*) !'; ****ḫali*** is then the object of the athematic *imperative* ***ḫaš-*** (instead of thematic ***ḫaš=i-***). The whole personal name ***qa-qa-ru*** (HT 93a.4-5; HT 111a.3; HT 118.2-3; HT 122b.3-4), Hurrian ***Ḫaš-ḫalu***, can be interpreted as an Akkadianizing *nominative* in ***-u***. The formation of ****ḫali*** may be compared with e.g. ***tari*** 'Feuer' ['fire'], cf. Th Richter, *BGH*, 444-445, s.v. ***tari*** I. Compare also Linear A ***qa-qa-ru*** with Linear A ***qa-ra₂-wa*** (HT 86a.3) from Hagia Triada.

The next Hurrian name ***a-we-su*** (HT 118.3) has already been discussed extensively (*supra*). Th. Richter (*BGH*, 41) tells that in a quadrilingual comparison (Ugarit) Hurrian ***abuškumme*** is equated with Sumerian KAR, Akkadian ***šūzubu*** and Ugaritic ***pullaṭu*** 'to save', cf. J. Huehnergard, *Ugaritic vocabulary in syllabic transcrip-tion* (Harvard Semitic Studies 32), Atlanta 1987[1], 82f., 168; G. Wilhelm, Zum hurritischen Infinitiv in Nuzi, *SCCNH 2 (1987)*, 331[3]. The form ***abuškumme*** can be analysed as {*av=ušk=umme*} consisting of the root ***ab/w-***, root-extension ***-ušk-*** and the Hurrian infinitive-suffix ***-umme***.

According to Th. Richter (*VHN*, 375-376, s.v. ***aw-*** II {*av-*}) the root ***aw-*** also occurs in *a-wu-um* {*av=o=m*} at Mari and Tuttul (Tall Bi'a). In onomastics the verbal element ***aw-*** mainly occurs in modal forms in ***ᵒ=i=ž*** and in imperative forms in ***ᵒ=i***. Since *a-wi/mi-iš-ta-e* at Nuzi and *a-bi-iš-ta-e/i* at Ugarit are certainly the same name, orthographies with [W], [M] and [B]/[P] are to be taken into account in accordance with time and place of reference. Richter has brought the root ***aw-*** and the stem ***ab=ušk-*** (= root + root-extension) in ***abuškumme*** together and has proposed that the meaning 'to save', that has been established for ***ab=ušk-*** can probably also be applied to the root ***aw-*** without root-extension, which fits well in personal names expressing a blessing to the child.

Th. Richter (*VHN*, 2016, 63, 375-376) offers two Hurrian personal names that can be equated with Linear A ***a-we-su*** (HT 118.3): ***Awizzu*** (wr. *a-wi-iz-zu*) from Mari may be considered an exact equivalent, analysis {*avišš(e)=u*[N.]}, lexicon *awizze* (→ *aw-* II), typology 3.1, translation 'Rettung' ['Rescue, Salvation, Saving']. [N.] refers to an Akkadianizing nominative in ***-u***.

The other is ***Awiš-una*** (wr. *a-wi-iš-ú-na*), name of two men from Mari, that Th. Richter analyses as {*av=i=ž-o/un(i)=a* [E.]}, typology 1.3.2.2, lexicon *aw-* II, *uni*, translation 'Er/Sie (*scil.* ein *Numen*) möge *uni* retten' ['He/she (*scil.* a *numen*) may save *uni*']. [E.] refers to the *essive* case in ***-a***. This analysis is not impossible, but Th. Richter mentions (*VHN*, 553) that the word ***uni*** has to date been isolated neither in context nor in onomastics and that ***Awiš-una*** (Mari) is to date the only possible attestation. In my view another solution is feasible, if one assumes that ***Awiš-una*** with single writing of ***-n-***, may stand for ***Awišunna*** with double ***-nn-*** (a phenomenon that occurs more often). The analysis is then {*av=i=ž=o=nna*}, typology 1.3.1.1.2.1, with an extra thematic vowel ***-o/u-*** between ***-ž-*** and ***-nna***, which may be a means to show that the suffix ***-nna*** is meant to distinguish the 3rd person singular of the personal pronoun 'him', yielding the translation 'He/she (*scil.* a *numen*) may save him (the boy)', from the form ***-Na***, hypocoristic of ***-Naja/-Naje***, as attested in ***ᶠAweš-na*** (wr. *ᶠA*-PI-*iš-na*) at Mari and (wr. *ᶠA-we-eš-na*) at Nuzi, and ***ᶠAwiš-naia/ᶠAweš-naia*** (wr. *ᶠA-wi-iš-na-a-a, ᶠA-we-eš-na-a-a*) at Nuzi, '*Na(je)* möge (Mädchen) retten' ['*Na(je)* may save (the girl)'], cf. Th. Richter, *VHN*, 62.

Since a final consonant is not expressed in Linear A and B, Linear A ***a-we-su*** (HT 118.3) may not only represent ***Awešu***, but also ***Awešun***. Since ***-n*** is a very common abbreviation of ***-nna***, ***Awešun*** can then be analysed as {*av=e=ž=o=n(na)*} and also be translated as 'He/she (*scil.* a *numen*) may save him/her (the child)'.

The cognate Linear A personal name ***a-we-||ni-ta*** (ZA 8.2-3) from Kato Zakro can probably be analysed as {*aw(=i)=en=i=tta*}, consisting of the root ***aw-*** + *jussive* indicator ***-i-*** that probably amalgamated with following ***-en-*** (cf. I. Wegner, *Einführung*, 103ff.) + indicator of the *jussive* 3rd person singular ***-en-*** (according to Wegner, *ibid.*) + thematic vowel ***-i-*** + the suffix of the enclitic personal pronoun 1st person singular ***-tta*** 'me'. I. Wegner uses the term *jussive*, whereas E. Laroche (*GLH*, 28) used the terms 'potentiel' ['subjunctive expressing possibility'] and 'optatif' ['optative'] for the suffix ***-en-*** indicating the 3rd person singular of that mood. Linear A ***a-we-||ni-ta*** (ZA 8.2-3) can be translated as 'May he/she (the *numen*) save me'.

Since ***we-ru-ma*** (HT 118.4) is the last of a series of personal names preceding ***ku-ro*** (HT 118.5) on tablet HT 118, Linear A ***-ma*** in ***we-ru-ma*** can be interpreted as the Hurrian enclitic connective suffix ***-ma*** 'and' (frequent at Boğazköy and Mâri, less frequent in the Tušratta letter). Cf. E.A. Speiser, *IH*, 177-179, § 212: ***-ma*** 'and, also, but'; cf. E. Laroche, *GLH*, 163: ***-ma*** 'et'. Conjonction enclitique. Mâri, Boğ., Msk. ***-ma*** et ***-m***; Ug. alph. ***-m***.

I. Wegner (*Einführung*, 78-79) mentions sub 2.2.7: Position 9: *the syntactical particles*: connective particle: ***-ma*** 'und, aber' ['and, but'] and ***/man/*** or ***/mân/*** 'und, aber, eben' ['and, but, even']. Consequenly the personal name may be ****Weru*** followed by the enclitic connective. Thus Linear A ***-ma*** in ***we-ru-ma*** may have the same function as in ***i-pi-na-ma*** (KO Za 1.c-d, *e.a.*); ***i-pi-na-ma*** is virtually always mentioned near the close of the 'Libation formula' and ***-ma*** in ***i-pi-na-ma*** (KO Za 1.c-d, *e.a.*) can be identified with the enclitic connective suffix ***-ma*** 'and' (*Chapter 11: 'Religious' Linear A inscriptions*).

In the 2016 edition of *Minoan Linear A* I still hesitated to assume an alternation of ***p/w***, phonologically of /***b/w***/, for the root ***wer-*** in Linear A ***we-ru-ma***, although such alternations are quite common in Hurrian cuneiform texts, e.g. ***pant*** / ***want*** as phonetic variants, cf. P.M. Purves, *NPN*, 274 s.v. ***want***. See also my interpretation of Linear A ***wa-du-ni-mi*** (HT 6b.1; HT 85b.4-5) as the Hurrian personal {*wad=u=n-irmi*} or {*wand=u=n-irmi*}, consisting of the Hurrian verbal root ***p/wand-*** or ***p/wad-*** 'to make good, just' + the marker of the transitive perfect form ***-o/u-*** + the suffix of the enclitic personal pronoun 3rd person sing. ***-n(na)*** marking the object of the transitive verb + the theophorous element ***irmi*** / ***ermi*** 'Lord', indicating the subject of the verb. Linear A ***wa-du-ni-mi*** can be translated as an *indicative* sentence name 'The Lord has made him/her [***-n(na)***] (the child) good, just', but also as an *imperative* 'Make him/her [***-n(na)***] (the child) good, just, oh Lord !'. As a matter of fact the ***w-/b-*** phenomenon is well-known in many languages.

Th. Richter (*BGH*, 312-314), s.v. ***p/wir-*** [Boğ.; Nuzi; PN] and (*VHN*, 483), s.v. ***pir-*** {*fir-*(?)}, has confirmed this alternation for the verbal root ***p/wir-*** that can now be translated as 'lösen (durch die gesprochene Beschwörung)' ['to liberate (by chanting incantations)'], i.e. /***fer-***/ (Haas/Thiel, 1978, 245), corresponding with Hittite ***lā-***, and Sumerogram DU_8; 'to loosen, undo' (Huehnergard 1987a, 92); 'liberare' (Giorgieri 2000a, 224[156]; 2000b, 292,294) ['to liberate']; cf. for the labial fricative Wilhelm, 2005a, 176[7].

There may also be a correlation with ***wir=wir=išt-***, *bi-ir-bi-ri-iš-du-up-pu-uš* (KBo 33.118 + = ChS I/5 Nr. 2 Vs. 40') 'lösen, befreien' (Haas/Thiel, 1978, 245; Wilhelm, 1983, 97). The noun ***p/wiradi***, */**firade**/*, may well contain the same root ***p/wir-*** and was explained as 'Edelmann' ['noble gentleman'], literally 'Ungebunde, Freie' ['unbound, freedman, free man'] (Haas/Thiel, 1978, 176, 246), 'nobleman' (Diakonoff, 1979, 41), 'noble ?' (Laroche, *GLH*, 297), but most recently as 'auswärtiger Gast(freund)' ['foreign guest'] (Wilhelm, 2005a, 184, a. o.). The noun is used as a personal name at Mari and Šušarrā.

This evidence enables us to compare ***we-ru-*** in Linear A ***we-ru-ma*** (HT 118.4) with personal names like *Be-ru, Be-i-ru, Bi-e-ru, Bi-ru, Bi-i-ru, Bi-i-ru(m), Bi-i-ru-ú* at Nuzi (cf. P.M. Purves, *NPN*, 245, s.v. ***pir***, ***piru***). As a result the last sequence ***we-ru-ma*** in the series of Linear A personal names can be translated as 'and *Weru*'. Interpretation of ***-ma*** as Hurrian enclitic connective suffix seems to be the easiest solution, especially because of the position of ***we-ru-ma*** as last sequence in a series of personal names. The name ***Βιρων***, mentioned by L. Zgusta, *Kleinasiatische Personennamen*, 124, § 171, might be a late parallel of the Nuzi name.

Other theoretical interpretations of ***-ma*** in Linear A ***we-ru-ma*** are:

1) Hurrian ***-ma*** may be a formative as in the Hurrian personal names ***Erima***, ***Šennima***, ***Taima*** at Nuzi (cf. P.M. Purves, *NPN*, 232, s.v. ***-ma***).

2) It would even be conceivable that ***-ma*** in personal names is a hypocoristic of ***-madi*** 'wisdom', 'wise' that occurs not only as first onomastic element, but also as second (*quasi*) theophorous element in personal names. It would in that case be comparable with ***-še*** as hypocoristic of ***-šena*** or ***-šen(n)i*** '(the) brother' or ***-te*** or ***-teja***, hypocoristics of ***-Tešub*** in personal names.

3) I. Wegner (*Einführung*, 93, Table 4: *Order of suffixes of the indicative, transitive-ergative, positive verb*) mentions ***-mma/-m***, enclitic personal pronoun 2nd person sing. (position 9); see also Th. Richter (*VHN*, 586, sub F): ***arijamma*** (wr. *a-ri-ia-am-ma*) {*ari=a=mma*} 'Er/Sie (scil. ein *Numen*) gibt dich' ['He/She (scil. a *numen*) gives you'], at Nippur (Hölscher, 1996, 38). The suffix ***-mma*** has in this case the function of object. The meaning of Linear A ***we-ru-ma***, analysis {*wer=u=mma*}, would then be 'He/She (scil. a *numen*) liberated you (by listening to the chanted incantations)'. This would in fact provide a plausible meaning for a personal name commemorating a happy delivery.

4) Th. Richter (*VHN*, 594) also mentions (sub 1.3.1.1.2.1: *Normal forms*) in more recent morphological descriptions of the transitive imperative the suffix ***°-m(ma)*** as absolutive enclitic marker of the 2nd person singular in the function of subject (cf. M. Giorgieri, Schizzo grammaticale della lingua hurrica, *La parola del Passato 55 (2000)*, 235: *"un pronome personale enclitico ... in funzione di soggetto"*). I gather that this possibility can be ruled out for the Linear A form ***we-ru-ma***, since it is very unlikely that 'you', referring to the newborn child, can be the *subject* of the 'liberation (by listening to the chanted incantations)' during the delivery. The suffix ***°-m(ma)*** is obviously the *object* (see sub 3).

5) I. Wegner (*Einführung*, 96, sub c: *Die Verneinung der 3. Pers. Sg.*; and 137, sub c, in the chapter on *Althurritisch*) explains the Old Hurrian form ***ar+i+a+(m)ma*** (wr. *a-ri-ja-am-ma*) {*ar=i=a=(m)ma*} from the Hurrian-Hittite bilingual ***Kirenze*** (KBo 32: 15 IV 16) (which incidentally looks exactly identical with the form from Nippur, mentioned by Th. Richter, *VHN*, 586, sub F) as 'er gibt (etwas) nicht' ['he does not give something'].

Her explanation clearly shows that we are not dealing with an error, but with a difference between Old Hurrian and Mitanni-Hurrian, because she explains (137, sub c) that in forms of the 3rd person singular, in which the morpheme of the negation ***-(m)ma*** is written at the end of the verbal form, this morpheme is in the Tušratta letter always written with single ***m***, but at Boğazköy apparently mainly with double ***mm***. She adds that it must not be confused with the enclitic particle ***-(m)ma*** 'and, but' and with the enclitic pronoun of the 2nd person singular ***-mma*** 'du' ['you (as subject)'] and 'dich' ['you (as object)'].

However, this possibility can be ruled out, because I. Wegner (*Einführung*, 96, sub c) explains that the negative morpheme ***-ma*** only occurs, if usage of the suffix ***-wa-*** would lead to a sequence of **i+wa+a* (3rd person transitive). It is to be considered *allomorph* of ***-wa-***, although ***-ma*** does not take the same position as ***-wa-*** in the chain of suffixes. The normal suffix ***-wa-*** marking a negation in transitive constructions takes position 6 between the marker of transitivity ***-i-*** and the marker of the 3rd person singular ***-a-***, whereas ***-ma*** follows ***-a-***, cf. also I. Wegner, *Einführung*, 95, Table 5. The *negative* morpheme ***-ma*** is not combined with the associative ***-an*** 'and' in order to avoid confusion with the particle ***-mân*** (*-ma-a-an*, cf. I. Wegner, *Einführung*, 117), cf. Chr. Girbal, *SMEA 34*, 1994, 83 f.

Consequently Linear A ***we-ru-ma*** (HT 118.4) contains ***-u-ma***, not ****-i+a+(m)ma*** (replacing **i(+wa)+a*), so that replacement of a negation ***-wa-*** by ***-ma-*** is not justifiable.
6) Since final consonants were not expressed in Linear A and B, one may also think of the onomastic element ***-mar*** as in the Hurrian Nuzi name ***Nu-du-mar***, cf. P.M. Purves, *NPN*, 233, s.v. ***-mar*** (2). Since ***wer-*** is verbal, the second element ***-mar*** must be nominal.

Th. Richter (*VHN*, 455) remarks that already Gustavs (1925, 301-302; 1929, 58[1]), considering the etymology of ***marijannu*** (cf. Th. Richter, *BGH*, 245-246), postulated a root ***mar-*** or ***mari-***, perhaps 'besitzen' ['to possess'] or 'nutznießen' ['to hold in usufruct']. Although the etymology remains problematic, the existence of the root cannot be denied. More recent suggestions such as 'von Unreinheit befreien' ['to free from impurities'] or 'töten' ['to kill'] need to be verified. The meaning of the nominal forms is not clear either. He also discusses the onomastic element ***mari*** that is possibly already known from Mari- and/or Ḫattuša-texts, as well as the new form ***maruḫ(ḫ)e***, {*mari»o=ġ/ḫḫe*}, 'zu mari/Mari gehörig' ['belonging to mari/Mari']. Perhaps ***°-mar/-ma-ar-ra*** can be connected that occurs in the same form at Nuzi (cf. *NPN*, 233). He mentions: (1) {*mar-*}: *Maratilla* (Mari); *Maruš-taḫe* (Mari). (2) {*marri*}: *ᶠTupi-marra* (Mari). (3) {*mari»o=ġ/ḫḫe*}: *ᶠMaruḫ(ḫ)e* (Mari).

Linear A tablet HT? 170 is probably from Hagia Triada, but the exact provenance is uncertain, because the tablet was donated by the family of a labourer who had participated in the Italian excavations in Crete. According to the donator the tablet came from the debris at Phaistos. *GORILA* 1, XX, n.1, followed this view considering the aspect of the tablet and material not very typical for Hagia Triada and labelled it PH? 31. J. Raison - M. Pope, however, considered provenance from Hagia Triada more likely in view of the text itself. A. Furumark (*Opuscula Romana XI.1*, 1976, 3, note 5, writes: "The tablet quoted by Godart-Olivier as 'PH(?) 31a' is actually from Hagia Triada, as clearly shown by its contents and as already rightly inferred by Raison and Pope in their Index, where it is cited as HT? 170." Probably Late Minoan I b.

HT (?) 170 = HM 1609. Sup. mut.

a.1.]CAP^{f} 2 OVIS^{f} 1[
2.]*ku-du-we* CAP^{m} 1 *tu-*[
3.]*ne* CAP^{m} 1 CAP^{f} 5 *te-we* OVIS^{m}[
4. CAP^{m}+*ku* 1 *we-ru-ma-ti* OVIS^{m} SUS+*si(+re)*[
5.] *a-mi-da-o* OVIS^{m} 1 [

Sup. mut.

b.1.]*-a-*[
2.]*ru* CAP^{m}+*ku* 1 *ma-di* OVIS^{m} 1 OVIS^{f}[
3.]' 1 *ku-pa$_3$-nu* SUS+*si*+*re* 1 *pa-ta-da* |
4.]1 *ku-ro* CAP^{m}+*ku* 1 OVIS^{m} 5 OVIS^{f} 3
5.] vacat

Linear A ***we-ru-ma*** (HT 118.4) seems cognate with ***we-ru-ma-ti*** (HT? 170a.4) from Hagia Triada, which means that the verbal root ***p/wir-*** [Boğ.; Nuzi; PN], {*fir-/fer-*}, 'to liberate (by chanting incantations)' (Th. Richter (*BGH*, 312-314; *VHN*, 483) is also the first element of ***we-ru-ma-ti*** (HT? 170a.4). The question is, how ***we-ru-ma-ti*** should be analysed and divided. Does ***-m-*** belong to the verbal form as first onomastic element, so that we are dealing with the Old Hurrian *past indicative* in ***-o/u=m-*** (cf. I. Wegner, *Einführung*, 126-127, 134) and the second element is Hurrian ***-ašti*** or ***-atti*** 'woman' (cf. Th. Richter, *VHN*, 382) ? The analysis is then {*wer=o/u=m-atti*} or {*wer=o/u=m-ašti*}, translation 'He/She (a *numen* / priest ?) liberated the woman (by chanting incantations)'.

Or are we dealing with consecutive verbal root-extensions ***-om-*** and ***-ar-*** (cf. I. Wegner, *Einführung*, 88: e.g. *tiḫan=ol=om-*, from *tiḫan-* 'to indicate'), so that the analysis is {*wer=o/um=ar=tti*} 'Liberate me (by chanting incantations) (oh *numen*) !'. According to the Linear A and B orthographic conventions ***-š-*** and ***-r-*** preceding an occlusive are not expressed in consonant clusters. The Minoan scribe no doubt knew the registered name.

Compare, for instance, the Linear A personal name ***ka-nu-ti*** (HT 97[+]109a.3) that can be interpreted as Hurrian ***Ḫanutti***, analysis {*ḫan=o/u=tti*}, consisting of the verbal root ***ḫan-*** 'to give birth to / to create' + the Old Hurrian suffix indicating the transitive perfect ***-u-*** + the suffix indicating the enclitic pronoun 1st person singular ***-tta*** (position 9), cf. I. Wegner, *Einführung*, 93 (Table 4), 126 (Althurritisch) or the suffix ***-tti***, cf. Th. Richter (*VHN*, 596, sub 1.3.1.1.2.2), who mentions that the suffix indicating the enclitic pronoun 1st person singular ***-tta*** can sometimes be replaced by an optional allomorphic suffix ***-tti***. He explains that the 'one-word names' with enclitic ***=tti***, ***=nni*** / ***=nnu***, ***=lle*** / ***=lli*** are *optional allomorphic forms* for ***=tta***, ***=nna***, ***=lla***, respectively. Compare also the Linear A personal name ***i-du-ti*** (HT 104.2-3) that can be analysed as Hurrian {*id=u=tti*} 'Beat, hit, strike me (oh *numen*) !' Th. Richter mentions ***Ullutti*** at Mari and Tigunāni as examples of a name with enclitic ***=tti*** (1st person sg.).

Linear A ***te-we*** (HT? 170a.3) from Hagia Triada can be compared with Hurrian personal names at Nuzi ***Tewi....***, wr. ***Te-wi-***[....], *JEN* 469: 16, as well as ***Te-wi-ia***; and ***Te-wi-e***, *JEN* 470: 6, 10. The last and possibly the first are in fact an exact equivalent to the Linear A form, since the last ***-e*** in cuneiform ***Te-wi-e*** confirms that ***-wi-*** has the value ***-we-*** (cf. I.J. Gelb, *NPN*, 155; P.M. Purves, *NPN*, 266, s.v. ***tew***, *Te-wi-ia*, *Te-wi-e*).

D.J. Wiseman, *The Alalakh Tablets* (Occasional publications of the British Institute of Archaeology at Ankara 2), London 1953, 149, mentions at Alalaḫ ***Te-wi-ia*** AT 293, 36, and ***Te-wa-at-ti*** AT 75, 9. 15. The latter name may possibly be compared with Linear B ***ti-wa-ti-ja*** (KN Ap 618+633+[X] 5922,2 Killen), with uncertain interpretation.

F. Gröndahl (*PNTU*, 295) mentions at Ugarit ***Te-wa-a***, ***Te-wa-an-na*** and ***Te-wa-ti***. She includes them, however, in her list of 'Anatolische Namen'. 'Anatolian' is a wide concept, which probably also includes Hurrian names from east Anatolia, especially from Kizzuwatna and Cappadocia. ***Te-wi-ia*** can be analysed as {*tew=i=a*} 'He/She speaks'.

The fact that names with the root ***tew-*** occur at Nuzi, Ugarit and Alalaḫ makes identification as Hurrian most likely. Linear A ***te-we*** can probably be analysed as ***tew=e***. P.M. Purves equates ***tew*** with ***tiw*** and compares ***tiw*** with ***tiwi*** 'word, thing' in the Tušratta letter (*NPN*, 268). If this comparison is correct, the common Hurrian term ***tiwi***, ***tiwe***, ***tewe*** is used as a caressing name. The term ***tiwe*** was first translated as 'word' by A.H. Sayce, 'The language of Mitanni', *Zeitschrift für Assyriologie V (1890)*, 264, and similarly by L. Messerschmidt (*Mitanni-Studien*, 21; 132). The term frequently occurs in the Tušratta letter, but also at Boğazköy in several grammatical forms, also with the suffix of the so-called singular definite article ***-ni*** and plural ***-na***, cf. E.A. Speiser, *IH*, 22, 74; E. Laroche, *GLH*, 267-268: ***tiwe*** 'mot, chose'.

However, Th. Richter (*BGH*, 453-455) mentions that ***ti-*** I, ***tiw-*** I [*passim*] can also be a verbal root 'sprechen' ['to speak'], which means that the personal name ***te-we*** (HT? 170a.3), analysis {*tew=e/i* / *tiw=e/i*} may well represent an *imperative* 'Speak !' or 'Say words/names (oh child or oh *numen*) !'. This is the most satisfactory interpretation.

Non-occlusives *σ, μ, ν, ρ, λ, ϝ* in Linear B are usually expressed before the sonantic consonants *μ, ν, ρ, λ, y, ϝ*. Linear A probably followed the same conventions. Consequently it is unlikely that Linear A ***te-we*** (HT? 170a.3) can be identified as ***Teswe*** (cf. P.M. Purves, *NPN*, 266, s.v. ***T(i)ešwa*** (wr. *Te-eš-wa*), since Linear A would have provided ****te-se-we*** instead. For the consonant cluster ***-σϝ-*** in Linear B one may compare e.g. ***po-ti-ni-ja a-si-wi-ja*** (PY Fr 1206: dative fem. sing. ?), which can be explained as ***Πότνια Ἀσϝίᾱ*** 'Asian Mistress' (possibly *Κυβέλη*) from the ethnic ***Ἄσϝιος***, or ***Πότνια Ἀσϝίᾱς*** 'Mistress of Asia' from the toponym ***Ἀσϝίᾱ*** (cf. *Aššuwa* in Hittite texts), cf. C.J. Ruijgh, *EGM*, §156.

Linear A orthography also offers another possibility. Since ***-r-*** preceding ***-m-***, ***-n-*** and ***-w-*** is usually not expressed in consonant clusters in Linear A and B, Linear A can also be identified as ***tirwe***. ***Tirwe*** is attested in the younger tradition as a deity of Azuḫinni, east of the Tigris, presumably northeast of Nuzi and Arrapḫa, in the direction of Šušarrā.

If the Linear A personal name ***te-we*** (HT? 170a.3) is a caressing name ***Tewe / Tiwe***, representing the same word in the singular form as ***di-we-na*** (HT 93a.1-2; HT 102.3) in the plural form, also used as a personal name, Linear A ***te-we*** and ***di-we-na*** would provide evidence for the allophonic character of the dentals in (Minoan-)Hurrian. Hurrian scribes were apparently not able to hear the phonological difference between voiced and voiceless stops properly or well-enough. Not only ***di-we-na***, but also many other examples in Linear A show that initial voicing of dental stops is to be accepted in the Minoan-Hurrian dialect and perhaps also in (some) other areas, where Hurrian written with syllabic cuneiform was the only source. Only at Ugarit the alphabetic cuneiform Hurrian texts seem to give evidence for initial voicelessness during the rather late period of existence of this script.

Since the Linear A sequence ***di-we-na*** (HT 93a.1-2; HT 102.3) occurs on two tablets from Hagia Triada, we have a good opportunity to compare its position in both texts and to see whether the structure of the texts reveals whether it may be a lexical term or a personal name. In my view ***di-we-na*** is a personal name in both cases.

HT 93a.1. *pa$_3$-ni-na* , GRA *pa$_3$* , *se+re* ↓ 12 *di-*
2. *we-na* , *se+re+da* ↓ 43 J *di-di-*
3. *ni* 5 JH *a-se* , *no* 3
4. GRA+*pa* 26 JE *sa-ra$_2$* 20 *qa-qa-*
5. *ru* , *no* GRA+*pa* 5 *wo-no*
6. 6 *de-96-ku* 1 J *o-ti-*
7. *ro* 3 *da-we-da* *115* 2 ARB 2
8. *pa$_3$-ni-na*[ ]*da-se-ja* 20
9. VIR 10 F '[ ]' 2 B ROTA 4

HT 93b.1. [*ku-ro*] 165 H , *ki-ro*
2. [ ] vacat and lines 3-9. Vacant

HT 102.1. *ka-pa* , *sa-ra$_2$* GRA 900
2. 76 *pa$_3$-ni* GRA+*pa* 33
3. VIR (*126*) GRA+*pa* 33 *di-we-na* 10 *ma-*
4. *do* 3 *wi* 10[ ] *i-ka* 5
5. *ku-ro* 1060 [
6. vacat

Comment: If the total number 1060 after *ku-ro* is complete, the dot after *wi* is probably a word divider instead of a *ten*. If the dot after *wi* is a *ten*, the total should be 1070.

Analysis I: The position of Linear A ***di-we-na*** (HT 93a.1-2) makes it theoretically possible that this sequence is a noun. If it may be compared with Hurrian ***ti-we-na***, plural of ***ti-we*** 'word, thing', with the plural suffix ***-na*** of the so-called definite article, for example, ***ti-we-e-na***^{MEŠ} Tuš. I 99 *et passim* (cf. E. Laroche, *GLH*, 267-268; E.A. Speiser, *IH*, 22,74; F.W. Bush, *GHL*, 139); ***tiwena*** can mean 'the things' or 'the words'. But since ***di-we-na*** (HT 102.3) likely belongs to a list of personal names, it is more likely that ***di-we-na*** (HT 93a.1-2) is a personal name as well. The meaning 'The words' is in that case also a caressing name and probably refers to the first words spoken by the child.

Analysis II: As a result of more recent research it has become clear that some roots are not only nominal, but also verbal, cf. Th. Richter, *BGH*, 453-455, s.v. ***ti-*** I, ***tiw-*** I [*passim*]; and *VHN*, 534-535, s.v. ***ti-*** / ***te-***. He mentions that I. Wegner (1988, 152) was the first who confirmed the meaning 'to speak', its relation to ***tiwe*** 'word', and who distinguished ***ti-*** I from ***tea*** 'great' and ***te-*** II (*BGH*, 455-456) and ***tel-*** I 'to be great' (cf. ***talm-***).

Th. Richter (*VHN*, 305-306) mentions the following Hurrian personal names with the root ***ti-*** I, ***tiw-*** I: ***Tiwar*** (wr. *ti-wa-ar*) at Tigunāni, typology 3.1, lexicon *tiwari* (→ *ti-*), translation 'Spruch(?)' ['motto, aphorism']; ***Tiwarri*** (wr. *ti-wa-ar-ri*) at Tuttul, typology 3.1, lexicon *tiwarni* (→ *ti-*), 'Spruch(?)'; ***Tiwiran*** (wr. *ti-wi-ra-an*) at Mari, analysis {*tiv=i=r(i)=a*[E.]*-n(na)*}, typology 3.2.1, lexicon *tiwiri* (→ *ti-*), 'Spruch(?)'. [E.] refers to the *essive* case in ***-a***. Th. Richter (*VHN*, 534-535) explains that ***tiwiri*** {*tiv=i=ri*} and ***tiwari*** {*tiv=a=ri*} are nominal and that the meaning 'Spruch(?)' ['proverb(?)'] can be guessed on the analogy of ***šid-*** 'verfluchen' ['to curse'] and ***šidarni*** 'Fluch' ['curse'].

He explains that the verbal root ***ti-*** / ***tiw-*** 'sprechen' ['to speak'] can in onomastics offer the specific meaning '(Namen) aussprechen' ['to say, pronounce (a name)'], especially in personal names containing a verbal form expressing mood, e.g. ***ti-ez-°***.

Verbal forms in personal names often miss the marker of transitivity ***-i/e-*** or of intransitivity ***-a-*** (e.g. ***Ar-Kaniš*** (*VHN*, 534) instead of Old Hurrian *{*ar=i=b-Kaniš*} or *{*ar=o(=m)-Kaniš*} [PGvS]; ***Ar-Teššub*** beside ***Arip-Tešub*** {*ar=i=b-Tešub*} at Nuzi 'Tešub gives' (cf. P.M. Purves, *NPN*, 203-204) and ***Un-Tešub*** beside ***Unap-Tešub*** {*un=a=b-Tešub*} 'Tešub comes' at Nuzi (P.M. Purves, *NPN*, 272). Th. Richter (*VHN*, 535) gives the following examples of personal names with the root {*ti-*}: ***ᶠTieš-Naje*** (Mari), ***ᶠTiš-naru*** (Mari), ***ᶠTiš-na***[..]x (Mari), ***ᶠTiš-nuri*** (Mari), ***Tiš-ulme*** (Mari); with the root {***te-***}: ***Teš-ḫuḫ*** (Tigunāni).

Th. Richter (*BGH*, 454) also mentions ***tie/tije*** [Bog.] 'Wort, Name' ['word, name'], cf. Urartian ***tiau-*** 'sagen' ['to say'] and ***tini*** 'Name' ['name']. It can, for instance, be recognized in the theonym ***Ti(ja)-pa/enti*** 'Er spricht das Gute' ['He says the right things'] (Wegner, 1988, 152), or ***Tiye-bendi*** 'Gutes sprechend' (V. Haas, 1994a, 310) and ***Tiya-bendi*** / ***Tiya-bandi*** (*ibidem*, 389). ***Tiya***, mentioned by E. Laroche, *NH*, 183, N° 1322, may also be added: Homme d'Ura: akk. *ᵐTi-ya*, RS 17.316 Vo 9 = PRU IV 190.

These forms are also interesting with regard to Linear A. Since Linear A and B ***ta₂*** is ***tia/tya***, Linear A ***ta₂-ti-te*** (PK 1.3) and ***ta₂-ta-re*** (PK 1.2) may well contain the same verbal root ***ti-*** I, stem ***ti(y)=a-*** or root + root-extension ***ti(y)=am-***.

So if ***di-we-na*** (HT 93a.1-2; HT 102.3) contains the verbal root ***ti-*** I, ***tiw-*** I, it can be analysed as {*d/tiw=e/i=nna*}, consisting of the verbal root ***d/tiw-*** + the indicator of transitivity ***-e/i-*** + the enclitic personal pronoun 3rd person ***-nna*** (position 9) expressing the object of action of the transitive verb, translation 'Say / Pronounce it (the name) !'. Whereas syllabic cuneiform has the means of expressing double writing (***-nn-***) by using two syllabic signs *VC-CV*, Linear A and B miss this possibility. This was obviously no problem for the scribes, because they knew what they had written, but for us it can be a problem that we sometimes do not know whether a Minoan scribe, who wrote ***-na***, meant ***-nna*** or ***-na***.

Analysis III: Since ***-na*** in onomastics can sometimes be an abbreviation of the name of the goddess ***Naja/Naje***, Linear A ***di-we-na*** can in principle also be an abbreviation or hypocoristic of *{*d/tiw=e-Naje/a*} 'Pronounce (the name), oh *Naje/a* !'.

Analysis IV: As we have seen sub analysis II, verbal forms in names often miss the marker of transitivity ***-i/e-*** and are consequently athematic, if the second (nominal) element in a sentence name begins with a consonant, but the marker of transitivity ***-i/e-*** can also be absorbed by the following vowel, if this element starts with a vowel.

Consequently, if Linear A ***di-we-na*** contains a theophorous element such as ***-enna*** < {*en(i)=na*} 'the Gods', the personal name ***di-we-na*** can be analysed as {*d/tiw(=e/i)-en(i)=na*} and be translated as 'Pronounce (the name), oh Gods !'.

Analysis V: As if four analyses are not enough, Linear A orthographic conventions and Hurrian onomastics allow for even more interpretations. In Linear B ***ρ*** and ***λ*** are usually not expressed before ***μ***, ***ν*** and ***ϝ*** (***pe-ma*** = ***σπέρμα***, ***ko-wa***= ***κόρϝā***). The same applies probably also to Linear A. So I wrote in the 2016 edition of *Minoan Linear A*, Vol. I:

"Linear A ***di-we-na*** can be interpreted as ****Tirwena***, phonologically ***/*Dirwena/***, a Hurrian personal name containing the theophorous element ***Tirwi-*** (cf. P.M. Purves, *NPN*, 267, s.v. ***Tirwi***, ***dTi-ir-wi***, ***Tirwiia*** (wr. *Ti-ir-wi-ia* and *fTi-ir-w-ia*), ***Tirwin-atal*** (wr. *Ti-ir-wi-na-tal*, *Ti-ir-wi-na-a-tal*), ***fTirwin-elli*** (wr. *fTi-ir-wi-ni-el-li*) and the Hurrian formative ***-na*** as in *Taena* and *Zikena* (cf. P.M. Purves, *NPN*, 236, s.v. ***-na***). P.M. Purves, *NPN*, 267: "Hurrian. Cf. ***dTi-ir-wi***, *AASOR XVI*, 47:7 and 50:8, name of a deity worshipped at Nuzi. On its appearance in personal names see Speiser, *ibid.* 101 and Oppenheim in *AOF XII*, 30, n. 5. A Nippur personal name is ***Ḫut-tirme***, Clay, *PNCP*, 81. A personal name occurring in Egyptian sources as ***Trwsr*** may be ****Tirwi-šarri*** rather than **Tariw-šarri* as proposed by Gustavs in *ZAS LXIV (1929)*, 56." The name ***Ḫut-tirwi*** is also attested at Nuzi (wr. *Ḫu-ut-ti-ir-wi*). Cf. for voicing of the dental also ***Ar-tirwi*** (wr. *Ar-ti-ir-wi*, *Ar-di-ir-wi*, *Ar-ti-ir-mi*) 'Giving is Tirwi' at Nuzi (Purves, *ibidem*). Another possibility is that we are dealing with ****Tirw-enna***, ***/*Dirw-enna/***, cf. ***Ḫuti-l-enna*** (wr. *Ḫu-ti-le-en-na*) next to ***Ḫuti-l-enni*** (wr. *Ḫu-ti-le-en-ni*). In that case the form ****Tirw-enna*** (***/*Dirw-enna/***) would be a form with apocope of ***-i*** or of contraction of ***-i-e-> e*** instead of inclusion of the root-complement ***-l-*** as in ***Ḫuti-l-enna***." Now I analyse ***Ḫuti-l-enna*** as {*ḫud=i=l(la)-en(=i)=na*} 'Bless them [***-l(la)***], oh Gods !', ***Ḫuti-l-enni*** as {*ḫud=i=l(la)-en(=i)=ni*} 'Bless them, oh God !'.

If analysis IV is correct, it is tempting to assume that ***tirwe*** cannot only be substantival, but also adjectival and maybe even verbal, cf. e.g. ***madi*** 'wisdom, wise' and the verbal root ***mad-*** 'to give wisdom to (somebody)' in transitive constructions (cf. Th. Richter, *BGH*, 248-249, and *VHN*, 456). ***Madi*** can also be deified, cf. E. Laroche, *GLH*, 163-164). Since the meaning of ***tirwe/i*** is not known, the meaning of the personal name ****Tirw-enna*** ***/ *Dirw-enna/*** remains equally enigmatic.

Th. Richter (*VHN*, 537, s.v. ***tirwe*** {*tirve*}, ***tirme***) mentions that ***Tirwe*** (*ti-ir-we/me*) is attested in the younger tradition as a deity of Azuḫinni, east of the Tigris, presumably northeast of Nuzi and Arrapḫa, in the direction of Šušarrā. This corresponds with occurrence of ***Tirwen-šenni*** at Šušarrā, cf. ***Tirmen-šenni*** at Šubat-Enlil, ***Tirwe-šenni*** (provenance unknown) and ***Tirwi-i***[…] at Mari. Nevertheless he thinks that the names in *VHN* hardly contain this theonym, because expressions like '(God) *Tirwe* is the brother' cannot be detected in his *corpus*. Suffixing of a theophorous element with ***°=n(na)*** does not occur elsewhere either. In spite of these objections he maintains (*VHN*, 537[804]) that we are dealing with nominal sentence names, since the same word occurs in an *appellative* function and in that of *numina*. He explains (*VHN*, 614, sub 2.2: *Formations extended with* ***°=n(na)***, and sub 2.2.1: *Absolutive with enclitic*, that personal names with a nominal first element with the shortened form ***°=n*** of the absolutive enclitic personal pronoun 3rd person singular ***°=n(na)*** belong to the group of nominal sentence names. Since we find personal names like ***fTirwin-elli*** 'The sister …' at Nuzi beside ***Tirwen-šenni*** at Šušarrā, ***Tirmen-šenni*** at Šubat-Enlil, ***Tirwe-šenni*** (provenance unknown) 'The brother …', we may conclude that ***tirwe*** can be used for male and female persons alike.

Analysis VI: If ***Tirwin-*** {*tirw=e/i=n*} in ***Tirwin-atal*** 'The strong one …..', ***fTirwin-elli***, ***Tirwen-šenni***, ***Tirmen-šenni*** contains the shortened form ***°=n*** of the enclitic personal pronoun 3rd person singular ***°=n(na)***, then it is also conceivable that Linear A ***di-we-na*** can be analysed as Hurrian {*tirw=e/i=nna*}, with the suffix ***°=nna*** in full writing. I should not be surprised, if the root ***tirw-*** turns out to be nominal and verbal after all.

If ***tirw-*** is indeed also verbal, ***Tirwin-atal***, ***ᶠTirwin-elli***, ***Tirwen-šenni***, ***Tirmen-šenni*** can also be interpreted as *jussive* sentence names, with *jussive* suffix ***-en-*** (*jussive* indicator of the 3rd person singular), cf. I. Wegner, *Einführung*, 103. In other words ***Tirwen-šenni***, analysed as {*tirve=n(na)-šen(a)=ni*} by Th. Richter (*VHN*, 306), can then also be analysed as {*tirv=(i)=en-šen(a)=ni*}, consisting of the root ***tirv-*** + the *jussive* indicator (***-i-***), that disappeared under influence of the following suffix ***-en-*** (*jussive* indicator of the 3rd person singular) 'He may .... the brother'. Compare an example from the Tušratta letter: ***še-e-ni-iw-wu-uš ḫa-ši-en-na-an*** (Mit. III 42), analysis ***ḫaš + i + en + (n)na + an*** 'and (***an***) may he (my brother, ***še-e-ni-iw-wu-uš***) hear it' (cf. also I. Wegner, *Einführung*, 104.

Comparison of HT 93a with HT 102 shows that ***di-we-na*** is preceded by ***pa₃-ni-na*** , GRA ***pa₃*** , ***se+re*** ↓ 12 (HT 93a.1) and by ***pa₃-ni*** GRA+***pa*** 33 VIR (*126*) GRA+***pa*** 33 (HT 102.2-3). ***Pa₃-ni*** (HT 85a.2) is a personal name. Linear A ***pa₃*** may have been ***bha***.

It is tempting to assume that ***pa₃-ni*** and ***pa₃-ni-na*** represent the same persons, which is even likely, if we realize that ***pa₃-ni-na*** can be analysed as Hurrian {*pann=i=nna*} and that ***pa₃-ni*** cannot only represent Hurrian {*pann=i*}, but also {*pann=i=n*}, because a final consonant is not expressed in Linear A and B. The suffix ***-nna*** also has a shortened form ***-n*** representing the enclitic personal pronoun 3rd pers. sing. (position 9), indicating the object of the transitive verb (meaning unknown) and the subject of the intransitive verb. Such verbal forms are frequently attested as personal names in Hurrian, cf. Th. Richter, *VHN*, 584 ff. ***Panni / Wanni*** (wr. *pa-an-ni, wa-an-ni, wa-an-na*) is a correspondence clerk of Kuwari at Šušarrā and his name is (because of the ***p/w*** alternation) analysed as {*fanni*} and {*fann(i)=a*} by Th. Richter (*VHN*, 222), typology 3.1, lexicon *wanni*.

Linear A ***pa₃-ni-wi*** (SY Za 4) on a round serpentine Libation Table from the Peak Sanctuary of Symi Viannou seems *prima facie* the genitive ***Panni=wi***, but analysis as ***pann(=i)-i/erwi***, '..... oh Lord !' is more likely after ***a-ta-i-jo-wa-ja*** , ***ja-i-nwa-za*** ,

At Nippur ***Panni*** (wr. *pa-an-ni*) is attested as well, cf. Th. Richter, *VHN*, 222; cf. M. Hölscher, *Die Personennamen der kassitenzeitlichen Texte aus Nippur*, IMGULA 1, Münster 1996, 166). At Ḫattuša ***Wanni*** is a priest, cf. E. Laroche, *NH*, 204, N° 1489: 1. Prêtre: nom. *ᵐWa-an-ni-i-iš*, XII 2 I 24; 2. Prêtre: abs. *ᵐWa-an-ni*, XVIII 9 II 22; KBo XXXI 51 Rs 7'. E. Laroche also mentions a stone-cutter ***Wana*** (*NH*, 204, N° 1488) in Luwian Hieroglyphic: *Wa-na-s* SCRIBE-*la-š*, Karaburun. At Alalaḫ VII we find ᶠIŠ₈-TÁR-*ba-an-ni* (*AT* *178 = *UF 38*, 90: 33), cf. Th. Richter, *VHN*, 222. At Mari *wa-na*, *wa-ni* occur (Mari 3, 19; 2, 8), cf. E. Laroche, *GLH*, 293; Th. Richter, *BGH*, 293.

It has occurred to me that ***Ἥρᾱ*** and ***Ἥρως*** may not be derived from *just a* Pre-Greek language, but from Hurrian. Hera's epithet ***βοῶπις*** 'with the eyes of a cow' (*βοῦς* 'ox, cow' and *ὤψ* 'eyes') in the Homeric formula ***βοῶπις πότνια Ἥρη*** (*Iliad* Α 551, Θ 471, Ο 49, Σ 357) has astonished me ever since I read Homer. But we must not forget that ***Tešub*** and his 'guardian companions' ***Ḫurri***, ***Tilla*** and ***Šerri*** were often depicted as bulls and that *Zeus* himself sometimes acted in the appearance of a bull. Could ***Ἥρως*** and ***Ἥρᾱ*** be derived from ***Šerri*** or ***Šeri***. We must realize that the form ***Šerri*** owes its double ***-rr-*** to assimilation of the ***-n-*** of the so-called definite article ***-ni***: ***Šerri < šer(i)=ni < šeri=ni***. Forms with single ***-r-*** and double ***-rr-*** are attested as well as ***Šera*** (wr. *še-e-ra*).

E. Laroche (*GLH*, 227, s.v. ***šeri***. Nom. *še-e-ri*, KUB XXVII 1 II 61; 42 Ro 16; XXXII 52 III 13; XLVII 10, 12; KBo XXI 23 Vo 9. - *ši-i-ri*, RS h. 5, 12; KUB XLVII 78 IV 14. – Erg. ? *še-re-eš*, KUB XLV 21 Ro 2. - *še-e-ra*, KUB XLVII 31 I 10. Dir. *še-e-ri-da*, KUB XXXII 19+ II 34. Onom. ***šeri***, *NPN*, 256.

E. Laroche (*GLH*, 227), s.v. ***šerri***. Peut être le thème déterminé de ***šeri***: ****šeri=ni*** > ***šerri***.Sg. nom. *še-er-ri-e*, KUB XXIX 8 III 52. - *ši-ir-ri*, RS h. 18, 1. - *še-er-ri-in*, IBoT II 39 Ro 45; etc. Erg. *še-er-re-eš*, KBo XIX 139 III 3. - *še-e-er-ra-a-tan*, Mit. IV 115 (abl.?). - *še-e-er-re-e-wi-i-in*, Mit. III 67. - ***Šerri***. Un des taureaux de Tešub; v. ***Ḫurri*** et ***Tilla***: *še-er-ri ḫu-ur-ri* GUD$^{hi.a}$*-ri*, KBo XX 119 IV 26, I 15 = KBo XVII 86+ I 4; dét. par GUD, souvent par DINGIR (^{d}***Šerri***). Graphies *še-(e)-ri* et *še-er-ri*. Flexion hitt. nom. *Še(r)riš*, acc. *Še(r)rin*, abs. *Še(r)ri*. Aussi GUD/^{d}*Še-ri-šu-(un)*, cf. JCS 6, 40, et *še-ri-šu-uš*, KBo XXII 33 IV 7.

With regard to my hypothesis about derivation of ***Ἥρως*** and ***Ἥρᾱ*** from ***Šere/i*** / ***Šerri*** it may be significant that the Linear A ligature ***se+re*** ↓ 12 (HT 93a.1), read from top to bottom, can be equated with the *absolutive* Hurrian theonym ***Šere/Šeri***, and that the ligature ***se+re+da*** ↓ 43 J (HT 93a.2) in the next line can be equated with the *directive* case ***Šere=da*** of the same theonym, 'for *Šere*', with directive suffix ***-da***. The other option is the *ablative* case ***Šere=dan*** ↓ 43 J (HT 93a.2), 'from *Šere*', with the ablative suffix ***dan***. Linear A ***se+re*** ↓ (HT 93a.1) can be compared with absolutive *še-er-ri-e*, KUB XXIX 8 III 52 or with ergative *še-er-re-eš*, KBo XIX 139 III 3. Linear A ***se+re+da*** ↓ (HT 93a.2) can be compared with directive *še-e-ri-da*, KUB XXXII 19+ II 34. The fact that ***se+re*** ↓ (HT 93a.1) and ***se+re+da*** ↓ (HT 93a.2) are written as ligatures instead of normal sequences is not a disadvantage, but a recommendation, because there are more theonyms written as ligatures with Linear A: e.g. Linear A ***qe+pa₃*** (HT 33.4) = *Ḫeba(t)*, preceded by NUBES+*pi* = genitive *Tešuppi* < *Tešub=wi* 'of *Tešub*'; Linear A ***si+me-ki*** TAL 1 JE (HT 24b.1-2) and ***ka+ja*** TAL 1 (HT 24b.2) = the Hurrian Sun-god *Šimegi* and *Gaia* 'Earth'.

Now ***Ἥρᾱ*** is not only attested as a theonym, but also as a toponym in Crete derived from the theonym. This can also have been the case with Hurrian ***Šere/i/a***, if that is the theonym from which ***Ἥρᾱ*** is derived. In that case ***se+re+da*** (HT 93a.2) could also indicate the ablative 'from ***Šere/i***' or, if the sequence indicates a person, '(the one) from ***Šere/i***'. Attestation of ***da-we-da*** (HT 93a.7), {*daw(a)=e=dan*}, '(the one) from Dawa', a toponym also attested as ***da-wo*** on the Linear B Knossos tablets, corroborates the identification.

It is known that the Indo-European initial [***s-***] developed > [***h-***] in Greek, cf. e.g. Greek ***ἑπτά*** 'seven' < ***septm̥*** : Latin ***septem*** : Sanskrit ***saptá***; cf. Greek ***ἕξ*** 'six' : Latin ***sex***.

One usually assumes that this did not apply to the non-Indo-European initial [***s-***] as I have assumed with regard to the Pre-Greek name of the ***Σειρῆνες*** (*Sirens*, plural of ***Σειρήν***), of which I have proposed that it contains the Hurrian root ***šir-*** 'to sing'.

Can it be accidental that the queenly sorceress *Circe* (***πότνια Κίρκη***) with a Hurrian name ***Kirka*** (wr. *Ki-ir-qa*), attested at Nuzi (cf. I.J. Gelb, *NPN*, 88), warns Odysseus for the ***Σειρῆνες*** (the *Sirens*) in *Odyssey μ* 36 ff.: *"To the Sirens first thou shalt come, who beguile all men whosoever comes to them. Whosoever in ignorance draws near to them and hears the Sirens' voice, he nevermore returns, that his wife and little children may stand at his side rejoicing, but the sirens beguile him with their clear-toned voice ... ."*

P. Chantraine (*DELG*, 993-994) mentions s.v. ***Σειρήν***: "f. (***σει-*** *IG* II^2, 1629, 687, mais ***σιρ-*** sur les vases). .... « sirènes », génies mi-oiseaux-mi-femmes. ..... On admet en mycénien l'existence d'un composé (instrum.) *seremokaraore* « à tête de sirène », cf. L. Baumbach, *Glotta 49*, 1971, 170. .... Étymologie: Obscure." All attempts cited by him are unsatisfactory. Hurrian, however, offers a satisfactory etymology, because ***Šir-ene/i*** can be analysed as {*šir(e/i)-ene/i*} 'Sing, oh God !' (with ***šir-*** as *athematic imperative*) and the plural ***Šir-enna*** as {*šir=(e/i)-en=(i)=na*} 'Sing, oh Gods !'.

It is conceivable that a phoneme in a word adopted from another language was so close to a similar phoneme of the own language that the *phonetic law*, effective at the time of adoption or shortly after the adoption, had also effect on the adopted non-Indo-European word/name.

Actually *phonetic laws* are usually only *at work* during a certain period of the process of change within a language. It is conceivable that ***šere/i/a***, the basis of ***Ἥρως*** and ***Ἥρᾱ***, was earlier adopted into Mycenaean Greek than the prototype of ***Σειρήν*** and ***Σειρῆνες***, so that the phonetic law concerning initial [***s-***] developing > [***h-***] worked for ***Ἥρως*** and ***Ἥρᾱ***, but was no longer effective for ***Σειρήν*** and ***Σειρῆνες***, because the period of effectiveness of the phonetic law in question had already passed. Perhaps other factors, such as the frequency of usage and popularity of a loan-word or foreign name adopted into an idiom, may have had some influence on the process as well. Such matter is difficult to assess.

The Linear A personal names]***ku-du-we*** (HT? 170a.2),] ***a-mi-da-o*** (HT? 170a.5), ***ku-pa₃-nu*** (HT? 170b.3) and ***pa-ta-da*** (HT? 170b.3) have been discussed before.

Linear A ***tu-ma*** (HT 94[+ HT 154 I + Fr.]b.1) at Hagia Triada is no doubt a personal name, since it occurs in a list of five personal names following ***ki-ro*** **,** (HT 94[+ HT 154 I + Fr.]b.1). The join has been made by L. Godart.

All these names, ***tu-ma*** 1, ***pa-ta-ne*** 1, ***de-di*** 1, ***ke-ki-ru*** 1, ***sa-ru*** 1 (HT 94[+ HT 154 I + Fr.]b.1-2), are each followed by 1 unit. Then follows the total: ***ku-ro*** 5 (HT 94[+ HT 154 I + Fr.]b.3). The ethnic ***pa-ta-ne*** 'Spartan' used as a personal name has already been discussed as well as the personal name ***sa-ru***.

Linear A ***tu-ma*** (HT 94[+ HT 154 I + Fr.]b.1) is equivalent to the Hurrian personal name ***Tumma*** (wr. *tu-um-ma*) at Nuzi, cf. I.J. Gelb, *NPN*, 157; P.M. Purves, *NPN*, 268.

Th. Richter (*BGH*, 468) mentions ***tum-*** [Süd-B.] 'schlängeln(?)' ['to squirm, to wriggle (like a snake)'] (Prechel/Richter, 2001, 358). If that meaning is correct, the name can be interpreted as an intransitive *imperative* 2nd person singular {*tum=a*} ['Squirm / Wriggle (like a snake) (oh child) !' or as an intransitive *indicative* 3rd person singular {*tum=a*} 'He/She (the child) squirms / wriggles (like a snake)'.

Linear A ***de-di*** (HT 94[+ HT 154 I + Fr.]b.1) at Hagia Triada is a personal name that may contain the verbal root ***tid-*** I [Boğ.] 'to share out, to separate', cf. I.M. Diakonoff – S.E. Starostin, *Hurro-Urartian as an Eastern Caucasian language* (Münchener Studien zur Sprachwissenschaft, Beiheft 12, Neue Folge), München 1986, 27; I.M. Diakonoff, On some new trends in Urartian philology and some new Urartian texts, *Archäologische Mitteilungen aus Iran. Neue Folge 22*, Berlin 1989, 100) and 'zählen' ['to count'], cf. Th. Richter , *BGH*, 464; cf. I. Wegner, *Einführung*, 212, 287.

I. Wegner (*ibid.*, 210-212) analyses ***ti-i-ti-wa**$_a$**-a-te*** in the Hurrian-Hittite bilingual ***kirenze*** (KBo 32: 13 Vs I 18) as {*tid=i=bade*} and compares it with the Hittite parallel ***kapuwauwar*** 'das Zählen, das Gezählte' ['count(ing)']; ***tid=i=bade*** consists of the verbal root ***tid-*** 'to count' and the suffix ***-i-bade*** that forms *abstracta*. Compare for ***kapuwauwar*** e.g. Th. van den Hout, *The elements of Hittite*, Cambridge 2013[3], 192: ***kappuwa(e)-*** 'to count, take care of' ***kappuwauwar***, neuter 'count(ing)'. I. Wegner also attributes the first element in the personal name ***Tí-tí-na-tal*** {*Titin-atal*} on a tablet from Kültepe (KT 90/k, 223 9) to this verbal root. In my view the Urartian root ***did-*** 'to share?' must certainly be compared with this Hurrian verbal root (cf. M. Salvini - I. Wegner, *Einführung in die urartäische Sprache*, Wiesbaden 2014, 108).

Morphologically the Linear A personal name ***de-di*** (HT 94[+ HT 154 I + Fr.]b.1) can easily be analysed as a Hurrian transitive *imperative* {*ded=i*} 'Share !, Count !' and I must say that the Urartian root ***did-*** 'to share?' helps in this respect. It has to be emphasized that it is unlikely that all initial consonants were voiceless in all Hurrian dialects. It certainly was not the case in the Minoan Hurrian dialect, at least with regard to the dentals, as can be proved by the many words and names beginning with ***da-***, ***de-***, ***di-***, ***do-***, ***du-*** in Linear A. I consider it likely that voicing of the initial consonant was influenced by a voiced consonant of the following syllable. I am therefore convinced that ***de-di*** should be analysed as {*ded=i*} and not be normalised to {*ted=i*}, for there is no reason to assume that the phonetic value of the Linear A ***d-*** signs differs from that of the Linear B ***d-*** signs.

The Hurrian personal name ***de-di*** (HT 94[+ HT 154 I + Fr.]b.1) may be compared with ***di-de-ru*** (HT 86a.3; HT 95+149a.4; HT 95+149b.4) and ***di-de-***[(HT 86b.3), that is also a 'one-word' Hurrian personal name. The ending of Linear A ***di-de-ru*** may be considered an Akkadianizing nominative in ***-u***, so that the underlying Hurrian form is probably ****di-de-ri***. I. Wegner (*Einführung*, 113) sub 5.8 (participles): ***-i=ri*** is the suffix for the transitive participles and ***-a=uri*** for the intransitive. She gives the example ***tab=i=ri*** 'someone who pours/casts (metal, bronze)' > '(bronze)smith'. So ***di-de-ru*** {*did=e/i=r(i)=u*} can be translated as 'The one who counts, shares (out), takes care of' > 'caretaker'.

Th. Richter (*BGH*, 464-465) mentions another verbal root ***tid-*** II [Boğ.; Mitt.], ***titt-*** [Boğ.] 'angreifen' ['to attack'] and possibly also ***te-t*** ^{o}. Th. Richter (*VHN*, 541) mentions s.v. ***ted-/tid-*** that it is uncertain which of the two roots ***tid-*** I 'to count' or ***tid-*** II 'to attack' was used in personal names or whether they were both used. He mentions apart from the personal names from Nuzi (*NPN*, 155 and 268, s.v. *ti-ti*) also: (a) {*ted-*}: ***Tetija*** (Š). (b) {*tid-*}: ***^{f}Tita-ki*** (Mari); ***Titikkan*** (Mari). If Linear A ***de-di*** {*ded=i*} belongs to the verbal root ***tid-*** II 'to attack', it can be translated as 'Attack !'.

Linear A ***ti-ti-ku*** (HT 35.1; ZA Zb 3.2) can be analysed as {*titt=i=kk=u=n(ni)*}, based on the root ***tid- / titt-*** and the nominal suffixes ***-kk=u/o=nni***, cf. I. Wegner, *Einführung*, 55-56. This formant ***-kk-*** (often occurring in descriptions of persons: possibly *nomina actoris*) should not be confused with the negation-suffix (***-kk*** + vowel) in *intransitive* and *antipassive* verbal forms. ***Titikun*** {*tid=i=kk=u/o=n*} at Alalaḫ is the shortened form of {*tid=i=kk=u/o=nni*} (root ***tid-***), with voiced second dental, whereas the Linear A names ***ti-ti-ku*** and ***ti-ti-ku-ni*** (root ***titt-***) have voiceless initial and second dentals. The Linear A personal names ***ti-ti-ku*** (HT 35.1; ZA Zb 3.2) and ***ti-ti-ku-ni*** (HT 96a.1) as well as ***Titiku*** and ***Titikun*** at Alalaḫ can now be translated as 'Attacker'.

Since final ***-n*** of ***Ti-di-ku-un*** at Alalaḫ (AT 189, 17) is not expressed in Linear A, ***ti-ti-ku*** (HT 35.1; ZA Zb 3.2) can represent {*titt=i=kk=u/o*} or {*titt=i=kk=u/o=n*}. Linear A ***ti-ti-ku-ni*** (HT 96a.1) represents {*titt=i=kk-u/o=nni*}, see for the examples from Alalaḫ D.J. Wiseman, *The Alalakh Tablets*, London 1953, 149, and A. Draffkorn, *HHA*, 57, 109.

The personal name ***ke-ki-ru*** (HT 94[+ HT 154 I + Fr.]b.2) is almost a copy of the Hurrian name ***Kirgiri*** (wr. *Ki-ir-ki-ri*), husband of Ikrukitam at Šušarrā, typology 3.1, lexicon *kirgiri*. It is a total copy of ***Kirkirum*** (wr. *ki-ir-ki-ru-um*) in Old Babylonian Nērebtum (*University of California Publications in Semitic Philology 10/1*, Berkeley, 91, Siegel [*Bibliotheca Mesopotamica 19* (Malibu), 205]) and of ***Kirkiru*** *ki-ir-ki-ru* at Nuzi (E. Cassin - J.-J. Glassner, *Anthroponymie et Anthropologie de Nuzi*, Vol. I: *Les anthroponymes*, Malibu 1977, 84), cf. Th. Richter, *VHN*, 166. The liquid ***-r-*** preceding an occlusive is not expressed in Linear A consonant clusters. Final ***-m*** is not expressed either.

Th. Richter (*VHN*, 441) mentions, s.v. ***kirgiri***, that the (at that time isolated and inassignable) personal name ***Kirka*** (wr. *Ki-ir-qa*) at Nuzi (cf. P.M. Purves, *NPN*, 228) contains the same root ***kirg-*** as ***Kirgiri*** from Šušarrā and ***Kirkiru*** (with Akkadianizing nominative in ***-u***) from Nuzi and ***Kirkirum*** from OB Nērebtum. Reduplication of the root seems unlikely, if *Kirka*, *Kirgiri*, *Kirkiru* and *Kirkirum* belong together.

Incidentally, the Hurrian name ***Kirka*** is identical with that of the divine sorceress ***Κίρκη*** (*Kirkè*) from the island of *Aia*, where Odysseus stayed for a year, see Homer's *Odyssey* κ, 135-136: *Αἰαίην δ' ἐς νῆσον ἀφικόμεθ'· ἔνθα δ' ἔναιε Κίρκη ἐυπλόκαμος, δεινὴ θεὸς αὐδήεσσα,..* - *And we arrived at the island of Aia; and there fair-tressed Circe dwelt, a dread goddess of human speech ..* So Hurrian ***Kirka*** may well be the prototype of the Pre-Greek and epic name. There is a Cretan town ***Gergeri*** between *Zaros* and *Hagia Barbara*.

Since the Hurrian names ***Kirkiri***, ***Kirkiru*** and ***Kirkirum*** are attested at Šušarrā, Nuzi and OB Nērebtum, respectively, and Linear A ***ke-ki-ru*** (HT 94[+ HT 154 I + Fr.]b.2) from Hagia Triada can be identified with these names, it is not too farfetched to propose that the name of the island of *Κέρκυρα* (Herodotus III, 48, 53, VII 145, Thucydides) shows the same formation. The ***o*** in the later name *Κόρκυρα* is the result of assimilation of ***ε*** under the influence of following ***υ*** (Schwyzer, Gr. Gr. 1, 255). The ethnics *Κερκυραῖος* (*Κορ-*) and *Κερκυραικός* are derived from the toponym. Alcman uses *Κέρκυρ*, cf. D.L. Page, *Poetae Melici Graeci*, Oxford 1962, 70, fragment 114 (Etym. Mag. 506.20 = Hdn. II 212. 15 L): *Κέρκυρ· .... Ἀλκμάν φησι·* etc., cf. also P. Chantraine (*DELG*, 520), who mentions (sub *Et.*) that one supposes Illyrian forms *Κέρκυρ* and *Κέρκυρες*, cf. A. Mayer, *KZ* 70, 1951, 76 ff., and A. Mayer, *Die Sprache der Illyrier*, Wien 1957, 186-187. About the hypothesis that the names refer to "l'île aux chênes" ["island of the oaks"], cf. Latin *quercus*, Chantraine rightfully states that it cannot be proved (hypothèse indémontrable).

Indeed that popular etymology can be disproved, since an Indo-European labio-velar preceding ***e*** or ***i*** changed in Ionic and Attic > ***τ*** and in Aeolic to ***π***, not to ***κ***, cf. Latin ***quis*** 'who ?' = Greek ***τίς***; Mycenaean Greek ***k^w^e*** and Latin ***-que*** 'and' = Greek ***τε***.

Linear A ***ka-ki*** (HT 37.1) from Hagia Triada, preceding ***su-wa-re-su***, but probably recurring as ***ka-ki*** 11 (HT 37.5) after ***ki-ro***, may be identified with the Hurrian personal name ***Kakki*** (wr. *Qa-ak-ki, Ka-ak-ki, Qa-ag-ge, Ga-ak-ki, Qa-ak-ki-im*) at Nuzi.

Also the variants with the nasal ***-n-***, *Qa-an-ge, Qa-an-ki*, *Ka-an-ge*, would according to the orthographic conventions of Linear A and B be written as ***ka-ki***, cf. P.M. Purves, *NPN*, 222, s.v. ***kakk*** and ***kakki***. He comments that L. Oppenheim, *RHA V, fasc. 33 (1938)*, 20, considers *kakk* Hurrian on the basis of its frequent occurrence in Nuzi personal names. Purves also provides other variants at Nuzi with the same root ***kakk*** and possibly ***kak***: *Qa-ak-ki-ia, Ka-ki-ia, Ka-ak-ki-še, ᶠQa-ak-ki-še, Qa-ak-ku, Ka-an-ku, Qa-an-ku* (a variant form that also seems to occur in Linear A as ***ka-ku*** in HT 62.2), *Qa-ak-ku-uz-zi, Ka-[ak-ku-uz]-zi, Qa-ku-zi, Ga-ku-zi, Qa-an-qa,* ⸢*Ka*⸣*-an-ka, ᶠQa-an-qa-a-a, Ka-gu-ia, Ka-ku-ia,* cf. also Gelb's list in *NPN.*

According to Th. Richter (*VHN*, 425-426, s.v. ***kakk-***) we find in personal names at Nuzi the element ***kakki*** that can be combined with derivational suffixes such as ***ᵒ=o/u=zzi*** as in ***Kakkuzzi*** (wr. *Qa-ak-ku-uz-zi, Ka-*[*ak-ku-uz*]*-zi, Qa-ku-zi, Ga-ku-zi*), '*kakki* angemessen' ['suitable for/to *kakki*, appropriate to *kakki*'], so that a stem {*kakk=i*} can be postulated. The meaning of ***kakk-*** is not yet known. Th. Richter (*VHN*, 127, 145-146, 426) mentions: {*kakk-*}: ***ᶠKakka*** (wr. *ᶠKa-ak-ka*) from Mari, Alalaḫ VII (AT *80: 13; cf. A. Draffkorn, *HHA*, 37), Ekalte (Mayer, 2001, 58), Emar (wr. *Ka/Kà-ak-ka*) (Pruzsinszky, 2003/2, 543), Ḫattuša (wr. *Ka-ag-ga*) (E. Laroche, *NH*, 83, nᵒ 481.1), analysis {*kakk=a=Ø*}, typology 1.1.1.3.3; ***ᶠKakkanna*** (wr. *ᶠKa-ak-ka-an-na, ᶠKa-ka-na*) from Mari (cf. *Ka-ka-ni* at Emar), analysis {*kakk=a=nna*}, typology 1.1.1.3.3.1; ***Kakki*** (wr. *Ka-ak-ki*) from Mari, analysis {*kakk=i*}, typology 1.3.1.2.1; {*kakk=ar-*}: ***Kakkarukkum*** (wr. *Ka-ak-ka-ru-kum, Ka-ak-ka-ru-uk-ki-im*) from Mari, analysis {*kakk=ar=o=kk(=o)=um*[N.]}, typology 1.2.2.1; {*kakki*}: ***Ḫazi-Kakku*** (wr. *Ḫa-zi-ga-ak-ku*) from Šubat-Enlil, analysis {*ḫaz=i-kakk(i)=u*[N.]}, typology 1.3.1.2.1, translation 'Erhöre (Person oder Gebet), oh *Kakku* !' ['Hear/Listen to (the person or prayer), oh *Kakku* !']; ***Ḫazip-Kakka*** from Mari, analysis {*ḫaz=i=b-Kakka*} '*Kakka* heard/listened to (the person or prayer)' (indicative).

Before appearance of Th. Richter's *Bibliographisches Glossar des Hurritischen* (Wiesbaden 2012), the only feasible Hurrian equivalent to Linear A ***ka-ki*** (HT 37.1) and ***ka-ki*** 11 (HT 37.5) seemed to be the Hurrian personal name ***Kakki*** or ***Kanki*** at Nuzi.

However, there is another explanation feasible, perhaps even preferable because of its position in the heading of the tablet. E. Laroche, *GLH*, 139, s.v. ***kaška***: Nuzi, gén. du dét. *qa-aš-gi-ni-we*; terme relatif à l'agriculture (hourrite ??); bibl. dans *CAD* K 290. Boğazköy, KUR ᵘʳᵘ*Gašga*, KBo XXIII 35,3, 8, 14.

Th. Richter, *BGH*, 193: s.v. ***kaška***, ***kaškiniwe***, ***kaš(a)ku*** [Nuzi]: 'eine Art Grundstückpfand' (W. von Soden, *Akkadisches Handwörterbuch* = *AHw*, Lfg. 5 [1963] 462 [hu. Fremdwort]); 'a right to a part of a field in feudal tenure' (*The Assyrian Dictionary of the Oriental Institute of the University of Chicago* = *CAD* K [1971] 290 [hu. Wort / Hurrian word]); 'terme relatif à l'agriculture (hourrite ??)' (Laroche, *GLH*: 139 [*kaška*]); wörtl. 'appezzamento', d.i. 'ein unveräußerlicher Teil eines Grundstücks', entspricht akk. ***niksu*** (Negri Scafa 1982: 139); 'separated plot(?)', d.i. ***kaš=ki*** (?) (Fincke 1998 d: 384); 'a kind of land holding' (J. Black, A. George, N. Postgate, *A Concise Dictonary of Akkadian* = *CDA*² [Wiesbaden 2000] 152 [hu. Lehnwort / Hurrian loan-word]). Nominalform: Zu *kaškiniwe* als *kašku* mit hu. Endung siehe *CAD* K l.c.; dort genanntes *kaškaniwe* existiert vermutlich nicht (Tippfehler für *kaškiniwe* ? [typographic error for *kaškiniwe* ?]).

Since according to Linear A and B orthographic conventions ***-s-*** preceding an occlusive is always omitted in consonant clusters, the Linear A rendering of the Hurrian *absolutive* ***kaš=ki*** 'a part of land held in feudal tenure' is ***ka-ki***.

Linear B offers parallels referring to different types of land holding: For instance at Pylos the Eb and Ep series register ***ko-to-na ke-ke-me-na*** = ***κτοίνᾱ χεχεμένᾱ*** 'plot of land left barren / not cultivated' belonging to the community (***pa-ro da-mo***), whereas the En and Eo series register ***ko-to-na ki-ti-me-na*** = ***κτοίνᾱ κτιμένᾱ*** 'plot of cultivated land', used by individual persons indicated by their personal names. Both ***κτοίνᾱ*** and ***κτιμένᾱ*** are connected with the root ****κτει-*** 'to build, to cultivate', cf. Homer's *Iliad* B 501, 505: *ἐυκτίμενον πτολίεθρον* 'the well-built city' and Homer's *Odyssey* ω 226: *ἐυκτιμένῃ ἐν ἀλωῇ* 'in a well-cultivated vineyard'. The perfect participle ***ke-ke-me-na*** may well represent phase zero of verbal root *χη-* < **gheə₁-* (cf. Sanskrit *jáhāti* 'leave'), with present **χίχημι*'. In Homer the present is *κιχάνω* (< **κιχάνϝω*) and the aorist *ἐκίχην* (cf. *φθάνω* : *ἔφθην*), cf. for an extensive explanation C.J. Ruijgh, *EGM*, § 327-328; cf. L.R. Palmer, *The interpretation of Mycenaean Greek texts*, Oxford 1963, 188-190.

Before I continue the discussion on tablet HT 37, I consider it relevant to discuss Linear A ***ka-ku*** (HT 62[+]73.2) on the heavily damaged tablet HT 62[+]73 (join by M. Pope) and Linear A ***ka-ku-pa*** (HT 16.1; HT Wc 3015a; HT Wc 3016a).

Linear A ***ka-ku*** (HT 62[+]73.2) from Hagia Triada may well be identified with the Hurrian personal names from Nuzi ***Qa-ak-ku***, ***Ka-an-ku***, ***Qa-an-ku***, cf. P.M. Purves, *NPN*, 222, s.v. ***kakk***. See also the names mentioned by Th. Richter (*VHN*, 127, 145-146, 426) with regard to ***ka-ki*** (HT 37.1) and ***ka-ki*** (HT 37.5).

However, there is another feasible explanation. Since according to Linear A and B orthographic conventions ***-s-*** preceding an occlusive is always omitted in consonant clusters, the Linear A rendering of Hurrian ***kaš=ku*** 'a part of land held in feudal tenure' would be ***ka-ku*** as attested in HT 62.2. In view of the context it may be significant that the ideograms VIN [(HT 62.1) and GRA 15 E (HT 62.2) both precede ***ka-ku*** (HT 62[+]73.2), if *GORILA*'s reading of [.]-***na*** followed by the ideogram GRA 15 E is correct as it may well be. J. Raison – M. Pope read sign ***-re*** instead of GRA: ***u-na-re*** 15 E. Obviously a context of wine and grain makes interpretation of ***ka-ku*** as Hurrian ***kaš=ku*** relevant.

Nevertheless interpretation of ***ka-ku*** as a Hurrian personal name ***Qa-ak-ku***, ***Ka-an-ku*** or ***Qa-an-ku*** (as attested at Nuzi) cannot be ruled out, because several other personal names are also mentioned on the same tablet: *vide* e.g. the first entry ***a-du-sa-ra*** (HT 62.1) and on HT 73 (joined to HT 62 by M. Pope) ***pa-i-ki*** (HT 73.2) and ***sa-ro-qe-***[(HT 73.2), which is an ethnic name (with the Hurrian ethnic suffix ***-ḫe***) or an ethnic used as a personal name, derived from the toponym ***sa-ro***.

No doubt the scribe knew whether ***ka-ku*** represented a personal name or a noun, but because of the ambiguity resulting from the orthographic conventions of Linear A and B we do not, so that we have to rely on the indications provided by the context.

As a matter of fact Linear A ***ka-ku-pa*** (HT 16.1; HT Wc 3015; HT Wc 3016) from Hagia Triada offers three times a form that may well contain the dative of Hurrian ***kaš=ku*** 'a part of land held in feudal tenure', with dative suffix ***-pa/-wa***.

On two roundels from Hagia Triada we find the form ***ka-ku-pa*** in combination with the ideogram HORD(eum) 'barley': HT Wc 3015 (= HM 78), side a: ***ka-ku-pa***; side b: HORD; on the edge (side c): three badly legible seal impressions. HT Wc 3016 (= HM 68), side a: ***ka-ku-pa* ,** (word-divider); side b: 2 ***zo*** HORD+D; on the edge (side c): two seal impressions (Doro Levi: type 112). On a tablet from Hagia Triada we find ***ka-ku-pa*** (HT 16.1) as first entry followed by a word divider and ***di-na-u*** (HT 16.1-2) 'for the part of land held in feudal tenure I make', so that ***di-na-u*** (HT 16.1-2) may here be a grammatical form in context 'I make, I build'. The function of ***di-na-u*** (HT 16.1-2) differs in that case from the personal names ***di-na-u*** (HT 9a.3; HT 9b.5) 'I make, build' (v. *supra*).

HT 16.1. *ka-ku-pa* , *di-*
2. *na-u* F TELA
3. B *87+ku* EF
4. *sa-po* , ZE K
5. vacat

So the form ***ka-ku-pa*** occurs twice in combination with the ideogram HORD(eum) 'barley'. It may contain Hurrian ***kaš=k(i)=u-***. Since ***p-*** and ***w-*** can often be exchanged in Hurrian and since ***-p-/-w-*** (with single writing in cuneiform) is regarded as voiced **[*v*]**, whereas ***-pp-/-ww-*** (with double writing in cuneiform) is considered voiceless **[*f*]**, it is attractive to consider Linear A ***ka-ku-pa*** equivalent to Old Hurrian ****kaš=ku=pa*** (= ****kaš=ku=va***), dative of ***kaš=k(i)=u*** 'for a part of land held in feudal tenure', cf. the attested genitive form ***kaškiniwe*** (with the suffix ***-we*** = **[*ve*]** of the singular genitive and the suffix ***-ni-*** of the so-called 'definite article'). The ***-u-*** in the dative ***ka-ku-pa*** (Old Hurrian ****kaš=k(i)u=pa***) may well be due to the following labial ***-p/w-***, since ***u*** and ***w*** are cognate.

Linear A ***da-na-si*** (HT 126(+Fr)a.1) may possibly be equated with a personal name from Nuzi *Da-an-na-ši* (JENu 356; 977), but this identification is impossible, if I.J. Gelb is right in restoring the name to *Da-an-na-*[ta-á]š*-*ši*, cf. I.J. Gelb, *NPN*, 147, s.v. *Tanna-tašši*, and P.M. Purves, *NPN*, 262, s.v. *tanna-* and *-tašši*, (wr. *Ta-an-na-taš-ši, Da-an-na-taš-ši* and *Da-an-na-*[*ta-á*]š*-*ši*). P.M. Purves considers them Kassite because of the element *-taš-ši*. E. Laroche (*GLH*, 255, s.v. ***dani-***) mentions, but does not explain the form *da-a-ni-ya-aš-ši* (KUB XXXII 27 II 12).

The personal name ***Tan-atal*** (wr. *Ta-na-ta-al*) at Tigunāni is analysed as {*Tan-adal*}, typology 1.4, lexicon *tan-*, *adal*, translation 'The strong one made/created (the boy)', cf. Th. Richter, *VHN*, 297, 529, s.v. ***tan-*** 'machen, erschaffen' ['to make, to create']; cf. Th. Richter, *BGH*, 436-438, s.v. ***tan-*** [*passim*] 'machen, tun'. The forms with ***tan=i-*** (with marker of transitivity ***-i-***) show that the forms without this marker should probably also be considered transitive. The meaning of Hurrian ***tan-*** is confirmed by Urartian ***tan=u***.

Th. Richter (*BGH*, 437) mentions, that M. Salvini - I. Wegner (2004, 182) interpret ***da-a-nu-še*** [Boğ.] as adjective / abstract. According to I. Wegner (*Einführung*, 55) the suffix ***-(a)=šše*** forms abstract notions. She gives the examples ***ašt=a=šše*** 'femininity', ***all=a=šše*** 'ladyship', ***šarr=a=šše*** 'kingship'. It is conceivable that ***d/tann=a=šše*** means 'creation'.

However, if we compare Linear A ***da-na-si*** with the formation of ***Tan-atal***, it is tempting to interpret ***da-na-si*** as Hurrian ***d/tan-azzi*** < ***tan-aždi/ašti***, the athematic *imperative* 'Make/Create (the child), oh woman !', which would be quite acceptable in view of Hurrian name-giving.

It is remarkable that Linear A seems to offer evidence with regard to the root ***dan-*** / ***tan-*** that the initial dental occlusive in these Minoan-Hurrian roots can be both voiced and voiceless. This confirms the allophonic character of Hurrian occlusives, also at the beginning of a word or name, at least in the Hurrian dialect of Minoan Crete.

I have suggested that the character of the following consonant (cf. e.g. Linear A ***da-du-ma-ta***) might influence whether an initial occlusive is voiced or not, but that at the same time the phenomenon of (restoration by) analogy might play a role. Compare for a voiceless initial ***tan-*** in Linear A, for instance, ***ta-na-te*** (ZA 10a.1). See also my general remarks on the alleged voicelessness of initial Hurrian occlusives on the basis of alphabetic cuneiform of Ugarit. In my view this evidence can only be considered proof for the Hurrian dialect of the area of Ugarit and only for the rather late period to which this evidence belongs. It cannot indiscriminately be applied to other places and periods of Hurrian residence, where syllabic cuneiform was the only source. With regard to Linear A occlusives it is important that only the dentals show separate series for ***d-*** and ***t-*** and that initial voiced dental stops are attested in Linear A. For the labials ***p-/b-*** and palatals / velars ***k-/g-*** there are no separate series for voiceless and voiced stops in Linear A and B.

One may compare the personal name ***ta-ni-ia*** at Alalaḫ IV (*AT* 189: 19), that can be interpreted as either a hypocoristic name (with the Hurrian hypocoristic suffix ***-ya***) or as a name formed as the indicative form ***ta-ni-a*** {*tan=i=a*} (3rd person sing.) 'He/She made/created (the child)', cf. Th. Richter, *VHN*, 585. At Boğazköy ^{f}***Tanu-ḫepa*** (cf. E. Laroche, *NH*, 174, N° 1244): 1. Reine, femme de Muwatalli: hiér. *Tà-nú-he-pa*, SBo I 42.
2. Reine, femme de Urḫi-Tešub: hiér. *Tà-nú-he-pa*, SBo I 43-44.
3. Reine, femme d'un Mursili (II ou III ?): hiér. *Tà-nú-he-pa*, SBo I 24-29.
4. Sources cunéiformes: abs. nom. ^{f}*Da/Ta-nu-ḫé-pa-(aš)*, XIV 7 + XXI 19 I 16, 17, 20; XXI 33, 19; XXXI 66 III 15; XV 5 I 7, III 4, 9; XVI 16 Vo 1; 32 II 1, 4; KBo IX 151, 5.

Linear A ***a-na-qa*** (HT 126(+Fr)a.2) from Hagia Triada cannot be identified with the Nuzi personal name ***Anaka*** (wr. *A-na-ka*), son of *A-mi-li-ia*, JEN 560: 102 (cf. I.J. Gelb, *NPN*, 21; P.M. Purves, *NPN*, 200), because Linear A ***q-*** does not reflect a cuneiform emphatic, c.q. a voiced palatal ***g***, but a voiced velar fricative ***-ḫ-*** in the cuneiform syllabary and ***ġ*** in the cuneiform alphabet of Ugarit. So Linear A ***-qa*** represents Hurrian ***-ḫa***.

P.M. Purves has observed that ***-ḫa*** at Nuzi seems to be a shortened form of ***-ḫai̯a*** in personal names such as *A-ri-ḫa* and *A-ri-iḫ-ḫa* (< **Ari-p-ḫa*) beside *A-ri-ḫa-a-a* and *A-ri-iḫ-ḫa-a-a* (< **Ari-p-ḫai̯a*), cf. P.M. Purves, *NPN*, 212, s.v. ***-ḫa*** and ***-ḫai̯a***.

According to Th. Richter (*BGH*, 26f.; *VHN*, 373) the meaning of the Hurrian verbal root ***an(n)-*** '(sich) freuen' is established. So *intransitive* ***an(n)=a-*** (theme-vowel ***-a-*** marking intransitivity) means 'to enjoy, rejoice, be delighted' and *transitive* ***an(n)=i-*** (theme-vowel ***-i-*** marking transitivity) means 'to give joy'. Consequently the Linear A name ***a-na-qa*** can be interpreted as Hurrian {*an(n)=a-ḫa*}, hypocoristic of {*an(n)=a-ḫai̯a*}, '*Ḫai̯a* rejoices, is delighted'. It is unlikely that ***-ḫai̯a*** can be equated with the verbal root ***ḫai-*** 'prendre' (cf. E. Laroche, *GLH*, 89) and ***ḫa-*** I [*passim*] 'nehmen', 'prendre', 'attraper (un animal)' ['to take, to catch (an animal)'] (cf. Th. Richter, *BGH*, 117), since a Hurrian personal name cannot contain two verbal roots. This means that ***-ḫai̯a*** and the alleged abbreviation ***-ḫa*** are probably nominal.

Linear A ***si-di-ja*** (HT 126(+Fr)a.3) from Hagia Triada can be identified as a Hurrian hypocoristic personal name (with the hypocoristic suffix ***-ya***) or as a Hurrian verbal 'one-word' name, built on the root ***še/id-*** I 'to curse' (see Th. Richter, *BGH*, 398-400, s.v. ***še/id-*** I [Boğ.; Tiš-atal] 'verfluchen'; *VHN*, 516, s.v. ***šid-***) or perhaps ***šed-*** II 'to fatten, to feed' (cf. Th. Richter, *BGH*, 400, s.v. ***šed-*** II [Boğ.] 'fett machen, mästen'; and *VHN*, 516, s.v. ***šed-***), but also on the verbal root ***šind-*** 'to make seven', (in personal names) 'to create the seventh (child)' (see Th. Richter, *BGH*, 387-388, s.v. ***šind-*** [PN] 'sieben'; *VHN*, 512, s.v. ***šind-/šend-***, 'sieben', in *intransitive* verbal forms 'sieben sein', in transitive forms 'sieben (Kinder) / ein siebtes (Kind) vorhanden sein lassen').

Indeed ***si-di-ja*** (HT 126(+Fr)a.3) can be equated with the Hurrian personal name ***Šetija*** (wr. *še-di-ia*) from Mari, analysis *{šed=i=ia}*, typology 1.1.1.2.4, translated by Th. Richter (*VHN*, 279) as 'Er/Sie (scil. ein *Numen*) machte (Jungen) fett' ['He/She (scil. a *numen*) made (the boy) fat, fed (the boy)']. However, the meaning can also be 'He/She (scil. a *numen*) cursed (the older deceased child)'. Since the Linear A form may well contain the root ***šid-*** (not ***šed-***), the latter translation may be preferred for Linear A ***si-di-ja*** (HT 126(+Fr)a.3). Linear A ***si-di-ja*** (HT 126(+Fr)a.3) can also be equated with ***Šintiḭa*** (wr. *Ši-en-ti-ia*, *Ši-in-ti-ia*) from Nuzi, phonologically ***/šindiḭa/***, that P.M. Purves considers hypocoristic for ***Šintip-tešup*** (wr. *Ši-in-di-ip-te-šup*, *Ši-in-ti-ip-te-šup*), because a man of each name is son of *Eḫli-tešup* (*NPN*, 257, s.v. ***šint*** and ***šintiḭa***). The dental may be considered voiced as the Linear A name confirms. In Linear A and B a nasal ***-n-*** preceding a dental stop is not expressed in consonant clusters.

P.M. Purves: "Occurrences as personal name element with ***-p*** added imply verbal use. Yet in *šint-arpu*, e.g. JEN 102:12 and 25, *šint* seems to be primarily a numeral; see Speiser in *AASOR XVI (1936)*, 132, and Oppenheim in *OLZ XL*, cols. 1-6. That *šint* may not necessarily be identical with Hurrian *šin*, 'two', is suggested by Friedrich, *KBCG*, 34, who mentions a letter in which Von Brandenstein proposes tr. 'seven'."

E. Laroche, *GLH*, 235-236, distinguished verbal ***šinti*** (1) from the numeral ***šinti*** (2). Sub ***šinti*** (2) 'sept' [seven]: ***šintarbu*** 'de sept ans' [seven years old], Nuzi; cf. Speiser, *AASOR XVI*, 133; *AW* 1243; v. sous *Šidarbu*. - *ši-in-ta-(ta)-a-i* 'par sept, septuple ans' [seven times], KUB XXVII 23 II 10; XLVII 31 I 13, 15; instr. adv. comme *kigatae*. […] - D'après les parallèles hittites, ***7 widar*** 'les sept eaux / fleuves', on interprête ainsi ***šintatai šiyai***, [According to Hittite parallels, ***7 widar*** 'the seven waters / rivers', one interprets ***šintatai šiyai*** likewise], cf. C.-G. von Brandenstein, *ZA 46*, 94 n.1; E.A. Speiser, *IH*, 82.

Šintip-tešup can be analysed as *{šind=i=b-tešub}*, consisting of the verbal root ***šind-*** 'to create the seventh (child)' + the marker of transitivity ***-i-*** + the Old Hurrian marker of the 3rd person singular ***-b-*** + ***Tešub***, subject of the transitive verb, translation 'Tešub, he created the seventh (child)' > 'Tešub made it possible that the seventh (child) was born'. The Old Hurrian form ***šind=i=b*** would be ***šind=i=a*** in the Tušratta letter. Actually the transitive form ***šind=i=a*** in so-called Mitanni-Hurrian, often provided with a transitional glide ***-y-*** (written ***-i-***) between the vowels [***i***] and [***a***], is almost identical with the hypocoristic form with the hypocoristic suffix ***-ya*** (written ***-ia***).

Within Linear A we may compare ***si-da-te*** (AK 2.1) from Arkhanes, ***si-du-mina ̦ ku-mi*** (HT 110a.1) from Hagia Triada and the second sequence ***si-di-jo-pi*** in the inscription ***a-re-ne-si-di-jo-pi-ke-pa-ja-su-ra-i-te-ra-me-a-ja-ku*** (KN Zf 13) from Mavro Spilio.

Linear A]***ta-nu-ri-ja***[(PK Zc 13) from Palaikastro may be compared with]***nu-ri***[(NE Zc 1) from Nerospilios. The Linear A inscription]***ta-nu-ri-ja***[(PK Zc 13) occurs on a sherd of a cup from Palaikastro, now in the Ashmolean Museum at Oxford.

Another Linear A inscription]***nu-ri***[(NE Zc 1) painted in black on a yellow sherd of an amphora or pithos, found by P. Faure in the Cave of Nerospilios (*Νεροσπήλιος*), a toponym that owes its name to the fact that there is water in the cave during the winter, can be read as]***ri-nu***[, if it is read as published, but if the sherd is turned upside-down, so that ***-ri-*** is shown in the same position as the same sign ***-ri-*** on the sherd from Palaikastro, the result is]***nu-ri***[(NE Zc 1), that can possibly be restored to ***ta-***]***nu-ri***[***-ja***. Although Palaikastro in northeast Crete is far away from Nerospilios in northwest Crete, both places may have yielded the same type of inscription, possibly the same personal names.

Formerly]***ta-nu-ri-ja***[(PK Zc 13) and possibly restored ***ta-***]***nu-ri***[***-ja*** (NE Zc 1) would have been divided into ***tanu-*** and ***-ri-ja***. P.M. Purves (*NPN*, 248), for instance, writes, s.v. ***-rija***: "Hurrian ? Seems to consist of ***-ri+-ja*** in *Kuzzarija* and *Turarija*."

I.J. Gelb, *NPN*, 147, mentions, for instance, a man from Nuzi ***Tanu*** (wr. *Ta-a-nu*, var. *Ta-ni*, *Ta-a-ni*) as the brother of *Wa-aḫ-ri-še-ni*, whose name can be recognized as an irrefutable Hurrian name. In spite of this P.M. Purves fails to mention *Tanu* as a Hurrian name in *NPN*. The name is probably derived from the Hurrian verbal root ***tan-*** 'do, make'. Cf. also the Hurrian feminine sentence name ***fTanuḫepa*** attested at Boğazköy.

According to Th. Richter (*BGH*, 436-438, s.v. ***tan-*** [*passim*], *tin-* [Ugarit]), ***tan-*** 'to make, do' is usually transitive. He mentions that Hurrian ***tan-*** corresponds with Hittite ***ija-*** 'to make', Akkadian ***epēšu*** and Urartian ***tanu-*** 'to make'.

In recent research more attention has been paid to the so-called root-extensions taking the first position in the order of suffixes after the root. Root-extension ***-u/ol-*** is according to I. Wegner (*Einführung*, 88) *reflexive* and causing intransitivity. The exact meaning of the root-extension ***-ol-*** is not yet clear. For instance, Hurrian ***salḫ-*** is 'to hear', but ***salḫ=ol-*** also means 'to hear'; Hurrian ***ar-*** is 'to give', but ***ar=ol-*** also means 'to give', but also 'to bring away', so that the formant might express a spatial relation, cf. E. Neu, *StBoT 32*, 1996, 361: ***-ol-*** 'hin' ['away']. See for the Urartian verbal forms with the formant ***-ul-*** also M. Salvini, *ZA 81 (1991)*, 122 ff.

Consequently,]***ta-nu-ri-ja***[(PK Zc 13) and restored ***ta-***]***nu-ri***[***-ja*** (NE Zc 1) can be analysed as {*tan=ul=i=(j)a*}, consisting of the verbal root ***tan-*** 'to make, create' + root-extension ***-u/ol-*** (position 1) + the marker of transitivity ***-i-*** (position 5) + the marker of the subject of action of the transitive verb 3rd person singular ***-a*** (position 7).

Since the sequences are in both cases the only entries, it is uncertain whether we are dealing with a verbal form 'he/she makes' or a verbal 'one-word' personal name 'He/She (a *numen*) creates/created (the child)' or with a hypocoristic name with the suffix ***-ya***.

The Linear A personal name ***a-ru-ra-ta***[(HT 11a.1-2) provides a useful parallel with the root-extension ***-u/ol-***. It can be analysed as a sentence name {*ar=o/ul-atta*} with a double meaning 'Give (the child), oh (God the) Father !' and at the same time 'Give (the child), oh Father (of the child) !', consisting of the verbal root ***ar-*** 'to give' + root-extension ***-u/ol-*** + ***atta(i)*** 'father' that can also have the function of theophorous element, *(Eni) Attanni* '(God) the Father' who can probably be identified with the Stormgod Tešub. This kind of name-giving combines the domestic and divine sphere in a splendid way.

In some cases one may think of a so-called replacement-name (the newborn child replaces a deceased member of the family). Cf. Linear A ***da-du-ma-ta*** (HT 95+149a.1), analysed as Old Hurrian {*dad=o/u=m-atta*} and translated as '(God the) Father loves / loved the child'.

Since there is also an Old Hurrian root-extension ***-o/ur-***, of which the meaning is not clear, Linear A]***ta-nu-ri-ja***[(PK Zc 13), restored ***ta-***]***nu-ri***[***-ja*** (NE Zc 1) and ***a-ru-ra-ta***[(HT 11a.1-2) can also contain this root-extension. The translations would be more or less the same. I. Wegner (*Einführung*, 89) offers the following examples, s.v. ****-o/ur-***: *kul=o/ur=o=m* 'er sprach' ['he spoke'] from ***kul-*** 'to speak', *ar=o/ur=o=m* 'er gab' ['he gave'] from ***ar-*** 'to give'.

su - ki-ni-|ma 7 or ***wa-su - ki-ni-|ma*** 7 (ZA 5.1-2) from Kato Zakro.
The analysed structure of the first lines of text of text ZA 5a reads:

ZA 5a.1:	*79 - 85* 1	or: *79* TAL 1
ZA 5a.1-2:	*wa-su - ki-ni-|ma* 7	or: VINa *su - ki-ni-|ma* 7
ZA 5a.2-3:	*o - ta-ni-za-|se* 6	*sa-mi-da-e*

The scribe of Linear A tablet ZA 5 has not made it easy for us to read the text properly, since he left much space between some signs, so that we sometimes wonder, whether he used this space in order to avoid writing a word divider. He left much space between signs ***79*** and ***85***, between signs ***su*** and ***ki*** in ***su - ki-ni-|ma 7*** (ZA 5.1-2) or ***wa-su - ki-ni-|ma*** 7 (ZA 5.1-2) and also between signs ***o*** and ***ta*** in ***o - ta-ni-za-|se*** (ZA 5.2-3). The fact that the scribe shows this idiosyncratic way of writing in various sequences and that separating ****o*** from ****ta-ni-za-se*** does not make sense, because there is no evidence for usage of sign ***o*** as a monosyllable, has convinced me that ***su - ki-ni-|ma*** or ***wa-su - ki-ni-|ma*** may be one sequence as well. The tablet begins with *79* TAL 1 or 79 TAL **,** (word divider) followed by VINa ***su - ki-ni-|ma*** 7 or ***wa-su - ki-ni-|ma*** 7.

The signs ***79 - 85*** or ***79*** TAL (ZA 5a.1) also occur in ZA 14.1, where they are written closer together and are followed by 1 unit, which makes it likely that we must also read 1 unit (instead of a word divider) after ***79 - 85*** or ***79*** TAL (ZA 5a.1).

Sign ***85*** usually indicates the ideogram TAL(entum) = Linear B sign *L, but is by some scholars also regarded as a syllabic sign. Sign ***79*** (with 3 legs) resembles sign ***633*** = OVIS^{f} (with 2 legs) and is by some scholars regarded as syllabic sign ***qi***. In this respect it is treated as sign ***48b***, which is the general ideogram OVIS and was by J. Raison – M. Pope (*Index transnuméré du linéaire A*, 1977, 60) considered equivalent to Linear B sign ****21*** = OVIS / ***qi***. In *chapter 12: From undeciphered to deciphered Linear A signs*, I argue that Linear A ***48b*** is only identical with Linear B ideogram OVIS, but is not a syllabic sign.

I prefer reading ***79*** TAL, especially because of the distance between the two signs in ZA 5.1. Raison-Pope (1994) read, however, in ZA 5.1-2 (= their tablet ZA 13.1-2) ***79 - 85*** **,** ***82a su - ki-ni-|ma*** 7 = ***79 - 85*** **,** VINa ***su - ki-ni-|ma*** 7.

If this reading *79* TAL 1 VINa ***su - ki-ni-|ma*** 7 is correct, ***su-ki-ni-|ma*** can *prima facie* be identified with Hurrian ***šu-uk-ki-ni*** (KUB XXVII 35,5) with the suffix of the so-called singular article ***-ni***, followed by the Hurrian enclitic connective particle ***-ma*** 'and', but a connective ***-ma*** does not make sense syntactically, since it seems to be the first personal name and ***o - ta-ni-za-|se*** and ***sa-mi-da-e*** are not followed by ***-ma***.

So it seems more likely that ***-ma*** in ***su - ki-ni-|ma*** is e.g. a hypocoristic of the (*quasi*) theophorous onomastic element ***-madi*** 'wisdom, wise'.

E. Laroche, *GLH*, 241, s.v. ***šukki***: Sg. nom. *šu-u-ug-gi*, KBo VIII 143,5; KUB XXXII 19 I 18. Nom. dét. *šu-uk-ki-ni*, KUB XXVII 35,5; *šu-uk-ki-ne-e-il*, KBo XI 19 Vo 15; cf. KBo XIX 144 IV 13. At the time of Laroche the meaning of Hurrian ***šukki*** was not known.

If the suffix of the so-called definite article ***-ni*** is used, this may show, that Linear A ***su-ki-ni-*** designates a Hurrian noun, but it is not certain that the definite article is involved.

Th. Richter (*BGH*, 406-408) mentions the root ***šug-*** I, ***šukk-*** 'eins' ['one'], also as verbal root (intr.) 'to be(come) one' and (trans.) 'to make one', also with root-extensions, e.g. ***šug=am(m)-*** [Boğ.] 'to unite (?)' (Campbell, 2007a, 170^{+94}, 171); ***šug=ar=umma*** *epēšu* [Nuzi] 'zu Tausch geben, Ausgleichzahlungen leisten' ['to compensate']. In names the latter meaning may be useful, if a newborn child is considered to offer compensation for a lost child.

If Linear A ***su - ki-ni-|ma*** is a personal name, it could be Hurrian ***Šuk(k)innima***, analysis *{šug/kk=i=nni-ma(di)}*, consisting of verbal root ***šug-*** I, ***šukk-*** + marker of transitivity ***-i-*** + *optional allomorphic* suffix ***-nni*** (instead of *normal* ***-nna***) of the enclitic personal pronoun 3rd person singular indicating the object of action of the transitive verb + ***madi***, 'Make him/her (***-nna/-nni***) (the newborn child) number one, oh *Madi* / oh Wisdom !' > 'Make him/her the first-born child, oh *Madi*, oh Wisdom !' or possibly 'Let him / her give compensation (for the lost child), oh *Madi* !'.

However, Th. Richter (*BGH*, 408; *VHN*, 517-518) mentions interesting Hurrian nouns: ***šugi*** I [Boğ.] 'Türsturz(?)' ['lintel(?)'] (cf. Akkadian ***šukû***); 'Dachkonstruktion(?)' ['roof-construction(?)'], 'building'. ***zugi*** II [Ugarit] 'petit' ['small'], RS voc. II 19 = Hh II 131: Sumerian TAR.RA = Hurrian ***zu-gi*** (Akkadian ***ṣîḫru***), cf. E. Laroche, *GLH*, 306; ***zugi*** = Akkadian ***ṣeḫru*** 'Junge' ['boy'].

Th. Richter (*VHN*, 280-281) mentions the following personal names: ***Zukan*** (wr. *Zu-ga-an*) from Mari, analysis *{Zo/ug(i)=a*[E.]*=n(na)}*, typology 3.2.1, lexicon *zugi* II, translation 'Er (Junge) ist als Kleiner (geboren)' ['He (the boy) is (born) as a small one']. [E.] refers to the *essive* case in ***-a***. Cf. *zu-ga* at Alalaḫ IV (AT 192: 28); *zu-ku* at Alalaḫ IV (AT 148: 19); *zu-ú-kum* at Ekalte (*WVDOG* 102, 23: 21, 26); ***Zuku*** (wr. *zu-ú-ku*, *zu-uk-ku*) and *ᶠzu-ku-ni-ge* at Nuzi (I.J. Gelb, *NPN*, 181; P.M. Purves, *NPN*, 279); ***Zukašši*** (?) (wr. *Zu-ga-aš*(?)*-ši*) from Mari, typology 3.1, lexicon *zugašše* (→ *zugi* II), 'Kleinkind-schaft (?)' ['Young childhood']; ***Zuki*** (wr. *zu-ki*) at Ašnakkum, typology 3.1, lexicon *zugi* II, ***Zuki-zuki*** (wr. *zu-gi-zu-ki*) at Mari, typology 5.1, lexicon *zugi* II; ***Šukšeija*** (wr. ***Šu-uk-ši-ja***) at Mari, *{šukše=ja}*, typology 3.3, lexicon *šukše*, 'Erstgeborener/s (Sohn, Kind)' ['Firstborn (son, child)'], etc. Observing all these names the Linear A personal name ***su - ki-ni-|ma*** can also be Hurrian ***Zukini***, analysis *{zugi=ni-ma(di)}*, consisting of ***zugi*** II 'small child/boy' + the suffix of the so-called singular definite article or individualising suffix ***-ne/-ni*** + ***madi***, 'The small child/boy is wise'.

Raison-Pope's reading of ***82a*** (= VINa) is graphically certainly correct, since the sign is neatly drawn, but it is strange that in that case the 'wine' ideogram is not immediately followed by a number. The number 7 follows ***su-ki-ni-|ma***.

This problem may be solved, if sign ***82a*** is not read as the ideogram VINa, but as the resembling sign ***75a = wa*** that may ultimately be derived from this ideogram.

As a result we can read the sequence ***wa-su - ki-ni-|ma***, which resembles the name of the capital of Mitanni, ***Waššukkanni*** and the enclitic connective particle ***-ma*** 'and', but that sounds too wonderful to be true. So I'll try to analyse ***wa-su - ki-ni-|ma*** (ZA 5.1-2).

Although there is no word divider visible between ***wa-su*** and ***ki-ni-|ma***, *GORILA 3* (152-153) reads ***wa-su*** separate from ***ki-ni-|ma***, which would in principle offer two Hurrian sequences. If the reading ***wa-su ki-ni-|ma*** (*GORILA 3*) or ***wa-su - ki-ni-|ma*** is correct, it may be interesting that the ***p/w*** alternation occurring in the Hurrian verbal roots ***paš-/waš-*** and ***pašš-/wašš-*** also occurs in Linear A. I only explain the roots briefly, since they have already been treated extensively in the discussion on Linear A ***pa-sa-ri-ja*** (HT 24a.4), ***pa-se*** (HT 18.1; HT 27+48b.4), ***pa-si-a*** (HT 45b.3), ***pa-se-ja*** (HT Wc 3001a, HT Wc 3002) from Hagia Triada and ***pa-za-ku*** [(ZA 6b.4) from Kato Zakro.

E. Laroche, *GLH*, 294-295, s.v. ***waš-***, 'apporter ?', *waši-*, *wašu-*: *wa$_a$-a-šu*, KUB XXIX 8 II 38; *wa$_a$-a-šu-uš*, *ib.* II 43, 44. The *transitive* meaning of the root was recognized first.

Th. Richter (*BGH*, 302-304), s.v. ***w/paš-*** I [*passim*] *intr.* 'to come in, to enter' (corresponds with Hittite ***andan uwa-***) and *trans.* 'to bring in, to introduce'; s.v. ***p/wašš-*** [Boğ.; Mitt.; PN] 'to send' (corresponding with ***šapâru*** in Akkadian letters from Mitanni, cf. E. Laroche, *GLH*, 197, s.v. ***pašš-***). According to Th. Richter (*VHN*, 482), s.v. ***paš-/paz-*** *{faž}*, ***pazz-***, the translation 'to enter' for *intr.* *{faž}* is established by the rendering with Hittite ***andan uwa-*** in the bilingual ***kirenze***, by comparisons with Sumerian KU4 and Akkadian ***erēbu*** in a vocabulary from Ugarit and again with Akkadian ***erēbu*** in a glossary from Qaṭna. Hittite ***anda(n)*** means 'in, into, inside', and ***uwa-*** [Ii] 'to come'.

If we read ***wa-su ki-ni-|ma***, the form ***wašu*** can be analysed as an Old Hurrian *imperative* *{w/paš(š)=u}* 'bring in' or as personal name ***Wašun*** *{w/paš(š)=u=n(na)}* 'Bring him/her (the child) in', since a final consonant is not expressed in Linear A and B.

Linear A ***ki-ni-|ma*** can then possibly represent ***ḫinim(a)***, that means 'ferner' ['further'] according to Haas/Thiel (1978, 13[23]; 1979, 345-346) and 'now' according to Campbell (2007a, 339), cf. Th. Richter, *BGH*, 151, s.v. ***ḫenne/i*** [Boğ.; Mit.], 'zu diesem Zeitpunkt' ['at this moment'], 'jetzt, damals' ['now, then'], corresponds with Akkadian ***inanna*** and Urartian ***ḫini*** 'jetzt' ['now']. I do not know, whether the personal name ***Ḫini***, a man of Temiya: nom. ***^{m}Ḫi-i-ni-iš***, KUB XXVI 62 IV 36 (cf. E. Laroche, *NH*, 68) can be associated with this adverb.

If we read ***wa-su - ki-ni-|ma*** as one sequence, the form is probably a personal name followed by the number 7, but the analysis *{w/paš(š)=u=n(na)=ḫinima}*, translation 'Bring him/her (the child) *now* in (oh *numen*) !' seems very unusual, but not impossible.

Th. Richter (*BGH*, 207) mentions several forms ***kin(n)-*** and ***ken(n)-***, but all without translation: ***kin(n)-*** [PN] o.Ü. [ohne Übersetzung]; ***keni*** I [Boğ.] o.Ü.; ***ke-e-ni*** II [Boğ.] o.Ü.; ***ki-ni-wa$_a$*** [Emar] o.Ü.; ***kenniwe*** [Nuzi] o.Ü. 'a term describing certain horses or the royal retinue'; ***kin(n)idi*** [Boğ.] o.Ü. 'divine attribute of Ḫepat and IŠTAR'.

Unfortunately too many questions remain to be answered, but sometimes one must be content with signalizing the problems without being able to solve them all.

I have for now to dismiss the tempting thought that Linear A ***wa-su - ki-ni-|ma*** could be taken as one sequence, since a word divider fails, and that the name ***wa-su-ki-ni***, provided with the Hurrian enclitic connective particle ***-ma***, resembles the name of the capital of Mitanni, ***Waššukkanni / Uššukani***.

It does not do any harm to ponder on the fact that this legendary city has still not been found and that we are still missing the Royal Archives of the Empire of Mitanni with all knowledge on the Imperial society and administration and the relations with other areas such as Minoan Crete, where Hurrian was the written and spoken vernacular. That is more interesting than the question whether Linear A ***wa-su-ki-ni*** could be an orthographic variant of *Waššukkanni*.

I translate some passages from G. Wilhelm, *Grundzüge der Geschichte und Kultur der Hurriter*, Darmstadt 1982, 37-38, but I have quoted his German text in the Linear A *indices* s.v. ***Waššukkanni / Uššukani***: "The residence of *Šauštatar* was the city *Waššukkanni*. One has assumed, that this name developed in the Middle-Assyrian period to *Uššukani* and then to *Sikāni* (Opitz 1927). The latter place lies according to an Assyrian inscription (Grayson 1976: 90) in the area of 'the source of the Ḫābūr', i.e. near present *Ra's al-^{c}Ain*, and could recently at last be identified with Tall *Faḫḫārīya*.

That the name *Sikāni* is a younger form of *Waššukkanni / Uššukani*, may be doubted on account of the fact that already in the Ur III-period a town *Sigan* existed in the region of the Ḫābūr (Edzart/Farber 1974). Moreover as a result of a neutron-activation analysis of the Tušratta letter, allegedly written at *Waššukkanni* by order of the King of Mitanni, the characteristics of elements occurring in these clay tablets deviate strongly from the tablets found in Tall *Faḫḫārīya* itself and dating from the Middle-Assyrian period (Dobel e.a. 1977). Probably *Waššukkanni* is to be sought farther to the north, approximately in the region of Mardin (Goetze 1957: 67) or even more likely, to the west or northwest of Mardin. [….] Two tablets found at Alalaḫ, containing *Šauštatar's* judicial decisions, received his royal assent with the so-called 'dynastic seal'. It is the seal of a predecessor that was reused for reasons not yet clarified. The same practice is known from Alalaḫ, Ugarit and Amurru (Klengel 1965:175). The so-called 'dynastic seal' of Mitanni bears the legend '*Šuttarna*, son of *Kirta*, King of Maitani' and thus hands down the names of two otherwise unknown kings. The name *Šuttarna* returns several times in the dynastic line of Kings of Mitanni and one has regarded King *Kirta* as prototype of the legendary King *Krt* in an Ugaritic epic (Albright 1968:103, Astour 1973:32) which remains unprovable. It is uncertain when the two have reigned."

My comment: *Šaušsatatar* seals are found on tablets 13 (ATT/8/52) and 14 (ATT/8/44) from Alalaḫ, cf. D.J. Wiseman, *The Alalakh tablets*, London 1953, 39. Cf. also *supra* the discussion on Alalaḫ text 108. ATT/8/251 with a similar seal impression on the reverse: a letter from a king to *Utti.* The accumulating evidence of Hurrians and Hurrian in Minoan Crete may confirm the theory that the epic hero *krt* from Ugarit may well be equated with a historical king *Kirta* of Mitanni. The name of *krt*'s wife *Ḫurrai* is in that case not surprising (see *supra*). The direct reference to king *Kirta* himself closes the triangle of Mitanni – *KRT* / Ugarit – Minoan Crete and suggests an explosion of power at the time of the creation and rise of Mitanni culminating in tremendous expansion that included Crete.

The name ***Kirta*** may now be analysed as a verbal 'one-word' name of birth {*kir=tta*}, consisting of the verbal root ***kir-*** 'to liberate, to set free' + the *enclitic* personal pronoun 1st person singular ***-tta***, indicating the object of the transitive verb, translation 'Set me free, Liberate me (from the womb) (oh *numen*) !' The *imperative* ***kir-*** is here used athematically.

Linear A ***a-||ra-tu*** (ZA 7a.1-2) from Kato Zakro offers two feasible interpretations: I) It may be ***Allatum***, Akkadianized form in ***-tum*** of Hurrian ***allay***. E. Laroche, *GLH*, 43, s.v. *Allani*: "Déesse associée à IŠTAR-*Šauška* dans les listes syro-kizouvatniennes; le nom signifie 'la Dame'; cf. *Allai*. *Allani* semble être l'équivalent de l'akk. *Allatum* = *Ereškigal*, déesse des enfers; cf. Yazīlīkaya N° 49. *Allatum*, à son tour, n'est peut-être que l'akkadisation en *-tum* de h. *allai*; cf. *BiOr*. 21, 321." ***Allay*** 'Lady', c.q. ***Allani*** 'the Lady', is epithet of *Ḫebat* and IŠTAR-*Šauška* and is sometimes also associated with other goddesses such as *Naja/e*, but she is also mentioned as a goddess in her own right in lists of Hurrian divinities at Ugarit.

The theonym ***Allatum*** may also be used as a personal name. Cf. the Hurrian personal names ***ᶠAlla*** (wr. *ᶠAl-la*) at Ešnunna, Mari, Nuzi; ***ᶠAllai*** (wr. *ᶠAl-la-i*) at Ekalte; ***ᶠAllanni*** (wr. *ᶠAl-la-an-ni*) at Mari and Nippur, cf. Th. Richter, *VHN*, 49-51, 369-370, s.v. ***alla / allae / allai / alli***, 'Herrin' ['Lady']. Cf. also the sentence names ***ᶠAllaiš-arum*** (wr. *al-la-iš-a-rum, al-la-i-ša-rum, al-la-jí-ša-rum*), name of three ladies at Mari, {*allai=ž-ar=o=m*}, typology 1.1.1.1.5, lexicon *allai, ar-*, translation '*The Lady* gave (the girl)'; ***Allaš-arum*** (wr. *al-la-aš-a-rum, al-la-aš-a-ru-um*), name of 3 men at Mari and one man at Qaṭṭarā (Tall ar-Rimaḫ), {*alla=ž-ar=o=m*}, typology 1.1.1.1.5, lexicon *alla, ar-*, '*The Lady* gave (the boy)'; ***ᶠAllaš-arum*** (wr. *al-la-aš-a-rum, al-la-aš-a-ru-um*), name of two ladies at Mari, {*alla=ž-ar=o=m*}, typology 1.1.1.1.5, lexicon *allai, ar-*, translation '*The Lady* gave (the girl)'; ***ᶠAlla-tatum*** (wr. *al-la-ta-dum*), name of a lady at Mari, {*alla-tad=o=m*}, typology 1.1.1.1.5, lexicon *alla, tad-*, translation '*The Lady* loved (the girl)', ***ᶠAllai-Ḫebat*** (wr. *ᶠAl-la-i-ḫé-bat*) at Mari, {*allai-Ḫebat*}, typology 2.1, '*Ḫebat* is the Lady'; ***ᶠAllae-kijaze*** (wr. *ᶠAl-la-e-ki-ia-ze*) at Mari, {*allae-kijaze*}, typology 2.1, 'The Lady is the sea'; ***ᶠAllae-mata*** (wr. *ᶠAl-la-e-ma-da*) at Mari, {*allae-mad(i)=a*[E.]}, typology 2.1, 'The Lady is like wisdom [*essive*]' > 'The Lady is wise'; ***ᶠAlla-Naje*** (wr. *ᶠAl-la-na-a-ie*) at Mari, {*alla-Naje*}, typology 2.1, '*The Lady* is Naje', cf. ***ᶠAllai-Naja*** (wr. *ᶠAl-la-i-na-a-a*) at Nuzi (*NPN*, 18; *AAN* I, 22), cf. Th. Richter, *VHN*, 49-52.

II) Since signs transliterated with ***r-*** in Linear A and B can be read as ***l-*** or ***r-***, Linear A ***a-||ra-tu*** might also be equivalent to the personal name ***Arattu*** from Nuzi (wr. *A-ra-at-tu(m)*), father of *Ta-i-qa*, *HSS* V 13:14 , cf. I.J. Gelb, *NPN*, 24, and P.M. Purves, *NPN*, 204, who compares the name with Nuzian ***Arratta*** (wr. *Ar-ra-at-ta*), cautiously identified as Hurrian s.v. ***arr*** (*NPN*, 205).

Linear A ***a-re-tu-||mi***[(ZA 7a.2-3) follows ***a-||ra-tu*** (ZA 7a.1-2) from Kato Zakro. A large part of the tablet is missing after the first sign ***-mi*** in line 3. If this name is completed to ***a-re-tu-||mi***[***-ni***, it yields a perfect Linear A rendering of a Hurrian name with the Hurrian numeral ***tumni*** 'four', analysis {*are/i-tumni*}, consisting of the verbal root ***ar-*** 'to give' + the marker of the transitive *imperative* ***-i/e*** + numeral ***tumni*** 'four', translation 'Give four (oh *numen*) !' > 'Give the fourth child (oh *numen*) !'.

According to the Linear A and B orthographic conventions ***m*** preceding ***n*** is expressed in consonant clusters, since non-occlusives (*σ, μ, ν, ρ, λ, ϝ*) preceding sonantic consonants (*μ, ν, ρ, λ, ϝ, y*) were expressed: cf. Linear B ***a-mi-ni-so*** = Ἀμνῑσός; ***de-so-mo*** = δεσμός. The ***-i-*** of ***-mi-*** in ***a-re-tu-||mi***[***-ni*** and in ***a-mi-ni-so*** is therefore a mute vowel.

Th. Richter (*BGH*, 468-469) mentions s.v. ***tumn-*** 'vier sein' ['to be four'] (Th. Richter, Ein Ḫurriter wird geboren … und benannt, in: J. Becker, R. Hempelmann, E. Rehm (eds.), *Kulturlandschaft Syrien – Zentrum und Peripherie*. Festschrift für Jan-Waalke Meyer, *AOAT 371*, Münster 2010, 503-528, esp. 519); ***tumni*** [Boğ.; Mitt.; PN] meaning 'four' unanimously confirmed; corresponds with Hittite ***mijaweš*** 'four'.

tum(u)narbu, tumunarbe [Nuzi] {*tumn(i)=arbu*} 'four years old'; - ***tumnatala*** [Alalaḫ IV] '(chair) with four legs', Hurrian etymology, with Von Dassow (2008, 322[146]) translation gloss corresponding with Sumerogram 4.TA.ÀM; - ***tumnadi*** [Boğ.], ***tumnātu*** [Nuzi] {*tumn(i)=ade*}: two meanings are given based on the original meaning of 'a group/number of four': '(a chariot) having four-spoked wheels' or 'a wagon / carriage with four wheels'. Since a chariot usually has two wheels with four spokes, which is shown on the poros-sarcophagus from a chamber-tomb near the Palace of Hagia Triada, most scholars consider the meaning '(a chariot) having four-spoked wheels' most likely. This seems to be confirmed by Sumerian ^{giš}GIGIR corresponding with Hurrian *du-um-na-du.* ^{giš}GIGIR is 'wagon, cart' according to Th. van den Hout, *The elements of Hittite*, 200.

On the other side of the same tablet from Kato Zakro Linear A ***a-ma*** (ZA 7b.1) is the first entry, probably containing the verbal root ***amm-***, {*amm=a*} 'He/She arrives' or 'Arrive !'. It can be identified with the Hurrian name ^{f}***Amma*** (wr. ^{f}*Am-ma*) from Nuzi, cf. I.J. Gelb, *NPN,* 20; P.M. Purves, *NPN,* 200), already discussed extensively. Linear A ***a-ma*** (HS Zg 1.2) also occurs on a schist plaque from Hagios Stephanos (Lakonia).

Linear A ***a-ra-na-re*** 105 (HT 1a.4) at Hagia Triada is the last legible entry of a list of personal names, all followed by high numbers. The name may well be analysed as Hurrian {*alla(i)=n(i)-ar=e*} '*Allani*, give (the child/girl) !', consisting of the theophorous element *Allai/y, Allan(n)i*, '(the) Lady' and the imperative 2nd person singular of ***ar-*** 'to give'.

It is interesting that the personal name ***a-ra-na-ro*** (KN As 1516, 11) occurs before VIR 1, in a Linear B list of masculine personal names at Knossos, cf. A. Morpurgo(-Davies) (*Mycenaeae Graecitatis Lexicon*, Incunabula Graeca, Vol. III, Rome 1963, 32), who mentions about the context of ***a-ra-na-ro***: ante VIR 1 in catalogo virorum qui ad -2 *ko-no-si-ja ra-wa-ke-ja* spectant. It seems that ***a-ra-na-ro*** at Knossos is equivalent to the Minoan-Hurrian name ***a-ra-na-re*** from Hagia Triada, but with the Greek ending in ***-ος***.

In a vast majority of Hurrian personal names consisting of verbal and nominal elements the verbal element is the first and the nominal the second, but in a number of names the elements occur in a reverse order: e.g. ^{f}***Allaiš-arum*** (wr. *al-la-iš-a-rum, al-la-i-ša-rum, al-la-ji-ša-rum*), name of three ladies at Mari, analysis {*allai=ž-ar=o=m*}, typology 1.1.1.1.5, lexicon *allai, ar-*, translation '*The Lady* gave (the girl)'; ***Allaš-arum*** (wr. *al-la-aš-a-rum, al-la-aš-a-ru-um*), name of 3 men at Mari and one man at Qaṭṭarā (Tall ar-Rimaḫ), analysis {*alla=ž-ar=o=m*}, typology 1.1.1.1.5, lexicon *alla, ar-*, '*The Lady* gave (the boy)'; ^{f}***Allaš-arum*** (wr. *al-la-aš-a-rum, al-la-aš-a-ru-um*), name of two ladies at Mari, analysis {*alla=ž-ar=o=m*}, typology 1.1.1.1.5, lexicon *allai, ar-*, translation '*The Lady* gave (the girl)'; ^{f}***Alla-tatum*** (wr. *al-la-ta-dum*), name of lady at Mari, {*alla-tad=o=m*}, typology 1.1.1.1.5, lexicon *alla, tad-*, translation '*The Lady* loved (the girl)', cf. Th. Richter, *VHN*, 50-52.

The incomplete Linear A forms]**, *a-ra***[(AK 1a.2) from Arkhanes, and ***a-ra-***[(PH 14b) from Phaistos may well contain (forms of) Hurrian ***allay*** 'Lady' or ***allani*** 'the Lady'. epithet of the goddesses *Ḫebat* and *IŠTAR-Šauška*, but also mentioned as a goddess in her own right in lists of Hurrian divinities at Ugarit.

Since the sequences are probably not complete, they may also reflect Hurrian personal names with ***Allay*** or ***Allani*** as a theophorous element. This may even be the most likely possibility in the case of the tablet from Arkhanes, since the next sequences on the same side of the tablet, ***a-su-mi*** (AK 1a.4), ***a-pa-ru***[(AK1a.5) and ***mi-ki-sa-ne*** (AK 1a.6), are probably Hurrian personal names as well. On the clay bar from the Palace of Phaistos it is not clear whether ***a-ra-***[(PH 14b) may contain the theonym or an anthroponym.

Linear A ***a-pa-ru***[or possibly ***a-pa-re***[(?) (AK 1a.5) from Arkhanes follows]***-ne*** 2 J (first entry of AK 1a.5) that can probably be regarded as the last syllable of a sequence that started at the end of the preceding line of the missing right side of the text. It may be either the Hurrian suffix ***-ne*** representing the so-called singular definite article or the optional allomorphic enclitic personal pronoun 3rd person singular ***-nne/-nni*** instead of ***-nna***.

Only the first two signs of ***a-pa-ru***[are clearly legible. The third sign is only partly visible, since the right side of the tablet is broken off. *GORILA 3* shows that at least one sign follows ***a-pa-***, whereas J. Raison - M. Pope (1994), 33, indicate that this sign might be ***ru***. If the reading ***a-pa-ru***[is correct and if the sequence is complete, it may well represent the Hurrian personal name ***Apalu*** (wr. *a-pa-lu*), the name of a *dimtu* at Nuzi (JEN 580:8), cf. I.J. Gelb, *NPN*, 22; cf. P.M. Purves, *NPN*, 202, s.v. *apa*, *apa-*. Both Gelb and Purves mention, however, that this Nuzi name might be a scribal error for Akkadian *A-wi-lu* (?). Anyway, since only a very small part of the left top curve of the sign is visible, it is also conceivable that ***a-pa-re***[should be read, because the signs for ***ru*** and ***re*** are very similar. In that case the Hurrian personal names ***A-pa-ri*** (wr. *A-ba-ri*) and ***Apparika*** (wr. *Ap-pa-ri-qa*), attested at Nuzi (cf. I.J. Gelb, *NPN*, 22; P.M. Purves, *NPN*, 202), are a good option. Hurrian **[*e*]** is very close and interchangeable with **[*i*]**.

Th. Richter (*VHN*, 374-375) also mentions ***A-pa-ri*** (wr. *A-ba-ri*) and ***Apparika*** (wr. *Ap-pa-ri-qa*) at Nuzi and attributes them to the root ***ab-*** I and ***app-***, which he for the time being cautiously distinguishes from the root ***aw-*** II {*av-*}, probably 'retten' ['to save'], which we have already encountered in the Linear A personal names ***a-we-su*** (HT 118.3) from Hagia Triada and ***a-we-||ni-ta*** (ZA 8.2-3) from Kato Zakro. As long as an equation of ***ab-*** I / ***app-*** with ***aw-*** II {*av-*} cannot be confirmed, the meaning of ***ab-*** I / ***app-*** remains unknown. However, an equation may be feasible, if *a-w[a(?)-r]i(?)-*DIŠKUR (AL VII: AIT *411 = *UF 38*, 124: 23) contains the same form as first element that we have as 'one-word' name ***Abari*** (wr. *A-ba-ri*) at Mari and Nuzi. He adds, however, that [BA] = {VA} is very rare at Mari. As a result only after confirmation of an equation of ***ab-*** I / ***app-*** with ***aw-*** II {*av-*} we are permitted to analyse Linear A ***a-pa-re***[as {*ap/w=ar=e/i*} and to translate 'Save (the child) (oh *numen*), again and again !'. The name probably contains the *factitive* or *iterative* root-extension ***-ar-*** (cf. I. Wegner, *Einführung*, 88).

Th. Richter (*VHN*, 376) mentions, s.v. ***Abari*** (GNf), that the personal name ***Apari*** (wr. *A-ba-ri*) from Mari may not only represent the 'one-word' name {*ab=ar=i*} but also the name of a goddess ^{D}*a-ba/pa-(a-)r*^{o}, who appears in the entourage of *Ištar/Ša(w)uška* of Šamuḫa taking the second place in the hierarchy after *Ša(w)uška*, cf. Th. Richter, *BGH*, 35.

L.C. Meijer, *Eine strukturelle Analyse der Hagia Triada-Tafeln*, 134, reads Linear A [ ]***di-za-ke*** (HT la.2-3), although he erroneously mentions [ ] *L51-34-24* instead of [ ] *L51-23-24* on page 7 of his book, but this is probably a printer's error, since he reads ***di-za-ke*** on page 134. However, this reading may well be a hoax, since L. Godart - J.-P. Olivier, *GORILA Vol. 1*, read *di-di-za-ke*, whereas J. Raison - M. Pope, *BCILL 18*, 33, and *BCILL 74*, 44 seem to waver between these readings. If **[ ]*di-za-ke*** is not a hoax, this sequence, which is probably a personal name, was formerly compared with the Thracian name *Dizzaca* in inscriptions from Worms (*CIL XIII, 6231*: *Aur. Dizzaca leg. II Part.*) and from Troesmis (*CIL III, 6189*: *Iulius Dizzace* (gen.)), but because of the doubtful reading, that identification has become unlikely. A Thracian or Proto-Thracian provenance has become very doubtful anyway, because it would be extremely exceptional in the Linear A *corpus* of personal names that is almost exclusively Hurrian. If *GORILA*'s reading ***di-di-za-ke*** (HT la.2-3) is correct (and I think it is), ***di-di-*** may be compared with names from Cappadocia such as ***Tí-tí-a*** (CCT V 25 c 4; Garelli N° 63, 8; E. Laroche, *NH*, 186. n° 1342) and ***Tí-tí-na-ri*** (EL 1, 2; 284, 3; E. Laroche, *NH*, 186. n° 1343). This name is also mentioned by P.M. Purves, *NPN*, 268, s.v. ***titi***: "Hurrian. Cf. perhaps *ti-i-ti*, Tuš. iii 121, and *ti-i-ti-pa*⌈*a*⌉, VBoT 59 ii 8. Perhaps in personal name ***Titinari/atal*** from Anatolia, wr. *Tí-tí-na*-RI, TCL IV 67:2, cited as Hurrian by Götze, *Kleinasien*, 69, n. 4; Gelb, IAV, 14; and Ungnad, Subartu, 151. The personal name ***Tette*** adduced by Gustavs in *AOF XI*, 149, is probably not involved." The new reading by *GORILA* seems preferable and consequently a Hurrian interpretation of ***di-di-za-ke*** seems more likely than a 'Thracian' or 'Proto-Thracian' of ***di-za-ke***. Single writing of the cuneiform intervocalic dental in *ti-i-ti-* proves that it is voiced.

The Hurrian personal name ***di-di-za-ke*** (HT la.2-3) may be compared with ***de-di*** (HT 94[+ HT 154 I + Fr.]b.1), ***di-de-ru*** (HT 86a.3; HT 95+149a.4; HT 95+149b.4) and ***di-de-***[(HT 86b.3), and possibly also with Linear A ***ti-ti-ku*** (HT 35.1; ZA Zb 3.2) and ***ti-ti-ku-ni*** (HT 96a.1). In the discussion on these names I have quoted Th. Richter (*VHN*, 541, s.v. ***ted- / tid-***) who remarks that to date two roots ***tid-*** are lexically confirmed: 'to share, count' (cf. *BGH*, 464: ***tid-*** I [Boğ.]) and 'to attack' (cf. *BGH*, 464-465: ***tid-*** II [Boğ; Mitt.] / ***titt-*** [Boğ.]). He tells that it is not certain which of the two is used in personal names.

On the basis of the voiceless dental stops in Linear A ***ti-ti-ku*** (HT 35.1; ZA Zb 3.2) and ***ti-ti-ku-ni*** (HT 96a.1) I assume that these names contain the root ***tid-*** II / ***titt-*** and can provisionally be translated as 'Attacker'. Although the Hurrian names ***Titiku*** and ***Titikun*** at Alalaḫ contain a voiced intervocalic dental, I interpret these names in the same way as Linear A ***ti-ti-ku*** and ***ti-ti-ku-ni*** because of the obvious resemblance between these names.

With regard to the root ***ted- / tid-*** I. Wegner (*ibid.*, 210-212) analyses ***ti-i-ti-wa***$_{a}$***-a-te*** in the Hurrian-Hittite bilingual ***kirenze*** (KBo 32: 13 Vs I 18) as {*tid=i=bade*} and compares it with the Hittite parallel ***kapuwauwar*** 'das Zählen, das Gezählte' ['count(ing)']; ***tid=i=bade*** consists of the verbal root ***tid-*** 'to count' and the suffix ***-i-bade*** that forms *abstracta*. Compare for ***kapuwauwar*** e.g. Th. van den Hout, *The elements of Hittite*, Cambridge 2013[3], 192: ***kappuwa(e)-*** 'to count, take care of', ***kappuwauwar***, neuter 'count(ing)'. I. Wegner also attributes the first element in the personal name ***Tí-tí-na-tal*** {*Titin-atal*} on a tablet from Kültepe (KT 90/k, 223 9) to this verbal root. In my view the Urartian root ***did-*** 'to share?' must certainly be compared with this Hurrian verbal root (cf. M. Salvini - I. Wegner, *Einführung in die urartäische Sprache*, Wiesbaden 2014, 108).

Prima facie Linear A ***-za-ke*** in ***di-di-za-ke*** can be compared with the onomastic element ***šagi / šekki*** {*šagi / šekki*}, mentioned by Th. Richter (*BGH*, 343-344; *VHN*, 495-496). He mentions that a transitive verbal root ***šag-*** was first interpreted as 'reinigen, verzieren' ['to clean, purify, adorn, embellish'], but was later regarded as equivalent to ***šagr-*** 'schützen' ['to protect'] by I. Wegner (Zum Namen des *Udibšarri*, *AoF 30 (2003)*, 342[8]), that she analysed as {*šag=r-*} = root ***šag-*** + root-extension ***°=r***.

However, if ***di-di-*** {*d/tid-*} in ***di-di-za-ke*** (HT la.2-3) is to be interpreted as verbal, ***-za-ke*** must be nominal, since a Hurrian personal name cannot contain two verbal roots.

Th. Richter (*VHN*, *ibidem*) thinks that in personal names the form ***šagi*** {*šag=i*} is nominal. He probably refers to the usage of ***-šagi*** as second onomastic element. He also tells that ***šagi*** is almost without exception written with [KI]. Only ***ᶠŠakija*** and ***Šakijān*** show [GI]. Whereas the orthography of ***°za-ki*** in ***ᶠAšmun-šaki*** M2 can plausibly be explained (see *VHN*, section D/0.1.2 sub B2), the alternation of ***°-šagi / °-za-ki*** with ***°-ta-***[***ki*** (?) *ibidem* as well as of ***°-ta-ki / °-te-ki*** and ***°-šagi*** in ***ᶠAštar-taki*** M1 can only be explained by confusion of ***šagi*** with ***tagi*** 'beautiful, pure, beaming' (***tag-/takk-***).

E. Laroche (*GLH*, 249-250), s.v. ***tagi*** 'beau'. "Lecture du sum. ZALAG; épithète de l'argent. RS voc. II 24 = Ḫḫ II 134 ; sum. ki.lam.zalag.ga = h. MIN ***te-gi-še*** 'beau prix'; cf. Friedrich, HW 325 : 'schön'. - *inu-me ušḫuni šiḫala ḫišma tagi-ma kiraši-ma* 'comme l'argent (est) pur, brillant, et beau, et long (durable)', KUB XXIX 8 IV 27." He also mentions (*GLH*, 250): "***tagi*** 'attribut de Ḫebat', *da-(a)-ki, da-a-ki-it-ti*, KUB XXV 44 II 19; KBo XX 113 IV 16; KUB XXXII 59 II 3; etc."

If ***ti-i-ti-wa$_a$-a-te*** {*tid=i=bade*} in the Hurrian-Hittite bilingual ***kirenze*** (KBo 32: 13 Vs I 18) can be compared with the Hittite parallel ***kapuwauwar*** 'count(ing)' and if the root ***tid-*** I / ***ted-*** can be compared with Hittite ***kappuwa(e)-*** 'to count, take care of' (cf. Th. van den Hout, *The elements of Hittite*, Cambridge 2013[3], 192), we can interpret ***di-di-za-ke*** (HT la.2-3) as 'Take care of the beauty / the beautiful child !'.

However, since *da-(a)-ki* is 'attribute of Ḫebat' according to E. Laroche and probably an epithet of this goddess, ***°za-ki/e = °d/ta-ki/e*** 'the beautiful, beauty' in Linear A ***di-di-za-ke*** may well refer to *Ḫebat* herself, so that ***°za-ki/e = °d/ta-ki/e*** can be regarded as a (*quasi*) theophorous element. The meaning of ***di-di-za-ke*** may then be 'Take care of (the child), oh beautiful (goddess) !'. If ***°za-ki/e = °d/ta-ki/e*** is interpreted as a *vocative*, the other root ***tid-*** II / ***titt-*** 'to attack' may be involved as well. The meaning of ***di-di-za-ke*** may then be 'Attack, oh beautiful (goddess) !'. Compare also my interpretation of Linear A ***a-di-da-ki-ti ₁ pa-ku*** (KN Zc 6.2), see *chapter 11: 'Religious' Linear A inscriptions.*

Th. Richter (*VHN*, 496) mentions the following examples: (a) {*šaki*}: ***ᶠAšmun-šaki*** (Mari), [variants *ᶠAšmu-šaki, ᶠAšmen-šaki, ᶠAšmut-ta*[*ki* (?)]], ***ᶠAtal-šaki*** (Ašnakkum), ***ᶠElan-šaki*** (Mari), ***ᶠElen-šaki*** (Mari), ᶠIŠTAR-***šaki*** (Mari), ***ᶠḪazip-šaki*** (Mari), ***ᶠKun-šaki*** (Šušarrā), ***ᶠKupe-šaki*** (Tigunāni), ***ᶠMemen-šaki*** (Mari), ***ᶠPirḫen-šaki*** (M), ***ᶠŠakija*** (M) and ***Šakijān*** (M), ***ᶠŠewen-šaki*** (M), ***ᶠŠewlu(?)-šaki*** (M), variant *iš$_8$-tár-ša-ki* with ***ᶠAštar-taki*** M1; (b) {*šekki*}: ***ᶠKun-šekki*** (?) (Tigunāni). According to Th. Richter (*VHN*, 496[652]) we are here certainly not dealing with Akkadian ***šaqî*** 'arrose'. I may perhaps add the Hurrian name ***Zizzakke*** (wr. *Zi-iz-za-ag-ge*) from Nuzi (cf. P.M. Purves, *NPN*, 278) as a parallel to Linear A ***di-di-za-ke*** or [ ]***di-za-ke***.

The personal name ***a-ki-ro*** (AK 4b.4) can morphologically be compared with Linear A ***a-ka-ru*** (HT 2.1; HT 86a.1; HT 86b.1) from Hagia Triada. Only the root-extensions are different. Both names may be Old Hurrian *imperatives* in ***-o/u***, built on the verbal root ***ag- / akk-***, which is frequent in personal names (cf. Th. Richter, *VHN*, 366-368), (transitive) 'to bring (up), lead', (remarkably with the same meaning as the Indo-European root ***ag-***), (intransitive) 'to appear'. The meaning of the transitive Hurrian root ***ak-***, */ag-/*, 'guide', 'direct' was first established on account of comparison with Urartian ***agu*** 'guide', 'direct', cf. E.A. Speiser, *JAOS LIX (1939)*, 298 and n. 36. The 'one-word' name ***a-ka-ru*** (HT 2.1; HT 86a.1; HT 86b.1) may represent an Old Hurrian *imperative* in ***-u*** and be analysed as *{ag=al=u}* or *{ag=ar=u}*, with the root-extension ***-al-*** of unknown meaning (cf. I. Wegner, *Einführung*, 87) or with the *factitive* or *iterative* root-extension ***-ar-*** (cf. I. Wegner, *Einführung*, 88) and be translated 'Bring (the child) (up) (oh *numen*) !'. Analysis as an Old Hurrian perfect form 3rd pers. sing. *{ag=al=o/u=m}* or *{ag=ar=o/u=m}* is also possible, 'He/She (a *numen*) brought (the child) (up)'.

The 'one-word' name ***a-ki-ro*** (AK 4b.4) may be analysed as the Old Hurrian *imperative* in ***-o/u*** *{ag=ill=o/u}* with Old Hurrian *inchoative* or *ingressive* root-extension ****-ill-*** indicating the beginning of action (cf. I. Wegner, *Einführung*, 89) and be translated 'Begin to bring (the child) (up) (oh *numen*) !'. This Old Hurrian root-extension (marked with *) occurs in the Hurrian-Hittite bilingual ***Kirenze*** (KBo 32): *šid=ar=ill=o=m* 'er begann zu verfluchen' ['he began to curse']; *am=ar=ill=o=m* 'er begann Böses zuzufügen' ['he began to inflict evil'] (cf. E. Neu, *Orientalia 59 (1990)*, 223-233; E. Neu, *StBoT* 32, 1996, 104.

Since Linear A (and B) sign ***ro*** can be ***ro*** or ***lo***, Linear A ***a-ki-ro*** (AK 4b.4) may also be analysed as *{ag=ir=o/u}*, with the root-extension ***-ir-*** (cf. I. Wegner, *Einführung*, 89). The meaning of this root-extension is not clear. She offers the example *maz=ir=i* from *maz-* 'helfen' ['to help'] and adds that it is not easy to distinguish this very rare root-extension from the participial formant ***=i=ri***. In case of ***a-ki-ro*** I consider a participial form unlikely, because for the form *{ag=i=ri)* with Akkadianized nominative in ***-u*** *{ag=i=r(i)=u)* I should have expected Linear A ****a-ki-ru*** instead of attested ***a-ki-ro***.

It is important to observe the orthographic conventions of Linear A and B with regard to ***a-si-ki-ra*** , HORD+E [ ] B | (KH 20+48.2) from Khania. The ***-i-*** of ***a-si-*** cannot be mute. So it is impossible to read † ***aškira***, for the sibilant ***š*** preceding an occlusive would not have been expressed in a consonant cluster. Consequently, if we are dealing with two onomastic elements ***a-si-*** and ***-ki-ra***, we must conclude that the ***-i-*** of ***a-si-*** belongs to the stem. The sequence ***a-si-ki-ra*** is probably a personal name. The only other sequence on this tablet [.]***du-re-za*** , HORD+E J FIC E, may well be completed to [***a-***]***du-re-za***, because ***a-du-re-za*** (KH 11.1) is already attested as a personal name at Khania as well as the assimilated form of that name]***a-se-re-za***|[(KH 13.2). Linear A ***a-si-ki-ra*** may well contain the assimilated onomastic element ***azzi-*** (< ***ašti*** = */ašdi/* or */aždi/*) 'woman' or ***arši/e/ə*** 'young lad, boy' and the adjective ***kira / kera*** 'long', probably in the sense of 'tall', when said of a 'woman/girl' (***az(z)i***) or 'boy' (***arši/ə***), although the adjective is usually interpreted as 'long-lasting, durable', especially if it is applied to a metal such as silver. It provides a perfectly acceptable personal name, particularly since it probably appealed to an aesthetic ideal, also for girls as is known, for instance, from Greek antiquity.

E. Laroche, *GLH*, 143, s.v. ***keri*** 'long': 1. RS voc. IV 28: sum. gíd.da = h. ***ki-ra-i*** 'long'. Épithète de l'argent: *taki-ma ke-ra-(a)-ši-ma*, KUB XXIX 8 IV 28 = KBo XXI 24, 3; cf. KUB XXVII 24 I 7; KBo XX 131 II 23. Etc. – 2. Thème ***kiri / keri-***, *ke-e-ri,* KUB XXVII 34 I 12. Instr. adv. *ki-ra-a-e,* KUB XXIX 8 III 5, 14 = KBo XX 142, 9; cf. RS l.c. – 3. Thème ***kiraši*** 'allongé'. Erg. *ke-e-ra-šu-uš,* KBo XX 126 + III 53. Onom. ***Keraše***, ***^{f}Meni-geraše***, *NPN*, 225. Th. Richter (*BGH*, 211-212; *VHN*, 440) describes the root ***kir- / ker-*** discussed by Purves and Laroche as ***ke/ir-*** II [Boğ.; PN] 'andauernd' ['lasting'] and 'dauerhaft, lang (sein)' ['(to be) long-lasting']. The emphasis seems to be on 'long-lasting' in time, but this does not exclude the possibility that the notion 'long' can be used in time and space. If the root is used in personal names, it is in my view more likely that namegivers paid attention to the actual appearance of a child (especially if it was taller than usual) than to a long lasting life, however desirable. If ***ke/ir-*** II only means '(long) lasting', Linear A ***a-si-ki-ra*** (KH 20.1) {*az(z)=i-kir=a*} means 'The woman has a long life' or 'Live long, woman !' or {*arš=i-kir=a*}, 'The young lad has a long life' or 'Live long, boy !'.

In that case ***-kir=a=Ø*** is the third person singular of *intransitive* ***kir-***, with the marker of intransitivity ***-a***. If we translate 'The woman (girl) is like a tall girl' or 'The young lad is like a tall boy', final ***-a*** may be due to the *essive* case. This appears to be in accordance with Th. Richter's remark (*VHN*, 440) that ***ker-*** II can mean '(intr.) lang sein, (trans.) lang machen' ['(intr.) to be long, (trans.) to make long']. He also mentions that KI-***ra-ẓi*** reminds of *(°-)ge-ra-še* at Nuzi. Then {*ker-*} is preferable and we are probably dealing with the well-known word ***keraš(š)e*** 'lang, dauerhaft' ['long-lasting'] in names. This also applies to *ke-ri-(iz-)zi/zu* {*ker=i=šše*} 'Länge' ['length, duration']: (1) {*kerašše*}:*^{f}Kerazze* (Mari). - (2) {*kerišše*}: *Kerizze* (Mari); *Kerizzu* (Mari).

However, since publication of the Hurrian-Hittite bilingual ***Kirenze*** (KBo 32) another important root ***ke/ir-*** I [Boğ.; PN(?)] 'to release, liberate, set free, manumit (especially with respect to slaves)', corresponding with Hittite ***para tarna-***, has been confirmed, cf. Th. Richter, *BGH*, 210-211; *VHN*, 440.

If the second element of Linear A ***a-si-ki-ra*** (KH 20.1) contains the root ***ke/ir-*** I [Boğ.; PN(?)] (*BGH*, 210-211) = ***kir-/kirr-*** I (*VHN*, 440), ***a-si-ki-ra*** can be analysed as either {*az(z)=i-kir(r)=a=Ø*} 'The woman (girl) is released, liberated, set free, manumitted' or {*arš=i-kir(r)=a=Ø*} 'The young lad / boy is released, liberated, set free, manumitted'. Alternatively, if the name consists of two nominal elements, ***a-si-ki-ra*** can be analysed as either {*az(z)=i-kir(r)=a*} and translated as 'The woman (girl) is (like a) freed woman' or {*arš=i-kir(r)=a*} 'The young lad / boy is (like a) freedman'. If the act of manumission in fact refers to the parents instead of the child, the result might be that the girl or boy is free-born by law, which is a memorable fact indeed.

It is not easy to choose which of the roots is the most likely for Linear A ***a-si-ki-ra***, since both seem to play an important part in Hurrian names. According to Th. Richter (*VHN*, 440) the following personal names can be attributed to ***kir-/kirr-*** I: (a) {***kir-***} *Kirija* (ŠE); *Kirip-Aranziḫ* (M, T), *Kirip-atal* (M), *^{f}Kirip-elli* (AŠ), *Kirip-ewri* (M), *Kirip-Kalli* (T), *Kirip-šarri* (M), *Kirip-šenni* (M), *Kirip-Šerriš* (M, ŠE), *Kirip-Teššub* (M), *Kirip-ulme* (AŠ, M), *Kir-tuk* (T). - (b) {***kirr-***} *Kirri* (AŠ, M), *Kirru* (M), possibly also *Kirpaia* (M).

I. Wegner (*Einführung*, 138) mentions in her section E '*Old Hurrian*' sub '*The jussive and other forms of mood in the bilingual*' the form ***kir=o*** (wr. *ki-i-ru*), KBo 32: 15 IV 3, which she translates as 'er soll freigelassen sein/werden' ['he must be set free / released / liberated / manumitted']. However, in accordance with the usage at Nuzi (and probably also in the bureaucratic setting of the Minoan palace administration expressed through the Linear A tablets) Hurrian ***kir=o***, exact equivalent to Linear A ***ki-ro***, probably also means 'it (the debt) must be redeemed', 'he must redeem/pay back his debt'.

There is even a root ***ker-*** III (intr.) '(to be) eight', (trans.) 'to make it happen that eight (children) will be present', so that {*az(z)=i-kir=a*} means 'The woman is the eighth child' and {*arš=i-kir=a*} 'The young lad is the eighth child'.

However, all other verbally used numerals are very rare in personal names and it probably does not often happen either that eight children are born in one family, but it is not impossible, and if it happens, it might be such a memorable event that it is worth remembering. Anyway ***ke/ir-*** I and ***ke/ir-*** II seem the better candidates.

Linear A ***a-si-su-po-a*** (KH 9.1) from Khania is followed by VIR or MULIER [+] [and (in line 2) by other ideograms and fraction signs. In the first edition of *Minoan Linear A*, (Vol. II: *Corpus of transliterated Linear A texts*, Part II, 2016) I read the ideogram VIR+[, following J. Raison - M. Pope, *Corpus transnuméré du linéaire A*, Louvain-la Neuve 1994, 165, who read ideogram ***657***[= ***99***+[= VIR+[. It may depend on the interpretation of the first element of ***a-si-su-po-a***, whether we should read VIR or MULIER [+] [.

Since ***-r-*** preceding a sibilant is not expressed in Linear A consonant clusters, we may interpret Linear A ***a-si-*** as ***arši/e*** 'young lad, boy'. According to Th. Richter (*BGH*, 48) ****arš-*** is a reconstructed Hurro-Urartian root on the basis of Urartian ***aršə*** 'adolescents, young boys'. W.G.E. Watson (Ugaritic onomastics (1), *Aula Orientalis 8*, 1990, 115) presumes in the alphabetic cuneiform ***åršm*** 'young boy(?)'. If Linear A ***a-si-*** is ***arši-***, the ideogram is probably VIR, but if ***a-si-*** represents ***azzi-*** 'woman', it is probably MULIER.

Linear A ***a-si-su-po-a*** (KH 9.1) from Khania seems morphologically similar to the sequence ***a-su-pu-wa*** (AK 2.5) from Arkhanes, occurring in a list of personal names. One of these names, ***a-si-da-to|-i̯*** (AK 2.2-3), has ***a-si-*** as first onomastic element as well.

Both ***a-si-su-po-a*** and ***a-su-pu-wa*** seem to contain the Hurrian singular dative suffix ***-wa*** 'for'. The distinction between ***-uwa*** and ***-oa*** is probably only orthographic. This way of writing ***a-si-da-to|-i̯*** (AK 2.2-3) and ***a-si-su-po-a*** (KH 9.1) in Linear A reminds us of cuneiform usage, where the genitive ***-wi/-we*** is often written as ***-ú-e*** and the dative ***-wa*** as ***-ú-a***, especially after ***-o/u-***: e.g. the genitive KUR *Lu-lu-ú-e*, Nuzi; cf. Lacheman, *BASOR 78*, 22 f; Speiser, *IH*, 51 ff., 89, etc.; cf. E. Laroche, *GLH*, 161, s.v. *Lullu*, pays au Nord-Est de la Mésopotamie. Cf. also *attai-fe* 'my father' and the genitive: *at-ta-iw-wu-ú-e*, Mit. III 35, 37, 71; and the dative: *at-ta-iw-wu-ú-a*, Mit. III 68. So ***a-si-su-po-a*** {*Azz=i-šub=(e/i)o/u(w)a*} would be 'for {**Azz=i-šub=e/i*}' (< **Ažd=i-sub=e/i*).

The onomastic element ***šup*** was already considered Hurrian by P.M. Purves, *NPN*, 259, s.v. ***šup***. He mentions: *šu-u-pu-ga-*.[…], at Boğazköy KUB VII 58 III 16, and at Nuzi the personal names ***Šupui̯a*** (wr. *Šu-pu-ia*), ***Šupuka*** (see also Gelb's list), ***Šupukii̯a*** (wr. *Šu-pu-ki-ia*), possibly variant of ***Šupuka***, since a man of each name is father of *Ar-tei̯a*, ***Šupukka*** (wr. *Šu-pu-uq-qa*, *Šu-pu-qa*, or two different names).

Th. Richter (*BGH*, 415-417, 421) mentions several roots and themes s.v. ***šub-*** I [Boğ.; Mitt.(?)], without translation; (possibly) ***šuw-*** II [Boğ.] 'tagen, Tag werden' ['to dawn']; ***šuwi*** or ***šuwa*** [Boğ.] 'Tag' ['daylight, dawn']; ***zub-*** III, *zub=umma epēšu* [Nuzi] 'zurückgeben, erstatten' ['to give back, return, restitute']; ***šubi*** I, also *šuppi I* [Boğ.], without translation; ***šu-bé-e*** II [loan-word into Hurrian] probably derived from Sumerian (NA_4.)ŠUBA via Akkadian *šubûm*, e.g. *CAD* Š/III 185 ['a stone, perhaps agate']; ***zuwi*** III [Boğ.; Mari], without interpretation; [...]***(-)zubi*** IV [Boğ.] 'Opferterminus, unklar' ['term with regard to sacrifice, not clear']; ***zuppi*** II [Boğ.], E. Laroche, *GLH*, 308-309, s.v. ***zuppi*** (Nom. *zu-up-pí*, KUB XXVII 6 I 9 'une arme ?' ['a weapon ?']); ***zubinni*** [Ug.] 'a tool', corresponds with Sumerian BA and Akkadian ***supinnu*** (W.H. van Soldt, Review of "J. Huehnergard, *Ugaritic vocabulary in syllabic transcription*, HSS 32, Atlanta 1987", in *Bibliotheca Orientalis 47*, Leiden 1990, 731); ***šubi*** VI [Boğ.; Ug.], RS quadr. 137 II 40, 42: *šu-bi* = oug. *ḫarimu* 'séparé' (E. Laroche, *GLH*, 238); *šu-ú-bi-i-ni-wa*$_a$, KUB XLVII 1 III 7', 'evil'; ***šurw-***, *šurw=ušt-* [Mitt.] 'Schlechtes tun, Böses tun' ['to do evil']; ***šurwe*** I [Mitt.; PN]. The last items are also mentioned by Th. Richter (*VHN*, 520-521) s.v. ***šub-*** {*šo/ub-*}, ***šurw-*** {*šo/urv-*}, but he doubts that e.g. ***ᶠŠupal-enna*** could mean 'Die Götter sind böse' ['The gods are evil'] (see *VHN*, 520, note 736).

Indeed some roots provide unlikely meanings in personal names, but some are quite conceivable. The absolute form {**Azz=i-šub=e/i*} of the Linear A dative ***a-si-su-po-a*** {*Azz=i-šub=(e/i)o/u(w)a*} could mean 'The woman (girl) is the daylight / dawn' (***šuwi*** or ***šuwa*** [Boğ.] 'daylight, dawn') or 'The woman (girl) is a precious stone, an agate' (***šu-bé-e*** II) or, if the newborn girl is regarded as substituting a child that passed away, the meaning could be 'Give back / Return the woman (girl), oh *numen* !' (***zub-*** III). It is evident that in all cases, where we have interpreted ***a-si-su-po-a*** with ***azzi-*** as first element, we have to change the translation 'woman' into 'young lad', if we choose ***arši*** as first element.

The sequence ***a-su-pu-wa*** (AK 2.5) from Arkhanes occurs in a list of personal names and seems morphologically similar to the personal name ***a-si-su-po-a*** VIR or MULIER+[(KH 9.1) from Khania. One of the other names on AK 2 is ***a-si-da-to|-i̱*** (AK 2.2-3) that has ***a-si-*** as first onomastic element as well.

The dative ***a-su-pu-wa*** (AK 2.5) from Arkhanes may contain the same elements as ***a-si-su-po-a*** from Khania, but with ***azz-*** < ***/ažd-/*** in ***a-su-pu-wa*** instead of ***azzi-*** < ***/aždi-/*** in ***a-si-su-po-a***, or with ***arš-*** instead of ***arši-***, possibly due to *syncope* of ***-i-*** or *haplology* or *haplography*. This interpretation is not inconceivable.

Perhaps ***a-su-pu-wa*** (AK 2.5) consists of the root ***ar-*** 'to give' + the same element ***-su-pu-wa*** as in ***a-si-su-po-a*** (KH 9.1). Then dative ***a-su-pu-wa*** (AK 2.5) means 'for *Ar-šubi*'.

Yet another interpretation is conceivable: Linear A ***a-su-pu-wa*** (AK 2.5) can be analysed as {*azzu=(i)ff=u=wa*} and may consist of Hurrian ***azzu-*** < ***/aždu-/*** 'woman/wife' + the enclitic possessive pronoun 1st person singular ***-(i)pp=u-*** + the singular dative suffix ***-wa***, translation 'for my wife / woman', cf. *aš-ti-iw-wu-ú-un-na* 'my wifes' (Mit. I 51), cf. E. Laroche, *GLH*, 62, s.v. ***ašte*** 'femme'; cf. *šen(a)=iff=u=ve ašte* (Mit. III 21) 'the wife of my Brother', I. Wegner, *Einführung*, 70; cf. *ibidem*, 62, sub 2.2.2: *The enclitic possessive pronouns*. The thematic vowel ***-u-*** occurs before genitive ***-we*** and dative ***-wa***.

I prefer to read]|***a-su-mi*** TAL to reading]|***a-su-mi-85*** (AK 1a.3-4) on tablet AK 1a from Arkhanes, because it seems better to identify Linear A sign ***85*** with the TAL(entum) ideogram than to assume that it represents a syllabic sign. Since the right side of the tablet is missing, sign]-***ne*** (first entry of AK 1a.4), which is followed by 2 units and the fraction J, can be regarded as the last syllable of a sequence that started at the end of the preceding line of the missing right side of the text. It may be the suffix ***-ne*** of the so-called singular definite article, but it can also be the *optional allomorphic* enclitic personal pronoun 3rd person singular ***-nne/i*** instead of ***-nna***. Linear A ***a-su-mi*** is probably a personal name and can be identified with the feminine Hurrian name ***ᶠAs-su-me*** from Nippur. P.M. Purves, *NPN*, 208, s.v. ***az(z)***: "Cf. *ᶠAzzu*, Gadd in *Iraq VII* 37, from Chagar Bazar. From Nippur cf. *As-su-e* and *ᶠAs-su-me*, Clay, *PNCP*, 59, also *As-sul-la*, *ibidem*, beside Nuzi *ᶠAzuli.*"

It is attractive to assume that the first onomastic element of Linear A ***a-su-mi*** is Hurrian ***azzu-*** (< ***aždu-***) 'woman' and the second an abbreviation or hypocoristic form of ***-mina*** in Linear A, either ***-mi*** or ***-min***. Both forms are possible, because final consonants are not expressed according to the orthographic conventions of Linear A and B. Compare for the Hurrian forms: ***mena***, ***menni*** (< **mena=ni*), ***men***, ***me/mi***, ***minna***, ***minni***, e.g. Th. Richter, *VHN*, 457-458. If this analysis is correct, Linear A ***a-su-mi*** can be analysed as {*azzu-mi(n)*} meaning 'The woman is a twin'. The Linear A personal names ***a-ku-mi-na*** (ZA 10a.1-2) and ***a-du-|ku-mi-na*** (ZA 10a.3-4) from Kato Zakro, which have been discussed extensively before, may well contain the same element ***-mina***.

Linear A ***a-ra-96*** occurs in the interesting combination ***a-ra-96 a-tu*** (HT 87.5) from Hagia Triada. Transliteration with the value ***ḫi*** for signs ***96*** and ***68*** offers the sequences ***a-ra-ḫi*** that can be interpreted as ***Alla(i)=ḫi*** 'pertaining to the queen', 'belonging to the mistress, queen'. Th. Richter (*BGH*, 12-14) mentions ***all-*** II 'herrschen' ['to be lord, to rule'], that can be compared with Urartian ***alae*** and ***aluse*** 'Herrscher' ['ruler'] and ***al-*** 'herrschen' ['to be lord, to rule']. Hurrian ***allai***, ***alla***, ***alli*** [*passim*] unanimously interpreted as 'Herrin' ['Lady'] or 'Königin' ['queen'], also occurs as ***alli*** in lists of personal names.

It is remarkable that ***a-ra-96 a-tu*** 1 (HT 87.5) consist of two entries followed by 1 unit, whereas all preceding sequences, *pi-ta-ka-se* 1, *ja-re-mi* 1, *di-ki-se* 1, *qe-su-pu* 1, *ku-ru-ku* 1, are personal names each followed by 1 unit. The explanation may be that ***a-ra-96 a-tu*** can be interpreted as ***alla(i)=ḫi aštu*** 'the woman belonging to the queen', which we may understand as 'the female servant belonging to the queen'. This means that in this case the lady was not mentioned with her proper name, but with her function as the queen's servant. This combination may remind us of ***da-qe-ra , qe-pi-ta*** (HT 6a.6) = ***d/taḫe=ra Ḫebitta*** (< ****Ḫebit=wa***) 'with a man (a priest ?) for *Ḫebit* / *Ḫebat*'. Although ***alla(i)=ḫi aštu*** can theoretically also be interpreted as 'the woman belonging to the goddess *Allai* / *Allani*', so that we may be dealing with 'a priestess of *Allai* / *Allani*', I prefer the more secular meaning of 'the female servant belonging to the queen' in view of comparison with the role of the queen and practices at the Hittite court.

Incidentally, interpretation of ***a-tu*** as ***aštu*** {*ašt=u*} (with a voiceless dental) next to other Linear A forms like ***a-de*** {*ažd=e*}, ***a-di*** {*ažd=i*}, ***a-di-na*** {*ažd=i=na*}, etc. (with voiced dental) can be explained from the allophonic character of Hurrian consonants. Otherwise it is possible that ***a-tu*** (HT 87.5) reflects the form ***attu***, variant of ***aštu*** and ***azzu*** elsewhere.

Linear A ***a-ra-ḫi*** (HT 97a+109a.4; HT 122b.3) = ***Alla(i)=ḫi*** may, for instance, be compared on the one hand with the (shortened) variant ***Alḫi*** at Boğazköy (cf. I. Wegner, 2004, 9; De Martino/Giorgieri, 2008, 67; M. Salvini / I. Wegner, 2004, 83) and the theonym ^{D}***Alḫé*** (Van Gessel, 1998/1, 22), on the other with the more common form ***allanuḫḫi*** 'propre à la reine' ['proper to the queen, characteristic of the queen'], *al-la-an-nu-(u)-uḫ-ḫi*, KBo XIV 132 II 6, 9; KBo XX 134 + 9; KBo XX 129 + II 5. Adj. de qualité, dérivé en ***-(u)ḫḫi*** de ***allani***; comparer ***šennuḫḫa***, cf. E. Laroche, *GLH*, 42-43, s.v. ***allai*** 'dame, reine', ***Allani*** 'la Dame'. ***Allanuḫḫi*** analysed as {*alla=nu<ni=(ḫ)ḫi(=ni=ja)*} is epithet of Ḫebat, cf. M. Cl. Trémouille, 1997, 133, 156[+522]; {*alla=n(i)=ō=ḫḫe*}, cf. M. Giorgieri, 1999a, 81[78]; 'belonging to the mistress, queen', cf. Van Gessel, 2001, 174; 'Herrinnenwürde', cf. I. Wegner, *Einführung*, 246. See Th. Richter, *BGH*, 13. The context of Linear A] ***a-ra-96*** 123 = ***a-ra-ḫi*** 123 (HT 97a+109a.4) is interesting, because it follows] ***ku-ro*** 129. We may conclude that of the total number of 129 units 123 are 'belonging to the queen'.

The context of]|***a-ra-68*** (HT 122b.3), probably also ***Alla(i)=ḫi***, is also interesting, because it is (unlike the other entries in the list) not directly followed by a numeral or number of units, but by ***u-de-za*** (HT 122b.3) that is followed by 2 units. Moreover, this form ***u-de-za*** can also be seen in the heading of the *a*-side of the same tablet where it appears in the combination]***ra-ri*** , ***u-de-za*** 2 (HT 122a.1). Due to a large *lacuna*, since the left top corner of the *a*-side (right top corner of the *b*-side) is missing,]***ra-ri*** is incomplete.

I analyse ***u-de-za*** (HT 122a.1; HT 122b.3) as {*ud=e=zz(i)=a*}, consisting of the Hurrian verbal root ***ud-*** 'to protect' (cf. Th. Richter, *BGH*, 507) + the marker of transitivity ***-e/i-*** + the nominal suffix ***-šše/-zze/i*** or adjectival suffix ***-(š)še/-(z)ze/i***, cf. I. Wegner, *Einführung*, 55, 69. She gives some examples of abstract forms in ***-(i)=šše***: ***šar=i=šše*** 'Wünsch' ['wish'] from ***šar-*** 'wünschen' ['to wish, demand'], Ugarit vocabulary RS 94-2939, col. II 5; ***nir=i=šše*** 'Güte' ['goodness'], derived from ***niri*** 'gut' ['good']; ***kib=i=šše*** 'das Sitzen (auf dem Thron)' ['being seated (on the throne)'], derived from ***keb-*** 'setzen, stellen, legen' ['to set, put, lay down'], cf. *Einführung*, 55. If this analysis is correct, the lexeme {*ud=e=zze/i*} may mean 'protection' and {*ud=e=zz(i)=a*} may be the *essive* form in ***-a***, that can be translated 'as protection'.

If]***ra-ri*** (HT 122a.1) can be completed to ***a***]***ra-ri***, this conjectural form may be interpreted as Hurrian ***alali*** 'garment, garb, robe (of state)'. Th. Richter (*BGH*, 15) mentions that since publication of the Hurrian-Hittite bilingual ***Kirenze*** (KBo 32), and in particular KBo 32.15 Vs I 12', ***alali*** 'Umhang', 'Gewand' is classified as Hurrian. In the Hittite version it corresponds with (TÚG.)***kušiši-*** ntr. He also mentions that (GADA.)***alalu-*** ntr. is considered a loan-word into Hittite, cf. (GADA.)***alalu(ša)*** 'ein Tuch, Gewand ?'.

If interpretation of ***a***]***ra-ri*** , ***u-de-za*** (HT 122a.1) as {*alali*} {*ud=e=zz(i)=a*} is correct, the meaning is 'garment/garb/robe as protection'.

Likewise]|***a-ra-ḫi u-de-za*** (HT 122b.3), that still may refer to ***a***]***ra-ri*** (HT 122a.1), can be analysed as ({*alali*}) {*alla(i)=ḫi*} {*ud=e=zz(i)=a*} '(garment) belonging to the queen as protection'. The reason, why it is justifiable to combine ***a***]***ra-ri*** , ***u-de-za*** (HT 122a.1) with]|***a-ra-ḫi u-de-za*** (HT 122b.3), is not only the repetition of ***u-de-za***, but also the fact that tablet HT 122 is one of the tablets with ***po-to-ku-ro*** (HT 122b.6), twice preceded by ***ku-ro*** (HT 122a.8) and ***ku-ro*** (HT 122b.5), which means that the *a*- and *b*-sides of the tablet comprise one continuous text.

Linear A ***a-tu*** [(THE Zb 3) on an amphora from Thera (Nat. Museum at Athens, 1364), excavated at Akrotiri in 1970 by Sp. Marinatos, is the reading by Raison-Pope (1994, 290), but the reading by *GORILA 4* (103) and Younger is ***a-ne***[[ ]]. *GORILA*: ***-ne*** en partie effacé. The problem is that on the photograph in *GORILA 4* (103) the sign in question (***tu*** or ***ne***) is not really visible. ***a-tu*** [or ***a-ne***[[ ]] is the only entry on this vessel.

I first discuss the reading ***a-tu*** [. If ***a-tu*** [is the correct reading and if it is complete, it can be the lexeme ***aštu*** 'woman' as in the combination ***a-ra-96 a-tu*** 1 = ***a-ra-ḫi a-tu*** 1 (HT 87.5) that I have interpreted as ***alla(i)=ḫi aštu*** 1 'one woman belonging to the queen'.

Since the lexeme ***aštu*** 'woman' is also commonly used as a personal name throughout the Hurrian lands, it can also be the anthroponym ***Aštu*** 'Woman'. Three interpretations are feasible because of the orthographic conventions of Linear A and B:

1. Linear A ***a-tu*** [can be identified with the Hurrian personal name ***ᶠAttu*** (wr. *ᶠAt-tu*) 'Woman' at Mari and Ašnakkum (Tall Šaġīr Bāzār / 'Chagar Bazar'), typology 3.1 (cf. Th. Richter, *VHN*, 91-92).

2. Since ***-s-*** preceding an occlusive is not expressed in consonant clusters in Linear A and B, Linear A ***a-tu*** [can be identified with the Hurrian personal name ***ᶠAštu*** (wr. *ᶠAš-tu*, *ᶠAš-tu-ú*) 'Woman' at Mari and Tuttul (Tall Bi'a), ***ᶠAštu*** (wr. *ᶠAš-du*) at Nuzi (cf. I.J. Gelb, *NPN*, 37), ***ᶠAš-du*** (wr. *ᶠAš-du-uš*, KBo X 10 III 37) at Boğazköy (cf. E. Laroche, *NH*, 46, nº 182), ***áš-tù*** at Kaniš, ***aš-tu*** at Nippur, typology 3.1 (cf. Th. Richter, *VHN*, 79).

3. Since final consonants are not expressed in Linear A an B, Linear A ***a-tu*** [can be identified with the Hurrian personal name ***ᶠAštun*** (wr. *ᶠAš-tu-un*) at Mari, analysis {*ašto/u=n(na)*} typology 3.1, 'She [*n(na)*] (scil. the girl) is a woman' (cf. Th. Richter, *VHN*, 80), cf. also the element ***ᶠAštun-*** in ***ᶠAštun-Naja*** (wr. *ᶠAš-du-un-na-a-a*) at Nuzi, {*ažd(e)/ažd(o/u)=n(na)-Naj(e)=a*[E.]}, 'She [*n(na)*] (scil. the girl) is a woman like Naje' (cf. I.J. Gelb, *NPN*, 37), comparable with ***ᶠAzza-Naje*** (wr. *ᶠAz-za-na-a-ie*) at Mari, analysis {*azz(e)/azz(o/u)=a*[E.]*-Naje*}, typology 2.1, lexicon *azze*, *Naje*, translation 'Like a woman is Naje', cf. Th. Richter, *VHN*, 75. [E.] refers to the *essive* form in ***-a***. Or we are dealing with an *a*-stem ***azza***, in which case the translation is 'The woman is Naje'.

If Linear A ***a-tu*** (HT 87.5) and ***a-tu*** [(THE Zb 3) represent ***aštu***, respectively ***ᶠAštu***, with voiceless dental, we must admit that it is an allophonic doublet of ***a-du-*** in Linear A ***a-du-sa-ra*** (Hurrian ***Ašdu-šara***, possibly phonologically ***/ažduzara/*** and with the *essive* ending in ***-a***) and of Linear A ***a-de*** (Hurrian ***ašde*** 'woman', possibly phonologically ***/ažde/***), Linear A ***a-di-ne*** (Hurrian ***ašdine*** 'the woman', possibly phonologically ***/aždine/***) and Linear A ***a-di-na*** (Hurrian plural ***ašdina*** 'the women', possibly phonologically ***/aždina/***).

In his discussion on the onomastic elements ***ašte*** and ***aštu*** {*ašto/u*} on the one hand and ***azze*** and ***azzu*** {*azzo/u*} on the other, Th. Richter (*VHN*, 381-385) also mentions occurrence of the elements ***atte*** and ***attu***, mainly in personal names. He points out that usage of the onomastic element ***atte*** correlates so extensively with that of ***azze*** and ***ašte*** that this is only conceivable, if the forms are semantically similar or even identical. Therefore he translates ***ašte***, ***azze*** and ***atte*** as 'woman' and the personal names ***ᶠAšte***, ***ᶠAzze***, ***ᶠAtte*** and ***ᶠAštu***, ***ᶠAzzu***, ***ᶠAttu*** as 'Woman'. In diminutive forms such as ***ᶠAštakki*** {*ašt(e)=a=kk=i*} 'Little woman' and in ***ᶠAzza*** + noun such as ***ᶠAzza-Naje*** (Mari) one also finds ***ašt(e)=a-*** and ***azz(e)=a-***.

For the forms *ᶠAštu*, *ᶠAzzu*, *ᶠAttu* he gives different explanations for final ***-u*** (*VHN*, 382): - 1. It might be due to an Akkadianizing nominative in ***-u***. - 2. For ***ᶠAzzu*** in particular confusion with Amorite ***ᶜazzum*** 'strong' may have played a role, especially, of course, in places like Mari, where Amorites had taken a dominant position. - 3. Since, however, the synonyms ***aštu*** {*ašto/u*} and ***attu*** show the same phenomenon, one may also accept a second form of the stem: ***azzu*** {*azzo/u*}; it varies with ***azze*** in ***ᶠAzze*** M 1. Decisive are the extended formations ***azzukki*** {*azzo/u=(a=)kk=i*} 'little woman', cf. ***ᶠAzzukki*** at Mari, ***ᶠAzzukka*** at Ašnakkum (Tall Šaġīr Bāzār / 'Chagar Bazar') and its extended form ***ᶠAzzukkanni*** {*azzo/u=(a=)kk=(i=)a=nni*} 'She is like a little woman', cf. ***ᶠAzzukkanni*** at Mari, and ***azzu-zari*** {*azzo/u=žari*}, cf. ***ᶠAzzuzari*** at Mari.

He also provides the required parallels for the Linear A personal name ***a-du-sa-ra*** (HT 62.1) = ***Ašdu-šara*** (possibly with the essive ending in ***-a***): namely ***ᶠAštuzar*** (wr. *aš-tu-za-ar*), typology 3.1, lexicon *aštuzari* (→ *ašte*), a female weaver from Ašnakkum (Tall Šaġīr Bāzār, 'Chagar Bazar') and a lady from Mari (cf. Th. Richter, *VHN*, 80), as well as ***ᶠAzzuzari*** (wr. *az-zu-*IZ*-za-ri*), typology 3.1, lexicon *azzuzari* (→ *azze*), Admattum[KI], 'wife' of Kulmiš, and female weaver from Mari (cf. Th. Richter, *VHN*, 84).

Th. Richter accepts that ***-za-ri*** in ***ᶠAštuzar*** and ***ᶠAzzuzari*** reflects an abstract or collective suffix, because he translates both names as 'Frauen(?)' ['women(?)'].

I should like to propose the translation 'Womanhood' or 'Woman *par excellence*' for the personal names ***ᶠAštuzar*** at Ašnakkum and Mari, ***ᶠAzzuzari*** at Mari, ***ᶠAš-du-a-šar*** at Nuzi and Linear A ***a-du-sa-ra*** (HT 62.1) = ***Ašdu-šara*** at Hagia Triada.

Attestation of ***ᶠAš-du-a-šar*** from Nuzi, ***ᶠAš-tu-za-ar*** from Ašnakkum and ***ᶠAzzuzari*** at Mari makes it unlikely that ***-sa-ra*** in Linear A ***a-du-sa-ra*** represents Hurrian ***šala*** 'daughter'. So one may assume that one is dealing with ***Ašdu-šar(i)=a***. ***ᶠAš-du-a-šar*** and ***ᶠAš-tu-za-ar*** could be unassimilated and abbreviated forms.

I. Wegner (*Einführung*, 57) explains ***-zari*** / ***-šari*** as a possibly abstract or collective suffix, offering the examples: ***enzari*** (< ***en(i)*** + ***šari***) 'Gottheit' ['divinity'], derived from ***eni*** 'God'; ***tipšari*** (< ***tiv(e)*** + ***šari***) 'Wort, Sache, Erzählung' ['word, thing, story'], derived from ***tive*** 'Wort'; ***furulzari*** (< ***fur*** + ***(u)l(i)*** + ***šari***) 'Opferschauer' ['interpreter of sacrifices'], derived from ***fur-*** 'to see'.

As regards ***a-sa-sa-ra-me*** it should be noted, that I have finally come to the conclusion that ***a-sa-*** in ***a-sa-sa-ra-me*** is not to be interpreted as ***azza-***, but most likely as ***arša-***, and that ***a-sa-sa-ra-me*** is ***Arša-Šarra(m)me*** meaning 'The young lad is *Šarra(m)me*', a description of *Šarru(m)ma*, the son of Tešub and Ḫebat, in a poetic sentence name based on ***arše/a*** 'young lad' (see for an extensive analysis *chapter 11: 'Religious' Linear A texts*).

It is surprising that all forms ***ᶠAšte***, ***ᶠAzze***, ***ᶠAtte***, ***ᶠAtti*** and ***ᶠAštu***, ***ᶠAzzu***, ***ᶠAttu*** are found at Mari, so in one and the same place, so that one can hardly assume that the distinction between ***ᶠAšt***, ***ᶠAzz-***, ***ᶠAtt-***, is due to dialectal differences.

If, for instance, a phonetic law is at work during a certain period, it is possible that one finds during the process older forms beside the younger ones. At the end of or after the process one sometimes finds forms that are expected on phonetic grounds next to forms restored on the analogy of another cognate form that was not subjected to the same process.

A good example is the process of *palatalization* and *assibilation* of the voiceless dental occlusives ***τ*** and ***θ*** before ***ι*** in Mycenaean Greek (except in initial syllables and in a position immediately after ***σ***). The process of ***ti*** > $t^{y}i$ > $t^{sy}i$ > $t^{s}i$ > ***si*** was probably already completed before the time of destruction of the Mycenaean palaces, when the Linear B tablets were baked and preserved by the fires, since the use of the sign ***si*** in the Mycenaean texts actually suggests that the stage $t^{s}i$ had already been passed. Thus we find e.g. the phonetically expected ethnic names ***ko-ri-si-ja*** (PY Ep 212,4; Eb 347,1; En 74, 18, 24; *alibi*, fem.) ***Κορινσίᾱ*** and ***ko-ri-si-jo*** (PY An 209,1; 207,15, masc.), derived from the toponym ***ko-ri-to*** (PY Ad 921) ***Κόρινθος*** (Corinth); ***ka-pa-si-ja*** (PY Vn 851, 12), feminine dative of ***Καρπασίᾱ*** derived from the toponym ***Κάρπαθος*** (Karpathos), next to the ethnics ***ka-pa-ti-ja*** (PY Ep 704,7; 539,9; Eb 338,1; Un 443,3, fem.) ***Καρπαθίᾱ***, with ***θ*** restored on the analogy of ***Κάρπαθος***, and ***mi-ra-ti-ja*** (PY Aa 1180; Ab 573; *alibi*), feminine of ***Μῑλάτιος*** with ***τ*** restored on the analogy of the toponym ***Μίλᾱτος*** (Miletus), cf. for more examples and an extensive discussion on the matter P.G. van Soesbergen, The coming of the Dorians, *Kadmos XX.1 (1981)*, 42-44.

There can be no doubt that the Hurrian forms ***atte*** and ***attu*** 'woman' and the personal names ***ᶠAtte*** and ***ᶠAttu*** 'Woman' must have led to confusion with ***atta(i)*** 'father' and the personal name ***Atta(i)*** 'Father'. The need for a clear distinction between the two may well explain why usage of ***ašte*** was preferred for the plain word 'woman' and the variants ***azze*** and ***atte*** were primarily used beside ***ašte*** as (elements in) personal names.

Linear A ***a-se*** (HT 81.1; HT 93a.3; HT 132.1; ZA Zb 3.1), three times attested at Hagia Triada and once in an inscription on a large pithos from the Minoan villa or farmhouse near Epano Zakros, magazine Θ, where it immediately follows Linear A ***a-sa-mu-ne*** (ZA Zb 3.1). Linear A ***a-se*** can be identified with ***azze*** 'woman' or the name ***ᶠAzze*** 'Woman'.

The alternative reading ***a-ne***[[ ]] (THE Zb 3) by *GORILA 4*, 103 and by J.G. Younger can be interpreted as an *imperative* of the verbal root ***an-*** or ***ann-*** (transitive) 'to give joy (to somebody)', 'to delight', 'to make (somebody) happy', (intransitive) 'to rejoice'. The form can be analysed as *{an(n)=e/i}* 'make (somebody) happy !', if the sequence is complete. It can also be a 'one-word' personal name with approximately the same meaning 'Make (the parents) happy (oh *numen*) !'.

According to I. Wegner (*Einführung*, 22, 247) the Hurrian name of a king ***Ann-atal*** 'Rejoice, oh strong one !' was found on one of the more than 600 sealings discovered by G. Buccellati and M. Kelly-Buccellati at Urkeš (modern Tell Mōzān), cf. also Th. Richter, *BGH*, 26-27, s.v. ***an-***, *ana-*, (trans.) '(jdn.) erfreuen', (intr.) 'sich freuen'.

The identical Linear A ligatures ***a+ti*** (HT 94a.2; HT 100.2) at Hagia Triada may be equated with e.g. Hurrian ***Atti*** (wr. *At-ti-*.[..]) at Nuzi (*JEN* 539:24) and be compared with the hypocoristic name ***Attiia*** (wr. *At-ti-ia*), son of *In-ni-qa-a-a* (HSS IX 126:2, rev.1), with double writing of the dental, so voiceless, cf. I.J. Gelb, *NPN*, 39-40.

The context of the first lines of HT 94a shows ideograms of VIR, CAPSUS (wagon-body of a chariot) and VIR HASTATUS or VIR ARMATUS and the context of the first lines of HT 100 shows ideograms of VIR PARMATUS (Man armed with a small round shield) and VIR HASTATUS or VIR ARMATUS.

Consequently the similar context of warriors and their arms on these tablets makes it likely that ***a+ti*** (HT 94a.2; HT 100.2) represents a masculine personal name and has nothing to do with ***atti*** 'woman' or the feminine personal name *ᶠ**Atti***.

P.M. Purves, *NPN*, 207, s.v. ***att*** (1) ascribed names with this root to ***attai*** 'father' and compared the masculine personal names ***Attaḭa*** (wr. *At-ta-a-a*), ***Attanu*** (wr. *At-ta-nu*), ***Attiḭa*** (wr. *At-ti-ia*) and ***Attuḭa*** (wr. *Ad-du-ia*) at Nuzi, but also the feminine personal names *ᶠAt-ta-i-ni-ir-ze* and *ᶠAt-tap-ki-ia-ze* at Chagar Bazar, *Iraq VII*, 36. In modern literature 'Chagar Bazar' is now described as Ašnakkum (Tall Šaġīr Bāzār).

According to Th. Richter (*VHN*, 386, s.v. ***att-*** {*att-*}) A. Goetze, (1963, 6) was the first to offer evidence for the 'Hurricity' of the verbal root ***att-*** (see Th. Richter, *BGH*, 66, s.v. ***att-*** [Boğ.]). He observed that personal names with ***att-*** are widely spread, but not frequent. Personal names such as *(a)-at-ta-ra/ru* are probably based on a noun ***attari*** {*att=a=ri*}. He mentions (*VHN*, 386) the following names: (1) {*att-*}: ***Attaja*** (Mari) [with variant ***Attija***]; ***Attan*** (Tigunāni); ***ᶠAttap-kijaze*** (Ašnakkum); ***ᶠAttap-Na*** (Mari); ***ᶠAttap-Naje*** (Mari, Qaṭṭarā, Šubat-Enlil); ***Attija*** (Mari, Šušarrā); ***Attijān*** (Terqa); ***[A]ttuja*** (Mari). (2) {*att=a=ri*}: ***Attara*** (Qaṭṭarā, Šubat-Enlil); ***Attaru*** (Šušarrā); (3) {*att=i=zzi*}: ***Attizzi*** (Mari).

In my view the element {*att=a=b-*} in the names ***ᶠAttap-kijaze***, ***ᶠAttap-Na***, ***ᶠAttap-Naje*** clearly shows that ***att-*** is verbal, because ***-b-*** is in Old Hurrian and in archaic or archaizing Hurrian personal names the suffix indicating the subject (3rd person sing.) of the verbal form, for instance, in Old Hurrian ***pašš=i=b*** 'he sends' that would in later Mitanni-Hurrian be ****pašš=i=a***, cf. *pa-aš-ši-a-(ma)*, Mit. IV 55 (present 3rd person sing.); and in Old Hurrian ***un=a=b*** 'he comes' that is in Mitanni-Hurrian ***un=a=Ø***, cf. I. Wegner, *Einführung*, 126.

In view of this evidence one may reasonably infer that Old Hurrian ***ᶠAttap-Na*** {*att=a=b-Na*} and ***ᶠAttap-Naje*** {*att=a=b-Naja/e*} could in Mitanni-Hurrian be ****ᶠAtta-Na*** {*att=a-Na*} and ****ᶠAtta-Naje*** {*att=a-Naja/e*}, respectively. The latter names would then probably also contain the verbal root ***att-***, of which the meaning is unfortunately not yet established. This might also have consequences for the Pre-Greek theonym ***Ἀθάνᾱ*** and its doublet form ***Ἀθηναίη*** (Attic ***Ἀθηναία***), cf. Hurrian ***-Naḭa/e*** and ***-Na***. Th. Richter (*BGH*, 66) mentions, s.v. ***att-*** [Boğ.], the meaning 'to conspire (?)', which does not seem satisfactory.

On the other hand, if ***atta-*** in ****ᶠAtta-Na*** {*att=a-Na*} and ****ᶠAtta-Naje*** {*att=a-Naja/e*} is nominal, the meaning can also be '*Naia/e* is like her father'.

At Mari ***Atta*** (wr. *at-ta, a-at-ta, ad-da, ad-da-a*) is attested as personal name of four men, typology 3.1, lexicon *atta*, translation 'Vater' ['father'], at Tigunāni as name of two men and at Qaṭṭarā (Tall ar-Rimaḥ) and Terqa (Tall 'Ašara) as name of one man, cf. Th. Richter, *VHN*, 84. See *ibid.*, 84-85, also for sentence names with the onomastic element ***atta(i)***, such as ***ᶠAttai-nirze*** 'Der Vater ist das Gute' ['The father is the good thing'], ***Attai-šarri*** 'Der Vater ist Götterkönig' ['The Father is King of Gods'], ***Attakkuzzi*** 'Einem kleinen Vater angemessen' ['In accordance with a small father'], and hypocoristic ***Attaja*** {*att=a=ja*} and ***Attija*** {*att=i=ja*}, etc.

The reading ***a-te*** (ZA 26a.1) at Kato Zakro is preferred by J. Raison - M. Pope (1994, 316), although they admit that reading ***si-te*** is possible as well; according to *GORILA 3*, 202-203, reading ***si-te*** is to be preferred.

Since the first sign is really very close to Linear B sign ****41 = si***, I have also preferred to read ***si-te*** in *Minoan Linear A*, Vol. II: *Corpus of transliterated Linear A texts*, Part II, 450-451.

Since ***-r-*** or ***-l-*** preceding an occlusive is not expressed in consonant clusters in Linear A and B, it is conceivable that ***si-te*** represents ***Šir-te*** or ***Šil-te***, consisting of the athematic verbal stem ***šir-*** or ***šil-***, probably representing an *imperative*, comparable with the frequent thematic form ***si-ru-te*** at the end of many Linear A libation formulas.

Th. Richter (*BGH*, 374) offers, s.v. ***šel-*** I [Boğ.] and ***šil-*** II, and s.v. ***šer-/šir-*** [Boğ.; Mitt.] the meaning 'angenehm sein' ['to be pleasant'] and 'gut' ['good'] and, s.v. *šel=ab-*, *šel=b-* 'in gutem Sinne (in Gute) betrachten (behandeln)' ['to treat in a good / kind way'], corresponding with Urartian ***silua*** 'wohlwollend gesinnt sein' ['to be kind, benevolent, benign, well-disposed'].

Correspondence of Hurrian ***šilu*** with Hurrian ***šilwa*** in personal names (especially in combination with ***-te*** and ***-tešub***) and with Urartian ***silua*** has convinced me that Linear A ***si-lu-te*** is probably equivalent to a Hurrian proverbial expression at the close of the prayer. The libation formula turns out to be a prayer addressing Tešub as 'Our Father' in his role of *eni attanni* 'God the Father' and closing off with 'Tešub is good, benevolent' or (transitively) 'treat (us) well / benevolently, oh Tešub !', which is semantically similar to 'be beneficent, oh Tešub !', close to *Kyrie eleison !* in prayers for God's mercy, and close to '*erbarme dich !*' in J.S. Bach's St. Matthew Passion.

If the reading ***si-te*** (ZA 26a.1) from Kato Zakro is correct, the Hurrian personal name ***Šil-te*** may be translated 'Treat (the child) well / benevolently, oh Tešub !'.

What has been said about the sequence ***a-tu*** (HT 87.5), may also be applied to ***a-te*** (ZA 26a.1), but only if the reading ***a-te*** by Raison-Pope is correct. Due to the orthographic conventions of Linear A (and B) we cannot be sure, whether Linear A ***a-te*** (ZA 26a.1), if it is the correct reading, is Hurrian ***atte*** or ***ašte*** 'woman' or the personal name ^{f}***Atte*** or ^{f}***Ašte***, since ***-s-*** preceding an occlusive is not expressed in consonant clusters in Linear A and B.

On a tablet from Khania ***a-ta-83a|-jo*** 1 or ***a-ta-83a| 66*** 1 (KH 11.5-6) is enigmatic. If sign ***66*** (IUGUM) is the correct reading, registration of IUGUM 1 means 'one yoke'.

Only the first two signs ***a-ta-*** can be identified with certainty. J. Raison - M. Pope (1994) read ***a-ta***[.] (or -[.]-) at the end of line 5 and qualify the sign following ***a-ta-*** as 'fort obscure'. L. Godart - J.-P. Olivier (*GORILA 3*) only transcribe the sign. I consider the sign similar to sign ***83a*** that also occurs as monogram ***83a*** 4 (KH 11.3) and ***83a*** 1 (KH 11.6) after ***-jo*** 1 or IUGUM 1. As long as the phonetic value of sign ***83a*** remains obscure, one can only speculate about the meaning of ***a-ta-83a|-jo*** 1 or ***a-ta-83a| 66*** (= IUGUM) 1.

An inscription on a serpentine ladle from the Peak Sanctuary of Hagios Georgios on Kythera (Piraeus Museum 6588) offers ***da-ma-te*** (KY Za 2). Because of the sacred object and site where it was found, the meaning of {*d/talm=a-te*} 'Teš(š)ub is great' is excellent.

According to J.G. Younger (*Linear A texts in phonetic transcription, other texts (not Hagia Triada)* the word curves around the upper point of a ladle, but reads from the point of view of the person holding the ladle in cupped hands. Sign ***da*** occurs to the left of the ladle's point, ***ma-te*** at the point itself.

There is no reason to assume that the inscription is incomplete and should be completed to ***[i]-da-ma-te***, for which I refer to the discussion on ***i-da-ma-te*** (AR Zf 1; AR Zf 2).

Although formations like ****talma-te*** are frequently used to form personal names, I consider it likely that the inscription on the ladle is not a personal name, but means exactly what it says, 'Teš(š)ub is great', and can morphologically be compared with ***si-ru-te***: 'Teš(š)ub is benevolent' or 'Be benevolent, oh Teš(š)ub !' on many libation tables.

Nevertheless it can be helpful to compare the religious Linear A inscription ***da-ma-te*** (KY Za 2) with so-called sentence names, which comprise a large part of our material. ****Talma-Te***, phonologically ***/Dalma-te/***, analysis *{d/talm=a-te}*, 'Teš(š)ub is great', with verbal root ***d/talm-*** + marker of intransitivity ***-a-*** and theophorous onomastic element ***-te*** as hypocoristic of ***-tešup***. Since Hurrian ***talmi*** can be the adjective 'great, powerful', but can also be the transitive verbal root ***talm-*** + marker of transitivity ***-i***, the personal name ***Talmi-Tešub*** can mean 'Teš(š)ub is great', but also 'Make (the child) great, oh Teš(š)ub !'.

Talmi-Tešub (wr. *talmi/tal-mi-Tešub*^{ub}) occurs at Ugarit (cf. F. Gröndahl, *PNTU*, 260) and Boğazköy (cf. E. Laroche, *NH*, 172, N° 1230.1-2. ***Talmi-Tešub***, King of Kargamis, son of *Ini-Tešub*; N° 1230.3. ***Talmi-Tešub***, *Qardabbu* of the Hittite king. Other notable person: ***Talmi-Šarruma*** (*NH* n° 1229), king of Aleppo, grandson of *Suppiluliuma I.*

E. Laroche, *GLH*, 253, s.v. *talmi* 'grand': "Thureau-Dangin, *Syria XII*, 246; J. Lewy, *Rev. Et. Sém. 1938*, 62; von Brandenstein, *ZA 46*, 106, n. 2; Laroche, *Ugar. III*, 128. Lecture du sum. GAL dans le nom de *Talmi-Tešub*, écrit GAL-^{d}U-*ub*, *NH* n° 1230. [...] 1. Thème *talmi* et *talami.* [..] - *ta-al-ma*, KUB XXXII 19+ II 38; XXXII 22 Ro 4. 2. Onomastique. *Talmi-, Talmu-, Talma-*, premiers termes de composés théophores; alph. *tlmyn* = *Talmiyana*; *-talma*, second terme de composés: cf. *NPN*, 262; *AT* p. 149 et passim; *PNTU* 259 sq.; *NH* n°s 1228 sqq."

In Linear B the liquids ***ρ*** and ***λ*** preceding ***μ***, ***ν*** and ***ϝ*** were usually omitted: e.g. ***pe-ma*** = ***σπέρμα***; ***ko-wa*** = ***κόρϝᾱ***. Since the Linear B orthographic conventions were probably inherited from Linear A, all evidence shows that ***l*** was not expressed before ***m*** in Linear A either. For the existence of initial voicing of dentals in the Hurrian vernacular of Minoan Crete I may refer to Linear A ***da-ku-na*** (HT 103.4), ***da-ku-se-ne*** (HT 103.2; HT 103.4-5), ***da-ku-|se-ne-ti*** (HT 104.1-2) and ***da-<u>ku</u>*** (SE Zf 1). Compare also e.g. the sequence *Da-al-mu* at Nuzi, I.J. Gelb, *NPN*, 146.

According to Th. Richter (*VHN*, 527-528) several proposals for use of a verbal root ***talm-/talb-*** were at last recommended (see also *BGH*, 432-435, s.v. ***talm-***, ***talb-***, ***tal-*** II, ***tel-*** I). The meaning of *transitive* forms in personal names seems to be 'to make great, powerful' and that of the *intransitive* forms 'to be/become great, powerful'. Accordingly the simple form ***talme/i*** means 'great' or 'the great'. Th. Richter prefers the view that all personal names with ***talm°/talp°*** as first onomastic element may be considered verbal sentence names (Verbalsatznamen). A parallel for the fact that no indicatives occur in these formations can be found in ***teḫ-*** 'to grow, to bring up, to nurse somebody' (cf. *BGH*, 457-458, s.v. ***teḫ-*** I, 'wachsen, gedeihen lassen, großziehen, etc.'). This can be explained from the desire to express best wishes for the future of the child.

Anyway, most forms with ***talma*** are found as second element of Hurrian personal names: at Nuzi ^{f}***Allai-talma*** (wr. ^{f}*Al-la-i-tal-ma*) 'The Lady is great, powerful' and ***Erwi-talma*** (wr. *Er-wi-tal-ma, Er-wi-ta-al-ma*) 'The Lord is great, powerful'.

P.M. Purves (*NPN*, 262) compared ***Erwi-talma*** (with metathesis of ***-wr-*** > ***-rw-***) at Nuzi to ***Ewri-talma*** (wr. *ew-ri-ta-al-ma*) at Ebla and Mari. Th. Richter (*VHN*, 111) analyses ***Ewri-talma*** as {*evri-talm(i)=a*[E.]}, typology 2.1, lexicon *ewri, talmi* (→ *talm-*) and translates 'Der Herr ist groß' ['The Lord is great']. His marking with [E.] shows that he regards the element ***-talma*** as a nominal form ***-talmi*** in the *essive* case. This may be right, but although it is true that the majority of verbal forms in Hurrian sentence names occur as first element, inversion of the order of onomastic elements is quite normal in many languages, Hurrian and Greek included. Consequently, the possibility that ***-talma*** as second onomastic element represents the intransitive form {*talm=a*} of the verbal root ***talm-***, should not be ruled out. Moreover, A. Draffkorn (*HHA*, 107) mentions s.v. ***talmi*** 'great' and ***talma-***, ***-talma***, ***-dalma***: ***Talma-mu*** (or ***Talm-ammu*** ?), ***Muš-talma***, and ***Wəri-dalma***.

Cf. also A. Draffkorn, *HHA*, 55, s.v. ***Talm-Ammu*** (1) (wr. **Tal-ma-am-mu*) *203:6. (2) (wr. **Tal/Ta-al-ma-am-mu*) *18:16; *27:10; *35:2; *36:3; *37:2; *38:15; *44:3; *53:5; *59:4; *61:21; *97:4; 119:15. (D.J. Wiseman (*AT*) and A. Draffkorn (*HHA*) marked the finds in layer VII with * and those in layer IV without *.) In my discussion on the onomastic elements ***muš-***, ***muša-***, ***-muša***, ***-muše***, ***-mušni*** I have mentioned P.M. Purves's hypothesis (*NPN*, 235, s.v. ***-mu***) that the Hurrian onomastic element ***-mu*** might be a shortened form of elements formed on ***muš***. Occurrence of ***Muš-talma*** beside an inversed ***Talma-mu*** at Alalaḫ seems to corroborate this view.

On the other hand interpretation as ***Talm-Ammu*** is interesting for several reasons. Th. Richter (*VHN*, 293) analyses a personal name ***Ta<l>m(i)-Ammi*** (wr. *ta-<al->ma-am-mi*) from Ebla (Tall Mardiḫ) as {**talm=i-^{c}amm=i*}, lexicon *talm-*, *^{c}ammu*, typology 1.3.1.2.1, and translates the name as 'Mache (Jungen) groß, oh Vatersbruder !' ['Make (the boy) great, oh brother of the father !']. The conjecture ***<l>*** and analysis are based on the attestations at Alalaḫ VII and IV, cf. A. Draffkorn, *HHA*, 55.

According to Th. Richter (*VHN*, 372-373, and note 145) the Amorite lexeme ***^{c}ammu*** 'Vatersbruder' ['brother of the father'] is well-known. He explains its usage in hybrid Hurrian-Semitic names from the fact that there was no proper Hurrian lexeme for the notion 'brother of the father' available and that it was one of the most common elements in onomastics of the Semitic world in the second millennium B.C. Moreover, *^{c}ammu* could allegedly in contexts also have a more general meaning 'older kinsman, relative' and even 'grandfather'.

The latter remark is in my view important with regard to the Hurrian form ***ammade***, analysis {*amm=ade*}, 'grandfather' (cf. I. Wegner, *Einführung*, 53, 'Großvater'; the form {*amm=ad(e)=iff=u-*} 'my grandfather', with the possessive pronoun 1st person singular; the ergative singular {*amm=ad(e)=iff=uš*} (*ibid.* 148, 165, 167); the genitive sg. + enclitic pronoun 3rd person sg. {*amm=ad(e)=iff=u=ve=n(na)*} (*ibid.* 161-162); the dative sg. {*amm=ad(e)=iff=u=va*} (*ibid.* 192-193); the absolutive plural (Boğazköy) {*amatte=na*} (*ibid.* 213, 215). If ***ammade*** is indeed derived from the Amorite lexeme ***^{c}ammu***, the form ***ammade*** with the Hurrian suffix ***-ade*** proves that ***^{c}ammu*** has become embedded in the Hurrian vernacular and may have been Hurrianized > ***ammi***.

As a result {*amm=ade*} is semantically close to ***attarde***, analysis {*atta(i)=arde*}, 'forefather, ancestor' (cf. I. Wegner, *Einführung*, 58, 251: 'Vorväter, Vorfahren').

Significantly ***a-ma-wa-si*** (KT Zf 1) is the first and ***a-ta-de*** the last sequence of a Linear A inscription of 18 signs in one line on one side of a gold pin (11 cm), with floral decoration on the other side. Exact provenance of the pin is uncertain. It probably comes from Crete. The pin appeared on the European Antiquities Market in 1980 and is now in the Museum of Hagios Nikolaos (inv. nr. 9675), see *chapter 10: Linear A inscriptions on metal objects*.

Although I consider the interpretation of Linear A ***da-ma-te*** (KY Za 2) as *{d/talm=a-te}* 'Teš(š)ub is great' most satisfactory, it is necessary to examine all interpretations that Linear A orthography theoretically allows, especially since at Nuzi at least 27 persons with the name ***Tarmi-Tešub*** (wr. *Tar-mi-te-šup, Tar-mi-te-eš-šup*) are attested (cf. I.J. Gelb, *NPN*, 149, s.v. *Tarmi-Tešub*), so that a variant ***Tarma-te*** (phonologically ***/Darma-te/***) of hypocoristic ***Tarmi-te***, would be conceivable.

In my 2016 edition of *Minoan Linear A*, Volume I, I mentioned that there are indications that there is no phonemic distinction between the liquids ***r*** and ***l*** in Hurrian (a phenomenon that might explain the fact that there are no separate signs in Linear A for ***ra*** and ***la***, for ***re*** and ***le***, for ***ri*** and ***li***, for ***ro*** and ***lo***, for ***ru*** and ***lu***, a phenomenon that Linear B must have inherited from its predecessor, since it cannot be explained from Mycenaean Greek, where distinction between ***r*** and ***l*** was phonemic). It seemed therefore conceivable that ***talmi*** and ***tarmi*** as well as ***talma*** and ***tarma*** might be approximately the same elements. However, recent research has shown that the roots ***talm-*** and ***tarm-*** have to be distinguished.

E. Laroche already mentioned the Hurrian noun ***tarmani*** 'source' ['well, spring, source'] and ***tarmanni*** 'la source'. The meaning was confirmed by the RS quadrilingual 137 III 8: Sumerian IDIM = Hurrian ***tar-m[a]-ni*** = Akkadian ***nagbu*** = Ugaritic ***nap-ku***; and by ***tar-ma-ni*** = Sumerogram TÚL, KUB XXVII 1 II 68-69 (cf. for further information E. Laroche, *Ugar. V*, 461; *GLH*, 257). However, at present there are more and more indications that both ***talm-*** and ***tarm-*** can be used as nominal and verbal roots. As dicussed before transitive ***talm=i-*** means 'to make great, powerful' and *intransitive* ***talm=a-*** 'to be/become great, powerful'. Semantically transitive ***tarm=i-*** can be placed into the same category of name-giving as ***talm=i-***, but the meaning is different. According to Th. Richter (*BGH*, 446, s.v. ***tarm-*** [PN], and *VHN*, 531, s.v. ***tarm-***) the meaning 'tränken, zu trinken geben' ['to give to drink, to nurse, to nourish, to (breast)feed (a child)'] is established. He also mentions the *infinitive* ***tarm-umma*** *epēšu* [Nuzi].

However, interpretation of Linear A ***da-ma-te*** (KY Za 2) as an intransitive imperative ****Tarma-te***, *{d/tarm=a-te}*, does not offer a satisfactory meaning. Moreover a meaning like 'Let (the child) suck, be nursed, nourished, oh *Tešub*', seems to require a form with the *final debitive* suffix ***-ae-/-ai-***, according to the grammatical rules described by I. Wegner (*Einführung*, 111-112). She analyses *it-ta-in-na-a-an* (Mit. IV 53) in the Tušratta letter as: *itt+ai+nna+ân* = 'und damit er gehen möge/kann' ['and that he may go'], see *ibidem*, 111, Table 12: *Die Suffixfolge beim sog. Debitiv-Finalis*. This ultimately makes interpretation of Linear A ***da-ma-te*** as an intransitive imperative ****Tarma-te***, *{d/tarm=a-te}*, unlikely.

However, Linear A orthographic conventions allow for more solutions: Since consonants ***-l-***, ***-m-***, ***-n(n)-***, ***-r-*** or ***-š-*** are not expressed preceding an occlusive in consonant clusters written with Linear A, ***da-ma-te*** may contain a root-extension ***-al-*** (function not clear), *factitive* ***-am-***, *causative* ***-an(n)-***, *factitive* and *iterative* ***-ar-*** or *intensive* ***-aš-***.

The scribe no doubt knew what he meant to write, but for us it is not so easy to make the right choice, if there are more possibilities due to the orthographic conventions. At least one personal name with the verbal root ***tarm-*** and root-extension ***-ar-*** is attested at Mari.

It is ***Tarmariš*** (wr. *ta-ar-ma-ri-iš*), analysis {*tarm=ar=i=ž*}, typology 1.3.2.2, lexicon *tarm-*, that Th. Richter (*VHN*, 299, 531) translates as 'Er/Sie (scil. ein *Numen*) möge (Jungen) wiederholt tränken' ['He/She (namely a *numen*) may nurse, nourish, (breast)feed (the boy) repeatedly'].

Another Hurrian combination of onomastic elements is conceivable. Comparing the Hurrian personal names ***ᶠTamar-elli*** (wr. *ᶠTa-ma-re-el-li*), ***Tamar-tae*** (wr. *Ta-mar-ta-e*) and ***Tamar-taḫe*** (wr. *Ta-mar-ta-ḫe*) at Nuzi (P.M. Purves, *NPN*, 262, s.v. ***tamar, tamar-***), ****Tamar-te*** (phonologically ***/Damar-te/***), hypocoristic of ****Tamar-tešup*** is feasible as well. Th. Richter (*VHN*, 296,) mentions the Hurrian personal names ***ᶠTamar-elli*** (wr.*ᶠta-mar-e-li*) at Mari and Nuzi, {*tam=ar-el(a)=ni*}, typology 1.4, lexicon *tam-*, *ela* 'sister', ***ᶠTa-mar-ᴰḪé-bat*** at Ugarit, ***Tamar-taḫe*** (wr. *ta-mar-ta-ḫe*) at Mari and Nuzi {*tam=ar-taġe*}, typology 1.4, lexicon *tam-*, *taḫe* 'man' and offers for ***Tamar-*** the analysis {*tam=ar-*}, i.e. root ***tam-*** + root-extension ***-ar-***, see *VHN*, 528, s.v. ***tam-***.

He mentions that words starting with ***tamᵒ*** are not very well attested (see also *BGH*, 435-436). Both ***tamari*** '(Opfer)Grube, Kanal' ['(sacrificial) pit, canal'] (see *BGH*, 460) and the term ***ta-me*** 'Floh (?)' ['flea (?)'] that is compared with Akkadian *pur(?)-ḫu-šu* in a lexical list at Ugarit, offer no clear meaning for the root. One may refer to some words at Ḫattuša such as ***ta-mar-ra*** (*ChS* I/7, 30 Rs. V 1), ***ta-mar-re-e-eš*** (I/5, 146: 6') and ***ta-mar-***[…] (I/1, 13 Rs. III 24'') that show similarities with ***ta-mar/ma-arᵒ-*** in personal names. He considers derivation from ***tamr-*** 'neun sein' ['to be nine, the ninth child'] not likely in personal names. Unfortunately the meaning of ***tam-*** is not yet clear. I may cautiously suggest a development ***tam-*** < ***tamm-*** < ***talm-***, but must admit that proof for such an etymology fails as yet. A disadvantage would be that such a hypothesis would even increase the number of variants we already know: see Th. Richter, *BGH*, 432-435: ***talm-***, ***talb-***, ***tal-*** II, ***tel-*** I [*passim*], ***talam(m)e/i*** [Boğ., Mitt., Ugarit], ***telamae*** [Ugarit] in: KI.LAM GU.LA = MIN ***te-la-ma-e*** 'grand prix', cf. E. Laroche, *GLH*, 253, s.v. ***talmi***. On the other hand it happens more often that frequently used terms are liable to change.

Anyway, if Richter's analysis of {*tam=ar-*} is correct, I assume that the root ***tam-*** is probably verbal, at least originally, cf. also the verbal usage of ***talm=i-*** 'to make great, powerful', ***talm=a-*** 'to be great, powerful'.

Whatever the meaning of ***d/tamar*** may be, interpretation of Linear A ***da-ma-te*** as ****Tamar-te*** (phonologically ***/Damar-te/***), hypocoristic of ****Tam=ar-te-šup***, is not only feasible, but attractive on the basis of ***ᶠTa-mar-ᴰḪé-bat*** at Ugarit.

So far we have investigated all possible interpretations of ***da-ma-te*** (KY Za 2) from the perspective of Linear A and Hurrian as *the* vernacular of Minoan Crete, but we also have to take into account the geographical position and demographic composition of the island Kythera, where the inscription was found. Apart from a Linear A inscription <u>GRA</u> + <u>E</u> (KY Zg 1) on a fragment of a clay weight, ***da-ma-te*** (KY Za 2) is to date the only Linear A inscription from that island.

Since we have too little evidence of the demographic composition of the island Kythera in Minoan times, we simply do not know whether the island was a Minoan colony and its inhabitants spoke a Minoan vernacular or whether the majority of its inhabitants (so close to the Peloponnese) consisted of Mycenaean Greeks, possibly with a superstrate Minoan aristocracy or with a small adstrate group of Minoan traders from Crete.

Since the Linear A sequence ***da-ma-te*** in KY Za 2 is identical with the Linear B form at Pylos, ***da-ma-te*** (KY Za 2) could theoretically be the Greek singular dative ***δαμάρτει*** or the plural nominative ***δάμαρτες*** written with Linear A or it could be one of the Hurrian personal names discussed before. Many scholars accept the view that Linear B **DA** might be the abbreviation of ***δάμαρ*** 'official, steward', especially because persons indicated with DA receive larger rations than others in the *personnel tablets* from Pylos. It is even conceivable that the Hurrian onomastic element ***tamar*** (phonologically ***/damar/***) is the basis for Mycenaean ***δάμαρ***, which is suspected to be Pre-Greek. A Hurrian etymology of 'a great or powerful person' would be in accordance with the powerful position of the ***δάμαρ*** in Mycenaean society. P.M. Purves (*NPN*, 262) and Th. Richter (*VHN*, 528) do not doubt the Hurricity of ***tamar***, so it does not seem necessary either to assume that ***tamar*** is a loan-word in Hurrian from e.g. Indo-Iranian, derived from the Indo-European root **dᵒm-* 'house'. Still I consider a Hurrian analysis {*d/talm=a-te*} 'Teš(š)ub is great' by far the best.

Linear A ***da-na-tu*** , (AK 6.1) is the first entry of this tablet from Arkhanes, followed by a clear word divider, that is followed by the sign ***ku-***, probably the first syllable of a sequence that is continued in the next line: possibly ***ku-*[.]*te-we*** (AK 6.1-2). Only one fragment belonging to the upper part of the tablet is preserved. Only the top parts of the signs, read as **]*te-we*** (AK 6.2), are preserved. Since the sign after ***te-*** is not complete, ***-we*** (without dot) might also be ***-ri*** (with dot). Linear A ***da-na-tu*** is most likely a Hurrian personal name. It is clear that initial voicing of dentals and probably also of the other occlusives in the Minoan-Hurrian dialect was normal. Interpretation of ***da-na-tu*** depends on its division.

The first element probably contains the Hurrian verbal root ***tan-/dan-*** 'to make, to do', cf. Th. Richter, *BGH*, 436-438, s.v. ***tan-*** [*passim*], ***tin-*** [Ug.] (I translate the German text): "Unanimously interpreted as 'to make, do'. [...] Corresponds with Hittite ***ija-*** 'to make' and Akkadian ***epēšu***. [...] Etymology: cf. Urartian ***tanu-*** 'to make'."

According to Th. Richter (*VHN*, 529) the transitive form ***tan-*** is (apart from 'machen' ['to make']) used with the meaning 'erschaffen' ['to create'] in personal names. He analyses the personal name ***Tan-atal*** (wr. *Ta-na-ta-al*) from Tigunāni as {*tan-adal*}, typology 1.4, translation 'Der Starke machte (Jungen)' ['The strong one made/created (the boy)']. Another interpretation is an *athematic imperative* 'Make/Create (the boy), oh strong one !'. Compare at Ḫattuša Old Hurrian ᶠ***Tanu-ḫepa*** (cf. E. Laroche, *NH*, 174, N° 1244):

1. Reine, femme de Muwatalli: hiér. *Tà-nú-he-pa*, SBo I 42.
2. Reine, femme de Urḫi-Tešub: hiér. *Tà-nú-he-pa*, SBo I 43-44.
3. Reine, femme d'un Mursili (II ou III ?): hiér. *Tà-nú-he-pa*, SBo I 24-29.
4. Sources cunéiformes: abs. nom. *ᶠDa/Ta-nu-ḫé-pa-(aš)*, XIV 7 + XXI 19 I 16, 17, 20; XXI 33, 19; XXXI 66 III 15. - XV 5 I 7, III 4, 9. - XVI 16 Vo 1; 32 II 1, 4 - KBo IX 151, 5.

Translation of ᶠ***Tanu-ḫepa***: 'Create (the girl), oh *Ḫepa(t)* !' or '*Ḫepa(t)* created (the girl)'.

Not only sentence names like ***Tan-atal*** and ***ᶠTanu-ḫepa*** were used, but also so-called 'one-word' names as ***Tania*** (wr. *Ta-ni-ia*) at Alalaḫ IV (*AT* 189: 19), that can be analysed as a transitive indicative 3rd person singular {*tan=i=a*} 'He/She makes/creates, made/ created (the child)', which cannot easily be distinguished from a hypocoristic name (with the Hurrian hypocoristic suffix ***-ya***), cf. Th. Richter, *VHN*, 585.

Linear A ***da-na-tu*** (AK 6.1) may well be such a 'one-word' name, if we assume that the root ***dan-/tan-*** was extended with the root-extension ***-Všt-*** [V = vowel], of which the vowel is adapted to the vowel in the root, cf. I. Wegner (*Einführung*, 88-89), who actually gives the example ***tan / tan=ašt-*** 'machen' ['to make'], ***an- / an=ašt-*** 'to enjoy', ***mad- / mad=ašt-*** 'to be wise', ***teḫ- / teḫ=ešt-*** 'to elevate, to grow, to become great', ***šurv=ušt-*** 'to do evil, to cause evil, to bring about evil'.

If this root-extension is involved, Linear A ***da-na-tu*** (AK 6.1) can be analysed as Old Hurrian {*dan/tan=ašt=o/u=m*} 'He/She (a *numen*) has made/created (the child)'. This form is interesting, since I. Wegner (*ibid.*) tells that there are indications that the formants ***-ol-*** and especially ***-Všt-*** in combination with verbal forms in ***=o=m*** may show other grammatical differentiations (aspect or type of action), cf. G. Wilhelm, *Festschrift Heger*, 1992, 670. The 'Old Hurrian' formant ***-Všt-*** seems to express the end or result of an action, e.g. ***pa=ašt=o=m*** 'he has built'. The analysis {*dan/tan=ašt=o/u=m*} of Linear A ***da-na-tu*** is possible, since ***-s-*** preceding an occlusive is not expressed in consonant clusters and final ***-m*** is not expressed in Linear A and B either. This analysis seems preferable because of the combination of the root-extension ***=Všt=*** with the Old Hurrian perfect form ***=o/u=m***.

However, I. Wegner (*Einführung*, 147) also mentions the jussive *ta-a-na-aš-ti-en* (Mit. I 82, III 75, 78) in the Tušratta letter, analysis ***tan=ašt=i=en***, consisting of the root ***tan-*** 'to make' + the root-extension ***-ašt-*** + the marker of the *jussive* ***-i-*** + the marker of the 3rd person singular of the *jussive* ***-en***, translation 'he may make'. This makes an Old Hurrian *imperative* in ***-o/u-*** also a likely option. Consequently Linear A ***da-na-tu*** (AK 6.1) can also be analysed as {*dan/tan=ašt=o/u*}, 'Make/Create (the child) (oh *numen*) !'

An analysis of Linear A ***da-na-tu*** (AK 6.1) as {*d/tan(i)=attu*} or {*d/tan(i)=aštu*} 'Create (the child), oh woman !' is theoretically possible, since ***ᶠaštu***, ***ᶠattu*** and ***ᶠazzu*** (with a stem in ***-u***) are variants of ***ᶠašte***, ***ᶠatte*** and ***ᶠazze***. Th. Richter (*VHN*, 391) writes, s.v. ***atte/atti*** and ***attu*** {*atto/u*}, that Hurrian ***att°*** in the meaning 'father' or sometimes 'direct male ancestor' is known through ***atta*** and the root ***att-***, but that it should be separated from ***atte*** 'woman' because of an extensive usage of the same type of feminine personal names built on ***atte*** as on ***azze*** and ***ašte*** (also with a stem in ***-u***), cf. Th. Richter, *VHN*, 381-382.

However, the 'one-word' names with the root-extension ***-Všt-*** seem preferable. No doubt the Linear A scribe knew exactly which interpretation of ***da-na-tu*** was meant, but we have to deal with different interpretations that are possible due to the orthographic conventions of Linear A (and B).

In view of the allophonic character of Hurrian occlusives comparison of Linear A ***da-na-tu*** with Linear A ***ta-na-ti*** (HT 10b.4) and ***ta-na-te*** (ZA 10a.1) may be significant. Recent literature, especially Th. Richter, *VHN*, Wiesbaden 2016, has thrown new light on the structure and possible interpretations of Hurrian onomastics. If the Linear A sequence ***ta-na-ti*** (HT 10b.4) is equivalent to ***ta-na-te*** (ZA 10a.1) from Kato Zakro, several interpretations are feasible, see *supra* for these analyses.

Linear A ***ku-*[.]*-te-we*** (AK 6.1-2) following ***da-na-tu* ,** (AK 6.1) is the second entry on this fragmentary tablet from Arkhanes. The word divider **(,)** following ***da-na-tu*** is clear. Since Linear A ***da-na-tu*** is most likely a Hurrian name, ***ku-*** (line 1) is probably the first syllable of a sequence that is continued in the next line: possibly ***ku-*[.]*-te-we*** (AK 6.1-2).

Only one fragment belonging to the upper part of the tablet is preserved. Only the top parts of the signs read as **]*-te-we*** (AK 6.2) are preserved. Since the sign after ***te-*** is not complete, ***-we*** might also be ***-ri***. There is possibly space for a sign preceding ***-te-we*** in the second line, but the reading remains uncertain and conjectural.

If ***ku-te-we*** (AK 6.1-2) is the correct reading, interpretation as ***Ḫut-te-we***, genitive of the Hurrian personal name ****Ḫut-te*** (with the Hurrian suffix ***-we*** for the singular genitive), hypocoristic of ***Ḫut-tešub*** (wr. *Ḫu-ut-te-šup*), would be feasible, cf. I.J. Gelb, *NPN*, 64, who mentions 8 persons at Nuzi named ***Ḫut-tešup***; cf. P.M. Purves, *NPN*, 265, s.v. ***-tešup***, ***Ḫut-tešup***. Linear A ***ku-te-we*** could then be analysed as {*ḫud=te(šub)=we*} and be interpreted as 'The one of *Ḫut-te*', probably a patronymic form: 'The son of *Ḫut-te*'.

Cf. ***ᵈḪutena ᵈḪutellura***, occurring as ***ḫdn ḫdlr*** at Ugarit. E. Laroche (1948, 125) proposed 'écrire, marquer' ['to write, to express'] for the root ***ḫud-***, but in his *Glossaire de la langue hourrite*, 110, he abandoned that suggestion, s.v. ***ḫud-***, 'verbe de sens inconnu'.

I shall not repeat all meanings proposed for the root ***ḫud-*** [*passim*] in the older literature, cf. Th. Richter, *BGH*, 175-177, see *supra*. Th. Richter (*VHN*, 424-425) mentions, s.v. ***ḫud-*** {*ḫo/ud-*}, that in more recent literature the meaning 'Schicksal entscheiden' ['to destine a fate'] was at first attributed to the root, but that since publication of the Hurrian-Hittite bilingual ***Kirenze*** (KBo 32) ***ḫud-*** can be translated as 'beten, huldigen, erhöhen, preisen, segnen' ['to pray, to pay homage to, to exalt, to praise, to bless'], since it corresponds with Hittite ***šarlāi***. The root is relatively rare in the *VHN*-corpus, but at Nuzi (P.M. Purves, *NPN*, 218-219) and Ugarit (F. Gröndahl, *PNTU*, 233) it is a popular onomastic element.

P.M. Purves (*ibid.*) also mentioned ***Ḫut-tirwi*** (wr. *Ḫu-ut-ti-ir-wi, Ḫu-ti-ir-wi*). He attributed the second variant *Ḫu-ti-ir-wi* to *Ḫut-tirwi*, but since there is only one ***-t-*** in that name, it could better be read as ***Ḫut-irwi***, with the onomastic element ***irwi*** (Nuzi) = ***erwi*** (Nuzi) = ***ewri / ibri*** (elsewhere) 'Lord'. Incidentally, ***ᵈTirwi*** is a god at Nuzi according to P.M. Purves, *NPN*, 267, cf. also Th. Richter, *VHN*, 537, s.v. ***tirwe*** {*tirve*}, ***tirme***.

If we regard Hurrian ***Ḫut-irwi*** (wr. *Ḫu-ti-ir-wi*) at Nuzi (which P.M. Purves assigned erroneously to ***Ḫut-tirwi***) as equivalent to Linear A ***ku-te-we*** (AK 6.1-2), the Linear A name can be analysed as {*ḫud/ḫutt=erwe*}, since ***-r-*** preceding ***-w-*** was omitted in Linear A an B consonant clusters (***ḫud-*** and ***ḫutt-*** occur at Nuzi and Tigunāni), translation 'Praise/ Bless the Lord !' or 'Bless (the child), oh Lord !'. The latter meaning seems the most appropriate interpretation of this personal name. Moreover, ***Ḫut-tešub*** and ***Ḫut-irwi*** are comparable names, since ***ewri*** is an epithet of Tešub in the Tušratta letter (Mit. IV 118).

However, if there is a sign to be read before ***-te-we*** and if this sign is ****-i-***, interpretation as ****Ḫui-te-we*** would be feasible, (patronymic ?) genitive of the Hurrian personal name ***Ḫui-te*** (wr. *Ḫu-i-te*, *Ḫu-i-te-e*, *Ḫu-e-te*, *Ḫu-i-ti*), 9 times attested at Nuzi and hypocoristic of ***Ḫui-tešub*** (wr. *Ḫu-i-te-šup*), 11 times attested at Nuzi, cf. I.J. Gelb, *NPN*, 62, s.v. ***Ḫui-te*** and ***Ḫui-tešub***; cf. P.M. Purves, *NPN*, 264-265, s.v. ***-te***, ***Ḫui-te***, ***-tešup***, ***Ḫui-tešup***. Compare also Linear A]***ku-du-we*** (HT? 170a.2) from Hagia Triada.

All editors agree that the entire inscription on two adjoining fragments of a 'corded' pithos from the Palace of Phaistos reads: ***si-ma* , *i-ja-te*** [(PH Zb 4). The inscription was found in 1900 (HM 1620) in magazine 27 of the west wing of the palace. F. Halbherr identified it in 1901 among the material of the preceding campaign.

The Linear A sequence ***i-ja-te*** [(PH Zb 4) from Phaistos shows only homographic identity with Linear B ***i-ja-te*** (PY Eq 146) from Pylos, for the Mycenaean form ***i-ja-te*** can be explained as a perfectly Greek term (with Indo-European etymology) ***ἰᾱτήρ*** (nom. sing.) 'physician', cf. Homer *Iliad* B, 732, *ἰητήρ* in dual form; cf. Classical Cypriot acc. *to-ni-ja-te-ra-ne, τὸν ἰᾱτεραν* (cf. M. Ventris - J. Chadwick, *Documents*, 547). Morphologically the Linear A sequence ***i-ja-te*** can be compared with Linear A ***da-du-te*** (HT 34.1) from Hagia Triada and probably also with ***i-da-ma-te*** (AR Zf 1; AR Zf 2) on a gold and a silver double axe-head from the Cave of Arkalokhori, since it probably contains the same theophorous element ***-te***, hypocoristic of ***-Tešub***, that occurs very frequently in personal names. So one may infer that ***i-ja-te*** belongs to the category of 'sentence names'.

Th. Richter (*BGH*, 73) offers, s.v. ***i-***(?) or ***ij-*** [Mitt.], the meaning 'taugen, wert sein' ['to be reliable'] or 'Taugliches, Gutes tun' ['to treat well']. Th. Richter (*VHN*, 393) offers, s.v. ***ij-*** {*ij-*} or ***i-***, ***ej-*** {*ej-*} only the meaning 'taugen, wert sein' ['to be reliable'].

He assumes that the personal names ***Ijuḫul*** from Tigunāni and ***^{f}Ijuzzi*** from Tigunāni and Mari and the name of King Tušratta's wife ***^{f}I-ú-ni*** contain the verbal root ***ij-***, whereas ***^{f}Ejan-elli*** from Mari probably contains the root ***ej-*** (*VHN*, 393, n. 238). Since Hurrian ***ela*** 'sister' is not connected with theonyms in his corpus, he considers it unlikely that the first element of ***^{f}Ejan-elli*** has anything to do with the Hurrian form of the feminine theonym ***Aja*** that appears as ***Ajan*** in the list of deities at Emar and as ***Ejan*** in the quadrilingual 137 IV a 19 at Ugarit: [***^{d}A-a***] = h. ***e-ya-an*** = oug. ***Ku-ša-ru***, cf. E. Laroche, *GLH*, 39-40.

If Linear A ***i-ja-te*** is analysed as {*ij=a-te*}, the verbal root ***ij-*** as first onomastic element is most likely, so that the meaning of the personal name may well be 'Tešub is reliable'. But if the analysis is ***ij=ar=(i/u)-Te(šub)***, with the *factitive / iterative* root-extension ***-ar-***, the verbal element may well be transitive: 'Make (the child) good, oh *Tešub* !'.

The sequence ***si-ma*** (PH Zb 4), preceding ***i-ja-te***, may well be a Hurrian personal name as well. In many archives personal names with the root ***šim-*** are preserved such as *Ši-mi-ik-ku* at Alalaḫ IV (*AT*, 136: 39), ***^{f}Šimaia*** (wr. *^{f}Ši-ma-a-a*), ***Šimiia*** (wr. *Ši-mi-ia*), ***Šimi-Tilla*** (wr. *Ši-mi-til-la*), ***^{f}Šim-Te*** (wr. *^{f}Ši-im-Te*, *^{f}Ši-im-Te-e*), ***Šimšar*** (wr. *Ši-im-šar*) at Nuzi (I.J. Gelb, *NPN*, 134-135). ***Šimšar*** at Nuzi probably correlates with ***Šimšari*** (wr. *Ši-im-ša(?)-ri*) at Mari, analysis {*šim(i)=žari*}, typology 3.1. Also attested at Mari are ***^{f}Šima-ewri*** (wr. *^{f}Ši-ma-ew-ri*), analysis {*šim=a=Ø-evri*}, typology 1.1.1.3.3, ***Šimiš-ewri*** (wr. *^{f}Ši-mi-iš-ew-ri, ^{f}Ši-mi-i-iš-ew-ri*), analysis {*šim=i=ž-evri*}, typology 1.3.2.2, ***Šimiš-šarri*** (wr. *Ši-im-iš-šar-ri*), analysis {*šim=i=ž-šarri*}, typology 1.3.2.2, ***^{f}Šim-kintiri*** (wr. *^{f}Ši-im-gi-in-di-ri*), analysis {*šim-kindiri*}, typology 1.4 (Th Richter, *VHN*, 267-268 and 508, s.v. ***šim-***).

According to Th. Richter (*VHN*, 508) lexical terms based on ***šim-*** are rare (see *BGH*, 378-379). For a great deal they are morphologically and lexically not clear. E. Laroche (*GLH*, 232) booked *ši-mi*[!](LUM)*-i-ki* (Mit. III 46) as *ši-mi-i-ki* under ***Šimigi*** 'soleil'. At Ugarit (RS voc. III 13) Hurrian ***ši-ma-ni-šu-ḫi*** is compared with Sumerian MA.NA.LÁ, which suggests a meaning 'hängen (lassen)' ['to (let) hang'] or 'bezahlen' ['to pay'] for ***ši-m***^{o} or ***ši-ma-n***^{o}, but this meaning seems not easily applicable elsewhere.

Prima facie one tends to regard ***di-ra-di-na 133*** HL (PH la.1) from Phaistos and ***di-re-di-na*** (HT 98.2-3) from Hagia Triada as writing variants, but it seems wise to analyse them separately. Both sequences are probably personal names. ***]di-ra-di-na*** is followed by a rare cereal ideogram ***133*** and 2 fraction signs HL. The other ideograms on the tablet are OLIVA according to J. Raison and M. Pope on the *a*-side and ***79*** , ***67*** and FIC on the *b*-side. *GORILA 1* reads HORDEUM instead of OLIVA on the *a*-side.

Since the Linear A and B ***r-*** series of syllabic signs can also reflect ***l-***, there is theoretically more than one analysis possible, but the orthographic conventions with regard to consonant clusters give rise to more possibilities as well:

Analysis I: {*d/til=ad=i=nna*} consisting of the root ***t/dil-*** II 'to destroy, crush, trample down' + root-extension ***-ad-*** + marker of transitivity ***-i-*** (position 5) + enclitic personal pronoun 3rd person singular ***-nna*** 'him, her', indicating the object of action (position 9). The one-word name probably expresses the *imperative* 'Destroy / Crush / Trample him / her (the child) down, oh *numen* !'. Cf. for the root Th. Richter, *BGH*, 459, s.v. ***til-*** II [Boğ.; Mari; PN] 'zerstampfen, zertrampeln, vernichten'. Compare for the root-extension ***-ad-*** I. Wegner, *Einführung*, 88, ***šir=ad-*** '(be)singen' ['to sing (of), chant, celebrate (in song)'], cf. ***šir-*** 'to sing'. Cf. *supra* and *infra* my 3 Hurrian etymologies of the names of the sorceress *Kirke* (***πότνια Κίρκη***) who warned *Odysseus* (***Ὀδυσσεύς*** / ***Ὀλυσσεύς***) for the *Sirens* (***Σειρῆνες***), Homer's *Odyssey* μ 36 ff.

Th. Richter (*VHN*, 535-536, s.v. ***tel-/til-***) mentions that in more recent research two roots, ***tel-*** as variant of ***talm-*** (*intransitive*) 'to be great', (*transitive*) 'to make great' (cf. *BGH*, 432-435) and ***til-*** 'to destroy' (cf. *BGH*, 459), are examined. He thinks (*VHN*, 535-536) that ***Telum-atal*** (wr. *te-lum-a-tal*), analysis {*tel=o=m-adal*} 'Der Starke vernichtete (älteres Kind)' ['The strong one destroyed (the older child)'] could, for instance, offer a good meaning as a 'substitute name', but he prefers (*VHN*, 305) the other root ***tel- / talm-*** and translates ***Telum-atal*** as 'Der Starke vergrößerte(?) (Jungen)' ['The strong one made (the child) great']. Cf. also ***telame / talame / talm*** 'great'; see also s.v. Linear A ***te-ra-me*** (KN Zf 13) on the gold signet-ring with spiral inscription from Mavro Spilio. Since an ***a/e*** alternation in ***tel- / talm-*** and ***telame / talame / talm*** is firmly established, an ***i/e*** alternation seems unacceptable for ***tel-*** 'to be great' and 'to make great', because an ***i/e*** alternation presupposes that such an [***e***] is close, which is incompatible with an ***e/a*** alternation. This makes it unlikely that Linear A ***]di-ra-di-na*** (PH la.1) and ***di-re-di-na*** (HT 98.2-3) contain the root ***tel-*** 'to make great'.

Analysis II of ***di-ra-di-na***: {*d/tir=ad=i=nna*}, consisting of the root ***t/dir-***, of which the meaning has not yet been established. The one-word name may express the *imperative* and can only partly be translated: '.... him, her (the child), oh *numen* !'. The root occurs in the names ***Tirija*** {*Tir=i=ja*}, ***Tirikka*** {*Tir=i=kk=i»a=Ø*} and ***Terikka*** {*ter=i=kk=i»a=Ø*}, ***Terikkan*** {*ter=i=kk=i»a=n(na)*}, ***Terip-Teššub*** {*ter=i=b-Teššob*}, cf. Th. Richter, *VHN*, 306. Th. Richter (*VHN*, 537, n. 800) discusses attempts to compare the Hurrian root with Urartian ***ter=u*** 'festsetzen, bestimmen, stellen' and 'to put, to establish'.

Analysis III: {*d/til-ažd=i=na*}, consisting of the root ***t/dil-*** II 'to destroy, crush, trample down' + ***ašte/i / ažde/i*** 'woman' [*passim*] + the suffix of the so-called plural definite article ***-na*** (***ž/š*** preceding a dental or other occlusive is not expressed in Linear A and B consonant clusters), translation 'Destroy, crush, trample down (the deceased child), oh women !'.

Analysis IV: {*d/til=ard=i=na*}, consisting of the root ***t/dil-*** II 'to destroy, crush, trample down' + ***arde/i*** 'town, city' [passim] + the suffix of the so-called plural definite article ***-na*** (***-r-*** preceding a dental or other occlusive is not expressed in Linear A and B consonant clusters), translation 'Destroy, crush, trample down the cities !'

As for *analysis III*: {*d/til-ažd=i=na*} and *analysis IV*: {*d/til=ard=i=na*} comparison with Linear A ***o-ra₂-di-ne*** (HT 6a.4) {*o/ull=i-ažd=i=ne*} 'Destroy the woman !' and {*o/ull=i-ard=i=ne*} 'Destroy the city !' offers in fact the same type of Hurrian personal names in Linear A with two verbal roots ***d/til-*** and ***o/ull-*** that both mean 'to destroy', ***d/til-*** in the sense of 'to crush, trample down' and, if the root ***o/ull-*** is related to Hurrian ***ulme*** {*ul=me*} 'weapon, lance, axe', ***o/ull-*** might mean 'to destroy with a weapon' (cf. Th. Richter, *BGH*, 485, s.v. ***ul-*** IV and ***ulme*** I; cf. also *ibidem*, 484-486, s.v. ***ul-*** I, ***ul-*** II, ***ul-*** III and ***ull-***).

Linear A ***di-re-di-na*** (HT 98.2-3) from Hagia Triada is like]***di-ra-di-na*** (PH la.1) from Phaistos probably a personal name. The name ***di-re-di-na*** is preceded by ***ta-na-ti*** (analysed before) and 2 fraction signs JE (HT 98.2) and followed by ***te-jo*** and again 2 fraction signs JE. Ideograms are missing on the *a*-side of HT 98, which is probably due to the fact that the upper part of the tablet is missing. Only the *b*-side has 2 ideograms, sign ***87*** (possibly a chariot-frame) and VIN.

Since the Linear A and B ***r-*** series of syllabic signs can also reflect ***l-***, there is again theoretically more than one analysis possible, but the orthographic conventions with regard to consonant clusters give rise to more possibilities as well:

Analysis I: {*d/til=ed=i=nna*} consisting of the root ***t/dil-*** II 'to destroy, crush, trample down' + suffix marking the *future* tense ***-ed-*** (position 2) + marker of transitivity ***-i-*** (position 5) + enclitic personal pronoun 3rd person singular ***-nna*** 'him, her', indicating the object of action (position 9). This one-word name expresses the future tense 'He/she (a *numen*) will destroy / crush / trample him/her (the child) down', cf. Th. Richter, *BGH*, 459, s.v. ***til-*** II [Boğ.; Mari; PN] 'zerstampfen, zertrampeln, vernichten'. Compare for the suffix ***-ed-*** (marking the *future* tense) I. Wegner, *Einführung*, 93, Table 4: *The order of suffixes of the indicative, transitive-ergative positive verb* [I have translated the German text]. Single writing of the dental ***-t-*** in ***-et-*** indicates that it is voiced /***d***/.

Analysis II of ***di-re-di-na***: {*d/tir=ed=i=nna*}, consisting of the Hurrian root ***t/dir-***, of which the meaning has not yet been established. The form can only partly be translated: 'He/she (a *numen*) will .... him, her (the child)'. Cf. the names ***Tirija*** {*Tir=i=ja*}, ***Tirikka*** {*Tir=i=kk=i»a=Ø*}, ***Terikka*** {*Ter=i=kk=i»a=Ø*}, ***Terikkan*** {*Ter=i=kk=i»a=n(na)*}, ***Terip-Teššub*** {*Ter=i=b-Teššob*}, cf. Th. Richter, *VHN*, 306. Cf. Urartian ***ter=u*** 'stellen, festsetzen, bestimmen' and 'to put, to establish', cf. Th. Richter, *VHN*, 537, n. 800.

Analysis III: {*d/til-ed=i=na*}, consisting of the root ***t/dil-*** II 'to destroy, crush, trample down' + ***edi/idi*** 'body, person' [*passim*] + the suffix of the so-called plural definite article ***-na***, translation 'Destroy, crush, trample down the bodies / persons !'.

E. Laroche, *GLH*, 73-74, s.v. ***edi / idi*** 'corps, personne'. Mit. ***edi***; Mâri, RS, Boğ. ***edi*** ou ***idi***; ***idi*** = akk. ***pagru*** 'corps', RS bil. 15-10, 7; cf. PRU III 311, 315. Dir. ***idi-da*** 'à la personne de, à' = akk. ***ana*** 'à, pour': RS 20.149 III 15, [MU] = ***a-na*** = ***idi-da*** = oug. ***le-e***; cf. Laroche, *Ugar. V* 232, 457; *RA* 54, 198; *edi-da*, directif postposé au datif: 'à l'égard de, au sujet de'; d'où, par affaiblissement, 'à, pour'.

dŠimigi-ni-wa e-ti-i-ta 'à l'égard du Soleil', Mit. I 106. - ***i-ti pa-a-ḫi*** etc. 'corps, tête' et autres parties du corps; cf. Laroche, *RA 67*, 120. Cf. Th. Richter, *BGH*, 112-113, s.v. ***e/idi*** [*passim*] 'Körper, Person', etc. Compare also Urartian ***edi=ni*** 'per, a causa di' (cf. M. Salvini, Il lessico delle lingue hurrica e urartea. Progressi di interpretazione e problemi particolari, *Studi epigrafici e linguistici sul Vicino Oriente antico 12*, Verona 1995, 164. See for the Hurrian noun ***p/waḫi*** Th. Richter, *BGH*, 287-288, s.v. ***p/waḫi*** I [Boğ.; Mari; Mitt.; Ug.], ***paḫi-*** [Lw/He], analysis {*paġ=e*} 'Kopf, Haupt' ['head'], compared with Sumerian SAG and Akkadian *qaqqadu*.

Unfortunately the Linear A inscription **]*i-ja-re-di-ja i-ja-pa*[** (IO Za 5) from Mount Ioukhtas is broken off after ***i-ja-pa***[, so that we cannot be sure, whether the latter sequence can be completed to ***i-ja-pa***[**-qe-ja* = cuneiform ****i-ja-pa***[***-ḫe-ja(š)***, or to ***i-ja-pa***[****-96-ja*** = cuneiform ****i-ja-pa***[***-ḫi-ja(š)***. Because of the vicinity of ***-e-di-ja*** it is tempting, for Linear A]***i-ja-re-di-ja i-ja-pa***[****-qe-ja / -96-ja*** would offer a splendid parallel of the Hurrian phrase ***i-ti pa-a-ḫi***, with proclitic ***i-ja-re*** = Hurrian ***ya-lle-*** (wr. *i-i-al-le-*) and ***i-ja-*** = Hurrian ***ya-*** (wr. *i-ya* or *i-i-a*), and the possessive suffixes ***-ya*** 'his' or ***-yaš*** 'theirs' (E. Laroche) and ***-i***, 'his' or ***-i + aš*** > ***-iaš*** 'theirs' (I. Wegner, *Einführung*, 63). Single writing of Hurrian ***-t-*** in cuneiform ***e-ti-*** and ***i-ti*** shows a voiced dental ***/d/***.

Analysis IV: {*d/til=erd=i=na*}, consisting of the root ***t/dil-*** II 'to destroy, crush, trample down' + ***e/irdi*** 'part of the body, breast (?), tongue (?)' + the suffix of the so-called plural definite article ***-na*** (***-r-*** preceding a dental or other occlusive is not expressed in Linear A and B consonant clusters), 'Destroy, crush, the (evil) tongues (?) !'. E. Laroche, *GLH*, 125, s.v. ***irti*** ou ***irdi***: nom de partie du corps, suivi de ***karši***, probablement identique à l'akkadien ***irtu*** 'poitrine' ['breast'], cf. Laroche, *RA 67*, 121. Nom. *ir-ti*, KBo XX 126+III 11, IV 10, 29; e.a.; *e-erti*, KBo XV 1 IV 11. Th. Richter, *BGH*, 101, s.v. ***e/irde*** [Boğ.], first quotes Laroche (*GLH*, 125) and other scholars opting for the meaning 'breast', then (since Girbal, 1992b, 173) a new option 'not breast, rather tongue' and the example of ***irde paḫrubade*** 'evil tongue' (Haas, 2003a, 151), → *waḫrubade* [*p/waḫr-*].

Linear A ***qa-ku-re , di-83a*** (HT Wc 3017a.1-2) appears on a roundel from Hagia Triada. For the nodules, sealings and roundels I have followed the classification as proposed by L. Godart - J.-P. Olivier, *GORILA 2*: HT Wc 3017a.1-2. J. Raison and M. Pope had classified this inscription as HT W 217a.1-2. The *b*-side of the roundel reads: HORD+D , ***zo*** .

The c-side (edge) has five seal impressions (D. Levi; type 112).

According to Th. Richter (*BGH*, 120), s.v. ***ḫalgi*** [Lw/ Hu], ***ḫalgi*** is a loan-word into Hurrian and can be compared with Hittite ***ḫalki-*** (common) 'Korn, Getreide' ['corn, grain'] that may well be a cultural word (Wanderwort).

The deity ***Ḫalki*** may (according to some scholars) originally have belonged to the Hattic pantheon, but has been adopted into the Hurrian as well. His name was also used as epithet to *Kumarbi* and *Nisaba*. The name may or may not be connected with ***ḫalgi***.

If the theonym ***Ḫalki*** can be connected with ***ḫalki-*** 'corn, grain', *Kumarbi* may (in his appearance of ***Ḫalki***) represent a vegetation god or a 'barley' god, if the combination with the ideogram HORDEUM (HT Wc 3017b) 'barley' has any significance in this respect.

If Linear A ***qa-ku-re*** is analysed as {*ḫalg(i)»=u=le*}, combination of ***ḫalgi*** with the nominal suffix ***-li/-le*** marking professions offers the meaning 'a man working with 'corn'.

An objection may be that I. Wegner (*Einführung*, 56) mentions that the nominal suffix ***-li/-le*** marking professions is usually athematically attached to the root, cf. ***keb+li*** 'hunter' < ***keb-*** 'to set (a trap)', and ***tab/v+li*** '(copper)smith' < ***tab/v-*** 'to cast (metal, copper)'.

However, one may perhaps compare the formation of the Hurrian 'one-word' name ***Ḫaluli*** (wr. *Ḫa-lu-li*), from Qaṭṭarā and Kaniš, probably with root-extension ***-ul-***, typology 3.1, 'Weintraube, Wein(rebe)' ['Grape, Wine, Vine'], and ***ᶠḪalulāja*** (wr. *ᶠḪa-lu-la-a-ia*) from Mari and Nuzi, analysis {*ḫalo/ul(i)=āya*}, typology 3.1/4.2, 'Kleine Weintraube / rebe' ['Small grape, Small vine'], cf. Th. Richter, *VHN*, 119. Cf. E. Laroche (*GLH*, 90), s.v. ***ḫalul-***: *ḫa-a-lu-(u)-la*, KBo XIX 139 III 13; An. 10595, 4; *ḫa-a-lu-u-li*, KBo XX 126+ III 47 (without translation). According to Th. Richter (*BGH*, 122) ***ḫaluli*** [Boğ; EN], ***ḫalulu*** [Nuzi], first interpreted as 'a fruit', later as 'Weintraube' (V. Haas, 1989a, 269^{+44}, 2003a, 254), alphabetic cuneiform ***ḫll*** (also ***ġll***) as rendering of ***ḫalulu*** 'a fruit', referring to Urartian ***ḫaluli*** 'wine' (Watson, 1996d, 99; 2001a, 120; 2004a, 121; ***ḫlln*** 2007a, 166, 199. Corresponds with Hittite ***muri(n)-*** and ***muriyan-*** com. as well as Sumerogram (GIŠ.)GEŠTIN and (GIŠ.)GEŠTIN *KÀ-RA-A-AN* (V. Haas, 2003a, 254). Also toponym *ḫa-lu-ul-li-we*, cf. Fincke, 1993a, 85, sub ***Ḫalulli(we)*** and ***til-ḫa-lu-li-na*** in Nuzi texts.

On the basis of these formations analysis of Linear A ***qa-ku-re*** as {*ḫalg(i)»=ul=e*}, possibly with root-extension ***-ul-***, seems conceivable, but needs to be verified.

Another interpretation seems conceivable as well. Th. Richter (*BGH*, 119) mentions, s.v. ***ḫal-*** I [Boğ.] 'singen(?)', also the form ***ḫalikkuli*** [Boğ.] that is explained as 'Ritual, Zeremonie' ['ceremony, ritual'] (V. Haas, 1988d, 138[23]) or 'Sänger(?)' ['singer'] (De Martino, 1993, 125), possibly {*ḫali=i=kk=uḫ(u)li*}. If we compare the form ***ḫalikkuli*** [Boğ.] with Linear A ***qa-ku-re***, interpretation as athematic ***ḫalkuli*** < ***ḫalikkuli*** as a result of *syncope* of ***-i-*** seems feasible.

According to I. Wegner (*Einführung*, 57-58) *nomina actoris* are formed with the very productive combination of suffixes ***=o/u=ḫ(e)li*** (graphically ***uḫli*** or ***uḫuli***, the latter is the usual form at Alalaḫ and the western Hurrian area). The real suffix of the *nomen actoris* is ***-li***, for the designations of professions in ***uḫli / uḫuli*** are based on nouns becoming attributive adjectives with the adjectival suffix ***-ḫe*** to which the suffix ***-li*** indicating professions is added, at Alalaḫ also with the derivational vowel ***-o/u-***, elsewhere without ***-o/u-***, but with syncope of the vowel ***-e*** of ***-ḫe***.

Substantival designations of professions built on Hurrian and non-Hurrian stems are:
emand=o/uḫlu (Akkadianized nominative in ***-u***) 'Zehnerschaftsführer' ['commander of a group of ten'] < ***eman*** 'Zehn' ['ten'] + ***ti*** > ***emandi*** 'Zehnerschaft' ['group of ten'] > ***emand(i)=o=ḫe*** 'zu Zehnerschaft gehörig' ['belonging to a group of ten'] + ***-li*** > ***emand(i)=o=ḫ(e)-li***.
ḫalz=uḫli [Nuzi, Alalaḫ, Boğazköy] 'Bürgermeister' ['Lord Mayor'] ('derjenige, der berufsmäßig mit den zum (Militär-)Bezirk Gehörigen befaßt ist' ['someone who has a professional interest in those who belong to the (military) district'], cf. G. Wilhelm, *SMEA 29 (1992)*, 239 ff. - ***zil=ikk=uḫli*** 'Zeuge' ['witness'].
ambann=uḫli 'someone who is profesionally engaged in burning firewood', ***ambane*** 'Feuerholz' ['firewood'], root ***am-*** 'verbrennen' ['to burn'].
mardad=uḫuli 'Teppichknüpfer' ['carpet-maker']. Th. Richter (*AoF 32 (2005)*, 39 ff.) takes Hurrian etymology into consideration: analysis {*mardad(i)=o=ḫ(e)=o/u=li*}.

mašk=uḫuli [Alalaḫ] 'Lederarbeiter' ['tanner'], (Akkadian ***mašku*** 'Haut' ['hide, skin, fell, pelt']).

Compare Linear A ***qa-ki-se ̣ nu-ti*** or ***za-ki-se ̣ nu-ti*** (KT Zf 1) or ***qa-ki-se-nu-ti*** or ***za-ki-se-nu-ti*** (KT Zf 1) from Crete (see the Chapter on *inscriptions on metal objects*).

M. Pope - J. Raison (Linear A: changing perspectives, in: Y. Duhoux (ed.), *Études minoennes I*, BCILL 14, 20) presumed in the sequences ***qa-ku-re*** (HT Wc 3017a.1-2) and ***qe-ku-re*** (HT 20.2-3) from Hagia Triada an interlocking pattern of values. There are indeed examples of ***a/e*** alternations in Hurrian as, for instance, in the variants ***talme / talame / telame*** 'great' and ***tag- / teg-*** 'beautiful', but a seeming correspondence between ***qa-ku-re*** and ***qe-ku-re*** can also be accidental. The analysed structure of tablet HT 20 is as follows:

HT 20.1:	*pa-ro-su* ,		
HT 20.1-2:	*ku-ma-96*		E
HT 20.2-3:	*qe-ku-re* , *di*		JGF
HT 20.4:	*sa-re-96*		F
HT 20.4-5:		TELA	E
HT 20.5:		*87+ku*	J

Linear A ***qe-ku-re*** is actually equivalent to the Hurrian personal name ***ᶠḪikulla*** (wr. *ᶠḪi-gu-la, ᶠḪi-gu-ul-la*) name of three women at Mari, analysis {*ḫe/ig=o=lla*}, typology 1.3.1.1.2.1, lexicon *ḫig-*, cf. Th. Richter (*VHN*, 134, 413). He assumes that ***Ḫekaịa*** (wr. *Ḫé-qa-a-a*) at Nuzi (cf. I.J. Gelb, *NPN*, 59) and ***Ḫi-ku*** at Nuzi (see *AAN I*, 58, *SANTAG 4*, 261) contain the same root ***ḫeg-/ḫig-***. Unfortunately the meaning of the verbal root ***ḫeg-/ḫig-*** is not yet known. Linear A ***qe-ku-re*** can be analysed as {*ḫe/ig=o=lle*}, consisting of the verbal root ***ḫeg-/ḫig-*** + the marker of the *imperative* ***-o/u-*** + the *optional allomorphic* enclitic personal pronoun 3rd person plural ***-lle/-lli***, replacing the regular form ***-lla*** (them), indicating the object of the transitive verb. This *imperative* is graphically identical with the *indicative* paradigm, cf. Th. Richter, *VHN*, 593: sub 1.3.1.1: *names with transitive imperative in* {*o*}; *VHN*, 594, sub 1.3.1.1.2.1: *normal forms*; *VHN*, 596, sub 1.3.1.1.2.2: *with optional allomorphic forms*.

Linear A]***-ta-pi*** , (AK 1a.1) from Arkhanes is the first sequence in the top left corner of tablet AK 1 (= HM 1668+1669+fr.) from Arkhanes. The sequence is followed by a word divider (,) and ***qa***[that probably is the first syllabic sign of the next sequence. I shall first discuss the possibility that the sequence]***-ta-pi*** is complete, subsequently that a sign might be missing at the beginning.

a) Since]***-ta-pi*** is the first entry of the text, it is not easy to determine whether we are dealing with a proper name, in particular a personal name as e.g. ***mi-ki-sa-ne***[(AK 1a.6), or e.g. a noun. If the form is complete, one may refer to two feasible Hurrian roots:

1) ***tab/w-*** I 'to pour out metal' or 'to melt metal'. Compare for '(Metall) gießen': E. Neu, *Das Hurritische*: *eine altorientalische Sprache in neuem Licht*, Akademie der Wissenschaften und der Literatur Mainz, 1988/3, 27[83]. He also assumes (*ibidem*, 36) an original spirant second consonant following the labial stop of the root ***tab-***, cf. Th. Richter's ***tapš-*** II 'to pour' (*BGH*, 2012, 443: Aus der Bilingue heraus deutbare Wurzel für 'gießen'), which may well suggest a possible relation with Linear A]***ta-pi-si-di*** (HT 4.3), see *supra*.

M. Salvini - I. Wegner: *Die mythologischen Texte*, Corpus der hurritischen Sprachdenkmäler. I. Abteilung: Die Texte aus Boğazköy, Band I/6, Rome 2004, 182; I. Wegner, *Einführung in die hurritische Sprache*, Wiesbaden 2007[2], 283. Compare for '(Metall) schmelzen': E. Neu, *Das hurritische Epos der Freilassung. I: Untersuchungen zu einem hurritisch-hethitischen Textensemble aus Ḫattuša* (Studien zu den Boğazköy Texten 32), Wiesbaden 1996, 144. See Th. Richter, *BGH*, 2012, 438-440, s.v. ***tab/w-*** I.

If **]-*ta-pi*** is a lexical term, it may be the *imperative* {*tab=i*} 'cast (metal) !'. If **]-*ta-pi*** is a personal name, the meaning is 'Cast (the child) (oh *numen*) !'.

2) A second feasible Hurrian root is ***tapp-*** 'to strengthen', 'to fortify (a town)', cf. Th. Richter, *BGH*, 2012, 440, s.v. ***tapp-*** [Boğazköy (?); Nuzi (?); Qaṭna; PN] '(Stadt) befestigen, verstärken', corresponds with Akkadian *dunnunu.* Among several references he mentions at Boğazköy ***ta-ap-pi*** and at Nuzi ***tap-pi-pi***.

b) If the placing of the fragment with **]-*ta-pi*** on the photograph by L. Godart - J.-P. Olivier (*GORILA 3*) is correct, there may well be space for one syllabic sign preceding the sequence on a missing piece left of the fragment. If that sign is ***a***], which is just a hypothesis, the sequence would offer *****a*]-*ta-pi*** that can be identified with the Hurrian Warrior God ***Aštabi***, since according to the orthographic conventions of Linear A an B ***š*** before (dental or other) occlusive is not expressed in consonant clusters. See for ***Aštabi*** e.g. E. Laroche, *GLH*, 61: "*Aštabi.* Dieu guerrier, identifié à Ninurta." In Akkadian texts the theonym is written as *ᵈAš-ta-bi-nu* (CT XXV 11 II 31), in Hittite texts as *ᵈAštabiš* (nom.), *ᵈAštabin* (acc.), *ᵈAš-ta-(a)-bi, ᵈAš-ta-(a)-wi* (abs.), in hieroglyphic texts as ***ᵈAštabi***, in Hurrian texts at Ugarit as ***Aštb*** (abs.), CTA 166, 29, 31; cf. Hrozný, *ArchOr. 4*, 123; ***Aštb-d*** (directive), *Ugar. V*, 519 ff. The quadriligual RS 137 IV b 16 = *Ugar. V*, 249, offers: *Aš-ta-bi-*[*i*] = Ugaritic *Aštaru*. The Warrior God ***Aštabi*** has, of course, nothing to do with the personal name ***ᶠAš-du(-)*** 'Woman'. See for the onomastic element ***Aš-ta-bi(-)*** in Hurrian names ***Aštabi-šarra*** '*Aštabi* (is) as the King of Gods' at Alalaḫ (***šarra*** with *essive* in ***-a***): A. Draffkorn, *HHA*, 25): (1) **Aš-ta-bi*-LUGAL, son of *Ammi-eda,* *270 2. (2) **Aš-ta-bi*-LUGAL-*ra*, son of *I-lu-ra,* *374 3. (3) *Aš-ta-bi*-LUGAL, son of *Ku*-[ ], 171. Cf. also D.J. Wiseman, *The Alalaḫ tablets*, 130; and for Boğazköy: E. Laroche, *NH*, 46, nº 178: ***Aštabi-šarri,*** auteur de rituel: *ᵐA-aš-ta-bi*-LUGAL (abs.), XXX 51 I 17 = KBo XIV 68 I 14.

Linear A ***qa***[(AK 1a.1) is the first syllabic sign of the second sequence of this tablet from Arkhanes. It follows]***ta-pi*** and a word divider (,).

I have considerable doubt that the tiny fragment with the syllabic sign]***ki***, assigned to the right top corner of AK 1a.1 by *GORILA 3* and J. Raison - M. Pope (1994), 33, belongs to that tablet. J. Raison - M.Pope remark: "Disposition des fragments non entièrement sûr; nombre de lignes incertain." It is also important to realize that all fragments that have been assigned to AK 1 by *GORILA 3* do not touch each other and that the tablets AK 1, AK 2 and AK 3 have been inscribed by the same scribe according to L. Godart and J.-P. Olivier (cf. Ἀ. Λεμπέση, J.-P. Olivier, L. Godart, *AE 1974*, 164-165, and *GORILA 5*, 83): Scribe *1 ARKH.* For that reason I have proposed the following conjecture in *Minoan Linear A*, Vol. II, Part I: *Corpus of transliterated Linear A texts*, 15: "If the little fragment in the left top corner of AK 1b (with the syllabic sign ***a***[) could be joined to the top left of AK 3a, the heading of AK 3a.1 would provide ***a***]***-ka-ne*** followed by the grain ideogram.

According to Linear A and B orthographic conventions ***-r-*** before occlusive is not expressed in consonant clusters. A final consonant is not expressed either.

The Linear A join ***a*]-*ka-ne*** GRA [ ]D OLIVA 3D VINb 2[(AK 3a+1b.1-2) is first entry of the tablet, offers the exact place-name of the Minoan Villa of ***Arkhanes*** and is followed by the 'grain' ideogram and ideograms of other agricultural commodities. This is not only a close parallel to the position of the toponym ***ka-pa***, often at the beginning of tablets from Hagia Triada, but also reminds us of the fact that in Linear B many *Knossos tablets* begin with ***ko-no-so*** and many *Pylos tablets* with ***pu-ro/lo***, indicating the place of residence of the scribe and the place where goods and persons were registered.

The Linear A toponym ***a*]-*ka-ne*** can actually be analysed as {*ar=ḫane/i*} 'Give a child (oh God(s)) !'. Arkhanes is situated in the foothills of Mount Ioukhtas and may have been used as a starting point for those who wished to visit the Peak Sanctuary of Ioukhtas and pray.

We know that pious worshippers or priests brought 'libation tables' with incised prayers to the Peak Sanctuaries. Some 'libation formulas' from Ioukhtas contain ***u-na-ka-na-si*** (IO Za 2.1; IO Za 9) as well as ***u-na-ru-ka-***[(IO Za 16.b) that can be completed to ***u-na-ru-ka-***[***na-si***. Linear A ***u-na-ka-na-si*** can be interpreted as {*un=a-ḫ(ḫ)an(i)=a=šše/i*} 'come offspring, childhood, childbirth', and ***u-na-ru-ka-***[***na-si*** as {*un=al=u-ḫ(ḫ)an(i)=a=šše/i*} or {*un=ar=u-ḫ(ḫ)an(i)=a=šše/i*} 'bring offspring, childhood, childbirth (oh God(s) !' (***un=a-*** is *intransitive* 'to come'; ***un=al=u-*** or ***un=ar=u-*** *transitive* 'to bring', with the root-extensions ***-al-*** and ***-ar-***), see *Chapter 11: 'Religious' Linear A inscriptions.*

Consequently, if fragment ***a-***] (AK 1b.1) is joined to AK 3a.1, we should no longer read]***<u>ki</u>*** at the end of AK 1a.1, but]***<u>ki</u>*** should be placed at the end of AK 3b.1, so that we should read the sequence [***ki-***]***pi-163a*** GRA 1 (AK 3b.1-2+AK 1a.1)." If sign ***163a*** (consisting of 3 parallel curved lines) is a graphic variant of ***58*** (consisting of 2 parallel curved lines) = ***ra_2*** = ***ria/lia***, [***Ki-***]***pi-ria*** would represent a perfect Hurrian personal name, see *supra*.

Since the right side of tablet AK 1a from Arkhanes is missing, sign **]*-ne*** (first entry of AK 1a.4), which is followed by **2** units and the fraction J, can be regarded as the last syllable of a sequence that started at the end of the preceding line of the missing right side of the text. It may be the Hurrian suffix ***-ne*** of the so-called singular definite article or the *optional allomorphic* enclitic personal pronoun 3rd person singular ***-nne/-nni*** (instead of ***-nna***).

Linear A] [[***-na*** <u>9</u>]] (AK 1b.4) is probably a palimpsest inscription occurring on the largest fragment in the bottom right corner of AK 1b from Arkhanes. It is interesting that this piece of text shows sign ***-na***, followed by 8 or 9 units, probably as last syllable of a sequence, because the fragment is broken off at its left side. Since ***-na*** may well be the Hurrian suffix of the so-called plural "definite article" and therefore an indicator of a plural form, one may conclude that this is entirely in accordance with the following number 8 or 9. Cf. e.g. Linear A]***<u>a-di</u>-na*** 5 (KH 59.3) = Hurrian ***ašdina*** 'the women 5', with suffix ***-na*** (plural definite article), cf. ***ašde*** 'woman', ***ašdi=ne*** 'the woman', cf. Th. Richter, *BGH*, 59-61, s.v. ***ašte/i***. But Linear A ***-na*** can also represent a 'one-word' personal name ending with the enclitic personal pronoun 3rd person singular ***-nna***, but there are other possibilities as well, e.g. a personal name with ***-mi-na*** 'twin' as second onomastic element, cf. Linear A ***a-du-|ku-mi-na*** (ZA 10a.3-4) and ***a-ku-|mi-na*** (ZA 10a.1-2) from Kato Zakro.

Coming to the close of this chapter the reader may have noticed that I have started to discuss some fragmentary Linear A texts. The reason is that I have started to transform the *Indices* to a *Glossary of Minoan Linear A*, in which every inscription, however fragmentary and tiny, will eventually be discussed. The purpose is that this *Glossary of Minoan Linear A* will be comparable with A. Morpurgo's *Mycenaean Graecitatis Lexicon*, Incunabula Graeca III, Rome 1963, in which all Linear B inscriptions, found upto 1963, are assembled.

The decipherment of Linear A has by now reached a stage, that there can no longer be any doubt that the Minoan vernacular written with Linear A is a Hurrian dialect and cannot be anything else. The Linear A *Indices* in this revised and extended edition of *The Decipherment of Minoan Linear A*, Volume I: *Hurrians and Hurrian in Minoan Crete*, Parts III - VI, Amsterdam 2022, are now called *Indices and glossaries*, and will possibly also be published as E-book. Therefore the *lemmata* of the Linear A *indices and glossaries* are more elaborate than they would have been, if they had only been references to the main text of Volume I. The systematic incorporation into the *Glossary* of all entries in all Linear A texts published in the *Corpus of transliterated Linear A texts* has started with the Linear A texts from Arkhanes, which are the first of the *Corpus*.

Reading ***do-161-se* | *de-162*** TAL 6 (AK 2.3-4) at Arkhanes is to be preferred to ***do-161-se*|*-de-162-85*** 6. According to *GORILA*: ***-161-*** over [[ ]]; ***-162-*** over [[ ]]. Raison-Pope: |***de-79-85***. In my view ***162*** may be a variant of ***93*** = ***du*** (or of ***79***). I prefer identification of ***85*** with the ideogram TAL(entum), since the position of TAL is in accordance with the following number 6. Linear A ***a-si-da-to*|*-i*** 22 (AK 2.2-3) and ***a-su-pu-wa*** 4 (AK 2.5-6) may be Hurrian personal names, but ***a-su-pu-wa***, if analysed as {*azzu=(i)ff=u=wa*}, may also mean 'for my wife' (see *supra*). Due to the unknown phonetic values of signs ***161*** and ***79***, interpretation of Linear A ***do-161-se*| *de-du*** or ***de-79*** (AK 2.3) as ***do-ḫo-še* | *de-du*** or ***de-79*** may tentatively be equated with the Hurrian theonym **ᴰ*Tuḫuši*** (wr. ᴰ*Tu-(u-)ḫu-(u)-ši-*) [Boğ.] (cf. E. Laroche, *GLH*, 270; Van Gessel, 1998/1, 525f.) or Hurrian ***tuḫulzi*** [Boğ] and loan-word into Hittite ***tuḫulzi(-)*** and ***tuḫalzi(-)***{*tuḫ=u=lzi*} com./ntr. 'sacrificial rite, term, tool' (cf. Th. Richter, *B*, 465-466) and ***de-du*** may be interpreted as Old Hurrian *imperative* ***tid=u*** 'share out (6 talents) !' from ***tid-*** I [Boğ.] 'to share out' (cf. Th. Richter, *BGH*, 464). If ***de-79*** is, for instance, ***de-ḫu***, the *imperative* ***teḫ=u*** may mean 'let grow !' from ***teḫ-*** I [Mit.; PN] 'wachsen, gedeihen lassen' (cf. Th. Richter, *BGH*, 457-458).

Linear A ***ru-mi-***[ ] vestigia (AK 2.6) is the last incomplete entry on this tablet from Arkhanes. Although the tablet is broken into four pieces, it is almost complete. Only a small part of the lower right corner (containing this entry) is missing. The end of the line is written over a palimpsest [[ ]]. According to Godart and Olivier AK 2 was written by the same scribe as AK 1 (cf. Ἀ. Λεμπέση, J.-P. Olivier, L. Godart, *AE 1974*, 164-165). *GORILA 5*, 83: Scribe *1 ARKH*. The incomplete sequence ***ru-mi-***[may be personal name. Since it begins with ***ru-*** or ***lu-***, it may not be Hurrian, but an adstrate name or Pre-Hurrian. In a cuneiform text one might have thought of Sumerogram LÙ 'man' ***mi-***[***na*** 'twin', but that would be very exceptional in Linear A, especially because Linear A has an ideogram VIR and the Hurrian lexemes ***da-ḫi*** (PH 3b.1) ***d/taḫi*** and ***d/ture*** 'man'

Tablet AK 3 from Arkhanes is incomplete and consists of three fragments [see also *GORILA 5*, 83: Scribe *1 ARKH* (?)]. The first entry ***a***]***-ka-ne***, GRA[ ] D OLIVA 3 D VIN*b* 2[2 [[*136* 2 vest.]] [(AK 3a.1-3), the toponym ***Arkhanes***, has been discussed extensively.

The first personal name after ***a*]-*ka-ne*** (AK 3a.1) is **]|*ki-nu*** or]|***-ki-nu*** GRA 13[ ][(AK 3a.4) at the beginning of line 4 of this tablet. If it is complete, it may be identified with the Hurrian personal name ***Kinnu*** (wr. *ki-in-nu, ki-in-nu-ú*) at Šušarrā and Šubat-Enlil, analysis {*kinn=o*}, typology 1.3.1.1.1, lexicon *kinn-*, cf. Th. Richter, *VHN*, 162.

Th. Richter (*VHN*, 437), mentions, s.v. ***kin-/kinn-***, that in Hurrian several words are attested beginning with ***ke/in°***. Most of them are, however, lexically and semantically not clear, cf. *BGH*, 207. Since single writing with ***-n-*** and double writing with ***-nn-*** are both attested in names of the same persons at Nuzi, there is no distinction between ***kin-*** and ***kinn-***. Th. Richter mentions: (a) {***kin-***}: *ᶠKinam-turi* (Ašnakkum); *Kinija* (Mari); *Kinip-šarri* (Mari); *Kinum-atal* (Mari). (b) {***kinn-***}: *Kinnija* (Qaṭṭarā); *Kinikku* (Mari); *Kinnu* (Šubat-Enlil; Šušarrā).

If Linear A]|***-ki-nu*** GRA 13[ ][(AK 3a.4) is not complete, it may offer the last two syllabic signs of a Hurrian personal name ending in ***-kinu***, e.g. ***Araš-kenu*** (wr. *A-ra-aš-ge-nu*), a Hurrian personal name attested at Nuzi, see P.M. Purves, *NPN*, 225, s.v. ***ken***, ***-kenu***: Hurrian. Possibly phonetic and dialectal variant of ***kin***. Cf. ***kenn***. Cf. also at Nuzi ***ᶠAzze-kena*** (wr. *ᶠAz-ze-ge-na*), cf. ***Ašta-kina***, see Purves, *ibidem*. The missing first element of the personal name, of which |***-ki-nu*** may be the second element, was in that case probably written at the end of the preceding line in a missing part of the text.

Linear A [ ]***-te*** 2 (AK 3a.5) follows]|***-ki-nu*** GRA 13[ ][(AK 3a.4) and is probably the second onomastic element of a personal name. It may represent either the theophorous element ***-Te***, hypocoristic of ***-Tešub***, in a sentence name or the *optional allomorphic* enclitic personal pronoun 1st person singular ***-tte/-tti*** (instead of normal ***-tta***) in a verbal 'one-word' name, indicating the object of a transitive or the subject of an intransitive verb.

Linear A **]-*ku*** 3 [(AK 3a.6) is the last entry on the *a*-side of this fragmentary tablet from Arkhanes. It is probably the last syllable of a name ending in ***-ku*** in a list of personal names.

According to P.M. Purves (*NPN*, 228) there are many Hurrian personal names at Nuzi with a formative ***-ku***: *Ammaku, Ellaku, Etaku?, Ḫaniku, Ḫinziku, Inniku, Išaku?, Miniku, Niziku, Pazaku, Piriku, Taiku, Tarpaku?, Tiriku, Unuku, Wiriku, Wunnuku, Wurruku*; and with a formative ***-kku*** (according to P.M. Purves apparently with assimilation by ***k*** of an immediately preceding consonant): *ᶠAttakku?, Naikku, Paikku, Watikku.*

For now it is interesting to mention some attestations in the Linear A texts: e.g. ***ku-ru-ku*** (HT 87.4), a Linear A personal name that may well be identified with the Nuzi personal name ***Kuruzku*** (wr. *Ku-ru-uz-ku*), which is probably Hurrian, built on the root ***kur-***, cf. I.J. Gelb, *NPN*, 92, s.v. ***Kuruzku*** (wr. *Ku-ru-uz-ku*) son of *Gur-mi-še-en-ni*, HSS IX 27: 24, 33, and P.M. Purves, *NPN*, 230, s.v. ***kur*** and ***kuruzku***. According to the Linear A and B orthographic conventions ***-z*** preceding an occlusive is not expressed in consonant clusters.

Another possibility is ***ti-ti-ku*** (HT 35.1; ZA Zb 3.2) occurring twice in Linear A and on two different sites, Hagia Triada and Epano Zakro, cf. also ***ti-ti-ku-ni*** (HT 96a.1). These names have been discussed extensively.

Another is ***ka-ku*** (HT 62.2) that may be identified with the Hurrian personal names from Nuzi ***Qa-ak-ku***, ***Ka-an-ku***, ***Qa-an-ku***, cf. P.M. Purves, *NPN*, 222, s.v. ***kakk***. But Hurrian ***kaš=ku*** 'a part of land held in feudal tenure' is also possible, cf. Th. Richter, *BGH*, 193.

Another is ***da-<u>ku</u>***, Linear A inscription on a bronze double axe, bought by Evans at Kritsa near Lato, but reported to be from Selakonos (or rather Selakanos). If complete, it may be analysed as *{d/tag=o/u=n(na)}* identified as the Hurrian hypocoristic name from Alalaḫ ***Tagu-n*** *(Ta-ku-un)* with the abbreviated enclitic personal pronoun 3rd person sing. ***-n*** instead of ***-nna*** (phonologically probably */Dagu-n/*) on AT 189: 59, cf. D.J. Wiseman, *AT,* 149; cf. A. Draffkorn, *HHA*, 54 and 106.

Tablet AK 4 from Arkhanes consists of two fragments. Thanks to the join with the smaller fragment, one may infer that there is space for one syllabic sign preceding]***-ta-re*** 5 ***a-***[(AK 4a.2). Considering the repertoire of complete Linear A sequences containing ***-ta-re*** there are several options for completion:

1) ***a***]***-ta-re***, cf. ***a-ta-re*** (ZA 8.1), personal name from Zakros. Two interpretations as Hurrian names are possible, because neither ***-n-*** nor ***-s-*** preceding a dental in consonant clusters are expressed in Linear A. So both Hurrian ***antare*** and ***aštare*** are feasible options. It seems very difficult to establish the degree of voicing of the dentals in these consonant clusters. Since voicing was not phonemic in Hurrian, the Hurrian scribes were probably not even aware of using allophonic variants. The phonological representation of the Hurrian anthroponym ***Aštari*** (wr. *Aš-ta-ri*), attested at Nuzi as son of *Pa-pa-an-te* (HSS IX 13:26), may well be ***/aštare/*** in accordance with Linear A ***a-ta-re***. Compare at Nuzi ***Aštar-teįa*** (wr. *Aš-tar-te-ia, Aš-tar-te-e-a, Aš-tar-te-e*), ***Aštar(i)-tešub*** (wr. *Aš-tar-te-šup, Aš-ta-ri-te-šu-up, A-aš-ta-ri-te-šup, Aš-ta-ri-te-šup*), ***Aštar-tilla*** (wr. *Aš-tar-til-la*), see I.J. Gelb, *NPN*, 37. P.M. Purves, *NPN*, 206, s.v. *Aštar, Aštar-, Aštari, Aštari-*.

Aštari has certainly nothing to do with Hurrian ***ašta***, ***ašte***, ***ašti***, ***aštu*** 'woman' and the onomastic elements ***ašta-***, ***ašte-***, ***ašti-***, ***aštu-*** in Hurrian feminine personal names as attestation of ***Aštari*** as son of *Pa-pa-an-te* at Nuzi proves as well as the combination with ***-tešub***, ***-teįa***, ***-tilla*** in other masculine personal names. P.M. Purves (*NPN*, 206, s.v. *Aštar, Aštari, Aštar-, Aštari-*) tells that Hurrian *Aštar, Aštari* has nothing to do with *Ištar* and can according to I.J. Gelb possibly be explained by dissimilation: *aštar* < *artar*.

Th. Richter (*BGH*, 58) writes that the transitive verbal root ***ašt-*** I [Boğ.] means 'entsprechen lassen' ['to let agree / correspond with, to let respond / answer / conform to'] and the intransitive root 'entsprechen' ['to agree / correspond with, to respond / answer / conform to'] (De Martino - Giorgieri, 2007a, 142, 2008, 132). According to G. Wilhelm (1991b, 164[34]) ***ašt-*** may be a denominalisation of ***ašte-***, ***ašti-***. According to De Martino - Giorgieri, 2007a, 128[11]) ***ašt-*** should be distinguished from ***ašte-***, ***ašti-***. The meaning of *iterative / frequentative* ***ašt=ar-*** [PN] is 'immer wieder entsprechen lassen' ['to let agree, correspond with again and again, to let respond, answer, conform to again and again'], cf. De Martino - Giorgieri, 2007a, 143f, 2008, 133. See for the *factitive / iterative* root-extension ***-ar-*** I. Wegner, *Einführung*, 88. According to Th. Richter (*BGH*, 58) the anthroponym ***Aštari*** is either a single verbal form without theophorous element [→ see ***ašt=ar-***] or a nominalized form 'Der Entsprechende' ['The (cor)responding one'], 'Die Entsprechung' ['The agreement, correspondence'].

The scribe no doubt knew, whether he wrote the name of ***Aštari / Aštare*** or of ***Attari / Attare***, but we cannot be sure, since Linear A orthographic conventions offer more than one possibility.

Thanks to Th. Richter's *Vorarbeiten zu einem hurritischen Namenbuch*, Erster Teil, Wiesbaden 2016, 89, the Hurrian personal name ****Attari/e*** can now be confirmed on the basis of ***Attara*** (wr. *a-at-ta-ra*), analysis {*attar(i)=a*[E.]}, typology 3.2.1, lexicon *attari* (→ *att-*) at Qaṭṭara (Tall ar-Rimaḫ) and at Šubat-Enlil / Šeḫna (Tall Leilān), and on the basis of ***Attaru*** (wr. *at-ta-ru*), analysis {*attar(i)=u*[N.]}, typology 3.1, lexicon *attari* (→ *att-*) at Šušarrā (Tall Shemshara); -***a***[E.] refers to the *essive* case-ending in -***a***; -***u***[N.] refers to the Akkadian(izing) *nominative* case-ending in -***u***. Th. Richter assumes (*VHN*, 386, s.v. ***att-*** {*att-*}) that a noun ***attari*** {*att=a=ri*} can be inferred on the basis of *(a-)at-ta-ra/u* and similar personal names. Although identification of Linear A ***a-ta-re*** (ZA 8.1) with Hurrian ***Aštari*** is certainly possible (compare, for instance, Linear A and B ***pa-i-to*** that reflects most likely the name of the Palace of *Phaistos*; see for a Hurrian etymology of Linear A ***pa-i-to*** *sub voce*), we may now conclude that Linear A ***a-ta-re*** (ZA 8.1) is an exact equivalent to the Hurrian personal name ***Attari / Attare***.

2) ***da*]*-ta-re***, cf. ***da-ta-re*** (HT 88.6), after ***sa-ma-ro*** in a list of personal names.

It is likely that Linear A ***da-ta-re*** and ***da-ta-ra*** contain the verbal root ***tad-/tatt-*** 'to love', which is frequent in personal names. If ***a-si-da-to|-i̯*** is a *genitive* (perhaps in the sense of *matronymic*), the *absolutive* may be ****Azzi-datti*** 'The woman is a darling' or ****Azzi-datta*** {*Azzi-datt(i)=a*} 'The woman is like a darling', since ***o/u*** in ***a-si-da-to|-i̯*** is probably due to -***w***- of the *genitive* -***wi***. The Hurrian feminine personal name ***Allai-tatta*** from Nuzi (wr. *ᶠAl-la-i-ta-at-ta*), phonologically ***/Allai-datta/*** because of single writing of the first dental, is semantically a parallel to ****Azzi-datta***. ***Azzi*** < ***aždi*** 'woman' is semantically close to ***allay*** 'lady'. Other names with the element ***-tatta*** (phonologically ***/datta/***) are the names from Nippur ***Ir-me/mi-ta-at-ta*** and ***Ir-me-ta-ta***, Clay, *PNCP*, 93, to be read ***Erme/i-tatta*** (according to P.M. Purves, *NPN*, 263, s.v. *tatt*), i.e. ****Erwi-tatta***. Cf. also ***Ta-at-ta***, *ibid*., 138, and ***Ta-ad-du*** at Nuzi, as well as ⌈***ta***⌉***-ad-du*** at Boğazköy KUB XXVII 42 obv. 15, 16."

Although the variants ***Ir-me/mi-ta-at-ta*** and ***Ir-me-ta-ta*** from Nippur had made it quite clear that the roots ***tad-*** 'to love' and ***tatt-*** could probably be brought together, my hesitations completely disappeared after publication of Th. Richter's *Vorarbeiten zu einem hurritischen Namenbuch*, Erster Teil, 2016. In *BGH*, 2012, 451, s.v. ***tad-*** [*passim*] he had already casually referred to the variant ***tatt-***, discussed in his Ergänzungen zum hurritischen Wörterbuch, *Altorientalische Forschungen 34 (2007)*, 92[60].

Th. Richter (*VHN*, 533-534), s.v. ***tad- / tatt-***, confirmed that starting from the variant ***ta-at-t*** ***°*** for ***tadubadi*** one may assume that other forms in ***tatt-*** may be connected as well. In accordance with the function of the morpheme-group ***°=o=bade*** one may understand ***tadubadi*** (as well as *ta-at-tu-ba-di*) as 'ungeliebt' ['not loved']. According to I. Wegner (*Einführung*, 59-60 and 137: sub E 'Old Hurrian') the suffix-combination ***-ubad-*** in expressions such as ***naḫḫ=ubad(e)=uš*** 'nicht besiedelt' ['not inhabited'], ***kul=ubad=e*** 'nicht genannt' ['not mentioned'], ***faḫr=ubad=e*** 'ungut' ['not good'] or ***nir=ubad=e*** 'ungut, schlecht' ['not good, bad'] (Ugarit-Vocabulary RS 94-2939, col. V 11', published by B. André-Salvini - M. Salvini, in *SCCNH 9*, 1998, 3 ff. and 14) may be segmented into ***-uw(a)+ade*** and ***-uw(a)*** may reflect the morpheme ***-wa-*** indicating negation. The Tušratta letter also offers abstract forms in ***-ubad-*** without an apparent negative meaning, cf. I. Wegner, Die "genannten" und die "nicht-genannten" Götter in den hethitisch-hurritischen Opferlisten, *Studi micenei ed egeo-anatolici 36 (1995)*, 97 ff..

The variant root ***tatt-*** occurs frequently: ***Tattip-papni*** (wr. *ta-at-ti-ip-pa-ap-ni*), at Nuzi (cf. I.J. Gelb, *NPN*, 150), analysis {*tatt=i=b-fabni*}; ***ᶠTattiri*** (wr. *ᶠta-at-te-ri*), {*tatt=i=ri*} (Ekalte: WVDOG 192, 75: 19). He also refers (in note 789) to a comparable verbal root ***tid-*** 'to attack' that also occurs as ***titt-*** (cf. *BGH*, 464), which may well be significant for the interpretation of Linear A ***ti-ti-ku*** (2 times) and ***ti-ti-ku-ni*** (see *supra*).

Cuneiform ***tatt-*** may well be significant for the orthography of Linear A ***da-ta-re*** and ***da-ta-ra***, of which the second dental is voiceless, whereas in ***da-du-ma-ta*** (HT 95a.1), ***da-du-te*** (HT 34.1), ***da-du-mi-ne*** (KN Zf 31) the second dental is voiced as in ***tad-***.

I. Wegner (*Einführung*, 88) offers s.v. the *factitive* or *iterative* root-extension ***-ar-*** the examples ***tad=ar-*** 'lieben' ['to love'], ***šid=ar-*** 'verfluchen' ['to curse']; cf. also Th. Richter, *BGH*, 451, s.v. ***tad-*** [*passim*] and ***tad=ar-*** 'lieben'. Consequently ***da-ta-re*** (HT 88.5) can be analysed as {*d/tatt=ar=e/i*} and may contain the Hurrian root ***d/tad- / d/tatt-*** 'to love' (frequent in onomastics) + the *factitive* or *iterative* root-extension ***-ar-*** + the *jussive* or *imperative* 2nd person singular in ***-e/i***, cf. I. Wegner, *Einführung*, 103-104 and Table 9: *The order of suffixes of the positive jussive*. Consequently the name can be translated as 'Love again and again !'.

If Linear A ***da-ta-ra*** (HT 6a.1) is likewise explained and analysed as {*d/tatt=ar=a*}, the form would be intransitive and can perhaps be translated as 'Be loving / Be a loving person again and again !' or {*d/tatt(=i)-Alla*} 'Love (the child), oh Lady !'. E. Laroche assumed that ***Tatta*** or ***Dada*** is the most probable etymology of the divine name ***ᵈTatta*** (cf. *NH*, 241). He adds (*NH*, 291): "*ᵈTatta* ou *Datta*: nom divin auparavant déduit du seul nom propre *Arma-*ᵈU = *Arma-Datta*. Il est maintenant attesté: *ᵈTattas*, Bo 3254 Ro 14 = MIO 8, 205. Mais ce texte unique ne dit pas que *Tatta* est un dieu de l'orage." If Linear A ***ta-ta*** (KH 7a.3) indeed represents the divine Hurrian name ***ᵈTatta***, it may well be the basis of Linear A ***da-ta-ra*** (HT 6a.1) 'With ***ᴰTatta/Datta***' (with the comitative suffix ***-ra***), marking the month in which tablet HT 6 was written and the described transactions took place.

Th. Richter mentions (*VHN*, 533) in his discussion of the *month-name* ? and personal name ***ta-da-ra*** (R. Pruzsinszky 2003/1, 240[152]) that it remains uncertain, how we must understand the intransitive forms. He remarks (*Ibidem*, note 788) that ***tá-da-ar-ri***, at Emar (Pruzsinszky 2003/2, 767) and ***ta-da-ra*** may only be harmonized on the assumption of a participle ****tadari*** {*tad=a=ri*}, cf. ***tiwarri*** for a comparable formation.

3) ***ta₂]-ta-re***, cf. ***ta₂-ta-re*** 1 (PK 1.2) that is followed by ***ta₂-ti-te*** 1 (PK 1.3).

If Linear A ***ta₂-ta-re*** is to be interpreted as the Hurrian personal name ***Ti=am-tale***, the meaning may be (*imperative*) 'Make / Let (the child) speak, oh wood / tree !'. If Linear A ***ta₂-ta-re*** is to be interpreted as the personal name ***Ti(j)=a-tale***, the meaning may be (*indicative*) 'The tree / wood speaks, says words' or perhaps 'He/She (the child) speaks / says words, oh wood / tree !'. Th. Richter (*VHN*, 534-535) mentions that the verbal root ***te-/ti-/ tiw-*** means 'to speak, to pronounce names'. Th. Richter (*VHN*, 527) mentions, that the onomastic element ***tali*** may well have the meaning 'Holz, Baum' ['wood, tree'] or be a sacrificial term (see *BGH*, 431). He mentions (*VHN*, 59, 527) the personal name ***Ani[š(?)]-tali*** (wr. *a-ni-*[...]*-ta-li*) from Mari, analysis {*an=i*[*=ž*]*-tali*}, lexicon *an-*, *tali*, typology 1.3.2.2, translation 'Der Baum(?) möge erfreuen' ['The tree may delight, make happy'].

However, if Linear A ***ta₂-ta-re*** is to be interpreted as the Hurrian personal name ***Ti=am-tare***, the meaning may be (*imperative*) 'Make / Let (the child) speak, oh fire / oh power !'.

If Linear A ***ta₂-ta-re*** is to be interpreted as the personal name ***Ti(j)=a-tare***, the meaning may be (*indicative*) 'The fire / power speaks' or perhaps 'He/She (the child) speaks / says words, oh fire / power !'. I have no doubt that the scribe of tablet PK 1 has deliberately combined the personal names ***ta₂-ta-re*** 1 (PK 1a.2) and ***ta₂-ti-te*** 1 (PK 1a.3) in his list of personal names.

On a damaged tablet from Arkhanes we read ***de-su-***[.]***-*** or possibly ***de-su-ke*** (AK 4a.3). *GORILA 3* reads: ***de-su-***[, peut-être ***de-su-109-***; J. Raison - M. Pope (1994): ***de-su-ke-***. Due to considerable damage to the right side of this tablet from Arkhanes, identification of the last sign(s) of line 3 is uncertain. It is also uncertain whether ***de-su-***[.]***-*** should or should not be connected with ***154-te*** 5 at the beginning of the next line, so that we should read ***de-su-***[.]***-|154-te*** 5 (AK 4a.3-4). Sign ***154*** is a very rare sign anyway in Linear A.

If the reading ***de-su-ke-*** is correct and complete, and in that case probably followed by a number of units as is the case with the other sequences on this tablet, reading of a Hurrian personal name with ***-uke/-uki*** or ***-ukki*** as its second element would be feasible, cf. e.g. at Nuzi ***Ḫaši-úki*** (wr. *Ḫa-ši-ú-ki*), ***Kulip-uki*** (wr. *Ku-ú-li-pu-ki*), ***Tai-uki*** (wr. *Ta-a-a-ú-ki, Ta-i-ú-ki, Ta-a-ú-ki, Ta-ú-ki, Ta-a-a-ú-ge, Da-a-ú-ki, Da-ú-ki, Ta-a-i-ú-ki, Ta-ù-ki, Ta-a-a-ù-ki*), ***Uke*** (wr. *Ú-ge, Ú-ge-e*), cf. P.M. Purves, *NPN*, 270-271, s.v. ***uk***, ***-uki***; and ***Ari-ukki*** (wr. *A-ri-ú-uk-ki*), cf. Purves, *NPN*, 271.

However, since according to Linear A and B orthographic conventions ***-r-*** preceding an occlusive is not expressed in consonant clusters, an interpretation as ***Dešurḫe < Teš-urḫe*** should *a priori* not be excluded, although a Linear A orthography of ****Te-su-qe*** instead of ***de-su-ke*** would have been expected and more in line with Linear A ***u-qe-ti*** (PL Zf 1). If ***de-su-ke*** is, however, ***Dešurḫe***, we may be dealing with a rare form of metathesis, since the initial dental seems to have become voiced and the ***-ḫ-*** in ***-urḫe*** that is supposed to be voiced (cf. alphabetic cuneiform ***urġtṯb*** = ***Urḫi-tešub*** at Ugarit), seems to have become voiceless. At Nuzi ***Teš-urḫe*** (wr. *Te-eš-ur-ḫe*) and ***Tieš-urḫe*** (wr. *Ti-e-eš-ur-ḫé, Ti-e-eš-ur-ḫe, Ti-eš-ur-ḫé, Ti-šu-ur-ḫé, Ti-i-e-eš-ur-ḫé, Ti-a-aš-ur-ḫé*) are attested.

Such an interpretation would be attractive, because the forms with ***-urḫe*** are much more frequent than those with ***-uke/-uki*** or ***-ukki*** in Hurrian personal names. Basically ***Teš-urḫe*** is the same name (written in reverse order) as ***Urḫi-tešup*** (wr. *Ur-ḫi-te-šup*) 'True is Tešub', 16 times attested at Nuzi, cf. I.J. Gelb, *NPN*, 166-167 and P.M. Purves, *NPN*, 273. ***Urḫi-Tešub*** is also the Hurrian birth-name of the Hittite king ***Muršiliš III***, son of the famous Hittite emperor ***Muwatalli*** who fought the battle of Qadeš with the Egyptian king ***Rameses II***. He was dethroned by his uncle, Muwatalli's brother, general ***Ḫattušiliš III***. The name ***Urḫi-Tešub*** is attested at Boğazköy (KBo I 14 Vo 15; KBo IV 12 Ro 20, 24 = Ḫatt. 42; KBo IV 14 I 54; Ḫatt. III 41, 74, IV 19,24, 30; KUB III 22, 9; XVI 32, 14, 27, 29; XXI 14, 5, 8; 37, 7, 14, 16, 18; XXIII 1 II 21, 22; XXVI 58, 5 a; 70, 2; XXXI 23 Vo; KBo VII 73 Vo 8; at Ugarit RS 17.346, 7, 10 = PRU IV 176; in hieroglyphic Hittite *Ur-ḫí-Tešub*[ba], SBo I 43-44), cf. E. Laroche, *NH*, 198-199, N° 1443.

The hypocoristic form of this name, ***Urḫi-te*** (wr. *Ur-ḫi-te*), is also attested at Nuzi, and probably also in Linear A ***u-qe-ti*** (PL Zf 1), read by all editors as second sequence of the Linear A inscription on a silver hairpin from Tholos A at Platanos in the Messara-valley, if the inscription is read from right to left.

If the interpretation of Linear A ***de-su-<u>ke</u>-*** as ****Deš-urḫe*** < ***Teš-urḫe*** is correct, the form shows that at least some scribes took the liberty of some overlap in the usage of some consonants within the script of Linear A. It is feasible that at least some Linear A scribes used the ***k-*** signs also for the voiced velar fricatives or this velar fricative may have sounded voiceless to them because it was part of a consonant cluster. Voicing of ***Deš-*** in ****Deš-urḫe***, if its identification is right, is certainly exceptional as compared to the normal voicelessness of the dental in the Linear A personal names with onomastic elements derived from the theonym ***Tešub***, but the exception may be explained by analogy, cf. alphabetic cuneiform ***agdṯb*** = ***Agi-tešub***, and ***akdṯb*** = ***Akku-tešub***.

The spelling of ***o-ka-*** in the Linear A personal name ***o-ka-mi-za*** (PK 1a.3) from Palaikastro may well corroborate the interpretation of ***de-su-<u>ke</u>-*** as ***Dešurḫe***. If Hurrian ***Karmišá / Karmiše*** (wr. *Qar-mi-šá, Qar-mi-še, Qar-me-še, Ka-ar-mi-še*) is to be divided into ***kar-*** + ***-mišá / -miše*** (cf. P.M. Purves, *NPN*, 223, s.v. ***kar***) and ***o-ka-mi-za*** consists of ***Urḫa-*** + ***-mišá***, cf. e.g. ***Urḫa-tarmi***, (wr. *Ur-ḫa-tar-mi, Ur-ḫa-tar-me*); and ***Urḫa-tati*** (wr. *Ur-ḫa-ta-ti*, at Nuzi), the Hurrian element ***Urḫa-*** could be rendered into Linear A ***o-ka-***.

Eventually the voicelessness of the dental of ***Tešub*** seems to have prevailed as may be inferred from Linear B ***te-se-u*** (PY En 74, 5; PY Eo 276, 4: ***te-o-jo do-e-ro*** 'servant of a god') interpreted as ***Θησεύς***. The voiceless Hurrian dental even appears to have sounded as an aspirate voiceless dental in the ears of Mycenaean Greeks, since the name was rendered with ***Θ-*** instead of ***T-*** in alphabetic Greek.

The name attested at Pylos is clearly Pre-Greek, because an Indo-European intervocalic ***-s-*** would have changed into ***-h-*** and ultimately have disappeared in Greek. P. Chantraine, *DELG*, 436, s.v. ***Θησεύς***. Étymologie: Inconnue. Was *Θησεύς* originally a Cretan name derived from the Hurrian hypocoristic name ***Teššuia*** (wr. *Te-eš-šu-ia, Te-šu-ia, Te-iš-šu-ia, Ti-iš-šu-ú-ia*), attested at Nuzi (cf. I.J. Gelb, *NPN*, 154), comparable to ***a-pa-je-u*** (PY Jn 845, 5) ***Ἀφαιεύς*** 'celebrant of *Ἀφαίᾱ*', and was the Minoan myth about Theseus and Ariadna later connected with the Greek mainland, so that Theseus could become an Athenian prince and hero with a name that contained an onomastic element referring to the head of the Hurrian pantheon ? Only ***Tešub*** knows: ***Talmi-Teš(š)ub*** 'Teš(š)ub is Great' !

Combination of ***te-se-u*** with ***te-o-jo do-e-ro*** 'servant of a god' (probably the description of a priest) in PY En 74, 5 and PY Eo 276, 4 is intriguing, because the 'Greek' word ***θεός*** is suspected to be of 'Pre-Greek' origin as well. P. Chantraine, *DELG*, 429-430, s.v. ***θεός***: "m., f. (Hom., ion.-att., etc.), béot., chypr., crét. ***θιός***, lacon. ***σιός***. Adjectifs dérivés: *θεῖος* 'divin'….. probablement de ****θέσ-yος***; le mycénien a le féminin ***teija***; la forme ***θήιος*** chez Alc. et chez Balbilla n'est pas expliquée. … Étymologie inconnue. Le rapprochement avec lat. *deus*, skr. *devá-*, est bien entendue impossible. D'une façon plus générale, la chute d'un *ϝ* intervocalique dans ***θεός*** ne peut être supposée en raison du mycénien ***teo*** et de la forme crétoise ***θιός***. Dans ces conditions, on a amené à admettre la chute d'un sigma intervocalique et à évoquer les composés d'ailleurs obscurs ***θέσ-κελος***, ***θεσ-πέσιος***, ***θέσ-φατος***." He also rejects two other hypotheses and concludes: "Finalement l'ensemble reste incertain." The Homeric compounds ***θέσ-κελος*** 'miraculous', ***θεσ-πέσιος*** 'formidable, divine' and ***θέσ-φατος*** 'said/announced by a god' prove that ***θεός*** is the result of change from intervocalic ***-s-*** (****θεσός***) > intervocalic ***-h-*** (Mycenaean ***θεὅς***) > (later) ***θεός***.

C.J. Ruijgh (*EGM*, § 233) explains Mycenaean ***te-o*** as ***θεὅς*** (with intervocalic ***h***) < ****θεσός***, mot d'origine probablement préhellénique, cf. ***te-i-ja***." *Ibidem*, § 175, he writes: "***te-i-ja*** (PY Fr 1202: dat. sg. f.): ***θέἱος*** 'des dieux', dérivé de ***te-o θεὅς*** (PY Ep 704, 5: acc. ? sg.; *al.*). Plus tard, on trouve la forme ***θεῖος***. L'expression ***ma-te-re te-i-ja Μᾱτρεῖ θεἵᾳ*** ('pour la Mère des dieux' ou 'pour la Mère divine') rappelle *Μήτηρ* = *Δημήτηρ* (cf. aussi *Ῥέᾱ*, *Κυβέλη*) et, d'autre part, ***Θεία̃***, nom d'une soeur de Rhéa d'après Hésiode."

There is a correlation between ***Ḫebat*** in her appearance of ***Allani*** 'the Lady' and the goddess ***Hera*** and between the theonym ***Ḫebat / Ḫebet*** and the goddess ***Ἥβη*** who had to become 'daughter of Zeus and Hera' instead of 'consort of Teš(š)ub / Zeus', because her name was later associated by the Greeks with the Greek noun ***ἥβη*** 'youth, vigour, puberty'.

Remarkably the "goddess" ***Θεία̃*** is mentioned by Hesiod in his *Theogony* as the sister of ***Ῥέᾱ***, who is consort of Kronos and mother of Zeus. The struggle for power between ***Ouranos***, ***Kronos*** and ***Zeus*** is a close copy of that between the Hurrian ***Anu***, ***Kumarbi*** and ***Teš(š)ub***. Teš(š)ub's place in the Mycenaean pantheon had been taken by the Indo-European Zeus. But Hurrian and Cretan ***Teš(š)ub***, possibly Linear A ***te-zu***, survived in personal names such as Linear B ***te-se-u Θησεύς***. The Hurrian onomastic element ***-teḭa***, hypocoristic of ***-teš(š)ub***, may have survived as the deity ***Θεία̃*** in Hesiod, but because the position of the Head of the pantheon had already been taken by Zeus and since most words and names in ***-α*** in Greek are feminine, ***Θεία̃*** had to become a female deity and became sister of ***Ῥέᾱ*** instead of her son. ***Teš(š)-*** may also be the basis of ****θεσός*** > (Mycenaean) ***θεὅς*** that was treated as if it was a common Indo-European noun (intervocalic ***-s-*** > ***-h-***).

On the *b*-side of the same tablet from Arkhanes the beginning of the sequence]***-<u>du</u>-re*** 10 (AK 4b.2) is missing. L. Godart – J.-P. Olivier (*GORILA 3*):]***-re***: trace à gauche pas entierement incompatible avec ***<u>79</u>***; J. Raison - M. Pope:]***-<u>du</u>-re***. Linear A]***-<u>du</u>-re*** 10 (AK 4b.2) may be a Hurrian personal name ending with ***-ri / -re*** or ***-li / -le***. If the reading of]***-<u>du</u>*** by Raison-Pope is correct, completion to ***a***]***-<u>du</u>-re*** , Hurrian ***Ar-d/ture*** 'Give a man', is conceivable, since there seems to be space for only one syllabic sign before]***-<u>du</u>-re*** and one may compare Linear A ***a-du-re***[(KH 4.1) at Khania. However, it also appears attractive to complete ***a-du-re***[(KH 4.1) at Khania to ***a-du-re-***[***za***, because on another tablet from Khania ***a-du-<u>re</u>-za*** HORD K (KH 11.1) is attested.]***-<u>du</u>-re*** 10 (AK 4b.2) can certainly not be completed to ***a-du-re-za***, because the number 10 follows immediately after]***-<u>du</u>-re***.

Another option is to complete]***-<u>du</u>-re*** 10 to ***u***]***-<u>du</u>-re*** 10, that can be analysed as an *imperative* 'one-word' personal name ***Ud=ul=e*** or ***Ud=ur=e***, consisting of the root ***ud-*** 'to protect' + root-extension ***-ul-*** or ***-ur-*** (cf. Th. Richter, *BGH*, 507, s.v. ***ud-***, ***ud=ul-*** and ***ud=ur-*** [Boğ.]) + marker of transitivity ***-i/e-***. However, ***u***]***-<u>du</u>-re*** may also be the Linear A equivalent to the Hurrian personal name ***ᶠUr-duri*** (wr. *ᶠUr-du-ri*, *ᶠÚ-ur-tu-ri*) at Nuzi (cf. P.M. Purves, *NPN*, 269), since ***-r-*** is not expressed before occlusives in Linear A and B consonant clusters. Purves compares the Hurrian element ***tu-ri*** with Sumerian KI.TA 'below', Ug. Voc. IV 5. Cf. E. Laroche, *GLH*, 273: 'inférieur'; cf. Th. Richter, *BGH*, 477: s.v. ***tu-ri*** II [Boğ., Nuzi, Ug.] 'unten', which must not be confused with ***tu-ri*** I 'man' and the adjective ***turaḫ(ḫ)e*** [Boğ.; PN] and ***turuḫḫe*** [Boğ., Ug.] 'male', cf. Th. Richter, *BGH*, 476-477. On the other hand, if Linear A ****U***]***-du-re*** refers to a man, Hurrian ***Ur-dure/i*** 'The man is present' would provide a good meaning, cf. ***ur-*** 'to be present', ***tu-ri*** I 'man'.

Also on the *b*-side of this tablet from Arkhanes we find ***u***[.]***-de-mi*** 10 ***i-154-***[.] | 9 (AK 4b.3-4). Only two fragments of this incomplete tablet are preserved. The sequences ***u***[.]***-de-mi*** 10 ***i-154-***[.] 9, followed by numbers, are possible readings, but it is not certain that ***u***[and]***-de-mi*** form one sequence. Since the right side of this tablet from Arkhanes is damaged, there are two possibilities: ***u***[(AK 4b.2) is either part of a sequence of two signs, followed by some units or 'ten(s)' at the end of line 2, or it is the beginning of a sequence that is continued in the next line with]***-de-mi*** 10 ***i-154-***[.] | 9, so that one can read ***u***[.]***-de-mi*** 10 ***i-154-***[.] | 9 (AK 4b.2-4).

If ***u***[.]***-de-mi*** is a complete sequence and if there is no sign missing between ***u***[(AK 4b.2) and]***-de-mi*** (AK 4b.3), the analysis may be {*ud=(e/i)-ermi*}, consisting of the root ***ud-*** 'to protect' + marker of *transitivity* ***-e/i-*** (at the same time marker of the *imperative*) that contracted with the initial vowel of ***ermi / irmi / erwi / ewri / ibri*** 'Lord', translation 'Protect (the child), oh Lord !'. It would in that case be equivalent to and almost identical with the Linear A personal name ***u-di-mi*** (HT 117a.4) from Hagia Triada.

Although Linear A sign ***154*** (= Linear B sign ****47***) is a rare sign, it occurs twice on this tablet from Arkhanes: |***154-te*** 5 (AK 4a.4) and ***i-154-***[.] | 9 (AK 4b.3-4). If sign ***154*** might reflect one of the missing values in the grids of Linear A and B, ***wu*** might be a good candidate, since that value offers good Hurrian personal names in both cases.

Linear A ***i-154-***[.] | 9 (AK 4b.3-4) may possibly be identified as ***i-wu-***[.], which might be compared with the Hurrian personal name ***Iwuk***[ ] (wr. *I-ú-uk-*[x]) at Alalaḫ (71:7), cf. A. Draffkorn, *HHA*, 36, s.v. ***Iwuk***[ ] and the personal names ***Iuki*** (wr. *I-ú-ki*), son of *Ma-zi-ilu*, father of *ᶠŠi-lu-ia* (JEN 26:3,15), or ***Iuzzi*** (wr. *I-ú-uz-zi*), father of *Gu-duq-qa* (JENu 414) at Nuzi, cf. I.J. Gelb, *NPN*, 77; P.M. Purves, *NPN*, 221, s.v. ***Iw***, ***Iuki*** (wr. *I-ú-ki*, perhaps < **Iwuki*) and ***Iuzzi*** (wr. *I-ú-uz-zi*, perhaps < **Iwuzzi*).

If ***de-su-ke-***| (AK 4a.3) and |***154-te*** 5 (AK 4a.4) on the *a*-side are separate sequences, which is quite feasible, and if sign ***154*** may reflect ***wu***, Linear A ***154-te*** may be ***wu-te***. If that value can be confirmed, interpretation as a Hurrian personal name would be possible. Since ***-te*** and ***-teia*** are frequent hypocoristics of the onomastic element ***-tešub***, ***Wur-te*** or ***Wul-te*** would offer a perfect Hurrian name, because ***Wur-tešup*** (wr. *Wu-ur-te-šup*, *Wu-ur-te-šup*$_x$(RUM)) is 6 times, ***Wur-teia*** (wr. *Wu-ur-te-ia*) 4 times and ***Wul-tešup*** (wr. *Wu-ul-te-šup*) 1 time attested at Nuzi, cf. I.J. Gelb, *NPN*, 174; P.M. Purves, *NPN*, 275-276. ***Wur-teia*** and ***Wur-tešup*** can now be interpreted as 'Tešub sees' or 'See / Look, Tešub !', cf. I. Wegner, *Einführung*, 274, s.v. ***wur- / pur-*** {*fur-*} 'sehen' ['to see'].

Linear A ***za-si-ni***[ ] 3 (AK 4b.5) is probably the last entry on the last line of this tablet from Arkhanes, which is read as ***za-si-ni***[ ] 3 by Raison-Pope (1994, 35-36), and as ***za-si-do***[ ] 3 by *GORILA 3* (1976, 14-15). I consider the reading of ***-si-*** quite certain, although the bottom edge of the tablet is severely damaged. If ***za-si-ni***[is the correct reading and if the sequence is complete, it may well be a Hurrian personal name (like the other sequences on the tablet), containing the verbal onomastic element ***Zaz***, ***Zazi*** as in ***Zaziia*** (wr. *Za-zi-ia*) at Nuzi, who is mentioned as the father of 5 persons with clearly Hurrian names (cf. I.J. Gelb, *NPN*, 126, 175; P.M. Purves, *NPN*, 277, s.v. ***zaz***), probably followed by the *optional allomorphic* enclitic personal pronoun 3rd person singular ***-nni***.

We may also compare ᶠ**Šaš-kiaše** (wr. ᶠ*Ša-aš-ki-ia-še,* ᶠ*Ša-aš-ki-a-še*); **Šaš-kuli** (wr. ᶠ*Ša-aš-ku-li*); **Šaš-naiḫe** (wr. ᶠ*Ša-aš-na-i-ḫé*); **Šaš-tae** (wr. ᶠ*Ša-aš-ta-e*); ᶠ**Šašuḭa** (wr. ᶠ*Ša-šu-ú-ia,* ᶠ*Ša-šu-ia*); ᶠ**Šašuri** (wr. ᶠ*Ša-šu-ri*); **Šašu-Tešup** (wr. *Ša-šu-te-šup*), cf. I.J. Gelb, *NPN*, 126; P.M. Purves, *NPN*, 252, s.v. **šaš**.

Th. Richter (*BGH*, 360-361) mentions, s.v. **zaš-** I [Boğ.; PN], and (*VHN*, 502), s.v. **šaz-** {**šaž-**} and **zaz-/zazz-**, that the meaning 'zu essen geben, verköstigen, ernähren', 'to feed' is known since publication of the Hurrian-Hittite bilingual *Kirenze* (KBo 32). One assumes that the root with root-extensions has more or less the same meaning as that without them.

We find **zaš=ul-** [Boğ.; Mitt.] and **zaz=ul=umma** *epēšu* [Nuzi], corresponding with Hittite **adanna pāi-** in the bilingual (cf. E. Neu, 1990, 230[17]) '(jem.) zu essen geben, verköstigen, ernähren', 'to nourish'; and **zaz=ul=il-** [Boğ.] 'zu essen geben, ernähren, bewirten', corresponding with Hittite **adanna pe/išk-**, and **zaz=ul=ušt-** {**zaž=ol=ošt-**} (same meaning). The nominal stem **zazzi** {*zazz=i*} means 'Ernährung' ['nourishment'] and **zazzari** {*zazz=ar=i*} in context 'Schlemmer(?)' ['carouser, reveller(?)'] (cf. M. Dijkstra, The myth of *apši* 'the (sea)dragon in the Hurrian tradition, *UF 37*, 2005, 319).

Th. Richter (*VHN*, 251-254) mentions the Hurrian personal names **Zazza-Naje** (wr. *Za-za-na-ie, Za-az-za-na-ie*) at Mari and ᶠ**Zazza-Naje** (wr. ᶠ*Za-za-na-ie*) at Mari, typology 2.1, analysis {*zazz(i)=a*[E.]*-Naje*}, translation 'Wie die Ernährung ist Naje' ['Like nourishment is Naje']. Th. Richter prefers here a nominal sentence name, since an intransitive meaning of **zaz(z)-** is not likely; ᶠ**Zazaraja** (wr. ᶠ*Za-za-ra-ia,* ᶠ*Za-za-ra-a-ia*) at Mari and Qaṭṭarā, analysis {*zaž=ar=(i)=aja*}, typology 1.3.1.2.1, translation 'Verköstige (das Mädchen) wiederholt !' ['Nourish (the girl) again and again !']; **Zazari** (wr. *Za-za-ri*) at Šubat-Enlil, analysis {*zaž=ar=i*}, typology 1.3.1.2.1, translation 'Verköstige (den Jungen) wiederholt!' ['Nourish (the boy) again and again !']; **Zazzari** (wr. *Za-az-za-ri*) at Mari and Nuzi, analysis {*zazz=ar=i*}, typology 1.3.1.2.1, translation 'Verköstige (den Jungen) wiederholt !' ['Nourish (the boy) again and again !']; **Zazi** (wr. *Za-az-zi, Za-zi*) at Tigunāni, Alalaḫ IV, Emar, Kurruḫanni, Puzriš-Dagan, analysis {*zaž=i*}, typology 1.3.1.2.1, translation 'Verköstige (den Jungen) !' ['Nourish (the boy) !']; **Zazija** (wr. *Za-zi-ia*) at Ašnakkum, Mari, Qaṭṭarā, Šušarrā, Šubat-Enlil and Tuttul, analysis {*zaž=i=ja*}, typology 1.1.1.2.4, translation 'Er/Sie (scil. ein *Numen*) verköstigte (den Jungen)' ['He/She (scil. a *numen*) nourished (the boy)'].

If Linear A **za̱-si̱-ni̱**[(AK 4b.5) is the correct reading and if the sequence is complete, we may conclude that a verbal or nominal analysis is possible. The verbal analysis as {*zaš=i=nni*} is preferable, translation 'Nourish him/her (**-nni**) (the child) (oh *numen*) !'.

Since the nominal stem **zazzi** {*zazz=i*} 'nourishment' has also been identified, analysis as {*zazz=i=ni*}, with the suffix of the so-called definite article **-ni / -ne** is also possible. So theoretically the name can also be translated as 'The nourishment', but semantically and also in view of the popularity of verbal personal names {*zaš=i=nni*} seems the winner.

-.-.-.-.-.-

CHAPTER 14
LINEAR B ONOMASTICS

The names discussed in this chapter do not have a Greek etymology and are to be considered adstrate forms in the wide sense in Mycenaean Greek. Many substrate names and some lexical terms in Mycenaean and ancient Greek sources, appear to have a Hurrian etymology, which is not surprising in the light of the Minoan-Hurrian legacy of Minoan Crete.

Although the forms ***pi-we-ri-ja-ta***, ***pi-we-re***, ***pi-we-ri-si***, ***pi-we-ri-di*** have a good Greek and Indo-European etymology (cf. P. Chantraine, *Dictionnaire étymologique de la langue grecque*, 898-899, s.v. ***πῖαρ***), they are also discussed here, since a relation of the names in question with Thrace and Macedonia seems feasible as well. In this chapter I shall discuss data that appear to be particularly relevant to the subject of this monograph. Some results may also be of interest for Anatolian and Thracian studies. Some names formerly assigned to Lycian or its Bronze Age predecessor Luwian and some assigned to Proto-Thracian are now more likely of Hurrian origin. Special attention will be paid to the significance of some theonyms.

To start with, it may be useful to stress a point of methodology. Although ancient sources used the term 'Thracian' without reservation when referring to those peoples and tribes who dwelled in the northern Balkans and on the Greek mainland itself in a very remote past and who were considered the ancestors of those whom the Greeks knew as 'the Thracians' in historic times, it may be preferable to use the term 'Proto-Thracian' when we refer to the Bronze Age, since the Thracians just as the Greeks themselves had not yet passed the threshold of history in Mycenaean times.

Linear B ***pu-zo*** (KN Ap 5748+5901+5923+8558.2) has been recognized as the Thracian personal name ***Buzo*** by P.Hr. Ilievski, 'Myc. *PU-ZO*', *Živa Antika 19 (1969)*, 149.

D. Detschew, *Die thrakischen Sprachreste*, 94-95, has previously suggested a Thracian origin for personal names such as ***Βύζος***, ***Βύζας***, ***Βύζης***. P. Kretschmer (Das *-nt-* Suffix, *Glotta 14, 1925*, 94-95) assumed on the basis of occurrence of the name *Beuzas* in Dalmatia that Byzantium was founded by an Illyrian *Βύζας*, but the *Etymologicum Magnum* tells: *Βυζάντιον· ἡ πόλις, διὰ τὸν Βύζαντα τὸν Θρᾴκης βασιλέα.*

Actually, it is a very common mistake, also often made by H. Krahe and A. Mayer, to attribute an Illyrian origin to names that were in fact Thracian. C. Patsch demonstrated already in 1907 in his article on 'Thrakische Spuren an der Adria', Österreichische Jahreshefte 10, 169-174, that there was a Pre-Illyrian substrate of Thracian onomastics in Dalmatia and Epirus. Moreover, isoglosses of substrate words in Albanian, Bulgarian and Rumanian can probably best be explained as relics of Thracian and cognate Dacian.

Thracian ***Βύζος*** and ***Βύζας*** may be compared with Awestian *buza* 'billy-goat', Persian *buz* 'goat' and 'billy-goat' and Armenian ***buz*** 'lamb', from I.-E. ****bhug-yo-s***, cf. I. Duridanov, Die Stellung des Thrakischen im Kreise der indoeuropäischen Sprachen, *Thracia I* (Academia Litterarum Bulgarica, Primus Congressus Studiorum Thracicorum), Serdicae 1972, 242.

Although I am convinced that the toponym *Βυζάντιον* is derived from Thracian *Βύζας*, I am now less certain about the same origin of the Linear B name from Knossos, since also at Nuzi the name *Pu-ú-za* is attested, cf. P.M. Purves, *NPN*, 248, s.v. *puza*, whose verdict is 'unidentified'. P.M. Purves agrees with L. Oppenheim in opposing the opinion of others who maintain that this personal name is Hurrian. He compares the Nuzi name with ***Bu-zi*** from Gasur, HSS X 190: 1, and with ***Bu-za*** from the Ur III period, cf. Schneider in *Orientalia* No. 23, No. 523, also cited by Meyer in *AOF XII* 368. Also ***Bu-za*** and perhaps ***Bu-zi*** from Anatolia, cf. Stephens, *PNC*, 28, former cited by Ungnad, *Subartu*, 150. See for more examples from Anatolia Gustavs in *AOF XI* 147 and Oppenheim in *RHA V, fasc. 33*, 16. References of *Bu-za* from Middle Assyrian texts are listed by Ebeling in *MAOG XIII.1*, 35. From Susa cf. perhaps [*Bu*]-*ú-zi*, Mém. XXIII 248:3. I conclude that the range of occurrences of ***Bu-za*** and ***Bu-zi*** is widely spread over Anatolia and the Near East as well, so that it would be unwise to point to only one source.

However, recently formations with the Hurrian verbal root ***puz-*** 'eintauchen' ['to dive, to dip in(to), to plunge in, to submerge'] could be shown, e.g. the Old Hurrian forms in ***=o=m*** and ***=o=b*** beside each other in the Hurrian-Hittite bilingual *Kirenze* (KBo 32: 14 Rs. 23-24) *pu-ú-zi-ḫu-um* {*puz=iḫ=o=m*} corresponding with Hittite *an-da šu-ú-ni-at* 'er (hund) tauchte ein' ['he (the dog) submerged in(to)'] and *pu-ú-zi-ḫu-ub* {*puz=iḫ=o=b*}, cf. E. Neu, *StBoT 32*, 1996, 169; cf. I. Wegner, *Einführung*, 128.

Th. Richter (*BGH*, 331) ***puz-*** I: *puz=iḫ(ḫ)-* [Boğ.] 'eintauchen' ['to dive, to plunge in, to submerge'], corresponds with Hittite *anda šunna-/šunije-*, and ***puz-*** II [Emar; Mari; PN] onomastic element (no translation). Th. Richter (*VHN*, 491-492) has assembled several names s.v. ***puš-*** I {*po/už-*}: *Pušaja* (Mari), *Pušan* (Tuttul), *Pušepḫe* (Šušarrā); and s.v. ***puz-*** II {*po/uz-*} / ***puzz-*** {*po/uzz-*} 'eintauchen': *ᶠPuzakki* (Šubat-Enlil), *ᶠPuzi* (Ašnakkum, Mari), *ᶠPuzija* (Mari), *ᶠPuzum-ki* (Qaṭṭarā), *ᶠPuzunna* (Mari), *Puzunni* (Mari), *Puzzaja* (Šubat-Enlil), *Puzzi* (Mari, Qaṭṭarā), *ᶠPuzni* (Mari), *Puzunze* (Mari).

Frankly I consider it now more likely that in Mycenaean Knossos the Pre-Greek Linear B name ***pu-zo*** (KN Ap 5748+5901+5923+8558.2) is derived from Minoan-Hurrian ***Puzo/u*** or ***Puzun*** (with not-expressed final ***-n***), shortened form for ***Puzunna*** or ***Puzunni***, than from a (Proto-)Thracian name. A problem with disyllabic names is that there is a chance that we are dealing with homographs derived from different origins. It may have been a different matter, if Linear B ***pu-zo*** had not been attested at Knossos, but on the Greek mainland.

Some personal names in Linear B appear to contain a root ***διζ-***, e.g. ***di-za-so*** (KN Pp 493+500+5813; Dv 1505) = e.g. ****Διζασ(σ)ος***, ***di-za***[(KN Dv 1506) = e.g. ***Δίζας*** (or perhaps also ****Διζασ(σ)ος***, since we do not know whether the name is complete or not) and ***di-zo*** (KN V(3) 479a.1; As(2) 1520.5; V(7) 1523.4b), ****Δίζος*** or ****Δίζων*** or ****Δίζως*** (with the same ending as *Τρώς* and *Μίνως*).

In historical times this root is frequently attested in Thracian personal names such as *Δίζας, Δίζα, Δίζης, Δείζας, Δείζης, Diszas, Disza, Diza, Dizza* (gen. *Δίζα, Διζαδος, Διζανος*), extended forms as *Διζαλας, Διζουλος, Διζαπης* and compounds as *Διζα-ζελμις, Diza-poris, Disa-centus, Disza-tralis, Δισα-τραλις*, cf. D. Detschew, *Die thrakischen Sprachreste*, 132-135; 143; cf. V. Beševliev, *Untersuchungen über die Personennamen bei den Thrakern*, Amsterdam 1970, 42.

We may see a parallel to Thracian *Δίζας* in the Lithuanian name *Dižas*, in the Latvian family name *Dižais* and in Latvian *dīža*, cf. I. Duridanov, Die Stellung des Thrakischen im Kreise der indoeuropäischen Sprachen, *Thracia I* (Academia Litterarum Bulgarica, Primus Congressus Studiorum Thracicorum), Serdicae 1972, 239.

P. Chantraine, *DELG* I, 281, accepted A. Fick's correction of Hesychius's gloss of *δίζα· αἴξ Λάκωνες* into *δίζα· αἴξ Καύκωνες*. He compared Thracian *δίζα* with Armenian *tik* 'leather sack' (< I.-E. **digā*) and Old High German *ziga* 'goat', of which the dorsal stop may go back to I.-E. *k* or *gh*. *Kaukones* are mentioned by Herodotus I, 147; IV 118, in Homer's *Odyssey* γ 366 and by Strabo VII, 7, 1-2; VIII, 3, 11; XII, 8, 3, as living in the Peloponnese west of Arcadia; in *Iliad* K 429 and Y 329, and by Strabo XI, 3, 2-5; XIV, 5, 23-28, and Ptolemy *Geog.* V, 1, 3, as a people in Paphlagonia in Asia Minor. Ptolemy Geog. III, 8, 3, mentions Dacian *Καυκοήνσιοι*, and in an inscription from Mauretania Caesariensis (CIL VIII, 9390) we read: [d.] m. *Saeci Cauce<n>sis* [*equitis*] *alae II Thracum.*

L.C. Meijer (*Eine strukturelle Analyse der Hagia Triada-Tafeln*, 134) reads Linear A [ ]***di-za-ke*** (HT la.2-3). He erroneously mentions [ ]*L51-34-24* instead of [ ]*L51-23-24* on page 7 of his book, but this is probably a printer's error, since he reads ***di-za-ke*** on p. 134.

This reading might, however, be a hoax, since L. Godart - J.-P. Olivier, *GORILA 1*, read ***di-di-za-ke***, whereas J. Raison - M. Pope, *BCILL 18*, 33, and *BCILL 74*, 44, seem to waver between these readings. If [ ]***di-za-ke*** is not a hoax, this sequence, which is probably a personal name, could perhaps be compared with the (very late) Thracian name *Dizzaca* in inscriptions from Worms (*CIL XIII,* 6231: *Aur. Dizzaca leg. II Part.*) and from Troesmis (*CIL III,* 6189: *Iulius Dizzace* (gen.)). But if *di-di-za-ke* is the correct reading, the first onomastic element ***di-di-*** may be compared with names from Cappadocia such as ***Tí-tí-a*** (CCT V 25 c 4; Garelli N° 63, 8; E. Laroche, *NH*, 186. n° 1342) and ***Tí-tí-na-ri*** (EL 1, 2; 284, 3; E. Laroche, *NH*, 186. n° 1343). This name is also mentioned by P.M. Purves, *NPN*, 208, s.v. ***titi***: "Hurrian. Cf. perhaps *ti-i-ti*, Tuš. iii 121, and *ti-i-ti-pa*⌈*a*⌉, VBoT 59 ii 8. Perhaps in personal name ***Titinari/atal*** from Anatolia, wr. *Tí-tí-na*-RI, TCL IV 67:2, cited as Hurrian by Götze, *Kleinasien*, 69, n. 4; Gelb, *IAV*, 14; and Ungnad, *Subartu*, 151. The personal name ***Tette*** adduced by Gustavs in *AOF XI*, 149, may not be involved." Single writing of the cuneiform intervocalic dental in *ti-i-ti-* proves that it is voiced.

The new reading ***di-di-za-ke*** by *GORILA* (HT la.2-3) seems preferable, since ***di-di-*** is legible. Consequently a Hurrian interpretation of ***di-di-za-ke*** seems more likely than a 'Thracian' or 'Proto-Thracian' of ***di-za-ke***. Th. Richter (*VHN*, 541, s.v. ***ted-/tid-***) remarks that to date two roots ***tid-*** are lexically confirmed: 'zählen' ['to count'] (cf. *BGH*, 464: ***tid-*** I [Boğ.]) and 'angreifen' ['to attack'] (cf. *BGH*, 464-465: ***tid-*** II [Boğ.; Mitt.]/ ***titt-*** [Boğ.]), but he adds that it is not certain which of the two is used in personal names. Theoretically there may also be a root that is as yet not recognized. Furthermore the question of whether a root ***ted-***, on which ***Tetija*** (wr. *te-di-ia*) at Šušarrā and other personal names at Nuzi are based, exists next to ***tid-***, is not yet solved. Names with the root {*tid-*} are ***Tita-ki*** (Mari) and Titikkan (Mari), cf. Th. Richter, *VHN*, 541. Compare also Linear A ***ti-ti-ku*** (HT 35.1; ZA Zb 3.2) and ***ti-ti-ku-ni*** (HT 96a.1). M. Pope has compared these Linear A personal names with Hurrian ***Titiku*** and ***Titikun*** at Alalaḫ, cf. M. Pope, *Aegean writing and Linear A* (*Studies in Mediterranean Archaeology, Vol. VIII*), Lund 1964, 5.

Linear A ***ti-ti-ku-ni*** can now be analysed as {*Titt=i=kk=u=nni*}, based on the root ***tid- / titt-*** and the nominal suffixes ***-kk=u/o=nni***, cf. I. Wegner, *Einführung*, 55-56. She warns that this formant ***-kk-*** (often occurring in descriptions of persons: possibly *nomina actoris*) should not be confused with the negation-suffix (***-kk***+vowel) in intransitive and antipassive verbal forms. ***Titikun*** {*tid=i=kk-u/o=n*} with voiced second dental at Alalaḫ is a shortened form of {*tid=i=kk=u/o=nni*} (root ***tid-***), whereas the Linear A names ***ti-ti-ku*** and ***ti-ti-ku-ni*** have voiceless initial and second dentals (root ***titt-***). It seems justifiable that (because of ***tid- / titt-*** that can be identified with ***tid-*** II / ***titt-*** 'to attack') the Linear A personal names ***ti-ti-ku*** (HT 35.1; ZA Zb 3.2) and ***ti-ti-ku-ni*** (HT 96a.1) as well as ***Titiku*** and ***Titikun*** at Alalaḫ can now provisionally be translated as 'Attacker'. I refer to a parallel in Urartian mentioned by I. Wegner, *Einführung*, 56: In Urartian we find ^{LÚ}***urb=i=ka*** 'Schlachtopfer, Priester (?)' ['victim, priest (?)'] from Urartian and Hurrian ***urb-*** 'to slaughter, sacrifice'.

Linear A ***-za-ke*** in ***d̲i̲-di-za-ke*** can now most likely be compared with the onomastic element ***šagi / šekki*** {*šagi / šekki*} mentioned by Th. Richter (*BGH*, 343-344; *VHN*, 495-496). He mentions that a transitive verbal root ***šag-*** was first interpreted as 'reinigen, verzieren' ['to clean, purify, adorn, embellish'], but was later regarded as equivalent to ***šagr-*** 'schützen' ['to protect'] by I. Wegner (Zum Namen des *Udibšarri*, *AoF 30 (2003)*, 342[8]), that she analysed as {*šag=r-*} = root ***šag-*** + root-extension ***°=r***. According to A. Mouton (La vieille femme hourrite *Aštu* et son rituel: quelque réflexions autour d'un ouvrage récent, *Bibliotheca Orientalis 68 (2011)*, 243-254, 248) the root ***šag-*** can mean 'attraper, capturer'. Th. Richter (*VHN*, *ibidem*) thinks that in personal names the form ***šagi*** {*šag=i*} is nominal. He probably refers to the usage of ***-šagi*** as second onomastic element. He also tells that ***šagi*** is almost without exception written with [KI]. Only ***ᶠŠakija*** and ***Šakijān*** show [GI]. Whereas the orthography of ***°za-ki*** in ***ᶠAšmun-šaki*** M2 can plausibly be explained (see *VHN*, section D/0.1.2 sub B2), the alternation of ***°-šagi / °-za-ki*** with ***°-ta-[ki*** (?) *ibidem* as well as of ***°-ta-ki / °-te-ki*** and ***°-šagi*** in ***ᶠAštar-taki*** M1 can only be explained by confusion of ***šagi*** with ***tagi*** 'beautiful, pure, beaming' (***tag-/takk-***).

E. Laroche (*GLH*, 249-250), s.v. ***tagi*** 'beau'. "Lecture du sum. ZALAG; épithète de l'argent. RS voc. II 24 = Ḫḫ II 134 ; sum. ki.lam.zalag.ga = h. MIN *te-gi-še* 'beau prix'; cf. Friedrich, *HW* 325 : 'schön'. - *inu-me ušḫuni šiḫala ḫišma tagi-ma kiraši-ma* 'comme l'argent (est) pur, brillant, et beau, et long (durable)', KUB XXIX 8 IV 27." He also mentions (*GLH*, 250): "***tagi*** 'attribut de Ḫebat', *da-(a)-ki, da-a-ki-it-ti*, KUB XXV 44 II 19; KBo XX 113 IV 16; KUB XXXII 59 II 3; etc." Since *da-(a)-ki* is 'attribute of Ḫebat' according to E. Laroche and probably an epithet of this goddess, ***°za-ki/e = °d/ta-ki/e*** 'the beautiful, beauty' in Linear A ***d̲i̲-di-za-ke*** may well refer to *Ḫebat* herself, so that ***°za-ki/e = °d/ta-ki/e*** can be regarded as a (*quasi*) theophorous element. The meaning of ***d̲i̲-di-za-ke*** may be 'Attack, oh beautiful (goddess) !'. Compare also my interpretation of Linear A ***a-di-da-ki-ti-p̲a̲-ku*** (KN Zc 6.2).

Th. Richter (*VHN*, 496) mentions the following examples: (a) {*šaki*}: ***ᶠAšmun-šaki*** (Mari), [variants *ᶠAšmu-šaki, ᶠAšmen-šaki, ᶠAšmut-ta*[*ki* (?)]], ***ᶠAtal-šaki*** (Ašnakkum), ***ᶠElan-šaki*** (Mari), ***ᶠElen-šaki*** (Mari), ᶠIŠTAR-***šaki*** (Mari), ***ᶠḪazip-šaki*** (Mari), ***ᶠKun-šaki*** (Šušarrā), ***ᶠKupe-šaki*** (Tigunāni), ***ᶠMemen-šaki*** (Mari), ***ᶠPirḫen-šaki*** (M), ***ᶠŠakija*** (M) and ***Šakijān*** (M), ***ᶠŠewen-šaki*** (M), ***ᶠŠewlu(?)-šaki*** (M), variant *iš₈-tár-ša-ki* with ***ᶠAštar-taki*** M1; (b) {*šekki*}: ***ᶠKun-šekki*** (?) (Tigunāni).

According to Th. Richter (*VHN*, 496[652]) we are here certainly not dealing with Akkadian ***šaqî*** 'arrose'. If the roots ***tak-*** and ***šag-/zak-*** are indeed basically the same, the forms with ***šag-/zak-*** are in my view the youngest, since we probably have to deal with a process of palatalization and assibilation from $t > t^y > t^s > s$.

We may conclude that Linear A ***di-di-za-ke*** (HT la.2-3) has nothing to do with Linear B ***di-za-so*** (KN Pp 493+ 500+5813; Dv 1505), ***di-za***[(KN Dv 1506) and ***di-zo*** (KN V(3) 479a.1; As(2) 1520.5; V(7) 1523.4b).

The ethnic ***i-ta-ra-jo*** (PY Jn 431.10), probably ***Ἰστραῖος***, used as a personal name, is derived from ****Ἴστρᾱ***, that can be compared with ***Ἴστρος***, the name of the river Danube mentioned by Herodotus (*IV*, 48) as the greatest of all rivers we know: *Ἴστρος μὲν ἐὼν μέγιστος ποταμῶν πάντων τῶν ἡμεῖς ἴδμεν*.

According to Stephanus of Byzantium (*341, 3*) *Ἴστρος* occurs not only as a toponym in Thrace, but also as one in Crete, in the area of Knidos in Asia Minor and in that of the Iapyges, a tribe in the east of Italy. Stephanus Byzantinus, *341, 3*: *Ἴστρος, πόλις Κρήτης, ἣν Ἀρτεμίδωρος Ἰστρῶνά φησι. δευτέρα πόλις Ἴστρος ἐν τῷ Πόντῳ. τὸ ἐθνικὸν Ἴστριος καὶ Ἰστριεύς. Ἀρριανὸς δὲ Ἰστρίαν ὡς Ὀλβίαν αὐτήν φησι. τὸ ἐθνικὸν ταύτης Ἰστριανός ὡς Ὀλβιανός, καὶ κατὰ τροπὴν Ἰστριηνὸς λιμὴν καὶ Τριόπιον τῆς Κνιδίας. τετάρτη πόλις τῆς Ἰαπυγίας, ὡς Ἔφορος εἰκοστῷ ἐνάτῳ.* Steph. Byz., *648, 5,* also mentions a Thracian tribe called ***Istroi***: *Ἀπολλόδωρος* [...] *ἐν τῷ περὶ γῆς δευτέρῳ "ὑπὲρ δὲ τοὺς Ὕλλους Λιβυρνοὶ καί τινες Ἴστροι λεγόμενοι Θρᾷκες".*

Although D. Detschew (*Die thrakischen Sprachreste*, Wien 1957, 217-219) considers ***Ἴστρος*** Thracian on the argument that the name and its derivatives are attested as Thracian in ancient sources, Stephanus Byzantinus already pointed out that the name also occurs far beyond the Thracian area. The name of the river ***Ἴστρος*** may be cognate with that of other rivers in Europe such as the ***Isère***, ***Isar***, etc., cf. A. Walde - J. Pokorny, *Vergleichendes Wörterbuch der indogermanischen Sprachen,* Berlin 1927-1932, 299-300. The original meaning of the Indo-European adjectives ***$*H_1$isrós*** > (Greek) ***ἰρός***; ***$*H_1$iserós*** > (Greek) ***ἱερός***; *$*H_1$eysr̥rós* > (Greek) ***εἰαρός***, cf. Doric ***ἰαρός***, meaning 'provided with supernatural power'. The name of the ***Istros*** river in Thrace and Dacia may be considered a piece of evidence for the Indo-European character of the Thracian and Dacian languages. At the same time we must realize that these ancient Indo-European languages probably also contained many substrate words and names of (non-Indo-European) predecessors, just like the Greek and Anatolian languages did. The ethnic ***Θρᾷκες*** 'Thracians' is probably inherited from a non-Indo-European substrate language just as the Greeks inherited the ethnic ***Ἀχαιϝοί*** from such a language, in the same way as the Anglo-Saxon British inherited their name from the Celtic *Britons* inhabiting South Britannia before the Roman conquest, cf. Middle English and Old French *Breton*, Latin *Britto, -onis*, Old Celtic **Britto(s)*.

The toponym from Knossos ***o-du-ru-we*** (KN C 902.6), probably dative-locative of ****Ὄδρυς***, and the ethnic ***o-du-ru-wi-jo*** (KN C 902.2), probably ***Ὀδρύιος***, and feminine ***o-du-ru-wi-ja*** (KN Ai(3) 982.1), as well as ***o-du-ru-wi-jo*** on a stirrup-jar found in Thebes (TH Z 839), but imported from Crete (on the evidence of clay analysis), recall the tribal name of the Thracian ***Ὀδρύσαι***, with the adjectival forms ***Ὀδρύσιος*** and ***Ὀδρυσαῖος***.

Herodotus (IV, 92) tells that the river *Ἀρτησκός* (a tributary of the Maritsa) flowed through the area of the Odrysae: *Δαρεῖος δὲ ἐνθεῦτεν ὁρμηθεὶς ἀπίκετο ἐπ' ἄλλον ποταμὸν τῷ οὔνομα Ἀρτησκός ἐστι, ὃς διὰ Ὀδρυσέων ῥέει.*

According to a gloss by Hesychius: *ὄθρυν · Κρῆτες τὸ ὄρος*, the toponym ***Ὄθρυς*** is attested in Crete. It might well be considered a doublet of **** Ὄδρυς***. A ***δ/θ*** alternation can be explained by the non-Greek origin of the name.

M. Lejeune, 'Doublets et complexes', *Proceedings of the Cambridge Colloquium on Mycenaean Studies* (ed. L.R. Palmer - J. Chadwick), Cambridge 1966, 140: "Dans certains emprunts 'préhelléniques' du grec, il a pu se produire des flottements entre (douces) aspirées et (douces) sonores; un exemple en est peut-être fourni par confrontation de la glose d'Hésychius ***ὄθρυν · Κρῆτες τὸ ὄρος*** et du toponyme ***oduru*** de nos tablettes cnossiennes; s'il s'agit du même mot (ce qui est plausible, mais non démontrable), ce flottement entre ***δ*** et ***θ*** serait du même ordre que le flottement entre ***β*** et ***φ*** impliqué par une lecture ****Δαφύρινθος*** où ***pu₂*** (comme dans tous les autres examples contrôlables) vaudrait ***φυ***." According to F.M.J. Waanders ***βυ/φυ*** may be derived from Linear A ***pu₂*** that may have represented ***bhu***. The value ***bhu*** seems a good starting point for a development to either ***βυ*** or ***φυ***.

There is also a mount ***Ὄθρυς*** in Thessaly situated to the north of Phthiotis according to Herodotus (VII, 129) and Strabo (VIII, 3, 32; IX, 5, 8; IX, 5, 14), cf. P. Chantraine, *Dictionnaire étymologique de la langue grecque III,* Paris 1974, 778, s.v. ***Ὄθρυς***.

In Homer's (*Iliad* N 363, 374, 772) ***Ὀθρυονεύς*** is mentioned as coming from Thracian *Καβησσός* or *Καβησός* to Troy hoping to marry Kassandra, but slain by Idomeneus instead (cf. Strabo *XIII,* 1, 40). Stephanus Byzantinus *344, 12*: *Καβασσός, πόλις ἐν Καππαδοκίᾳ, πατρὶς Ὀθρυονέως. Ὅμηρος "Καβησσόθεν ἔνδον ἐόντα". Ἑκαταῖος δ' ὁ Μιλήσιος Καβασσὸν πόλιν εἶναί φησιν ὑπερβάντι τὸν Θρᾴκιον Αἶμον. καὶ συμφωνεῖ καὶ ἡ τοῦ γάμου ἐλπὶς τῶν Θρᾳκῶν ἀκολασίᾳ. Ἑλλάνικος δὲ τῆς Λυκίας πόλιν Καβησσόν. Ἀπίων δὲ ἀληθέστερόν φησι κώμην εἶναί Καππαδοκίας μεταξὺ Ταρσοῦ καὶ Μαζάκων.* Cf. also Eust. and *Scholium ad Iliad N* 363. If all these names are somehow related, their geographic occurrence is spread over a large area. They may be substrate names that have nothing to do with the language(s) of the populations inhabiting these areas in later times.

L.R. Palmer (Mycenaean inscribed vases, II. The mainland finds, *Kadmos XI, 1972*, 27-46) examined clusters of Cretan place names and ethnics mentioned by Linear B scribes at Knossos and established their interrelations discovering patterns of Cretan geography. His hypothesis that the stirrup-jars found at Thebes, Eleusis and Mycenae, bearing Cretan toponyms or ethnics, were imported from Cretan centres to the mainland, was proved by the close contextual relations between e.g. ***wa-to*** and ***o-du-ru-we*** (c.q. ***o-du-ru-wi-jo***) in the Knossos tablets, but also by archaeological and spectrographic research by H.W. Catling - A. Millett, A study of the inscribed stirrup-jars from Thebes, *Archaeometry 8 (1965)*, 3-85; Theban stirrup-jars: Questions and answers, *Archaeometry 11 (1969)*, 3-20. I quote L.R. Palmer, *Kadmos XI (1972)*, 45: "As for the pinpointing of the exporting centres, the recent spectrographic analysis of the clay from some of the Theban jars has suggested the conclusion that ***wa-to*** is to be identified with Palaikastro and ***o-du-ru-wi-jo*** with Zakro.

The factual basis for this is that the clay of the ***o-du-ru-wi-jo*** jar closely resembles samples taken from Zakro, while clay from the ***wa-to*** group bears a similar relationship to a sample from Palaikastro." The Linear B toponym ***wa-to*** (KN Ch 902,3^{bis}; KN Co 903,1 and on several Theban jars) may be interpreted as Greek ***Ϝαστός***, probably derived from Linear B ***wa-tu*** (KN X 114; PY Eq 887, 1; PY Tn 316, v., 1) = Greek ***ἄστυ*** n. 'town, city', an old word that corresponds with Sanskrit Vedic ***vāstu*** n. 'residence', perhaps Messapian ***vastei*** (dative, cf. H. Krahe, *Sprache der Illyrier I*, 28), Tocharian A ***waṣt***, B ***ost*** 'house'. A connection with Sanskrit ***vásati*** 'to reside', Gothic ***wisan*** and Greek ***ἄεσα*** seems possible, cf. P. Chantraine, *DELG*, 129-130.

J. Chadwick, 'Linear B tablets from Thebes', *Minos 10 (1969)*, 119, also regards the evidence as decisive. He compares ***Odrus*** with (the Thracian) ***Ὀδρύσαι*** in the same section. Cf. M. Ventris - J. Chadwick, *Documents in Mycenaean Greek,* Cambridge 1973^2, 211-213 and 438. But C.J. Ruijgh, *EGM*, § 156, n. 439, finds a relation between ****Ὄδρυς*** and the name of the Thracian tribe of the ***Ὀδρύσαι*** more difficult to explain. Probably he refers to the intervocalic ***-σ-*** in *Ὀδρύσαι*, which is not found in the Linear B forms of the ethnics. Since names with the root *Ὀδρύ-* / *Ὀθρυ-* show connections with Crete, Thrace, Lycia and Cappadocia, it is likely that the name of the Thracian *Ὀδρύσαι* was derived from a *non-Indo-European* substrate language just like the name of the *Θρᾷκες* themselves.

Since the cluster ***odr-*** is not very common, it may be interesting to compare the Hurrian verbal root ***udr-*** [Qaṭna; Ugarit] 'protéger' ['to protect'], corresponding with Sumerian ŠEŠ and ÚR and Akkadian ***naṣāru***, cf. B. André-Salvini – M. Salvini, Un nouveau vocabulaire trilingue sumérien-akkadien-hourrite de Ras Shamra, *Studies on the civilization and culture of Nuzi and the Hurrians 9 (1998)*, 22; B. André-Salvini – M. Salvini, Le liste lessicali e i vocabulari plurilingui di Ugarit. Una chiave per l'interpretazione della lingua hurrica, *Parola del Passato 55 (2000)*, 328; D.R.M. Campbell, *Mood and modality in Hurrian*, Dissertation University of Chicago, Chicago 2007, 109; Akkadian ***šullumum*** corresponds in the Ugarit bilingual (G. Wilhelm, Bemerkungen zu der akkadisch-hurritischen Bilingue aus Ugarit, *Festschrift* Cl. Wilcke, 343[11]). Compare Hurrian *udr=ašt=e=š* (*imperative* 2nd person plural), consisting of the root ***udr-*** 'schützen' ['to protect'] + root-extension ***-ašt-*** + marker of the *jussive* ***-e-*** + pluralizer ***-š***, translation 'protect !; you must protect !' (Qaṭna), cf. Th. Richter, *AoF 32*, 2005, 27 f.; I. Wegner, *Einführung*, 104; Th. Richter, *BGH*, 509. According to I. Wegner the root ***udr-*** may be a shortened form of ***ud=ur-***.

According to Th. Richter (2005, 27 f.) the root ***udr-*** means 'militärischen Schutz leisten' ['to offer military protection'] in the Qaṭna-letters. This is exactly the meaning one may expect in ethnic names (cf. the etymology of the root ***ḫur-*** as compared to ***ḫur=adi*** 'Wachsoldat' ['guarding soldier'] by G. Wilhelm, *Grundzüge der Geschichte und Kultur der Hurriter*, Darmstadt 1982, 1). Also a mountain such as ***Ὄθρυς*** in Crete (cf. *ὄθρυν · Κρῆτες τὸ ὄρος*) offers protection in many ways. A modal form like Hurrian ****Udr=o/u=ž*** 'He/She (the Mountain-God) may protect (us) !' may be the basis for Linear B ****Ὄδρυς***.

I have no problem to derive Linear B ***o-du-ru-we*** (KN C 902.6), probably dative-locative of ****Ὄδρυς***, from Hurrian ***o/udr-*** 'to protect', nor the ethnic ***o-du-ru-wi-jo*** (KN C 902.2), probably ***Ὀδρύιος***, nor feminine ***o-du-ru-wi-ja*** (KN Ai(3) 982.1), nor ***o-du-ru-wi-jo*** on a stirrup-jar found in Thebes (TH Z 839), but imported from Crete.

However, it is less easy to understand presence of mount ***Ὄθρυς*** in Thessaly situated to the north of Phthiotis. If that name has a Hurrian origin as well, how far up north into the Aegean did (Minoan-)Hurrian power reach ? Mountains often have substrate names.

The toponym ***tu-ni-ja*** = e.g. ***Θῡνίᾱ*** on several Knossos tablets (KN Ap 629.1; Db 1246; Dv 1511+7193+7198+fr.; Le 641+fr.; X 7750.2; X 7633; Xd 149+8121.3); ***tu-ni-ja-de*** (KN Fh 373), acc. + ***-δε***, and the ethnic ***tu-ni-jo*** = e.g. ***Θύνιος*** at Pylos (PY Cn 4.4; Xa 1419.2), are possibly derived from the Thracian ethnic ***Θῡνός***. Herodotus (*I*, 28) mentions: *Θρήικες οἱ Θυνοί τε καὶ Βιθυνοί*, and Stephanus of Byzantium (*320, 8*): *Θυνία, χώρα τῶν Θυνῶν. τὸ ἐθνικὸν Θυνὸς ὁμοφώνως τῷ οἰκιστῇ τῆς Θυνίας*. J. Chadwick now compares Linear B *tu-ni-ja* with *Ἐλτυνία* (now Kunávi) south of Knossos ? (see M. Ventris - J. Chadwick, *Documents in Mycenaean Greek*, Cambridge 1973[2], 317, 588). Chadwick himself has placed a question mark after his equation. If it is correct, which seems doubtful, the toponym might have nothing to do with the Thracian Thynians. L.R. Palmer, however, has argued from the Knossos tablets and the 'Theban' jar, imported from Crete, for a link between ***tu-ni-ja*** on the one hand and ***o-du-ru-we*** and ***o-du-ru-wi-jo/ja*** on the other.

As we have just seen in the discussion on **Ὄδρυς* and its derivatives, L.R. Palmer has been able to establish certain groupings of toponyms in the Knossos tablettes. In one of these groupings a close relationship between ***tu-ni-ja*** and ****Ὄδρυς*** can be identified, cf. L.R. Palmer, Mycenaean inscribed vases, II. The mainland finds, *Kadmos XI (1972)*, 37 and 41.

The question is whether the close relationship between the two Cretan place names in Mycenaean times is just accidental or not. In historic times the *Odrysian* and *Thynian* tribes, the latter mentioned as inhabiting the region of Salmydessos in the first millennium B.C., lived close together. The Thynians even claimed ***Odrysos*** (eponymic hero of the largest Thracian tribe) as their ancestor, cf. A. Fol, Thrako-Bithynische Parallelen im vorrömischen Zeitalter II. Bevölkerungs- und Gesellschaftsstrukturen, *Thracia I*, Academia Litterarum Bulgarica, Primus Congressus Studiorum Thracicorum, Serdicae 1972, 198.

If toponyms such as ***o-du-ru-we*** and ***tu-ni-ja*** in Crete may account for presence of ancestors of the Odrysian and Thynian tribes on the island at some time during the Bronze Age, could they perhaps be identified with the *Πελασγοί* in Crete mentioned in *Odyssey* τ 177 ? We have unfortunately not the slightest idea of whether our ancient sources based their statements about *Πελασγοί* and, for instance, 'Thracians' on real traditions from centuries in the past or whether they just tried to figure out how similar names found in different places could be explained in the most logical way. I regard casual information in Homer about Thracian chieftains and tribes helping the Trojans as their allies as historically more reliable than the information provided by later scholars from antiquity.

Authors like Dionysios of Halicarnassus, Pausanias, Hesychius Alexandrinus, Strabo resemble to a large extent philologists of our time. They only had potentially more sources at their disposal, sources lost to us. They could read Hecataeus and quote him themselves and in their time they were much closer to their past than we are to theirs. But we have better facilities for communication and can rely on an immense amount of easily accessible data. It is difficult to pinpoint our identifications, partly since orthographic conventions of Linear B make more than one interpretation possible (e.g. ***τ*** or ***θ*** in ***tu-ni-ja***).

Apart from this ambiguity of orthography, even if we assume that * *Ὀδρυς*, *Ὀθρυς* and *Ὀθρυονεύς* are all related, it must be admitted that the scope of occurrences of these names is very wide: from Crete to Thessaly and from Cappadocia to Thrace. As far as toponyms are concerned, assignment of these names to the category of substrate names appears more likely than to that of adstrates in the narrow sense.

C.J. Ruijgh (*EGM,* § 144, n. 367) remarks: "À vrai dire, ***Θῡνίᾱ*** est attesté plus tard comme nom du pays des ***Θῡνοί***, c'est-à-dire d'une tribu thrace. Évidemment, s'il s'agit d'un nom d'origine thrace, il est difficile de l'admettre pour la Crète mycénienne.

Cependant, il est possible qu'il s'agisse d'un nom préhellénique emprunté par des Thraces." C.J. Ruijgh's hesitation to accept presence of Thracian toponyms in Crete in the Mycenaean era is understandable, especially if they are regarded as adstrate names in the narrow sense. Doubt may increase, if other feasible equations are compared. E. Laroche, *GLH*, 271, mentions a possible Hurrian connection s.v. ***tuni***. "Attribut de divinités; le plus souvent avec *tabri.* Graphies *tu/du-(u)-ni*. Sg. nom. ***tuni*** *(tabri)*, KUB XX 93+ VI 7; XXV 44 II 4; 45, 7; XXVII 1 II 30-31; XV 37 II 6; XXXII 84 IV 18; XLV 2 II 6; etc., etc. Gén. du poss. ***tu-ni-ib-bi-na***, KUB XXV 45, 3-4. Dir. ***tu-u-ni-da***, KUB XLVII 29 Ro 5, Vo 3, 6. ***tuniya*** *(tabriya)*, IBoT III 148 II 64, IV 13; KUB XXXII 50, 21; KBo VIII 89 Ro 4."

The latter form ***tuniya*** provides an exact equivalent to Linear B ***tu-ni-ja*** (KN Ap 629.1; Db 1246; Dv 1511+7193+7198+fr.; Le 641+fr.; X 7750.2; X 7633; Xd 149 + 8121.3). E. Laroche, *NH*, 257 and 270, also mentions a toponym ***D/Tunna*** (KBo IV 10 Ro 36; HT 2 VI 7; KBo XII 140 b.g. 3; Bo 595 III 15 = MIO 8, 195) in the 'Pays-Bas' of Asia Minor.

The Minoan site of Tylissos has to date only yielded 2 Linear A tablets, 1 roundel, 1 graffito incised on the shoulder of a corded pithos and 1 inscribed incomplete male figurine. None of these inscriptions contains the name of the site Tylis(s)os, known from the Linear B texts from Knossos: ***tu-ri-so*** (KN C 59,3; al.) ***Τυλῑσός***, with the ethnics ***tu-ri-si-jo*** (KN E 668,2; Og 833,5; B 807,1, mut.) ***Τυλίσιος***, and ***tu-ri-si-ja*** (KN Lc 533) ***Τυλίσια***, derived from the toponym. The genitive ***tu-ri-si-jo-jo*** (PY Sa 758) of the ethnic ***tu-ri-si-jo***, used as a personal name, is attested at Pylos, cf. C.J. Ruijgh, *EGM*, § 127, 149.

To date the etymology of the Pre-Greek toponym ***Τυλῑσός*** and ethnic ***Τυλίσιος*** was not known, but it is in my view justifiable to propose a Hurrian etymology, since (GIŠ.)***tuli*** [Boğ.] 'vine, vine-mountain' (cf. Th. Richter, *BGH*, 467, s.v. (GIŠ.)***tuli*** [Boğ.] 'Weinstock, Weinberg'), corresponds with Urartian (GIŠ.)***uldi*** (V. Haas 1989a, 269^{+44}) and with Hittite ***wiyan(a)-*** com./ntr., Luwian ***maddu-*** ntr., Ḫattic ***tefušne***(?), ***karam***, ***karamu***, ***karan***, Akkadian ***karānu***, ***kirānu*** and Sumerogram (GIŠ)GEŠTIN (cf. V. Haas 2003a, 251). See for etymologically cognate Urartian (GIŠ.)***uldi/e*** 'Weingarten' ['vineyard'] M. Salvini 1979b, 121; I.M. Diakonoff, 1989, 86. The Sumerogram GEŠTIN means 'wine'.

Since the Hurrian suffix ***=(i)=šše*** builds abstract forms (cf. I. Wegner, *Einführung*, 55) the Hurrian abstract ***tuli=(i)=šše*** probably means 'vineculture, viniculture, viticulture' that is an excellent name for a place suitable for growing wine on the sunny slope of a Cretan mountain. I. Wegner (*Einführung*, 55, 69) offers the following examples of abstracts formed with ***=(i)=šše***: ***šar=i=šše*** 'wish' from ***šar-*** 'to wish, demand', Ugarit vocabulary RS 94-2939, col. II 5; ***nir=i=šše*** 'goodness', derived from ***niri*** 'good'; ***kib=i=šše*** 'being seated (on the throne)', derived from ***keb-*** 'to set, put, lay down'.

The question about etymology of the toponym *Knossos* is not easy to answer. According to A. Fick (*Vorgriechische Ortsnamen als Quelle für die Vorgeschichte Griechenlands*, Göttingen 1905, 26, 126) the epigraphic evidence only offers ***Κνωσός*** and ***Κνώσιος*** with one ***σ***, but he adds that the names from Asia Minor with a similar formation usually show double ***σσ***. He compares ***Κνωσός*** with the West-Cilician name ***Κνῶς***. *Cilicia*, originally called *Kizzuwatna*, had a Hurrian and Luwian population in the 2nd millennium B.C., and probably a Lycian population in the 1st millennium B.C., but that does not mean that the etymology of ***Κνωσός*** is Luwian, the predecessor of Lycian.

P. Chantraine (*DELG*), mentions the verb ***κνώσσω*** (*Odys*. δ 809) 'dormir' ['to sleep'], 'dit d'un sommeil profond où apparaît un songe' ['said about a deep sleep, in which a dream appears'], but adds that a Greek or other etymology fails. He does not discuss the etymology of ***Κνωσός***. The excavations of Knossos have to date yielded only a few Linear A tablets that are quite fragmentary. They show no indication that the Linear A name of Knossos was similar to Linear B ***ko-no-so***, of which the ***-o-*** in ***ko-*** is supposed to be a mute vowel, needed to express the consonant cluster ***kno-***. It is conceivable that the first ***-o-*** of ***ko-no-so*** was originally not mute and that shortening of the first syllables ***kono- > kno-*** occurred under influence of the accent on the last syllable. As far as I know, consonant clusters such as initial ***kno-*** are not attested in Hurrian. So if this initial consonant cluster was already present in the Minoan name, the toponym may well be Pre-Hurrian.

If the ***-o-*** in ***ko-*** was not mute in the Minoan predecessor of Mycenaean ***ko-no-so***, a Hurrian 'one-word' name {**ko/un=o/uš=a*} 'He/She (a god/*numen*) has .... (the palace)' is conceivable, consisting of the Hurrian verbal root ***kun-*** + the suffix of the past or perfect tense ***-oš-*** + the marker of the subject of the transitive verb 3rd person singular ***-a***. Unfortunately the meaning of Hurrian ***kun-*** is not yet known, cf. Th. Richter, *VHN*, 446-447, s.v. ***kun-/kunn-*** {*ko/un-*}. Theoretically the 2nd person sing. in ***-o/u*** {**ko/un=o/uš=o*} 'You (a god/*numen*) have .... (the palace)' is also possible.

The root can also be nominal as in the personal name ***fKunnuzzi*** (wr. *fKu-un-nu-zi*) at Mari, {*ko/unn(i)=o=zzi*}, typology 3.1, (cf. Th. Richter, *VHN*, 177), with adjective suffix ***-(u)=zzi*** (cf. I. Wegner, *Einführung*, 56). Possibly {*ko/unn(i)=o=zzi*} is the Minoan-Hurrian prototype of Linear B ***ko-no-so***, that has a Greek ending in ***-ος***, but verification and confirmation of one of these possibilities would be welcome. Th. Richter (*VHN*, 174-178, 447) offers the following names with the root {*ko/un-*}: ***fKuniš-Naja*** (wr. *fKu-ni-iš-na-a*) at Mari, {*ko/un=i=ž-Naja/e*}, typology 1.3.2.2; ***fKunuš-Na*** (wr. *fKu-nu-úš-na*) at Mari, {*ko/un=o=ž-Na*}, typology 1.3.2.1, lexicon *kun-*, *Na/Naja/e*; ***Kun-šaki*** (wr. *fKu-un-ša-ki*) at Šušarrā, {*ko/un-šagi*}, typology 1.4; lexicon *kun-*, *šagi*; ***Kun-šekki*** (wr. *fKu-un-še-ek-ki*) at Tigunāni, {*ko/un-šekki*}, typology 1.4; lexicon *kun-*, *šekki* (→ *šagi*); ***Kun-šen*** (wr. *fKu-un-še-en*) at Mari, {*ko/un-šen*}, typology 1.4; lexicon *kun-*, *šen*; ***Kun-šenni*** (wr. *fKu-un-še-ni*) at Tigunāni, {*ko/un-šen(a)=ni*}, typology 1.4; lexicon *kun-*, *šena*; ***fKunukki*** (wr. *fKu-nu-uk-ki*) at Mari, {*ko/un=o=kk=i*}, typology 1.2.2.3, lexicon *kun-*; ***Kunum*** (wr. *Ku-nu-um*) at Mari, {*ko/un=o=m*}, typology 1.1.1.1.1, lexicon *kun-*; with root {*ko/unn-*}: ***Kunni*** (wr. *Ku-un-ni*) at Mari, Alalaḫ VII (AlT *54: 27), Ugarit (F. Gröndahl, *PNTU*, 340), Ḫattuša (E. Laroche, *NH*, 98, N° 629), {*ko/unn=i*}, typology 1.3.1.2.1, lexicon *kunn-*; ***Kunnunna*** (wr. *Ku-un-nu-na, ku-nu-na*) at Mari, {*ko/unn=o=nna*}, typology 1.3.1.1.2.1, lexicon *kunn-*; etc.

Linear A ***ku-ni-su*** (HT 10a.1; HT 86a.1-2; HT 86b.1-2; HT 95+149a.3; HT 95+149b.3) may contain the same verbal root ***kun-/kunn-*** {*ko/un-*}. Sign ***-ni-*** following ***ku-*** shows that the ***-u-*** of ***ku-*** is certainly not mute. I have concluded that ***ku-ni-su*** is probably not the agricultural commodity 'emmer-wheat', variant of Akkadian ***kunāšu(m)***, alleged by C.H. Gordon and J.G.P. Best, but a Hurrian personal name analysed as a 'one-word' (*optative*) name {*ko/un=i=ž=u=n(na)*}, 'He/She (a *numen*) may ... it (the child)'.

The feminine ethnics from Pylos ***ka-pa-si-ja*** (PY Vn 851.12), e.g. ***Καρπασίᾱ*** (with ***-σ-*** which we expect on phonetic grounds), and ***ka-pa-ti-ja*** (PY Eb 338.A; Ep 539.9; Ep 704.7; Un 443.3), e.g. ***Καρπαθίᾱ*** (with ***-θ-*** restored on the analogy of the toponym), are both derived from Pre-Greek ***Κάρπαθος***, a name which reminds us not only of the island ***Κάρπαθος*** between Crete and Rhodes, a toponym ***Καρπασίᾱ*** on Cyprus (cf. P. Chantraine, *DELG*, 500, s.v. ***κάρπασον*** 'nom d'une plante vénéneuse'), but also of ***τὸ Καρπάθιον ὄρος***, the Karpathian mountains in Rumania mentioned by Ptolemy *III*, 8, 1 and *III*, 5, 8, cf. W. Pape - G.E. Benseler, *Wörterbuch der griechischen Eigennamen*, Braunschweig 1884, reprint of the 3rd ed., Graz 1959, 627. These names establish a link between the Aegean and the northern Balkan area. The root of ***Κάρπαθος*** may go back to Indo-European ***(s)qerp-*** 'to cut' (cf. Lithuanic ***kerpù*** 'cut'). Since Bulgarian ***karpa*** and Albanian ***karpë*** both mean 'rock', ***Κάρπαθος*** could signify 'rocky island' and ***τὸ Καρπάθιον ὄρος*** 'the Rocky Mountain(s)'. The formant ***-θ-*** in ***Κάρπαθος*** has a Pre-Greek appearance and may be observed in toponyms such as *Κάνηθος, Κικύνηθος, Πεπάρηθος, Σκίαθος, Σώπηθος* and *Ὑρνάθιον*. We may consider whether ***Κικύνηθος*** might contain the same root as occurs in the name of the Thracian ***Κίκονες*** (*Iliad* B 846; P 73 and *Odyssey* ι 165). Herodotus (*VII*, 110) tells: - *ἔθνεα δὲ Θρηίκων δι' ὧν τῆς χώρης ὁδὸν ἐποιέετο τοσάδε, Παῖτοι Κίκονες Βίστονες Σαπαῖοι Δερσαῖοι Ἠδωνοὶ Σάτραι*. On the other hand names showing a reduplication or a *quasi*-reduplication are common in some languages, cf. E. Laroche, *NH*, 240: 'Lallnamen' Type II: base I redoublée: *Kaka/Gaga, Kiki, Kuku, Lala, Lili, Lulu, Mama, Μιμμι(ς), Nana, Nini, Nunu, Papa/Baba, Tata/Dada, Tete/Didi, Tutu/Dudu, Zuzu.* Cas particulier du type II: la série en *A-, Aba, Ada, Aga, Aka, Aya, Αμμα, Ana, Apa, Ata.* [Note 4: Les noms cunéiformes orthographiés selon l'usage cappadocien, sans la gémination consonantique hittite. Par ex.: *Kuku* = capp. *Ku-ku-ú*, hitt. *Ku-uk-ku*; *Ana* = capp. *A-na-(a)*, hitt. *A-an-na*, etc.]

A reflection of the Pre-Greek ethnic name ***Ὕαντες*** may be found in the dative-locative ***u-wa-si*** (PY An 656.15), ***Ὕανσι*** serving as a topographic indication. Pausanias (*X*, 35, 5) mentions Boeotian ***Ὑάμπολις*** as a city of the ***Ὕαντες*** who lived at Thebes before they had to flee from Kadmos and his army. Strabo (*IX*, 2, 3) mentions them with Aones, Temmikes and Leleges as barbarian inhabitants of Boeotia before the coming of the Phoenicians with Kadmos who fortified the Kadmeia. Further on, in the same section, he seems either to associate ***Ὕαντες*** with Thracians and Pelasgoi or to identify them as Thracians themselves. He mentions that Thracians were driven out of Boeotia to Parnassos and that the ***Ὕαντες*** founded a city ***Ὕᾱ*** in Phocis. Such stories about migrating and resettling peoples in our ancient sources point to the substrate character of these populations and their names. It is clear that the authors in antiquity were aware of that character. An expressive ethnic derived from this toponym may occur in Linear B ***u-wa-ta*** (KN Dd 1286.B), possibly ***Ὑάτᾱς***.

The patronymic ***u-wa-si-jo*** (KN Ai(1) 115) may be explained as either a derivative from this name, e.g. *Ὑάσιος*, or a derivative from ***Ὑαυς*, later attested as a personal name **Ὑᾶς**, e.g. *Ὑάνσιος*, cf. C.J. Ruijgh, *EGM,* § 126, n. 283; cf. W. Pape - G.E. Benseler, *Wörterbuch der griechischen Eigennamen*, 1573.

However, ***u-wa-ta*** (KN Dd 1286.B) from Knossos can also be interpreted as a Hurrian 'one-word' name ***Uw=a=tta***, consisting of ***uw-/urb-*** 'to slaughter (large cattle)' {*o/uv-*} + the marker of intransitivity ***-a-*** + the enclitic personal pronoun ***-tta***, translation 'I am engaged in sacrifices'. The root ***uw-/urb-*** was already known from Nuzi, but the bilingual ***kirenze*** made the meaning 'to slaughter (large cattle)' and the professional designation of ***uwuḫule*** {*o/uv=o=ġ(e)=o=le*} 'butcher' possible, cf. ***fUwaja*** (wr. *fú-wa-ia, fú-wa-a-ia*) at Mari, {*o/uv=a=ja* 'He/She (a priest ?) is engaged in sacrifices' [PGvS] and ***fUwuḫule*** (wr. *fú-wu-ḫu-le, fú-wu-ḫu-ul-le*} at Mari, '(female) butcher', cf. Th. Richter, *VHN*, 336, 554.

Another tribal name containing the same formant as we find in ***Ὕαντες***, is ***Ἄβαντες***. They are mentioned in Homer's *Iliad* B 536 ff. as inhabitants of Euboea where they lived in Chalcis, Eretria, Histiaia, Kèrinthos, Dios, Karystos and Styra. Strabo (*X*, 1, 3) tells that the old name of Euboea was not only *Makris*, but also ***Ἀβαντίς***. He also mentions that Aristotle says that Thracians setting out from ***Aba*** in Phocis, recolonised the island and renamed those who held it ***Ἄβαντες***. In Eustathius's commentary on Dionysius *Periegeta* 520 we read: *ὁ ποιητὴς .. τὴν Εὔβοιαν Ἀβαντιάδα λέγει, ἀπὸ τοῦ ἐν αὐτῇ ἔθνους τῶν Ἀβάντων, Θρᾳκίου ἔθνους, ὥς φησιν Ἀρριανός*; cf. *IG XII*, 8 no. 181 (from Samothrake): *Ἀβαῖος*. F. Bechtel, *Die historischen Personennamen des Griechischen bis zur Kaiserzeit*, Halle 1917, 530. Cf. D. Detschew, *Die thrakischen Sprachreste*, Wien 1957, 1.

On Linear B tablets from Knossos and Pylos we find the name ***wa-na-ta-jo*** (KN V(3) 466.2; PY Eb 369.A; En 609.15; Eo 211.2.3.5; Eo 224.5; Ep 301.3; Jn 832.7), probably ***Ϝαρνᾱταῖος***, patronymic of ****Ϝαρνάτᾱς***, expressive ethnic of ****Ϝάρνᾱ*** (cf. *Iliad* B 507: *πολυστάφυλον Ἄρνην*). The Greeks themselves, following popular etymology, probably connected this name with ***(ϝ)ἀρήν***, genitive ***(ϝ)ἀρνός***, 'lamb', but phonetically this is impossible, since vocalisation of ***-r̥-*** resulted in Mycenaean Greek ***ϝορνός*** or ***ϝρονός*** < ****wr̥n-***, which is attested in Linear B ***wo-ro-ne-ja*** (MY Oe 111) ***ϝρονέyα*** 'lamb's wool'. Thus ***Ἄρνη < Ϝάρνᾱ***, must contain a different, probably Pre-Greek root, cf. C.J. Ruijgh, *EGM*, § 191 and n. 68. There is still a town called ***Varna*** on the Black Sea coast of Bulgaria.

The name ***Ἄρνη*** is mentioned by Stephanus of Byzantium (123, 18) as a polis in Boeotia, Thessaly, Mesopotamia and Thrace. Ptolemy (*Geog. III*, 12, 17) mentions the town ***Ἄρνισσα*** near Dyrrhachium. D. Detschew (*Die thrakischen Sprachreste*, 25-26) was unaware of the original digamma in ***Ἄρνη***: "Vgl. den luvischen Ortsname ***Arinna***, der Forrer, *GL. 26, 1937*, 193, als 'Quelle' deutet und zu ai. ***rịṇati*** 'lässt fliessen, entlässt', abg. ***rinąti*** 'fliessen', gall. ***Renos*** 'Rhein', got. ***rinno*** 'Bach' stellt. Nach Kretschmer, *Gl. 28, 1939*, 115, wäre möglich, dass der luvische Ortsname mit Syncope des *i*-Lautes auch in den lykischen Ortsnamen ***Arñna, Ἄρνα, Ἀρνέαι*** (Steph. Byz. 123, 12) vorliege, während der griech. Ortsname ***Ἄρνη***, m.E. sicher thrakischen Ursprungs ist, und der ital. Flussname *Arnus* (Liv. 22, 2,2; Tac. Ann. I, 79) von dem luvischen Worte ferngehalten werden soll." So Detschew opts for a Thracian origin of the toponym *Ἄρνη* in Boeotia, Thessaly and Thrace (a 'Mesopotamian' *Ἄρνη* could have been founded by Alexander the Great).

The Mycenaean patronymic ***wa-na-ta-jo*** (KN V(3) 466.2; PY Eb 369.A; En 609.15; Eo 211.2.3.5; Eo 224.5; Ep 301.3; Jn 832.7), ***Ϝαρνᾱταῖος***, shows that ***Ἄρνη*** contained a digamma, which is confirmed by the existence of the Bulgarian toponym ***Varna***.

The occurrence of the toponym in Greece and Thrace pleads for a substrate character of the name which is likely Pre-Greek and Pre-Thracian, or, if one prefers the ancient name, 'Pelasgian'. The original ***Ϝ-*** in the Mycenaean name also proves that the toponym ***Ἄρνη*** in Greece and Thrace has nothing to do with the Luwian toponym ***Arinna***, because Luwian, as Mycenaean Greek, faithfully recorded the ***w***-sounds. Since Lycian is derived from Luwian, it is likely that Lycian ***Arñna*** is directly derived from Luwian ***Arinna*** and did not contain a ***w***-sound either. If E. Forrer's etymology of Luwian ***Arinna*** as 'well' (German 'Quelle') is correct and if it is related to Sanskrit *riṇati* 'let flow', ancient Bulgarian *rinąti* 'flow', Gallic *Renos* 'Rhine', Gothic *rinno* 'brook', then Detschew's view that "der ital. Flussname *Arnus* (Liv. 22, 2,2; Tac. Ann. I, 79) von dem luvischen Worte ferngehalten werden soll" is evidently wrong and the name of the Italian *Arno* river (Latin *Arnus*) corresponds etymologically with Luwian *Arinna*.

Since [***w***] and [***b***] are phonetically close, I may propose the hypothesis that ****Ϝάρνᾱ*** > ***Ἄρνη*** may have survived in the element ***-βερνα*** / ***-περνα*** in *Μηκύβερνα*, *Μηκύπερνα*, *Mecyberna*, *Megyperna*, a town on the east coast of *Pallene* (cf. for toponym and ethnics Herodotus *VII*, 122; Thucydides *V*, 39, 1; Skylax *66*; Steph. Byz. *450, 5*; Strabo *VII*, fragm. 29; Pliny, *Naturalis Historia IV*, 37; D. Detschew, *Die thrakischen Sprachreste*, 302-303).

If so, it is not inconceivable that there is also a correlation of ***-βερνα*** / ***-περνα*** with Hittite and Luwian ***parna*** 'house', which contains according to L.R. Palmer (*supra*) the same root as ***Παρνασσός*** in Greece and ***Parnašša*** in Anatolia.

The toponym ***Πέρνη*** in Thrace across the sea from Thasos (Steph. Byz. 517, 24: *Πέρνη, πόλις Θρᾴκης ἀντικρὺ Θάσου. τὸ ἐθνικὸν Περναῖος καὶ Περναία*) is identical with the name of an island in Caria and may be compared with the personal name ***Πέρνας*** in Isauria, cf. J. Sundwall, *Die einheimischen Namen der Lykier* (Klio Beiheft XI), Leipzig 1913, 288, 175; cf. D. Detschew, *Die thrakischen Sprachreste*, 364. Detschew, *ibidem*, 359, refers to the personal name ***Πάρνος*** from Olbia (*IPE 1*, 55), but adds that the name is according to Vasmer, *ISR* 48, related to the Iranian tribal name ***Πάρνοι***. Detschew, *ibid.*, mentions a castle ***Παρνοῦστα*** in Thrace.

On a Linear B tablet from Knossos (KN C 902.11) one previously read **(†)** ***re-na-jo***, which could be interpreted as ***Λερναῖον***, an ethnic used as a toponym derived from the toponym ***Λέρνᾱ***. The Pre-Greek ethnic ***Λερναῖος*** is later attested, cf. C.J. Ruijgh, *EGM*, § 194 and n. 86. However, the reading ***re-na-jo*** must now be abandoned, for the corrected reading is ***re-ri-jo***, possibly the ethnic ***Λέριος***, derived from the name of the island of ***Λέρος***, cf. J. Chadwick - L. Godart - J.T. Killen - J.-P. Olivier - A. Sacconi - I.A. Sakellarakis 1986, *Corpus of Mycenaean Inscriptions from Knossos, Volume I (1-1063)*, Incunabula Graeca Vol. LXXXVIII, Cambridge, London, New York, New Rochelle, Melbourne, Sydney, Roma 1986, 366. I refer to the Hittite texts for the ***-rn-*** cluster in Anatolian toponyms: *Ašurnaš, Au̯arna, Gurna, Kau̯arna, Karna, Kurna, Zišparna*, cf. H. Ertem, *Boğazköy metinlerinde geçen coğrafya adları dizini* (*Çivi yazılı metin yerleri ve Bibliyografya ile birlikte*), Ankara 1973. See the names s.v. in the alphabetical list with references to the Boğazköy texts in question. Cf. also Hittite and Luwian ***parna*** 'house'.

In Pamphylia we find the personal names ***Ϝαρνοπας*** and ***Ϝαρνις*** (cf. L. Zgusta, *Kleinasiatische Personennamen*, Prag 1964, 177, § 373) and in Phrygia and Pisidia ***Δαρνος*** (*ibidem*, 143, § 253). We find several names with the ***-rn-*** cluster in Greece, Anatolia and Thrace, e.g. ***Πρόερνα*** or ***Πρόαρνα*** (< * ***Πρό-ϝαρνα*** ?), a town in Phthiotis, ***Τάρνη*** (cf. *Iliad* E 44), a town in Lydia and in Achaia. Stephanus Byzantinus (347, 20) mentions the Macedonian polis ***Κάλαρνα***. It may be interesting to compare the name of the island ***Κάρνος*** along the Acarnanian coast and ***Ἁλικαρνησός*** in Caria with ***Κύρνος*** in Asia Minor and ***Ἁλίκυρνα*** south of the mountain ***Arakynthos*** in Aetolia.

The cluster was productive in Thrace where we find beside *Μηκύβερνα* (*vide supra*), *Δίερνα / Dierna, Tierna, statio Tsiernensis, colonia Zernensis, Zernae, Ζέρνης* (cf. D. Detschew, *Die thrakischen Sprachreste*, 132). We also find *Θέρνη, πόλις Θρᾴκης, τὸ ἐθνικὸν Θερναῖος* (Stephanus of Byzantium 310, 7), *Κόρνας*, a personal name from Bithynia, to be compared with the Pisidian personal name *Κόρνος* and the Cappadocian and Lykaonian toponym *Κόρνη* (D. Detschew, *Die thrakischen Sprachreste*, 254).

Ἐλευθέρνα with the ***-rn-*** cluster is a toponym in Crete. C.J. Ruijgh has been so kind as to draw my attention to this name which may contain the same 'Pre-Greek' root as the Mycenaean theonym ***e-re-u-ti-ja*** (KN Gg(3) 705.1; *alibi*), dative of ***Ἐλευθίᾱ***, at Knossos.

Compare also the toponym ***Ἐλευσίς***, with 'Pre-Greek' suffix ***-īν-***, ***Ἐλευσ-ίν-*** < ****Ἐλευθ-ίν-***, cf. C.J. Ruijgh, *EGM*, §101. P. Chantraine, *DELG*, 318, s.v. ***Εἰλείθυια***: "f. nom de la déesse des accouchements, souvent employé au pluriel (Hom. ion.-att.). Nombreuses variations orthographiques. .. Le mycénien fournit de façon certaine ***Ereutija*** = ***Ἐλευθίᾱ*** à Cnossos, à côté de ***aminiso*** = ***Ἀμνισος*** pour une offrande de miel, cf. J. Chadwick - L. Baumbach, 188. Étymologie: La forme ancienne, comme le prouve le mycénien, est ***Ἐλεύθυια***, d'où par dissimilation (et influence de *Ὠρείθυια* ?), ***Ἐλείθυια***, cf. Kalén, *Quaest. Gramm. Graecae* 8, n. 1; l'hom. ***Εἰλείθυια*** peut s'expliquer par un allongement métrique (Schulze, *Q.E.* 260 sq.). Deux voies sont ouvertes pour l'étymologie: ou bien on tire le mot du thème ***ἐλευθ-*** de *ἐλεύσομαι, ἤλυθον*, avec le même suffixe f. que dans ***Ἅρπυιαι***: 'celle qui vient' ou 'celle qui fait venir'. ... Ou bien terme indigène non grec (cf. p.-ê. le nom de lieu ***Ἐλευθέρνα***), Wackernagel apud Nilsson, *Gr. Rel.* 1, 313; le mot aurait pu être rapproché par étymologie populaire de *ἐλεύσομαι*, etc."

If comparison of the theonym with the verbal forms *ἐλεύσομαι, ἤλυθον* is indeed due to popular etymology and the theonym is Pre-Greek, a Hurrian origin may well be feasible. Feminine names with the Hurrian onomastic element ***-tuḭa*** are attested at Nuzi, e.g. ***ᶠApattuḭa*** (wr. *ᶠA-ba-ad-du-ia*), cf. I.J. Gelb, *NPN*, 22, with double writing of the dental indicating its voicelessness), and ***ᶠUntuḭa*** (wr. *ᶠUn-tu-ia* and *ᶠUn-du-ia*), cf. I.J. Gelb, *NPN*, 165), which might explain the unusual ending ***-θυια*** of the theonym. The first element ***Ἐλευ-*** / ****Elew-*** may be the result of metathesis < Hurrian ***Elwi-***, e.g. in the feminine name ***ᶠElwi-kui*** (wr. *ᶠEl-wi-ku-i* and variant *ᶠIl-mi-ku-i*), cf. I.J. Gelb, *NPN*, 44; P.M. Purves, *NPN*, 209. The name ****ᶠElwi-tuḭa*** can only be reconstructed from two separate Hurrian onomastic elements, which makes the identification less certain. If ***Ἐλεύθυια*** (**Ἐλέϝθυια*) is derived from ****ᶠElwi-tuḭa*** (through metathesis), we must also accept that a feminine personal name was first used as an epithet of a deity in Minoan times, probably in the manifestation or function of the Goddess of Birth, to become the goddess ***Ἐλεύθυια*** or ***Ἐλευθίᾱ***, ***e-re-u-ti-ja*** (KN Gg(3) 705.1; *al.*), in her own right in Mycenaean times.

Incidentally, a (double) formative ***-tiịa***, consisting of ***-ti*** + ***-ịa***, is attested at Nuzi in *Ikatiịa*, *Intatiịa*, *Kutatiịa* and *Tampatiịa*, cf. P.M. Purves, *NPN*, 266.

A derivation of ***Ἐλεύθυια*** or ***Ἐλευθίᾱ*** from Hurrian ****fElwi-tuịa / *fElew-tuịa*** is only feasible, if an original division of the onomastic elements *Ἐλεύ-* and *-θυια* is admitted instead of the usual division *Ἐλεύθ-υια*, which is based on an alleged Greek etymology.

Those who may consider the Hurrian option plausible, could argue that the Mycenaean Greeks after their conquest of Crete, soon established their own language as a superstrate language on the island and soon lost all knowledge of the Minoan vernacular, which differed so much from their own. Loan-words and non-Greek names were adapted by providing them with Greek formants and case endings, and sometimes the meaning was adapted with the help of popular etymology. They could also argue that the various orthographies of the name, mentioned by P. Chantraine, *DELG*, 318 (of which I have quoted only a few), may plead for a non-Greek origin, whether Hurrian or not. Though I have proposed the hypothesis myself, I am not yet convinced that an explanation of the theonym ***Ἐλεύθυια*** through Hurrian is preferable, partly because there are still too many unanswered questions and partly because a semantic connection between ***Ἐλεύθυια / Ἐλευθίᾱ*** and the ancient adjective ***ἐλεύθερος*** 'free' is quite strong.

Ἐλεύθυια (Hom. ***Εἰλείθυια***) is the Goddess of Birth. She liberates mother and child from each other by her support during the delivery of a baby. Dutch 'verlossen' means 'to release, liberate, deliver at childbirth'. Unfortunately the etymology of *ἐλεύθερος* is not easy either, cf. P. Chantraine, *DELG*, 336-337.

The name of female demons ***Ἅρπυιαι*** (usually in the plural form) mentioned by P. Chantraine in his comparison of the suffix ***-υια*** of that name with that of ***Ἐλεύθ-υια***, resembles the Hurrian personal name ***Arpuịa*** (wr. *Ar-pu-ja*), father of *Mu-uš-te-šup* at Nuzi, cf. I.J. Gelb, *NPN*, 31; P.M. Purves, *NPN*, 205, s.v. ***arp***. The name from Nuzi is masculine, so if ***Ἅρπυια*** is derived from that Hurrian name, the demon(s) had to become female, because names and words in ***-α*** are usually feminine in Greek, which is not necessarily the case in Hurrian. Comparison with Greek ***ἐρέπτομαι***, alluded to in *Odyssey* ξ 371: *Ἅρπυιαι ἀνηρείψαντο* (*ἀν-ερέπτομαι*), may be due to popular etymology, but may also indicate that the name *Ἅρπυια* originally missed initial ***h-***. Comparison with ***ἁρπάζω*** (cf. Chantraine, *DELG*, 114-115, s.v. ***Ἅρπυια***), may be due to popular etymology as well, but the ***h-*** of ***Ἅρπυια*** may yet have been caused by this comparison. Apparently [***h***] did not exist in the phonological system of Hurrian. O. Szemerényi, *Syncope in Greek and Indo-European and the nature of Indo-European accent*, Naples 1964, 203-213, and probably P. Chantraine as well, consider ***Ἅρπυια*** (and variant *Ἁρέπυια*) a loan-word.

Hesychius mentions the Carian polis ***Ἰδάρνας*** with the ***-rn-*** cluster, cf. P. Chantraine, *Dictionnaire étymologique de la langue grecque*, 455. This Carian toponym analysed as Hurrian ***id=ar=nna-***, consists of the root ***id-*** 'to beat, strike' + *factitive* and *iterative* root-extension ***-ar-*** + enclitic personal pronoun 3rd person singular ***-nna*** (single writing of ***-n-*** after ***-r-***) 'Beat him/her again and again'. If this analysis is correct, ***Ἰδάρνας*** did not contain an initial digamma ***F*** and has nothing to do with an alleged I.E. root in Greek ***ϝίδᾱ > ἴδη*** 'wood', 'forest', which used to provide the popular etymology for the name of the ***Ἴδᾱ*** mountains in Crete and Troas and possibly of the polis ***Ἴδη*** on the Thracian Chersonese.

Scylax 67: *μετὰ δὲ τὸν Μέλανα κόλπον ἐστὶν ἡ Θρᾳκία Χερρόνησος καὶ πόλεις ἐν αὐτῇ αἵδε· Καρδία, Ἴδη, Παιών, Ἀλωπεκόννησος*, cf. D. Detschew, *Die thrakischen Sprachreste*, 214; D.A. Hester, Pelasgian - a new Indo-European language ?, *Lingua 13 (1965)*, 372-373.

Since ***w-*** was faithfully and consistently written with the scripts of Linear A and B, it can be proved that Linear A ***i-da*** (ZA 21b.1; ZA 27a.1) from Kato Zakro, ***i-da*** (PK Za 17) and ***i-da-ja*** (PK Za 18) from Mount Petsophas near Palaikastro, ***i-da-a*** (KO Za 1.b-c) from Mount Kophinas, | ***i-da-da*** | (KT Zg 2.b) from Crete, ***i-da-ma-te*** (AR Zf 1; AR Zf 2) from Arkalokhori, ***i-da-mi*** (SY Za 1) from Symi Viannou, ***i-do-ri-ni-ta*** (PH 6.2) from Phaistos, ***i-da-pa$_3$-i-sa-ri*** (PH 6.4) from Phaistos and Linear B ***i-da-i-jo*** (KN K 875,4; PY An 661,2) from Knossos and Pylos did not contain an initial ***w-***.

Nevertheless Linear B has preserved a few names that may have been derived from I.-E. ***ϝίδᾱ*** > ***ἴδη*** 'wood', 'forest': e.g. ***wi-da-jo*** (KN V(2) 60+151.3), a personal name ***Ϝῑδαῖος*** with *F-*. According to D. Detschew (*Die thrakischen Sprachreste*, 558) existence of a root ***ϝίδᾱ*** is confirmed by the second element of a Dacian plant-name ***ῥαθιβίδα*** 'Schamkraut'. Linear B ***wi-da-jo*** (KN V(2) 60+151.3) may be translated as 'forester, woodman', *not* 'God of Mount Ida', that is represented by Linear B ***i-da-i-jo*** (KN K 875,4; PY An 661,2) ***Ἰδαῖος***, the Mycenaean equivalent to Linear A ***i-da-a*** (KO Za 1.b-c) and ***i-da-ja*** (PK Za 18).

The Linear B anthroponym ***wi-da-ma-ro*** (KN V(3) 479, 2; KN Do 919+921.B) may contain the element ***ϝίδᾱ-*** combined with ***-μαρος*** occurring in Thracian names such as *Βηρι-μαρος, Ἴσ-μαρος, Καρσι-μαρος, Κατο-μαρος, Ζμερτο-μαρος*, cf. Detschew, *Die thrakischen Sprachreste*, 289. It may be significant that the personal name ***di-zo*** (KN V(3) 479, 1) occurs in the first line of the same tablet, identified as possibly 'Proto-Thracian'.

For a better understanding of the formation of the apparently non-Greek personal name ***wi-da-ka-so*** (KN Dd 1402+1593+2007.B), e.g. **Ϝῑδάκασος*, it may be useful to make the following equation: ****Ϝίδακος*** (toponym *Ἴδακος* on the Thracian Chersonese is mentioned by Thucydides VIII, 104, 2) relates to ****Ϝῑδάκασος*** as ***Ἴμβρος*** (name of an island of Thrace according to Stephanus of Byzantium 331, 14: *Ἴμβρος, νῆσος ἐστι Θρᾴκης*) to ***Ἴμβρασος*** (cf. Stephanus of Byzantium 331, 12: *Ἴμβρασος, ἡ Σάμος, ἀπὸ τοῦ ποταμοῦ. τὸ ἐθνικὸν Ἰμβράσιος καὶ Ἰμβρασία.* Cf. also the patronymic *Ἰμβρασίδης* in *Iliad* A 519-520: *βάλε δὲ Θρῃκῶν ἀγὸς ἀνδρῶν, Πείρως Ἰμβρασίδης, ὃς ἄρ' Αἰνόθεν εἰληλούθει.*).

The Linear A sequences ***i-da-a*** (KO Za 1.b-c) from Kophinas and ***i-da-ja*** (PK Za 18) from Petsophas can be interpreted as a divine epithet ***Idaia*** 'God of Mount Ida', originally 'He (Our Father, Tešub) thunders', possibly hypocoristic (with hypocoristic suffix ***-ya***) of ***i-da-ma-te*** (AR Zf 1; AR Zf 2) from Arkalokhori. If we take ***i-da-a*** and ***i-da-ja*** as divine epithets, it belongs to ***a-ta-i-jo-wa-ja***. ***Ida*** (*Ἴδη*) mountains in central Crete, mentioned in Linear A texts from Kato Zakro and Petsophas as ***i-da*** (ZA 21b.1; ZA 27a.1; PK Za 17), but also known from Phrygia and Mysia, was originally an *intransitive* form ***id=a*** meaning 'He (the mountain-god or mountain) thunders', later became the name of the mountain.

Linear B provides ***i-da-i-jo*** (KN K 875,4; PY An 661,2), probably ***Ἰδαῖος***, that may well be equivalent to Linear A ***i-da-a*** and ***i-da-ja***. ***Ἰδαῖος*** is an epithet of Zeus who has an altar on Mount Ida near Troy (*Iliad* Π 605; Ω 291). But Zeus is also ***Κρηταγενής*** 'born in Crete' and is called '***Zeus Idaios***' in Euripides, *Cretans, Fragm. Trag. Gr.* No. 472.

Here the priests in the cult of the ***Kourètes*** (***Κουρῆτες***) call themselves *mystai* of ***Zeus Idaios*** and *Bakkhantes* of the *Kourètes*, and say that they have accomplished the *omophagia* of *Zagreus* and brandished the torches of the Mountain Mother (cf. M.P. Nilsson, *The Minoan-Mycenaean religion*, Lund 1968, 578). There is also a charioteer of King Priamos called ***Ἰδαῖος*** (*Iliad* Γ 248; Ω 325) and a Trojan, son of Dares, saved by Hephaistos (*Iliad* E 11, 20). Incidentally, *Ζαγρεύς* reminds us of the *Zagros* mountains on the border of Iran and Iraq, but also of *Zakros* in Crete.

In Linear B the masculine form ***i-do-me-ni-jo***, dative of ***Ἰδομένιος*** (PY Gn 428,5; PY Fn 324,7 mut.) and the feminine ***i-do-me-ne-ja*** (PY Eb 498,1; Ep 212,9), ***Ἰδομένεια***, feminine form of ***Ἰδομενεύς***, are attested (cf. C.J. Ruijgh, *EGM*, § 118 and 219). ***Ἰδομενεύς*** is, of course, also known as son of Deukalion, grandson of Minos and King of Knossos who joined Agamemnon's army in the Trojan war and is mentioned as a hero in the Iliad several times. Since I suspect that Mycenaean ***Ἰδομενεύς*** may well be derived from the Old Hurrian 'sentence name' ***id=o=m-en(n)i***, consisting of the Hurrian verbal root ***id-*** 'to beat, strike, crush' + the Old Hurrian suffix marking the (transitive) past tense ***-o-***, + the Old Hurrian marker of the subject (3rd person singular of the verb) ***-m*** + the theophorous element ***eni*** 'God' or ***enni*** < ***en(i)=ni*** 'the God', 'He (*-m*), the God crushed (the enemy ?)', cf. I. Wegner, *Einführung*, 126-127. The formation of ***id=o=m-en(n)i*** is similar to Linear A ***da-du-ma-ta*** (HT 95a.1), analysis {*dad=o/u=m-atta*}, 'He, (God the) Father loved (the child)', with ***atta(i)*** in the double meaning of 'the (natural) father' and '(God the) Father'.

The Linear B personal name ***e-da-e-u***, e.g. ***Ἐδαεύς*** (PY Qa 1298), genitive ***e-da-e-wo*** (PY Eb 495.1; Ep 613.1), ***Ἐδαῆϝος*** (cf. C.J. Ruijgh, *EGM*, § 280, n.121, and § 299), might well be of the same Pre-Greek, c.q. Minoan-Hurrian, origin as ***i-da-i-jo***. C.J. Ruijgh has been so kind as to draw my attention to a possible ***i/e*** alternation in the Pre-Greek roots of these names, provided that ***i/e*** comprises a short vowel. A relation with *Ἰδομενεύς* (Homer: - ᵕ ᵕ -) is then only possible, if one assumes metrical lengthening for this form. Possible examples of this Pre-Greek root may be found in anthroponyms mentioned by E. Laroche, *NH*, 82, no. 478. *Idari* 1. Cappadocia: *I-d*[*a*]*-ri-iš*, TCL XX 191, 7. 2. 'Roi de montagne': nom. ^{m}*I-da-ri-iš*, IBoT I 1 V 12; no. 479. *Itarzia*. Cappadocia: *I-da-ar-zi-a*, EL 186, 4.

Although P. Chaintraine (*Dictionnaire étymologique de la langue grecque*, 455) writes s.v. ***ἴδη***: "dor. ***ἴδᾱ*** f. 'bois, forêt' (Hdt., Théocr.). Vieux mot qui fournit le toponyme ***Ἴδη***, massif montagneux en Mysie occidentale (Iliade etc.) et en Crète (D.P., Paus.), d'où ***Ἴδηθεν***, ***Ἰδαῖος*** (Iliade etc.)", he also adds: "Comme le confirme le toponyme, doit être un terme indigène préhellénique, donc sans étymologie établie." Linear A and B attestations of all these names without ***w-*** and the fact that there is no trace of ***ϝ-*** in these names in Homer prove conclusively that the root of *Ida, Idaia, Idaios, Idomeneus, Idomeneia* is Pre-Greek and has nothing to do with *ἴδη*, Doric *ἴδᾱ* < Indo-European *ϝίδᾱ* 'wood', 'forest'. Apparently, Chantraine may have overlooked the possibility that we are dealing with two different roots, one Indo-European with digamma (*ϝίδᾱ* 'wood', 'forest') and one probably non-Indo-European without digamma. This observation is in fact confirmed by coexistence of the Linear B personal name ***wi-da-jo*** (KN V 60,3) = ***Ϝῑδαῖος*** with ***w-***, which is derived from *ϝίδᾱ* > *ἴδη* 'wood', 'forest' and Linear B ***i-da-i-jo*** (KN K 875,4; PY An 661,2), ***Ἰδαῖος*** that can be equated with Linear A ***i-da-a*** (KO Za 1.b-c) from Mount Kophinas and ***i-da-ja*** (PK Za 18) from Mount Petsophas.

A perforated sealstone of black-green steatite in the form of a bobbin / reel (*CMX* XI, n° 96), donated by R.B. Seager to the Metropolitan Museum in New York (26.31.158), probably from Crete (exact provenance uncertain), bears a Linear A inscription (KT Zg 2): a. | ꜗ *te-ro-a*| (← as read from the sealstone), but | *a-ro-te* ꜗ | (→ as read from the seal-impression) and b. | *da-da-i*| (← as read from the sealstone), but | *i-da-da* | (→ as read from the seal-impression). The form *i-da-da* probably consists of the name of mount **Ida** + the Hurrian *directive* suffix -*da* 'to' (cf. Greek *Ἴδαν-δε) or the Hurrian *ablative* suffix -*dan* 'from' (cf. Greek *Ἴδηθεν* <*Ἴδᾱ-θεν).

Linear A *a-ro-te* can be identified with the Hurrian personal name *Allu-te. The Hurrian personal name **Allu-teіa** (wr. *Al-lu-te-e-a*) is attested at Nuzi (JEN 518:10; cf. I.J. Gelb, *NPN*, 20, s.v. **Allu-teіa**; P.M. Purves, *NPN*, 199, s.v. **all, allu-**). Since -*teіa* and -*te* are both very common hypocoristic forms of -*tešup* in Hurrian theophorous sentence names, *Allu-te is equivalent to **Allu-teіa**. Phonologically it is probably /*Allote*/. According to Th. Richter (*BGH*, 12-14) the verbal root **all-** II means 'to rule', cf. Urartian *alae* and *aluse* 'ruler' and the Urartian root **al-** 'to be lord, to rule'. Cf. also Hurrian **allai** 'Lady, Mistress' or 'Queen'. If this verbal root is chosen, the whole phrase *a-ro-te* ꜗ *i-da-da* (KT Zg 2.a-b) can be analysed as **all=o-te ida=dan** and can be rendered as 'Tešub ruled and rules from (Mount) Ida'. This would be the Old Hurrian version of Homeric *Ἴδηθεν μεδέων* "ruling from Ida" in *Iliad* Ω 308, where Priam prays to Zeus: "*Ζεῦ πάτερ, Ἴδηθεν μεδέων, κύδιστε μέγιστε*", "*Father Zeus, that rulest from Ida, most glorious, most great*".

Since -*m*- preceding an occlusive is not expressed in consonant clusters in Linear A and B, analysis of *a-ro-te* as **all=o=m-te**, consisting of the root **all-** + the marker of the Old Hurrian past tense (with durative aspect) -*o*- + the Old Hurrian marker of the subject 3rd person singular -*m* and the hypocoristic theophorous element -*te*, is also feasible: 'Tešub, he ruled and rules (from Ida)'. Since there is no object mentioned, we may conclude that the verb is used as an *antipassive*. Since *a-ro-te* occurs on a sealstone (not on a clay-tablet) **all=o-te** or **all=o=m-te** need not be a personal name, but can be a proverbial expression.

In my view a closer parallel between the Hurrian *ablative* suffix -*dan* and the Greek *separative* suffix -*θεν* can hardly be found. I even consider it possible that thanks to strong Minoan influence on Mycenaean society, Mycenaean Greek may well have derived enclitic -*θεν* from the Minoan-Hurrian *ablative* suffix -*dan*. Likewise it is also likely that the Mycenaean Greek enclitic *directive* suffix -*δε* is derived from the Minoan-Hurrian *directive* suffix -*da*. The double parallels make accidental correspondence less likely. It may seem odd that an Indo-European language may have derived such a grammatical feature from an agglutinative language, but miracles have also happened *vice-versa*. For instance, the former city of Constantine, *Κωνσταντινούπολις*, is now called *Istanbul*, which is not a Turkish name. It is derived from *εἰς τὴν πόλιν* 'to the city'. Moreover, suffixes such as -*δε* and -*θεν* are basically anomalous in an inflexional language such as Greek and were largely replaced by prepositions, but they are characteristic for an agglutinative language such as Hurrian, cf. also *Ἴδηθεν μεδέων* (*Iliad* Γ 276), where Agamemnon uses the same epic formula as Priam in *Iliad* Ω 308: "*Ζεῦ πάτερ, Ἴδηθεν μεδέων ! κύδιστε ! μέγιστε !*".

According to Th. Richter (*BGH*, 10-11; *VHN*, 368) **al-** I, *alu-* [*passim*] means 'sagen, sprechen, antworten' ['to say, speak, answer']. If Linear A *a-ro-te* contains this verbal root **al-** I, *al=o=(m)-te ida=dan* can be rendered 'Tešub (he) spoke and speaks from Ida'.

Th. Richter (*VHN*, 602) also mentions ***Aruš-Ḫeba*** (wr. *a-ru-uš-ḫé-ba*), analysed as a *jussive* form {*ar=o=ž-Ḫeba*} and translated 'May *Ḫeba* give (the girl)', a form that can be considered parallel to Linear A ***a-ro-te***, interpreted as Hurrian ***Aruš-te***. If the theophorous element ***-Ḫeba*** is exchanged for ***-Te***, hypocoristic of ***-Teš(š)ub***, the result would be 'May *Teš(š)ub* give (the boy)', quite an acceptable name for a boy.

Since ***a-ro-te*** in the phrase ***a-ro-te ₂ i-da-da*** (KT Zg 2.a-b) is probably not a personal name, the forms analysed as ***ar=o=ž-Te(šub) ida=dan*** may be rendered as 'May *Teš(š)ub* from (Mount) Ida give !', cf. *chapter 11: Religious Linear A inscriptions.*

C.J. Ruijgh (*EGM*, § 191) interpreted Linear B ***i-ta-ja*** (KN Ap 769, 2) from Knossos (nom. fem. personal name, ante MULIER 1) as a Greek name: e.g. ***Ἱσταίᾱ***, patronymique de **Ἵστᾱς*, lui-même sobriquet dérivé de *ἱστός* 'métier de tisserand'.

However, Linear A ***i-ta-ja*** OLE+***di*** 10 (HT 28b.6) from Hagia Triada can be interpreted as a Hurrian hypocoristic name, that can be analysed as {*itt=a=ja*}, consisting of the Hurrian verbal root ***itt-*** 'to go' + the marker of intransitivity ***-a-*** + hypocoristic suffix ***-ya***, 'He/She goes', cf. Th. Richter, *BGH*, 110-111, s.v. ***itt-*** I [Boğ.; Mitt.] 'to go, to depart'. The orthographic conventions of Linear A and B make it not easy to determine, whether Linear B ***i-ta-ja*** (KN Ap 769, 2) from Knossos represents the Hurrian name {*itt=a=ja*} as attested at Hagia Triada or a personal name *Ἱσταίᾱ* with a Mycenaean Greek etymology.

Some names might have a relation with both Macedonia and Thrace. In Pylos we find an expressive ethnic used as a personal name ***pi-we-ri-ja-ta*** (PY Jn 389.3), e.g. ***Πῑϝεριάτᾱς***, derived from ****Πῑϝερίᾱ***, itself derived from the toponym ***Πίϝερος*** of which the locative form is attested at Pylos ***pi-we-re*** (PY Aa 1182), probably ***Πῑϝερεῖ***, cf. C.J. Ruijgh, *EGM*, § 167. The geographical names *Πίερος*, *Πῑέρᾱ*, *Πῑερίᾱ* and *Πίων*, which are found later on, can be explained etymologically from the adjectives signifying the notion of fertility, ***πῑερός*** < ****πῑϝερός*** and ***πίων*** < ****πίϝων***, respectively. The original forms, showing the ***-ϝ-***, can be compared with Old Indian ***pívan-***, ***pívari*** and display a perfect Indo-European (c.q. Indo-Iranian) etymology, cf. P. Chantraine, *Dictionnaire étymologique de la langue grecque II*, 898-899, s.v. ***πῖαρ***; cf. also C.J. Ruijgh, *EGM*, § 167 and note 486.

Another explanation for ***pi-we-re*** might be the plural nominative of the ethnic ***Πίϝερες*** serving as a toponym on this Pylos tablet (cf. C.J.Ruijgh, *ibidem*). However, since the toponyms in the Aa, Ab, Ad series of the Pylos tablets seem to appear in the locative or instrumental forms (cf. e.g. ***po-to-ro-wa-pi***), the locative ***Πῑϝερεῖ*** (from athematic ***πῑϝερ-***) seems more likely than the plural nominative ***Πίϝερες***. At Mycenae ***pi-we-ri-ṣị*** (MY Fo 101,5) occurs, probably ***Πῑϝερίσ(σ)ι***, plural dative of the feminine ethnic ***Πῑϝερίς***, derived from ***Πίϝερος***. The dative singular ***pi-we-ri-di*** (MY Oe 103,5) occurs as well, probably serving as a personal name, cf. C.J. Ruijgh, *EGM*, § 167, n. 486. C.J. Ruijgh has been so kind as to point out to me that J.T. Killen has convincingly demonstrated that ***pi-we-ri-ṣị*** (MY Fo 101,5) is probably to be interpreted as 'for ***Πῑϝερίς*** and the person belonging to her (probably her daughter)', as later ***Δημήτερσι*** means 'for Demeter and her daughter'. This can be inferred from the portions attributed to the persons mentioned in MY Fo 101, which begins with ***a-ne-a₂*** = dative of ***Ἀνέᾳ***, (nickname derived from ****ἄνος***, neuter attested in ***ἀπηνής***, ***προσηνής***, ***αἰᾱνής***, see Frisk s.v.) who receives V 3, then follow six women who each get V 1, then ***pi-we-ri-ṣị*** who receive S 1 (= V 6), then again six women receiving each V 1.

Ἀνέᾱ receives thrice as much as the other women, because she is presumably a forewoman in charge of a group of women. Since ****pi-we-ri*** (dative ***pi-we-ri-di*** in MY Oe 103,5), who probably has the same rank as ***Ἀνέᾱ***, receives twice as much as her (V 6), one may conclude that ***pi-we-ri-ṣị*** means 'for *Πῑϝερίς* and the person belonging to her (probably her daughter)'.

The same root occurs in the ethnic name of the Thracian tribe of the ***Πίερες***, mentioned by Herodotus (*VII*, 112) and Thucydides (*II*, 99, 3) as living in the area of the Pangaean mountains beyond the Strymon, but who allegedly lived originally in Pieria on the Thessalian border near mount Olympus. Strabo, *VII*, frg. 11: *Θρᾳκῶν δὲ Πίερες μὲν ἐνέμοντο τὴν Πιερίαν καὶ τὰ περὶ τὸν Ὄλυμπον*, ... (*X*, 3, 17): *Πιερία γὰρ καὶ Ὄλυμπος καὶ Πίμπλα καὶ Λείβηθρον τὸ παλαιὸν ἦν Θρᾴκια χωρία καὶ ὄρη, νῦν δὲ ἔχουσι Μακεδόνες·*

According to Hesiod, *Aspis*, 205-206, 'Pierides' serves as epithet of the Muses: *θεαὶ δ' ἐξῆρχον ἀοιδῆς Μοῦσαι Πιερίδες, λιγὺ μελπομένης ἐικυῖαι*. They were born in Pieria as the daughters of Zeus (Hesiod, *Theogony*, 50-62) and according to Homer (*Iliad* B 595) they found the Thracian singer and musician *Θάμυρις* 'Thamyris' in the kingdom of Pylos and stopped him singing and playing the cither. The spelling of ***μοῦσα*** (Homer, Attic-Ionic, etc.), ***μοῖσα*** (Aeolic), ***μῶσα*** (Doric, Alkman, *passim*), shows that we are probably dealing with a seeming diphthong ***-οῦ-*** (probably representing a long close [***ō***] in Homer and Attic-Ionic), a real diphthong ***-οῖ-*** in Lesbian and a long open ***-ῶ-*** in Doric.

Aristophanes (*Lysistrata*, 1296-1300) relentlessly mocks at the Lakonian pronunciation, that sounded funny in the ears of the Athenian public. With some comic exaggeration he lets a Lakonian recite: *Ταΰγετον αὖτ' ἐραννὸν ἐκλιπῶα, Μῶά μόλε Λάκαινα πρεπτὸν ἁμὶν κλέωα τὸν Ἀμύκλαις σιὸν καὶ χαλκίοικον Ἀσάναν·* (Attic: *ἐκλιποῦσα, Μοῦσα, ἡμῖν κλείουσα, θεόν, χαλκέοικον Ἀθηνᾶν*) 'Come, Lakonian Muse, after having left lovely Taygetos, praising for us the splendid god of Amyclae (Apollo) and bronze-domed Athena'.

P. Chantraine, *DELG*, 716, s.v. ***μοῦσα***, rejects most etymologies discussed by him. The least sceptical he is about the etymology proposed by Ehrlich: "Ehrlich, *KZ 41*, 1947, 287, part de ****μόνθya***, ce qui lui permet d'évoquer *μενθήρη, μανθάνω*, lesquels pourraient être rattachés à la racine ****men-***, cf. s.v. *μανθάνω*, mais non à skr. *mánthati* 'agiter, troubler'; cette analyse est peut-être possible. Dans une toute autre direction, on a voulu voir dans la Muse, ****montya*** une 'nymphe de la montagne', cf. lat. ***mōns*** (Wackernagel, *KZ 33*, 1895, 571 sq.): cette hypothèse qui sémantiquement n'est pas absurde se heurte à la difficulté que la famille de lat. ***mōns*** n'est pas représentée en grec; cf. sur ce mot Ernout-Meillet."

Ehrlich's Indo-European etymology, based on ****μόνθya***, cannot be ruled out on phonetic grounds, since the dialectal variation of ***μοῦσα*** (Homer, Attic-Ionic, etc.), ***μοῖσα*** (Aeolic), ***μῶσα*** (Doric), shows that the seeming diphthong ***-οῦ-*** (probably representing a long close [***ō***] in Homer and Attic-Ionic) and the long open ***-ῶ-*** in Doric, are probably caused by compensatory lengthening of the vowel as a result of loss of following ***-ν-***, whereas the ***-ν-*** changed into ***-y-*** before ***-σ-*** in Lesbian, cf. West-Greek *ἄγοντι* (3rd person plural), Arcadian *ἄγονσι*, Att.-Ion. *ἄγουσι*, Lesbian *ἄγοισι*; **ἄγοντ-yă* (part. fem.) > Arc. *ἄγονσα*, Lac. *ἄγωσα*, Att.-Ion. *ἄγουσα*, Lesbian *ἄγοισα*. However, semantically a relation between *μοῦσα, μοῖσα, μῶσα* and *μανθάνω* seems less likely, which may well explain Chantraine's hesitation to accept the etymology ("peut-être possible").

If etymologies based on Indo-European roots are so unsatisfactory, the problem may be solved by derivation from a non-Indo-European source. Hurrian ***muš***, ***muša-***, ***-muša***, 'august, sublime, righteous, pure' is epithet of divinities, especially *Ḫebat*, but also applied to road and river. It is an element in theophorous personal names. P.M. Purves, *NPN*, 235, s.v. ***muš***: "Hurrian. Cf. *mu-úš*, Mari 6: 11, 15, 19, *mu-šu-un-na*, KUB XXVII 46 IV 24, translated 'auguste, sublime' by F. Thureau-Dangin in *RA XXXVI (1939)*, 22f. Adjectival and substantival roles are evident for ***muša***. Occurrences of ***muš(u)ni***, formed on ***muš*** and identical with the personal name element ***mušni*** are more common in Hurrian texts." The substantivated forms ***mušni*** with the so-called singular definite article ***-ni***, and ***mušna*** with the plural definite article ***-na***, both occur at Boğazköy as ***mu-u-uš-ni/na***, KUB XXXII 19 IV 43, 44. The Mycenaeans may have adopted the plural form ***mušna*** (wr. *mu-u-uš-na*), 'the august ones', phonologically /***mosna***/, into the Greek vernacular from Minoan Crete, but they may well have adapted the form to ****monsa*** through metathesis, yielding the form which later developed into ***μοῦσα***, ***μοῖσα*** and ***μῶσα***, respectively. Semantically 'the august ones', 'the pure ones' seems much more in accordance with the identity of the Greek divine Muses than the notion attached to *μανθάνω*. The Hurrian form ***mušna*** was probably not recognized as a plural form by most Mycenaean Greeks who were not familiar with the Hurrian language. Since the form with metathesis ****monsa*** < ***mušna*** was probably by most Greeks associated with their singular feminine forms in ***-α***, they adapted the form to the Greek plural feminine case ending ***-αι***.

Thus they completely hellenized the adopted form. As a matter of fact the plurals ***μοῦσαι***, ***μοῖσαι*** and ***μῶσαι*** are more common in later Greek than the singulars.

E. Laroche, *GLH*, 173, s.v. ***muš(u)*** 'juste': "Il faut noter maintenant l'équation de RS 21.62 Ro 7 (*Ugar. V* 238): sum. [D]U = akk. ***qe-en-nu*** = h. ***mu-u[š-x]***. S'il s'agit bien d'une graphie pour akk. ***kênu***, ***kînu*** 'ferme, juste', on obtient un sens applicable partout; le nom ***Ibri-muša***, par exemple, sérait la réplique hourrite de l'akkadien ***Šarru-kînu***. Cf. aussi oug. ***muṣ*** = ***kînu***." The plural 'nominative' ***mu-šu-un-na šiye-[na]*** 'pure rivers, waters', KUB XXVII 46 + IV 24, with the suffix ***-na*** of the plural definite article, is attested at Boğazköy (***šiye*** = river, water, cf. E. Laroche, *GLH*, 173 and 230-231). Since the Muses are divine, Hurrian forms with the divine determinative deserve attention. E. Laroche, *GLH*, 173: ***^{d}Mušuni***, forme de *Ḫebat*. *^{d}Ḫé-bat-mu-uš-ni*, KUB V 27 I 17; XXVII 1 II 37 = 3 III 19; KBo XI 28 V 25, etc. - *^{d}Ḫé-bat-mu-šu-(un)-ni*, KUB XII 12 V 33; XXVII 22 I 19; XXXII 52, 3, etc. - *^{d}Mu-šu-ni*, VBoT 16 Ro 13. Erg. *^{d}Ḫé-bat-^{d}mu-šu-un-ni-iš*, KUB XXIX 8 III 32. Dat. *^{d}Mu-šu-u-ni-pa*, KBo XX 129 + III 23. – Onomastique: Nuzi, *NPN*, 236; Alalaḫ ***Arammušuni***; Hatti: ***^{f}Mušu-ḫepa***, *NH* N° 825. – Nom divin ***^{d}Ebri-muša***, v. ***ewri***. To these names may be added *Mu-zu-um-a-dal* and *^{f}A-we-eš-mu-zi* from Chagar Bazar, analogous to Nuzi ***^{f}Aweš-muše***, in *Iraq VII*, 40 and 36. At Nuzi occur *Muš-apu, Muš-tešup, Muš-teḭa, Muš-te, Muš-tilla, ^{f}Muša-teni, ^{f}Muša-til, Aki-muša, Enna-muša, En-muša, Muša-l-enni, Ir-muša, Tanni-muša, Danni-muša, Wanti-muša, Wandi-muša, Wadi-muša, Ari-muše, ^{f}Aweš-muša, ^{f}Awiš-muša, ^{f}Musu-p-šaḭa, ^{f}Musu-p-šaḭu, Muš-šen(n)i, Mušuš-šenni, Mušuš-še* (*-še* is hypocoristic of *-šen(n)i*), hypocoristics *Muše-ia* and *Mušu-ia*, and with the suffix of the definite article *-ni, Akam-mušni, Šatam-mušni, Šeḫra(m)-mušni, Tiša(m)-mušni, Warim-mušni*, cf. P.M. Purves, *NPN*, 235-236, with all variant writings.

Homer tells that the goddess *Hera* jumped down from mount Olympos to lovely Pieria and Emathia: *Ἥρη δ' ἀΐξασα λίπεν ῥίον Οὐλύμποιο, Πιερίην δ' ἐπιβᾶσα καὶ Ἠμαθίην ἐρατεινὴν* (*Iliad* E 225-226). Is Hera's interest in Pieria, domain of the Muses, accidental or did the epic tradition preserve her relation with ***dḪé-bat-mu-uš-ni*** ? Anyway, reversing Homer's statement, it is not a big step either to move from the Pierian Muses up to the Olympian gods.

Herodotus (*V,* 7) tells that the only gods worshipped by the Thracians were Ares, Dionysus and Artemis: *θεοὺς δὲ σέβονται* (*οἱ Θρήικες*) *μούνους τούσδε, Ἄρεα καὶ Διόνυσον καὶ Ἄρτεμιν*. The problem with such statements is how they should be interpreted. Since most peoples or tribes were used to waging war in antiquity, there is virtually none that did not worship some martial god. Did the Thracians have their own 'war god' whom the Greeks could identify with their god *Ares* or did the Thracians have a theonym built on the same root as that of the Greek god's name ? D. Detschew (*Die thrakischen Sprachreste*, 24), s.v. ***Ἀρεύς***, ***Ἄρης***: [I translate the German text] "However, since the Thracians in contrast with the Greeks imagined *Ares* as a horseman, he could easily be identified with *Heros*, since dedications to the latter in Thessaly and Boiotia are usually connected with equestrian reliefs. In this way it can be explained that dedications to Ares are rare in Thrace, whereas worship of the horseman-heros is attested in a great number of monuments."

Ares's name occurs in various forms in the Mycenaean texts. The epic flection of this non-Greek theonym is rather complicated, because it is built on three different roots: ***Ἀρη-***, ***Ἀρεσ- / Ἀρεh-*** and ***ἈρηϜ-***, all derived from 'Pre-Greek' ****Arē-***. To date no trace has been found of ***ἈρηϜ-*** in the Mycenaean texts (cf. C.J. Ruijgh, *EGM*, § 67). At Knossos we find ***a-re*** (KN Fp(1) 14+27+28+fr.2; Mc 462+5792+5808+5816+8450+fr.B) ***Ἄρῃ***, dative of ***Ἄρης***, derived from the root ***Ἀρη-***. At Knossos the personal name]***a-re-jo*** (KN Vc(1) 208) occurs, probably ***Ἄρεῖος*** 'the martial man', also derived from the root ***Ἀρη-***. The doublet form ***a-re-i-jo*** occurring at Knossos and Pylos (KN Le 641+fr.1; PY An 656.6), probably ***Ἀρέἰος***, however, is derived from the root ***Ἀρεσ- / Ἀρεh-***. Likewise, on some Theban jars the compound personal name ***a-re-me-ne*** is attested (TH Z 852; al.), probably ***Ἀρῃμένης***, besides ***a-re-i̯-me-ne*** (TH Z 849), probably ***Ἀρέἰμένης***, derived from ***Ἀρη-*** and ***Ἀρεσ- / Ἀρεh-***, respectively. The personal name ***pa-na-re-jo*** (nominative KN As 1516,15; KN U 4478,5,19; KN V 1004; *al.*; dative PY Fn 867,2), may be explained as ***Παναρεῖος***, comparable with ***Παναθήναιος*** (cf. ***Παναθήναια***).

The combination ***e-ma-a₂ a-re-ja*** (PY Tn 316 r. 7) can be interpreted as singular dative ***Ἑρμάᾳ Ἀρείᾳ*** 'for *Ἑρμάας Ἀρείāς*', 'for Hermes, the Martial' (Hermes as protector on the roads and in war). ***Ἀρείāς*** may be considered a substantivated adjective placed in apposition to ***Ἑρμάας*** (cf. C.J. Ruijgh, *EGM*, § 229). M. Lejeune (*Mémoires de philologie mycénienne*, 210, n. 20) regards ***a-re-ja***, however, as a feminine theonym: une déesse …dans une même offrande (à laquelle Hermès imprime un caractère dominant masculin). Interpretation of ***Ἀρείāς*** as 'the Martial' is in fact corroborated by an Arcadian inscription (*Del.* 665 C): *τὸν Δία τὸν Ἄρηα, τὰν Ἀθάνāν τὰν Ἀρείāν* etc., showing that the special domain of Ares is shared by Zeus the Martial and Athena the Martial (cf. C.J. Ruijgh, *EGM*, § 229, n. 154).

Th. Richter (*VHN*, 378) mentions a theonym ***Ara***, that was to date only known from Ḫattuša as the theonym ***Da-a-ra(o)***, that is attested in CTH 492 among Hurrian deities.

It now also occurs as subject of Old Hurrian verbal 'sentence names' as ***°-a-ra***, e.g. in ***Arum-Ara*** (wr. *A-rum-a-ra*) at Tigunāni, analysis *{ar=o/um-Ara}*, typology 1.1.1.1.1, 'Ara gab (Jungen)' ['Ara gave (the boy)'], cf. Th. Richter, *VHN*, 73; and ***Ḫašip-Ara*** (wr. *Ḫa-ši-ip-a-ra*) at Tigunāni, analysis *{ḫaž=i=b-Ara}*, typology 1.1.1.2.1, 'Ara erhörte (Person oder Gebet)' ['Ara heard (and answered person or prayer)'], cf. Th. Richter, *VHN*, 128. See for the theonym V. Haas, *Geschichte der hethitischen Religion, Handbuch der Orientalistik I/15*, Leiden 1994, 257-258 + note 37. Unfortunately it is not known whether ***Ara*** is a martial god, whose name might be related to 'Pre-Greek' ****Arē-***.

There is another Hurrian god, ***Aštabi***, described by E. Laroche (*GLH*, 61) as 'Dieu guerrier, identifié à Ninurta' ['Martial God identified with Ninurta']. In Akkadian texts: ^{D}*Aš-tu-u-bi-nu*, CT XXV 11 II 31; cf. Ungnad, *Subartu*, 65, etc. In Hittite texts: nom. ^{D}*Aštabiš*; acc. ^{D}*Aštabin*; abs. ^{D}*Aš-ta-(a)-bi*, ^{D}*Aš-ta-(a)-wi*; hieroglyphic ^{D}*As-ta-bi*. In Hurrian texts: abs. *Aštb*, CTA 166, 29, 31; Hrozný, *ArchOr. 4*, 123. RS quadr. 137 IV b 16 = *Ugar. V*, 249: ***Aš-ta-bi-i[n]*** = Ugaritic ***Aštaru***. Dir. *Aštb-d*, *Ugar. V*, 519 ff. Onom.: *AT*, 130 *et passim*; *NH* N° 178.

According to Th. Richter (*BGH*, 59) ***Aštabi*** I [Alalaḫ VII] is used as name of a month at Alalaḫ, according to F. Zeeb (*Die Palastwirtschaft in Altsyrien nach den spätaltbabylonischen Getreidelieferlisten aus Alalaḫ (Schicht VII), AOAT 282*, Münster 2001, 163, 653), the second month (October/November). Ugaritic ***Aštaru*** (RS quadr. 137 IV b 16) has an Akkadianizing nominative in ***-u***, whereas ***Aštari-*** in the Nuzi personal name ***Aštar(i)-tešub*** (wr. *Aš-tar-te-šup, Aš-ta-ri-te-šu-up, A-aš-ta-ri-te-šup, Aš-ta-ri-te-šup*) shows the Hurrian absolutive ending in ***-i***. Linear A ***a-ta-re*** (ZA 8.1) from Kato Zakro may well be equivalent to the Hurrian personal name ***Aštari*** (wr. *Aš-ta-ri*), attested at Nuzi as son of *Pa-pa-an-te* (HSS IX 13:26), phonologically */aštare/*, see for an extensive discussion *chapter 13*.

The name of Dionysus is twice attested at Pylos in the genitive ***di-wo-nu-so-jo*** (PY Xa 102) and ***di-wo-nu-so***[(PY Xa 1419.1), probably both to be interpreted as ***Διϝονύσοιο***. Since tablet PY Xa 102: ***di-wo-nu-so-jo*** is now joined with PY Ea 107:] ***e-ka-ra*** GR 2 T 6, the new text offers the combination ***di-wo-nu-so-jo , e-ka-ra = Διϝονύσοιο ἐσχάρᾱ*** GR 2 T 6 = 'altar of Dionysos for burnt sacrifices, 2 talents and 6 T of grain'.

A Linear B text from Khania: 1. ***di-wi-jo-de di-we***...2. ***di-wo-nu-so***..., ***Δίϝyονδε Διϝεῖ Διϝονύσῳ***, points to 'a sanctuary of Zeus (***Δίϝyον*** + *directive* suffix ***-δε***, cf. *di-u-jo*, PY Tn 316 v. 8) for Zeus (*dative* ***Διϝεῖ***, cf. ***di-we***, PY Tn 316 v. 9, *al.*) and Dionysos, showing that the two deities shared a cult and a sanctuary at Cretan Khania.

The theonym Dionysos was explained by P. Kretschmer as Thracian ****Διοσ-νύσος*** 'son of Zeus', ****νύσος*** 'son', the masculine equivalent to ***νύση***, synonym of ***νύμφη***. The meaning 'son of Zeus' seems very plausible and may be confirmed by the Linear B text ***di-wo , i-je-we = Διϝὸς ἱυέϝει*** (PY Tn 316 v. 10) 'for the son of Zeus'. The etymology ***Διόνυξος*** (cf. ***νύσσω*** 'to stab', 'to pierce'), coined by the *Etymologicum Magnum* 277.35, is obviously to be considered a popular etymology (cf. P. Kretschmer, *Einleitung in die Geschichte der griechischen Sprache*, 242-243; cf. D. Detschew, *Die thrakischen Sprachreste*, 141).

M.P. Nilsson, *The Minoan-Mycenaean religion and its survival in Greek religion*, Lund 1950, 567-568, tells that P. Kretschmer, *Aus der Anomia*, 1890, 17, also proposed the etymology of the name of Dionysos's mother ***Σεμέλη*** '*Semelè*' as '(Mother) earth' on the basis of Russian *zemlya* 'earth'.

P. Chantraine, *DELG*, 996: "**Σεμέλη**: dor. **-ā**, fille de Cadmos, mère de Dionysos qu'elle a eue de Zeus. On rapproche la formule du néo-phrygien ***δεως ζεμελως κε*** 'aux dieux du ciel et de la terre' et on admet qu'il s'agit d'une déesse thraco-phrygienne de la terre; cf. A. Heubeck, *Praegraeca* 77; O. Haas, *Ling. Balk. 10*, 1966, 92-93."

About Kretschmer's explanation of the theonym Dionysos as 'Thracian' M.P. Nilsson (*ibidem*) is more sceptical: "Professor Kretschmer, to whom these important discoveries are due, presents them as evidence for the Thracian origin of Dionysos; but the inscriptions from which he draws his material are Phrygian, and this distinction is not to be lightly passed over. The Phrygians were a Thracian tribe, but they immigrated early, about 1200 B.C., to Asia Minor, where they overthrew the Hittite Empire. In the centuries after the migration the Phrygians and the Thracians had very different fates. The latter persisted in their savagery, the former were subjected to the influence of the old civilization and religions of Asia Minor. These they took over. The cult of the *Magna Mater*, for example, is often called Phrygian, but is of course native to Asia Minor. The question raised by the provenance of the inscriptions, whether the child Dionysos is really Phrygian and not Thracian, is therefore of more far-reaching importance than appears from a first glance. Phrygia was, at that early time, when the cult of Dionysos was imported, a highly civilized country, from which the Greeks received many impulses."

According to ancient sources the *Φρύγες 'Phrygians'* moved from Europe into Asia Minor after the Trojan War. They were called *Βρίγες 'Briges'*, while they still lived in Europe (Strabo, *Geogr.* VII, 3, 2). Their migration probably took place at the same time as the southward migration of the Dorians from areas in north-western Greece, according to Thucydides (I, 12, 3) in the eightieth year after the Trojan War (cf. P.G. van Soesbergen, 'The Coming of the Dorians', *Kadmos XX.1, 1981*, 38-51). Whatever caused these migrations, it is likely that the causes were correlated. The name '*Dionysos*' is attested everywhere in the Mycenaean world, now also at Khania. The adoption of the deity and his cult into Greek religion had probably already taken place before the migration of the Phrygians into Asia Minor.

The suggestion of later Greek authors that the Greeks adopted the cult of Dionysos from the Thracians or Phrygians may be based on an erroneous reconstruction. The Mycenaean Greeks could have adopted the cult either directly from Minoan Crete or from Asia Minor, but in the latter case from the civilizations preceding the arrival of the Phrygians. Kretschmer's etymology of the element ***-nūs-*** 'son' may be accepted, but his arguments for a Thracian origin are no longer valid. For the time being a designation of Pre-Greek is more appropriate for the element ***-nūs-***. ***Διϝο-*** can be the Greek equivalent to Hurrian Tešub. The most logical conclusion is that *Dionysos* 'the son of Zeus' has taken the place in the Greek religion, that *Šarrum(m)a* had in the Hurrian pantheon.

The root ***nuz-/nuzz-*** and variant ***nazz-*** occurs in Hurrian personal names (cf. Th. Richter, *BGH*, 284), but its meaning is to date not identified. Th. Richter (*VHN*, 475) mentions that the root ***nuz-/nuzz-*** {*no/uz(z)-*} in contexts is only found in *nu-(uz-)za-a-i* at Ḫattuša (ChS I/5, 46 Rs. IV 9'; 47 Vs. II 16'; 48 Rs. III 13'), cf. E. Laroche, *GLH*, 189.

Th. Richter (*VHN*, 475) mentions the following personal names: *Nuzakku* (Š), *Nuzukka*, with variant *Nuzukkānu* (M), Nuzza (T), *Nuzukkulla* and *Nuzukkulli* (M), *Nazzakku* (Š), *Nazzakkulla* (Q), *Nazzukku* (M), *Nuzānu* ([Q], ŠE), *Nuzzan* (M), *Nuzama* (Q).

Linear B ***e-ka-ra*** 'altar for burnt sacrifices' in ***di-wo-nu-so-jo* , *e-ka-ra*** (PY Xa 102 + PY Ea 107) **= *Διϝονύσοιο ἐσχάρᾱ* =** 'altar of Dionysos for burnt sacrifices, is intriguing.

According to P. Chantraine (*DELG*, 379-380) the exact meaning of Greek ***ἐσχάρᾱ***, Ionic ***ἐσχάρη***, is 'foyer bas, brasier' ['low hearth, fireplace'], (*Il.*, *Od.*, Ar., etc.), employé notamment pour des foyers de sacrifice, distingués des *βῶμοι* plus élevés [particularly used for sacrificial fireplaces, distinguished from the higher *βῶμοι*]. He adds with regard to the etymology: Terme technique et dans une certaine mesure religieux des plus anciens. Apparemment dérivé en ***-ρᾱ***; pas d'étymologie [technical term and to a certain degree one of the oldest religious terms. Apparently derivative in ***-ρᾱ***.].

Since there is no Greek or I.-E. etymologie, it is not farfetched, if I assume that (Mycenaean) Greek ***e-ka-ra*** = ***ἐσχάρᾱ*** could refer to a charcoal hearth/fireplace in the kitchen or, for instance, in the throne-room of the Palace of Nestor at Pylos, where the king could kebab his meat with his guests, but first and foremost it is the sacrificial altar for burnt sacrifices to propitiate the gods. E. Laroche (*GLH*, 125) mentions s.v. ***išḫarini*** 'cuisinier'. RS quadr. 130 Vo 4: *nuḫatimu* = h. *iš-ḫa-ri-ni*.

According to I. Wegner (*Einführung*, 55) the suffix ***-i=nni*** forms adjectives into substantives designating professions. She derives the Hurrian term ***išḫ=ar=i=nni*** 'baker' from ****išḫ=ar=i***, from the root ****išḫ-***, with root-extension ***-ar-***, which is most interesting, if we compare it with Mycenaean Greek ***e-ka-ra*** = ***ἐσχάρᾱ***. It is in my view clear that the Mycenaean Greeks adopted the Hurrian lexeme ****išḫ=ar=i*** and only had to change the Hurrian ending in ***-i*** into the Greek feminine ending ***-a***. Other Hurrian forms in ***-i=nni*** are:
urb=ar=i=nni 'butcher' from *u(r)b/v-* 'to slaughter' (*Einführung*, 55, 211).
far=i=nni (*warin(n)i*) 'baker of bread', root *par-*, */far=/*; *far=i=nni=na=ma*, absolutive plural + enclitic particle ***-ma*** (*ibid.* 129, 213).
fand=ar=i=nni (*p/wandarinni*) 'cook'; *fand=ar=i=n(n)i=na=ma*, absolutive plural + particle ***-ma*** (*ibid.* 129, 134, 213-214).
tab=(i)=r(i)=i=nni (*tabrinni*) '(copper)smith', agens-orientated participial form + suffix ***=i=nni*** designating professions, from *tab/v-* 'to cast (metal)' (*ibid.* 21, 55-56, 283), cf. ***tab=ašt=o=m***, 3rd person sing. (Old Hurrian), (*ibid.* 128, 216, 218), cf. ***ta/ibira/i*** 'someone who casts (metal), copperworker' (*ibid.* 21).

Th. Richter (*BGH*, 102) s.v. ***išḫ-***: o.Ü. [without translation] (Giorgieri 2000a, 211; Wegner 223; *Einführung*, 256: ****išḫ-*** Verbalwurzel [verbal root]). ****išḫari*** 'kitchen' (Diakonoff/Starostin 1986, 39); ***išḫarinni*** [Ug.] 'cuisinier' corresponds with Akkadian *nuḫatimmu* (E. Laroche, *GLH*, 125); 'baker' corresponds with Sumerian [MU], Akkadian *nuḫatimmu*, Ugaritic *'āpiyūma* (*CAD* N/II [1980] 313; Huehnergard 1987a, 52, 108); 'cuoco' ['cook'], i.e. ***išḫ=ar=i=nni*** (Giorgieri 2000a, 211; 'Bäcker', i.e. ***išḫ=ar=i=nni*** (Wegner 2000, 223; *Einführung*, 256). So I do not believe that ****išḫari*** means 'kitchen', but 'low hearth, fireplace', indeed for domestic usage the most important utensil in the kitchen, but also fireplace for sacrificial usage, altar for burnt sacrifices. It is also likely that (Mycenaean) Greek ***e-ka-ra*** = *ἐσχάρᾱ* is derived from it.

I also think that the name of the Syrian goddess ***Išḫara*** (Akkadian ***išḫara*** < older ***ešḫara***) of unknown provenance, attested since the Ur III-period, is derived from it. Her qualifications seem to reflect her relation with the altar for burnt sacrifices, for she is the 'Lady of the verdict and the sacrificial altar'.

She is also 'Mistress of the inhabited regions / residences' and has some militant features. Her festivals with peculiar rites are celebrated in spring and autumn: for instance, a sculpture of the Goddess is carried through *two fireplaces* for purification, a cathartic rite that only appears in this festival. She is also connected with otherwise completely unknown gods such as Ḫalma, Tangara and Tuḫḫiura who are possibly all of Syrian provenance (KUB X 37+, elaborated by H.G. Güterbock, Some stray Boghazköy tablets, *Florilegium Anatolicum*, 137 ff.). A priest of *Išḫara* in *Kummanni* (Hurrian centre of cult and culture and the place where the struggle between Kumarbi and Tešub was staged) was *Ammiḫatna*, of whom several cathartic rituals were handed down in Hittite, that partly go back to Hurrian traditions (CTH 471-473, cf. also KBo XXIII I). There are also rituals for the goddess described in Luwian (LTU, 88-89). Temple of *Išḫara* and sacrificial actions are also attested in rituals of the *(Ḫ)išuwa*-festival, see for more information V. Haas, *Hethitische Berggötter and hurritische Steindämonen. Riten, Kulte und Mythen*, Mainz 1982, 100-102. She was also worshipped by the Hittites and at Ugarit, where her name was also spelled as ***Ušḫara*** and in the list of Hurrian divinities (RS. 24.295) as ***užḫrd***, with *directive* suffix ***-d*** in alphabetic cuneiform.

Whether ***Išḫara*** is originally Hurrian or not, it is clear that she belonged to the Hurrian pantheon and that with the increase of southeast Anatolian influence (especially from Kizzuwatna and Cappadocia) on religious thought at Ḫattuša from the time of Šuppiluliuma I onwards the significance of *Išḫara* grew in the documents from Boğazkale as well. I have no doubt that the Mycenaean Greeks inherited the lexeme ***ἐσχάρᾱ*** from Minoan-Hurrian in Minoan Crete.

In his search of the child Dionysos in the Phrygian religion M.P. Nilsson found a Phrygian god *Sabazios*, commonly identified with Dionysos (*The Minoan-Mycenaean religion and its survival in Greek religion*, 568), but had to conclude that the Phrygian inscriptions call him ***Zeus Sabazios***. His mysteries, which came to Greece in the 5th and 4th centuries B.C., comprised purifications and other ceremonies, and the snake took a prominent place in them. Two inscriptions from the Maeonian district with a mixed Lydo-Phrygian population, are dedicated to ***Mètèr Hipta*** and ***Zeus Sabazios***, *Denkschr. d. Akad., Wien, LIV*, 1911, No. II, 96, No. 188: *Μητρὶ Ἵπτᾳ, καὶ Διεὶ Σα[βαζίῳ*; (on a round altar from Gjölde near Kula) *Denkschr., l.c.*, 85, No. 169: *Με[λ]τίνη Μητρᾶ Μητρὶ Ἵπτᾳ εὐχήν*. According to M.P. Nilsson (*ibidem*, 568, n. 22) P. Kretschmer (*Glotta XV*, 1926, 76 f.) connects the name ***Hipta*** with the element ***-hepa*** of some Mitannian feminine names, which he derived from a goddess ***Hepa***, and thinks that this deity appears in the Boğazköy texts under the name of ***Hebe*** or ***Hepit***.

In *Hymn. Orph.*, 49, 1-4, ***Hipta*** is called the nurse of Bacchos and ***χθονίη μῆτερ*** (voc.). Proklos, *in Timaeum*, II, 124 C, relates that ***Hipta*** carried the child Dionysos on her head in a *liknon*, surrounded by a snake, cf. M.P. Nilsson, *ibidem*, 569 and n. 23. The vocative ***χθονίη μῆτερ*** is a literal translation of the name ***Semelè*** (cf. Russian *zemlya* 'earth') into Greek. If ***Hipta*** is indeed to be equated with the Hurrian goddess ***Ḫebat***, spouse of ***Teš(š)ub***, Zeus Sabazios can be associated with *Teš(š)ub* or a later form of that god. Their son is ***Šarru(m)ma***. E. Laroche, *GLH*, 218, s.v. *Šarru(m)ma*: "Dieu d'origine hittite, formant triade avec *Tešub* et *Ḫebat* au Kizuwatna, importé en Syrie au 14ème siècle.

Sarrumma a survécu en Asie Mineure sous les formes *Sarma* et *-zarma*; cf. Laroche, *Syria 40*, 277 sqq. – *Šarrumma* = LUGAL-*ma* 'veau / garçon de *Tešub*.'

Πῡθώ is the ancient name of Delphi. At Delphi Dionysos is associated with the chthonic *Πύθων* 'the snake Python', killed by Apollo. Ancient etymologies of the toponym were already rejected by Strabo *Geogr. IX*, 419; cf. P. Chantraine, *DELG*, 953, s.v. *Πῡθώ*: toponyme sans étymologie.

Interesting are the so-called snaketubes found in Minoan peak sanctuaries, e.g. at Koumasa (M.P. Nilsson, *The Minoan-Mycenaean Religion*, 103, fig. 28) as well as Symi Viannou, which no doubt played a part in the cult of the gods revered. *Hermes* and *Aphrodite* are the gods who were later worshipped at Symi Viannou, but although there seems to have been a remarkable and rare continuity of a cult in the sanctuary, the character of the deities worshipped at the site may have changed in the course of time.

We have seen that e.g. *Hermes* appears to have been a *Martial god* in Mycenaean times. A martial aspect has at least been one of his features. M.P. Nilsson, *o.c.*, 515-516: "It is very likely that Hermes has appropriated some Minoan-Mycenaean elements, but he was, more than Artemis, an essentially Greek god."

The question "What is essentially Greek about Hermes ?" is difficult to answer. He is certainly a god with many human aspects and features, but is that proof of his Greekness ? Is the Cave on Mount *Κυλλήνη* in southern Arkadia, where he was born, proof of his Greekness ? In M.P. Nilsson's days many scholars believed that the etymology of his name was Greek. Important is that his name is attested in the Mycenaean texts. At Knossos occurs ***e-mi-ja-ta*** (KN V 831,1), ***Ἑρμιάτᾱς***, ethnic in ***-ιάτᾱς***, used as a personal name. It may be derived from a toponym ****Ἑρμίᾱ*** (cf. the adjective ***Ἕρμιος***, derived from the hydronym ***Ἕρμος***. C.J. Ruijgh, *EGM*, § 167, n. 482: "Il est possible qu'à ce nom préhellénique se rattache le théonyme ***Ἑρμῆς*** < ***Ἑρμάάς*** (***e-ma-a₂*** PY Tn 316 r 7: dat.), dont la finale est visiblement non grecque; noter que le thème *Ἑρμο-* survit dans les anthroponymes composés du type ***Ἑρμογένης*** et du type ***Εὔερμος*** (Bechtel, *H.P.*, p. 164-166)."

My hypothesis that the theonym ***Ἑρμῆς*** < ***Ἑρμάάς*** < ****Ἑρμάάς*** is derived from Hurrian ***Ermi-*** 'Lord, King', variant at Nippur of ***Erwi-*** at Nuzi and ***Ewri*** (in Tušratta letter and elsewhere), is corroborated by the fact that ***ewri/erwi/ermi*** could not only refer to a king of flesh and blood, but also to a deity as is confirmed by ***dEb-ri-muša***, KUB XXV 50 II 11 sq.; KBo XXIII 25, 2, 5; and ***dIr-bi-ti-ig(a)***, provided with the divine determinative (cf. E. Laroche, *GLH*, 85-87, s.v. ***ewri*** 'seigneur, roi'), that I interpret as 'The Lord is beautiful' (***tag-/takk-/teg-***). Cf. compounds of ***dḪébat*** and ***dMuš(u)ni*** with the divine determinative, mentioned by E. Laroche, *GLH*, 173: ***dMušuni***, forme de ***Ḫebat***. *dḪé-bat-mu-uš-ni*, KUB V 27 I 17; XXVII 1 II 37 = 3 III 19; KBo XI 28 V 25, etc. - *dḪé-bat-mu-šu-(un)-ni*, KUB XII 12 V 33; XXVII 22 I 19; XXXII 52, 3, etc. - *dMu-šu-ni*, VBoT 16 Ro 13. Erg. *dḪé-bat-dmu-šu-un-ni-iš*, KUB XXIX 8 III 32. Dat. *dMu-šu-u-ni-pa*, KBo XX 129 + III 23. ***dEwri***, if used as a divine name, primarily refers to Tešub, but could perhaps refer to a limited number of prominent gods, just as the epithet *Allani* refers to *dḪébat* or *dŠa-uš-ka* (*Ištar*). The noun ***ewri / ibri*** (Tušratta *et alibi*) = ***erwi*** (at Nuzi) = ***irmi / ermi*** (at Nippur and in Linear A) can be used as title of a King (e.g. of Mitanni) or as an epithet of Tešub, cf. *ergative* of the possessive 1st pers. plur. ***eb-ri-iw-wa-šu-uš*** (Mit. IV 118) 'Our Lord'.

In that passage King Tušratta addresses *Tešub* as ***^{d}Te-e-eš-šu-pa-aš*** (*ergative*) ………. ***eb-ri-iw-wa-šu-uš at-ta-iw-wa-šu-uš*** 'Tešub .. Our Lord, Our Father' (Mit. IV 118), cf. my discussion on Linear A ***a-ta-i-jo-wa-ja*** = Hurrian ****at-ta-(i)-iw-wa-(j)-aš*** 'Our Father', reconstructed *absolutive* (and *vocative*) on the analogy of the attested *absolutive* ***at-ta-a-ar-ti-iw-wa-aš^{meš}*** {*att(a)=ardi=iwwa=aš*} 'our ancestors, our grandfathers'.

It is significant that the theophorous elements ***Ermi-/Irmi-*** and ***-ermi/-irmi*** are several times attested in Linear A. The Linear A personal name ***i-mi-sa-ra*** (HT 27+HT 48a.3) from Hagia Triada contains the theophorous element ***Irmi-*** 'Lord' as first onomastic element. It can be interpreted as the Hurrian personal name ****Irmi/Ermi-šarra*** 'The Lord is like the King of Gods', which is in fact almost equivalent to ***Erwi-šarri*** at Nuzi and to ***ibri-šarri***, ***ibri***(EN)***-šarri***(LUGAL), ***ibrḏr / iwrḏr*** at Ugarit; ***ibri-šarri*** [AL 137] at Alalaḫ. Cf. also ***Ir-me/mi-ta-at-ta*** and ***Ir-me-ta-ta*** at Nippur, cf. Clay *PNCP*, 93, to be read ***Erme/i-tatta***, i.e. ****Erwi-tatta***, according to Purves, *NPN*, 263. Since ***Erwi-šarri*** 'the Lord is King of Gods' is the name of 29 persons at Nuzi (cf. I.J. Gelb, *NPN*, 48; P.M. Purves, *NPN*, 211) and since it is also well attested elsewhere, interpretation of Linear A ***i-mi-sa-ra*** as ****Irmi/Ermi-šarra*** is to be preferred to that of a sentence name with ***Ilmi-/Elmi-***, that is considerably less frequent. The ending ***-a*** of ***-šarra*** may well be due to the *essive* case, which explains my translation of the Linear A personal name as 'The Lord (is) *like* the King of Gods'.

Linear A ***u-di-mi*** (HT 117a.4) may be analysed as {*ud=(e/i)-e/irmi*}, consisting of the root ***ud-*** 'to protect' + marker of *transitivity* ***-e/i-*** that contracted with the initial vowel of ***ermi / irmi / erwi / ewri / ibri*** 'Lord' (the *imperative* does not have its own marker), translation 'Protect (the child), oh Lord !'. It may be equivalent to and almost identical with the Linear A personal name ***u*[.]*-de-mi*** (AK 4b.2-3) at Arkhanes, if ***u*[.]*-de-mi*** is a complete sequence and if there is no sign missing between ***u***[(AK 4b.2) and]***-de-mi*** (AK 4b.3).

Linear A ***wa-du-ni-mi*** can be analysed as {*wad=u=n-irmi*} or {*wand=u=n-irmi*}, consisting of the Hurrian verbal root ***p/wad-*** or ***p/wand-*** + the marker of the transitive perfect form ***-u-*** + the enclitic personal pronoun 3rd pers. sing. ***-n(na)*** marking the object of the transitive verb + the theophorous element ***irmi*** / ***ermi*** (at Nippur and in Linear A) 'Lord', indicating the subject of the verb. Linear A ***wa-du-ni-mi*** can be translated as 'The Lord has made him/her [*-n(na)*] (the child) good, just', cf. Th. Richter, *BGH*, 293-295, s.v. ***p/wand-***, *p/wend-* I [*passim*]; *VHN*, 477-478, s.v. ***p/wand-***, *p/wend-* {*fa/end-*}; *VHN*, 482-483, s.v. ***pad-/patt-***. Compare for the interpretation of the ***-n-*** in ***wa-du-ni-mi*** forms like ***Wantin-muša*** {*fand=i=n-muša*} 'Make him [*n(na)*] (the boy) good / just, oh *Muša* !' and ***Wantin-Ugur*** {*fand=i=n-Ugur*} 'Make him [*n(na)*] (the boy) good / just, oh *Ugur* !'.

The Linear A personal name ***ja-re-mi*** (HT 87.3) at Hagia Triada can be compared with the Hurrian personal name ***ia-ru-ḫé-pa***. Th. Richter (*BGH*, 74) does not translate ***iar-/ijar-*** [PN] in ***ia-ru-ḫé-pa***, used in a transitive way, cf. M. Popko, Eine "schwarze Tafel" aus Boğazköy (KUB LX 121), *AoF 18 (1991)*, 244; G. Wilhelm, Name, Namengebung. D. Bei den Hurritern, in: D.O. Edzard (ed.), *Reallexikon der Assyriologie und Vorderasiatischen Archäologie*, Berlin - New York, Band 9/1-2, 1998, 123. But he provides the meaning 'to be good, worthy' and 'to make good, worthy' for the root ***i-/ij-*** (*BGH*, 73; *VHN*, 393).

Since ***iar-/ijar-*** may well consist of ***i-/ij-*** + *factitive* or *iterative* root-extension ***-ar-***, Old Hurrian ***I(j)=ar=u-Ḫeba*** means either 'Ḫeba(t) made (the child) good / worthy' or 'Make (the child) good / worthy, oh Ḫeba(t) !'.

Likewise Linear A ***ja-re-mi*** (HT 87.3) can be analysed as a sentence name ***I(j)=ar-Ermi***, with athematic imperative ***i(j)=ar-*** + absolutive vocative ***ermi / erwi / ewri***. 'Make (the child) good / worthy, oh Lord !'.

The number and variety of aspects and functions ascribed to *Hermes* surprised M.P. Nilsson, but the phenomenon may well be explained from the character of the divine name *ᵈEwri* 'Lord' that could in principle be epithet of any prominent male deity. Tasks that would have been inappropriate for some specific gods could be attributed to him. At Symi Viannou he could be *Hermes Dendrites*. His *κηρύκειον* (Latin *caduceus*) with two snakes may remind of the snakes seen on either side of the snaketubes found at the Minoan site of the sanctuary and in other Peak Sanctuaries. He has features of a shepherd god, but could also be *Ἀργειφόντης* 'killer of Argos', *ψυχοπομπός* 'companion of souls' to the underworld, god of commerce and thiefs and help gods, heroes and mortals at many occasions.

The Linear A inscription ***te-we-mi*** (↓) (PS Zf 1) among the repoussé designs on a bronze tablet from the Dictaean Cave of Psykhro (discussed in chapter 11: *'Religious' Linear A inscriptions*) is probably not a personal name. It can be analysed as {*tew-ermi*}, 'speak, oh Lord !', consisting of ***ti-/te- / tiw-/tew-*** 'to speak, say words' + ***ermi*** = ***erwi/ewri*** 'Lord'. It may well represent the prayer of the dancing supplicant on the tablet.

Which deities were exactly worshipped in Minoan times at different sites is as yet not known. ***Teš(š)ub*** and his spouse ***Ḫebat*** were mountain gods, and their son ***Šarrumma*** as well. It is likely that at least in some Minoan Peak Sanctuaries they were revered as a Holy Trinity: in a fixed poetic order as ***A-ta-i-jo-wa-ja***, ***A-di-<da->ki-ti/e(-te)***, ***A-sa-sa-ra-me***.

Teš(š)ub and *Eni attanni* 'God the Father' may probably be equated as is suggested by the parallels of **Dyēu-s* $pə_2$*ter* > *Ζεὺς πἄτήρ*, Sanskrit *dyāuḥ pitā*, Latin *Dies-piter* (Latin *Iuppiter* corresponds with the vocative *Ζεῦ πάτερ*). The Sanskrit form ***dyáuḥ*** corresponds with Greek ***Ζεύς*** as genitive ***Δι(ϝ)ός*** corresponds with ***diváḥ***.

As extensively explained in the discussion on Linear A ***a-ta-i-jo-wa-ja***, *Teš(š)ub* is called 'Our Lord' and 'Our Father' in the Tušratta letter. ***Eni Attanni*** appears at the top of lists of Hurrian divinities at Ugarit. In these lists *Teš(š)ub* is mentioned as well, but even if *Eni attanni* and *Teš(š)ub* are essentially the same, mentioning both may be due to a desire of the pious faithful not to forget any deity or divine power whose wrath may be expected, if he or she is ignored. One could better keep on the safe side and address *Eni attanni* or *Ewri*, if the god was male, or *Allani*, if a female deity was involved.

V. Haas (*Hethitische Berggötter und hurritische Steindämonen, Riten, Kulte und Mythen*, Mainz 1982, 10, Abb.1) shows in the middle of the picture (I translate): "Teššub and Hebat, the two highest gods of the Hittite Pantheon, next to their retinue; idealised image of the rock-reliefs of Yazılıkaya (see p. 52), after Charles Texier, *Description de l'Asie Mineure I*, Paris 1839)". He writes (*ibidem*, 30): "The most famous goddess, during more than three millennia worshipped in North-Syria, is ***Hebat***; she is already mentioned in the earliest texts from Syria, the texts of Ebla, the city-state from the end of the third millennium B.C. near Aleppo, in the forms *Heba*, *Hapatu* und *Kapatu*. She is the oldest ancestor of the later *Μήτηρ Ἵππα* and is still attested in Lycian inscriptions as ***ḫba-ẽni*** 'Mother-*Hepa*'. The name was also (through the Semitic form ***Ḥawwat***) transformed to biblical *Eva*. .... She formed a close pair with the Cilician mountain god and bull *Šarruma*".

V. Haas reads *"Ιππα*; P. Kretschmer and M.P. Nilsson *"Ιπτα*; the Lycian inscription ***ḫba-ẽni*** is translated as '*Ḫebat* (is) mother', since Lycian ***ẽnẽ* = *annan*** (cf. Ph.H.J. Houwink ten Cate, *The Luwian population groups of Lycia and Cilicia Aspera during the Hellenistic period,* Leiden 1965, 172). Hittite ***anna-*** and Luwian ***anni-*** = 'mother' (cf. e.g. E. Laroche, *NH*, 337; J. Friedrich, *Hethitisches Wörterbuch*, Heidelberg 1952-1954, 21). Lycian ***ẽnẽ*** should not be confused with Hurrian ***eni*** 'god' / ***enni*** 'the god'.

Teš(š)ub, *Ḫebat* and *Šarru(m)ma* were not the only mountain deities. V. Haas (*ibidem*, 30-31) continues: "When the Hittites under their successful king *Ḫattušiliš I* made their first raids into North-Syria in the middle of the second millennium B.C., they seized at *Ḫaššu*(*wa*) on the upper Orontes not far from Aleppo the statues of the following gods: "Weathergod, Lord of *Armaruk*; Weathergod, Lord of *Ḫalap* (Aleppo); ***Allatum***, ***Adalur***, ***Liluri***, two silver oxen, three statues of silver and gold, two *ḫamri*-(cult-)-houses. The daughter of ***Allatum***, [***Ḫebat***, three] statues of silver, two statues of gold." (KBo X 1 Vs. 37-46.) .... "The seized statue of ***Allatum***, whose Hurrian name is ***allai*** 'Lady, Mistress', represents an Earth-Goddess. A local mountain god is ***Adalur***, whose name contains the Hurrian word ***adali*** 'strong'. The two divine silver oxen, the goddesses ***Liluri*** and ***Ḫebat***, will also be discussed." We may have encountered ***Allatum*** in Linear A ***a-||ra-tu*** (ZA 7a.1-2) at Kato Zakro, but due to the fact that the signs transliterated with ***r-*** in Linear A and B can be read as ***l-*** and ***r-***, Linear A ***a-||ra-tu*** might also be equivalent to the Hurrian personal name ***Arattu*** from Nuzi (wr. *A-ra-at-tu(m)*), father of *Ta-i-qa*, *HSS* V 13:14 , cf. I.J. Gelb, *NPN,* 24; P.M. Purves, *NPN*, 204.

The Hurrian mountain goddess ***Liluri*** is very likely represented by Linear A ***ra₂-ro-re*** (ZA 10b.5), with palatalized ***l*** (> ***l^y***) in the first syllable, **=** ***L^yaluri*** **=** ***/L^yalore/*** or ***Lialuri*** = ***/Lialore/*** (with Hurrian [***o***] and [***e***]). Linear A and B ***ra_2*** **=** ***ria/r^ya*** or ***lia/l^ya***, see *supra*.

The Hurrian mountain god ***Adalur*** may be represented in Linear A as ***a-da-ro*** GRA 40[ ] VINb 6 (AK 5.2-3) at Arkhanes, phonologically ***/Adalor/***, that may well be this theonym used as a personal name, since it is preceded by another personal name ***a-du-ni-ta-na*** 41.

Th. Richter (*VHN*, 387-389), s.v. ***adal*** 'stark, der Starke' ['strong, the strong one'], and his very long list of compounds with ***adal-*** and ***-adal***. He mentions that the meaning has been known for a long time thanks to a vocabulary comparison *a-da-al-lu* = *ga-áš-ru* (cf. *AHw*, 10; *CAD* A/I, 94).

The goddess ***Λητώ***, Doric ***Λᾱτώ*** (< **Lātō*), *Lātōna* in Latin, is interesting, since she is not only the mother of Apollo and Artemis, but there is also a toponym ***Λᾱτώ*** / *Lātō* in Crete. The modern place *Lātō* lies between Hagios Nikolaos and *Κριτσά* / *Kritsá*.

C.J. Ruijgh, *EGM*, § 151: "***ra-ti-jo*** (KN E 668,2; X 7754): ethn., pr. ***Λάτιος***, dérivé de ***ra-to*** (KN Da 1191 al.). Il est probable que ce toponyme avait la forme de *Λᾱτός*, qui doit être rapprochée du théonyme *Λᾱτώ* (> ion. *Λητώ*). Il est vrai que plus tard on trouve le toponyme crétois *Λᾱτώς* (*SGDI* 5075) ou *Λᾱτώ* (Étienne de Byzance), mais à partir de *Λᾱτώ*, on attendrait comme dérivé *Λᾱτόϊος*, non *Λάτιος*. Après tout, il se peut que *Λᾱτώς* repose sur la contamination de *Λᾱτώ* avec *Λᾱτός*, dont le locatif *Λᾱτοῖ* et la forme *Λᾱτόθεν* sont encore attestés (*SGDI* 5149,6 al.; 5171,25). La forme *Λάτιος* présente le *τ* restauré."

According to P. Chantraine (*DELG*, 638) the etymology of ***Λητώ***, Doric ***Λᾱτώ*** is obscure. One has tried to find the provenance of this 'Mother Goddess' in Asia Minor and has thought of the Lycian term ***lada*** 'spouse, woman', but the name of ***Λήδη***, mother of Kastōr and Polydeukès (*Odyssey* λ 298), is also derived from that Lycian term.

Consequently it is tempting, if ***Λητώ*** and ***Λήδη*** can each be associated with the Lycian term ***lada***, to recognize the same correlation in the Linear A personal names ***ra-ti-se*** (HT 6b.2) and ***re-di-se*** (HT 85b.4). According to I. Wegner (*Einführung*, 54-55) ***-še / -šše*** may be a Hurrian adjectival morpheme. She offers the examples: ***talav(i)=o=še*** 'great' [root *tal(mi)-*] (with derivational vowel *o* < *i*); ***šav=o=še*** 'great, high, august'; ***faḫr(i)=o=še*** 'good' [*waḫri* {*faḫri*} 'good']; ***ker=a=šše*** 'long' [*keri-* 'long']. The suffix ***-(a)+šše*** also forms abstract nouns: ***ašt=a=šše*** 'femininity' [*ašti* 'woman']; ***all=a=šše*** 'ladyship' [*allai-* 'Lady']; ***šarr=a=šše*** 'kingship' [*šarri* 'King']. The suffix ***-(i)+šše*** also forms abstract nouns: ***šar=i=šše*** 'wish' [*šar-* 'to wish']; ***nir=i=šše*** 'goodness' [*niri* 'good']; ***kib=i=šše*** 'being seated (on the throne)' [*kib-/keb-* 'to set, place'].

The name ***Hera*** occurs as a toponym ***e-ra*** at Knossos (KN Da 1333.A; al.), ***Ἥρᾱ***, and as a theonym ***e-ra*** at Pylos (PY Tn 316, 9), ***Ἥρᾳ***, dative of *Ἥρᾱ*. The ethnic ***e-ra-jo*** (KN Fh 1059; V(3) 431.1) occurs at Knossos: ***Ἡραῖος***, derived from the toponym *Ἥρᾱ*; the feminine form is ***e-ra-ja*** (KN Ap 639, 5; Lc(1) 528.B; al.), cf. C.J. Ruijgh, *EGM*, § 195. As regards the usage of the name *Hera* as both theonym and toponym one may compare the names of *Athena* and *Lato*.

In fact the theonym ***e-ra*** (PY Tn 316, 9), ***Ἥρᾳ***, dative of ***Ἥρᾱ***, occurs immediately after ***di-we*** (PY Tn 316, 9), ***Διϝεῖ***, dative of ***Ζεύς***. What is more interesting, elsewhere on the same tablet we find the theonym ***di-u-ja*** in the dative form (PY Tn 316, 6), ***Δίϝyᾳ***, which could mean either 'for the wife of Zeus' or 'for the daughter of Zeus'. If the meaning of ***di-u-ja*** (PY Tn 316, 6), ***Δίϝyă***, is 'spouse of Zeus', the close connection between ***Διϝεῖ*** and ***Ἥρᾳ*** on this tablet seems to imply that the so-called ***ἱερὸς γάμος*** 'the sacred wedding' between Zeus and Hera had already taken place by the time of the Mycenaean tablets, whereas Zeus's former Indo-European wife ***Δίϝyă*** had moved into the background. On other tablets from Pylos we find ***di-wi-ja do-e-ro*** (PY Cn 1287, 6), ***Δίϝyᾱς δόἑλος*** 'male servant of ***Δίϝyă*** = *Diwia*' (spouse of Zeus) and ***di-wi-ja do-e-ra*** (PY An 607, 5), ***Δίϝyᾱς δοἕλᾱ*** 'female servant of ***Δίϝyă***'. ***Δίϝyᾱς*** is genitive of ***Δίϝyă***. ***Δίϝyă*** 'wife / spouse of Zeus' has a short ***-ă*** (cf. ***λέαινᾰ*** < ****λέϝ^{o}νyă*** 'lioness' : ***λέ(ϝ)ων*** 'lion').

Instead of the theonym ***Δίϝyă*** (with short ***-ă***) 'spouse of Zeus' one may also choose the patronymic form ***Δίϝyᾱ*** (with long ***-ᾱ***) for the interpretation of ***di-u-ja*** (PY Tn 316, 6: dat.), 'daughter of Zeus'. ***Ἥβη***, daughter of Zeus and Hera, is qualified as ***Δίᾱ*** at Phlius and Sicyon by Strabo, *Geography VIII*, 6, 24: *τιμᾶται δ' ἐν Φλιοῦντι καὶ Σικυῶνι τὸ τῆς Δίας ἱερόν· καλοῦσι δ' οὕτω τὴν Ἥβην* (C.J. Ruijgh, *EGM*, § 108). The current etymology of the theonym ***Ἥβη*** is that the name of the goddess is derived from the Greek word ***ἥβη*** 'youth, vigour, puberty'. In modern Greek it still has the meaning of 'puberty' (cf. P. Chantraine, *DELG*, 404-405, s.v. ***ἥβη*** : dor. ***ἥβᾱ***). In Pamphylian ***ἡβοτά*** 'youth' occurs. Chantraine compares Greek ***ἥβη*** with forms in the Baltic languages, Lithuanian *jegà* and Latvian *jega* 'strength': "Bien que le baltique soit loin et qu'il n'y ait pas d'autre témoignage dans une langue indo-européenne, il n'est pas absurd de rapprocher, comme on le fait ordinairement, lit. *jegà* 'force', lette *jega*, même sens. Aucun rapport avec *ἁβρός*." Mycenaean ***δόἑλος*** > ***δοῦλος***.

Indo-European ***Ζεύς*** as 'Weather God' and 'Head of the Pantheon' may well be a Greek rendering of Hurrian *Teš(š)ub*. P. Chantraine, *DELG*, 399, s.v. *Ζεύς*: "Zeus est le vieux dieu i.-e. du ciel, de la lumière, bien connu en skr., en grec, en italique, également en hittite. S'il a fourni en latin le nom du jour *diēs*, on observe ce sens dans des termes grecs comme *ἔνδιος*, *εὐδία*. Étymologie: *Ζεύς* répond exactement au skr. *dyáuḥ*, comme gén. ***Δι(ϝ)ός*** à *diváḥ*, etc. Pour latin *Juppiter*, *Jovis* v. Ernout-Meillet s.v.; le hittite a **šiuš*, *šiun(i)*.

La flexion ancienne repose sur un thème **dy-ēu-*, au nom. sg. *Ζεύς* et anciennement à l'accusatif, *Ζῆν* de **dyē(u)m*, qui se retrouve dans lat. *diem*, skr. véd. *dyām*, alternant avec **diw-* de *Διϝός*. Sur le plan de l'étymologie i.-e. il faut donc poser un thème I **dei-w-* qui a fourni le nom du 'dieu', lat. *dīvos*, skr. *devá-*, et avec le vocalisme zéro radical, le gén. grec *Δι(ϝ)ός*, skr. *diváḥ*, d'autre part un thème II: **dy-eu*, **dy-ēu-* avec l'allongement des monosyllables de *Ζεύς*, *Ζῆν* et des forms skr. correspondantes. Cette analyse permet de retrouver la racine **dei-* 'briller' de skr. *dī-de-ti*, grec *δέατο* (v. ce mot)."

Teš(š)ub's spouse ***Ḫebat***, ***Ḫebet*** was also called ***Allani*** 'The Lady' (Hurrian ***allay*** 'lady', ***allani*** 'the lady', with the suffix of the so-called definite article ***-ni/-ne***). ***Allani*** was *Ḫebat*'s epithet, but she was also mentioned separately in lists of deities belonging to the Hurrian pantheon. Consequently one has thought of the possibility that the Mycenaean Greeks may have rendered the name ***Allani*** into a form with the same meaning, Pre-Greek ***Ἥρᾱ*** 'mistress', feminine form of Pre-Greek ***Ἥρως*** 'Lord, master'.

The name ***Ḫebat***, ***Ḫebet*** may have been adapted to a form similar to Greek ***Ἥβη***. After the Mycenaean conquest of Knossos the whole island of Crete was gradually hellenized and the original meaning of the theonym ***Ḫebat***, ***Ḫebet*** was completely forgotten and associated with the Greek word ***ἥβη*** 'youth, vigour, puberty'. No longer was it possible to associate ***Ἥβη***, as she was now called, with a concept like 'consort of Zeus (*Teš(š)ub*)', because *ἥβη* 'youth, puberty' required a young goddess. So ***Hèbè*** became the daughter of Zeus and Hera.

On a tablet from Hagia Triada Linear A ***da-qe-ra*** **,** ***qe-pi-ta*** (HT 6a.6) occurs, which may be explained as Hurrian ****daḫera*** ****Ḫebitta*** 'with a man for *Ḫépét*/*Ḫebat*'. Linear A ***da-qe-ra*** *{t/daḫe=ra}* is the *comitative* of *t/daḫe* 'man' (wr. *da-aḫ-e*, KBo XIX 145 IV 43; KUB XLV 60, 3), with *comitative* suffix ***-ra***, referring to a 'man' taking part in Ḫebat's cult. Linear A ***da-qe-ra*** also occurs as first entry of two other tablets: HT 57a.1 and HT 120.1.

I have compared this Linear A sequence with Linear B ***di-wi-ja do-e-ro*** (PY Cn 1287,6) on a tablet from Pylos, ***Δίϝyᾱς δόἐλος*** 'male servant of ***Δίϝyᾰ*** (consort of Zeus)' or 'male servant of ***Δίϝyᾱ*** (daughter of Zeus)'. Linear A ***qe-pi-ta*** may well be equated with the Hurrian dative form of *Ḫépét*/*Ḫebat*, consort of *Teš(š)ub*, (Hittite Hieroglyphic *^{d}He-ba-tu*, Yaz. N°. 43). P.M. Purves, *NPN*, 215-216, s.v. *ḫepet*: "Hurrian female deity mentioned frequently under form ***Ḫé-pét*** in rituals from Boğazköy, often followed in the Hurrian passages by the epithet ***muš(u)ni***, *q.v.* under ***muš***. For position of *Ḫepet* in this pantheon, where she seems to be the consort of *Tešup*, see Götze, *Kleinasien*, pp. 58, 123 f., 129. [....] In Ugarit wr. ***ḫbt*** [....] Outside of Nuzi ***^{f}Ḫepet-naịa***, wr. *^{f}Ḫé-be-et-na-a-a*, cf. for this element *Um-mi-^{d}ḫe-bi-it*, CT XXXIII 41:1, cited by Ungnad, *Subartu*, p. 100, and *^{f}Me-e-na-ḫe-bi* from Nippur, Clay, *PNCP*, p. 106. The form ***ḫepa***, commonly taken as variant of ***ḫepet***, is found in many personal names; cf. e.g. *^{f}Kelu-ḫepa*, *^{f}Putu-ḫepa*, *^{f} Tatu-ḫepa*, *^{f}Keluš-ḫepa(š)* and ERUM-*ḫé*/*ḫe-ba*. Etc."

I have explained Linear A ***qe-pi-ta*** as the Hurrian dative form ***Ḫebitta*** as a result of the process of assimilation < ****Ḫebit-wa***, with the Hurrian singular dative suffix ***-wa***. The comparable assimilated genitive form with the singular genitive suffix ***-wi/-we*** is attested at Boğazköy: *ᵈḪé-pa-at-ti*, KBo XIX 129 Ro 33, cf. E. Laroche, *GLH*, 100-101, s.v. *Ḫebat*.

E.A. Speiser (*IH*, 63, § 82) writes: "This assimilation of *w*- is not restricted to instances with a preceding labial. We find it again in *ᵈḪé-bat-te/i* XXVII 1 ii 55, 38 iii 8 and *ᵈḪé-bat-te-na* XXV 45.7, XXIX 8 ii 30, alongside the unassimilated forms [*ᵈḪé*]*-bat-wiᵢ* XXVII 4. 5, and with a following *-na* in XXV 44 ii 2, 4, XXVII 4. 4, 8 obv. 16, rev. 1, 4, 5, 7."

Association of ***Ἥρᾱ*** with ***Ἥρως***, already suggested by M.P. Nilsson and accepted by P. Chantraine, is attractive and probably correct. P. Chantraine, *DELG*, 417, s.v. ***ἥρως***: "Il ne s'agit pas d'un thème *ἡρωϝ*- comme on l'enseignait souvent, puisque le mycénien *tiriseroe*, si l'interprétation qu'on en donne est correcte, écarte cette analyse. Un rapport avec lat. *servāre* est malaisé. Un rapprochement avec *Ἥρᾱ* sérait plausible. Peut-être racine **ser*- variante de **swer*- et **wer*-, cf. *servāre*. Ou emprunt." Since the form ***Ἥρως / ἥρως*** (vocative *ἥρως*, so root in ***-ōs-/-ōh-***) reminds of Pre-Greek *Μίνως* and *Τρώς*, the term 'Pre-Greek' seems appropriate for *Ἥρως / ἥρως*.. L.R. Palmer has suggested that the formula ***πότνια Ἥρη*** contains both the Pre-Greek title ***ἥρᾱ*** 'mistress' and the Greek translation ***πότνια***. If the name of the god ***Ἑρμῆς < Ἑρμάὰς < *Ἑρμάὰς*** 'Hermes' is indeed derived from Hurrian ***Ermi / Erwi / Ewri*** 'Lord', which is in fact the male counterpart of ***Allani*** 'the Lady', there was no need for ***Ἥρως*** as equivalent to ***Ἥρᾱ*** in the Greek pantheon.

Ἥρως played a significant part as a 'Horseman God' in the Thracian religion according to literary and iconographic evidence, cf. D. Detschew, *Die thrakischen Sprachreste*, 200, s.v. *Ἥρως*, *Ἥρος*; G.I. Kazarov, *RE*, *Suppl. 3*, 1132 ff.; G.I. Kazarov, *Die Denkmäler des thrakischen Reitergottes in Bulgarien*, Dissertationes Pannonicae, ser. II, fasc. 14, Budapest 1938, *passim*; A. Fol - I. Marazov, *Thrace and the Thracians,* London 1977, 13, 17, 110, 138.

In my paper "Thracian" onomastica in Mycenaean Linear B, *Ancient Bulgaria* (Papers presented to the International Symposium on the Ancient History and Archaeology of Bulgaria, University of Nottingham, 1981, ed. A.G. Poulter, Part 1, Nottingham 1983), I expressed the view that the Greeks might have derived Pre-Greek ***Ἥρᾱ*** and ***Ἥρως / ἥρως*** from a 'Proto-Thracian' substrate. My position has changed, because it seems most likely that ancient Indo-European languages such as Thracian, Dacian, Macedonian and Illyrian, of which our knowledge is only fragmentary, contained many substrate words and names of non-Indo-European predecessors, probably to the same extent as can be detected in Greek and Anatolian languages.

Comparison of ***Ἥρως / ἥρως*** with Pre-Greek ***Μίνως*** and ***Τρώς*** leads to the conclusion that ***Ἥρως / ἥρως*** may belong to the same non-Indo-European substrate. On two tablets from Pylos a compound of ***Ἥρως / ἥρως*** occurs in the form of ***ti-ri-se-ro-e*** (PY Tn 316, 5; PY Fr 1204), probably ***Τρισ-ἡρώέι***. It may be interpreted as 'Three times Lord'. ***Τρισ-ἥρως*** seems to refer to a deceased gentleman enjoying a burial-cult, perhaps the ancestor of a royal or at least an aristocratic family. According to Homer ***ἥρως*** 'Lord' may have been the title of aristocrats in Mycenaean times. Later the term was used for those who could boast on a pedigree and who enjoyed an ancestral burial-cult.

Although the title *῞Ηρως* did not acquire the same position in the Greek pantheon as its feminine counterpart *῞Ηρᾱ*, the term *ἥρως* was reserved for the epic heroes and the aristocrats in society who could prove at the Olympic, Pythian, Nemean or Isthmian Games that they were not only the *aristoi* 'the best' of their polis, but also of the Greek commonwealth and fully deserved their aristocratic status.

It has occurred to me that *῞Ηρᾱ* and *῞Ηρως* may not be derived from *just a* Pre-Greek language, but from Hurrian. Hera's epithet ***βοῶπις*** 'with the eyes of a cow' (*βοῦς* 'ox, cow' and *ὤψ* 'eyes') in the Homeric formula ***βοῶπις πότνια ῞Ηρη*** (*Iliad* A 551, Θ 471, O 49, Σ 357) has astonished me ever since I read Homer. But we must not forget that ***Tešub*** and his 'guardian companions' ***Ḫurri***, ***Tilla*** and ***Šerri*** were often depicted as bulls and that *Zeus* himself sometimes acted in the appearance of a bull. Could *῞Ηρως* and *῞Ηρᾱ* be derived from ***Šerri*** or ***Šeri***. Hurrian initial ***š-*** must have behaved as the Indo-European [***s-***] that developed > [***h-***] in Greek, cf. Greek *ἑπτά* 'seven' < ***septm̥*** : Latin ***septem*** : Sanskrit ***saptá***; cf. Greek *ἕξ* 'six' : Latin ***sex***. The time of transmission of ***Šer(r)i*** into Greek must also have coincided with the time that the phonetic law in question was still at work. We must realize that the form ***Šerri*** owes its double ***-rr-*** to assimilation of the ***-n-*** of the so-called definite article ***-ni***: ***Šerri*** < ***šer(i)=ni*** < ***šeri=ni***. Forms with single ***-r-*** and double ***-rr-*** are attested.

E. Laroche (*GLH*, 227, s.v. ***šeri***. Nom. *še-e-ri*, KUB XXVII 1 II 61; 42 Ro 16; XXXII 52 III 13; XLVII 10, 12; KBo XXI 23 Vo 9. - *ši-i-ri*, RS h. 5, 12; KUB XLVII 78 IV 14. – Erg. ? *še-re-eš*, KUB XLV 21 Ro 2. - *še-e-ra*, KUB XLVII 31 I 10. Dir. *še-e-ri-da*, KUB XXXII 19+ II 34. Onom. ***šeri***, *NPN*, 256. E. Laroche (*GLH*, 227-228), s.v. ***šerri***. Peut être le thème déterminé de ***šeri***: ****šeri=ni*** > ***šerri***. Sg. nom. *še-er-ri-e*, KUB XXIX 8 III 52. - *ši-ir-ri*, RS h. 18, 1. - *še-er-ri-in*, IBoT II 39 Ro 45; etc. Erg. *še-er-re-eš*, KBo XIX 139 III 3. - *še-e-er-ra-a-tan*, Mit. IV 115 (abl.?). - *še-e-er-re-e-wi-i-in*, Mit. III 67.

E. Laroche (*GLH*, 227-228), s.v. ***Šerri***. Un des taureaux de Tešub; v. ***Ḫurri*** et ***Tilla***. *še-er-ri ḫu-ur-ri* GUD$^{hi.a}$*-ri*, KBo XX 119 IV 26, I 15 = KBo XVII 86+ I 4; dét. par GUD, souvent par DINGIR (^{d}***Šerri***). Graphies *še-(e)-ri* et *še-er-ri*. Flexion hitt. nom. *Še(r)riš*, acc. *Še(r)rin*, abs. *Še(r)ri*. GUD/^{d}*Še-ri-šu-(un)*, cf. JCS 6, 40, et *še-ri-šu-uš*, KBo XXII 33 IV 7.

One usually assumes that the Greek phonetic law (initial ***s-*** > ***h-***) did not apply to the non-Indo-European initial [***s-***] as I have assumed with regard to the Pre-Greek name of the ***Σειρῆνες*** (*Sirens*, plural of ***Σειρήν***) that contains in my view the Hurrian root ***šir-*** 'to sing'.

Can it be accidental that the queenly sorceress *Kirke* (***πότνια Κίρκη***) with a Hurrian name ***Kirka*** (wr. *Ki-ir-qa*), attested at Nuzi (cf. I.J. Gelb, *NPN*, 88), warns Odysseus for the ***Σειρῆνες*** (the *Sirens*) in *Odyssey μ* 36 ff.: *"To the Sirens first thou shalt come, who beguile all men whosoever comes to them. Whosoever in ignorance draws near to them and hears the Sirens' voice, he nevermore returns, that his wife and little children may stand at his side rejoicing, but the sirens beguile him with their clear-toned voice ..."*

The name of the ***Σειρῆνες*** (*Sirens*, plural of ***Σειρήν***) is Pre-Greek for the reason just mentioned. P. Chantraine (*DELG*, 993-994) mentions s.v. ***Σειρήν***: "f. (***σει-*** *IG* II^2, 1629, 687, mais ***σιρ-*** sur les vases). .... « sirènes », génies mi-oiseaux-mi-femmes. ..... On admet en mycénien l'existence d'un composé (instrum.) *seremokaraore* « à tête de sirène », cf. L. Baumbach, *Glotta 49*, 1971, 170. .... Étymologie: Obscure."

All etymological attempts cited by him are unsatisfactory. Hurrian, however, offers a satisfactory etymology, because ***Šir-ene/i*** can be analysed as {*šir=(e/i)-ene/i*} 'Sing, oh God !' (with ***šir-*** as *athematic imperative*) and the plural ***Šir-enna*** as {*šir=(e/i)-en=(i)=na*} 'Sing, oh Gods !'. It is conceivable that a phoneme in a word adopted from another language was so close to a similar phoneme of the own language that the *phonetic law*, effective at the time of adoption or shortly after the adoption, had also effect on the adopted non-Indo-European word/name. Actually *phonetic laws* are usually only *at work* during a certain period of the process of phonetic change within a language. It is conceivable that ***šere/i***, the basis of ***Ἥρως*** and ***Ἥρᾱ***, was earlier adopted into Mycenaean Greek than the prototype of ***Σειρήν*** and ***Σειρῆνες***, so that the phonetic law concerning initial [***s-***] developing > [***h-***] worked for ***Ἥρως*** and ***Ἥρᾱ***, but was no longer effective for ***Σειρήν*** and ***Σειρῆνες***, because the period of effectiveness of the phonetic law in question had already passed. Perhaps other factors, such as the frequency of usage and popularity of a loan-word or foreign name adopted into an idiom, may have had some influence on the process as well. Such matter is difficult to assess.

If my hypothesis about derivation of ***Ἥρως*** and ***Ἥρᾱ*** from ***Šere/i*** / ***Šerri*** is correct, it is interesting to see, whether ***Šere/i*** occurs in Linear A. This may well be the case on tablet HT 93a from Hagia Triada, where the ligature ***se+re*** ↓ 12 (HT 93a.1) can be read from top to bottom and ***se+re+da*** ↓ 43 J (HT 93a.2) in the next line. Linear A ***se+re*** (HT 93a.1) can be equated with the *absolutive* Hurrian theonym ***Šere/Šeri*** and ***se+re+da*** (HT 93a.2) with the *directive* case ***Šere=da*** of the same theonym, 'for *Šere/Šeri*', with directive suffix ***-da***. Linear A ***se+re*** ↓ (HT 93a.1) can be compared with *absolutive še-er-ri-e*, KUB XXIX 8 III 52 or with *ergative še-er-re-eš*, KBo XIX 139 III 3. Linear A ***se+re+da*** ↓ (HT 93a.2) can be compared with *directive še-e-ri-da*, KUB XXXII 19+ II 34. The fact that ***se+re*** ↓ (HT 93a.1) and ***se+re+da*** ↓ (HT 93a.2) are written as ligatures instead of normal sequences is not a disadvantage, but a recommendation, because there are more theonyms written as ligatures with Linear A: e.g. Linear A ***qe+pa₃*** (HT 33.4) = *Ḫeba(t)*, preceded by NUBES+*pi* = *genitive Tešuppi* < *Tešub=wi* 'of *Tešub*'; Linear A ***si+me-ki*** TAL 1 JE (HT 24b.1-2) and ***ka+ja*** TAL 1 (HT 24b.2) = the Hurrian Sun-god *Šimegi* and *Gaia* 'Earth'.

Kirka at Nuzi is son of *Ge-ni-ia* (JEN 118: 24, 30). Hurrian does not have gender (*genera*), so no distinction between masculine, feminine and neuter gender. Thus men and women can sometimes bear the same name. In cuneiform a man's name is indicated by the Sumerogram LÚ as a determinative (*ᵐ*) at the beginning of the name, a woman's name by the Sumerogram MUNUS as a determinative (*ᶠ*) at the beginning of the name. It is conceivable that ***Kirka*** could indicate equally a man or a woman in Hurrian and Minoan society. ***Kirka*** may have been a sorcerer or sorceress in an original Hurrian myth.

If ***Kirka*** was a man in the Minoan-Hurrian fairy tale, the ending of the name in ***-a*** made it necessary that he became a woman in the Mycenaean (and later Homeric) tale after transmission from the Minoan to the Mycenaean tradition, because (singular) words and names in ***-a*** are usually feminine in Greek.

The name ***Ὀδυσσεύς / Odysseus*** might be derived from Hurrian {*o/ud=o/u=z=i=ja*} 'May he/she (a *numen*) protect (the child)', consisting of ***o/ud-*** 'to protect' + the transitive form with ***°=o=z*** (see Th. Richter, *VHN*, 601-602) + theme-vowel ***-i-*** + hypocoristic ***-ya***. Are ***Ὀδυσσεύς*** and ***Ὀλυσσεύς*** originally different names with different verbal roots ?

P. Chantraine (*DELG*, 775-776, s.v. ***Ὀδυσσεύς***) points to a popular etymology going back to antiquity and to the Odyssey itself. The most explicit passage, based on ***Ὀδυσσεύς*** (not on ***Ὀλυσσεύς***), is ***ὀδυσσάμενος*** (*Odyssey* τ 407), where Autolykos, the father of Odysseus's mother, being asked to propose a name for the child, answers, *Od.* τ 406-409:

"Γαμβρὸς ἐμὸς θυγάτηρ τε, τίθεσθ' ὄνομ', ὅττι κεν εἴπω·
πολλοῖσιν γὰρ ἐγώ γε ὀδυσσάμενος τόδ' ἱκάνω,
ἀνδράσιν ἠδὲ γυναιξὶν ἀνὰ χθόνα πουλυβότειραν·
τῷ δ' Ὀδυσεὺς ὄνομ' ἔστω ἐπώνυμον· ...." etc.

"My daughter's husband and my daughter, give him whatsoever name I say.
Lo, inasmuch as I am come hither as one that has been angered with many,
both men and women, over the fruitful earth,
therefore let the name by which the child is named be Odysseus."

The suggestion given by this popular etymology is according to P. Chantraine that *Odysseus* means 'enfant de la haine' ['child of hatred'], since ***ὀδύσσομαι*** means 'to hate, to be angry' (the term is mainly used with regard to gods).

I think that the ***d/l*** alternation is a strong indication that ***Ὀδυσσεύς / Ὀλυσσεύς*** (*Odysseus / Olysseus*) and the variant ***Οὐλίξης*** (cf. latin ***Ulixes***) is a Pre-Greek substrate name with a phoneme that sounded peculiar to native speakers of the Greek vernacular. Chantraine concludes that the real etymology is not known (Frisk mentions numerous hypotheses). Anyway the variations of the form suggest adoption from an Anatolian or Aegean substrate. Certain Mycenaean orthographies (cf. *λαβύρινθος*) suggest that in the language written with Linear A ***l*** was pronounced close to [***d***], cf. M. Lejeune, *Mémoires I*, 327; A. Heubeck, *Praegraeca*, 25, with other details. It is in my view exactly in such circumstances that graphic and phonic variants can be observed.

The question of how graphic variants in Linear B should be explained was raised in the discussion between John Chadwick and me on the 11th of April 1983 during the Colloquio Internazionale *Dori e mondo egeo: I termini della questione dorica* (Roma, 11-13 Aprile 1983). In my article 'The coming of the Dorians' (*Kadmos XX.1*, 1981, 38-51) I had already pointed out that J. Chadwick's theory (since 1975) that there had not been a migration of Dorian tribes into the Peloponnese at the transition from Late Helladic IIIB to IIIC (ca. 1200-1180 B.C), but a revolt by 'lower class' subjects against their 'upper class' rulers and that the Mycenaean documents showed evidence for two coexisting Mycenaean dialects, a 'standard Mycenaean' (Proto-Arcado-Cypriot) and a 'substandard Mycenaean' (Proto-Doric) in all Mycenaean centres, was untenable. My thesis was and is that all evidence brought forward by J. Chadwick has to be explained differently and points to the existence of only one Mycenaean dialect, the predecessor of the Arcadian and Cypriote dialects.

Since my arguments on the basis of linguistic, historical and archaeological evidence had already been described extensively in 'The Coming of the Dorians', I only discussed a part of the linguistic evidence in my paper 'Il valore fonetico dei segni micenei per *z-* ai fini della questione dorica' (The phonetic value of the Mycenaean *z-* signs in view of the Dorian question), given to the Colloquio Internazionale *Dori e mondo egeo: I termini della questione dorica* (Roma, 11-13 Aprile 1983), published in *Le origini dei Greci. Dori e mondo egeo*, a cura di Domenico Musti, Roma 1985, 323-327, with my discussion with John Chadwick, 365-368.

Part of J. Chadwick's theory concerned interchange of the Linear B signs ***ke*** and ***ze*** in some Mycenaean forms. J. Chadwick ascribed, for instance, ***ke-i-ja-ka-ra-na*** (PY Nn 228, 3) and ***a-ke-ti-ri-ja*** (KN Ai 739,1; al.) to 'standard Mycenaean' (Proto-Arcado-Cypriot) and ***ze-i-ja-ka-ra-na*** (PY Xa 70), and ***a-ze-ti-ri-ja*** (KN Ap 694,3; al.) to 'substandard Mycenaean' (Proto-Doric), whereas I argued that it is preferable to regard ***a-ze-ti-ri-ja*** and ***ze-i-ja-ka-ra-na*** *not* as an alternative 'substandard' orthography of ***ἀσκήτριαι*** and ***Κηΐᾱ κράνᾱ***, but as a graphic and phonetic variant with different reflection of the non-Greek affricate. These variants can be explained better through the probably non-Greek origin of the forms in question than by assuming contemporary use of 'standard and 'substandard' dialects within all Mycenaean palatial centres. I illustrate this with a quotation from a passage (in Italian) from *Dori e mondo egeo* (325), followed by the English translation: Ma allora come andrebbero spiegate apparenti varianti grafemiche quali *a-ke-ti-ri-ja* e *a-ze-ti-ri-ja* o *ke-i-ja-ka-ra-na* (PY Nn 228.3) e *ze-i-ja-ka-ra-na* (PY Xa 70) ? Si è osservato che varianti grafemiche si riscontrano specialmente in imprestiti e in nomi 'pre-greci' come *da-pu$_2$-ri-to-jo* (KN Gg(1) 702, 2), probabilmente *δαβυρίνθοιο*, gen. sing. di *δαβύρινθος* (probabile doppione di *λαβύρινθος*), cfr. *Ὀδυσσεύς* e *Ὀλυσσεύς* (cfr. latino *Ulixes*). È del tutto giustificato considerare nello stesso modo il primo elemento dei toponimi composti *ke-i-ja-ka-ra-na* e *ze-i-ja-ka-ra-na*. In quanto toponimi essi potrebbero certamente contenere un elemento non greco, e, se vanno considerati doppioni, le loro consonanti iniziali potrebbero essere state in origine una qualche affricata non riconosciuta dal sistema fonologico del greco. *Ke-i-ja-ka-ra-na* può quindi venir letto come *Κηΐᾱ κράνᾱ* e *ze-i-ja-ka-ra-na* in accordo col valore fonetico ricostruito dei segni per *z-*, come *^{T}σσηΐᾱ κράνᾱ*.

But how should apparent graphemic variants such as *a-ke-ti-ri-ja* and *a-ze-ti-ri-ja* or *ke-i-ja-ka-ra-na* (PY Nn 228.3) and *ze-i-ja-ka-ra-na* (PY Xa 70) then be explained ? One has observed that graphemic variants can be found especially in loan-words and 'Pre-Greek' names such as *da-pu$_2$-ri-to-jo* (KN Gg(1) 702, 2), probably *δαβυρίνθοιο*, gen. sing. of *δαβύρινθος* (probably a doublet of *λαβύρινθος*), cf. *Ὀδυσσεύς* and *Ὀλυσσεύς* (cf. Latin *Ulixes*). It is quite justifiable to regard the first element in the compound topographic names *ke-i-ja-ka-ra-na* and *ze-i-ja-ka-ra-na* in the same way. As toponyms they might well contain a non-Greek element, and if they are to be considered doublets, their initial consonants might originally have been some affricate not established in the phonological system of Greek. *Ke-i-ja-ka-ra-na* may then be read as *Κηΐᾱ κράνᾱ* and *ze-i-ja-ka-ra-na*, in accordance with the reconstructed phonetic value of the *z-* signs, as *^{T}σσηΐᾱ κράνᾱ*.

In my view Homer may well have been aware of another etymology, not based on ***ὀδύσσομαι*** 'to hate, to be angry', but on another Greek verb ***ὄλλῡμι*** 'to destroy' that may be concealed in the variant spelling ***Ὀλυσσεύς***. In both *Iliad* B 278 and *Odyssey* ϑ 3 we encounter ***πτολίπορϑος Ὀδυσσεύς*** 'the destroyer of cities Odysseus' and Homer clearly alludes to the epithet right in the first two verses of the Odyssey α 1-2:

Ἄνδρα μοι ἔννεπε, Μοῦσα, πολύτροπον, ὃς μάλα πολλὰ
πλάγχθη, ἐπεὶ Τροίης ἱερὸν πτολίεθρον ἔπερσε·
Tell me, o Muse, of the man of many devices, who wandered
full many ways after he had sacked the sacred citadel of Troy.

Homer has been playing with words, for he knew that ***ὄλλῡμι*** and ***πέρθω*** are synonyms.

The Greek verb ***ὄλλῡμι*** 'to destroy', ***-μαι*** 'to destroy oneself, to perish' is intriguing, since the root ***ὀλ-*** is formally and semantically equal to the Hurrian root ***o/ull-*** 'to destroy'. P. Chantraine (*DELG*, 792-793), s.v. ***ὄλλῡμι, -μαι*** 'perdre, détruire', 'se perdre, périr', mentions about the etymology: "Il faut partir d'un radical ***ὀλ-*** alternant avec ***ὀλε-*** (pour *ὤλεσα, ὄλεθρος, ὀλοός*). On pose donc *ὄλ-νῡ-μι* à côté de *ὤλεσα*, comme *στόρνυμι* à côté de *στορέσαι* : pour ce dernier le skr. fournit un vocalisme zéro, au présent *str̥ṇōti*, le vocalisme du grec étant difficile à expliquer, cf. s.v. Celui de *ὄλλῡμι* n'est pas plus clair. .... R. Beekes, *Laryngeals*, 131, 236, pose *ə₃el-ə₁*. Quant à l'aor. *ὠλόμην* on ne peut démontrer qu'il est refait sur un **ὠλέμᾱν, ὤλετο* qui serait athématique. Voir encore *οὖλος*. Pas de rapprochement étymologique plausible hord du grec : celui avec lat. *aboleō, deleō* est inacceptable. Hypothèses chez Pokorny, 306."

It is significant that the Hurrian root ***ull-***, phonologically */oll-/*, 'to destroy', completely corresponds with the Greek transitive verb ***ὄλλῡμι*** 'to destroy' (root *ὀλ-, ὀλε-*). So I am not surprised that P. Chantraine (*DELG*, 792-793) concludes s.v. ***ὄλλῡμι*** that there is no plausible etymological comparison outside Greek and that comparisons with Latin *aboleō* and *deleō* are unacceptable. The only conclusion is: Greek transitive ***ὄλλῡμι*** and *ὀλ-, ὀλε-* are directly derived from Minoan-Hurrian ***ull-/oll-*** with exactly the same meaning and Greek ***ὄλλῡμαι*** 'to perish' corresponds with Hurrian ***ull=ul-/oll=ol-*** (with reflexive ***-u/ol-***), e.g. *Kummi-ni-m ulluliš* 'et que Kummi périsse !', cf. Laroche, *GLH*, 279, s.v. *Ullikummi.*

The Hurrian root ***o/ull-*** 'to destroy' may in my view provide a good external etymology for Greek ***ὄλλῡμι***, cf. Th. Richter, *BGH*, 486, s.v. ***ull-*** [Boğ.; Mitt.; PN], 'to destroy', cf. G. Wilhelm, A Hurrian letter from Tell Brak, *Iraq 53 (1991)*, 161-162: /***ull-***/ or /***oll-***/.

Etymologically it is also comparable with Urartian ***ul(u)-*** 'vernichten' ['to destroy'], cf. also Hurrian ***ull=ul-*** [Boğ.] 'distruggere' ['to destroy'] with Urartian ***ulu=le-***, see M. Salvini, Sui testi mitologici in lingua ḫurrica, *SMEA 18 (1977)*, 84.

However, since the Nuzi name ***Ulušiḭa*** (wr. *Ú-lu-ši-ia*) and ***Ὀλυσσεύς*** and ***Ulixes*** contain only one ***-l-***, one may also think of the verbal root ***ul-*** II [Boğ.; Mit.] 'to change', 'to bring from one situation into another' corresponding with Hittite ***arḫa dā-*** 'to take away', cf. Hittite ***dā-*** 'to take, seize', cf. Th. Richter, *BGH*, 484-485, s.v. ***ul-*** II. The option of Hurrian ***ul-*** II 'to take, seize' with single liquid ***l*** will do as well, for the sacking of a city is only possible after it has been seized. Confusion of ***o/ull-*** and ***ul-*** II is conceivable.

The Pre-Greek name of the hero ***Ὀδυσσεύς*** / ***Ὀλυσσεύς*** (*Odysseus / Olysseus*) and the variant ***Οὐλίξης*** (cf. latin ***Ulixes***) may be derived from a Hurrian prototype ***Ulušiḭa*** (wr. *ú-lu-ši-ia*), personal name of the father of *Am-ma-ku* at Nuzi, HSS V 62: 19; *Am-ma-a-ku*, HSS IX 95:4, cf. I.J. Gelb, *NPN*, 163. The name has the appearance of a hypocoristic like ***Ulluḭa*** (wr. *Ul-lu-ia*), the name of 5 persons at Nuzi, cf. I.J. Gelb, *NPN*, 162; P.M. Purves, *NPN*, 271, s.v. ***ul-*** and ***ull-***. Th. Richter (*VHN*, 326) refers for ***Ulluḭa*** at Nuzi also to SCCNH 6, 413 and RGTC 10: 323. He analyses ***Ulluja*** (wr. *ul-lu-ú-ia*) at Tigunāni as {*o/ull=o=ja*}, typology 1.1.1.1.4, lexicon *ull-*, translation 'Er / Sie (*scil.* ein *Numen*) zerstörte (älteres Kind)' ['He/She (a *numen*) destroyed (the older child ?)'], so that it can be explained as a substitute name. He likewise explains and translates the name ***Ullija*** (wr. *ul-li-ia*) at Mari, analysis {*o/ull=i=ja*}, typology 1.1.1.2.4, lexicon *ull-*. He also mentions that ***Ulluja*** is at Ḫattuša the Hurrian personal name equivalent to Akkadian ***Ūta-napišti*** in the Gilgameš-epos, cf. V. Haas, 2006, 273.

An analysis of ***Ulušiia*** as {*o/ull=o/uš=i=a*} 'He/She (a *numen*) destroyed (the older child?)' faces, however, a serious objection, since I. Wegner's remarks (*Einführung*, 93, Table 4) that the indicator of transitivity ***-i-*** (position 5) only occurs in the 2nd and 3rd persons singular of the present tense. Consequently, the 3rd person sing. of the past or perfect tense in ***-o/uš-*** should have been {*o/ull=o/uš=a*} instead of {*o/ull=o/uš=i=a*}, which makes in this case explanation of the name as a hypocoristic more likely.

Hypocoristic ***Ulušiia*** might be derived from a name such as ***Ulluštaia*** (wr. *ul-lu-úš-ta-ia, ul-lu-úš-ta-a-ia*) at Mari. Th. Richter (*VHN*, 329) analyses ***Ulluštaia*** as {*o/ull=o=ž-Taja*} 'Taia may destroy', which means that he divides the name into a verbal (modal) element ***o/ull=o=ž-*** and a theophorous element ***Taja***. He treats the first element as a *jussive* form, which I may compare with the 3rd person singular of the *jussive / imperative* forms from the Hurrian-Hittite bilingual ***kirenze***: *za-am-ma-la-aš-du-uš* (KBo 32: 14 I 57), analysed as {*zamm=al=ašt=o=š*} 'soll abgerissen sein/werden' ['should be torn off'] and *bar-nu-uš-du-uš* (*ChS* I/5 Nr.2 64'), analysed as {*parn=ošt=o=š*} 'er soll/möge rein sein' ['he must be pure !' / 'may he be pure !'] by I. Wegner, *Einführung*, 138.

Th. Richter (*VHN*, 525) writes, s.v. ***Taja***, that the element *-ta-(a-)ia* is certainly identical with the theonym ***Dāja***, sometimes ***dai***, listed by E. Laroche, *GLH*, 252. The context (KUB 27, 1 = ChS I/3-1, 1 Vs. II 60 and 47, 64 + IBoT 2, 50 = Rs. III 10') consists of descriptions of festivities dedicated to the cult of *Ša(w)uška* of the area of the town *Šamuḫa* (cf. I. Wegner, 1995a, 11). Other names with the theophorous element ***-taia*** are SUM-*ta-ia* at Ugarit (cf. F. Gröndahl, *Die Personennamen der Texte aus Ugarit*, Rome 1967, 258) and possibly *fḪa-bur-ta(?)-ia* at Kār-Tukultī-Ninurta = modern Tulūl cAqīr (cf. H. Freydank - M. Salvini, 'Zu den hurritischen Personennamen aus Kār-Tukultī-Ninurta', *Studi micenei ed egeo-anatolici 24 (1984)*, 50. According to Th. Richter (*VHN* I, 525, n. 758) it is conceivable that some personal names at Nuzi with an element ***tai*** or ***-taia*** (P.M. Purves, *NPN*, 261) also belong to this element. He also tells (*VHN* I, 523-524), s.v. ***taḫe / taḫḫe*** {*taġ/ḫḫe*), ***Ta(')e***, that on the basis of equations with Sumerian **lú** and Akkadian ***amīlu*** in vocabularies the meaning 'man' is certain.

Richter's interpretation of ***Ulluštaia*** is morphologically the best candidate for the name, from which hypocoristic ***Ulušiia*** is derived, because the first elements {*o/ull=o=ž-*} and {*o/ul=o=ž-*} are virtually the same.

Nevertheless ***Ulluštaia*** may theoretically also be interpreted as {*o/ull=(i/e)-uštai=a*} 'Destroy, as a hero !', 2nd person singular of the *iussive / imperative* ***o/ul(l)=i/e-*** (with vowel absorbtion of the *transitive imperative* suffix ***-i/e-***) + theophorous nominal element ***-uštai*** 'hero' in the *essive* case in ***-a*** 'as a hero'. Semantically 'Destroy, as a hero !' would have provided a meaning of the prototype of ***Ὀδυσσεύς* / *Ὀλυσσεύς*** worthy of a great warlord.

But if ***Ulluštaia*** is divided into {*o/ull=(i/e)-uštai=a*}, the verbal element is {*o/ull-*}, not {*o/ull=o=ž-*}, so that the hypocoristic form derived from it would have been Hurrian ***Ullija*** {*o/ull=i=ja*} at Mari or ***Ulluia/Ulluja*** at Nuzi, Tigunāni and Ḫattuša, not Hurrian ***Ulušiia***, which is indeed a hypocoristic of ***Ulluštaia***, but analysed as {*o/ull=o=ž-Taja*} '*Taia* may destroy (the deceased child or perhaps a city ?)'. It is, of course, conceivable that instead of ***-Taja*** other theophorous elements (e.g. ***-Tešub*** or ***-Tilla***) could have been combined with {*o/ull=o=ž-*}. Hypocoristic ***Ulušiia*** is very likely the prototype of hypocoristic ***Ὀλυσσεύς***.

Some scholars brought ***ull-*** and ***ul-*** together, e.g. P.M. Purves, *NPN*, 271, s.v. *ul*, *ull*; cf. Th. Richter (*BGH*, 486), s.v. *ull-* [Boğ; Mitt; PN] 'détruire (?)' (Laroche, *GLH*, 279 sub *ulli-* 2); 'zerstören' (Salvini 1988b, 158); 'to destroy, sack', i.e. ***ull-***, /***oll-***/, (Wilhelm, o.c., 161f.). Though ***ul-*** II 'to take, seize' is semantically close to ***ull-*** 'to destroy', most scholars distinguish the roots. The root ***ull-/-oll-*** 'to destroy' seems most appropriate for ***Ὀλυσσεύς* / *Ὀδυσσεύς***, since one of his epithets in Homer is ***πτολίπορθος*** 'destroyer of cities'. But seizure of a city precedes the sacking of it, which does not exclude ***ul-*** II 'to take, seize'.

Other Nuzi names with the roots ***ull-*** and ***ul-*** are: *Ullunzi* (wr. *Ul-lu-un-zi*), *Uluniki* (wr. *Ú-lu-ni-ki*), *Ulluia̯* (wr. *Ul-lu-ia*), *Ulukka* (wr. *Ú-lu-uq-qa, Ú-lu-uk-ka*), *Ululiia̯* (wr. *Ú-lu-li-ia, Ú-lu-li-a*), cf. I.J. Gelb, *NPN*, 162-163. Hurrian personal names with the root ***ull-***, /***oll-***/, are also frequent elsewhere, cf. e.g. Th. Richter, *VHN* I, 325-329: *Ullaja* (Mari), ^{f}*Ulli* (Mari), *Ullija* (Mari), ^{f}*Ullen* (Mari), *Ullu* (Šubat-Enlil), *Ullu-ewri* (Mari), *Ulluja* (Tigunāni), *Ullukki* (Mari), ^{f}*Ullum-ki* (Mari), *Ullum-tišni* (Mari), variant *Ullam-tašni* (Šušarrā), *Ullum-tišti* (Mari), *Ullum-*[...] (Mari), *Ullun* (Mari), *Ullunna* (Mari), *Ullunni* (Mari), *Ullup-atal* (Šušarrā), *Ulluš-Taja* (Mari), *Ullutta* (Šušarrā), *Ullutti* (Mari, Tigunāni), *Ulluri* (Ašnakkum, Mari). ***Ullu-ewri*** (*ul-lu-ew-ri, ul-lu-ew-ru*) at Mari, analysis {*o/ull=o-evri, o/ull=o-evr(i)=u*[Akkadianizing nominative]} may well be identified with Linear A ***u-re-wi*** (HT 25a.2) = Hurrian ***Ull(=u)-erwi***, 'Destroy (the deceased child),oh Lord !', with vowel absorption and the same (dialectical) metathesis of ***ewri*** > ***erwi*** as in Nuzi names.

Incidentally, Linear A ***u-re-wi*** can be interpreted as ***Ur-erwi*** 'Be present, oh Lord !' as well, cf. Th. Richter, *BGH*, 495-496, s.v. ***ur-*** I [Boğ.; Mit.; PN] 'to be present, appear'.

Notorious is the Hurrian name of the monster created by *Kumarbi*, ***Ullikummi*** 'Destroy Kumme !', and indeed Linear A ***o-ra$_2$-di-ne*** (HT 6a.4) {*o/ull=i-ažd=i=ne*} 'Destroy the woman !', Hurrian prototype of the name of the Cretan hero ***Perseus***, who killed ***Μέδουσα*** (*Medusa*). Linear A and B ***ra$_2$*** = ***ria/rya*** or ***lia/lya***. Since the Hurrian root ***o/ull-*** is attested in Linear A ***o-ra$_2$-di-ne*** (HT 6a.4), direct derivation from Minoan-Hurrian into Mycenaean Greek is more likely than derivation from Mitanni-Hurrian or Syrian Hurrian into Greek.

According to M. Ventris - J. Chadwick (*Documents in Mycenaean Greek*, 126) ***Apollo*** does not appear in the Mycenaean texts. However, the incomplete theonym may be attested at Knossos in the form]***pe-ro$_2$-***[(KN E 842, 3). C.J. Ruijgh, *EGM*, § 237: "Si on admet la lecture possible]***pe-ro$_2$-ne***, il serait tentant de lire [***a-***]***pe-ro$_2$-ne*** et de voir dans cette forme le datif du théonyme ***Ἀπέλγων*** (plus tard dor. ***Ἀπέλλων***, chypr. ***Ἀπείλων***). La forme ***Ἀπόλλων*** peut résulter de l'assimilation régressive de voyelles non contiguës. Une telle interprétation serait corroborée par ***te-o-i*** *θεοῖς* à la ligne 1. De même, ***me-na*** (ligne 2) peut être le datif de ***Μήνᾱ*** 'Lune'." If Ruijgh's conjecture is correct, the Mycenaean form ***Ἀπέλγων*** is of course the oldest, preserved in Cypriot ***Ἀπείλων*** and Doric ***Ἀπέλλων***. The assembly of Spartan citizens (the *Σπαρτιᾶται* 'Spartiates' or *ὅμοιοι* 'equals' / 'peers') was called *Ἀπέλλα*, probably because the citizens met in the assembly under the auspices or the patronage of ***Ἀπέλλων***. A gloss by Hesychius tells: *ἀπέλλαι · σηκοί, ἐκκλησίαι, ἀρχαιρεσίαι.*

The equation with *ἐκκλησίαι* obviously refers to the Lakonian *Ἀπέλλα*, but that with *σηκοί* 'sheds' may indicate that *Ἀπέλγων* was originally a shepherd god and perhaps also a hunting **πότνιος θηρῶν* 'master of wild animals' as his twin sister *Artemis* represented the *πότνια θηρῶν* 'mistress of wild animals'. The twins were both armed with bow and arrows.

It is attractive to associate the root ***Ἀπέλ-*** with the word ***apellu*** 'arrow(head)' from Nuzi, which is suspected to be Hurrian according to V. Haas – H.-J. Thiel, 'Die Beschwörungs-rituale der Allaiturah(h)i und verwandte Texte', *Alter Orient und Altes Testament 31 = Hurritologische Studien II*, Kevelaer/Neukirchen-Vluyn 1978, 262; cf. Th. Richter, *BGH*, 39. If this etymology is correct, Mycenaean *Ἀπέλγων* was originally a Hurrian *hunting god*, worshipped in Crete. M.P. Nilsson (*The Minoan-Mycenaean religion*, 513-516) coined the notion ****πότνιος θηρῶν*** on account of iconographic evidence, arguing that there was no need for two deities with the same function, so that Apollo could move on to other areas important for Greek society, but his original features were never completely wiped out.

The name of ***Ἄρτεμις*** is represented in the genitive ***a-te-mi-to*** (PY Es 650, 5), ***Ἀρτέμιτος*** (with East Greek declension in ***τ*** instead of ***δ***) and in the dative ***a-ti-mi-te*** (PY Un 219, 5), ***Ἀρτιμίτει*** (with ***e/i*** alternation) at Pylos. The form ***]-mi-te*** (KN X 7887, 1) at Knossos is likely to be completed to the dative of the same theonym. Linear A has not yet yielded an equivalent to the Linear B theonym. The ***e/i*** alternation in the Linear B forms ***Ἀρτέμιτος*** and ***Ἀρτιμίτει*** make a Greek origin of the theonym unlikely.

P. Chantraine (*DELG*, 117) s.v. ***Ἄρτεμις***: "À la différence du nom d'Apollon, le nom d'Artémis, quelle qu'en soit l'origine, semble bien attesté dans des inscriptions lydiennes: *artimuś ibśimsis* répondrait à *Ἄρτεμις Ἐφεσία* à Larissa du Caystre, etc., cf. A. Heubeck, *Lydiaka*, 22-25. Il est bien vrai qu'Artémis peut être considérée comme une déesse asiatique (cf. Wilamowitz, *Glaube der Hellenen 1*, 324; M.P. Nilsson, *Gr. Rel. 1*, 451, sqq.). Il est vrai d'autre part qu'elle joue un grand rôle dans le monde dorien, ce qui a conduit à chercher une étymologie illyrienne, d'un illyr. **artos* (M.S. Ruiperez, *Emerita 15*, 1-60, et *Zephyrus 2*, 89 sqq. avec bibliographie). Cette hypothèse qui s'accorde mal avec les données homériques se heurte maintenant à une difficulté, puisque la déesse est connue en mycénien. C'est l'explication par l'Asie Mineure qui semble la plus probable.

Les étymologies par le grec reposent toutes plus ou moins sur des jeux de mots. Le rapprochement avec *ἄρτος* 'ours' se heurte à la difficulté que *ἄρτος* est en grec une forme secondaire. Celui avec *ἄρταμος* 'boucher' est retenue par Kretschmer, *Gl. 27*, 34, mais la graphie *Ἄρταμις* avec le second *α* doit reposer sur une étymologie populaire, cf. Schwyzer, *Gr. Gr. 1*, 256, ce que confirme le mycénien. Quant à un rapprochement avec *ἀρτεμής*, il consiste à expliquer *obscura per obscuriora*. Nous ne savons pas s'il existe un rapport entre ces deux termes, ni lequel des deux serait tiré de l'autre."

The Lydian form ***Artimuś*** equated with ***Ἄρτεμις*** may perhaps be compared with the Hurrian personal name ***Ar-ta-mu-zi***, son of *Ut-ḫap-še*, attested at Nuzi HSS V 69: 22, 24; father of *Ta-a-a*, grandfather of *Ar-ti-ir-wi*, *AASOR XVI* 28:3, cf. I.J. Gelb, *NPN*, 33; P.M. Purves (*NPN*, 203), s.v. ***ar-***, and (262), s.v. ***tamuzi***. Gelb and Purves prefer to divide the name into the elements ***ar-*** 'give' and ***tamuzi***, because Hurrian ***tamuzi*** (perhaps derived from Akkadian) is identical with the Nuzi month name ***Tamuzi***. The name is cognate with Babylonian ***dûzu***. The months so named are equated by Gordon and Lacheman in *AOr X (1938)*, 55 and 60. Th. Richter mentions an abstract form ***tammunze*** {*tamm=o/u=n=že*} that reminds of *da-a-am-mu-u-zi-*[…] (Ḫattuša: ChS I/5, 88: 6) and equals the personal name ***ᶠTammunze*** (wr. *ᶠTa-am-mu-un-ze*) at Mari, cf. *VHN*, 297,529.

If the interpretation of the masculine personal name ***Ar-ta-mu-zi*** as 'Give (the child), oh Tamuzi !' is correct, we may infer that ***Tamuzi*** is not only the name of a month at Nuzi, but probably also a theonym. *Ar-ta-mu-zi* is a rare name and it is unknow whether it could also be used as a feminine name. The name could explain the ending ***-muś*** in Lydian ***Artimuś***, equated with Greek ***Ἄρτεμις***. If the name *Ar-ta-mu-zi* consists of the elements ***arta-*** and ***-muzi*** and if ***-muzi*** may be equated with Hurrian adjectival ***muš***, ***muša-***, ***-muša***, ***-muše***, ***mušu-*** and substantival ***-mušni***, we know that this element was feminine, if connected with ***^{d}Hebat***, and masculine, if connected with ***^{d}Ewri***.

We should examine, whether the Hurrian root ***ard-*** in ***arde*** 'town, city, settlement', that can be compared with Sumerogram URU, Akkadian ***ālu***, Ugaritic ***qarītu*** < **qariytu* and Hittite ***ḫappirija-***, cf. Th. Richter, *BGH*, 48-49, s.v. ***arde*** [*passim*]) may be involved in spite of the alleged voiced dental occlusive, which is voiceless in ***Ἄρτεμις***. Th. Richter (*ibid.*) offers interesting derivatives: the name of a river ***Artamašša*** [Nuzi], see J. Fincke, *Die Orts- und Gewässernamen der Nuzi-Texte* (RGTC 10), 1993, 375; ***artamašše***, Nuzi: HSS XIII 31, 9; XV 56, 10. - obscure (cf. E. Laroche, *GLH*, 56; cf. also *CAD* A/II [1968] 310 [*HW*]; *CDA*^{2} [2000] 25 [*HLW*]); *ar-du-ma-an-zi* = uru.ki (cf. Pirinkir), Msk. (cf. E. Laroche, *GLH*, 54); ***ardumašše***, ***ardumanzi***, *ar-ta-ma-an-zi* [Emar] 'belonging to the city', ≈ Lydian ***Artimi-*** and Greek ***Artemis*** as 'the goddess of the *polis*' (Ivanov 1998, 148ff.[+37], 1999a, 204ff. [zur Etym. des GN s.a. Szemerényi 1994].

It is true that *Artemis* had later famous temples at Sparta and Ephesos, but semantically it seems strange that a goddess, known as a *huntress* and *πότνια θηρῶν* 'Mistress of wild animals', would in Minoan and Mycenaean times be depicted as a sort of 'patroness of the city'. That seems a *contradictio in terminis*, especially since ***arde*** 'town, city, settlement' and ***awari*** 'field, steppe' are proverbial antipoles in Hurrian. Moreover, the dental of ***arde*** is allegedly voiced, whereas the dental of *Artemis* is certainly voiceless.

P.M. Purves (*NPN*, 203) divided ***Ar-ti-mu-ri*** at Nuzi into ***Ar-timuri*** that also seems close to the Lydian form ***Artimuś*** and the Mycenaean forms of ***Ἄρτεμις*** and ***Ἄρτιμις***, but the meaning of the (probably nominal) onomastic element ***timuri*** is unknown.

Th. Richter (*VHN*, 380-381[+176]) mentions that there are now also indications for a verbal usage of the Hurrian root ***ard-***, of which the meaning is not yet certain. G. Wilhelm (A Hurrian letter from Tell Brak, *Iraq 53*, 1991, 164[20]) refers to Urartian ***ard-*** 'to give', and Girbal (2010, 156) to 'übereignen, übergeben, (ab)liefern' ['to hand over, to deliver'].

I. Wegner (*Einführung*, 89) assumes a Hurrian root-extension ***-t-*** (meaning not clear) in ***tan=d-*** 'to celebrate a festival' from ***tan-*** 'to do, make', ***kul=d-*** from ***kul-*** 'to say, speak', ***pal=d-*** from ***pal-*** 'to know', cf. Urartian forms with ***-d-***: *ar=d(u)-ilana* from ***ar-*** 'to give', cf. M. Salvini, *SMEA 29*, 1992, 217-218, with reference to G. Steiner, *RHA 36*, 1978, 184, n. 49, who assumes a meaning with centrifugal force 'away'. This means that the root ***ar=d-*** might mean 'to give away'. ***Ar-ti-mu-ri*** at Nuzi could then be analysed as ***Ar=d=i-muri*** 'Give (the girl), oh *muri* !', cf. ***^{f}Arummura*** (wr. *^{f}A-ru-(um)-mu-ra-(aš)*), XV 5 I 11; XXVI 43 Ro 51, cf. E. Laroche, *NH*, 43, n° 155; cf. Th. Richter, *VHN*, 459-460, s.v. ***mur-***: *{ar=o=m-mur(i)=a}* '*muri* gave (the girl)'. Since ***Arta-*** *{ar=d=a-}* in ***Ar-ta-mu-zi*** would then yield an inexplicable intransitive form, a division of ***ar-*** + ***tamuzi*** would become more likely in the Nuzi personal name, as P.M. Purves thought.

The most simple solution to an etymology of ***Ἄρτεμις / Ἄρτιμις*** (with ***i/e*** alternation in the Linear B examples) may be a combination of the *athematic imperative* ***ar-*** 'give !' with the Hurrian *ominous sign* ***tem(m)i / tim(m)i***, of which I presume that it is derived from the Hurrian verbal root ***te- / ti-*** and ***tew- / tiw-*** 'to speak', in this case with a ***m/w*** alternation ***tem- / tim-*** (as in ***ermi / erwi*** 'Lord' in Minoan-Hurrian and at Nippur) or with the nominal formant ***-me*** (as in ***ul=me*** 'weapon', ***taš=me*** 'gift' and ***ḫud=me*** 'prayer', cf. I. Wegner, *Einführung*, 59): ***te(m)me < te(w)=me***. In the sphere of *ominous signs* the meaning may be 'oracle' or 'verdict', which happen to be translations of ***θέμις*** in Homer.

E. Laroche (*GLH*, 262) mentions Hurrian ***te(m)mi***: signe omineux. Nom. hittite ***te-em-mi-iš, te-me-eš***, cf. *RA 64*, 135. He also mentions the adjective ***te(m)miḫi***: *te-mi-ḫi*, KUB XXXII 26 II 35. – *tim-mi-ḫi-(ya)*, KUB XXXII 50, 3. - *te-mi-ḫa*, IBoT II 39 Vo 14. - *te-em-me-ḫi*, KBo XXIII 23, 73, without translation. Th. Richter (*BGH*, 460; *VHN*, 536) mentions: ***temmi-*** com. [loan-word into Hittite] 'un signe omineux' (Laroche, *GLH*, 262; De Martino, 1992a, 155); 'Vertiefung?', 'Terminus im Omen' (Tischler, 1993, 308, 2001b, 174). He interprets the adjective ***te/imm=e/i=ḫi*** as 'das zu *temmi* Gehörige' ['belonging to *temmi*']. The name of a *ḫabiru* ***Temmiḫe*** (wr. *Te-em-mi-ḫe*) occurs at Tigunāni, typology 3.1, cf. Th. Richter, *VHN*, 305. Even if a Hurrian etymology is not accepted, the Mycenaean theonym *Artemis* is several centuries earlier than the Lydian inscriptions, which makes provenance from Crete more likely than from Anatolia. Since *Apollo*'s name is probably represented in the Linear B texts from Knossos and the name of *Artemis* in texts from Pylos and Knossos, they likely had a Minoan origin as their mother *Lato* (cf. also the toponym *Lato* in Crete). Provenance from Anatolia is not impossible, but not necessarily preferable.

The theonym ***Ἀθήνη*** is to date unexplained. P. Chantraine, *DELG*, 27-28: "***Ἀθήνη***: ép., poètes; ***Ἀθάνᾱ*** (attesté en mycénien, dial. non ioniens), déesse grecque que l'on suppose une ancienne déesse minoenne, qui serait issue d'une déesse au serpent protégeant le palais. C'est probablement d'après la déesse qu'a été dénommée la cité attique ***Ἀθῆναι***.

Le mycénien connaît le nom de la déesse dans l'expression ***atanapotinija***, cf. J. Chadwick – L. Baumbach 167. Dérivé: ***Ἀθηναῖος***, 'athénien', mais le fém. ***Ἀθηναίη*** sert aussi de nom de la déesse (88 ex. chez Hom.), att. ***Ἀθηναία*** et par contraction l'usuel ***Ἀθηνᾶ***. Ét.: Théonyme inexpliqué, cf. Nilsson, *Griech. Rel. 1*, 405 sqq. *Lex. Ep.* 208."

It is intriguing that the Linear B texts from Knossos provide both ***a-ta-na-po-ti-ni-ja*** (KN V 52+52bis+[X] 8285, join by J.-P. Olivier), the dative ***Ἀθάνᾳ Ποτνίᾳ*** 'for the Mistress Athena', and ***da-pu$_2$-ri-to-jo po-ti-ni-ja*** (KN Gg 702,2), ***δαβυρίνθοιο Ποτνίᾳ*** 'for the Mistress of the labyrinth'. If the hypothesis that these deities are the same is correct, the goddess ***Ἀθάνᾱ*** was the deity protecting the labyrinth, which may have been the name of the palace. She may have been the Minoan deity portrayed as the 'goddess with the snakes' and she played a special role, disguised as *Ariadne*, helping *Theseus* to slay the *Minotauros* and to escape from the labyrinth.

An indication for a Hurrian origin of the Mycenaean theonym ***Ἀθάνᾱ*** is the parallel form ***Ἀθηναίη***, Attic ***Ἀθηναία***. Apart from the frequent suffix ***-na*** of the plural article, there is a Hurrian onomastic element ***-na*** occurring in feminine personal names, which may well be a shortened / hypocoristic form of ***-naịa***, cf. at Nuzi: ***fAru-na***, ***fAweš-na*** and ***fAwiš-naịa***, ***fAẓe-na***, ***fMinen-na*** and ***fMinen-naịa***, cf. P.M. Purves, *NPN*, 236-237, s.v. ***-na*** and ***-naịa***.

P.M. Purves adds: Hurrian element apparently found exclusively in feminine personal names. See Speiser in *AASOR XVI (1936)*, p. 75, n. 1, and Oppenheim in *AOF XII (1937-39)*, 36. P.M. Purves, *NPN*, 237, offered a long list of feminine personal names with the theophorous element ***-nai̯a*** at Nuzi: ^{f}*Allai-nai̯a*, ^{f}*Ašmun-nai̯a*, ^{f}*Aštun-nai̯a* (wr. ^{f}*Aš-du-un-na-a-a*), ^{f}*Awiš-nai̯a*, ^{f}*Azun-nai̯a*, ^{f}*Ḫašun-nai̯a*, ^{f}*Ḫepet-nai̯a*, ^{f}*Ḫumer-nai̯a*, ^{f}*Ilim-nai̯a*, ^{f}*Imšen-nai̯a*, ^{f}*Iwin-nai̯a*, ^{f}*Minen-nai̯a*, ^{f}*Našmun-nai̯a*, ^{f}*Nupen-nai̯a*, ^{f}*Šalḫun-nai̯a*, ^{f}*Šatum-nai̯a*, ^{f}*Šeltun-nai̯a*, ^{f}*Šewir-nai̯a*, ^{f}*Šinen-nai̯a*, ^{f}*Šuḫur-nai̯a*, ^{f}*Šunšun-nai̯a*, ^{f}*Tatun-nai̯a*, ^{f}*Teḫeš-nai̯a*, ^{f}*Teššen-nai̯a*, ^{f}*Tilun-nai̯a*, ^{f}*Tulpun-nai̯a*, ^{f}*Uššen-nai̯a*, ^{f}*Zilim-nai̯a*, and with the variation *-nai̯e*: ^{f}*Ammi-nai̯e*.

If the etymology of Mycenaean ***Ἀθάνᾱ*** (later ***Ἀθήνη*** with the doublet form ***Ἀθηναίη***) from Minoan ****Attānā / *Attānāia*** is Hurrian, the analysis is *{Att(a)=a-Nai̯a}*, '*Nai̯a* is *like* her Father'. I deliberately do not analyse the name as *{Atta-Nai̯a}*, which would mean '*Nai̯a* is her Father', but with the *essive* form *{Att(a)=a-Nai̯a}*, '*Nai̯a* is *like* her Father'. The myth about '*Athena born from her father's head*' may help to explain the meaning of her name. Hephaistos's axe certainly helped to cure the headache of her father Zeus.

P.M. Purves (*NPN*, 236-237) had already isolated ***-nai̯a*** and the shortened form ***-na*** in personal names as an onomastic, probably theophorous, element. Th. Richter (*VHN*, 461-462 and notes 516-523) mentions, s.v. ***Naje*** and ***Na***, that this theonym only occurs in onomastics and very frequently in names of women. This may not be decisive, but it is likely that we are dealing with a goddess. At Nuzi the theonym was mainly written as ***°na-A+A*** and rarely as ***°na-IA***, so that it was normalized as ***Naja***. But in the area of *Kašijari* and elsewhere the orthography was also ***°na-ie-e***.

Th. Richter (*VHN*, 462) offers a long list of names with ***Naje*** and ***Na***: (1) *{Na}* ^{f}*Awiš-Na* (Mari); ^{f}*Attap-Na* (Mari); ^{f}*Ilip-Na* (ŠE); ^{f}*Elul-Na* (Mari); ^{f}*Ḫazip-Na* (Mari); ^{f}*Kunuš-Na* (Mari); ^{f}*Nakaš-Na* (AŠ); ^{f}*Šatum-Na* (Mari); ^{f}*Šeḫlum-Na* (ŠE); ^{f}*Šelwi(?)-Na* (AŠ, Mari); ^{f}*Šerwi(?)-Na* (Mari); ^{f}*Taḫiz-Na* (Mari); ^{f}*Talmeš-Na* (Mari); ^{f}*Tulup-Na* (Mari); ^{f}*Tuza-Na* (Mari); ^{f}*Uniš-Na* (AŠ); ^{f}*Unzi-Na* (AŠ); ^{f}*Unuš-Na* (Mari). (2) *{Naje}* ^{f}*Alla-Naje* (Mari); ^{f}*Allum-Naje* (Q); ^{f}*Azza-Naje* (Mari); ^{f}*Attap-Naje* (Mari, Q, ŠE); ^{f}*Elip-Naje* (Mari); ^{f}*Ilip-Naje* (Mari); ^{f}*Inip-Naje* (Q); ^{f}*Innu-Naje* (Mari); ^{f}*Kanzuš-Naje* (AŠ); ^{f}*Maška-Naje* (Mari); ^{f}*Memen-Naje* (AŠ); ^{f}*Naktum-Naje* (Mari); ^{f}*Nanip-Naje* (Mari); ^{f}*Neniš-Naje* (Mari); ^{f}*Nupin-Naje* (Mari); ^{f}*Zazza-Naje* (Mari); ^{f}*Šatam-Naje* (Mari); ^{f}*Šatum-Naje* ([AŠ], Mari); ^{f}*Šatu-Naje* (Mari); ^{f}*Šiḫlum-Naje* (Mari); ^{f}*Šeḫra-Naje* (Mari); ^{f}*Šerum-Naje* (Mari); ^{f}*Šunzu-Naje* (AŠ); ^{f}*Tieš-Naje* (Mari); ^{f}*Tulup-Naje* (Mari); ^{f}*Tuza-Naje* (Mari); ^{f}*Unuš-Naje* (Mari), and some incomplete names. I have underscored the names with doublets of ***-Na*** and ***-Naja/e***.

Among these names ***^{f}Attap-Na*** occurs at Mari and ***^{f}Attap-Naje*** at Mari, Qaṭṭarā and Šubat-Enlil, which suggests a verbal analysis of the first element *att=a=b-*. But the first element is not always verbal. The first element of ^{f}*Alla-Naje* (Mari) and ^{f}*Azza-Naje* (Mari) is nominal: ***Alla(i)*** 'Lady' and ***azza*** 'woman', respectively.

Th. Richter (*VHN*, 88) analyses ***Attan*** (wr. *at-ta-an*) as *{att=a=n(na)}*, typology 1.1.1.3.3.1, lexicon *att-*, name of 2 *ḫabiru* on *Prisma* II 39 and *Prisma* V 24 at Tigunāni.

So he assumes in this case that ***Attan*** is a verbal 'one-word' name, but in the discussion he mentions that one can alternatively think of a form of ***attani*** 'father' without final vowel or of {*atta(i)=a*[E.]=*n(na)*} 'He (the boy) is like the (deceased ?) father'. [E.] refers to the *essive* case. The enclitic personal pronoun 3rd person singular ***-nna*** is the subject 'he' (in the *absolutive* case) of an alleged (intransitive) 'is'.

The latter analysis is comparable with my analysis of the Minoan theonym ****Attana*** (prototype of Mycenaean ***Ἀθάνᾱ*** that I analyse as '*Na* (= *Naịa*) is like her Father (Tešub)'. This analysis is in accordance with the fact that ***-νᾱ*** and ***-ναίη*** < ***-nāía*** in ***Ἀθάνᾱ*** > ***Ἀθήνη*** and ****Attānāía*** > ***Ἀθηναίη*** are always written with single ***-n-***, whereas the enclitic personal pronoun 3rd person singular ***-nna*** is written with double ***-nn-***. It also shows that ***atta-*** can be analysed as the *essive* ***att(a)=a***.

According to Th. Richter (*VHN*, 386, s.v. ***att-*** {*att-*}) A. Goetze, (1963, 6) was the first to offer evidence for the 'Hurricity' of the verbal root ***att-*** (cf. Th. Richter, *BGH*, 66, s.v. ***att-*** [Boğ.]). He also observed that personal names with ***att-*** are widely spread, but not very frequent. Names such as *(a)-at-ta-ra/ru* are probably based on a noun ***attari*** {*att=a=ri*}.

He mentions (*VHN*, 386) the following names: (1) {*att-*}: ***Attaja*** (Mari) [with variant ***Attija***]; ***Attan*** (Tigunāni); ***ᶠAttap-kijaze*** (Ašnakkum); ***ᶠAttap-Na*** (Mari); ***ᶠAttap-Naje*** (Mari, Qaṭṭarā, Šubat-Enlil); ***Attija*** (Mari, Šušarrā); ***Attijān*** (Terqa); ***[A]ttuja*** (Mari). (2) {*att=a=ri*}: ***Attara*** (Qaṭṭarā, Šubat-Enlil); ***Attaru*** (Šušarrā); (3) {*att=i=zzi*}: ***Attizzi*** (Mari).

In my view the element {*att=a=b-*} in the names ***ᶠAttap-kijaze***, ***ᶠAttap-Na***, ***ᶠAttap-Naje*** clearly shows that ***att-*** is verbal in these names, since ***-b-*** is in Old Hurrian and in archaic or archaizing Hurrian personal names the suffix indicating the subject (3rd person sing.) of the verbal form, for instance, in Old Hurrian ***pašš=i=b*** 'he sends' that would in later Mitanni-Hurrian be ****pašš=i=a***, cf. *pa-aš-ši-a-(ma)*, Mit. IV 55 (present 3rd person sing.); and in Old Hurrian ***un=a=b*** 'he comes' that is in later Mitanni-Hurrian ***un=a=Ø***, cf. I. Wegner, *Einführung*, 126. In view of this evidence one may reasonably infer that Old Hurrian ***ᶠAttap-Na*** {*att=a=b-Na*} and ***ᶠAttap-Naje*** {*att=a=b-Naja/e*} could in Mitanni-Hurrian be ****ᶠAtta-Na*** {*att=a=Ø-Na*} and ****ᶠAtta-Naje*** {*att=a=Ø-Naja/e*}, respectively.

The latter names would then also contain the verbal root ***att-***, of which the meaning is unfortunately not yet established. This might also have consequences for the Pre-Greek theonym ***Ἀθάνᾱ*** and its doublet form ***Ἀθηναίη*** (Attic ***Ἀθηναία***), cf. Hurrian ***-Naịa / e*** and ***-Na***. Th. Richter (*BGH*, 66, s.v. ***att-*** [Boğ.]) mentions with hesitation the meaning 'to conspire (?)', which does not seem satisfactory. As long as the meaning of verbal ***att-*** is not known, we do not know whether a verbal interpretation of ***att-*** in the theonym ****Attana*** would be as satisfactory as the nominal analysis with ***atta(i)*** in the *essive* case ***att(a)=a*** is.

It is unlikely that Mycenaean ***Ἀθάνᾱ*** and probably Minoan-Hurrian ***Attana*** can be equated with the Hurrian personal names ***A-da-na*** at Kaniš and ***A-ta-na*** at Nuzi, phonologically /***adana***/, since single writing of the dental indicates that it is voiced. The personal name ***a-ta-na*** seems identical with the toponym ***Adana*** in south-east Anatolia, cf. also *a-da/ta-(a)-ni*, KUB XXV 44 ii? 5; XXVII 1 ii 31 and 70; XXVII 6 i 31, cf. P.M. Purves, *NPN*, 207, s.v. ***atan***. Although there are apparently variants attested with single and double writing of the dentals such as ***Ataja / Attaja***, ***Atakku / Attakku***, ***Atija / Attija***, ***Atan / Attan***, and even *a-ta-ia / a-at-ta-a-ia* (see Th. Richter, *VHN*, 386, s.v. ***att-***), the verbal roots ***ad-*** and ***att-*** are usually distinguished from each other.

To keep on the safe side it is for the present preferable to equate ***Ἀθάνᾱ*** and probably Minoan-Hurrian ****Attana*** only with the Hurrian forms with voiceless dentals. Th. Richter (*VHN*, 390, n. 227) mentions that because of consistent single writing of the dental it is hardly possible to connect the personal names ***A-da-na*** at Kaniš and ***A-ta-na*** at Nuzi with the Hurrian month-names ***Attana*** and ***Attanašwe***, since these are connected with ***atta/attai*** 'father' (see also *BGH*, 67).

E. Laroche (*GLH*, 64), s.v. ***attana***, ***attanašwe***, nom d'un mois à Nuzi et à Alalaḫ, cf. *CAD* A II 510; *AW* 87. According to Th. Richter (*BGH*, 67) ***attana*** is the first month at Alalaḫ VII, September / October (cf. also ***attannatim*** {*atta(i)=nn(i)=ade*} at Alalaḫ IV) that can be compared with the 7th month at Nuzi ***attanašwe***. Th. Richter analyses the name of the month ***Attana*** as {*atta(i)=na*} and translates it as 'The fathers', which is in accordance with ***Attanašwe***, analysed as plural genitive {*attan(i)=n(a)=aš=ve*} by G. Wilhelm (*Das Archiv des Šilwa-Teššup*. Heft 3: *Rationenlisten 2*, Wiesbaden 1985, 84) and as {*atta(i)=na=aš=we*} by J.-P. Vita (Zur Menologie und zum Kalender von Alalaḫ, *AoF 27*, 2000, 298) that can be translated as '(Month) of the fathers'. Incidentally, this form from Nuzi with the ending ***-na=aš=we*** (consisting of the suffix of the so-called plural definite article ***-na*** + pluralizing suffix ***-aš-*** + the genitive suffix ***-we/-wi***) can also be used to prove that the so-called plural genitive in ***-še / -ši*** (cf. E. Laroche, *GLH*, 26) was actually derived from < ***=(a)š=(w)e/(w)i*** < ***=(a)š=we/wi***.

In the 2016 edition of *Minoan Linear A* I had expressed the view that the month ***Attana*** at Alalaḫ was probably derived from a divine name just as some Roman month-names are derived from Roman theonyms: e.g. (mensis) *Martius* (< Mars), *Iunius* (< Iuno). I also expressed the view that the Pre-Greek theonym *Athena* was probably equivalent to the Hurrian month-name ***Attana***. Theoretically that view is still possible, but comparison of the Hurrian month-name ***Attana*** at Alalaḫ with ***Attanašwe*** at Nuzi, that can only be explained as a plural genitive '(Month) of the fathers', makes explanation of the month-name ***Attana*** at Alalaḫ as 'The fathers' obviously the most likely option.

At the same time it does not make sense to interpret the theonym ***Attana*** (Hurrian prototype of Mycenaean ***Ἀθάνᾱ***) as 'The fathers'. Consequently the etymology of the Pre-Greek theonym ***Ἀθάνᾱ*** and its doublet form ***Ἀθηναίη*** (Attic ***Ἀθηναία***) as '*Na* (= *Na̯ia*) is like her Father (namely Tešub/Zeus)' remains the most likely option.

The resemblance of the goddess to her father reminds us of her dramatic and spectacular mythological birth. The severe headache of her father Zeus had to be cured by Hephaistos's axe. When the axe cleaved his head, Athena jumped out in full armour. Athena was also her father's darling. The name of ***Ἀθάνᾱ / Ἀθηναία*** (later *Ἀθήνη* with the doublet form *Ἀθηναίη*) in fact tells the myth of her birth in a nutshell. The Minoan-Hurrian etymology of her name may still have been known in Mycenaean times, since the Minoan-Mycenaean religion as well as mythology and iconography had so much in common. In my view the real *caesura* and serious loss of Minoan and Hurrian traditions probably came only with the end of the Mycenaean era and the arrival of the Dorians in Crete. They came from the north-west of mainland-Greece from areas that had been beyond the sphere of influence of the southern Mycenaean centres, let alone the Minoan civilization.

Since the theonym was in alphabetic Greek written with *theta* (***θ***), the Hurrian voiceless dental may have sounded as a voiceless dental with aspiration **[t^h]** in Greek ears.

Returning to P. Chantraine's analysis (*DELG*, 27-28), s.v. ***Ἀθήνη***: "….. ***Ἀθηναῖος***, 'athénien', mais le fém. ***Ἀθηναίη*** sert aussi de nom de la déesse (88 ex. chez Hom.), att. ***Ἀθηναία*** et par contraction l'usuel ***Ἀθηνᾶ***. Ét.: Théonyme inexpliqué.", we may now conclude that his explanation of ***Ἀθήνη*** as the result of contraction of ***Ἀθηναία*** > ***Ἀθηνᾶ*** was understandable from the perspective of Greek morphology. Nobody could have suspected that Greek morphology had preserved the doublets of the Hurrian theonym ***Naja/e*** in Pre-Geek ***Ἀθηναία*** and shortened or hypocoristic ***Na*** in Mycenaean ***Ἀθάνᾱ***.

The connection of ***Ἀθάνᾱ*** / ***Ἀθηναία*** analysed as '*Na* / *Naja* is like her Father (Tešub)' is corroborated by her epithet ***Παλλάς***, ***-άδος*** (*Pallas*), *Iliad* A 200; *Odyssey* α 125; *alibi*.

P. Chantraine (*DELG*, 853) provided no separate *lemma* for ***Παλλάς***, but only briefly mentioned, s.v. ***παλλακή*** 'concubine': "Autre suffixe féminin ***-αδ-***, cf. *δρυάς*, etc., dans ***Παλλάς***, ***-άδος***, épithète d'Athéna (Hom., ion.-att., etc.), employé par Eub. pour une monnaie portant l'effigie de Pallas." Athena's association with ***παλλακή*** is almost an insult, since she is also called ***παρθένος*** 'young girl, virgin'. ***Παλλὰς Ἀθήνη*** is the goddess of *wisdom* and the *arts* and she has also Martial features in Greek mythology. The epithet ***Παλλάς*** probably means 'The goddess who knows', 'Goddess of wisdom'.

The Hurrian verbal root ***pal-*** I / ***pall-*** I means 'to know'. Th. Richter (*BGH*, 291), s.v. root ***pal-*** I / ***pall-*** I [*passim*]: Einhellig als 'wissen, kennen' aufgefaßt [unanimously interpreted as 'to know']. Hurrian ***pal-/pall-*** corresponds with Akkadian ***idû*** (E. Laroche, *GLH*, 194), resp. ***edû*** (Dijkstra, 1993b, 167, Wilhelm, 2003b, 341[3]) and Hittite ***šak(k)-*** 'wissen, kennen' (E. Neu, 1996a, 408[30]).

One may infer that the root ***pall-*** is in fact the result of an extra formant ***-il-***, especially in the forms of the *final debitive* mood, cf. I. Wegner, *Einführung*, 111-112 and *table 12*: *The chain of suffixes of the* so-called *final debitive*.

Root+root-extension	formant	formant	pluralizer	enclitic pronoun	syntactic particle
	(-il-)	***-ae/-ai***	***-š(a)***	***-tta***	***-an***, etc.
				-mma	
				-nna, etc.	
pal	+ ***(i)l***	+ ***-ae***	+	***-n(na)***	

(*pal-la-(a-)en*, Mit. IV 56, 59) 'in order that he (My Brother) may know it'.

pal	+ ***(i)l***	+ ***-ai***	+	***-n(na)***	

(*pal-la-in*, Mit. IV 64) 'in order that he may know it'.

The daughter of king Minos, ***Ἀριάδνη***, played a very peculiar role by helping the Athenian hero ***Theseus*** escaping from the labyrinth after he had killed the Minotaur. After Theseus had left her on the island of Naxos, Dionysos took her to Mount Olympos. One can only conclude that the Minoan princess must have had some godlike features. She did not only play the part of a goddess by helping heroes as, for instance, Athena did several times with Odysseus and other heroes, but she also became the consort of a god.

However, the myth does not show what actually happened, because it was not ***Ἀριάδνη*** behaving like a goddess, but in reality the Goddess Athena helping the hero Theseus in the appearance of the princess, thus concealing that an immortal God was interfering in the affairs of mortal human beings. The element ***ἀρι-*** in the name of Ariadna was later probably understood as the augmentive particle which we find e.g. in Homer in ***ἀριδείκετος*** 'very excellent, eminent' and ***ἀρίζηλος*** 'very clear'.

However, if the name was originally Minoan, the element ***ari-*** may well represent the Hurrian verbal root ***ar-*** 'to give'; ***ar=i-*** is the *transitive imperative* in ***-i-***, of which ***-i-*** is in fact the marker of transitivity (the *imperative* does not have its own marker). The indicative 3rd person singular in 'Mitanni' Hurrian would be ***ar=i=a***, consisting of the root ***ar-*** + the marker of transitivity ***-i-*** + the marker ***-a*** of the subject of the transitive verb 3rd pers. sing. In many personal names we find Old Hurrian forms with the Old Hurrian marker of the subject of the transitive verb 3rd pers. sing. ***-b***, which was formerly called a 'root-complement' ***-p/b-***, but is now considered the suffix indicating the 3rd person singular: e.g. ***Ari-p-ḫurra***, ***Ari-p-šarri***, ***Ari-p-šeriš***, ***Ari-p-tešup***, ***Ari-p-tilla***, etc... at Nuzi.

Old Hurrian ***ar=i=b-*** = 'Mitanni' Hurrian ***ar=i=a***. The Hurrian personal name ***Ariḭa*** can be a 'one word' personal name ***Ar=i=a*** 'He gives' or the hypocoristic form ***Ar=i=ya***, in which the hypocoristic suffix ***-ya*** replaces, for instance, a theophorous element like ***-šarri***, ***-tešup***. The name of the princess ***Ἀριάδνη*** may be explained from the Hurrian prototype ****Ari-attānā*** > Minoan ****Ari-atʰānā*** 'Give, oh Attana /Athana !' > ****Ari-atʰnā*** (syncope) > ****Ari-adnā*** (voicing of the dental under influence of nasal in Hurrian) > (Greek) ****Ἀριάδνᾱ*** > ***Ἀριάδνη***. The name ***Ἀριάδνη*** may be interpreted as a theophorous sentence name.

The Pre-Greek name ***Θησεύς*** is attested at Pylos as ***te-se-u*** (PY En 74, 5; Eo 276, 4: ***te-o-jo do-e-ro*** 'servant of a god'). The name is clearly Pre-Greek, because an Indo-European intervocalic ***-s-*** would have changed into ***-h-*** and ultimately have disappeared in Greek. To date an etymology of the name ***Θησεύς*** is failing, cf. P. Chantraine, *DELG*, 436, s.v. ***Θησεύς***: "Étymologie: Inconnue." Was ***Θησεύς*** originally a Cretan name derived from the Hurrian hypocoristic theophorous name ***Teššuḭa*** (wr. *Te-eš-šu-ia*, *Te-šu-ia*, *Te-iš-šu-ia*, *Ti-iš-šu-ú-ia*), attested at Nuzi (cf. I.J. Gelb, *NPN*, 154), comparable to e.g. ***a-pa-je-u*** (PY Jn 845, 5), probably ***Ἀφαιεύς*** 'celebrant of ***Ἀφαίᾱ***', and was the Minoan myth about Theseus and Ariadna later connected with the Greek mainland, so that Theseus could become an Athenian prince and hero with a name that contained an onomastic element referring to the head of the Hurrian pantheon ? Only Teš(š)ub knows: *Talmi-Teš(š)ub* 'Teš(š)ub is Great'!

P.M. Purves (*NPN*, 265) about Hurrian ***teššu***: "Since ***Teššuḭa*** is evidently hypocoristic for personal names beginning with ***Tešup-*** (cf. ***Tešup-erwi***, ***Tešup-nirari*** in name-list) and ***Teššu-mati*** occurs as variant of ***Tešup-mati***, this element may belong to the same root as the name of the deity ***Tešup***, which would imply that what is generally understood as ***Tešup*** is actually ***Teššup***." Th. Richter (*BGH*, 461-462) mentions ***teš-*** as a reconstructed root that can be accepted for *te-ša/i-ḫi*, *ti-iš-šu-uḫ-ḫi*, *te-šu-ḫa-ar-ḫi-ta*, *ti-i-šu-wa-ar-ḫa-a-am-ma*, ***tešuḫarḫi***, ***tešuḫi*** as well as the theonym ***Teššup***; ***tešuḫi***, ***tešaḫi***, ***tešiḫi*** [Boğ.; Ug.] 'chef' ['chief'] corresponds with Sumerian UGULA, Akkadian ***aklu***. He mentions (*BGH*, 462) that ***tešš-*** [Boğ; GN] may be the same root in the theonym ***Teššob***; ***tešši*** [Boğ; South-Bab.] is now interpreted as 'erhaben' ['great, august, sublime, grand'], 'ehrwürdig, angesehen' ['honourable, notable, prominent, distinguished'], 'noble'.

The combination of ***te-se-u*** with ***te-o-jo do-e-ro*** 'servant of a god' (probably the description of a priest) in PY En 74, 5 and PY Eo 276, 4 is intriguing, since the 'Greek' word ***θεός*** is suspected to be of 'Pre-Greek' origin. P. Chantraine, *DELG*, 429-430, s.v. ***θεός***: "m., f. (Hom., ion.-att., etc.), béot., chypr., crét. ***θιός***, lacon. ***σιός***. Adjectifs dérivés: ***θεῖος*** 'divin'... probablement de ****θέσ-yος***; le mycénien a le féminin ***teija***.

La forme ***θήιος*** chez Alc. et chez Balbilla n'est pas expliquée. ... Étymologie inconnue. Le rapprochement avec lat. *deus*, skr. *devá-*, est bien entendue impossible. D'une façon plus générale, la chute d'un *ϝ* intervocalique dans ***θεός*** ne peut être supposée en raison du mycénien ***teo*** et de la forme crétoise ***θιός***. Dans ces conditions, on a amené à admettre la chute d'un sigma intervocalique et à évoquer les composés d'ailleurs obscurs ***θέσ-κελος***, ***θεσ-πέσιος***, ***θέσ-φατος***." He also rejects two other hypotheses and concludes: "Finalement l'ensemble reste incertain." The Homeric compounds ***θέσκελος*** 'miraculous', ***θεσπέσιος*** 'divine, formidable', ***θέσφατος*** 'said/announced by a god' prove that ***θεός*** is the result of change from intervocalic ***-s-*** (****θεσός***) > intervocalig ***-h-*** (Mycenaean ***θεὅς***) > (later) ***θεός***.

C.J. Ruijgh (*EGM*, § 233) explains Mycenaean ***te-o*** as ***θεὅς*** (with intervocalic ***h***) < ****θεσός***, a word of probably Pre-Greek origin, cf. ***te-i-ja*** (§ 175). In § 175 he writes: "***te-i-ja*** (PY Fr 1202: datif sg. f.): ***θεἵος*** 'des dieux', dérivé de ***te-o θεὅς*** (PY Ep 704, 5: acc. ? sg.; *al.*). Plus tard, on trouve la forme ***θεῖος***. L'expression ***ma-te-re te-i-ja Μᾱτρεῖ θεἵᾳ*** ('pour la Mère des dieux' ou 'pour la Mère divine') rappelle ***Μήτηρ = Δημήτηρ*** (cf. aussi ***Ῥέᾱ***, ***Κυβέλη***) et, d'autre part, ***Θεία̅***, nom d'une soeur de Rhéa d'après Hésiode." We may conclude that according to C.J. Ruijgh Linear B ***ma-te-re te-i-ja*** (PY Fr 1202, dative), ***Μᾱτρεῖ θεἵᾳ***, can be interpreted in various ways as 'for the Mother of the gods' or 'for the divine Mother' or 'for Mother ***Θεία̅*** (*Theia*) ?'.

We have discussed the correlation between ***Ḫebat*** in her appearance of ***Allani*** 'the Lady' and the goddess ***Hera*** (cf. also the discussion on Linear A ***se+re*** and ***se+re+da***) and between the theonym ***Ḫebat / Ḫebet*** and the goddess ***Ἥβη*** (*Hèbè*) who had to become 'daughter of Zeus and Hera' instead of 'consort of Teš(š)ub / Zeus', because her name was later associated by the Greeks with the Greek term ***ἥβη*** 'youth, vigour, puberty'. Remarkably the "goddess" ***Θεία̅*** is mentioned by Hesiod in his *Theogony* as the sister of ***Ῥέᾱ*** (*Rhea*) who is consort of Kronos and mother of Zeus.

The struggle for power between *Ouranos* (*Οὐρανός*), *Kronos* and *Zeus* is a close copy of that between the Hurrian *Anu* (< Sum. AN), *Kumarbi* and *Tešub*. Tešub's place in the Mycenaean pantheon had been taken by the Indo-European Zeus. But Hurrian and Cretan ***Tešub***, possibly Linear A ***te-zu***, survived in names such as Linear B ***te-se-u Θησεύς***.

The Hurrian onomastic element ***-teḭa***, hypocoristic of ***-teš(š)ub***, may have survived as the deity ***Θεία̅*** in Hesiod, but because the place of the Head of the pantheon had already been taken by Zeus and since most words and names in ***-a*** in Greek are feminine, ***Θεία̅*** had to become a female deity and became sister of ***Ῥέᾱ*** instead of her son, cf. also the discussion on Linear A ***re-za***.

Teš- may also be the basis for ****θεσός*** > (Mycenaean) ***θεὅς*** > ***θεός*** that was treated as if it was a common Indo-European noun. Frequent usage of the 'loan-word' in the Greek vernacular may have led to the process just described, whereas the intervocalic ***-s-*** in ***Θησεύς*** (Linear B ***te-se-u***) was preserved, possibly because the Hurrian prototype ***Teššuḭa*** was usually written with double ***-šš-***. Attestation of [***θ***] in ***Ἀθάνᾱ***, ***Ἀθηναία***, ***Θησεύς***, ***Θεία̅***, ***θεός*** suggests that the (Mycenaean) Greeks may have understood the Minoan-Hurrian voiceless dental as a voiceless dental with aspiration.

CONCLUSIONS AND SUMMARY

In this monograph I have reviewed attempts to decipher the script of Linear A and have concluded that none could be accepted as presenting consistent phonological, morphological and syntactical evidence, necessary in the case of decipherment of a script, if the idiom written with it is unknown. Using phonological and morphological evidence I have shown by linguistic methods that Linear A reflects the notation of an idiom with very specific phonological features and with a morphology of agglutinative character. I have identified this idiom as Hurrian or rather a Hurrian dialect that can be described as Minoan-Hurrian.

This new revised and extended edition of *Minoan Linear A* offers irrefutable linguistic evidence showing that the idiom written with Minoan Linear A is a Minoan branch of the Hurrian language. E. Neu's publication of the Hurrian-Hittite bilingual ***Kirenze*** (KBo 32) has offered a great contribution to Hurrian studies.

As a result I. Wegner's completely revised her Hurrian grammar, *Einführung in die hurritische Sprache* (Wiesbaden 2007^2), and two important publications by Th. Richter, *Bibliographisches Glossar des Hurritischen* (Wiesbaden 2012) and *Vorarbeiten zu einem hurritischen Namenbuch*, Erster Teil: *Personennamen altbabylonischer Überlieferung vom Mittleren Euphrat und aus dem nördlichen Mesopotamien* (Wiesbaden 2016) made a revision of my 2016 edition of *Minoan Linear A*, Volume I: *Hurrians and Hurrian in Minoan Crete*, inevitable, since it was largely based on studies of the *pre-Kirenze* period. These works also contained so much more elaborate grammatical evidence and better understanding of lexical terms, that they offered a great opportunity to improve my Hurrian identifications of Linear A sequences and to triple the number of identifications.

The quantity and quality of the evidence make it now justifiable to officially announce *the decipherment of the idiom of Minoan Linear A as Hurrian.*

Since the text of Volume I had grown to 3100 pages, the indices and glossaries included, I had to increase the number of parts from two to six and to use a smaller letter-font as well. I have also slightly changed the title of *Minoan Linear A*, Volume I, into ***The decipherment of Minoan Linear A: Hurrians and Hurrian in Minoan Crete***.

Overall there is a great unity of evidence visible in all Minoan palatial centres, villas and farm-houses. The administrative clay tablets with Linear A inscriptions offer mainly lists of personal names, consisting of Hurrian 'sentence names' and so-called 'one-word' names comparable with those from Near-Eastern and Anatolian centres. It is significant that we find both 'Old Hurrian' names and 'Mitanni-Hurrian' names in the Minoan centres as in the Near East and Anatolia. The 'Old Hurrian' names contain 'Old Hurrian' verbal forms and the 'Mitanni-Hurrian' show verbal forms that we know from the Tušratta letter.

It is clear that Linear B inherited many features from Linear A, especially the majority of syllabic and ideographic signs, signs for weights, measures and numerals (that show a decimal system). Linear A used, however, also many ligatures, of which some turn out to represent theonyms, notably NUBES+***pi*** 100 (HT 33.4) = 'Cloud'+***pi***, which appears to be a *rebus-like* notation of the 'God of clouds' = Tešub+***pi*** > ***Tešuppi*** (genitive) 'of Tešub' followed by ***qe+pa$_3$*** = ***ḫe+pa$_3$*** 100 (HT 33.4) = (Tešub's wife) *Ḫebat*, both followed by the high number of 100. Linear A has also signs for fractions that Linear B seems to miss.

So there are many resemblances between Linear A and B, but also some differences. Most remarkable is the apparent lack of syllabic sequences describing products as we sometimes encounter in Linear B. The most likely reason is the very small size of the Linear A tablets, on which the Minoan scribes used ideograms that clearly and simply indicated vessels, commodities, animals, people, etc., whereas the Linear B scribes had enough space to add more detailed information to the ideograms. An exception may well be tablet HT 31 from Hagia Triada, where syllabic sequences are written on top of vessel-ideograms.

Other exceptions are, of course, grammatical combinations like ***da-qe-ra* , *qe-pi-ta*** 22 JE FIC 15 J | (HT 6a.6-7) 'with a man (probably a priest) for *Ḫebat/Ḫebe/it*'.

It is significant that at least three Hurrian toponyms can be recognized in the Messara-valley that all have a Hurrian origin. The oldest is Linear A ***pa-i-to*** (HT 97a.3; HT 120.6). It is a genuine Hurrian toponym meaning 'He/She (a God/the King) has built (the palace)' and it is equivalent to Old Hurrian ***ba-'à-áš-to/um*** in the Tiš-atal inscription, analysed and normalised as ***pa=ašt=o=m***, and translated as 'He (Tiš-atal) has built (a temple)', cf. Th. Richter (*BGH*, 285-286), s.v. ***pa-***, *paḫ-* II [*passim*] '(er)bauen' ['to build'], *pa('/h)-*, cf. G. Wilhelm, 1988b, 55. In my view the following phases of phonetic development are likely: ***ba-'à-áš-to/um** = **pa('/h)=ašt=o=m** > **pa=j=ašt=o=m** > **pa=j=(a)št=o=m** > **pa=j=št=o=m*** (wr. ***pa-i-to*** in Linear A). Transitional glide ***-j-*** (***-i-*** in Linear A ***pa-i-to***) distinguished ***-a-*** of the root ***pa-*** from the ***-a-*** of root-extension ***-ašt-*** and eventually the ***-a-*** of ***-ašt-*** disappeared as a result of *syncope*. For Linear B ***pa-i-to*** (KN Da 1163+1400, *al.*) the Old Hurrian ending in ***=o=m*** had to be changed into a Hellenized form in ***-ος*** (***-os***): ***Φαιστός*** (Phaistos).

The ancient name of the palace of Hagia Triada, ***ka-pa*** (frequent in Linear A, but only at Hagia Triada), was the first Hurrian toponym that I detected in Linear A and interpreted as ***Ḫalba***, the Hurrian name of Aleppo (***Ḫalab*** in Semitic) with the Linear A ethnic ***ka-pa-qe*** (HT 6a.4-5) = syllabic cuneiform ***Ḫalbaḫe*** = alphabetic cuneiform ***Ḫlbġ*** 'Man of ***Ḫalba***', 'Man of Aleppo'. The toponym ***ka-pa*** and ethnic ***ka-pa-jo*** (with Greek ethnic suffix ***-yος***) were already known from the Linear B tablets from Knossos.

Linear A ***ku-mi*** (HT 110a.1) may well be the Minoan-Hurrian toponym ***Kummi***, present ***Kommos***, the Minoan harbour of Phaistos and Hagia Triada on the south coast of Crete, recently excavated by the Canadian G. Cadogan and his team. It can be recognized as the second sequence of the entry ***si-du-69*** ₗ ***ku-mi*** that is followed by HORD+E 20 ***ku-pa*** 1 [ ] (HT 110a.2) and ***ku-ro*** 100 [(HT 110a.3). The Cretan toponym ***Kummi*** is probably derived from the name of the city of ***Kumma/e/i*** or ***Kummiya*** in Anatolia. Both names may well be derived from the Hurrian root ***kum-*** 'to build / erect / pile up'. If this identification is correct, it would after ***ka-pa* = *Ḫalba*** (present Hagia Triada) be the second Cretan site named after a famous predominantly Hurrian city in the Near East, centre of the cults of *Kumarbi* and *Tešub*. Identification of ***ku-|ma-ḫi*** (HT 20.1-2) as Hurrian ethnic 'Man of *Kumma*', derived from the toponym, is confirmed by occurrence of Linear A ***sa-re-ḫi*** (HT 20.4) 'Man of Saro' on the same tablet, derived from the Linear A toponym ***sa-ro*** (HT 9a.1; HT 17.2) that may well be ***Zaros*** north of Phaistos and Hagia Triada. ***Sa-re-ḫi*** (HT 20.4) 'Man of Saro' is probably equivalent to Linear A ***sa-ro-qe*** (HT 62+73.3), also Hurrian ethnic of toponym ***sa-ro***, with the Hurrian ethnic suffix ***-ḫe***, conventionally spelled as ***sa-ro-qe*** as if there is no distinction between Linear A and B. My proposal to identify Linear A sign ***96/68*** as ***ḫi*** has yielded a lot of new confirmatory Hurrian identifications.

The theonym *Kumarbi* has also been connected with the verbal root ***kum-*** 'errichten, auftürmen' ['to build / erect / pile up'] and has been interpreted as ***kum=ar=we*** '(der) des Errichtens / Auftürmens' ['(the one) of building > active as a builder'] or '(quello) di Kumar' ['(the one) of (toponym) Kumar'], cf. Th. Richter, *BGH*, 221-222, s.v. ***kum-*** [EN; Nuzi]. Both etymologies are possible, but in my view not very satisfactory.

It is tempting to interpret ***-bi*** or ***-wi*** in ***Kumarbi / Kumarwi*** not as the genitive suffix ***-bi / -wi***, but as part of the Nuzian variant ***erwi*** (as a result of metathesis) of ***ibri / iwri / ebri / ewri*** 'Lord', so that the meaning of ***Kumarbi/wi*** < ****Kum(m)a-erwi*** (as a result of contraction of ***a+e***) is 'Lord of Kumma' and that of ***Kumarbi-ni*** is 'The Lord of Kumma'.

The variant ***erwi*** may not be limited to Nuzi. One may, for instance, also compare ***ermi/irmi*** at Nippur, cf. P.M. Purves, *NPN*, 210-211, s.v. ***erw***, *erwi-*, *-erwi*. In this way the etymology of *Kumarbi* contributes to a better understanding of the mythological struggle between Kumarbi as 'Lord of Kumma' and his son Tešub who conquered (and mutilated) his father, but also succeeded him as the new Lord of Kumma and is therefore called ***Kummeni***, cf. E. Laroche, *GLH*, 154, s.v. ***Kummeni***: Épithète de Tešub. ^{d}U-*ub* ^{uru}*Arrapḫi-ni* ^{uru}*Kum-me-ni*, KBo XX 128, 8 = XXII 165, 14; cf. KUB XXV 47 I 7 = XXXII 44 Vo 9. *Tešuba(m) ku-um-me-ni-en*, Mâri 1, 34; Hitt. ^{uru}*Kummiyas* ^{d}U-*as* 'Tešub de Kummi'. Gén. *alla-ni Ku-um-me-ni-we*, litt. 'la dame de Kummi' (Ḫebat ?), RS h. 10, 4 = *Ugar. V* 467.

Of course, the name of the city of ***Kumma/e/i*** may still be derived from the root ***kum-*** 'to build / erect / pile up'. The name of the monster ***Ullikummi*** (***^{d}Ul-li-kum-mi***) also fits very well into this mythological tradition. It was formerly translated as 'Destroyer of Kummi', but if ***ulli-*** is interpreted as *imperative* of ***ull-*** 'to destroy', now preferably, as 'Destroy Kummi (oh monster) !'. Old Hurrian variant ***Ullukummi*** (***^{d}Ul-lu-kum-mi***) can at present be translated as *indicative* 'He (the monster) destroyed Kummi' or as *imperative* 'Destroy Kummi, (oh monster) !' So ***Kumma/e/i*** plays an essential role in the name of *Kumarbi*, in the epithet of Tešub, *Kummeni*, and in the name of the monster *Ullikummi*. The monster is created by Kumarbi to annihilate the kingdom of Teš(š)ub (Storm-god rules, Kumarbi is displaced, but foments new rebellion using Ullikummi, product of his seed and a rock), cf. E. Laroche, *GLH*, 279, s.v ***Ullikummi***.

In *Minoan Linear A* (Vol. II, Part 1, 15) I have proposed: "If the little fragment in the left top corner of AK 1b (with the syllabic sign ***a***]) could be joined to the top left of AK 3a, the heading of AK 3a.1 would provide ***a***]***-ka-ne*** followed by the grain ideogram. According to Linear A and B orthographic conventions ***-r-*** before occlusive is not expressed in consonantal clusters. A final consonant would not be expressed either."

The Linear A join ***a***]***-ka-ne*** GRA [ ]D OLIVA 3D VINb 2[(AK 3a+1b.1-2) is first entry of the tablet, offers the exact place-name of the Minoan Villa of ***Arkhanes*** and is followed by the 'grain' ideogram and ideograms of other agricultural commodities. This is not only a close parallel to the position of the toponym ***ka-pa***, often at the beginning of tablets from Hagia Triada, but also reminds us of the fact that in Linear B many Knossos tablets begin with ***ko-no-so*** and many tablets from Pylos with ***pu-ro/lo***, indicating the place of residence of the scribe and the place where goods and persons were registered.

The Linear A toponym ***a***]***-ka-ne*** can actually be analysed as {*ar=ḫane/i*} 'Give a child (oh God(s)) !'. Arkhanes is situated in the foothills of Mount Ioukhtas and may have been used as a starting point for those who wished to visit the Peak Sanctuary of Ioukhtas and pray.

We know that pious worshippers or priests brought 'libation tables' with incised prayers to the Peak Sanctuaries. Some 'libation formulas' from Ioukhtas contain ***u-na-ka-na-si*** (IO Za 2.1; IO Za 9) as well as ***u-na-ru-ka-***[(IO Za 16.b) that can be completed to ***u-na-ru-ka-***[***na-si***. Linear A ***u-na-ka-na-si*** can be interpreted as {*un=a-ḫ(ḫ)an(i)=a=šše/i*} 'come offspring, childhood, childbirth', and ***u-na-ru-ka-***[***na-si*** as {*un=al=u-ḫ(ḫ)an(i)=a=šše/i*} or {*un=ar=u-ḫ(ḫ)an(i)=a=šše/i*} 'bring childhood, childbirth (oh God(s)) !' (***un=a-*** is *intransitive* 'to come'; ***un=al=u-*** or ***un=ar=u-*** *transitive* 'to bring', with the root-extensions ***-al-*** and ***-ar-***), see *chapter 11: 'Religious' Linear A inscriptions*.

The formation of Hurrian toponyms is sometimes similar to that of personal names. Compare also my Hurrian interpretation of the toponym ***Khania*** that has not yet appeared in the Linear A texts from Khania, but which is an exact equivalent to the Hurrian personal names ***Ḫani(j)a*** (wr. *Ḫa-ni-ia*) from Ašnakkum, Mari (5 persons), Emar, Nippur and Šušarrā (cf. Th. Richter, *VHN*, 407) and Nuzi (*NPN*, 53, *Ḫa-ni-a*; AAN I, 51, *Ḫa-ni-ia*), analysis {*ḫan=i=ja*}, 'She (the woman) gave birth to (the child)'. The identical name of the Palace of Khania would be 'He/She (a God/the King) created (the palace)'. The creation of a palace could be compared with the creation of a living organism. A palace was not only made of stones and wood, but was the home of a whole community of human beings.

The Minoan site of Tylissos has to date only yielded 2 Linear A tablets, 1 roundel, 1 graffito incised on the shoulder of a corded pithos and 1 inscribed incomplete male figurine. None of these inscriptions contains the name of the site *Tylis(s)os*, known from the Linear B texts from Knossos: ***tu-ri-so*** (KN C 59,3; al.) ***Τυλῖσός***, with the ethnics ***tu-ri-si-jo*** (KN E 668,2; Og 833,5; B 807,1, mut.) ***Τυλίσιος***, and ***tu-ri-si-ja*** (KN Lc 533) ***Τυλίσια***, derived from the toponym. The genitive of the ethnic ***tu-ri-si-jo*** (PY Sa 758) is attested at Pylos.

To date the etymology of the Pre-Greek toponym ***Τυλῖσός*** and ethnic ***Τυλίσιος*** was not known, but it is in my view justifiable to propose a Hurrian etymology, since (GIŠ.)***tuli*** [Boğ.] 'vine, vine-mountain' (cf. Th. Richter, *BGH*, 467, s.v. (GIŠ.)***tuli*** [Boğ.] 'Weinstock, Weinberg') corresponds with Urartian (GIŠ.)***uldi*** (V. Haas 1989a, 269[+44]) and with Hittite ***wiyan(a)-*** com./ntr., Luwian ***maddu-*** ntr., Ḫattic ***tefušne***(?), ***karam***, ***karamu***, ***karan***, Akkadian ***karānu***, ***kirānu*** and Sumerogram (GIŠ)GEŠTIN (cf. V. Haas, 2003a, 251). See for etymologically cognate Urartian (GIŠ.)***uldi/e*** 'Weingarten' ['vineyard'] M. Salvini 1979b, 121; I.M. Diakonoff, 1989, 86.

Since the Hurrian suffix ***=(i)=šše*** builds abstract forms (cf. I. Wegner, *Einführung*, 55) the Hurrian abstract ***tuli=(i)=šše*** probably means 'vineculture, viniculture, viticulture' that is an excellent name for a place suitable for growing wine on the sunny slope of a mountain.

Th. Richter (*BGH*, 240), s.v. ***ma-la-še*** [Ug.] and (*VHN*, 454), s.v. ***mal-***, mentions that the vocabulary *SCCNH 9*, 7 IV 12' (Ugarit) offers Sumerian **ŠEŠ** = Akkadian ***ma-ra-ru*** = Hurrian ***ma-la-še***, so that the meaning 'bitterness' can be assumed for Hurrian ***malaš(š)e***, from which a verbal root ***mal-*** 'to be bitter, to make bitter' can be derived. It cannot yet be established whether this or a homographic root is used in onomastics and whether this or the other is cognate with the purification terms ***mali*** and ***maldi*** in the tradition of Ḫattuša. The personal name ***Malija*** (wr. *Ma-li-ia*) at Emar, Kurruḫanni and Šubat-Enlil can be a hypocoristic formation on a verbal or nominal root or a theonym as a one-word name.

At Puzriš-Dagan the name is written ***Ma-li-a***. Th. Richter (*VHN*, 189) analyses the name as {*mal=i=ja*}, typology 1.1.1.2.4. The personal name ***Mali̯a*** (wr. *Ma-li-ia, Ma-li-a*) is the name of 29 persons at Nuzi, cf. I.J. Gelb, *NPN*, 95. The vegetation goddess ***Malija*** belongs to the local pantheon of Kaniš / Neša (modern Kültepe), but the linguistic provenance is not clarified according to Th. Richter, *VHN*, 454, note 494.

Some scholars assume a Luwian origin, but in view of the popularity of the personal name ***Mali̯a*** at Nuzi I consider a Hurrian identity much more likely than a Luwian, though a homonymic theonym with another identity at Kaniš / Neša cannot be ruled out.

With respect to the qualification of 'vegetation goddess' one readily associates the name with the Greek word *τὸ μῆλον* and Doric and Aeolic *μᾶλον* < *μᾱλον* 'apple' and 'each fruit from a tree that resembles an apple', but P. Chantraine (*DELG*, 694) mentions, s.v. 1. *μῆλον*: "Mot méditerranéen qui s'est substitué au nom i.-e. de la pomme, cf. Ernout-Meillet s.v. *Abella*. Il a été emprunté par le latin sous la forme *mālum*, puis *mēlum*, avec *mālinus* et *mēlinus*." Since a commodity is involved, there is a good chance that we are indeed dealing with a so-called 'Wanderwort'.

In the spectrum of onomastics we should not forget that ***Malia*** is also a toponym. It is the name of the Minoan palace (excavated by the French School of Archaeology), a few miles east of the small town of Malia on the north coast of Crete. If the name ***Malia*** is a one-word verbal name, analysis {*mal=i=a*}, consisting of the verbal root ***mal-*** + the marker of transitivity ***-i-*** + the marker of the subject of action 3rd person singular in ***-a***, the name has exactly the same structure as the Hurrian personal name ***Ḫania*** {*Ḫan=i=a*}, just discussed. If ***Malia*** in Crete is called after a goddess ***Malija***, it is not the only toponym formed in that way: There are places in Crete called after the goddesses ***Lato*** and ***Hera*** and the great city of Athens is called after ***Athena*** (probably Hurrian ***Atta-na / Atta-Naia/e*** '*Naia/e* is like her father', a name that can be explained from the myth about the dramatic birth of Athena, born from the head of her father Zeus (Tešub).

The question about the origin and etymology of the toponym Knossos is not easy to answer. According to A. Fick (*Vorgriechische Ortsnamen als Quelle für die Vorgeschichte Griechenlands*, Göttingen 1905, 26, 126) the epigraphic evidence only offers ***Κνωσος*** and ***Κνωσιος*** with one ***σ***, but he adds that the names from Asia Minor with a similar formation usually show double ***σσ***. He compares ***Κνωσός*** with the West-Cilician name ***Κνῶς***. *Cilicia*, originally called *Kizzuwatna*, had a Hurrian and Luwian population in the 2nd millennium B.C., and probably a Lycian population in the 1st millennium B.C., but that does not mean that the etymology of ***Κνωσός*** is Luwian, the predecessor of Lycian.

P. Chantraine (*DELG*), mentions the verb ***κνώσσω*** (*Odys*. δ 809) 'dormir' ['to sleep'], 'dit d'un sommeil profond où apparaît un songe' ['said about a deep sleep, in which a dream appears'], but adds that a Greek or other etymology fails. He does not discuss the etymology of ***Κνωσός***. The excavations of Knossos have to date yielded only a few Linear A tablets that are quite fragmentary. They show no indication that the Minoan Linear A name of Knossos was identical with or similar to Linear B ***ko-no-so***, of which the ***-o-*** in ***ko-*** is supposed to be a mute vowel, needed to express the consonant cluster ***kno-***. As far as I know, such an initial consonant cluster is not attested in Hurrian. If this consonant cluster was already present in the Minoan name, the toponym may be Pre-Hurrian.

If the *-o-* in ***ko-*** was not mute in the Minoan predecessor of Mycenaean ***ko-no-so***, a Hurrian 'one-word' name {**ko/un=o/uš=a*} 'He/She (a god/*numen*) has .... (the palace)' is conceivable, consisting of the Hurrian verbal root ***kun-*** + the suffix of the past or perfect tense ***-oš-*** + the marker of the subject of the transitive verb 3rd person singular ***-a***. Unfortunately the meaning of Hurrian ***kun-*** is not yet known, cf. Th. Richter, *VHN*, 446-447, s.v. ***kun-/kunn-*** {*ko/un-*}. Theoretically the 2nd person sing. in ***-o/u*** {**ko/un=o/uš=o*} 'You (a god/*numen*) have .... (the palace)' is also possible.

The root can also be nominal as in the personal name ***fKunnuzzi*** (wr. *fKu-un-nu-zi*) from Mari, analysis {*ko/unn(i)=o=zzi*}, typology 3.1, (cf. Th. Richter, *VHN*, 177), with adjectival suffix ***-(u)=zzi*** (cf. I. Wegner, *Einführung*, 56). Possibly {*ko/unn(i)=o=zzi*} is the Minoan-Hurrian prototype of Linear B ***ko-no-so***, that has a Greek ending in ***-ος***, but verification and confirmation of one of these possibilities would be welcome.

My recent 'decipherment' of the spiral Linear A inscription on a gold signet-ring from Mavro Spilio ***a-re-ne-si-di-jo-pi-ke-pa-ja-su-ra-i-te-ra-me-a-ja-ku*** (KN Zf 13) probably consisting of six sequences: *a-re-ne* (,) *si-di-jo-pi* (,) *ke-pa-ja* (,) *su-ra-i* (,) *te-ra-me* (,) *a-ja-ku* can be analysed as {*Ar-ene=š*} or {*Ar-en(i)=ne=š*} {*Šid=i-j=o/umbi*} or {*Šind=i-(j)o/umpi*} {*Kebaja*} {*zul(l)=ai*} {*Telame*} (*Telame/Talame/Talme*) {*Aya=k(k)=un*}, that can be translated as: 'In order that (the priest) *Aren(n)e* may connect (final debitive *zul(l)=ai*) *Ši(n)dijombi* and *Kebaja* (in wedlock with this wedding-ring), oh *Great Ajak(k)un* (vocative) !'. Can it be accidental that the sequence ***te-ra-me*** = *telame / talame / talme* 'great' precedes ***a-ja-ku*** in this inscription ? Can it be accidental that we have here the Linear A prototypes of ***Τελαμών*** and his father ***Αἰακός***, grandfather of the 'Great' ***Αἴας***, together in one inscription ? *A-ya-ku-un* is a Hurrian divine name, cf. E. Laroche, *GLH*, 40, s.v. *ayakki*: Nom divin: *a-ya-ku-un* = oug. *a-ya-ku*, RS quadr. 137 IV b 15 (Série An, No 48); cf. Nougayrol, *Ugar.* V 249, n. 1; E. Laroche, *ibid.*, 460. The Hurro-Minoan meaning of ***telame*** (root *telam-, talam-, talm-*) 'great' or 'The Great' was probably forgotten during or after the Mycenaean age and the name was probably connected with Greek *τελαμών* 'band, bandage, belt' through popular etymology. So on the basis of the original Hurrian adjective a whole new personal name was created in Greek mythology, *Τελαμών*, who became the son of *Αἰακός* and father of the 'Great' *Αἴας*, king of Salamis, and bravest of the Greeks after Achilles in the Trojan war.

One feature of Minoan-Hurrian appears to corresponds specifically with the evidence from Nippur, where Hurrian personal names are attested with the theophorous element ***irmi / ermi*** as a variant of ***erwi*** at Nuzi and ***ewri / ibri*** 'Lord' and 'king' in the Tušratta letter and elsewhere, cf. ***Ir-me/mi-ta-at-ta*** and ***Ir-me-ta-ta*** at Nippur (Clay *PNCP*, 93), to be read ***Erme/i-tatta***, i.e. ****Erwi-tatta***, according to Purves (*NPN*, 263). But Linear A ***erwi*** also occurs.

Several personal names with the element ***e-mi / i-mi*** are attested in Linear A. They can be identified with ***ermi / irmi***, since according to Linear A and B orthographic conventions ***-r-*** preceding ***-m-*** is not expressed in consonant clusters: e.g.

Long ago Linear A ***wa-du-ni-mi*** has been interpreted as Lycian *Badunimi* by P. Meriggi, *Primi Elementi di Minoico A (Minos Suppl.)*, 65. In the 2016 edition of *Minoan Linear A* (Vol. I) I still followed that view, but my position has changed.

Although *Badunimi* may have been found in Lycian context in the first millennium B.C. (It is neither mentioned by Ph.H.J. Houwink ten Cate, *The Luwian population groups of Lycia and Cilicia Aspera during the Hellenistic period*, Leiden 1965, nor by L. Zgusta, *Kleinasiatische Personennamen*, Prague 1964), it is probably of Hurrian origin.

Linear A ***wa-du-ni-mi*** (HT 6b.1; HT 85b.4-5) at Hagia Triada can be analysed as an Old Hurrian *indicative* sentence name {*wad=u=n-irmi*} or {*wand=u=n-irmi*} 'The Lord has made him/her [***n(na)***] (the child) good, just', consisting of the Hurrian verbal root ***p/wand-*** or ***p/wad-*** 'to make good, just' + the marker of the Old Hurrian transitive perfect form ***-u-*** + the enclitic personal pronoun 3rd person sing. ***-n(na)*** marking the object of the transitive verb + theophorous element ***irmi*** / ***ermi*** 'Lord', indicating the subject of the verb.

But Linear A ***wa-du-ni-mi*** can also be an Old Hurrian *imperative* in ***-u***. Compare for interpretation of the ***-n-*** in ***wa-du-ni-mi*** forms like ***Wantin-muša*** {*fand=i=n-muša*} 'Make him [*n(na)*] (the boy) good / just, oh *Muša* !' and ***Wantin-Ugur*** {*fand=i=n-Ugur*} 'Make him [*n(na)*] (the boy) good/just, oh *Ugur* !'. Consequently Linear A ***wa-du-ni-mi*** {*fand=u=n(na)-irmi*} can also be translated 'Make him/her [*n(na)*] good / just, oh Lord !'.

Linear A ***|i-mi-sa-ra*** (HT 27+HT 48a.3), Hurrian ****Irmi/Ermi-šarra***, 'The Lord is like the King of Gods'. Linear A ***|i-mi-sa-ra***, Hurrian ****Irmi/Ermi-šarra***, 'The Lord is like the King of Gods' contains two epithets to Tešub.

Linear A ***ja-re-mi*** (HT 87.3) from Hagia Triada is the second sequence in a list of 7 personal names. Context and linguistic analysis show that it is a Hurrian personal name. Linear A ***ja-re-mi*** can be compared with the Hurrian personal name ***ia-ru-ḫé-pa***.

According to Th. Richter (*BGH*, 74, s.v. ***iar-/ijar-*** [PN]) the verbal root ***iar-/ijar-*** (without translation) in ***ia-ru-ḫé-pa***, is used in a transitive way. No doubt he refers to the theme-vowel ***-u-*** that follows the root. Consequently it can be analysed as a transitive *indicative* or *imperative* sentence name {*iar/ijar=u-ḫé-pa*} 'Ḫebat ....' or '..., oh Ḫebat !'. If we assume that ***iar-/ijar-*** consists of a root ***i-*** or ***ij-*** 'to be good' or 'to make good' + *factitive* or *iterative* root-extension ***-ar-***, Linear A ***ja-re-mi*** (HT 87.3) can be analysed as ***i=ar-/ij=ar-Ermi*** 'Make (the child) good, oh Lord !', cf. Th. Richter, *BGH*, 73.

The Linear A inscription ***te-we-mi*** (↓) (PS Zf 1), read from top to bottom, among the repoussé designs on a bronze tablet from the Dictaean Cave of Psykhro (discussed in *chapter 11: 'Religious' Linear A inscriptions*) can be analysed as {*tew-ermi*}, 'speak, oh Lord !', consisting of ***ti-/te- / tiw-/tew-*** 'to speak, say words' + ***ermi*** = ***erwi/ewri*** 'Lord'. The *imperative* 'speak, oh Lord !' may well reflect the prayer pronounced by the dancing supplicant / worshipper portrayed on the bronze tablet.

Concluding: Linear A ***-e-mi / -i-mi*** = Hurrian ***ermi / irmi*** is the form in which the Mycenaean Greeks inherited the name of their god ***Ἑρμῆς*** < ***Ἑρμάάς*** < ***Ἑρμάhάς*** (form with intervocalic ***-h-***), cf. Linear B ***e-ma-a₂ a-re-ja*** (PY Tn 316 r. 7), interpreted as singular dative ***Ἑρμάᾳ Ἀρείᾳ*** 'for ***Ἑρμάάς Ἀρείᾱς***', 'for Hermes the Martial'. *Hermes* means 'Lord'.

H.G. Güterbock (*Kumarbi, Mythen vom churritischen Kronos aus den hethitischen Fragmenten zusammengestellt, übersetzt und erklärt*, Zürich - New York 1946) had clearly shown that the struggle for power between the generations of Chief Gods in the Greek pantheon, *Ouranos*, *Kronos* and *Zeus*, as described in Hesiod's *Theogony*, was in fact a close copy of the struggle between *Anu*, *Kumarbi* and *Teš(š)ub* in the Hurrian pantheon.

The details in the narrative of corresponding descriptions made it very likely that the correlations were not accidental. It is an important achievement that it can be demonstrated that the influence of Minoan-Hurrian religious traditions on the Mycenaean Greek religion went far beyond the struggle for dominance between *Anu – Ouranos*, *Kumarbi – Kronos* and *Teš(š)ub – Zeus*. In this monograph an attempt has been made to make the transition from Minoan to Mycenaean religious traditions more transparent by discussing the names and nature of Minoan, c.q. Hurrian, deities and their Mycenaean Greek counterparts.

There was also a correlation between *Ḫebat* in her appearance of *Allani* 'the Lady' and the goddess *Hera* and between the theonym *Ḫebat / Ḫebet* and the goddess *Hèbè* who had to become 'daughter of Zeus and Hera' instead of 'consort of Teš(š)ub / Zeus', because her name was later associated by the Greeks with the Greek term *ἥβη* 'youth, vigour, puberty'.

The name of *Hermes* may be derived from Hurrian *ermi*, *irmi*, *erwi*, *irwi*, *ewri*, *ibri* 'Lord, King', but also 'Lord' in the divine sense, when the divine determinative is added. The root *Ἀπέλ-* of the name of *Apollo* in its Mycenaean appearance of *Ἀπέλγων* may well be derived from Hurrian *apellu* 'arrow(head)'. I have also discussed the names of *Ares*, *Dionysos*, *Artemis*, *Leto* and other gods.

The most likely etymology of the Pre-Greek theonym *Ἀθάνᾱ* and its doublet *Ἀθηναίη* (Attic *Ἀθηναία*) is *{atta(i)=a-Na(ja/e)}*, '*Na / Naja* is like her Father (Tešub / Zeus)'. The goddess *Athena*, mentioned on a Linear B tablet from Knossos as *a-ta-na-po-ti-ni-ja* (KN V 52+52bis+[X] 8285, Olivier), *Ἀθάνᾳ Ποτνίᾳ*, '(for) the Mistress *Athena*' can probably be identified with *da-pu₂-ri-to-jo po-ti-ni-ja* (KN Gg 702,2), *δαβυρίνθοιο Ποτνίᾳ* '(for) the Mistress of the labyrinth'. The myth of Athena, Ariadna, Theseus and Minotauros was very much alive in Mycenaean Knossos, but goes back to the Minoan age.

Virtually all Hurrian theonyms also represent a theophorous element in Hurrian personal names, a phenomenon not entirely unknown in Greek names such as *Διογένης*, *Διοκλέης*, *Διομήδης*, *Ἡρακλῆς* and *Ἡράκλειτος*, but far less popular than in Hurrian and e.g. Akkadian onomastics. I have proposed a Hurrian etymology for the name of *Ἀριάδνη*, who adopted the role of the goddess *Ἀθάνᾱ* helping the hero Theseus or (more likely) who was actually the goddess helping the Athenian prince by acting in the appearance of *Ἀριάδνη*, for that is the normal way of acting of a god that he or she assumes the disguise of a mortal, concealing that a god is interfering in mortal affairs. The etymology of Hurrian **Ari-Attana* > Minoan **Ari-athānā* 'Give, oh Attana/Athana' > **Ari-athnā* (syncope) > **Ari-adnā* (voicing of the dental under influence of nasal in Hurrian) > (Greek) **Ἀριάδνᾱ* > *Ἀριάδνη* reveals the Hurrian and Minoan kernel of the myth. The Hurro-Minoan cycle is completed with the Hurrian etymology of the Pre-Greek name of *Θησεύς* (Theseus), derived from the Hurrian hypocoristic theophorous name *Teššuja* (wr. *Te-eš-šu-ia*, *Te-šu-ia*, *Te-iš-šu-ia*, *Ti-iš-šu-ú-ia*), attested at Nuzi (cf. I.J. Gelb, *NPN*, 154).

Finally, I have identified Linear A sequences with both Hurrian lexical terms and Hurrian onomastics. The Hurrian idiom written with Linear A has shown some 'dialectal' features as compared to variations between second millennium Hurrian written at Boğazköy / Boğazkale (Ḫattuša), Tell Açana (Alalaḫ), Ras Shamra (Ugarit), Tell Hariri (Mâri), Kirkuk (Nuzi), Nippur (Nuffar), Ašnakkum (Tall Šaġīr Bāzār, formerly 'Chagar Bazar'), Dilbat, Tell Taᶜannak in Palestine, the Tušratta letter (discovered at Tell el Amarna) and many other places.

If one takes into account that on the one hand the Hurrian language itself is still in a process of decipherment, that many features of its grammar can be recognized, though they are not yet all fully understood, that the number of words in the Hurrian vocabulary that can be recognized and understood is still quite limited, and that on the other hand the corpus of Linear A texts is still small as compared to the corpus of Linear B texts and that many Linear A sequences are not complete, it is quite remarkable how many words can be recognized as Hurrian in Linear A, and what is even more important, how many words can be recognized in a grammatical form characteristic of Hurrian.

As regards the onomastics, which were the starting point of my research, a remarkable number of Hurrian personal, ethnic and topographic names could be recognized and analysed. The main categories are the Hurrian theophorous personal names (c.q. the *quasi*-theophorous names), the so-called 'one-word' names and the typical hypocoristic names, which appear in great numbers in Near Eastern archives and approximately in the same percentages in Minoan Linear A. From the beginning it appeared to be a great advantage that the structure of Hurrian names, especially of theophorous personal names, is very clear and can easily be recognized. Therefore the identification of Hurrian names in Linear A attains a high degree of certainty.

It is significant that finally the epithets, c.q. poetic descriptions, of the Holy Trinity of *Tešub*, *Ḫebat* and their son *Šarruma* could be identified and analysed in the so-called 'libation formulas'. They appear in a fixed order of importance. Most clear is Tešub's epithet ***a-ta-i-jo-wa-ja*** 'Our Father' that always appears as first entry in the most complete inscriptions on 'libation tables' from the Peak Sanctuaries. Then *Ḫebat*'s epithet appears as ***a-di-<da->ki-ti/e(-te)*** 'The woman is a beauty / beautiful' > 'The (most) beautiful woman' and then that of *Šarruma* as ***a-sa-sa-ra-me*** 'The young man/boy, he is like the King of Gods'. See for an extensive analysis *chapter 11: 'Religious' Linear A inscriptions*.

The contents of the prayers in the 'libation formulas' appear to have the same subject as many personal names, in which the birth of healthy children, sometimes after the death of older children, is always in the minds of the parents. Linear A ***u-na-ka-na-si*** {*un=a-ḫ(ḫ)an=a=šši*} 'come childhood, childbirth' (or some variants of it) is an essential term occurring in almost every formula.

The bulk of Linear A material dates from the destruction levels of Late Minoan IB with the typical Marine style of pottery of ca. 1450 / 1400 B.C. This is about the same time as the reign of King *Tušratta* of Mitanni (ca. 1410-1375 B.C.), when Mitanni's power was still unchallenged and Tušratta was Pharaoh Amenhotep's equal, before the new rise to power of the Hittite empire under *Suppiluliuma I* (1372-1345 B.C.). The bulk of our epigraphic evidence of Linear A dates from a period about four to five centuries after the founding of the First Palaces. So it is not without historical significance that one of the earliest Linear A tablets in Crete, PH 6, found beneath the concrete of phase 2 in room XXVIII in the south-west section of the Palace of Phaistos, belonging to the end of Doro Levi's local phase 1b of the protopalatial period (2nd architectural period of the First Palace) and dated to the transition of MM II a/b, also contains Hurrian words and personal names. This accounts for Hurrian presence in Crete at a very early date and most interesting, apparently even before the zenith of power of the Mitannian Kingdom.

Regarding the chronology of the Palace of Phaistos I quote the cautious explanation by Doro Levi, 'The recent excavations at Phaistos', *Studies in Mediterranean Archaeology, Vol. XI*, Lund 1964, 13-14: *"Therefore bearing in mind the dates mentioned above for the foundation of the first Palace of Phaistos, and making use also of other synchronisms recently given by Minoan objects exported abroad (e.g. a conical cup of the first protopalatial phase found in a Cypriote tomb containing objects of the Middle Cypriote I period, corresponding to about the 18th century B.C.) and leaving a wide margin of error for the as yet uncertain extent of the phases of civilization preceding the foundation of the Palaces, we are inclined to propose the following chronological chart as the highest now acceptable:*

		Approx. date B.C.	
Chalcolithic period			
Prepalatial period		2000	
Protopalatial period	Phase 1 a	1850	
	Phase 1 b		
	Phase 2 (a – b ?)....		
	Phase 3	1700	
Late-palatial period	(a – b ?)	1550	
Mycenaean period		1400 "	Doro Levi

Since Hurrians indeed played a significant and dominant part in Minoan civilization, it may be preferable and more satisfactory to explain the most striking parallels between Hesiod's *Theogony* and the Hurrian myths of '*the Kingdom in Heaven*' and '*the Song of Ullikummi*' (first described by H.G. Güterbock, *Kumarbi* (*Mythen vom churritischen Kronos aus den hethitischen Fragmenten zusammengestellt, übersetzt und erklärt*, Zürich - New York 1946) through close contacts between Mycenaean Greeks and 'Hurrian' Minoans in Crete during the Bronze Age than by later contacts of Greeks with the Near East and Asia Minor in historical times. This explanation is even more likely, if one realizes that the stories told by Hesiod do not give the impression of a recent transmission through contacts of colonisation and commerce during the eighth century B.C., but suggest that they were already deeply embedded in Greek religion and daily life. When I visited Cambridge (during the Falkland crisis) to give an extensive paper on '*Progress in Linear A research*' to the Field Club of the Department of Archaeology of the University of Cambridge, I got the opportunity (in the company of Dr. R. Janko) of discussing this matter with Prof. G.S. Kirk of Trinity College, and we agreed upon the issue.

Here follow the most striking parallels between Hesiod's *Theogony* and the Hurrian myths of '*the Kingdom in Heaven*' and '*the Song of Ullikummi*' (first described by H.G. Güterbock, *Kumarbi* (*Mythen vom churritischen Kronos aus den hethitischen Fragmenten zusammengestellt, übersetzt und erklärt*, Zürich - New York 1946). I quote the parallels as described by G.S. Kirk, *Myths. Its meaning and functions in ancient and other cultures*, Cambridge 1971, 217.

Hurrian version	*Greek versions*
	Ouranos keeps his children in Gaia by persistent mating.
Anu is castrated by Kumarbi as he flees up to the sky.	Ouranos is castrated by Kronos from within Gaia's vagina.
Kumarbi swallows Anu's phallus, is made pregnant by it; has embryos in his belly	Kronos swallows his children as they are born from Gaia; has children in his belly.
Spits out some of them, which are brought to birth (probably) by earth.	Blood from Ouranos's wound impregnates earth with Erinyes, Giants, Melian nymphs; phallus falls in sea, engenders Aphrodite.
Storm-god discusses with Anu how to be born from Kumarbi.	
(Kumarbi wants to eat his son?)	Kronos is persuaded by Rhea to swallow stone instead of infant Zeus.
Storm-god is born from 'good place'.	Kronos vomits up children through his mouth.
(something about a stone in the text?)	Stone comes up first, is worshipped at Delphi.
Storm-god rules, Kumarbi is displaced, but foments new rebellion using Ullikummi, product of his seed and a rock.	Zeus rules, Kronos is displaced to Tartarus with Titans, but Gaia bears Typhoeus, source of new rebellion-product of Kronos's seed according to the B-scholium on *Iliad* II, 783, or of Tartarus according to Hesiod.

It is significant that the legend of King *Krt* (eponymous hero of Crete) and his lady *Ḫurrai*, attested at Ugarit, may be traced back to the first historical King *Kirta* of Mitanni, father of *Šuttarna*. Hurrian expansion in the area of the Fertile Crescent may have taken place much earlier than was held possible by many scholars. Early presence of Hurrians in Syria, Palestine and Kizzuwatna (Cilicia) might well account for their early arrival in Crete (and Cyprus ?). The excavations at *Urkiš / Tell Mozan* (northeast Syria) have even pushed back Hurrian presence in northeast Syria, east Turkey and north Iraq for at least half a millennium, suggesting that Hurrians may have been as indigenous in north Mesopotamia and north Syria as the Sumerians were in south Iraq. If Hurrians were indigenous in *Urkiš* in northeast Syria from at least 2300 B.C., this may well account for the proportion of 50% Hurrian names in the archives of Alalaḫ VII (ca. 1640 B.C.) in northwest Syria. The Amorite names at Alalaḫ VII might then offer the names of the most recent newcomers in the area and the increase of Hurrian names upto 75 % in Alalaḫ IV (ca. 1460 B.C.) might reflect the growth of Mitannian power in Syria. So if Hurrians were indigenous in north Syria right upto the Mediterranean coast in a much earlier period than was ever thought before, their early arrival in Crete would be more likely as well.

Although frescoes and pottery found in the Minoan palaces may give an impression of thorough peacefulness of the Minoan society, I have never believed that there has ever been a contrast between the Minoan and Mycenaean world in a fierceful and warlike attitude. Frescoes found in Akrotiri on Thera and King Minos's *thalassokratia* 'dominance of the sea', described by Thucydides (*History of the Peloponnesian war* I, iv) should have warned scholars that throughout antiquity there is no example of any people that could maintain its power without using or displaying force. The evidence of Linear A ideograms on tablets from different sites showing wheels and other parts of chariots, as well as other arms and armed men, definitely proves that Minoan society probably was a *charioteers' aristocracy* like the Hittite kingdom, Mitanni, Babylonia, the Syrian states, Egypt since the Hyksos occupation, and the Mycenaean kingdoms.

Since presence of Hurrian names in Linear A is overwhelming (only a few names such as *ku-pa*$_3$*-nu* and *ku-pa*$_3$*-na-tu* may be Semitic, although a Hurrian interpretation is now more probable), it is likely that the Minoan society of Crete reveals strong relations with the Kingdom of Yamḫad (Aleppo and Alalaḫ) in Syria and directly or indirectly with Mitanni, possibly also with the area of second millennium Kizzuwatna (later Cilicia) and parts of Cappadocia. Hurrian presence was widespread at all Cretan sites and on some Aegean islands. Since Minoan society was thoroughly Hurrian, I get the impression that 'colonisation' of the Minoan world was an almost exclusively Hurrian enterprise, initiated and accomplished from a powerful centre such as Ḫalba (Aleppo) or Waššukkanni during the rise of Mitanni or even earlier from a city like Urkiš. Palatial centres in Crete may from the very start have become independent from the Near Eastern metropoleis, whence the settlers came, though they may have kept commercial, cultural and religious contacts.

From a cultural point of view the Minoan palace civilization with the First palaces dating (according to Doro Levi) from the middle of the nineteenth century B.C. onwards (from ca. 1850 B.C.), can probably be best associated with the palaces of Mâri and Alalaḫ. Certainly frescoes and ceramics from Alalaḫ (*Açana* style) bear a close resemblance with Minoan frescoes and pottery, especially the Kamares-style and later the Palace-style. Unfortunately we do not know how the palaces of Aleppo and Waššukkanni looked like.

Since Crete was populated from Neolithic times and through the Early Bronze Age, the Neolithic and Early Minoan periods may well have yielded Pre-Hurrian topographic, ethnic and personal names. Evidence from the Greek mainland shows, how the so-called Pre-Greek onomastics proved to persist through centuries of Greek occupancy and domination. It would be unwise to assume that with identifying the language written with Linear A, all problems with identifying Pre-Greek substrata would be solved. After the Mycenaean conquest of Crete, the island was largely Hellenized as the Linear B tablets show.

As regards Linear B it has been shown that Indo-European and non-Indo-European adstrates have played a significant part in Mycenaean onomastics. Relations of the Mycenaean world with Asia Minor have been discussed by scholars as S. Hiller, '*RA-MI-NI-JA*: Mykenisch-Kleinasiatische Beziehungen und die Linear B-Texte', *Živa Antika 25.1-2 (1975),* 388-412, and J.C. Billigmeijer, 'An inquiry into the non-Greek names on the Linear B tablets from Knossos and their relationship to languages of Asia Minor', *Minos 10 (1969),* 177-183, and occasionally by other scholars as well.

The decipherment of Minoan Linear A as a Minoan-Hurrian dialect has opened up a large source of evidence that may offer an important contribution to the interpretation and understanding of many Pre-Greek words and names. And *vice versa* the meaning of some Pre-Greek words such as (Mycenaean) Greek ***e-ka-ra*** = *ἐσχάρᾱ* 'charcoal hearth/fireplace in the kitchen (or in the throne-room of the Palace of Nestor at Pylos)', but foremost 'the sacrificial altar for burnt sacrifices to propitiate the gods' shows that Hurrian **išḫ=ar=i*, from which the Hurrian term *išḫ=ar=i=nni* 'baker' is derived, does not mean 'kitchen', but 'hearth' and 'sacrificial altar'. It also throws light on the true meaning of the theonym *Išḫara* and may explain some peculiar features of festivals in honour of that goddess. The results may encourage scholars in Greek diachronic linguistics and scholars in Hurrian studies to cooperate more closely in this new field of research.

One may wonder how the Hurrian language could be wiped off the face of the earth as if it had never existed. It had after all taken a prominent position in Mitanni, one of the greatest powers in the Near East for several centuries during the second millennium B.C.. Hurrian culture and religion had exercised considerable influence on the cities in adjacent areas such as Syria, Phoenicia, Palestine, Kizzuwatna, Ḫattuša, possibly (partly) Egypt during the Hyksos occupation, Cyprus (if Cypro-Minoan 2 is indeed Hurrian) and Minoan Crete, all far beyond the borders of Mitanni proper. In the first millennium B.C. Urartian, the language of the kingdom of Urartu (9th – 7th century B.C.), was cognate with second millennium Hurrian. Urartian was probably not a direct successor of Hurrian, but, as Gernot Wilhelm thinks, both languages had a common ancestor.

The historical events can explain a lot. After the Hittite emperor *Suppiluliuma I* had reduced Mitanni to the status of a vassal state and had annexed the western parts of the former Empire of Mitanni, Assyria took the opportunity to annexe eastern parts of Mitanni and to become the new great power in the Near East and eventually in the first millennium B.C. Aramaic, belonging to the northern branch of Semitic languages, became the language of Syria and was used as *lingua franca* by Jews and others, e.g. in the time of Christ.

Minoan Crete was the first great civilization in Europe. The Mycenaeans had lived in close contact with the Minoans and had been thoroughly influenced by them during the centuries before they occupied Knossos. That process was only intensified after they conquered Knossos. They adopted and adapted the Minoan script for their own purposes, inherited religious and other traditions, but since they started to dominate the island from the palace of Knossos, they also started a gradual process of Hellenization of the entire island. We do not know whether that process had already been completed at the end of the Mycenaean era. The Mycenaeans at Knossos used the same South Greek dialect as the Mycenaeans of the Greek mainland (Mycenae, Pylos, Thebes), predecessor of the Arkadian and Cypriot dialects, which is coined 'Proto-Arcado-Cypriot'.

The great *caesura* probably came with the arrival of the Dorians in southern Greece (best characterized as a secondary migration within Greece), according to Thucydides eighty years after the Trojan war, i.e. ca. 1180 B.C., if the end of the Trojan war can be dated to 1260 B.C. at the end of Troy VI. The Dorians also arrived in Crete bringing their own dialect and traditions.

The Mycenaeans had integrated and embedded Minoan traditions in their own system, but the Mycenaeans in Crete were now dominated themselves by fellow-Greeks coming from the North-West of Greece who had probably had no or virtually no contact with the southern Mycenaean centres and their high civilization.

Typical for the beginning of the Dark Ages in Greece, Crete and elsewhere is not only the destruction of the palatial centres, but the loss of the highly organized social and economic infrastructure and organisation, which meant that life was in every respect reduced to a local standard: agricultural and commercial activities were limited to a small and local scale. Agriculture was largely replaced by 'transhumance' husbandry, as was demonstrated by S. Georgoudi, (Quelques problèmes de la transhumance dans la Grèce ancienne, *Revue des études grecques LXXXVII (1974)*, 155-185) and A.M. Snodgrass (*The Dark Age of Greece*, Edinburgh 1971, and *Archaic Greece, the age of experiment*, London 1980).

The coming of the Dorians in Crete brought a breach of Bronze Age traditions and caused the preceding Mycenaean and Minoan civilizations to fall into oblivion. The Mycenaean age was kept alive thanks to the epic tradition, but about the Minoan age one had only a vague idea. Apart from the stories about king Minos residing at Knossos, and his *thalassokratia*, one knew that a few pockets of *Eteocretans* were present in Crete commemorating the fact that it was once inhabited by a non-Greek population.

The decipherment of Minoan Linear A has yielded some interesting Hurrian phrases that reveal that Homer preserved - especially in his epic formulas - not only clear relations with specific Mycenaean vocabulary, but also with particular Minoan-Hurrian expressions. The Minoan and Mycenaean legacies show a remarkable degree of continuity, especially in the field of religion, rituals and the names of gods and heroes. A considerable number of Pre-Greek words and names can now be identified as Hurrian. The parallels between Hesiod's *Theogony* and the Hurrian myths of '*the Kingdom in Heaven*' and '*the Song of Ullikummi*', recognized by H.G. Güterbock, were only the tip of the iceberg. Mythological parallels between the Hurrian and Greek religions go far beyond that realm.

Especially during the last decades it has become evident that the Hurrian civilization has played a much more prominent role in the Near East than was ever considered possible. It is of historical significance that the Minoan civilization of Crete was part of that Hurrian heritage. The Minoan-Hurrian civilization was also the first great civilization bringing literacy to Europe. Its contribution to the cultural and historical development of Europe should not be underestimated.

ABBREVIATIONS OF NEAR EASTERN SITES

Names of ancient sites are followed by those of modern sites

AL	Alalaḫ	Tell / Tall Açana
AL VII	Alalaḫ VII, (late) Old Babylonian period (texts marked by *)	
AL IV	Alalaḫ IV, Middle Babylonian period	
Ass	Assur	Qal^{c}at Šerqāt
AŠ	Ašnakkum	Tell Šaġīr Bāzār (ŠB) / "Chagar Bazar"
Boğ.	Ḫattuša	Boğazköy / Boğazkale
Brak		Tell Brak
DurK	Dūr-Katlimmu	Tell Šēḫ Ḥamad
EA	Achet-Aten	Tell el Amarna (EA 24 = Tušratta letter)
EB	Ebla	Tell Mardiḫ
EK	Ekalte	Tell Munbaqa
EM	Emar	Meskene (Msk)
HT		Hamam et-Turkmān
Ḫana	(Texts from the kingdom of) Ḫana (around Terqa)	
Ḫatt.	Ḫattuša	Boğazköy / Boğazkale (Boğ.)
KAḪ	Kaḫat	Tell Barri
Kay		Kayalıpınar
KRḪ / Kurr	Kurruḫanni	Tell al-Faḫḫar
KT	Kaneš	Kültepe
KTN	Kār-Tukultī-Ninurta	Tulūl ^{c}Aqīr
Lid		Lidar Höyük
M	Mari / Mâri	Tell Hariri
Nip	Nippur	Nuffar
Nuzi	Nuzi	Yorġan/Yolġan Tepe (texts from Kirkuk included)
PD	Puzriš-Dagan	Drēḥem
Q	Qaṭṭarā	Tell ar-Rimaḥ
Qa	Qaṭna	Mišrife (West-Syria)
QH		Tell Qal'at al-Hādī
Š or Šu	Šušarrā	Tell Shemshara (on the lower Zab)
Šap	Šapinuwa	Ortaköy
ŠE	Šubat-Enlil / Šeḫna	Tell Leilān (Leilan)
Taan		Tell Taanach
T or Tig	Tigunāni / Tigunānum	
TQ	Terqa (in Ḫana)	Tell 'Ašarā
TU or Tu	Tuttul	Tell Bi^{c}a
ṬA	Ṭabatum	Tell Ṭabān
Ug.	Ugarit	Ras Šamra (RS)

CPSIA information can be obtained
at www.ICGtesting.com
Printed in the USA
BVHW020042100223
658263BV00005B/127

9 789083 275413